LITERATURE

For additional information on Intel products in the U.S. or Canada, call Intel's Literature Center at (800) 548-4725 or write to:

Intel Literature
P.O. Box 7641
Mt. Prospect, Il 60056-7641

To order literature outside of the U.S. and Canada contact your local international sales office.

CURRENT DATABOOKS

Product line databooks contain datasheets, application notes, article reprints, and other design information. Databooks can be ordered in the U.S. and Canada by calling TAB/McGraw-Hill at 1-800-822-8158; outside of the U.S. and Canada contact your local international sales office.

Title	Intel Order Number	ISBN
Automotive Products	231792	N/A
Embedded Applications (2 vol. set)	270648	1-55512-242-6
Embedded Microcontrollers	270646	1-55512-230-2
Embedded Microprocessors	272396	1-55512-231-0
Flash Memory (2 vol. set)	210830	1-55512-232-9
Intel486™ Microprocessors and Related Products	241731	1-55512-235-3
i960® Processors and Related Products	272084	1-55512-234-5
Military and Special Products	210461	N/A
Networking	297360	1-55512-236-1
OEM Boards, Systems and Software	280407	1-55512-237-X
Packaging	240800	1-55512-238-8
Pentium™ Processors and Related Products	241732	1-55512-239-6
Peripheral Components	296467	1-55512-240-X

A complete set of this information is available on CD-ROM through Intel's Data on Demand program, order number 240897. For information about Intel's Data on Demand ask for item number 240952.

24-HOUR AUTOMATED TECHNICAL SUPPORT*

Intel's Application Bulletin Board System (BBS) and FaxBack System are at your service, 24-hours a day, at no charge, and the information is updated frequently.

FaxBack SYSTEM

Technical and product information are available 24-hours a day! Order documents containing:

- Product Announcements
- Product Literature
- Intel Device Characteristics

- Design/Application Recommendations
- Stepping/Change Notifications
- Quality and Reliability Information

Information on the following subjects is also available:

- Microcontroller and Flash
- OEM Branded Systems
- Multibus/BBS Listing
- Multimedia

- Development Tools
- Quality and Reliability/Change Notification
- Microprocessor/PCI/Peripheral
- Intel Architecture Lab

To use FaxBack for Intel components and systems, dial **(800) 628-2283** or (916) 356-3105 (U.S. and Canada) or +44{0} 1793-496646 (Europe) and follow the automated voice-prompt menu. Document orders will be faxed to the fax number you specify. Catalogs are updated twice a month, so call for the latest information!

BULLETIN BOARD SYSTEM

Intel's Application Bulletin Board System (BBS) enables file retrieval 24-hours a day. The following can be located on the BBS:

- Software Drivers
- Tool Information
- Software/Application Utilities

- Product/Technical Documentation
- Firmware Upgrades
- Quality and Reliability Data

To use the Intel Application BBS (components and systems), dial **(916) 356-3600** for download access (U.S. and Canada) or +44{0} 1793-496340 (Europe). The BBS will support 1200–19200 baud rate modem. *Typical modem configuration: 9600 baud rate, No Parity, 8 Data Bits, 1 Stop Bit.* A directory listing of BBS files is also available through FaxBack or our 800 BBS (800-897-2536).

Retail Products

Information on Intel's retail products (Coprocessors and wireless, video, personal conferencing and network products) is available through the following services:

Internet : ftp.intel.com (143.185.65.2)
CompuServe : GO INTELFORUM (modem settings: E-7-1, up to 14.4 Kbps)

Country	BBS (N-8-1, up to 14.4 Kbps)	FaxBack
North America	(503) 264-7999	(800) 525-3019 or (503) 264-6835
Europe	+44 1 793-432955	+44 1 793-432509
Australia	+61 2 975-3066	+61 2 975-3922
Taiwan	+886 2 718-6422	+886 2 514-0815
Singapore	+65 256-4776	+65 256-5350
Hong Kong	+852 530-4116	+852 844-4448
Korea	+822 784-3430	+822 767-2594

*Support services provided courtesy of Intel Application Support

intel®

Embedded
Applications
Volume 2

1995

Information in this document is provided solely to enable use of Intel products. Intel assumes no liability whatsoever, including infringement of any patent or copyright, for sale and use of Intel products except as provided in Intel's Terms and Conditions of Sale for such products.

Intel Corporation makes no warranty for the use of its products and assumes no responsibility for any errors which may appear in this document nor does it make a commitment to update the information contained herein.

Intel retains the right to make changes to these specifications at any time, without notice.

Contact your local Intel sales office or your distributor to obtain the latest specifications before placing your product order.

MDS is an ordering code only and is not used as a product name or trademark of Intel Corporation.

Intel Corporation and Intel's FASTPATH are not affiliated with Kinetics, a division of Excelan, Inc. or its FASTPATH trademark or products.

*Other brands and names are the property of their respective owners.

Additional copies of this document or other Intel literature may be obtained from:

>
> Intel Corporation
> Literature Sales
> P.O. Box 7641
> Mt. Prospect, IL 60056-7641
>
> or call 1-800-879-4683

©INTEL CORPORATION, 1995

DATASHEET DESIGNATIONS

Intel uses various datasheet markings to designate each phase of the document as it relates to the product. The markings appear in the lower inside corner of each datasheet page. Following are the definitions of each marking:

Datasheet Marking	Description
Product Preview	Contains information on products in the design phase of development. Do not finalize a design with this information. Revised information will be published when the product becomes available.
Advanced Information	Contains information on products being sampled or in the initial production phase of development.*
Preliminary	Contains preliminary information on new products in production.*
No Marking	Contains information on products in full production.*

* Specifications within these datasheets are subject to change without notice. Verify with your local Intel sales office that you have the latest datasheet before finalizing a design.

intel.

MCS® 48 Microcontroller Family	1
MCS® 51 Microcontroller Family	2
RUPI Family	3
80186/80188 Microprocessor Family	4
MCS® 96 Microcontroller Family	5
Embedded Intel386™ Processors	6
General Microcontroller	7

CONTENTS

Table of Contents

Alphanumeric Index xi

CHAPTER 1
MCS® 48 Microcontroller Family
APPLICATION NOTES
- AP-24 Application Techniques for the MCS-48 Family 1-1
- AP-40 Keyboard/Display Scanning with Intel's MCS-48 Microcomputers 1-25
- AP-49 Serial I/O and Math Utilities for the 8049 Microcomputer 1-50
- AP-55A A High-Speed Emulator for Intel MCS-48 Microcomputers 1-73
- AP-91 Using the 8049 as an 80 Column Printer Controller 1-173

CHAPTER 2
MCS® 51 Microcontroller Family
APPLICATION NOTES
- AP-69 An Introduction to the Intel MCS-51 Single-Chip Microcomputer Family 2-1
- AP-70 Using the Intel MCS 51 Boolean Processing Capabilities 2-31
- AP-223 8051 Based CRT Terminal Controller 2-77
- AP-252 Designing With The 80C51BH 2-154
- AP-410 Enhanced Serial Port on the 83C51FA 2-179
- AP-415 83C51FA/FB PCA Cookbook 2-187
- AP-425 Small DC Motor Control 2-232
- AP-429 83C152 Global Serial Channel in CSMA/CD Mode 2-247
- AP-476 How to Implement I²C Serial Communication 2-316

APPLICATION BRIEFS
- AB-12 Designing a Mailbox Memory for Two 80C31 Microcontrollers Using EPLDs . 2-343
- AB-38 Interfacing the 82786 Graphics Coprocessor to the 8051 2-352
- AB-39 Interfacing the Densitron LCD to the 8051 2-359
- AB-40 32-Bit Math Routines for the 8051 2-367
- AB-41 Software Serial Port Implemented with the PCA 2-377
- AB-44 Using the 87C51GB 2-401

ARTICLE REPRINTS
- AR-517 Using the 8051 with Resonant Transducers 2-429
- AR-526 Analog/Digital Processing with Microcontrollers 2-434

CHAPTER 3
RUPI Family
APPLICATION NOTES
- AP-281 UPI-452 Accelerates iAPX 286 Bus Performance 3-1
- AP-283 Flexibility in Frame Size with the 8044 3-23

CHAPTER 4
80186/80188 Microprocessor Family
APPLICATION NOTES
- AP-258 High Speed Numerics with the 80186/80188 and 8087 4-1
- AP-286 80186/188 Interface to Intel Microcontrollers 4-19
- AP-468 Quick Upgrade from the 80C186 to the 80C186EA 4-51
- AP-477 Low Voltage Embedded Design 4-79
- AP-484 Interfacing a Floppy Disk Drive to an 80C186EX Family Processor 4-91
- AP-502 Quick Upgrade from the 80C186XL to the 80C186EA 4-158
- AP-503 Add-In Flash Memory Card for an 80C186EA Application 4-188

APPLICATION BRIEFS
- AB-31 The 80C186XL/80C188XL Integrated Refresh Control Unit 4-219
- AB-35 DRAM Refresh/Control with the 80186/80188 4-234

CONTENTS

Table of Contents (Continued)

AB-36 80186/80188 DMA Latency	4-243
AB-37 80186/80188 EFI Drive and Oscillator Operation	4-247

CHAPTER 5
MCS® 96 Microcontroller Family
APPLICATION NOTES

AP-248 Using The 8096	5-1
AP-275 An FFT Algorithm for MCS 96 Products Including Supporting Routines and Examples	5-106
AP-406 MCS 96 Analog Acquisition Primer	5-183
AP-428 Distributed Motor Control Using the 80C196KB	5-284
AP-466 Using the 80C196KB	5-314
AP-475 Using the 8XC196NT	5-358

APPLICATION BRIEFS

AB-32 Upgrade Path from 8096-90 to 8096BH to 80C196	5-396
AB-33 Memory Expansion for the 8096	5-401
AB-34 Integer Square Root Routine for the 8096	5-414
AB-45 Converting from the 8X9XBH or 8X9XJF to the 8XC196KB	5-419
AB-46 Serial Port Mode 0, 8X9XBH/KB/KC/KD Application Brief	5-425

ARTICLE REPRINT

AR-515 A Single-Chip Image Processor	5-435

DIAGNOSTIC LIBRARY

MCS 96 Diagnostic Library	5-440

CHAPTER 6
Embedded Intel386™ Processors
APPLICATION NOTES

AP-442 33 MHz Intel386 System Design Considerations	6-1
AP-513 Intel386 EX CPU POS Terminal Reference Design	6-112
AP-514 Hamilton Hallmark H4T Intel 386 Embedded Microprocessor Reference Design	6-146

CHAPTER 7
General Microcontroller
APPLICATION NOTES

AP-125 Designing Microcontroller Systems for Electrically Noisy Environments	7-1
AP-155 Oscillators for Microcontrollers	7-24

Alphanumeric Index

AB-12 Designing a Mailbox Memory for Two 80C31 Microcontrollers Using EPLDs	2-343
AB-31 The 80C186XL/80C188XL Integrated Refresh Control Unit	4-219
AB-32 Upgrade Path from 8096-90 to 8096BH to 80C196	5-396
AB-33 Memory Expansion for the 8096	5-401
AB-34 Integer Square Root Routine for the 8096	5-414
AB-35 DRAM Refresh/Control with the 80186/80188	4-234
AB-36 80186/80188 DMA Latency	4-243
AB-37 80186/80188 EFI Drive and Oscillator Operation	4-247
AB-38 Interfacing the 82786 Graphics Coprocessor to the 8051	2-352
AB-39 Interfacing the Densitron LCD to the 8051	2-359
AB-40 32-Bit Math Routines for the 8051	2-367
AB-41 Software Serial Port Implemented with the PCA	2-377
AB-44 Using the 87C51GB	2-401
AB-45 Converting from the 8X9XBH or 8X9XJF to the 8XC196KB	5-419
AB-46 Serial Port Mode 0, 8X9XBH/KB/KC/KD Application Brief	5-425
AP-125 Designing Microcontroller Systems for Electrically Noisy Environments	7-1
AP-155 Oscillators for Microcontrollers	7-24
AP-223 8051 Based CRT Terminal Controller	2-77
AP-24 Application Techniques for the MCS-48 Family	1-1
AP-248 Using The 8096	5-1
AP-252 Designing With The 80C51BH	2-154
AP-258 High Speed Numerics with the 80186/80188 and 8087	4-1
AP-275 An FFT Algorithm for MCS 96 Products Including Supporting Routines and Examples	5-106
AP-281 UPI-452 Accelerates iAPX 286 Bus Performance	3-1
AP-283 Flexibility in Frame Size with the 8044	3-23
AP-286 80186/188 Interface to Intel Microcontrollers	4-19
AP-40 Keyboard/Display Scanning with Intel's MCS-48 Microcomputers	1-25
AP-406 MCS 96 Analog Acquisition Primer	5-183
AP-410 Enhanced Serial Port on the 83C51FA	2-179
AP-415 83C51FA/FB PCA Cookbook	2-187
AP-425 Small DC Motor Control	2-232
AP-428 Distributed Motor Control Using the 80C196KB	5-284
AP-429 83C152 Global Serial Channel in CSMA/CD Mode	2-247
AP-442 33 MHz Intel386 System Design Considerations	6-1
AP-466 Using the 80C196KB	5-314
AP-468 Quick Upgrade from the 80C186 to the 80C186EA	4-51
AP-475 Using the 8XC196NT	5-358
AP-476 How to Implement I2C Serial Communication	2-316
AP-477 Low Voltage Embedded Design	4-79
AP-484 Interfacing a Floppy Disk Drive to an 80C186EX Family Processor	4-91
AP-49 Serial I/O and Math Utilities for the 8049 Microcomputer	1-50
AP-502 Quick Upgrade from the 80C186XL to the 80C186EA	4-158
AP-503 Add-In Flash Memory Card for an 80C186EA Application	4-188
AP-513 Intel386 EX CPU POS Terminal Reference Design	6-112
AP-514 Hamilton Hallmark H4T Intel 386 Embedded Microprocessor Reference Design	6-146
AP-55A A High-Speed Emulator for Intel MCS-48 Microcomputers	1-73
AP-69 An Introduction to the Intel MCS-51 Single-Chip Microcomputer Family	2-1
AP-70 Using the Intel MCS 51 Boolean Processing Capabilities	2-31
AP-91 Using the 8049 as an 80 Column Printer Controller	1-173
AR-515 A Single-Chip Image Processor	5-435
AR-517 Using the 8051 with Resonant Transducers	2-429

ALPHANUMERIC INDEX

Alphanumeric Index (Continued)

AR-526 Analog/Digital Processing with Microcontrollers 2-434
MCS 96 Diagnostic Library 5-440

intel.

MCS® 96 Microcontroller Family

5

AP-248

APPLICATION NOTE

Using The 8096

IRA HORDEN
MCO APPLICATIONS ENGINEER

September 1987

Order Number: 270061-002

Using The 8096

CONTENTS
PAGE

- 1.0 INTRODUCTION 5-5
- 2.0 8096 OVERVIEW 5-5
  - 2.1. General Description 5-5
    - 2.1.1. CPU Section 5-6
    - 2.1.2. I/O Features 5-8
  - 2.2. The Processor Section 5-8
    - 2.2.1. Operations and Addressing Modes 5-8
    - 2.2.2. Assembly Language 5-11
    - 2.2.3. Interrupts 5-12
  - 2.3. On-Chip I/O Section 5-14
    - 2.3.1. Timer/Counters 5-14
    - 2.3.2. HSI 5-15
    - 2.3.3. HSO 5-16
    - 2.3.4. Serial Port 5-17
    - 2.3.5. A to D Converter 5-20
    - 2.3.6. PWM Register 5-21
- 3.0 BASIC SOFTWARE EXAMPLES 5-23
  - 3.1. Using the 8096's Processing Section 5-23
    - 3.1.1. Table Interpolation 5-23
    - 3.1.2. PL/M-96 5-26
  - 3.2. Using the I/O Section 5-28
    - 3.2.1. Using the HSI Unit 5-28
    - 3.2.2. Using the HSO Unit 5-29
    - 3.2.3. Using the Serial Port in Mode 1 5-33
    - 3.2.4. Using the A to D 5-35
- 4.0 ADVANCED SOFTWARE EXAMPLES 5-35
  - 4.1. Simultaneous I/O Routines under Interrupt Control 5-35
  - 4.2. Software Serial Port Using the HSIO Unit 5-38
  - 4.3. Interfacing an Optical Encoder to the HSI Unit 5-43
- 5.0 HARDWARE EXAMPLE 5-55
  - 5.1. EPROM Only Minimum System 5-55
  - 5.2. Port Reconstruction 5-57
- 6.0 CONCLUSION 5-58
- 7.0 BIBLIOGRAPHY 5-58

CONTENTS

APPENDICES

	PAGE
Appendix A. Basic Software Examples	5-59
A.1. Table Lookup 1	5-59
A.2. Table Lookup 2	5-61
A.3. PLM-96 Code with Expansion	5-63
A.4. Pulse Measurement	5-69
A.5. Enchanced Pulse Measurement	5-71
A.6. PWM Using the HSO	5-73
A.7. Serial Port	5-77
A.8. A to D Converter	5-79
Appendix B. HSO and A to D Under Interrupt Control	5-81
Appendix C. Software Serial Port	5-85
Appendix D. Motor Control Program	5-91

Figures

- 2-1. 8096 Block Diagram 5-5
- 2-2. Memory Map 5-6
- 2-3. SFR Layout 5-7
- 2-4. Major I/O Functions 5-8
- 2-5. Instruction Summary 5-9
- 2-6. Instruction Format 5-11
- 2-7. Interrupt Sources 5-12
- 2-8. Interrupt Vectors and Priorities 5-12
- 2-9. Interrupt Structure Block Diagram ... 5-13
- 2-10. The PSW Register 5-14
- 2-11. HSI Unit Block Diagram 5-15
- 2-12. HSI Mode Register 5-15
- 2-13. HSO Command Register 5-16
- 2-14. HSO Block Diagram 5-16
- 2-15. Serial Port Control/Status Register ... 5-17
- 2-16. Baud Rate Formulas 5-18
- 2-17. Baud Rate Values for 10, 11, 12 MHz ... 5-19
- 2-18. Multiprocessor Communication 5-20
- 2-19. A to D Result/Command Register ... 5-21
- 2-20. PWM Output Waveforms 5-22
- 2-21. PWM to Analog Conversion Circuitry ... 5-22
- 3-1. Using the HSIO to Monitor Rotating Machinery ... 5-32
- 3-2. Serial Port Level Conversion 5-34
- 4-1. 10-Bit Asynchronous Frame 5-39
- 4-2. Optical Encoder and Waveforms .. 5-43
- 4-3. Filtered Encoder Waveforms 5-44
- 4-4. Schematic of Optical Encoder to 8096 Interface ... 5-45
- 4-5. Motor Driver Circuitry 5-45
- 4-6. Mode State Diagram 5-48
- 4-7. Motor Control Modes 5-53
- 5-1. Minimum System Configuration 5-56

Listings

- 3-1. Include File DEMO96.INC 5-23
- 3-2. ASM-96 Code for Table Lookup Routine 1 ... 5-24
- 3-3. ASM-96 Code for Table Lookup Routine 1 ... 5-25
- 3-4. PLM-96 Code for Table Lookup Routine 1 ... 5-27
- 3-5. 32-Bit Result Multiply Procedure for PLM-96 ... 5-27
- 3-6. Measuring Pulses Using the HSI Unit ... 5-28
- 3-7. Enhanced HSI Pulse Measurement Routine ... 5-29
- 3-8. Generating a PWM with the HSO .. 5-30
- 3-9. Changes to Declarations for HSO Routine ... 5-31
- 3-10. Driver Module for HSO PWM Program ... 5-31
- 3-11. Using the Serial Port in Mode 1 5-33
- 3-12. Scanning the A to D Channels 5-35
- 4-1. Using Multiple I/O Devices 5-36
- 4-2. Software Serial Port Declarations ... 5-39
- 4-3. Software Serial Port Interface Routines ... 5-40
- 4-4. Software Serial Port Initialization Routine ... 5-40
- 4-5. Software Serial Port Transmit Process ... 5-41
- 4-6. Receive Process 5-41
- 4-7. Motor Control HSO.0 Timer Routine ... 5-46
- 4-8. Motor Control HSI Data Available Routine ... 5-48
- 4-9. Motor Control Mode 1 Routines ... 5-49
- 4-10. Motor Control Mode 0 Routines ... 5-50
- 4-11. Motor Control Software Timer 1 Routine ... 5-51
- 4-12. Motor Control Next Position Lookup ... 5-53
- 4-13. Motor Control Timer Interrupt Routine ... 5-54
- 4-14. Motor Control Software Timer Interrupt Handler ... 5-54
- 4-15. Motor Control Software Timer 2 Routine ... 5-55

AP-248

1.0 INTRODUCTION

High speed digital signals are frequently encountered in modern control applications. In addition, there is often a requirement for high speed 16-bit and 32-bit precision in calculations. The MCS®-96 product line, generically referred to as the 8096, is designed to be used in applications which require high speed calculations and fast I/O operations.

The 8096 is a 16-bit microcontroller with dedicated I/O subsystems and a complete set of 16-bit arithmetic instructions including multiply and divide operations. This Ap-note will briefly describe the 8096 in section 2, and then give short examples of how to use each of its key features in section 3. The concluding sections feature a few examples which make use of several chip features simultaneously and some hardware connection suggestions. Further information on the 8096 and its use is available from the sources listed in the bibliography.

2.0 8096 OVERVIEW

2.1. General Description

Unlike microprocessors, microcontrollers are generally optimized for specific applications. Intel's 8048 was optimized for general control tasks while the 8051 was optimized for 8-bit math and single bit boolean operations. The 8096 has been designed for high speed/high performance control applications. Because it has been designed for these applications the 8096 architecture is different from that of the 8048 or 8051.

There are two major sections of the 8096; the CPU section and the I/O section. Each of these sections can be subdivided into functional blocks as shown in Figure 2-1.

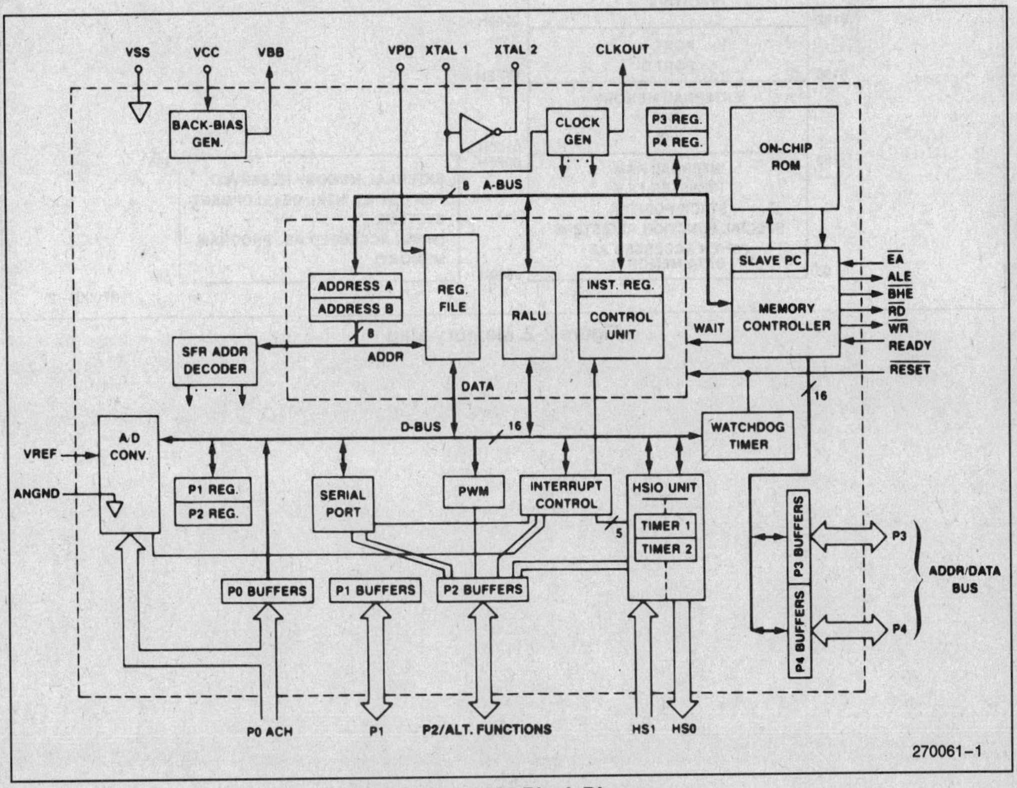

Figure 2-1. 8096 Block Diagram

AP-248

2.1.1. CPU SECTION

The CPU of the 8096 uses a 16-bit ALU which operates on a 256-byte register file instead of an accumulator. Any of the locations in the register file can be used for sources or destinations for most of the instructions. This is called a register to register architecture. Many of the instructions can also use bytes or words from anywhere in the 64K byte address space as operands. A memory map is shown in Figure 2-2.

In the lower 24 bytes of the register file are the register-mapped I/O control locations, also called Special Function Registers or SFRs. These registers are used to control the on-chip I/O features. The remaining 232 bytes are general purpose RAM, the upper 16 of which can be kept alive using a low current power-down mode.

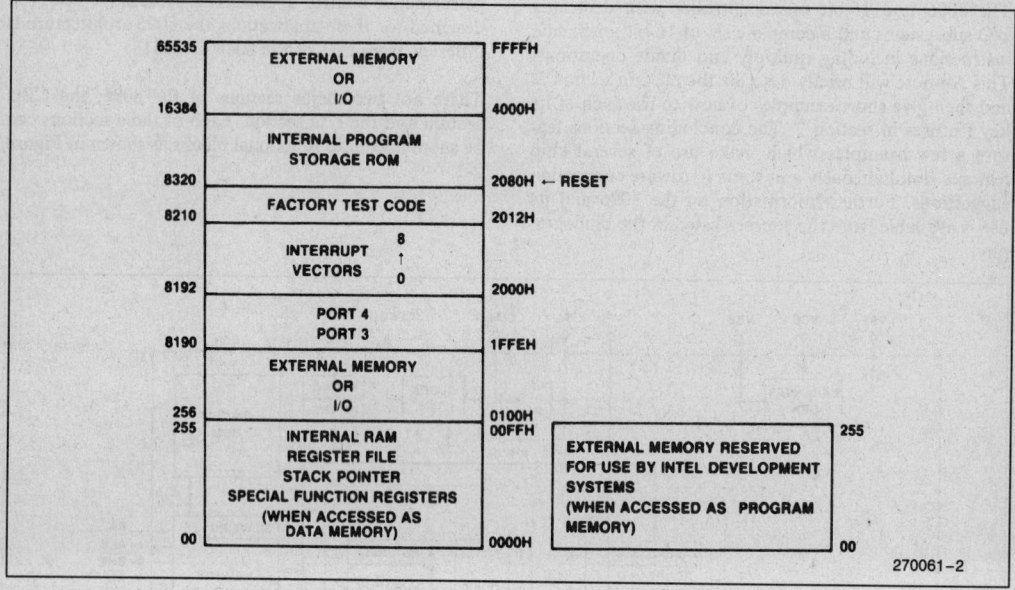

Figure 2-2. Memory Map

AP-248

Figure 2-3 shows the layout of the register mapped I/O. Some of these registers serve two functions, one if they are read from and another if they are written to. More information about the use of these registers is included in the description of the features which they control.

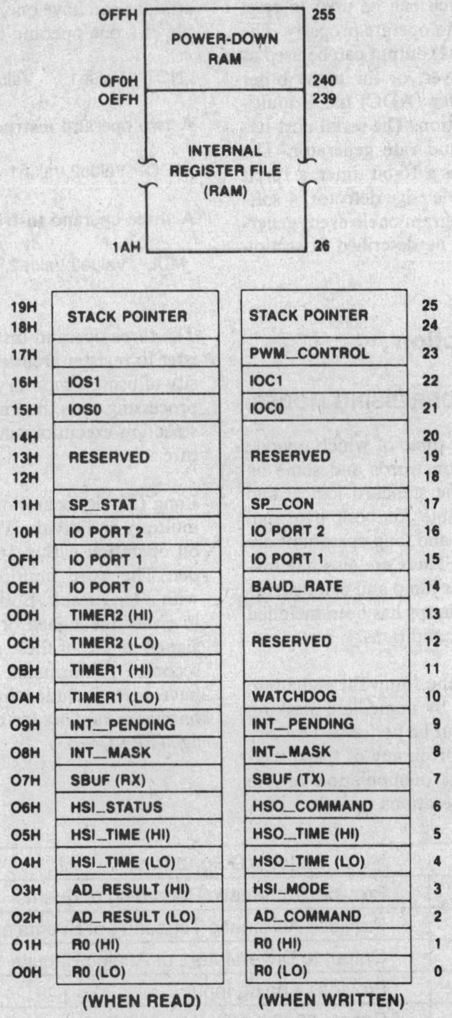

Addr	(WHEN READ)	(WHEN WRITTEN)	#
OFFH–OF0H	POWER-DOWN RAM		255–240
OEFH–1AH	INTERNAL REGISTER FILE (RAM)		239–26
19H / 18H	STACK POINTER	STACK POINTER	25 / 24
17H		PWM_CONTROL	23
16H	IOS1	IOC1	22
15H	IOS0	IOC0	21
14H / 13H / 12H	RESERVED	RESERVED	20 / 19 / 18
11H	SP_STAT	SP_CON	17
10H	IO PORT 2	IO PORT 2	16
0FH	IO PORT 1	IO PORT 1	15
0EH	IO PORT 0	BAUD_RATE	14
0DH	TIMER2 (HI)		13
0CH	TIMER2 (LO)	RESERVED	12
0BH	TIMER1 (HI)		11
0AH	TIMER1 (LO)	WATCHDOG	10
09H	INT_PENDING	INT_PENDING	9
08H	INT_MASK	INT_MASK	8
07H	SBUF (RX)	SBUF (TX)	7
06H	HSI_STATUS	HSO_COMMAND	6
05H	HSI_TIME (HI)	HSO_TIME (HI)	5
04H	HSI_TIME (LO)	HSO_TIME (LO)	4
03H	AD_RESULT (HI)	HSI_MODE	3
02H	AD_RESULT (LO)	AD_COMMAND	2
01H	R0 (HI)	R0 (HI)	1
00H	R0 (LO)	R0 (LO)	0

270061-3

Figure 2-3: SFR Layout

AP-248

2.1.2. I/O FEATURES

Many of the I/O features on the 8096 are designed to operate with little CPU intervention. A list of the major I/O functions is shown in Figure 2-4. The Watchdog Timer is an internal timer which can be used to reset the system if the software fails to operate properly. The Pulse-Width-Modulation (PWM) output can be used as a rough D to A, a motor driver, or for many other purposes. The A to D converter (ADC) has 8 multiplexed inputs and 10-bit resolution. The serial port has several modes and its own baud rate generator. The High Speed I/O section includes a 16-bit timer, a 16-bit counter, a 4-input programmable edge detector, 4 software timers, and a 6-output programmable event generator. All of these features will be described in section 2.3.

2.2. The Processor Section

2.2.1. OPERATIONS AND ADDRESSING MODES

The 8096 has 100 instructions, some of which operate on bits, some on bytes, some on words and some on longs (double words). All of the standard logical and arithmetic functions are available for both byte and word operations. Bit operations and long operations are provided for some instructions. There are also flag manipulation instructions as well as jump and call instructions. A full set of conditional jumps has been included to speed up testing for various conditions.

Bit operations are provided by the Jump Bit and Jump Not Bit instructions, as well as by immediate masking of bytes. These bit operations can be performed on any of the bytes in the register file or on any of the special function registers. The fast bit manipulation of the SFRs can provide rapid I/O operations.

A symmetric set of byte and word operations make up the majority of the 8096 instruction set. The assembly language for the 8096 (ASM-96) uses a "B" suffix on a mnemonic to indicate a byte operation, without this suffix a word operation is indicated. Many of these operations can have one, two or three operands. An example of a one operand instruction would be:

NOT Value1 ;   Value1 : = 1's complement (Value1)

A two operand instruction would have the form:

ADD Value2,Value1 ;   Value2 : = Value2 + Value1

A three operand instruction might look like:

MUL Value3,Value2,Value1 ;
                                  Value3 : = Value2* Value1

The three operand instructions combined with the register to register architecture almost eliminate the necessity of using temporary registers. This results in a faster processing time than machines that have equivalent instruction execution times, but use a standard architecture.

Long (32-bit) operations include shifts, normalize, and multiply and divide. The word divide is a 32-bit by 16-bit operation with a 16-bit quotient and 16-bit remainder. The word multiply is a word by word multiply with a long result. Both of these operations can be done in either the signed or unsigned mode. The direct unsigned modes of these instructions take only 6.5 microseconds. A normalize instruction and sticky bit flag have been included in the instruction set to provide hardware support for the software floating point package (FPAL-96).

	Major I/O Functions
High Speed Input Unit	Provides Automatic Recording of Events
High Speed Output Unit	Provides Automatic Triggering of Events and Real-Time Interrupts
Pulse Width Modulation	Output to Drive Motors or Analog Circuits
A to D Converter	Provides Analog Input
Watchdog Timer	Resets 8096 if a Malfunction Occurs
Serial Port	Provides Synchronous or Asynchronous Link
Standard I/O Lines	Provide Interface to the External World when other Special Features are not needed

Figure 2-4. Major I/O Functions

AP-248

Mnemonic	Operands	Operation (Note 1)	Z	N	C	V	VT	ST	Notes
ADD/ADDB	2	D ← D + A	✔	✔	✔	✔	↑	—	
ADD/ADDB	3	D ← B + A	✔	✔	✔	✔	↑	—	
ADDC/ADDCB	2	D ← D + A + C	↓	✔	✔	✔	↑	—	
SUB/SUBB	2	D ← D − A	✔	✔	✔	✔	↑	—	
SUB/SUBB	3	D ← B − A	✔	✔	✔	✔	↑	—	
SUBC/SUBCB	2	D ← D − A + C − 1	↓	✔	✔	✔	↑	—	
CMP/CMPB	2	D − A	✔	✔	✔	✔	↑	—	
MUL/MULU	2	D, D + 2 ← D * A	—	—	—	—	—	?	2
MUL/MULU	3	D, D + 2 ← B * A	—	—	—	—	—	?	2
MULB/MULUB	2	D, D + 1 ← D * A	—	—	—	—	—	?	3
MULB/MULUB	3	D, D + 1 ← B * A	—	—	—	—	—	?	3
DIVU	2	D ← (D, D + 2)/A, D + 2 ← remainder	—	—	—	✔	↑	—	2
DIVUB	2	D ← (D, D + 1)/A, D + 1 ← remainder	—	—	—	✔	↑	—	3
DIV	2	D ← (D, D + 2)/A, D + 2 ← remainder	—	—	—	?	↑	—	2
DIVB	2	D ← (D, D + 1)/A, D + 1 ← remainder	—	—	—	?	↑	—	3
AND/ANDB	2	D ← D and A	✔	✔	0	0	—	—	
AND/ANDB	3	D ← B and A	✔	✔	0	0	—	—	
OR/ORB	2	D ← D or A	✔	✔	0	0	—	—	
XOR/XORB	2	D ← D (excl. or) A	✔	✔	0	0	—	—	
LD/LDB	2	D ← A	—	—	—	—	—	—	
ST/STB	2	A ← D	—	—	—	—	—	—	
LDBSE	2	D ← A; D + 1 ← SIGN(A)	—	—	—	—	—	—	3, 4
LDBZE	2	D ← A; D + 1 ← 0	—	—	—	—	—	—	3, 4
PUSH	1	SP ← SP − 2; (SP) ← A	—	—	—	—	—	—	
POP	1	A ← (SP); SP ← SP + 2	—	—	—	—	—	—	
PUSHF	0	SP ← SP − 2; (SP) ← PSW; PSW ← 0000H I ← 0	0	0	0	0	0	0	
POPF	0	PSW ← (SP); SP ← SP + 2; I ← ✔	✔	✔	✔	✔	✔	✔	
SJMP	1	PC ← PC + 11-bit offset	—	—	—	—	—	—	5
LJMP	1	PC ← PC + 16-bit offset	—	—	—	—	—	—	5
BR (indirect)	1	PC ← (A)	—	—	—	—	—	—	
SCALL	1	SP ← SP − 2; (SP) ← PC; PC ← PC + 11-bit offset	—	—	—	—	—	—	5
LCALL	1	SP ← SP − 2; (SP) ← PC; PC ← PC + 16-bit offset	—	—	—	—	—	—	5
RET	0	PC ← (SP); SP ← SP + 2	—	—	—	—	—	—	
J (conditional)	1	PC ← PC + 8-bit offset (if taken)	—	—	—	—	—	—	5
JC	1	Jump if C = 1	—	—	—	—	—	—	5
JNC	1	Jump if C = 0	—	—	—	—	—	—	5
JE	1	Jump if Z = 1	—	—	—	—	—	—	5

Figure 2-5. Instruction Summary

NOTES:
1. If the mnemonic ends in "B", a byte operation is performed, otherwise a word operation is done. Operands D, B, and A must conform to the alignment rules for the required operand type. D and B are locations in the register file; A can be located anywhere in memory.
2. D, D + 2 are consecutive WORDS in memory; D is DOUBLE-WORD aligned.
3. D, D + 1 are consecutive BYTES in memory; D is WORD aligned.
4. Changes a byte to a word.
5. Offset is a 2's complement number.

AP-248

Mnemonic	Operands	Operation (Note 1)	Flags						Notes
			Z	N	C	V	VT	ST	
JNE	1	Jump if Z = 0	—	—	—	—	—	—	5
JGE	1	Jump if N = 0	—	—	—	—	—	—	5
JLT	1	Jump if N = 1	—	—	—	—	—	—	5
JGT	1	Jump if N = 0 and Z = 0	—	—	—	—	—	—	5
JLE	1	Jump if N = 1 or Z = 1	—	—	—	—	—	—	5
JH	1	Jump if C = 1 and Z = 0	—	—	—	—	—	—	5
JNH	1	Jump if C = 0 or Z = 1	—	—	—	—	—	—	5
JV	1	Jump if V = 1	—	—	—	—	—	—	5
JNV	1	Jump if V = 0	—	—	—	—	—	—	5
JVT	1	Jump if VT = 1; Clear VT	—	—	—	—	0	—	5
JNVT	1	Jump if VT = 0; Clear VT	—	—	—	—	0	—	5
JST	1	Jump if ST = 1	—	—	—	—	—	—	5
JNST	1	Jump if ST = 0	—	—	—	—	—	—	5
JBS	3	Jump if Specified Bit = 1	—	—	—	—	—	—	5, 6
JBC	3	Jump if Specified Bit = 0	—	—	—	—	—	—	5, 6
DJNZ	1	D ← D − 1; if D ≠ 0 then PC ← PC + 8-bit offset	—	—	—	—	—	—	5
DEC/DECB	1	D ← D − 1	✓	✓	✓	✓	↑	—	
NEG/NEGB	1	D ← 0 − D	✓	✓	✓	✓	↑	—	
INC/INCB	1	D ← D + 1	✓	✓	✓	✓	↑	—	
EXT	1	D ← D; D + 2 ← Sign (D)	✓	✓	0	0	—	—	2
EXTB	1	D ← D; D + 1 ← Sign (D)	✓	✓	0	0	—	—	3
NOT/NOTB	1	D ← Logical Not (D)	✓	✓	0	0	—	—	
CLR/CLRB	1	D ← 0	1	0	0	0	—	—	
SHL/SHLB/SHLL	2	C ← msb ————— lsb ← 0	✓	?	✓	✓	↑	—	7
SHR/SHRB/SHRL	2	0 → msb ————— lsb → C	✓	?	✓	0	—	✓	7
SHRA/SHRAB/SHRAL	2	msb → msb ————— lsb → C	✓	✓	✓	0	—	✓	7
SETC	0	C ← 1	—	—	1	—	—	—	
CLRC	0	C ← 0	—	—	0	—	—	—	
CLRVT	0	VT ← 0	—	—	—	—	0	—	
RST	0	PC ← 2080H	0	0	0	0	0	0	8
DI	0	Disable All Interrupts (I ← 0)	—	—	—	—	—	—	
EI	0	Enable All Interrupts (I ← 1)	—	—	—	—	—	—	
NOP	0	PC ← PC + 1	—	—	—	—	—	—	
SKIP	0	PC ← PC + 2	—	—	—	—	—	—	
NORML	2	Left Shift Till msb = 1; D ← shift count	✓	?	0	—	—	—	7
TRAP	0	SP ← SP − 2; (SP) ← PC PC ← (2010H)	—	—	—	—	—	—	9

Figure 2-5. Instruction Summary (Continued)

NOTES:
1. If the mnemonic ends in "B", a byte operation is performed, otherwise a word operation is done. Operands D, B, and A must conform to the alignment rules for the required operand type. D and B are locations in the register file; A can be located anywhere in memory.
5. Offset is a 2's complement number.
6. Specified bit is one of the 2048 bits in the register file.
7. The "L" (Long) suffix indicates double-word operation.
8. Initiates a Reset by pulling RESET low. Software should re-initialize all the necessary registers with code starting at 2080H.
9. The assembler will not accept this mnemonic.

One operand of most of the instructions can be used with any one of six addressing modes. These modes increase the flexibility and overall execution speed of the 8096. The addressing modes are: register-direct, immediate, indirect, indirect with auto-increment, and long and short indexed.

The fastest instruction execution is gained by using either register direct or immediate addressing. Register-direct addressing is similar to normal direct addressing, except that only addresses in the register file or SFRs can be addressed. The indexed mode is used to directly address the remainder of the 64K address space. Immediate addressing operates as would be expected, using the data following the opcode as the operand.

Both of the indirect addressing modes use the value in a word register as the address of the operand. If the indirect auto-increment mode is used then the word register is incremented by one after a byte access or by two after a word access. This mode is particularly useful for accessing lookup tables.

Access to any of the locations in the 64K address space can be obtained by using the long indexed addressing mode. In this mode a 16-bit 2's complement value is added to the contents of a word register to form the address of the operand. By using the zero register as the index, ASM96 (the assembler) can accept "direct" addressing to any location. The zero register is located at 0000H and always has a value of zero. A short indexed mode is also available to save some time and code. This mode uses an 8-bit 2's complement number as the offset instead of a 16-bit number.

2.2.2. ASSEMBLY LANGUAGE

The multiple addressing modes of the 8096 make it easy to program in assembly language and provide an excellent interface to high level languages. The instructions accepted by the assembler consist of mnemonics followed by either addresses or data. A list of the mnemonics and their functions are shown in Figure 2-5. The addresses or data are given in different formats depending on the addressing mode. These modes and formats are shown in Figure 2-6.

Additional information on 8096 assembly language is available in the MCS-96 Macro Assembler Users Guide, listed in the bibliography.

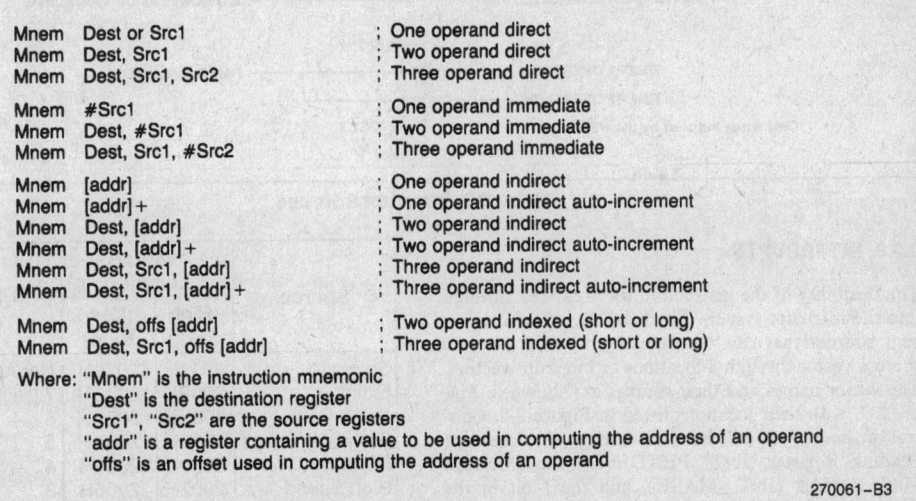

Figure 2-6. Instruction Format

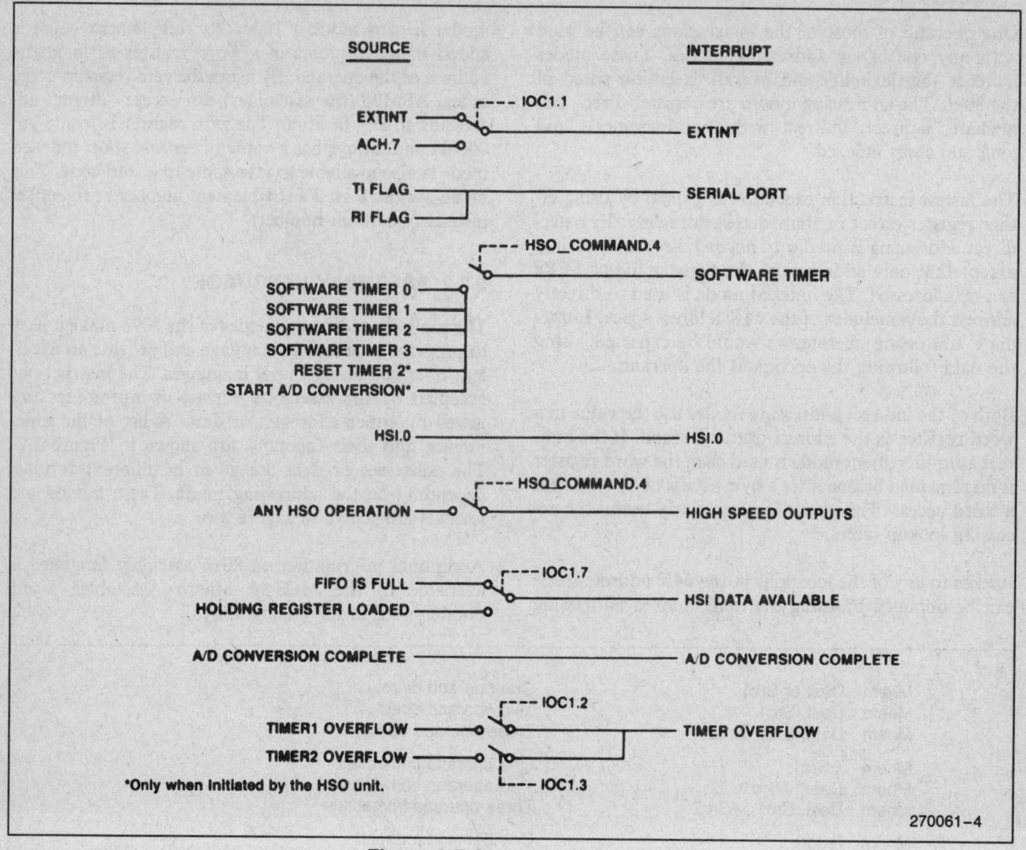

AP-248

Figure 2-7. Interrupt Sources

2.2.3. INTERRUPTS

The flexibility of the instruction set is carried through into the interrupt system. There are 20 different interrupt sources that can be used on the 8096. The 20 sources vector through 8 locations or interrupt vectors. The vector names and their sources are shown in Figure 2-7, with their locations listed in Figure 2-8. Control of the interrupts is handled through the Interrupt Pending Register (INT_PENDING), the Interrupt Mask Register (INT_MASK), and the I bit in the PSW (PSW.9). Figure 2-9 shows a block diagram of the interrupt structure. The INT_PENDING register contains bits which get set by hardware when an interrupt occurs. If the interrupt mask register bit for that source is a 1 and PSW.9 = 1, a vector will be taken to the address listed in the interrupt vector table for that

Source	Vector Location		Priority
	(High Byte)	(Low Byte)	
Software	2011H	2010H	Not Applicable
Extint	200FH	200EH	7 (Highest)
Serial Port	200DH	200CH	6
Software Timers	200BH	200AH	5
HSI.0	2009H	2008H	4
High Speed Outputs	2007H	2006H	3
HSI Data Available	2005H	2004H	2
A/D Conversion Complete	2003H	2002H	1
Timer Overflow	2001H	2000H	0 (Lowest)

Figure 2-8. Interrupt Vectors and Priorities

5-12

AP-248

source. When the vector is taken the INT_PENDING bit is cleared. If more than one bit is set in the INT_PENDING register with the corresponding bit set in the INT_MASK register, the Interrupt with the highest priority shown in Figure 2-8 will be executed.

The software can make the hardware interrupts work in almost any fashion desired by having each routine run with its own setup in the INT_MASK register. This will be clearly seen in the examples in section 4 which change the priority of the vectors in software. The

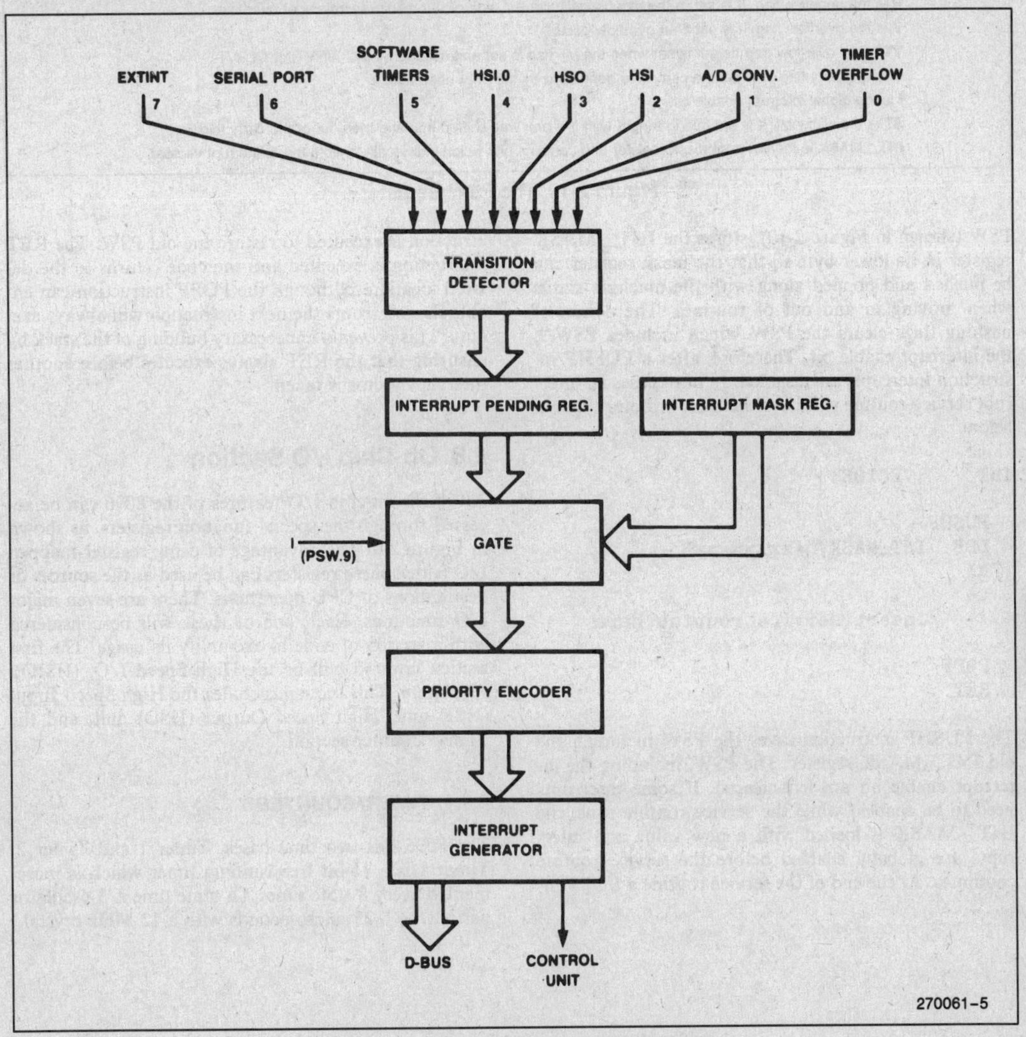

Figure 2-9. Interrupt Structure Block Diagram

270061-5

5-13

AP-248

15	14	13	12	11	10	09	08	07	06	05	04	03	02	01	00
Z	N	V	VT	C	—		I	ST				INT_MASK			

WHERE:

Z is the zero flag. It is set when the result of an operation is zero.

N is the negative flag. It is set to the algebraically correct sign of the result regardless of overflows.

V is the overflow flag. It is set if an overflow occurs.

VT is the overflow trap flag. It is set when the VT flag is set and cleared by JVT, JNVT, or CLRVT.

C is the carry flag. It is set if a carry was generated by the prior operation.

I is the global interrupt enable bit.

ST is the sticky bit. It is set during a right shift if a one was shifted into and then out of the carry flag.

INT_MASK is the interrupt mask register and contains bits which individually enable the 8 interrupt vectors.

Figure 2-10. The PSW Register

PSW (shown in Figure 2-10), stores the INT_MASK register in its lower byte so that the mask register can be pushed and popped along with the machine status when moving in and out of routines. The action of pushing flags clears the PSW which includes PSW.9, the interrupt enable bit. Therefore, after a PUSHF instruction interrupts are disabled. In most cases an interrupt service routine will have the basic structure shown below.

```
INT     VECTOR:

        PUSHF
        LDB     INT_MASK, #xxxxxxxxB
        EI
        -
        -       ;Insert service routine here
        -
        POPF
        RET
```

The PUSHF instruction saves the PSW including the old INT_MASK register. The PSW, including the interrupt enable bit are left cleared. If some interrupts need to be enabled while the service routine runs, the INT_MASK is loaded with a new value and interrupts are globally enabled before the service routine continues. At the end of the service routine a POPF instruction is executed to restore the old PSW. The RET instruction is executed and the code returns to the desired location. Although the POPF instruction can enable the interrupts the next instruction will always execute. This prevents unnecessary building of the stack by ensuring that the RET always executes before another interrupt vector is taken.

2.3. On-Chip I/O Section

All of the on-chip I/O features of the 8096 can be accessed through the special function registers, as shown in Figure 2-3. The advantage of using register-mapped I/O is that these registers can be used as the sources or destinations of CPU operations. There are seven major I/O functions. Each one of these will be considered with a section of code to exemplify its usage. The first section covered will be the High Speed I/O, (HSIO), subsystem. This section includes the High Speed Input (HSI) unit, High Speed Output (HSO) unit, and the Timer/Counter section.

2.3.1. TIMER/COUNTERS

The 8096 has two time bases, Timer 1 and Timer 2. Timer 1 is a 16-bit free running timer which is incremented every 8 state times. (A state time is 3 oscillator periods, or 0.25 microseconds with a 12 MHz crystal.)

AP-248

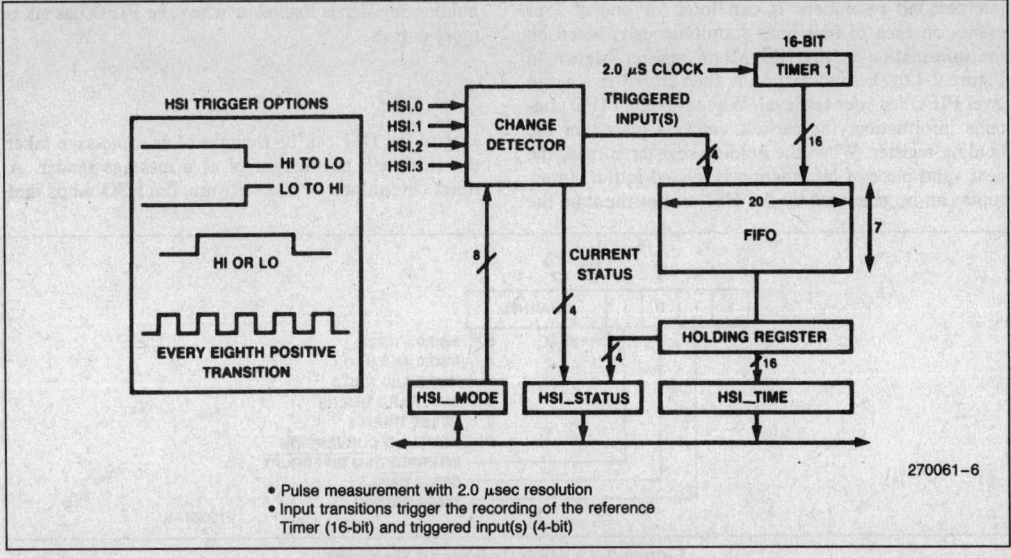

Figure 2-11. HSI Unit Block Diagram

Its value can be read at any time and used as a reference for both the HSI section and the HSO section. Timer 1 can cause an interrupt when it overflows, and cannot be modified or stopped without resetting the entire chip. Timer 2 is really an event counter since it uses an external clock source. Like Timer 1, it is 16-bits wide, can be read at any time, can be used with the HSO section, and can generate an interrupt when it overflows. Control of Timer 2 is limited to incrementing it and resetting it. Specific values can not be written to it.

Although the 8096 has only two timers, the timer flexibility is equal to a unit with many timers thanks to the HSIO unit. The HSI enables one to measure times of external events on up to four lines using Timer 1 as a timer base. The HSO unit can schedule and execute internal events and up to six external events based on the values in either Timer 1 or Timer 2. The 8096 also includes separate, dedicated timers for the baud rate generator and watchdog timer.

2.3.2. HSI

The HSI unit can be thought of as a message taker which records the line which had an event and the time at which the event occurred. Four types of events can trigger the HSI unit, as shown in the HSI block diagram in Figure 2-11. The HSI unit can measure pulse widths and record times of events with a 2

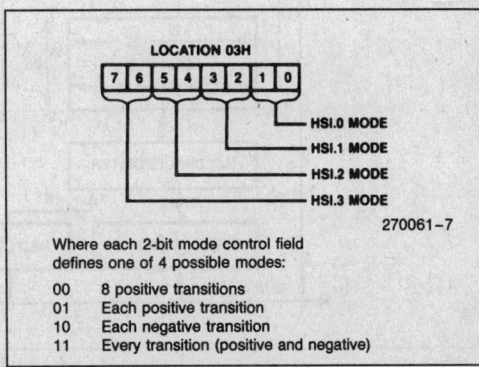

Figure 2-12. HSI Mode Register

AP-248

microsecond resolution. It can look for one of four events on each of four lines simultaneously, based on the information in the HSI Mode register, shown in Figure 2-12. The information is then stored in a seven level FIFO for later retrieval. Whenever the FIFO contains information, the earliest entry is placed in the holding register. When the holding register is read, the next valid piece of information is loaded into it. Interrupts can be generated by the HSI unit at the time the holding register is loaded or when the FIFO has six or more entries.

2.3.3. HSO

Just as the HSI can be thought of as a message taker, the HSO can be thought of as a message sender. At times determined by the software, the HSO sends mes-

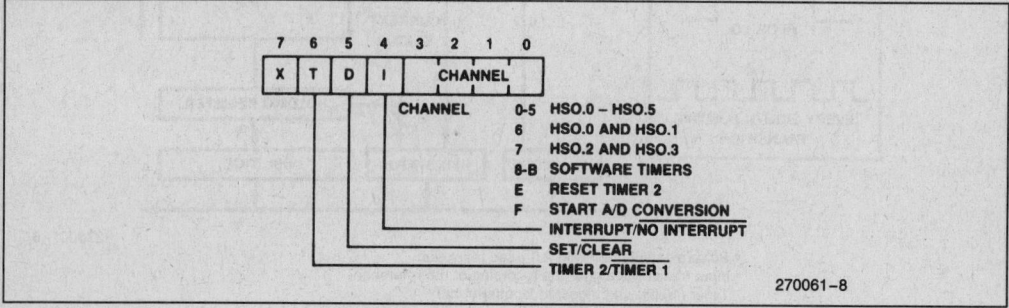

Figure 2-13. HSO Command Register

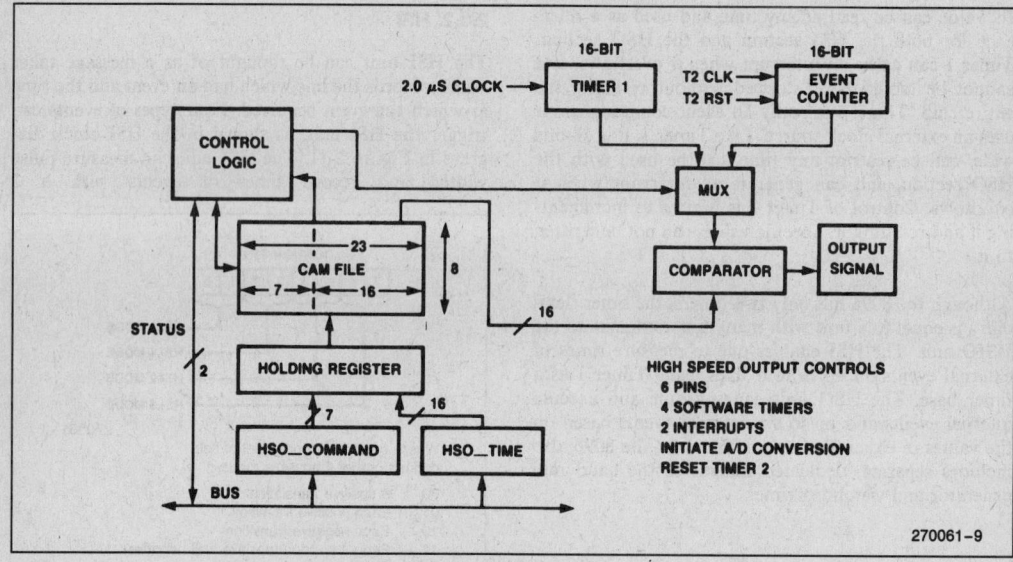

Figure 2-14. HSO Block Diagram

sages to various devices to have them turn on, turn off, start processing, or reset. Since the programmed times can be referenced to either Timer 1 or Timer 2, the HSO makes the two timers look like many. For example, if several events have to occur at specific times, the HSO unit can schedule all of the events based on a single timer. The events that can be scheduled to occur and the format of the command written to the HSO Command register are shown in Figure 2-13.

The software timers listed in the figure are actually 4 software flags in I/O Status Register 1 (IOS1). These flags can be set, and optionally cause an interrupt, at any time based on Timer 1 or Timer 2. In most cases these timers are used to trigger interrupt routines which must occur at regular intervals. A multitask process can easily be set up using the software timers.

A CAM (Content Addressable Memory) file is the main component of the HSO. This file stores up to eight events which are pending to occur. Every state time one location of the CAM is compared with the two timers. After 8 state times, (two microseconds with a 12 MHz clock), the entire CAM has been searched for time matches. If a match occurs the specified event will be triggered and that location of the CAM will be made available for another pending event. A block diagram of the HSO unit is shown in Figure 2-14.

2.3.4. Serial Port

Controlling a device from a remote location is a simple task that frequently requires additional hardware with many processors. The 8096 has an on-chip serial port to reduce the total number of chips required in the system.

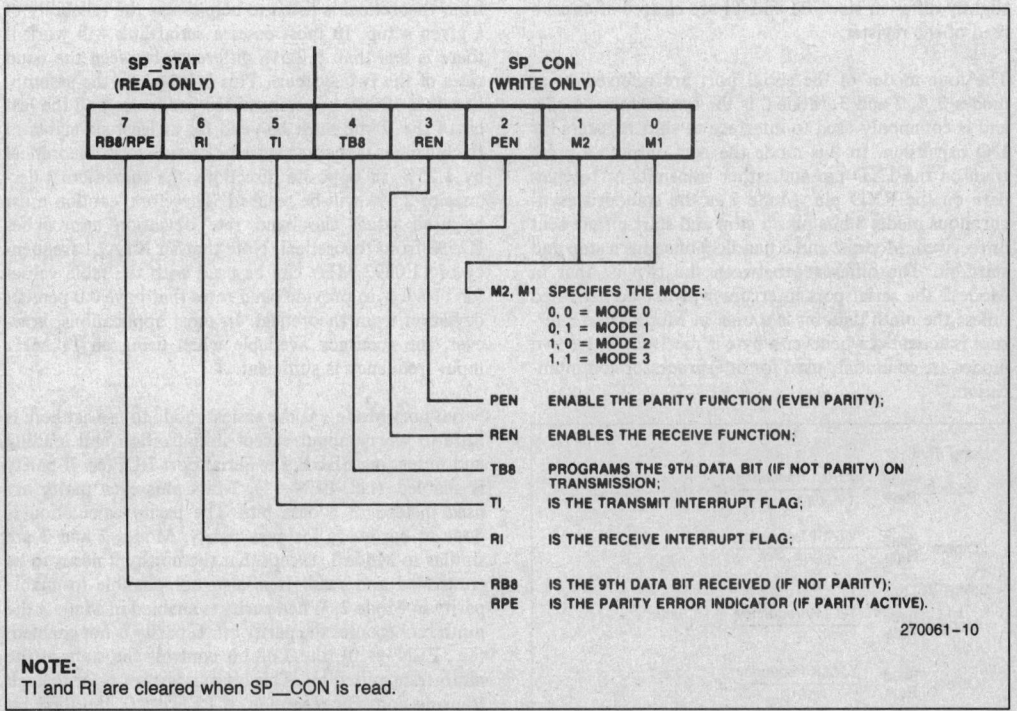

NOTE:
TI and RI are cleared when SP_CON is read.

Figure 2-15. Serial Port Control/Status Register

The serial port is similar to that on the MCS-51 product line. It has one synchronous and three asynchronous modes. In the asynchronous modes baud rates of up to 187.5 Kbaud can be used, while in the synchronous mode rates up to 1.5 Mbaud are available. The chip has a baud rate generator which is independent of Timer 1 and Timer 2, so using the serial port does not take away any of the HSI, HSO or timer flexibility or functionality.

Control of the serial port is provided through the SPCON/SPSTAT (Serial Port CONtrol/Serial Port STATus) register. This register, shown in Figure 2-15, has some bits which are read only and others which are write only. Although the functionality of the port is similar to that of the 8051, the names of some of the modes and control bits are different. The way in which the port is used from a software standpoint is also slightly different since RI and TI are cleared after each read of the register.

The four modes of the serial port are referred to as modes 0, 1, 2 and 3. Mode 0 is the synchronous mode, and is commonly used to interface to shift registers for I/O expansion. In this mode the port outputs a pulse train on the TXD pin and either transmits or receives data on the RXD pin. Mode 1 is the standard asynchronous mode, 8 bits plus a stop and start bit are sent or received. Modes 2 and 3 handle 9 bits plus a stop and start bit. The difference between the two is, that in Mode 2 the serial port interrupt will not be activated unless the ninth data bit is a one; in Mode 3 the interrupt is activated whenever a byte is received. These two modes are commonly used for interprocessor communication.

Baud rates for all of the modes are controlled through the Baud Rate register. This is a byte wide register which is loaded sequentially with two bytes, and internally stores the value as a word. The least significant byte is loaded to the register followed by the most significant. The most significant bit of the baud value determines the clock source for the baud rate generator. If the bit is a one, the XTAL1 pin is used as the source, if it is a zero, the T2 CLK pin is used. The formulas shown in Figure 2-16 can be used to calculate the baud rates. The variable "B" is used to represent the least significant 15 bits of the value loaded into the baud rate register.

The baud rate register values for common baud rates are shown in Figure 2-17. These values can be used when XTAL1 is selected as the clock source for serial modes other than Mode 0. The percentage deviation from theoretical is listed to help assess the reliability of a given setup. In most cases a serial link will work if there is less than a 2.5% difference between the baud rates of the two systems. This is based on the assumption that 10 bits are transmitted per frame and the last bit of the frame must be valid for at least six-eights of the bit time. If the two systems deviate from theoretical by 1.25% in opposite directions the maximum tolerance of 2.5% will be reached. Therefore, caution must be used when the baud rate deviation approaches 1.25% from theoretical. Note that an XTAL1 frequency of 11.0592 MHz can be used with the table values for 11 MHz to provide baud rates that have 0.0 percent deviation from theoretical. In most applications, however, the accuracy available when using an 11 MHz input frequency is sufficient.

Serial port Mode 1 is the easiest mode to use as there is little to worry about except initialization and loading and unloading SBUF, the Serial port BUFfer. If parity is enabled, (i.e., PEN = 1), 7 bits plus even parity are used instead of 8 data bits. The parity calculation is done in hardware for even parity. Modes 2 and 3 are similar to Mode 1, except that the ninth bit needs to be controlled and read. It is also not possible to enable parity in Mode 2. When parity is enabled in Mode 3 the ninth bit becomes the parity bit. If parity is not enabled, (i.e., PEN = 0), the TB8 bit controls the state of the ninth transmitted bit. This bit must be set prior to each transmission. On reception, if PEN = 0, the RB8 bit indicates the state of the ninth received bit. If parity is enabled, (i.e., PEN = 1), the same bit is called RPE (Receive Parity Error), and is used to indicate a parity error.

Using XTAL1:

Mode 0: $\dfrac{\text{Baud}}{\text{Rate}} = \dfrac{\text{XTAL1 frequency}}{4*(B+1)}$; $B \neq 0$

Others: $\dfrac{\text{Baud}}{\text{Rate}} = \dfrac{\text{XTAL1 frequency}}{64*(B+1)}$

Using T2CLK:

Mode 0: $\dfrac{\text{Baud}}{\text{Rate}} = \dfrac{\text{T2CLK frequency}}{B}$; $B \neq 0$

Others: $\dfrac{\text{Baud}}{\text{Rate}} = \dfrac{\text{T2CLK frequency}}{16*B}$; $B \neq 0$

Note that B cannot equal 0, except when using XTAL1 in other than mode 0.

Figure 2-16. Baud Rate Formulas

AP-248

Baud Rate	Baud Register Value	Percent Error
XTAL1 Frequency = 12.0 MHz		
19.2K	8009H	+2.40
9600	8013H	+2.40
4800	8026H	−0.16
2400	804DH	−0.16
1200	809BH	−0.16
300	8270H	0.00
XTAL1 Frequency = 11.0 MHz		
19.2K	8008H	+0.54
9600	8011H	+0.54
4800	8023H	+0.54
2400	8047H	+0.54
1200	808EH	−0.16
300	823CH	+0.01
XTAL1 Frequency = 10.0 MHz		
19.2K	8007H	−1.70
9600	800FH	−1.70
4800	8020H	+1.38
2400	8040H	−0.16
1200	8081H	−0.16
300	8208H	+0.03

Figure 2-17. Baud Rate Values for 10, 11, 12 MHz

The software used to communicate between processors is simplified by making use of Modes 2 and 3. In a basic protocol the ninth bit is called the address bit. If it is set high then the information in that byte is either the address of one of the processors on the link, or a command for all the processors. If the bit is a zero, the byte contains information for the processor or processors previously addressed. In standby mode all processors wait in Mode 2 for a byte with the address bit set. When they receive that byte, the software determines if the next message is for them. The processor that is to receive the message switches to Mode 3 and receives the information. Since this information is sent with the ninth bit set to zero, none of the processors set to Mode 2 will be interrupted. By using this scheme the overall CPU time required for the serial port is minimized.

A typical connection diagram for the multi-processor mode is shown in Figure 2-18. This type of communicaton can be used to connect peripherals to a desk top computer, the axis of a multi-axis machine, or any other group of microcontrollers jointly performing a task.

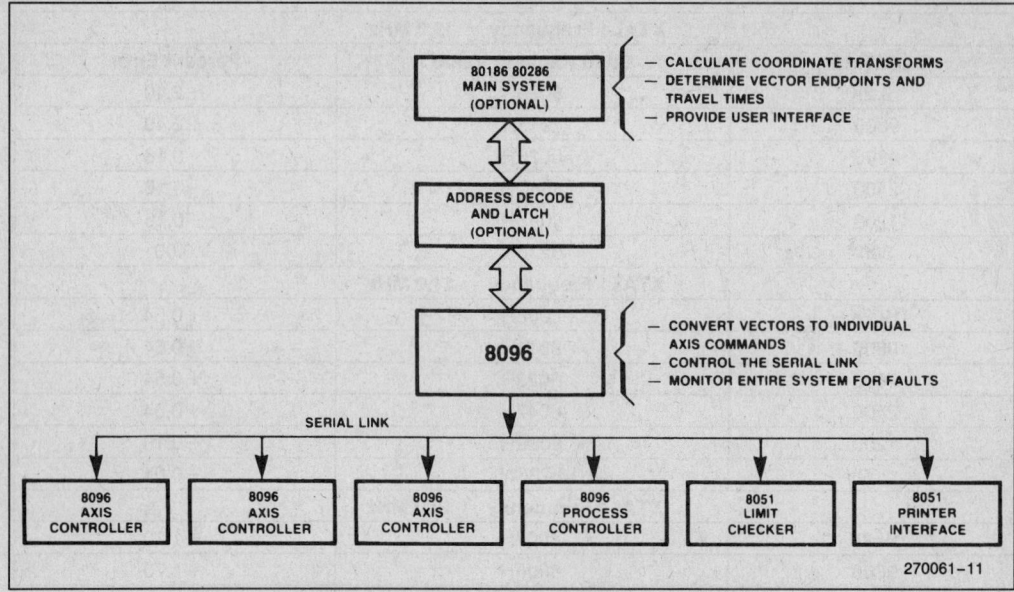

Figure 2-18. Multiprocessor Communication

Mode 0, the synchronous mode, is typically used for interfacing to shift registers for I/O expansion. The software to control this mode involves the REN (Receiver ENable) bit, the clearing of the RI bit, and writing to SBUF. To transmit to a shift register, REN is set to zero and SBUF is loaded with the information. The information will be sent and then the TI flag will be set. There are two ways to cause a reception to begin. The first is by causing a rising edge to occur on the REN bit, the second is by clearing RI with REN = 1. In either case, RI is set again when the received byte is available in SBUF.

2.3.5. A to D CONVERTER

Analog inputs are frequently required in a microcontroller application. The 8097 has a 10-bit A to D converter that can use any one of eight input channels. The conversions are done using the successive approximation method, and require 168 state times (42 microseconds with a 12 MHz clock).

The results are guaranteed monotonic by design of the converter. This means that if the analog input voltage changes, even slightly, the digital value will either stay the same or change in the same direction as the analog input. When doing process control algorithms, it is frequently the changes in inputs that are required, not the absolute accuracy of the value. For this reason, even if the absolute accuracy of a 10-bit converter is the same as that of an 8-bit converter, the 10-bit monotonic converter is much more useful.

Since most of the analog inputs which are monitored by a microcontroller change very slowly relative to the 42 microsecond conversion time, it is acceptable to use a capacitive filter on each input instead of a sample and hold. The 8097 does not have an internal sample and hold, so it is necessary to ensure that the input signal does not change during the conversion time. The input to the A/D must be between ANGND and VREF. ANGND must be within a few millivolts of VSS and VREF must be within a few tenths of a volt of VCC.

Using the A to D converter on the 8097 can be a very low software overhead task because of the interrupt and HSO unit structure. The A to D can be started by the HSO unit at a preset time. When the conversion is complete it is possible to generate an interrupt. By using these features the A to D can be run under complete interrupt control. The A to D can also be directly

AP-248

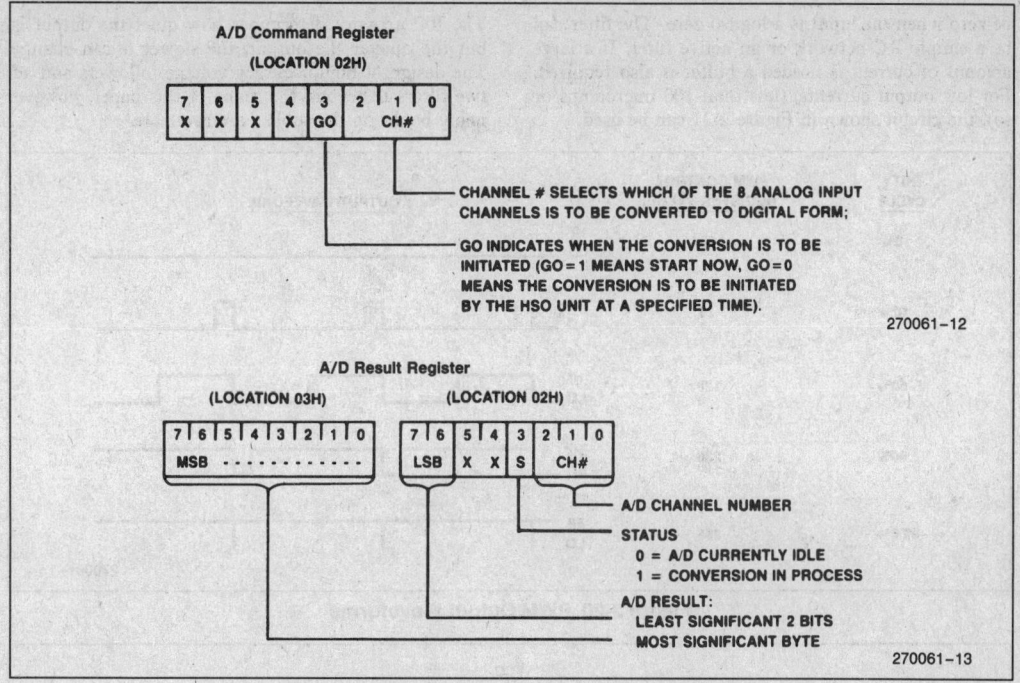

Figure 2-19. A to D Result/Command Register

controlled by software flags which are located in the AD_RESULT/AD_COMMAND Register, shown in Figure 2-19.

2.3.6. PWM REGISTER

Analog outputs are just as important as analog inputs when connecting to a piece of equipment. True digital to analog converters are difficult to make on a microprocessor because of all of the digital noise and the necessity of providing an on chip, relatively high current, rail to rail driver. They also take up a fair amount of silicon area which can be better used for other features. The A to D converter does use a D to A, but the currents involved are very small.

For many applications an analog output signal can be replaced by a Pulse Width Modulated (PWM) signal. This signal can be easily generated in hardware, and takes up much less silicon area than a true D to A. The signal is a variable duty cycle, fixed frequency waveform that can be integrated to provide an approximation to an analog output. The frequency is fixed at a period of 64 microseconds for a 12 MHz clock speed. Controlling the PWM simply requires writing the desired duty cycle value (an 8-bit value) to the PWM Register. Some typical output waveforms that can be generated are shown in Figure 2-20.

Converting the PWM signal to an analog signal varies in difficulty, depending upon the requirements of the system. Some systems, such as motors or switching power supplies actually require a PWM signal, not a true analog one. For many other cases it is necessary only to amplify the signal so that it switches rail-to-rail, and then filter it. Switching rail-to-rail means that the output of the amplifier will be a reference value when the input is a logical one, and the output will be zero when the input is a logical zero. The filter can be a simple RC network or an active filter. If a large amount of current is needed a buffer is also required. For low output currents, (less than 100 microamps or so), the circuit shown in Figure 2-21 can be used.

The RC network determines how quiet the output is, but the quieter the output, the slower it can change. The design of high accuracy voltage followers and active filters is beyond the scope of this paper, however many books on the subject are available.

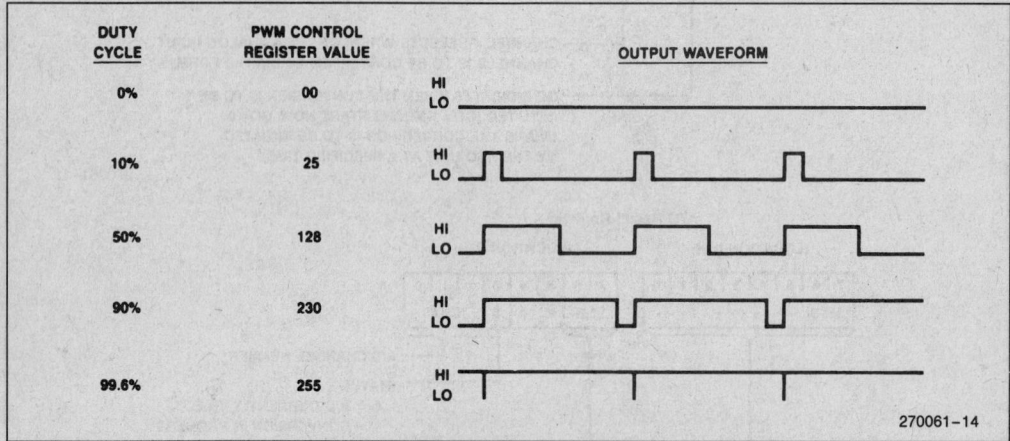

Figure 2-20. PWM Output Waveforms

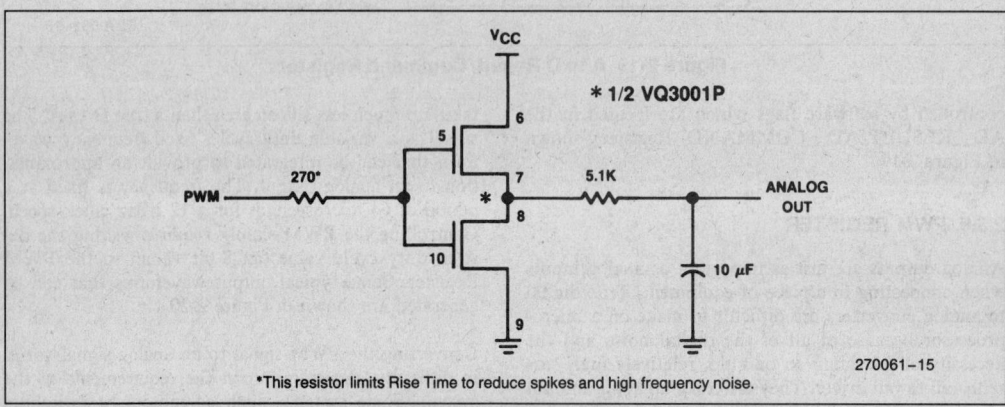

*This resistor limits Rise Time to reduce spikes and high frequency noise.

Figure 2-21. PWM to Analog Conversion Circuitry

AP-248

3.0 BASIC SOFTWARE EXAMPLES

The examples in this section show how to use each I/O feature individually. Examples of using more than one feature at a time are described in section 4. All of the examples in this ap-note are set up to be used as listed. If run through ASM96 they will load and run on an SBE-96. In order to insure that the programs work, the stack pointer is initialized at the beginning of each program. If the programs are going to be used as modules of other programs, the stack pointer initialization should only be used at the beginning of the main program.

To avoid repetitive declarations the "include" file "DEMO96.INC", shown in Listing 3-1, is used. ASM-96 will insert this file into the code file whenever the directive "INCLUDE DEMO96.INC" is used. The file contains the definitions for the SFRs and other variables. The include statement has been placed in all of the examples. It should be noted that some of the labels in this file are different from those in the file 8096.INC that is provided in the ASM-96 package.

3.1. Using the 8096's Processing Section

3.1.1. TABLE INTERPOLATION

A good way of increasing speed for many processing tasks is to use table lookup with interpolation. This can eliminate lengthy calculations in many algorithms. Frequently it is used in programs that generate sine waveforms, use exponents in calculations, or require some non-linear function of a given input variable. Table lookup can also be used without interpolation to determine the output state of I/O devices for a given state of a set of input devices. The procedure is also a good example of 8096 code as it uses many of the software features. Two ways of making a lookup table are described, one way uses more calculation time, the second way uses more table space.

```
;****************************************************************
;
; DEMO96.INC - DEFINITION OF SYMBOLIC NAMES FOR THE I/O REGISTERS OF THE 8096
;
;****************************************************************
;
ZERO            EQU     00H:WORD        ; R/W
AD_COMMAND      EQU     02H:BYTE        ;   W
AD_RESULT_LO    EQU     02H:BYTE        ; R
AD_RESULT_HI    EQU     03H:BYTE        ; R
HSI_MODE        EQU     03H:BYTE        ;   W
HSO_TIME        EQU     04H:WORD        ;   W
HSI_TIME        EQU     04H:WORD        ; R
HSO_COMMAND     EQU     06H:BYTE        ;   W
HSI_STATUS      EQU     06H:BYTE        ; R
SBUF            EQU     07H:BYTE        ; R/W
INT_MASK        EQU     08H:BYTE        ; R/W
INT_PENDING     EQU     09H:BYTE        ; R/W
SPCON           EQU     11H:BYTE
SPSTAT          EQU     11H:BYTE
WATCHDOG        EQU     0AH:BYTE        ;   W  WATCHDOG TIMER
TIMER1          EQU     0AH:WORD        ; R
TIMER2          EQU     0CH:WORD        ; R
PORT0           EQU     0EH:BYTE        ; R
BAUD_REG        EQU     0EH:BYTE        ;   W
PORT1           EQU     0FH:BYTE        ; R/W
PORT2           EQU     10H:BYTE        ; R/W
IOC0            EQU     15H:BYTE        ;   W
IOS0            EQU     15H:BYTE        ; R
IOC1            EQU     16H:BYTE        ;   W
IOS1            EQU     16H:BYTE        ; R
PWM_CONTROL     EQU     17H:BYTE        ;   W
SP              EQU     18H:WORD        ; R/W  STACK POINTER


RSEG at 1CH
        AX:     DSW     1
        DX:     DSW     1
        BX:     DSW     1
        CX:     DSW     1

        AL      EQU     AX        :BYTE
        AH      EQU     (AX+1)    :BYTE
```

Listing 3-1. Include File DEMO.96.INC

AP-248

In both methods the procedure is similar. Values of a function are stored in memory for specific input values. To compute the output function for an input that is not listed, a linear approximation is made based on the nearest inputs and nearest outputs. As an example, consider the table below.

If the input value was one of those listed then there would be no problem. Unfortunately the real world is never so kind. The input number will probably be 259 or something similar. If this is the case linear interpolation would provide a reasonable result. The formula is:

$$\text{Delta Out} = \frac{\text{UpperOutput-Lower Output}}{\text{Upper Input-Lower Input}} * (\text{Actual Input-Lower Input})$$

Actual Output = Lower Output + Delta Out
For the value of 259 the solution is:

$$\text{Delta Out} = \frac{900-400}{300-200} * (259-200) = \frac{500}{100} * 59 = 5 * 59 = 295$$

Actual Output = 400 + 295 = 695

To make the algorithm easier, (and therefore faster), it is appropriate to limit the range and accuracy of the function to only what is needed. It is also advantageous to make the input step (Upper Input-Lower Input) equal to a power of 2. This allows the substitution of multiple right shifts for a divide operation, thus speeding up throughput. The 8096 allows multiple arithmetic right shifts with a single instruction providing a very fast divide if the divisor is a power of two.

For the purpose of an example, a program with a 12-bit output and an 8-bit input has been written. An input step of 16 (2**4) was selected. To cover the input range 17 words are needed, 255/16 + 1 word to handle values in the last 15 bytes of input range. Although only 12 bits are required for the output, the 16-bit architecture offers no penalty for using 16 instead of 12 bits.

The program for this example, shown in Listing 3-2, uses the definitions and equates from Listing 3-1, only the additional equates and definitions are shown in the code.

Input Value	Relative Table Address	Table Value
100	0001H	100
200	0002H	400
300	0003H	900
400	0004H	1600

```
$TITLE('INTER1.APT: Interpolation routine 1')
;;;;;;;    8096 Assembly code for table lookup and interpolation
$INCLUDE(:F1:DEMO96.INC)      ; Include demo definitions

    RSEG  at 22H
            IN_VAL:       dsb    1
            TABLE_LOW:    dsw    1
            TABLE_HIGH:   dsw    1
            IN_DIF:       dsw    1          ; Actual Input Value
            IN_DIFB       equ    IN_DIF  ;byte  ; Upper Input - Lower Input
            TAB_DIF:      dsw    1
            OUT:          dsw    1          ; Upper Output - Lower Output
            RESULT:       dsw    1
            OUT_DIF:      dsl    1          ; Delta Out

    CSEG at 2080H
            LD    SP, #100H
```

270061-17

Listing 3-2. ASM-96 Code for Table Lookup Routine 1

AP-248

```
look:      LDB      AL, IN_VAL          ; Load temp with Actual Value
           SHRB     AL, #3              ; Divide the byte by 8
           ANDB     AL, #11111110B      ; Insure AL is a word address
                                        ; This effectively divides AL by 2
                                        ; so AL = IN_VAL/16

           LDBZE    AX, AL              ; Load byte AL to word AX
           LD       TABLE_LOW, TABLE[AX]    ; TABLE_LOW is loaded with the value
                                            ; in the table at table location AX

           LD       TABLE_HIGH, (TABLE+2)[AX]  ; TABLE_HIGH is loaded with the
                                              ; value in the table at table
                                              ; location AX+2
                                              ; (The next value in the table)

           SUB      TAB_DIF, TABLE_HIGH, TABLE_LOW
                                        ; TAB_DIF=TABLE_HIGH-TABLE_LOW

           ANDB     IN_DIFB, IN_VAL, #0FH   ; IN_DIFB=least significant 4 bits
                                            ; of IN_VAL
           LDBZE    IN_DIF, IN_DIFB     ; Load byte IN_DIFB to word IN_DIF
           MUL      OUT_DIF, IN_DIF, TAB_DIF
                                        ; Output_difference =
                                        ; Input_difference*Table_difference
           SHRAL    OUT_DIF, #4         ; Divide by 16 (2**4)
           ADD      OUT, OUT_DIF, TABLE_LOW ; Add output difference to output
                                            ; generated with truncated IN_VAL
                                            ; as input
           SHRA     OUT, #4             ; Round to 12-bit answer
           ADDC     OUT, zero           ; Round up if Carry = 1
no_inc:    ST       OUT, RESULT         ; Store OUT to RESULT
           BR       look                ; Branch to "look:"

cseg       AT 2100H
table:     DCW      0000H, 2000H, 3400H, 4C00H   ; A random function
           DCW      5D00H, 6A00H, 7200H, 7800H
           DCW      7B00H, 7D00H, 7600H, 6D00H
           DCW      5D00H, 4B00H, 3400H, 2200H
           DCW      1000H
END
```

Listing 3-2. ASM-96 Code for Table Lookup Routine 1 (Continued)

If the function is known at the time of writing the software it is also possible to calculate in advance the change in the output function for a given change in the input. This method can save a divide and a few other instructions at the expense of doubling the size of the lookup table. There are many applications where time is critical and code space is overly abundant. In these cases the code in Listing 3-3 will work to the same specifications as the previous example.

```
$TITLE('INTER2.APT: Interpolation routine 2')
;;;;;;;    8096 Assembly code for table lookup and interpolation
;;;;;;;    Using tabled values in place of division

$INCLUDE(:F1:DEMO96.INC) ; Include demo definitions

RSEG    at 24H
        IN_VAL:      dsb    1           ; Actual Input Value
        TABLE_LOW:   dsw    1           ; Table value for function
        TABLE_INC:   dsw    1           ; Incremental change in function
        IN_DIF:      dsw    1           ; Upper Input - Lower Input
        IN_DIFB      equ    IN_DIF :byte
        OUT:         dsw    1
        RESULT:      dsw    1
        OUT_DIF:     dsl    1           ; Delta Out
```

Listing 3-3. ASM-96 Code For Table Lookup Routine 2

AP-248

```
        CSEG at 2080H
                LD      SP, #100H         ; Initialize SP to top of reg. file
    look:       LDB     AL, IN_VAL        ; Load temp with Actual Value
                SHRB    AL, #3            ; Divide the byte by 8
                ANDB    AL, #11111110B    ; Insure AL is a word address
                                          ; This effectively divides AL by 2
                                          ; so AL = IN_VAL/16
                LDBZE   AX, AL            ; Load byte AL to word AX
                LD      TABLE_LOW, VAL_TABLE[AX] ; TABLE_LOW is loaded with the value
                                          ; in the value table at location AX
                LD      TABLE_INC, INC_TABLE[AX] ; TABLE_INC is loaded with the value
                                          ; in the increment table at
                                          ; location AX
                ANDB    IN_DIFB, IN_VAL, #0FH ; IN_DIFB=least significant 4 bits
                                          ; of IN_VAL
                LDBZE   IN_DIF, IN_DIFB   ; Load byte IN_DIFB to word IN_DIF
                MUL     OUT_DIF, IN_DIF, TABLE_INC
                                          ; Output_difference =
                                          ; Input_difference*Incremental_change
                ADD     OUT, OUT_DIF, TABLE_LOW ; Add output difference to output
                                          ; generated with truncated IN_VAL
                                          ; as input
                SHR     OUT, #4           ; Round to 12-bit answer
                ADDC    OUT, zero         ; Round up if Carry = 1
    no_inc:     ST      OUT, RESULT       ; Store OUT to RESULT
                BR      look              ; Branch to "look:"
        cseg    AT 2100H
        val_table:
                DCW     0000H, 2000H, 3400H, 4C00H  ; A random function
                DCW     5D00H, 6A00H, 7200H, 7800H
                DCW     7B00H, 7D00H, 7600H, 6D00H
                DCW     5D00H, 4B00H, 3400H, 2200H
                DCW     1000H
        inc_table:
                DCW     0200H, 0140H, 0180H, 0110H  ; Table of incremental
                DCW     00D0H, 0080H, 0060H, 0030H  ; differences
                DCW     00020H, 0FF90H, 0FF70H, 0FF00H
                DCW     0FEE0H, 0FE90H, 0FEE0H, 0FEE0H
        END
                                                                  270061-20
```

Listing 3-3. ASM-96 Code for Table Lookup Routine 2 (Continued)

By making use of the second lookup table, one word of RAM was saved and 16 state times. In most cases this time savings would not make much of a difference, but when pushing the processor to the limit, microseconds can make or break a design.

3.1.2. PL/M-96

Intel provides high level language support for most of its micro processors and microcontrollers in the form of PL/M. Specifically, PL/M refers to a family of languages, each similar in syntax, but specialized for the device for which it generates code. The PL/M syntax is similar to PL/1, and is easy to learn. PLM-96 is the version of PL/M used for the 8096. It is very code efficient as it was written specifically for the MCS-96 family. PLM-96 most closely resembles PLM-86, although it has bit and I/O functions similar to PLM-51. One line of PL/M-code can take the place of many lines of assembly code. This is advantageous to the programmer, since code can usually be written at a set number of lines per hour, so the less lines of code that need to be written, the faster the task can be completed.

If the first example of interpolation is considered, the PLM-96 code would be written as shown in Listing 3-4. Note that version 1.0 of PLM-96 does not support 32-bit results of 16 by 16 multiplies, so the ASM-96 procedure "DMPY" is used. Procedure DMPY, shown in Listing 3-5, must be assembled and linked with the compiled PLM-96 program using RL-96, the relocator and linker. The command line to be used is:

RL96 PLMEX1.OBJ, DMPY.OBJ, PLM96.LIB & to PLMOUT.OBJ ROM (2080H-3FFFH)

5-26

AP-248

```
/* PLM-96 CODE FOR TABLE LOOK-UP AND INTERPOLATION */
PLMEX:   DO;
DECLARE IN_VAL           WORD     PUBLIC;
DECLARE TABLE_LOW        INTEGER  PUBLIC;
DECLARE TABLE_HIGH       INTEGER  PUBLIC;
DECLARE TABLE_DIF        INTEGER  PUBLIC;
DECLARE OUT              INTEGER  PUBLIC;
DECLARE RESULT           INTEGER  PUBLIC;
DECLARE OUT_DIF          LONGINT  PUBLIC;
DECLARE TEMP             WORD     PUBLIC;

DECLARE TABLE(17)        INTEGER DATA (
        0000H, 2000H, 3400H, 4C00H,         /* A random function */
        5D00H, 6A00H, 7200H, 7800H,
        7B00H, 7D00H, 7600H, 6D00H,
        5D00H, 4B00H, 3400H, 2200H,
        1000H);

DMPY:    PROCEDURE (A,B) LONGINT EXTERNAL;
         DECLARE (A,B) INTEGER;
END DMPY;

LOOP:
    TEMP=SHR(IN_VAL,4);          /* TEMP is the most significant 4 bits of IN_VAL */

    TABLE_LOW=TABLE(TEMP);       /* If "TEMP" was replaced by "SHR(IN_VAL,4)"   */
    TABLE_HIGH=TABLE(TEMP+1);    /* The code would work but the 8096 would      */
                                 /* do two shifts                               */

    TABLE_DIF=TABLE_HIGH-TABLE_LOW;

    OUT_DIF=DMPY(TABLE_DIF,SIGNED(IN_VAL AND 0FH)) /16;

    OUT=SAR((TABLE_LOW+OUT_DIF),4); /* SAR performs an arithmetic right shift, */
                                    /*    in this case 4 places are shifted   */

    IF CARRY=0 THEN RESULT=OUT;     /* Using the hardware flags must be done   */
       ELSE     RESULT=OUT+1;       /* with care to ensure the flag is tested  */
                                    /* in the desired instruction sequence    */
GOTO LOOP;

/* END OF PLM-96 CODE */

END;
```

Listing 3-4. PLM-96 Code For Table Lookup Routine 1

```
         $TITLE('MULT.APT: 16*16 multiply procedure for PLM-96')

         SP      EQU     18H:word
rseg
         EXTRN   PLMREG  :long
cseg
         PUBLIC  DMPY            ; Multiply two integers and return a
                                 ; longint result in AX, DX registers
DMPY:    POP     PLMREG+4        ; Load return address
         POP     PLMREG          ; Load one operand
         MUL     PLMREG,[SP]+    ; Load second operand and increment SP
         BR      [PLMREG+4]      ; Return to PLM code.
END
```

Listing 3-5. 32-Bit Result Multiply Procedure For PLM-96

AP-248

Using PLM, code requires less lines, is much faster to write, and easier to maintain, but may take slightly longer to run. For this example, the assembly code generated by the PLM-96 compiler takes 56.75 microseconds to run instead of 30.75 microseconds. If PLM-96 performed the 32-bit result multiply instead of using the ASM-96 routine the PLM code would take 41.5 microseconds to run. The actual code listings are shown in Appendix A.

3.2. Using the I/O Section

3.2.1. USING THE HSI UNIT

One of the most frequent uses of the HSI is to measure the time between events. This can be used for frequency determination in lab instruments, or speed/acceleration information when connected to pulse type encoders. The code in Listing 3-6 can be used to determine the high and low times of the signals on two lines. This code can be easily expanded to 4 lines and can also be modified to work as an interrupt routine.

Frequently it is also desired to keep track of the number of events which have occurred, as well as how often they are occurring. By using a software counter this feature can be added to the above code. This code depends on the software responding to the change in line state before the line changes again. If this cannot be guaranteed then it may be necessary to use 2 HSI lines for each incoming line. In this case one HSI line would look for falling edges while the other looks for rising edges. The code in Listing 3-7 includes both the counter feature and the edge detect feature.

The uses for this type of routine are almost endless. In instrumentation it can be used to determine frequency on input lines, or perhaps baud rate for a self adjusting serial port. Section 4.2 contains an example of making a software serial port using the HSI unit. Interfacing to some form of mechanically generated position information is a very frequent use of the HSI. The applications in this category include motor control, precise positioning (print heads, disk drives, etc.), engine control and

```
        $TITLE('PULSE.APT: Measuring pulses using the HSI unit')
        $INCLUDE(DEMO96.INC)
        rseg    at  28H

                HIGH_TIME:      dsw     1
                LOW_TIME:       dsw     1
                PERIOD:         dsw     1
                HI_EDGE:        dsw     1
                LO_EDGE:        dsw     1


        cseg    at  2080H

                LD      SP, #100H
                LDB     IOC0, #00000001B        ; Enable HSI 0
                LDB     HSI_MODE, #00001111B    ; HSI 0 look for either edge
        wait:   ADD     PERIOD, HIGH_TIME, LOW_TIME
                JBS     IOS1, 6, contin         ; If FIFO is full
                JBC     IOS1, 7, wait           ; Wait while no pulse is entered

        contin: LDB     AL, HSI_STATUS          ; Load status; Note that reading
                                                ;    HSI_TIME clears HSI_STATUS

                LD      BX, HSI_TIME            ; Load the HSI_TIME

                JBS     AL, 1, hsi_hi           ; Jump if HSI.0 is high

        hsi_lo: ST      BX, LO_EDGE
                SUB     HIGH_TIME, LO_EDGE, HI_EDGE
                BR      wait

        hsi_hi: ST      BX, HI_EDGE
                SUB     LOW_TIME, HI_EDGE, LO_EDGE
                BR      wait
                END
```

Listing 3-6. Measuring Pulses Using The HSI Unit

AP-248

transmission control. The HSI unit is used extensively in the example in section 4.3.

3.2.2. USING THE HSO UNIT

Although the HSO has many uses, the best example is that of a multiple PWM output. This program, shown in Listing 3-8, is simple enough to be easily understood, yet it shows how to use the HSO for a task which can be complex. In order for this program to operate, another program needs to set up the on and off time variables for each line. The program also requires that a HSO line not change so quickly that it changes twice between consecutive reads of I/O Status Register 0, (IOS0).

A very eye catching example can be made by having the program output waveforms that vary over time. The driver routine in Listing 3-10 can be linked to the above program to provide this function. Linking is accomplished using RL96, the relocatable linker for the 8096. Information for using RL96 can be found in the "MCS-96 Utilities Users Guide", listed in the bibliography. In order for the program to link, the register dec-

```
        $TITLE ('ENHSI.APT: ENHANCED HSI PULSE ROUTINE')
        $INCLUDE(DEMO96.INC)
        RSEG AT 28H

                TIME:           DSW  1
                LAST_RISE:      DSW  1
                LAST_FALL:      DSW  1
                HSI_S0:         DSB  1
                IOS1_BAK:       DSB  1
                PERIOD:         DSW  1
                LOW_TIME:       DSW  1
                HIGH_TIME:      DSW  1
                COUNT:          DSW  1

        cseg    at      2080H
        init:   LD      SP,#100H

                LDB     IOC1,#00100101B  ; Disable HSO.4,HSO.5, HSI_INT-first,
                                         ; Enable PWM,TXD,TIMER1_OVRFLOW_INT

                LDB     HSI_MODE,#10011001B  ; set hsi.1 -; hsi.0 +
                LDB     IOC0,#00000111B      ; Enable  hsi 0,1
                                             ; T2 CLOCK=T2CLK, T2RST=T2RST
                                             ; Clear timer2

        wait:   ANDB    IOS1_BAK,#01111111B  ; Clear IOS1_BAK.7
                ORB     IOS1_BAK,IOS1        ; Store into temp to avoid clearing
                                             ; other flags which may be needed
                JBC     IOS1_BAK,7,wait      ; If hsi is not triggered then
                                             ; jump to wait

                ANDB    HSI_S0,HSI_STATUS,#01010101B
                LD      TIME, HSI_TIME

                JBS     HSI_S0,0,a_rise
                JBS     HSI_S0,2,a_fall
                BR      no_cnt

        a_rise: SUB     LOW_TIME, TIME, LAST_FALL
                SUB     PERIOD, TIME,LAST_RISE
                LD      LAST_RISE, TIME
                BR      increment

        a_fall: SUB     HIGH_TIME, TIME, LAST_RISE
                SUB     PERIOD, TIME,LAST_FALL
                LD      LAST_FALL, TIME

        increment:
                INC     COUNT

        no_cnt: BR      wait

                END
```

270061-24

Listing 3-7. Enhanced HSI Pulse Measurement Routine

5-29

AP-248

```
        $TITLE ('HSOPWM.APT: 8096 EXAMPLE PROGRAM FOR PWM OUTPUTS')

        ; This program will provide 3 PWM outputs on HSO pins 0-2
        ; The input parameters passed to the program are:
        ;
        ;               HSO_ON_N        HSO on time for pin N
        ;               HSO_OFF_N       HSO off time for pin N
        ;
        ;       Where:  Times are in timer1 cycles
        ;               N takes values from 0 to 3

        ;;;;;;;;;;;;;;;;;;;;;;;;;;;;;;;;;;;;;;;;;;;;;;;;;;;;;;;;;

        $INCLUDE(DEMO96.INC)

        RSEG AT 28H

                HSO_ON_0:       DSW     1
                HSO_OFF_0:      DSW     1
                HSO_ON_1:       DSW     1
                HSO_OFF_1:      DSW     1
                OLD_STAT:       dsb     1
                NEW_STAT:       dsb     1


        cseg    AT 2080H

                LD      SP,#100H
                LD      HSO_ON_0, #100H         ; Set initial values
                LD      HSO_OFF_0, #400H        ; Note that times must be long enough
                LD      HSO_ON_1, #280H         ; to allow the routine to run after each
                LD      HSO_OFF_1, #280H        ; line change.
                ANDB    OLD_STAT, IOS0, #0FH
                XORB    OLD_STAT, #0FH

        wait:   JBS     IOS0, 6, wait           ; Loop until HSO holding register
                NOP                             ; is empty

                        ; For operation with interrupts 'store_stat:' would be the
                        ; entry point of the routine.
                        ; Note that a DI or PUSHF might have to be added.

        store_stat:
                ANDB    NEW_STAT, IOS0, #0FH    ; Store new status of HSO
                CMPB    OLD_STAT, NEW_STAT
                JE      wait                    ; If status hasn't changed
                XORB    OLD_STAT, NEW_STAT


        check_0:
                JBC     OLD_STAT, 0, check_1    ; Jump if OLD_STAT(0)=NEW_STAT(0)
                JBS     NEW_STAT, 0, set_off_0

        set_on_0:
                LDB     HSO_COMMAND, #00110000B ; Set HSO for timer1, set pin 0
                ADD     HSO_TIME, TIMER1, HSO_OFF_0 ; Time to set pin = Timer1 value
                BR      check_1                 ;     + Time for pin to be low

        set_off_0:
                LDB     HSO_COMMAND, #00010000B ; Set HSO for timer1, clear pin 0
                ADD     HSO_TIME, TIMER1, HSO_ON_0 ; Time to clear pin = Timer1 value
                                                ;     + Time for pin to be high
        check_1:
                JBC     OLD_STAT, 1, check_done ; Jump if OLD_STAT(1)=NEW_STAT(1)
                JBS     NEW_STAT, 1, set_off_1

        set_on_1:
                LDB     HSO_COMMAND, #00110001B ; Set HSO for timer1, set pin 1
                ADD     HSO_TIME, TIMER1, HSO_OFF_1 ; Time to set pin = Timer1 value
                BR      check_done

        set_off_1:
                LDB     HSO_COMMAND, #00010001B ; Set HSO for timer1, clear pin 1
                ADD     HSO_TIME, TIMER1, HSO_ON_1 ; Time to clear pin = Timer1 value
                                                ;     + Time for pin to be high
        check_done:
                LDB     OLD_STAT, NEW_STAT      ; Store current status and
                                                ; wait for interrupt flag

                BR      wait
                        ; use RET if "wait" is called from another routine

                END
```

Listing 3-8. Generating a PWM with the HSO

AP-248

laration section (i.e., the section between "RSEG" and "CSEG") in Listing 3-8 must be changed to that in Listing 3-9.

The driver routine simply changes the duty cycle of the waveform and sets the second HSO output to a frequency twice that of the first one. A slightly different driver routine could easily be the basis for a switching power supply or a variable frequency/variable voltage motor driver. The listing of the driver routine is shown in Listing 3-10.

```
        ;   NOTE: Use this file to replace the declaration section of
        ;         the HSO PWM program from "$INCLUDE(DEMO96.INC)" through
        ;         the line prior to the label "wait". Also change the last
        ;         branch in the program to a "RET".
        RSEG
            D_STAT:     DSB      1
            extrn   HSO_ON_0  :word , HSO_OFF_0 :word
            extrn   HSO_ON_1  :word , HSO_OFF_1 :word
            extrn   HSO_TIME  :word , HSO_COMMAND :byte
            extrn   TIMER1    :word , IOS0        :byte
            extrn   SP        :word
            public  OLD_STAT
            OLD_STAT:   dsb      1
            NEW_STAT:   dsb      1
        cseg
            PUBLIC  wait
```

Listing 3-9. Changes to Declarations for HSO Routine

```
        $TITLE('HSODRV.APT: Driver module for HSO PWM program')
        HSODRV          MODULE  MAIN, STACKSIZE(8)

                PUBLIC  HSO_ON_0 , HSO_OFF_0
                PUBLIC  HSO_ON_1 , HSO_OFF_1
                PUBLIC  HSO_TIME , HSO_COMMAND
                PUBLIC  SP , TIMER1 , IOS0

        $INCLUDE(DEMO96.INC)

        rseg at 28H

                EXTRN   OLD_STAT        :byte

                HSO_ON_0:       dsw     1
                HSO_OFF_0:      dsw     1
                HSO_ON_1:       dsw     1
                HSO_OFF_1:      dsw     1
                count:          dsb     1

        cseg at 2080H

                EXTRN   wait    :entry

        strt:   DI
                LD      SP, #100H
                ANDB    OLD_STAT, IOS0, #0FH
                XORB    OLD_STAT, #0FH

        initial:
                LD      CX, #0100H

        loop:   LD      AX, #1000H
                SUB     BX, AX, CX
                LD      AX, CX

                ST      AX, HSO_ON_0
                ST      BX, HSO_OFF_0
```

Listing 3-10. Driver Module for HSO PWM Program

```
           SHR      AX,#1
           SHR      BX,#1
           ST       AX, HSO_ON_1
           ST       BX, HSO_OFF_1

           CALL     wait

           INC      CX
           CMP      CX, #00F00H
           BNE      loop

           BR       initial
           END
                                          270061-28
```

Listing 3-10. Driver Module for HSO PWM Program (Continued)

Since the 8096 needs to keep track of events which often repeat at set intervals it is convenient to be able to have Timer 2 act as a programmable modulo counter. There are several ways of doing this. The first is to program the HSO to reset Timer 2 when Timer 2 equals a set value. A software timer set to interrupt at Timer 2 equals zero could be used to reload the CAM. This software method takes up two locations in the CAM and does not synchronize Timer 2 to the external world.

To synchronize Timer 2 externally the T2 RST (Timer 2 ReSeT) pin can be used. In this way Timer 2 will get reset on each rising edge of T2 RST. If it is desired to have an interrupt generated and time recorded when Timer 2 gets reset, the signal for its reset can be taken from HSI.0 instead of T2RST. The HSI.0 pin has its own interrupt vector which functions independently of the HSI unit.

Another option available is to use the HSI.1 pin to clock Timer 2. By using this approach it is possible to use the HSI to measure the period of events on the input to Timer 2. If both of the HSI pins are used instead of the T2RST and T2CLK pins the HSIO unit can keep track of speed and position of the rotating device with very little software overhead. This type of setup is ideal for a system like the one shown in Figure 3-1, and similar to the one used in section 4.3.

In this system a sequence of events is required based on the position of the gear which represents any piece of rotating machinery. Timer 2 holds the count of the number of tooth edges passed since the index mark. By using HSI.1 as the input to Timer 2, instead of T2 CLK, it is possible to determine tooth count and time information through the HSI. From this information instantaneous velocity and acceleration can be calculated. Having the tooth edge count in Timer 2 means

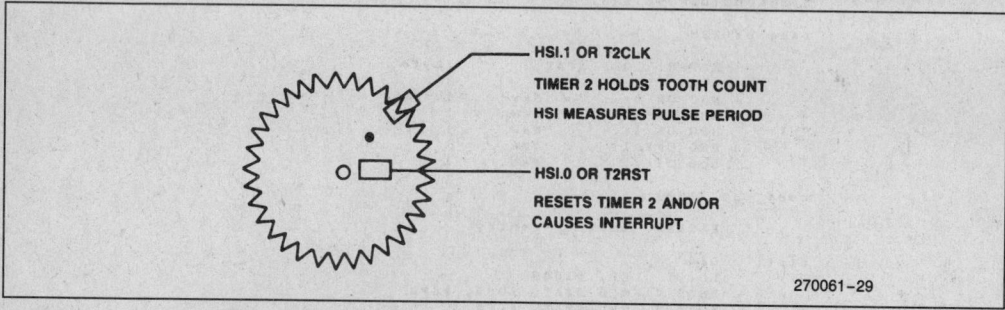

Figure 3-1. Using the HSIO to Monitor Rotating Machinery

AP-248

that the HSO unit can be used to initiate the desired tasks at the appropriate tooth count. The interrupt routine initiated by HSI.0 can be used to perform any software task required every revolution. In this system, the overhead which would normally require extensive software has been done with the hardware on the 8096, thus making more software time available for control programs.

3.2.3. USING THE SERIAL PORT IN MODE 1

Mode 1 of the serial port supports the basic asynchronous 8-bit protocol and is used to interface to most CRTs and printers. The example in Listing 3-11 shows a simple routine which receives a character and then transmits the same character. The code is set up so that minor modifications could make it run on an interrupt basis. Note that it is necessary to set up some flags as initial conditions to get the routine to run properly. If it was desired to send 7 bits of data plus parity instead of 8 bits of data the PEN bit would be set to a one. Interprocessor communication, as described in section 2.3.4, can be set up by simply adding code to change RB8 and the port mode to the listing below. The hardware shown in Figure 3-2 can be used to convert the logic level output of the 8096 to ±12 or 15 volt levels to connect to a CRT. This circuit has been found to work with most RS-232 devices, although it does not conform to strict RS-232 specifications. If true RS-232 conformance is required then any standard RS-232 driver can be used.

```
        $TITLE('SP.APT: SERIAL PORT DEMO PROGRAM')
        $INCLUDE(DEMO96.INC)
        rseg    at 28H

                CHR:      dsb   1
                SPTEMP:   dsb   1
                TEMP0:    dsb   1
                TEMP1:    dsb   1
                RCV_FLAG:       dsb   1

        cseg    at 200CH

                DCW     ser_port_int

        cseg    at 2080H

                LD      SP, #100H
                LDB     IOC1, #00100000B        ; Set P2.0 to TXD

                ; Baud rate = input frequency / (64*baud_val)
                ; baud_val  = (input frequency/64) / baud rate

        baud_val        equ     39              ; 39 = (12,000,000/64)/4800 baud
        BAUD_HIGH       equ     ((baud_val-1)/256) OR 80H    ; Set MSB to 1
        BAUD_LOW        equ     (baud_val-1) MOD 256

                LDB     BAUD_REG, #BAUD_LOW
                LDB     BAUD_REG, #BAUD_HIGH

                LDB     SPCON, #01001001B       ; Enable receiver, Mode 1
                ; The serial port is now initialized

                STB     SBUF, CHR               ; Clear serial Port
                LDB     TEMP0, #00100000B       ; Set TI-temp

                LDB     INT_MASK, #01000000B    ; Enable Serial Port Interrupt
                EI
        loop:   BR      loop                    ; Wait for serial port interrupt

        ser_port_int:
                PUSHF
        rd_again:
                                                ; This section of code can be replaced
                LDB     SPTEMP, SPSTAT          ; with "ORB TEMP0, SP_STAT" when the
                ORB     TEMP0, SPTEMP           ; serial port TI and RI bugs are fixed
                ANDB    SPTEMP,#01100000B
                JNE     rd_again                ; Repeat until TI and RI are properly cleared
```

Listing 3-11. Using the Serial Port in Mode 1

AP-248

```
get_byte:
    JBC     TEMP0, 6, put_byte      ; If RI-temp is not set
    STB     SBUF, CHR               ; Store byte
    ANDB    TEMP0, #10111111B       ; CLR RI-temp
    LDB     RCV_FLAG, #0FFH         ; Set bit-received flag

put_byte:
    JBC     RCV_FLAG, 0, continue   ; If receive flag is cleared
    JBC     TEMP0, 5, continue      ; If TI was not set
    LDB     SBUF, CHR               ; Send byte
    ANDB    TEMP0, #11011111B       ; CLR TI-temp

    ANDB    CHR, #01111111B         ; This section of code appends
    CMPB    CHR, #0DH               ; an LF after a CR is sent
    JNE     clr_rcv
    LDB     CHR, #0AH
    BR      continue

clr_rcv:
    CLRB    RCV_FLAG                ; Clear bit-received flag
continue:
    POPF
    RET

    END
```

Listing 3-11. Using the Serial Port in Mode 1 (Continued)

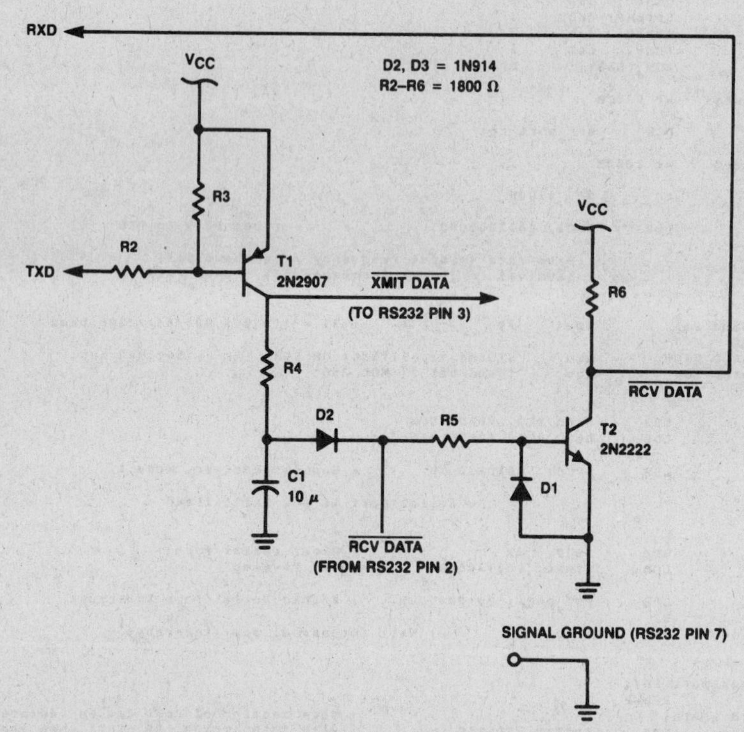

Figure 3-2. Serial Port Level Conversion

3.2.4. USING THE A TO D

The code in Listing 3-12 makes use of the software flags to implement a non-interrupt driven routine which scans A to D channels 0 through 3 and stores them as words in RAM. An interrupt driven routine is shown in section 4.1. When using the A to D it is important to always read the value using the byte read commands, and to give the converter 8 state times to start converting before reading the status bit.

Since there is no sample and hold on the A to D converter it may be desirable to use an RC filter on each input. A 100Ω resistor in series with a 0.22 uf capacitor to ground has been used successfully in the lab. This circuit gives a time constant of around 22 microseconds which should be long enough to get rid of most noise, without overly slowing the A to D response time.

4.0 ADVANCED SOFTWARE EXAMPLES

Using the 8096 for applications which consist only of the brief examples in the previous section does not really make use of its full capabilities. The following examples use some of the code blocks from the previous section to show how several I/O features can be used together to accomplish a practical task. Three examples will be shown. The first is simply a combination of several of the section 3 examples run under an interrupt system. Next, a software serial port using the HSIO unit is described. The concluding example is one of interfacing the HSI unit to an optical encoder to control a motor.

4.1. Simultaneous I/O Routines under Interrupt Control

A four channel analog to PWM converter can easily be made using the 8096. In the example in Listing 4 analog channels are read and 3 PWM waveforms are generated on the HSO lines and one on the PWM pin. Each analog channel is used to set the duty cycle of its associated output pin. The interrupt system keeps the whole program humming, providing time for a background task which is simply a 32 bit software counter. To show which routines are executing and in which

```
        $TITLE('ATOD.APT: SCANNING THE A TO D CHANNELS')
        $INCLUDE(DEMO96.INC)
        RSEG    at  28H
                BL      EQU     BX:BYTE
                DL      EQU     DX:BYTE
        RESULT_TABLE:
                RESULT_1:   dsw     1
                RESULT_2:   dsw     1
                RESULT_3:   dsw     1
                RESULT_4:   dsw     1

        cseg    at  2080H

start:  LD      SP, #100H           ; Set Stack Pointer
        CLR     BX
next:   ADDB    AD_COMMAND,BL, #1000B   ; Start conversion on channel
                                        ; indicated by BL register
        NOP                             ; Wait for conversion to start
        NOP
check:  JBS     AD_RESULT_LO, 3, check  ; Wait while A to D is busy
        LDB     AL, AD_RESULT_LO        ; Load low order result
        LDB     AH, AD_RESULT_HI        ; Load high order result
        ADDB    DL, BL, BL              ; DL=BL*2
        LDBZE   DX, DL
        ST      AX, RESULT_TABLE[DX]    ; Store result indexed by BL*2
        INCB    BL                      ; Increment BL modulo 4
        ANDB    BL, #03H
        BR      next
        END
```

Listing 3-12. Scanning the A to D Channels

AP-248

order, Port 1 output pins are used to indicate the current status of each task. The actual code listing is included in Appendix B.

The initialization section, shown in Listing 4-1a, clears a few variables and then loads the first set of on and off times to the HSO unit. Note that 8 state times must be waited between consecutive loads of the HSO. If this is not done it is possible to overwrite the contents of the CAM holding register. An A/D interrupt is forced by setting the bit in the Interrupt Pending register. This causes the first A/D interrupt to occur just after the Interrupt Mask register is set and interrupts are enabled.

Listing 4-1. Using Multiple I/O Devices

```
        $TITLE ('8096 EXAMPLE PROGRAM FOR PWM OUTPUTS FROM A TO D INPUTS')
        $PAGEWIDTH(130)
        ; This program will provide 3 PWM outputs on HSO pins 0-2
        ; and one on the PWM.
        ;
        ; The PWM values are determined by the input to the A/D converter.
        ;
        ;;;;;;;;;;;;;;;;;;;;;;;;;;;;;;;;;;;;;;;;;;;;;;;;;;;;;;;;;;;;;;
        $INCLUDE(DEMO96.INC)
        RSEG AT 28H

                DL          EQU         DX:BYTE
        ON_TIME:
                PWM_TIME_1: DSW         1
                HSO_ON_0:   DSW         1
                HSO_ON_1:   DSW         1
                HSO_ON_2:   DSW         1

        RESULT_TABLE:
                RESULT_0:   DSW         1
                RESULT_1:   DSW         1
                RESULT_2:   DSW         1
                RESULT_3:   DSW         1

                NXT_ON_T:   DSW         1
                NXT_OFF_0:  DSW         1
                NXT_OFF_1:  DSW         1
                NXT_OFF_2:  DSW         1
                COUNT:      DSL         1
                AD_NUM:     DSW         1       ; Channel being converted
                TMP:        DSW         1
                HSO_PER:    DSW         1
                LAST_LOAD:  DSB         1

        cseg    AT 2000H

                DCW         start               ; Timer_ovf_int
                DCW         Atod_done_int
                DCW         start               ; HSI_data_int
                DCW         HSO_exec_int


        cseg    AT 2080H

        start:  LD          SP, #100H           ; Set Stack Pointer
                CLR         AX
        wait:   DEC         AX                  ; wait approx. 0.2 seconds for
                JNE         wait                ; SBE to finish communications
                CLRB        AD_NUM

                LD          PWM_TIME_1, #080H
                LD          HSO_PER, #100H
                LD          HSO_ON_0, #040H
                LD          HSO_ON_1, #080H
                LD          HSO_ON_2, #0C0H
                ADD         NXT_ON_T, Timer1, #100H
```

Listing 4-1a. Initializing the A to D to PWM Program

```
            LDB     HSO_COMMAND, #00110110B    ; Set HSO for timer1, set pin 0,1
            LD      HSO_TIME, NXT_ON_T         ; with interrupt
            NOP
            NOP
            LDB     HSO_COMMAND, #00100010B    ; Set HSO for timer1, set pin 2
            ADD     HSO_TIME, NXT_ON_T         ; without interrupt

            ORB     LAST_LOAD, #00000111B      ; Last loaded value was set all pins
            LDB     INT_MASK, #00001010B       ; Enable HSO and A/D interrupts
            LDB     INT_PENDING, #00001010B    ; Fake an A/D and HSO interrupt
            EI
loop:       ORB     Port1, #00000001B          ; set P1.0
            ADD     COUNT, #01
            ADDC    COUNT+2,zero
            ANDB    Port1, #11111110B          ; clear P1.0
            BR      loop
```

Listing 4-1a. Initializing the A to D to PWM program (Continued)

```
;;;;;;;;;;;;;;;;;;;;;;;;;;;;;;;;;;;;;;;;;;;;;;;;;;;;;;;;;;;;;;;;
;;;;;;;;;;;;;;;;;;       HSO  EXECUTED  INTERRUPT       ;;;;;;;;;;;;;;;;;;;;;
;;;;;;;;;;;;;;;;;;;;;;;;;;;;;;;;;;;;;;;;;;;;;;;;;;;;;;;;;;;;;;;;

HSO_exec_int:
       PUSHF
       ORB     Port1, #00000010B          ; Set p1.1

       SUB     TMP,TIMER1, NXT_ON_T
       CMP     TMP,ZERO
       JLT     set_off_times

set_on_times:
       ADD     NXT_ON_T, HSO_PER
       LDB     HSO_COMMAND, #00110110B    ; Set HSO for timer1, set pin 0,1
       LD      HSO_TIME, NXT_ON_T
       NOP
       NOP
       LDB     HSO_COMMAND, #00100010B    ; Set HSO for timer1, set pin 2
       LD      HSO_TIME, NXT_ON_T

       ORB     LAST_LOAD, #00000111B      ; Last loaded value was all ones

       LDB     PWM_CONTROL, PWM_TIME_1    ; Now is as good a time as any
                                          ; to update the PWM reg

       BR      check_done

set_off_times:
       JBC     LAST_LOAD, 0, check_done

       ADD     NXT_OFF_0, NXT_ON_T, HSO_ON_0
       LDB     HSO_COMMAND, #00010000B    ; Set HSO for timer1, clear pin 0
       LD      HSO_TIME, NXT_OFF_0

       NOP
       ADD     NXT_OFF_1, NXT_ON_T, HSO_ON_1
       LDB     HSO_COMMAND, #00010001B    ; Set HSO for timer1, clear pin 1
       LD      HSO_TIME, NXT_OFF_1

       NOP
       ADD     NXT_OFF_2, NXT_ON_T, HSO_ON_2
       LDB     HSO_COMMAND, #00010010B    ; Set HSO for timer1, clear pin 2
       LD      HSO_TIME, NXT_OFF_2

       ANDB    LAST_LOAD, #11111000B      ; Last loaded value was all 0s

check_done:
       ANDB    Port1, #11111101B          ; Clear P1.1
       POPF
       RET
```

Listing 4-1b. Interrupt Driven HSO Routine

AP-248

```
;;;;;;;;;;;;;;;;;;;;;;;;;;;;;;;;;;;;;;;;;;;;;;;;;;;;;;;;;;;;;;;;;;;;;;;;;;;;;
;;;;;;;;;;;;;;;;;;              A TO D COMPLETE INTERRUPT           ;;;;;;;;;;;;;;;;;;;;;;;;
;;;;;;;;;;;;;;;;;;;;;;;;;;;;;;;;;;;;;;;;;;;;;;;;;;;;;;;;;;;;;;;;;;;;;;;;;;;;;

ATOD_done_int:
        PUSHF
        ORB     Port1, #00000100B           ; Set P1.2

        ANDB    AL, AD_RESULT_LO,#11000000B ; Load low order result
        LDB     AH, AD_RESULT_HI            ; Load high order result
        ADDB    DL, AD_NUM, AD_NUM          ; DL= AD_NUM *2
        LDBZE   DX, DL
        ST      AX, RESULT_TABLE[DX]        ; Store result indexed by DX

        CMPB    AL, #01000000B
        JNH     no_rnd                      ; Round up if needed
        CMPB    AH,#0FFH                    ; Don't increment if AH=0FFH
        JE      no_rnd
        INCB    AH

no_rnd: LDB     AL, AH                      ; Align byte and change to word
        CLRB    AH
        ST      AX, ON_TIME[DX]

        INCB    AD_NUM
        ANDB    AD_NUM, #03H                ; Keep AD_NUM between 0 and 3

next:   ADDB    AD_COMMAND, AD_NUM, #1000B  ; Start conversion on channel
                                            ; indicated by AD_NUM register
        ANDB    Port1, #11111011B           ; Clear P1.2
        POPF
        RET

        END
```

Listing 4-1c. Interrupt Driven A to D Routine

The HSO routine shown in Listing 4-1b is slightly different than the one in section 3. All of the HSO lines turn on at the same time, only the turn-off-time is varied between lines. This action is what is most commonly required for multiple PWM outputs and simplifies the software. A comparison is made between Timer1 and the next HSO turn on time at the beginning of the routine. If the next turn on time has passed, then the on-times are loaded into the CAM, otherwise the off times are loaded.

The maximum number of events in the CAM at any given time is 7. This occurs when the first line to turn off does so, causing the off-times for all of the lines to be loaded. For two of the lines there will be an offtime, an on-time, and the just loaded off-time. The other line (the one that just turned off) will have only the on-time and the just loaded off-time.

A/D conversions are performed by the code in Listing 4-1c about every 60 microseconds, 42 for the conversion, the rest for overhead. The A/D routine sets up the HSO and PWM on and off times. Since the A/D has a ten bit output, the most significant 8 bits are rounded up or down based on the least significant two bits.

4.2. Software Serial Port Using the HSIO Unit

There are many systems which require more than one serial port, an example is a system which must communicate with other computers and have an additional port for a local console. If the on-board UART is being used as an inter-processor link, the HSIO unit can be used to interface the 8096 to an additional asynchronous line.

Figure 4-1 shows the format of a standard 10-bit asynchronous frame. The start bit is used to synchronize the receiver to the transmitter; at the leading edge of the START bit the receiver must set up its timing logic to sample the incoming line in the center of each bit. Following the start bit are the eight data bits which are transmitted least significant bit first. The STOP bit is set to the opposite state of the START bit to guar-

AP-248

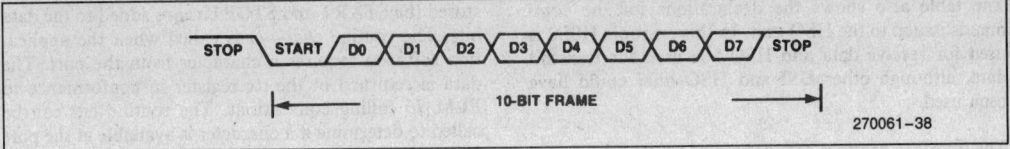

Figure 4-1. 10-bit Asynchronous Frame

antee that the leading edge of the START bit will cause a transition on the line; it also provides for a dead time on the line so that the receiver can maintain its synchronization.

The remainder of this section will show how a full-duplex asynchronous port can be built from the HSIO unit. There are four sections to this code:

1. Interface routines. These routines provide a procedural interface between the interrupt driven core of the software serial port and the remainder of the application software.
2. Initialization routine. This routine is called during the initialization of the overall system and sets up the various variables used by the software port.
3. Transmit ISR. This routine runs as an ISR (interrupt service routine) in response to an HSO interrupt interrupt. Its function is to serialize the data passed to it by the interface routines.
4. Receive ISRs. There are two ISRs involved in the receive process. One of them runs in response to an HSI interrupt and is used to synchronize the receive process at the leading edge of the start bit. The second receive ISR runs in response to an HSO generated software timer interrupt, this routine is scheduled to run at the center of each bit and is used to deserialize the incoming data.

The routines share the set of variables that are shown in Listing 4-2. These variables should be accessed only by the routines which make up the software serial port.

```
;
;            VARIABLES NEEDED BY THE SOFTWARE SERIAL PORT
;            ------------------------------------------------
;
             rseg

rcve_state:    dsb  1
  rxrdy        equ  1        ; indicates receive done
  rxoverrun    equ  2        ; indicates receive overflow
  rip          equ  4        ; receive in progress flag
rcve_buf:      dsb  1        ; used to double buffer receive data
rcve_reg:      dsb  1        ; used to deserialize receive
sample_time:   dsw  1        ; records last receive sample time

serial_out:    dsw  1        ; Holds the output character+framing (start and
                             ;   stop bits) for transmit process.
baud_count:    dsw  1        ; Holds the period of one bit in units
                             ;   of T1 ticks.
txd_time:      dsw  1        ; Transition time of last Txd bit that was
                             ;   sent to the CAM
char:          dsb  1        ; for test only
;
;            COMMANDS ISSUED TO THE HSO UNIT
;            -------------------------------
;
mark_command    equ   0110101b    ; timer1,set,interrupt on 5
space_command   equ   0010101b    ; timer1,clr,interrupt on 5
sample_command  equ   0011000b    ; software timer 0

$eject
```

Listing 4-2. Software Serial Port Declarations

5-39

AP-248

The table also shows the declarations for the commands issued to the HSO unit. In this example HSI.2 is used for receive data and HSO.5 is used for transmit data, although other HSI and HSO lines could have been used.

The interface routines are shown in Listing 4-3. Data is passed to the port by pushing the eight-bit character into the stack and calling *char__out*, which waits for any in-process transmission to complete and stores the character into the variable *serial__out*. As the data is stored the START and STOP bits are added to the data bits. The routine *char—in* is called when the application software requires a character from the port. The data is returned in the *ax* register in conformance to PLM 96 calling conventions. The routine *csts* can be called to determine if a character is available at the port before calling *char__in*. (If no character is available *char__in* will wait indefinitely).

The initialization routine is shown in Listing 4-4. This routine is called with the required baud rate in the

```
;
char_out:
; Output character to the software serial port
;
        pop     cx                      ; the return address
        pop     bx                      ; the character for output
        ldb     (bx+1),#01h             ; add the start and stop bits
        add     bx,bx                   ; to the char and leave as 16 bit
wait_for_xmit:
        cmp     serial_out,0            ; wait for serial_out=0 (it will be cleared by
        bne     wait_for_xmit           ;   the hso interrupt process)
        st      bx,serial_out           ; put the formatted character in serial_out
        br      [cx]                    ; return to caller
;
csts:
; Returns "true" (ax<>0) if char_in has a character.
;
        clr     ax
        bbc     rcve_state,0,csts_exit
        inc     ax
csts_exit:
        ret
;
char_in:
; Get a character from the software serial port
;
                                        ; wait for character ready
        bbc     rcve_state,0,char_in
        pushf                           ; set up a critical region
        andb    rcve_state,#not(rxrdy)
        ldbze   al,rcve_buf
        popf                            ; leave the critical region
        ret
```

Listing 4-3. Software Serial Port Interface Routines

```
;
setup_serial_port:
; Called on system reset to intiate the software serial port.
;
        pop     cx                      ; the return address
        pop     bx                      ; the baud rate (in decimal)
        ld      dx,#0007h               ; dx:ax:=500,000 (assumes 12 Mhz crystal)
        ld      ax,#0A120h
        divu    ax,bx                   ; calculate the baud count (500,000/baudrate)
        st      ax,baud_count
        st      0,serial_out            ; clear serial out
        ldb     iocl,#01100000b         ; Enable HSO.5 and Txd
        bbs     ios0,6,$                ; Wait for room in the HSO CAM
                                        ; and issue a MARK command.
        add     txd_time,timer1,20
        ldb     hso_command,#mark_command
        ld      hso_time,txd_time
        clrb    rcve_buf                ; clear out the receive variables
        clrb    rcve_reg
        clrb    rcve_state
        call    init_receive            ; setup to detect a start bit
        br      [cx]                    ; return
```

Listing 4-4. Software Serial Port Initialization Routine

AP-248

stack; it calculates the bit time from the baud rate and stores it in the variable *baud_count* in units of TIMER1 ticks. An HSO command is issued which will initiate the transmit process and then the remainder of the variables owned by the port are initialized. The routine *init_receive* is called to setup the HSI unit to look for the leading edge of the START bit.

The transmit process is shown in Listing 4-5. The HSO unit is used to generate an output command to the transmit pin once per bit time. If the *serial_out* register is zero a MARK (idle condition) is output. If the *serial_out* register contains data then the least significant bit is output and the register shifted right one place. The framing information (START and STOP bits) are appended to the actual data by the interface routines. Note that this routine will be executed once per bit time whether or not data is being transmitted. It would be possible to use this routine for additional low resolution timing functions with minimal overhead.

The receive process consists of an initialization routine and two interrupt service routines, *hsi_isr* and *software_timer_isr*. The listings of these routines are shown in Listings 4-6a, 4-6b, and 4-6c respectively. The

```
;
hso_isr:
; Fields the hso interrupts and performs the serialization of the data.
; Note: this routine would be incorporated into the hso service strategy for an
;       actual system.

        cseg    at 2006h
        dcw     hso_isr         ; Set up vector

        cseg
        pushf
        add     txd_time,baud_count
        cmp     serial_out,0    ; if character is done send a mark
        be      send_mark
        shr     serial_out,#1   ; else send bit 0 of serial_out and shift
        bc      send_mark       ; serial_out left one place.
send_space:
        ldb     hso_command,#space_command
        ld      hso_time,txd_time
        br      hso_isr_exit
send_mark:
        ldb     hso_command,#mark_command
        ld      hso_time,txd_time

hso_isr_exit:
        popf
        ret
$eject
```

Listing 4-5. Software Serial Port Transmit Process

Listing 4-6. Receive Process

```
;
init_receive:
; Called to prepare the serial input process to find the leading edge of
; a start bit.
;
        ldb     ioc0,#00000000b         ; disconnect change detector
        ldb     hsi_mode,#00100000b     ; negative edges on HSI.2
flush_fifo:
        orb     iosl_save,iosl
        bbc     iosl_save,7,flush_fifo_done
        ldb     al,hsi_status
        ld      ax,hsi_time             ; trash the fifo entry
        andb    iosl_save,#not(80h)     ; clear bit 7.
        br      flush_fifo
flush_fifo_done:
        ldb     ioc0,#00010000b         ; connect HSI.2 to detector
        ret
```

Listing 4-6a. Software Serial Port Receive Initialization

AP-248

```
;
hsi_isr:
; Fields interrupts from the HSI unit, used to detect the leading edge
; of the START bit
; Note: this routine would be incorporated into the HSI strategy of an actual
; system.
;
        cseg at 2004h
        dcw     hsi_isr                 ; setup the interrupt vector

        cseg
        pushf
        push    ax
        ldb     al,hsi_status
        ld      sample_time,hsi_time
        bbc     al,4,exit_hsi
        bbs     ios0,7,$                ; wait for room in HSO holding reg
        ld      ax,baud_count           ; send out sample command in 1/2
        shr     ax,#1                   ; bit time
        add     sample_time,ax
        ldb     hso_command,#sample_command
        st      sample_time,hso_time
        ldb     ioc0,#00000000b         ; disconnect hsi.2 from change detector
exit_hsi:
        pop     ax
        popf
        ret
```

Listing 4-6b. Software Serial Port Start Bit Detect

```
;
software_timer_isr:
; Fields the software timer interrupt, used to deserialize the incoming data.
; Note: this routine would be incorporated into the software timer stategy
; in an actual system.
;
        cseg at 200ah
        dcw     software_timer_isr      ; setup vector

        cseg
        pushf
        orb     ios1_save,ios1
        andb    ios1_save,#not(01h)     ; clear bit 0
        andb    0,rcve_state,#0fch      ; All bits except rxrdy and overrun=0
        bne     process_data
process_start_bit:
        bbc     hsi_status,5,start_ok
        call    init_receive
        br      software_timer_exit
start_ok:
        orb     rcve_state,#rip         ; set receive in progress flag
        br      schedule_sample

process_data:
        bbs     rcve_state,7,check_stopbit
        shrb    rcve_reg,#1
        bbc     hsi_status,5,datazero
        orb     rcve_reg,#80h           ; set the new data bit
datazero:
        addb    rcve_state,#10h         ; increment bit count
        br      schedule_sample

check_stopbit:
        bbc     hsi_status,5,$          ; DEBUG ONLY
        ldb     rcve_buf,rcve_reg
        orb     rcve_state,#rxrdy
        andb    rcve_state,#03h         ; Clear all but ready and overrun bits
        call    init_receive
        br      software_timer_exit

schedule_sample:
        bbs     ios0,7,$                ; wait for holding reg empty
        ldb     hso_command,#sample_command
        add     sample_time,baud_count
        st      sample_time,hso_time

software_timer_exit:
        popf
        ret
```

Listing 4-6c. Software Serial Port Data Reception

5-42

start is detected by the *hsi_isr* which schedules a software timer interrupt in one-half of a bit time. This first sample is used to verify that the START bit has not ended prematurely (a protection against a noisy line). The software timer service routine uses the variable *rcve_state* to determine whether it should check for a valid START bit, deserialize data, or check for a valid STOP bit. When a complete character has been received it is moved to the receive buffer and *init_receive* is called to set up the receive process for the next character. This routine is also called when an error (e.g., invalid START bit) is detected.

Appendix C contains the complete listing of the routines and the simple loop which was used to initialize them and verify their operation. The test was run for several hours at 9600 baud with no apparent malfunction of the port.

4.3. Interfacing an Optical Encoder to the HSI Unit

Optical encoders are among one of the more popular devices used to determine position of rotating equipment. These devices output two pulse trains with edges that occur from 2 to 4000 times a revolution.

Frequently there is a third line which generates one pulse per revolution for indexing purposes. Figure 4-2 shows a six line encoder and typical waveforms. As can be seen, the two waveforms provide the ability to determine both position and direction. Since a microcontroller can perform real time calculations it is possible to determine velocity and acceleration from the position and time information.

Interfacing to the encoder can be an interesting problem, as it requires connecting mechanically generated electrical signals to the HSI unit. The problems arise because it is difficult to obtain the exact nature of the signals under all conditions.

The equipment used in the lab was a Pittman 9400 series gearmotor with a 600 line optical encoder from Vernitech. The encoder has to be carefully attached to the shaft to minimize any runout or endplay. Fortunately, Pitmann has started marketing their motors with ball bearings and optical encoders already installed. It is recommended that the encoder be mounted to the motor using the exact specifications of the encoder manufacturer and/or a good machine shop.

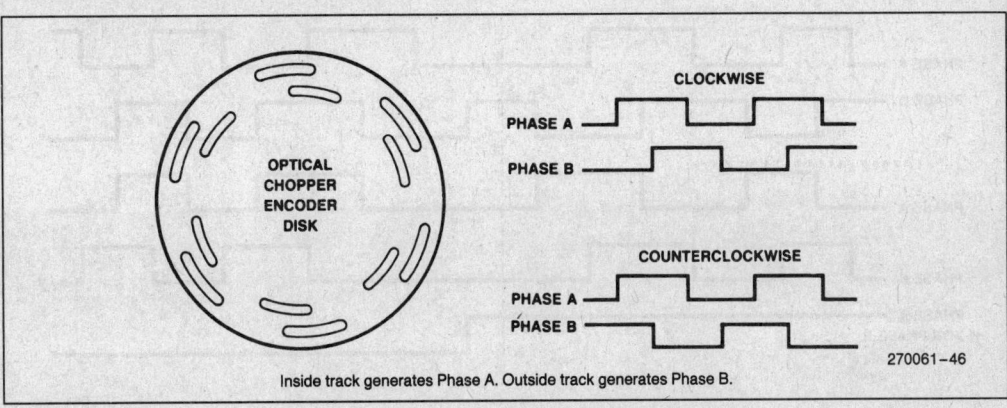

Inside track generates Phase A. Outside track generates Phase B.

Figure 4-2. Optical Encoder and Waveforms

AP-248

Digital filtering external to the 8096 is used on the encoder signals. The idealized signals coming from the encoder and after the digital filter are shown in Figure 4-3. The circuitry connecting the encoder to the 8096 requires only two chips. A one-shot constructed of XOR gates generates pulses on each edge of each signal. The pulses generated by Phase A are used to clock the signal from Phase B and vice versa. The hardware is shown in Figure 4-4. CMOS parts are used to reduce loading on the encoder so that buffers are not needed. Note that T2CLK is clocked on both edges of both filtered phases.

By using this method repetitive edges on a single phase without an edge on the other phase will not be passed on to the 8096. Repetitive edges on a phase can occur when the motor is stopped and vibrates or when it is changing direction. The digital filtering technique causes a little more delay in the signal at slow speeds than an analog filter would, but the simplicity trade off is worthwhile. The net effect of digital filtering is losing the ability to determine the first edge after a direction change. This does not affect the count since the first edge in both directions is lost.

If it is desired to determine when each edge occurs before filtering, the encoder outputs can be attached directly to the 8096. As these would be input signals, Port 0 is the most likely choice for connection. It would not be required to connect these lines to the HSI unit, as the information on them would only be needed when the motor is going very slowly.

The motor is driven using the PWM output pin for power control and a port pin for direction control. The 8096 drives a 7438 which drives 2 opto-isolators. These in turn drive two VFETs. A MOV (Metal Oxide Varistor, a type of transient absorber) is used to protect the VFETs, and a capacitor filters the PWM to get the best motor performance. Figure 4-5 shows the driver circuitry. To avoid noise getting into the 8096 system, the ±15 volt power supply is isolated from the 8096 logic power supply.

This is the extent of the external circuitry required for this example. All of the counting and direction detection are done by the 8096. There are two sections to the example: driving the motor and interfacing to the encoder. The motor driver uses proportional control with

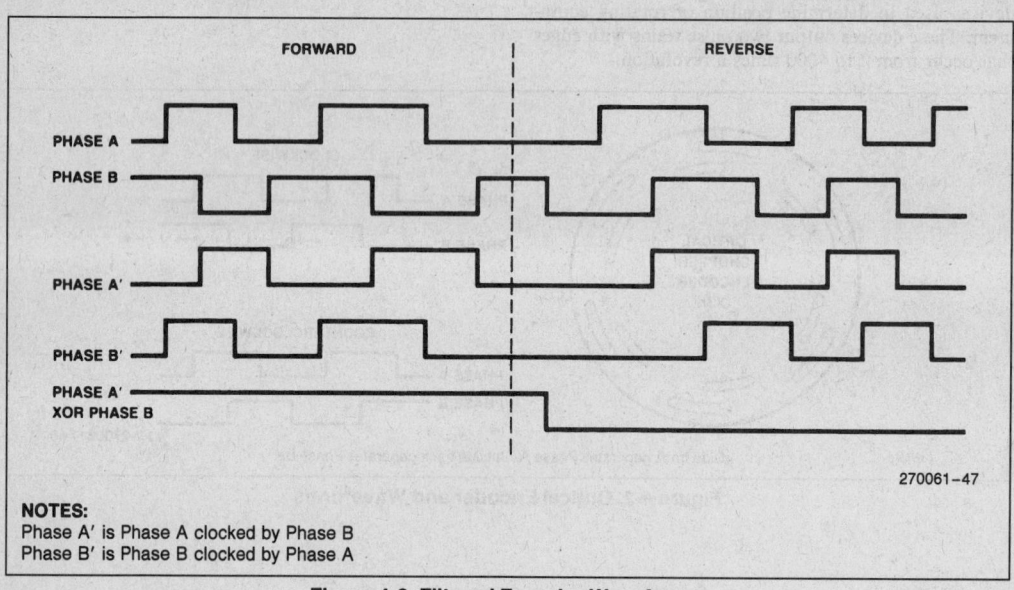

Figure 4-3. Filtered Encoder Waveforms

AP-248

some modifications and a braking algorithm. Since the main point of this example is I/O interfacing, the motor driver will be briefly described at the end of this section.

In order to interface to the encoder it is necessary to know the types of waveforms that can be expected. The motor was accelerated and decelerated many times using different maximum voltages. It was found that the

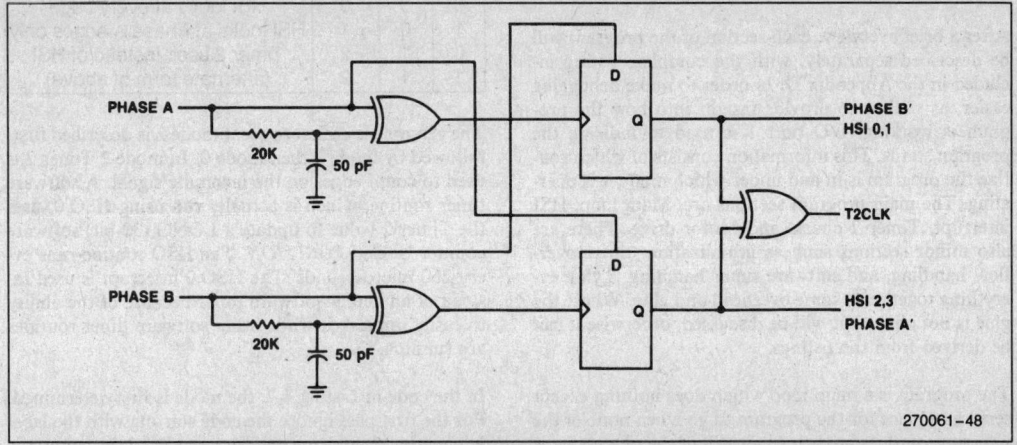

Figure 4-4. Schematic of Optical Encoder to 8096 Interface

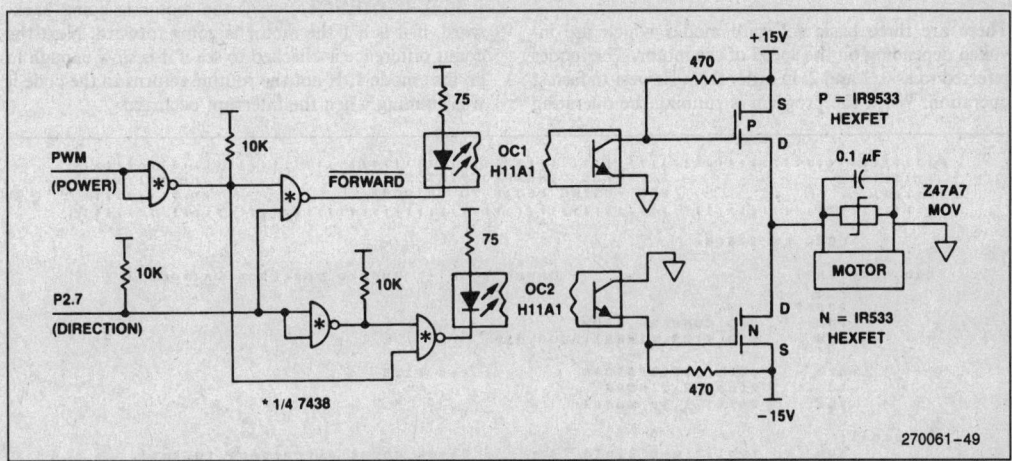

Figure 4-5. Motor Driver Circuitry

5-45

AP-248

motor would decelerate smoothly until the time between encoder edges was around 100 microseconds. At this point the motor would either continue to decelerate slowly, or would suddenly stop and reverse. The latter case is the one that was most problematic.

After a brief overview, each section of the program will be described separately, with the complete listing included in the Appendix D. In order to make debugging easier, as well as to provide insight into how the program is working, I/O port 1 is used to indicate the program status. This information consists of which routine the program is in and under which mode it is operating. The main program sections are: Main loop, HSI interrupt, Timer 2 check, and Motor drive. There are also minor sections such as initialization, timer overflow handling, and software timer handling. Tying everything together is some overhead and glue. Where the glue is not obvious it will be discussed, otherwise it can be derived from the listings.

The program is a main loop which does nothing except serve as a place for the program to go when none of the interrupt routines are being run. All of the processing is done on an interrupt basis.

There are three basic software modes which are invoked depending on the speed of the motor. The modes referred to as 0, 1 and 2, in order from slowest to fastest operation. When the program is running the operating mode is indicated by the lower 2 bits of Port 1, with the following coding:

P1.0	P1.1	Mode	Description
0	0	0	HSI looks at every edge
1	0	1	HSI looks at Phase A edges only
0	1	2	Timer 2 used instead of HSI
1	1	2	(alternate form of above)

The example is easiest to see if mode 2 is described first, followed by mode 1 then mode 0. In mode 2 Timer 2 is used to count edges on the incoming signal. A software timer routine, which is actually run using HSO.0, uses the Timer 2 value to update a LONG (32-bit) software counter labeled *POSITION*. The HSO routine runs every 260 microseconds. The HSO.0 interrupt is used instead of an actual software timer because of the ability to easily unmask it while other software timer routines are running.

In the code in Listing 4-7, the mode is first determined. For the first pass ignore the code starting with the label *in__mode__1*. Starting with *in__mode__2* the counter is incremented or decremented based on bit zero of DIRECT. If DIRECT.0 = 0 the motor is going backward, if it is a 1 the motor is going forward. Next the count difference is checked to see if it is slow enough to go into mode 1. If not the routine returns to the code it was running when the interrupt occurred.

```
;;;;;;;;;;;;;;;;;;;;;;;;;;;;;;;;;;;;;;;;;;;;;;;;;;;;;;;;;;;;;;;;;;;;;;;;;
;;;;;;                  SOFTWARE TIMER ROUTINE 0                  ;;;;;;;;;;
;;;;;;                NOW  USING HSO.0 TO TRIGGER                 ;;;;;;;;;;
;;;;;;;;;;;;;;;;;;;;;;;;;;;;;;;;;;;;;;;;;;;;;;;;;;;;;;;;;;;;;;;;;;;;;;;;;

        CSEG AT 2280H

hso_exec_int:                      ; Check mode - Update position in mode 2
        PUSHF
        ldb     HSO_COMMAND,#30H
        add     HSO_TIME,TIMER1,HSO0_dly
        orb     port1,#00100000B       ; set P1.5
        ld      Timer_2,TIMER2
        jbs     Port1,1,in_mode2

in_mode1:
        sub     tmp1,Timer_2,old_t2    ; Check count difference in tmp1
        cmp     tmp1,#2
        jh      end_swt0
set_mode0:
        jbc     Port1,0,end_swt0       ; if already in mode 0
        andb    Port1,#11111100B       ; Clear P1.0, P1.1 (set mode 0)
        ldb     IOC0,#01010101B        ; enable all HSI
        ldb     last_stat,zero
        br      end_swt0
```

270061-50

Listing 4-7. Motor Control HSO.0 Timer Routine

```
in_mode2:
        sub     delta_p,timer_2,tmr2_old    ; get timer2 count difference
        ld      tmr2_old,timer_2

        jbc     direct,0,in_rev

in_fwd: add     position,delta_p
        addc    position+2,zero
        br      chk_mode

in_rev: sub     position,delta_p
        subc    position+2,zero

chk_mode:
        sub     tmp1,Timer_2,old_t2         ; Check count difference in tmp1
        cmp     tmp1,#5                     ; set mode1 if count is too low
        jgt     end_swt0                    ; count <= 5

set_mode1:
        andb    Port1,#11111101B            ; Clear P1.1, set P1.0 (set mode 1)
        orb     Port1,#00000001B
        ldb     IOC0,#00000101B             ; enable HSI 0 and 1
        ld      zero, HSI_TIME
        sub     last1_time,Timer1,min_hsi1
                                            ; set up so (time-last2_time)>min_hsi1 on next HSI
clr_hsi:
        ld      ZERO, HSI_TIME
        andb    ios1_bak,#01111111B         ; clear bit 7
        orb     ios1_bak,ios1
        jbs     ios1_bak,7,clr_hsi          ; If hsi is triggered then clear hsi

end_swt0:
        ld      old_t2,TIMER_2
        andb    port1,#11011111B            ; clear P1.5
        POPF
        ret
                                                                       270061-51
```

Listing 4-7. Motor Control HSO.0 Timer Routine (Continued)

If the pulse rate is slow enough to go to mode 1, the transition is made by enabling HSI.0 and HSI.1. Both of these lines are connected to the same encoder line, with HSI.0 looking for rising edges and HSI.1 looking for falling edges. The *HSI_TIME* register is read to speed up clearing the HSI FIFO and the *LAST1_TIME* value is set up so the mode 1 routine does not immediately put the program into another mode. The HSI FIFO is then cleared, the Timer 2 value used throughout this routine is saved, and the routine returns.

This routine still runs in modes 0 and 1, but in an abbreviated form. The section of code starting with the label *in__mode1* checks to see if the pulses are coming in so slowly that both HSI lines can be checked. If this is the case then all of the HSIs are enabled and the program returns. This routine is the secondary method for going from mode 1 to mode 0, the primary method is by checking the time between edges during the HSI routine, which will be described later.

The HSO routine will enable mode 0 from mode 1 if two edges are not received every 260 microseconds. The primary method, (under the HSI routine), can only enable mode 0 after an edge is received. This could cause a problem if the last 2 edges on Phase A before the encoder stops were too close to enable mode 0. If this happened, mode 0 would not be enabled until after the encoder started again, resulting in missed edges on Phase B. Using the HSO routine to switch from mode 1 to mode 0 eliminates this problem.

Figure 4-6 shows a state diagram of how the mode switching is done. As can be seen, there are two sources for most of the mode decisions. This helps avoid problems such as the one mentioned above.

When either Mode 1 or Mode 0 is enabled the HSI interrupt routine performs the counting of edges, while the HSO routine only ensures that the correct mode is running. The routines for modes 0 and 1 share the same initialization and completion sections, with the main body of code being different.

The initialization routine is similar to many HSI routines. The flags are checked to ensure that the HSI FIFO data is valid, and then the FIFO is read. Next, the main body of code (for either mode 0 or mode 1) is

AP-248

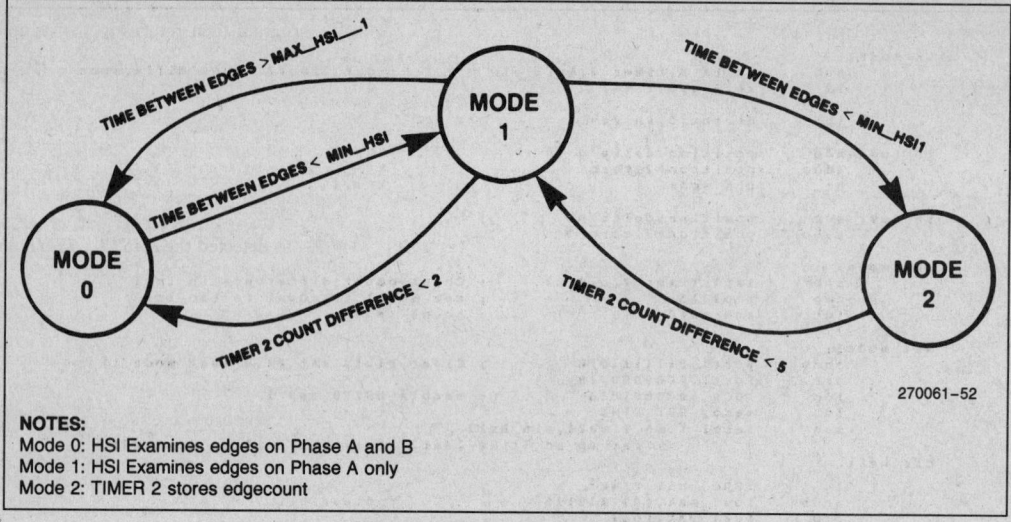

NOTES:
Mode 0: HSI Examines edges on Phase A and B
Mode 1: HSI Examines edges on Phase A only
Mode 2: TIMER 2 stores edgecount

Figure 4-6. Mode State Diagram

```
;;;;;;;;;;;;;;;;;;;;;;;;;;;;;;;;;;;;;;;;;;;;;;;;;;;;;;;;;;;;;;;;;;;;;;;;;;;;
;;;;;              HSI DATA AVAILABLE INTERRUPT ROUTINE            ;;;;;;;;;;;;;;
;;;;;;;;;;;;;;;;;;;;;;;;;;;;;;;;;;;;;;;;;;;;;;;;;;;;;;;;;;;;;;;;;;;;;;;;;;;;
; This routine keeps track of the current time and position of the motor.
; The upper word of information is provided by the timer overflow routine.

           CSEG AT 2400H
now_mode_1: br     in_mode_1         ; used to save execution time for
no_int1:    br     no_int            ; worst case loop

hsi_data_int: pushf
           orb    port1,#01000000B
           andb   ios1_bak,#01111111B    ; set P1.6
           orb    ios1_bak,ios1          ; Clear ios1_bak.7
           jbc    ios1_bak,7,no_int1     ; If hsi is not triggered then
                                         ; jump to no_int
get_values:
           ld     timer_2,TIMER2
           andb   hsi_s0,HSI_STATUS,#01010101B
           ld     time,HSI_TIME

           jbs    port1,0,now_mode_1     ; jump if in mode 1

in_mode_0:


;;;;;;;;;;;;;;;;;;;;
;;;;;;;;;;;;;;;;;;;;              INSERT  BODY  OF  ROUTINE
;;;;;;;;;;;;;;;;;;;;


load_lasts:
           ld     tmr2_old,timer_2
no_cnt:    andb   ios1_bak,#01111111B    ; clr bit 7
           orb    ios1_bak,ios1
           jbc    ios1_bak,7,no_int
again:     br     get_values

no_int:    andb   port1,#10111111B       ; Clear P1.6
           popf
           ret    ; end of hsi_data interrupt routine
                  ; Routine for mode 1 follows and then returns to "load_lasts"
$EJECT
```

Listing 4-8. Motor Control HSI Data Available Routine

AP-248

run. At the end time and count values are saved and the holding register is checked for another event. Listing 4-8 contains the initialization and completion sections of the HSI routine.

Listing 4-9 is the main body of the Mode 1 routine. Before any calculations are done in Mode 1, the incoming pulse period is measured to see if it is too fast or too slow for mode 1. The time period between two edges is used so that the duty cycle of the waveform will not affect mode switching. If it is determined that Mode 2 should be set, Port 1.1 is set, all of the HSI lines are disabled, and the HSI fifo is cleared. If Mode 0 is to be set all of the HSI lines are enabled and the variable *LAST__STAT* is cleared. LAST__STAT = 0 is used as a flag to indicate the first HSI interrupt in Mode 0 after Mode 1. After the mode checking and setting are complete the incremental value in Timer 2 is used to update

POSITION. The program then returns to the completion section of the routine.

There is a lot more code used in Mode 0 than in Mode 1, most of which is due to the multiple jump statements that determine the current and previous state of the HSI pins. In order to save execution time several blocks of code are repeated as can be seen in Listing 4-10. The first determination is that of which edge had occurred. If a Phase A edge was detected the *LAST1__TIME* and *LAST2__TIME* variables are updated so a reference to the pulse frequency will be available. These are the same variables used under Mode 1. A test is also made to see if the edges are coming fast enough to warrant being in Mode 1, if they are, the switch is made. If the last edge detected was on Phase B, the information is used only to determine direction.

```
In_mode_1:                  ; mode 1 HSI routine

        andb    tmp1,hsi_s0,#01010000B
        jne     no_cnt
cmp_time:                                   ; Procedure which sets mode 1 also
                                            ; sets times to pass the tests
        ld      last2_time,last1_time
        ld      last1_time,time

cmp1:   sub     tmp1,time,last2_time
        cmp     tmp1,min_hsi
        jh      check_max_time

set_mode_2:
        orb     Port1,#00000010B            ; Set P1.1 (in mode 2)
        ldb     IOC0,#00000000B             ; Disable all HSI
mt_hsi: ld      zero,hsi_time               ; empty the hsi fifo
        andb    ios1_bak,#01111111B         ;    clear bit 7
        orb     ios1_bak,ios1
        jbs     ios1_bak,7,mt_hsi           ; If hsi is triggered then clear hsi
        br      done_chk

check_max_time:
        sub     tmp1,time,last2_time
        cmp     tmp1,max_hsi                ; max_hsi = addition to min_hsi for
                                            ; total time
        jnh     done_chk

set_mode_0:
        andb    Port1,#11111100B            ; clear P1.0,1 set mode 0)
        ldb     IOC0,#01010101B             ; Enable all HSI
        ldb     last_stat,zero

done_chk:
        sub     delta_p,timer_2,tmr2_old    ; get timer2 count difference
        jbc     direct,0,add_rev
add_fwd:
        add     position,delta_p
        addc    position+2,zero
        br      load_lasts
add_rev:
        sub     position,delta_p
        subc    position+2,zero
        br      load_lasts

$eject
```

Listing 4-9. Motor Control Mode 1 Routines

AP-248

```
In_mode_0:
        jbs     hsi_s0,0,a_rise
        jbs     hsi_s0,2,a_fall
        jbs     hsi_s0,4,b_rise
        jbs     hsi_s0,6,b_fall
        br      no_cnt

a_rise: ld      last2_time,last1_time
        ld      last1_time,time
        sub     time,last2_time
        cmp     time,min_hsi
        jh      tst_statr
;set mode1-
        orb     Port1,#00000001B        ; Set P1.0 (in mode 1)
        ldb     IOC0,#00000101B         ; Enable HSI 0 and 1
tst_statr:
        jbs     last_stat,6,going_fwd
        jbs     last_stat,4,going_rev
        jbs     last_stat,2,change_dir
        cmpb    last_stat,zero
        je      first_time              ; first time in mode0
        br      inp_err

a_fall: ld      last2_time,last1_time
        ld      last1_time,time
        sub     time,last2_time
        cmp     time,min_hsi
        jh      tst_statf
;set mode1-
        orb     Port1,#00000001B        ; Set P1.0 (in mode 1)
        ldb     IOC0,#00000101B         ; Enable HSI 0 and 1
tst_statf:
        jbs     last_stat,4,going_fwd
        jbs     last_stat,6,going_rev
        jbs     last_stat,0,change_dir
        cmpb    last_stat,zero
        je      first_time              ; first time in mode0
        br      inp_err

b_rise: jbs     last_stat,0,going_fwd
        jbs     last_stat,2,going_rev
        jbs     last_stat,6,change_dir
        cmpb    last_stat,zero
        je      first_time              ; first time in mode0
        br      inp_err

b_fall: jbs     last_stat,2,going_fwd
        jbs     last_stat,0,going_rev
        jbs     last_stat,4,change_dir
        cmpb    last_stat,zero
        je      first_time              ; first time in mode0
        br      inp_err

first_time:
        stb     hsi_s0,last_stat
        br      done_chk                ; add delta position
inp_err:
        br      no_int


change_dir:
        notb    direct
no_inc: jbc     direct,0,going_rev

going_fwd:
        orb     PORT2,#01000000B        ; set P2.6
        ldb     direct,#01              ; direction = forward
        add     position,#01
        addc    position+2,zero
        br      st_stat
going_rev:
        andb    PORT2,#10111111B        ; clear P2.6
        ldb     direct,#00              ; direction = reverse
        sub     position,#01
        subc    position+2,zero

st_stat:
        stb     hsi_s0,last_stat
```

270061-55

Listing 4-10. Motor Control Mode 0 Routines

AP-248

After mode correctness is confirmed and the *LAST x_TIME* values are updated the *LAST_STAT* (Last Status) variable is used to determine the current direction of travel. The POSITION value is then updated in the direction specified by the last two edges and the status is stored. Note that the first time in Mode 0 after being in Mode 1, the Mode 1 *done_chk* routine is used to update POSITION, instead of the routines *going_fwd* and *going_rev* from the Mode 0 section of code. The completion section of code is then executed.

Providing the PWM value to drive the motor is done by a routine running under Software Timer 1. The first section of code, shown in Listing 4-11a, has to do with calculating the position and timer errors. Listing 4-11b shows the next section of code where the power to be supplied to the motor is calculated. First the direction is checked and if the direction is reverse the absolute value of the error is taken. If the error is greater than 64K counts, the PWM routine is loaded with the maximum value. The next check is made to see if the motor is close enough to the desired location that the power to it should be reversed, (i.e., enter the Braking mode). If the motor is very close to the position or has slowed to the point that is likely to turn around, the *Hold_Position* mode is entered.

The determination of which modes are selected under what conditions was done empirically. All of the parameters used to determine the mode are kept in RAM so they can be easily changed on the fly instead of by re-assembling the program. The parameters in the listing have been selected to make the motor run, but have not been optimized for speed or stability. A diagram of the modes is shown in Figure 4-7.

In the *Hold_Position* mode power is eased onto the motor to lock it into position. Since the motor could be stopped in this mode, some integral control is needed, as proportional control alone does not work well when the error is small and the load is large. The BOOST variable provides this integral control by increasing the output a fixed amount every time period in which the

Listing 4-11. Motor Control Software Timer 1 Routine

```
;;;;;;;;;;;;;;;;;;;;;;;;;;;;;;;;;;;;;;;;;;;;;;;;;;;;;;;;;;;;;;;;;;;;;;;;
;;;;;;                  SOFTWARE TIMER ROUTINE 1                 ;;;;;;;;;;
;;;;;;;;;;;;;;;;;;;;;;;;;;;;;;;;;;;;;;;;;;;;;;;;;;;;;;;;;;;;;;;;;;;;;;;;

        CSEG AT 2600H

        swt1_expired:
                pushf
                orb     port1,#10000000B        ; set port1.7

                ldb     int_mask,#00001101B     ; enable HSI, Tovf, HSO

                ldb     HSO_COMMAND,#39H
                add     HSO_TIME,TIMER1,swt1_dly

                ld      time_err+2,des_time+2   ; Calculate time & position error
                ld      pos_err+2,des_pos+2
                sub     time_err,des_time,time  ; values are set
                subc    time_err+2,time+2
                sub     pos_err,des_pos,position
                subc    pos_err+2,position+2

                EI

                sub     time_delta,last_time_err,time_err
                ld      last_time_err,time_err

                sub     pos_delta,last_pos_err,pos_err
                ld      last_pos_err,pos_err

;;;;;           Time_err  = Desired time to finish - current time
;;;;;           Pos_err   = Desired position to finish - current position
;;;;;           Pos_delta = Last position error - Curent position error
;;;;;           Time_delta = Last time error - Current time error
;;;;;                note that errors should get smaller so deltas will be
;;;;;                positive for forward motion (time is always forward)
```

Listing 4-11a. Motor Control Software Position Counter

AP-248

```
chk_dir:
        cmp     pos_err+2,zero
        jge     go_forward
go_backward:
        neg     pos_err             ; Pos_err = ABS VAL (pos_err)
        ldb     pwm_dir,#00h
        cmp     pos_err+2,#0ffffH
        jne     ld_max
        br      chk_brk
go_forward:
        ldb     pwm_dir,#01H
        cmp     pos_err+2,zero
        je      chk_brk
ld_max: ldb     pwm_pwr,max_pwr
        br      chk_sanity

Chk_brk:                            ; Position_Error now = ABS(pos_err)
        cmp     pos_err,pos_pnt
        jnh     hold_position       ; position_error<position_control_point
        cmp     pos_err,brk_pnt
        jh      ld_max              ; position_error>brake_point

braking:
        cmp     pos_delta,zero
        jge     chk_delta
        neg     pos_delta
chk_delta:
        cmp     pos_delta,vel_pnt   ; velocity = pos_delta/sample_time
        jnh     hold_position       ; jmp if ABS(velocity) < vel_pnt
brake:  ldb     pwm_pwr,max_brk
        ldb     tmp,direct          ; If braking apply power in opposite
        notb    tmp                 ; direction of current motion
        ldb     pwm_dir,tmp
        br      ld_pwr

Hold_position:                      ; position hold mode
        cmp     pos_err,#02
        jh      calc_out            ; if position error < 2 then turn off power
        clr     tmp+2
        clr     boost
        BR      output

calc_out:
        mulub   tmp,max_hold,#255
        mulu    tmp,pos_err         ; Tmp = pos_err * max_hold
        cmp     pos_delta,zero
        jne     no_bst
        add     boost,#04           ; Boost is integral control
        add     tmp+2,boost         ; TMP+2 = MSB(pos_err*max_hold)
        br      ck_max
no_bst: clr     boost
ck_max: cmp     tmp+2,max_hold
        jnh     output
maxed:  ld      tmp+2,max_hold
output: ldb     pwm_pwr,tmp+2

chk_sanity:
        br      ld_pwr

ld_pwr:
        ldb     rpwr,pwm_pwr
        notb    rpwr
        jbs     pwm_dir,0,p2fwd
p2bkwd: DI
        andb    port2,#01111111B    ; clear P2.7
        ldb     pwm_control,rpwr
        EI
        br      pwrset
p2fwd:  DI
        orb     port2,#10000000B    ; set P2.7
        ldb     pwm_control,rpwr
        EI
```

Listing 4-11b. Motor Control Power Algorithm

AP-248

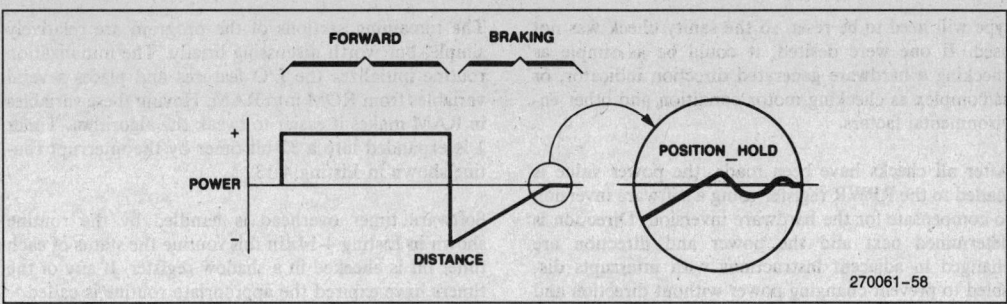

Figure 4-7. Motor Control Modes

error does not get smaller. Once the error does get smaller, usually because the motor starts moving, BOOST is cleared.

A sanity check can be performed at this point to double check that the 8096 has proper control of the motor. In the example the worst that can happen is the proto-

```
        pwrset:
                cmp     time_err+2,zero       ; do pos_table when err is negative
                jgt     end_p
        ;;;     br      end_p

                cmp     nxt_pos,#(32+pos_table)
                jlt     get_vals              ; jump if lower
                ld      nxt_pos,#pos_table
                clr     time+2
        get_vals:
                ld      des_pos,[nxt_pos]+
                ld      des_pos+2,[nxt_pos]+
                ld      des_time+2,[nxt_pos]+
                ld      max_pwr,[nxt_pos]+
                ld      max_brk,max_pwr
                add     des_pos,offset
                addc    des_pos+2,zero
                sub     last_pos_err,des_pos,position

        end_p:  andb    port1,#01111111B      ; clear P1.7
                popf
                ret

        pos_table:
                dcl     00000000H             ; position 0
                dcw     0020H, 0080H          ; next time, power
                dcl     0000C000H             ; position 1
                dcw     0040H, 0040H          ; next time, power
                dcl     00000000H             ; position 2
                dcw     0060H, 00C0H          ; next time, power
                dcl     0FFFF8000H            ; position 3
                dcw     0080H, 0080H          ; next time, power

                dcl     00000800H             ; position 4
                dcw     0058H, 0080H          ; next time, power
                dcl     00003000H             ; position 5
                dcw     0070H, 00ffH          ; next time, power
                dcl     00000000H             ; position 6
                dcw     0090H, 00f0H          ; next time, power
                dcl     00000000H             ; position 7
                dcw     0091H, 00f0H          ; next time, power
```

Listing 4-12. Motor Control Next Position Lookup

AP-248

type will need to be reset, so the sanity check was not used. If one were desired, it could be as simple as checking a hardware generated direction indicator, or as complex as checking motor condition and other environmental factors.

After all checks have been made, the power value is loaded to the RPWR register using a software inversion to compensate for the hardware inversion. Direction is determined next and the power and direction are changed in adjacent instructions with interrupts disabled to prevent changing power without direction and vice versa.

To exercise the program logic the desired position is changed based on the time value using the code and lookup table shown in Listing 4-12.

The remaining sections of the program are relatively simple, but worth discussing briefly. The initialization routine initializes the I/O features and places several variables from ROM into RAM. Having these variables in RAM makes it easier to tweak the algorithm. Timer 1 is expanded into a 32-bit timer by the interrupt routine shown in Listing 4-13.

Software timer overhead is handled by the routine shown in Listing 4-14. In this routine the status of each timer bit is checked in a shadow register. If any of the timers have expired the appropriate routine is called.

```
;;;;;;;;;;;;;;;;;;;;;;;;;;;;;;;;;;;;;;;;;;;;;;;;;;;;;;;;;;;;;;;;;;;;
;;;;;;                  TIMER     INTERRUPT     SERVICE              ;;;;;;;;;;;;
;;;;;;;;;;;;;;;;;;;;;;;;;;;;;;;;;;;;;;;;;;;;;;;;;;;;;;;;;;;;;;;;;;;;

            CSEG AT 2200H

timer_ovf_int:
            pushf

            orb         ios1_bak,IOS1
chk_t1:     jbc         ios1_bak,5,tmr_int_done
            inc         time+2
            andb        ios1_bak,#11011111B      ; clear bit 5
tmr_int_done:
            popf
            ret                  ; End of timer interrupt routine
```

Listing 4-13. Motor Control Timer Interrupt Routine

```
;;;;;;;;;;;;;;;;;;;;;;;;;;;;;;;;;;;;;;;;;;;;;;;;;;;;;;;;;;;;;;;;;;;;
;;;;;            SOFTWARE TIMER INTERRUPT SERVICE ROUTINE           ;;;;;;;;;
;;;;;;;;;;;;;;;;;;;;;;;;;;;;;;;;;;;;;;;;;;;;;;;;;;;;;;;;;;;;;;;;;;;;

            CSEG AT 2220H

soft_tmr_int:
            pushf
            orb         ios1_bak,IOS1
chk_swt0:
            jbc         ios1_bak,0,chk_swt1
            andb        ios1_bak,#11111110B      ; Clear bit 0 - end swt0
chk_swt1:   call        swt0_expired
            jbc         ios1_bak,1,chk_swt2
            andb        ios1_bak,#11111101B      ; Clear bit 1
            call        swt1_expired
chk_swt2:
            jbc         ios1_bak,2,chk_swt3
            andb        ios1_bak,#11111011B      ; Clear bit 2
            call        swt2_expired
chk_swt3:
            jbc         ios1_bak,4,swt_int_done
            andb        ios1_bak,#11110111B      ; Clear bit 3
,           call        swt3_expired

swt_int_done:
            popf
            ret         ; END OF SOFTWARE TIMER INTERRUPT ROUTINE

$eject
```

Listing 4-14. Motor Control Software Timer Interrupt Handler

AP-248

```
;;;;;;;;;;;;;;;;;;;;;;;;;;;;;;;;;;;;;;;;;;;;;;;;;;;;;;;;;;;;;;;;;;;;;;;;;;;;
;;;;;;                 SOFTWARE TIMER ROUTINE 2                  ;;;;;;;;;;;
;;;;;;;;;;;;;;;;;;;;;;;;;;;;;;;;;;;;;;;;;;;;;;;;;;;;;;;;;;;;;;;;;;;;;;;;;;;;

        CSEG AT 2380H

swt2_expired:
        pushf
        ldb     hso_command,#3AH        ; set swt_2
        add     hso_time,timer1,swt2_dly

        orb     port1,#00000100B        ; set port 1.2
        cmp     out_ptr,#7ffH
        bnh     pulsing
        ld      out_ptr,#1f0H

pulsing:
        jbc     tr_col,0,swt2_done

        st      position+2,[out_ptr]+   ; position high, position low
        st      position,[out_ptr]+

        st      direct,[out_ptr]+
        st      pwm_pwr,[out_ptr]+

                                        ; store 8 bytes externally

swt2_done:
        sub     tmp1,timer1,last1_time
        cmp     tmp1,#1800H
        jnh     swt2_ret                ; keep (time_last4_time)<7000H

        add     last1_time,#1000H
swt2_ret:
        andb    port1,#11111011B        ; clear port1.2
        popf
        ret
```

Listing 4-15. Motor Control Software Timer 2 Routine

The last routine, shown in Listing 4-15, is the Software Timer 2 routine which outputs some variables to external RAM. It also keeps LAST1__Time within 1800H of Timer1 to prevent overflows from occurring when the Mode 0 and Mode 1 software check this variable.

A complete listing of the program as it is used in our lab can be found in Appendix D. For a given motor or encoder it will probably be necessary to change some of the time constants on the first page of the listing. With the motor used in our experimentation, pulses are missed from time to time when direction changes quickly. If the motor were not as fast to turn around or the encoder were mounted better these problems should disappear. The missing pulses occur when switching from Mode 1 to Mode 0, other than that no anomalies were found in the lab.

Prior to the version of code just discussed, several attempts were made, one of which could be used under certain constraints. It is possible to use only modes 2 and 0 to monitor the encoder, provided the encoder always operates smoothly and provides at least 200 microseconds between the last several edges of Phase A before reversing. This idea was originally tried because the motor was not characterized thoroughly at first, and caused problems because of the motors tendency to stop suddenly when its speed was low.

If an encoder has a lower line count and therefore more time between output pulses the two mode solution can be used. The software for the two mode version can be easily extracted form the three mode version, so it will not be presented.

5.0 HARDWARE EXAMPLE

5.1. EPROM Only Minimum System

The diagram in Figure 5-1 illustrates how to connect an 8096 in a minimum configuration system. Either 2764s or 27128s can be used in the system. Note that the lower EPROM contains the even bytes while the upper

AP-248

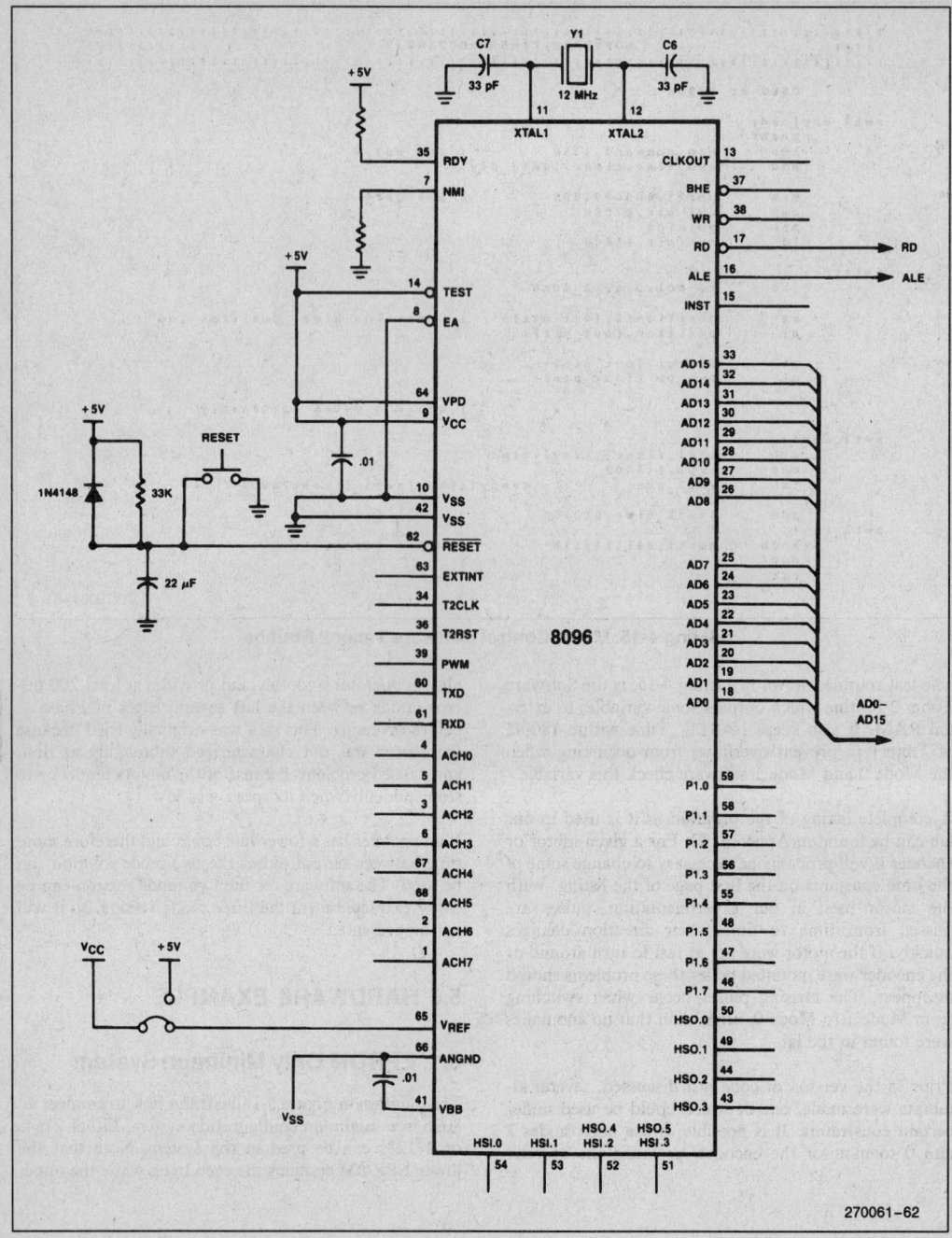

Figure 5-1 (1 of 2).

one contains the odd bytes, and the addressing is not fully decoded. This means that the addressing on a 2764 will be such that the lower 4K of each EPROM is mapped at 0000H and 4000H while the upper 4K is mapped at 2000H. If the program being loaded is 16 Kbytes long the first half is loaded into the second half of the 2764s and vice versa. A similar situation exists when using 27128s.

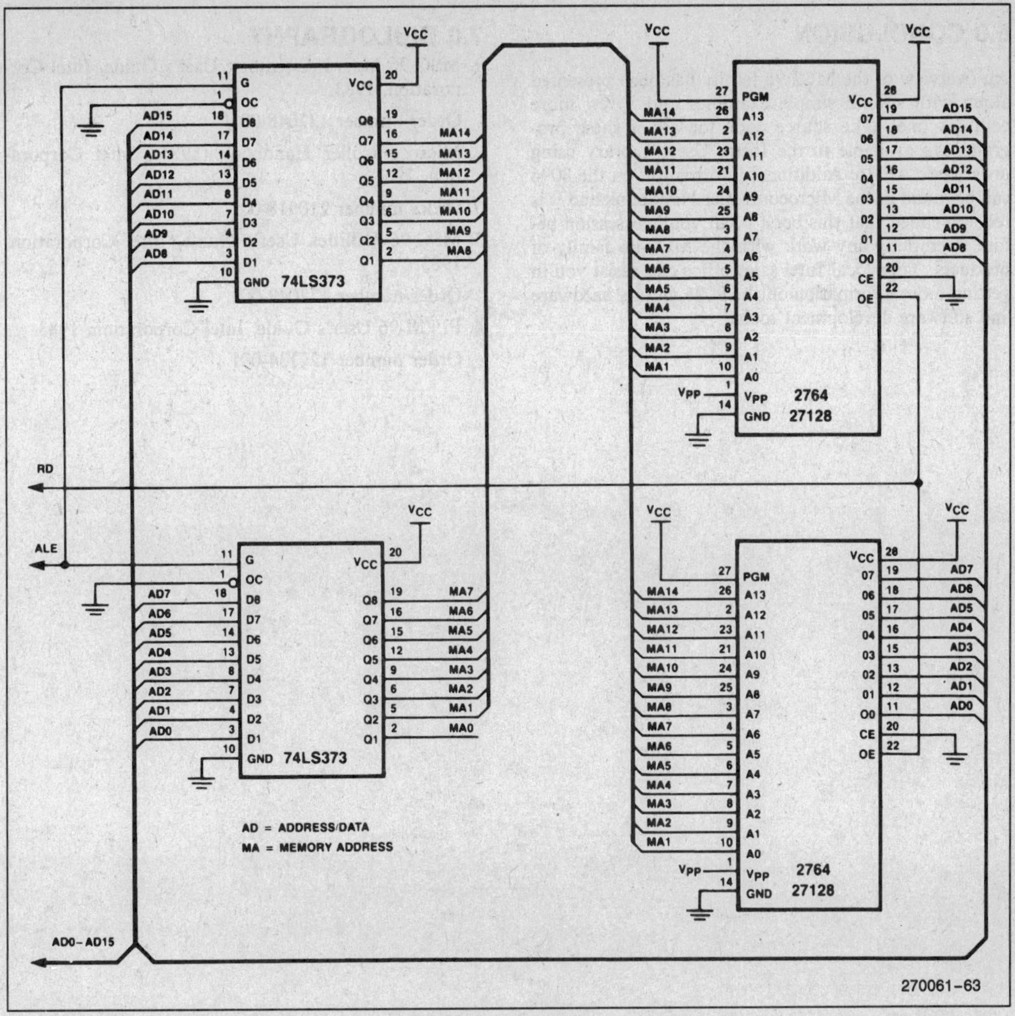

Figure 5-1 (2 of 2).

This circuit will allow most of the software presented in this ap-note to be run. In a system designed for prototyping in the lab it may be desirable to buffer the I/O ports to reduce the risk of burning out the chip during experimentation. One may also want to enhance the system by providing RC filters on the A to D inputs, a precision VREF power supply, and additional RAM.

5.2. Port Reconstruction

If it is desired to fully emulate a 8396 then I/O ports 3 and 4 must be reconstructed. It is easiest to do this if the usage of the lines can be restricted to inputs or outputs on a port by port rather than line by line basis. The ports are reconstructed by using standard memory-mapped I/O techniques, (i.e., address decoders and latches), at the appropriate addresses. If no external RAM is being used in the system then the address decoding can be partial, resulting in less complex logic.

The reconstructed I/O ports will work with the same code as the on chip ports. The only difference will be the propagation delay in the external circuitry.

AP-248

6.0 CONCLUSION

An overview of the MCS-96 family has been presented along with several simple examples and a few more complex ones. The source code for all of these programs are available in the Insite Users Library using order code AE-16. Additional information on the 8096 can be found in the Microcontroller Handbook and it is recommended that this book be in your possession before attempting any work with the MCS-96 family of products. Your local Intel sales office can assist you in getting more information on the 8096 and its hardware and software development tools.

7.0 BIBLOGRAPHY

1. MSC-96 Macro Assembler User's Guide, Intel Corporation, 1983.

   Order number 122048-001.

2. Microcontroller Handbook (1985), Intel Corporation, 1984.

   Order number 210918-002.

3. MSC-96 Utilities User's Guide, Intel Corporation, 1983.

   Order number 122049-001.

4. PL/M-96 User's Guide, Intel Corporation, 1983.

   Order number 122134-001.

APPENDIX A
BASIC SOFTWARE EXAMPLES

```
SERIES-III MCS-96 MACRO ASSEMBLER, V1.0

SOURCE FILE:    :F3:INTER1.A96
OBJECT FILE:    :F3:INTER1.OBJ
CONTROLS SPECIFIED IN INVOCATION COMMAND:  NOSB

ERR LOC  OBJECT          LINE        SOURCE STATEMENT
                          1          $TITLE('INTER1.A96: Interpolation routine 1')
                          2          ;;;;;;;    8096 Assembly code for table lookup and interpolation
                          3
                          4          $INCLUDE(:F0:DEMO96.INC)   ; Include demo definitions
                     =1   5          $nolist     ; Turn listing off for include file
                     =1  53                      ; End of include file
                         54
                         55          RSEG at 22H
                         56
0022                     57          IN_VAL:     dsb    1          ; Actual Input Value
0024                     58          TABLE_LOW:  dsw    1
0026                     59          TABLE_HIGH: dsw    1
0028                     60          IN_DIF:     dsw    1          ; Upper Input - Lower Input
002A                     61          IN_DIFB     equ    IN_DIF :byte
002A                     62          TAB_DIF:    dsw    1          ; Upper Output - Lower Output
002C                     63          OUT:        dsw    1
002E                     64          RESULT:     dsw    1
0030                     65          OUT_DIF:    dsl    1          ; Delta Out
                         66
                         67
2080                     68          CSEG at 2080H
                         69
2080 A1000118            70                      LD     SP, #100H
                         71
2084 B02210              72  look:   LDB    AL, IN_VAL            ; Load temp with Actual Value
2087 1B031C              73          SHRB   AL, #3                ; Divide the byte by 8
208A 71FE1C              74          ANDB   AL, #11111110B        ; Insure AL is a word address
                         75                                       ; This effectively divides AL by 2
                         76                                       ; so AL = IN_VAL/16
                         77
208D AC1C1C              78          LDBZE  AX, AL                ; Load byte AL to word AX
2090 A31D002124          79          LD     TABLE_LOW, TABLE[AX]  ; TABLE_LOW is loaded with the value
                         80                                       ; in the table at table location AX
                         81
```

A.1. Table Lookup 1

AP-248

```
2095 A31D022126        82              LD      TABLE_HIGH, (TABLE+2)(AX) ; TABLE_HIGH is loaded with the
                       83                                                ;   value in the table at table
                       84                                                ;   location AX+2
                       85                                                ; (The next value in the table)
                       86                                                ; TAB_DIF=TABLE_HIGH-TABLE_LOW
209A 4824262A          87              SUB     TAB_DIF, TABLE_HIGH, TABLE_LOW
                       88
                       89
209E 510F2228          90              ANDB    IN_DIFB, IN_VAL, #0FH    ; IN_DIFB=least significant 4 bits
                       91                                                ;   of IN_VAL
20A2 AC2828            92              LDBZE   IN_DIF, IN_DIFB          ; Load byte IN_DIFB to word IN_DIF
                       93
20A5 FE4C2A2B30        94              MUL     OUT_DIF, IN_DIF, TAB_DIF
                       95                                                ; Output_difference =
                       96                                                ;   Input_difference*Table_difference
20AA 0E0430            97              SHRAL   OUT_DIF, #4              ; Divide by 16 (2**4)
                       98
20AD 4424302C          99              ADD     OUT, OUT_DIF, TABLE_LOW  ; Add output difference to output
                      100                                                ;   generated with truncated IN_VAL
                      101                                                ;   as input
20B1 0A042C           102              SHRA    OUT, #4                  ; Round to 12-bit answer
20B4 A4002C           103              ADDC    OUT, zero                ; Round up if Carry = 1
                      104
20B7 C02E2C           105     no_inc:  ST      OUT, RESULT              ; Store OUT to RESULT
                      106
20BA 27C8             107              BR      look                     ; Branch to "look:"
                      108
                      109
                      110              cseg    AT 2100H
                      111
2100                  112     table:
2100 000000020034004C 113              DCW     0000H, 2000H, 3400H, 4C00H ; A random function
2108 005D006A00720078 114              DCW     5D00H, 6A00H, 7200H, 7800H
2110 007B007D0076006D 115              DCW     7B00H, 7D00H, 7600H, 6D00H
2118 005D004B00340022 116              DCW     5D00H, 4B00H, 3400H, 2200H
2120 0010             117              DCW     1000H
                      118              END
2122

ASSEMBLY COMPLETED,    NO ERROR(S) FOUND.
```

A.1. Table Lookup 1 (Continued)

AP-248

```
SERIES-III MCS-96 MACRO ASSEMBLER, V1.0

SOURCE FILE:   F3:INTER2.A96
OBJECT FILE:   F3:INTER2.OBJ
CONTROLS SPECIFIED IN INVOCATION COMMAND:  NOSB

ERR LOC  OBJECT              LINE        SOURCE STATEMENT
                              1          $TITLE('INTER2 A96 Interpolation routine 2')
                              2
                              3          ;;;;;;;;    8096 Assembly code for table lookup and interpolation
                              4          ;;;;;;;;    Using tabled values in place of division
                              5
                              6          $INCLUDE(:F0:DEMO96.INC)  ; Include demo definitions
                    =1        7          $nolist   ; Turn listing off for include file
                    =1       55                    ; End of include file
                             56
0024                         57          RSEG at 24H
0024                         58
0024                         59          IN_VAL:       dsb    1          ; Actual Input Value
0026                         60          TABLE_LOW:    dsw    1          ; Table value for function
0028                         61          TABLE_INC:    dsw    1          ; Incremental change in function
002A                         62          IN_DIF:       equ    IN_DIFB    ; Upper Input - Lower Input
002A                         63          IN_DIFB       dsw    1      :byte
002C                         64          OUT:          dsw    1
002E                         65          RESULT:       dsw    1
0030                         66          OUT_DIF:      dsl    1          ; Delta Out
                             67
                             68
2080                         69          CSEG at 2080H
                             70
2080 A1001118                71                    LD     SP, #100H      ; Initialize SP to top of reg. file
                             72
2084 B0241C                  73          look:     LDB    AL, IN_VAL     ; Load temp with Actual Value
2087 18031C                  74                    SHRB   AL, #3         ; Divide the byte by 8
208A 71FE1C                  75                    ANDB   AL, #11111110B ; Insure AL is a word address
                             76                                         ; This effectively divides AL by 2
                             77                                         ; so AL = IN_VAL/16
208D AC1C1C                  78                    LDBZE  AX, AL         ; Load byte AL to word AX
                             79
2090 A31D002126              80                    LD     TABLE_LOW, VAL_TABLE[AX] ; TABLE_LOW is loaded with the value
                             81                                                   ; in the value table at location AX
                             82
2095 A31D222128              83                    LD     TABLE_INC, INC_TABLE[AX] ; TABLE_INC is loaded with the value
                             84                                                   ; in the increment table at
                             85                                                   ; location AX+2
                             86
```

A.2. Table Lookup 2

AP-248

```
209A  510F242A           87            ANDB    IN_DIFB, IN_VAL, #0FH   ; IN_DIFB=least significant 4 bits
                         88                                            ;   of IN_VAL
209E  AC2A2A             89            LDBZE   IN_DIF, IN_DIFB         ; Load byte IN_DIFB to word IN_DIF
                         90
20A1  FE4C2B2A30         91            MUL     OUT_DIF, IN_DIF, TABLE_INC
                         92                                            ; Output_difference =
                         93                                            ;   Input_difference*Incremental_change
                         94
20A6  4426302C           95            ADD     OUT, OUT_DIF, TABLE_LOW ; Add output difference to output
                         96                                            ;   generated with truncated IN_VAL
                         97                                            ;   as input
20AA  080420             98            SHR     OUT, #4                 ; Round to 12-bit answer
20AD  A4002C             99            ADDC    OUT, zero               ; Round up if Carry = 1
                        100
20B0  C02E2C            101   no_inc:  ST      OUT, RESULT             ; Store OUT to RESULT
20B3  27CF              102            BR      look                    ; Branch to "look:"
                        103
                        104
2100                    105            cseg    AT 2100H
                        106
2100                    107   val_table:
2100  000000200034004C  108            DCW     0000H, 2000H, 3400H, 4C00H   ; A random function
2108  005D006A00720078  109            DCW     5D00H, 6A00H, 7200H, 7800H
2110  007B007D00760060  110            DCW     7B00H, 7D00H, 7600H, 6D00H
2118  005D004B00340022  111            DCW     5D00H, 4B00H, 3400H, 2200H
2120  0010              112            DCW     1000H
2122                    113   inc_table:
2122  0002400180011001  114            DCW     0200H, 0140H, 0180H, 0110H   ; Table of incremental
212A  D000800060003000  115            DCW     00D0H, 0080H, 0060H, 0030H   ;   differences
2132  2000090FF70F00FF  116            DCW     0020H, 0FF90H, 0FF70H, 0FF00H
213A  E0FE90FEE0FEE0FE  117            DCW     0FEE0H, 0FE90H, 0FEE0H, 0FEE0H
                        118
2142                    119            END

ASSEMBLY COMPLETED.  NO ERROR(S) FOUND.
```

A.2. Table Lookup 2 (Continued)

```
SERIES-III PL/M-96 V1.0 COMPILATION OF MODULE PLMEX
OBJECT MODULE PLACED IN :F3:PLMEX1.OBJ
COMPILER INVOKED BY:   PLM96 86 :F3:PLMEX1.P96 CODE


            $TITLE('PLMEX1:   PLM-96 Example Code for Table Lookup')

            /* PLM-96 CODE FOR TABLE LOOK-UP AND INTERPOLATION */

  1         PLMEX:  DO;

  2   1       DECLARE IN_VAL          WORD        PUBLIC;
  3   1       DECLARE TABLE_LOW       INTEGER     PUBLIC;
  4   1       DECLARE TABLE_HIGH      INTEGER     PUBLIC;
  5   1       DECLARE TABLE_DIF       INTEGER     PUBLIC;
  6   1       DECLARE OUT             INTEGER     PUBLIC;
  7   1       DECLARE RESULT          INTEGER     PUBLIC;
  8   1       DECLARE OUT_DIF         LONGINT     PUBLIC;
  9   1       DECLARE TEMP            WORD        PUBLIC;

 10   1       DECLARE TABLE(17)       INTEGER DATA (       /* A random function */
                  0000H, 2000H, 3400H, 4C00H,
                  5D00H, 6A00H, 7200H, 7800H,
                  7B00H, 7D00H, 7600H, 6D00H,
                  5D00H, 4B00H, 3400H, 2200H,
                  1000H);

 11   1       DMPY:   PROCEDURE (A,B) LONGINT EXTERNAL;
 12   2         DECLARE (A,B) INTEGER;
 13   1       END DMPY;

 14   1       LOOP:
                TEMP=SHR(IN_VAL,4);         /* TEMP is the most significant 4 bits of IN_VAL */
                                            /* If "TEMP" was replaced by "SHR(IN_VAL,4)"    */
                                            /* The code would work but the 8096 would       */
                                            /* do two shifts                                */
 15   1         TABLE_LOW=TABLE(TEMP);
 16   1         TABLE_HIGH=TABLE(TEMP+1);

 17   1         TABLE_DIF=TABLE_HIGH-TABLE_LOW;

 18   1         OUT_DIF=DMPY(TABLE_DIF,SIGNED(IN_VAL AND OFH)) /16;

 19   1         OUT=SAR((TABLE_LOW+OUT_DIF),4); /* SAR performs an arithmetic right shift, */
                                                /*   in this case 4 places are shifted    */
```

A.3. PLM-96 Code with Expansion

AP-248

```
20    1           IF CARRY=0 THEN RESULT=OUT;      /* Using the hardware flags must be done  */
22    1           ELSE RESULT=OUT+1;                /* with care to ensure the flag is tested */
                                                    /* in the desired instruction sequence    */
23    1       GOTO LOOP;

              /* END OF PLM-96 CODE */

24    1    END;


PL/M-96 COMPILER    PLMEX1:  PLM-96 Example Code for Table Lookup
                    ASSEMBLY LISTING OF OBJECT CODE

                                        ;       STATEMENT   14
  0022                    PLMEX:
  0022  A1000018              PLMEX:     LD      SP,#STACK
  0026                    LOOP:
  0026  A00010          R    LD      TEMP,IN_VAL
  0029  0B0410          R    SHR     TEMP,#4H
                                        ;       STATEMENT   15
  002C  4410101C        R    ADD     TMP0,TEMP,TEMP
  0030  A31D000002      R    LD      TABLE_LOW,TABLE[TMP0]
                                        ;       STATEMENT   16
  0035  A31D020004      R    LD      TABLE_HIGH,TABLE+2H[TMP0]
                                        ;       STATEMENT   17
  003A  48020406        R    SUB     TABLE_DIF,TABLE_HIGH,TABLE_LOW
                                        ;       STATEMENT   18
  003E  CB06                 PUSH    TABLE_DIF
  0040  410F00001C      R    AND     TMP0,IN_VAL,#0FH
  0045  C81C                 PUSH    TMP0
  0047  EF0000          E    CALL    DMPY
  004A  0E041C               SHRAL   TMP0,#4H
  004D  A01E0E          R    LD      OUT_DIF+2H,TMP2
  0050  A01C0C          R    LD      OUT_DIF,TMP0
                                        ;       STATEMENT   19
  0053  A00220          R    LD      TMP4,TABLE_LOW
  0056  0620                 EXT     TMP4
  0058  641C20               ADD     TMP4,TMP0
  005B  641E22               ADDC    TMP6,TMP2
  005E  0E0420               SHRAL   TMP4,#4H
  0061  A0200B          R    LD      OUT,TMP4
                                        ;       STATEMENT   20
  0064  B1FF1C               LDB     TMP0,#0FFH
  0067  DB02                 BC      @0003
  0069  111C                 CLRB    TMP0
  006B                  @0003:
```

A.3. PLM-96 Code with Expansion (Continued)

```
006B  981C00              CMPB    R0,TMP0
006E  D705                BNE     @0001
                        ;   STATEMENT   21
0070  A0200A          R   LD      RESULT,TMP4
0073  2005                BR      @0002
                        ;   STATEMENT   22
0075              @0001:
0075  A0080A        R     LD      RESULT
0078  070A          R     INC     RESULT
                        ;   STATEMENT   23
007A              @0002:
007A  27AA                BR      LOOP
                        ;   STATEMENT   24
                          END

MODULE INFORMATION:

    CODE AREA SIZE          = 005AH      90D
    CONSTANT AREA SIZE      = 0022H      34D
    DATA AREA SIZE          = 0000H       0D
    STATIC REGS AREA SIZE   = 0012H      18D

PL/M-96 COMPILER    PLMEX1   PLM-96 Example Code for Table Lookup
                    ASSEMBLY LISTING OF OBJECT CODE

    OVERLAYABLE REGS AREA SIZE = 0000H    0D
    MAXIMUM STACK SIZE         = 0006H    6D
    48 LINES READ

PL/M-96 COMPILATION COMPLETE.   0 WARNINGS,   0 ERRORS
```

A.3. PLM-96 Code with Expansion (Continued)

```
MCS-96 MACRO ASSEMBLER    MULT.APT: 16*16 multiply procedure for PLM-96

SERIES-III MCS-96 MACRO ASSEMBLER, V1.0

SOURCE FILE: :F3:MULT.A96
OBJECT FILE: :F3:MULT.OBJ
CONTROLS SPECIFIED IN INVOCATION COMMAND: NOSB

ERR LOC  OBJECT            LINE         SOURCE STATEMENT
                             1          $TITLE('MULT.APT: 16*16 multiply procedure for PLM-96')
                             2
                             3
     0018                    4           SP      EQU     18H:word
                             5      rseg
                             6           EXTRN   PLMREG :long
     0000                    7
                             8      cseg
     0000                    9
                            10           PUBLIC  DMPY    ; Multiply two integers and return a
                            11                           ; longint result in AX, DX registers
                            12
     0000 CC04              13   DMPY:   POP     PLMREG+4   ; Load return address
     0002 CC00              14           POP     PLMREG
     0004 FE6E1900          15           MUL     PLMREG,[SP]+  ; Load second operand and increment SP
                            16
     0008 E304              17           BR      [PLMREG+4]    ; Return to PLM code.
     000A                   18           END
                            19

ASSEMBLY COMPLETED,  NO ERROR(S) FOUND.
```

A.3. PLM-96 Code with Expansion (Continued)

AP-248

```
SERIES-III MCS-96 RELOCATOR AND LINKER, V2.0
Copyright 1983 Intel Corporation

INPUT FILES:  :F3:PLMEX1.OBJ,  :F3:MULT.OBJ, PLM96.LIB
OUTPUT FILE:  :F3:PLMOUT.OBJ
CONTROLS SPECIFIED IN INVOCATION COMMAND:
    ROM(2080H-3FFFH)

INPUT MODULES INCLUDED:
    :F3:PLMEX1.OBJ(PLMEX)  12/25/84
    :F3:MULT.OBJ(MULT)     12/25/84
    PLM96.LIB(PLMREG)      11/02/83

SEGMENT MAP FOR :F3:PLMOUT.OBJ(PLMEX):

            TYPE    BASE    LENGTH   ALIGNMENT   MODULE NAME
            ----    ----    ------   ---------   -----------
**RESERVED*         0000H   001AH
*** GAP ***         001AH   0002H
            REG     001CH   000BH    ABSOLUTE    PLMREG
            REG     0024H   0012H    WORD        PLMEX
            STACK   0036H   0006H    WORD
*** GAP ***         003CH   2044H
            CODE    2080H   0003H    ABSOLUTE    PLMEX
*** GAP ***         2083H   0001H
            CODE    2084H   007CH    WORD        PLMEX
            CODE    2100H   000AH    BYTE        MULT
*** GAP ***         210AH   DEF6H
```

A.3. PLM-96 Code with Expansion (Continued)

```
SYMBOL TABLE FOR :F3:PLMOUT.OBJ(PLMEX).

ATTRIBUTES      VALUE    NAME
----------      -----    ----
                         PUBLICS:
REG   WORD      0024H    IN_VAL
REG   INTEGER   0026H    TABLE_LOW
REG   INTEGER   0028H    TABLE_HIGH
REG   INTEGER   002AH    TABLE_DIF
REG   INTEGER   002CH    OUT
REG   INTEGER   002EH    RESULT
REG   LONGINT   0030H    OUT_DIF
REG   WORD      0034H    TEMP
CODE  ENTRY     2100H    DMPY
REG   LONG      001CH    PLMREG
NULL  NULL      003CH    MEMORY
NULL  NULL      1FC4H    ?MEMORY_SIZE

                         MODULE: PLMEX

                         MODULE: MULT

                         MODULE: PLMREG

RL96 COMPLETED.   0 WARNING(S),   0 ERROR(S)
```

A.3. PLM-96 Code with Expansion (Continued)

AP-248

```
SERIES-III MCS-96 MACRO ASSEMBLER, V1.0

SOURCE FILE:  :F3:PULSE.A96
OBJECT FILE:  :F3:PULSE.OBJ
CONTROLS SPECIFIED IN INVOCATION COMMAND: NOSB

ERR LOC  OBJECT              LINE        SOURCE STATEMENT
                              1          $TITLE('PULSE A96: Measuring pulses using the HSI unit')
                              2
                              3          $INCLUDE(DEMO96.INC)
                         =1   4          $nolist  ; Turn listing off for include file
                         =1   52                  ; End of include file
                              53
                              54                  rseg    at 28H
     0028
                              55
     0028                     56          HIGH_TIME:  dsw     1
     002A                     57          LOW_TIME:   dsw     1
     002C                     58          PERIOD:     dsw     1
     002E                     59          HI_EDGE:    dsw     1
     0030                     60          LO_EDGE:    dsw     1
                              61
                              62
                              63
                              64                  cseg    at 2080H
     2080                     65
                              66
                              67                  LD      SP, #100H
     2080 A1000118            68                  LDB     IOC0, #00000001B   ; Enable HSI 0
     2084 B10115              69                  LDB     HSI_MODE, #00001111B ; HSI 0 look for either edge
     2087 B10F03              70
                              71          wait:   ADD     PERIOD, HIGH_TIME, LOW_TIME
     208A 442A282C            72                  JBS     IOS1, 6, contin    ; If FIFO is full
     208E 3E1603              73                  JBC     IOS1, 7, wait      ; Wait while no pulse is entered
     2091 3716F6              74
                              75          contin: LDB     AL, HSI_STATUS     ; Load status; Note that reading
                              76                                             ;   HSI_TIME clears HSI_STATUS
     2094 B0061C              77
                              78                  LD      BX, HSI_TIME       ; Load the HSI_TIME
     2097 A00420              79
                              80                  JBS     AL, 1, hsi_hi      ; Jump if HSI.0 is high
     209A 391C09               81
                              82          hsi_lo: ST      BX, LO_EDGE
     209D C03020              83                  SUB     HIGH_TIME, LO_EDGE, HI_EDGE
     20A0 482E302B            84                  BR      wait
     20A4 27E4                85
                              86
     20A6 C02E20              87          hsi_hi: ST      BX, HI_EDGE
```

A.4. Pulse Measurement

```
20A9 48302E2A          88    SUB   LOW_TIME, HI_EDGE, LO_EDGE
20AD 27DB              89    BR    wait
20AF                   90    END
                       91

ASSEMBLY COMPLETED, NO ERROR(S) FOUND.
```

270061-76

A.4. Pulse Measurement (Continued)

```
SERIES-III MCS-96 MACRO ASSEMBLER, V1.0

SOURCE FILE      :F3:ENHSI.A96
OBJECT FILE      :F3:ENHSI.OBJ
CONTROLS SPECIFIED IN INVOCATION COMMAND:  NOSB


ERR LOC  OBJECT            LINE        SOURCE STATEMENT
                             1         $TITLE ('ENHSI A96 ENHANCED HSI PULSE ROUTINE')
                             2         $INCLUDE(DEMO96.INC)
                        =1   3     +   $nolist  ; Turn listing off for include file
                        =1   4     +            ; End of include file
                            52
                            53         RSEG AT 28H
     0028                   54
     0028                   55         TIME        DSW  1
     002A                   56         LAST_RISE   DSW  1
     002C                   57         LAST_FALL   DSW  1
     002E                   58         HSI_SO      DSB  1
     002F                   59         IOS1_BAK    DSB  1
     0030                   60         PERIOD      DSW  1
     0032                   61         LOW_TIME    DSW  1
     0034                   62         HIGH_TIME   DSW  1
     0036                   63         COUNT       DSW  1
                            64
     2080                   65         cseg  at  2080H
                            66
     2080 A1000118          67         init:  LD   SP,#100H
                            68
     2084 B12516            69         LDB  IOC1,#00100101B  ; Disable HSO.4,HSO.5, HSI_INT=first,
                            70                               ; Enable PWM,TXD,TIMER1_OVRFLOW_INT
                            71
     2087 B19903            72         LDB  HSI_MODE,#10011001B  ; set hsi 1 -, hsi 0 +
     208A B10715            73         LDB  IOC0,#00000111B      ; Enable hsi 0,1
                            74                                   ; T2 CLOCK=T2CLK, T2RST=T2RST
                            75                                   ; Clear timer2
                            76
                            77
     208D 717F2F            78         wait: ANDB  IOS1_BAK,#01111111B  ; Clear IOS1_BAK.7
     2090 90162F            79               ORB   IOS1_BAK,IOS1         ; Store into temp to avoid clearing
                            80                                           ; other flags which may be needed
     2093 372FF7            81               JBC   IOS1_BAK,7,wait       ; If hsi is not triggered then
                            82                                           ; jump to wait
                            83
     2096 5155062E          84         ANDB  HSI_SO,HSI_STATUS,#01010101B
     209A A00428            85         LD    TIME,HSI_TIME
```

A.5. Enhanced Pulse Measurement

```
209D  382E05              88           JBS   HSI_S0,0,a_rise
20A0  3A2E0F              89           JBS   HSI_S0,2,a_fall
20A3  201A                90           BR    no_cnt
                          91
20A5  482C2832            92   a_rise: SUB   LOW_TIME,TIME,LAST_FALL
20A9  482A2830            93           SUB   PERIOD,TIME,LAST_RISE
20AD  A0282A              94           LD    LAST_RISE,TIME
20B0  200B                95           BR    increment
                          96
20B2  482A2834            97   a_fall: SUB   HIGH_TIME,TIME,LAST_RISE
20B6  482C2830            98           SUB   PERIOD,TIME,LAST_FALL
20BA  A0282C              99           LD    LAST_FALL,TIME
                         100
                         101   increment:
20BD  0736               102           INC   COUNT
20BF  27CC               103   no_cnt: BR    wait
                         104
20C1                     105           END

ASSEMBLY COMPLETED,    NO ERROR(S) FOUND.
```

A.5. Enhanced Pulse Measurement (Continued)

```
SERIES-III MCS-96 MACRO ASSEMBLER, V1.0

SOURCE FILE:  :F3:HSODRV.A96
OBJECT FILE:  :F3:HSODRV.OBJ
CONTROLS SPECIFIED IN INVOCATION COMMAND: NOSB

ERR LOC  OBJECT           LINE        SOURCE STATEMENT

                             1   $TITLE('HSODRV.A96: Driver module for HSO PWM program')
                             2
                             3   HSODRV       MODULE MAIN, STACKSIZE(8)
                             4
                             5
                             6                PUBLIC   HSO_ON_0 , HSO_OFF_0
                             7                PUBLIC   HSO_ON_1 , HSO_OFF_1
                             8                PUBLIC   HSO_TIME , HSO_COMMAND
                             9                PUBLIC   SP , TIMER1 , IOS0
                            10
                            11   $INCLUDE(DEMO96.INC)
                       =1   12   $nolist ; Turn listing off for include file
                       =1   60           ; End of include file
                            61
                            62   rseg at 28H
                            63
  0028                      64                EXTRN    OLD_STAT      :byte
                            65
  0028                      66                HSO_ON_0:       dsw   1
  002A                      67                HSO_OFF_0:      dsw   1
  002C                      68                HSO_ON_1:       dsw   1
  002E                      69                HSO_OFF_1:      dsw   1
  0030                      70                count:          dsb   1
                            71
                            72   cseg at 2080H
                            73
  2080                      74                EXTRN    wait     :entry
                            75
  2080 FA                   76   strt:        DI
  2081 A1000118             77                LD       SP, #100H
  2085 510F1500           E 78                ANDB     OLD_STAT, IOS0, #0FH
  2089 950F00             E 79                XORB     OLD_STAT, #0FH
                            80
                            81   initial:
  208C                      82
  208C A1000122             83                LD       CX, #0100H
                            84
  2090 A100101C             85   loop:        LD       AX, #1000H
  2094 48221C20             86                SUB      BX, AX, CX
  2098 A0221C               87                LD       AX, CX
```

A.6. PWM Using the HSO

```
209B C0281C              88        ST    AX, HSO_ON_0
209E C02A20              89        ST    BX, HSO_OFF_0
                         90
20A1 08011C              91        SHR   AX, #1
20A4 080120              92        SHR   BX, #1
20A7 C02C1C              93        ST    AX, HSO_ON_1
20AA C02E20              94        ST    BX, HSO_OFF_1
                         95
20AD EF0000      E       96        CALL  wait
                         97
20B0 0722                98        INC   CX
20B2 B9000F22            99        CMP   CX, #00F00H
20B6 D7D8               100        BNE   loop
                        101
20B8 27D2               102        BR    initial
                        103
20BA                    104        END

ASSEMBLY COMPLETED.  NO ERROR(S) FOUND
```

A.6. PWM Using the HSO (Continued)

```
SERIES-III MCS-96 MACRO ASSEMBLER, V1.0

SOURCE FILE : F3:HSOMOD.A96
OBJECT FILE : F3:HSOMOD.OBJ
CONTROLS SPECIFIED IN INVOCATION COMMAND: NOSB

ERR LOC   OBJECT           LINE      SOURCE STATEMENT
                             1       $TITLE('HSOMOD.A96: 8096 PWM PROGRAM MODIFIED FOR DRIVER')
                             2       $PAGEWIDTH(130)
                             3
                             4       ; This program will provide 3 PWM outputs on HSO pins 0-2
                             5       ; The input parameters passed to the program are:
                             6       ;
                             7       ;              HSO_ON_N     HSO on time for pin N
                             8       ;              HSO_OFF_N    HSO off time for pin N
                             9       ;
                            10       ;    Where:    Times are in timer1 cycles
                            11       ;              N takes values from 0 to 3
                            12       ;
                            13       ;;;;;;;;;;;;;;;;;;;;;;;;;;;;;;;;;;;;;;;;;;;;;;;;;;;;;;;;;;;;;
                            14       ;
                            15       ; NOTE: Use this file to replace the declaration section of
                            16       ;       the HSO PWM program from "$INCLUDE(DEMO96.INC)" through
                            17       ;       the line prior to the label "wait".  Also change the last
                            18       ;       branch in the program to a "RET".
                            19       ;
                            20               RSEG
                            21
0000                        22       D_STAT:   DSB      1
                            23               extrn    HSO_ON_0    :word , HSO_OFF_0   :word
                            24               extrn    HSO_ON_1    :word , HSO_OFF_1   :word
                            25               extrn    HSO_TIME    :word , HSO_COMMAND :byte
                            26               extrn    TIMER1      :word , IOS0        :byte
                            27               extrn    SP          :word
                            28
                            29               public  OLD_STAT
0001                        30       OLD_STAT:         dsb     1
0002                        31       NEW_STAT:         dsb     1
                            32
                            33
0000                        34               cseg
                            35
                            36               PUBLIC  wait
                            37
0000 3E00FD     E           38       wait:   JBS    IOS0, 6, wait     ; Loop until HSO holding register
0003 FD                     39               NOP                       ; is empty
                            40
                            41       ; For operation with interrupts 'store_stat:' would be the
                            42       ; entry point of the routine.
                            43       ; Note that a DI or PUSHF might have to be added.
                            44
```

A.6. PWM Using the HSO (Continued)

AP-248

```
                              store_stat:
0004                       45             ANDB    NEW_STAT, IOS0, #0FH
0004 510F0002           E  46             CMPB    OLD_STAT, NEW_STAT      ; Store new status of HSO
0008 9B0201             R  47             JE      wait
000B DFF3                  48             XORB    OLD_STAT, NEW_STAT
000D 940201             R  49
                           50
                           51  check_0:
0010                       52             JBC     OLD_STAT, 0, check_1
0010 300113             R  53             JBS     NEW_STAT, 0, set_off_0  ; Jump if OLD_STAT(0)=NEW_STAT(0)
0013 3B0209             R  54
                           55
                              set_on_0:
0016                       56             LDB     HSO_COMMAND, #00110000B ; Set HSO for timer1, set pin 0
0016 B13000                57             ADD     HSO_TIME, TIMER1, HSO_OFF_0 ; Time to set pin = Timer1 value
0019 44000000              58             BR      check_1                 ; + Time for pin to be low
001D 2007                  59
                           60
                              set_off_0:
001F                       61             LDB     HSO_COMMAND, #00010000B ; Set HSO for timer1, clear pin 0
001F B11000                62             ADD     HSO_TIME, TIMER1, HSO_ON_0 ; Time to clear pin = Timer1 value
0022 44000000              63                                             ; + Time for pin to be high
                           64
                           65  check_1:
0026                       66             JBC     OLD_STAT, 1, check_done
0026 310113             R  67             JBS     NEW_STAT, 1, set_off_1  ; Jump if OLD_STAT(1)=NEW_STAT(1)
0029 390209             R  68
                           69
                              set_on_1:
002C                       70             LDB     HSO_COMMAND, #00110001B ; Set HSO for timer1, set pin 1
002C B13100                71             ADD     HSO_TIME, TIMER1, HSO_OFF_1 ; Time to set pin = Timer1 value
002F 44000000              72             BR      check_done
0033 2007                  73
                           74
                              set_off_1:
0035                       75             LDB     HSO_COMMAND, #00010001B ; Set HSO for timer1, clear pin 1
0035 B11100                76             ADD     HSO_TIME, TIMER1, HSO_ON_1 ; Time to clear pin = Timer1 value
0038 44000000              77                                             ; + Time for pin to be high
                           78
                           79  check_done:
003C                       80             LDB     OLD_STAT, NEW_STAT      ; Store current status and
003C B00201             R  81                                             ; wait for interrupt flag
                           82
003F F0                    83             RET     ; use "BR wait" if this routine is used with the driver
                           84
0040                       85             END

ASSEMBLY COMPLETED,  NO ERROR(S) FOUND.
```

A.6. PWM Using the HSO (Continued)

AP-248

```
SERIES-III MCS-96 MACRO ASSEMBLER, V1.0

SOURCE FILE    F3 SP A96
OBJECT FILE    F3 SP OBJ
CONTROLS SPECIFIED IN INVOCATION COMMAND NOSB

ERR LOC  OBJECT              LINE      SOURCE STATEMENT

                              1        $TITLE('SP.A96: SERIAL PORT DEMO PROGRAM')
                              2
                              3        $INCLUDE(DEMO96.INC)
                         =1   4        $nolist  ; Turn listing off for include file
                         =1  53                 ; End of include file
                             54
0028                         55        rseg    at 28H
                             56
0028                         57   CHR:       dsb  1
0029                         58   SPTEMP:    dsb  1
002A                         59   TEMP0:     dsb  1
002B                         60   TEMP1:     dsb  1
002C                         61   RCV_FLAG:  dsb  1
                             62
200C                         63        cseg    at 200CH
                             64
200C 9C20                    65        DCW     ser_port_int
                             66
2080                         67        cseg    at 2080H
                             68
2080 A1001180                69        LD      SP, #100H
                             70
2084 B12016                  71        LDB     IOC1, #00100000B   ; Set P2.0 to TXD
                             72
                             73        ; Baud rate = input frequency / (64*baud_val)
                             74        ; baud_val = (input frequency/64) / baud rate
                             75
0027                         76   baud_val   equ   39            ; 39 = (12,000,000/64)/4800 baud
                             77
0080                         78   BAUD_HIGH  equ   ((baud_val-1)/256) OR 80H   ; Set MSB to 1
0026                         79   BAUD_LOW   equ   (baud_val-1) MOD 256
                             80
                             81
2087 B1260E                  82        LDB     BAUD_REG, #BAUD_LOW
208A B1800E                  83        LDB     BAUD_REG, #BAUD_HIGH
                             84
                             85
```

A.7. Serial Port

AP-248

```
208D  B14911              86              LDB     SPCON, #01001001B   ; Enable receiver, Mode 1
                          87                                          ; The serial port is now initialized
                          88
                          89
                          90
2090  C42807              91              STB     SBUF, CHR           ; Clear serial Port
2093  B1202A              92              LDB     TEMPO, #00100000B   ; Set TI-temp
                          93
2096  B14008              94              LDB     INT_MASK, #01000000B ; Enable Serial Port Interrupt
2099  FB                  95              EI
209A  27FE                96              BR      loop                ; Wait for serial port interrupt
                          97
                          98      loop:
                          99              PUSHF
                         100      ser_port_int:
209C  F2                 101      rd_again:
209D  B01129             102              LDB     SPTEMP, SPSTAT      ; This section of code can be replaced
20A0  90292A             103              ORB     TEMPO, SPTEMP       ;   with "ORB TEMPO, SP_STAT" when the
20A3  716029             104              ANDB    SPTEMP,#01100000B   ;   serial port TI and RI bugs are fixed
20A6  D7F5               105              JNE     rd_again            ; Repeat until TI and RI are properly cleared
                         106
                         107      get_byte:
20A8  362A09             108              JBC     TEMPO, 6, put_byte
20AB  C42807             109              STB     SBUF, CHR           ; Store byte
20AE  71BF2A             110              ANDB    TEMPO, #10111111B   ; CLR RI-temp
20B1  B1FF2C             111              LDB     RCV_FLAG, #0FFH     ; Set bit-received flag
                         112
                         113      put_byte:
20B4  302C1B             114              JBC     RCV_FLAG, 0, continue  ; If receive flag is cleared
20B7  352A15             115              JBC     TEMPO, 5, continue     ; If TI was not set
20BA  B02807             116              LDB     SBUF, CHR              ; Send byte
20BD  71DF2A             117              ANDB    TEMPO, #11011111B      ; CLR TI-temp
                         118
20C0  717F2B             119              ANDB    CHR, #01111111B        ; This section of code appends
20C3  990D2B             120              CMPB    CHR, #0DH              ;   an LF after a CR is sent
20C6  D705               121              JNE     clr_rcv
20C8  B10A2B             122              LDB     CHR, #0AH
20CB  2002               123              BR      continue
                         124
                         125      clr_rcv:
20CD  112C               126              CLRB    RCV_FLAG                ; Clear bit-received flag
                         127      continue:
20CF  F3                 128              POPF
20D0  F0                 129              RET
                         130
20D1                     131              END
                         132

ASSEMBLY COMPLETED,  NO ERROR(S) FOUND.
```

A.7. Serial Port (Continued)

AP-248

```
SERIES-III MCS-96 MACRO ASSEMBLER, V1.0

'SOURCE FILE  :F3:ATOD.A96
OBJECT FILE  :F3:ATOD.OBJ
CONTROLS SPECIFIED IN INVOCATION COMMAND: NOSB

ERR LOC  OBJECT              LINE      SOURCE STATEMENT
                               1       $TITLE('ATOD.A96: SCANNING THE A TO D CHANNELS')
                               2
                               3       $INCLUDE(DEM096.INC)
                          =1   4       $nolist  ; Turn listing off for include file
                          =1  52                ; End of include file
                              53
            0028          54       RSEG    at 28H
                          55
            0028          56           BL          EQU     BX:BYTE
            001E          57           DL          EQU     DX:BYTE
                          58
            0028          59       RESULT_TABLE:
            0028          60           RESULT_1:   dsw 1
            002A          61           RESULT_2:   dsw 1
            002C          62           RESULT_3:   dsw 1
            002E          63           RESULT_4:   dsw 1
                          64
                          65
            2080          66       cseg    at 2080H
                          67
                          68
  2080 A100011B           69       start:  LD      SP, #100H          ; Set Stack Pointer
  2084 0120                70               CLR     BX
                          71
  2086 55082002            72       next:   ADDB    AD_COMMAND,BL, #1000B  ; Start conversion on channel
                          73                                               ;  indicated by BL register
                          74
  208A FD                 75               NOP                         ; Wait for conversion to start
  208B FD                 76               NOP
  208C 3B02FD             77       check:  JBS     AD_RESULT_LO, 3, check  ; Wait while A to D is busy
                          78
  208F B0021C             79               LDB     AL, AD_RESULT_LO    ; Load low order result
  2092 B0031D             80               LDB     AH, AD_RESULT_HI    ; Load high order result
                          81
  2095 5420201E           82               ADDB    DL, BL, BL          ; DL=BL*2
  2099 AC1E1E             83               LDBZE   DX, DL
  209C C31E281C           84               ST      AX, RESULT_TABLE[DX]; Store result indexed by BL*2
                          85
  20A0 1720                86               INCB    BL                  ; Increment BL modulo 4
```

A.8. A to D Converter

20A2 710320	87	ANDB	BL, #03H
20A5 27DF	88	BR	next
20A7	89	END	
	90		
	91		

ASSEMBLY COMPLETED, NO ERROR(S) FOUND.

A.8. A to D Converter (Continued)

APPENDIX B
HSO AND A TO D UNDER INTERRUPT CONTROL

```
SERIES-III MCS-96 MACRO ASSEMBLER, V1.0

SOURCE FILE:  :F3:A2DHSO.A96
OBJECT FILE:  :F3:A2DHSO.OBJ
CONTROLS SPECIFIED IN INVOCATION COMMAND: NOSB

ERR LOC  OBJECT         LINE            SOURCE STATEMENT
                          1      $TITLE('A2DHSO.A96: GENERATING PWM OUTPUTS FROM A TO D INPUTS')
                          2      ;
                          3      ; This program will provide 3 PWM outputs on HSO pins 0-2
                          4      ; and one on the PWM.
                          5      ;
                          6      ; The PWM values are determined by the input to the A/D converter.
                          7      ;
                          8      ;;;;;;;;;;;;;;;;;;;;;;;;;;;;;;;;;;;;;;;;;;;;;;;;;;;
                          9
                         10      $INCLUDE(DEMO96.INC)
                    =1   11      $nolist  ; Turn listing off for include file
                    =1   59               ; End of include file
                         60
  0028                   61               RSEG AT 28H
                         62
  001E                   63      DL       EQU      DX:BYTE
                         64
                         65      ON_TIME:
  0028                   66      PWM_TIME_1:    DSW   1
  0028                   67      HSO_ON_0:      DSW   1
  002A                   68      HSO_ON_1:      DSW   1
  002C                   69      HSO_ON_2:      DSW   1
  002E                   70
                         71      RESULT_TABLE:
  0030                   72      RESULT_0:      DSW   1
  0030                   73      RESULT_1:      DSW   1
  0032                   74      RESULT_2:      DSW   1
  0034                   75      RESULT_3:      DSW   1
  0036                   76
                         77      NXT_ON_T:      DSW   1
  0038                   78      NXT_OFF_0:     DSW   1
  003A                   79      NXT_OFF_1:     DSW   1
  003C                   80      NXT_OFF_2:     DSW   1
  003E                   81      COUNT:         DSL   1
  0040                   82      AD_NUM:        DSW   1      Channel being converted
  0044                   83      TMP:           DSW   1
  0046                   84      HSO_PER:       DSW   1
  0048                   85      LAST_LOAD:     DSB   1
  004A                   86
```

AP-248

APPENDIX B
HSO AND A TO D UNDER INTERRUPT CONTROL

```
                        87          cseg    AT 2000H
                        88
2000                    89
2000  8020              90                  DCW     start           ; Timer_ovf_int
2002  1D21              91                  DCW     Atod_done_int
2004  8020              92                  DCW     start           ; HSI_data_int
2006  CC20              93                  DCW     HSO_exec_int
                        94          $EJECT
                        95
2080                    96          cseg    AT 2080H
                        97
2080  A1000118          98   start:  LD     SP, #100H       ; Set Stack Pointer
2084  011C              99          CLR     AX
2086  051C             100   wait:   DEC     AX              ; wait approx. 0.2 seconds for
2088  D7FC             101          JNE     wait            ; SBE to finish communications
                       102
208A  1144             103          CLRB    AD_NUM
                       104
208C  A180002B         105          LD      PWM_TIME_1, #080H
2090  A1000148         106          LD      HSO_PER, #100H
2094  A140002A         107          LD      HSO_ON_0, #040H
2098  A180002C         108          LD      HSO_ON_1, #080H
209C  A1C0002E         109          LD      HSO_ON_2, #0C0H
                       110
20A0  4500010A38       111          ADD     NXT_ON_T, Timer1, #100H
                       112
20A5  B13606           113          LDB     HSO_COMMAND, #00101100B   ; Set HSO for timer1, set pin 0, 1
20A8  A03B04           114          LDB     HSO_TIME, NXT_ON_T         ; with interrupt
20AB  FD               115          NOP
20AC  FD               116          NOP
20AD  B12206           117          LDB     HSO_COMMAND, #00100010B   ; Set HSO for timer1, set pin 2
20B0  643B04           118          ADD     HSO_TIME, NXT_ON_T         ; without interrupt
                       119
20B3  91074A           120          ORB     LAST_LOAD, #00000111B     ; Last loaded value was set all pins
20B6  B10A08           121          LDB     INT_MASK, #00001010B      ; Enable HSO and A/D interrupts
20B9  B10A09           122          LDB     INT_PENDING, #00001010B   ; Fake an A/D and HSO interrupt
20BC  FB               123          EI
                       124
20BD  91010F           125   loop:   ORB    Port1, #00000001B         ; set P1.0
20C0  65010040         126          ADD     COUNT, #01
20C4  A40042           127          ADDC   COUNT+2, zero
20C7  71FE0F           128          ANDB   Port1, #11111110B         ; clear P1.0
20CA  27F1             129          BR      loop
                       130
                       131          $EJECT
```

```
                    132   ;;;;;;;;;;;;;;;;;;;;;;;;;;;;;;;;;;;;;;;;;;;;;;;;
                    133   ;;;;;;;;;;;;;;;;;;;;;;;;;;;;;;;;;;;;;;;;;;;;;;;;
                    134   ;                HSO  EXECUTED  INTERRUPT
                    135   ;;;;;;;;;;;;;;;;;;;;;;;;;;;;;;;;;;;;;;;;;;;;;;;;
                    136   ;;;;;;;;;;;;;;;;;;;;;;;;;;;;;;;;;;;;;;;;;;;;;;;;
                    137   HSO_exec_int:
20CC     F2         138         PUSHF
20CC                139         ORB     Port1, #00000010B    ; Set p1.1
20CD 91020F         140
                    141         SUB     TMP,TIMER1, NXT_ON_T
20D0 4B380A46       142         CMP     TMP,ZERO
20D4 8B0046         143         JLT     set_off_times
20D7 DE19           144
                    145   set_on_times:
20D9 644B3B         146         ADD     NXT_ON_T, HSO_PER
20DC B13606         147         LDB     HSO_COMMAND, #00110110B   ; Set HSO for timer1, set pin 0.1
20DF A03804         148         LD      HSO_TIME, NXT_ON_T
20E2 FD             149         NOP
20E3 FD             150         NOP
                    151         LDB     HSO_COMMAND, #00100010B   ; Set HSO for timer1, set pin 2
20E4 B12206         152         LD      HSO_TIME, NXT_ON_T
20E7 A03804         153
20EA 91074A         154         ORB     LAST_LOAD, #00000111B     ; Last loaded value was all ones
                    155
20ED B02817         156         LDB     PWM_CONTROL, PWM_TIME_1   ; Now is as good a time as any
                    157                                           ; to update the PWM reg
20F0 2026           158         BR      check_done
                    159
                    160   set_off_times:
20F2 304A23         161         JBC     LAST_LOAD, 0, check_done
                    162
20F5 442A3B3A       163         ADD     NXT_OFF_0, NXT_ON_T, HSO_ON_0
20F9 B11006         164         LDB     HSO_COMMAND, #00010000B   ; Set HSO for timer1, clear pin 0
20FC A03A04         165         LD      HSO_TIME, NXT_OFF_0
                    166
20FF FD             167         NOP
2100 442C3B3C       168         ADD     NXT_OFF_1, NXT_ON_T, HSO_ON_1
2104 B11106         169         LDB     HSO_COMMAND, #00010001B   ; Set HSO for timer1, clear pin 1
2107 A03C04         170         LD      HSO_TIME, NXT_OFF_1
                    171
210A FD             172         NOP
210B 442E3B3E       173         ADD     NXT_OFF_2, NXT_ON_T, HSO_ON_2
210F B11206         174         LDB     HSO_COMMAND, #00010010B   ; Set HSO for timer1, clear pin 2
2112 A03E04         175         LD      HSO_TIME, NXT_OFF_2
                    176
2115 71F84A         177         ANDB    LAST_LOAD, #11111000B     ; Last loaded value was all 0s
                    178
2118                179   check_done:
2118 71FD0F         180         ANDB    Port1, #11111101B         ; Clear P1.1
                    181
```

```
211B F3                    182            POPF
211C F0                    183            RET
                           184
                           185   $EJECT
                           186   ;;;;;;;;;;;;;;;;;;;;;;;;;;;;;;;;;;;;;;;;;;;;;;;;;;;;;;;;;;;;
                           187   ;;                                                         ;;
                           188   ;;                A TO D COMPLETE INTERRUPT                ;;
                           189   ;;                                                         ;;
                           190   ;;;;;;;;;;;;;;;;;;;;;;;;;;;;;;;;;;;;;;;;;;;;;;;;;;;;;;;;;;;;
211D                       191   ATOD_done_int:
211D F2                    192            PUSHF
211E 91040F                193            ORB     Port1, #00000100B   ; Set P1.2
                           194
2121 51C0021C              195            ANDB    AL, AD_RESULT_LO, #11000000B  ; Load low order result
2125 B0031D                196            LDB     AH, AD_RESULT_HI              ; Load high order result
2128 5444441E              197            ADDB    DL, AD_NUM, AD_NUM            ; DL= AD_NUM *2
212C AC1E1E                198            LDBZE   DX, DL
212F C31E301C              199            ST      AX, RESULT_TABLE[DX]          ; Store result indexed by DX
                           200
2133 99401C                201            CMPB    AL, #01000000B
2136 D107                  202            JNH     no_rnd                        ; Round up if needed
2138 99FF1D                203            CMPB    AH, #0FFH                     ; Don't increment if AH=0FFH
213B DF02                  204            JE      no_rnd
213D 171D                  205            INCB    AH
                           206
213F B01D1C                207   no_rnd:  LDB     AL, AH                        ; Align byte and change to word
2142 111D                  208            CLRB    AH
2144 C31E281C              209            ST      AX, ON_TIME[DX]
                           210
2148 1744                  211            INCB    AD_NUM
214A 710344                212            ANDB    AD_NUM, #03H                  ; Keep AD_NUM between 0 and 3
                           213
214D 55084402              214   next:    ADDB    AD_COMMAND, AD_NUM, #1000B    ; Start conversion on channel
                           215                                                  ;  indicated by AD_NUM register
2151 71FB0F                216            ANDB    Port1, #11111011B             ; Clear P1.2
2154 F3                    217            POPF
2155 F0                    218            RET
                           219
2156                       220            END
                           221

ASSEMBLY COMPLETED, NO ERROR(S) FOUND.
```

APPENDIX C
SOFTWARE SERIAL PORT

```
SERIES-III MCS-96 MACRO ASSEMBLER, V1.0

SOURCE FILE: :F3:SWPORT.A96
OBJECT FILE: :F3:SWPORT.OBJ
CONTROLS SPECIFIED IN INVOCATION COMMAND: NOSB

ERR LOC  OBJECT           LINE         SOURCE STATEMENT
                            1          $TITLE('SWPORT.A96 ; SOFTWARE IMPLEMENTED ASYNCHRONOUS SERIAL PORT')
                            2
                            3          ; This module provides a software implemented asynchronous serial port
                            4          ; for the 8096.  HSO.5 is used for transmit data.  HSI.2 is used for
                            5          ; receive data. Note: the choice of HSO.5 and HSI.2 is arbitrary).
                            6
                            7          $INCLUDE(DEMO96.INC)
                      =1    8          $nolist ;  Turn listing off for include file
                      =1   56                  ;  End of include file
                           57
                           58          ;       VARIABLES NEEDED BY THE SOFTWARE SERIAL PORT
                           59          ;       ==============================================
                           60          ;
                           61                  rseg
                           62
     0000                  63          ios1_save:      dsb 1   ; Used to save contents of ios1
     0000                  64          rcve_state:     dsb 1
     0001                  65          rxrdy           equ 1   ; indicates receive done
     0002                  66          rxoverrun       equ 2   ; indicates receive overflow
     0004                  67          rip             equ 4   ; receive in progress flag
     0002                  68          rcve_buf:       dsb 1   ; used to double buffer receive data
     0003                  69          rcve_reg:       dsb 1   ; used to deserialize receive
     0004                  70          sample_time:    dsw 1   ; records last receive sample time
                           71
     0006                  72          serial_out:     dsw 1   ; Holds the output character+framing (start and
                           73                                  ;  stop bits) for transmit process.
     0008                  74          baud_count:     dsw 1   ; Holds the period of one bit in units
                           75                                  ;  of T1 ticks.
     000A                  76          txd_time:       dsw 1   ; Transition time of last Txd bit that was
                           77                                  ;  sent to the CAM
     000C                  78          char:           dsb 1   ; for test only
                           79
                           80          ;       COMMANDS ISSUED TO THE HSO UNIT
                           81          ;       =================================
                           82
     0035                  83          mark_command    equ 01101011b   ; timer1:set:interrupt on 5
     0015                  84          space_command   equ 00101011b   ; timer1:clr:interrupt on 5
     0018                  85          sample_command  equ 00110000b   ; software timer 0
                           86
                           87          $eject
```

270061-91

AP-248

```
                                        cseg at 2080h
2080
                            ;reset_loc:
                            ; The 8096 starts executing here on reset, the program will initialize the
                            ; the software serial port and run a simple test to excercize it.
2080 FA                             di
2081 A1F00018                       ld      sp,#0F0h
2085 C9C012                         push    #4800
2088 EF0000    R                    call    setup_serial_port
208B B16C08                         ldb     int_mask,#01101100b    ; serial, swt,hso,hsi
208E FB                             ei
                            ;
                            ;test1:
                            ; A simple test of the serial port routines.
                            ; While no characters are received an incrementing pattern is sent to the
                            ; serial output. When a character is received the incrementing pattern
                            ; "jumps" to the character recved and proceeds from there.
                            ;
        000D                CR      equ     0DH                    ; Carriage return
208F B10D0C                         ldb     char,#CR
2092 AC0C1C   R     testloop:
2092 AC0C1C   R             idbze   ax,char
2095 C81C                           push    ax
2097 EF3000   R                     call    char_out
209A 990D0C   R                     cmpb    char,#CR               ; Pause on Carriage return
209D D706                           bne     nopause
209F 011C                           clr     ax
20A1                        pause:
20A1 071C                           inc     ax
20A3 D7FC                           bne     pause
20A5                        nopause:
20A5 170C                           incb    char
20A7                        test2:
20A7 EF4400   R                     call    csts                   ; char ready?
20AA 9B001C                         cmpb    al,0
20AD DFE3                           be      testloop               ; loop if not
20AF EF4C00   R                     call    char_in
20B2 B01C0C   R                     ldb     char,al
20B5 27DB                           br      testloop
                                    $eject
```

270061-92

5-86

AP-248

270061-93

```
                          cseg
                  ;
                  ; setup_serial_port
                  ; Called on system reset to intiate the software serial port
                  ;
0000 CC22                 pop     cx              ; the return address
0002 CC20                 pop     bx              ; the baud rate (in decimal)
0004 A107001E             ld      dx,#0007h       ; dx:ax =500,000 (assumes 12 Mhz crystal)
0008 A120A11C             ld      ax,#0A120h      ; calculate the baud count (500,000/baudrate)
000C 8C201C                divu    ax,bx
000F C0081C              R st      0,serial_out    ; clear serial out
0012 C00600              R ldb     ioc1,#01100000b ; Enable HSO.5 and Txd
0015 B16016                ldb     ios0,6,$        ; Wait for room in the HSO CAM
0018 3E15FD                bbs                      ; and issue a MARK command

001B 44140A0A            R add     txd_time,timer1,20
001F B13506                ldb     hso_command,#mark_command
0022 A00A04              R ld      hso_time,txd_time
0025 1102                  clrb    rcve_buf        ; clear out the receive variables
0027 1103                  clrb    rcve_reg
0029 1101                  clrb    rcve_state
002B EF4800                call    init_receive    ; setup to detect a start bit
002E E322                  br      [cx]            ; return

                  $eject
                  ; char_out
                  ; Output character to the software serial port
                  ;
0030 CC22                 pop     cx              ; the return address
0032 CC20                 pop     bx              ; the character for output
0034 B10121               ldb     (bx+1),#01h     ; add the start and stop bits
0037 642020               add     bx,bx           ; to the char and leave as 16 bit
003A                 wait_for_xmit:
003A B80006              R cmp     serial_out,0    ; wait for serial_out=0 (it will be cleared by
003D D7FB                  bne     wait_for_xmit   ;   the hso interrupt process)
003F C00620              R st      bx,serial_out   ; put the formatted character in serial_out
0042 E322                  br      [cx]            ; return to caller

0044              csts:
                  ; Returns "true" (ax<>0) if char_in has a character.
                  ;
0044 011C                  clr     ax
0046 300102              R bbc     rcve_state,0,csts_exit
0049 071C                  inc     ax
004B                 csts_exit:
004B F0                    ret
004C              char_in:
```

AP-248

```
                              181          ; Get a character from the software serial port
                              182          ;
                              183                              bbc     rcve_state.0,char_in  ; wait for character ready
004C 3001FD                   184                              pushf
004F F2                       185                              andb    rcve_state,#not(rxrdy) ; set up a critical region
0050 71FE01         R         186                              ldbze   al,rcve_buf            ; leave the critical region
0053 AC021C         R         187                              popf
0056 F3                       188                              ret
0057 F0                       189
                              190          $eject
                              191          hso_isr:
                              192          ; Fields the hso interrupts and performs the serialization of the data.
                              193          ; Note: this routine would be incorporated into the hso service strategy
                              194          ;       for an actual system.
                              195
                              196                              cseg    at 2006h
0058                          197                              dcw     hso_isr                ; Set up vector
                              198
2006                          199                              cseg
2006 5800                     200                              pushf
                              201                              add     txd_time,baud_count
0058 F2             R         202                              cmp     serial_out,0           ; if character is done send a mark
0059 64080A         R         203                              be      send_mark              ; else send bit 0 of serial_out and shift
005C 880006                   204                              shr     serial_out,#1          ; serial_out left one place
005F DF0D           R         205                              bc      send_mark
0061 080106                   206          send_space:
0064 DB08                     207                              ldb     hso_command,#space_command
                              208                              ld      hso_time,txd_time
0066 B11506         R         209                              br      hso_isr_exit
0069 A00A04                   210          send_mark:
006C 2006                     211                              ldb     hso_command,#mark_command
                              212                              ld      hso_time,txd_time
006E B13506         R         213          hso_isr_exit:
0071 A00A04                   214                              popf
                              215                              ret
                              216          $eject
0074 F3                       217          init_receive:
0074 F0                       218          ; Called to prepare the serial input process to find the leading edge of
                              219          ; a start bit.
                              220                              ldb     ioc0,#00000000b
                              221                              ldb     hsi_mode,#00100000b    ; disconnect change detector
0076                          222          flush_fifo:                                         ; negative edges on HSI.2
                              223                              orb     iosi_save,iosi
                              224                              bbc     iosi_save,7,flush_fifo_done
0076 B10015                   225                              ldb     al,hsi_status
0079 B12003                   226                              ld      ax,hsi_time            ; trash the fifo entry
007C 901600
007F 370008
0082 B0061C
0085 A0041C         R
                    R
```

270061-94

```
0088  717F00        R       231             andb    ios1_save,#not(80h)      ; clear bit 7.
008B  27EF                  232             br      flush_fifo
008D  B11015                233     flush_fifo_done:
                            234             ldb     ioc0,#00010000b          ; connect HSI.2 to detector
0090  F0                    235             ret
                            236
                            237
                            238
0091                        239     hsi_isr:
                            240     ; Fields interrupts from the HSI unit, used to detect the leading edge
                            241     ; of the START bit
                            242     ; Note: this routine would be incorporated into the HSI strategy of an actual
                            243     ; system.
                            244
2004                        245             cseg    at 2004h
2004  9100          R       246             dcw     hsi_isr                  ; setup the interrupt vector
                            247
0091                        248             cseg
0091  F2                    249             pushf
0092  C81C                  250             push    ax
0094  B0061C                251             ldb     al,hsi_status
0097  A00404        R       252             ld      sample_time,hsi_time
009A  341C15                253             bbc     al,4,exit_hsi
009D  3F15FD                254             bbs     ios0,7,$                 ; wait for room in HSO holding reg
00A0  A0081C        R       255             ld      ax,baud_count            ; send out sample command in 1/2
00A3  08011C                256             shr     ax,#1                    ; bit time
00A6  641C04        R       257             add     sample_time,ax
00A9  B11806                258             ldb     hso_command,#sample_command
00AC  C00404        R       259             st      sample_time,hso_time
00AF  B10015                260             ldb     ioc0,#00000000b          ; disconnect hsi.2 from change detector
00B2                        261     exit_hsi:
00B2  CC1C                  262             pop     ax
00B4  F3                    263             popf
00B5  F0                    264             ret
                            265     $eject
                            266
                            267     software_timer_isr:
                            268     ; Fields the software timer interrupt, used to deserialize the incoming data.
                            269     ; Note: this routine would be incorporated into the software timer stategy
                            270     ; in an actual system.
                            271
200A                        272             cseg    at 200ah
200A  B600          R       273             dcw     software_timer_isr       ; setup vector
                            274
00B6                        275             cseg
00B6  F2                    276             pushf
00B7  901600                277             orb     ios1_save,ios1
00BA  71FE00                278             andb    ios1_save,#not(01h)      ; clear bit 0
00BD  51FC0100              279             andb    0,rcve_state,#0fch       ; All bits except rxrdy and overrun=0
00C1  D70C                  280             bne     process_data
```

```
00C3                    281     process_start_bit:
00C3  350604            282             bbc     hsi_status,5,start_ok
00C6  2FAE              283             call    init_receive
00C8  2032              284             br      software_timer_exit
00CA                    285     start_ok:
00CA  910401     R      286             orb     rcve_state,#rip ; set receive in progress flag
00CD  2021              287             br      schedule_sample
                        288
00CF                    289     process_data:
00CF  3F010E            290             bbs     rcve_state,7,check_stopbit
00D2  180103            291             shrb    rcve_reg,#1
00D5  350603            292             bbc     hsi_status,5,datazero
00D8  918003     R      293             orb     rcve_reg,#80h   ; set the new data bit
                        294
00DB                    295     datazero:
00DB  751001     R      296             addb    rcve_state,#10h ; increment bit count
00DE  2010              297             br      schedule_sample
                        298
00E0                    299     check_stopbit:
00E0  3506FD            300             bbc     hsi_status,5,$ ; DEBUG ONLY
00E3  B00302            301             ldb     rcve_buf,rcve_reg
00E6  910101     R      302             orb     rcve_state,#rxrdy
00E9  710301     R      303             andb    rcve_state,#03h ; Clear all but ready and overrun bits
00EC  2F88              304             call    init_receive
00EE  200C              305             br      software_timer_exit
                        306
00F0                    307     schedule_sample:
00F0  3F15FD            308             bbs     ios0,7,$        ; wait for holding reg empty
00F3  B11806            309             ldb     hso_command,#sample_command
00F6  640804     R      310             add     sample_time,baud_count
00F9  C00404     R      311             st      sample_time,hso_time
                        312
00FC                    313     software_timer_exit:
00FC  F3                314             popf
00FD  F0                315             ret
                        316
00FE                    317             end

ASSEMBLY COMPLETED,  NO ERROR(S) FOUND.
```

APPENDIX D
MOTOR CONTROL PROGRAM

```
SERIES-III MCS-96 MACRO ASSEMBLER, V1.0

SOURCE FILE : :F3:MOTCON.A96
OBJECT FILE : :F3:MOTCON.OBJ
CONTROLS SPECIFIED IN INVOCATION COMMAND: NOSB

ERR LOC  OBJECT          LINE        SOURCE STATEMENT
                           1         $TITLE ('MOTCON.A96: Motor Control Example Program')
                           2         ;
                           3         ;        USE WITH C-STEP or later parts
                           4         ;
                           5         ;                                    December 20, 1984
                           6         ;
                           7         $INCLUDE(DEMO96.INC)
                    =1     8         $nolist  ; Turn listing off for include file
                    =1    56         ;        ; End of include file
                          57
                          58         ;;;;;;;;;; Initial Values
                          59
 001E                     60         min_hsil_t      equ    30      ; min period for PHA edges in mode1 before mode2
                          61
 003C                     62         min_hsil_t      equ    2*min_hsil_t
                          63                                        ; min period for PHA edges in mode0 before mode1
                          64
 0069                     65         max_hsil_t      equ    3*min_hsil_t + min_hsil_t/2
                          66                                        ; max period for PHA edges in mode0 before mode0
                          67
                          68
 006E                     69         HSO0_dly_period equ    110     ; delay for HSO timer 0 (timed count of pulses)
                          70                                        ; min period for 5 T2 clocks before mode 1
                          71
 00FA                     72         swt1_dly_period equ    250     ; delay for software timer 1
 00FA                     73         swt2_dly_period equ    250     ; delay for software timer 2
 00FF                     74         max_power       equ    0ffh
 00FF                     75         max_brake       equ    0ffh
 0080                     76         maximum_hold    equ    080H
 04B0                     77         brake_pnt       equ    1200
 0064                     78         position_pnt    equ    100
 0010                     79         velocity_pnt    equ    16
                          80
                          81
 0024                     82         RSEG at 024H
                          83
 0024                     84         tmp:            dsl    1
 0028                     85         timer_2:        dsl    1
```

APPENDIX D
MOTOR CONTROL PROGRAM

```
002C    86              tmr2_old:       dsl 1
0030    87              position:       dsl 1
0034    88              des_pos:        dsl 1
0038    89              pos_err:        dsl 1
003C    90              delta_p:        dsl 1
0040    91              time:           dsl 1
0044    92              des_time:       dsl 1
0048    93              time_err:       dsl 1
        94
        95      $EJECT
        96
004C    97              last_time_err:  dsw 1
004E    98              last_pos_err:   dsw 1
0050    99              pos_delta:      dsw 1
0052    100             time_delta:     dsw 1
0054    101             last_pos:       dsw 1
0056    102             last1_time:     dsw 1
0058    103             last2_time:     dsw 1
005A    104             boost:          dsw 1
005C    105             tmp1:           dsw 1
005E    106             out_ptr:        dsw 1
0060    107             offset:         dsw 1
0062    108             nxt_pos:        dsw 1
0064    109             rpwr:           dsw 1
0066    110             old_t2:         dsw 1
        111
0068    112             direct:         dsb 1   ; 1=forward, 0=reverse
0069    113             pwm_dir:        dsb 1
006A    114             hsi_s0:         dsb 1
006B    115             last_stat:      dsb 1
006C    116             pwm_pwr:        dsb 1
006D    117             ios1_bak:       dsb 1
006E    118             TR_COL          DSB 1   ; COLLECT TRACE IF TR_COL=00
006F    119             main_dly:       dsb 1
        120
0070    121             max_pwr:        dsw 1
0072    122             max_brk:        dsw 1
0074    123             max_hold:       dsw 1
0076    124             vel_pnt:        dsw 1
0078    125             brk_pnt:        dsw 1
007A    126             pos_pnt:        dsw 1
007C    127             HSO0_dly:       dsw 1
007E    128             swt1_dly:       dsw 1
0080    129             swt2_dly:       dsw 1
0082    130             min_hsi:        dsw 1
0084    131             min_hsi1:       dsw 1
0086    132             max_hsi1:       dsw 1
        133
        134             dseg at 100H
0100    135
```

```
                                                    FLAG USAGE
136                mode_view:    dsb     1
137                count_out:    dsw     1
138                err_view:     dsw     1
139
140
141
142        $eject
143
144                ;          PIN#    PORT       FLAG USAGE
145                ;
146                ;           22     P1.0       mode0 0       mode1 1    mode2 1 or 0
147                ;           23     P1.1              0             0          1
148                ;           24     P1.2       software timer 2 routine enter/leave
149                ;           25     P1.3       Main program toggle
150                ;           26     P1.4       HSI overflow toggle
151                ;           37     P1.5       software timer 0 routine enter/leave
152                ;           38     P1.6       hsi_int enter/leave
153                ;           39     P1.7       software timer 1 routine enter/leave
154                ;           40     P2.6       Input direction (0=reverse, 1=forward)
155                ;           45     P2.7       direction 0=rev, 1=fwd
156
157                   cseg    at     2000H
2000 0022          timer_ovf_int   dcw    timer_ovf_int
2002 1020          atod_done_int   dcw    atod_done_int
2004 0424          hsi_data_int    dcw    hsi_data_int
2006 8022          hso_exec_int    dcw    hso_exec_int
2008 1020          hsi_0_int       dcw    hsi_0_int
200A 2022          soft_tmr_int    dcw    soft_tmr_int
200C 1020          ser_port_int    dcw    ser_port_int
200E 1020          external_int    dcw    external_int
167
2010               atod_done_int:
2010               hsi_0_int:
2010               ser_port_int:
2010               external_int:
171
172                   cseg    at     2080H
173
2080 A1F00018      init:     ld      sp,#0F0H
2084 B1FF17                  ldb     pwm_control,#0FFH
176
2087 1168                    clrb    direct
2089 A170175C                ld      tmp1,#6000
208D 055C          delay:    ld      tmp1                      ; wait about 3 seconds for motor
208F E068FD                  dec     direct.$                  ;   to come to a stop
2092 88005C                  djnz    tmp1,zero                 ; wait 0.512 milliseconds
2095 D2F6                    jgt     delay
183
2097 B1FF0F                  ldb     port1,#0FFH
209A B1FF10                  ldb     port2,#0FFH
```

AP-248

```
209D B12516          186          ldb    IOC1,#00100101B  ; Disable HSO 4, HSO 5, HSI_INT=first,
                     187                                  ;   Enable PWM, TXD, TIMER1_OVRFLOW_INT
                     188
20A0 71FC0F          189          andb   Port1,#11111100B ; clear P1.0,1 (set mode 0)
20A3 B19903          190          ldb    HSI_mode,#10011001B ; set hsi1,3 -; hsi.0,2 +
20A6 B15715          191          ldb    IOCO,#01010111B  ; Enable all hsi
                     192                                  ; T2 CLOCK=T2CLK, T2RST=T2RST
                     193                                  ; Clear timer2
                     194  $eject
                     195
20A9 A00400          196          ld     zero,hsi_time
20AC 0140            197          clr    time
20AE 0142            198          clr    time+2
20B0 0128            199          clr    timer_2
20B2 012A            200          clr    timer_2+2
20B4 0130            201          clr    position
20B6 0132            202          clr    position+2
20B8 0154            203          clr    last_pos
20BA 0134            204          clr    des_pos
20BC 0136            205          clr    des_pos+2
20BE 0144            206          clr    des_time
20C0 0146            207          clr    des_time+2
20C2 A00A56          208          ld     last1_time,Timer1
20C5 490008565B      209          sub    last2_time,last1_time,#800H
20CA 116D            210          clrb   int_pending
20CC 1109            211          clrb   iost_bak
20CE A1F0015E        212          ld     out_ptr,#1F0H
20D2 A13C00B2        213          ld     min_hsi,#min_hsi_t
20D6 A11E00B4        214          ld     min_hsi1,#min_hsi1_t
20DA A16900B6        215          ld     max_hsi1,#max_hsi1_t
20DE A16E007C        216          ld     HSO0_dly,#HSO0_dly_period
20E2 A1FA007E        217          ld     swt1_dly,#swt1_dly_period
20E6 A1FA00B0        218          ld     swt2_dly,#(swt2_dly_period)
20EA A1FF0070        219          ld     max_pwr,#max_power
20EE A1FF0072        220          ld     max_brk,#max_brake
20F2 A1B00074        221          ld     max_hold,#maximum_hold
20F6 A1B00478        222          ld     brk_pnt,#brake_pnt
20FA A164007A        223          ld     pos_pnt,#position_pnt
20FE A1100076        224          ld     vel_pnt,#velocity_pnt
2102 A1002762        225          ld     nxt_pos,#pos_table
2106 B0006C          226          ldb    pwm_pwr,zero
2109 B10169          227          ldb    pwm_dir,#01h                    ; FORWARD
                     228
210C B12D0B          229          ldb    int_mask,#00101101B  ; Enable tmr_ovf, hsi, swt, HSO interrupts
210F B13006          230          ldb    hso_command,#30H      ; set HSO_0
2112 447C0A04        231          add    hso_time,timer1,HSO0_dly
2116 FD              232          nop
2117 FD              233          NOP
2118 B13906          234          ldb    hso_command,#39H      ; set swt_1
211B 447E0A04        235          add    hso_time,timer1,swt1_dly
```

270061-A0

```
211F  FD                      236              nop
2120  FD                      237              nop
2121  B13A06                  238              ldb    hso_command,#3AH     ; set swt_2
2124  44800A04                239              add    hso_time,timer1,swt2_dly
                              240
2128  A00A40                  241              ld     time,TIMER1
212B  A00C2C                  242              ld     tmr2_old,timer2
212E  FB                      243              ei
                              244
212F  E7CE06                  245              br     main_prog
                              246
                              247   $eject
                              248   ;;;;;;;;;;;;;;;;;;;;;;;;;;;;;;;;;;;;;;;;;;;;;;;;;;;;;;;;;;;;;;;;;;;;;;;;;;
                              249   ;;;;;
                              250   ;;;;;                TIMER INTERRUPT SERVICE
                              251   ;;;;;
                              252   ;;;;;;;;;;;;;;;;;;;;;;;;;;;;;;;;;;;;;;;;;;;;;;;;;;;;;;;;;;;;;;;;;;;;;;;;;;
                              253
2200                          254              CSEG AT 2200H
                              255
2200  F2                      256   timer_ovf_int
                              257              pushf
2201  90166D                  258              orb    ios1_bak,IOS1
2204  356D05                  259   chk_t1:    jbc    ios1_bak,5,tmr_int_done
2207  0742                    260              inc    time+2
2209  71DF6D                  261              andb   ios1_bak,#11011111B  ; clear bit 5
                              262
220C                          263   tmr_int_done
220C  F3                      264              popf
220D  F0                      265              ret                         ; End of timer interrupt routine
                              266
                              267   ;;;;;;;;;;;;;;;;;;;;;;;;;;;;;;;;;;;;;;;;;;;;;;;;;;;;;;;;;;;;;;;;;;;;;;;;;;
                              268   ;;;;;
                              269   ;;;;;           SOFTWARE TIMER INTERRUPT SERVICE ROUTINE
                              270   ;;;;;
                              271   ;;;;;;;;;;;;;;;;;;;;;;;;;;;;;;;;;;;;;;;;;;;;;;;;;;;;;;;;;;;;;;;;;;;;;;;;;;
                              272
2220                          273              CSEG AT 2220H
                              274
                              275   soft_tmr_int
2220  F2                      276              pushf
2221  90166D                  277              orb    ios1_bak,IOS1
                              278
                              279   chk_swt0:
2224  306D03                  280              jbc    ios1_bak,0,chk_swt1
2227  71FE6D                  281              andb   ios1_bak,#11111110B  ; Clear bit 0 - end swt0
                              282              call   swt0_expired
                              283   chk_swt1:
222A  316D06                  284              jbc    ios1_bak,1,chk_swt2
222D  71FD6D                  285              andb   ios1_bak,#11111101B  ; Clear bit 1
```

AP-248

```
286              call     swt1_expired
287     chk_swt2:
2230 EFCD03    288              jbc      ios1_bak.2,chk_swt3
2233 326D06    289              andb     ios1_bak,#11110111B    ; Clear bit 2
2236 71FB6D    290              call     swt2_expired
2239 EF4401    291     chk_swt3:
223C 346D03    292              jbc      ios1_bak.4,swt_int_done
223F 71F76D    293              andb     ios1_bak,#11101111B    ; Clear bit 3
                294              call     swt3_expired
                295
                296     swt_int_done:
2242 F3        297              popf
2243 F0        298              ret
                299                     ; END OF SOFTWARE TIMER INTERRUPT ROUTINE
                300     $eject
                301     ;;;;;;;;;;;;;;;;;;;;;;;;;;;;;;;;;;;;;;;;;;;;;;;;;;;;;;;;;
                302     ;;;;;                 SOFTWARE TIMER ROUTINE 0        ;;;;;
                303     ;;;;;              NOW USING HSO 0 TO TRIGGER         ;;;;;
                304     ;;;;;;;;;;;;;;;;;;;;;;;;;;;;;;;;;;;;;;;;;;;;;;;;;;;;;;;;;
                305
                306
2280            307              CSEG AT 2280H
                308
2280            309     hso_exec_int:                    ; Check mode -- Update position in mode 2
2280 F2         310              PUSHF
2281 B13006     311              ldb      HSO_COMMAND,#30H
2284 447C0A04   312              add      HSO_TIME,TIMER1,HSO0_dly
                313
2288 91200F     314              orb      port1,#00100000B       ; set P1.5
228B A00C28     315              ld       Timer_2,TIMER2
228E 390F18     316              jbs      Port1,1,in_mode2
                317
2291            318     in_mode1:
2291 4866285C   319              sub      tmp1,Timer_2,old_t2    ; Check count difference in tmp1
2295 8902005C   320              cmp      tmp1,#2
2299 D94C       321              jh       end_swt0
                322
229B            323     set_mode0:
229B 300F49     324              jbc      Port1.0,end_swt0       ; if already in mode 0
229E 71FC0F     325              andb     Port1,#11111100B       ; Clear P1.0, P1.1 (set mode 0)
22A1 B15515     326              ldb      IOC0,#01010101B        ; enable all HSI
22A4 B0006B     327              ldb      last_stat,zero
22A7 203E       328              br       end_swt0
                329
22A9            330     in_mode2:
22A9 482C283C   331              sub      delta_p,timer_2,tmr2_old  ; get timer2 count difference
22AD A0282C     332              ld       tmr2_old,timer_2
                333
22B0 306B08     334              jbc      direct.0,in_rev
                335
```

```
2283 643C30          336      in_fwd:  add     position,delta_p
22B6 A40032          337               addc    position+2,zero
22B9 2006            338               br      chk_mode
                     339
22BB 683C30          340      in_rev:  sub     position,delta_p
22BE A80032          341               subc    position+2,zero
                     342
22C1                 343      chk_mode:
22C1 4866285C        344               cmp     tmp1,Timer_2,old_t2     ; Check count difference in tmp1
22C5 B905005C        345               cmp     tmp1,#5                 ; set model if count is too low
22C9 D21C            346               jgt     end_swt0                ; count <= 5
                     347
22CB                 348      set_model:
22CB 71FD0F          349               andb    Port1,#11111101B        ; Clear P1.1, set P1.0 (set mode 1)
22CE 91010F          350               orb     Port1,#00000001B
22D1 B10515          351               ldb     IOC0,#00000101B         ; enable HSI 0 and 1
22D4 A00400          352               ld      zero, HSI_TIME
22D7 4B840A56        353               sub     last1_time,Timer1,min_hsil
                     354                                               ; set up so (time-last2_time)>min_hsil on next HSI
                     355      $EJECT
                     356
                     357      clr_hsi:
22DB A00400          358               ld      ZERO, HSI_TIME
22DE 717F6D          359               andb    ios1_bak,#01111111B     ; clear bit 7
22E1 90166D          360               orb     ios1_bak,ios1
22E4 3F6DF4          361               jbs     ios1_bak,7,clr_hsi      ; If hsi is triggered then clear hsi
                     362
                     363      end_swt0:
22E7 A02866          364               ld      old_t2,TIMER_2
22EA 71F0F           365               andb    Port1,#10111111B        ; clear P1.5
22ED F3              366               POPF
22EE F0              367               ret
                     368
                     369      ;;;;;;;;;;;;;;;;;;;;;;;;;;;;;;;;;;;;;;;;;;;;;;;;;;;;;;;;;;;;
                     370      ;;;;;                                                   ;;;;
                     371      ;;;;;               SOFTWARE TIMER ROUTINE 2            ;;;;
                     372      ;;;;;                                                   ;;;;
                     373      ;;;;;;;;;;;;;;;;;;;;;;;;;;;;;;;;;;;;;;;;;;;;;;;;;;;;;;;;;;;;
                     374
2380                 375               CSEG AT 23B0H
                     376
                     377      swt2_expired:
2380 F2              378               pushf
2381 B13A06          379               ldb     hso_command,#3AH        ; set swt_2
2384 44B00A04        380               add     hso_time,timer1,swt2_dly
                     381
2388 91040F          382               orb     port1,#00000100B        ; set port 1.2
238B 89FF075E        383               cmp     out_ptr,#7ffH
238F D104            384               bnh     pulsing
2391 A1F0015E        385               ld      out_ptr,#1f0H
```

AP-248

```
2395                                                  pulsing:
2395  30␣E0C                                                    jbc     tr_col.0,swt2_done
2398  C25F32                                                    st      position+2,[out_ptr]+    ; position high, position low
239B  C25F30                                                    st      position,[out_ptr]+
239E  C25F68                                                    st      direct,[out_ptr]+
23A1  C25F6C                                                    st      pwm_pwr,[out_ptr]+       ; store 8 bytes externally
                                                     swt2_done:
23A4  48560A5C                                                  sub     tmp1,timer1,last1_time
23A8  B9001B5C                                                  cmp     tmp1,#1B00H
23AC  D104                                                      jnh     swt2_ret                 ; keep (Timer1-last1_time)<2000H
23AE  65001056                                                  add     last1_time,#1000H
                                                     swt2_ret:
23B2  71FB0F                                                    andb    port1,#11111011B         ; clear port1.2
23B5  F3                                                        popf
23B6  F0                                                        ret

                                                     $EJECT
                                                     ;;;;;;;;;;;;;;;;;;;;;;;;;;;;;;;;;;;;;;;;;;;;;;;;;;;;;;;;;;
                                                     ;               HSI DATA AVAILABLE INTERRUPT ROUTINE
                                                     ;;;;;;;;;;;;;;;;;;;;;;;;;;;;;;;;;;;;;;;;;;;;;;;;;;;;;;;;;;
                                                     ; This routine keeps track of the current time and position of the motor.
                                                     ; The upper word of information is provided by the timer overflow routine.
                                                     
                                                             CSEG AT 2400H
2400                                                 now_mode_1:
2400  20CE                                                    br      in_mode_1
2402  20C7                                          no_int:   br      no_int                    ; worst case loop
2404  F2                                            hsi_data_int:
2404  F2                                                      pushf
2405  91400F                                                  orb     port1,#01000000B          ; set P1.6
2408  717F6D                                                  andb    ios1_bak,#01111111B       ; Clear ios1_bak.7
240B  90166D                                                  orb     ios1_bak,ios1
240E  376DF1                                                  jbc     ios1_bak.7,no_int1        ; If hsi is not triggered then
                                                                                                ; Jump to no_int
2411                                                 get_values:
2411  A00C28                                                   ld      timer_2,TIMER2
2414  5155066A                                                 andb    hsi_s0,HSI_STATUS,#01010101B
2418  A00440                                                   ld      time,HSI_TIME

241B  380FE2                                                   jbs     port1.0,now_mode_1       ; jump if in mode 1
241E                                                 in_mode_0:
241E  386A0B                                                   jbs     hsi_s0.0,a_rise
```

5-98

```
2421  3A6A2C                  436             jbs    hsi_so,2,a_fall
2424  3C6A4D                  437             jbs    hsi_so,4,b_rise
2427  3E6A5A                  438             jbs    hsi_so,6,b_fall
242A  2094                    439             br     no_cnt
                              440
242C  A05658                  441  a_rise:    ld     last2_time,last1_time
242F  A04056                  442             ld     last1_time,time
2432  685840                  443             sub    time,last2_time
2435  888240                  444             cmp    time,min_hsi
2438  D906                    445             jh     tst_statr
                              446  ;set model-
243A  91010F                  447             orb    Port1,#00000001B      ; Set P1.0 (in mode 1)
243D  B10515                  448             ldb    IOCO,#00000101B       ; Enable HSI 0 and 1
                              449  tst_statr:
2440  3E6B5B                  450             jbs    last_stat,6,going_fwd
2443  3C6B67                  451             jbs    last_stat,4,going_rev
2446  3A6B50                  452             jbs    last_stat,2,change_dir
2449  98006B                  453             cmpb   last_stat,zero
244C  DF46                    454             je     first_time            ; first time in mode0
244E  27B2                    455             br     no_int1
                              456
2450  A05658                  457  a_fall:    ld     last2_time,last1_time
2453  A04056                  458             ld     last1_time,time
2456  685840                  459             sub    time,last2_time
2459  888240                  460             cmp    time,min_hsi
245C  D906                    461             jh     tst_statf
                              462  ;set model-
245E  91010F                  463             orb    Port1,#00000001B      ; Set P1.0 (in mode 1)
2461  B10515                  464             ldb    IOCO,#00000101B       ; Enable HSI 0 and 1
                              465  $EJECT
                              466  tst_statf:
2464  3C6B37                  467             jbs    last_stat,4,going_fwd
2467  3E6B43                  468             jbs    last_stat,6,going_rev
246A  386B2C                  469             jbs    last_stat,0,change_dir
246D  98006B                  470             cmpb   last_stat,zero
2470  DF22                    471             je     first_time            ; first time in mode0
2472  2057                    472             br     no_int
                              473
2474  386B27                  474  b_rise:    jbs    last_stat,0,going_fwd
2477  3A6B33                  475             jbs    last_stat,2,going_rev
247A  3E6B1C                  476             jbs    last_stat,6,change_dir
247D  98006B                  477             cmpb   last_stat,zero
2480  DF12                    478             je     first_time            ; first time in mode0
2482  2047                    479             br     no_int
                              480
2484  3A6B17                  481  b_fall:    jbs    last_stat,2,going_fwd
2487  386B23                  482             jbs    last_stat,0,going_rev
248A  3C6B0C                  483             jbs    last_stat,4,change_dir
248D  98006B                  484             cmpb   last_stat,zero
2490  DF02                    485             je     first_time            ; first time in mode0
```

```
2492  2037                  486             br      no_int
                            487
2494  C46B6A     first_time:488
2494  C46B6A                489             stb     hsi_s0,last_stat
2497  2072                  490             br      done_chk    ; add delta position
                            491
                            492
2499                        493  change_dir:
2499  1268                  494             notb    direct
249B  30680F                495  no_inc:    jbc     direct.0,going_rev
                            496
249E                        497  going_fwd:
249E  914010                498             orb     PORT2,#01000000B   ; set P2.6
24A1  B10168                499             ldb     direct,#01         ; direction = forward
24A4  65010030              500             add     position+2,zero
24A8  A40032                501             addc    position+2,zero
24AB  200D                  502             br      st_stat
24AD                        503
24AD  71BF10                504  going_rev: andb   PORT2,#10111111B   ; clear P2.6
24B0  B10068                505             ldb     direct,#00         ; direction = reverse
24B3  69010030              506             sub     position+2,zero
24B7  A80032                507             subc    position+2,zero
                            508
24BA                        509  st_stat:
24BA  C46B6A                510  load_lasts: stb   hsi_s0,last_stat
24BD  A02B2C                511             ld      tmr2_old,timer_2
24C0  717F6D                512  no_cnt:    andb   ios1_bak,#01111111B  ; clr bit 7
24C3  901b6D                513             orb     ios1_bak,ios1
24C6  376D02                514             jbc     ios1_bak.7,no_int
24C9  2746                  515  again:     br      get_values
                            516
24CB  71BF0F                517  no_int:    andb   port1,#10111111B   ; Clear P1.6
24CE  F3                    518             popf
24CF  F0                    519             ret
                            520             ; end of hsi_data interrupt routine
                            521             ; Routine for mode 1 follows and then returns to "load_lasts"
                            522  $EJECT
                            523
                            524
24D0                        525  In_mode_1:                          ; mode 1 HSI routine
                            526
24D0  51506A5C              527             andb    tmp1,hsi_s0,#01010000B
24D4  D7EA                  528             jne     no_cnt
24D6                        529  cmp_time:                           ; Procedure which sets mode 1 also
                            530                                     ; sets times to pass the tests
24D6  A0565B                531             ld      last2_time,last1_time
24D9  A04056                532             ld      last1_time,time
                            533
24DC  4B58405C              534  cmp1:     sub     tmp1,time,last2_time
24E0  8BB45C                535             cmp     tmp1,min_hsi1
```

```
24E3 D914                     536               jh      check_max_time
                              537
                              538       set_mode_2:
24E5 91020F                   539               orb     Port1,#00000010B    ; Set P1.1 (in mode 2)
24E8 B10015                   540               ldb     IOCO,#00000000B     ; Disable all HSI
24EB A00400                   541               ld      zero,hsi_time       ; empty the hsi fifo
24EE 717F6D                   542       mt_hsi: andb    iosi_bak,#01111111B ; clear bit 7
24F1 90166D                   543               orb     iosi_bak,iosi
24F4 3F6DF4                   544               jbs     iosi_bak,7,mt_hsi   ; If hsi is triggered then clear hsi
24F7 2012                     545               br      done_chk
                              546
                              547       check_max_time:
24F9 4858405C                 548               sub     tmp1,time,last2_time
24FD 8B865C                   549               cmp     tmp1,max_hsi        ; max_hsi = addition to min_hsi for
                              550                                           ; total time
2500 D109                     551               jnh     done_chk
                              552
                              553       set_mode_0:
2502 71FCOF                   554               andb    Port1,#11111100B    ; clear P1.0,1 set mode 00
2505 B15515                   555               ldb     IOCO,#01010101B     ; Enable all HSI
2508 B0006B                   556               ldb     last_stat,zero
                              557
                              558       done_chk:
250B 482C283C                 559               sub     delta_p,timer_2,tmr2_old ; get timer2 count difference
250F 306808                   560               jbc     direct.0,add_rev
2512 643C30                   561       add_fwd:add     position,delta_p
2515 A40032                   562               addc    position+2,zero
2518 27A3                     563               br      load_lasts
                              564
251A 683C30                   565       add_rev:sub     position,delta_p
251D A80032                   566               subc    position+2,zero
2520 279B                     567               br      load_lasts
                              568
                              569       $eject
                              570       ;;;;;;;;;;;;;;;;;;;;;;;;;;;;;;;;;;;;;;;;;;;;;;;;;;;;;;;;;;
                              571       ;;;;;;                  SOFTWARE TIMER ROUTINE 1
                              572       ;;;;;;;;;;;;;;;;;;;;;;;;;;;;;;;;;;;;;;;;;;;;;;;;;;;;;;;;;;
                              573
                              574
2600                          575               CSEG AT 2600H
                              576       swt1_expired:
2600                          577               pushf
2600 F2                       578               orb     port1,#10000000B    ; set port1.7
2601 91800F                   579
                              580
2604 B10D08                   581               ldb     int_mask,#00001101B ; enable HSI, Tovf, HSO
                              582
2607 B13906                   583               ldb     HSO_COMMAND,#39H
260A 447E0A04                 584               add     HSO_TIME,TIMER1,swt1_dly
                              585
```

```
586                              ld      time_err+2,des_time+2    ; Calculate time & position error
587                              ld      pos_err+2,des_pos+2
588                              subc    time_err,des_time,time
589                              subc    time_err+2,time+2        ; values are set
590                              subc    pos_err,des_pos,position
591                              subc    pos_err+2,position+2
592
593
594                              EI
595
596                              sub     time_delta,last_time_err,time_err
597                              ld      last_time_err,time_err
598
599                              sub     pos_delta,last_pos_err,pos_err
600                              ld      last_pos_err,pos_err
601
602      ;;;;;            Time_err   = Desired time to finish - current time
603      ;;;;;            Pos_err    = Desired position to finish - current position
604      ;;;;;            Pos_delta  = Last position error - Current position error
605      ;;;;;            Time_delta = Last time error - Current time error
606      ;;;;;                note that errors should get smaller so deltas will be
607      ;;;;;                positive for forward motion (time is always forward)
608
609
610      chk_dir:
611                              cmp     pos_err+2,zero
612                              jge     go_forward
613
614      go_backward:
615                              neg     pos_err                   ; Pos_err = ABS VAL (pos_err)
616                              ldb     pwm_dir,#00h
617                              cmp     pos_err+2,#0FFFFH
618                              jne     ld_max
619                              br      chk_brk
620
621      go_forward:
622                              ldb     pwm_dir,#01H
623                              cmp     pos_err+2,zero
624                              je      chk_brk
625      $EJECT
626
627      ld_max:  ldb             pwm_pwr,max_pwr
628                              br      chk_sanity
629
630      Chk_brk:
631                              cmp     pos_err,pos_pnt           ; Position_Error now = ABS(pos_err)
632                              jnh     hold_position             ; position_error<position_control_point
633                              cmp     pos_err,brk_pnt
```

```
2658 D9F1                        jh              ld_max          ; position_error>brake_point

                       braking:
265A B80050                      cmp             pos_delta,zero
265D D602                        jge             chk_delta
265F 0350                        neg             pos_delta
                       chk_delta:
2661 B87650                      cmp             pos_delta,vel_pnt ; velocity = pos_delta/sample_time
2664 D10D                        jnh             hold_position   ; jmp if ABS(velocity) < vel_pnt

2666 B0726C            brake:    ldb             pwm_pwr,max_brk ; If braking apply power in opposite
2669 B06824                      ldb             tmp,direct      ; direction of current motion
266C 1224                        notb            tmp
266E B02469                      ldb             pwm_dir,tmp

2671 2030                        br              ld_pwr

                       Hold_position:                            ; position hold mode
2673 89020038                    cmp             pos_err,#02
2677 D906                        jh              calc_out        ; if position error < 2 then turn off power
2679 0126                        clr             tmp+2
267B 015A                        clr             boost
267D 201F                        BR              output

                       calc_out:
267F 5DFF7424                    mulub           tmp,max_hold,#255
2683 6C3824                      mulu            tmp+2,pos_err
2686 B80050                      cmp             pos_delta,zero
2689 D709                        jne             no_bst
268B 6504005A                    add             boost,#04
268F 645A26                      add             tmp+2,boost     ; Tmp = pos_err * max_hold
2692 2002                        br              ck_max
2694 015A            no_bst:     clr             boost           ; Boost is integral control
2696 B87426         ck_max:      cmp             tmp+2,max_hold  ; TMP+2 = MSB(pos_err*max_hold)
2699 D103                        jnh             output
269B A07426         maxed:       ld              tmp+2,max_hold
269E B0266C         output:      ldb             pwm_pwr,tmp+2

                       chk_sanity:
26A1 2000                        br              ld_pwr
                       ;;
                       ;;
                       $EJECT
                       ld_pwr:
26A3 B06C64                      ldb             rpwr,pwm_pwr
26A6 1264                        notb            rpwr
26A8 3B690A                      jbs             pwm_dir,0,p2fwd
```

```
684           p2bkwd: DI
26AB FA
26AC 717F10   685           andb    port2,#01111111B    ; clear P2.7
26AF B06417   686           ldb     pwm_control,rpwr
26B2 FB       687           EI
26B3 2008     688           br      purset
26B5 FA       689   p2fwd:  DI
26B6 918010   690           orb     port2,#10000000B    ; set P2.7
26B9 B06417   691           ldb     pwm_control,rpwr
26BC FB       692           EI
              693
26BD BB004A   694   purset: cmp     time_err+2,zero  ; do pos_table when err is negative
26BD          695           jgt     end_p
26C0 D225     696           br      end_p
              697   ;;;
              698
26C2 89202962 699           cmp     nxt_pos,#(32*pos_table)
26C6 DE06     700           jlt     get_vals             ; jump if lower
26C8 A1002962 701           ld      nxt_pos,#pos_table
26CC 0142     702           clr     time+2
              703   get_vals:
26CE A26334   705           ld      des_pos,[nxt_pos]+
26D1 A26336   706           ld      des_pos+2,[nxt_pos]+
26D4 A26346   707           ld      des_time+2,[nxt_pos]+
26D7 A26370   708           ld      max_pwr,[nxt_pos]+
26DA A07072   709           ld      max_brk,max_pwr
26DD 646034   710           add     des_pos,offset
26E0 A40036   711           addc    des_pos+2,zero
26E3 4830344E 712           sub     last_pos_err,des_pos,position
              713
26E7 717F0F   714   end_p:  andb    port1,#01111111B    ; clear P1.7
              715
26EA F3       716           popf
26EB F0       717           ret
              718           $EJECT
              719   ;;;;;;;;;;;;;;;;;;;;;;;;;;;;;;;;;;;;;;;;;;;;;;;;;;;;;;;;;;;;
              720   ;;;;;;;;;;;;;;;;;;;;;;;;;       main program       ;;;;;;;;;
              721   ;;;;;;;;;;;;;;;;;;;;;;;;;;;;;;;;;;;;;;;;;;;;;;;;;;;;;;;;;;;;
              722
              723
              724
2800          725           CSEG at 2800H
              726
              727   MAIN_PROG:
2800 90166D   728           orb     iosi_bak,iosi
2803 366D09   729           jbc     iosi_bak,6,control
2806 71BF6D   730           andb    iosi_bak,#10111111B  ; clear iosi_bak 6
2809 95100F   731           xorb    Port1,#00010000B     ; Compl Bit P1.4
280C EFF5FB   732           call    HSI_DATA_INT         ; prevent lockup
```

AP-248

```
280F              control:
280F 912D08                 orb   int_mask,#00101101B    ; enable hsi, hso, swt, tovf interrupts
2812 FD                     nop
2813 FD                     nop
2814 FD                     nop
2815 E06FFD                 djnz  main_dly,$
2818 FD                     nop
2819 95080F                 xorb  port1,#00001000B       ; compliment p1.3
281C 27E2                   BR    MAIN_PROG

2900              CSEG AT 2900H

2900              pos_table:
2900 00000000               dcl   00000000H,00B0H        ; position 0
2904 20008000               dcw   0020H,00B0H            ; next time, power
2908 00C00000               dcl   0000C000H              ; position 1
290C 40004000               dcw   0040H,0040H            ; next time, power
2910 00000000               dcl   00000000H              ; position 2
2914 6000C000               dcw   0060H,00C0H            ; next time, power
2918 00B0FFFF               dcl   0FFFFB000H             ; position 3
291C B0008000               dcw   00B0H,00B0H            ; next time, power
2920 00B08000               dcl   00000800H              ; position 4
2924 5B008000               dcw   005BH,00B0H            ; next time, power
2928 00300000               dcl   00003000H              ; position 5
292C 7000FF00               dcw   0070H,00FFH            ; next time, power
2930 00000000               dcl   00000000H              ; position 6
2934 9000F000               dcw   0090H,00F0H            ; next time, power
2938 00000000               dcl   00000000H              ; position 7
293C 9100F000               dcw   0091H,00F0H            ; next time, power

2940                        END

ASSEMBLY COMPLETED,  NO ERROR(S) FOUND.
```

270061-B1

intel.

AP-275

APPLICATION NOTE

An FFT Algorithm For MCS®-96 Products Including Supporting Routines and Examples

IRA HORDEN
ECO APPLICATIONS ENGINEER

October 1988

Order Number: 270189-002

AN FFT ALGORITHM FOR MCS®-96 PRODUCTS INCLUDING SUPPORTING ROUTINES AND EXAMPLES

CONTENTS	PAGE
1.0 INTRODUCTION	5-109
2.0 PROGRAM OVERVIEW	5-109
3.0 FOURIER TRANSFORMS	5-110
4.0 THE FFT ALGORITHM	5-114
5.0 USING THE FFT	5-115
6.0 BASIC PROGRAM FOR FFTS	5-118
7.0 ASM96 PROGRAM FOR FFTS	5-122
8.0 BACKGROUND CONTROL PROGRAM	5-136
9.0 ANALOG TO DIGITAL CONVERTER MODULE	5-147
10.0 DATA PLOTTING MODULE	5-158
11.0 USING THE FFT PROGRAM	5-166
12.0 APPENDIX A	5-167
13.0 APPENDIX B	5-168
BIBLIOGRAPHY	5-182

Figures

1. Timing of the FFT Program 5-110
2. Rectangular Pulse and its Fourier Transform 5-111
3. Graphical Summation of Sine Waves 5-111
4. Square Waves from Sinusoids 5-112
5. Discrete Transform of a Square Wave 5-113
6. Bin Windows 5-115
7. Waveform is a Multiple of the Window 5-116
8. Waveform is Not a Multiple of the Window 5-116
9. Effect of Hanning Window on FFT Input 5-117
10. Bin Windows after Using Hanning Input Window 5-117
11. Flowchart of Basic Program 5-119
12. Butterflies with N = 8 5-122
13. FFT Output for a Square Wave Input 5-147

Listings

1. BASIC FFT Program 5-120
2. ASM96 FFT Program 5-123
3. Main Routine 5-137
4. A to D Converter Routine 5-148
5. The Plot Module 5-159

AP-275

1.0 INTRODUCTION

Intel's 8096 is a 16-bit microcontroller with processing power sufficient to perform many tasks which were previously done by microprocessors or special building block computers. A new field of applications is opened by having this much power available on a single chip controller.

The 8096 can be used to increase the performance of existing designs based on 8051s or similar 8-bit controllers. In addition, it can be used for Digital Signal Processing (DSP) applications, as well as matrix manipulations and other processing oriented tasks. One of the tasks that can be performed is the calculation of a Fast Fourier Transform (FFT). The algorithm used is similar to that in many DSP and matrix manipulation applications, so while it is directly applicable to a specific set of applications, it is indirectly applicable to many more.

FFTs are most often used in determining what frequencies are present in an analog signal. By providing a tool to identify specific waveforms by their frequency components, FFTs can be used to compare signals to one another or to set patterns. This type of procedure is used in speech detection and engine knock sensors. FFTs also have uses in vision systems where they identify objects by comparing their outlines, and in radar units to detect the dopler shift created by moving objects.

This application note discusses how FFTs can be calculated using Intel's MCS®-96 microcontrollers. A review of fourier analysis is presented, along with the specific code required for a 64 point real FFT. Throughout this application note, it is assumed that the reader has a working knowledge of the 8096. For those without this background the following two publications will be helpful:

1986 Microcontroller Handbook

Using the 8096, AP-248

These books are listed in the bibliography, along with other good sources of information on the MCS-96 product family and on Fast Fourier Transforms.

2.0 PROGRAM OVERVIEW

This application note contains program modules which are combined to create a program which performs an FFT on an analog signal sampled by the on-board ADC (Analog to Digital Converter) of the 8097. The results of the FFT are then provided over the serial channel to a printer or terminal which displays the results. In the applications listed in the previous section, the data from this FFT program would be used directly by another program instead of being plotted. However, the plotted results are used here to provide an example of what the FFT does. There are four program modules discussed in this application note:

FFTRUN - Runs a 64 point FFT on its data buffer. It produces 32 14-bit complex output values and 32 14-bit output magnitudes. A fast square root routine and log conversion routine are included.

A2DCON - Fills one of two buffers with analog values at a set sample rate. The sample time can be as fast as 50 microseconds using 8x9xBH components.

PLOTSP - Plots the contents of a buffer to a serially connected printer. Routines are provided for console out and hexadecimal to decimal conversion and printing.

FTMAIN - The main module which controls the other modules.

Each of the modules will be described separately. In order to better understand how the programs work together, a brief tutorial on FFTs will be presented first, followed by descriptions of the programs in the order listed above.

The final program uses 64 real data points, taken from either a table or analog input 1. Each of the data points is a 16-bit signed number. The processing takes 12.5 milliseconds when internal RAM is used as the data space. If external RAM is used, 14 milliseconds are required. Larger FFTs can be performed by slightly modifying the programs. A 256-point FFT would take approximately 65 milliseconds, and a 1024-point version would require about 300 milliseconds.

In the program presented, the analog sampling time is set for 1 sample every 100 microseconds, providing the 64 samples in 6.4 milliseconds. The sampling time can be reduced to around 60 microseconds per point by changing a variable, and less than 50 microseconds by using the 8x9xBH series of parts, since they have a 22 microsecond A to D conversion time.

The programs are set up to be run in a sequence instead of concurrently. This provides the fastest operation if the sampling speed were reduced to the minimum possible. For the fastest operation above about 80 microseconds a sample, the programs could be run concurrently, but this would require some minor modifications of the program. Figure 1 shows the timing of the program as presented.

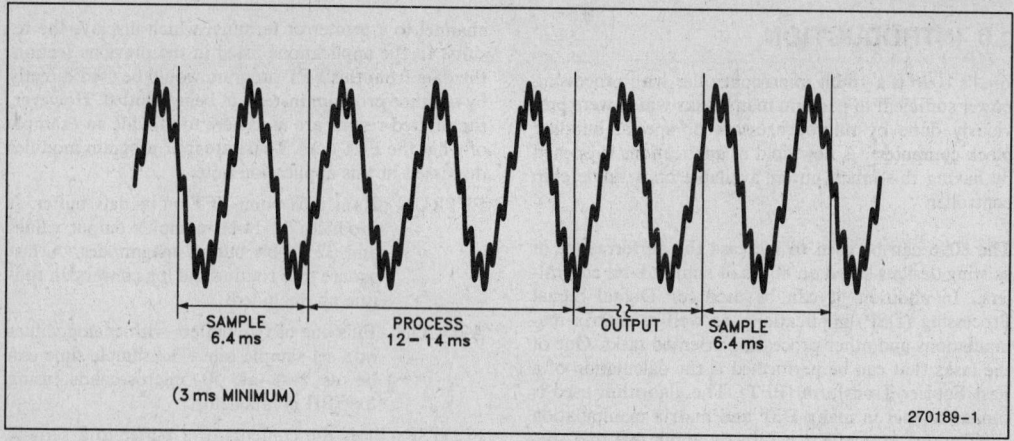

Figure 1. Timing of the FFT Program

These programs have run in the Intel Microcontroller Operation Application's Lab and produced the results presented in this application note. Since the programs have not undergone any further testing, we cannot guarantee them to be bug proof. We, therefore, recommend that they be thoroughly tested before being used for other than demonstration purposes.

3.0 FOURIER TRANSFORMS

A Fourier Transform is a useful analytical tool that is frequently ignored due to its mathematically oriented derivations. This is unfortunate, since Fourier transforms can be used without fully understanding the mathematics behind them. Of course, if one understands the theory behind these transforms, they become much more powerful.

The majority of this application note deals with how a Fast Fourier Transform (FFT) can be used for spectrum analysis. This procedure takes an input signal and separates it into its frequency components. One can almost treat the FFT as a black box, which has as its output, the frequency components and magnitudes of the input signal, much like a spectrum analyzer.

From a mathematical standpoint, Fourier Transforms change information in the time domain into the frequency domain. The theory behind the Fourier transform stems from Fourier analysis, also called frequency analysis.

There are many books on the topic of Fourier analysis, several of which are listed in the bibliography. In this application note, only the pertinent formulas and uses will be presented, not their derivations.

The main idea in Fourier analysis is that a function can be expressed as a summation of sinusoidal functions of different frequencies, phase angles, and magnitudes. This idea is represented by the Fourier Integral:

$$H(f) = \int_{-\infty}^{\infty} h(t) e^{-j2\pi ft} dt \qquad (1)$$

Where: $H(f)$ is a function of frequency
$h(t)$ is a function of time

Since

$$e^{-j\theta} = \cos\theta - j\sin\theta \qquad (2)$$

$$H(f) = \int_{-\infty}^{\infty} h(t)(\cos(2\pi ft) - j\sin(2\pi ft)) dt \qquad (3)$$

Figure 2 shows a rectangular pulse and its Fourier transform. Note that the results in the frequency domain are continuous rather than discrete. The horizontal axis in Figure 2a is frequency, while that of Figure 2b is time.

In a simplified case, the varying phase angles can be removed, and the integral changed to a summation, known as a Fourier Series. All periodic functions can be described in this way. This series, as shown below, can help provide a more graphical understanding of Fourier analysis.

$$y(t) = \frac{a_0}{2} + \sum_{n=1}^{\infty} [a_n \cos(2\pi n f_0 t) + b_n \sin(2\pi n f_0 t)] \qquad (4)$$

for $n = 1$ to ∞

Where $f_0 = \dfrac{1}{T_0}$, the fundamental frequency.

AP-275

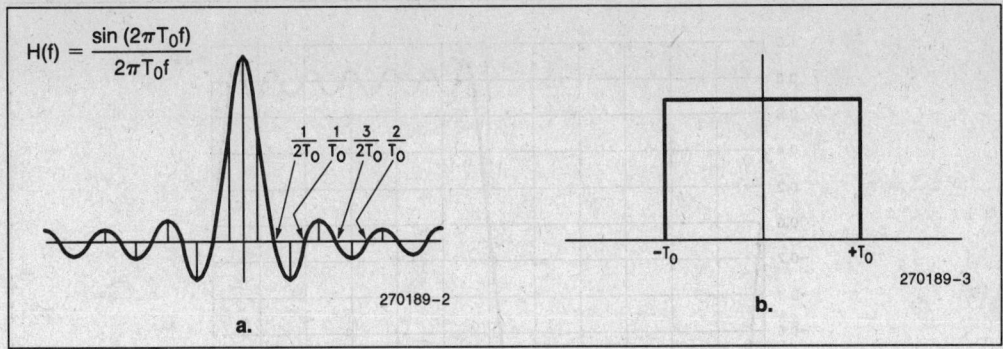

Figure 2. Rectangular Pulse and Its Fourier Transform

This formula can also be represented in complex form as:

$$\sum_{n=-\infty}^{\infty} \alpha_n e^{j2\pi n f_0 t} \quad (5)$$

The Fourier series for a square wave is

$$\sum_{K=0}^{\infty} \frac{\sin((2k+1)2\pi f_0 t)}{(2k+1)} \quad (6)$$

If these sinusoids are summed, a square wave will be formed. Figure 3 shows the graphical summation of the first 3 terms of the series. Since the higher frequencies contribute to the squareness of the waveform at the corners, it is reasonable to compare only the flatness of the top of the waveform. The sharpness or risetime of the waveform can be determined by the highest frequency term being summed. With rise and fall times of 10% of the period, the waveform generated by the first 3 terms is within 20% of ideal. At 7 terms it is within 10%, and at 20 terms it is within 5%. With a 5% risetime, it is within 20% of ideal after 5 terms, 10% after 13 terms and 5% after 32 terms. Figure 4 shows the resultant waveforms after the summation of 7, 15 and 30 terms.

Fourier analysis can be used on equation 4 to find the coefficients a_n and b_n. To make this process easier to use with a computer, a discrete form, rather than a continuous one, must be used. The discrete Fourier transform, shown in Equation 7, is a good approximation to the continuous version. The closeness of the approximation depends on several conditions which will be discussed later. The input to this transform is a set of N equally spaced samples of a waveform taken over a period of NT. The period NT is frequently referred to as the "Sampling Window".

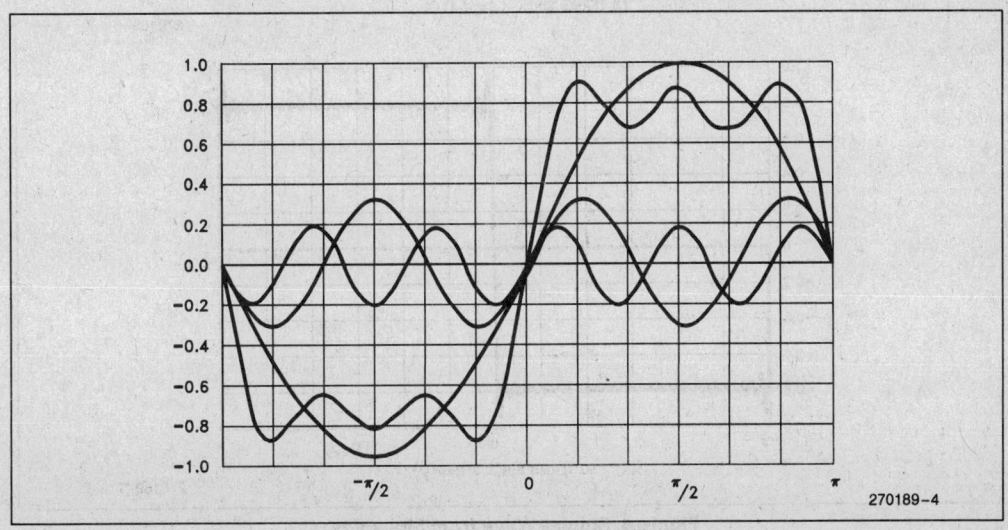

Figure 3. Graphical Summation of Sinewaves

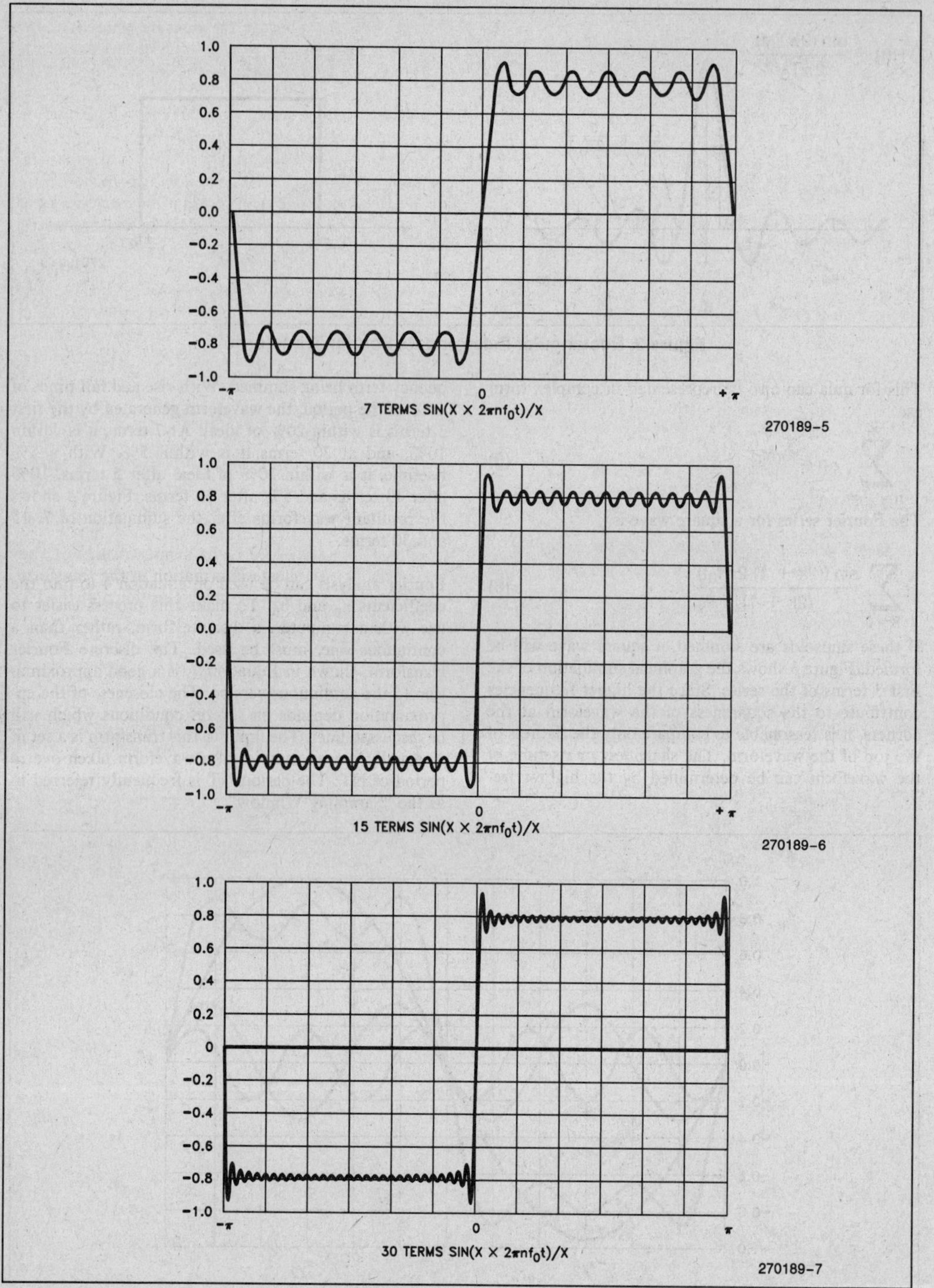

Figure 4. Square Wave from Sinusoids

AP-275

$$H\left(\frac{n}{NT}\right) = \sum_{k=0}^{N-1} h(kT)e^{-j2\pi nk/N}$$

$n = 0, 1, \ldots, N-1$ \hfill (7)

Where: $H(f)$ is a function of frequency

$h(t)$ is a function of time

T is the time span between samples

N is the number of samples in the window

$n = 0, 1, 2 \ldots N-1$

This transform is used for many applications, including Fourier Harmonic Analysis. This procedure uses the transform to calculate the coefficients used in Equation 5. In order to do this, the factor T/NT must be added to the transform as follows:

$$H\left(\frac{n}{NT}\right) = \frac{T}{(NT)} \sum_{k=0}^{N-1} h(kT)\, e^{-j2\pi nk/N}$$

$n = 0, 1, 2, 3, \ldots, N-1$ \hfill (8)

The factor provides compensation for the number of samples taken. Note that the functions $H(f)$ and $h(t)$ are complex variables, so the simplicity of the equation can be misleading. Once the values of $h(t)$ are known, (ie. the value of the input at the discrete times (t)), the Fourier Transform can be used to find the magnitude and phase shift of the signal at the frequencies (f).

A spectrum analyzer can provide similar information on an analog input signal by using analog filters to separate the frequency components. Regardless of its source, the information on component frequencies of a signal can be used to detect specific frequencies present in a signal or to compare one signal to another. Many lab experiments and product development tests can make use of this type of information. Using these methods, the purity of signals can be measured, specific harmonics can be detected in mechanical equipment, and noise bursts can be classified. All of this information can be obtained while still treating the FFT process as a black box.

Consider the discrete transform of a square wave as shown in Figure 5. Note that the component magnitudes, as shown in the series of Equation 6, are shown in a mirrored form in the transform. This will happen whenever only real data is used as the FFT input, if both real and imaginary data were used the output would not be guaranteed to be symmetrical. For this reason, there is duplicate information in the transform for many applications. Later in this section a method to make the most of this characteristic is discussed.

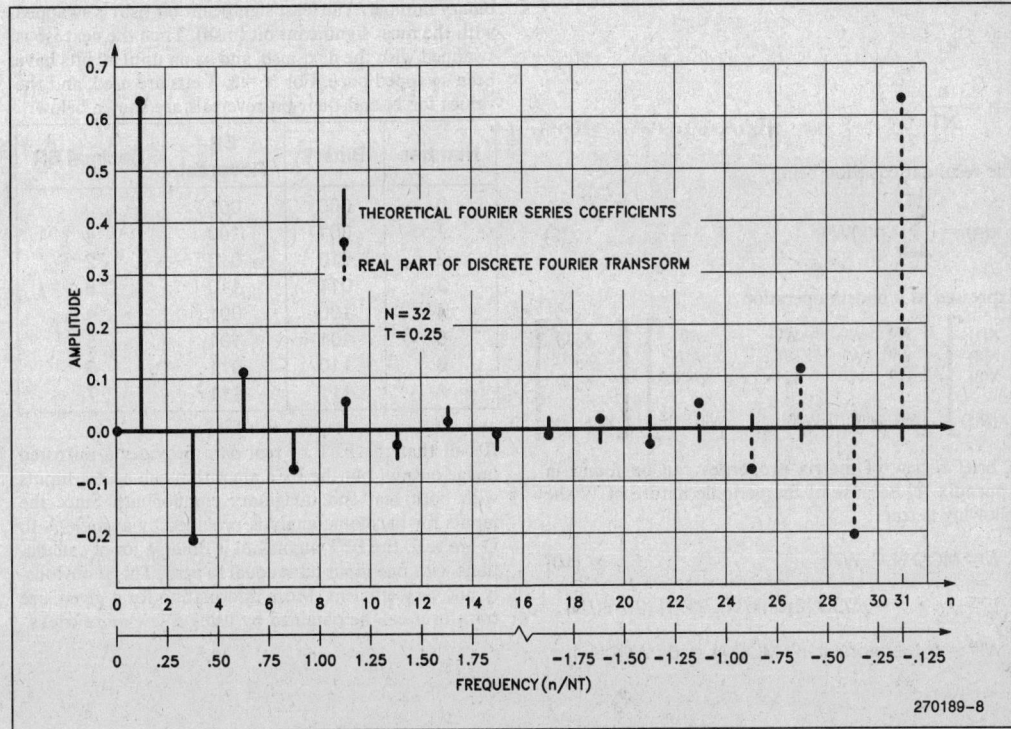

Figure 5. Discrete Transform of a Square Wave

AP-275

If one looks at Equation 8, it can be seen that the calculation of a discrete Fourier transform requires N squared complex multiplications. If N is large, the calculation time can easily become unrealistic for real-time applications. For example, if a complex multiplication takes 40 microseconds, at N = 16, 10 milliseconds would be used for calculation, while at N = 128, over half a second would be needed. A Fast Fourier Transform is an algorithm which uses less multiplications, and is therefore faster. To calculate the actual time savings, it is first necessary to understand how a FFT works.

4.0 THE FFT ALGORITHM

The FFT algorithm makes use of the periodic nature of waveforms and some matrix algebra tricks to reduce the number of calculations needed for a transform. A more complete discussion of this is in Appendix A, however, the areas that need to be understood to follow the algorithm are presented here. This information need not be read if the reader's intent is to use the program and not to understand the mathematical process of the algorithm.

To simplify notation the following substitutions are made in Equation 8.

$$W = e^{-j2\pi/N}$$

$$k = kT$$

$$n = \frac{n}{NT}$$

The resultant equation being

$$x(n) = \sum_{k=0}^{N-1} n(k) W^{nk} \qquad (9)$$

Expressed as a matrix operation

$$\begin{bmatrix} X(1) \\ X(2) \\ X(3) \\ \vdots \\ X(N-1) \end{bmatrix} = \begin{bmatrix} W^0 & W^0 & W^0 & \cdots & W^0 \\ W^0 & W^1 & W^2 & \cdots & W^N \\ W^0 & W^2 & W^4 & \cdots & W^{2N} \\ \vdots & & & & \\ W^0 & W^{(N-1)} & W^{2(N-1)} & \cdots & W^{(N-1)^2} \end{bmatrix} \begin{bmatrix} X_0(0) \\ X_0(1) \\ X_0(2) \\ \vdots \\ X_0(N-1) \end{bmatrix}$$

A brief review of matrix properties can be found in Appendix A. Because of the periodic nature of W the following is true:

$$W^{nk} \text{ MOD } N = W^{nk} \qquad (10)$$

$$= \cos(2\pi nk/N) - j \sin(2\pi nk/N)$$

$W^0 = 1$ therefore, if nk MOD $N = 0$, $W^{nk} = 1$

This reduces the calculations as several of the W terms go to 1 and the highest power of W is N. All of W values are complex, so most of the operations will have to be complex operations. We will continue to use only the W, X(n) and X0(k) symbols to represent these complex quantities.

The FFT algorithm we will use requires that N be an integral power of 2. Other FFT algorithms do not have this restriction, but they are more complex to understand and develop. Additionally, for the relatively small values of N we are using this restriction should not provide much of a problem. We will define EXPONENT as log base 2 of N. Therefore,

$$N = 2^{\text{EXPONENT}}$$

The magic of the FFT, (as detailed in Appendix A), involves factoring the matrix into EXPONENT matrices, each of which has all zeros except for a 1 and a W^{nk} term in each row. When these matrices are multiplied together the result is the same as that of the multiplication indicated in Equation 9, except that the rows are interchanged and there are fewer non-trivial multiplications. To reorder the rows, and thus make the information useful, it is necessary to perform a procedure called "Bit Reversal".

This process requires that N first be converted to a binary number. The least significant bit (lsb) is swapped with the most significant bit (msb). Then the next lsb is swapped with the next msb, and so on until all bits have been swapped once. For N = 8, 3 bits are used, and the values for N and their bit reversals are shown below:

Number	Binary	Bit Reversal	Decimal BR
0	000	000	0
1	001	100	4
2	010	010	2
3	011	110	6
4	100	001	1
5	101	101	5
6	110	011	3
7	111	111	7

Recall that the FFT of real data provides a mirrored image output, but the FFT algorithm can accept inputs with both real and imaginary components. Since the inputs for harmonic analysis provided by a single A to D are real, the FFT algorithm is doing a lot of calculations with one input term equal to zero. This is obviously not very efficient. More information for a given size transform can be obtained by using a few more tricks.

AP-275

It is possible to perform the FFT of two real functions at the same time by using the imaginary input values to the FFT for the second real function. There is then a post processing performed on the FFT results which separate the FFTs of the two functions. Using a similar procedure one can perform a transform on 2N real samples using an N complex sample transform.

The procedure involves alternating the real sample values between the real and imaginary inputs to the FFT. If, as in our example, the input to the FFT is a 2 by 32 array containing the complex values for 32 inputs, the 64 real samples would be loaded into it as follows:

N	00 01 02 03 04 05 06 07 ..... 30 31
REAL	00 02 04 06 08 10 12 14 ..... 60 62
IMAGINARY	01 03 05 07 09 11 13 15 ..... 61 63

This procedure is referred to as a pre-weave. In order to derive the desired results, the FFT is run, and then a post-weave operation is performed. The formula for the post-weave is shown below:

$$X_r(n) = \left[\frac{R(n)}{2} + \frac{R(N-n)}{2}\right] + \cos\frac{\pi n}{N}\left[\frac{I(n)}{2} + \frac{I(N-n)}{2}\right] -$$

$$\sin\frac{\pi n}{N}\left[\frac{R(n)}{2} - \frac{R(N-n)}{2}\right]. \quad n = 0, 1, \ldots, N-1$$

$$X_i(n) = \left[\frac{I(n)}{2} - \frac{I(N-n)}{2}\right] - \sin\frac{\pi n}{N}\left[\frac{I(n)}{2} + \frac{I(N-n)}{2}\right] -$$

$$\cos\frac{\pi n}{N}\left[\frac{R(n)}{2} - \frac{R(N-n)}{2}\right] \quad n = 0, 1, \ldots, N-1 \quad (11)$$

Where R(n) is the real FFT output value
I(n) is the imaginary FFT output value
Xr(n) is the real post-weave output
Xi(n) is the imaginary post-weave output

Note that the output is now one-sided instead of mirrored around the center frequency as it is in Figure 5. The magnitude of the signal at each frequency is calculated by taking the square root of the sum of the squares. The magnitude can now be plotted against frequency, where the frequency steps are defined as:

$$\frac{n}{NT} \quad n = 0, 1, 2, 3, \ldots, N-1$$

Where N is the number of complex samples (ie. 32 in this case) T is the time between samples

A value of zero on the frequency scale corresponds to the DC component of the waveform. Most signal analysis is done using Decibels (dB), the conversion is dB = 10 LOG (Magnitude squared). Decibels are not used as an absolute measure, instead signals are compared by the difference in decibels. If the ratio between two signals is 1:2 then there will be a 3 dB difference in their power.

5.0 USING THE FFT

There are several things to be aware of when using FFTs, but with the proper cautions, the FFT output can be used just like that of a spectrum analyzer. The

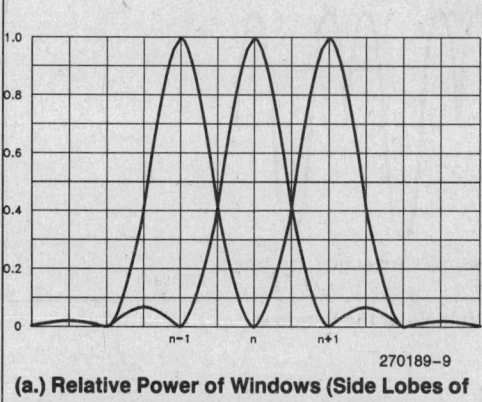

(a.) Relative Power of Windows (Side Lobes of Side Bins Removed for Clarity).

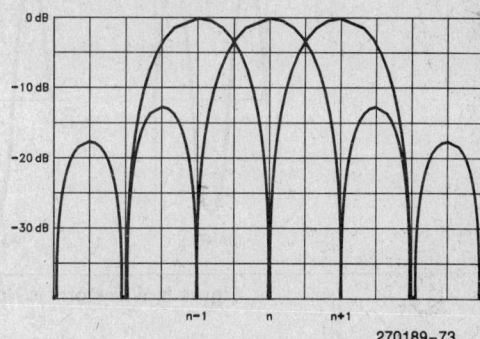

(b.) 10 Log Relative Power of Windows (Side Lobes of Side Bins Removed for Clarity).

Figure 6. Bin Windows

first precaution is that the FFT is a discrete approximation to a continuous Fourier Transform, so the output will seldom fit the theoretical values exactly, but it will be very close.

Since the programs in this application note generate a one-sided transform with N = 32, the frequency granularity is fairly course. Each of the frequency components output from the FFT is actually the sum of all energy within a narrow band centered on that frequency. This band of sensitivity is referred to as a "bin". The reported magnitude is the actual magnitude multiplied by the value of the bin window at the actual frequency. Figure 6 shows several bin windows. Note that these windows overlap, so that a frequency midway between the two center frequencies will be reported as energy split between both windows. Be careful not to confuse the *sampling window* NT with *bin windows* or with the *windowing function*.

Another area of caution is the relationship of the sampling window to the frequency of the waveform. For the best accuracy, the window should cover an exact multiple of the period of the waveform being analyzed. If it covers less than one period, the results will be invalid. Other variations from ideal will not produce invalid results, just additional noise in the output.

If the sampling window does not cover an exact multiple of all of the frequency components of a waveform, the FFT results will be noisy. The reason for this is the sharp edge that the FFT sees when the edges of the window cut off the input waveform. Figure 7 shows a waveform that is an exact multiple of the window and

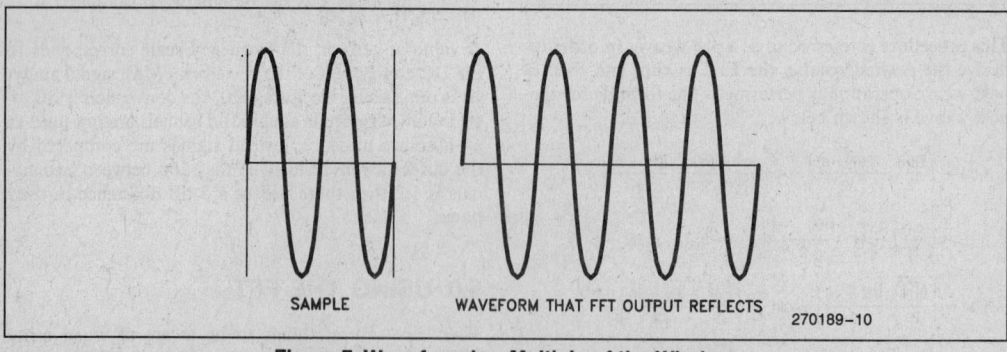

Figure 7. Waveform is a Multiple of the Window

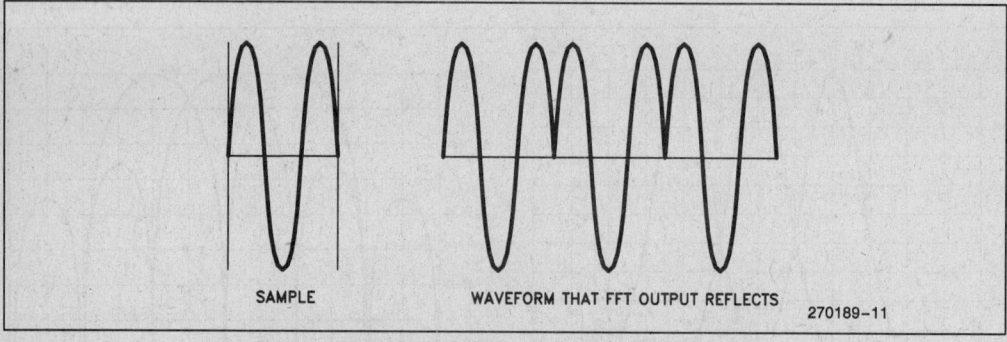

Figure 8. Waveform is Not a Multiple of the Window

AP-275

the periodic waveform that the FFT output reflects. In Figure 8, the waveform is not a multiple of the window and the waveform that the FFT output reflects has discontinuities. These discontinuities contribute to the noise in an FFT output. This noise is called "spectral leakage", or simply "leakage", since it is leakage between one frequency spectrum and another which is caused by digitization of an analog process.

To reduce this leakage, a process called windowing is used. In this procedure the input data is multiplied by specific values before being used in the FFT. The term "windowing" is used because these values act as a window through which the input data passes. If the input window goes smoothly to zero at both endpoints of the sampling window, there can be no discontinuities. Figure 9 shows a Hanning window and its effect on the input to an FFT. The Hanning window was named after its creator, Julius Von Hann, and is one of the most commonly used windows. More information on windowing and the types of windows can be found in the paper by Harris listed in the bibliography. As expected, the results of the FFT are changed because of the input windowing, but it is in a very predictable way.

Using the Hanning window results in bin windows which are wider and lower in magnitude than normal, as can be seen by comparing Figure 6 with Figure 10. For an input frequency which is equal to the center frequency of a bin window, the attenuation will be 6 dB on the center frequency. Since the bin windows are

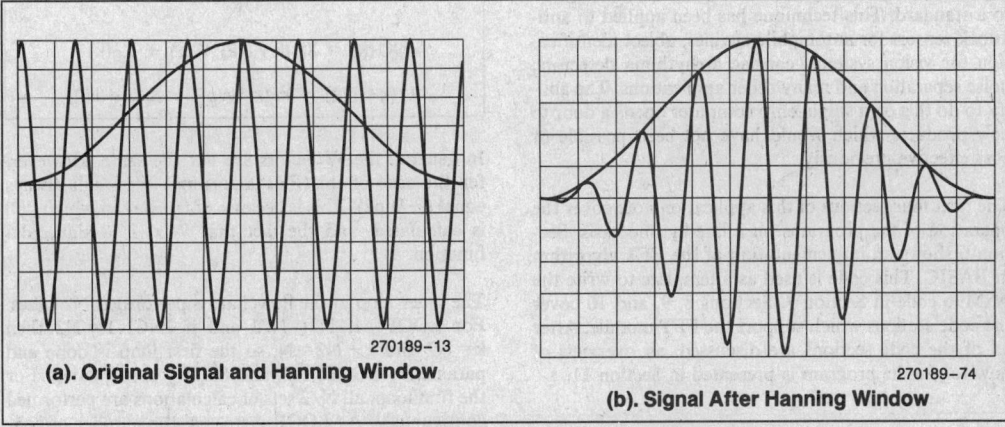

(a). Original Signal and Hanning Window

(b). Signal After Hanning Window

Figure 9. Effect of Hanning Window on FFT Input

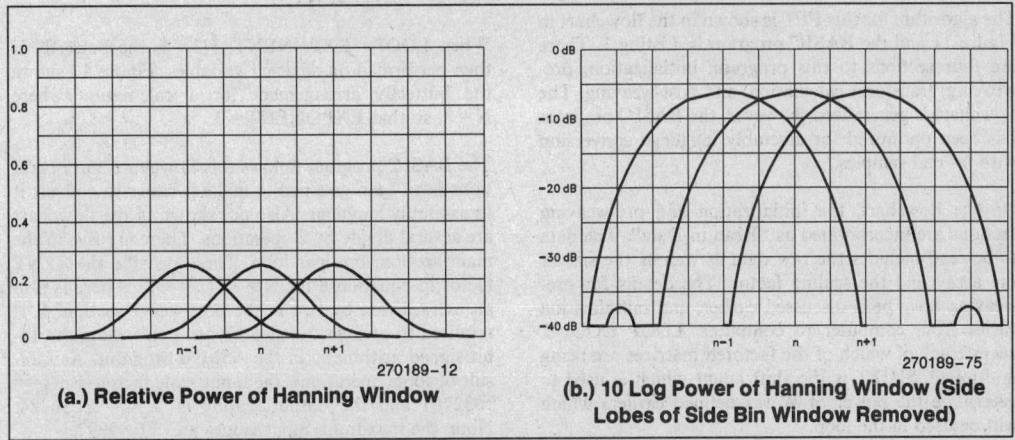

(a.) Relative Power of Hanning Window

(b.) 10 Log Power of Hanning Window (Side Lobes of Side Bin Window Removed)

Figure 10. Bin Windows after Using Hanning Input Window

wider than normal, the input frequency will also have energy which falls into the bins on either side of center. These side bins will show a reading of 6 dB below the center window. The disadvantage of this spreading is far less than the advantage of removing leakage from the FFT output.

A set of FFT output plots are included in the Appendix. These plots show the effect of windowing on various signals. There are examples of all of the cases described above. A brief discussion of the plots is also presented.

Applications which can make use of this frequency magnitude information include a wide range of signal processing and detection tasks. Many of these tasks use digital filtering and signature analysis to match signals to a standard. This technique has been applied to antiknock sensors for automobile engines, object identification for vision systems, cardiac arrhythmia detectors, noise separation and many other applications. The ability to do this on a single-chip computer opens a door to new products which would have not been possible or cost effective previously.

The next four sections of this application note cover the operation of the programs on a line by line basis. Section 6 shows an implementation of the FFT algorithm in BASIC. This code is used as a template to write the ASM96 code in Section 7. Sections 8, 9, and 10 cover the code sections which support the FFT module. After all of the code sections are discussed, an overview of how to use the program is presented in Section 11.

6.0 BASIC PROGRAM FOR FFTS

The algorithm for this FFT is shown in the flowchart in Figure 11 and the BASIC program in Listing 1. There are four sections to this program: initialization, pre-weaving, transform calculation, and post-weaving. The flowchart is generalized, however, the BASIC program has been optimized for assembly language conversion with 64 real samples.

On the flowchart, the initialization and pre-weaving sections are incorporated as "Read in Data". The data to be read includes the raw data as well as the size of the array and the scaling factor. The details for pre-weaving have been discussed earlier, and initialization varies from computer to computer. LOOP COUNT keeps track of which of the factored matrices are being multiplied. SHIFT is the shift count which is used to determine the power of W (as defined earlier) which will be used in the loop.

For each loop N calculations are performed in sets of two. Each calculation set is referred to as a butterfly and has the following form:

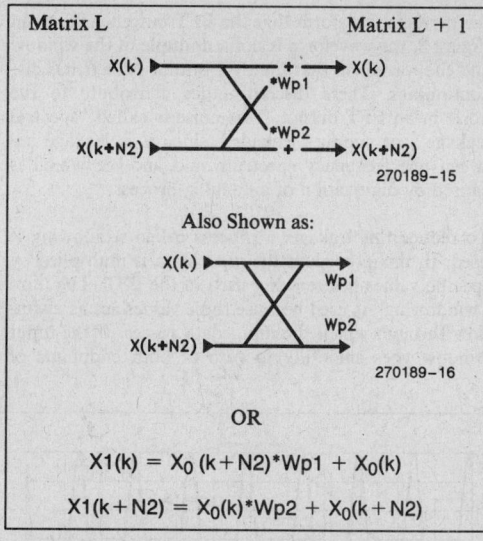

In general, the W factors are not the same. However, for the case of this FFT algorithm, Wp1 will always equal ($-$Wp2). This is because of the way in which "p" is calculated, and the fact that W(x) is a sinusoidal function.

The inner loop in the flowchart is performed N2 times. For LOOP=1, N2=N/2 and if INCNT=N2 then k=N2 and k+N2=N, so the first loop is done and parameters LOOP, N2, and SHIFT are updated. For the first loop, all N/2 sets of calculations are performed contiguously. As LOOP increases, the number of contiguous calculations are cut in half, until LOOP=EXPONENT.

When LOOP=EXPONENT, N2=1, the butterfly is then performed on adjacent variables. Figure 12 shows the butterfly arrangement for a calcuiation where N=8, so that EXPONENT=3.

The BASIC program follows this flowchart, but operations have been grouped to make it easier to convert it to assembly language. Also not shown in the flowchart are several divide by 2 operations. There are five in the main section, one per loop. These provide the T/NT factor in equation 8 for N=32 (2^5=32). There is also an extra divide by two in the post-weave section. It is required to prevent overflows when performing the 16-bit signed arithmetic in the ASM96 program. As a result of these operations, the input scale factor is $\pm 1 = \pm 32767$ and the output scaling is $\pm 1 = \pm 16384$. Note, the maximum input values are ± 0.99997.

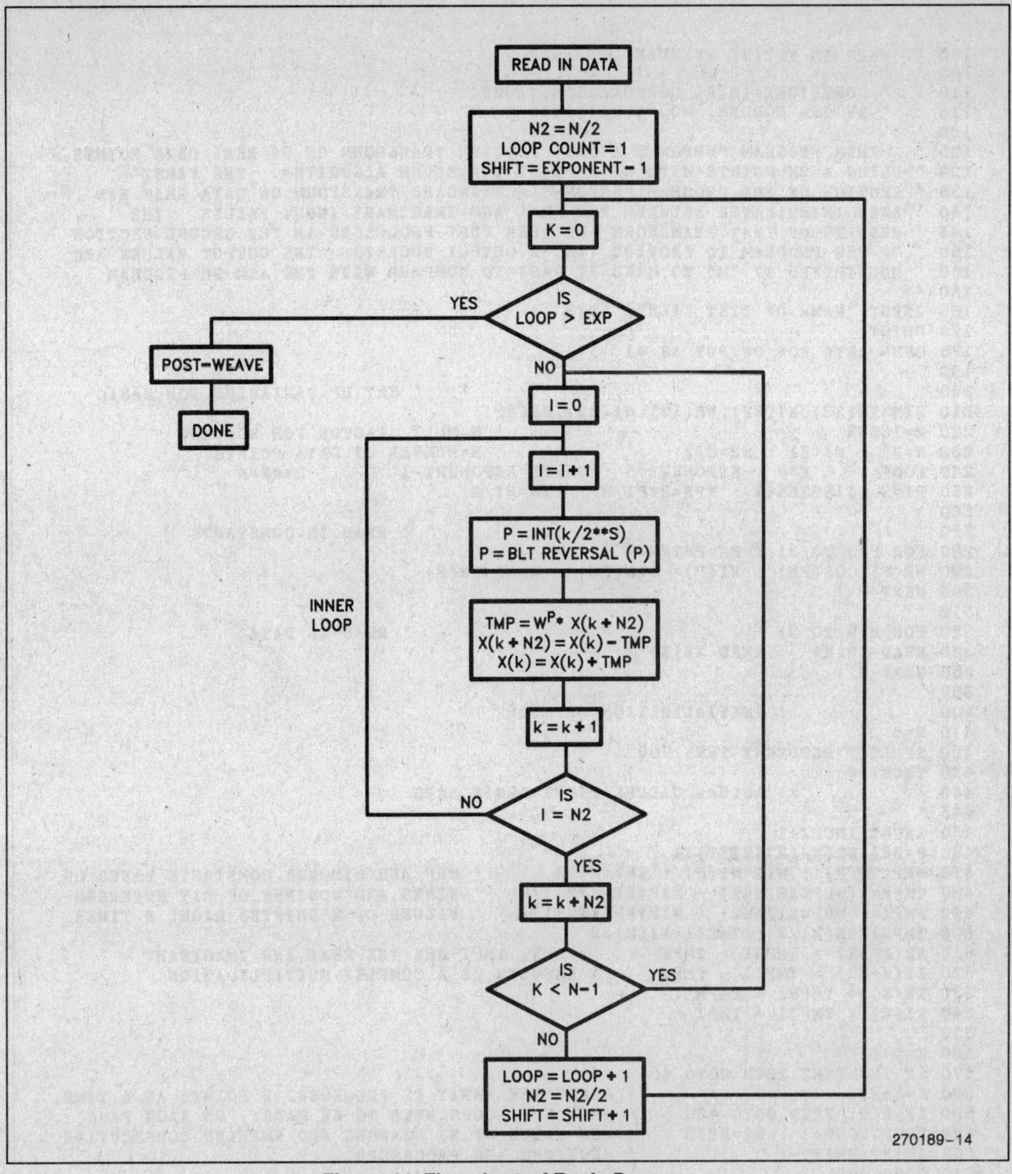

AP-275

Figure 11. Flowchart of Basic Program

5-119

AP-275

```
100 '   THIS IS FFT13, FEBRUARY 4, 1986
105 '
110     ' COPYRIGHT INTEL CORPORATION, 1985
115     ' BY IRA HORDEN, MCO APPLICATIONS
120 '
125 '   THIS PROGRAM PERFORMS A FAST FOURIER TRANSFORM ON 64 REAL DATA POINTS
130 ' USING A 2N-POINTS WITH AN N-POINT TRANSFORM ALGORITHM.  THE FIRST
135 ' SECTION OF THE PROGRAM PERFORMS A STANDARD TRANSFORM ON DATA THAT HAS
140 ' BEEN INTERLEAVED BETWEEN THE REAL AND IMAGINARY INPUT VALUES.  THE
145 ' RESULTS OF THAT TRANSFORM ARE THEN POST-PROCESSED IN THE SECOND SECTION
150 ' OF THE PROGRAM TO PROVIDE THE 32 OUTPUT BUCKETS.  THE OUTPUT VALUES ARE
155 ' MULTIPLIED BY "M" TO MAKE IT EASY TO COMPARE WITH THE ASM-96 PROGRAM
160 '
165 INPUT "NAME OF LIST FILE"; LST$
170 PRINT
175 OPEN LST$ FOR OUTPUT AS #1
180 '
200                                          ' SET UP VARIABLES FOR BASIC
210 DIM XR(32),XI(32),WR(32),WI(32),BR(32)
220 M=16383                         ' M=MULT. FACTOR FOR SCALING
230 N=32 : N1=31 : N2=N/2           ' N=NUMBER OF DATA POINTS
240 LOOP=1 : K=0 : EXPONENT=5 : SHIFT=EXPONENT-1    ' 2**E=N
250 PI=3.141592654# : TPN=2*PI/N : PIN=PI/N
260 '
270                                          ' READ IN CONSTANTS
280 FOR P=0 TO 31 : PN=P*TPN
290 WR(P)=COS(PN) : WI(P)=-SIN(PN) : READ BR(P)
300 NEXT P
310 '
320 FOR K=0 TO 31                            ' READ IN DATA
330 READ XR(K)  : READ XI(K)
350 NEXT K
360 '
400             ' INITIALIZATION OF LOOP
410 K=0
420 IF LOOP>EXPONENT THEN 700
430 INCNT=0
440             ' ACTUAL CALCULATIONS BEGIN HERE
445 '
450 INCNT=INCNT+1
460 P=BR(INT(K/(2^SHIFT)))
470 WRP=WR(P) : WIP=WI(P) : KN2=K+N2      ' WRP AND WIP ARE CONSTANTS BASED ON
480 TMPR= (WRP*XR(KN2) - WIP*XI(KN2))/2   ' SINES AND COSINES OF BIT REVERSED
490 TMPI= (WRP*XI(KN2) + WIP*XR(KN2))/2   ' VALUES OF K SHIFTED RIGHT S TIMES
500 TMPR1=XR(K)/2 : TMPI1=XI(K)/2
510 XR(K+N2) = TMPR1 - TMPR        ' TMPR, TMPI ARE THE REAL AND IMAGINARY
520 XI(K+N2) = TMPI1 - TMPI        ' RESULTS OF A COMPLEX MULTIPLICATION
530 XR(K) = TMPR1 + TMPR
540 XI(K) = TMPI1 + TMPI
550 '
560 K=K+1
570 IF INCNT<N2 THEN GOTO 450
580 K=K+N2                         ' SINCE THE ARRAY IS PROCESSED 2 POINTS AT A TIME,
590 IF K<N1 THEN GOTO 430          ' ONLY N/2 LOOPS NEED TO BE MADE.  ON EACH PASS,
600 LOOP=LOOP+1 : N2=N2/2          ' THE VALUE OF N2 CHANGES AND SMALLER CONSECUTIVE
605 SHIFT=SHIFT-1                  ' SECTIONS ARE PROCESSED.
610 GOTO 400
620 '
690 '
691 '
692 '
693 '
```

Listing 1—BASIC FFT Program

AP-275

```
694 '
695 '
696 '
697 '
700                              ' POST-PROCESSING AND REORDERING BEGIN HERE
710 '
720 FOR K = 0 TO 31
730 KPIN=K*PIN
740 XRBRK=XR(BR(K)) : XIBRK=XI(BR(K))   ' CONDENSED FOR EASE OF ASM PROGRAMMING
750 XRBRNK=XR(BR(N-K)) : XIBRNK=XI(BR(N-K))
760 TI = (XIBRK+XIBRNK)/2
770 TR = (XRBRK-XRBRNK)/2
780 XRT= (XRBRK+XRBRNK)/4
790 XIT= (XIBRK-XIBRNK)/4
800 OUTR= XRT + TI*COS(KPIN)/2 - TR*SIN(KPIN)/2
810 OUTI= XIT - TI*SIN(KPIN)/2 - TR*COS(KPIN)/2
820 '
830 MAGSQ = OUTR*OUTR+OUTI*OUTI     ' THE ASM-96 PROGRAM USES A TABLE LOOK-UP
840 MAG = SQR(MAGSQ)                ' ROUTINE TO CALCULATE SQUARE ROOTS
845 IF MAGSQ*M < .5 THEN DECIBEL=0 : GOTO 900
847 DBFACT=M/2/32767*M   ' M^2 / 64K
850 DECIBEL=10*LOG(MAGSQ*DBFACT)
860 DECIBEL=DECIBEL * .434294481#
900    GOTO 930
910 PRINT #1, USING "###### "; K,
920 PRINT #1, USING "\         \"; HEX$(M*OUTR), HEX$(M*OUTI), HEX$(M*MAG)
930 ' GOTO 950
942 PRINT #1, USING "##   "; K;
943 PRINT #1, USING "##.##### "; OUTR,OUTI,MAG;
945 PRINT #1, USING "###.### "; DECIBEL;
947 PRINT #1, USING "######   "; M*OUTR, M*OUTI, M*MAG
950 NEXT K
960 '
970 IF LST$<>"SCRN:" THEN PRINT #1, CHR$(12)
999 END
1000 END
1010             ' DATA FOR BR(P)  - BIT REVERSAL
1020 DATA 0,16,8,24,4,20,12,28,2,18,10,26,6,22,14,30
1030 DATA 1,17,9,25,5,21,13,29,3,19,11,27,7,23,15,31
1040            ' DATA FOR XR,XI
1050 DATA 2,2,2,2,2,2,2,2,2,2,2,2,2,2,2,2
1060 DATA 2,2,2,2,2,2,2,2,2,2,2,2,2,2,2,2
1070 DATA -2,-2,-2,-2,-2,-2,-2,-2,-2,-2,-2,-2,-2,-2,-2,-2
1080 DATA -2,-2,-2,-2,-2,-2,-2,-2,-2,-2,-2,-2,-2,-2,-2,-2
```

Listing 1—BASIC FFT Program (Continued)

Lines 165-175 set up the file for printing the data, this can be SCRN:, LPT1:, or any other file.

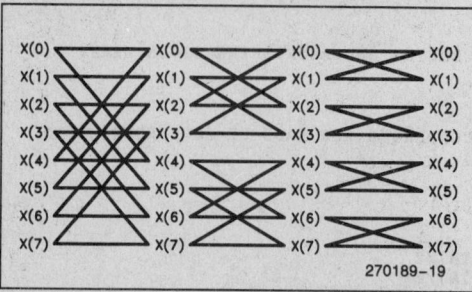

Figure 12. Butterflies with N = 8

Lines 200-310 set up the constants and calculate the WP terms which are stored in the matrices WR(p) and WI(p), for the real and imaginary component respectively.

Lines 320-350 read in the data, alternately placing it into the real and imaginary arrays. The data is scaled by 2 to make the data table simpler.

Lines 410-430 initialize the loop and test for completion.

Lines 450-620 perform the FFT algorithm. Note that all calculations are complex, with the suffixes "R" and "I" indicating real and imaginary components respectively.

The variables on line 470, TMPR1 and TMPI1 would normally not be used in a BASIC program as more than one operation can be performed on each line. However, indirect table lookups always use a separate line of assembly code, so separate lines have been used here.

Lines 700-810 perform the post-weave. This is not in the flowchart, but can be found in Equation 11. Once again, table look-ups are separated and additional variables are used for clarity. The variables BR(x) are the bit reversal values of x.

Line 830 calculates the magnitude of the harmonic components.

Lines 900-950 print the results of the calculations, with line 900 determining if the print-out should be in hex or decimal.

Lines 1000-1080 are the data for the bit reversal values and input datapoints. The input waveform is one cycle of a square-wave.

7.0 ASM96 PROGRAM FOR FFTS

The BASIC program just presented has been used as an outline for the ASM96 program shown in Listing 2. There are many advantages to using the BASIC program as a model, the main ones being debugging and testing. Since the BASIC program is so similar in program flow to the ASM96 program, it's possible to stop the ASM96 program at almost any point and verify that the results are correct.

AP-275

```
MCS-96 MACRO ASSEMBLER    FFT_RUN                                    02/18/86          PAGE    1

SERIES-III MCS-96 MACRO ASSEMBLER, V1.0

SOURCE FILE:  :F2:FFTRUN.A96
OBJECT FILE:  :F2:FFTRUN.OBJ
CONTROLS SPECIFIED IN INVOCATION COMMAND: NOSB

ERR LOC  OBJECT              LINE      SOURCE STATEMENT
                              1        $pagelength(50)
                              2
                              3        FFT_RUN MODULE STACKSIZE(6)
                              4
                              5        ; Intel Corporation, January 24, 1986
                              6        ; by Ira Horden, MCO Applications
                              7
                              8
                              9        ;       This module performs a fast fourier transform (FFT) on 64 real data
                             10        ; points using a 2N-point algorithm.  The algorithm involves using a standard
                             11        ; FFT procedure for 32 real and 32 imaginary numbers.  The real and imaginary
                             12        ; arrays are filled alternately with real data points, and the output of the
                             13        ; FFT is run through a post-processor.  The result is a one sided array with 32
                             14        ; output buckets.  The post processing includes a table lookup algorithm for
                             15        ; taking the square root of an unsigned 32-bit number.
                             16
                             17        ;       All of the calculations in the main FFT program are done using 16-bit
                             18        ; signed integers.  The maximum value of any frequency component is therefore
                             19        ; +/- 32K.  (Note that a square wave of +/- 32K has a fundamental component
                             20        ; greater than +/- 40K).  Wherever possible tables are used to increase the
                             21        ; speed of math operations.  The complete transform, including obtaining the
                             22        ; absolute magnitude of each frequency component, executes in 12
                             23        ; milliseconds with internal variables, 14 ms with external.
                             24
                             25        ;       The program requires two 32-word input arrays, with the sample values
                             26        ; alternated between the two.  These start at XREAL and XIMAG.  The resultant
                             27        ; magnitude will be placed in a 32-word array at FFT_OUT.  These are all
                             28        ; externally defined variables.  The external constant SCALE_FACTOR is used to
                             29        ; divide the output when averaging will be used.  Since the program averages
                             30        ; its output, it is necessary to clear the array based at FFT_OUT before
                             31        ; calling FFT_CALC to start the program.
                             32
                             33        ;       The program was originally written in BASIC for testing purposes.  The
                             34        ; comments include these BASIC statements to make it easier to follow the
                             35        ; algorithm.
                             36
                             37        $EJECT
```

Listing 2—ASM96 FFT Program

5-123

MCS-96 MACRO ASSEMBLER   FFT_RUN   02/18/86   PAGE 2

```
ERR LOC  OBJECT        LINE    SOURCE STATEMENT
                        38
                        39     RSEG
                        40     EXTRN port1, zero, error
                        41
                        42     OSEG at 24H
 0024                   43     TMPR:    dsl   1      ; Temporary register, Real
 0028                   44     TMPI:    dsl   1      ; Temporary register, Imaginary
 002C                   45     TMPRI:   dsl   1      ; Temporary register1, Real
 0030                   46     TMPII:   dsl   1      ; Temporary register1, Imaginary
 0034                   47     XTMPR:   dsl   1      ; Temporary data register, Real
 0038                   48     XTMPI:   dsl   1      ; Temporary data register, Imaginary
 003C                   49     XRRRK:   dsl   1
 0040                   50     XRRMK:   dsl   1
 0044                   51     XIRK:    dsl   1
 0048                   52     XIRMK:   dsl   1
 003C                   53     diff     equ   xrrk   :long ; Table difference for square root
 0040                   54     sqrt     equ   xrrmk  :long ; Square root
 0040                   55     log      equ   xrrmk  :long ; 10 Log magnitude^2
 0044                   56     nxtloc   equ   xirk   :long ; Next location in table
                        57
 003C                   58     WRP      equ   xrrk   :word ; Multiplication factor, Real
 003E                   59     WIP      equ   xrrk+2 :word ; Multiplication factor, Imaginary
 0040                   60     PWR      equ   xrrmk  :word
 0042                   61     IN_CNT   equ   xrrmk+2:word ; n divided by 2  (0 < n < N) #2
 0044                   62     NDIV2    equ   xirk   :word
                        63
 004C                   64     KPTR:    dsw   1      ; K for counter #2 to index words
 004E                   65     KN2:     dsw   1      ; KPTR + NDIV2
 0050                   66     N_SUB_K: dsw   1      ; N-K #2 to index words
 0052                   67     KK:      dsw   1      ; Bit reversed pointer of KPTR
 0054                   68     RNK:     dsw   1      ; Bit reversed pointer of N_SUB_K
 0056                   69     SHFT_CNT: dsw  1
 0058                   70     LOOP_CNT: dsw  1
 004E                   71     ptr      equ   kn2    :word ; Pointer for square root table
                        72     DSEG
                        73
                        74     EXTRN    FFT_MODE          ; FFT MODE: mode for FFT input and graphing
                        75     EXTRN    XRREAL, XIMAG     ; XRREAL, XIMAG: Base addresses for 32 16-bit signed
                        76                               ; entries for real and imaginary numbers respectively.
                        77     EXTRN    FFT_OUT           ; FFT_OUT: Starting address for 32 word array
                        78                               ; of magnitude information.
                        79
 0000                   80     OUT0:    dsw   32     ; Real component of fft
 0040                   81     OUT1:    dsw   32     ; Imaginary component of waveform
                        82     PUBLIC OUT0,OUT1
                        83
                        84     $EJECT
```

AP-275

```
MCS-96 MACRO ASSEMBLER    FFT_RUN                                      02/18/86    PAGE  3

ERR LOC  OBJECT            LINE     SOURCE STATEMENT
    2280                    85
                            86              CSEG at 2280H
                            87
                            88              PUBLIC fft_calc      ; Starting point for FFT algorithm
                            89
                            90              EXTRN scale_factor   ; Shift factor used to prevent overflow when averaging
                            91                                   ; fft outputs
                            92
                            93                                   ;;;;    START FOURIER CALCULATIONS
                            94                                   ;;;;    400 ' INITIALIZATION OF LOOP
                            95     FFT_CALC:
    2280 1100               96              clrb    error                        ;#### Indication Only
    2282 B10100             97              ldb     port1,#00000001b
                            98
    2285 FC                 99              clrvt
    2286 B10158            100              ldb     loop_cnt,#1
    2289 B10456            101              ldb     shft_cnt,#4
    228C A1200044          102              ld      ndiv2,#32
                           103
                           104     OUT_LOOP:
    2290 950400            105              xorb    port1,#00000100B             ;#### Indication Only
    2293 014C              106              clr     kptr
                           107     ;                                             ;;;;   410 K=0
    2296 990558            108              cmpb    loop_cnt, #5                 ;;;;   420 IF LOOP > EXP THEN 700
    2298 DA0220A3          109              bgt     UNWEAVE                      ; 32=2^5
                           110
                           111
                           112     MID_LOOP:                                     ;;;;   430 INCNT=0
    229C 0142              113              clr     in_cnt
                           114
                           115     IN_LOOP:                                      ;;;;   440 ' CALCULATIONS BEGIN HERE
    229E 65020042          116              add     in_cnt,#2                    ;;;;   450 INCNT=INCNT+1
                           117                                                   ;;;;   460 P=BR(INT(K/(2^SHIFT)))
    22A2 A04C40            118              ld      pwr,kptr                     ;; Calculate multiplication factors
    22A5 085640            119              shr     pwr,shft_cnt
    22A8 71F840            120              andb    pwr,#11111110B
    22AB A341003840        121              ld      pwr,brev[pwr]
                           122                                                   ;;;;   470 WRP=WR(P) : WIP=WI(P) : KN2=K+N2
    22B0 A341143393C       123     ;qw:     ld      wrp,wr[pwr]
    22B5 A341863393E       124              ld      wip,wi[pwr]
    22BA 4444404E          125              add     kn2,kptr,ndiv2
                           126
                           127     $eject
```

Listing 2—ASM96 FFT Program (Continued)

MCS-96 MACRO ASSEMBLER   FFT_RUN   02/18/86   PAGE   4

ERR LOC OBJECT   LINE   SOURCE STATEMENT
                           128   ;; Complex multiplication follows
                           129
                           130
22B8 F84F4F00003C24   E   131   mul   tmpr,wrp,xreal[km2]   ;;;; 480 TMPR= (WRP*XR(KN2) - WIP*XI(KN2))/2
22C5 F84F4F00003B28   E   132   mul   tmp1,wip,ximag[km2]
22CC 682A26   133   sub   tmpr+2,tmp1+2

22CF F84F4F00003C2C   E   135   mul   tmp1,wrp,ximag[km2]   ;;;; 490 TMPI= (WRP*XI(KN2) + WIP*XR(KN2))/2
22D6 F84F4F00003B28   E   136   mul   tmp1,wip,xreal[km2]
22DD 642E2A   137   add   tmp1+2,tmpr1+2
                           138
                           139   ;;   using the high byte only of a signed multiply
                           140   ;;   provides an effective divide by two
                           141
22E0 DC55   142   BVT   ERR1   ; Branch on error in complex multiplications
                           143
22E2 A34D00002C   E   144   ld   tmpr1,xreal[kptr]   ;;;;   500 TMPR1=XR(K)/2 :
22E7 0A012C   145   shra   tmpr1,#1   ;;;;   TMPI1=XI(K)/2 /2
22EA A34D0000030   E   146   ld   tmpi1,ximag[kptr]
22EF 0A0130   147   shra   tmpi1,#1
                           148
22F2 48262C34   149   gr2:   sub   xrtmp,tmpr1,tmpr+2   ;;;;   510 XR(KN2) = TMPR1 - TMPR
22F6 C34F000034   E   151   st   xrtmp,xreal[km2]
                           152
22FB 482A3038   153   ;gr2:   sub   xitmp,tmpi1,tmp1+2   ;;;;   520 XI(KN2) = TMPI1 - TMPI
22FF C34F000038   E   154   st   ximag[km2]
                           155
2304 44262C34   156   add   xrtmp,tmpr1,tmpr+2   ;;;;   530 XR(K) = TMPR1 + TMPR
2308 C34D000034   E   157   st   xrtmp,xreal[kptr]
                           158
230D 442A3038   159   gr: add   xitmp,tmpi1,tmp1+2   ;;;;   540 XI(K) = TMPI1 + TMPI
2311 C34D000038   E   160   st   ximag[kptr]
                           161
2316 DC23   162   BVT   ERR2   ; Branch on error in complex additions
                           163
                           164   $eject

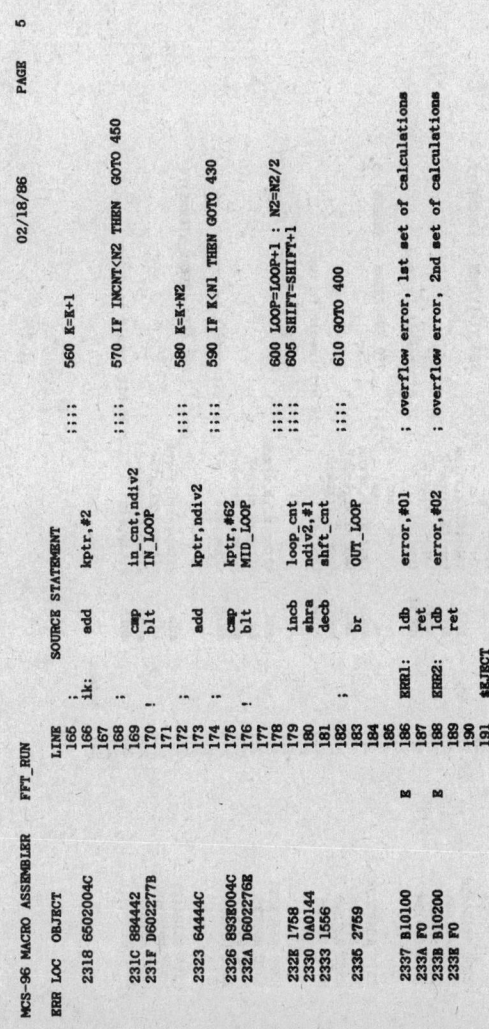

Listing 2—ASM96 FFT Program (Continued)

MCS-96 MACRO ASSEMBLER   FFT_RUN   02/18/86   PAGE   6

ERR LOC OBJECT   LINE   SOURCE STATEMENT
              192
              193   ;;;;   700 ' POST-PROCESSING AND REORDERING STARTS HERE
233F B10200   194 UNWRAVE: ldb   port1,#00000001b   ;****
              195
              196   ;;;;   720 FOR K=0 TO 31
2342 014C   197   clr   kptr
2344 A1400050 198   ld   n_sub_k,#64
2348   199 UN_LOOP:
              200   ;   ;;;;   740 XIBRK=XI(BR(K)) : XRBRK=XR(BR(K))
2348 A34D003852 201   ld   rk,brev[kptr]
234D A353000003C 202   ext   xrrk,xreal[rk]
2352 063C   203   xrrk
2354 A353000044 204   ld   xirk,ximag[rk]
2359 0644   205   ext   xirk
              206
              207   ;   ;;;;   760 XIBRNK=XI(BR(N-K)) : XRBRNK=XR(BR(N-K))
235B A351003854 208   ld   rnk,brev[n_sub_k]
2360 A355000040 209   ext   xrrnk,xreal[rnk]
2365 0640   210   xrrnk
2367 A355000048 211   ld   xirnk,ximag[rnk]
236C 0648   212   xirnk
              213   ;;;;   760 TI=(XIBRK + XIBRNK)/2
236E 44484428 214 ar: add   tmpi,xirk,xirnk
2372 A04A2A   215   ld   tmpi+2,xirnk+2
2375 A4462A   216   addc   tmpi+2,xirk+2
2378 0B0128   217   shral   tmpi,#1
              218   ; 16 bit result in tmpi
              219   ;;;;   770 TR=(XRBRK - XRBRNK)/2
237E 48403C24 220   sub   tmpr,xrrk,xrrnk
237F A03E26   221   ld   tmpr+2,xrrk+2
2382 A84226   222   subc   tmpr+2,xrrnk+2
2385 0B0124   223   shral   tmpr,#1
              224   ; 16 bit result in tmpr
              225   ;;;;   780 XRT= (XRBRK + XRBRNK)/4
2388 44403C34 226   add   xrtmp,xrrk,xrrnk
238C A03E36   227   ld   xrtmp+2,xrrk+2
238F A44236   228   addc   xrtmp+2,xrrnk+2
2392 0D0E34   229   shll   xrtmp,#l4
              230   ; 32 bit result in xrtmp
              231   ;;;;   790 XIT= (XIBRK-XIBRNK)/4
2395 48484438 232   sub   xitmp,xirk,xirnk
2399 A0463A   233   ld   xitmp+2,xirk+2
239C AB4A3A   234   subc   xitmp+2,xirnk+2
239F 0D0E38   235   shll   xitmp,#l4
              236   ; 32 bit result in xitmp
              237 $eject

Listing 2—ASM96 FFT Program (Continued)

AP-275

```
MCS-96 MACRO ASSEMBLER    FFT_RUN                         02/18/86   PAGE   7

ERR LOC  OBJECT             LINE   SOURCE STATEMENT
                             238   ;;;;
                             239   ;                          Multiply will provide effective divide by 2
                             240   ;;;;                   800 OUTR= (XRT + YI*COSFN(K)/2 - TR*SINFN(K)/2)
                             241
23A2 F84F4D4038242C          242         mul   tmpr,tmpr,sinfn[kptr]
23A9 F84F4DC23B82B30         243   mr:   mul   tmpi1,tmpi,cosfn[kptr]
23B0 643034                  244         add   xrtmp,tmpi1
23B3 A43236                  245         sub   xrtmp+2,tmpi1+2
23B6 682C34                  246         addc  xrtmp,tmpr1
23B9 A82E36                  247         subc  xrtmp+2,tmpr1+2
23BC C34D000036      R       248         st    xrtmp+2,outr[kptr]
                             249
                             250   ;;;;                   810 OUTI= (XIT - YI*SINFN(K)/2 - TR*COSFN(K)/2)
                             251
                             252   ;
23C1 F84F4DC23B82C4C         253   mi:   mul   tmpr1,tmpr,cosfn[kptr]
23C8 F84F4D403B2B30          254         mul   tmpi1,tmpi,sinfn[kptr]
23CF 683038                  255         sub   xitmp,tmpi1
23D2 A83238                  256         subc  xitmp+2,tmpi1+2
23D5 682C38                  257         sub   xitmp,tmpr1
23D8 682E38                  258         sub   xitmp+2,tmpr1+2
23DB C34D40003A      R       259         st    xitmp+2,outi[kptr]
                             260
                             261   ;;;;;                  OUTI = Imaginary Output values
                             262
                             263   ;;                     830 MAG =SQR(OUTR*OUTR + OUTI*OUTI)
                             264   GET_MAG:               ;; Get Magnitude of Vector
23E0 A03624                  265         ld    tmpr,xrtmp+2
23E3 A03A28                  266         ld    tmpi,xitmp+2
                             267
23E6 F86C2424                268         mul   tmpr,tmpr         ; tmpr = tmpi**2 + tmpi**2
23EA F86C2828                269         mul   tmpi,tmpi
23EE 642824                  270         add   tmpr,tmpi
23F1 A42A26                  271         addc  tmpr+2,tmpi+2
                             272
23F4 32004C                  273         bbc   FFT_MODE,2,CALC_SQRT
                             274
                             275   $eject
```

Listing 2—ASM96 FFT Program (Continued)

MCS-96 MACRO ASSEMBLER   FFT_RUN   02/18/86   PAGE   8

ERR LOC   OBJECT   LINE   SOURCE STATEMENT

                            276
                            277   ;;;; ### CALCULATE 10 log magnitude^2 ###
                            278   ;   x=1,2,3 ... 64K
                            279   ; Output = 512*10*LOG(x)
                            280   CALC_LOG:
     23F7 0156   281   clr   shft_cnt
     23F9 0F5624   282   normal tmpr,shft_cnt   ; Normalize and get normalization factor
     23FC 990F56   283   cmpb   shft_cnt,#15
     23FF DA04   284   jle   LOG_IN_RANGE   ; Jump if SHIFT_CNT <= 15
     2401 0140   285   clr   log
     2403 202C   286   br   LOG_STORE
                            287
                            288
     2405   289   LOG_IN_RANGE:
     2405 44565656   290   add   shft_cnt,shft_cnt,shft_cnt   ; Make shft_cnt a pointer
                            291
     2409 AC274E   292   ldbze ptr,tmpr+3   ; Most significant byte is table pointer
     240C 444BAB4E   293   add   ptr,ptr,ptr
     2410 650683A4E   294   add   ptr,# LOG_TABLE-256 ; ptr= Table + offset (offset=tmpr+3)
                            295   ; Use -256 since tmpr+3 is always >= 128
     2414 A24F40   296   ld   log,[ptr]+
     2417 A24E44   297   ld   mxtloc,[ptr]   ;; Linear Interpolation
                            298
     241A 694D044   299   sub   mxtloc,log   ; mxtloc = next log - log
                            300
     241D AC263C   301   ldbze diff,tmpr+2   ; diff+1 = mxtloc * tmpr+2 / 256
     2420 6C443C   302   mulu   diff,mxtloc
                            303
     2423 0C083C   304   shrl   diff,#8
     2426 643C40   305   add   log,diff   ; log = log + diff/256
     2429 080540   306   shr   log,#5   ; 8192/32 * 20LOG(x) = 256 * 20LOG(x)
                            307
     242C A7570A3C40   308   addc   log,log_offset[shft_cnt]   ; add log of normalization factor
                            309   ;; Log (M*N) = Log M + Log N
                            310
     2431   311   LOG_STORE:
     2431 080040   E 312   shr   log,#SCALE_FACTOR   ; Divide to prevent overflow during
     2434 A40040   E 313   addc   log,zero   ; averaging of outputs
     2437 674D000040   E 314   add   log,FFT_OUT[kptr]
     243C C34D000040   E 315   st   log,FFT_OUT[kptr]
                            316
     2441 2045   317   BR   ENDL
                            318
                            319    $eject

AP-275

```
MCS-96 MACRO ASSEMBLER    FFT_RUN                                          02/18/86    PAGE  9

ERR LOC  OBJECT            LINE    SOURCE STATEMENT
                            320            ;;;; *** CALCULATE SQUARE ROOT ***
    2443                    321    CALC_SQRT:
                            322
    2443 0156               323            clr     shft_cnt
    2445 0F5624             324    norml   tmpr,shft_cnt        ; Normalize and get normalization factor
                            325
    2448 D705               326            jne     SQRT_IN_RANGE ; Jump if tmpr > 0
    244A C04200    E        327            st      zero,sqrt+2
    244D 2029               328            br      SQRT_STORE
                            329
    244F                    330    SQRT_IN_RANGE:
    244F AC274B             331            ldbze   ptr,tmpr+3          ; Most significant byte is table pointer
    2452 444B4B4E           332            add     ptr,ptr,ptr
    2456 650B394E           333            add     ptr,# SQ_TABLE-256 ; ptr= Table + offset (offset=tmpr+3)
                            334                                       ; Use -256 since tmpr+3 is always >= 128
    245A A24F40             335            ld      sqrt, [ptr]+        ;; Linear Interpolation
    245D A24E44             336            ld      nxtloc, [ptr]
                            337
    2460 684044             338            sub     nxtloc,sqrt         ; nxtloc = sqrt - next sqrt
                            339
    2463 AC263C             340            ldbze   diff,tmpr+2         ; diff+1 = nxtloc * tmpr+2 / 256
    2466 6C443C             341            mulu    diff,nxtloc
                            342
    2469 AC3D3C             343            ldbze   diff,diff+1         ; sqrt = sqrt + delta   (diff < 0FFH)
    246C 643C40             344            add     sqrt,diff
                            345
    246F 44665656           346            add     shft_cnt,shft_cnt,shft_cnt
                            347
    2473 6F57C83940         348            mulu    sqrt,tab_sq+[shft_cnt] ; divide by normalization factor
                            349                                       ;; mulu acts as divide since if tab2=0FFFFH
                            350                                       ;; sqrt would remain essentially unchanged
                            351
    2478                    352    SQRT_STORE:
    2478 080042             353            shr     sqrt+2,#SCALE_FACTOR ; Divide to prevent overflow during
    247B A40042             354            addc    sqrt+2,zero          ; averaging of outputs
    247E 674D000042 E       355            add     sqrt+2,FFT_OUT[kptr]
    2483 C34D000042 E       356            st      sqrt+2,FFT_OUT[kptr]
                            357
                            358            ;       ;;;; *** END OF LOOP ***
                            359
    2488 65020004C          360    ENDL:   add     kptr,#2              ;;;;    950 NEXT K
    248C 690200050          361            sub     n_sub_k,#2
    2490 DF0228B4           362            bne     UN_LOOP
                            363    ;
    2494 F0                 364            RET
                            365
                            366            $eject
```

Listing 2—ASM96 FFT Program (Continued)

```
MCS-96 MACRO ASSEMBLER      FFT_RUN                                              02/18/86   PAGE 10

ERR LOC  OBJECT              LINE     SOURCE STATEMENT
                              367     $nolist
                              368              CSEG  AT  3800H       ;;;;   Use 2k for tables
     3800                     369
                              370
                              371     BREV:  ; 2bit reversal value
     3800  0000200010003000   372            DCW    2#0,  2#16, 2#8,  2#24, 2#4,  2#20, 2#12, 2#28
     3810  040024001400340    373            DCW    2#2,  2#18, 2#10, 2#26, 2#6,  2#22, 2#14, 2#30
     3820  02002200120032 00  374            DCW    2#1,  2#17, 2#9,  2#25, 2#5,  2#21, 2#13, 2#29
     3830  06002600160036 00  375            DCW    2#3,  2#19, 2#11, 2#27, 2#7,  2#23, 2#15, 2#31
                              376
                              377     SINFN:
     3840  0000BC0CF9182B25   378            DCW    0,     3212,  6393,  9612,  12539, 15446, 18204, 20787
     3850  B25AF1626D6AE270   379            DCW    23170, 25329, 27245, 28898, 30273, 31356, 32137, 32609
     3860  FF7F617F8977C7A    380            DCW    32767, 32609, 32137, 31356, 30273, 28898, 27245, 25329
     3870  B25A3351C47563C    381            DCW    23170, 20787, 18204, 15446, 12539, 9612,  6393,  3212
     3880  00007 4F307E7D6DA   382            DCW    0,     -3212, -6393, -9612, -12539, -15446, -18204, -20787
     3890  7EA50F9093961EBF   383            DCW    -23170, -25329, -27245, -28898, -30273, -31356, -32137, -32609
     38A0  01809F8077828485  384            DCW    -32767, -32609, -32137, -31356, -30273, -28898, -27245, -25329
     38B0  7EA5CDAEB4B8AAC3   385            DCW    -23170, -20787, -18204, -15446, -12539, -9612,  -6393,  -3212
     38C0  0000               386            DCW    0
                              387     COSFN:
     38C2  FF7F617F8977C7A    388            DCW    32767, 32609, 32137, 31356, 30273, 28898, 27245, 25329
     38D2  B25A3351C47563C    389            DCW    23170, 20787, 18204, 15446, 12539, 9612,  6393,  3212
     38E2  00074F307E7D6DA    390            DCW    0,     -3212, -6393, -9612, -12539, -15446, -18204, -20787
     38F2  7EA50F9093961EBF   391            DCW    -23170, -25329, -27245, -28898, -30273, -31356, -32137, -32609
     3902  01809F8077828485  392            DCW    -32767, -32609, -32137, -31356, -30273, -28898, -27245, -25329
     3912  7EA5CDAEB4B8AAC3   393            DCW    -23170, -20787, -18204, -15446, -12539, -9612,  -6393,  -3212
     3922  0000BC0CF9182B25   394            DCW    0,     3212,  6393,  9612,  12539, 15446, 18204, 20787
     3932  B25AF1626D6AE270   395            DCW    23170, 25329, 27245, 28898, 30273, 31356, 32137, 32609
     3942  FF7F               396            DCW    32767
                              397
                              398     WR:   ;;;;  WR = COS(K*2PI/N)
     3944  FF7F897D41766D6A   399            DCW    32767, 32137, 30273, 27245, 23170, 18204, 12539, 6393
     3954  00007E705CF4B4B8   400            DCW    0,     -6393, -12539, -18204, -23170, -27245, -30273, -32137
     3964  01807782BF899395   401            DCW    -32767, -32137, -30273, -27245, -23170, -18204, -12539, -6393
     3974  0000F918FB301C47  402            DCW    0,     6393,  12539, 18204, 23170, 27245, 30273, 32137
     3984  FF7F               403            DCW    32767
                              404
                              405     WI:   ;;;;  WI = -SIN(K*2PI/N)
     3986  0000007E705CF4BB   406            DCW    -0,    -6393, -12539, -18204, -23170, -27245, -30273, -32137
     3996  01807782BF899395   407            DCW    -32137, -32137, -30273, -27245, -23170, -18204, -12539, -6393
     39A6  0000F918FB301C47  408            DCW    0,     6393,  12539, 18204, 23170, 27245, 30273, 32137
     39B6  FF7F897D41766D6A   409            DCW    32767, 32137, 30273, 27245, 23170, 18204, 12539, 6393
     39C6  0000               410            DCW    0
                              411
                              412     $eject
```

Listing 2—ASM96 FFT Program (Continued)

AP-275

```
MCS-96 MACRO ASSEMBLER    FFT_RUN                                           02/18/86         PAGE 11

ERR LOC  OBJECT            LINE    SOURCE STATEMENT
                           413
                           414
                           415    TAB_SQR:    ; 65535/(square root of 2**SHFT_CNT)    0<=SHFT_CNT<32
                           416
     39C8                  417                ;    1       2       4       8      16      32      64     128
     39C8 FFFF04B50080825A 418                DCW  65535,  46340,  32768,  23170,  16384,  11685,  8192,  5793
                           419
                           420                ;   256     512    1024    2048    4096    8192   16384   32768
     39D8 0010500B0008AB05 421                DCW   256,   2896,   2048,   1448,   1024,    724,    512,    362
                           422
                           423                ; 65536, 131072, 262144, 524288, ...
     39E8 0001B500800005B00 424                DCW 65536, 181,    128,    91,     64,     45,     32,     23
     39F8 10000B0008000600 425                DCW   256,   16,     11,     8,      6,      4,      3,      1
                           426
                           427
                           428    SQ_TABLE:   ; square root of n * 2**24   N=128, 129, 130 ... 255
     3A08                  429
     3A08 05B5BAB56RB621B7 430                DCW  46341, 46522, 46702, 46881, 47059, 47237, 47415, 47591
     3A18 97BA46B3BF5BA3BC 431                DCW  47767, 47942, 48117, 48291, 48465, 48637, 48809, 48981
     3A28 0BC0AAC054C1FDC1 432                DCW  49152, 49322, 49492, 49661, 49830, 49998, 50166, 50332
     3A38 43C5E9C58BC633C7 433                DCW  50499, 50665, 50830, 50996, 51159, 51323, 51486, 51649
     3A48 63CA04CBA6CB46CC 434                DCW  51811, 51972, 52134, 52294, 52464, 52614, 52773, 52932
     3A58 62CF00D09D0D03AD1 435                DCW  53090, 53248, 53405, 53562, 53719, 53874, 54030, 54185
     3A68 44D4DED477D511D6 436                DCW  54340, 54494, 54647, 54801, 54954, 55106, 55258, 55410
     3A78 09D9A0D9D936DACCDA 437              DCW  55561, 55712, 55862, 56012, 56162, 56311, 56459, 56608
     3A88 B4DD47DEDBDE6BDF 438                DCW  56756, 56903, 57061, 57198, 57344, 57490, 57636, 57781
     3A98 46E2D7E267E3F7E3 439                DCW  57926, 58071, 58215, 58359, 58503, 58646, 58789, 58931
     3AA8 C1E64FE7DDE76AE8 440                DCW  59073, 59215, 59357, 59498, 59639, 59779, 59919, 60059
     3AB8 27EBB2EB3DECC7EC 441                DCW  60199, 60338, 60477, 60615, 60754, 60891, 61023, 61166
     3AC8 77EF00F08BF010F1 442                DCW  61303, 61440, 61576, 61712, 61848, 61984, 62119, 62254
     3AD8 B4F33BF4C1F446F5 443                DCW  62388, 62523, 62657, 62790, 62924, 63057, 63190, 63323
     3AE8 DFF763F8F7F86AF9 444                DCW  63455, 63587, 63719, 63850, 63982, 64113, 64243, 64374
     3AF8 F8FB7AFCFBFC7DFD 445                DCW  64504, 64634, 64763, 64893, 65022, 65151, 65280, 65408
                           446
                           447    $eject
```

Listing 2—ASM96 FFT Program (Continued)

```
MCS-96 MACRO ASSEMBLER    FFT_RUN                                                02/18/86   PAGE 12

ERR LOC  OBJECT                 LINE     SOURCE STATEMENT

3B08                            448
                                449
                                450      LOG_TABLE:  16384*10*LOG(n/128)          n=128,129,130 ... 256
3B08  00002A024F047006          451          DCW        0,   554,  1103,  1648,  2190,  2727,  3260,  3789
3B18  DA10E312E914EA16          452          DCW     4314,  4835,  5353,  5866,  6376,  6883,  7386,  7885
3B28  BD20A92292247B26          453          DCW     8381,  8873,  9362,  9848, 10330, 10810, 11286, 11758
3B38  C42F97316G333335          454          DCW    12228, 12696, 13158, 13619, 14076, 14531, 14983, 15432
3B48  063EC13F74A133043         455          DCW    15878, 16321, 16762, 17200, 17635, 18067, 18497, 18925
3B58  954B3C4D0F4EB150          456          DCW    19349, 19772, 20191, 20609, 21024, 21436, 21846, 22254
3B68  8458175AA85B365D          457          DCW    22660, 23063, 23464, 23862, 24259, 24653, 25045, 25435
3B78  DE64606680675D69          458          DCW    25822, 26208, 26592, 26973, 27353, 27730, 28106, 28479
3B88  B37024T294T300275         459          DCW    28851, 29220, 29588, 29954, 30318, 30680, 31040, 31399
3B98  OB7C8ETDCF71E2F80         460          DCW    31755, 32110, 32463, 32815, 33165, 33512, 33859, 34203
3BA8  F2864T85B85BED8A          461          DCW    34546, 34887, 35227, 35565, 35902, 36236, 36570, 36901
3BB8  7091B892FF934595          462          DCW    37232, 37560, 37887, 38213, 38537, 38860, 39181, 39501
3BC8  BB99C89C0A9E3E9F          463          DCW    39819, 40136, 40452, 40766, 41079, 41390, 41700, 42009
3BD8  4CA57EA6AFA7DEA8          464          DCW    42316, 42622, 42927, 43230, 43533, 43833, 44133, 44431
3BE8  B9AEE0AF07B12CB2          465          DCW    44729, 45024, 45319, 45612, 45905, 46196, 46486, 46774
3BF8  D6B7F4B811BA2DBB          466          DCW    47062, 47348, 47633, 47917, 48200, 48482, 48763, 49042
3C08  A9C0                      467          DCW    49321
                                468
                                469      LOG_OFFSET:  ; 512*10*LOG(2**(16-n))        n= 0,1,2,3 ... 15
                                470                   ; 512*10*LOG(0.5)              n= 16,17,18 ... 31
3C0A  4F5A4A54454E3F48          472          DCW    23119, 21578, 20037, 18495, 16954, 15413, 13871, 12330
3C1A  252A20241A1R1518          473          DCW    10789,  9248,  7706,  6165,  4624,  3083,  1541,     0
3C2A                            474
                                475      END

ASSEMBLY COMPLETED,  NO ERROR(S) FOUND.
```

Listing 2—ASM96 FFT Program (Continued)

The BASIC program is used as comments in the ASM96 program. Some of the variables in the ASM96 program have slightly different names than their counter-parts in the BASIC program. This was to make the comments fit into the ASM96 code. Highlights in this section of code are a table driven square root routine and log conversion routine which can easily be adapted for use by any program.

Both the square root routine and the log conversion routine use the 32-bit value in the variable TMPR. The square root routine calculates the square root of that value in the variable SQRT+2, a 16-bit variable. In this program, the square root value is averaged and stored in a table.

The log conversion routine divides the value in TMPR by 65536 (2^{16}) and uses table lookup to provide the common log. The result is a 16-bit number with the value 512 * 10 Log (TMPR/65536) stored in the variable LOG. This calculation is used to present the results of the FFT in decibels instead of magnitude. With an input of 63095, the output is 512*48 dB. The graph program, (Section 10), prints the output value of the plot as INPUT/512 dB.

The following descriptions of the ASM code point out some of the highlights and not-so-obvious coding:

Lines 1-104 initialize the code and declare variables. The input and output arrays of the program are declared external. Note that many of the registers are overlayable, use caution when implementing this routine with others with overlayable registers.

Lines 116-124 calculate the power of W to be used. Note that KPTR is always incremented by 2. The multiple right shift followed by the AND mask creates an even address and the indirect look to the BR (Bit Reversal) table quickly calculates the power PWR.

Lines 130-138 perform the complex multiplications. Since WIP and WRP range from -32767 to $+32767$, the multiplication is easy to handle. The automatic divide by two which occurs when using the upper word only of the 32-bit result is a feature in this case.

Lines 144-163 use right shifts for a fast divide, then add or subtract the desired variables and store them in the array. Note that the upper word of TMPR and TMPI is used, and the same array is used for both the input and output of the operations.

Lines 165-189 update the loop variables and then check for errors on the complex multiplications and additions. If there are no overflows at this time the data will run smoothly through the rest of the program.

Lines 200-212 load variables with values based on the bit reversed values of pointers.

Lines 214-236 perform additions and subtractions to prepare for the next set of formulas. Note that XITMP and XRTMP are 32-bit values.

Lines 240-260 perform multiplies and summations resulting in 32-bit variables. This saves a bit or two of accuracy. The upper words are then stored as the results.

Lines 263-272 generate the squared magnitude of the harmonic component as a 32-bit value.

Lines 278-310 calculate 10 Log (TMPR/65536). The 32-bit register TMPR is divided by 65536 so that the output range would be reasonable.

First, the number is normalized. (It is shifted left until a 1 is in the most significant bit, the number of shifts required is placed in SHFT_CNT.) If it had to be shifted more than 15 times the output is set to zero.

Next, the most significant BYTE is used as a reference for the look-up table, providing a 16-bit result. The next most significant BYTE is then used to perform linear interpolation between the referenced table value and the one above it. The interpolated value is added to the directly referenced one.

The 16-bit result of this table look-up and interpolation is then added to the Log of the normalization factor, which is also stored in a table. This table look-up approach works fast and only uses 290 bytes of table space.

Lines 321-357 calculate the square root of the 32-bit register TMPR using a table look-up approach.

First, the number is normalized. Next, the most significant BYTE is used as a reference for the look-up table, providing a 16-bit result. The next most significant BYTE is then used to perform linear interpolation between the referenced table value and the one above it. The interpolated value is added to the directly referenced one.

The 16-bit result of this table look-up and interpolation is then divided by the square root of the normalization factor, which is also stored in a table. This table look-up approach works fast and only uses 320 bytes of table space. The results are valid to near 14-bits, more than enough for the FFT algorithm.

Lines 352-360 average the magnitude value, if multiple passes are being performed, and then store the value in the array. The loop-counters are incremented and the process repeats itself.

This concludes the FFT routine. In order to use it, it must be called from a main program. The details for calling this routine are covered in the next section.

8.0 BACKGROUND CONTROL PROGRAM

The main routine is shown in Listing 3. It begins with declarations that can be used in almost any program. Note that these are similar, but not identical, to other 8096 include files that have been published. Comments on controlling the Analog to Digital converter routine follow the declarations.

```
MCS-96 MACRO ASSEMBLER    FFT_MAIN_APNOTE                                                02/18/86    PAGE    1

SERIES-III MCS-96 MACRO ASSEMBLER, V1.0

SOURCE FILE: :F2:FTMAIN.A96
OBJECT FILE: :F2:FTMAIN.OBJ
CONTROLS SPECIFIED IN INVOCATION COMMAND: NOSB


ERR LOC  OBJECT              LINE        SOURCE STATEMENT

                               1         $pagelength(50)
                               2
                               3         FFT_MAIN_APNOTE MODULE MAIN, STACKSIZE(6)
                               4
                               5         ; Intel Corporation, January 24, 1986
                               6         ; by Ira Horden, MCO Applications
                               7
                               8         ; This program performs an FFT on real data and plots it on a printer.
                               9         ; It uses the program modules A2DCON, PLOTSF, and FFTRUN. The adjustable
                              10         ; parameters of each of the programs are set by this main module.
                              11
                              12
                              13
                              14         $INCLUDE (:F0:DEMO96.INC)   ; Include SFR definitions
                              15         ;$nolist  ; Turn listing off for include file
                              16
                              17         ;********************************************************************
                              18                                       Copyright 1985, Intel Corporation
                              19                                             October 28,1985
                              20                                       by Ira Horden, MCO Applications
                              21
                              22         ; DEMO96.INC - DEFINITION OF SYMBOLIC NAMES FOR THE I/O REGISTERS OF THE 8096
                              23
                              24         ;********************************************************************
                              25
                              26
0000                      =1  27         ZERO            EQU     00h:WORD      ; R/W   Zero Register
0002                      =1  28         AD_COMMAND      EQU     02H:BYTE      ;   W   A to D command register
0002                      =1  29         AD_RESULT_LO    EQU     02H:BYTE      ;  R    Low byte of result and channel
0003                      =1  30         AD_RESULT_HI    EQU     03H:BYTE      ;  R    High byte of result
0003                      =1  31         HSI_MODE        EQU     03H:BYTE      ;   W   Controls HSI transition detector
0004                      =1  32         HSO_TIME        EQU     04H:WORD      ;   W   HSI time tag
0004                      =1  33         HSI_TIME        EQU     04H:WORD      ;  R    HSO time tag
0006                      =1  34         HSO_COMMAND     EQU     06H:BYTE      ;   W   HSO command tag
0006                      =1  35         HSI_STATUS      EQU     06H:BYTE      ;  R    HSI status register (reads fifo)
0007                      =1  36         SBUF            EQU     07H:BYTE      ; R/W   Serial port buffer
0008                      =1  37         INT_MASK        EQU     08H:BYTE      ; R/W   Interrupt mask register
0009                      =1  38         INT_PENDING     EQU     09H:BYTE      ; R/W   Interrupt pending register
0011                      =1  39         SPCON           EQU     11H:BYTE      ;   W   Serial port control register
0011                      =1  40         SPSTAT          EQU     11H:BYTE      ;  R    Serial port status register
000A                      =1  41         WATCHDOG        EQU     0AH:BYTE      ;   W   Watchdog timer
```

Listing 3—Main Routine

```
MCS-96 MACRO ASSEMBLER    FFT_MAIN_APNOTE                                         02/18/86    PAGE   2

ERR LOC  OBJECT      LINE         SOURCE STATEMENT

     000A          =1  42    TIMER1       EQU   0AH:WORD      ; R     Timer1 register
     000C          =1  43    TIMER2       EQU   0CH:WORD      ; R     Timer2 register
     000E          =1  44    PORT0        EQU   0EH:BYTE      ; R     I/O port 0
     000E          =1  45    BAUD_REG     EQU   0EH:BYTE      ; W     Baud rate register
     000F          =1  46    PORT1        EQU   0FH:BYTE      ; R/W   I/O port 1
     0010          =1  47    PORT2        EQU   10H:BYTE      ; R/W   I/O port 2
     0015          =1  48    IOC0         EQU   15H:BYTE      ; W     I/O control register 0
     0015          =1  49    IOS0         EQU   15H:BYTE      ; R     I/O status register 0
     0016          =1  50    IOC1         EQU   16H:BYTE      ; W     I/O control register 1
     0016          =1  51    IOS1         EQU   16H:BYTE      ; R     I/O status register 1
     0017          =1  52    PWM_CONTROL  EQU   17H:BYTE      ; W     PWM control register
     0018          =1  53    SP           EQU   18H:WORD      ; R/W   System stack pointer
                   =1  54
     000D          =1  55    CR           EQU   0DH
     000A          =1  56    LF           EQU   0AH
                   =1  57
                   =1  58    PUBLIC ZERO,AD_COMMAND,AD_RESULT_LO,AD_RESULT_HI,HSI_MODE,HSO_TIME,HSI_TIME
                   =1  59    PUBLIC HSO_COMMAND
                   =1  60    PUBLIC HSI_STATUS,SBUF,INT_MASK,INT_PENDING,WATCHDOG,TIMER1,TIMER2
                   =1  61    PUBLIC BAUD_REG,PORT0,PORT1,PORT2,SPSTAT,SPCON,IOC0,IOC1,IOS0,IOS1
                   =1  62    PUBLIC PWM_CONTROL,SP,CR,LF
                   =1  63
     001C          =1  64    RSEG at 1CH
                   =1  65
     001C          =1  66    AX:          DSW   1             ; Temp registers used in conformance
     001E          =1  67    DX:          DSW   1             ; with PLM-96(tm) conventions.
     0020          =1  68    BX:          DSW   1
     0022          =1  69    CX:          DSW   1
                   =1  70
     001C          =1  71    AL           EQU   AX     :BYTE
     001D          =1  72    AH           EQU   (AX+1) :BYTE
     0020          =1  73    BL           EQU   BX     :BYTE
                   =1  74
                   =1  75    public ax, bx, cx, dx, al, ah, bl
                   =1  76
                   =1  77    $list      ; Turn listing back on
                   =1  78               ; End of include file
                   =1  79
                   =1  80    ; A2D UTILITY COMMANDS/RESPONSES FOR "CONTROL_A2D"
                   =1  81
     0007          =1  82    busy         equ   7
     0010          =1  83    con_b0       equ   00010000b; convert to BUFF0
     0028          =1  84    dump_b0_p_s  equ   00101000b; download BUFF0 as PAIRED SIGNED data
                   =1  85    ;
                   =1  86
     0001          =1  87    AVR_NUM      equ   1         ; Number of times to average the waveform
                   =1  88                                 ;   AVR_NUM < 256
```

Listing 3—Main Routine (Continued)

AP-275

```
MCS-96 MACRO ASSEMBLER    FFT_MAIN_APNOTE                                         02/18/86   PAGE   3

ERR LOC  OBJECT           LINE      SOURCE STATEMENT
         0000              89
                           90       SCALE_FACTOR    equ     0           ; Number of rights shifts performed on
                           91                                           ; output of FFT. Used to prevent overflow
                           92                                           ; on summation
                           93
         0100              94       PLOT_RES        equ     256         ; Number of input units per plot unit
         0080              95       PLOT_RES_2      equ     plot_res/2
         9100              96       PLOT_MAX        equ     plot_res*145; 145 chrs/row
                           97
                           98       PUBLIC scale_factor, plot_res, plot_res_2, plot_max
                           99
         0024             101       OSEG at 24H     ; common oseg area
         0024             102
         0028             103       tmpreal:        dsl     1
         002C             104       tmpimag:        dsl     1
         002E             105       wndptr:         dsw     1
                         106       varptr:         dsw     1
                         107
         0000             108       RSEG
         0000             109       fft_mode:       dsb     1
         0001             110       error:          dsb     1
         0002             111       svr_cnt:        dsb     1
                         112       PUBLIC error, fft_mode
                         113
                         114       EXTRN sample_period, control_a2d
                         115
                         116
         0080             117       DSEG at 80h,
         0080             118       XREAL:
         00C0             119       DEST_BUFF_BASE: DSW     64          ; For FFT routine
                         120       XIMAG equ       XREAL+64
                         121
                         122       PUBLIC DEST_BUFF_BASE, XREAL, XIMAG
                         123
         0200             124       DSEG AT 200H
         0200             125       PLOT_IN:
         0200             126       FFT_OUT:        DSW     32          ; For FFT routine
         0240             127       BUFF0_BASE:     DSW     64          ; For A2D routine
         02C0             128       BUFF1_BASE:     DSW     64          ; For A2D routine
                         129
                         130       PUBLIC BUFF0_BASE, BUFF1_BASE, FFT_OUT, PLOT_IN
                         131
                         132       $eject
                         133
```

Listing 3—Main Routine (Continued)

MCS-96 MACRO ASSEMBLER   FFT_MAIN APNOTE   02/18/86   PAGE   4

ERR LOC   OBJECT   LINE   SOURCE STATEMENT

     2080   134   CSEG AT 2080H
                               135
                               136
                               137   EXTRN   INIT_OUTPUT, DRAW_GRAPH, CON_OUT   ; For Plot Routine
                               138   EXTRN   FFT_CALC   ; For FFT routine
                               139   EXTRN   A2D_BUFF_UTIL   ; For A2D routine
                               140
     2080 A1000018   141   LD   SP,#STACK
     2084 A301003010   R   142   LD   AX,3000H
                               143   SBE_WAIT:
     2089 E01CFD   144   djnz   al,sbe_wait   ; WAIT FOR SBE TO CLEAR SERIAL PORT INTERRUPTS
     208C E01DFA   145   djnz   ah,sbe_wait
                               146
     208F EF0000   B   147   BEGIN: CALL   INIT_OUTPUT   ; Initialize serial port
                               148
                               149   NEW_TRANSFORM_SET:
     2092 B10000   R   150   ldb   fft_mode,#0000B   ; Bit 0 - Real data / Tabled data#
                               151   ; Bit 1 - Windowed / Unwindowed#
                               152   ; Bit 2 - 10log Mag^2 / Magnitude#
                               153   ; Bit 3 - 256xdb plot / Normal Plot#
     2096 B10102   R   154   ldb   avr_cnt,#avr_num
     2098 0120   155   clr   bx
     209A C321000200   156   CLRRAM: st   zero,fft_out[bx] ; clear fft magnitude array
     209F 65020020   157   add   bx,#2
     20A3 89400020   158   cmp   bx,#64
     20A7 DEF1   159   blt   CLRRAM
                               160
     20A9 300004   R   161   C_load: bbc   fft_mode,0,do_tab ; Branch if real data is not used
     20AC 2819   162   CALL   LOAD_DATA
     20AE 2002   163   br   C_win
                               164
     20B0 282F   165   do_tab: CALL   TABLE_LOAD
                               166
     20B2 310002   R   167   C_win: bbc   fft_mode,1,calc   ; Branch if windowing is not used
     20B5 2BCB   168   CALL   DO_WINDOW
                               169
     20B7 EF0000   B   170   CALC: CALL   FFT_CALC
     20BA 980001   R   171   errtrp: cmpb   error,zero
     20BD D7FB   172   jne   errtrp
                               173
     20BF E00205   R   174   DJNZ   avr_cnt,LOAD_DATA ; repeat for AVR_NUM counts
                               175
     20C2 EF0000   B   176   CALL   DRAW_GRAPH
                               177
     20C5 27CB   178   BR   NEW_TRANSFORM_SET
                               179             $eject

```
MCS-96 MACRO ASSEMBLER    FFT_MAIN APNOTE                                02/18/86   PAGE  5

ERR LOC  OBJECT           LINE      SOURCE STATEMENT
                          180       ;::::      LOAD DATA INTO RAM        :::::  **** FOR INDICATION ONLY
                          181       ;
                          182       LOAD_DATA:
     20C7                 183           ldb     port1,#00
     20C7 B1000F          184
                          185       SET_A2D:
     20CA B11000          186           ldb     control_a2d,#con_b0        ; Set converter for buffer0
     20CD 910100      B   187           orb     control_a2d,#01            ; Convert channel 1
     20D0 A1320000    B   188           ld      sample_Period,#50          ; 100 us sample period
                          189
     20D4 EF0000          190           CALL    a2d_buff_util              ; Start the conversion process
     20D7 3F00FD      B   191           jbs     control_a2d,busy,$         ; wait for all conversions to be done
                          192
                          193       Down_load:
     20DA B12800       B  194           ldb     control_a2d,#dump_b0_p_s   ; download b0 paired/signed
     20DD EF0000       B  195           CALL    a2d_buff_util
     20E0 F0              196           RET
                          197
                          198       ;TABLE_LOAD:
     20E1 0120            199           clr     bx
     20E3 A102211C        200       load: ld    ax,#DATA0                  ; Load tabled data for testing
     20E7 A21D22          201           ld      dx,[ax]+
     20EA A21D1E          202           ld      cx,[ax]+
     20ED C321B00022      203           st      cx,xreal[bx]
     20F2 C321C0001E      204           st      dx,ximag[bx]
     20F7 650202020       205           add     bx,#2
     20FB 89400020        206           cmp     bx,#64
     20FF DEE6            207           blt     LOAD
     2101 F0              208           RET
                          209
                          210       ; SQUARE WAVE
     2102                 211       DATA0:
                          212
     2102 FF7FFF7FFF7FFF7F 213         DCW     32767,  32767,  32767,  32767
     2112 FF7FFF7FFF7FFF7F 214         DCW     32767,  32767,  32767,  32767
     2122 FF7FFF7FFF7FFF7F 215         DCW     32767,  32767,  32767,  32767
     2132 FF7FFF7FFF7FFF7F 216         DCW     32767,  32767,  32767,  32767
     2142 01800180018001 80 217        DCW    -32767, -32767, -32767, -32767
     2152 01800180018001 80 218        DCW    -32767, -32767, -32767, -32767
     2162 01800180018001 80 219        DCW    -32767, -32767, -32767, -32767
     2172 01800180018001 80 220        DCW    -32767, -32767, -32767, -32767
                          221
                          222       $eject
```

Listing 3—Main Routine (Continued)

AP-275

```
MCS-96 MACRO ASSEMBLER    FFT_MAIN_APNOTE                              02/18/86    PAGE   6

ERR LOC  OBJECT                    LINE    SOURCE STATEMENT

                                    223    ;
                                    224    ;;;; PERFORM HANNING WINDOW
                                    225    DO_WINDOW:
2182  012C                          226         wndptr                 ; Windowing provides an effective
2184  012E                          227         varptr                 ; divide by 2 because of the multiply
2186                                228    WINDOW:
2186  A32DBE211C                    229         ld    ax,hanning[wndptr]
218B  A32DC02120                    230         ld    bx,hanning+2[wndptr]
2190  FE4F2F80001C24                231         mul   tmpreal,ax,xreal[varptr]
2197  FE4F2FC0002028                232         mul   tmpimag,bx,ximag[varptr]
219E  0D0124                        233         shll  tmpreal,#1
21A1  0D0128                        234         shll  tmpimag,#1           ; Compensate for the divide by 2
21A4  C32FB00026                    235         st    tmpreal+2,xreal[varptr]
21A9  C32FC0002A                    236         st    tmpimag+2,ximag[varptr]
21AE  66040020                      237         add   wndptr,#4
21B2  65020020                      238         add   varptr,#2
21B6  8940002E                      239         cmp   varptr,#64
21BA  D7CA                          240         jne   window
21BC  F0                            241         RET
                                    242
21BE                                243    HANNING:      ; Windowing function
21BE  00004F003B01C102              244         DCW   0,    79,    315,    705,   1247,   1935,   2761,   3719
21C6  BF1266177110D421              245         DCW   4799, 5990,  7281,   8660,  10114,  11628,  13187,  14778
21CE  00404546704C9352              246         DCW   16384,17989, 19580,  21139, 22653,  24107,  25486,  26777
21E6  406D7871367570F8              247         DCW   27968,29048, 30006,  30832, 31520,  32062,  32452,  32688
21FE  FF7FB07FC47F3E7D              248         DCW   32767,32688, 32452,  32062, 31520,  30832,  30006,  29048
220E  46D99688E632B5E               249         DCW   27968,26777, 25486,  24107, 22653,  21139,  19580,  17989
221E  0040BA3983336C2D              250         DCW   16384,14778, 13187,  11628, 10114,   8660,   7281,   5990
222E  BF128F0BC90A8F07              251         DCW   4799, 3719,  2761,   1935,  1247,    705,    315,     79
223E  0000                          252         DCW   0
                                    253         $eject
                                    254
```

Listing 3—Main Routine (Continued)

AP-275

```
MCS-96 MACRO ASSEMBLER   FFT_MAIN APNOTE                                                             02/18/86   PAGE  7

ERR  LOC  OBJECT              LINE   SOURCE STATEMENT

                              255    CSEG AT 3D00H    ; ADDITIONAL TABLES FOR TESTING
     3D00                     256
                              257
     3D00                     258    DATA1:
     3D00  0000335189970E270  259           DCW         0,  20787,  32137,  28898,  12539,  -9512, -27245, -32609
     3D10  7EA574F31C477C7A   260           DCW     -23170,  -3212,  18204,  31356,  -9446,  15446, -6393,  -25329
     3D20  01800F90D08B75630  261           DCW     -32767, -25329,  -6392,  15446,  30273,  31356,  18204,  -3212
     3D30  7EA59F80939500BDA  262           DCW     -23170, -32609, -27245,  -9512,  12539,  28898,  32137,  20787
     3D40  0000C0AB77821EBF   263           DCW         -0, -20787, -32137, -28898, -12539,   9512,  27245,  32609
     3D50  8225A8C0C84B8B485  264           DCW      23170,  3212, -18204, -31356, -30273, -15446,   6393,  25329
     3D60  FF7FF162F818AAC3   265           DCW      32767,  25329,  6392, -15446, -30273, -31356, -18204,   3212
     3D70  8225A617F506A2825  266           DCW      23170,  32609,  27245,   9512, -12539, -28898, -32137, -20787
                              267
     3D80                     268    DATA2:                 ; SINE 7.5 X
                              269
     3D80  0000F555617FCF66   270           DCW         0,  22005,  32609,  26319,   6393, -16846, -31356, -29621
     3D90  05CF1F2BE270297C   271           DCW     -12539,  11039,  28898,  31785,  18204,  -4808, -25329, -32728
     3DA0  7EA5B8F9933519C7B  272           DCW     -23170,  -1608,  20787,  32412,  27245,   7962, -15446, -30852
     3DB0  BF8946C928825C960  273           DCW     -30273, -14010,   9512,  28105,  32137,  19519,  -3212, -24279
     3DC0  0180291A174F33F4C  274           DCW     -32767, -24279,  -3212,  19519,  28105,  32137,  19870,   9512, -14010
     3DD0  BF8979C87AAC31A1F  275           DCW     -30273, -30852, -15446,   7962,  24412,  20787,  -1608
     3DE0  7EA528B00F9D38BD   276           DCW     -23170, -32728, -25329,  -4808,  18205,  31785,  28898,  11039
     3DF0  05CF4BBC8485C33BE  277           DCW     -12539, -29621, -31356, -16845,   6393,  26319,  32609,  22005
                              278
     3E00                     279    DATA3:                 ; .707*SINE 7.5X
                              280
     3E00  0000C63C0F6AAF48   281           DCW         0,  15558,  23055,  18607,   4520, -11910, -22169, -20942
     3E10  5FDD7C1ECF4FC857   282           DCW      -8865,   7804,  20431,  22472,  12870,  -3399, -17908, -23138
     3E20  03C08FFB693984559  283           DCW     -16381,  -1137,  14697,  22916,  19262,   5629, -10921, -21812
     3E30  65AC4FD9451A9B84D  284           DCW     -21403,  -9905,   6725,  19870,  22721,  13800,  -2271, -17165
     3E40  82A5F3BC21F78E35   285           DCW     -23166, -17165,  -2271,  13800,  22721,  19870,   6725,  -9905
     3E50  65ACCCA58D5FD15    286           DCW     -21403, -21812, -10920,   5629,  19262,  22916,  14696,  -1137
     3E60  03C09EA50C8AB9F2   287           DCW     -16381, -23138, -17908,  -3399,  12871,  22472,  20431,   7804
     3E70  5FDD32AE67A97AD1   288           DCW      -8865, -20942, -22169, -11910,   4520,  18607,  23055,  15557
                              289
     3E80                     290    DATA4:                 ; .707*SINE(11x) /16
                              291
     3E80  0000FD0AB40472FF   292           DCW         0,   1277,   1204,  -1420,   -142,  -1338,  -1119,    282,   1386
     3E90  000450F874FA69FC   293           DCW      1024,   -420,  -1420,    804,   1441,    554,   1441,    804,   -683
     3EA0  58FA55FD2403A105   294           DCW     -1448,   -683,    804,   1441,   -919,  -1338,  -1420,   -919,   -420
     3EB0  00046A051A01A1FB   295           DCW      1024,   1386,    282,  -1277,  -1119,   -142,   1119,   1204,   1277
     3EC0  000003FB4CFB8B00   296           DCW        -0,  -1277,  -1204,   -142,   1338,   1119,   -142,  -1204,  -1386
     3ED0  001FCA4018C0059703 297           DCW     -1024,   1420,   1420,    919,   -554,  -1441,   -554,  -1441,    683
     3EE0  ABO5ABO2DCFC5FFA   298           DCW      1448,    683,   -804,  -1441,    919,   1338,   1420,    919,    420
     3EF0  00FC95FA86FB5F04   299           DCW     -1024,  -1386,   -282,   1119,   1338,    142,  -1119,  -1204,  -1277
                              300
     3F00                     301    DATA5:                 ; .707*(SINE 7.5X + 1/16 SINE 11X)
```

Listing 3—Main Routine (Continued)

5-143

MCS-96 MACRO ASSEMBLER   FFT_MAIN_APNOTE   02/18/86   PAGE 8

ERR LOC OBJECT   LINE   SOURCE STATEMENT

3F00 0000C241C35E2148   302   DCW   0, 16834, 24259, 18466, 3182,-13029,-21886,-19657
3F10 5EE1D81C434A3154   303   DCW   -7842, 7384, 19011, 21553, 13425, -1958,-17103,-23821
3F20 5BAE5F88D3C245F   304   DCW   -17829, -1819, 15501, 24356, 19816, 4710,-12341,-23232
3F30 65B0B90D85F1B3F49   305   DCW   -20379, -8519, 7007, 18751, 21383, 13658, -1067,-15888
3F40 82A5F6B75DF27636   306   DCW   -23166,-18442, -3475, 13942, 24059, 20990, 6442,-11290
3F50 65A870ACB4DA9A119   307   DCW   -22427,-21392, -9600, 6648, 18708, 21475, 13892, -454
3F60 ABC548ABB3B618BD   308   DCW   -14933,-22456,-18712, -4840, 12317, 23391, 21851, 8225
3F70 5FD9C8A84DA8BD9D5   309   DCW   -9889,-22328,-22451,-10791, 5857, 18749, 21851, 14281
                                310   END
3F80   311
                                312
                                313

ASSEMBLY COMPLETED, NO ERROR(S) FOUND.

AP-275

```
SERIES-III MCS-96 RELOCATOR AND LINKER, V2.0
Copyright 1983 Intel Corporation

INPUT FILES: :F2:FTMAIN.OBJ, :F2:FFTRUN.OBJ, :F2:PLOTSP.OBJ, :F2:A2DCON.OBJ
OUTPUT FILE: :F2:FFTOUT
CONTROLS SPECIFIED IN INVOCATION COMMAND:
  IX


INPUT MODULES INCLUDED:
  :F2:FTMAIN.OBJ(FFT_MAIN_APNOTE)   02/18/86
  :F2:FFTRUN.OBJ(FFT_RUN)           02/18/86
  :F2:PLOTSP.OBJ(PLOT_SERIAL)       02/18/86
  :F2:A2DCON.OBJ(A2D_BUFFERING_UTILITY)  02/18/86


SEGMENT MAP FOR :F2:FFTOUT(FFT_MAIN_APNOTE):

             TYPE    BASE    LENGTH  ALIGNMENT  MODULE NAME
             ----    ----    ------  ---------  -----------

**RESERVED*          0000H   001AH
             REG     001AH   0001H   BYTE       PLOT_SERIAL
*** GAP ***          001BH   0001H
             REG     001CH   0008H   ABSOLUTE   FFT_MAIN_APNOTE
             OVRLY   0024H   0035H   ABSOLUTE   FFT_RUN
**OVERLAP**  OVRLY   0024H   0010H   ABSOLUTE   PLOT_SERIAL
**OVERLAP**  OVRLY   0024H   000CH   ABSOLUTE   FFT_MAIN_APNOTE
*** GAP ***          0059H   0001H
             OVRLY   005AH   0006H   WORD       A2D_BUFFERING_UTILITY
             REG     0060H   000CH   WORD       A2D_BUFFERING_UTILITY
             REG     006CH   0003H   BYTE       FFT_MAIN_APNOTE
*** GAP ***          006FH   0011H
             DATA    0080H   0080H   ABSOLUTE   FFT_MAIN_APNOTE
             STACK   0100H   001EH   WORD
             DATA    011EH   0080H   WORD       FFT_RUN
*** GAP ***          019EH   0062H
             DATA    0200H   0140H   ABSOLUTE   FFT_MAIN_APNOTE
*** GAP ***          0340H   1CC2H
             CODE    2002H   0002H   ABSOLUTE   A2D_BUFFERING_UTILITY
*** GAP ***          2004H   007CH
             CODE    2080H   01C0H   ABSOLUTE   FFT_MAIN_APNOTE
*** GAP ***          2240H   0040H
             CODE    2280H   0215H   ABSOLUTE   FFT_RUN
*** GAP ***          2495H   006BH
             CODE    2500H   0168H   ABSOLUTE   PLOT_SERIAL
             CODE    2668H   00ECH   BYTE       A2D_BUFFERING_UTILITY
*** GAP ***          2754H   10ACH
             CODE    3800H   042AH   ABSOLUTE   FFT_RUN
*** GAP ***          3C2AH   00D6H
             CODE    3D00H   0280H   ABSOLUTE   FFT_MAIN_APNOTE
*** GAP ***          3F80H   C080H
```

270189-53

Listing 3—Main Routine (Continued)

AP-275

Several constants are then setup for other routines. The purpose of centrally locating these constants was the ease of modifying the operation of the routines. Note that AVR__NUM and SCALE__FACTOR must be changed at the same time. SCALE__FACTOR is the shift count used to divide each FFT output value before it is added to the output array. AVR__NUM must be less than 2**SCALE__FACTOR or an overflow could occur. Next, the public variables are declared for the arrays and a few other parameters.

The program then begins by setting the stack pointer and waiting for the SBE-96 to finish talking to the terminal. If this is not done, there may be serial port interrupts occurring for the first twenty five milliseconds of program operation.

Initialization of the plotter is next, followed by setting the FFT__MODE byte. This byte controls the graphing, loading and magnitude calculation of the FFT data. Since FFT__MODE is declared PUBLIC in this module, and EXTERNAL in the PLOT module and FFTRUN module, the extra bits available in this byte can be used for future enhancements.

The next step is to clear the FFT output array. Since the FFT program can be set to average its results by dividing the output before adding it to the magnitude array, the array must be cleared before beginning the program.

Data is then loaded into into the FFT input array by the code at LOAD__DATA, or the code at TABLE__LOAD, depending on the value of FFT__MODE bit 0. The tabled data located at DATA0 is a square wave of magnitude 1. This waveform provides a reasonable test of the FFT algorithm, as many harmonics are generated. The results are also easy to check as the pattern contains half zeros, imaginary values which are always the same, and real values which decrease. Figure 13 shows the output in fractions, hexadecimal and decimal. The hexadecimal and decimal values are based on an output of 16384 being equal to 1.00.

Note that the magnitude is

SQR (REAL^2 + IMAG^2)

and the dB value is

10 LOG ((REAL^2 + IMAG^2)/65536)

The divide by 65536 is used for the dB scale to provide a reasonable range for calculations. If this was not done, a 32-bit LOG function would have been needed.

After the data is loaded, the data is optionally windowed, based on FFT__MODE bit 1, and the FFT program is called. Once the loop has been performed AVR__CNT times, the graph is drawn by the plot routine.

Appended to the main routine is the FFTOUT.M96 Listing. This is provided by the relocator and linker, RL96. With this listing and the main program, it is possible to determine which sections of code are at which addresses.

Using the modular programming methods employed here, it is reasonably easy to debug code. By emulating the program in a relatively high level language, each routine can be checked for functionality against a known standard. The closer the high level implementation matches the ASM96 version, the more possible checkpoints there are between the two routines.

Once all of the program routines (modules) can be shown to work individually, the main program should work unless there is unwanted interaction between the modules. These interactions can be checked by verifying the inputs and outputs of each module. The assembly language locations to perform the program breaks can be retrieved by absolutely locating the main module. The other modules can be dynamically located by RL96.

The more interactive program modules are, the more difficult the program becomes to debug. This is especially true when multiple interrupts are occurring, and several of the interrupt routines are themselves interruptable. In these cases, it may be necessary to use debugging equipment with trace capability, like the VLSiCE-96. If this type of equipment is not available, then using I/O ports to indicate the entering and leaving of each routine may be useful. In this way it will be possible to watch the action of the program on an oscilloscope or logic analyzer. There are several places within this code that I/O port toggling has been used as an aid to debugging the program. These lines of code are marked "FOR INDICATION ONLY."

AP-275

K	Fractional			dB	Decimal			Hexadecimal		
	REAL	IMAG	MAG²		REAL	IMAG	MAG²	REAL	IMAG	MAG²
0	0.0000	0.0000	0.0000	0.000	0	0	0	0	0	0
1	0.0625	−1.2722	1.2738	38.225	1024	−20843	20868	400	AE95	5184
2	0.0000	0.0000	0.0000	0.000	0	0	0	0	0	0
3	0.0625	−0.4213	0.4260	28.710	1024	−6903	6978	400	E509	1B42
4	0.0000	0.0000	0.0000	0.000	0	0	0	0	0	0
5	0.0625	−0.2495	0.2572	24.329	1024	−4088	4214	400	F008	1076
6	0.0000	0.0000	0.0000	0.000	0	0	0	0	0	0
7	0.0625	−0.1747	0.1855	21.491	1024	−2862	3039	400	F4D2	BDF
8	0.0000	0.0000	0.0000	0.000	0	0	0	0	0	0
9	0.0625	−0.1321	0.1462	19.421	1024	−2165	2395	400	F78B	95B
10	0.0000	0.0000	0.0000	0.000	0	0	0	0	0	0
11	0.0625	−0.1043	0.1216	17.820	1024	−1708	1992	400	F954	7C8
12	0.0000	0.0000	0.0000	0.000	0	0	0	0	0	0
13	0.0625	−0.0843	0.1049	16.540	1024	−1381	1719	400	FA9B	6B7
14	0.0000	0.0000	0.0000	0.000	0	0	0	0	0	0
15	0.0625	−0.0690	0.0931	15.499	1024	−1130	1525	400	FB96	5F5
16	0.0000	0.0000	0.0000	0.000	0	0	0	0	0	0
17	0.0625	−0.0566	0.0844	14.645	1024	−928	1382	400	FC60	566
18	0.0000	0.0000	0.0000	0.000	0	0	0	0	0	0
19	0.0625	−0.0464	0.0778	13.944	1024	−759	1275	400	FD09	4FB
20	0.0000	0.0000	0.0000	0.000	0	0	0	0	0	0
21	0.0625	−0.0375	0.0729	13.374	1024	−614	1194	400	FD9A	4AA
22	0.0000	0.0000	0.0000	0.000	0	0	0	0	0	0
23	0.0625	−0.0296	0.0691	12.918	1024	−484	1133	400	FE1C	46D
24	0.0000	0.0000	0.0000	0.000	0	0	0	0	0	0
25	0.0625	−0.0224	0.0664	12.564	1024	−366	1088	400	FE92	440
26	0.0000	0.0000	0.0000	0.000	0	0	0	0	0	0
27	0.0625	−0.0157	0.0644	12.305	1024	−256	1056	400	FF00	420
28	0.0000	0.0000	0.0000	0.000	0	0	0	0	0	0
29	0.0625	−0.0093	0.0632	12.135	1024	−152	1035	400	FF68	40B
30	0.0000	0.0000	0.0000	0.000	0	0	0	0	0	0
31	0.0625	−0.0031	0.0626	12.051	1024	−50	1025	400	FFCE	401

Figure 13. FFT Output for a Square Wave Input

9.0 ANALOG TO DIGITAL CONVERTER MODULE

The module presented in Listing 4 is a general purpose one which converts analog values under interrupt control and stores them in one of two buffers. These buffers can then be downloaded to another buffer, such as the input buffer to the FFT program. During downloading, this module can convert the data into signed or unsigned formats, and fill a linear or a paired array. A paired array is like the one used in the FFT transform program. It requires N data points placed alternately in two arrays, one starting at zero and the other at N/2.

AP-275

```
MCS-96 MACRO ASSEMBLER    A2D_BUFFERING_UTILITY

SERIES-III MCS-96 MACRO ASSEMBLER, V1.0

SOURCE FILE: :F2:A2DCON.A96
OBJECT FILE: :F2:A2DCON.OBJ
CONTROLS SPECIFIED IN INVOCATION COMMAND: NOSB

                                                        02/18/86         PAGE    1

ERR LOC  OBJECT          LINE        SOURCE STATEMENT
                           1         $pagelength(50)
                           2
                           3         A2D_Buffering_Utility  module  stacksize(12)
                           4         ;
                           5         ;  Intel Corporation, July 16, 1985
                           6         ;  by Dave Ryan, Intel Applications Engineer
                           7         ;
                           8         ;  This utility fills a memory buffer with A/D conversion results. The
                           9         ;  conversions are done under interrupt control, and are initiated when
                          10         ;  A2D_BUFF_Util is called. The results of the conversions are placed
                          11         ;  in one of two buffers, called BUFF0 and BUFF1.
                          12         ;
                          13         ;  This utility provides options for the selection of the buffer lengths, data
                          14         ;  format, sample period, conversion channel and time base. The utility also
                          15         ;  has a download routine that will load either buffer into a register file
                          16         ;  buffer. Output formats can also be chosen for the downloaded buffer. The
                          17         ;  data can be formatted as signed or unsigned linear or paried arrays.
                          18         ;
                          19         ;  RUN-TIME OPTIONS
                          20         ;
                          21         ;  Rather than use the STACK to pass controls, this utility gets its directions
                          22         ;  from 2 control words in memory. The utility expects that its control words
                          23         ;  are valid at the time A2D_BUFF_Util is called and remain valid throughout
                          24         ;  A/D interrupt executions and downloads. The control words are:
                          25         ;
                          26         ;    Sample_Period  ; WORD ; The time between samples in timer counts
                          27         ;                          ; where the timer used has been specified
                          28         ;
                          29         ;
                          30         ;    Control_A2D    ; BYTE ; Control information for the utility:
                          31         ;                          BIT#
                          32         ;
                          33         ;                          : 0-2 : Channel Number
                          34         ;                          :  3  : Signed Result/Unsigned Result#
                          35         ;                          :  4  : Convert/Download#
                          36         ;                          :  5  : BUFF1/BUFF0# for conversions
                          37         ;                          :      : BUFF0/BUFF1# for downloads
                          38         ;                          :  6  : Linear/Paired#
                          39         ;                          :  7  : Converter BUSY/IDLE#
                          40         ;
                          41         $EJECT
```

Listing 4—A to D Converter Routine

AP-275

```
MCS-96 MACRO ASSEMBLER    A2D_BUFFERING_UTILITY                       02/18/86    PAGE    2


ERR LOC  OBJECT          LINE    SOURCE STATEMENT
                          42
                          43     ; The following is a table of equates that can be used to simplify the
                          44     ; bit diddling requirements. If you are not running conversions concurrently
                          45     ; with downloads, always LDB Control_A2D with the following command then
                          46     ; ORB Control_A2D with the channel number you wish to convert if you are
                          47     ; starting a conversion.
                          48     ;
                          49     ; Once the utility is called, care must be taken when Control_A2d is
                          50     ; modified. You can cause downloads to occur while conversions are running,
                          51     ; but you cannot start conversions during a download. To do this, ORB to the
                          52     ; control byte with the appropriate bits set. Do NOT change the BUFF bit or
                          53     ; the BUSY bit. Just set the download bit and set the data format bits to the
                          54     ; correct values.
                          55     ;
                          56     ; The BUFF bit has opposite definitions for conversions and downloads. This
                          57     ; allows conversions to be done into BUFF0 while downloads come from BUFF1, and
                          58     ; vice versa.
                          59     ;
                          60     ; A2D UTILITY COMMANDS
                          61     ;
                          62     con_b0          equ     00010000b;convert to BUFF0
                          63     con_b1          equ     00110000b; "            BUFF1
                          64
                          65     dump_b0_l_u     equ     01100000b; download     BUFF0  as LINEAR USIGNED data
                          66     dump_b1_l_u     equ     01000000b; "            BUFF1  "   "      "      "
                          67     dump_b0_p_u     equ     00100000b; "            BUFF0  "   PAIRED        "
                          68     dump_b1_p_u     equ     00000000b; "            BUFF1  "   "             "
                          69     dump_b0_l_s     equ     01101000b; download     BUFF0  as LINEAR SIGNED  data
                          70     dump_b1_l_s     equ     01001000b; "            BUFF1  "   "      "      "
                          71     dump_b0_p_s     equ     00101000b; "            BUFF0  "   PAIRED        "
                          72     dump_b1_p_s     equ     00001000b; "            BUFF1  "   "             "
                          73
                          74     $eject
```

Listing 4—A to D Converter Routine (Continued)

MCS-96 MACRO ASSEMBLER   A2D_BUFFERING_UTILITY   02/18/86   PAGE 3

ERR LOC OBJECT   LINE   SOURCE STATEMENT

                            75   ;
                            76   ; ASSEMBLY-TIME OPTIONS
                            77   ;
                            78   ; The base addresses and length of each conversion buffer and the destination
                            79   ; buffer are DECLARED EXTERNal in this utility. Other options such as selection
                            80   ; of the timer used as a timebase, the length of the buffer, and the effective
                            81   ; number of bits in the reported result are set at assembly time through use
                            82   ; of EQUates in this module.
                            83   ;
                            84   ; The following parameters need to be provided at assembly or link time.
                            85   ; The buffer bases are declared EXTERNal by this utility, while the buffer
                            86   ; length shift count and ESO commands are EQUated.
                            87   ;
                            88   ;   BUFF0_BASE   ; The starting address of BUFF0
                            89   ;   BUFF1_BASE   ; The starting address of BUFF1
                            90   ;   DEST_BUFF_BASE ; The starting address of the download
                            91   ;   ; target buffer.
                            92   ;
                            93   ;   BUFF_LENGTH   ; The number of SAMPLES that each
                            94   ;   ; buffer must hold. must be >1 and <256
                            95   ;
                            96   ;   Shift_count   ; The number of times that the conversion result is
                            97   ;   ; to be shifted right from its natural left justified
                            98   ;   ; position. Setting a shift count greater than 6 will
                            99   ;   ; result in lost bits to the right. Rounding is NOT
                           100   ;   ; done.
                           101   ;
                           102   ;   CLOCK   ; Specify as either TIMER1 or T2CLK. This is the
                           103   ;   ; timebase used for conversions.
                           104   ;
                           105   ; Samples are stored as words in the buffers. The program stores
                           106   ; conversions linearly in BUFF0 and BUFF1, and linearly or paired in the
                           107   ; destination buffer as selected. If the download is to be paired, the first
                           108   ; sample is placed in location DEST_BUFF_BASE, the second sample is placed in
                           109   ; location (DEST_BUFF_BASE + BUFF_LENGTH), the third in (DEST_BUFF_BASE + 2),
                           110   ; the fourth in (DEST_BUFF_BASE + 2 + BUFF_LENGTH), etc.
                           111   ;
                           112          $eject

Listing 4—A to D Converter Routine (Continued)

```
MCS-96 MACRO ASSEMBLER    A2D_BUFFERING UTILITY                    02/18/86    PAGE    4

ERR LOC  OBJECT           LINE        SOURCE STATEMENT

                          113
                          114         ;NOTES ON EXECUTION
                          115         ;
                          116         ; When a utility call directs the initiation of a set of A2D conversions, the
                          117         ; first conversion is begun at approximately one sample time plus 50 state
                          118         ; times from when the utility was called. This assumes that no interrupts are
                          119         ; present.
                          120         ;
                          121         ; The conversion busy bit is set approximately 50 state times after a call
                          122         ; to the utility, if the convert bit was set in the A2D Control byte. The
                          123         ; busy bit is cleared after all conversion results have been stored in the
                          124         ; result buffer designated (BUFF0 or BUFF1).
                          125         ;
                          126         ; Take great care in modifying the A2D_Control byte to do a download while
                          127         ; conversions are taking place. You can never download a buffer that is
                          128         ; being converted into. The results would be invalid.
                          129         $eject
```

Listing 4—A to D Converter Routine (Continued)

```
MCS-96 MACRO ASSEMBLER    A2D_BUFFERING_UTILITY                                    02/18/86   PAGE  5

ERR LOC  OBJECT           LINE     SOURCE STATEMENT
         0000             130             RSEG
                          131
                          132
                          133      EXTRN BUFF0_BASE, BUFF1_BASE, DEST_BUFF_BASE
                          134      EXTRN ad_command, ad_result_lo, ad_result_hi
                          135      EXTRN hso_command, hso_time, sp
                          136
    0040                  137      BUFF_LENGTH   EQU   64
    0001                  138      Shift_Count   EQU   1
    000A                  139      CLOCK         EQU   TIMER1
                          140
                          141      ; set up hso commands for correct timer *************************
                          142
    000A                  143      TIMER1        equ   0AH
    000C                  144      T2CLK         equ   0CH
                          145
    0000                  146      MASK          equ   (10b&CLOCK)AND(40h)
                          147
    000F                  148      Start_A2D     equ   (00001111b)OR(MASK)
                          149                          ;start a2d based on timer 1, no interrupt
    0000                  150
    0000                  151      HSO_0_Low     equ   (00000000b)OR(MASK)
                          152                          ; make hso.0 low based on timer1 no interrupt
    0020                  153
                          154      HSO_0_High    equ   (00100000b)OR(MASK)
                          155                          ; make hso.0 hi based on timer1 no interrupt
                          156
                          157      ; set up storage ************************************************
                          158
    0000                  159      sdudtemp0:    DSW   1  ; temp register for download calls
                          160
    0002                  161      sdudtemp1:    DSW   1  ; temp registers for conversion calls
    0004                  162      top_of_buffer:DSW   1
    0006                  163      sample_count: DSW   1
    0008                  164
    0009                  165      Control_A2D:  DSB   1  ; the byte that controls the utility execution
                          166
    0003                  167                    DForm   equ   3         ; Signed/Unsigned#
    0004                  168                    Con_Dwn equ   4         ; Convert/Download#
    0005                  169                    B0_B1   equ   5         ; Buff1/Buff0# for conversions
                          170                                            ; Buff0/Buff1# for downloads
    0006                  171                    Lin_Par equ   6         ; Linear/Paired#
    0080                  172                    Busy    equ   10000000B ; Bit 8
                          173
                          174      $eject
```

Listing 4—A to D Converter Routine (Continued)

AP-275

```
MCS-96 MACRO ASSEMBLER    A2D_BUFFERING_UTILITY                           02/18/86   PAGE  6

ERR LOC  OBJECT           LINE       SOURCE STATEMENT
                           175
                           176   Sample_Period:  DSW    1; the word that specifies the number of clock ticks
                           177                          ; that elapse between each sample
                           178
                           179   PUBLIC Control_A2D, Sample_Period
                           180
                           181        OSEG
                           182
    0000                   183   src_ptr:        DSW    1; some overlayable temp registers
                           184                   temp set src_ptr:WORD
    0000                   185   dest_ptr:       DSW    1
    0002                   186   loop_count:     DSW    1
    0004                   187
                           188
    2002                   189        CSEG  at  2002h
                           190
                           191   PUBLIC A2D_DONE_Vector
    2002 AC00          R   192   DCW    A2D_DONE_Vector
                           193
    0000                   194        CSEG
                           195
                           196   PUBLIC A2D_BUFF_Util
                           197
                           198   Load_HSO_Command MACRO var   ; Macro to load HSO
                           199        LDB   hso_command,#var
                           200        LD    hso_time,aductemp0
                           201        ENDM
                           202   $eject
```

Listing 4—A to D Converter Routine (Continued)

```
MCS-96 MACRO ASSEMBLER    A2D BUFFERING UTILITY                       02/18/86         PAGE    7

ERR LOC  OBJECT             LINE    SOURCE STATEMENT
         0000                207
                             208    A2D_BUFF_Util:
                             209
0000 3C0962                  210            JBS     Control_A2D, Con_Dwn, Convert   ; Select convert or download
0003 A1000000         B      211    Download:
0007 350904           R      212            LD      src_ptr,#BUFF1_BASE
                             213            JBC     Control_A2D, B0_B1,     Set_Data_Format
                             214
000A                         215    Download_BUFF0:
000A A1000000         B      216            LD      src_ptr,#BUFF0_BASE
                             217
                             218
000E                         219    Set_Data_Format:
000E A1000002         R      220            LD      dest_ptr, #DEST_BUFF_BASE
0012 B14004           R      221            LDB     loop_count,#BUFF_LENGTH
0015 3E091D           R      222            JBS     Control_A2D, Lin_Par,   Linear_data_loop
                             223
                             224
0018 1B0104                  225    PAIRED: SHRB    loop_count,#1           ; Choose linear or paired
                             226                                            ; The paired data routine uses 1/2
001B                         227    Paired_Data_loop:                       ; as many loops as the unpaired
001B A20000           R      228            LD      adudtemp0,[src_ptr]+
001E C20200           R      229            ST      adudtemp0,[dest_ptr]    ; Move even word
0021 65400002         R      230            ADD     dest_ptr,#BUFF_LENGTH   ; Length = # of words = 1/2 # of bytes
                             231
0025 A20000           R      232            LD      adudtemp0,[src_ptr]+
0028 C20200           R      233            ST      adudtemp0,[dest_ptr]+   ; Move odd word
002B 69400002         R      234            SUB     dest_ptr,#BUFF_LENGTH
                             235
002F E004E9                  236            DJNZ    loop_count, Paired_Data_loop    ; Loop until done
0032 28D                     237            CALL    Convert_Data
0034 F0                      238            RET
                             239
                             240
                             241
0035                         242    Linear_Data_loop:
0035 A20000           R      243            LD      adudtemp0,[src_ptr]+            ; Move data linearly
0038 C20200           R      244            ST      adudtemp0,[dest_ptr]+
                             245
003B E004F7           R      246            DJNZ    loop_count, Linear_Data_loop    ; Loop until done
                             247
003E 2801                    248            CALL    Convert_Data
0040 F0                      249            RET
                             250            $eject
```

AP-275

```
MCS-96 MACRO ASSEMBLER    A2D_BUFFERING_UTILITY                    02/18/86    PAGE    8

ERR LOC  OBJECT              LINE    SOURCE STATEMENT
         0041                251
                             252             ; Convert the data in the destination buffer
                             253     Convert_Data:
    0041 A1400004         R  254             LD      loop_count,#BUFF_LENGTH
    0045 A1000000         B  255             LD      src_ptr,#DEST_BUFF_BASE
                             256
    0049 A20000           R  257     Again:  LD      adudtemp0,[src_ptr]
    004C 71C000           R  258             ANDB    adudtemp0,#11000000b
    004F 330909           R  259             JBC     Control_A2D, DForm, Unsigned_Result
                             260
    0052                     261     Signed_Result:
    0052 69B07F00         R  262             SUB     adudtemp0,#7fe0H
    0056 0A0100           R  263             SHRA    adudtemp0,#Shift_Count
    0059 2003                264             BR      Replace_Sample
                             265
    005B                     266     Unsigned_Result:
    005B 080100           R  267             SHR     adudtemp0, #Shift_Count
                             268
    005E                     269     Replace_Sample:
    005E C20000           R  270             ST      adudtemp0,[src_ptr]+
    0061 E004B5           R  271             DJNZ    loop_count,Again    ; Loop until done
                             272
    0064 F0                  273             RET
                             274
                             275
    0065                     276     Convert:
    0065 F2                  277             PUSHF
                             278
                             279             ;; Prepare to Start Conversions
    0066 918009           R  280             ORB     Control_A2D, #Busy      ; set converter busy bit
    0069 B13708           R  281             LDB     sample_count,#BUFF_LENGTH - 1
    006C A1000006         B  282             LD      top_of_buffer,#BUFF0_BASE
    0070 A1800004         B  283             LD      aductempl,$(BUFF0_BASE + 2*BUFF_LENGTH)
                             284
    0074 350908           R  285             JBC     Control_A2D, B0_B1, Start Conversions
    0077 A1000006         B  286             LD      top_of_buffer,#BUFF1_BASE
    007B A1800004         B  287             LD      aductempl,$(BUFF1_BASE + 2*BUFF_LENGTH)
                             288
                             289     $eject
```

Listing 4—A to D Converter Routine (Continued)

```
MCS-96 MACRO ASSEMBLER    A2D_BUFFERING_UTILITY                              02/18/86    PAGE  9

ERR LOC  OBJECT          LINE       SOURCE STATEMENT
     007F                 290
                          291  Start_Conversions:
                          292
     007F 51070900   R    293          ANDB    ad_command,Control_A2D,#00000111b  ;load channel number
                          294
     0083 440AOA02   R    295          ADD     eductemp0,CLOCK,Sample_Period      ;start first conversion
                          296                                                     ;one sample time from
                          297                                                     ;now
                          298
     008D CC00            299          Load_HSO_Command Start_A2D                 ; Start A2D at time=eductemp0
                          303
                          304          POP     temp                               ; get a copy of the psw
                          305
                          306          Load_HSO_Command HSO_0_high                ; set hso.0 high at conversion
                          310                                                     ; start time for external S/H
                          311
     0095 81020200   R    312          OR      temp,#202h                         ; enable a2d interrupts
                          313
     0099 640A02    R    314          ADD     eductemp0,Sample_Period
                          315
                          316          Load_HSO_Command Start_A2D                 ; start second convertion one
                          320                                                     ; sample time from the first
                          321
     00A2 C800       R    322          PUSH    temp                               ; put psw back on stack
                          323
                          324          Load_HSO_Command HSO_0_low                 ;lower hso.0 for external S/H
                          328
     00AA F3              329          POPF
     00AB F0              330          RET
                          331   $eject
```

Listing 4—A to D Converter Routine (Continued)

intel. AP-275

```
MCS-96 MACRO ASSEMBLER    A2D_BUFFERING_UTILITY                              02/18/86    PAGE   10

ERR LOC  OBJECT                   LINE      SOURCE STATEMENT
                                  332       CSEG
    00AC                          333   A2D_DONE_Vector:
    00AC F2                       334                   PUSHF              ; A/D INTERRUPT ROUTINE
                                  335
                                  336
    00AD C60600                 B 337             STB    ad_result_lo,[top_of_buffer]+
    00B0 C60600                 B 338             STB    ad_result_hi,[top_of_buffer]+
    00B3 51070900               B 339             ANDB   ad_command,Control_A2D,#00000111b     ;load channel number
                                  340
    00B7 E00B09                 R 341             DJNZ   sample_count, Sample_Again
    00BA 1708                     342             INCB   sample_count
                                  343
    00BC 880406                 R 344             CMP    top_of_buffer,aductempl               ; Check top of buffer
    00BF DF26                     345             BE     Top_of_buffers
    00C1 F3                       346             POPF
    00C2 F0                       347             RET
                                  348
                                  349   Sample_Again:
    00C3 640A02                 R 350             ADD    aductemp0,Sample_Period               ; Set next sample time
    00C6 880406                 R 351             CMP    top_of_buffer,aductempl               ; Check top of buffer
                                  352                                                          ; for later jump
                                  353             Load_HSO_Command Start_A2D
                                  357
    00CF 30080B                 R 358             JBC    sample_count,0,Make_HSO_High
                                  359
                                  360   Make_HSO_low:
    00D2 FD                       361             nop                                          ; wait 8 states after HSO load
                                  362             Load_HSO_Command HSO_0_Low                   ; Load for change of HSO to trigger S/H
    00D9 DF0C                     367             BE     Top_of_buffers
    00DB F3                       368             POPF
    00DC F0                       369             RET
                                  370
                                  371   Make_HSO_high:
                                  372             Load_HSO_Command HSO_0_High                  ; Load for change of HSO to trigger S/H
                                  376
    00E3 DF02                     377             BE     Top_of_buffers
    00E5 F3                       378             POPF
    00E6 F0                       379             RET
                                  380
                                  381   Top_of_buffers:
    00E7 717F09                 R 382             ANDB   Control_A2D,#NOT(Busy)                ; Clear converter BUSY bit
    00EA F3                       383             POPF
    00EB F0                       384             RET
    00EC                          385   END

ASSEMBLY COMPLETED,    NO ERROR(S) FOUND.
```

Listing 4—A to D Converter Routine (Continued)

The listing contains a fairly complete description of what the program does. The block by block operations are shown below:

Lines 1-198 describe the program, declare the variables and set up equates. Several of these variables are declared as overlayable, so the user needs to be careful if using this module for other than the FFT program.

Lines 205-210 declare a macro which is used to load the HSO unit. This will be used repeatedly through the code.

Lines 212-253 determine whether a conversion or download has been requested. If a download has been requested, the data is downloaded to the destination array as either paired or linear data. Paired data has been described earlier.

Lines 255-278 contain a subroutine which converts the destination array to either signed or unsigned numbers. The numbers are also shifted right to provide the desired full-scale value as requested by SHIFT__COUNT.

Lines 279-334 initialize the conversion routine. HSO.0 is toggled with the start of each routine so that an external sample and hold can be used. The instructions in lines 308, 316, and 326 have been interweaved with the Load__HSO__Commands to provide the required 8 state delays between HSO loadings. If this was not done, NOPs would have been needed. It is easier to understand the code if these lines are thought of as being gathered at line 326.

Lines 337-353 are the actual A/D interrupt routine. The A/D results are placed BYTE by BYTE on the buffer, the A/D is reloaded, and then the number of samples taken is compared to the number needed. Note that the A/D command register needs to be reloaded even if the channel does not change. INCB on line 348 is used to insure that the DJNZ falls through on the next pass (if sample__count is not reset).

Lines 355-396 complete the routine. The HSO is set up to trigger the next conversion and provide the HSO.0 toggle for an external sample and hold. Once again, the time between consecutive loads of the HSO is 8 states minimum. Note that this section of code has been optimized for speed by reducing branches to an absolute minimum and duplicating code where needed.

This concludes the description of the A to D buffer module. In the FFT program, this module is run, then the FFT transform module, then the plot module. This allows variables to be overlaid, saving RAM space. The time cost for this is not bad, considering the printer is the limiting factor in these conversions. If more RAM was provided, and the FFT was run with its data in external RAM, this module could be run simultaneously with the other modules.

10.0 DATA PLOTTING MODULE

The plot module is relatively straight-forward, and is shown in Listing 5. After the declarations, which include overlayable registers, an initialization routine is listed. This separately called routine sets up the serial port on the 8096 to talk to the printer. In this case, the port has to be set for 300 baud.

A console out routine follows. This routine can also be called by any program, but it is used only by the plot routine in this example. The write to port 1 is used to trace the program flow. The character to be output is passed to this routine on the stack. This conforms to PLM-96 requirements.

Since all stack operations on the 8096 are 16-bits wide, a multiple character feature has been added to the console out routine. If the high byte it receives is non-zero, the ASCII character in that byte is printed after the character in the low byte. If the high byte has a value between 128 and 255, the character in the low byte is repeated the number of times indicated by the least significant 7 bits of the high byte.

The print decimal number routine is next. It is called with two words on the stack. The first word is the unsigned value to be printed. The second byte contains information on the number of places to be printed and zero and blank suppression. This routine is not overflow-proof. The user must declare a sufficient number of places to be printed for all possible numbers.

The DRAW__GRAPH routine provides the plot. It first sends a series of carriage return, line feeds (CRLFs) to clear the printer and provides a margin on the paper. Each row is started with the row number, 2 spaces, and a "+". Asterisks are then plotted until

Number of asterisks > FFT Value / PLOT__RES

Recall that PLOT__RES is a variable set by the main program. When the number of asterisks hits the desired value, the value of the line is printed. If the Decibel mode is selected, the line value is divided by 512 and printed in integer + decimal part form, followed by "dB". If the number of asterisks reaches PLOT__MAX, no value is printed. The next line is then started. A line with only a "!" is printed before the next plot line to provide a more aesthetic display on the printer. If a CRT was used, this extra line would probably not be wanted.

MCS-96 MACRO ASSEMBLER   PLOT_SERIAL   02/18/86   PAGE   1

SERIES-III MCS-96 MACRO ASSEMBLER, V1.0

SOURCE FILE: :F2:PLOTSP.A96
OBJECT FILE: :F2:PLOTSP.OBJ
CONTROLS SPECIFIED IN INVOCATION COMMAND: NOSB

```
ERR LOC  OBJECT          LINE        SOURCE STATEMENT
                           1    $pagelength(50)
                           2
                           3    PLOT_SERIAL MODULE STACKSIZE (6)
                           4
                           5    ; Intel Corporation, December 12, 1985
                           6    ; by Ira Horden, MCO Applications
                           7
                           8    ; This program produces a plot on serially connected printer. The
                           9    ; magnitude of each of the 32 input values is plotted horizontally, with one
                          10    ; "," followed by a linefeed between each plot line. Each plot line starts
                          11    ; with a "+" and the entire plot begins with 3 line feeds and ends with a form
                          12    ; feed. The values to be plotted are 32 unsigned words based at the externally
                          13    ; defined pointer PLOT_IN.
                          14
                          15    ; The routine INIT_OUTPUT must be run to set up the serial port when the
                          16    ; system is turned on. COM_OUT can be used by a program to output to the
                          17    ; serial port. DRAW_GRAPH is the routine that automatically plots the data.
                          18
                          19    ; Sizing of the graph can be done using PLOT_RES, which determines how many
                          20    ; units are needed for each dot, and PLOT_MAX, which is the maximum value the
                          21    ; program will be passed. Note that (PLOT_MAX/PLOT_RES) defines the maximum
                          22    ; number of columns the routine will print.
                          23
                          24          RSEG
                          25
                          26          EXTRN    locl, baud_reg, spcon, spstat, sbuf, portl
                          27          EXTRN    zero, ax, bx, cx, dx, FFT_MODE
                          28          sptmp:   dsb    1
                          29
                          30          DSEG at 24H
0000                      31          value:    dsl    1
0000                      32          divisor:  dsl    1
0024                      33          xptr:     dsw    1
0028                      34          yptr:     dsw    1
002C                      35          xval:     dsw    1
002E                      36          log_val:  dsw    1
0030                      37
0032                      38          DSEG
                          39          EXTRN    PLOT_IN
                          40
0000                      41    $eject
```

Listing 5—The Plot Module

```
MCS-96 MACRO ASSEMBLER    PLOT_SERIAL                                    02/18/86           PAGE    2

ERR LOC  OBJECT           LINE    SOURCE STATEMENT

                           42
                           43     CSEG at 2500H        ;;;;           PROGRAM MODULE BEGINS
    2500                   44
                           45     PUBLIC INIT_OUTPUT, CON_OUT, DRAW_GRAPH
                           46     EXTRN PLOT_RES, PLOT_RES_2, PLOT_MAX
                           47
                           48     INIT_OUTPUT:                ; INITIALIZE SERIAL PORT
                           49
    2500 B12000            50              ldb      iocl,#00100000B  ; set p2.0 to txd
                           51
    0270                   52     baud_val    equ    624         ; 624=300 baud (at 12 MHz)
                           53
    0082                   54     Baud_high   equ    ((baud_val-1)/256) OR 80H   ; set for XTAL1 clock
    006F                   55     baud_low    equ    (baud_val-1) MOD 256
                           56
    2503 B16F00          R 57              ldb      baud_reg,#baud_low
    2506 B18200          R 58              ldb      baud_reg,#baud_high
                           59
    2509 B14900          R 60              ldb      spcon,#01001001b    ; enable reciver mode 1
    250C B12000          R 61              ldb      sptmp,#00100000B    ; set TI-tmp
                           62
    250F F0                63              RET
                           64
                           65     $eject
```

Listing 5—The Plot Module (Continued)

```
MCS-96 MACRO ASSEMBLER    PLOT_SERIAL                                    02/18/86   PAGE   3

ERR LOC  OBJECT          LINE     SOURCE STATEMENT

                          66      ;----------------------------------------------------------------
                          67      ;                      CONSOLE OUT ROUTINE
                          68      ;
                          69      ;    Call with a word parameter on stack. The low byte has the character
                          70      ;    to be sent. If the high byte has a value between 81H and 8FEH, the
                          71      ;    character is repeated 1 to 126 times respectively. One repeat means
                          72      ;    that the character will be printed 2 times. If the high byte contains
                          73      ;    a value between 1 and 7FH, the character represented by that value will
                          74      ;    be printed after the character in the low byte. If the high byte
                          75      ;    contains a value of zero only the low byte will be printed.
                          76      ;
                          77      ;----------------------------------------------------------------
2510 CC00                 78      CON_OUT:  pop    ax              ; cx contains the calling adress
2512 CC00                 79                pop    dx
2514 3F011C               80                jbs    dx+1,7,onechr   ; If bit 7 is set print one character
2517 980001               81                cmpb   dx+1,zero
251A DF17                 82                je     onechr          ; if highbyte=0 print one character
                          83
                          84
251C 900000         M     85      twochr:   orb    sptmp,spstat    ; wait for TI
251F 3500FA         M     86                jbc    sptmp,5,twochr
2522 71DFF00        R     87                andb   sptmp,#11011111b ; clear TI-tmp
2525 900000         M     88                orb    zero,spstat     ; remove possible false TI
                          89
2528 B00000         M     90                ldb    sbuf,dx         ; Load second character
252B B00100         M     91                ldb    dx,dx+1
252E 1101           R     92                clrb   dx+1            ; clear count byte
2530 717F00         M     93                andb   dx,#07FH        ; mask MSB
                          94
2533 1701           M     95      onechr:  incb   dx+1
2536 717F01         M     96      wait1:   orb    sptmp,spstat    ; wait for TI
2538 900000         M     97                jbc    sptmp,5,wait1
253B 3500FA         M     98                andb   sptmp,#11011111b ; clear TI-tmp
253E 71DFF00        R     99                orb    zero,spstat     ; remove possible false TI
2541 900000         M    100
                         101
2544 B00000         M    102                ldb    sbuf,dx
2547 B001EE         M    103                DJNZ   dx+1,wait1
254A E300           M    104                BR     [ax]            ; Effectively a RET
                         105
                         106      $eject
```

Listing 5—The Plot Module (Continued)

AP-275

```
MCS-96 MACRO ASSEMBLER          PLOT_SERIAL                              02/18/86     PAGE   4

ERR LOC  OBJECT              LINE       SOURCE STATEMENT

                              107       ;-------------------------------------------------------------
                              108       ;              PRINT DECIMAL NUMBER ROUTINE
                              109       ;-------------------------------------------------------------
                              110       ;   Call with two words on stack. The first is the value to be printed.
                              111       ;   The second has mode information in the low byte.
                              112       ;          MODE:   000 = supress all zeros
                              113       ;                  001 = print all numbers
                              114       ;                  010 = supress all zeros except rightmost
                              115       ;                  1xx = do not print leading blanks
                              116       ;
                              117       ;   The high byte of the 2nd word = 2x the number of places to be printed
                              118       ;
                              119       ;
254C CC00                     120       PRINT_NUM:  pop   cx            ; Send Decimal number to CON OUT
254E CC00                     121                   pop   bx            ; bx is mode byte, bx+1 is divisor pointer
2550 A00100                   122                   ldbze dx,bx+1
2553 A3009E2528               123                   ld    divisor,divtab[dx]
2558 CC24                     124                   pop   value
                              125       ;
                              126       div_loop:
255A 0126                     126                   clr   value+2
255C 802824                   128                   divu  value,divisor  ; divide cx,dx by divisor
255F 380017                   129                   jbs   bx,0,chr_ok    ; print character regardless of value
2562 980024                   130                   cmpb  value,zero
2565 D70F                     131                   jne   non_0
                              132       ;
2567                          132       Val_0:                          ; Jump if value is non zero
2567 310003                   133                   jbc   bx,1,prntsp
256A 38280C                   134                   jbs   divisor,0,chr_ok ; Print space instead of 0
256D 3A0015                   135                   jbs   bx,2,cont      ; If in rightmost position print 0
2570 A1F00024                 136                   ld    value,#0F0H    ; Do not print space if bit is set
2574 2003                     137                   br    chr_ok         ; 0F0H+30H = 20H = space
                              138       ;
2576 910100                   139       non_0:      orb   bx,#0001B      ; Set flag so 0's will be printed
2579 65300024                 140       chr_ok:     add   value,#30h     ; 30h + n = 0 to 9 ascii
257D 617F0024                 141                   and   value,#7Fh     ; send least sig seven bits, clear upper word
2581 C824                     142                   push  value
2583 2F6B                     143                   call  con_out        ; output ascii result (result<9)
2585 A02624                   144       cont:       ld    value,value+2  ; load value with remainder
2588 012A                     145                   clr   divisor+2
258A 8D0A0028                 146                   divu  divisor,#10    ; next lower power of ten
258E 880028                   147                   cmp   divisor,zero
2591 D7C7                     148                   jne   div_loop
                              149       ;
2593                          149       div_done:
2593 E300                     150                   br    [cx]
                              151       ;
                              152       ;               Number of places for result
2596 0000010000A006400        153       DIVTAB:     dcw   0, 1, 10, 100, 1000, 10000 ; divisor table - 10#m
```

Listing 5—The Plot Module (Continued)

```
MCS-96 MACRO ASSEMBLER    PLOT_SERIAL                                  02/18/86   PAGE  5

ERR LOC   OBJECT           LINE    SOURCE STATEMENT
                           154
                           155
                           156
                           157
25A2                       158     DRAW_GRAPH:                         ; Graph drawing routine
25A2 C90D00                159             push    #0dh
25A5 2769                  160             call    con_out
25A7 C90A82                161             push    #820AH              ;;;    Clear 3 lines
25AA 2764                  162             call    CON_OUT
25AC C90000                163             push    #00
25AF 2F5F                  164             call    CON_out
                           165
25B1 012C                  166             clr     xptr
25B3 0130                  167             clr     xval
25B5                       168     NXT_ROW:
25B5 C90D0A                169             push    #0A0DH              ; CRLF
25B8 2F56                  170             call    CON_OUT
25BA C90000                171             push    #00H                ; nul
25BD 2F51                  172             call    CON_OUT
                           173
25BF C830                  174             push    xval
25C1 C9020A                175             push    #(0A00H or 0010b)   ; supress all zeros except rightmost
25C4 2F86                  176             call    PRINT_NUM
                           177
25C6 C92020                178             push    #2020H              ; Print 2 spaces
25C9 2F45                  179             call    CON_OUT
25CB C92B00                180             push    #2BH                ; +
25CE 2F40                  181             call    con_out
                           182
25D0 A1000002E             183             ld      yptr,#PLOT_RES_2    ; PLOT_RES_2 = PLOT_RES/2
                           184                                         ; PLOT_RES is defined 7 lines down
                           185
25D4                       186     NXT_COL:                            ; Next Column
25D4 8B2D00002E            187             cmp     yptr,PLOT_IN[xptr]
25D9 D911                  188             jh      PRT_NUM
25DB                       189     PRT_MK: push    #2AH                ; Print Mark
25DB C92A00                190             push    #2AH
25DE 2F30                  191             call    CON_OUT
25E0                       192     INC_CNT:
25E0 65000002E             193             add     yptr,#PLOT_RES
25E4 8900002E              194             cmp     yptr,#PLOT_MAX      ; PLOT_RES = number of inputs per output point
                           195                                         ; PLOT_max = maximum line length
25E8 D1EA                  196             jnh     nxt_col
25EA 204F                  197             br      NXTLN
                                   $eject
```

MCS-96 MACRO ASSEMBLER   PLOT_SERIAL   02/18/86   PAGE   6

```
ERR LOC  OBJECT              LINE      SOURCE STATEMENT
                              198
     25BC 8900002E            199 PRT_NUM:  cmp    yptr,#PLOT_RES_2    ; If value is less than minimum needed
     25F0 DF49                200           be     NXTLN               ; for a plot, do not print value
                              201
     2572 C92020              202           push   #2020H              ; print 2 spaces then value
     2575 2F19                203           call   con_out
     2577 3B000B              204           JBS    FFT_MODE,3,db_mode
                              205
                              206 norm_mode:
     257A C82D0000            207           push   PLOT_IN[xptr]
     257E C9000A              208           push   #(0A00H or 0000B)   ; supress all zeros
     2601 2F49                209           call   PRINT_NUM
     2603 2036                210           BR     NXTLN
                              211
                              212 db_mode:
     2605 A32D00002E          213           ld     yptr,plot_in[xptr]
     260A 080132              214           shr    yptr,#1             ; PLOT_IN = 512*10*LOG(x)
     260D AC2F00              215           ldbze  ax,yptr+1           ; yptr=256 * 10LOG(x)
                              216                                     ; ax= 10LOG(x) = yptr/256
                              217
     2610 C800                218           push   ax                  ; Print AX
     2612 C9020A              219           push   #(0A00H or 0010B)   ; supress all but rightmost zero
     2615 2F35                220           call   PRINT_NUM
     2617 C92E00              221           push   #2EH                ; Decimal point
     261A 2F4                 222           call   con_out
                              223
     261C B02E01              224           ldb    ax+1,yptr           ; high byte of ax = fractional portion of
     261F 1100                225           clrb   ax                  ;   10LOG(x)
                              226
     2621 6BE60300            227           mulu   ax,#3E6H            ; if ax=F700H then ax+2 now = 998 decimal
     2625 370102              228           jbc    ax+1,7,no_rnd       ; round value up
     2628 0700                229           inc    dx
                              230
                              231 no_rnd:   push   dx                  ; dx=ax+2
     262A C800                232           push   dx                  ; Print_num
     262C C90106              233           call   PRINT_NUM
     262F 2F1B                234           push   #(600H or 001B)     ; print all numbers to three places
     2631 C92000              235           call   PRINT_NUM
     2634 2E3A                236           push   #20H                ; space
     2636 C96442              237           push   #4264H               ; "dB"
     2639 2E05                238           call   con_out
                              239           $eject
```

Listing 5—The Plot Module (Continued)

intel. AP-275

```
MCS-96 MACRO ASSEMBLER    PLOT_SERIAL                                      02/18/86  PAGE  7

ERR LOC   OBJECT          LINE      SOURCE STATEMENT
                          240
                          241
     263B  C9D0A          242       NXTLN:  push    #0A0DH
     263E  2ED0           243               call    CON_OUT                 ; Setup for next line
     2640  C90000         244               push    #00H                    ; CRLF
     2643  2ECB           245               call    CON_OUT                 ; nul
     2645  C92086         246               push    #8620H
     2648  2EC6           247               call    CON_OUT                 ; 7 spaces
     264A  C92100         248               push    #21H
     264D  2EC1           249               call    con_out                 ; :
                          250
     264F  0730           251               inc     xval
     2651  65020002C      252               add     xptr,#2
     2655  893B0002C      253               cmp     xptr,#62
     2659  D2022758       254       ;       ble     nxt_row                 ; Start printing next row
                          255
     265D  C9D0A          256       Done:   push    #0A0DH
     2660  2EA8           257               call    CON_OUT                 ; CRLF ; Form feed for next graph
     2662  C9000C         258               push    #0C00H
     2665  2EA9           259               call    con_out                 ; null,FF
                          260
     2667  F0             261               RET
     2668                 262               END

ASSEMBLY COMPLETED,  NO ERROR(S) FOUND.
```

270189-70

Listing 5—The Plot Module (Continued)

AP-275

At the end of the plot, a form feed is given to set the printer up for the next graph. Our printer would frequently miss the character after a CRLF. To solve this problem, a null (ASCII 0) is sent after every CRLF to make sure the printer is ready for the next line. This has been found to be a problem with many devices running at close to their maximum capacity, and the nulls work well to solve it.

With the plot completed, the program begins to run again by taking another set of A to D samples.

11.0 USING THE FFT PROGRAM

The program can be used with either real or tabled data. If real data is used, the signal is applied to analog channel 1. The program as written performs A/D samples at 100 microsecond intervals, collecting the 64 samples in 6.4 milliseconds. This sets the sampling window frequency at 156 Hz. If tabled data is used, 64 words of data should be placed in the location pointed to by DATA0 in the TABLE_LOAD routine of the Main Module.

Program control is specified by FFT_MODE which is loaded in the main module. Also within the main module are settings which control the A to D buffer routine and the Plot routine. The intention was to have only one module to change and recompile to vary parameters in the entire program.

The program modules are set up to run one-at-a-time so that the code would be easy to understand. Additionally, the Plot routine takes so long relative to the other sections, that it doesn't pay to try to overlap code sections. If this code were to be converted to run a process instead of print a graph, it might be worthwhile to run the FFT and the A/D routines at the same time.

If the goal of a modified program is to have the highest frequency sampling possible, it might be desirable to streamline the A/D section and run it without interruption. When the A to D routine was complete the FFT routine could be started. The reasoning behind this is that at the fastest A/D speeds the processor will be almost completely tied up processing the A/D information and storing it away. Using an interrupt based A/D routine would slow things down.

A set of programs which will perform a FFT has been presented in this application note. These programs are available from the INSITE users library as program CA-26. More importantly, dozens of programing examples have been made available, making it easier to get started with the 8096. Examples of how to use the hardware on the 8096 have already appeared in AP-248, "Using The 8096". These two applications notes form a good base for the understanding of MCS-96 microcontroller based design.

12.0 APPENDIX A - MATRICES

Matrices are a convenient way to express groups of equations. Consider the complex discrete Fourier Transform in equation 9, with $N = 4$.

$$Y_n = \sum_{k=0}^{3} X(k) W^{nk} \quad n = 0, 1, 2, 3$$

This can be expanded to

$Y(0) = X(0) W^0 + X(1) W^0 + X(2) W^0 + X(3) W^0$
$Y(1) = X(0) W^0 + X(1) W^1 + X(2) W^2 + X(3) W^3$
$Y(2) = X(0) W^0 + X(1) W^2 + X(2) W^4 + X(3) W^6$
$Y(3) = X(0) W^0 + X(1) W^3 + X(2) W^6 + X(3) W^9$

In matrix notation, this is shown as

$$\begin{bmatrix} Y(0) \\ Y(1) \\ Y(2) \\ Y(3) \end{bmatrix} = \begin{bmatrix} W^0 & W^0 & W^0 & W^0 \\ W^0 & W^1 & W^2 & W^3 \\ W^0 & W^2 & W^4 & W^6 \\ W^0 & W^3 & W^6 & W^9 \end{bmatrix} \begin{bmatrix} X(0) \\ X(1) \\ X(2) \\ X(3) \end{bmatrix}$$

The first step to simplifying this is to reduce the center matrix. Recalling that

$$W^N = W^{N \bmod N} \quad \text{and} \quad W^0 = 1$$

The matrix can be reduced to have less non-trivial multiplications.

$$\begin{bmatrix} Y(0) \\ Y(1) \\ Y(2) \\ Y(3) \end{bmatrix} = \begin{bmatrix} 1 & 1 & 1 & 1 \\ 1 & W^1 & W^2 & W^3 \\ 1 & W^2 & W^0 & W^2 \\ 1 & W^3 & W^2 & W^1 \end{bmatrix} \begin{bmatrix} X(0) \\ X(1) \\ X(2) \\ X(3) \end{bmatrix}$$

The square matrix can be factored into

$$\begin{bmatrix} Y(0) \\ Y(2) \\ Y(1) \\ Y(3) \end{bmatrix} = \begin{bmatrix} 1 & W^0 & 0 & 0 \\ 1 & W^2 & 0 & 0 \\ 0 & 0 & 1 & W^1 \\ 0 & 0 & 1 & W^3 \end{bmatrix} \begin{bmatrix} 1 & 0 & W^0 & 0 \\ 0 & 1 & 0 & W^0 \\ 1 & 0 & W^2 & 0 \\ 0 & 1 & 0 & W^2 \end{bmatrix} \begin{bmatrix} X(0) \\ X(1) \\ X(2) \\ X(3) \end{bmatrix}$$

For this equation to work, the Y(1) and Y(2) terms need to be swapped, as shown above. This procedure is a Bit Reversal, as described in the text.

Multiplying the two rightmost matrices results in

$X(0) + X(2) W^0$
$X(1) + X(3) W^0$ requiring 4 complex multiplications
$X(0) + X(2) W^3$ & 4 complex additions
$X(1) + X(3) W^2$

Noting that $W^0 = -W^2$, 2 of the complex multiplications can be eliminated, with the following results

$X(0) + X(2) W^0$
$X(1) + X(3) W^0$ requiring 2 complex multiplications
$X(0) - X(2) W^0$ and 4 complex additions
$X(1) - X(3) W^0$

Since $W^1 = -W^3$, a similar result occurs when this vector is multiplied by the remaining square matrix. The resulting equations are:

$Y(0) = (X(0) + X(2) W^0) + W^0 (X(0) + X(3) W^0)$
$Y(2) = (X(0) + X(2) W^0) - W^0 (X(1) + X(3) W^0)$
$Y(1) = (X(0) - X(2) W^0) + W^1 (X(1) - X(3) W^0)$
$Y(3) = (X(0) - X(2) W^0) - W^1 (X(1) - X(3) W^0)$

The number of complex multiplications required is 4, as compared with 16 for the unfactored matrix.

In general, the FFT requires

$$\frac{N * \text{EXPONENT}}{2} \text{ complex multiplications}$$

and

$$N * \text{EXPONENT complex additions}$$

where

$$\text{EXPONENT} = \log_2 N$$

A standard Fourier Transform requires

$$N^2 \text{ complex multiplications}$$

and

$$N(N-1) \text{ complex additions}$$

13.0 APPENDIX B - PLOTS

The following plots are examples of output from the FFT program. These plots were generated using tabled data, but very similar plots have also been made using the analog input module. Typically, a plot made using the analog input module will not show quite as much power at each frequency and will show a positive value for the DC component. This is because it is difficult to get exactly a full-scale analog input with no DC offset.

Plot 1 is a Magnitude plot of a square wave of period NT.

Plot 2 is the same data plotted in dB. Note how the dB plot enhances the difference in the small signal values at the high frequencies.

Plot 3 shows the windowed version of this data. Note that the widening of the bins due to windowing shows energy in the even harmonics that is not actually present. For data of this type a different window other than Hanning would normally be used. Many window types are available, the selection of which can be determined by the type of data to be plotted.[3]

Plot 4 shows a sine wave of period NT/7 or frequency 7/NT.

Plot 5 shows the same input with windowing. Note the signal shown in bins 6 and 8.

Plot 6 shows a sine wave of period NT/7.5. Note the noise caused by the discontinuity as discussed earlier.

Plot 7 uses windowing on the data used for plot 6. Note the cleaner appearance.

Plot 8 shows a sine wave input of magnitude 0.707 and period NT/7.5.

Plot 9 shows same input with windowing.

Plot 10 shows a sine wave of magnitude 0.707/16 and period NT/11.

Plot 11 shows the same input with windowing. Note that there is no power shown in bins 10 and 12. This is because at 6 dB down from 3 dB they are nearly equal to zero.

Plot 12 uses the sum of the signals for plots 8 and 10 as inputs. Note that the component at period NT/11 is almost hidden.

Plot 13 uses the same signal as plot 12 but applies windowing. Now the period component at NT/11 can easily be seen. The Hanning window works well in this case to separate the signal from the leakage. If the signals were closer together the Hanning window may not have worked and another window may have been needed.

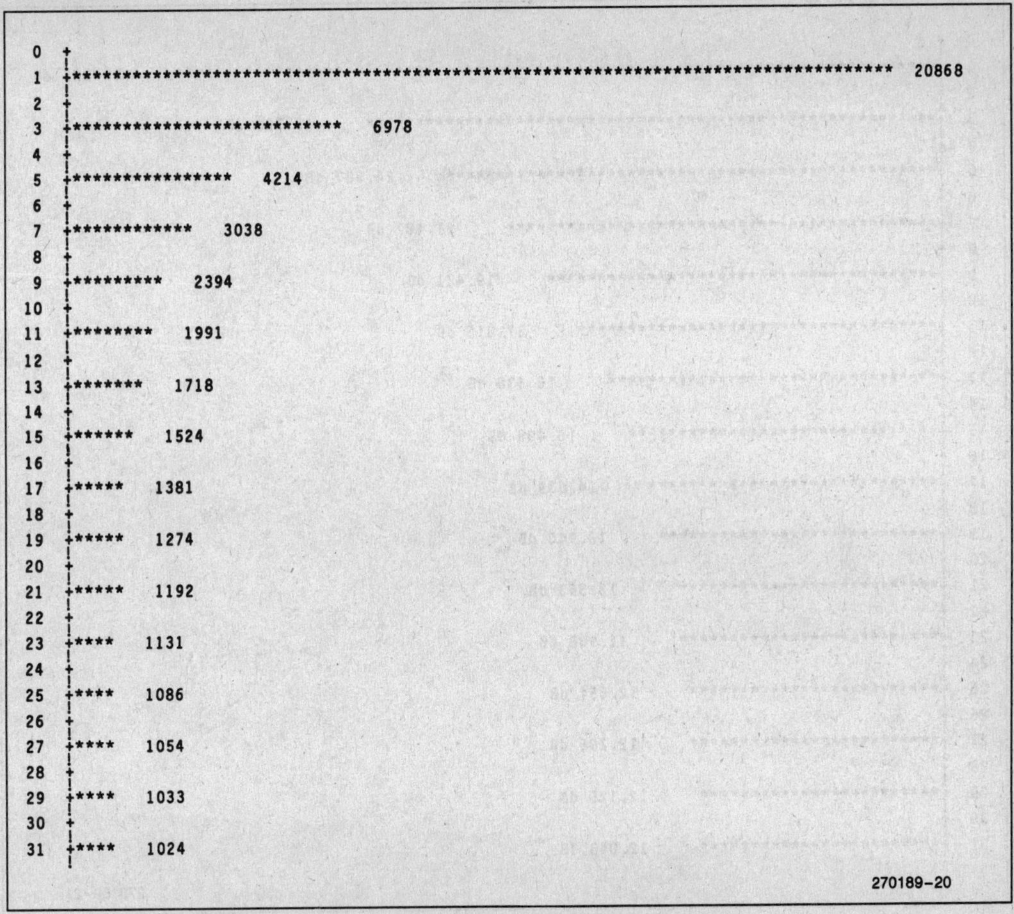

```
 0 +
 1 +************************************************************************  20868
 2 +
 3 +***********************  6978
 4 +
 5 +***************  4214
 6 +
 7 +***********  3038
 8 +
 9 +*********  2394
10 +
11 +********  1991
12 +
13 +*******  1718
14 +
15 +******  1524
16 +
17 +*****  1381
18 +
19 +*****  1274
20 +
21 +*****  1192
22 +
23 +****  1131
24 +
25 +****  1086
26 +
27 +****  1054
28 +
29 +****  1033
30 +
31 +****  1024
```

Plot 1—Magnitude Plot of Squarewave

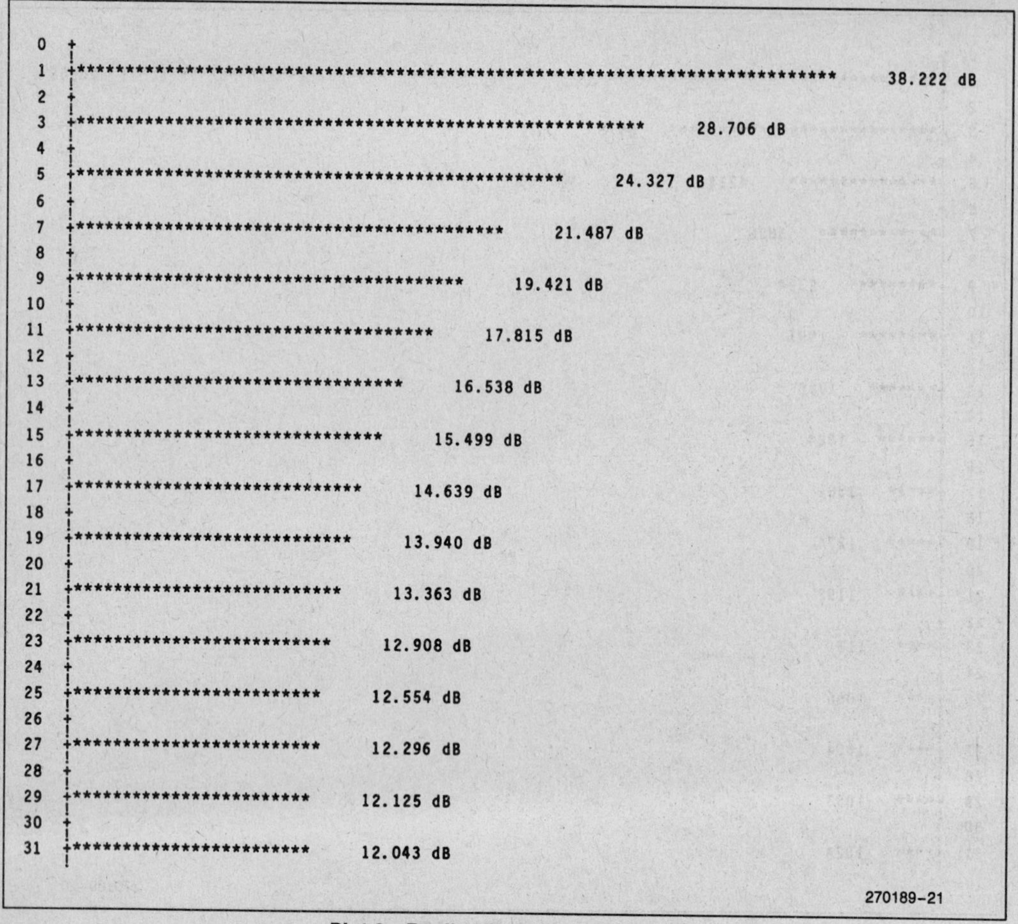

```
 0 +
 1 +*********************************************************************  38.222 dB
 2 +
 3 +*******************************************************  28.706 dB
 4 +
 5 +*********************************************  24.327 dB
 6 +
 7 +****************************************  21.487 dB
 8 +
 9 +************************************  19.421 dB
10 +
11 +**********************************  17.815 dB
12 +
13 +********************************  16.538 dB
14 +
15 +******************************  15.499 dB
16 +
17 +*****************************  14.639 dB
18 +
19 +****************************  13.940 dB
20 +
21 +***************************  13.363 dB
22 +
23 +**************************  12.908 dB
24 +
25 +**************************  12.554 dB
26 +
27 +*************************  12.296 dB
28 +
29 +*************************  12.125 dB
30 +
31 +*************************  12.043 dB
```

Plot 2—Decibel Plot of Squarewave

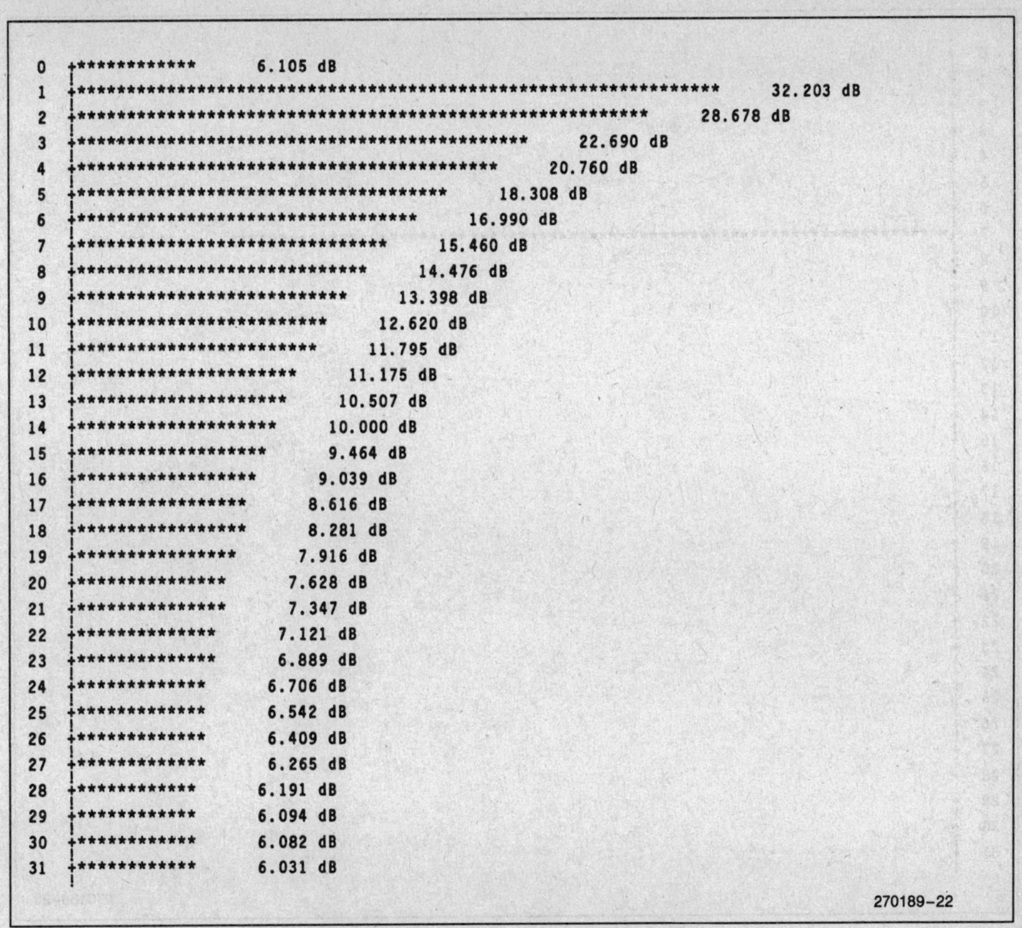

AP-275

```
 0 +************             6.105 dB
 1 +********************************************************** 32.203 dB
 2 +*******************************************************   28.678 dB
 3 +*************************************          22.690 dB
 4 +*******************************           20.760 dB
 5 +****************************         18.308 dB
 6 +***************************        16.990 dB
 7 +*************************       15.460 dB
 8 +***********************       14.476 dB
 9 +**********************       13.398 dB
10 +*********************        12.620 dB
11 +*********************     11.795 dB
12 +********************      11.175 dB
13 +*******************       10.507 dB
14 +******************        10.000 dB
15 +******************         9.464 dB
16 +*****************          9.039 dB
17 +*****************          8.616 dB
18 +****************           8.281 dB
19 +****************           7.916 dB
20 +***************            7.628 dB
21 +***************            7.347 dB
22 +**************             7.121 dB
23 +**************             6.889 dB
24 +*************              6.706 dB
25 +*************              6.542 dB
26 +*************              6.409 dB
27 +************               6.265 dB
28 +************               6.191 dB
29 +************               6.094 dB
30 +************               6.082 dB
31 +************               6.031 dB
```

Plot 3—Plot of Squarewave with Window

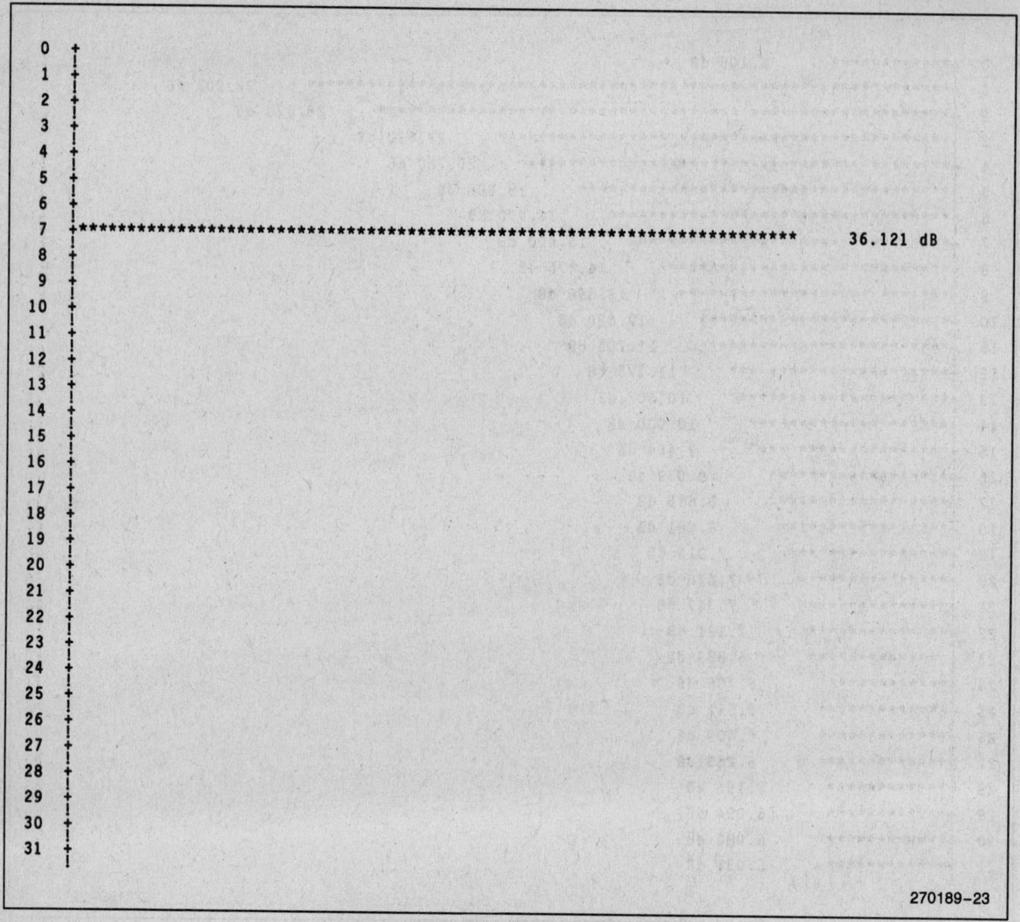

AP-275

```
 0 +
 1 +
 2 +
 3 +
 4 +
 5 +
 6 +
 7 +***********************************************************    36.121 dB
 8 +
 9 +
10 +
11 +
12 +
13 +
14 +
15 +
16 +
17 +
18 +
19 +
20 +
21 +
22 +
23 +
24 +
25 +
26 +
27 +
28 +
29 +
30 +
31 +
```

270189-23

Plot 4—Sin (7.0X) without Window

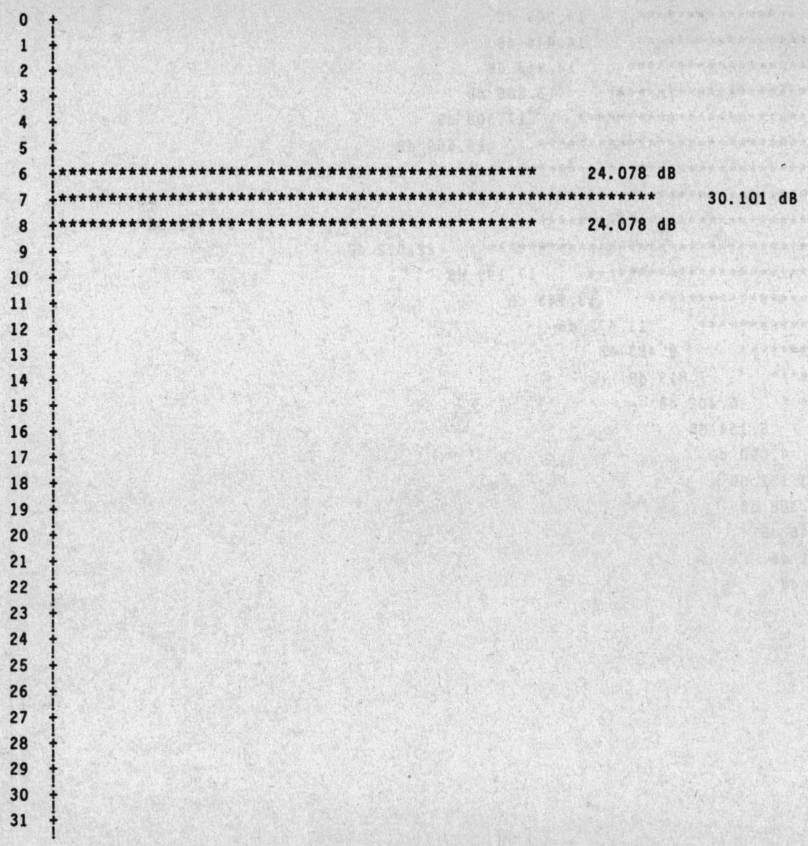

AP-275

```
 0 +
 1 +
 2 +
 3 +
 4 +
 5 +
 6 +***********************************************      24.078 dB
 7 +*************************************************             30.101 dB
 8 +***********************************************      24.078 dB
 9 +
10 +
11 +
12 +
13 +
14 +
15 +
16 +
17 +
18 +
19 +
20 +
21 +
22 +
23 +
24 +
25 +
26 +
27 +
28 +
29 +
30 +
31 +
```

Plot 5—Sin (7.0X) with Window

AP-275

```
 0 +*****************************       14.265 dB
 1 +****************************        14.444 dB
 2 +******************************      14.943 dB
 3 +********************************    15.865 dB
 4 +***********************************  17.308 dB
 5 +****************************************  19.569 dB
 6 +*************************************************  23.421 dB
 7 +*******************************************************************  32.441 dB
 8 +******************************************************************   31.971 dB
 9 +*******************************************  22.012 dB
10 +***********************************   17.199 dB
11 +****************************   13.943 dB
12 +***********************   11.472 dB
13 +*******************   9.483 dB
14 +****************   7.819 dB
15 +*************   6.402 dB
16 +**********   5.164 dB
17 +********   4.090 dB
18 +******   3.152 dB
19 +*****   2.308 dB
20 +***   1.546 dB
21 +**   0.901 dB
22 +*   0.300 dB
23 +
24 +
25 +
26 +
27 +
28 +
29 +
30 +
31 +
```

Plot 6—Sin (7.5X) without Window

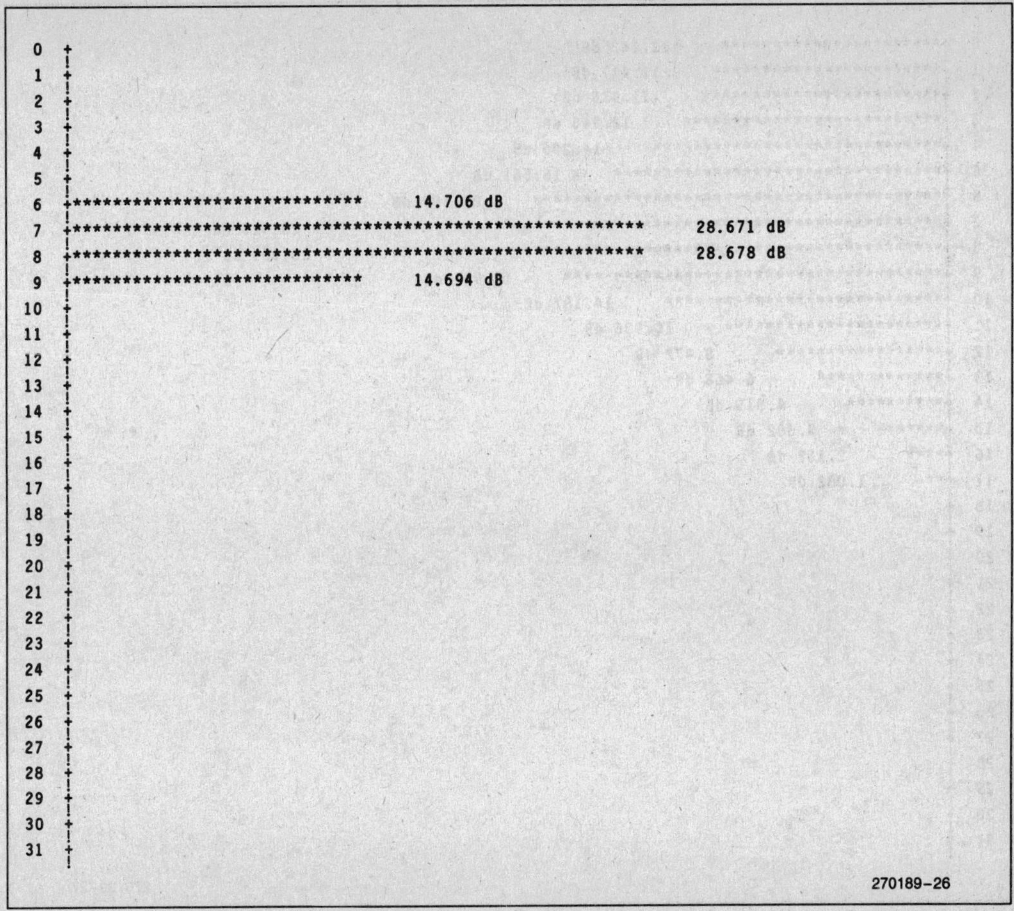

```
 0 +
 1 +
 2 +
 3 +
 4 +
 5 +
 6 +***************************     14.706 dB
 7 +*****************************************************    28.671 dB
 8 +*****************************************************    28.678 dB
 9 +***************************     14.694 dB
10 +
11 +
12 +
13 +
14 +
15 +
16 +
17 +
18 +
19 +
20 +
21 +
22 +
23 +
24 +
25 +
26 +
27 +
28 +
29 +
30 +
31 +
```

270189-26

Plot 7—Sin (7.5X) with Window

AP-275

```
 0 +**********************       11.242 dB
 1 +***********************      11.417 dB
 2 +************************     11.936 dB
 3 +**************************   12.846 dB
 4 +******************************  14.296 dB
 5 +***********************************   16.561 dB
 6 +*******************************************   20.409 dB
 7 +***************************************************************   29.425 dB
 8 +**************************************************************    28.959 dB
 9 +****************************************   18.994 dB
10 +******************************   14.187 dB
11 +***********************   10.936 dB
12 +******************    8.472 dB
13 +**************    6.468 dB
14 +**********    4.819 dB
15 +*******    3.382 dB
16 +****    2.152 dB
17 +**    1.082 dB
18 +
19 +
20 +
21 +
22 +
23 +
24 +
25 +
26 +
27 +
28 +
29 +
30 +
31 +
```

270189-27

Plot 8—0.707 ∗ Sin (7.5X) without Window

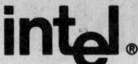

```
 0 +
 1 +
 2 +
 3 +
 4 +
 5 +
 6 +************************     11.694 dB
 7 +*****************************************************     25.663 dB
 8 +*****************************************************     25.667 dB
 9 +************************     11.674 dB
10 +
11 +
12 +
13 +
14 +
15 +
16 +
17 +
18 +
19 +
20 +
21 +
22 +
23 +
24 +
25 +
26 +
27 +
28 +
29 +
30 +
31 +
```

270189-28

Plot 9—0.707 * Sin (7.5X) with Window

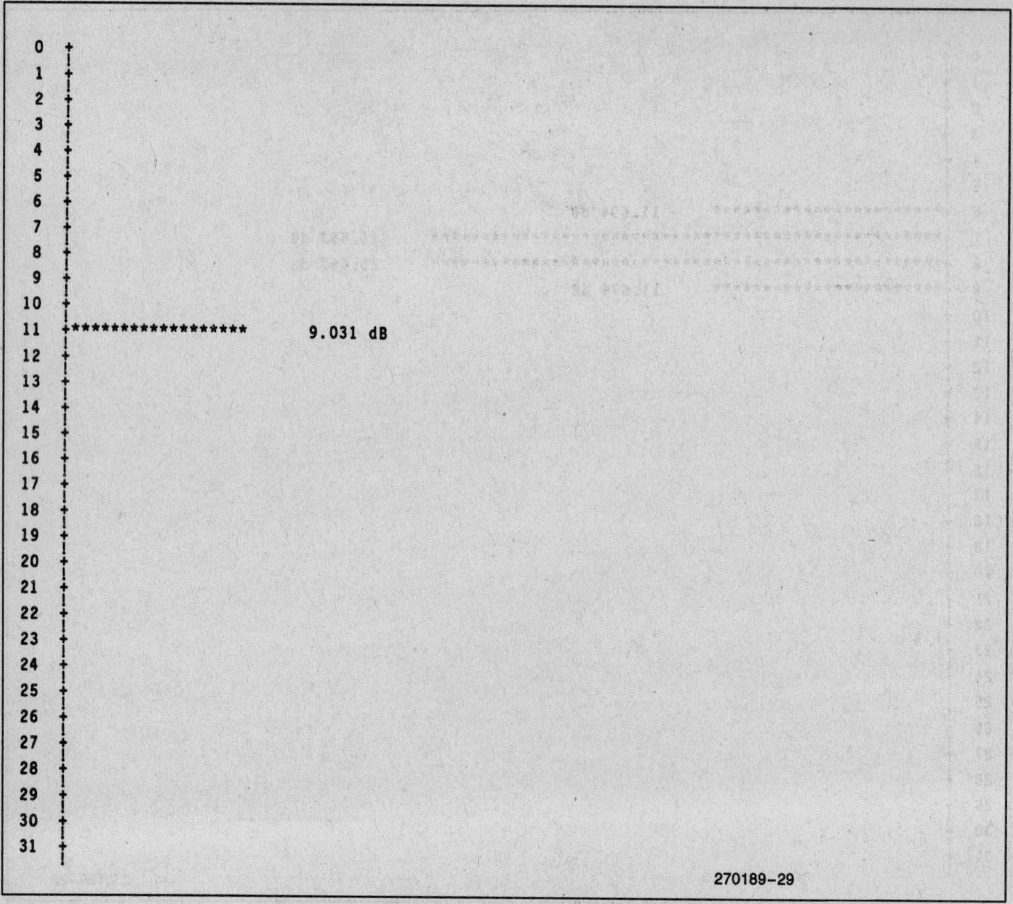

AP-275

```
 0 +
 1 +
 2 +
 3 +
 4 +
 5 +
 6 +
 7 +
 8 +
 9 +
10 +
11 +******************   9.031 dB
12 +
13 +
14 +
15 +
16 +
17 +
18 +
19 +
20 +
21 +
22 +
23 +
24 +
25 +
26 +
27 +
28 +
29 +
30 +
31 +
```

Plot 10—0.707/16 * Sin (11X) without Window

AP-275

```
 0 +
 1 +
 2 +
 3 +
 4 +
 5 +
 6 +
 7 +
 8 +
 9 +
10 +
11 +******   3.008 dB
12 +
13 +
14 +
15 +
16 +
17 +
18 +
19 +
20 +
21 +
22 +
23 +
24 +
25 +
26 +
27 +
28 +
29 +
30 +
31 +
                                    270189-30
```

Plot 11—0.707/16 * Sin (11X) with Window

AP-275

```
 0 +**********************       11.242 dB
 1 +***********************      11.425 dB
 2 +************************     11.936 dB
 3 +**************************   12.846 dB
 4 +*****************************    14.296 dB
 5 +*********************************    16.561 dB
 6 +*******************************************     20.409 dB
 7 +***************************************************************       29.425 dB
 8 +**************************************************************        28.959 dB
 9 +*****************************************    19.000 dB
10 +*****************************    14.187 dB
11 +***************************      13.105 dB
12 +*****************     8.472 dB
13 +*************    6.483 dB
14 +**********   4.819 dB
15 +*******  3.382 dB
16 +****    2.152 dB
17 +**   1.082 dB
18 +
19 +
20 +
21 +
22 +
23 +
24 +
25 +
26 +
27 +
28 +
29 +
30 +
31 +
```

270189-31

Plot 12—0.707 (Sin (7.5X) + 1/16 Sin (11X)) without Window

AP-275

```
 0 +
 1 +
 2 +
 3 +
 4 +
 5 +
 6 +***********************        11.702 dB
 7 +*****************************************      25.663 dB
 8 +*****************************************      25.667 dB
 9 +***********************        11.674 dB
10 +
11 +******    3.074 dB
12 +
13 +
14 +
15 +
16 +
17 +
18 +
19 +
20 +
21 +
22 +
23 +
24 +
25 +
26 +
27 +
28 +
29 +
30 +
31 +
```

270189–32

Plot 13—0.707 (Sin (7.5X) + 1/16 Sin (11X)) with Window

BIBLIOGRAPHY

1. Boyet, Howard and Katz, Ron, The 16-Bit 8096: Programming, Interfacing, Applications. 1985, Microprocessor Training Inc., New York, NY.

2. Brigham, E. Oran, The Fast Fourier Transform. 1974, Prentice-Hall, Inc., Englewood Cliffs, New Jersey.

3. Harris, Fredric J., On the use of Windows for Harmonic Analysis with the Discrete Fourier Transform. Proceedings of the IEEE, Vol. 66, No. 1, January 1978.

4. Weaver, H. Joseph, Applications of discrete and continuous Fourier analysis. 1983, John Wiley and Sons, New York.

INTEL PUBLICATIONS

1. 1986 Microcontroller Handbook, Order Number 210918-004

2. Using the 8096, AP-248, Order Number 270061-001

3. MCS-96 Macro Assembler User's Guide, Order Number 122048-001

4. MCS-96 Utilities User's Guide, Order Number 122049-001

AP-406

APPLICATION NOTE

MCS®-96
Analog Acquisition Primer

DAVID P. RYAN
INTEL CORPORATION

December 1987

Order Number: 270365-001

ANALOG ACQUISITION PRIMER

CONTENTS

	PAGE
INTRODUCTION	5-186
WHAT IS AN ANALOG ACQUISITION SYSTEM?	5-187
A/D CONVERTER	5-187
THE MULTIPLEXER	5-191
SAMPLE-AND-HOLD	5-193
THE MCS®-96 CONVERSION SEQUENCE	5-193
APPLICATION HINTS	5-195
ANALOG INPUTS	5-195
ANALOG REFERENCES	5-196
GETTING MORE RESOLUTION	5-197
CONCLUSION	5-199
APPENDIX A: A/D GLOSSARY OF TERMS	5-200
APPENDIX B: CAPACITIVE INTERPOLATION	5-202
APPENDIX C: ERROR FORMULAS	5-208
APPENDIX D: SAMPLE CONVERTER DATA	5-214
APPENDIX E: BIBLIOGRAPHY	5-283

CONTENTS

LISTING OF FIGURES

Figure 1. An Analog Acquisition System 5-187
Figure 2. Ideal A/D Characteristic 5-188
Figure 3. A Three-Bit D-to-A 5-189
Figure 4. Actual and Ideal Characteristics 5-190
Figure 5. Types of Linearity Errors 5-190
Figure 6. Undesirable Converter Operation 5-191
Figure 7. Terminal Based Characteristic 5-192
Figure 8. Repeatability Error 5-191
Figure 9. Sample-and-Hold Voltage 5-193
Figure 10. A/D Converter Block Diagram 5-194
Figure 11. Idealized A/D Sampling Circuitry 5-195
Figure 12. Suggested A/D Input Circuit 5-195
Figure 13. (a). Non-Inverting Buffer 5-196
Figure 13. (b). Inverting Buffer 5-196
Figure 14. Trimming Offset and Gain 5-196
Figure 15. Supply Decoupling 5-196
Figure 16. A Flexible Input Circuit 5-197
Figure 17. A Low-Cost Log Amplifier 5-198
Figure 18. A Low Pass Filter 5-198
Figure 19. Dither 5-199
Figure 20. Software Controlled Offset and Gain 5-199
Figure B1 (a). Connections During the Sample Window 5-203
Figure B1 (b). Connections After the Sample Window Closes 5-203
Figure B2. Superposition Analysis of Comparator Input Voltage 5-204
Figure B3. Initial Conditions 5-204
Table B1. Conversion Simulation 5-205
Table D1. Sample Converter Data 5-214

LISTINGS

Listing B1 A/D Converter Simulator 5-206
Listing C1 Error Formulas 5-209

AP-406

THE MCS®-96 ANALOG ACQUISITION PRIMER

INTRODUCTION

As technology advances, embedded control applications continue to reduce chip-count and demand microcontrollers with increased features to assist system-cost reduction. Since every embedded control application interfaces with the physical world, and the physical world is an analog process, it was inevitable that microcontrollers would include integrated analog acquisition capabilities.

The first such integration of standard microcontroller and A/D converter occurred on Intel's 8022 in 1978. This opened the door to cost reduction of high volume applications that required analog inputs. The device fit well into applications that needed processing of analog data. But this chip, with its 8-bit CPU, could not perform in high-end applications requiring analog inputs, or in applications that had computationally demanding analog tasks.

With the introduction of the MCS®-96 family of 16-bit microcontrollers in 1982, the combined CPU and A/D performance became available to greatly reduce the system cost of mid- and high-performance embedded control applications. These are applications which were customarily implemented with 16-bit microprocessor chip-sets teamed with analog acquisition chip sets.

There are less obvious avenues for system cost reduction when a 16-bit CPU is teamed with an on-chip analog acquisition system. For example, closed-loop servo control had been implemented almost exclusively by using analog methods. When an MCS-96 device is designed into such an application, it is not only replacing a microcontroller or microprocessor, but it also replaces closed-loop analog circuitry which never before came in contact with the digital system.

To take full advantage of this new level of integration, digital designers must become familiar with analog acquisition, and analog designers must become familiar with digital methods of processing analog signals. This Application Note assists with the first task—understanding of an analog acquisition system.

Designers experienced with analog design, or analog acquisition systems, may find no revelations herein. To those unfamiliar with analog acquisition systems, this Ap Note provides a tutorial on the subject and will serve as a handy reference.

Answering the limitless number of analog circuit design questions is beyond the scope of this Ap Note. Suffice it to say that the effort placed on the design of analog circuits should increase with a decreasing error budget.

At a minimum, the applications literature of op-amp manufacturers and analog design manuals are a good place to start. Furthermore, the applications literature of monolithic analog acquisition system manufacturers should be consulted since the suggestions presented therein are largely transportable to any A/D system.

This Ap Note is organized in the following sections. The components of an analog acquisition system and the errors associated with each is first explained. Then, interfacing suggestions and ideas for getting more resolution are presented. Finally, a set of appendices provides back-up information, a bibliography, actual converter data and some program listings.

The definitions of terms used, and the examples presented, are drawn from the body of applications literature publicly available on the components of an analog acquisition system. There is usually no single meaning for a particular term or specification used to describe analog acquisition. However, there is, in most cases, a generally accepted definition which is most often used. To the extent possible, we have adopted the most used definition. To avoid any ambiguity, Appendix A lists the dictionary of terms as used to refer to the analog acquisition systems of MCS-96 devices.

For any users of an MCS-96 analog acquisition system (experienced or not), this document contains very useful information. It should be considered mandatory reading in addition to the latest Embedded Controller Handbook and MCS-96 data sheet for the actual device in use prior to the actual design.

intel

AP-406

WHAT IS AN ANALOG ACQUISITION SYSTEM?

An analog acquisition system is a collection of individual units which, when logically configured, form a system capable of converting an analog input to a digital value.

The typical components of an Analog Acquisition Unit (Figure 1) include an Analog-to-Digital Converter (A/D), a Sample-and-Hold (S/H) and an Analog Multiplexer (MUX). The A/D converts the infinitely varying analog voltage present on the S/H into a digital representation for use by the digital system. The S/H is required so a "snapshot" of a changing analog input can be stored for conversion by the A/D. The MUX is used to leverage the investment in the A/D by allowing a large number of isolated analog input channels to use the same converter.

The conversion result of an MCS-96 device is a 10-bit ratiometric representation of the input voltage. This produces a stair-stepped transfer function when the output code is plotted versus input voltage. See Figure 2.

The resulting digital codes can be taken as simple ratiometric information, or they can be used to provide information about absolute voltages or relative voltage changes on the inputs. The more demanding the application is on the A/D converter, the more important it is to fully understand the converter's operation. For simple applications, knowing the absolute error of the converter is sufficient. However, controlling a closed loop with analog inputs necessitates a detailed understanding of an A/D converter's operation and errors.

The errors inherent in an analog-to-digital conversion process are many: quantizing error; zero offset; full-scale error; differential non-linearity; and non-linearity. These are "transfer function" errors related to the A/D converter. In addition, the S/H and MUX may induce channel dissimilarities and sampling error (described later).

Fortunately, one "Absolute Error" specification is available which describes the sum total of all deviations between the actual conversion process and an ideal converter. The various sub-components of error are, however, important in many applications. These error components are described in Appendix A and in the text below where ideal and actual converters are compared.

A/D Converter

There are at least three well-recognized methods for converting an analog voltage to a digital value—flash, dual slope and successive approximation.

Flash A/Ds are the fastest, and most expensive converters for a given accuracy. Flash converters typically resolve bits of the result in parallel to achieve fast conversions. Flash converter speeds are measured in tens-of-nanoseconds.

Dual slope converters are the slowest, but most accurate. Dual slope conversion is rather insensitive to noise on the input, but conversion times are measured in milliseconds.

Successive approximation converters provide a balanced tradeoff between speed and accuracy. Successive approximation conversion times are measured in tens-of-microseconds, and converter implementations are very economical for a given accuracy.

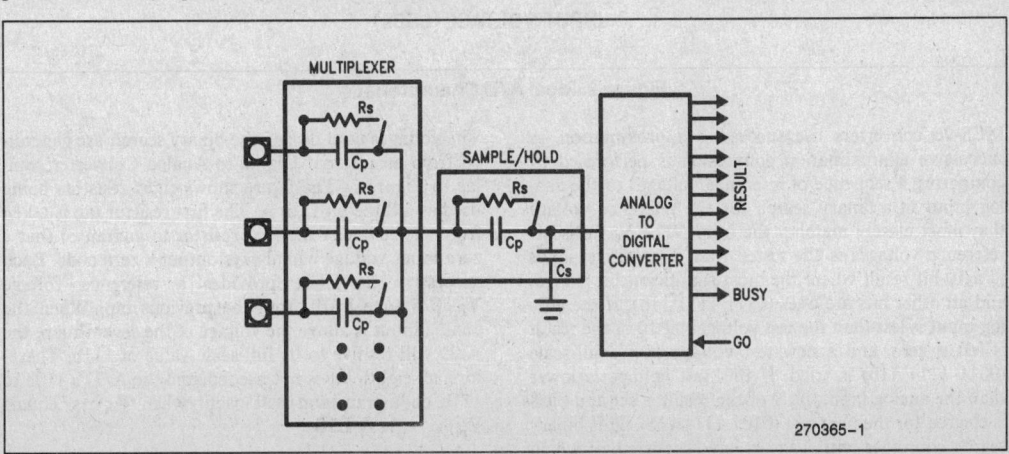

Figure 1. An Analog Acquisition System

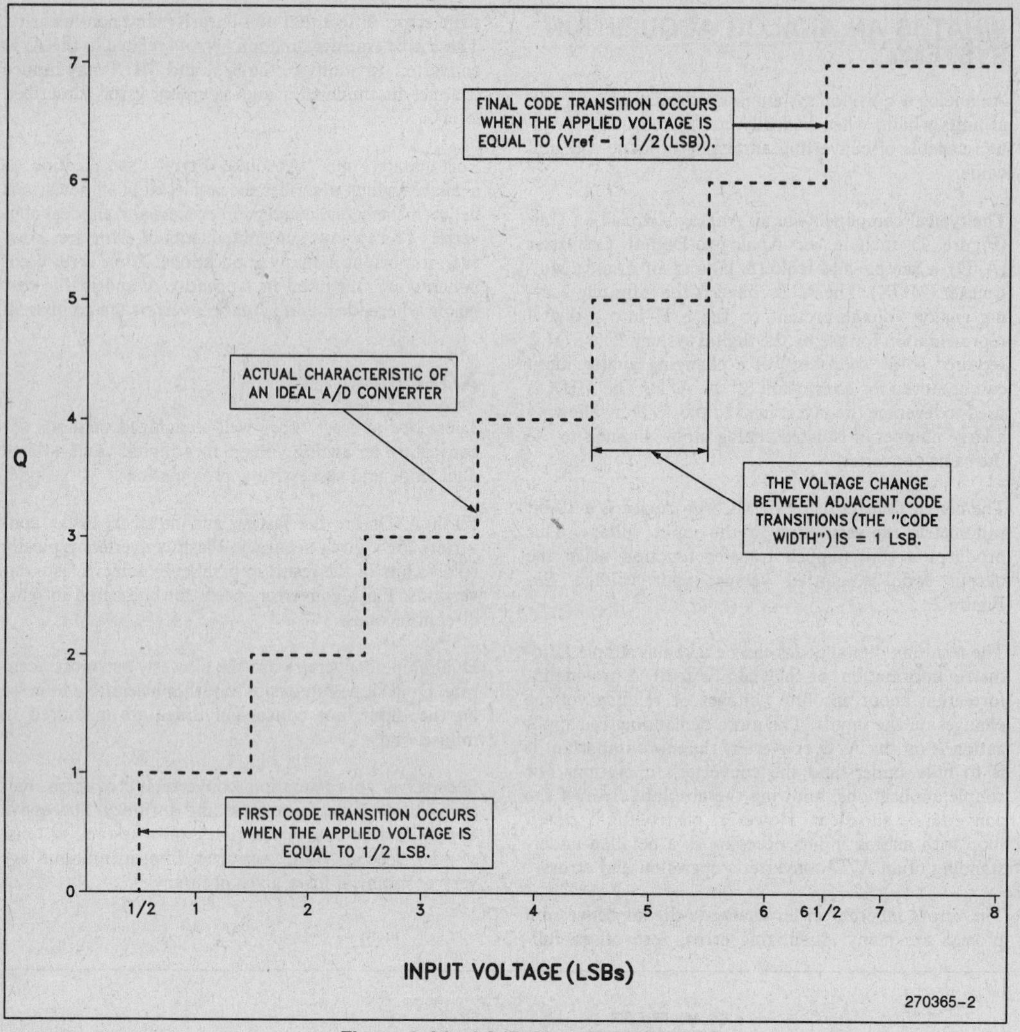

AP-406

Figure 2. Ideal A/D Characteristic

MCS-96 converters use successive approximation. A successive approximation conversion is performed by comparing a sequence of reference voltages to the analog input in a binary search for the reference voltage that most closely matches the input. The ½ full-scale reference voltages is the tested first. This corresponds to a 10-bit result where the most significant bit is zero, and all other bits are ones (0111 1111 11b). If the analog input is less than the test voltage, bit 10 of the result is left a zero, and a new test voltage of ¼ full-scale (0011 1111 11b) is tried. If this test voltage is lower than the analog input, bit 9 of the result is set and bit 8 is cleared for the next test (0101 1111 11b). This binary search continues until 10 tests have occurred, at which time the valid 10-bit conversion result resides in a register where it can be read by software.

The voltages used during the binary search are generated from an internal Digital-to-Analog Converter similar to Figure 3. The figure shows eight resistors being used as a three-bit D to A. The first resistor tap is taken from the center of the first resistor to guarantee that a zero input voltage will always output a zero code. Each successive tap then provides a reference voltage $V_{REF}/8$ (one LSB) from the previous tap. When the analog input is above the voltage of the seventh tap, the A/D will resolve to its full-scale value of 111b. Therefore, an eighth tap is not needed, and the A/D's 110b to 111b code transition will occur when V_{ANIN} equals $V_{REF} - 1\ ½$ LSB.

The first error seen in this process is unavoidable, and results from the conversion of a continuous voltage to

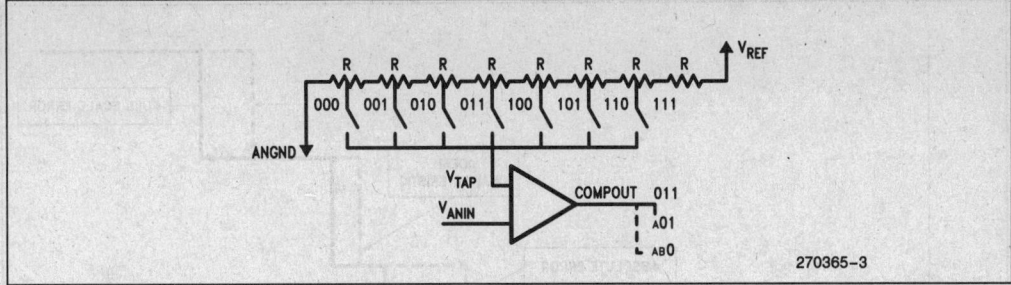

Figure 3. A Three-Bit D-to-A

an integer digital representation. This error is called quantizing error, and is always ±0.5 LSB. Quantizing error is the only error seen in a perfect A/D converter, and is obviously present in actual converters. Figure 2 shows the transfer function for an ideal 3-bit A/D converter (i.e. the Ideal Characteristic).

Note that in Figure 2 the Ideal Characteristic possesses unique qualities: it's first code transition occurs when the input voltage is 0.5 LSB; it's full-scale code transition occurs when the input voltage equals the full-scale reference minus 1.5 LSB; and it's code widths are all exactly one LSB. These qualities result in a digitization without offset, full-scale or linearity errors. In other words, a perfect conversion.

Figure 4 shows an Actual Characteristic of a hypothetical 3-bit converter which is not perfect. When the Ideal Characteristic is overlaid with the imperfect characteristic, the actual converter is seen to exhibit errors in the location of the first and final code transitions and code widths. The deviation of the first code transition from ideal is called "zero offset". The deviation of the final code transition from ideal is "full-scale error".

The deviation of the code widths from ideal causes two types of errors. Differential Non-Linearity and Non-Linearity. Differential Non-Linearity is a local linearity error measure, whereas Non-Linearity is an overall linearity error measure. For example, Figure 5a shows a transfer function with a large differential non-linearity and a little non-linearity. In contrast, Figure 5b shows a characteristic with small differential errors but a large overall linearity error.

Differential Non-Linearity is the degree to which actual code widths differ from the ideal width. Differential Non-Linearity gives the user a measure of how much the input voltage may have changed in order to produce a one count change in the conversion result.

If the absolute value of an input voltage is less important than the amount that the input changes, the differential non-linearity (DNL) specification of a converter is very important. For example, if the differential non-linearity of a converter is less than ± 0.5 LSB, a one count change in the digital result means that the input voltage changed at most 1.5 LSB (1 LSB ideal ± 0.5 LSB DNL). This is a much more accurate description of the input voltage change than would be available if the differential non-linearity of the converter was not known.

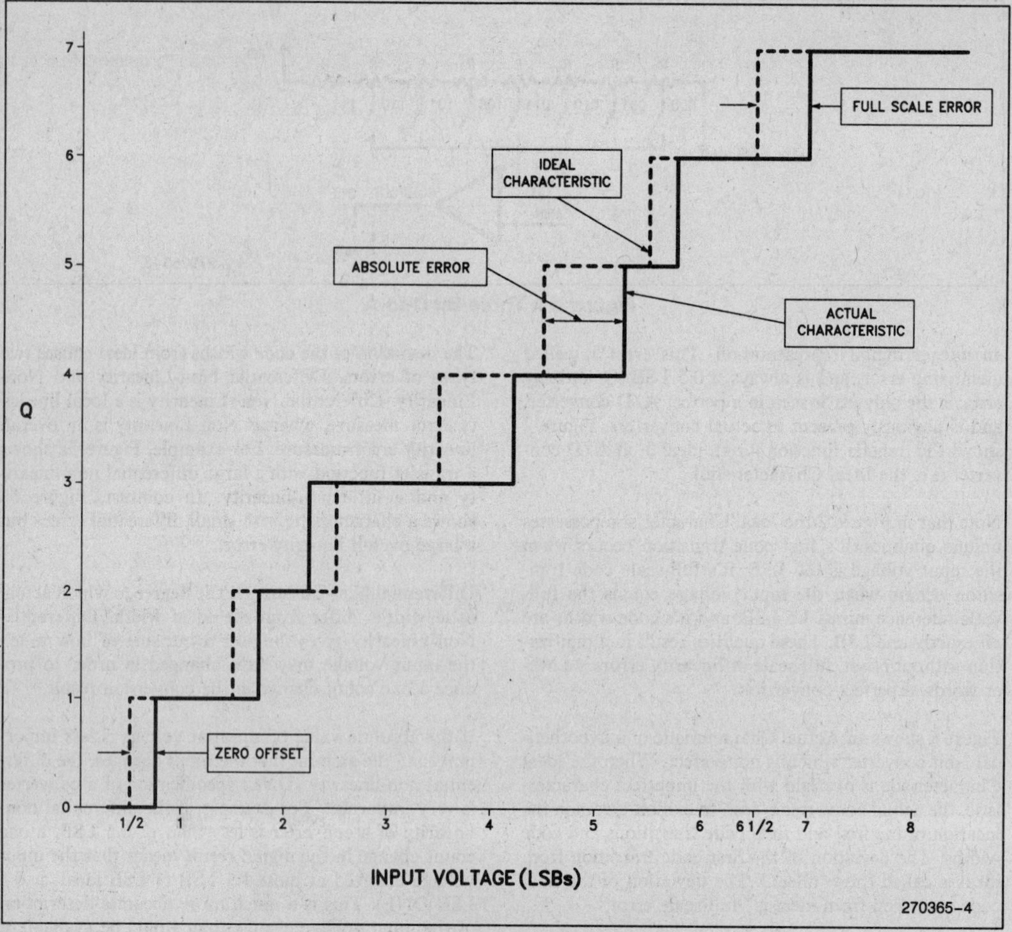

AP-406

Figure 4. Actual and Ideal Characteristics

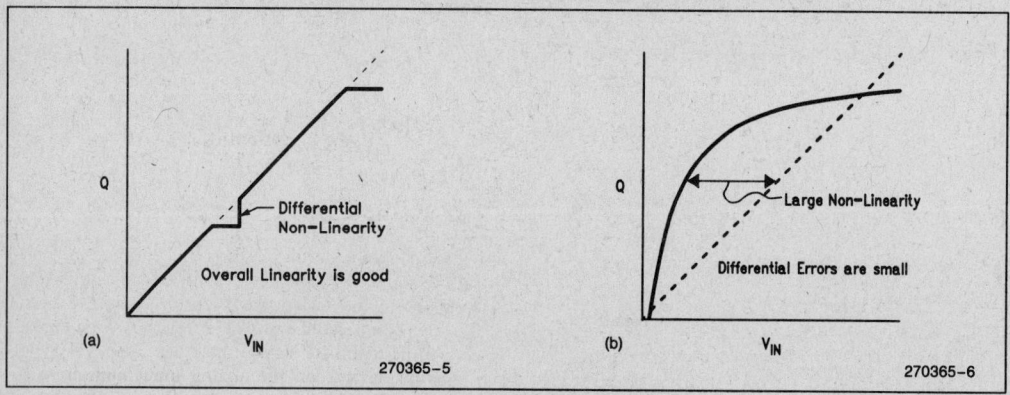

Figure 5. Types of Linearity Errors

AP-406

Non-Linearity is the worst case deviation of code transitions from the corresponding code transitions of the Ideal Characteristic. Non- Linearity describes how much Differential Non-Linearities could add to produce an overall maximum departure from a linear characteristic.

If the Differential Non-Linearity errors are large enough, it is possible for an A/D converter to miss codes or exhibit non-monotonicity. Neither behavior is desirable in a closed-loop system. A converter has no missed codes if there exists for each output code a unique input voltage range that produces that code only. A converter is monotonic if every subsequent code change represents an input voltage change in the same direction. Figure 6a shows a converter with missed codes. Figure 6b shows a non-monotonic converter.

Differential Non-Linearity and Non-Linearity are quantified by measuring the Terminal Based Linearity Errors. A Terminal Based Characteristic results when an Actual Characteristic is shifted and scaled to eliminate zero offset and full-scale error (see Figure 7). The Terminal Based Characteristic is similar to the Actual Characteristic that would be seen if zero offset and full-scale error were externally trimmed away. In practice, this is done by using input circuits which include gain and offset trimming. (See the Application Hints section for more details.)

An often overlooked characteristic of A/D converters is that code transitions do not really occur instantaneously at some finite set of input voltages. Specific code transitions can be analyzed by doing repeated conversions around the transition point using a high accuracy input voltage. When this is done, we find that there is actually a range of voltages around code transitions where both the lower and upper codes occur for repeated conversions on the same input voltage.

Figure 8 shows this "repeatability" error. At the lower end of the region of repeatability error the lower code is most prevalent, but the upper code will occur in a small percentage of the conversion attempts. As the input voltage increases slightly, a point is reached where both lower and upper codes occur with 50 percent probability. As the input voltage moves slightly higher, the upper code occurs most often with the lower code showing up in a small percentage of conversions.

The repeatability error is due to the fundamental ability of the comparator in the A/D to resolve very similar voltages. Random noise also contributes to repeatability errors. On MCS-96 devices, the width of the region of repeatability error has been found to be typically 1 mV to 1.25 mV. Since this error is specified, all other errors are specified assuming the code transitions occur at the voltage where adjacent codes are equally likely.

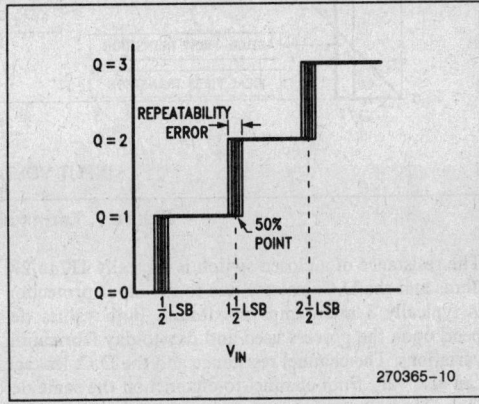

Figure 8. Repeatability Error

The Multiplexer

The eight channel multiplexer is implemented as a collection of eight MOS switches. Only one of eight can be closed at any instant in time. Figure 1 shows the multiplexer with the switches acting as resistors when closed and as small parasitic capacitors when open. The input protection devices on the analog input pins are also considered a part of the multiplexer.

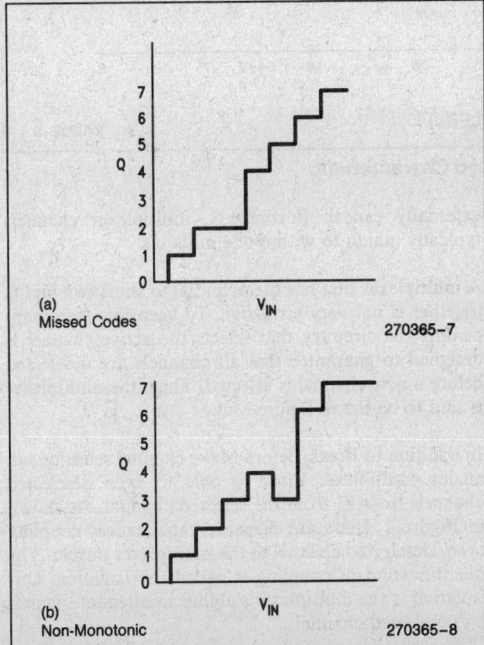

Figure 6. Undesirable Converter Operation

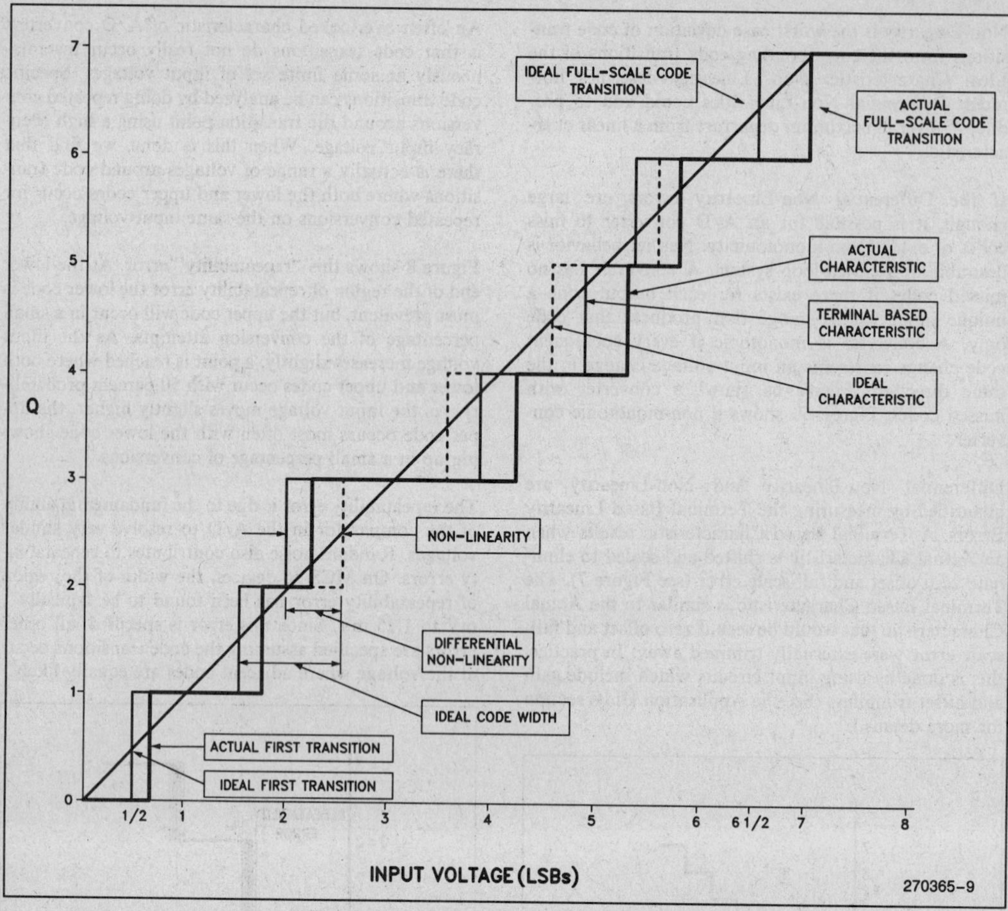

AP-406

Figure 7. Terminal Based Characteristic

The resistance of a closed switch is typically 1K to 2K ohms and the D.C. leakage due to the input protection is typically 3 microamps maximum. Both values depend upon the process used and day-to-day fabrication variations. The channel resistance and the D.C. leakage can also vary from channel-to-channel on the same device. These variations can be seen in the conversion process and are described by the channel- to-channel matching specification.

Channel-to-channel matching specifies the input voltage differences induced by mismatched elements of the multiplexer. This error is quantified by measuring the difference between the input voltages necessary to cause the same code transition to occur through different multiplexer channels under identical test conditions.

Matching errors are more complex than a simple voltage offset between channels, and thus are difficult to externally cancel. Fortunately, multiplexer channels typically match to within one millivolt.

A multiplexer that has the potential to short two inputs together is not very attractive. To keep this from happening, the circuitry that selects the active channel is designed to guarantee that all channels are deselected before a new channel is selected. Thus, the multiplexer is said to be Break-Before-Make.

In addition to Break-Before-Make channel selection, an analog multiplexer must be able to keep deselected channels isolated from the selected channel. As shown in Figure 1, there are parasitic capacitances coupling every deselected channel to the multiplexer output. The quantification of coupling is called Off-Isolation. Off-isolation is the multiplexer's ability to attenuate signals on deselected channels.

AP-406

Sample-and-Hold

The sample-and-hold of an analog acquisition system can be built using an analog switch and a sample capacitor. As with the multiplexer, there is also a parasitic capacitance coupling the switch input to the sample capacitor when the switch is open (Figure 1).

The resistance of the sample-and-hold switch combines with the series resistance of the multiplexer to impede the current necessary to charge the sample capacitor. For example, with a 5K ohm total input resistance from the pin to the 2 pf sample capacitor, the RC time constant is 10 nS (2 pf $\times$ 5K ohms).

During the one microsecond that the sample capacitor is connected to the input, 100 time constants elapse (1 microsecond/10 nS). This means that the sample capacitor is 100 percent of the voltage on the input pin ($1-e^{-100}$), assuming a zero source impedance.

If a source impedance of 2K ohms is assumed, the RC time constant of the sampling process would be 14nS (7K ohms $\times$ 2 pf). Thus, 71.4 time constants would pass in one microsecond resulting in the sample capacitor being charged to within 99.9 percent of its final value. Source impedances above 2K ohms would begin to degrade the conversion accuracy due to D.C. leakage (described later).

Figure 9 shows the actual input voltage and the sampled voltage approaching the input voltage. Once the sample-and-hold switch closes, the sample window begins. The sample window extends for four state times and ends with the sample-and-hold switch opening on MCS-96 devices (except 8X9X-90, which is 8 state times and has no sample-hold). Figure 9 also shows the sample delay, which is the delay from the time a start conversion signal is generated to the time a conversion process begins.

It is important to understand the uncertainties associated with the timing of the sample-and-hold. Digital signal processing algorithms rely upon the "spectral purity" of the sampling process. If the sample window jumps around with respect to the start conversion signal, or if the start conversion signal cannot be generated at precise times, consecutive samples of input data will not be equally spaced in time (i.e. sampling will be spectrally impure).

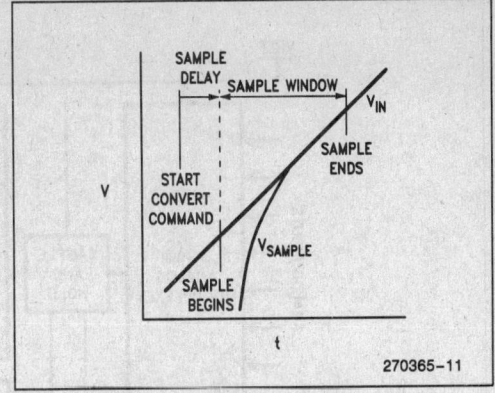

Figure 9. Sample-and-Hold Voltage

To improve the spectral purity of the sampling in digital signal processing applications, sequential MCS-96 start conversion signals can be generated with less than 50 nanoseconds of jitter using the HSO unit. The sample delay and sample time are also a constant number of state times to within 50 nanoseconds each.

Once the sample window closes, it is desired that all further changes on any input channel be isolated from the sample capacitor. The multiplexer's off-isolation is responsible for isolating deselected channels, while the sample-and-hold switch must attenuate changes on the selected channel. This source of error is described as Feedthrough. Feedthrough is quantified as the ability of the sample-and-hold to reject unwanted signals on its input.

Other factors that affect a real A/D Converter system include sensitivity to temperature. Temperature sensitivities are described by the change in typical specifications with a change in temperature.

The MCS®-96 Conversion Sequence

The MCS-96 Analog Acquisition System includes an eight channel analog multiplexer, sample-and-hold circuit and 10-bit analog to digital converter (Figure 10). An MCS-96 device can therefore select one of eight analog inputs, sample-and-hold the input voltage and convert the voltage into a digital value. Each conversion takes 22 microseconds (8097BH), including the time required for the sample-hold (with XTAL1 = 12 MHz). The method of conversion is successive approximation.

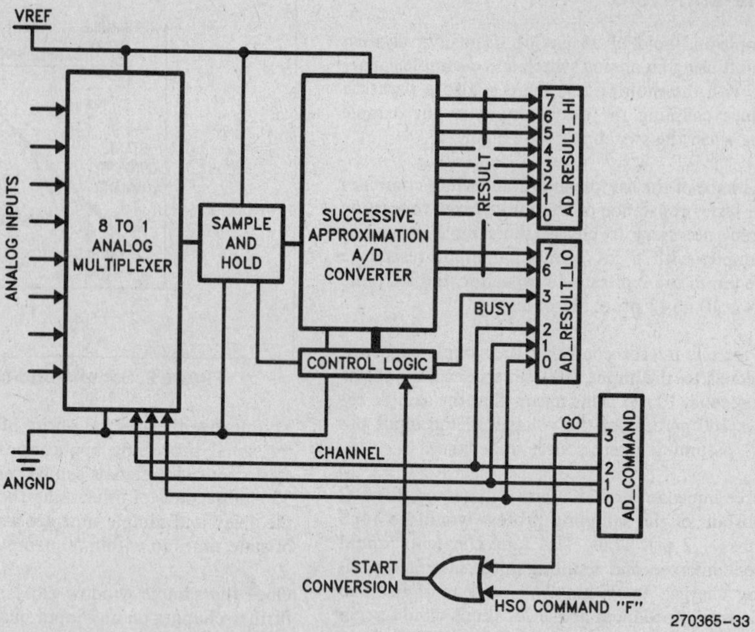

AP-406

NOTE:
1. Sample and hold not on 8X9X-90 devices.

Figure 10. A/D Converter Block Diagram

The conversion process is initiated by the execution of HSO command 0FH, or by writing a one to the GO Bit in the A/D Control Register. Either activity causes a start conversion signal to be sent to A/D control logic. If an HSO command was used, the conversion process will begin when Timer 1 increments. This aids applications attempting to approach spectrally pure sampling, since successive samples spaced by equal Timer 1 delays will occur with a variance of about ±50 ns (assuming a stable clock on XTAL1). However, conversion initiated by writing a one to the ADCON register GO Bit will start within three state times after the instruction has completed execution, resulting in a variance of about 0.75 µs (XTAL1 = 12 MHz).

Once the A/D unit receives a start conversion signal, there is a one state time delay before sampling (sample delay) while the successive approximation register is reset and the proper multiplexer channel is selected. After the sample delay, the multiplexer output is connected to the sample capacitor and remains connected for four state times (sample time). After this four state time "sample window" closes, the input to the sample capacitor is disconnected from the multiplexer so that changes on the input pin will not alter the stored charge while the conversion is in progress. The sample delay and sample time uncertainties are each approximately ±50 ns, independent of clock speed.

To perform the actual analog-to-digital conversion the MCS-96 implements a successive approximation algorigthm. The converter hardware consists of a 256-resistor ladder, a comparator, coupling capacitors and a 10-bit successive approximation register (SAR) with logic that guides the process. The resistor ladder provides 20 mV steps (V_{REF} = 5.12V), while capacitive coupling is used to create 5 mV steps within the 20 mV ladder voltages. Therefore, 1024 internal reference voltages are available for comparison against the analog input to generate a 10-bit conversion result. Appendix B contains a detailed description of the method used to generate 1024 voltages from a 256-resistor chain.

The total number of state times required for a 10-bit conversion varies from one MCS-96 version to the next. Attempting to short-cycle the 10-bit conversion process by reading A/D results before the done bit is set may work on some versions of MCS-96 devices, however it is not recommended. Short-cycling is not tested, nor is it guaranteed. Furthermore, it may not work on future MCS-96 devices.

AP-406

APPLICATION HINTS

The analog signals that must be converted by an analog acquisition system vary widely. The analog input may arrive at the controller as a voltage or current. The range may be 0 to 1 volt or ±30 volts, or some other arbitrary range. The input may be linear, logarithmic, non- linear, or perturbated in some bizarre fashion. Although interfacing to such signals could be considered an art form, some simple suggestions are contained in this section.

Analog Inputs

The external interface circuitry to an analog input is highly dependent upon the application, and can impact converter characteristics. In the external circuit's design, important factors such as input pin leakage, sample capacitor size and multiplexer series resistance from the input pin to the sample capacitor must be considered.

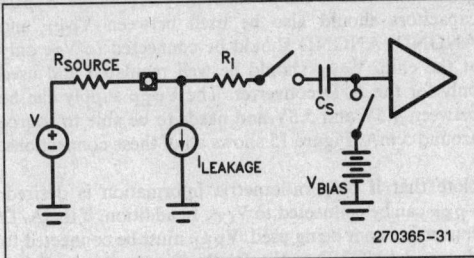

Figure 11. Idealized A/D Sampling Circuitry

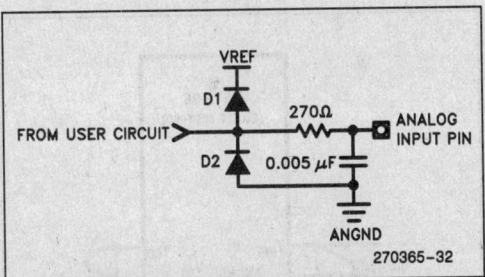

Figure 12. Suggested A/D Input Circuit

For the 8096BH, these factors are idealized in Figure 11. The external input circuit must be able to charge a sample capacitor (C_S) through a series of resistance (R_I) to an accurate voltage given a D.C. leakage (I_L). On the 8096BH, C_S is around 2 pF, R_I is around 5 KΩ and I_L is specified at 3 μA maximum. In determining the source impedance R_S, V_{BIAS} is not important.

External circuits with source impedances of 1 KΩ or less will be able to maintain an input voltage within a tolerance of about ±0.61 LSB (1.0 KΩ × 3.0 μA = 3.0 mV) given the D.C. leakage. Source impedances above 2 KΩ can result in an external error of at least one LSB due to the voltage drop caused by the 3 μA leakage. In addition, source impedances above 25 KΩ may degrade converter accuracy as a result of the internal sample capacitor not being fully charged during the 1 μs (12 MHz clock) sample window.

Placing an external capacitor on each analog input will reduce the sensitivity to noise, as the capacitor combines with source resistance in the external circuit to form a low-pass filter. In practice, one should include a small series resistance prior to an external low leakage capacitor on the analog input pin and choose the largest capacitor value practical, given the frequency of the signal being converted. This provides a low-pass filter on the input, while the resistor will also limit input current during over-voltage conditions.

Figure 12 shows a simple analog interface circuit based upon the discussion above. The circuit in the figure also provides limited protection against over-voltage conditions on the analog input (limits to 2.6 mA with 270Ω (0.7/270)). The circuit induces leakage from the diodes, which should be kept small.

The wide range of possible analog environments that must be interfaced to, or the existence of stringent accuracy requirements, makes the consideration of alternative input buffer configurations necessary. The most popular input buffer is a single op-amp in the non- inverting or inverting configurations of Figure 13.

In the non-inverting circuit of Figure 13 (a), the analog input is scaled by the buffer gain to output 5 volts when the input is at its maximum positive input. When the buffer input is 0 volts, the output will also be 0 volts.

In the inverting circuit of Figure 13 (b), a reference equal to the maximum possible input voltage is placed on the non-inverting input of the op-amp and the actual analog input is placed on the inverting input. The output voltage of the buffer is then proportional to the deviation of analog input from its maximum possible value. For example, when the analog input equals V_{MAX}, the buffer output will equal 0 zero volts. When the analog input equals its minimum value, the buffer output equals 5 volts. The digital result from the A/D converter might, of course, have to be complemented before being used.

The circuits of Figure 13 show only feedback resistors that set the gain of the buffer. In practice, it will often be necessary to include offset adjustments, gain trimming, temperature or frequency stability compensation, or components to build an active filter.

Figure 14 depicts a generalized non-inverting input buffer that offsets the analog input and scales the input to a 5 volt range. The course offset is set by the ratio of R_{BIG1} and R_{BIG2}, while offset fine tuning is done by adjusting R_{TRIM}. The course gain is set by the ratio of R_{G1} and R_{G2} while gain trimming is done with R_{GTRIM}.

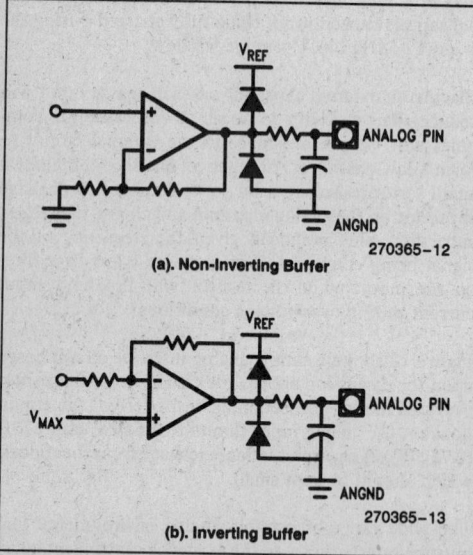

Figure 13

By trimming the offset and gain, not only can external component errors be zeroed out, but the offset and full scale error of the A/D converter can be nulled.

The procedure for nulling offset and gain is simple. First, a voltage is applied to V_{IN} which corresponds to the ideal first code transition of the A/D. R_{TRIM} is adjusted so that 50 percent of the conversion results are 0 while 50 percent are 1. Second, a voltage is applied to V_{IN} which corresponds to the ideal final code transition of the A/D converter. R_{GTRIM} is then adjusted until 50 percent of the conversion results are 3FEH and 50 percent are 3FFH. Once this adjustment is complete, the converter zero offset and full-scale errors are nulled, and could be ignored (except for temperature variation). This allows the system to rely upon the tighter, more descriptive converter specifications for Terminal Based Non- Linearity and Differential Non-Linearity.

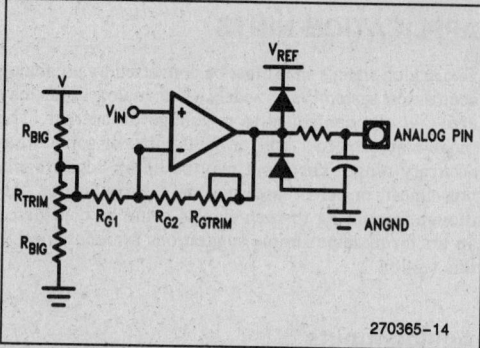

Figure 14. Trimming Offset and Gain

Analog References

Reference supply levels strongly influence the absolute accuracy of the conversion. For this reason, it is recommended that the ANGND pin be tied to a clean ground, as close to the power supply as possible. Bypass capacitors should also be used between V_{REF} and ANGND. ANGND should be connected to V_{SS} only at the chip. V_{REF} should be well regulated and used only for the A/D converter. The V_{REF} supply can be between 4.5V and 5.5V and needs to be able to source around 5 mA. Figure 15 shows all of these connections.

Note that if only ratiometric information is desired, V_{REF} can be connected to V_{CC}. In addition, if the A/D converter is not being used, V_{REF} must be connected to V_{CC} and ANGND to V_{SS} for Port0 to work as a digital port.

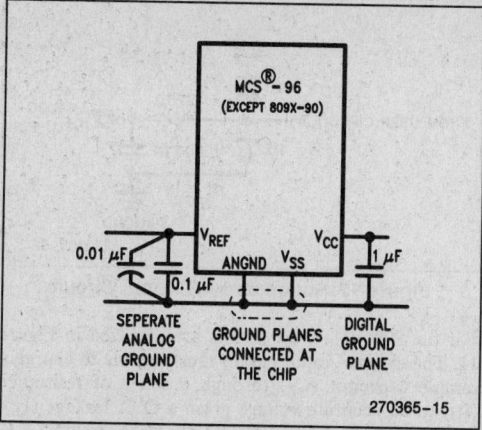

Figure 15. Supply Decoupling

Getting More Resolution

Given that the A/D converter can convert an analog input ranging from 0 volts to 5 volts into 1024 steps of 5 millivolts each, the desire for more resolution can come from three basic needs – need extra LSB, need extra MSB, need BOTH.

The configuration shown in Figure 16 can be used to solve each of the "more resolution" problems. This set-up requires the use of two input channels with different offsets and gains.

When the 5 millivolt step size of the A/D is too large for the application requirements, but the 5 volt range is sufficient, the system needs an "extra LSB". For example, an application requiring 2.5 millivolt steps over a 5 volt range needs an 11-bit conversion result. The 11th bit needs to be added to the least significant side of the 10-bit result (the "right"). This can be achieved using the circuit of Figure 16.

If both channels are set for a gain of 2, with channel 1 offset to 2.5 volts, the 5 volt input range is split into 2.5 volt ranges that are amplified by two before being input to the A/D. While V_{IN} is between 0 and 2.5 volts, channel 0 will be providing a proportional voltage between 0 volts and 5 volts to the A/D converter. Channel 1 will be clamped to 5 volts. When V_{IN} rises above 2.5 volts, channel 1 will begin to output a proportional voltage between 0 volts and 5 volts to the A/D converter and channel 0 will be clamped at 5 volts. Using this method, an 11-bit (2048 step) result is created with 2.5 millivolt steps (i.e. an extra LSB).

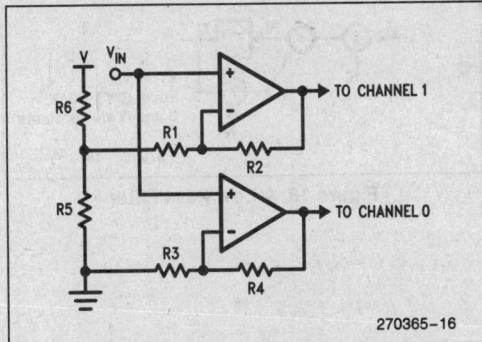

Figure 16. A Flexible Input Circuit

It is useful to note that only one conversion per sample will be required if the software keeps track of which channel is active. The only time that two conversions will be required for one sample is when the voltage crosses the midpoint.

The second reason that "more resolution" is requested is the need for an "extra MSB". When the converter's input voltage range is too small (5 volts when 10 volts is needed), but 5 millivolt steps over the actual input voltage range is sufficient, an extra bit is needed on the most significant ("left") side of the 10-bit result. The circuit of Figure 16 can also be used, with different gains and offsets, to satisfy this extra MSB need by splitting the 10 volt range into 5 volt ranges.

If both channels of Figure 16 are set for unity gain, and channel 1 is offset to 5 volts, an 11-bit conversion result with 5 millivolt steps is available. While V_{IN} is in the lower half of its range (0 volts to 5 volts), channel 0 will be active. While V_{IN} is in the upper half of its range (5 volts to 10 volts), channel 1 will be active. Thus, an extra MSB is created.

For applications requiring multiple extra bits of result, the solutions can become more "elegant" (i.e. elaborate). However, it is profitable to first squeeze the most out of the now familiar circuit in Figure 16.

Assume that the analog input, V_{IN}, ranges from 0 volts to 10 volts, and it is desired to measure this range in 2.5 millivolt steps. This requires two extra bits of result – one extra MSB and one extra LSB. A simple extrapolation of the preceding discussion of creating extra bits might have the designer planning to tieup four channels of the multiplexer needlessly. Needlessly, that is, if the application is a typical control application where the high accuracy requirements are only important in the "normal" operating range of the process. Outside of the normal operating range is the "possible" operating range which must be measured, but with less stringent requirements.

Since the requirements of the normal range set the necessary LSB weight, and the extent of the possible range sets the maximum voltage span, it follows that only two channels need to be used (Figure 16). Channel 0 would be set with a gain that compressed the possible V_{IN} range to 5 volts, while channel 1 would be offset to the normal operating range and would have a gain of two to expand this region of critical interest. With this approach, 100 percent of the normal operating range is digitized in 2.5 millivolt steps, while 100 percent of the possible range is digitized in 10 millivolt steps.

Unfortunately, not all high resolution applications can be described as a process with a small region of in-control operation, where the process is out-of-control outside of that small region. For example, it is necessary to measure airflow in an engine controlling carburetion. The air flow at idle is likely to be several orders-of-magnitude lower than the airflow at full RPM. The process needs to be in tight control over the entire range, not only when the engine is at half-speed.

When it is desired to measure a process with a fixed percent of error throughout a range spanning several orders-of-magnitude, a non-linear input buffer becomes attractive. For example, assume that the analog signal that needs to be digitized can vary from 1 millivolt to 25 volts and describes a physical process that must be represented digitally with 1 percent error at any point in the possible input range. A linear solution to this application would require a converter with a 10 microvolt LSB (1% × 1 mV), and a resolution of 22 bits (25 V/10 microvolts). This is clearly undesirable.

The use of a log input buffer to compress the 25 volt range logarithmically to 5 volts would satisfy the application requirements. The input would range from 1 millivolt to 25 volts with the output ranging from 0 volts to 5 volts proportionally to the log of $V_{IN}/1mV$. Each one-percent change in the input voltage would change the output voltage by 5 millivolts (one count). The antilog could be taken in software using a lookup table, or the control calculations could be performed in a log base.

Simple inexpensive log-amps can be built as in Figure 17, or high-accuracy, self-contained log-amps can be purchased. Which is chosen depends upon the application tradeoffs of price and performance.

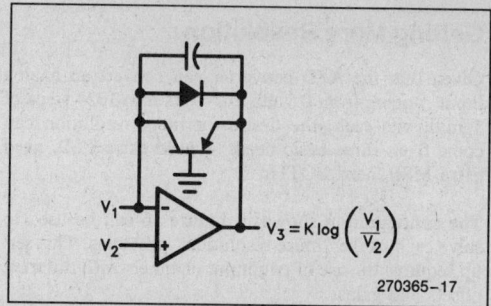

Figure 17. A Low-Cost Log Amplifier

Other techniques become available for consideration in systems that have slow sample rate requirements, but very high resolution requirements. In addition to the methods described above, which require external hardware, software filtering or other post-processing of the conversion results can be productive. Each method relies upon the ability to sample the analog input much faster than the system requires an analog input.

When resolution is limited by filterable noise, perhaps the most straightforward approach to post-processing is to oversample the input by a factor of N and digitally low-pass filter the data (i.e. weighted rolling average). A result would be reported to the rest of the system every N samples (Figure 18). A low-pass filter can increase the signal-to-noise ratio (SNR) by a factor of N (see bibliography). However, care must be taken to be certain that the input voltage varies slowly with respect to the sampling rate.

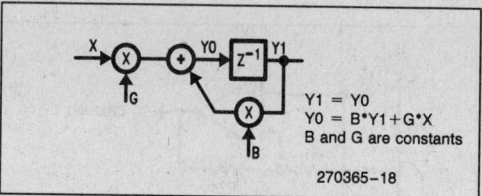

Figure 18. A Low Pass Filter

AP-406

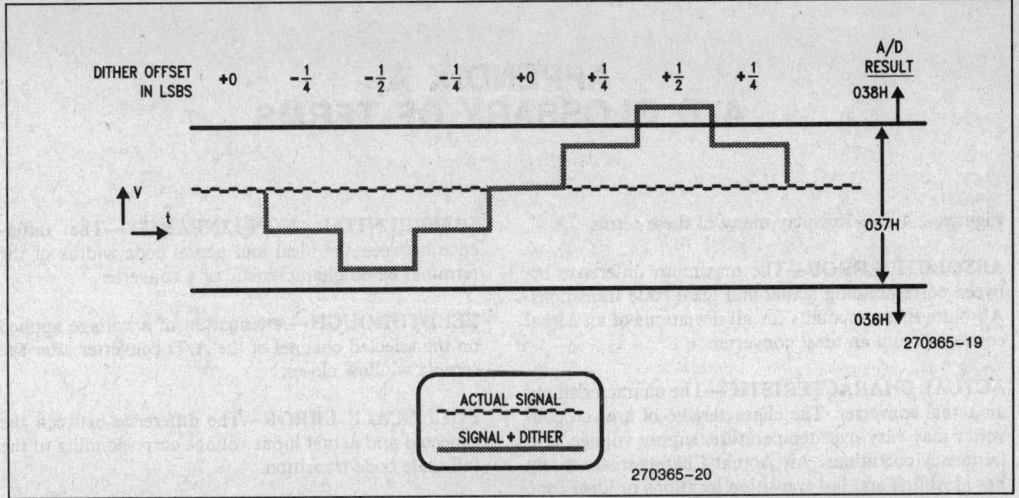

Figure 19. Dither

Another approach to creating more resolution is called "synchronized dither". Figure 19 shows an input voltage that is constant somewhere between two code transition points. This input is "dithered" by adding a small periodic waveform ($1/4$ LSB steps) to the input while performing an A/D conversion synchronized with each dither step. Every time the dither completes a full cycle, the eight conversion results are averaged to form one digitized value. Since the dither is periodic and symmetrical about 0 volts, its average impact on the input voltage is 0 volts.

The creation of extra resolution can be seen with the example shown in Figure 19. Without dither, the input voltage would always convert to 37H. With dither, one-eighth of the conversions would be 38H and $7/8$ of the conversions would be 37H. If every eight conversions were averaged, the result would be 37H + $1/8$ LSB. The possible results given a four level dither, where the input voltage was always within the 37H code width, would be

$$36H + 5/8$$
$$36H + 7/8$$
$$37H + 0$$
$$37H + 1/8$$
$$37H + 3/8$$

Hence, four new levels exist (two bits).

Dither will only create more resolution up to the limit of the A/D converter comparator's ability to distinguish voltages. Since MCS-96 converter repeatability error is typically around 1 millivolt to 1.25 millivolts, $1/4$ LSB dither is the practical limit if no other processing is done. Figure 20 shows a simple method by which the input voltage could be dithered under software control.

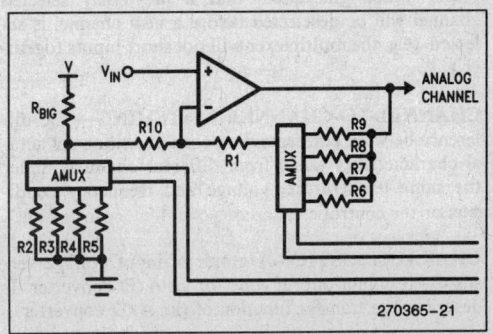

Figure 20. Software Controlled Offset and Gain

While only a few of the more obvious interfacing techniques were described here, there are as many innovative interfacing tricks as there are designers.

CONCLUSION

This application note provides a fundamental understanding of MCS-96 analog acquisition for the digital designer. Since answering the limitless number of analog circuit design questions is beyond the scope of this document, it is expected that analog design manuals and the large body of publicly available applications literature will be consulted for detailed design hints. Furthermore, the applications literature of monolithic analog acquisition system manufacturers should be consulted since the suggestions presented therein are largely transportable to any A/D system.

AP-406

APPENDIX A
A/D GLOSSARY OF TERMS

Figures 2, 4 and 7 display many of these terms.

ABSOLUTE ERROR—The maximum difference between corresponding actual and ideal code transitions. Absolute Error accounts for all deviations of an actual converter from an ideal converter.

ACTUAL CHARACTERISTIC—The characteristic of an actual converter. The characteristic of a given converter may vary over temperature, supply voltage, and frequency conditions. An Actual Characteristic rarely has ideal first and last transition locations or ideal code widths. It may even vary over multiple conversions under the same conditions.

BREAK-BEFORE-MAKE—The property of a multiplexer which guarantees that a previously selected channel will be deselected before a new channel is selected. (e.g. the multiplexer will not short inputs together.)

CHANNEL-TO-CHANNEL MATCHING—The difference between corresponding code transitions of actual characteristics taken from different channels under the same temperature, voltage and frequency conditions.

CHARACTERISTIC—A graph of input voltage versus the resultant output code for an A/D converter. It describes the transfer function of the A/D converter.

CODE—The digital value output by the converter.

CODE CENTER—The voltage corresponding to the midpoint between two adjacent code transitions.

CODE TRANSITION—The point at which the converter changes from an output code of Q, to a code of Q + 1. The input voltage corresponding to a code transition is defined to be that voltage which is equally likely to produce either of two adjacent codes.

CODE WIDTH—The voltage corresponding to the difference between two adjacent code transitions.

CROSSTALK—See "Off-Isolation".

D.C. INPUT LEAKAGE—D.C. Leakage current of an analog input pin.

DIFFERENTIAL NON-LINEARITY—The difference between the ideal and actual code widths of the terminal based characteristic of a converter.

FEEDTHROUGH—Attenuation of a voltage applied on the selected channel of the A/D converter after the sample window closes.

FULL-SCALE ERROR—The difference between the expected and actual input voltage corresponding to the full-scale code transition.

IDEAL CHARACTERISTIC—A characteristic with its first code transition at $V_{IN} = 0.5$ LSB, its last code transition at $V_{IN} = (V_{REF} - 1.5$ LSB) and all code widths equal to one LSB.

INPUT RESISTANCE—The effective series resistance from the analog input pin to the sample capacitor.

LSB - LEAST SIGNIFICANT BIT—The voltage value corresponding to the full-scale voltage divided by $2n$, where n is the number of bits of resolution of the converter. For a 10-bit converter with a reference voltage of 5.12 volts, one LSB is 5.0 mV. Note that this is different than digital LSBs, since an uncertainty of two LSBs, when referring to an A/D converter, equals 10 mV. (This has been confused with an uncertainty of two digital bits, which would mean four counts, or 20 mV.)

MONOTONIC—The property of successive approximation converters which guarantees that increasing input voltages produce adjacent codes of increasing value, and that decreasing input voltages produce adjacent codes of decreasing value.

NO MISSED CODES—For each and every output code, there exists a unique input voltage range which produces that code only.

NON-LINEARITY—The maximum deviation of code transitions of the terminal based characteristic from the corresponding code transitions of the actual characteristic of a converter.

OFF-ISOLATION—Attenuation of a voltage applied on a deselected channel of the A/D converter. (Also referred to as Crosstalk.)

AP-406

REPEATABILITY—The difference between corresponding code transitions from different actual characteristics taken from the same converter on the same channel at the same temperature, voltage and frequency conditions.

RESOLUTION—The number of input voltage levels that the converter can unambiguously distinguish between. Also defines the number of useful bits of information which the converter can return.

SAMPLE DELAY—The delay from receiving the start conversion signal to when the sample window opens.

SAMPLE DELAY UNCERTAINTY—The variation in the Sample Delay.

SAMPLE TIME—The time that the sample window is open.

SAMPLE TIME UNCERTAINTY—The variation in the sample time.

SAMPLE WINDOW—Begins when the sample capacitor is attached to a selected channel and ends when the sample capacitor is disconnected from the selected channel.

SUCCESSIVE APPROXIMATION—An A/D conversion method which uses a binary search to arrive at the best digital representation of an analog input.

TEMPERATURE COEFFICIENTS—Change in the stated variable per degree centigrade temperature change. Temperature coefficients are added to the typical values of a specification to see the effect of temperature drift.

TERMINAL BASED CHARACTERISTIC—An Actual Characteristic which has been rotated and translated to remove zero offset and full-scale error.

V_{CC} REJECTION—Attenuation of noise on the V_{CC} line to the A/D converter.

ZERO OFFSET—The difference between the expected and actual input voltage corresponding to the first code transition.

APPENDIX B
CAPACITIVE INTERPOLATION

A successive approximation A/D converter needs an internal D/A converter of the same resolution as the desired A/D result. A 10-bit D/A could have been made using a string of 1024 resistors connected from the analog reference at one end to ground at the other end. Although this would be technically ideal, such a circuit would be enormous. Therefore, a method was developed to generate the needed reference voltages using a small area of silicon so that an on-chip 10-bit A/D converter would be economical.

The method used relies upon a 256-resistor chain to generate reference voltages in 20mV (5.12V/256) steps while two ratioed capacitors are used to capacitively "interpolate" voltages in-between the resistor tap voltages. The area of the 256-resistor chain together with the capacitors is one-fourth the area of the would-be 1024 resistor chain.

Before beginning a detailed description of the capacitive part of the conversion process, it is necessary to understand a few details about the resistor chain.

There are 256 resistors connected in series from the analog reference to analog ground. The actual value of the resistors only impacts the current through the reference pin. If every resistor in the chain is the same value the converter will function properly.

To reduce resistor-to-resistor variation, the chain is folded in half, and then in an accordion fashion to produce a 16 × 16 block of resistors. This minimizes the sensitivity of the array to processing gradients, while also allowing the array to be addressed roughly similar to a 16 × 16 memory array.

As explained earlier, it is desired for the A/D converter to have its first code transition at ½ LSB followed by subsequent code widths 1 LSB wide.

To accomplish this, each resistor is tapped in its center rather than between resistors. For example, the first resistor tap is half-way up the first resistor. This means that the zero resistor tap will output 10mV (20mV/2). When calculating the voltage on a certain resistor tap, you must add 10mV to the product of the tap number and 20mV.

The internal connections while an analog input is being sampled are shown in Figure B1a. Once sampling is complete, the analog input is disconnected and the comparator inputs are no longer clamped to V_{BIAS} (Figure B1b).

During the sample window (Figure B1a), V_{ANIN} and V_{OFS} control the amount of charge stored in C_A and C_B (V_{OFS} controls the converter offset). Once the sample window closes (Figure B1b), voltages applied to V_{IN} and V_{IN2} will add or subtract charge proportional to ($V_{ANIN} - V_{IN}$) on C_A and ($V_{OFS} - V_{IN2}$) on C_B. Unless a voltage is applied to V_{IN} and V_{IN2}, the inverting comparator input of Figure B1b will remain at V_{BIAS} due to the charges on C_A and C_B. The non-inverting comparator input will always remain at V_{BIAS} and serves as a reference.

If a V_{IN}, V_{IN2} combination is applied which causes the non-inverting input to drop below V_{BIAS} the comparator will output to a 1 to indicate that the applied voltage was lower than the original V_{ANIN}. To better understand how the circuit works, Figure B2 shows the superposition analysis used to form the equation for V_{OUT}, given initial charge on C_A and C_B and new input voltages V_{IN} and V_{IN2}.

AP-406

Adding the independent effects shown in Figure B2 we have:

$V_{OUT} = V1 + V2 + V3 + V4$

$V_{OUT} = V_{IN}\left(\dfrac{C_A}{C_A+C_B}\right) + V_{IN2}\left(\dfrac{C_B}{C_A+C_B}\right) + V_{AI}\left(\dfrac{C_A}{C_A+C_B}\right) + V_{BI}\left(\dfrac{C_B}{C_A+C_B}\right)$

$V_{OUT} = (V_{IN} + V_{AI})\dfrac{C_A}{C_A+C_B} + (V_{IN2} + V_{BI})\dfrac{C_B}{C_A+C_B}$ (I)

The initial conditions on C_A and C_B are set-up as shown in Figure B3.

We can see that:

$V_{AI} = V_{BIAS} - V_{ANIN}$ (II)

$V_{BI} = V_{BIAS} - V_{OFS}$ (III)

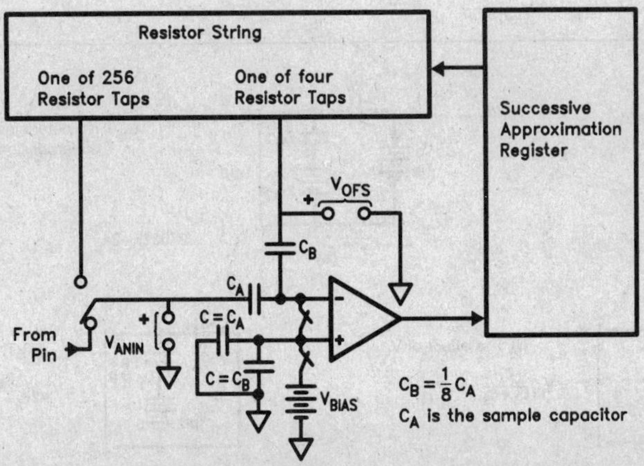

(a). Connections during the sample window

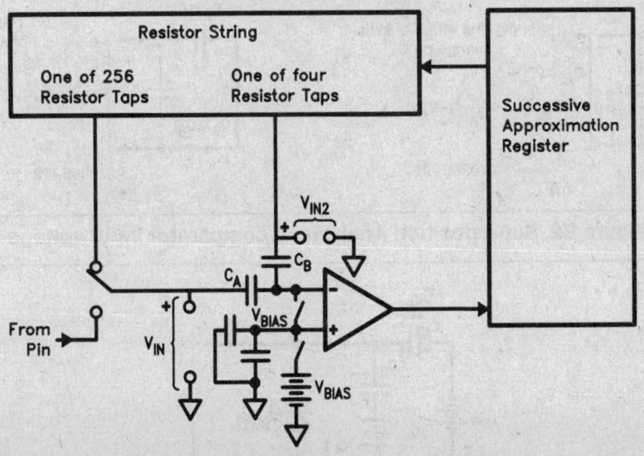

(b). Connections after the sample window closes

Figure B1

5-203

AP-406

Substituting II and III into I we get:

$$V_{OUT} = (V_{IN} + V_{BIAS} - V_{ANIN})\frac{C_A}{C_A + C_B} +$$

$$(V_{IN2} + V_{BIAS} - V_{OFS})\frac{C_B}{C_A + C_B} \quad \text{(IV)}$$

V_{OUT} becomes the input voltage to the comparator which ideally presents no load. The only way to make V_{OUT} approach the value of V_{BIAS} (after V_{BIAS} is removed) is to apply a voltage combination which makes equation IV evaluate to V_{BIAS}. If we had an infinitely variable internal voltage reference to use, we could just set the reference on V_{IN} to the value of V_{ANIN} and make $V_{INZ} = V_{OFS}$.

We would then have, from IV:

$$V_{IN} = V_{ANIN}, V_{IN2} = V_{OFS}$$

However, using a 256-resistor chain to provide references, we can find a V_{IN}, V_{INZ} combination which can bring V_{OUT} close to the value of V_{BIAS}. The 256-resistor chain provides a reference voltage in 20 mV steps. We can then take separate taps of the resistor chain and connect them to V_{IN} and V_{IN2}. The voltage attached to V_{IN} will couple to V_{OUT} by a factor of $C_A/(C_A + C_B)$ = 8/9 from EQN IV. The voltage attached to V_{IN2} will couple to V_{OUT} by a factor of $C_B/(C_A + C_B)$. The ratio of the impacts on V_{OUT} of V_{IN} versus V_{IN2} is:

$$\left(\frac{\partial V_{OUT}}{\partial V_{IN}}\right) \div \left(\frac{\partial V_{OUT}}{\partial V_{IN2}}\right) = (8/9)/(1/9) = 8$$

Therefore, a voltage change on V_{IN} will affect the voltage seen at V_{OUT} eight times more than the same change placed on V_{IN2}.

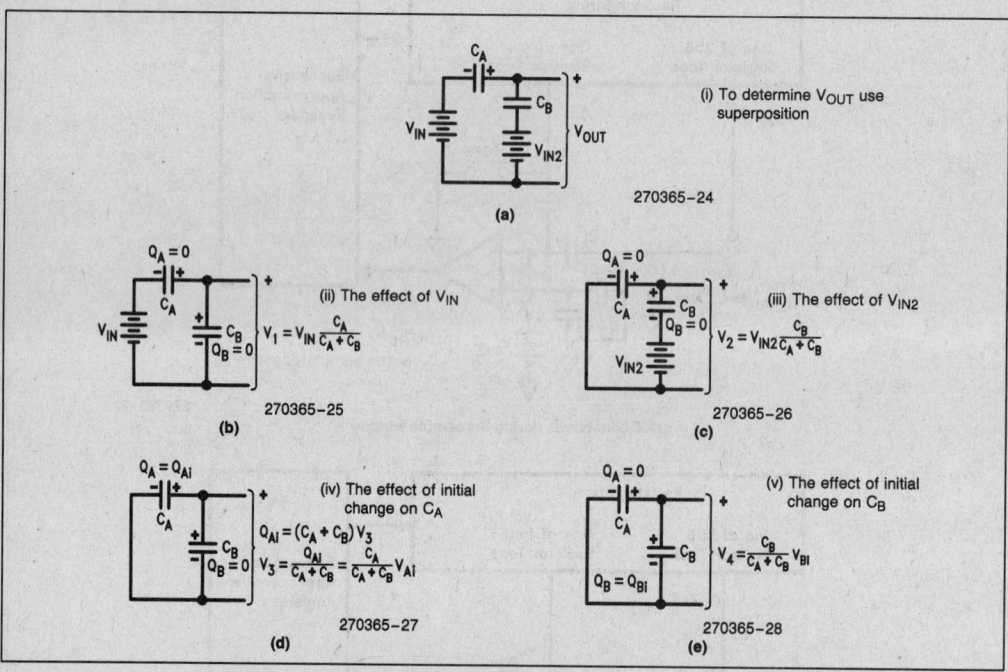

Figure B2. Superposition Analysis of comparator input voltage

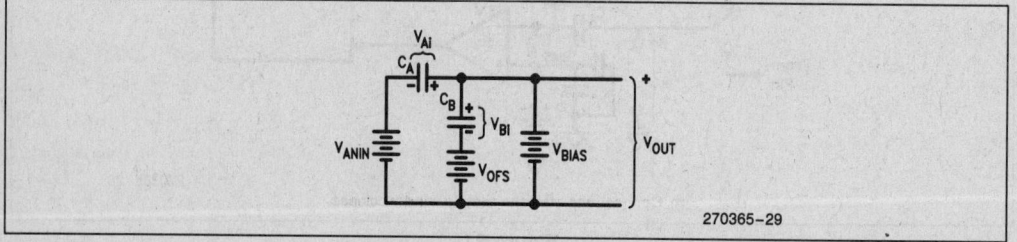

Figure B3. Initial Conditions

For example, assume the actual input voltage V_{ANIN} was 2.50mV during the sample window. Using EQN IV, and assuming $V_{BIAS} = 3V$ and $V_{OFS} = 70mV$, we substitute and find:

$$V_{OUT} = (V_{IN} + 2.9975) \times (8/9) + (V_{IN2} + 2.93) \times (1/9) \quad (V)$$

Using successive approximation, the first trial input voltage attempted corresponds to the digital code 0111 1111 11b ($127 \times 20mV + 10mV$). This means that the voltage applied to V_{IN} will be the 0111 1111b tap and the voltage applied to V_{IN2} will be the 0110b tap ($6 \times 20mV + 10mV = 3$ LSB). Substituting these values into EQN V we have:

$$V_{OUT} = (2.550 + 2.9975) \times (8/9) + (0.130 + 2.93) \times (1/9) \quad (V)$$
$$V_{OUT} = \quad 4.931 \quad + \quad 0.34 \quad = 5.271$$

Since the 3V reference is lower than V_{OUT} with these inputs, the comparator will output a 0 which is placed in the MSB of the successive approximation register. The next most significant bit of the SAR is then zero'd and the new ladder tap applied to V_{IN}. The result of this second comparison, and the subsequent comparisons are shown in Table B1. The C program used to generate Table B1 is listed in Listing B1.

The value selected for V_{OFS} during the sample window may not be obvious. The purpose of V_{OFS} is to inject a constant offset in the sampling process so that the converter's first code transition will occur at 2.5mV.

Using EQN IV we can quickly see why V_{OFS} is chosen to be the fourth resistor tap ($4 \times 20mV + 10mV = 70mV$). For $V_{ANIN} = 2.5mV$, we want V_{OUT} to evaluate to V_{BIAS} when the SAR is 0H.

$$V_{OUT} = \{(0.20\ mV + 10\ mV) + (V_{BIAS} - 2.5\ mV)\} \times (8/9) + \{(0.20\ mV + 10\ mV) + (V_{BIAS} - 70\ mV)\} \times (1/9)$$

$$V_{OUT} - V_{BIAS} = 7.5\ mV \times (8/9) - 60\ mV \times (1/9) = 0$$

Therefore, if $V_{OFS} = 70\ mV$, the converter's first code transition will be when $V_{ANIN} = 2.5\ mV$.

Table B1. Conversion Simulation

```
A to D simulator. (center taps) . . With
V_IN = 0.002500
V_CENT = 3.000000  V_OFF = 0.070000
SAR =  1FFH  ( 511)   V_OUT = 5.271111
SAR =   FFH  ( 255)   V_OUT = 4.133333
SAR =   7FH  ( 127)   V_OUT = 3.564444
SAR =   3FH  (  63)   V_OUT = 3.280000
SAR =   1FH  (  31)   V_OUT = 3.137778
SAR =    FH  (  15)   V_OUT = 3.066667
SAR =    7H  (   7)   V_OUT = 3.031111
SAR =    3H  (   3)   V_OUT = 3.013333
SAR =    1H  (   1)   V_OUT = 3.004444
SAR =    0H  (   0)   V_OUT = 3.000000
SAR =    1H  (   1)   which means 0.005000 volts
```

AP-406

```c
#include "CTYPE.H"
#include "STDIO.H"
/* example invocation lines

    a2dsim 0.0025   3.0     0.07          p
           Vin      Vbias   Vofs    print to screen and lp

    a2dsim 0.0075   3.0     0.07
           Vin      Vbias   Vofs    print to screen only
*/

int main(k, argv)
int k;
char *argv[];
    {                                       /* main */
    FILE *fp, *fopen();
    double initial_conditions, vin, vout, vcent, voff, v89, v19;
    unsigned int sar = 0x3FF;
    unsigned int mask = 0x200;
    unsigned int count = 0;
    unsigned int printon;
    if (strcmp(argv[0], "run") == 0)
            count++;
    if ((k != (4 + count)) & (k != (5 + count)))
            {
            printf("\nInvocation error!\n");
            return;
            }
    count++;
    sscanf(argv[count++], "%lf", &vin);
    sscanf(argv[count++], "%lf", &vcent);
    sscanf(argv[count++], "%lf", &voff);
    if (count == k)
            printon = 0;
    else printon = 1;

    printf("A to D simulator.(center taps)..");

    if (printon)
            {
            if ((fp = fopen("\prn:", "w")) == 0)
                    {
                    printf("\nCan't open printer\n");
                    return;
                    }
            }
    if (printon)
            fprintf(fp, "A to D simulator..");

    printf(" with \nVin = %f\nVcent = %f\nVoff = %f\n", vin, vcent, voff);
    if (printon)
            fprintf(fp, " with \nVin = %f\nVcent = %f\nVoff = %f\n",
                    vin, vcent, voff);

    initial_conditions = ((8.0 / 9.0) * (vcent - vin))
            + ((1.0 / 9.0) * (vcent - voff));
    v89 = 8.0 / 9.0;
    v19 = 1.0 / 9.0;
```

270365-A5

Listing B1. A/D Converter Simulator

```
            sar ^= mask;
            printf("SAR = %3xH (%4d)\t", sar, sar);
            if (printon)
                    fprintf(fp, "SAR = %3xH (%4d)\t", sar, sar);
            for (count = 0;  count < 10;  count++)
                    {

                    vout = (v89 * (((double) (sar )) 2)) * 0.02 + 0.01))
                            + (vl9 * (((double) ((sar & 3) << 1)) * 0.02 + 0.01))
                            + initial_conditions;
                    if (vout < vcent)
                            sar |= mask;
            mask ))= 1;
            sar ^= mask;
            printf("Vout = %f\nSAR = %3xH (%4d)\t", vout, sar, sar);
            if (printon)
                    fprintf(fp, "Vout = %f\nSAR = %3xH (%4d)\t",
                            vout, sar, sar);
                    }
            printf(" which means %f volts\n\n", (double) sar * 0.005);
            if (printon)
                    fprintf(fp, " which means %f volts\n\n", (double) sar * 0.005);
            return;
            }                                       /* main */
```

Listing B1. A/D Converter Simulator (Continued)

APPENDIX C
ERROR FORMULAS

The following C program listing contains the routines used to calculate A/D performance in the Embedded Controller Applications lab. Most of the routines require floating point arrays to operate upon. In the listings, the array x[ ] contains the input voltages corresponding to each code transition of the converter. The array dx[ ] contains the width of the region in which each code transition of the converter could occur. For example, an input voltage of 0.003V may cause code 0 and code 1 to be equally likely outputs. x[0] would then contain 0.0030000. However, 0-to-1 code transitions might be observed infrequently through a range of input voltages from 0.0025V to 0.0035V. dx[0] would then contain 0.0010000 to indicate that there is a 1 millivolt window in which either code could occur. x[ ] and dx[ ] are generated by hardware doing repeated conversions using precision voltage standards to provide the input voltages. The array dd[ ] is used throughout as temporary storage.

Generally, typical data is drawn from x[ ] only. When minimum and maximum data is desired, x[ ] and dx[ ] are used to find the range of possible input voltages that could cause each code. For example, typical zero offset is found by simply subtracting 0.5 LSB from the value of x[0]. But, the minimum and maximum zero offset would be calculated as x[0] - 0.5 LSB $\pm$ dx[0]/2.

The listings are provided to show exactly how performance data is calculated. They are not meant to be compiled by the reader. In fact, they are too incomplete to compile correctly, as some support routines and global data structures are not provided.

AP-406

```
#include "\DPR\ADTMAC.H"
#include "\DPR\TDBASE.H"
#include "\DPR\RDBASE.H"
#define LSB (nov.avcc/(pow(2,nbits)))
#define FCT (int)(pow(2,nbits) - 2)
#undef min
#undef max
#undef abs

double pow(a, b)
int a, b;
        {                               /* pow */
        double temp;
        int i;
        temp = 1.0;
        for (i = 1; i <= ((int) b); i++, temp = temp * a)
                ;
        return (temp);
        }                               /* pow */

double fabs(a)
double a;
        {
        if (a < 0)
                return (-a);
        else return (a);
        }

int min(a, b)
double a, b;
        {
        if (a < b)
                return (1);
        else if (a > b)
                return (2);
        else return (0);
        }

int max(a, b)
double a, b;
        {
        return (min(b, a));
        }

double typzoff(x, dx)
float x[], dx[];
        {
        double pow();
        return (x[0] - (0.5 * LSB));
        }

double maxzoff(x, dx)
float x[], dx[];
        {
        double pow();
        return (x[0] + (dx[0] / 2.0) - 0.5 * LSB);
        }

double minzoff(x, dx)
```

Listing C1. Error Formulas

```
        float x[], dx[];
            {
            double pow();
            return (x[0] - (dx[0] / 2.0) - 0.5 * LSB);
            }

    double typfse(x, dx)
    float x[], dx[];
            {
            double pow();
            return (x[FCT] - (now.avcc - (1.5 * LSB)));
            }

    double minfse(x, dx)
    float x[], dx[];
            {
            double pow();
            return ((x[FCT] - (dx[FCT] / 2.0)) - (now.avcc - (1.5 * LSB)));
            }

    double maxfse(x, dx)
    float x[], dx[];
            {
            double pow();
            return ((x[FCT] + (dx[FCT] / 2.0)) - (now.avcc - (1.5 * LSB)));
            }

    int xabserror(x, dx, dd, start, stop)    /* transition absolute error */
    float x[], dx[], dd[];
    unsigned int start, stop;
            {
            double pow(), fabs();
            int i, worst;
            for (i = worst = start;  i <= stop;  i++)
                    {
                    dd[i] = x[i] - ((double) i + 0.5) * LSB;
                    if (fabs(dd[i]) > fabs(dd[worst]))
                            worst = i;
                    }
            return (worst);
            }

    int xabserrordx(x, dx, dd, start, stop) /* transition absolute error w/dx */
    float x[], dx[], dd[];
    unsigned int start, stop;
            {
            double pow(), fabs();
            int i, worst;
            double t1, t2;
            for (i = worst = start;  i <= stop;  i++)
                    {
                    t1 = (x[i] - (dx[i] / 2.0)) - (((double) i + 0.5) * LSB);
                    t2 = (x[i] + (dx[i] / 2.0)) - (((double) i + 0.5) * LSB);
                    if (fabs(t1) > fabs(t2))
                            dd[i] = t1;
                    else dd[i] = t2;
                    if (fabs(dd[i]) > fabs(dd[worst]))
                            worst = i;
                    }
            return (worst);
            }
```

Listing C1. Error Formulas (Continued)

AP-406

```
int tbnonlin(x, dx, dd, start, stop)     /* tb nonlin using x only */
float x[], dx[], dd[];
unsigned int start, stop;
    {
    int i, worst;
    double pow(), typzoff(), typfse(), fabs();
    double oadj, qadj;

    oadj = typzoff(x, dx);
    qadj = 1.0 + ((typfse(x, dx) - oadj) / x[stop]);

    for (i = worst = start; i <= stop; i++)
        {
        dd[i] = (x[i] - oadj) * qadj - (((double) i + 0.5) * LSB);
        if (fabs(dd[i]) > fabs(dd[worst]))
            worst = i;
        }
    return (worst);
    }

int tbnonlindx(x, dx, dd, start, stop)    /* tb nonlin using x and dx */
float x[], dx[], dd[];
unsigned int start, stop;
    {
    int i, worst;
    double pow(), typzoff(), typfse(), fabs();
    double oadj, qadj, t1, t2;

    oadj = typzoff(x, dx);
    qadj = 1.0 + ((typfse(x, dx) - oadj) / x[stop]);
```

270365-A9

Listing C1. Error Formulas (Continued)

AP-406

```
                for (i = worst = start; i <= stop; i++)
                        {
                        t1 = (x[i] - (dx[i] / 2.0) - oadj) * gadj - (((double) i + 0.5) * LSB);
                        t2 = (x[i] + (dx[i] / 2.0) - oadj) * gadj - (((double) i + 0.5) * LSB);
                        if (fabs(t1) > fabs(t2))
                                dd[i] = t1;
                        else dd[i] = t2;
                        if (fabs(dd[i]) > fabs(dd[worst]))
                                worst = i;
                        }
                return (worst);
                }

int xdnl(x, dx, dd, start, stop)          /* using x only */
float x[], dx[], dd[];
int start, stop;
        {
        int i, worst;
        double pow(), fabs();
        double oadj, gadj;
        double typfse(), typzoff();

        oadj = typzoff(x, dx);
        gadj = 1.0 + ((typfse(x, dx) - oadj) / x[stop]);

        worst = start;
        if (start == 0)
                {
                dd[0] = 0.0;
                start++;
                }
        for (i = start; i <= stop; i++)
                {
                dd[i] = (x[i] - oadj) * gadj
                        - (x[i - 1] - oadj) * gadj
                        - LSB;
                if (fabs(dd[i]) > fabs(dd[worst]))
                        worst = i;
                }
        return (worst);
        }

int xdnldx(x, dx, dd, start, stop)        /* using x and dx */
float x[], dx[], dd[];
int start, stop;
        {
        int i, worst;
        double pow(), fabs();
        double t1, t2;
        double oadj, gadj;
        double typfse(), typzoff();

        oadj = typzoff(x, dx);
        gadj = 1.0 + ((typfse(x, dx) - oadj) / x[stop]);

        worst = start;
        if (start == 0)
                {
                dd[0] = dx[0] / 2.0;
```

Listing C1. Error Formulas (Continued)

270365-B0

AP-406

```
                    start++;
                    }
            for (i = start; i <= stop; i++)
                    {
                    t1 = (x[i] - (dx[i] / 2.0) - oadj) * gadj
                    -(x[i - 1] + (dx[i - 1] / 2.0) - oadj) * gadj
                    - LSB;
                    t2 = (x[i] + (dx[i] / 2.0) - oadj) * gadj
                    -(x[i - 1] - (dx[i - 1] / 2.0) - oadj) * gadj
                    - LSB;
                    if (fabs(t1) > fabs(t2))
                            dd[i] = t1;
                    else dd[i] = t2;
                    if (fabs(dd[i]) > fabs(dd[worst]))
                            worst = i;
                    }
            return (worst);
            }

int reslevels(x, dx)           /* finds resolution in levels */
float x[], dx[];
            {
            int i, levels, n;
            double pow();

            levels = 1;
            n = (int) pow(2, nbits) - 1;
            if ((x[0] - (dx[0] / 2.0) > 0.0))
                    levels++;

            for (i = 1; i < n; i++)
                    if ((x[i - 1] + (dx[i - 1] / 2.0))
                            < (x[i] - (dx[i] / 2.0) - tparms.fine_step))
                            levels++;
            return (levels);
            }
```
270365–B1

Listing C1. Error Formulas (Continued)

AP-406

APPENDIX D
SAMPLE CONVERTER DATA

The following pages include printouts describing the performance of an 8097BH. The data shown is for one device and is provided for illustrative purposes only. Users should only rely upon data sheet specifications for the exact device they are designing with.

Table D1 summarizes many performance measures for one converter at 25 C, 12 MHz, V_{CC} = 5.00 volts and V_{REF} = 5.120 volts. Following Table D2 are several error plots that describe Absolute Error, Terminal-based Non-Linearity, Differential Non-Linearity and Repeatability for the test device code-by-code. The y-axis in the plots is the error in volts for each code transition, where code transitions make up the x-axis.

Table D1. Sample Converter Data

```
Test ID = D0H
sN: 4130 (1022H)
T = 25.000000
Vcc = 5.000000, Avcc = 5.120000
Freq = 12.000000
Chan. = 3
States = 188    Mode = 0H
X0.15 1/28/87
Transition Characterization Parameter Listing
Large Step = 0.001000 V
Small Step = 0.000100 V
Endpoints when (1/100) are wrong

Center is 50 percent

Typical Offset Error = -0.001923
Maximum Offset Error = -0.002460
Maximum Offset Error = -0.001385

Typical FS Error = -0.000566
Maximum FS Error = -0.001254
Minimum FS Error = -0.000120

Absolute Error (typ) 40  = 0.004157
Absolute Error (max) 40  = 0.004795
Absolute Error (min) 325 = 0.001111

Diff. Non. Lin. Error (max) 40 = 0.003747
Diff. Non. Lin. Error (min) FF = -0.001071

Term. Non. Lin. Error (max) 325 = -0.004102
Term. Non. Lin. Error (min) 40  = 0.002148

Maximum Reliability Error 3D1 = 0.001875
Minimum Reliability Error 3A7 = 0.000974

Resolution is 1024 levels.
```

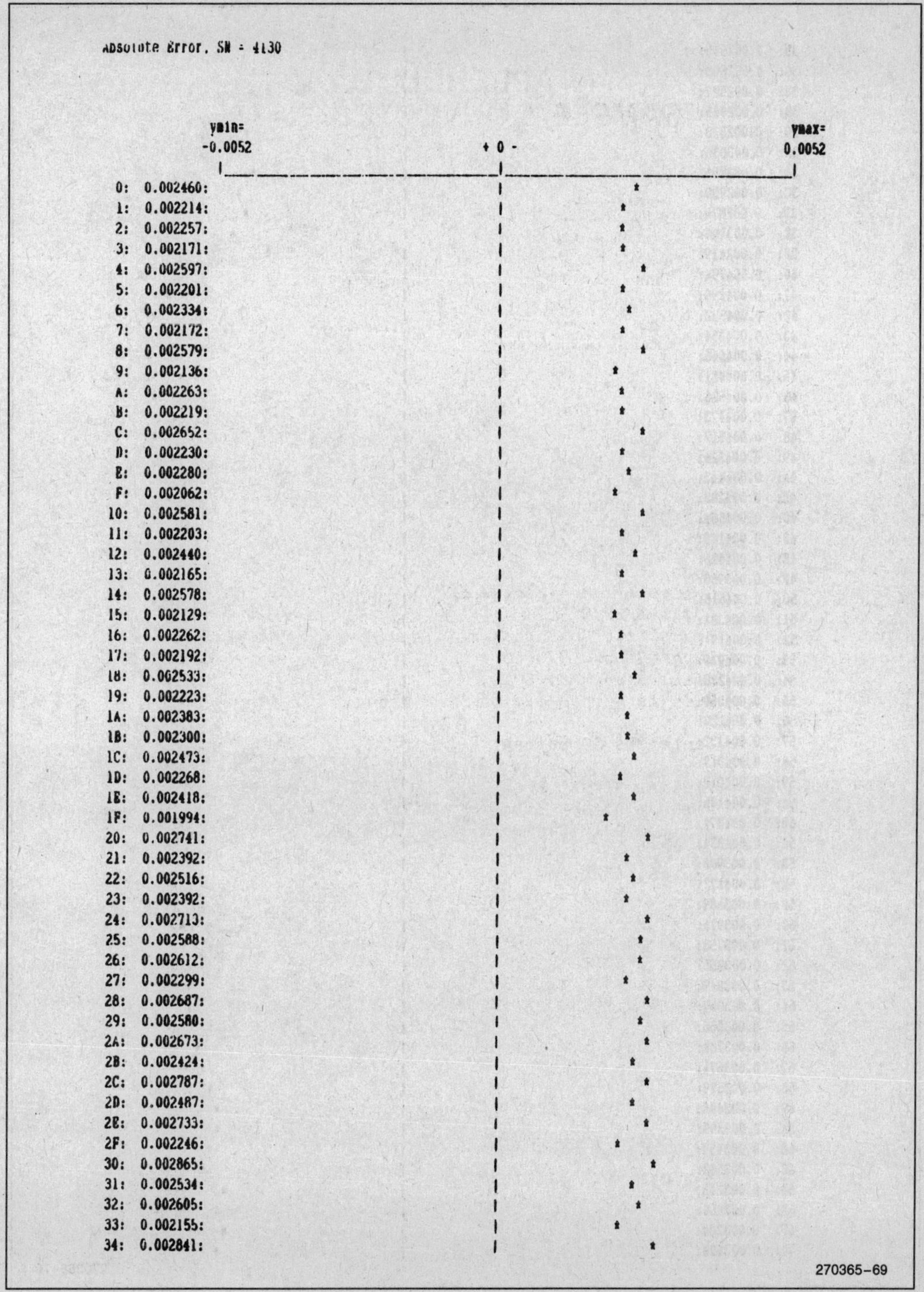

AP-406

```
Absolute Error, SN = 4130

                    ymin=                                              ymax=
                   -0.0052                    + 0 -                    0.0052
                      |_____|_____|
     0:  0.002460:                               |             *
     1:  0.002214:                               |             *
     2:  0.002257:                               |             *
     3:  0.002171:                               |             *
     4:  0.002597:                               |             *
     5:  0.002201:                               |             *
     6:  0.002334:                               |             *
     7:  0.002172:                               |             *
     8:  0.002579:                               |             *
     9:  0.002136:                               |             *
     A:  0.002263:                               |             *
     B:  0.002219:                               |             *
     C:  0.002652:                               |             *
     D:  0.002230:                               |             *
     E:  0.002280:                               |             *
     F:  0.002062:                               |             *
    10:  0.002581:                               |             *
    11:  0.002203:                               |             *
    12:  0.002440:                               |             *
    13:  0.002165:                               |             *
    14:  0.002578:                               |             *
    15:  0.002129:                               |             *
    16:  0.002262:                               |             *
    17:  0.002192:                               |             *
    18:  0.002533:                               |             *
    19:  0.002223:                               |             *
    1A:  0.002383:                               |             *
    1B:  0.002300:                               |             *
    1C:  0.002473:                               |             *
    1D:  0.002268:                               |             *
    1E:  0.002418:                               |             *
    1F:  0.001994:                               |            *
    20:  0.002741:                               |             *
    21:  0.002392:                               |             *
    22:  0.002516:                               |             *
    23:  0.002392:                               |             *
    24:  0.002713:                               |             *
    25:  0.002588:                               |             *
    26:  0.002612:                               |             *
    27:  0.002299:                               |             *
    28:  0.002687:                               |             *
    29:  0.002580:                               |             *
    2A:  0.002673:                               |             *
    2B:  0.002424:                               |             *
    2C:  0.002787:                               |             *
    2D:  0.002487:                               |             *
    2E:  0.002733:                               |             *
    2F:  0.002246:                               |             *
    30:  0.002865:                               |             *
    31:  0.002534:                               |             *
    32:  0.002605:                               |             *
    33:  0.002155:                               |             *
    34:  0.002841:                               |             *
```

Absolute Error, SN = 4130

AP-406

```
35:  0.002515:                                    |                    *
36:  0.002698:                                    |                    *
37:  0.002527:                                    |                    *
38:  0.002945:                                    |                     *
39:  0.002823:                                    |                    *
3A:  0.003036:                                    |                     *
3B:  0.002755:                                    |                    *
3C:  0.002959:                                    |                     *
3D:  0.002879:                                    |                     *
3E:  0.003106:                                    |                     *
3F:  0.002419:                                    |                   *
40:  0.004794:                                    |                         *
41:  0.004299:                                    |                       *
42:  0.004532:                                    |                        *
43:  0.004334:                                    |                        *
44:  0.004646:                                    |                         *
45:  0.004081:                                    |                       *
46:  0.004526:                                    |                        *
47:  0.004173:                                    |                       *
48:  0.004517:                                    |                        *
49:  0.004224:                                    |                       *
4A:  0.004443:                                    |                        *
4B:  0.004282:                                    |                       *
4C:  0.004584:                                    |                        *
4D:  0.004149:                                    |                       *
4E:  0.004486:                                    |                        *
4F:  0.003958:                                    |                      *
50:  0.004518:                                    |                        *
51:  0.004301:                                    |                       *
52:  0.004191:                                    |                       *
53:  0.004020:                                    |                      *
54:  0.004278:                                    |                       *
55:  0.004059:                                    |                       *
56:  0.004220:                                    |                       *
57:  0.004132:                                    |                       *
58:  0.004319:                                    |                       *
59:  0.004012:                                    |                      *
5A:  0.004185:                                    |                       *
5B:  0.004071:                                    |                       *
5C:  0.004334:                                    |                        *
5D:  0.003908:                                    |                      *
5E:  0.004172:                                    |                       *
5F:  0.003589:                                    |                     *
60:  0.003976:                                    |                      *
61:  0.003753:                                    |                     *
62:  0.003956:                                    |                      *
63:  0.003849:                                    |                      *
64:  0.003969:                                    |                      *
65:  0.003566:                                    |                     *
66:  0.003788:                                    |                     *
67:  0.003671:                                    |                     *
68:  0.003579:                                    |                     *
69:  0.003404:                                    |                    *
6A:  0.003399:                                    |                    *
6B:  0.003459:                                    |                    *
6C:  0.003583:                                    |                     *
6D:  0.003245:                                    |                    *
6E:  0.003450:                                    |                    *
6F:  0.003200:                                    |                    *
70:  0.003408:                                    |                    *
```

Absolute Error, SN = 4130 (Continued)

AP-406

```
71: 0.003203:
72: 0.003238:
73: 0.003201:
74: 0.003281:
75: 0.002882:
76: 0.003161:
77: 0.003112:
78: 0.003000:
79: 0.002833:
7A: 0.002989:
7B: 0.002932:
7C: 0.002924:
7D: 0.002716:
7E: 0.002759:
7F: 0.002027:
80: 0.003422:
81: 0.003129:
82: 0.003322:
83: 0.003169:
84: 0.003202:
85: 0.002953:
86: 0.003086:
87: 0.002897:
88: 0.003038:
89: 0.002446:
8A: 0.002983:
8B: 0.002623:
8C: 0.002813:
8D: 0.002593:
8E: 0.002485:
8F: 0.002415:
90: 0.002791:
91: 0.002647:
92: 0.002812:
93: 0.002576:
94: 0.002682:
95: 0.002514:
96: 0.002711:
97: 0.002405:
98: 0.002593:
99: 0.002268:
9A: 0.002550:
9B: 0.002340:
9C: 0.002412:
9D: 0.002118:
9E: 0.002303:
9F: 0.001754:
A0: 0.002191:
A1: 0.001893:
A2: 0.002259:
A3: 0.001986:
A4: 0.002103:
A5: 0.001881:
A6: 0.002071:
A7: 0.001933:
A8: 0.002059:
A9: 0.001792:
AA: 0.001967:
AB: 0.001776:
AC: 0.001864:
```

Absolute Error, SN = 4130 (Continued)

```
AD: 0.001592:                          |          *
AE: 0.001781:                          |           *
AF: 0.001538:                          |          *
B0: 0.001906:                          |            *
B1: 0.001724:                          |           *
B2: 0.001887:                          |            *
B3: 0.001773:                          |           *
B4: 0.001585:                          |          *
B5: 0.001598:                          |          *
B6: 0.001650:                          |          *
B7: 0.001554:                          |          *
B8: 0.001715:                          |           *
B9: 0.001545:                          |          *
BA: 0.001653:                          |          *
BB: 0.001474:                          |         *
BC: 0.001467:                          |         *
BD: 0.001384:                          |         *
BE: 0.001588:                          |          *
BF: 0.001028:                          |       *
C0: 0.003214:                          |                  *
C1: 0.002914:                          |                *
C2: 0.002966:                          |                *
C3: 0.002779:                          |               *
C4: 0.003087:                          |                 *
C5: 0.002717:                          |               *
C6: 0.003096:                          |                 *
C7: 0.002806:                          |               *
C8: 0.003030:                          |                *
C9: 0.002796:                          |               *
CA: 0.002642:                          |              *
CB: 0.002885:                          |                *
CC: 0.003040:                          |                *
CD: 0.002719:                          |               *
CE: 0.002878:                          |                *
CF: 0.002742:                          |               *
D0: 0.002845:                          |                *
D1: 0.002546:                          |              *
D2: 0.002790:                          |               *
D3: 0.002395:                          |             *
D4: 0.002848:                          |                *
D5: 0.002487:                          |             *
D6: 0.002768:                          |               *
D7: 0.002700:                          |              *
D8: 0.002681:                          |              *
D9: 0.002617:                          |              *
DA: 0.002755:                          |               *
DB: 0.002643:                          |              *
DC: 0.002684:                          |              *
DD: 0.002398:                          |             *
DE: 0.002553:                          |              *
DF: 0.002223:                          |            *
E0: 0.002483:                          |             *
E1: 0.001878:                          |            *
E2: 0.002439:                          |             *
E3: 0.002206:                          |            *
E4: 0.002083:                          |           *
E5: 0.002055:                          |           *
E6: 0.002288:                          |            *
E7: 0.002144:                          |           *
E8: 0.002356:                          |            *
```

Absolute Error, SN = 4130 (Continued)

```
E9:  0.002225:
EA:  0.002263:
EB:  0.002113:
EC:  0.002233:
ED:  0.002172:
EE:  0.002369:
EF:  0.002149:
F0:  0.002216:
F1:  0.001841:
F2:  0.002051:
F3:  0.001935:
F4:  0.001965:
F5:  0.001729:
F6:  0.001979:
F7:  0.001899:
F8:  0.001589:
F9:  0.001718:
FA:  0.001935:
FB:  0.001756:
FC:  0.001975:
FD:  0.001832:
FE:  0.001920:
FF:  0.001041:
100: 0.002291:
101: 0.002008:
102: 0.002296:
103: 0.001975:
104: 0.001946:
105: 0.001874:
106: 0.001884:
107: 0.001817:
108: 0.002135:
109: 0.001921:
10A: 0.002009:
10B: 0.001832:
10C: 0.001903:
10D: 0.001694:
10E: 0.001838:
10F: 0.001537:
110: 0.001681:
111: 0.001436:
112: 0.001730:
113: 0.001631:
114: 0.001636:
115: 0.001374:
116: 0.001550:
117: 0.001500:
118: 0.001530:
119: 0.001411:
11A: 0.001390:
11B: 0.001271:
11C: 0.001321:
11D: 0.001074:
11E: 0.001268:
11F: 0.000814:
120: 0.001401:
121: 0.001052:
122: 0.001193:
123: 0.001106:
124: 0.001253:
```

Absolute Error, SN = 4130 (Continued)

```
125:  0.000758:
126:  0.000953:
127:  0.000976:
128:  0.001080:
129:  0.000937:
12A:  0.001181:
12B:  0.001018:
12C:  0.000959:
12D:  0.000862:
12E:  0.000812:
12F:  0.000813:
130:  0.000933:
131:  0.000671:
132:  0.000811:
133:  0.000634:
134:  0.000929:
135: -0.000647:
136:  0.000888:
137:  0.000539:
138:  0.001027:
139:  0.000850:
13A:  0.000749:
13B:  0.000809:
13C:  0.001032:
13D:  0.000788:
13E:  0.000963:
13F: -0.000681:
140:  0.002218:
141:  0.002186:
142:  0.002327:
143:  0.002196:
144:  0.002447:
145:  0.002267:
146:  0.002435:
147:  0.002385:
148:  0.002554:
149:  0.002284:
14A:  0.002420:
14B:  0.002482:
14C:  0.002523:
14D:  0.002299:
14E:  0.002303:
14F:  0.002097:
150:  0.002267:
151:  0.002127:
152:  0.002312:
153:  0.002092:
154:  0.002264:
155:  0.001976:
156:  0.002034:
157:  0.002084:
158:  0.002235:
159:  0.001959:
15A:  0.002071:
15B:  0.002048:
15C:  0.002104:
15D:  0.001998:
15E:  0.002110:
15F:  0.001935:
160:  0.002075:
```

Absolute Error, SN = 4130 (Continued)

AP-406

```
161: 0.001755:
162: 0.001922:
163: 0.001706:
164: 0.001984:
165: 0.001481:
166: 0.001830:
167: 0.001812:
168: 0.001987:
169: 0.001880:
16A: 0.002022:
16B: 0.001736:
16C: 0.001873:
16D: 0.001595:
16E: 0.001620:
16F: 0.001649:
170: 0.001770:
171: 0.001492:
172: 0.001635:
173: 0.001572:
174: 0.001725:
175: 0.001534:
176: 0.001601:
177: 0.001527:
178: 0.001743:
179: 0.001443:
17A: 0.001623:
17B: 0.001578:
17C: 0.001528:
17D: 0.001386:
17E: 0.001466:
17F: 0.001457:
180: 0.001971:
181: 0.001741:
182: 0.001816:
183: 0.001707:
184: 0.001894:
185: 0.001598:
186: 0.001600:
187: 0.001498:
188: 0.001771:
189: 0.001478:
18A: 0.001654:
18B: 0.001591:
18C: 0.001732:
18D: 0.001404:
18E: 0.001536:
18F: 0.001411:
190: 0.001811:
191: 0.001467:
192: 0.001372:
193: 0.001370:
194: 0.001323:
195: 0.001306:
196: 0.001429:
197: 0.001025:
198: 0.001585:
199: 0.001281:
19A: 0.001465:
19B: 0.001323:
19C: 0.001540:
```

Absolute Error, SN = 4130 (Continued)

AP-406

```
19D:  0.001262:
19E:  0.001245:
19F:  0.001201:
1A0:  0.001413:
1A1:  0.001170:
1A2:  0.001361:
1A3:  0.001321:
1A4:  0.001181:
1A5:  0.000872:
1A6:  0.001086:
1A7:  0.001080:
1A8:  0.001195:
1A9:  0.001138:
1AA:  0.001204:
1AB:  0.001230:
1AC:  0.001210:
1AD:  0.000971:
1AE:  0.001083:
1AF:  0.001274:
1B0:  0.001211:
1B1:  0.001133:
1B2:  0.001069:
1B3:  0.001095:
1B4:  0.001065:
1B5:  0.001081:
1B6:  0.001124:
1B7:  0.001079:
1B8:  0.001040:
1B9:  0.001081:
1BA:  0.001183:
1BB:  0.001297:
1BC:  0.001124:
1BD:  0.001006:
1BE:  0.001046:
1BF:  0.001061:
1C0:  0.002475:
1C1:  0.002358:
1C2:  0.002538:
1C3:  0.002457:
1C4:  0.002712:
1C5:  0.002415:
1C6:  0.002579:
1C7:  0.002436:
1C8:  0.002796:
1C9:  0.002388:
1CA:  0.002368:
1CB:  0.002426:
1CC:  0.002661:
1CD:  0.002462:
1CE:  0.002497:
1CF:  0.002396:
1D0:  0.002617:
1D1:  0.002399:
1D2:  0.002503:
1D3:  0.002453:
1D4:  0.002623:
1D5:  0.002414:
1D6:  0.002423:
1D7:  0.002490:
1D8:  0.002606:
```

Absolute Error, SN = 4130 (Continued)

AP-406

```
1D9: 0.002351:                    |              *
1DA: 0.002439:                    |              *
1DB: 0.002382:                    |              *
1DC: 0.002426:                    |              *
1DD: 0.002376:                    |              *
1DE: 0.002443:                    |              *
1DF: 0.002531:                    |               *
1E0: 0.002583:                    |               *
1E1: 0.002038:                    |           *
1E2: 0.002371:                    |              *
1E3: 0.002043:                    |           *
1E4: 0.002350:                    |              *
1E5: 0.002166:                    |            *
1E6: 0.002351:                    |              *
1E7: 0.002363:                    |              *
1E8: 0.002455:                    |               *
1E9: 0.002002:                    |           *
1EA: 0.002299:                    |             *
1EB: 0.002146:                    |            *
1EC: 0.002279:                    |             *
1ED: 0.002072:                    |            *
1EE: 0.001960:                    |          *
1EF: 0.002221:                    |            *
1F0: 0.002314:                    |             *
1F1: 0.001940:                    |          *
1F2: 0.002086:                    |            *
1F3: 0.002310:                    |             *
1F4: 0.002188:                    |            *
1F5: 0.002075:                    |            *
1F6: 0.002065:                    |            *
1F7: 0.002267:                    |             *
1F8: 0.002187:                    |            *
1F9: 0.002002:                    |           *
1FA: 0.002120:                    |            *
1FB: 0.002133:                    |            *
1FC: 0.002158:                    |            *
1FD: 0.001937:                    |          *
1FE: 0.002079:                    |            *
1FF: 0.001409:                    |      *
200: 0.001879:                    |         *
201: 0.001707:                    |        *
202: 0.001905:                    |          *
203: 0.001557:                    |       *
204: 0.001658:                    |        *
205: 0.001661:                    |        *
206: 0.001683:                    |        *
207: 0.001595:                    |       *
208: 0.001535:                    |       *
209: 0.001179:                    |    *
20A: 0.001610:                    |       *
20B: 0.001454:                    |      *
20C: 0.001370:                    |     *
20D: 0.001262:                    |     *
20E: 0.001179:                    |    *
20F: 0.000983:                    |   *
210: 0.001405:                    |     *
211: 0.001074:                    |   *
212: 0.001168:                    |    *
213: 0.001193:                    |    *
214: 0.001420:                    |      *
```

Absolute Error, SN = 4130 (Continued)

AP-406

```
215:  0.001162:
216:  0.001323:
217:  0.001268:
218:  0.001296:
219:  0.001147:
21A:  0.001036:
21B:  0.001170:
21C:  0.001551:
21D:  0.001065:
21E:  0.001216:
21F:  0.000666:
220:  0.001304:
221:  0.000988:
222:  0.001207:
223:  0.001066:
224:  0.001079:
225:  0.001029:
226:  0.000971:
227:  0.000968:
228:  0.001203:
229:  0.000949:
22A:  0.001026:
22B:  0.001051:
22C:  0.001118:
22D:  0.000887:
22E:  0.001149:
22F:  0.000738:
230:  0.001214:
231:  0.000920:
232:  0.001203:
233:  0.000978:
234:  0.001203:
235:  0.001081:
236:  0.001003:
237:  0.001053:
238:  0.001235:
239:  0.000705:
23A:  0.001066:
23B:  0.000924:
23C:  0.001087:
23D:  0.001000:
23E:  0.001006:
23F: -0.000785:
240:  0.002137:
241:  0.001968:
242:  0.002196:
243:  0.002027:
244:  0.002162:
245:  0.001918:
246:  0.002075:
247:  0.001871:
248:  0.002060:
249:  0.002108:
24A:  0.002100:
24B:  0.002060:
24C:  0.002217:
24D:  0.002035:
24E:  0.002245:
24F:  0.002190:
250:  0.002415:
```

270365-78

Absolute Error, SN = 4130 (Continued)

```
251:  0.002013:
252:  0.002259:
253:  0.002068:
254:  0.002370:
255:  0.002213:
256:  0.002314:
257:  0.002207:
258:  0.002259:
259:  0.002090:
25A:  0.001956:
25B:  0.002095:
25C:  0.002377:
25D:  0.002086:
25E:  0.002090:
25F:  0.001972:
260:  0.002137:
261:  0.001808:
262:  0.002022:
263:  0.001944:
264:  0.002053:
265:  0.001856:
266:  0.002042:
267:  0.001940:
268:  0.002020:
269:  0.001762:
26A:  0.001820:
26B:  0.001773:
26C:  0.001850:
26D:  0.001685:
26E:  0.001910:
26F:  0.001794:
270:  0.001748:
271:  0.001653:
272:  0.001632:
273:  0.001540:
274:  0.001677:
275:  0.001356:
276:  0.001582:
277:  0.001630:
278:  0.001505:
279:  0.001403:
27A:  0.001464:
27B:  0.001402:
27C:  0.001620:
27D:  0.001106:
27E:  0.001437:
27F:  0.001276:
280:  0.001913:
281:  0.001950:
282:  0.002095:
283:  0.001620:
284:  0.002096:
285:  0.001850:
286:  0.001951:
287:  0.001836:
288:  0.001726:
289:  0.001690:
28A:  0.001743:
28B:  0.001775:
28C:  0.001551:
```

Absolute Error, SN = 4130 (Continued)

AP-406

```
28D:  0.001620:
28E:  0.001599:
28F:  0.001536:
290:  0.001558:
291:  0.001423:
292:  0.001437:
293:  0.001255:
294:  0.001423:
295:  0.001151:
296:  0.001336:
297:  0.001311:
298:  0.001308:
299:  0.001125:
29A:  0.001060:
29B:  0.001134:
29C:  0.001209:
29D:  0.000856:
29E:  0.001095:
29F:  0.000790:
2A0:  0.000988:
2A1:  0.000839:
2A2:  0.001122:
2A3:  0.000913:
2A4:  0.000971:
2A5:  0.000710:
2A6:  0.000879:
2A7:  0.000807:
2A8:  0.001102:
2A9:  0.000720:
2AA: -0.000620:
2AB:  0.000799:
2AC:  0.000991:
2AD:  0.000727:
2AE:  0.000684:
2AF:  0.000683:
2B0:  0.000713:
2B1: -0.000782:
2B2:  0.000601:
2B3: -0.000704:
2B4:  0.000647:
2B5: -0.000815:
2B6: -0.000685:
2B7: -0.000716:
2B8:  0.000688:
2B9: -0.000764:
2BA: -0.000661:
2BB: -0.000781:
2BC:  0.000904:
2BD:  0.000707:
2BE:  0.000763:
2BF:  0.000844:
2C0:  0.002248:
2C1:  0.001988:
2C2:  0.002117:
2C3:  0.002005:
2C4:  0.002275:
2C5:  0.002183:
2C6:  0.002092:
2C7:  0.002171:
2C8:  0.002366:
```

Absolute Error, SN = 4130 (Continued)

2C9:	0.002105:
2CA:	0.002047:
2CB:	0.002142:
2CC:	0.002308:
2CD:	0.002226:
2CE:	0.002106:
2CF:	0.001931:
2D0:	0.002298:
2D1:	0.001963:
2D2:	0.002106:
2D3:	0.002014:
2D4:	0.002136:
2D5:	0.001849:
2D6:	0.002152:
2D7:	0.002205:
2D8:	0.002087:
2D9:	0.001866:
2DA:	0.002304:
2DB:	0.002234:
2DC:	0.002308:
2DD:	0.001769:
2DE:	0.002155:
2DF:	0.002034:
2E0:	0.001801:
2E1:	0.001788:
2E2:	0.001813:
2E3:	0.001724:
2E4:	0.001537:
2E5:	0.001622:
2E6:	0.001797:
2E7:	0.001799:
2E8:	0.001720:
2E9:	0.001537:
2EA:	0.001715:
2EB:	0.001385:
2EC:	0.001687:
2ED:	0.001464:
2EE:	0.001508:
2EF:	0.001373:
2F0:	0.001488:
2F1:	0.001379:
2F2:	0.001508:
2F3:	0.001325:
2F4:	0.001385:
2F5:	0.001225:
2F6:	0.001381:
2F7:	0.001301:
2F8:	0.001168:
2F9:	0.001136:
2FA:	0.001032:
2FB:	0.000957:
2FC:	0.001102:
2FD:	0.001088:
2FE:	0.000999:
2FF:	0.001571:
300:	0.001484:
301:	0.001278:
302:	0.001463:
303:	0.001298:
304:	0.001282:

Absolute Error, SN = 4130 (Continued)

AP-406

```
305:  0.001267:
306:  0.001317:
307:  0.001154:
308:  0.001373:
309:  0.001001:
30A:  0.001208:
30B:  0.001134:
30C:  0.001258:
30D:  0.001135:
30E:  0.001168:
30F:  0.000971:
310:  0.001021:
311:  0.000689:
312:  0.000990:
313:  0.000857:
314:  0.000944:
315:  0.000651:
316:  0.000794:
317:  0.000744:
318:  0.000790:
319:  0.000702:
31A:  0.000724:
31B:  0.000613:
31C:  0.000823:
31D:  0.000691:
31E:  0.000789:
31F: -0.000870:
320: -0.000695:
321: -0.000923:
322: -0.000784:
323: -0.000845:
324: -0.000707:
325: -0.001111:
326: -0.000776:
327: -0.000991:
328: -0.000893:
329: -0.001089:
32A: -0.000888:
32B: -0.001001:
32C:  0.001505:
32D:  0.001350:
32E:  0.001438:
32F:  0.001358:
330:  0.001612:
331:  0.001368:
332:  0.001645:
333:  0.001482:
334:  0.001753:
335:  0.001664:
336:  0.001732:
337:  0.001582:
338:  0.001661:
339:  0.001472:
33A:  0.001472:
33B:  0.001522:
33C:  0.001702:
33D:  0.001371:
33E:  0.001545:
33F:  0.001281:
340:  0.002960:
```

Absolute Error, SN = 4130 (Continued)

AP-406

```
341: 0.002709:
342: 0.002828:
343: 0.002542:
344: 0.002784:
345: 0.002719:
346: 0.002590:
347: 0.002871:
348: 0.003014:
349: 0.003003:
34A: 0.002773:
34B: 0.002744:
34C: 0.003031:
34D: 0.002672:
34E: 0.002854:
34F: 0.002906:
350: 0.002960:
351: 0.002742:
352: 0.002836:
353: 0.002754:
354: 0.003072:
355: 0.002821:
356: 0.003011:
357: 0.003037:
358: 0.002763:
359: 0.002649:
35A: 0.002595:
35B: 0.002773:
35C: 0.002793:
35D: 0.002479:
35E: 0.002709:
35F: 0.002716:
360: 0.002505:
361: 0.002437:
362: 0.002451:
363: 0.002320:
364: 0.002448:
365: 0.002264:
366: 0.002375:
367: 0.002312:
368: 0.002421:
369: 0.002251:
36A: 0.002330:
36B: 0.002272:
36C: 0.002269:
36D: 0.001925:
36E: 0.002158:
36F: 0.002229:
370: 0.002246:
371: 0.001929:
372: 0.002095:
373: 0.002046:
374: 0.002085:
375: 0.001876:
376: 0.001926:
377: 0.002039:
378: 0.001967:
379: 0.001932:
37A: 0.002019:
37B: 0.001950:
37C: 0.001922:
```

Absolute Error, SN = 4130 (Continued)

AP-406

```
37D:  0.001815:
37E:  0.001689:
37F:  0.002200:
380:  0.002064:
381:  0.001764:
382:  0.001910:
383:  0.001945:
384:  0.001913:
385:  0.001866:
386:  0.001889:
387:  0.001800:
388:  0.001779:
389:  0.001454:
38A:  0.001584:
38B:  0.001477:
38C:  0.001469:
38D:  0.001268:
38E:  0.001562:
38F:  0.001268:
390:  0.001568:
391:  0.000946:
392:  0.001423:
393:  0.001232:
394:  0.001499:
395:  0.001255:
396:  0.001087:
397:  0.001265:
398:  0.001421:
399:  0.001169:
39A:  0.001269:
39B:  0.001245:
39C:  0.001440:
39D:  0.001153:
39E:  0.001402:
39F:  0.001260:
3A0:  0.001363:
3A1:  0.001145:
3A2:  0.001221:
3A3:  0.001155:
3A4:  0.001452:
3A5:  0.001302:
3A6:  0.001138:
3A7:  0.001079:
3A8:  0.001378:
3A9:  0.001043:
3AA:  0.001145:
3AB:  0.001207:
3AC:  0.001161:
3AD:  0.001133:
3AE:  0.001137:
3AF:  0.001175:
3B0:  0.001159:
3B1:  0.000747:
3B2:  0.000927:
3B3:  0.000883:
3B4:  0.001127:
3B5:  0.000784:
3B6:  0.001002:
3B7:  0.001058:
3B8:  0.000907:
```

Absolute Error, SN = 4130 (Continued)

AP-406

```
3B9: 0.000752:
3BA: 0.000941:
3BB: 0.000972:
3BC: 0.000949:
3BD: 0.000972:
3BE: 0.000996:
3BF: 0.001226:
3C0: 0.001963:
3C1: 0.001554:
3C2: 0.001804:
3C3: 0.001950:
3C4: 0.002170:
3C5: 0.001896:
3C6: 0.002087:
3C7: 0.001877:
3C8: 0.002183:
3C9: 0.002084:
3CA: 0.002163:
3CB: 0.002036:
3CC: 0.002131:
3CD: 0.002017:
3CE: 0.001908:
3CF: 0.001909:
3D0: 0.002159:
3D1: 0.002189:
3D2: 0.001986:
3D3: 0.001811:
3D4: 0.001939:
3D5: 0.001809:
3D6: 0.001920:
3D7: 0.001776:
3D8: 0.002066:
3D9: 0.001764:
3DA: 0.001874:
3DB: 0.001881:
3DC: 0.001942:
3DD: 0.001808:
3DE: 0.001838:
3DF: 0.001993:
3E0: 0.001739:
3E1: 0.001712:
3E2: 0.001616:
3E3: 0.001576:
3E4: 0.001812:
3E5: 0.001652:
3E6: 0.001872:
3E7: 0.001730:
3E8: 0.001548:
3E9: 0.001693:
3EA: 0.001857:
3EB: 0.001638:
3EC: 0.001738:
3ED: 0.001581:
3EE: 0.001579:
3EF: 0.001780:
3F0: 0.001451:
3F1: 0.001411:
3F2: 0.001342:
3F3: 0.001439:
3F4: 0.001508:                     270365-85
3F5: 0.001163:
3F6: 0.001341:
3F7: 0.001340:
3F8: 0.001373:
3F9: 0.001098:
3FA: 0.001106:
3FB: 0.001245:
3FC: 0.001320:
3FD: 0.001084:
3FE: 0.001254:
3FF: 0.000000:                     270365-86
```

Absolute Error, SN = 4130 (Continued)

AP-406

```
Non. Lin. Error, SN = 4130

                    vmin=                                                    ymax=
                   -0.0037                         + 0 -                     0.0037
                    |_____|_____|
         0: -0.000000:                              *
         1: -0.000297:                            * |
         2: -0.000256:                            * |
         3: -0.000343:                            * |
         4:  0.000031:                              *
         5: -0.000266:                            * |
         6: -0.000134:                             *|
         7: -0.000397:                            * |
         8:  0.000007:                              *
         9: -0.000386:                            * |
         A: -0.000210:                            * |
         B: -0.000256:                            * |
         C:  0.000075:                             |*
         D: -0.000247:                            * |
         E: -0.000199:                            * |
         F: -0.000468:                           *  |
        10: -0.000000:                              *
        11: -0.000330:                            * |
        12: -0.000094:                             *|
        13: -0.000320:                            * |
        14:  0.000040:                              *
        15: -0.000409:                            * |
        16: -0.000277:                            * |
        17: -0.000349:                            * |
        18: -0.000009:                              *
        19: -0.000270:                            * |
        1A: -0.000112:                             *|
        1B: -0.000296:                            * |
        1C: -0.000124:                             *|
        1D: -0.000281:                            * |
        1E: -0.000132:                             *|
        1F: -0.000607:                          *   |
        20:  0.000137:                             |*
        21: -0.000162:                            * |
        22: -0.000039:                              *
        23: -0.000215:                            * |
        24:  0.000104:                             |*
        25:  0.000028:                              *
        26:  0.000000:                              *
        27: -0.000313:                            * |
        28:  0.000123:                             |*
        29: -0.000085:                             *|
        2A:  0.000056:                             |*
        2B: -0.000143:                            * |
        2C:  0.000217:                             | *
        2D: -0.000083:                             *|
        2E:  0.000061:                             |*
        2F: -0.000276:                            * |
        30:  0.000290:                             | *
        31:  0.000008:                              *
        32:  0.000078:                             |*
        33: -0.000323:                            * |
        34:  0.000211:                             |*
```

270365-30

Non. Lin. Error, SN = 4130

```
35: -0.000065:              *|
36:  0.000165:               |*
37: -0.000106:              *|
38:  0.000409:               | *
39:  0.000186:               |*
3A:  0.000398:               | *
3B:  0.000166:               |*
3C:  0.000368:               | *
3D:  0.000287:               | *
3E:  0.000513:               | *
3F: -0.000275:            *  |
40:  0.002147:               |           *
41:  0.001651:               |        *
42:  0.001983:               |          *
43:  0.001784:               |         *
44:  0.001994:               |          *
45:  0.001478:               |       *
46:  0.001922:               |          *
47:  0.001617:               |        *
48:  0.001910:               |         *
49:  0.001616:               |        *
4A:  0.001833:               |         *
4B:  0.001621:               |        *
4C:  0.001872:               |         *
4D:  0.001585:               |        *
4E:  0.001771:               |         *
4F:  0.001392:               |       *
50:  0.001900:               |         *
51:  0.001682:               |        *
52:  0.001571:               |        *
53:  0.001498:               |       *
54:  0.001755:               |         *
55:  0.001485:               |       *
56:  0.001594:               |        *
57:  0.001455:               |       *
58:  0.001641:               |        *
59:  0.001382:               |       *
5A:  0.001604:               |        *
5B:  0.001489:               |       *
5C:  0.001650:               |        *
5D:  0.001323:               |      *
5E:  0.001536:               |       *
5F:  0.000952:               |    *
60:  0.001437:               |       *
61:  0.001163:               |     *
62:  0.001365:               |      *
63:  0.001156:               |     *
64:  0.001275:               |     *
65:  0.000971:               |    *
66:  0.001141:               |     *
67:  0.000923:               |    *
68:  0.000980:               |    *
69:  0.000803:               |   *
6A:  0.000797:               |   *
6B:  0.000806:               |   *
6C:  0.000928:               |    *
6D:  0.000589:               |  *
6E:  0.000793:               |   *
6F:  0.000592:               |  *
70:  0.000798:               |   *
```

Non. Lin. Error, SN = 4130 (Continued)

AP-406

```
71: 0.000442:
72: 0.000576:
73: 0.000537:
74: 0.000616:
75: 0.000216:
76: 0.000493:
77: 0.000393:
78: 0.000330:
79: 0.000111:
7A: 0.000216:
7B: 0.000158:
7C: 0.000148:
7D: -0.000060:
7E: 0.000081:
7F: -0.000601:
80: 0.000691:
81: 0.000447:
82: 0.000588:
83: 0.000434:
84: 0.000566:
85: 0.000265:
86: 0.000397:
87: 0.000157:
88: 0.000396:
89: -0.000196:
8A: 0.000339:
8B: -0.000021:
8C: 0.000166:
8D: -0.000104:
8E: -0.000163:
8F: -0.000285:
90: 0.000089:
91: -0.000055:
92: 0.000057:
93: -0.000129:
94: 0.000025:
95: -0.000194:
96: -0.000048:
97: -0.000255:
98: -0.000119:
99: -0.000445:
9A: -0.000214:
9B: -0.000376:
9C: -0.000305:
9D: -0.000650:
9E: -0.000467:
9F: -0.000967:
A0: -0.000481:
A1: -0.000830:
A2: -0.000416:
A3: -0.000790:
A4: -0.000574:
A5: -0.000848:
A6: -0.000709:
A7: -0.000898:
A8: -0.000774:
A9: -0.000892:
AA: -0.000768:
AB: -0.000911:
AC: -0.000824:
```

270365-35

Non. Lin. Error, SN = 4130 (Continued)

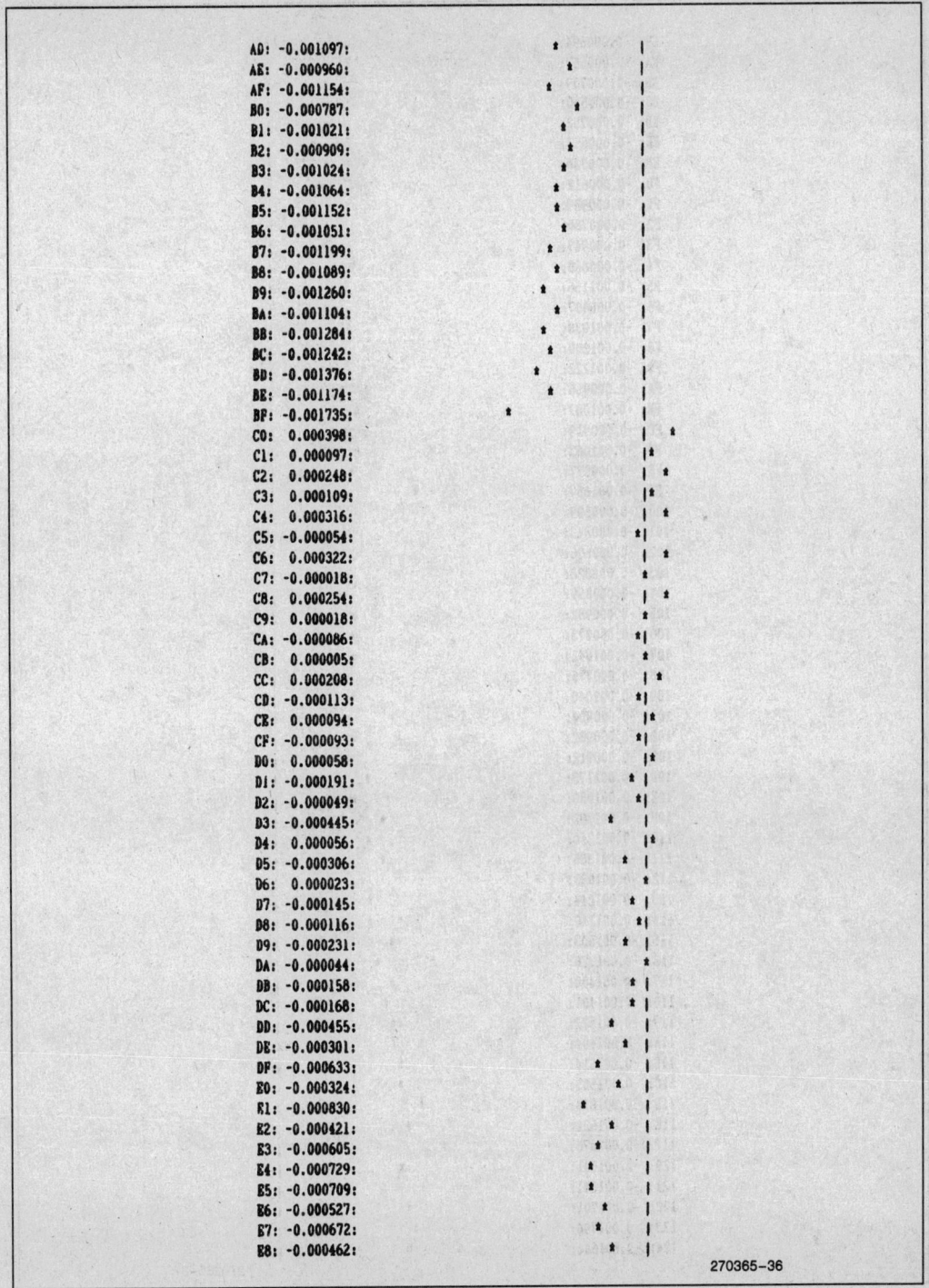

Non. Lin. Error, SN = 4130 (Continued)

AP-406

```
E9: -0.000694:
EA: -0.000557:
EB: -0.000709:
EC: -0.000540:
ED: -0.000752:
EE: -0.000557:
EF: -0.000728:
F0: -0.000612:
F1: -0.000989:
F2: -0.000780:
F3: -0.000947:
F4: -0.000868:
F5: -0.001156:
F6: -0.000807:
F7: -0.001038:
F8: -0.001200:
F9: -0.001222:
FA: -0.000956:
FB: -0.001087:
FC: -0.000919:
FD: -0.001063:
FE: -0.000977:
FF: -0.001857:
100: -0.000509:
101: -0.000843:
102: -0.000606:
103: -0.000828:
104: -0.000859:
105: -0.000982:
106: -0.000973:
107: -0.001042:
108: -0.000775:
109: -0.001040:
10A: -0.000904:
10B: -0.000982:
10C: -0.000912:
10D: -0.001173:
10E: -0.001030:
10F: -0.001382:
110: -0.001240:
111: -0.001386:
112: -0.001093:
113: -0.001244:
114: -0.001240:
115: -0.001503:
116: -0.001328:
117: -0.001480:
118: -0.001401:
119: -0.001521:
11A: -0.001494:
11B: -0.001614:
11C: -0.001565:
11D: -0.001814:
11E: -0.001621:
11F: -0.002076:
120: -0.001541:
121: -0.001841:
122: -0.001701:
123: -0.001790:
124: -0.001644:
```

270365-37

Non. Lin. Error, SN = 4130 (Continued)

```
125: -0.002140:              *           I
126: -0.001946:              *           I
127: -0.001975:              *           I
128: -0.001772:               *          I
129: -0.001967:              *           I
12A: -0.001774:               *          I
12B: -0.001888:               *          I
12C: -0.001948:              *           I
12D: -0.002097:             *            I
12E: -0.002048:             *            I
12F: -0.002148:             *            I
130: -0.001980:              *           I
131: -0.002243:            *             I
132: -0.002054:             *            I
133: -0.002233:            *             I
134: -0.002039:             *            I
135: -0.002342:           *              I
136: -0.002083:            *             I
137: -0.002333:           *              I
138: -0.001896:              *           I
139: -0.002125:             *            I
13A: -0.002177:            *             I
13B: -0.002168:            *             I
13C: -0.001897:              *           I
13D: -0.002142:             *            I
13E: -0.002018:             *            I
13F: -0.002490:          *               I
140: -0.000666:                      *   I
141: -0.000700:                      *   I
142: -0.000560:                       *  I
143: -0.000692:                      *   I
144: -0.000493:                       *  I
145: -0.000724:                      *   I
146: -0.000607:                       *  I
147: -0.000659:                      *   I
148: -0.000441:                        * I
149: -0.000712:                      *   I
14A: -0.000578:                       *  I
14B: -0.000517:                       *  I
14C: -0.000527:                       *  I
14D: -0.000753:                      *   I
14E: -0.000650:                      *   I
14F: -0.000857:                     *    I
150: -0.000688:                      *   I
151: -0.000880:                     *    I
152: -0.000746:                      *   I
153: -0.000917:                     *    I
154: -0.000747:                      *   I
155: -0.000986:                     *    I
156: -0.000929:                     *    I
157: -0.000931:                     *    I
158: -0.000731:                      *   I
159: -0.001008:                    *     I
15A: -0.000898:                     *    I
15B: -0.000972:                     *    I
15C: -0.000867:                     *    I
15D: -0.001075:                    *     I
15E: -0.000914:                     *    I
15F: -0.001140:                    *     I
160: -0.001002:                    *     I
```

Non. Lin. Error, SN = 4130 (Continued)

AP-406

```
161: -0.001273:
162: -0.001057:
163: -0.001275:
164: -0.001048:
165: -0.001502:
166: -0.001155:
167: -0.001274:
168: -0.001100:
169: -0.001259:
16A: -0.000968:
16B: -0.001205:
16C: -0.001170:
16D: -0.001449:
16E: -0.001375:
16F: -0.001347:
170: -0.001278:
171: -0.001557:
172: -0.001365:
173: -0.001430:
174: -0.001328:
175: -0.001520:
176: -0.001455:
177: -0.001480:
178: -0.001315:
179: -0.001617:
17A: -0.001338:
17B: -0.001484:
17C: -0.001486:
17D: -0.001679:
17E: -0.001500:
17F: -0.001611:
180: -0.001098:
181: -0.001379:
182: -0.001306:
183: -0.001366:
184: -0.001230:
185: -0.001478:
186: -0.001377:
187: -0.001480:
188: -0.001309:
189: -0.001553:
18A: -0.001378:
18B: -0.001493:
18C: -0.001353:
18D: -0.001682:
18E: -0.001502:
18F: -0.001678:
190: -0.001229:
191: -0.001624:
192: -0.001671:
193: -0.001674:
194: -0.001672:
195: -0.001841:
196: -0.001669:
197: -0.002024:
198: -0.001466:
199: -0.001871:
19A: -0.001688:
19B: -0.001782:
19C: -0.001516:
```

270365-39

Non. Lin. Error, SN = 4130 (Continued)

AP-406

```
19D: -0.001845:            *           |
19E: -0.001864:            *           |
19F: -0.001909:            *           |
1A0: -0.001698:             *          |
1A1: -0.001943:            *           |
1A2: -0.001803:            *           |
1A3: -0.001894:            *           |
1A4: -0.001936:            *           |
1A5: -0.002146:           *            |
1A6: -0.001983:            *           |
1A7: -0.002040:           *            |
1A8: -0.001877:            *           |
1A9: -0.002035:            *           |
1AA: -0.001921:            *           |
1AB: -0.001896:            *           |
1AC: -0.001867:            *           |
1AD: -0.002108:           *            |
1AE: -0.001997:           *            |
1AF: -0.001807:            *           |
1B0: -0.001822:            *           |
1B1: -0.002051:           *            |
1B2: -0.001916:            *           |
1B3: -0.001991:            *           |
1B4: -0.001973:            *           |
1B5: -0.002108:           *            |
1B6: -0.002067:           *            |
1B7: -0.002013:           *            |
1B8: -0.002053:           *            |
1B9: -0.002113:           *            |
1BA: -0.001913:            *           |
1BB: -0.001950:            *           |
1BC: -0.001974:            *           |
1BD: -0.002144:           *            |
1BE: -0.002055:           *            |
1BF: -0.002041:           *            |
1C0: -0.000629:                    *   |
1C1: -0.000747:                   *    |
1C2: -0.000569:                    *   |
1C3: -0.000701:                   *    |
1C4: -0.000497:                    *   |
1C5: -0.000746:                   *    |
1C6: -0.000533:                    *   |
1C7: -0.000677:                   *    |
1C8: -0.000419:                    *   |
1C9: -0.000728:                   *    |
1CA: -0.000699:                   *    |
1CB: -0.000643:                    *   |
1CC: -0.000509:                    *   |
1CD: -0.000759:                   *    |
1CE: -0.000676:                   *    |
1CF: -0.000678:                   *    |
1D0: -0.000508:                    *   |
1D1: -0.000778:                   *    |
1D2: -0.000675:                   *    |
1D3: -0.000726:                   *    |
1D4: -0.000558:                    *   |
1D5: -0.000768:                   *    |
1D6: -0.000760:                   *    |
1D7: -0.000645:                    *   |
1D8: -0.000580:                    *   |
```

Non. Lin. Error, SN = 4130 (Continued)

AP-406

```
1D9: -0.000836:
1DA: -0.000750:
1DB: -0.000758:
1DC: -0.000715:
1DD: -0.000816:
1DE: -0.000701:
1DF: -0.000714:
1E0: -0.000663:
1E1: -0.001060:
1E2: -0.000828:
1E3: -0.001107:
1E4: -0.000802:
1E5: -0.001037:
1E6: -0.000803:
1E7: -0.000843:
1E8: -0.000702:
1E9: -0.001156:
1EA: -0.000861:
1EB: -0.000965:
1EC: -0.000933:
1ED: -0.001142:
1EE: -0.001205:
1EF: -0.000995:
1F0: -0.000954:
1F1: -0.001179:
1F2: -0.001084:
1F3: -0.001061:
1F4: -0.001035:
1F5: -0.001099:
1F6: -0.001111:
1F7: -0.000960:
1F8: -0.000991:
1F9: -0.001178:
1FA: -0.001061:
1FB: -0.001099:
1FC: -0.001026:
1FD: -0.001248:
1FE: -0.001157:
1FF: -0.001828:
200: -0.001360:
201: -0.001583:
202: -0.001386:
203: -0.001636:
204: -0.001536:
205: -0.001584:
206: -0.001514:
207: -0.001703:
208: -0.001714:
209: -0.002021:
20A: -0.001592:
20B: -0.001799:
20C: -0.001884:
20D: -0.001994:
20E: -0.002028:
20F: -0.002225:
210: -0.001805:
211: -0.002137:
212: -0.001994:
213: -0.002071:
214: -0.001795:
```

Non. Lin. Error, SN = 4130 (Continued)

AP-406

```
215: -0.002104:
216: -0.001945:
217: -0.002001:
218: -0.001974:
219: -0.002175:
21A: -0.002187:
21B: -0.002104:
21C: -0.001725:
21D: -0.002212:
21E: -0.002012:
21F: -0.002564:
220: -0.002027:
221: -0.002294:
222: -0.002127:
223: -0.002269:
224: -0.002157:
225: -0.002308:
226: -0.002268:
227: -0.002372:
228: -0.002039:
229: -0.002344:
22A: -0.002218:
22B: -0.002244:
22C: -0.002179:
22D: -0.002361:
22E: -0.002101:
22F: -0.002463:
230: -0.002088:
231: -0.002333:
232: -0.002052:
233: -0.002328:
234: -0.002104:
235: -0.002278:
236: -0.002357:
237: -0.002259:
238: -0.002078:
239: -0.002559:
23A: -0.002199:
23B: -0.002343:
23C: -0.002181:
23D: -0.002369:
23E: -0.002265:
23F: -0.002833:
240: -0.001187:
241: -0.001357:
242: -0.001130:
243: -0.001301:
244: -0.001167:
245: -0.001462:
246: -0.001157:
247: -0.001412:
248: -0.001224:
249: -0.001278:
24A: -0.001187:
24B: -0.001278:
24C: -0.001023:
24D: -0.001256:
24E: -0.001147:
24F: -0.001204:
250: -0.000930:
```

270365-42

Non. Lin. Error, SN = 4130 (Continued)

AP-406

```
251: -0.001283:              *
252: -0.001088:              *
253: -0.001281:              *
254: -0.000930:               *
255: -0.001188:              *
256: -0.001039:               *
257: -0.001147:              *
258: -0.001096:              *
259: -0.001217:              *
25A: -0.001302:             *
25B: -0.001214:              *
25C: -0.001084:              *
25D: -0.001276:             *
25E: -0.001273:             *
25F: -0.001343:             *
260: -0.001229:             *
261: -0.001509:            *
262: -0.001297:             *
263: -0.001426:            *
264: -0.001318:             *
265: -0.001517:            *
266: -0.001282:             *
267: -0.001485:            *
268: -0.001357:             *
269: -0.001616:           *
26A: -0.001509:            *
26B: -0.001558:           *
26C: -0.001582:           *
26D: -0.001748:          *
26E: -0.001524:            *
26F: -0.001692:           *
270: -0.001589:           *
271: -0.001786:          *
272: -0.001708:          *
273: -0.001751:          *
274: -0.001716:          *
275: -0.001988:         *
276: -0.001813:          *
277: -0.001816:          *
278: -0.001943:         *
279: -0.002046:        *
27A: -0.001936:         *
27B: -0.002000:        *
27C: -0.001783:          *
27D: -0.002248:       *
27E: -0.001869:         *
27F: -0.002131:        *
280: -0.001496:            *
281: -0.001510:            *
282: -0.001316:             *
283: -0.001792:          *
284: -0.001318:             *
285: -0.001615:           *
286: -0.001465:            *
287: -0.001632:           *
288: -0.001643:           *
289: -0.001730:          *
28A: -0.001629:           *
28B: -0.001698:           *
28C: -0.001823:          *
```

Non. Lin. Error, SN = 4130 (Continued)

```
28D: -0.001855:                    *
28E: -0.001778:                    *
28F: -0.001942:                   *
290: -0.001871:                    *
291: -0.002008:                   *
292: -0.001945:                   *
293: -0.002128:                  *
294: -0.001962:                   *
295: -0.002235:                  *
296: -0.002101:                   *
297: -0.002178:                  *
298: -0.002132:                   *
299: -0.002366:                 *
29A: -0.002433:                 *
29B: -0.002360:                 *
29C: -0.002236:                  *
29D: -0.002541:                *
29E: -0.002403:                 *
29F: -0.002609:                *
2A0: -0.002413:                 *
2A1: -0.002563:                *
2A2: -0.002381:                 *
2A3: -0.002542:                *
2A4: -0.002435:                 *
2A5: -0.002697:               *
2A6: -0.002530:                *
2A7: -0.002653:               *
2A8: -0.002459:                *
2A9: -0.002742:               *
2AA: -0.002860:              *
2AB: -0.002666:               *
2AC: -0.002525:                *
2AD: -0.002741:               *
2AE: -0.002785:               *
2AF: -0.002737:               *
2B0: -0.002709:               *
2B1: -0.003031:             *
2B2: -0.002823:              *
2B3: -0.002906:              *
2B4: -0.002780:               *
2B5: -0.003019:             *
2B6: -0.002941:              *
2B7: -0.002923:              *
2B8: -0.002794:               *
2B9: -0.002973:              *
2BA: -0.002872:              *
2BB: -0.002943:              *
2BC: -0.002584:                *
2BD: -0.002832:              *
2BE: -0.002777:               *
2BF: -0.002698:               *
2C0: -0.001295:                       *
2C1: -0.001557:                     *
2C2: -0.001429:                      *
2C3: -0.001542:                     *
2C4: -0.001274:                       *
2C5: -0.001417:                      *
2C6: -0.001409:                      *
2C7: -0.001382:                      *
2C8: -0.001138:                        *
```

Non. Lin. Error, SN = 4130 (Continued)

AP-406

```
2C9: -0.001450:
2CA: -0.001409:
2CB: -0.001366:
2CC: -0.001201:
2CD: -0.001385:
2CE: -0.001406:
2CF: -0.001532:
2D0: -0.001166:
2D1: -0.001503:
2D2: -0.001411:
2D3: -0.001554:
2D4: -0.001334:
2D5: -0.001622:
2D6: -0.001370:
2D7: -0.001369:
2D8: -0.001438:
2D9: -0.001660:
2DA: -0.001324:
2DB: -0.001395:
2DC: -0.001273:
2DD: -0.001813:
2DE: -0.001428:
2DF: -0.001550:
2E0: -0.001685:
2E1: -0.001799:
2E2: -0.001725:
2E3: -0.001766:
2E4: -0.001954:
2E5: -0.001920:
2E6: -0.001747:
2E7: -0.001796:
2E8: -0.001776:
2E9: -0.002011:
2EA: -0.001834:
2EB: -0.002115:
2EC: -0.001915:
2ED: -0.002089:
2EE: -0.002046:
2EF: -0.002132:
2F0: -0.002069:
2F1: -0.002229:
2F2: -0.002101:
2F3: -0.002236:
2F4: -0.002177:
2F5: -0.002388:
2F6: -0.002284:
2F7: -0.002315:
2F8: -0.002449:
2F9: -0.002533:
2FA: -0.002538:
2FB: -0.002564:
2FC: -0.002471:
2FD: -0.002486:
2FE: -0.002576:
2FF: -0.002006:
300: -0.001994:
301: -0.002301:
302: -0.002168:
303: -0.002284:
304: -0.002251:
```

Non. Lin. Error, SN = 4130 (Continued)

AP-406

```
305: -0.002417:
306: -0.002269:
307: -0.002483:
308: -0.002265:
309: -0.002589:
30A: -0.002383:
30B: -0.002508:
30C: -0.002336:
30D: -0.002560:
30E: -0.002428:
30F: -0.002677:
310: -0.002528:
311: -0.002861:
312: -0.002612:
313: -0.002746:
314: -0.002710:
315: -0.002955:
316: -0.002813:
317: -0.002864:
318: -0.002770:
319: -0.002959:
31A: -0.002888:
31B: -0.002901:
31C: -0.002742:
31D: -0.002975:
31E: -0.002878:
31F: -0.003165:
320: -0.002991:
321: -0.003220:
322: -0.003083:
323: -0.003195:
324: -0.003109:
325: -0.003314:
326: -0.003130:
327: -0.003246:
328: -0.003301:
329: -0.003397:
32A: -0.003247:
32B: -0.003362:
32C: -0.002182:
32D: -0.002338:
32E: -0.002251:
32F: -0.002332:
330: -0.001979:
331: -0.002225:
332: -0.002099:
333: -0.002164:
334: -0.001894:
335: -0.002134:
336: -0.002018:
337: -0.002019:
338: -0.001991:
339: -0.002182:
33A: -0.002183:
33B: -0.002134:
33C: -0.002005:
33D: -0.002338:
33E: -0.002115:
33F: -0.002380:
340: -0.000653:
```

Non. Lin. Error, SN = 4130 (Continued)

AP-406

```
341: -0.001006:
342: -0.000888:
343: -0.001175:
344: -0.000834:
345: -0.000951:
346: -0.001030:
347: -0.000951:
348: -0.000710:
349: -0.000672:
34A: -0.000854:
34B: -0.000934:
34C: -0.000648:
34D: -0.001008:
34E: -0.000828:
34F: -0.000777:
350: -0.000774:
351: -0.000994:
352: -0.000901:
353: -0.000985:
354: -0.000618:
355: -0.000920:
356: -0.000731:
357: -0.000707:
358: -0.000832:
359: -0.001047:
35A: -0.001003:
35B: -0.000976:
35C: -0.000957:
35D: -0.001273:
35E: -0.000994:
35F: -0.001038:
360: -0.001150:
361: -0.001320:
362: -0.001257:
363: -0.001390:
364: -0.001263:
365: -0.001498:
366: -0.001388:
367: -0.001453:
368: -0.001295:
369: -0.001416:
36A: -0.001389:
36B: -0.001498:
36C: -0.001502:
36D: -0.001797:
36E: -0.001566:
36F: -0.001596:
370: -0.001531:
371: -0.001799:
372: -0.001684:
373: -0.001735:
374: -0.001647:
375: -0.001857:
376: -0.001809:
377: -0.001697:
378: -0.001770:
379: -0.001956:
37A: -0.001821:
37B: -0.001841:
37C: -0.001820:
```

Non. Lin. Error, SN = 4130 (Continued)

AP-406

```
37D: -0.001979:              *      |
37E: -0.002106:              *      |
37F: -0.001597:               *     |
380: -0.001784:              *      |
381: -0.002085:              *      |
382: -0.001840:              *      |
383: -0.001907:              *      |
384: -0.001890:              *      |
385: -0.001989:              *      |
386: -0.001867:              *      |
387: -0.001957:              *      |
388: -0.002029:              *      |
389: -0.002256:             *       |
38A: -0.002177:             *       |
38B: -0.002285:             *       |
38C: -0.002294:             *       |
38D: -0.002497:            *        |
38E: -0.002204:             *       |
38F: -0.002499:            *        |
390: -0.002201:             *       |
391: -0.002774:          *          |
392: -0.002398:            *        |
393: -0.002591:           *         |
394: -0.002325:            *        |
395: -0.002570:           *         |
396: -0.002590:           *         |
397: -0.002513:           *         |
398: -0.002409:           *         |
399: -0.002662:          *          |
39A: -0.002513:           *         |
39B: -0.002588:           *         |
39C: -0.002345:            *        |
39D: -0.002633:          *          |
39E: -0.002485:           *         |
39F: -0.002579:           *         |
3A0: -0.002427:           *         |
3A1: -0.002646:          *          |
3A2: -0.002572:           *         |
3A3: -0.002639:          *          |
3A4: -0.002393:            *        |
3A5: -0.002494:           *         |
3A6: -0.002609:          *          |
3A7: -0.002570:           *         |
3A8: -0.002522:           *         |
3A9: -0.002809:         *           |
3AA: -0.002658:          *          |
3AB: -0.002698:          *          |
3AC: -0.002645:          *          |
3AD: -0.002724:         *           |
3AE: -0.002721:         *           |
3AF: -0.002685:          *          |
3B0: -0.002752:         *           |
3B1: -0.003015:       *             |
3B2: -0.002837:        *            |
3B3: -0.002932:       *             |
3B4: -0.002689:         *           |
3B5: -0.003034:       *             |
3B6: -0.002817:        *            |
3B7: -0.002812:        *            |
3B8: -0.002965:       *             |
```

Non. Lin. Error, SN = 4130 (Continued)

AP-406

```
3B9: -0.003071:
3BA: -0.002884:
3BB: -0.002953:
3BC: -0.002878:
3BD: -0.002906:
3BE: -0.002784:
3BF: -0.002605:
3C0: -0.001870:
3C1: -0.002229:
3C2: -0.001980:
3C3: -0.001986:
3C4: -0.001668:
3C5: -0.001943:
3C6: -0.001804:
3C7: -0.001915:
3C8: -0.001660:
3C9: -0.001761:
3CA: -0.001633:
3CB: -0.001861:
3CC: -0.001768:
3CD: -0.001883:
3CE: -0.001943:
3CF: -0.001944:
3D0: -0.001795:
3D1: -0.001966:
3D2: -0.001921:
3D3: -0.002097:
3D4: -0.001970:
3D5: -0.002102:
3D6: -0.001992:
3D7: -0.002137:
3D8: -0.001848:
3D9: -0.002102:
3DA: -0.001942:
3DB: -0.002087:
3DC: -0.002028:
3DD: -0.002113:
3DE: -0.002034:
3DF: -0.001931:
3E0: -0.002086:
3E1: -0.002314:
3E2: -0.002311:
3E3: -0.002303:
3E4: -0.002068:
3E5: -0.002280:
3E6: -0.002111:
3E7: -0.002154:
3E8: -0.002338:
3E9: -0.002344:
3EA: -0.002181:
3EB: -0.002252:
3EC: -0.002153:
3ED: -0.002361:
3EE: -0.002264:
3EF: -0.002215:
3F0: -0.002445:
3F1: -0.002536:
3F2: -0.002507:
3F3: -0.002561:
3F4: -0.002493:
3F5: -0.002690:
3F6: -0.002563:
3F7: -0.002565:
3F8: -0.002533:
3F9: -0.002810:
3FA: -0.002753:
3FB: -0.002666:
3FC: -0.002592:
3FD: -0.002829:
3FE: -0.002710:
3FF:  0.000000:
```

270365-49

270365-50

Non. Lin. Error, SN = 4130 (Continued)

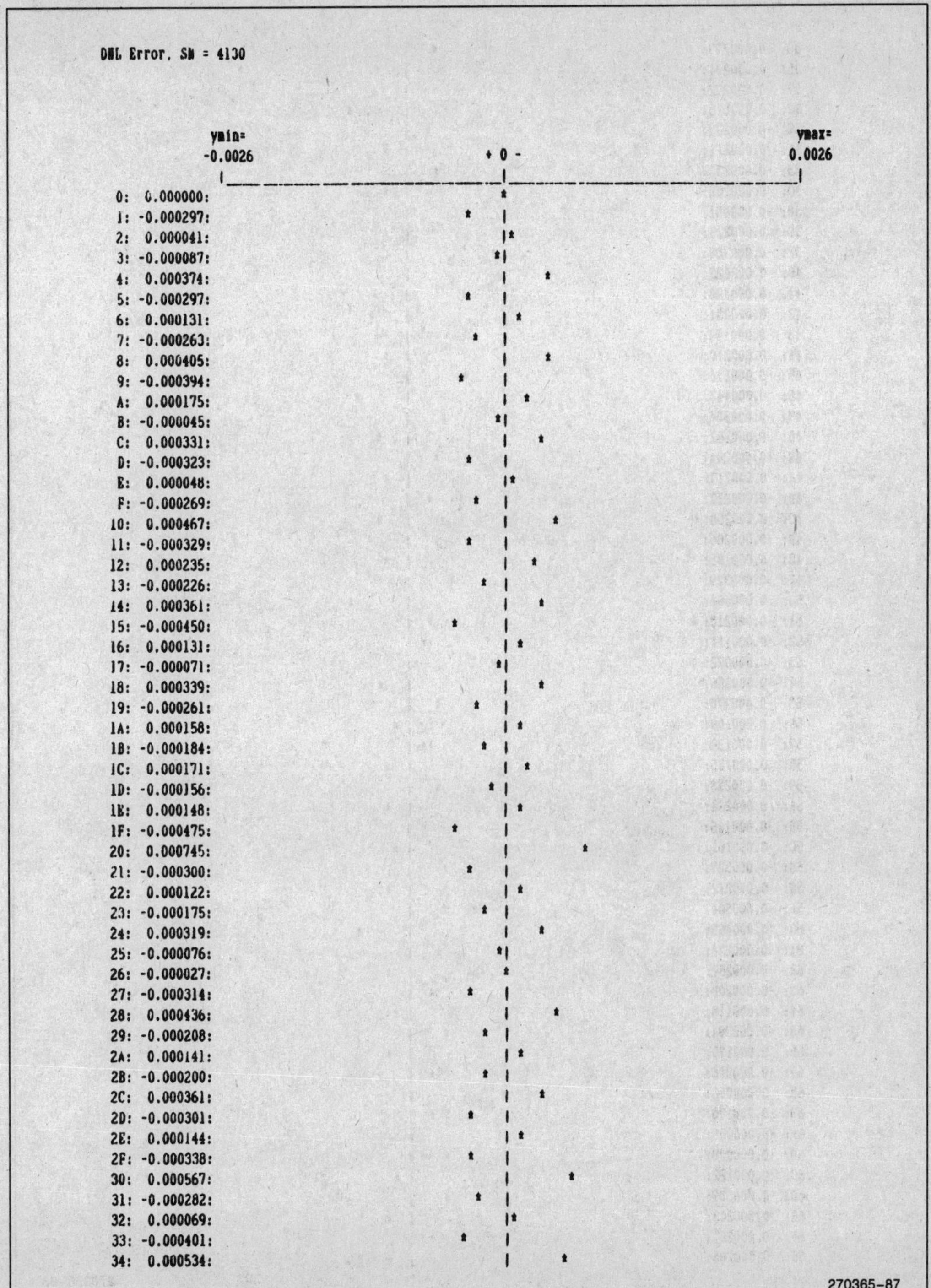

AP-406

DNL Error, SN = 4130

```
              ymin=                                          ymax=
              -0.0026                     + 0 -              0.0026
              |_____|
 0:  0.000000:                            *
 1: -0.000297:                           *|
 2:  0.000041:                            |*
 3: -0.000087:                           *|
 4:  0.000374:                            |   *
 5: -0.000297:                         *  |
 6:  0.000131:                            |*
 7: -0.000263:                          * |
 8:  0.000405:                            |   *
 9: -0.000394:                        *   |
 A:  0.000175:                            | *
 B: -0.000045:                           *|
 C:  0.000331:                            |  *
 D: -0.000323:                         *  |
 E:  0.000048:                            |*
 F: -0.000269:                          * |
10:  0.000467:                            |    *
11: -0.000329:                         *  |
12:  0.000235:                            |  *
13: -0.000226:                          * |
14:  0.000361:                            |   *
15: -0.000450:                        *   |
16:  0.000131:                            |*
17: -0.000071:                           *|
18:  0.000339:                            |   *
19: -0.000261:                          * |
1A:  0.000158:                            |*
1B: -0.000184:                          * |
1C:  0.000171:                            | *
1D: -0.000156:                          * |
1E:  0.000148:                            |*
1F: -0.000475:                        *   |
20:  0.000745:                            |      *
21: -0.000300:                         *  |
22:  0.000122:                            |*
23: -0.000175:                          * |
24:  0.000319:                            |  *
25: -0.000076:                           *|
26: -0.000027:                            *
27: -0.000314:                         *  |
28:  0.000436:                            |   *
29: -0.000208:                          * |
2A:  0.000141:                            |*
2B: -0.000200:                          * |
2C:  0.000361:                            |   *
2D: -0.000301:                         *  |
2E:  0.000144:                            |*
2F: -0.000338:                         *  |
30:  0.000567:                            |     *
31: -0.000282:                          * |
32:  0.000069:                            |*
33: -0.000401:                        *   |
34:  0.000534:                            |    *
```

270365-87

DNL Error, SN = 4130

AP-406

```
35: -0.000277:
36:  0.000231:
37: -0.000272:
38:  0.000516:
39: -0.000223:
3A:  0.000211:
3B: -0.000232:
3C:  0.000202:
3D: -0.000081:
3E:  0.000225:
3F: -0.000788:
40:  0.002423:
41: -0.000496:
42:  0.000331:
43: -0.000199:
44:  0.000210:
45: -0.000516:
46:  0.000443:
47: -0.000304:
48:  0.000292:
49: -0.000294:
4A:  0.000217:
4B: -0.000212:
4C:  0.000250:
4D: -0.000286:
4E:  0.000185:
4F: -0.000379:
50:  0.000508:
51: -0.000218:
52: -0.000111:
53: -0.000072:
54:  0.000256:
55: -0.000270:
56:  0.000109:
57: -0.000139:
58:  0.000185:
59: -0.000258:
5A:  0.000221:
5B: -0.000115:
5C:  0.000161:
5D: -0.000327:
5E:  0.000212:
5F: -0.000584:
60:  0.000485:
61: -0.000274:
62:  0.000201:
63: -0.000208:
64:  0.000118:
65: -0.000304:
66:  0.000170:
67: -0.000218:
68:  0.000056:
69: -0.000176:
6A: -0.000006:
6B:  0.000008:
6C:  0.000122:
6D: -0.000339:
6E:  0.000203:
6F: -0.000201:
70:  0.000206:
```

DNL Error, SN = 4130 (Continued)

270365-88

 **AP-406**

```
71: -0.000356:
72:  0.000133:
73: -0.000038:
74:  0.000078:
75: -0.000400:
76:  0.000277:
77: -0.000100:
78: -0.000063:
79: -0.000218:
7A:  0.000104:
7B: -0.000058:
7C: -0.000009:
7D: -0.000209:
7E:  0.000141:
7F: -0.000683:
80:  0.001293:
81: -0.000244:
82:  0.000141:
83: -0.000154:
84:  0.000131:
85: -0.000300:
86:  0.000131:
87: -0.000240:
88:  0.000239:
89: -0.000593:
8A:  0.000535:
8B: -0.000361:
8C:  0.000188:
8D: -0.000271:
8E: -0.000059:
8F: -0.000121:
90:  0.000374:
91: -0.000145:
92:  0.000113:
93: -0.000187:
94:  0.000154:
95: -0.000219:
96:  0.000145:
97: -0.000207:
98:  0.000136:
99: -0.000326:
9A:  0.000230:
9B: -0.000161:
9C:  0.000070:
9D: -0.000345:
9E:  0.000183:
9F: -0.000500:
A0:  0.000485:
A1: -0.000349:
A2:  0.000414:
A3: -0.000374:
A4:  0.000215:
A5: -0.000273:
A6:  0.000138:
A7: -0.000189:
A8:  0.000124:
A9: -0.000118:
AA:  0.000123:
AB: -0.000142:
AC:  0.000086:
```

DNL Error, SN = 4130 (Continued)

AP-406

```
AD: -0.000273:
AE:  0.000137:
AF: -0.000194:
B0:  0.000366:
B1: -0.000233:
B2:  0.000111:
B3: -0.000115:
B4: -0.000039:
B5: -0.000088:
B6:  0.000100:
B7: -0.000147:
B8:  0.000109:
B9: -0.000171:
BA:  0.000156:
BB: -0.000180:
BC:  0.000041:
BD: -0.000134:
BE:  0.000202:
BF: -0.000561:
C0:  0.002134:
C1: -0.000301:
C2:  0.000150:
C3: -0.000138:
C4:  0.000206:
C5: -0.000371:
C6:  0.000377:
C7: -0.000341:
C8:  0.000272:
C9: -0.000235:
CA: -0.000105:
CB:  0.000091:
CC:  0.000203:
CD: -0.000322:
CE:  0.000207:
CF: -0.000187:
D0:  0.000151:
D1: -0.000250:
D2:  0.000142:
D3: -0.000396:
D4:  0.000501:
D5: -0.000362:
D6:  0.000329:
D7: -0.000169:
D8:  0.000029:
D9: -0.000115:
DA:  0.000186:
DB: -0.000113:
DC: -0.000010:
DD: -0.000287:
DE:  0.000153:
DF: -0.000331:
E0:  0.000308:
E1: -0.000506:
E2:  0.000409:
E3: -0.000184:
E4: -0.000124:
E5:  0.000020:
E6:  0.000181:
E7: -0.000145:
E8:  0.000210:
```

DNL Error, SN = 4130 (Continued)

AP-406

```
E9: -0.000232:                    *  |
EA:  0.000136:                       | *
EB: -0.000151:                    *  |
EC:  0.000168:                       | *
ED: -0.000212:                    *  |
EE:  0.000195:                       | *
EF: -0.000171:                    *  |
F0:  0.000115:                       | *
F1: -0.000376:                   *   |
F2:  0.000208:                       | *
F3: -0.000167:                    *  |
F4:  0.000078:                       |*
F5: -0.000287:                   *   |
F6:  0.000348:                       |  *
F7: -0.000231:                    *  |
F8: -0.000161:                    *  |
F9: -0.000022:                       *
FA:  0.000265:                       |  *
FB: -0.000130:                    *  |
FC:  0.000167:                       | *
FD: -0.000144:                    *  |
FE:  0.000086:                       |*
FF: -0.000880:           *           |
100: 0.001348:                       |           *
101: -0.000334:                  *   |
102:  0.000236:                      | *
103: -0.000222:                   *  |
104: -0.000030:                      *
105: -0.000123:                   *  |
106:  0.000008:                      *
107: -0.000068:                     *|
108:  0.000266:                      |  *
109: -0.000265:                  *   |
10A:  0.000136:                      | *
10B: -0.000078:                     *|
10C:  0.000069:                      |*
10D: -0.000260:                  *   |
10E:  0.000142:                      | *
10F: -0.000352:                  *   |
110:  0.000142:                      | *
111: -0.000146:                   *  |
112:  0.000292:                      |  *
113: -0.000150:                   *  |
114:  0.000003:                      *
115: -0.000263:                  *   |
116:  0.000174:                      | *
117: -0.000151:                   *  |
118:  0.000078:                      |*
119: -0.000120:                   *  |
11A:  0.000027:                      *
11B: -0.000120:                   *  |
11C:  0.000048:                      |*
11D: -0.000248:                  *   |
11E:  0.000192:                      | *
11F: -0.000455:                 *    |
120:  0.000535:                      |   *
121: -0.000300:                  *   |
122:  0.000139:                      | *
123: -0.000088:                     *|
124:  0.000145:                      | *
```

270365-91

DNL Error, SN = 4130 (Continued)

AP-406

```
125: -0.000496:
126:  0.000193:
127: -0.000028:
128:  0.000202:
129: -0.000194:
12A:  0.000192:
12B: -0.000114:
12C: -0.000060:
12D: -0.000148:
12E:  0.000048:
12F: -0.000100:
130:  0.000168:
131: -0.000263:
132:  0.000188:
133: -0.000178:
134:  0.000193:
135: -0.000303:
136:  0.000259:
137: -0.000250:
138:  0.000436:
139: -0.000228:
13A: -0.000052:
13B:  0.000008:
13C:  0.000271:
13D: -0.000245:
13E:  0.000123:
13F: -0.000471:
140:  0.001823:
141: -0.000033:
142:  0.000139:
143: -0.000132:
144:  0.000199:
145: -0.000231:
146:  0.000116:
147: -0.000051:
148:  0.000217:
149: -0.000271:
14A:  0.000134:
14B:  0.000060:
14C: -0.000010:
14D: -0.000225:
14E:  0.000102:
14F: -0.000207:
150:  0.000168:
151: -0.000191:
152:  0.000133:
153: -0.000171:
154:  0.000170:
155: -0.000239:
156:  0.000056:
157: -0.000001:
158:  0.000199:
159: -0.000277:
15A:  0.000110:
15B: -0.000074:
15C:  0.000104:
15D: -0.000207:
15E:  0.000160:
15F: -0.000226:
160:  0.000138:
```

DNL Error, SN = 4130 (Continued)

AP-406

```
161: -0.000271:
162:  0.000215:
163: -0.000217:
164:  0.000226:
165: -0.000454:
166:  0.000347:
167: -0.000119:
168:  0.000173:
169: -0.000158:
16A:  0.000290:
16B: -0.000237:
16C:  0.000035:
16D: -0.000279:
16E:  0.000073:
16F:  0.000027:
170:  0.000069:
171: -0.000279:
172:  0.000191:
173: -0.000064:
174:  0.000101:
175: -0.000192:
176:  0.000065:
177: -0.000025:
178:  0.000164:
179: -0.000301:
17A:  0.000278:
17B: -0.000146:
17C: -0.000001:
17D: -0.000193:
17E:  0.000178:
17F: -0.000110:
180:  0.000512:
181: -0.000281:
182:  0.000073:
183: -0.000060:
184:  0.000135:
185: -0.000247:
186:  0.000100:
187: -0.000103:
188:  0.000171:
189: -0.000244:
18A:  0.000174:
18B: -0.000114:
18C:  0.000139:
18D: -0.000329:
18E:  0.000180:
18F: -0.000176:
190:  0.000448:
191: -0.000395:
192: -0.000046:
193: -0.000003:
194:  0.000001:
195: -0.000168:
196:  0.000171:
197: -0.000355:
198:  0.000558:
199: -0.000405:
19A:  0.000182:
19B: -0.000093:
19C:  0.000265:
```

270365-93

DNL Error, SN = 4130 (Continued)

AP-406

```
19D: -0.000329:
19E: -0.000018:
19F: -0.000045:
1A0:  0.000210:
1A1: -0.000244:
1A2:  0.000139:
1A3: -0.000091:
1A4: -0.000041:
1A5: -0.000210:
1A6:  0.000162:
1A7: -0.000057:
1A8:  0.000163:
1A9: -0.000158:
1AA:  0.000114:
1AB:  0.000024:
1AC:  0.000028:
1AD: -0.000240:
1AE:  0.000110:
1AF:  0.000189:
1B0: -0.000014:
1B1: -0.000229:
1B2:  0.000134:
1B3: -0.000075:
1B4:  0.000018:
1B5: -0.000135:
1B6:  0.000041:
1B7:  0.000053:
1B8: -0.000040:
1B9: -0.000060:
1BA:  0.000200:
1BB: -0.000037:
1BC: -0.000024:
1BD: -0.000169:
1BE:  0.000088:
1BF:  0.000013:
1C0:  0.001412:
1C1: -0.000118:
1C2:  0.000178:
1C3: -0.000132:
1C4:  0.000203:
1C5: -0.000248:
1C6:  0.000212:
1C7: -0.000144:
1C8:  0.000258:
1C9: -0.000309:
1CA:  0.000028:
1CB:  0.000056:
1CC:  0.000133:
1CD: -0.000250:
1CE:  0.000083:
1CF: -0.000002:
1D0:  0.000169:
1D1: -0.000269:
1D2:  0.000102:
1D3: -0.000051:
1D4:  0.000168:
1D5: -0.000210:
1D6:  0.000007:
1D7:  0.000115:
1D8:  0.000064:
```

DNL Error, SN = 4130 (Continued)

AP-406

```
1D9: -0.000256:
1DA:  0.000086:
1DB: -0.000008:
1DC:  0.000042:
1DD: -0.000101:
1DE:  0.000115:
1DF: -0.000013:
1E0:  0.000050:
1E1: -0.000396:
1E2:  0.000231:
1E3: -0.000279:
1E4:  0.000305:
1E5: -0.000235:
1E6:  0.000233:
1E7: -0.000039:
1E8:  0.000140:
1E9: -0.000454:
1EA:  0.000295:
1EB: -0.000104:
1EC:  0.000031:
1ED: -0.000208:
1EE: -0.000063:
1EF:  0.000209:
1F0:  0.000041:
1F1: -0.000225:
1F2:  0.000094:
1F3:  0.000023:
1F4:  0.000025:
1F5: -0.000064:
1F6: -0.000011:
1F7:  0.000150:
1F8: -0.000031:
1F9: -0.000186:
1FA:  0.000116:
1FB: -0.000038:
1FC:  0.000073:
1FD: -0.000222:
1FE:  0.000090:
1FF: -0.000671:
200:  0.000468:
201: -0.000223:
202:  0.000196:
203: -0.000249:
204:  0.000099:
205: -0.000048:
206:  0.000070:
207: -0.000189:
208: -0.000011:
209: -0.000307:
20A:  0.000429:
20B: -0.000207:
20C: -0.000085:
20D: -0.000109:
20E: -0.000034:
20F: -0.000197:
210:  0.000420:
211: -0.000332:
212:  0.000142:
213: -0.000076:
214:  0.000275:
```

270365-95

DNL Error, SN = 4130 (Continued)

AP-406

```
215: -0.000309:
216:  0.000159:
217: -0.000056:
218:  0.000026:
219: -0.000200:
21A: -0.000012:
21B:  0.000082:
21C:  0.000379:
21D: -0.000487:
21E:  0.000199:
21F: -0.000551:
220:  0.000536:
221: -0.000267:
222:  0.000167:
223: -0.000142:
224:  0.000111:
225: -0.000151:
226:  0.000040:
227: -0.000104:
228:  0.000333:
229: -0.000305:
22A:  0.000125:
22B: -0.000026:
22C:  0.000065:
22D: -0.000182:
22E:  0.000260:
22F: -0.000362:
230:  0.000374:
231: -0.000245:
232:  0.000281:
233: -0.000276:
234:  0.000223:
235: -0.000173:
236: -0.000079:
237:  0.000098:
238:  0.000180:
239: -0.000481:
23A:  0.000359:
23B: -0.000143:
23C:  0.000161:
23D: -0.000188:
23E:  0.000104:
23F: -0.000568:
240:  0.001646:
241: -0.000170:
242:  0.000226:
243: -0.000170:
244:  0.000133:
245: -0.000295:
246:  0.000305:
247: -0.000255:
248:  0.000187:
249: -0.000053:
24A:  0.000090:
24B: -0.000091:
24C:  0.000255:
24D: -0.000233:
24E:  0.000108:
24F: -0.000056:
250:  0.000273:
```

DNL Error, SN = 4130 (Continued)

AP-406

```
251: -0.000353:
252:  0.000194:
253: -0.000192:
254:  0.000350:
255: -0.000258:
256:  0.000149:
257: -0.000108:
258:  0.000050:
259: -0.000120:
25A: -0.000085:
25B:  0.000087:
25C:  0.000130:
25D: -0.000192:
25E:  0.000002:
25F: -0.000069:
260:  0.000113:
261: -0.000280:
262:  0.000212:
263: -0.000129:
264:  0.000107:
265: -0.000198:
266:  0.000234:
267: -0.000203:
268:  0.000128:
269: -0.000259:
26A:  0.000106:
26B: -0.000048:
26C: -0.000024:
26D: -0.000166:
26E:  0.000223:
26F: -0.000167:
270:  0.000102:
271: -0.000196:
272:  0.000077:
273: -0.000043:
274:  0.000035:
275: -0.000272:
276:  0.000174:
277: -0.000003:
278: -0.000126:
279: -0.000103:
27A:  0.000109:
27B: -0.000063:
27C:  0.000216:
27D: -0.000465:
27E:  0.000379:
27F: -0.000262:
280:  0.000635:
281: -0.000014:
282:  0.000193:
283: -0.000476:
284:  0.000474:
285: -0.000297:
286:  0.000149:
287: -0.000166:
288: -0.000011:
289: -0.000087:
28A:  0.000101:
28B: -0.000069:
28C: -0.000125:
```

DNL Error, SN = 4130 (Continued)

AP-406

```
28D: -0.000032:
28E:  0.000077:
28F: -0.000164:
290:  0.000070:
291: -0.000136:
292:  0.000062:
293: -0.000183:
294:  0.000166:
295: -0.000273:
296:  0.000133:
297: -0.000076:
298:  0.000045:
299: -0.000234:
29A: -0.000066:
29B:  0.000072:
29C:  0.000123:
29D: -0.000304:
29E:  0.000137:
29F: -0.000206:
2A0:  0.000196:
2A1: -0.000150:
2A2:  0.000181:
2A3: -0.000160:
2A4:  0.000106:
2A5: -0.000262:
2A6:  0.000167:
2A7: -0.000123:
2A8:  0.000193:
2A9: -0.000283:
2AA: -0.000117:
2AB:  0.000193:
2AC:  0.000140:
2AD: -0.000215:
2AE: -0.000044:
2AF:  0.000047:
2B0:  0.000028:
2B1: -0.000322:
2B2:  0.000207:
2B3: -0.000082:
2B4:  0.000125:
2B5: -0.000239:
2B6:  0.000078:
2B7:  0.000017:
2B8:  0.000128:
2B9: -0.000179:
2BA:  0.000101:
2BB: -0.000071:
2BC:  0.000359:
2BD: -0.000248:
2BE:  0.000054:
2BF:  0.000079:
2C0:  0.001402:
2C1: -0.000261:
2C2:  0.000127:
2C3: -0.000113:
2C4:  0.000268:
2C5: -0.000143:
2C6:  0.000007:
2C7:  0.000027:
2C8:  0.000243:
```

DNL Error, SN = 4130 (Continued)

```
2C9: -0.000312:              *  |
2CA:  0.000040:                 |*
2CB:  0.000043:                 |*
2CC:  0.000164:                 | *
2CD: -0.000183:              *  |
2CE: -0.000021:                *|
2CF: -0.000126:               * |
2D0:  0.000365:                 |   *
2D1: -0.000336:             *   |
2D2:  0.000091:                 |*
2D3: -0.000143:               * |
2D4:  0.000220:                 | *
2D5: -0.000288:             *   |
2D6:  0.000251:                 | *
2D7:  0.000001:                 *
2D8: -0.000069:                *|
2D9: -0.000222:              *  |
2DA:  0.000336:                 |   *
2DB: -0.000071:                *|
2DC:  0.000122:                 |*
2DD: -0.000540:         *       |
2DE:  0.000384:                 |   *
2DF: -0.000122:               * |
2E0: -0.000134:               * |
2E1: -0.000114:               * |
2E2:  0.000073:                 |*
2E3: -0.000040:                *|
2E4: -0.000188:              *  |
2E5:  0.000033:                 |*
2E6:  0.000173:                 | *
2E7: -0.000049:                *|
2E8:  0.000019:                 *
2E9: -0.000234:             *   |
2EA:  0.000176:                 | *
2EB: -0.000281:             *   |
2EC:  0.000200:                 | *
2ED: -0.000174:              *  |
2EE:  0.000042:                 |*
2EF: -0.000086:                *|
2F0:  0.000063:                 |*
2F1: -0.000160:              *  |
2F2:  0.000127:                 |*
2F3: -0.000134:               * |
2F4:  0.000058:                 |*
2F5: -0.000211:              *  |
2F6:  0.000104:                 | *
2F7: -0.000031:                *|
2F8: -0.000134:               * |
2F9: -0.000083:                *|
2FA: -0.000005:                 *
2FB: -0.000026:                 *
2FC:  0.000093:                 |*
2FD: -0.000015:                 *
2FE: -0.000090:                *|
2FF:  0.000570:                 |      *
300:  0.000011:                 *
301: -0.000307:             *   |
302:  0.000133:                 |*
303: -0.000116:               * |
304:  0.000032:                 *
```

DNL Error, SN = 4130 (Continued)

AP-406

```
305: -0.000166:              * |
306:  0.000148:              | *
307: -0.000214:              * |
308:  0.000217:              | *
309: -0.000323:           *  |
30A:  0.000205:              | *
30B: -0.000125:             *|
30C:  0.000172:              | *
30D: -0.000224:             *|
30E:  0.000131:              |*
30F: -0.000248:            *  |
310:  0.000148:              |*
311: -0.000333:           *   |
312:  0.000249:              |  *
313: -0.000134:             * |
314:  0.000035:              |*
315: -0.000244:            *  |
316:  0.000141:              | *
317: -0.000051:             *|
318:  0.000094:              |*
319: -0.000189:            *  |
31A:  0.000070:              |*
31B: -0.000012:              *
31C:  0.000158:              | *
31D: -0.000233:            * |
31E:  0.000096:              |*
31F: -0.000286:           *   |
320:  0.000173:              | *
321: -0.000229:            * |
322:  0.000137:              | *
323: -0.000112:             *|
324:  0.000086:              |*
325: -0.000205:            *  |
326:  0.000183:              | *
327: -0.000116:             *|
328: -0.000054:             *|
329: -0.000096:             *|
32A:  0.000149:              | *
32B: -0.000114:             *|
32C:  0.001180:              |       *
32D: -0.000156:             *|
32E:  0.000086:              |*
32F: -0.000081:             *|
330:  0.000352:              |  *
331: -0.000245:            *  |
332:  0.000125:              |*
333: -0.000064:             *|
334:  0.000270:              | *
335: -0.000240:            *  |
336:  0.000116:              |*
337: -0.000001:              *
338:  0.000027:              *
339: -0.000190:            *  |
33A: -0.000001:              *
33B:  0.000048:              |*
33C:  0.000128:              | *
33D: -0.000332:           *   |
33E:  0.000222:              | *
33F: -0.000265:           *   |
340:  0.001727:              |         *
```

DNL Error, SN = 4130 (Continued)

AP-406

```
341: -0.000352:            * |
342:  0.000117:            | *
343: -0.000287:           *  |
344:  0.000340:            |   *
345: -0.000116:           *|
346: -0.000079:           *|
347:  0.000078:            |*
348:  0.000241:            |  *
349:  0.000037:            |*
34A: -0.000181:           * |
34B: -0.000080:           *|
34C:  0.000285:            |  *
34D: -0.000360:          *  |
34E:  0.000180:            | *
34F:  0.000050:            |*
350:  0.000002:            *
351: -0.000219:          *  |
352:  0.000092:            |*
353: -0.000083:           *|
354:  0.000366:            |    *
355: -0.000302:          *  |
356:  0.000188:            | *
357:  0.000024:            *
358: -0.000125:           * |
359: -0.000215:          * |
35A:  0.000044:            |*
35B:  0.000026:            *
35C:  0.000018:            *
35D: -0.000315:          *  |
35E:  0.000278:            |  *
35F: -0.000044:           *|
360: -0.000112:           * |
361: -0.000169:           * |
362:  0.000062:            |*
363: -0.000132:           * |
364:  0.000127:            | *
365: -0.000235:          *  |
366:  0.000109:            | *
367: -0.000064:           *|
368:  0.000157:            | *
369: -0.000121:           * |
36A:  0.000027:            *
36B: -0.000109:           * |
36C: -0.000004:            *
36D: -0.000294:          *  |
36E:  0.000231:            |  *
36F: -0.000030:            *
370:  0.000065:            |*
371: -0.000268:          * |
372:  0.000114:            | *
373: -0.000050:           *|
374:  0.000087:            |*
375: -0.000210:          *  |
376:  0.000048:            |*
377:  0.000111:            | *
378: -0.000073:           *|
379: -0.000186:          * |
37A:  0.000135:            | *
37B: -0.000020:            *
37C:  0.000020:            *
```

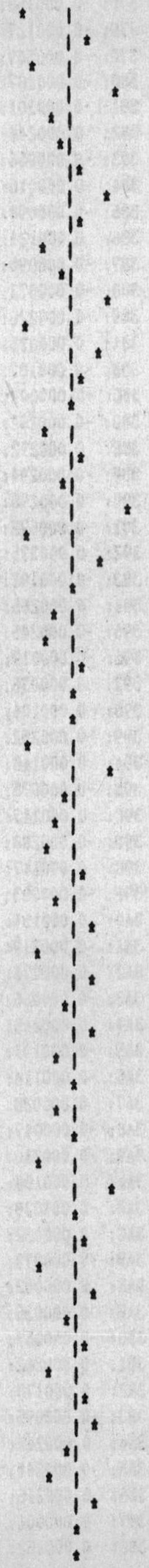

270365-A1

DNL Error, SN = 4130 (Continued)

AP-406

```
37D: -0.000158:
37E: -0.000127:
37F:  0.000509:
380: -0.000187:
381: -0.000301:
382:  0.000244:
383: -0.000066:
384:  0.000016:
385: -0.000098:
386:  0.000121:
387: -0.000090:
388: -0.000072:
389: -0.000226:
38A:  0.000078:
38B: -0.000107:
38C: -0.000009:
38D: -0.000202:
38E:  0.000292:
38F: -0.000294:
390:  0.000298:
391: -0.000572:
392:  0.000375:
393: -0.000192:
394:  0.000265:
395: -0.000245:
396: -0.000019:
397:  0.000076:
398:  0.000104:
399: -0.000252:
39A:  0.000148:
39B: -0.000075:
39C:  0.000243:
39D: -0.000288:
39E:  0.000147:
39F: -0.000093:
3A0:  0.000151:
3A1: -0.000219:
3A2:  0.000074:
3A3: -0.000066:
3A4:  0.000245:
3A5: -0.000101:
3A6: -0.000114:
3A7:  0.000038:
3A8:  0.000047:
3A9: -0.000286:
3AA:  0.000150:
3AB: -0.000039:
3AC:  0.000052:
3AD: -0.000079:
3AE:  0.000003:
3AF:  0.000036:
3B0: -0.000067:
3B1: -0.000262:
3B2:  0.000178:
3B3: -0.000095:
3B4:  0.000242:
3B5: -0.000344:
3B6:  0.000216:
3B7:  0.000004:
3B8: -0.000152:
```

270365–A2

DNL Error, SN = 4130 (Continued)

AP-406

```
3B9: -0.000106:
3BA:  0.000187:
3BB: -0.000069:
3BC:  0.000075:
3BD: -0.000028:
3BE:  0.000122:
3BF:  0.000178:
3C0:  0.000735:
3C1: -0.000359:
3C2:  0.000248:
3C3: -0.000005:
3C4:  0.000318:
3C5: -0.000274:
3C6:  0.000139:
3C7: -0.000111:
3C8:  0.000254:
3C9: -0.000100:
3CA:  0.000127:
3CB: -0.000228:
3CC:  0.000093:
3CD: -0.000115:
3CE: -0.000060:
3CF: -0.000000:
3D0:  0.000148:
3D1: -0.000171:
3D2:  0.000045:
3D3: -0.000176:
3D4:  0.000126:
3D5: -0.000131:
3D6:  0.000109:
3D7: -0.000145:
3D8:  0.000288:
3D9: -0.000253:
3DA:  0.000159:
3DB: -0.000145:
3DC:  0.000059:
3DD: -0.000085:
3DE:  0.000078:
3DF:  0.000103:
3E0: -0.000155:
3E1: -0.000228:
3E2:  0.000003:
3E3:  0.000008:
3E4:  0.000234:
3E5: -0.000211:
3E6:  0.000168:
3E7: -0.000043:
3E8: -0.000183:
3E9: -0.000005:
3EA:  0.000162:
3EB: -0.000070:
3EC:  0.000098:
3ED: -0.000208:
3EE:  0.000096:
3EF:  0.000049:
3F0: -0.000230:
3F1: -0.000091:
3F2:  0.000029:
3F3: -0.000054:
3F4:  0.000067:
3F5: -0.000196:
3F6:  0.000126:
3F7: -0.000002:
3F8:  0.000031:
3F9: -0.000276:
3FA:  0.000056:
3FB:  0.000087:
3FC:  0.000073:
3FD: -0.000237:
3FE:  0.000118:
3FF:  0.000000:
```

270365-A3

270365-A4

DNL Error, SN = 4130 (Continued)

AP-406

```
DX Array, SN = 4130

               ymin=
               -0.0020                         + 0 -                              ymax=
                                                                                  0.0020
               |_____|_____|
  0:  0.001074:                                  |                         *
  1:  0.001175:                                  |                         *
  2:  0.001175:                                  |                         *
  3:  0.001175:                                  |                         *
  4:  0.001275:                                  |                          *
  5:  0.001075:                                  |                        *
  6:  0.001075:                                  |                        *
  7:  0.001275:                                  |                          *
  8:  0.001275:                                  |                          *
  9:  0.001175:                                  |                         *
  A:  0.001075:                                  |                        *
  B:  0.001075:                                  |                        *
  C:  0.001275:                                  |                          *
  D:  0.001075:                                  |                        *
  E:  0.001075:                                  |                        *
  F:  0.001175:                                  |                         *
 10:  0.001275:                                  |                          *
 11:  0.001175:                                  |                         *
 12:  0.001175:                                  |                         *
 13:  0.001075:                                  |                        *
 14:  0.001175:                                  |                         *
 15:  0.001175:                                  |                         *
 16:  0.001175:                                  |                         *
 17:  0.001175:                                  |                         *
 18:  0.001175:                                  |                         *
 19:  0.001075:                                  |                        *
 1A:  0.001075:                                  |                        *
 1B:  0.001275:                                  |                          *
 1C:  0.001275:                                  |                          *
 1D:  0.001175:                                  |                         *
 1E:  0.001175:                                  |                         *
 1F:  0.001275:                                  |                          *
 20:  0.001275:                                  |                          *
 21:  0.001175:                                  |                         *
 22:  0.001175:                                  |                         *
 23:  0.001275:                                  |                          *
 24:  0.001275:                                  |                          *
 25:  0.001175:                                  |                         *
 26:  0.001275:                                  |                          *
 27:  0.001275:                                  |                          *
 28:  0.001175:                                  |                         *
 29:  0.001375:                                  |                           *
 2A:  0.001275:                                  |                          *
 2B:  0.001175:                                  |                         *
 2C:  0.001175:                                  |                         *
 2D:  0.001175:                                  |                         *
 2E:  0.001375:                                  |                           *
 2F:  0.001075:                                  |                        *
 30:  0.001175:                                  |                         *
 31:  0.001075:                                  |                        *
 32:  0.001075:                                  |                        *
 33:  0.000975:                                  |                       *
 34:  0.001275:                                  |                          *
```

Repeatability Error, SN = 4130

```
35: 0.001175:                          |                    *
36: 0.001075:                          |                   * *
37: 0.001275:                          |                    *
38: 0.001075:                          |                    *
39: 0.001275:                          |                     *
3A: 0.001275:                          |                    *
3B: 0.001175:                          |                    *
3C: 0.001175:                          |                    *
3D: 0.001175:                          |                    *
3E: 0.001175:                          |                    *
3F: 0.001375:                          |                      *
40: 0.001275:                          |                    *
41: 0.001275:                          |                    *
42: 0.001075:                          |                    *
43: 0.001075:                          |                    *
44: 0.001275:                          |                    *
45: 0.001175:                          |                    *
46: 0.001175:                          |                    *
47: 0.001075:                          |                    *
48: 0.001175:                          |                    *
49: 0.001175:                          |                    *
4A: 0.001175:                          |                    *
4B: 0.001275:                          |                    *
4C: 0.001375:                          |                     *
4D: 0.001075:                          |                    *
4E: 0.001375:                          |                     *
4F: 0.001075:                          |                    *
50: 0.001175:                          |                    *
51: 0.001175:                          |                    *
52: 0.001175:                          |                    *
53: 0.000975:                          |                  *
54: 0.000975:                          |                  *
55: 0.001075:                          |                    *
56: 0.001175:                          |                    *
57: 0.001275:                          |                     *
58: 0.001275:                          |                     *
59: 0.001175:                          |                    *
5A: 0.001075:                          |                    *
5B: 0.001075:                          |                    *
5C: 0.001275:                          |                     *
5D: 0.001075:                          |                    *
5E: 0.001175:                          |                    *
5F: 0.001175:                          |                    *
60: 0.000975:                          |                  *
61: 0.001075:                          |                    *
62: 0.001075:                          |                    *
63: 0.001275:                          |                     *
64: 0.001275:                          |                     *
65: 0.001075:                          |                    *
66: 0.001175:                          |                    *
67: 0.001375:                          |                      *
68: 0.001075:                          |                    *
69: 0.001075:                          |                    *
6A: 0.001075:                          |                    *
6B: 0.001175:                          |                    *
6C: 0.001175:                          |                    *
6D: 0.001175:                          |                    *
6E: 0.001175:                          |                    *
6F: 0.001075:                          |                    *
70: 0.001075:                          |                    *
```

Repeatability Error, SN = 4130 (Continued)

AP-406

```
71: 0.001375:
72: 0.001175:
73: 0.001175:
74: 0.001175:
75: 0.001175:
76: 0.001175:
77: 0.001275:
78: 0.001175:
79: 0.001275:
7A: 0.001375:
7B: 0.001375:
7C: 0.001375:
7D: 0.001375:
7E: 0.001175:
7F: 0.001075:
80: 0.001275:
81: 0.001175:
82: 0.001275:
83: 0.001275:
84: 0.001075:
85: 0.001175:
86: 0.001175:
87: 0.001275:
88: 0.001075:
89: 0.001075:
8A: 0.001075:
8B: 0.001075:
8C: 0.001075:
8D: 0.001175:
8E: 0.001075:
8F: 0.001175:
90: 0.001175:
91: 0.001175:
92: 0.001275:
93: 0.001175:
94: 0.001075:
95: 0.001175:
96: 0.001275:
97: 0.001075:
98: 0.001175:
99: 0.001175:
9A: 0.001275:
9B: 0.001175:
9C: 0.001175:
9D: 0.001275:
9E: 0.001275:
9F: 0.001175:
A0: 0.001075:
A1: 0.001175:
A2: 0.001075:
A3: 0.001275:
A4: 0.001075:
A5: 0.001175:
A6: 0.001275:
A7: 0.001375:
A8: 0.001375:
A9: 0.001075:
AA: 0.001175:
AB: 0.001075:
AC: 0.001075:
```

Repeatability Error, SN = 4130 (Continued)

270365–53

```
AD: 0.001075:
AE: 0.001175:
AF: 0.001075:
B0: 0.001075:
B1: 0.001175:
B2: 0.001275:
B3: 0.001275:
B4: 0.000975:
B5: 0.001175:
B6: 0.001075:
B7: 0.001175:
B8: 0.001275:
B9: 0.001275:
BA: 0.001175:
BB: 0.001175:
BC: 0.001075:
BD: 0.001175:
BE: 0.001175:
BF: 0.001175:
C0: 0.001275:
C1: 0.001275:
C2: 0.001075:
C3: 0.000975:
C4: 0.001175:
C5: 0.001175:
C6: 0.001175:
C7: 0.001275:
C8: 0.001175:
C9: 0.001175:
CA: 0.001075:
CB: 0.001375:
CC: 0.001275:
CD: 0.001275:
CE: 0.001175:
CF: 0.001275:
D0: 0.001175:
D1: 0.001075:
D2: 0.001275:
D3: 0.001275:
D4: 0.001175:
D5: 0.001175:
D6: 0.001075:
D7: 0.001275:
D8: 0.001175:
D9: 0.001275:
DA: 0.001175:
DB: 0.001175:
DC: 0.001275:
DD: 0.001275:
DE: 0.001275:
DF: 0.001275:
E0: 0.001175:
E1: 0.000975:
E2: 0.001275:
E3: 0.001175:
E4: 0.001175:
E5: 0.001075:
E6: 0.001175:
E7: 0.001175:
E8: 0.001175:
```

Repeatability Error, SN = 4130 (Continued)

AP-406

```
E9:  0.001375:
EA:  0.001175:
EB:  0.001175:
EC:  0.001075:
ED:  0.001375:
EE:  0.001375:
EF:  0.001275:
F0:  0.001175:
F1:  0.001175:
F2:  0.001175:
F3:  0.001275:
F4:  0.001175:
F5:  0.001275:
F6:  0.001075:
F7:  0.001375:
F8:  0.001075:
F9:  0.001375:
FA:  0.001275:
FB:  0.001175:
FC:  0.001275:
FD:  0.001275:
FE:  0.001275:
FF:  0.001275:
100: 0.001075:
101: 0.001175:
102: 0.001275:
103: 0.001075:
104: 0.001075:
105: 0.001175:
106: 0.001175:
107: 0.001175:
108: 0.001275:
109: 0.001375:
10A: 0.001275:
10B: 0.001075:
10C: 0.001075:
10D: 0.001175:
10E: 0.001175:
10F: 0.001275:
110: 0.001275:
111: 0.001075:
112: 0.001075:
113: 0.001175:
114: 0.001175:
115: 0.001175:
116: 0.001175:
117: 0.001375:
118: 0.001275:
119: 0.001275:
11A: 0.001175:
11B: 0.001175:
11C: 0.001175:
11D: 0.001175:
11E: 0.001175:
11F: 0.001175:
120: 0.001275:
121: 0.001175:
122: 0.001175:
123: 0.001175:
124: 0.001175:
```

Repeatability Error, SN = 4130 (Continued)

```
125:  0.001175:
126:  0.001175:
127:  0.001275:
128:  0.001075:
129:  0.001175:
12A:  0.001275:
12B:  0.001175:
12C:  0.001175:
12D:  0.001275:
12E:  0.001075:
12F:  0.001275:
130:  0.001175:
131:  0.001175:
132:  0.001075:
133:  0.001075:
134:  0.001275:
135:  0.001275:
136:  0.001275:
137:  0.001075:
138:  0.001175:
139:  0.001275:
13A:  0.001175:
13B:  0.001275:
13C:  0.001175:
13D:  0.001175:
13E:  0.001275:
13F:  0.001075:
140:  0.001075:
141:  0.001075:
142:  0.001075:
143:  0.001075:
144:  0.001175:
145:  0.001275:
146:  0.001375:
147:  0.001375:
148:  0.001275:
149:  0.001275:
14A:  0.001275:
14B:  0.001275:
14C:  0.001375:
14D:  0.001375:
14E:  0.001175:
14F:  0.001175:
150:  0.001175:
151:  0.001275:
152:  0.001375:
153:  0.001275:
154:  0.001275:
155:  0.001175:
156:  0.001175:
157:  0.001275:
158:  0.001175:
159:  0.001175:
15A:  0.001175:
15B:  0.001275:
15C:  0.001175:
15D:  0.001375:
15E:  0.001275:
15F:  0.001375:
160:  0.001375:
```

Repeatability Error, SN = 4130 (Continued)

AP-406

```
161:  0.001275:
162:  0.001175:
163:  0.001175:
164:  0.001275:
165:  0.001175:
166:  0.001175:
167:  0.001375:
168:  0.001375:
169:  0.001475:
16A:  0.001175:
16B:  0.001075:
16C:  0.001275:
16D:  0.001275:
16E:  0.001175:
16F:  0.001175:
170:  0.001275:
171:  0.001275:
172:  0.001175:
173:  0.001175:
174:  0.001275:
175:  0.001275:
176:  0.001275:
177:  0.001175:
178:  0.001275:
179:  0.001275:
17A:  0.001075:
17B:  0.001275:
17C:  0.001175:
17D:  0.001275:
17E:  0.001075:
17F:  0.001275:
180:  0.001275:
181:  0.001375:
182:  0.001375:
183:  0.001275:
184:  0.001375:
185:  0.001275:
186:  0.001075:
187:  0.001075:
188:  0.001275:
189:  0.001175:
18A:  0.001175:
18B:  0.001275:
18C:  0.001275:
18D:  0.001275:
18E:  0.001175:
18F:  0.001275:
190:  0.001175:
191:  0.001275:
192:  0.001175:
193:  0.001175:
194:  0.001075:
195:  0.001375:
196:  0.001275:
197:  0.001175:
198:  0.001175:
199:  0.001375:
19A:  0.001375:
19B:  0.001275:
19C:  0.001175:
```

Repeatability Error, SN = 4130 (Continued)

```
19D: 0.001275:
19E: 0.001275:
19F: 0.001275:
1A0: 0.001275:
1A1: 0.001275:
1A2: 0.001375:
1A3: 0.001475:
1A4: 0.001275:
1A5: 0.001075:
1A6: 0.001175:
1A7: 0.001275:
1A8: 0.001175:
1A9: 0.001375:
1AA: 0.001275:
1AB: 0.001275:
1AC: 0.001175:
1AD: 0.001175:
1AE: 0.001175:
1AF: 0.001175:
1B0: 0.001075:
1B1: 0.001375:
1B2: 0.000975:
1B3: 0.001175:
1B4: 0.001075:
1B5: 0.001375:
1B6: 0.001375:
1B7: 0.001175:
1B8: 0.001175:
1B9: 0.001375:
1BA: 0.001175:
1BB: 0.001475:
1BC: 0.001175:
1BD: 0.001275:
1BE: 0.001175:
1BF: 0.001175:
1C0: 0.001175:
1C1: 0.001175:
1C2: 0.001175:
1C3: 0.001275:
1C4: 0.001375:
1C5: 0.001275:
1C6: 0.001175:
1C7: 0.001175:
1C8: 0.001375:
1C9: 0.001175:
1CA: 0.001075:
1CB: 0.001075:
1CC: 0.001275:
1CD: 0.001375:
1CE: 0.001275:
1CF: 0.001075:
1D0: 0.001175:
1D1: 0.001275:
1D2: 0.001275:
1D3: 0.001275:
1D4: 0.001275:
1D5: 0.001275:
1D6: 0.001275:
1D7: 0.001175:
1D8: 0.001275:
```

Repeatability Error, SN = 4130 (Continued)

AP-406

```
1D9:  0.001275:
1DA:  0.001275:
1DB:  0.001175:
1DC:  0.001175:
1DD:  0.001275:
1DE:  0.001175:
1DF:  0.001375:
1E0:  0.001375:
1E1:  0.001075:
1E2:  0.001275:
1E3:  0.001175:
1E4:  0.001175:
1E5:  0.001275:
1E6:  0.001175:
1E7:  0.001275:
1E8:  0.001175:
1E9:  0.001175:
1EA:  0.001175:
1EB:  0.001075:
1EC:  0.001275:
1ED:  0.001275:
1EE:  0.001175:
1EF:  0.001275:
1F0:  0.001375:
1F1:  0.001075:
1F2:  0.001175:
1F3:  0.001574:
1F4:  0.001275:
1F5:  0.001175:
1F6:  0.001175:
1F7:  0.001275:
1F8:  0.001175:
1F9:  0.001175:
1FA:  0.001175:
1FB:  0.001275:
1FC:  0.001175:
1FD:  0.001175:
1FE:  0.001275:
1FF:  0.001275:
200:  0.001275:
201:  0.001375:
202:  0.001375:
203:  0.001175:
204:  0.001175:
205:  0.001275:
206:  0.001175:
207:  0.001375:
208:  0.001275:
209:  0.001175:
20A:  0.001175:
20B:  0.001275:
20C:  0.001175:
20D:  0.001275:
20E:  0.001175:
20F:  0.001175:
210:  0.001175:
211:  0.001175:
212:  0.001075:
213:  0.001275:
214:  0.001175:
```

Repeatability Error, SN = 4130 (Continued)

AP-406

```
215:  0.001275:
216:  0.001275:
217:  0.001275:
218:  0.001275:
219:  0.001375:
21A:  0.001175:
21B:  0.001275:
21C:  0.001275:
21D:  0.001275:
21E:  0.001175:
21F:  0.001175:
220:  0.001375:
221:  0.001275:
222:  0.001375:
223:  0.001375:
224:  0.001175:
225:  0.001375:
226:  0.001175:
227:  0.001375:
228:  0.001175:
229:  0.001275:
22A:  0.001175:
22B:  0.001275:
22C:  0.001275:
22D:  0.001175:
22E:  0.001175:
22F:  0.001075:
230:  0.001275:
231:  0.001175:
232:  0.001175:
233:  0.001275:
234:  0.001275:
235:  0.001375:
236:  0.001375:
237:  0.001275:
238:  0.001275:
239:  0.001175:
23A:  0.001175:
23B:  0.001175:
23C:  0.001175:
23D:  0.001375:
23E:  0.001175:
23F:  0.001275:
240:  0.001275:
241:  0.001175:
242:  0.001275:
243:  0.001275:
244:  0.001275:
245:  0.001375:
246:  0.001075:
247:  0.001175:
248:  0.001175:
249:  0.001375:
24A:  0.001175:
24B:  0.001275:
24C:  0.001075:
24D:  0.001175:
24E:  0.001375:
24F:  0.001375:
250:  0.001275:
```

Repeatability Error, SN = 4130 (Continued)

AP-406

```
251: 0.001175:
252: 0.001275:
253: 0.001275:
254: 0.001175:
255: 0.001375:
256: 0.001275:
257: 0.001275:
258: 0.001275:
259: 0.001175:
25A: 0.001075:
25B: 0.001175:
25C: 0.001475:
25D: 0.001275:
25E: 0.001275:
25F: 0.001175:
260: 0.001275:
261: 0.001175:
262: 0.001175:
263: 0.001275:
264: 0.001275:
265: 0.001275:
266: 0.001175:
267: 0.001375:
268: 0.001275:
269: 0.001275:
26A: 0.001175:
26B: 0.001175:
26C: 0.001375:
26D: 0.001375:
26E: 0.001375:
26F: 0.001475:
270: 0.001175:
271: 0.001375:
272: 0.001175:
273: 0.001075:
274: 0.001275:
275: 0.001175:
276: 0.001275:
277: 0.001375:
278: 0.001375:
279: 0.001375:
27A: 0.001275:
27B: 0.001275:
27C: 0.001275:
27D: 0.001175:
27E: 0.001075:
27F: 0.001275:
280: 0.001275:
281: 0.001375:
282: 0.001275:
283: 0.001275:
284: 0.001275:
285: 0.001375:
286: 0.001275:
287: 0.001375:
288: 0.001175:
289: 0.001275:
28A: 0.001175:
28B: 0.001375:
28C: 0.001175:
```

Repeatability Error, SN = 4130 (Continued)

AP-406

```
28D: 0.001375:
28E: 0.001175:
28F: 0.001375:
290: 0.001275:
291: 0.001275:
292: 0.001175:
293: 0.001175:
294: 0.001175:
295: 0.001175:
296: 0.001275:
297: 0.001375:
298: 0.001275:
299: 0.001375:
29A: 0.001375:
29B: 0.001375:
29C: 0.001275:
29D: 0.001175:
29E: 0.001375:
29F: 0.001175:
2A0: 0.001175:
2A1: 0.001175:
2A2: 0.001375:
2A3: 0.001275:
2A4: 0.001175:
2A5: 0.001175:
2A6: 0.001175:
2A7: 0.001275:
2A8: 0.001475:
2A9: 0.001275:
2AA: 0.001175:
2AB: 0.001275:
2AC: 0.001375:
2AD: 0.001275:
2AE: 0.001275:
2AF: 0.001175:
2B0: 0.001175:
2B1: 0.001175:
2B2: 0.001175:
2B3: 0.001275:
2B4: 0.001175:
2B5: 0.001275:
2B6: 0.001175:
2B7: 0.001275:
2B8: 0.001275:
2B9: 0.001275:
2BA: 0.001275:
2BB: 0.001375:
2BC: 0.001275:
2BD: 0.001375:
2BE: 0.001375:
2BF: 0.001375:
2C0: 0.001375:
2C1: 0.001375:
2C2: 0.001375:
2C3: 0.001375:
2C4: 0.001375:
2C5: 0.001475:
2C6: 0.001275:
2C7: 0.001375:
2C8: 0.001275:
```

Repeatability Error, SN = 4130 (Continued)

AP-406

```
2C9:  0.001375:
2CA:  0.001175:
2CB:  0.001275:
2CC:  0.001275:
2CD:  0.001475:
2CE:  0.001275:
2CF:  0.001175:
2D0:  0.001175:
2D1:  0.001175:
2D2:  0.001275:
2D3:  0.001375:
2D4:  0.001175:
2D5:  0.001175:
2D6:  0.001275:
2D7:  0.001375:
2D8:  0.001275:
2D9:  0.001275:
2DA:  0.001475:
2DB:  0.001475:
2DC:  0.001375:
2DD:  0.001375:
2DE:  0.001375:
2DF:  0.001375:
2E0:  0.001175:
2E1:  0.001375:
2E2:  0.001275:
2E3:  0.001175:
2E4:  0.001175:
2E5:  0.001275:
2E6:  0.001275:
2E7:  0.001375:
2E8:  0.001175:
2E9:  0.001275:
2EA:  0.001275:
2EB:  0.001175:
2EC:  0.001375:
2ED:  0.001275:
2EE:  0.001275:
2EF:  0.001175:
2F0:  0.001275:
2F1:  0.001375:
2F2:  0.001375:
2F3:  0.001275:
2F4:  0.001275:
2F5:  0.001375:
2F6:  0.001475:
2F7:  0.001375:
2F8:  0.001375:
2F9:  0.001475:
2FA:  0.001275:
2FB:  0.001175:
2FC:  0.001275:
2FD:  0.001275:
2FE:  0.001275:
2FF:  0.001275:
300:  0.001075:
301:  0.001275:
302:  0.001375:
303:  0.001275:
304:  0.001175:
```

Repeatability Error, SN = 4130 (Continued)

AP-406

```
305:  0.001475:
306:  0.001275:
307:  0.001375:
308:  0.001375:
309:  0.001275:
30A:  0.001275:
30B:  0.001375:
30C:  0.001275:
30D:  0.001475:
30E:  0.001275:
30F:  0.001375:
310:  0.001175:
311:  0.001175:
312:  0.001275:
313:  0.001275:
314:  0.001375:
315:  0.001275:
316:  0.001275:
317:  0.001275:
318:  0.001175:
319:  0.001375:
31A:  0.001275:
31B:  0.001075:
31C:  0.001175:
31D:  0.001375:
31E:  0.001375:
31F:  0.001375:
320:  0.001375:
321:  0.001375:
322:  0.001375:
323:  0.001275:
324:  0.001174:
325:  0.001575:
326:  0.001275:
327:  0.001475:
328:  0.001174:
329:  0.001375:
32A:  0.001275:
32B:  0.001275:
32C:  0.001375:
32D:  0.001375:
32E:  0.001375:
32F:  0.001375:
330:  0.001174:
331:  0.001174:
332:  0.001475:
333:  0.001275:
334:  0.001275:
335:  0.001575:
336:  0.001475:
337:  0.001174:
338:  0.001275:
339:  0.001275:
33A:  0.001275:
33B:  0.001275:
33C:  0.001375:
33D:  0.001375:
33E:  0.001275:
33F:  0.001275:
340:  0.001174:
```

Repeatability Error, SN = 4130 (Continued)

```
341:  0.001375:
342:  0.001375:
343:  0.001375:
344:  0.001174:
345:  0.001275:
346:  0.001174:
347:  0.001575:
348:  0.001375:
349:  0.001275:
34A:  0.001174:
34B:  0.001275:
34C:  0.001275:
34D:  0.001275:
34E:  0.001275:
34F:  0.001275:
350:  0.001375:
351:  0.001375:
352:  0.001375:
353:  0.001375:
354:  0.001275:
355:  0.001375:
356:  0.001375:
357:  0.001375:
358:  0.001074:
359:  0.001275:
35A:  0.001074:
35B:  0.001375:
35C:  0.001375:
35D:  0.001375:
35E:  0.001275:
35F:  0.001375:
360:  0.001174:
361:  0.001375:
362:  0.001275:
363:  0.001275:
364:  0.001275:
365:  0.001375:
366:  0.001375:
367:  0.001375:
368:  0.001275:
369:  0.001174:
36A:  0.001275:
36B:  0.001375:
36C:  0.001375:
36D:  0.001275:
36E:  0.001275:
36F:  0.001475:
370:  0.001375:
371:  0.001275:
372:  0.001375:
373:  0.001375:
374:  0.001275:
375:  0.001275:
376:  0.001275:
377:  0.001275:
378:  0.001275:
379:  0.001575:
37A:  0.001475:
37B:  0.001375:
37C:  0.001275:
```

Repeatability Error, SN = 4130 (Continued)

AP-406

```
37D:  0.001375:
37E:  0.001375:
37F:  0.001375:
380:  0.001475:
381:  0.001475:
382:  0.001275:
383:  0.001475:
384:  0.001375:
385:  0.001475:
386:  0.001275:
387:  0.001275:
388:  0.001375:
389:  0.001174:
38A:  0.001275:
38B:  0.001275:
38C:  0.001275:
38D:  0.001275:
38E:  0.001275:
38F:  0.001275:
390:  0.001275:
391:  0.001174:
392:  0.001375:
393:  0.001375:
394:  0.001375:
395:  0.001375:
396:  0.001074:
397:  0.001275:
398:  0.001375:
399:  0.001375:
39A:  0.001275:
39B:  0.001375:
39C:  0.001275:
39D:  0.001275:
39E:  0.001475:
39F:  0.001375:
3A0:  0.001275:
3A1:  0.001275:
3A2:  0.001275:
3A3:  0.001275:
3A4:  0.001375:
3A5:  0.001275:
3A6:  0.001174:
3A7:  0.000974:
3A8:  0.001475:
3A9:  0.001375:
3AA:  0.001275:
3AB:  0.001475:
3AC:  0.001275:
3AD:  0.001375:
3AE:  0.001375:
3AF:  0.001375:
3B0:  0.001475:
3B1:  0.001174:
3B2:  0.001174:
3B3:  0.001275:
3B4:  0.001275:
3B5:  0.001275:
3B6:  0.001275:
3B7:  0.001375:
3B8:  0.001375:
```

Repeatability Error, SN = 4130 (Continued)

```
3B9:  0.001275:
3BA:  0.001275:
3BB:  0.001475:
3BC:  0.001275:
3BD:  0.001375:
3BE:  0.001174:
3BF:  0.001275:
3C0:  0.001275:
3C1:  0.001174:
3C2:  0.001174:
3C3:  0.001475:
3C4:  0.001275:
3C5:  0.001275:
3C6:  0.001375:
3C7:  0.001174:
3C8:  0.001275:
3C9:  0.001275:
3CA:  0.001174:
3CB:  0.001375:
3CC:  0.001375:
3CD:  0.001375:
3CE:  0.001275:
3CF:  0.001275:
3D0:  0.001475:
3D1:  0.001875:
3D2:  0.001375:
3D3:  0.001375:
3D4:  0.001375:
3D5:  0.001375:
3D6:  0.001375:
3D7:  0.001375:
3D8:  0.001375:
3D9:  0.001275:
3DA:  0.001174:
3DB:  0.001475:
3DC:  0.001475:
3DD:  0.001375:
3DE:  0.001275:
3DF:  0.001375:
3E0:  0.001174:
3E1:  0.001575:
3E2:  0.001375:
3E3:  0.001275:
3E4:  0.001275:
3E5:  0.001375:
3E6:  0.001475:
3E7:  0.001275:
3E8:  0.001275:
3E9:  0.001575:
3EA:  0.001575:
3EB:  0.001275:
3EC:  0.001275:
3ED:  0.001375:
3EE:  0.001174:
3EF:  0.001475:
3F0:  0.001275:
3F1:  0.001375:
3F2:  0.001174:
3F3:  0.001475:
3F4:  0.001475:
3F5:  0.001174:
3F6:  0.001275:
3F7:  0.001275:
3F8:  0.001275:
3F9:  0.001275:
3FA:  0.001174:
3FB:  0.001275:
3FC:  0.001275:
3FD:  0.001275:
3FE:  0.001375:
```

Repeatability Error, SN = 4130 (Continued)

APPENDIX E
BIBLIOGRAPHY

A/D Processing with Microcontrollers, Katausky, Horden, Smith

Apfel, R., et. al., "Signal-Processing Chips enrich telephone line- card Architecture". Electronics, May 5, 1982.

Analog Devices - Data-Acquisition Databook 1984, Volume 1

Blahut, Richard E., "Fast algorithms for digital signal processing", Addison Wesley Publishing Company, Inc., 1985.

Boyes, ed. - Syncro and Resolver Conversion, 1980

Brown, Robert Grover, "Introduction to random signal analysis and Kalman filtering". John Wiley \& Sons, Inc., 1983.

Burr-Brown Application Note, Testing of Analog-to-Digital Converters

Burton and Dexter - Microprocessor Systems Handbook, 1977

Candy, J., et. al., "The Structure of Quantization Noise from Sigma-Delta Modulation", IEEE Transaction on Comm. Vol. Com. 29, No. 9, Sept. 1981.

Candy, J., et. al., "Using Triangularly Weighted Interpolation to Get 13-Bit PCM from a Sigma-Delta Modulator", IEEE Transaction on Comm., Nov. 1976.

Electronic Analog-to-Digital Converters, Seitzer, Pretzl, Handy

Handbook of Electronic Calculations, Chapter 15, Analog-Digital Conversion

Harris Analog and Telecom Data Book

IEEE 162

IEEE STD. 746-1984

Intel Application Note AP-124 - High-Speed Digital Servos for Motor Control Using the 2920/21 Signal Processor

Intel Application Note AP-125 - Designing Microcontroller Systems for Electrically Noisy Environments

Irwensen, J., "Calculated Quantization Noise of Single - Integration Delta Modulation Coders" BSTJ Sept. 1969.

ITT Digital 2000 VLSI Digital TV System, MAA 2300 Audio A/D Converter, Edition 1983/9.

MIL-M-38510/135 June 4, 1984

MIL-M-38510/135 May 6, 1985

Modern Electronic Circuits Reference Manual

NBS Staff Reports, May/June 1981 P.22/23

Sheingold, ed. - Analog-Digital Conversion Handbook, 1972

Sheingold, ed. - Analog-Digital Conversion Notes, 1977

Sheingold, ed. - Non-Linear Circuits Handbook, 1974

Sheingold, ed. - Transducer Interfacing Handbook, 1980

Steele, R., "Delta Modulation Systems", Pentech Press Limited, 1975.

Taylor, Fred U., "Digital filter design handbook", Marcel Dekker, Inc., 1983.

Terminology Related to the Perf of S/H, A/D, D/A Circuits, IEEE Transactions

intel.

AP-428

APPLICATION NOTE

Distributed Motor Control Using the 80C196KB

TIM SCHAFER
MICHAEL CHEVALIER
80C196KB APPLICATIONS

December 1993

Order Number: 270701-001

DISTRIBUTED MOTOR CONTROL USING THE 80C196KB

CONTENTS

1.0 INTRODUCTION 5-286

2.0 HARDWARE 5-287
   2.1 Optical Encoders 5-287
   2.2 Interfacing to TIMER2 5-290
   2.3 Interfacing to the HSI 5-290
   2.4 Driving a DC Servo Motor 5-291
   2.5 Using the Dedicated PWM Output 5-291
   2.6 Using the HSO to Generate PWMs 5-293
   2.7 Current Limiting 5-294

3.0 SOFTWARE 5-296
   3.1 Main Initialization Routine 5-297
   3.2 Software Timer Interrupt Routine 5-297
   3.3 PID Control Algorithm 5-299
   3.4 Position PID Software 5-299
   3.5 Velocity Profile 5-301
   3.6 Trapezoidal Profile Calculation .. 5-302
   3.7 Fast Execution of Control Algorithms 5-303

4.0 DISTRIBUTED CONTROL 5-305
   4.1 Receive Interrupt Service Routine 5-306
   4.2 Manual Positioning 5-306
   4.3 Motor Positioning 5-306
   4.4 Master Polling of Position 5-307

5.0 DISTRIBUTED CONTROL OF A SIX AXIS ROBOT 5-309
   5.1 Hardware Interface 5-309
   5.2 Human Interface 5-311
   5.3 Control Screen for the Robot 5-311
   5.4 Programmed Modes 5-311

6.0 CONCLUSION 5-312

AP-428

1.0 INTRODUCTION

Distributed control of servo motors has a wide range of applications including industrial control, factory automation and robotics. The tasks involved in controlling a servo motor include position and velocity measurement, implementation of control algorithms, detection of overrun and stress conditions, and communication back to a central controller. The 80C196KB high performance microcontroller provides a low cost solution for handling these required control tasks.

The 80C196KB microcontroller is a highly integrated and high performance member of the MCS®-96 family. The part is available in ROM (83C196KB) and EPROM (87C196KB) versions. A block diagram of the 80C196KB is shown in Figure 2. The availability of a variety of on board peripherals such as timer/counters, A/D, PWM, Serial Port and High Speed Input and Output capture/compare timer subsystem provides for a flexible architecture for control applications at a reasonable cost.

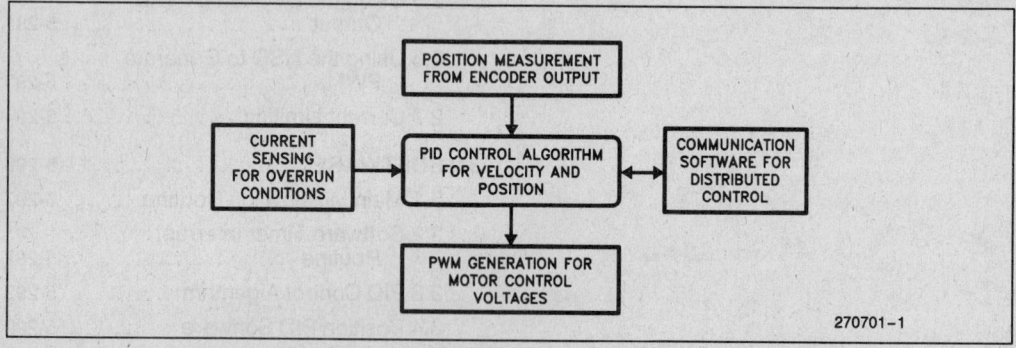

Figure 1. Control Tasks for Distributed Control of a Servo Motor

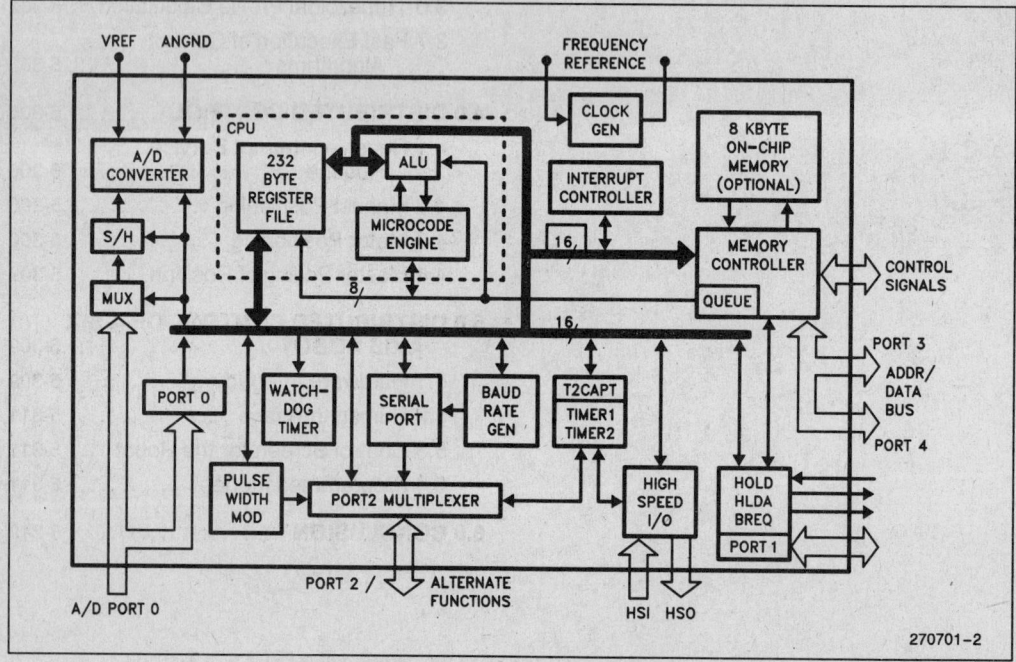

Figure 2. 80C196KB Block Diagram

AP-428

This application note describes several different methods for motor control using the on board peripherals of the 80C196KB. Hardware and Software techniques are addressed to generate PWMs for driving motors and to measure position from the output of precision optical encoders.

A Proportional, Integral and Differential (PID) algorithm controls both the position and velocity of the motor. The PID algorithm employs proportional, integral and differential feedback to control the system characteristics of the motor. The motor can be moved either manually or under the control of a velocity profile. The mode used to position the motor is determined by commands received from a master controller.

Communication to the master controller was implemented using the onboard serial port of the 80C196KB. The application of distributed control to position and program a six axis robot arm using six separate motors will be described. Each 80C196KB motor controller acts as a slave under control of the master. An IBM PC was selected as the master controller for the robot. Turbo Prolog was used to develop the human interface. A robot programming language and control screen was produced to program movements of each individual motor.

The motor control hardware, taking full advantage of the peripheral features of the 80C196KB, will be discussed first. The control software will be discussed later.

2.0 HARDWARE

The hardware tasks required to control a servo motor under the command of a centralized controller include the following:

1) Feedback of the motor position and direction.
2) Control of the motor speed and direction.
3) Detection of motor overrun conditions.
4) Communication from/to a master controller.

Two different hardware interface examples for controlling a servo motor are shown in Figures 3 and 4. The first example controls one motor using TIMER2 and the dedicated PWM unit on the 80C196KB and would best fit a high performance, high resolution application. Example number 2 uses the HSI (High Speed Inputs) and the HSO (High Speed Outputs) to control two motors. The second method can control up to four motors by trading off some performance and resolution.

This section deals with the hardware and software requirements of acquiring position feedback from incremental shaft encoders and generating outputs to drive DC servo motors. A current limiting circuit which is useful in determining when the motor has stalled is also presented. Current monitoring can also control the torque to prevent the motor from crushing an object. The closed loop digital control algorithms are discussed in the software section.

2.1 Optical Encoders

Optical encoders can be used to measure the position of rotating equipment. They provide a cost effective solution for digital position and velocity feedback to a microcontroller. Encoders produce two pulse trains which give an incremental position count. Velocity and acceleration may be calculated by measuring the number of counts in a given sample period. Or, in a slow speed system, velocity and acceleration can be measured directly from the time between edges of the pulse train. Acceleration and velocity calculations are discussed in detail in the software section.

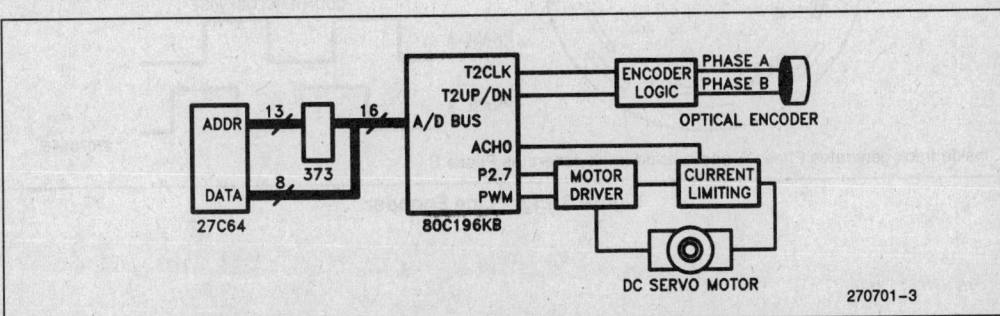

Figure 3. Block Diagram of Motor Control Hardware using PWM and TIMER2

AP-428

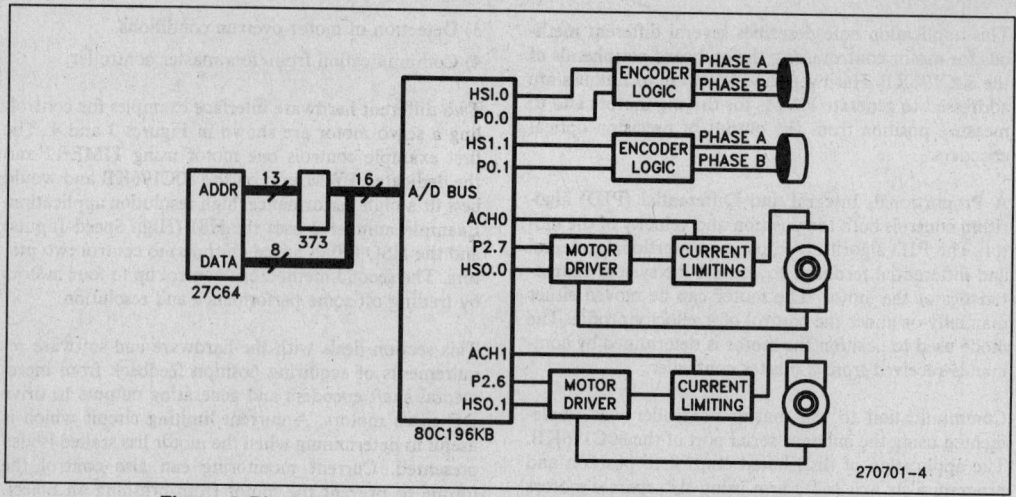

Figure 4. Block Diagram of Motor Control Hardware using HSO and HSI

Pulse trains from an encoder can vary from two pulses per revolution for low cost applications, to over 5000 pulses per revolution for high resolution requirements. Figure 5 shows an eight line encoder along with the associated waveforms. A small amount of external logic and a few discrete components decode a position count and a direction indication from phase A and phase B.

External logic for encoders is shown in Figure 6. Figure 7 shows a timing diagram of the circuit. Bold type denotes the input and desired output waveforms. The phases from an encoder are mechanically produced electrical signals. When the motor rotates slowly, the phases inherently exhibit slow rise and fall times. The four Schmitt triggers in the circuit protect against oscillation in the digital circuit due to these long rise and fall times.

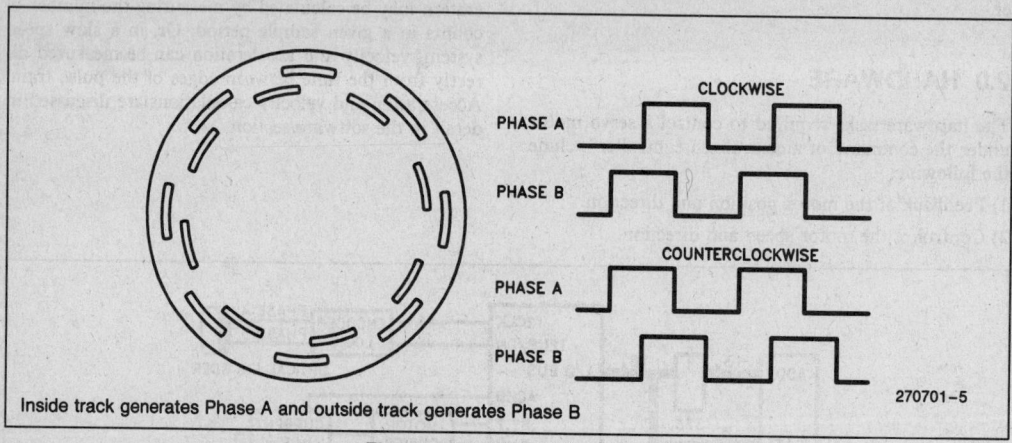

Inside track generates Phase A and outside track generates Phase B

Figure 5. Eight Line Encoder

AP-428

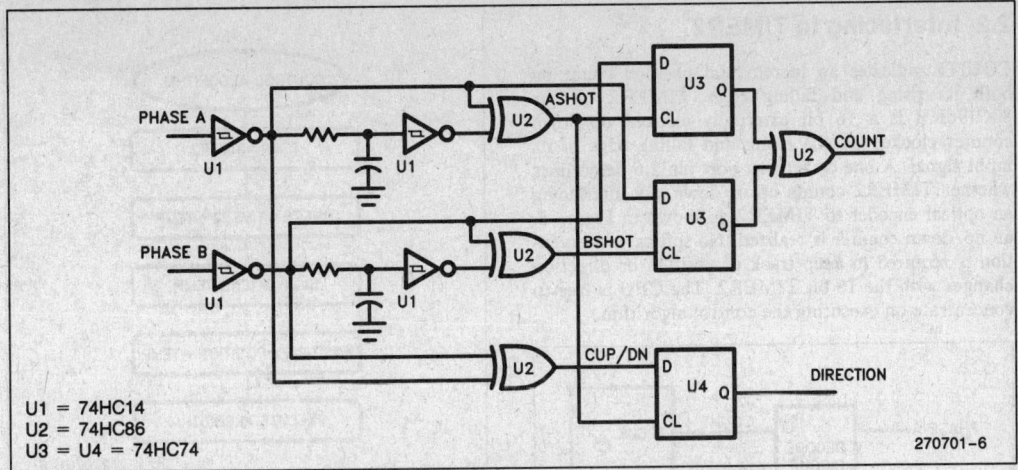

Figure 6. External Logic for Encoders

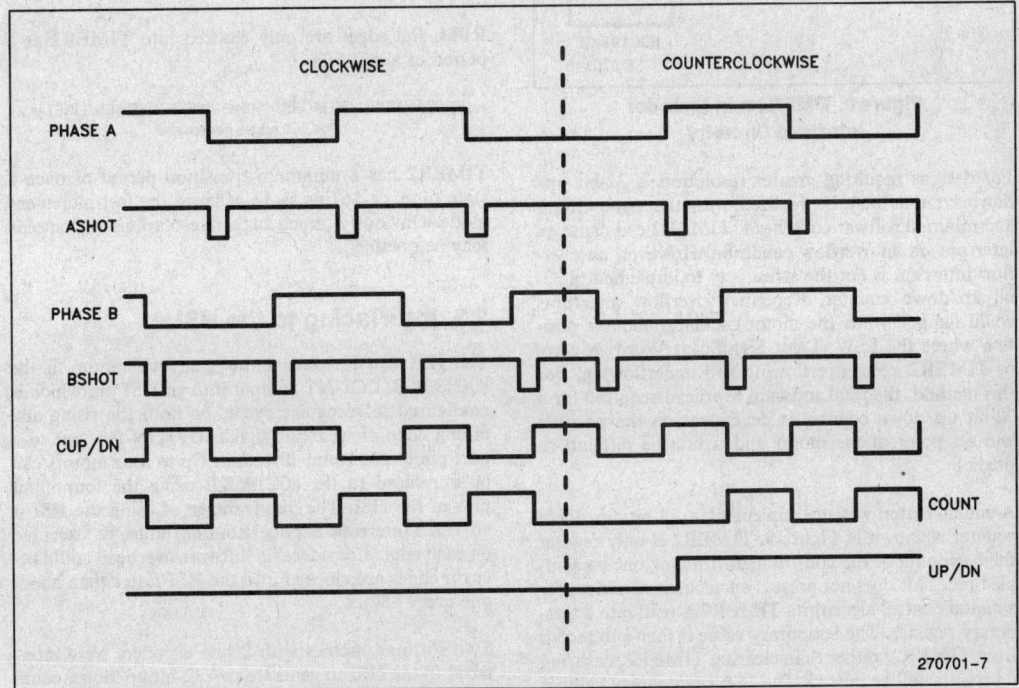

Figure 7. Timing Diagram for Logic Circuit

A simple one-shot is constructed with an RC circuit and an XOR gate to generate a pulse on each edge of each phase. ASHOT clocks phase B and BSHOT clocks phase A. This technique of digital filtering insures repetitive edges on a single phase without an edge on the other phase are not passed on to the processor. Repetitive edges occur when the motor changes direction.

Further logic obtains a direction or UP/DN bit. Note the first edge after a direction change is lost. A lost edge does not affect the count since the first transition is lost in both directions. Since an edge is lost in each direction, the circuit has an absolute resolution of one edge.

2.2 Interfacing to TIMER2

COUNT indicates an incremental position count on both its rising and falling edge. TIMER2 on the 80C196KB is a 16 bit externally clocked up/down counter clocked on the rising and falling edge of its input signal. A one or zero on port pin 2.6 determines whether TIMER2 counts up or down. By interfacing an optical encoder to TIMER2 as shown in Figure 8, an up/down counter is realized. No software intervention is required to keep track of position or direction changes with the 16 bit TIMER2. The CPU is free to concentrate on executing the control algorithm.

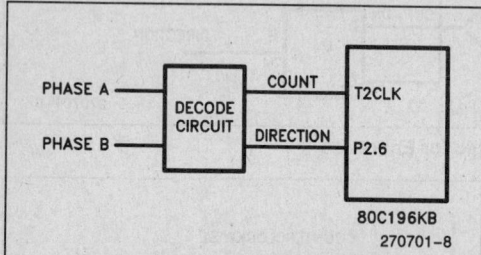

Figure 8. TIMER2 and Encoder Interface Circuitry

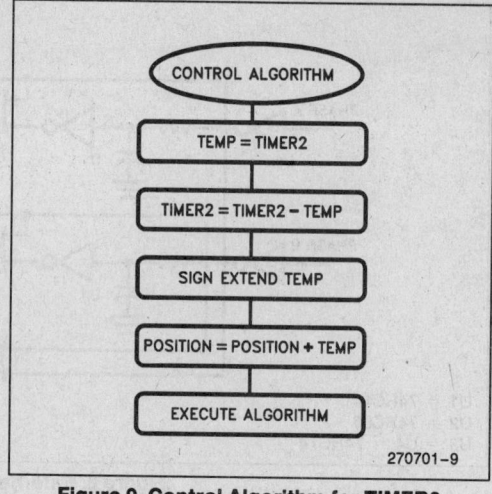

Figure 9. Control Algorithm for TIMER2

For designs requiring greater resolution, a 32-bit up/down counter may be realized with the same circuit and minimal software overhead. TIMER2 can cause an interrupt on an overflow condition. However, an overflow interrupt is not the safest way to implement a 32-bit up/down counter. Repetitive overflow interrupts could happen when the motor oscillates about a position where the LSW (Least Significant Word) is zero, or TIMER2 keeps overflowing and underflowing. For this method, the total software overhead required for a 32-bit up/down counter is dependent on the position and set point of the motor and would be difficult to predict.

A much better way to implement a 32-bit up/down counter is shown in Figure 9. TIMER2 is only read at the beginning of the control algorithm, or once a sample time. This does not present an accuracy problem for a digital control algorithm. TIMER2 is read into a temporary register. The temporary value is then subtracted from TIMER2, rather than clearing TIMER2, ensuring no counts will be missed. The 16-bit temporary value is sign extended to form a two's complement 32-bit value and added to the old 32-bit position value to form the current position value. This 32-bit up/down counter provides the accuracy needed for a control loop while keeping software overhead constant under all conditions.

A Pittman motor with a Hewlett Packard HEDS - 5310 512 line incremental shaft encoder was interfaced to TIMER2. Even at a maximum shaft rotation of 6000 RPM, the edges are only clocked into TIMER2 at a period of about 5 μs.

(6000 R/M) * (1/60 M/SEC) * (512 LINE) * (4 EDGES/LINE) = 204,800 edges per second

TIMER2 has a minimum transition period of once a state time, or 167 ns @ 12 Mhz, in the fast increment mode. Obviously, much higher resolutions and speeds may be obtained.

2.3 Interfacing to the HSI

The HSI can interface more than one motor to the 80C196KB. COUNT is input into an HSI pin which is configured to recognize events on both the rising and falling edge of its input signal. UP/DN is input to a port pin to determine direction. Up to four motors can be interfaced to the 80C196KB using the four input pins of the HSI. The disadvantage of using the HSI is an ISR (Interrupt Service Routine) must be executed on each edge. Considerable software overhead could occur if edges are clocked into the HSI faster than about one every 150 μs.

Two Pittman motors with 2 line encoders were interfaced to the HSI to generate two 32-bit up/down counters as an example. With both motors turning at a maximum velocity of 6000 RPM, an edge will occur every 625 μs. The ISR in Figure 10 processes the edges from the encoders and updates the position values and executes in about 15 μs @ 12 MHZ on the 80C196KB. This still allows 97.6% (1 − 15/1250) of the total processing time to implement control algorithms and other I/O functions.

AP-428

```
;;;;;;;;;;;;;;;;;;;;;;;;;;;;;;;;;;;;;;;;;;;;;;;;;;;;;;;;;;;;;;;;;;
;;;;;          HSI INTERRUPT SERVICE ROUTINE               ;;;;;;;;;
;;;;;;;;;;;;;;;;;;;;;;;;;;;;;;;;;;;;;;;;;;;;;;;;;;;;;;;;;;;;;;;;;;
hsi_data_int:
        pushf
        orb   ios1_bak,ios1              ;test for any data received
        jbc   ios1_bak,7,no_data
more_in_fifo:
        andb  ios1_bak,#01111111b
mot_4_cnt:
        jbc   hsi_status,0,mot_5_cnt     ;test for count of motor 4
        jbs   port1,0,mot_4_up           ;test for up/dn bit
        sub   mot_4_pos,#1               ;decrement motor 4 position
        subc  mot_4_pos+2,#0
        br    mot_5_cnt
mot_4_up:
        add   mot_4_pos,#1               ;increment motor 4 position
        addc  mot_4_pos+2,#0
mot_5_cnt:
        jbc   hsi_status,4,test_again
        jbs   port1,1,mot_5_up
        sub   mot_5_pos,#1               ;decrement motor 5 position
        subc  mot_5_pos+2,#0
        br    test_again
mot_5_up:
        add   mot_5_pos,#1               ;increment motor 5 position
        addc  mot_5_pos+2,#0
test_again:
        ld    ax,hsi_time                ;read hsi_time to step fifo
        nop                              ;wait 8 state times for
        nop                              ;holding register to be loaded
        nop
        nop
        orb   ios1_bak,ios1              ;make sure fifo is flushed
        jbs   ios1_bak,7,more_in_fifo
no_data:
        popf
        ret
```

270701-10

Figure 10. HSI Interrupt Service Routine

The HSI approach does add flexibility. Since the HSI records a TIMER1 value with each transition, velocity and acceleration can be calculated on every edge.

2.4 Driving a DC Servo Motor

Figure 11 shows the circuit used to drive the motors. A digital output from the 80C196KB is converted into an analog signal capable of driving a DC servo motor. POWER is a PWM output from the 80C196KB. DIRECTION is a port bit which qualifies the +15 or −15 supply. A signal diagram is shown in Figure 12. Isolation between the motor power supply and the digital supply is provided by the two optical isolators preventing any inductive glitches caused by the motor turning on and off from effecting the digital circuit. The optical isolators in turn drive the two V_{FET}s. Size of the V_{FET}s was determined by the current specifications of the motors. Heat sinks were used to protect the V_{FET}s. The V_{FET}s are protected from voltage spikes by the MOV, (Metal Oxide Varistor), a type of transient absorber.

2.5 Using the Dedicated PWM Output

The PWM output unit on the 80C196KB is an 8 bit counter which increments every state time. The output is driven high when the counter equals zero and driven low when the counter matches the value in the PWM_CONTROL register. Typical PWM waveforms are given in Figure 13. A prescaler can allow the PWM counter to increment every two state times. With a 12 Mhz crystal, the PWM has a fixed output frequency of 23.6 Khz, or 11.8 Khz with the prescaler enabled.

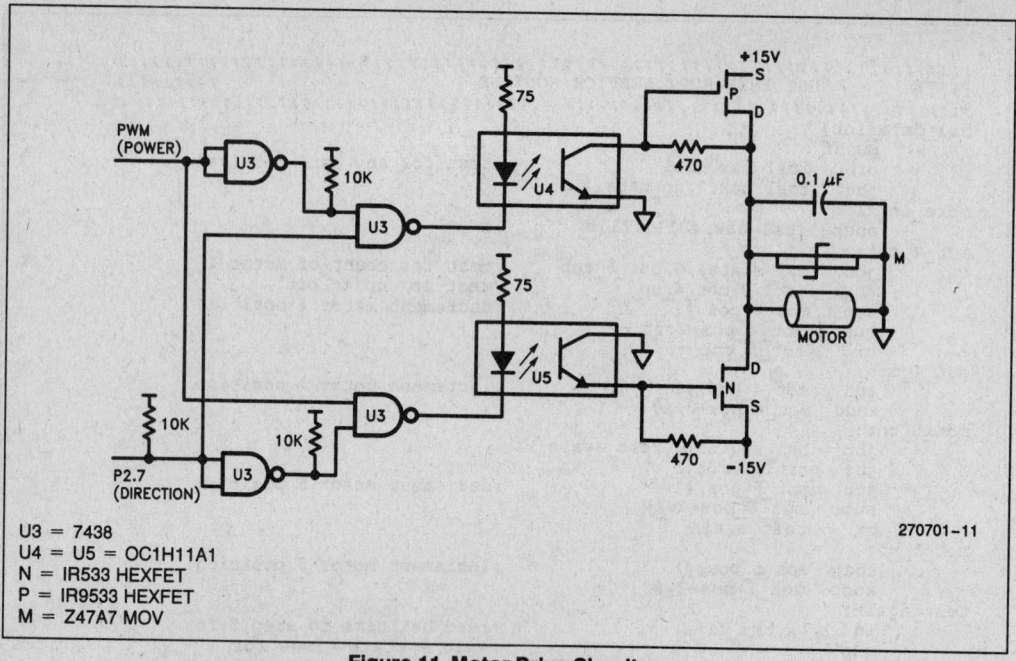

Figure 11. Motor Drive Circuitry

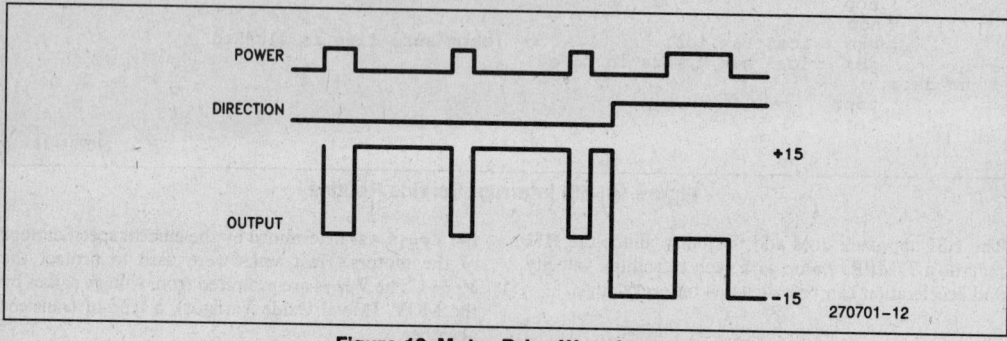

Figure 12. Motor Drive Waveforms

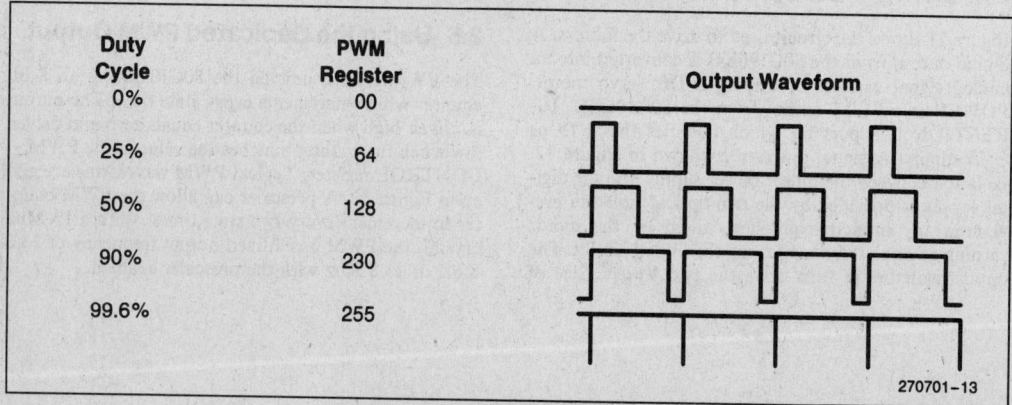

Figure 13. PWM Output Waveforms

AP-428

The PWM unit along with pin 2.7 was used to drive one motor at a fixed output frequency of 23.6 Khz. By driving the motor at this frequency, motor whine in the audible range was eliminated. Note that a 00 value in the PWM register applies full power to the motor; the desired 8 bit output value must be inverted before it is loaded into the PWM_CONTROL register to obtain the correct output.

2.6 Using the HSO to Generate PWMs

The HSO (High Speed Outputs) of the 80C196KB can generate up to four PWMs. The HSO triggers events at specified times based on TIMER1 or TIMER2. For the specific purpose of generating PWMs, the event is driving an output pin high or low. HSO commands are loaded onto the CAM, (Content Addressable Memory), which specify the time and event to take place. The CAM is eight positions deep. The HSO triggers the event on a successful compare with the associated timer.

The 80C196KB can optionally lock commands onto the CAM. This feature is very useful for generating PWMs using TIMER2 as the time base. Figure 14 shows an example of two PWM outputs using locked commands in the CAM. TIMER2 is clocked externally at a frequency which determines the resolution of the PWMs. TIMER2 can be clocked at a maximum frequency of once every eight state times (1.33μs @ 12 Mhz) when used with the HSO. The RESET TIMER2 @ T4 command specifies the output frequency of the PWMs. By changing the external TIMER2 clock frequency and the value of T4, the HSO can generate a wide range of PWMs.

T0 and T1 specify when the output pins will be driven low. By varying T0 and T1, the duty cycle of the output waveforms are changed. Both pins are driven high by the same command at the same time TIMER2 is reset. Since there are still four positions open in the CAM, two more PWMs could be generated and one position would still be left open in the CAM.

For this ap-note, two Pittman motors were controlled using the HSO along with port pins 2.6 and 2.7. It was desired to keep the output frequency the same as the output frequency of the on-board PWM. To accomplish this, TIMER2 was clocked every 8 state times and reset when it reached 31 counts. This makes the output frequency 23.6 Khz @ 12 Mhz with 5 bits of resolution. CLKOUT was externally divided by 16 and input into TIMER2. Since TIMER2 counts on both the positive and negative edge of its input signal, a square wave with a 16 state period clocks TIMER2 every 8 state times.

The ISR used to load commands onto the CAM is shown in Figure 15. When the control algorithm determines an output has changed, a RESET TIMER2 command gets loaded onto the CAM to generate an interrupt. The interrupt vectors to this routine and updates the CAM. To clear a locked entry from the CAM, the entire CAM must be flushed by setting IOC2.7. Care must be taken to reload all of the commands. This includes any commands not locked on the CAM.

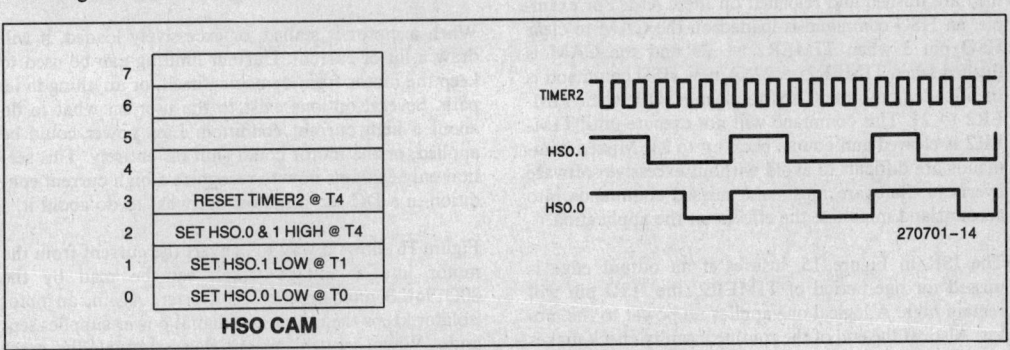

Figure 14. Two PWMs Using HSO Locked Entries

AP-428

```
timer2_reset:
        ldb     IOC2,#11000000b                 ;clear the CAM
        ld      hso_command,#11001110b          ;load reset timer2 command
        ld      hso_time,#31
        nop
        nop
        ldb     hso_command,#11100110b          ;this command will set both
        ld      hso_time,#31                    ;hso lines for the PWM

                                                ;load mot_4_power value
        cmpb    mot_4_power,#31                 ;if power is 1fh, do not load
        je      check_4                         ;this command, it will cancel
        ldb     hso_command,#11000000b          ;with the set command
        ldbze   hso_time,mot_4_power
check_4:
                                                ;load mot_5_power value
        cmpb    mot_5_power,#31                 ;if power is 1fh, do not load
        je      sanity_check                    ;this command, it will cancel
        ldb     hso_command,#11000001b          ;with set command
        ldbze   hso_time,mot_4_power
sanity_check:
        cmp     TIMER2,#32                      ;sanity check to make sure
        jnh     sane                            ;TIMER2 is not greater than 31
        clr     TIMER2
sane:
        ldb     hso_command,#39h                ;reload software timer 1
        add     swt1_period_bak,#swt1_dly_period
        ld      hso_time,swt1_period_bak
        ldb     port2,port2_bak                 ;load direction bits
        popf
        ret
```

Figure 15. HSO Interrupt Service Routine

There is the potential for commands to be missed when they are flushed and reloaded on the CAM. For example, an HSO command is loaded on the CAM to clear HSO pin 3 when TIMER2 = 23 and the CAM is flushed when TIMER2 = 22. A new HSO command is then loaded onto the CAM to clear HSO.3 when TIMER2 = 21. This command will not execute until TIMER2 is cleared and counts back up to 21. Missed commands are difficult to avoid without excessive software overhead. Software must take missed commands into account and minimize the effects on the application.

The ISR in Figure 15, insures if an output edge is missed for one period of TIMER2, the HSO pin will remain high. A logical one applies no power to the motor. Also, at the end of the routine a sanity check makes sure TIMER2 is not greater than 31.

2.7 Current Limiting

When a motor is stalled, or excessively loaded, it will draw a lot of current. Current limiting can be used to keep the motor from damaging itself, or anything in its path. Several options exist to the user on what to do about a high current condition. Less power could be applied, or the motor could shut off entirely. This section only explains how to recognize a high current condition in a DC servo motor, not what to do about it.

Figure 16 shows a way to convert the current from the motor into a voltage which can be read by the 80C196KB onboard A/D converter. Again, an opto-isolator keeps the motor and digital power supplies separate. When enough current flows through the opto-isolator, the A/D input voltage will drop down to about .7 volts. The current to the opto-isolator is varied by changing the values of the two resistors, R1 and R2 which split the current flow. By changing R1 and R2, this circuit can be adjusted to work properly with different motors and load conditions.

AP-428

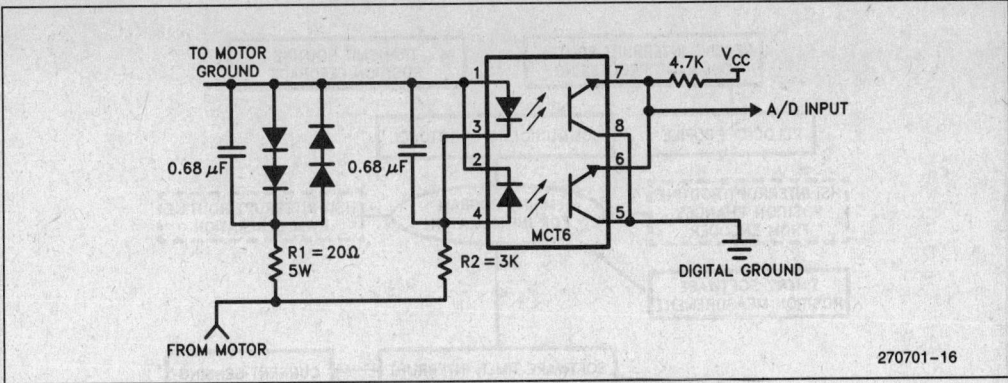

Figure 16. Current Sensing Circuitry

Motor startup current must be considered when testing for a high current condition. When a motor is started, it will draw a great deal of current. This current surge can last for a few milliseconds. Software must decide if the motor is drawing excessive current because it is stalled, or just starting. The section of code in Figure 17 executes during the control algorithm. The current must be above ad_limit for 30 sample times before software recognizes a high current condition. Of course, these values must be adjusted up or down depending on the motor and load conditions.

```
;do a current limit check
        jbs    ad_command,3,motor_around  ;if A/D still running,skip
        cmpb   ad_result_hi,ad_limit
        jh     current_ok
        incb   ad_count                   ;want to do 30h A/D conversions
        cmpb   ad_count,#30               ;before acting because of motor
                                          ;startup current
        jne    current_maybe_ok
;here is where the user inserts his code on what to do
;about a high current condition

current_ok:
        clrb   ad_count
current_maybe_ok:
        ldb    ad_command,#00001001b      ;start another a/d conversion
motor_around:
```

Figure 17. Current Sensing Software

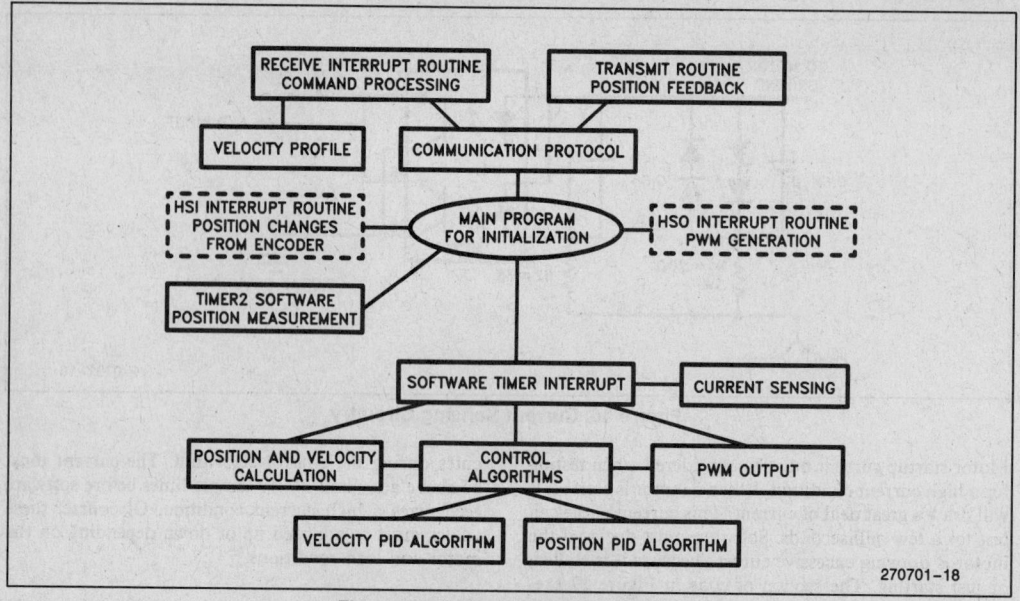

Figure 18. Software Block Diagram

3.0 SOFTWARE

A block diagram of the software is shown in Figure 18. The software consists of a main program for hardware and software initialization of the 80C196KB peripherals and programming of control tasks. The control tasks include tracking the motor position and direction, control of the motor speed and direction, detection of overrun conditions and communication to the master controller. After initialization is complete, the 80C196KB enters idle mode to preserve power while not performing control tasks. Interrupt service routines for the serial port, HSI, HSO and software timer perform the various control tasks.

The communication protocol to the main controller is implemented in the serial receive and transmit routines. Commands from the master controller move the motor in one of two modes, manual or automatic, depending on the command. The commands are listed in Figure 28.

Manual mode moves the motor clockwise or counterclockwise with a preset maximum control voltage applied. Manual mode commands include MOTOR UP, MOTOR DOWN and STOP. The MOTOR UP and MOTOR DOWN commands send the motor into manual mode. The motor continues to run in the desired direction until a STOP command is issued from the master controller. The STOP command loads the destination position with the current position and enters automatic mode.

Automatic mode positions the motor using either a position or velocity PID algorithm. The position PID algorithm is applied after reception of the STOP command or when the desired position is reached. The destination position can be changed by a POSITION command from the master controller.

The maximum motor velocity and the destination position are contained in the POSITION command. If the maximum velocity is zero, a position PID is applied to move the motor to the destination position. A non zero maximum velocity will position the motor using a velocity PID algorithm. Position and velocity input to the algorithms are calculated based on position input from the encoder.

Position information for the PID algorithms can be provided by using the High Speed Inputs or TIMER2. The HSI interrupt routine processes the direction and position information incoming from the encoder to provide current motor position. Alternatively, TIMER2 directly measures the position when used as an up/down counter. Velocity information can be calculated using the position information given a constant sampling rate. The position and velocity information are used by the PID control algorithms.

The control algorithm uses a software timer interrupt to generate the sampling rate of the control software. The main portion of the software timer routine calculates the current position and velocity, senses the motor

AP-428

current for overrun conditions, calls the PID control algorithm and generates the PWM control voltage to the motor.

The speed of the motor can be controlled using the PWM or the HSO. If the HSO is used, the HSO interrupt routine generates a PWM output to control the voltage applied to the motor. Otherwise, the PWM unit controls the voltage applied to the motor.

Each of the major software routines is covered in detail in this section.

3.1 Main Initialization Routine

The main initialization routine executes immediately following reset to initialize the 80C196KB peripherals and enable the interrupt driven control tasks. A flow chart for the main initialization routine is shown in Figure 19. The constants and variables for the control algorithms and software routines are loaded into register space for fast execution.

Next, the various peripherals are programmed to handle the control tasks. The PWM for voltage control of the servo motor is initialized. TIMER2 is programmed as an up/down counter with T2CLK as the clock source. The serial port is set to 19.2 Kbaud and programmed for mode 2 to receive incoming commands. An A/D conversion is started to check for initial stress conditions. Before the motor can be accurately positioned, an initial reference point must be established.

In order to find the reference point, an I/O port is connected to a limit switch. The motor is driven in a preset direction until the limit switch is activated. The initial position is then loaded and position PID control is applied to keep the motor stable. Position commands from the master controller can now precisely position the motor from the established reference point.

Finally, the software timer, timer overflow, receive and transmit interrupt routines are enabled and the idle mode is entered to conserve power. The routines will execute as each individual interrupt control task requires servicing. Discussion of the control tasks of each software routine is contained in the following sections.

3.2 Software Timer Interrupt Routine

The software timer interrupt service routine executes every 500 µs and determines the sampling rate of the PID control algorithm. Figure 20 shows the flow chart for the software timer interrupt routine. The routine determines the operating mode, calculates the current velocity and position and tests for overrun of preset boundary conditions and stress conditions.

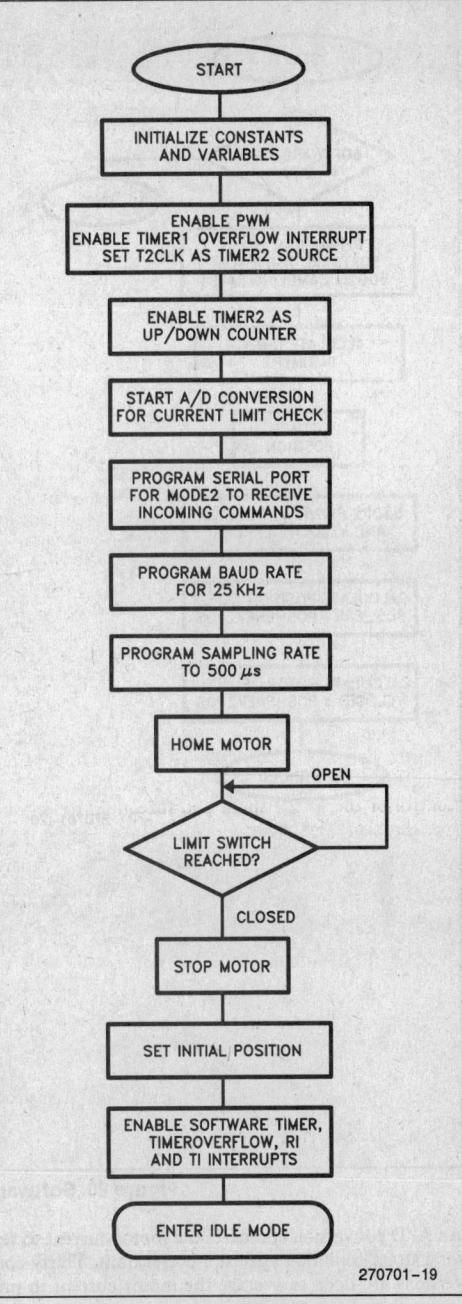

Figure 19. Motor Initialization Routine

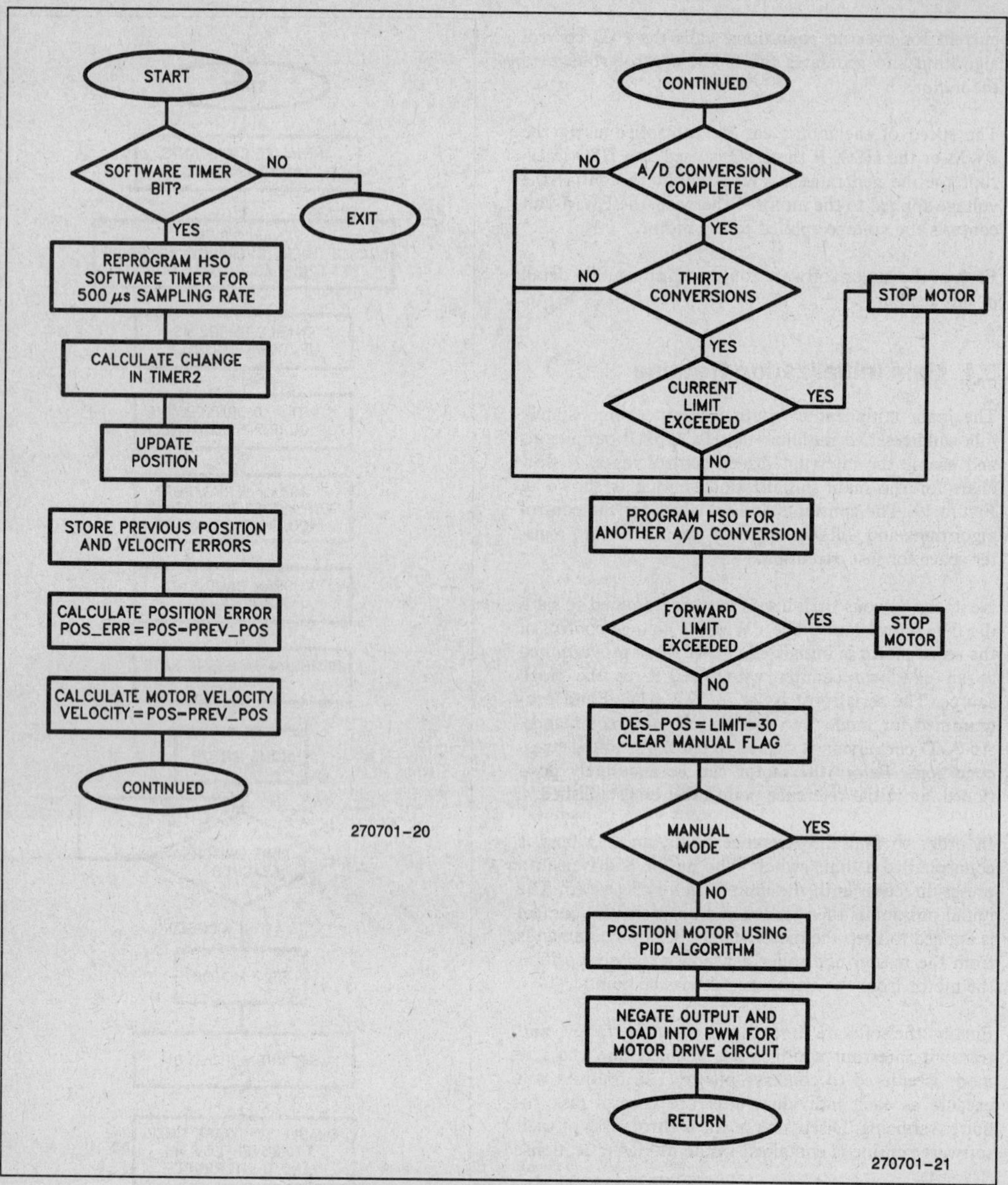

AP-428

Figure 20. Software Timer Interrupt Routine

An A/D conversion compares the motor current to test for a stress condition against a preset limit. Thirty conversions are done to average the motor current to prevent a false trigger due to a large current surge when the motor starts up. If the preset limit indicating a stress condition is exceeded, the motor is stopped.

The motor is also stopped if the current position exceeds the preset boundary limits. In the case of the robot, the movement of joints are limited to prevent positions which may cause stress conditions or damage the robot. The positioning of the robot is dependent on the mode of operation.

A manual flag is tested to determine if the automatic or manual mode should position the motor. The manual mode moves the motor either up or down with a preset maximum motor control voltage until a STOP command is issued. The automatic mode positions the motor using either the position PID for accurate positioning or the velocity PID for long positioning.

The software timer interrupt routine calculates and stores the current position and velocity of the motor for use by the appropriate PID algorithm. The current velocity is calculated given the sampling rate, the current position and the previous position. The calculated velocity and position information is stored in the 80C196KB register space for use by the PID algorithm software.

Recall that either a position PID or a velocity PID control algorithm will be executed depending on the maximum velocity value passed by the master controller. If the value is zero, a position PID is employed, otherwise, the velocity profile is employed. The velocity profile PID is ideal for large maneuvers while the position PID is better for shorter movements or maintaining the current position. The generated output from the control algorithm is then loaded into the PWM control register and a return is executed.

3.3 PID Control Algorithm

The algorithm used to control the angular position and velocity of the motor is a common PID algorithm. The algorithm uses proportional, integral and differential feedback to control the output to a motor. The PID algorithm controls the important system characteristics of the motor: settling time, steady state error, and system stability. Each term in the control algorithm affects each system characteristic differently. A block diagram of the PID algorithm is illustrated in Figure 21.

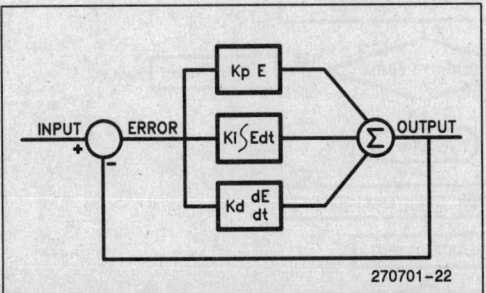

Figure 21. Block Diagram of PID Algorithm

The PID algorithm consists of three terms: a proportional term, integral term and differential term. The proportional term drives the motor with an output directly proportional to the error between the desired and measured position. The integral term consists of the integral of the position errors multiplied by an integral constant. The differential term is the change in error multiplied by a differential constant. The sum of the terms is then scaled to provide a control voltage to the motor. The system characteristics of the motor are tuned by the selection of appropriate constants.

The settling time, steady state error and system stability are impacted by the amount of proportional gain selected. To accurately control a small change in motor position, a large gain is desired. Faster system response is attained by selecting a large gain but at the cost of greater overshoot and longer settling time. The effect of varying loads on the motor makes proportional control in itself inadequate because of system instability and large steady state error.

Application of integral feedback drives the steady state error to zero by increasing the output in response to a steady state error. The integral term increases as the sum of the steady state error increases causing the error to eventually be driven to zero. The integral term, although driving the steady state error to zero, can cause overshoot and ringing if it is too large. This has the undesirable affect of poorer system response. Applying PI control works very well, however a faster system response can be acheived by applying a PID algorithm.

System response can be improved by adding a differential term. Addition of this term improves the response time by providing a output proportional to the rate of change in error. When the motor has a large change in error, the term produces a large output to the motor. Therefore, the system responds faster to disturbances in the system. Most of the system instability is caused by too high of a differential constant. The size of the proportional, integral and differential constants provide tradeoffs to the desired system characteristics.

Selection of the three gain constants is critical in providing fast system response with good system characteristics. A slightly modified PID algorithm controls the motor which improves both the system response and the system stability. Two modifications were made to improve the control algorithm. First, the size of the integral term was clamped to prevent instability caused by an extremely large integral term which could occur after a long time with large errors. Second, the integral term was cleared when the error changed sign to further improve the system stability. The PID control algorithm is written in PL/M-96 for ease of development.

3.4 Position PID Software

The software flow chart for the PID algorithm is shown in Figure 22. Upon entering the routine, the position

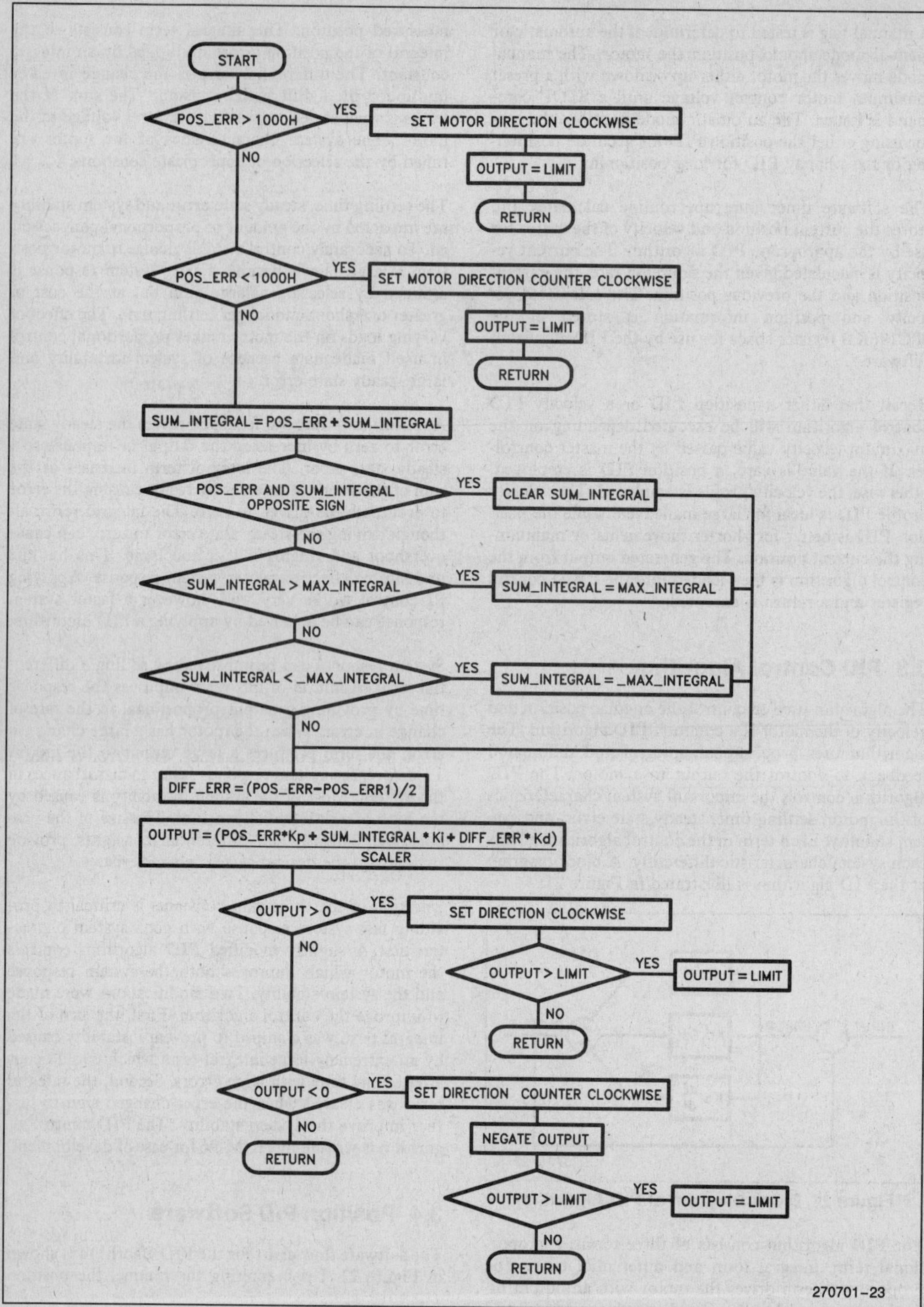

AP-428

Figure 22. Position PID Algorithm

error is checked for a minimum value before applying the position PID algorithm. If the minimum position error is exceeded, the maximum PWM output is applied to move the motor as rapidly as possible.

Current position error is added to the integral sum. Position error and integral sum are tested to clear the integral sum if they are opposite in sign. This improves the system stability by preventing the integral term from applying a correction opposite to the desired output.

If the integral sum is greater than the maximum sum allowed, the integral sum is clamped. This prevents the integral sum from becoming too large if the error is large for several samples. Differential error is then calculated from the current and previous position errors.

Output for the PID algorithm is calculated from the proportional, integral and differential terms multiplied by their individual gain constants. The output is then scaled and tested for the preset PWM output limit. If the limit is exceeded, the output to the PWM is set to the maximum value. The appropriate motor direction is set depending on the sign of the output. The final output to the PWM control is ready and the software returns.

3.5 Velocity Profile

Positioning of a servo motor using only a position PID algorithm wastes power and gives poor system performance when moving between two positions. A velocity profile provides a smooth transition between two angular positions and improves the energy consumption of the motor. Three different velocity profiles which can be applied are trapezoidal, triangular and parabolic.

The parabolic profile is the most power efficient and provides smooth acceleration and deceleration at the end points. However, a large amount of processor time is needed to calculate the profile in real time. The triangular profile provides ease of calculation versus the parabolic but generates a rough transition at the peak of the profile. A trapezoidal profile provides energy efficiency, ease of calculation and relatively smooth acceleration and deceleration throughout the velocity profile. For these reasons, the trapezoidal profile was selected.

A trapezoidal profile consists of an acceleration period, run period and deceleration period. The variables ACCEL_TIME, RUN_TIME and END_TIME represent the periods. Figure 23 shows the trapezoidal profile. Acceleration and deceleration rates for the motor are fixed according to the optimum values found through testing. The master controller sends a position command containing the maximum velocity (MAX_VELOCITY) and the desired end position (DES_POSITION). The DES_POSITION is equal to the integral of the velocity profile (i.e., the final position can be determined by integrating the velocity over the period of the profile. Therefore, the ACCEL_TIME, RUN_TIME and END_TIME can be calculated based on the DES_POSITION, ACCELERATION, DECELERATION and MAX_VELOCITY.

The destination position should be reached if the velocity profile was ideally tracked. However, a certain amount of position error can be expected as the motor travels from one point to another. This error is eliminated by applying the position PID at the end of the velocity profile. This modified control algorithm has both good motor performance and accurate angular positioning.

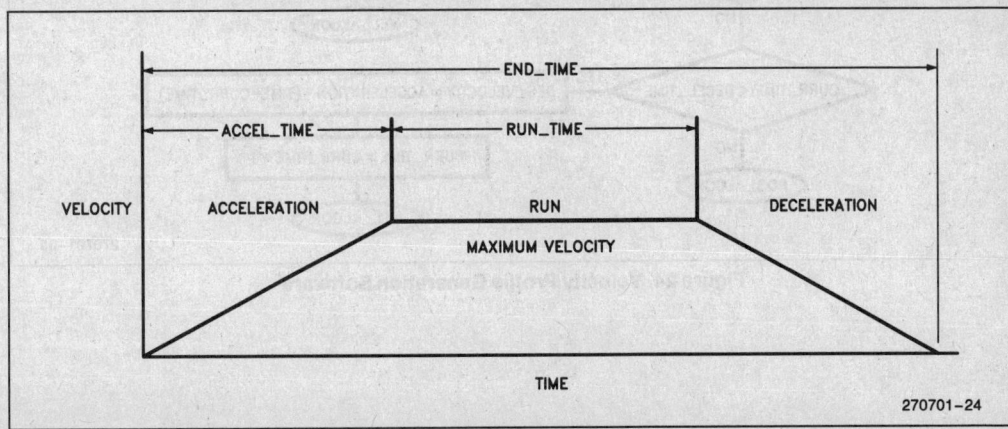

Figure 23. Trapezoidal Velocity Profile

AP-428

3.6 Trapezoidal Profile Calculation

The trapezoidal velocity profile is calculated when a position command with a nonzero maximum velocity is passed from the master controller. The master passes the desired end position and the maximum velocity of the motor. A reasonable acceleration (deceleration) rate was found through experimentation to be 1 position count/sampling rate (500 μs). ACCEL_TIME, RUN_TIME and END_TIME can be easily calculated given the relative acceleration rate of one, the end position and the maximum velocity.

The acceleration and deceleration time is equal to the maximum velocity since the acceleration/deceleration rate is one. RUN_TIME is the difference between the desired position and current position minus the distance covered during the acceleration and deceleration times. END_TIME is the RUN_TIME added to two times the ACCEL_TIME. With the velocity profile calculated, the velocity PID algorithm will be applied until the END_TIME is reached.

The velocity profile software generates the appropriate velocity depending on the current time. Figure 24 shows the velocity profile generation software. The TIME variable is incremented every software timer interrupt at the sampling rate if it is less then the end time (END_TIME) of the profile. Three different velocities are calculated during the profile. DES_VELOCITY equals the ACCELERATION multiplied by the TIME until the ACCEL_TIME is reached. The DES_VELOCITY equals the maxiumum velocity until the RUN_TIME is exceeded. Once the RUN_TIME is exceeded, the velocity is equal to the ACCELERATION (same as deceleration rate) multiplied by the TIME-CURR_TIME. When the end of the profile is reached (which is approximately the desired end position), the time equals the END_TIME and the position PID controls the motor. If the maximum velocity passed by the master controller is zero, the CURRENT_TIME is set to the END_TIME and the position PID controls the motor.

The velocity control algorithm employs the PID algorithm. The algorithm is similar to the position algorithm used to control the position. The velocity control algorithm is shown in Figure 25.

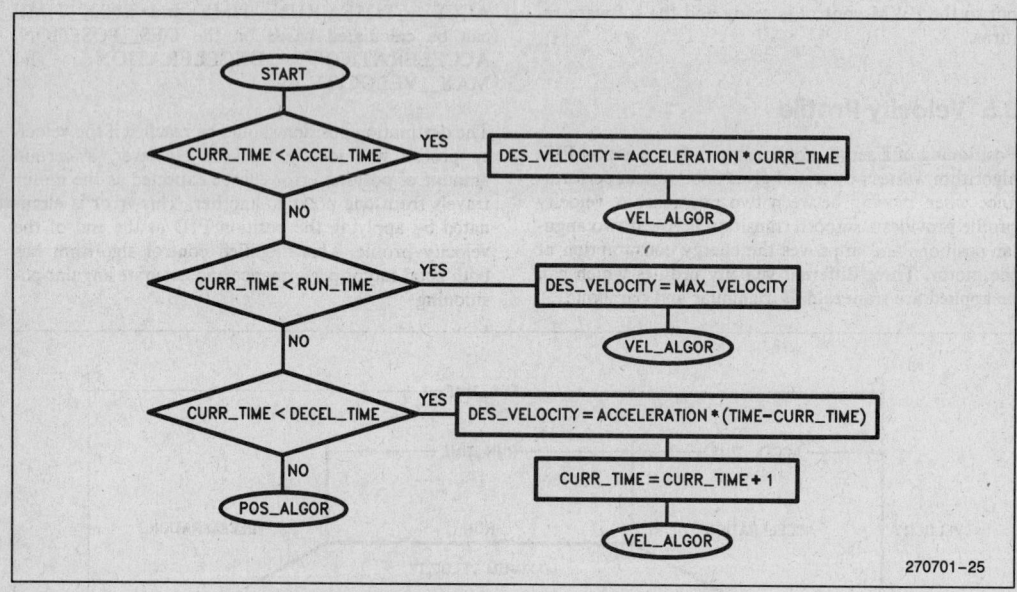

Figure 24. Velocity Profile Generation Software

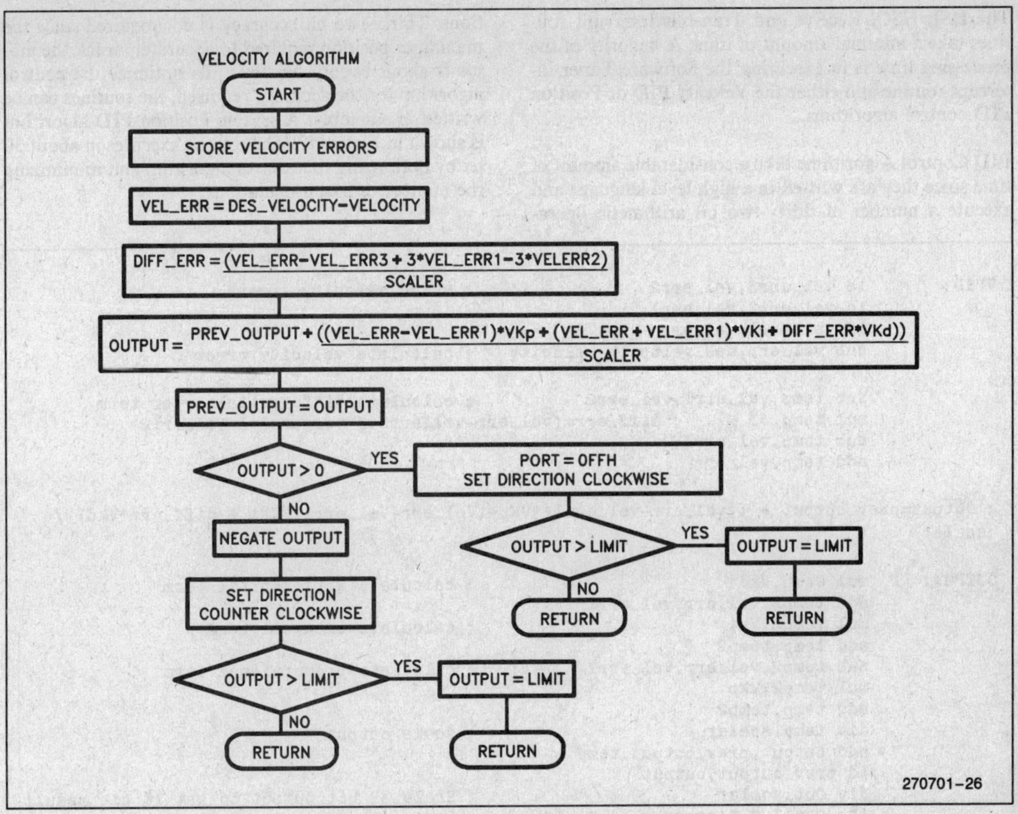

AP-428

Figure 25. Velocity Control Algorithm

3.7 Fast Execution of Control Algorithms

The high speed arithmetic operations capability, availability of three operand instructions and large register space of the 80C196KB provide for fast execution of control algorithms. The 80C196KB running at 12 Mhz can execute a 16 × 16 Multiply in 2.3 μs and 32/16 divide in 4.0 μs. Three operand instructions operate on two variables without modification and store the result in the third variable. This eliminates the need for executing load and store operations as required by accumulator bound architectures. The large register space can store all of the constants and variables for the control algorithm without the use of load and store operations. In addition, procedures do not need to pass parameters or store results since they can permanently reside in register space.

A summary of the execution times for the main software routines is shown in Figure 26.

	Execution Time
Software Timer Interrupt Routine	40 μs
PID Control Algorithms:	
Velocity PID (PL/M-96/ASM-96)	300 μs/30 μs
Position PID (PL/M-96/ASM-96)	240 μs/40 μs
Velocity Profile Generation	71 μs
HSI Interrupt Processing	22 μs
HSO Generate PWM Routine	16 μs
Receive Interrupt and Command Processing	26 μs
Transmit Interrupt Routine	11 μs

Figure 26. Execution Times for Main Software Routines

AP-428

The HSI, HSO, Receive and Transmit Interrupt routines take a minimal amount of time. A majority of the processing time is in executing the Software Timer interrupt routine and either the Velocity PID or Position PID control algorithms.

PID Control Algorithms take a considerable amount of time since they are written in a high level language and execute a number of thirty-two bit arithmetic operations. Thirty-two bit accuracy is not required since the maximum position required to accurately track the motor is about twenty four bits. To optimize the control algorithm for the accuracy required, the routines can be written in assembly. A sample Position PID algorithm is shown in Figure 27. The routine executes in about 30 μs by optimizing the control algorithm and minimizing the number of 32-bit operations.

```
VPID:       ld vel_err3,vel_err2              ; store velocity errors
            ld vel_err2,vel_err1
            ld vel_err1,vel_err
            sub vel_err,des_velocity,velocity ; calculate velocity error

            sub temp,vel_err1,vel_err2        ; calculate differential error term
            mul temp,#3      ; diff_err=(vel_err-vel_err3+3*vel_err1-3*vel_err2)
            sub temp,vel_err3
            add temp,vel_err

; Output=prev_output + ((vel_err-vel_err1)*VKp+(Vel_err+Vel_err1)*Vki + diff_err*Vkd))/
;scaler

OUTPUT:     mul temp,Vkd                      ; calculate differential term
            add temp2,vel_err,vel_err1
            mul temp2,Vki                     ; calculate integral term
            add temp,temp2
            sub temp2,vel_err,vel_err1        ; calculate proportional term
            mul temp2,Vkp
            add temp,temp2
            div temp,scaler                   ; scale output
            add output,prev_output,temp
            ld prev_output,output
            div Out_scaler                    ; Scale 32 bit output to get 16 bit result
            jbc Out+3,7,forward               ; test output for direction
REVERSE:    neg Out+2                         ; negate output
            ldb p2,#07fh                      ; set direction down(p2.0=0)
            sjmp scaleout
FORWARD:    ldb p2,#0FFh                      ; set direction up(P2.0=1)

SCALEOUT:   cmp Out,#0ffh                     ; scale output for maximum pwm value
            jgt exit                          ; if Out > maximum pwm output
            ld Out,#0ffh                      ; then clamp output to max pwm value
EXIT:       ldb pwm,Out
            ret
```

Figure 27. Position and Velocity PID Assembly Routine

5-304

```
PID:        add sum_int, pos_err       ; sum position errors
            div sum_int,decay          ; limit effect of old position errors
            sub diff_err, pos_err      ; differential error = (pos_err - pos_err1)/2
            div diff_err, #2
;           Out = Kp*pos_err + Ki*interr + Kd*differr
OUTPUT:     mul Out pos_err, Kp        ; Calculate proportional term
            mul temp, Ki interr        ; Calculate integral term
            add Out, temp              ; add integral term to Output
            addc Out+2, temp+2         ; 32 bit add to maintain full 32 bit accuracy
            div Out, scaler            ; Scale output
            jbc Out+3,7,forward        ; test output for direction
REVERSE:    neg Out+2                  ; negate output
            ldb p2,#07fh               ; set direction down (P2.7=0)
            sjmp scaleout
FORWARD:    ldb Port2,#0ffh            ; set direction up(P2.7=1)
SCALEOUT:   cmp Out,#0ffh              ; scale output for maximum pwm value
            jgtexit                    ; if Out > maximum pwm output
            ld Out,#0ffh               ; then limit output to maximum value
EXIT:       ldb pwm, Out               ; load pwm with Output value
            ret
```

Figure 27. Position and Velocity PID Assembly Routine (Continued)

4.0 Distributed Control

Distributed control of servo motors requires the passing of commands and data from a master to a slave. The master passes commands to report position, start and stop the motor, or position the motor to an exact location using a position PID or velocity profile. The slave needs to report current position and acknowledge incoming commands from the master. This protocol requires addressing of slaves and the distinction between incoming commands and transmission of data. The 80C196KB serial port provides a multiprocessor communication mode for implementing the protocol.

The 80C196KB provides a ninth bit in Mode 2 and Mode 3 that can assist communication between multiple processors. If the received ninth bit is zero in mode 2, the serial port interrupt will not occur. Each motor is initially programmed for this mode to distinguish receiving a command versus a data byte. With the ninth bit set, indicating a command byte has been received, all the slaves interrupt and process the incoming byte. The address of the motor being controlled is embedded in the command byte. All processors will process the command byte if the motor address matches.

A motor receiving a poll command from the master controller will enter mode 3. The polled motor then receives the data bytes which are sent with the ninth bit cleared. Therefore, only the processor receiving data will interrupt for serial reception while the other processors await another command byte with the ninth bit set. A list of available commands and the format for each is shown in Figure 28.

AP-428

Command Table

Command	Code	Operation
Position	01	Position motor using either position PID or Velocity profile.
Poll	05	Polls motor for current position.
Motor Up	08	Enters manual mode turning motor clockwise.
Motor Down	09	Enters manual mode turning motor counter clockwise.
Stop	10	Exits manual mode setting the desired position to the current position.

Position Command

Command	Position	Maximum Velocity
01	4 bytes	2 bytes

Poll Command

Command	Position
05	4 bytes

Figure 28. Master Commands and Format

4.1 Receive Interrupt Service Routine

Communication between the 80C196KB and the main controller is handled by the serial port routine. Figure 29 shows the flow for the receive interrupt service routine. Upon reception of a byte from the main controller, a receive interrupt will occur. The RI bit is tested to ensure a byte has been received. If a byte has not been received, an error is generated and a return from the routine is executed. After a valid reception, the ninth bit is tested to determine if the incoming byte is a command byte or incoming data sent after reception of a POSITION command.

If the byte is a command byte, the motor address is checked by each slave for its own address. The command byte is then echoed back to the master controller by the appropriate slave. The routine is exited if the command byte is not for the motor. Since each motor has a unique address, only the motor receiving the command will respond. Reception of a POSITION command will switch the serial port to mode 3.

Desired position and maximum velocity is sent by the master to each slave by a POSITION command. Received data for the position command is stored in a buffer. After all data has been received, MAX_VELOCITY and DES_POSITION is loaded with the values stored in the buffer and the serial port is switched back to mode 2.

Each command is then checked and appropriate action taken depending on the received command. Commands include POSITION, POLL, UP MOTOR, MOTOR DOWN and STOP. The commands are summarized in Figure 28.

4.2 Manual Positioning

The receive routine will check for one of three manual commands: MOTOR UP, DOWN MOTOR or STOP. A manual flag is used by the software determine if the motor should be positioned using either a position or velocity PID algorithm or by manual control. The motor up and motor down commands set the manual flag which will cause the PWM control to be loaded with a constant value during the software interrupt routine. The direction port bit is set to the appropriate value depending on whether the command is up or down. The motor will continue to move up or down until a STOP command is issued by the master controller or the motor's preset limits are reached.

A stop command will reset the manual flag and set the controller in automatic mode which employs the PID algorithm. The destination position gets loaded with the current position and a return from the receive interrupt is executed. The manual position mode is used by the master controller to position the motor under keyboard or switch control. This is instead to precise position control of the motor by sending a position command.

4.3 Motor Positioning

Either position control or a velocity profile can be used to position each motor. The maximum velocity information stored in the POSITION command determines the type of method employed. If the maximum velocity value is nonzero, the velocity PID algorithm will be applied to position the motor. If the maximum velocity is zero, position control using the PID algorithm will be used. This provides for two alternative methods for positioning the motor.

AP-428

Once a POSITION command is received, the processor enters serial mode 3 to receive the incoming position and maximum velocity information. The four bytes of position data and two bytes of maximum velocity are retrieved from a six byte storage buffer. A receive count keeps track of the number of incoming bytes until all bytes of the six byte frame have been received. If a frame or overrun error occurs, the motor will shut off and a 0FFH will be transmitted back to the master controller to indicate an error condition has occurred. Otherwise, an 88 is returned to indicate the valid transmission of position and maximum velocity. The manual flag will be turned off and the appropriate PID algorithm will be applied on the next software interrupt.

4.4 Master Polling of Position

The master controller can poll each motor controller for position with a poll command. After reception of the poll command, a transmit buffer is loaded with four bytes of position information. Each byte is then transmitted using the transmit interrupt routine.

The flowchart for the routine is shown in Figure 30. The routine simply tests the TI flag and continues to transmit a byte from the buffer until the transmit count goes to zero. After the count goes to zero, the transmission is complete and processing continues.

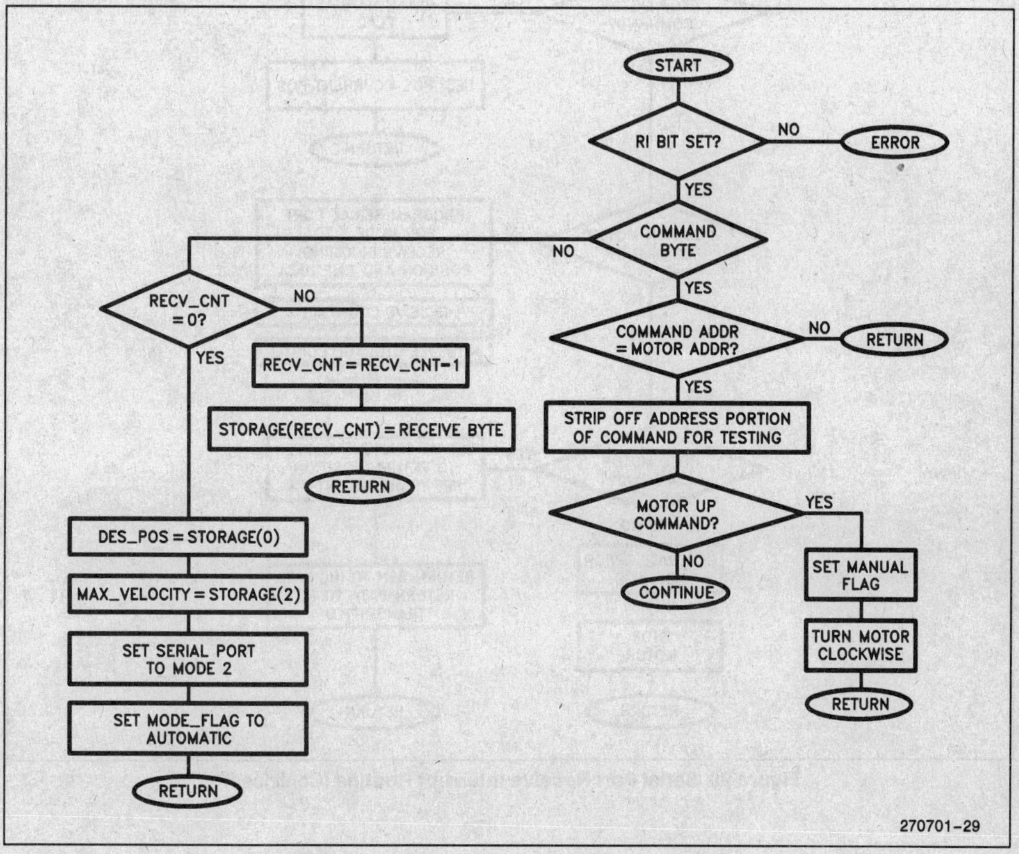

Figure 29. Serial Port Receive Interrupt Routine

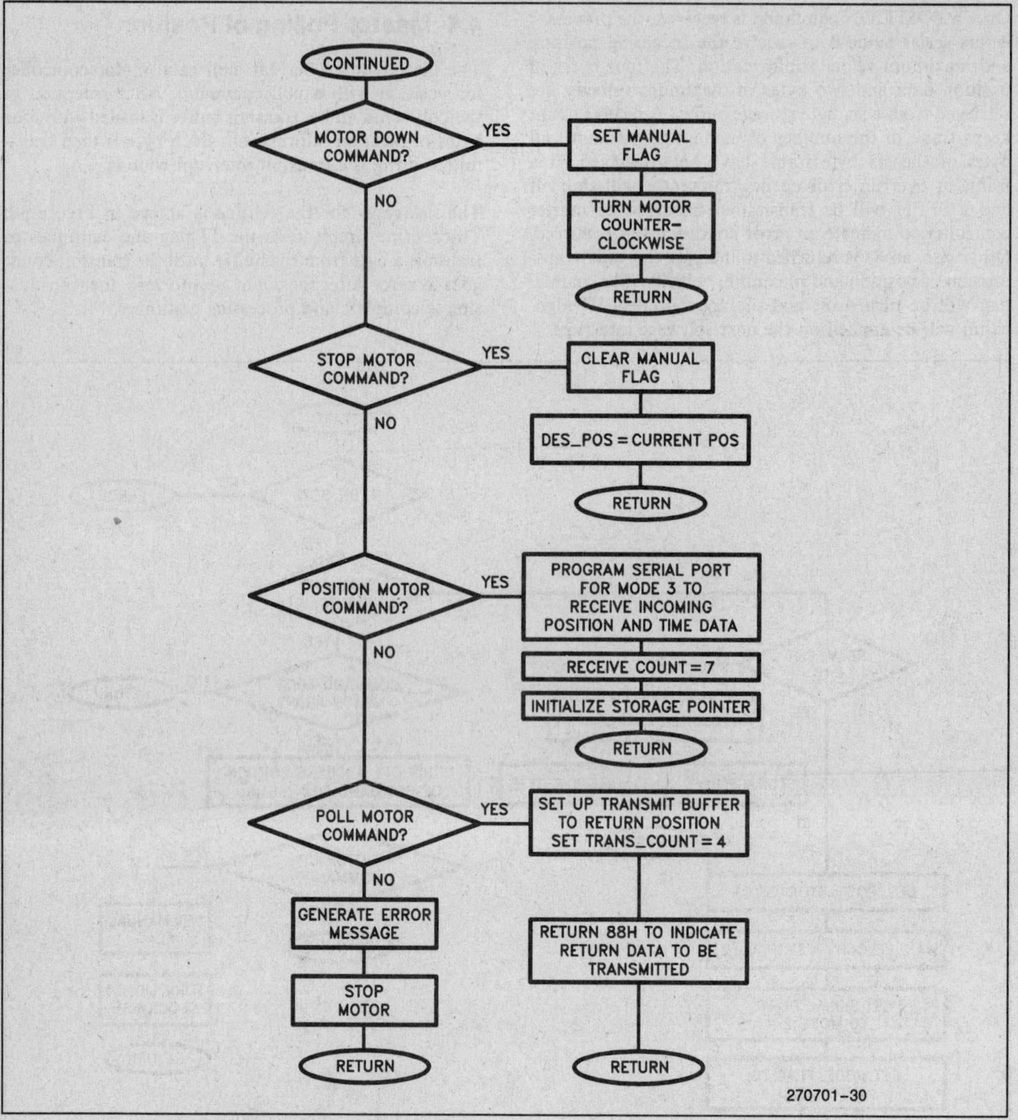

AP-428

Figure 29. Serial Port Receive Interrupt Routine (Continued)

270701-30

5-308

AP-428

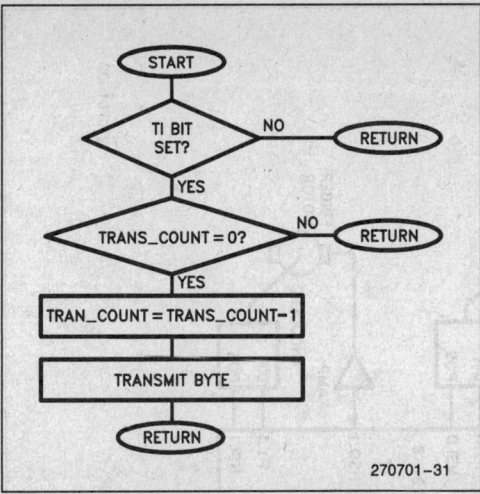

Figure 30. Serial Transmit Routine

5.0 DISTRIBUTED CONTROL OF A SIX AXIS ROBOT

A six axis robot demonstration system was built using distributed control of its six motors. The robot is a RHINO XR-1 prototype robot designed by SANDHU Machine Design Inc. Robot motors were replaced with similar models with high resolution encoders. The robot allows movement along six joints: base, shoulder, elbow, wrist, hand and fingers. Each joint is connected to a motor. The system used an IBM PC acting as a master controller.

The software used to develop the human interface was Turbo Prolog and the Turbo Prolog Toolbox. The human interface allowed for the programming and movement of the robot by individually controlling each joint motor. The IBM PC controlled each axis of the robot by passing commands serially.

The IBM PC provides a flexible master controller for positioning the robot. There are a large number of software languages for developing the control algorithms and human interface of the master controller. Turbo Prolog was selected for its low cost and ease of implementation. The control screen and robot programming language were rapidly developed using the Turbo Prolog. The software and hardware implementation easily provide for programming and controlling the robot through a variety of repetitive tasks. A robot using this control system could easily perform assembly or manufacturing tasks as shown in Figure 31.

5.1 Hardware Interface

The hardware interface to the robot is shown in Figure 32. Each major joint, elbow wrist, base and shoulder were controlled with a single 80C196KB using the PWM and TIMER2 as an up/down counter. The hand and finger motors used the HSI to track position and the HSO to generate PWM motor control voltages.

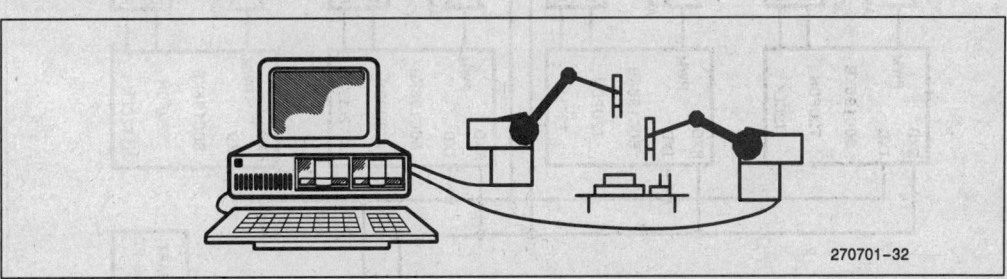

Figure 31. Automated Assembly using Distributed Control

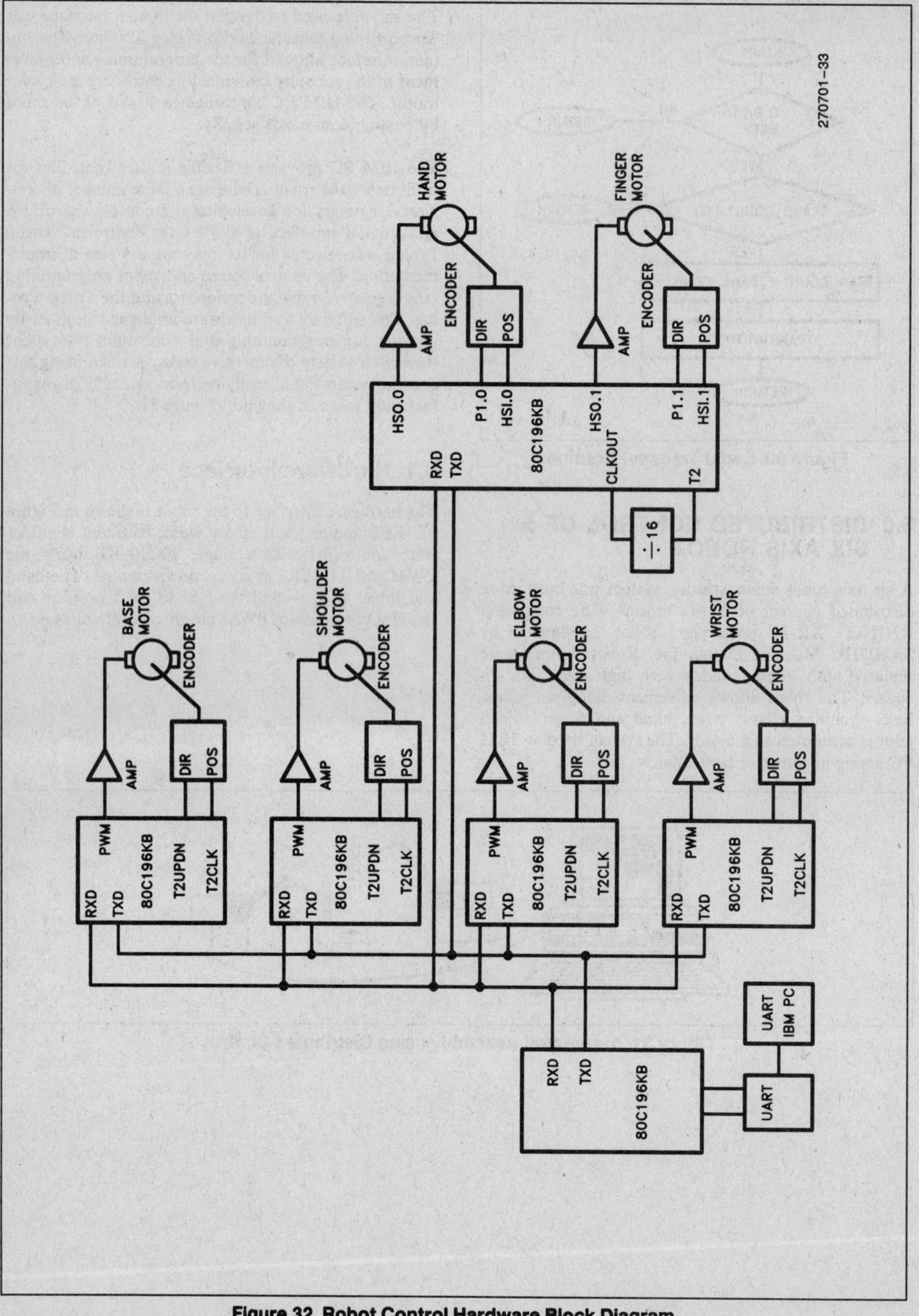

AP-428

Figure 32. Robot Control Hardware Block Diagram

5-310

AP-428

Switches on the robot were fed into 80C196KB I/O ports to provide a reference position when each motor starts up. Current sensing for each motor was fed back to the analog channels to provide an indication of any overrun or stress conditions. Limits were set for each motor to prevent the robot joints from entering positions where obstacles or mechanical limitations were reached.

Each motor was given a unique programming address for communication back to the master controller. The master controller sent commands with the address of whichever joint motor needed to be positioned or polled. The master 80C196KB communicated through a UART to the IBM-PC.

5.2 Human Interface

To control the robot, the human interface provided a variety of programming options.

The software features included:

Manual control via the keyboard
Editing robot command files
A Motor Control Command language
Table Display of motor position and status
Manual Programming mode
Table Positioning mode

The software front end developed only the basic features of robotic control to demonstrate the distributed control of servo motors.

5.3 Control Screen for the Robot

The screen for the control of the robot is shown in Figure 33. The screen displays a table of the position and status of each motor, shows the function keys used to execute commands or enter different modes and displays the keyboard keys for moving each robot joint up or down. The software has various modes for positioning and programming the robot.

5.4 Programmed Modes

The software provides for movement of the robot through table entry, execution of include command files or manually using the keyboard. The robot is positioned manually by entering the function key for manual mode and then pressing the predefined key for each joint motor to move up or down. As each key is released, a STOP command is issued to each motor. The motors are then polled and the current position updated in the table.

The table function allows for direct entry of the desired position and maximum velocity to position the motor when the table function key (F1) is pressed. After the

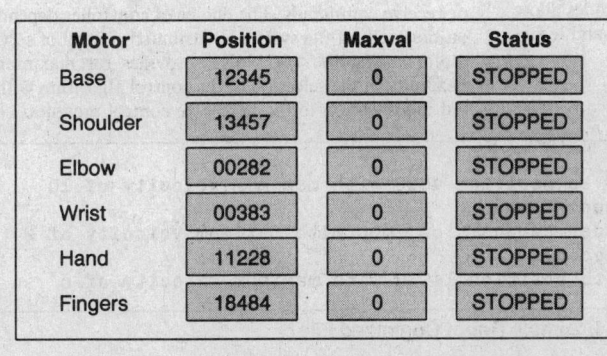

Figure 33. Robot Control Screen

AP-428

key is pressed, individual positioning commands are sent to each motor. With maximum velocity set to zero, the motor is positioned using a position PID. A non-zero maximum velocity would position the motor using a velocity profile. The final method of positioning allowed for the sending of commands (MOTOR UP, MOTOR DOWN, STOP, POSITION or POLL) to each joint in the robot from an include file.

The include mode function key (F6) executes commands stored in a file. The command file can be entered using an external editor or using the on board editor, Turbo Prolog. A sample command file is shown in Figure 34. The command file allows for programming of the robot through a sequence of programmed tasks. The task of programming the robot is eased by a manual program mode.

The manual program mode generates a command file while manually positioning the robot. After pressing the program key (F4), the program mode is entered and the robot is moved by pressing the appropriate motion key for each joint motor. When the robot stops, the position of the robot is polled and translated into a position command and stored in a file. As the programmed task is executed, each position of the robot and the time delay between joint movements is recorded. When the task is complete, the file contains all the stored position commands necessary to execute the programmed task. The file can be edited with by entering the edit mode (F5) to fine tune the programmed task or execute the command file directly. The manual program, command file execution and editing modes allow for a variety of robotic tasks to be developed and tested easily.

6.0 CONCLUSION

Use of an 80C196KB in distributed control of servo motors has been demonstrated with the effective utilization of the onboard peripherals and high speed math capability of the 80C196KB. The high performance and integration of the 80C196KB minimized the hardware interface. The task of controlling the motor resided in the 80C196KB with the control algorithm residing in the master. With this approach, the centralized controller can be adapted to the performance requirements of the system.

Although not implemented, a learn mode could be added to the robot to provide programming using AI techniques. The IBM PC and Turbo Prolog software provided the demonstration vehicle for testing the control of the robot using distributed control. Use of artificial intelligence programming to position the robot could be incorporated with the Turbo Prolog package. The application of a vision system or a more complex control algorithm could be realized without modification to the hardware controlling the robot. A more cost effective solution is obtained by replacing the IBM-PC with one 80C196KB or 80C186 acting as a master controller.

Repetitive tasks programmed using the robot command language could be stored in tables in the master 80C196KB. The controller would send the stored commands to each motor and communicate, through a serial UART, to the rest of the manufacturing system. The master 80C196KB controller would then report status or receive commands. The choice of controller depends on the needs of the system. Distributed control of servo motors using the 80C196KB provides for maximum flexibility in the selection of the control algorithm without modification to the hardware control modules.

```
pos(3,4000,10)    ; move elbow to position 4000 with maximum velocity of 10
time(10)          ; delay 10 seconds
pos(1,1000,2)     ; move shoulder to position 1000 with maximum velocity of 2
time(20)          ; delay 20 seconds
pos(0,14000,5)    ; move base to position 14000 with maximum velocity of 5
```

Figure 34. Sample Robot Command File

AP-428

REFERENCES

1. Michael Brady, *Robot Motion: Planning and Control* (MIT Press, 1982).
2. C. S. G. Lee, *Tutorial on Robotics* (2nd edition) (IEEE Computer Society Press, 1989)
3. Electro Craft Corporation, "DC Motors Speed Controls Servo Systems", 1978.
4. Proceedings of Conferences on Applied Motion Control, University of Minnesota, 1986.

AP-466

APPLICATION NOTE

Using the 80C196KB

ROBIN SHEER
EMD APPLICATIONS

November 1991

Order Number: 272116-001

Using the 80C196KB

CONTENTS	PAGE
1.0 INTRODUCTION	5-317
2.0 THE CPU	5-318
3.0 THE ARCHITECTURE	5-321
3.1 Addressing Modes	5-321
3.2 Program Status Word	5-326
4.0 INTERRUPTS	5-327
5.0 TIMERS/COUNTERS	5-329
6.0 HIGH SPEED INPUT UNIT	5-331
7.0 HIGH SPEED OUTPUT UNIT	5-333
8.0 PULSE WIDTH MODULATION OUTPUT	5-335
9.0 ANALOG OUTPUTS	5-336
10.0 ANALOG TO DIGITAL CONVERTER	5-337
11.0 SERIAL PORT	5-338
12.0 SOFTWARE EXAMPLES	5-342
12.1 Example 1—Table Look-Up and Interpolation	5-343
12.2 Example 2—Using the High Speed Input Unit	5-345
12.3 Example 3—Using the High Speed Input Unit and Pulse Width Modulation Output	5-347
12.4 Example 4—Using the High Speed Output Unit to Generate Multiple PWMs	5-349
12.5 Example 5—Using the High Speed Output Unit to Generate a Single PWM	5-351
12.6 Example 6—Using the A/D Converter	5-352
12.7 Example 7—Using the Serial Port	5-353
13.0 HARDWARE EXAMPLES	5-354
14.0 PORT RECONSTRUCTION	5-357
15.0 CONCLUSION	5-357

CONTENTS	PAGE
FIGURES	
Figure 1-1. 80C196KB Block Diagram	5-317
Figure 2-1. Block Diagram of the Register File, RALU, Interrupt Controller and Memory Controller	5-318
Figure 2-2. Special Function Registers	5-319
Figure 2-3. Special Function Register Descriptions	5-320
Figure 3-1. Instruction Format	5-321
Figure 3-2. The Program Status Word Register	5-326
Figure 4-1. 80C196KB Interrupt Sources	5-327
Figure 4-2. 80C196KB Interrupt Structure Block Diagram	5-328
Figure 4-3. Interrupt Mask and Pending Registers	5-328
Figure 5-1. Timer Block Diagram	5-329
Figure 5-2. I/O Control Register 1 (IOC1)	5-330
Figure 5-3. I/O Status Register 1 (IOS1)	5-330
Figure 5-4. I/O Control Register 2 (IOC2)	5-330
Figure 5-5. Timer2 Clock and Reset Options	5-330
Figure 6-1. High Speed Input Unit	5-331
Figure 6-2. High Speed Input Mode Register (HSI_MODE)	5-332
Figure 6-3. High Speed Input Status Register (HSI_STATUS)	5-332
Figure 6-4. I/O Control Register 0 (IOC0)	5-332
Figure 7-1. High Speed Output Block Diagram	5-333
Figure 7-2. High Speed Output Command Register (HSO_COMMAND)	5-334
Figure 7-3. I/O Status Register 1 (IOS1)	5-334
Figure 7-4. I/O Status Register 2 (IOS2)	5-334

CONTENTS

		PAGE
Figure 8-1.	PWM Block Diagram	5-335
Figure 8-2.	Typical PWM Outputs	5-335
Figure 9-1.	D/A Buffer Block Diagram	5-336
Figure 9-2.	PWM to Analog Conversion Circuitry	5-336
Figure 10-1.	A/D Converter Block Diagram	5-337
Figure 10-2.	A/D Command Register (AD__COMMAND)	5-338
Figure 10-3.	A/D Result High Register (AD__RESULT(HI))	5-338
Figure 10-4.	A/D Result Low Register (AD__RESULT(LO))	5-338
Figure 11-1.	Serial Port Control and Status Registers (SP__CON and SP__STAT)	5-339
Figure 11-2.	Mode 0 Timing	5-339
Figure 11-3.	Typical Shift Register Circuit	5-340
Figure 11-4.	Serial Port Frames, Mode 1, 2 and 3	5-340
Figure 11-5.	Multiprocessor Communication	5-341
Figure 11-6.	Baud Rate Formulas	5-341
Figure 12-1.	Example Input Signals and the Resulting PWM Outputs	5-347
Figure 12-2.	Example PWMs	5-349
Figure 13-1.	8-Bit System with EPROM and RAM	5-354
Figure 13-2.	16-Bit System with EPROM	5-354
Figure 13-3.	16-Bit System with Dynamic Bus Width	5-355
Figure 13-4.	Schematic of 16-Bit System with Dynamic Bus Width	5-356
Figure 14-1.	I/O Port Reconstruction	5-357

CONTENTS

		PAGE
TABLES		
Table 3-1.	Instruction Summary	5-323
Table 3-2.	Status Flag Descriptions	5-326
Table 4-1.	80C196KB Interrupt Vector Locations	5-328
Table 5-1.	Timer2 Control Bits	5-331
Table 8-1.	PWM Frequencies	5-336
Table 11-1.	Common Baud Rate Values	5-341
Table 12-1.	Table of Input and Output Values	5-343
LISTINGS		
Listing 12-0.	Include File 80C196KB.INC	5-342
Listing 12-1.	Table Look-Up and Interpolation—INTERP.A96	5-344
Listing 12-2.	Using the High Speed Input Unit—HSIA.A96	5-346
Listing 12-3.	Using the High Speed Input Unit and the Pulse Width Modulation Output—HSIB.A96	5-348
Listing 12-4.	Using the High Speed Output Unit to Generate Multiple PWMs—HSOA.A96	5-350
Listing 12-5.	Using the High Speed Output Unit to Generate a Single PWM—HSOB.A96	5-351
Listing 12-6.	Using the A/D Converter—AD.A96	5-352
Listing 12-7.	Using the Serial Port—SP.A96	5-353

AP-466

1.0 INTRODUCTION

The MCS®-96 family members are all high performance microcontrollers with a 16-bit CPU and at least 230 bytes of on chip RAM. The Intel MCS-96 family of 16-bit embedded controllers easily handles high speed calculations and fast input/output (I/O) operations. Typical applications using the MCS-96 products include closed-loop control and mid-range digital signal processing. Modems, motor control system, printers, engine control system, photocopiers, anti-lock brakes, air conditioner control systems, disk drives and medical instrumentation all use MCS-96 products.

The 80C196KB is a CHMOS member of the MCS-96 family. All of the MCS-96 components share a common instruction set and architecture. However, the CHMOS components have enhancements to provide higher performance with lower power consumption. To further decrease power usage, idle and power-down modes are available on these devices. The 80C196KB contains a dedicated I/O subsystem and can perform 16-bit arithmetic instructions including multiply and divide operations.

This application note briefly describes the 80C196KB, and provides software examples using its key features. For further information on the 80C196KB and its use consult the sources listed in the bibliography. Figure 1-1 shows a block diagram of the 80C196KB. Included in this application note are descriptions of the CPU and architecture, the interrupt structure and the peripherals. These peripherals include a Pulse Width Modulation output, an A/D Converter, a Serial Port and High Speed I/O Unit with two 16-bit timer/counters.

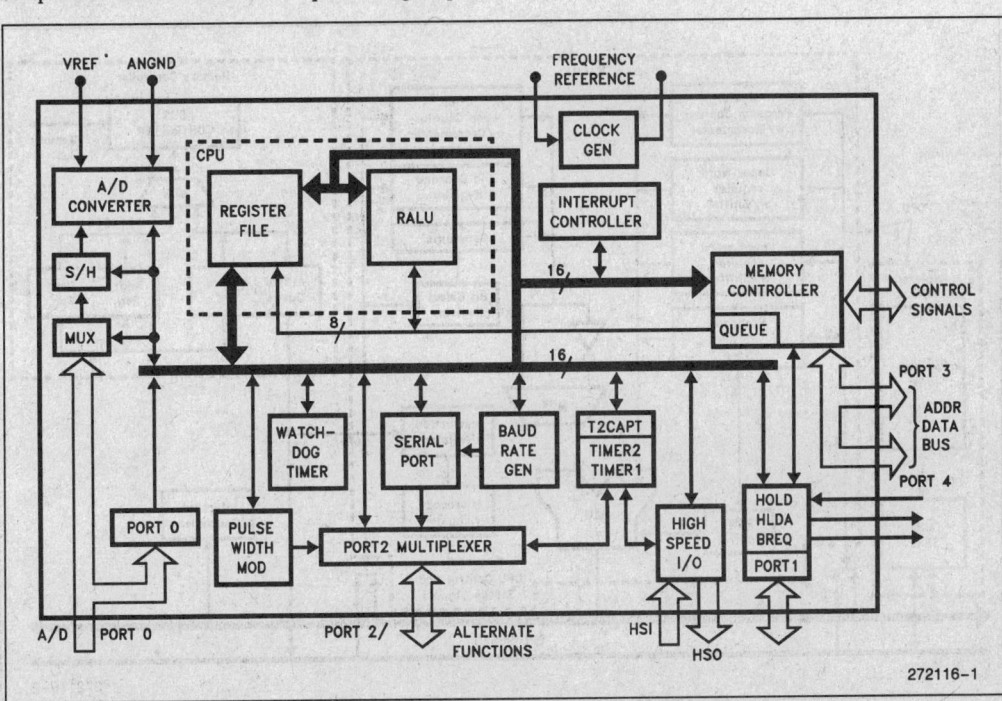

Figure 1-1. 80C196KB Block Diagram

5-317

AP-466

2.0 THE CPU

The major components of the 80C196KB CPU are the Register File and the Register/Arithmetic Logic Unit (RALU). The Register File contains 256 internal register locations (00H through 0FFH), all of which remain alive during power-down mode. Locations 00H through 17H are the I/O control registers or Special Function Registers (SFRs). Locations 18H and 19H contain the stack pointer, which can serve as general purpose RAM when not performing stack operations. The remaining 230 bytes serve as general purpose RAM, accessible as bytes, words or double-words.

Calculations performed by the 80C196KB take place in the RALU. The RALU shown in Figure 2-1 contains a 17-bit ALU, the Program Status Word (PSW), the Program Counter (PC), a loop counter, and three temporary registers. The RALU operates directly on the Register File, thus eliminating accumulator bottleneck and providing for direct control of I/O operations through the SFRs.

The SFRs control all the 80C196KB peripheral devices except Ports 3 and 4. Figure 2-2 shows the layout of these registers. Three SFR windows exist on the 80C196KB. The value in the Window Select Register (WSR) determines the SFR window; WSR = 0 selects Window 0 and WSR = 15 selects Window 15. Window 0 consists of 24 SFRs. Some of these registers serve one function when read and another function when written. The read-only registers in Window 0 become write-only registers in Window 15; and the write-only registers in Window 0 become read-only registers in Window 15. Figure 2-3 contains descriptions of the SFRs.

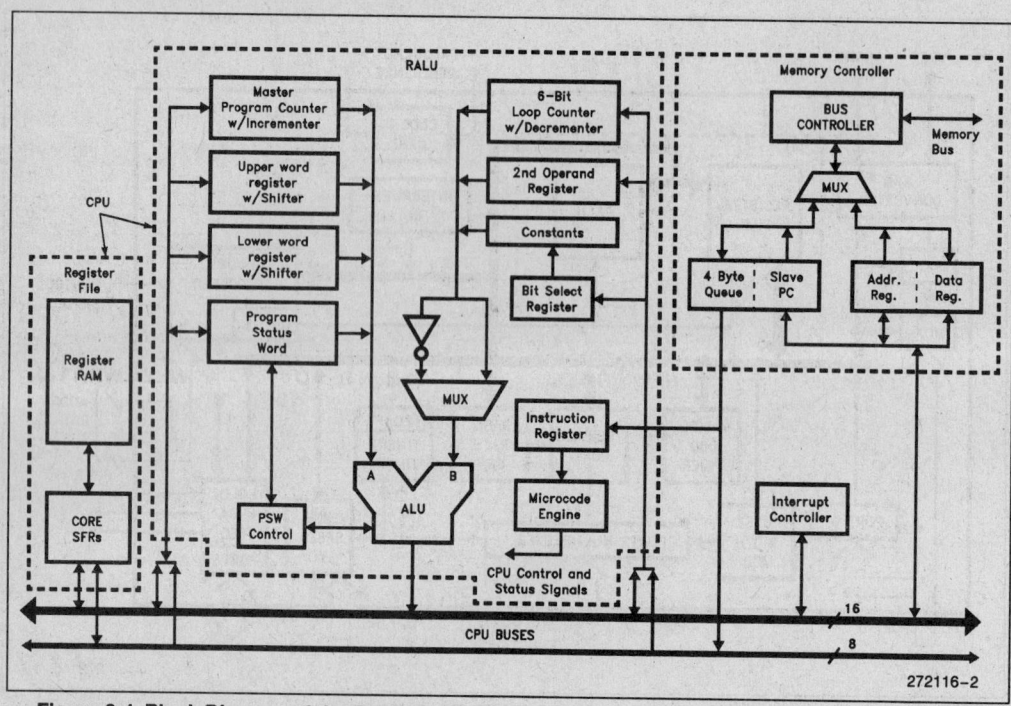

Figure 2-1. Block Diagram of the Register File, RALU, Interrupt Controller and Memory Controller

AP-466

Addr	WHEN READ WSR = 0	Addr	WHEN WRITTEN	Addr	WHEN READ WSR = 15	Addr	WHEN WRITTEN
19H	STACK POINTER	19H	STACK POINTER	19H	STACK POINTER	19H	STACK POINTER
18H		18H		18H		18H	
17H	*IOS2	17H	PWM_CONTROL	17H	PWM_CONTROL	17H	*IOS2
16H	IOS1	16H	IOC1	16H	IOC1	16H	IOS1
15H	IOS0	15H	IOC0	15H	IOC0	15H	IOS0
14H	*WSR	14H	*WSR	14H	*WSR	14H	*WSR
13H	*INT_MASK1	13H	*INT_MASK1	13H	*INT_MASK1	13H	*INT_MASK1
12H	*INT_PEND1	12H	*INT_PEND1	12H	*INT_PEND1	12H	*INT_PEND1
11H	*SP_STAT	11H	*SP_CON	11H	*SP_CON	11H	*SP_STAT
10H	PORT2	10H	PORT2	10H	RESERVED**	10H	RESERVED**
0FH	PORT1	0FH	PORT1	0FH	RESERVED**	0FH	RESERVED**
0EH	PORT0	0EH	BAUD RATE	0EH	RESERVED**	0EH	RESERVED**
0DH	TIMER2(HI)	0DH	TIMER2(HI)	0DH	T2CAPTURE(HI)	0DH	T2CAPTURE(HI)
0CH	TIMER2(LO)	0CH	TIMER2(LO)	0CH	T2CAPTURE(LO)	0CH	T2CAPTURE(LO)
0BH	TIMER1(HI)	0BH	*IOC2	0BH	*IOC2	0BH	TIMER1(HI)
0AH	TIMER1(LO)	0AH	WATCHDOG	0AH	WATCHDOG	0AH	TIMER1(LO)
09H	INT_PEND	09H	INT_PEND	09H	INT_PEND	09H	INT_PEND
08H	INT_MASK	08H	INT_MASK	08H	INT_MASK	08H	INT_MASK
07H	SBUF(RX)	07H	SBUF(TX)	07H	SBUF(TX)	07H	SBUF(RX)
06H	HSI_STATUS	06H	HSO_COMMAND	06H	HSO_COMMAND	06H	HSI_STATUS
05H	HSI_TIME(HI)	05H	HSO_TIME(HI)	05H	HSO_TIME(HI)	05H	HSI_TIME(HI)
04H	HSI_TIME(LO)	04H	HSO_TIME(LO)	04H	HSO_TIME(LO)	04H	HSI_TIME(LO)
03H	AD_RESULT(HI)	03H	HSI_MODE	03H	HSI_MODE	03H	AD_RESULT(HI)
02H	AD_RESULT(LO)	02H	AD_COMMAND	02H	AD_COMMAND	02H	AD_RESULT(LO)
01H	ZERO_REG(HI)	01H	ZERO_REG(HI)	01H	ZERO_REG(HI)	01H	ZERO_REG(HI)
00H	ZERO_REG(LO)	00H	ZERO_REG(LO)	00H	ZERO_REG(LO)	00H	ZERO_REG(LO)

NOTES:
*New or changed register function from 8096BH
**Reserved registers should not be written or read

Figure 2-2. Special Function Registers

Register	Description
ZERO_REG	Zero Register - Always reads as a zero, useful for a base when indexing and as a constant for calculations and compares.
AD_RESULT	A/D Result Hi/Low - Low and high order results of the A/D converter
AD_COMMAND	A/D Command Register - Controls the A/D
HSI_MODE	HSI Mode Register - Sets the mode of the High Speed Input unit.
HSI_TIME	HSI Time Hi/Lo - Contains the time at which the High Speed Input unit was triggered.
HSO_TIME	HSO Time Hi/Lo - Sets the time or count for the High Speed Output to execute the command in the Command Register.
HSO_COMMAND	HSO Command Register - Determines what will happen at the time loaded into the HSO Time registers.
HSI_STATUS	HSI Status Registers - Indicates which HSI pins were detected at the time in the HSI Time registers and the current state of the pins. In Window 15 - Writes to pin detected bits, but not current state bits.
SBUF(TX)	Transmit buffer for the serial port, holds contents to be outputted. Last written value is readable in Window 15.
SBUF(RX)	Receive buffer for the serial port, holds the byte just received by the serial port. Writable in Window 15.
INT_MASK	Interrupt Mask Register - Enables or disables the individual interrupts.
INT_PEND	Interrupt Pending Register - Indicates that an interrupt signal has occurred on one of the sources and has not been serviced. (also INT_PENDING)
WATCHDOG	Watchdog Timer Register - Written periodically to hold off automatic reset every 64K state times. Returns upper byte of WDT counter in Window 15.
TIMER1	Timer 1 Hi/Lo - Timer1 high and low bytes.
TIMER2	Timer 2 Hi/Lo - Timer2 high and low bytes.
IOPORT0	Port 0 Register - Levels on pins of Port 0. Reserved in Window 15.
BAUD_RATE	Register which determines the baud rate, this register is loaded sequentially. Reserved in Window 15.
IOPORT1	Port 1 Register - Used to read or write to Port 1. Reserved in Window 15
IOPORT2	Port 2 Register - Used to read or write to Port 2. Reserved in Window 15
SP_STAT	Serial Port Status - Indicates the status of the serial port.
SP_CON	Serial Port Control - Used to set the mode of the serial port.
IOS0	I/O Status Register 0 - Contains information on the HSO status. Writes to HSO pins in Window 15.
IOS1	I/O Status Register 1 - Contains information on the status of the timers and of the HSI.
IOC0	I/O Control Register 0 - Controls alternate functions of HSI pins, Timer 2 reset sources and Timer 2 clock sources.
IOC1	I/O Control Register 1 - Controls alternate functions of Port 2 pins, timer interrupts and HSI interrupts.
PWM_CONTROL	Pulse Width Modulation Control Register - Sets the duration of the PWM pulse.
INT_PEND1	Interrupt Pending register for the 8 new interrupt vectors (also INT_PENDING1)
INT_MASK1	Interrupt Mask register for the 8 new interrupt vectors
IOC2	I/O Control Register 2 - Controls new 80C196KB features
IOS2	I/O Status Register 2 - Contains information on HSO events
WSR	Window Select Register - Selects register window

Figure 2-3. Special Function Register Descriptions

3.0 THE ARCHITECTURE

The 80C196KB supports 106 instructions. This instruction set includes bit operations, byte operations, word operations, double-word operations (unsigned 32-bit) long operations (signed 32-bit), flag manipulations as well as jump and call instructions. All the standard logical and arithmetic instructions function as both byte and word operations. The Jump Bit Set and Jump Bit Clear instructions can operate on any of the SFRs or bytes in the register file. These fast bit manipulations allow for rapid I/O functions.

Byte and word operations make-up most of the 80C196KB instruction set. The assembly language for the 80C196KB (ASM-96) uses a "B" suffix on a mnemonic for a byte operation, otherwise the mnemonic refers to a word operation. One, two or three operand forms exist for many of the instructions.

A one operand instruction has the form:

```
NOT Value1        ;Value1 = 1's complement (Value1)
```

A two operand instruction has the form:

```
ADD Value2, Value1 ;Value2 = Value2 + Value1
```

A three operand instruction has the form:

```
MUL Value3, Value2, Value1 ;Value3 = Value2 * Value1.
```

Long and double-word operations include shifts, normalize, multiply and divide. The divide instruction functions as a 32-bit by 16-bit divide that generates a 16-bit quotient and 16-bit remainder. The word multiply operates as a 16-bit by 16-bit multiply with a 32-bit result. Both operations can function in either the signed or unsigned mode. The direct unsigned modes of these instructions take only 3.0 μs (at 16 MHz) for divide and 1.75 μs (at 16 MHz) for multiply. The normalize instruction and sticky bit flag provide hardware support for the software floating point package (FPAL-96).

3.1 Addressing Modes

The 80C196KB instruction set supports the following addressing modes: register-direct, indirect, indirect with auto-increment, immediate, short-indexed and long-indexed. These modes increase the flexibility and overall execution speed of the 80C196KB. Each instruction uses at least one of the addressing modes. These modes and formats are shown in Figure 3-1.

Mnem	Dest or Src1	;One Operand Direct
Mnem	Dest, Src1	;Two Operand Direct
Mnem	Dest, Src1, Src2	;Three Operand Direct
Mnem	#Src1	;One Operand Immediate
Mnem	Dest, #Src1	;Two Operand Immediate
Mnem	Dest, Src1, #Src2	;Three Operand Immediate
Mnem	[addr]	;One Operand Indirect
Mnem	[addr]+	;One Operand Indirect Auto-Increment
Mnem	Dest, [addr]	;Two Operand Indirect
Mnem	Dest, [addr]+	;Two Operand Indirect Auto-Increment
Mnem	Dest, Src1, [addr]	;Three Operand Indirect
Mnem	Dest, Src1, [addr]+	;Three Operand Indirect Auto-Increment
Mnem	Dest, offs[addr]	;Two Operand Indexed (Short or Long)
Mnem	Dest, Src1, offs[addr]	;Three Operand Indexed (Short or Long)

Where:
Mnem = Instruction Mnemonic
Dest = Destination Register
Src1, Src2 = Source Registers
addr = Word register used in computing the address of an operand
offs = Offset used in computing the address of an operand

Figure 3-1. Instruction Format

AP-466

The register-direct and immediate addressing modes execute faster than the other addressing modes. The register-direct addressing mode provides access to the addresses in the register file and the SFRs. The indexed modes provide for direct access to the remainder of the 64K address space. Immediate addressing uses the data following the opcode as the operand.

Both of the indirect addressing modes use the value in a word register as the address of the operand. The indirect auto-increment mode increments a word address by one after a byte operation and two after a word operation. This addressing mode provides easy access into look-up tables.

The long-indexed addressing mode provides direct access to any of the locations in the 64K address space.

This mode forms the address of the operand by adding a 16-bit 2's complement value to the contents of a word register. Indexing with the zero register allows "direct" addressing to any location. The short-indexed addressing mode forms the address of the operand by adding an 8-bit 2's complement value to the contents of a word register.

The multiple addressing modes of the 80C196KB make it easy to program in assembly language and provide an excellent interface to high level languages. The instructions accepted by the assembler consist of mnemonics followed by either addresses or data. Table 3-1 lists the mnemonics and their functions. The MCS-96 Macro Assembler Users Guide, listed in the bibliography, contains additional information on 80C196KB assembly language.

AP-466

Table 3-1. Instruction Summary

Mnemonic	Operands	Operation (Note 1)	Z	N	C	V	VT	ST	Notes
ADD/ADDB	2	D ← D + A	✔	✔	✔	✔	↑	–	
ADD/ADDB	3	D ← B + A	✔	✔	✔	✔	↑	–	
ADDC/ADDCB	2	D ← D + A + C	↓	✔	✔	✔	↑	–	
SUB/SUBB	2	D ← D − A	✔	✔	✔	✔	↑	–	
SUB/SUBB	3	D ← B − A	✔	✔	✔	✔	↑	–	
SUBC/SUBCB	2	D ← D − A + C − 1	↓	✔	✔	✔	↑	–	
CMP/CMPB	2	D − A	✔	✔	✔	✔	↑	–	
MUL/MULU	2	D,D + 2 ← D × A	–	–	–	–	–	–	2
MUL/MULU	3	D,D + 2 ← B × A	–	–	–	–	–	–	2
MULB/MULUB	2	D,D + 1 ← D × A	–	–	–	–	–	–	3
MULB/MULUB	3	D,D + 1 ← B × A	–	–	–	–	–	–	3
DIVU	2	D ← (D,D + 2) /A,D + 2 ← remainder	–	–	–	✔	↑	–	2
DIVUB	2	D ← (D,D + 1) /A,D + 1 ← remainder	–	–	–	✔	↑	–	3
DIV	2	D ← (D,D + 2) /A,D + 2 ← remainder	–	–	–	✔	↑	–	
DIVB	2	D ← (D,D + 1) /A,D + 1 ← remainder	–	–	–	✔	↑	–	
AND/ANDB	2	D ← D AND A	✔	✔	0	0	–	–	
AND/ANDB	3	D ← B AND A	✔	✔	0	0	–	–	
OR/ORB	2	D ← D OR A	✔	✔	0	0	–	–	
XOR/XORB	2	D ← D (excl. or) A	✔	✔	0	0	–	–	
LD/LDB	2	D ← A	–	–	–	–	–	–	
ST/STB	2	A ← D	–	–	–	–	–	–	
LDBSE	2	D ← A; D + 1 ← SIGN(A)	–	–	–	–	–	–	3,4
LDBZE	2	D ← A; D + 1 ← 0	–	–	–	–	–	–	3,4
PUSH	1	SP ← SP − 2; (SP) ← A	–	–	–	–	–	–	
POP	1	A ← (SP); SP + 2	–	–	–	–	–	–	
PUSHF	0	SP ← SP − 2; (SP) ← PSW; PSW ← 0000H; I ← 0	0	0	0	0	0	0	
POPF	0	PSW ← (SP); SP ← SP + 2; I ← ✔	✔	✔	✔	✔	✔	✔	
SJMP	1	PC ← PC + 11-bit offset	–	–	–	–	–	–	5
LJMP	1	PC ← PC + 16-bit offset	–	–	–	–	–	–	5
BR [indirect]	1	PC ← (A)							
SCALL	1	SP ← SP − 2; (SP) ← PC; PC ← PC + 11-bit offset	–	–	–	–	–	–	5
LCALL	1	SP ← SP − 2; (SP) ← PC; PC ← PC + 16-bit offset	–	–	–	–	–	–	5

AP-466

Table 3-1. Instruction Summary (Continued)

Mnemonic	Operands	Operation (Note 1)	Z	N	C	V	VT	ST	Notes
RET	0	PC ← (SP); SP ← SP + 2	—	—	—	—	—	—	
J (conditional)	1	PC ← PC + 8-bit offset (if taken)	—	—	—	—	—	—	5
JC	1	Jump if C = 1	—	—	—	—	—	—	5
JNC	1	Jump if C = 0	—	—	—	—	—	—	5
JE	1	Jump if Z = 1	—	—	—	—	—	—	5
JNE	1	Jump if Z = 0	—	—	—	—	—	—	5
JGE	1	Jump if N = 0	—	—	—	—	—	—	5
JLT	1	Jump if N = 1	—	—	—	—	—	—	5
JGT	1	Jump if N = 0 and Z = 0	—	—	—	—	—	—	5
JLE	1	Jump if N = 1 or Z = 1	—	—	—	—	—	—	5
JH	1	Jump if C = 1 and Z = 0	—	—	—	—	—	—	5
JNH	1	Jump if C = 0 or Z = 1	—	—	—	—	—	—	5
JV	1	Jump if V = 1	—	—	—	—	—	—	5
JNV	1	Jump if V = 0	—	—	—	—	—	—	5
JVT	1	Jump if VT = 1; Clear VT	—	—	—	—	0	—	5
JNVT	1	Jump if VT = 0; Clear VT	—	—	—	—	0	—	5
JST	1	Jump if ST = 1	—	—	—	—	—	—	5
JNST	1	Jump if ST = 0	—	—	—	—	—	—	5
JBS	3	Jump if Specified Bit = 1	—	—	—	—	—	—	5,6
JBC	3	Jump if Specified Bit = 0	—	—	—	—	—	—	5,6
DJNZ/DJNZW	1	D ← D − 1; If D ≠ 0 then PC ← PC + 8-bit offset	—	—	—	—	—	—	5, 10
DEC/DECB	1	D ← D − 1	✓	✓	✓	✓	↑	—	
NEG/NEGB	1	D ← 0 − D	✓	✓	✓	✓	↑	—	
INC/INCB	1	D ← D + 1	✓	✓	✓	✓	↑	—	
EXT	1	D ← D; D + 2 ← Sign (D)	✓	✓	0	0	—	—	2
EXTB	1	D ← D; D + 1 ← Sign (D)	✓	✓	0	0	—	—	3
NOT/NOTB	1	D ← Logical Not (D)	✓	✓	0	0	—	—	
CLR/CLRB	1	D ← 0	1	0	0	0	—	—	
SHL/SHLB/SHLL	2	C ← msb ----- lsb ← 0	✓	✓	✓	✓	↑	—	7
SHR/SHRB/SHRL	2	0 → msb ----- lsb → C	✓	✓	✓	0	—	✓	7
SHRA/SHRAB/SHRAL	2	msb → msb ----- lsb → C	✓	✓	✓	0	—	✓	7
SETC	0	C ← 1	—	—	1	—	—	—	
CLRC	0	C ← 0	—	—	0	—	—	—	

AP-466

Table 3-1. Instruction Summary (Continued)

Mnemonic	Operands	Operation (Note 1)	Z	N	C	V	VT	ST	Notes
CLRVT	0	VT ← 0	–	–	–	–	0	–	
RST	0	PC ← 2080H	0	0	0	0	0	0	8
DI	0	Disable All Interrupts (I ← 0)	–	–	–	–	–	–	
EI	0	Enable All Interrupts (I ← 1)	–	–	–	–	–	–	
NOP	0	PC ← PC + 1	–	–	–	–	–	–	
SKIP	0	PC ← PC + 2	–	–	–	–	–	–	
NORML	2	Left shift till msb = 1; D ← shift count	✔	✔	0	–	–	–	7
TRAP	0	SP ← SP – 2; (SP) ← PC; PC ← (2010H)	–	–	–	–	–	–	9
PUSHA	1	SP ← SP-2; (SP) ← PSW; PSW ← 0000H; SP ← SP-2; (SP) ← IMASK1/WSR; IMASK1 ← 00H	0	0	0	0	0	0	
POPA	1	IMASK1/WSR ← (SP); SP ← SP+2 PSW ← (SP); SP ← SP+2	✔	✔	✔	✔	✔	✔	
IDLPD	1	IDLE MODE IF KEY=1; POWERDOWN MODE IF KEY =2; CHIP RESET OTHERWISE	–	–	–	–	–	–	
CMPL	2	D-A	✔	✔	✔	✔	↑	–	
BMOV	2	[PTR_HI]+ ← [PTR_LOW]+ ; UNTIL COUNT=0	–	–	–	–	–	–	

NOTES:
1. If the mnemonic ends in "B" a byte operation is performed, otherwise a word operation is done. Operands D, B and A must conform to the alignment rules for the required operand type. D and B are locations in the Register File; A can be located anywhere in memory.
2. D,D + 2 are consecutive WORDS in memory; D is DOUBLE-WORD aligned.
3. D,D + 1 are consecutive BYTES in memory; D is WORD aligned.
4. Changes a byte to word.
5. Offset is a 2's complement number.
6. Specified bit is one of the 2048 bits in the register file.
7. The "L" (Long) suffix indicates double-word operation.
8. Initiates a Reset by pulling RESET low. Software should re-initialize all the necessary registers with code starting at 2080H.
9. The assembler will not accept this mnemonic.
10. The DJNZW instruction is not guaranteed to work. See Functional Deviations section.

Flag Settings. The modification to the flag setting is shown for each instruction. A checkmark (✔) means that the flag is set or cleared as appropriate. A hyphen (-) means that the flag is not modified. A one or zero (1) or (0) indicates that the flag will be in that state after the instruction. An up arrow (↑) indicates that the instruction may set the flag if it is appropriate but will not clear the flag. A down arrow (↓) indicates that the flag can be cleared but not set by the instruction.

AP-466

3.2 Program Status Word

The Program Status Word (PSW) is a collection of Boolean flags which contain information concerning the state of the user's program. The high byte of the PSW contains status flags and the low byte contains an interrupt mask register. The PSW high byte is shown in Figure 3-2. Table 3-2 contains descriptions of the status flags.

Table 3-2. Status Flag Descriptions

Flag	Name	Function
ST	Sticky Bit	Indicates whether any 1's were lost due to a right shift operation; primarily used for floating-point routines.
I	Interrupt Enable	Master control for 80C196KB interrupts
C	Carry Flag	Set if there is a carry (or no borrow), and otherwise cleared, as a result of an ADD or SUB instruction.
VT	Overflow Trap Flag	Set whenever overflow flag is set; cleared only by a CLRVT, JVT or JNVT instruction.
V	Overflow Flag	Set if result is out of range for signed arithmetic operation.
N	Negative Flag	Holds the algebraically correct sign as the result of an operation.
Z	Zero Flag	Set if the result of an operation is zero.

PSW:

15	14	13	12	11	10	9	8
Z	N	V	VT	C		I	ST

Figure 3-2. The Program Status Word Register (High Byte)

AP-466

4.0 INTERRUPTS

There are 28 different interrupt sources available on the 80C196KB. The 28 sources vector through 18 locations or interrupt vectors. The vector names and their sources are shown in Figure 4-1, and their locations are listed in Table 4-1. The four registers that control the interrupt system are: INT_PEND, INT_PEND1, INT_MASK, INT_MASK1. The Program Status Word (PSW) contains a global disable bit, I, which is set or cleared using the EI or DI instructions. Figure 4-2 shows a block diagram of the interrupt structure.

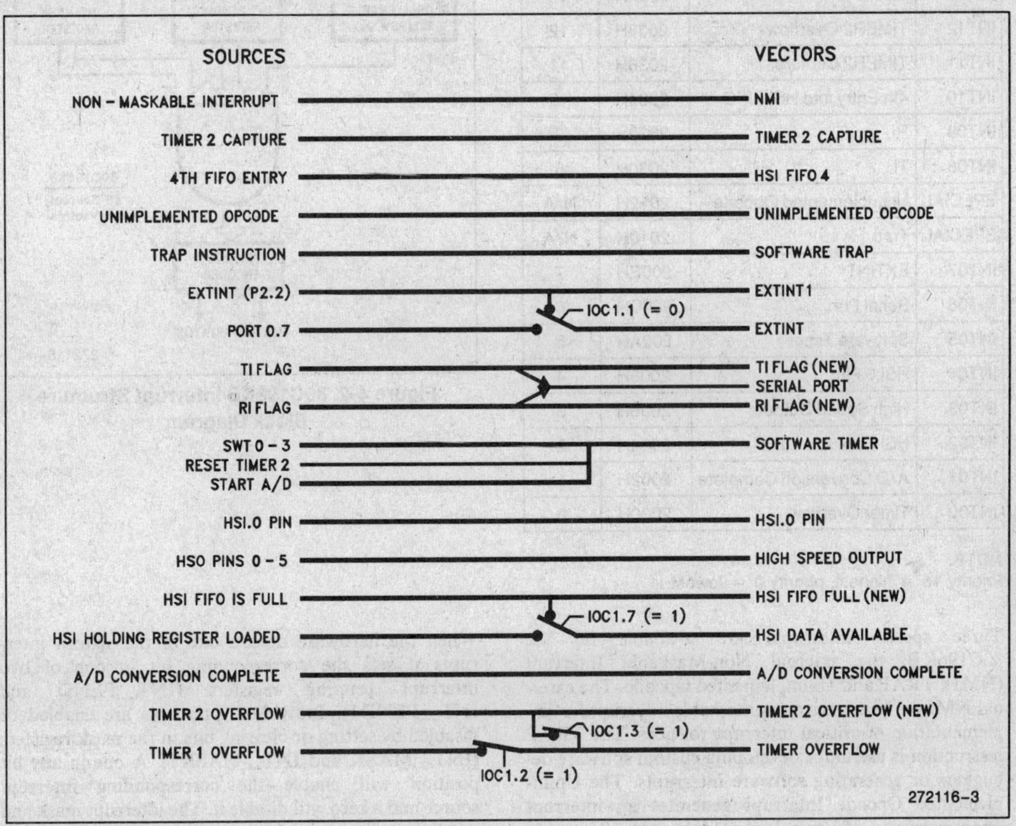

Figure 4-1. 80C196KB Interrupt Sources

AP-466

Table 4-1. 80C196KB Interrupt Vector Locations

Number	Vector Name	Vector Location	Priority
INT15	NMI	203EH	15
INT14	HSI FIFO Full	203CH	14
INT13	EXTINT1	203AH	13
INT12	TIMER2 Overflow	2038H	12
INT11	TIMER2 Capture	2036H	11
INT10	4th Entry into HSI FIFO	2034H	10
INT09	RI	2032H	9
INT08	TI	2030H	8
SPECIAL	Unimplemented Opcode	2012H	N/A
SPECIAL	Trap	2010H	N/A
INT07	EXTINT	200EH	7
INT06	Serial Port	200CH	6
INT05	Software Timer	200AH	5
INT04	HSI.0 Pin	2008H	4
INT03	High Speed Outputs	2006H	3
INT02	HSI Data Available	2004H	2
INT01	A/D Conversion Complete	2002H	1
INT00	Timer Overflow	2000H	0

NOTE:
Priority 15 = highest, priority 0 = lowest

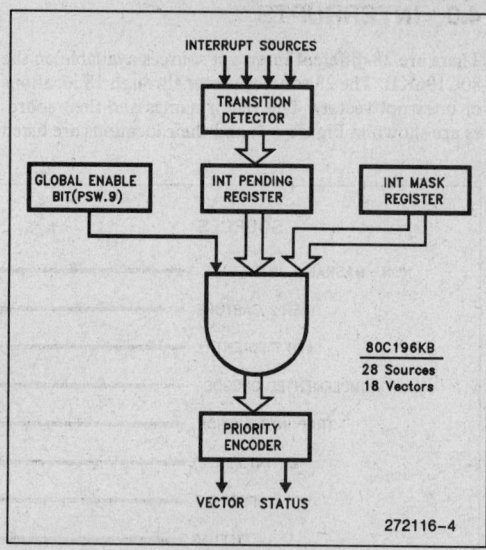

Figure 4-2. 80C196KB Interrupt Structure Block Diagram

Three special interrupts are available on the 80C196KB: the external Non-Maskable Interrupt (NMI), TRAP and Unimplemented Opcode. The external NMI pin generates an unmaskable interrupt for implementation of critical interrupt routines. The TRAP instruction is useful for developing custom software debuggers or generating software interrupts. The Unimplemented Opcode Interrupt generates an interrupt upon execution of unimplemented opcodes. This provides software recovery from random execution during hardware or software failures.

When the hardware detects one of the sixteen interrupts it sets the corresponding bit in one of two interrupt pending registers (INT_PEND and INT_PEND1). Individual interrupts are enabled or disabled by setting or clearing bits in the mask registers (INT_MASK and INT_MASK1). A one in any bit position will enable the corresponding interrupt source and a zero will disable it. The interrupt mask and pending registers are shown in Figure 4-3.

		7	6	5	4	3	2	1	0
12H	INT_PEND1:	NMI	FIFO FULL	EXT INT1	T2 OVF	T2 CAP	HSI4	RI	TI
13H	INT_MASK1:								

		7	6	5	4	3	2	1	0
09H	INT_PEND:	EXT INT	SER PORT	SOFT TIMER	HSI.0 PIN	HSO PIN	HSI DATA	A/D DONE	TIMER OVF
08H	INT_MASK:								

Figure 4-3. Interrupt Mask and Pending Registers

AP-466

The priority encoder looks at all the interrupts that are both pending and enabled, and selects the one with the highest priority. The priorities are shown in Table 4-1 (15 is highest, 0 is lowest). When the interrupt controller decides to process an interrupt, it executes a "call" to an Interrupt Service Routine (ISR). The address of the ISR is contained in the corresponding interrupt vector location. The interrupt controller clears the associated pending bit then pushes the return address onto the stack. The ISR should use the PUSHA instruction to save the PSW, INT_MASK, INT_MASK1 and WSR on the stack. The PUSHA instruction also clears the PSW and interrupt mask registers, disabling all interrupts. The ISR software must then implement the interrupt priority structure desired for that routine by enabling only the desired interrupts. At the end of the ISR, the POPA instruction restores the PSW, INT_MASK, INT_MASK1 and WSR to their original states and restores the original priority structure. In most cases an Interrupt Service Routine will have the basic structure shown below.

```
INT_VECTOR:   PUSHA                        ; Save the PSW, INT_MASK,
                                           ;INT_MASK1, and WSR
              LDB INT_MASK, #xxxxxxxxB     ;Set-up New Interrupt
              LDB INT_MASK1,#xxxxxxxxB     ;Priorities
              EI                           ;Enable Interrupts Again
              -
              -                            ;Service the Interrupt
              -
              POPA                         ;Restore
              RET
```

5.0 TIMERS/COUNTERS

The 80C196KB has two 16-bit timers, Timer1 and Timer2, shown in Figure 5-1. Timer1 is readable in Window 0 and writable in Window 15 while Timer2 is readable and writable in Window 0. The 80C196KB also includes separate, dedicated timers for the baud rate generator and watchdog timer. The watchdog timer is an internal timer that can be used to reset the system if the software fails to operate properly.

The Timer1 value is incremented by the 80C196KB internal clock every 8 state times. (A state time is 2 oscillator periods, or 0.167 μs with a 12 MHz crystal.) Timer1 generates a Timer Overflow Interrupt (INT00) when crossing the 0FFFFH/0000H boundary. I/O Control Register 1 (IOC1) controls the Timer1 overflow interrupt. As shown in Figure 5-2, setting IOC1.2 enables Timer1 overflow to INT00. The status of Timer1 Overflow Interrupt is read in I/O Status Register 1 (IOS1) shown in Figure 5-3.

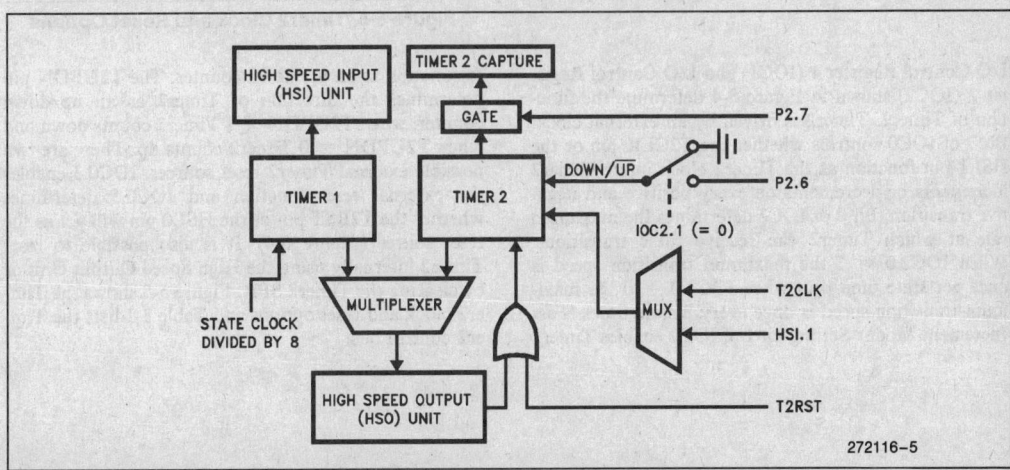

Figure 5-1. Timer Block Diagram

5-329

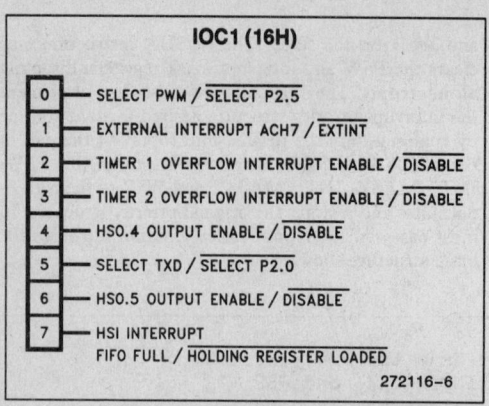

Figure 5-2. I/O Control Register 1 (IOC1)

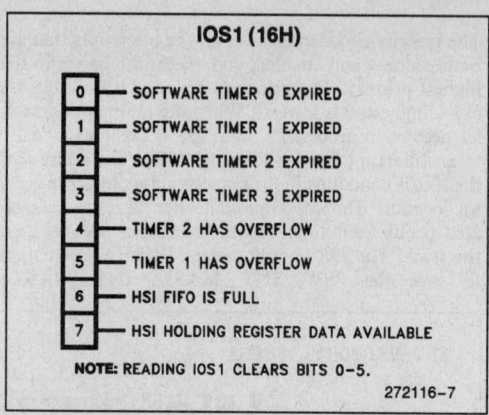

Figure 5-3. I/O Status Register 1 (IOS1)

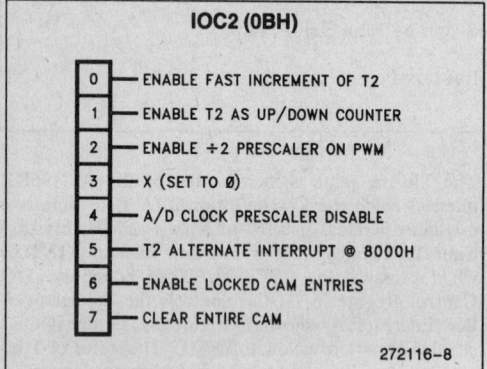

Figure 5-4. I/O Control Register 2 (IOC2)

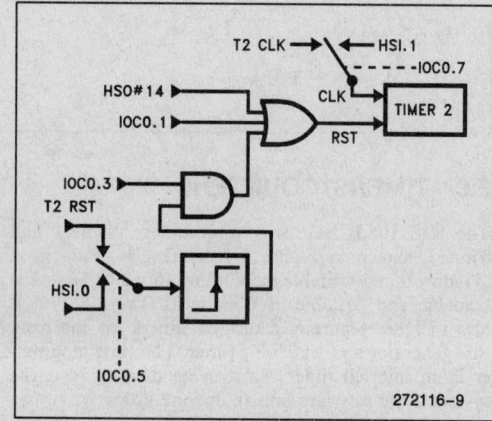

Figure 5-5. Timer2 Clock and Reset Options

I/O Control Register 1 (IOC1) and I/O Control Register 2 (IOC2) shown in Figure 5-4 determine the function of Timer2. Timer2 is driven by an external clock. Bit 7 of IOC0 controls whether the T2CLK pin or the HSI.1 pin function as the Timer2 clock input. Timer2 increments or decrements on every positive and negative transition. Bit 0 of IOC2 determines the maximum rate at which Timer2 can receive these transitions. When IOC2.0 = 1 the maximum transition speed is once per state time, and when IOC2.0 = 0 the maximum transition speed is once every 8 state times (Fast Increment Mode). Setting bit 1 of IOC2 enables Timer2 to function as an up/down counter. The T2UPDN pin determines the direction of Timer2 as an up/down counter; when T2UPDN = 1 Timer2 counts down and when T2UPDN = 0 Timer2 counts up. There are two possible external Timer2 reset sources. IOC0.3 enables the external reset function and IOC0.5 determines whether the T2RST pin or the HSI.0 pin will act as the reset source (Figure 6-4). It is also possible to reset Timer2 internally using the High Speed Output Unit or by clearing the Timer2 SFR. Figure 5-5 shows the Timer2 clock and reset options and Table 5-1 lists the Timer2 control bits.

AP-466

Table 5-1. Timer2 Control Bits

	Bit = 1	Bit = 0
IOC0.1	Reset Timer2 each write	No action
IOC0.3	Enable external reset	Disable
IOC0.5	HSI.0 is ext. reset source	T2RST is reset source
IOC0.7	HSI.1 is T2 clock source	T2CLK is clock source
IOC1.3	Enable Timer2 overflow int.	Disable overflow interrupt
IOC2.0	Enable fast increment	Disable fast increment
IOC2.1	Enable downcount feature	Disable downcount
P2.6	Count down if IOC2.1 = 1	Count up
IOC2.5	Interrupt on 7FFFH/8000H	Interrupt on 0FFFFH/0000H
P2.7	Capture Timer2 into T2CAPTURE on rising edge	

Timer2 can generate three interrupts: The Timer Overflow Interrupt (INT00), The Timer2 Overflow Interrupt (INT12), and The Timer2 Capture Interrupt (INT11). IOC1 determines whether Timer1 and/or Timer2 will generate INT00. Timer2 generates an overflow interrupt when crossing the 0FFFFH/0000H boundary or the 7FFFH/8000H boundary as determined by IOC2.5. A Timer2 overflow interrupts through INT00 if IOC1.3 and INT_MASK.0 are set. Alternatively, Timer2 interrupts through INT12 if INT_MASK1.3 is set. Bit 4 of I/O Status Register 1 (IOS1.4), shown in Figure 5-3, indicates that status of Timer2 Overflow Interrupt.

6.0 HIGH SPEED INPUT UNIT

The High Speed Input Unit (HSI) can record times of external events with an 8 state time (1.33 μs at 12 MHz) resolution. It can capture the value of Timer1 when an event takes place on one of the four HSI lines (HSI.0 through HSI.3). The four types of events that can trigger a capture are: rising edges only, falling edges only, rising or falling edges, or every eighth rising edge. As shown in Figure 6-2, the four input lines are independently configurable via the HSI_MODE register. This register determines the capture modes of the four inputs. A block diagram of the HSI unit is shown in Figure 6-1.

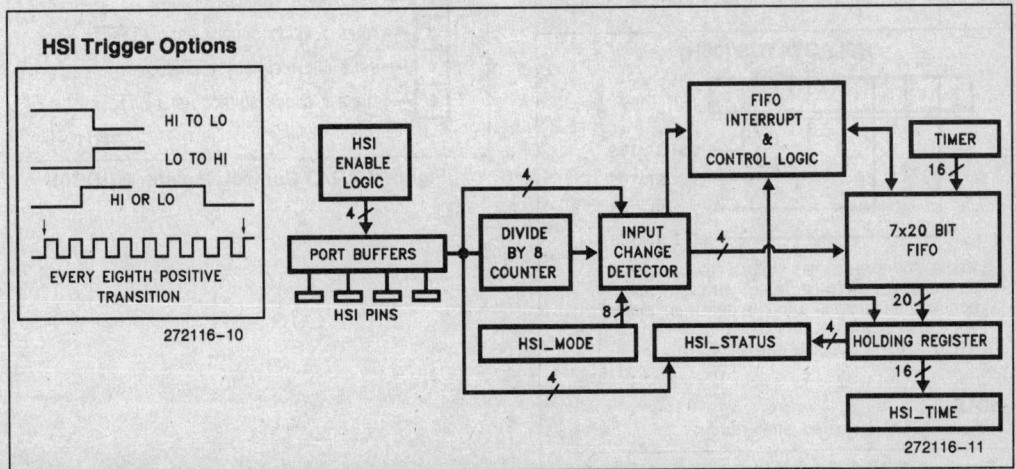

Figure 6-1. High Speed Input Unit

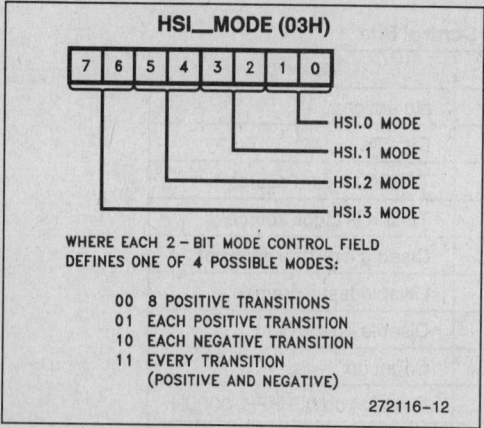

Figure 6-2. High Speed Input Mode Register (HSI_MODE)

The HSI unit stores the Timer1 value and 4 status bits in a 7 x 20 level FIFO and holding register. It is possible to store 8 entries, 7 in the FIFO and 1 in the holding register. The HSI unit will not store events occurring after the FIFO is full. The HSI holding register contains the earliest entry placed in the FIFO. Reading the holding register unloads one level of the FIFO. The HSI unit then places the next entry into the holding register.

The contents of the HSI holding register are obtained by first reading the HSI_STATUS register and then the HSI_TIME register. The HSI_TIME register returns the event time tag. The HSI_STATUS register returns a status and an input bit for each of the four HSI lines (see Figure 6-3). The status bit indicates

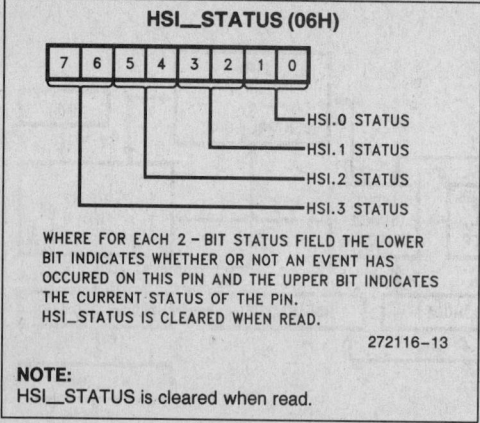

NOTE:
HSI_STATUS is cleared when read.

Figure 6-3. High Speed Input Status Register (HSI_STATUS)

which line(s) caused the event and the input bit indicates the **current** input level of the line, not the level when the event occurred. Reading the HSI_TIME register unloads one level of the FIFO.

To start the HSI use the following steps: 1) Flush the FIFO, 2) Enable the HSI interrupts, 3) Initialize and enable the HSI pins. The following section of code will flush the FIFO:

```
FLUSH:  LD ZERO_REG,        ;Unload one level of
        HSI_TIME            the FIFO
        SKIP ZERO_REG       ;Wait 4 state times
        SKIP ZERO_REG       ;Wait 4 state times
        JBS IOS1, 7, FLUSH  ;Check whether FIFO
                            is empty
```

I/O Control Register 0 (IOC0), shown in Figure 6-4, can individually enable or disable the four HSI lines (HSI.0 through HSI.3). Disabling an input line disconnects it from the FIFO, changing its function from an HSI line to a general purpose input line. However, the corresponding HSI_STATUS input bits indicate the current state of the line regardless of whether the line functions as an HSI input line or as a general purpose input line.

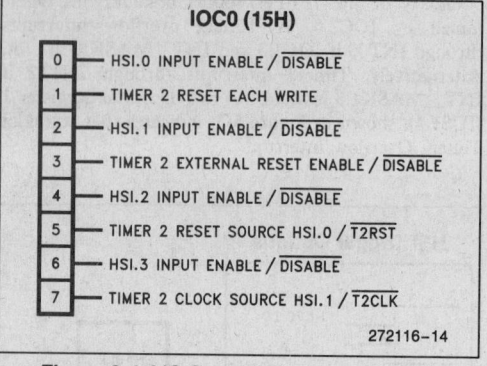

Figure 6-4. I/O Control Register 0 (IOC0)

AP-466

The HSI unit can generate three interrupts: The HSI Data Available Interrupt (INT02), the HSI_FIFO_4 Interrupt (INT10) and the HSI FIFO FULL Interrupt (INT14). Bit 7 of I/O Control Register 1 (IOC1) controls the INT02 source. If IOC1.7 = 0 loading the holding register will cause INT02; otherwise if IOC1.7 = 1 loading the sixth entry into the FIFO (not including the holding register) will cause INT02. After INT02 occurs bits 6 and 7 of I/O Status Register 1 (IOS1) indicate which source caused the interrupt. The sources for INT10 and INT14 are independent of IOC1. Loading the fourth entry into the FIFO causes INT10 and loading the sixth entry into the FIFO causes INT14. Note if IOC1.7 is set, loading the sixth entry into the FIFO will cause both INT02 and INT14.

7.0 HIGH SPEED OUTPUT UNIT

The HSO unit can trigger events at specified times based on Timer1 or Timer2. These programmable events include: starting an A/D conversion, resetting Timer2, generating up to four software time delays and setting or clearing one or more of the 6 output lines (HSO.0 through HSO.5). The HSO unit stores pending events and their specified times in a CAM (Content Addressable Memory) file. Figure 7-1 shows a block diagram of the HSO unit.

The CAM file is the main component of the HSO. This file stores up to eight commands. Each CAM register is 24 bits wide. Sixteen bits specify the action time, and 8 bits specify the nature of the action and whether Timer1 or Timer2 is the reference. Timer2 transitions should not occur faster than once every 8 state times when it is used as a reference for the HSO. Commands for the HSO first enter the HSO holding register. They then enter the CAM when an empty CAM register is available. Commands must be in the CAM to execute; commands in the holding register will not execute. It takes one state time to compare each CAM location, so 8 state times (1.33 µs with a 12 MHz clock) are necessary for a complete CAM search. The HSO unit triggers the specified event when it finds a time match.

Writing to the HSO_COMMAND register and the HSO_TIME register loads the HSO holding register. When the next opening in the CAM file is available the contents of the HSO holding register move into it. The HSO_COMMAND register shown in Figure 7-2 specifies the event type, whether an interrupt is to occur, and the reference timer. The I/O Status Register 0 (IOS0) bits 6 and 7 indicate the status of the HSO unit. If IOS0.6 equals 0, the holding register is empty and at least one CAM register is empty. If IOS0.7 equals 0, the holding register is empty. The holding register must be empty before writing the action time to the HSO_TIME registers. If the holding register is not empty, writing to the HSO will overwrite the current holding register value. Always write the command byte first, followed by the time word.

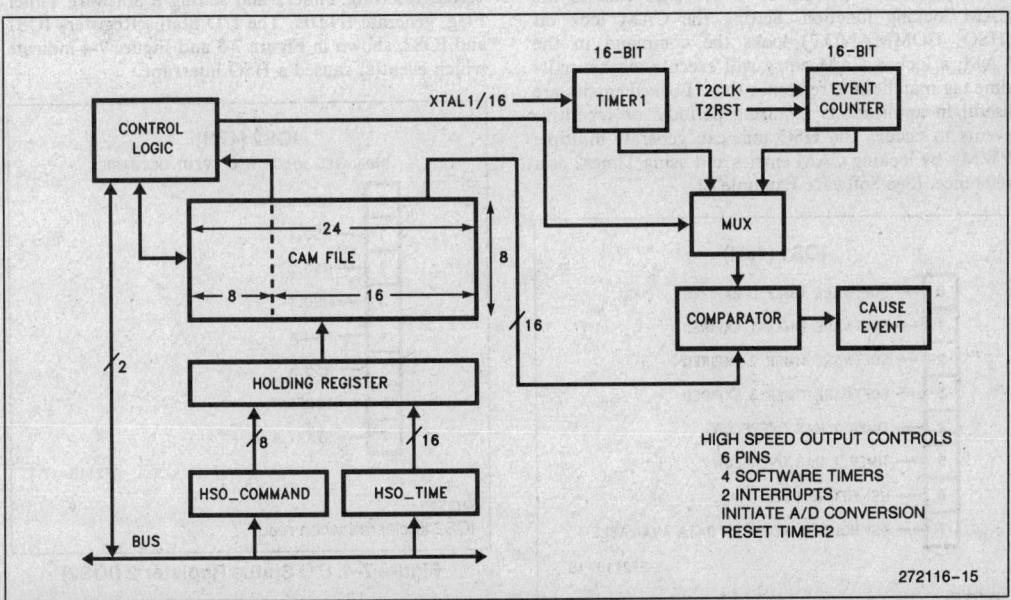

Figure 7-1. High Speed Output Block Diagram

AP-466

```
                              HSO_COMMAND (06H)
              ┌──────┬──────┬──────┬──────┬──────┬──────┬──────┬──────┐
              │  7   │  6   │  5   │  4   │  3   │  2   │  1   │  0   │
   HSO_       │ CAM  │TMR2/ │ SET/ │ INT/ │      │                    │
  COMMAND     │ LOCK │ TMR1 │CLEAR │ INT  │           CHANNEL         │
              └──────┴──────┴──────┴──────┴──────┴──────┴──────┴──────┘
```

CAM Lock   — Locks event in CAM if this is enabled by IOC2.6 (ENA_LOCK)
TMR/TMR1   — Events Based on Timer2/Based on Timer1 if 0
SET/CLEAR   — Set HSO pin/Clear HSO pin if 0
INT/INT   — Cause interrupt/No interrupt if 0
CHANNEL: 0–5: HSO pins 0–5 separately
(in Hex)   6:   HSO pins 0 and 1 together
             7:    HSO pins 2 and 3 together
             8–B: Software Timers 0–3
             C–D: Unflagged Events (Do not use for future compatibility)
             E: Reset Timer2
             F: Start A to D Conversion

Figure 7-2. High Speed Output Command Register (HSO_Command)

An entry placed in the CAM remains there until its execution unless a chip reset occurs or the CAM clear bit (IOC2.7) is set. It is possible to cancel an external pending event by writing the opposite event with the same time tag to the CAM. However, both events remain in the CAM until their time tag is matched or the CAM is cleared. Setting bit 2 of IOC2 enables the CAM locking function. Setting the CAM lock bit (HSO_COMMAND.7) locks the command in the CAM; a locked CAM entry will execute whenever its time tag matches the reference time. Locked entries are useful in applications requiring periodic or repetitive events to occur. The HSO unit can generate multiple PWM's by locking CAM entries and using Timer2 as a reference. (See Software Example 4)

The HSO unit can generate two interrupts (providing HSO_COMMAND.4 is set): The High Speed Output interrupt (INT03) and The Software Timer interrupt (INT05). The High Speed Output interrupt occurs as a result of changes on one or more of the six output pins. The other HSO commands, triggering the A/D Converter, resetting Timer2 and setting a Software Timer Flag, generate INT05. The I/O Status Registers IOS1 and IOS2, shown in Figure 7-3 and Figure 7-4 indicate which event(s) caused a HSO interrupt.

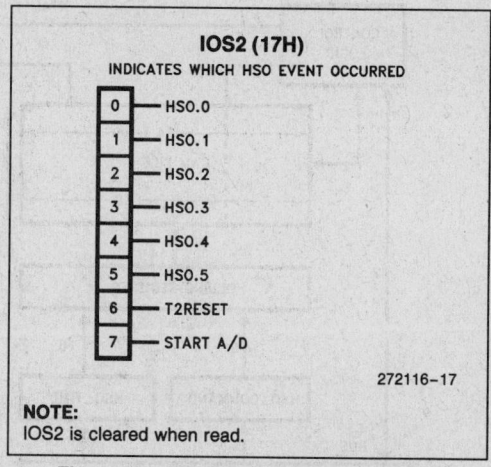

```
                IOS1 (16H)
   ┌───┬──────────────────────────────────┐
   │ 0 │ SOFTWARE TIMER 0 EXPIRED         │
   │ 1 │ SOFTWARE TIMER 1 EXPIRED         │
   │ 2 │ SOFTWARE TIMER 2 EXPIRED         │
   │ 3 │ SOFTWARE TIMER 3 EXPIRED         │
   │ 4 │ TIMER 2 HAS OVERFLOW             │
   │ 5 │ TIMER 1 HAS OVERFLOW             │
   │ 6 │ HSI FIFO IS FULL                 │
   │ 7 │ HSI HOLDING REGISTER DATA AVAILABLE │
   └───┴──────────────────────────────────┘
                                    272116-16
```

NOTE:
IOS1 is cleared when read.

Figure 7-3. I/O Status Register 1 (IOS1)

Figure 7-4. I/O Status Register 2 (IOS2)

The HSO unit can generate interrupts at preset times via four "Software Timers". Software Timer Flags are set in the I/O Status Register 1 (IOS1) at the prepro-

AP-466

grammed times. If the interrupt bit in the HSO command register is set, a Software Timer Interrupt will also occur at the designated time. The interrupt service routine can then examine IOS1 to determine which software timer expired and caused the interrupt. The most common use of the software timers is to trigger interrupt routines that must occur at regular intervals.

8.0 PULSE WIDTH MODULATION OUTPUT

The Pulse Width Modulator of the 80C196KB, when used with external hardware, can provide useful signals for a variety of applications. The PWM output can perform digital to analog conversions and drive several types of motors which require a PWM waveform for more efficient operation. A block diagram of the PWM circuit is shown in Figure 8-1. Three registers control the PWM: I/O Control Register 1 (IOC1), I/O Control Register 2 (IOC2) and the PWM Register (PWM_CONTROL). The PWM output shares a pin with Port 2; setting IOC1.0 selects the PWM function rather then the standard port function.

The PWM output waveform is a variable duty cycle pulse that repeats every 256 state times (42.75 μs @ 12 MHz) or 512 state times (85.5 μs @ 12 MHz) if the prescaler bit (IOC2.2) is set. The PWM frequencies for different clock speeds are shown in Table 8-1. Writing a value between 0 and 255 to the PWM_CONTROL register will change the duty cycle. The PWM unit has an 8-bit counter that is incremented every state time or every other state time if the prescaler bit is set. When

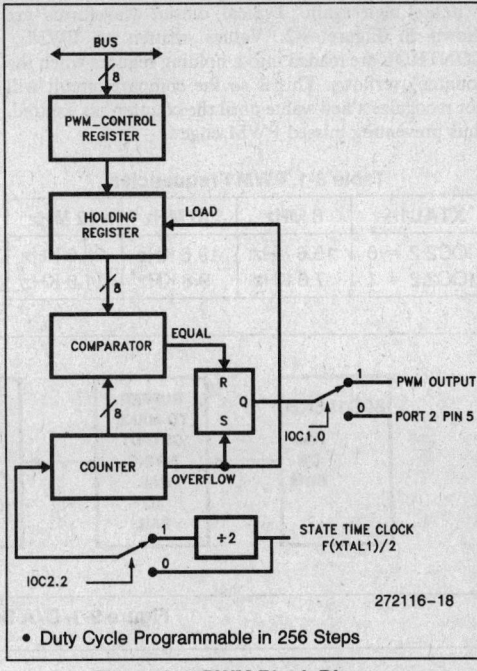

- Duty Cycle Programmable in 256 Steps

Figure 8-1. PWM Block Diagram

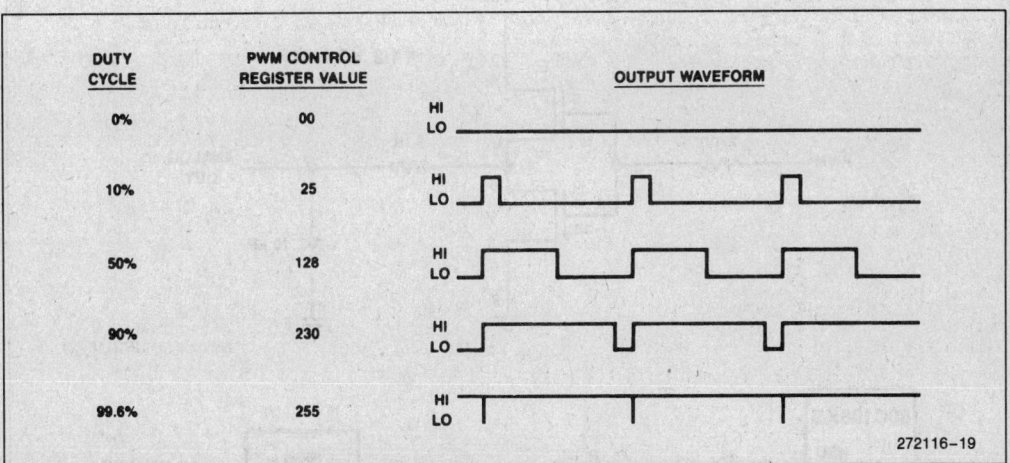

Figure 8-2. Typical PWM Outputs

AP-466

the counter equals 0 the PWM output switches high; when the counter matches the value in the PWM_CONTROL register the PWM output switches low; and when the counter overflows the PWM output switches high again. Typical output waveforms are shown in Figure 8-2. Values written to PWM_CONTROL are loaded into a holding register when the counter overflows. This is so the compare circuit will not recognize a new value until the counter has expired, thus preventing missed PWM edges.

Table 8-1. PWM Frequencies

XTAL1 =	8 MHz	10 MHz	12 MHz
IOC2.2 = 0	15.6 KHz	19.6 KHz	23.6 KHz
IOC2.2 = 1	7.8 KHz	9.8 KHz	11.8 KHz

9.0 ANALOG OUTPUTS

Both the PWM output and the HSO unit can generate analog outputs. Either peripheral will generate a rectangular pulse train that varies in duty cycle and period. Filtering the output will create a smooth analog signal. This filtering is typically done after the signal is buffered to make it swing over the desired analog output voltage range. A block diagram of the type of circuit needed is shown in Figure 9-1. The filter can be a simple RC network or an active filter. Shown in Figure 9-2 is a circuit used for low output currents, (less than 100 μA or so). The PWM unit can generate these waveforms if a fixed period on the order of 42.75 μs or 85.5 μs (at 12 MHz) is acceptable. The HSO unit can generate waveforms with a period of up to 87.5 ms (using Timer1 at 12 MHz).

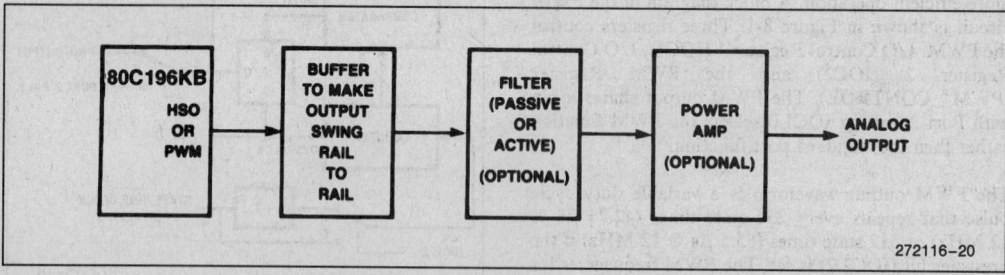

Figure 9-1. D/A Buffer Block Diagram

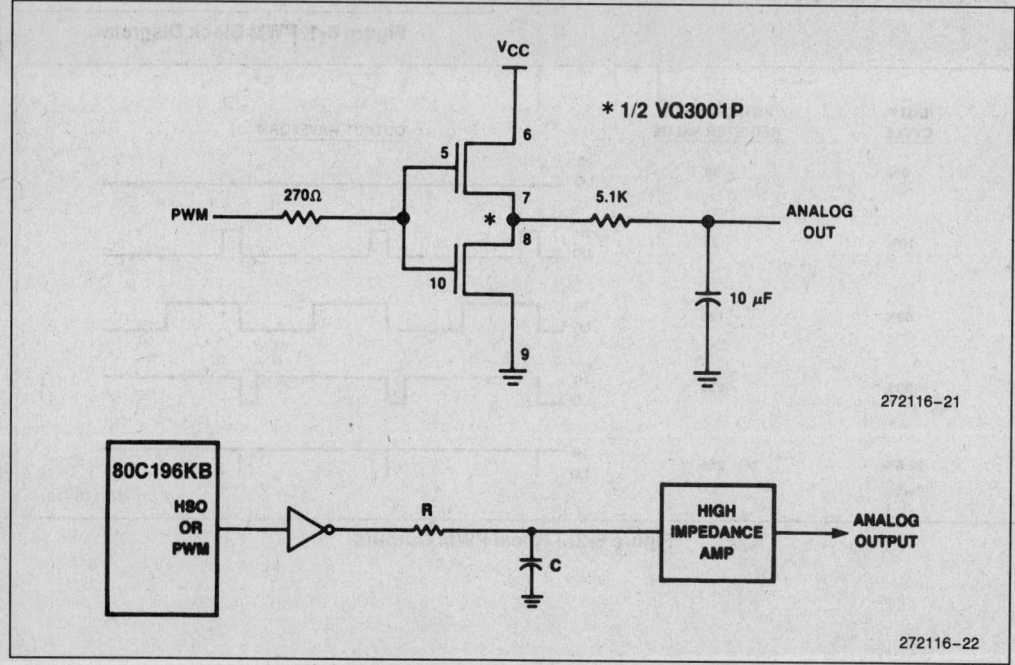

Figure 9-2. PWM to Analog Conversion Circuitry

AP-466

10.0 ANALOG TO DIGITAL CONVERTER

The 80C196KB analog interface consists of a sample-and-hold, an 8 channel multiplexer, and a 10-bit analog-to-digital converter. A block diagram of the A/D converter is shown in Figure 10-1. Port 0, an input-only port, shares the analog inputs ACH0 through ACH7. The A/D Converter uses the successive approximation method to perform an A/D conversion on one input at a time. Three SFRs control the A/D Converter. The AD_COMMAND register controls which channel and when a conversion will start, and the AD_RESULT (low and high) registers store the 10-bit conversion result. Bit 4 of the I/O Control Register 2 (IOC2.4) controls the number of state times required for the conversion.

To set-up an analog-to-digital conversion load the desired analog input channel into the lower three bits of the AD_COMMAND register. The GO bit, bit 4 of the AD_COMMAND register, controls when the conversion will start. If the GO bit is set the conversion will start immediately, otherwise the HSO unit will trigger the conversion. The AD_COMMAND register is shown in Figure 10-2. The A/D result registers (AD_RESULT(hi) and AD_RESULT(lo)), shown in Figure 10-3 and Figure 10-4 contain the 10-bit conversion result. The AD_RESULT(hi) register contains the most significant 8 bits of the result. Bits 6 and 7 of the AD_RESULT(lo) register contain the remaining least significant bits (LSB's) of the result. Also, the lower four bits of the AD_RESULT(lo) register contain the A/D channel number and the A/D status as shown in Figure 10-3. The AD_RESULT(lo) status bit, when set, indicates that an A/D conversion is in progress. It takes 8 state times to set this bit after the start of an A/D conversion.

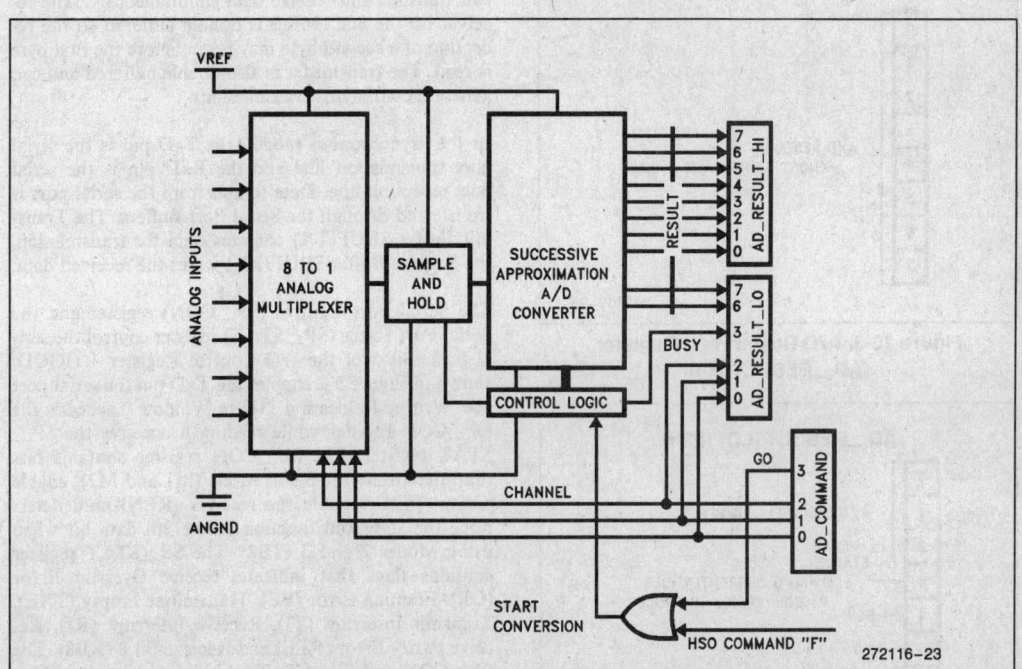

Figure 10-1. A/D Converter Block Diagram

AP-466

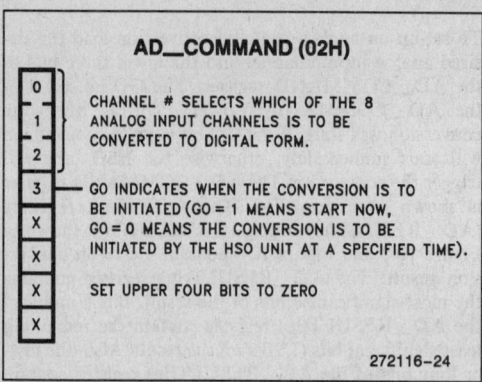

Figure 10-2. A/D Command Register (AD_COMMAND)

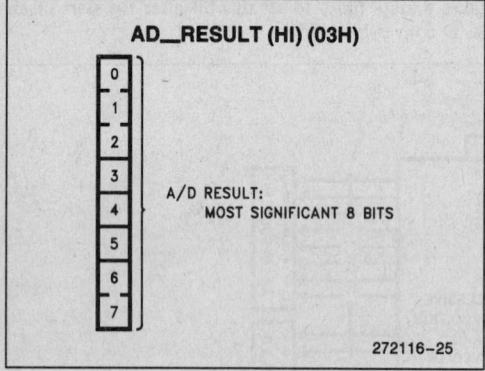

Figure 10-3. A/D Result High Register (AD_RESULT(HI))

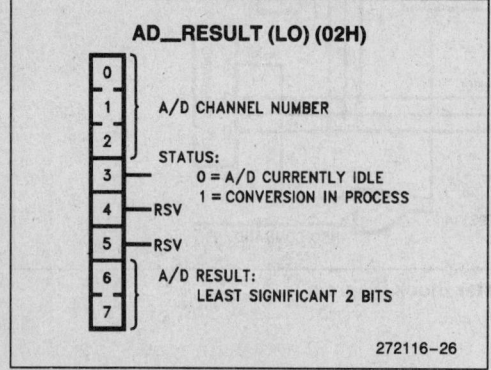

Figure 10-4. A/D Result Low Register (AD_RESULT(LO))

The clock prescaler bit of I/O Control Register 2 (IOC2.4) determines the number of state times required for an A/D conversion. High crystal frequencies require more states to complete a conversion to allow enough settling time for the internal comparator. When IOC2.4 = 1 the A/D conversion time is 91 state times (22.75 μs for an 8 MHz crystal) otherwise the A/D conversion time is 158 state times (26.33 μs for a 12 MHz crystal). An A/D Conversion Complete Interrupt (INT01) occurs on completion of an A/D conversion. It is possible to generate a Software Timer Interrupt (INT05) at the start of an A/D conversion by using the HSO unit to trigger the conversion.

11.0 SERIAL PORT

The Serial Port on the 80C196KB has one synchronous (Mode 0) and three asynchronous modes (Modes 1–3). The asynchronous modes are full duplex, meaning they can transmit and receive data simultaneously. The receiver on the 80C196KB is double buffered so the reception of a second byte may begin before the first byte is read. The transmitter is also double buffered and can generate continuous transmissions.

In the asynchronous modes, the TxD pin is the serial port transmission line and the RxD pin is the serial port reception line. Data to and from the serial port is transferred through the Serial Port Buffers. The Transmit Buffer SBUF(TX) contains data for transmission, the Receive Buffer SBUF(RX) stores the received data.

The Serial Port Control (SP_CON) register and the Serial Port Status (SP_STAT) register control the serial port. Bit 5 of the I/O Control Register 1 (IOC1), shown in Figure 5-2 enables the TxD pin for serial port use. Writing to location 11H in Window 0 accesses the SP_CON register while reading it accesses the SP_STAT register. The SP_CON register contains bits that: determine the Serial Mode (M1 and M2), enable parity (PEN), enable the receiver (REN), and determine the state and function of the 9th data bit when using Modes 2 and 3 (TB8). The SP_STAT register contains flags that indicate: receive Overrun Error (OE), Framing Error (FE), Transmitter Empty (TXE), Transmit Interrupt (TI), Receive Interrupt (RI), Receive Parity Error (RPE) and Receive Bit 8 (RB8). The SP_CON and SP_STAT registers are shown in Figure 11-1.

AP-466

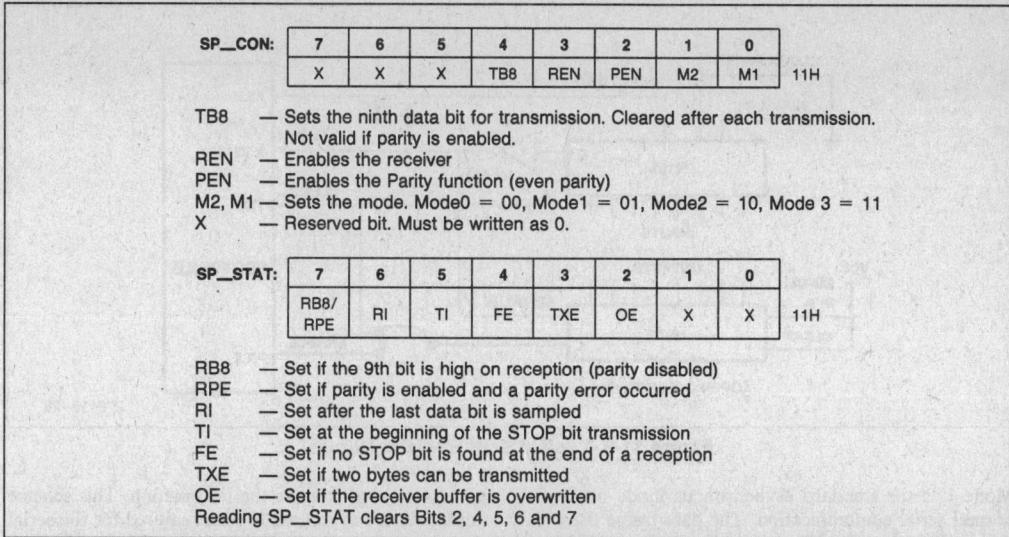

Figure 11-1. Serial Port Control and Status Registers (SP_CON and SP_STAT)

The most common use of Mode 0, the synchronous mode, is to expand the I/O capability of the 80C196KB using shift registers. In this mode the port outputs a set of 8 clock pulses on the TxD pin and either transmits or receives data synchronously on the RxD pin. Data is transferred 8 bits at a time with the LSB first. A diagram of the relative timing of these signals is shown in Figure 11-2. A schematic of a typical circuit that uses shift registers is shown in Figure 11-3. Since this circuit inverts the input data bits, software must re-invert them. The users software routine must control two pins (PX.X) to load data into the 74165 and to enable the shift clock on the 74164.

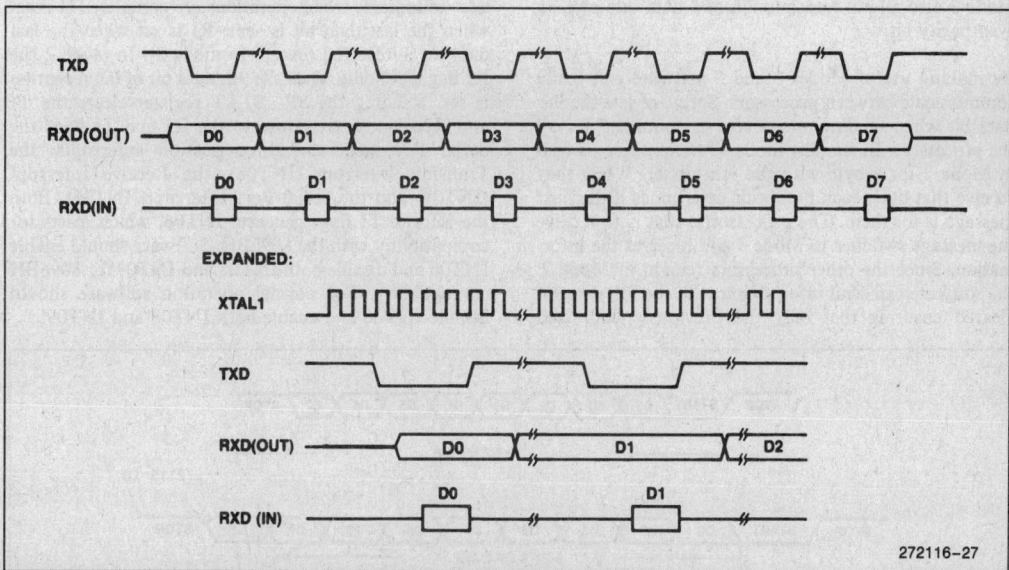

Figure 11-2. Mode 0 Timing

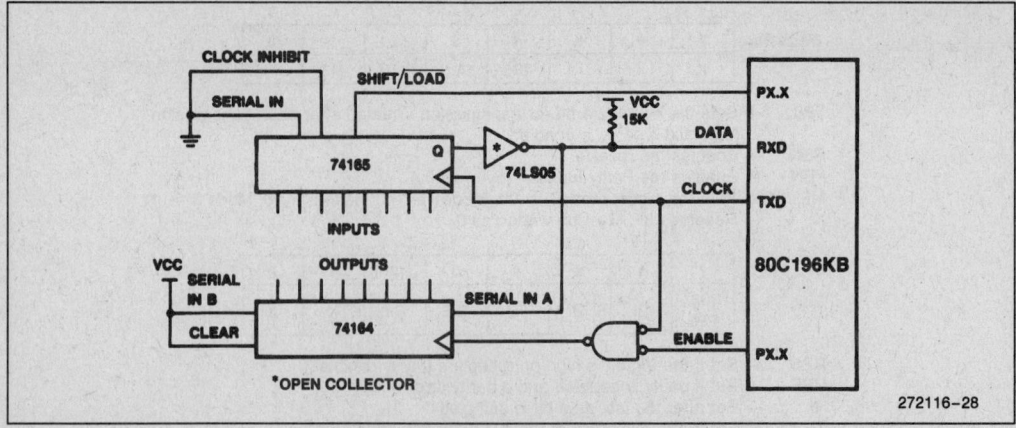

Figure 11-3. Typical Shift Register Circuit

Mode 1 is the standard asynchronous mode used for normal serial communication. The data frame used in this mode is shown in Figure 11-4. It consists of 10 bits: a start bit, 8 data bits (LSB first) and a stop bit. If parity is enabled (PEN = 1), an even parity bit is sent instead of the 8th data bit. Modes 2 and 3 are 9-bit modes commonly used for multi-processor communications. The data frame used in these modes, shown in Figure 11-4, consists of 11 bits: a start bit, nine data bits (LSB first) and a stop bit. Devices in Mode 2 will interrupt upon reception only if the 9th data bit is set. Devices in Mode 3 will always interrupt upon reception. Mode 3 also allows transmission of 8 data bits plus an even parity bit.

By making use of Modes 2 and 3 software can easily communicate between processors. Software sets the 9th data bit when sending an address or command for all the processors. In standby mode all the processors wait in Mode 2 for a byte with the 9th bit set. When they receive that byte, each processor determines if the next message is for them. The processor(s) that is to receive the message switches to Mode 3 and receives the information. Since the other processors remain in Mode 2, the software can send information with the 9th data bit cleared ensuring that only the previously addressed processor(s) will receive the information. This scheme minimizes the overall CPU time required for the serial port.

A typical connection diagram for multiprocessor communication is shown in Figure 11-5. This type of communication can connect peripherals to a desk top computer, an axis controller of a multi-axis machine, or any other group of microcontrollers.

The Serial Port sets the Transmit Interrupt (TI) and the Receive Interrupt (RI) flags in the SP_STAT register to indicate when operations are complete. TI is set when the last data bit is sent. RI is set when the last data bit is received (except in mode 2). In mode 2 the RI flag is set only when the 9th data bit of the reception is set. Reading the SP_STAT register clears the TI and RI flags. In response to the RI and TI flags the Serial Port generates three possible interrupts: the Transmit Interrupt (INT08), the Receive Interrupt (INT09) and the Serial Port Interrupt (INT06). Both the RI and TI flags generate INT06, which exists for compatibility with the 8096BH. Software should enable INT06 and disable both INT08 and INT09 for 8096BH compatibility. For normal operation software should disable INT06 and enable both INT08 and INT09.

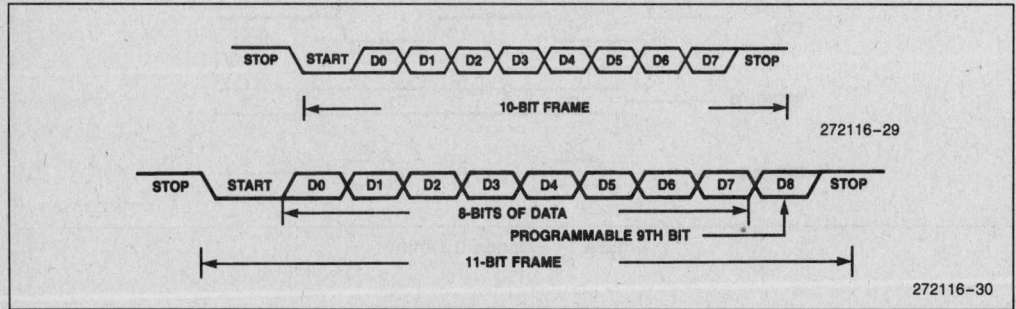

Figure 11-4. Serial Port Frames, Mode 1, 2 and 3

AP-466

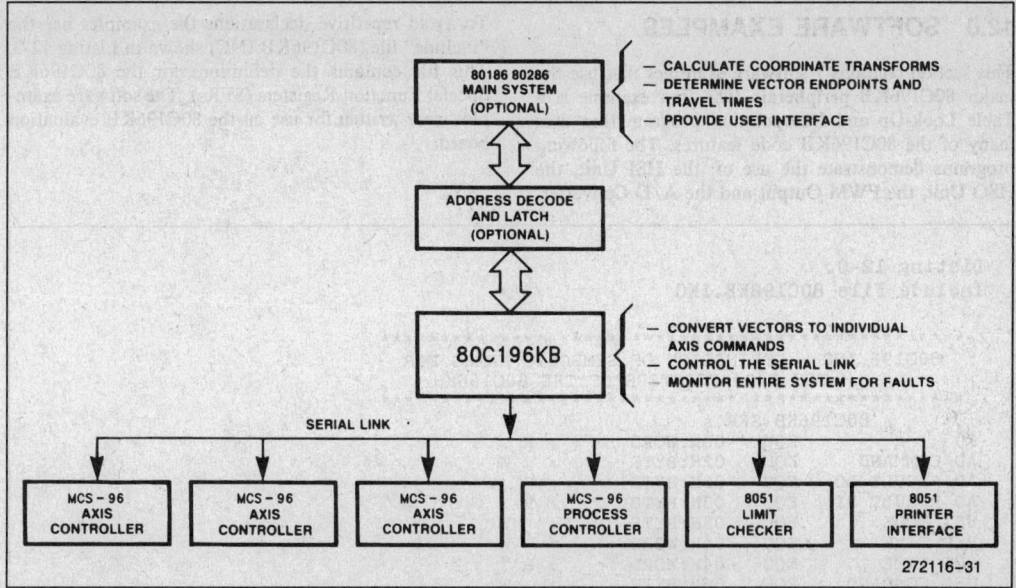

Figure 11-5. Multiprocessor Communication

The Baud Rate Register (BAUD__REG) controls the baud rates for the serial modes. This is a byte wide register that is loaded sequentially with two bytes, and internally stores the value as a word. The least significant byte is loaded to the register followed by the most significant byte. The most significant bit of the baud value determines the clock source for the baud rate generator. Setting this bit will select the XTAL1 pin as the clock, otherwise the T2CLK pin will function as the clock. To determine the baud value use the formulas shown in Figure 11-6. The baud values for common baud rates when using XTAL1 as the clock source are shown in Table 11-1. In most cases a serial link will work with up to 5.0% difference between baud rates.

Common baud rate values, using XTAL1 at 16 MHz, are shown below.

Asynchronous Modes 1, 2 and 3:

$$BAUD\_REG = \frac{XTAL1}{Baud\ Rate * 16} - 1 \text{ OR } \frac{T2CLK}{Baud\ Rate * 8}$$

Synchronous Mode 0:

$$BAUD\_REG = \frac{XTAL1}{Baud\ Rate * 2} - 1 \text{ OR } \frac{T2CLK}{Baud\ Rate}$$

B must only equal 0 in modes 1, 2 or 3, when using XTAL1 as the clock source. Do not use B = 0 in mode 0.

Figure 11-6. Baud Rate Formulas

Table 11-1. Common Baud Rate Values

Baud Rate	Baud Register Value	
	Mode 0	Others
9600	8340H	8067H
4800	8682H	80CFH
2400	8D04H	81A0H
1200	9A0AH	8340H
300	E82BH	8D04H

AP-466

12.0 SOFTWARE EXAMPLES

This section contains 7 software examples that use the major 80C196KB peripherals. The first example is a Table Look-Up and Interpolation program that uses many of the 80C196KB code features. The following programs demonstrate the use of: the HSI Unit, the HSO Unit, the PWM Output and the A/D Converter.

To avoid repetitive declarations the examples use the "include" file (80C196KB.INC) shown in Listing 12-0. This file contains the definitions for the 80C196KB Special Function Registers (SFRs). The software examples were written for use on the 80C196KB evaluation board.

```
Listing 12-0.
Include File 80C196KB.INC

;*****************************************************
;   80C196.INC - DEFINITION OF SYMBOLIC NAMES FOR
;            THE I/O REGISTERS OF THE 80C196KB
;*****************************************************
;            80C196KB SFR's
R0              EQU     00H:WORD        ; R
AD_COMMAND      EQU     02H:BYTE        ;   W
AD_RESULT_LO    EQU     02H:BYTE        ; R
AD_RESULT_HI    EQU     03H:BYTE        ; R
HSI_MODE        EQU     03H:BYTE        ;   W
HSO_TIME        EQU     04H:WORD        ;   W
HSI_TIME        EQU     04H:WORD        ; R
HSO_COMMAND     EQU     06H:BYTE        ;   W
HSI_STATUS      EQU     06H:BYTE        ; R
SBUF            EQU     07H:BYTE        ; R/W
INT_MASK        EQU     08H:BYTE        ; R/W
INT_PENDING     EQU     09H:BYTE        ; R/W
WATCHDOG        EQU     0AH:BYTE        ;   W
TIMER1          EQU     0AH:WORD        ; R
IOC2            EQU     0BH:BYTE        ;   W
TIMER2          EQU     0CH:WORD        ; R
BAUD_RATE       EQU     0EH:BYTE        ;   W
IOPORT0         EQU     0EH:BYTE        ; R
IOPORT1         EQU     0FH:BYTE        ; R/W
IOPORT2         EQU     10H:BYTE        ; R/W
SP_CON          EQU     11H:BYTE        ;   W
SP_STAT         EQU     11H:BYTE        ; R
IPEND1          EQU     12H:BYTE        ; R/W
IMASK1          EQU     13H:BYTE        ; R/W
WSR             EQU     14H:BYTE        ; R/W
IOC0            EQU     15H:BYTE        ;   W
IOS0            EQU     15H:BYTE        ; R
IOC1            EQU     16H:BYTE        ;   W
IOS1            EQU     16H:BYTE        ; R
IOS2            EQU     17H:BYTE        ; R
PWM_CONTROL     EQU     17H:BYTE        ;   W
SP              EQU     18H:WORD        ; R/W
```

272116-32

AP-466

12.1 Example 1—Table Look-Up and Interpolation

A good way to increase speed for many processing tasks is to use table look-up with interpolation. The program shown in Listing 12-1 uses 17 points at evenly spaced intervals to characterize a function. Example 1 stores the 17 points as output values in a table of words. These values correspond to 17 input values (0, 20D, 40D, ... 340D): an input = 0 returns the first output word, an input = 20D returns the second output word, and so on. Listed in Table 12-1 are the corresponding input and output values. To compute the output value for any intermediate input value (i.e., 28D) the program uses a linear approximation based on the nearest function values. Given below is a description of the interpolation process.

Table 12-1. Table of Input and Output Values

Input Value	Output Value
00D	0000H
20D	1900H
40D	2EE0H
60D	41A0H
80D	5140H
100D	5DC0H
120D	6720H
140D	6D60H
160D	7080H
180D	7080H
200D	6D60H
220D	6720H
240D	5DC0H
260D	5140H
280D	41A0H
300D	2EE0H
320D	1900H
340D	0000H

The linear interpolation formula:

RESULT = OUT_LOW + (OUT_DIF/SCALE) • (IN_VAL − IN_LOW)

IN_VAL	= The intermediate input value.
SCALE	= The difference between the nearest table input values.
IN_LOW	= The nearest table input value that is lower than IN_VAL.
OUT_DIF	= The difference between the nearest table output values.
OUT_LOW	= The lower table output value.
OUT_HIGH	= The higher table output value.

For example, if IN_VAL = 68D (44H) then OUT_LOW = 41A0H, OUT_HIGH = 5140H, OUT_DIF = 0FA0H, SCALE = 20D (14H), and INT_LOW = 60D (3CH)

RESULT = 41A0H + 0FA0H/14H • (44H − 3CH) = 75C0H

AP-466

```
Listing 12-1.
Table Look-Up and Interpolation - INTERP.A96

$DEBUG ERRORPRINT NOSYMBOLS
;***********************************************************************
;    INTERP.A96 -         TABLE-LOOKUP AND INTERPOLATION
;***********************************************************************
INTERPOLATION   MODULE MAIN,STACKSIZE(20)
$NOLIST INCLUDE (C:\INTEL\INCLUDE\80C196.INC)
$LIST

CSEG

;The table values below are 18 points for the function Y = 340*X - X*X
;Max_in_val equals the outer bound of the input values

TABLE:      DCW     0000H, 1900H, 2EE0H, 41A0H
            DCW     5140H, 5DC0H, 6720H, 6D60H
            DCW     7080H, 7080H, 6D60H, 6720H
            DCW     5DC0H, 5140H, 41A0H, 2EE0H
            DCW     1900H, 0000H

MAX_IN_VAL  EQU  340D
SCALE       EQU  MAX_IN_VAL/((($-TABLE)/2)-1)

RSEG AT 30H
RSV:        DSW 8                           ;Reserved space in RISM

RSEG
VALUE:      DSL 1                           ;Temporary value
OUT_LOW:    DSW 1                           ;Low table output value
OUT_HIGH:   DSW 1                           ;High table output value
IN_LOW:     DSW 1                           ;Low table input value
RESULT:     DSW 1                           ;Interpolated output value
TAB_PTR:    DSW 1                           ;Pointer into output table
IN_VAL:     DSW 1                           ;Actual input must be less
                                            ;than max_in_val

CSEG AT 2080H
INIT:       LD SP, #100H                    ;Load stack pointer
            LD IN_VAL, #320D                ;Load actual value must be
                                            ;less than max_in_val
POINTER:    LD TAB_PTR, IN_VAL              ;Table ptr=actual value
            DIVB TAB_PTR, #SCALE            ;Table ptr = table ptr\scale
            AND TAB_PTR, #00FFH             ;Discard remainder

            MULB IN_LOW, TAB_PTR, #SCALE    ;Determine the lower table
                                            ;input
            SUB IN_VAL, IN_VAL, IN_LOW      ;In_val = in_low - in_val

OUT_VALUES: SHL TAB_PTR, #1                 ;Multiple pointer by 2
            LD OUT_LOW, TABLE[TAB_PTR]      ;Out_low = low output value
            LD OUT_HIGH, (TABLE+2)[TAB_PTR] ;Out_high = hi output value
            SUB OUT_HIGH, OUT_LOW           ;out_high = out_high-out_low

;Calculate result using interpolation formula -
;result = out_low + (out_high - out_low)\scale * (in_val - in_low)

CAL_RESULT: LD VALUE, IN_VAL                ;Value = (in_val - in_low)
            MUL VALUE, OUT_HIGH             ;value * (out_high-out_low)
            DIV VALUE, #SCALE               ;Value = value \ scale
            AND VALUE, #0000FFFFH           ;Discard remainder
            ADD RESULT, VALUE, OUT_LOW      ;Result = value + value
            BR $
END                                         ;Last line must be end
```

272116-33

12.2. Example 2— Using the High Speed Input Unit

A common use of the HSI Unit is to monitor a signal and measure the time between positive and negative transitions. Example 2 shown in Listing 12-2 uses the pins HSI.0 and HSI.1 to monitor a signal. HSI.0 captures negative transition times and HSI.1 captures positive transition times. The program then calculates and stores transition time differences in a time table (TIME__TABLE). The value of TABLE__SIZE determines the size of TIME__TABLE. Once TIME__TABLE contains the designated number of values the software disables the HSI pins. Note the program discards the first transition time capture because the signal is input on the HSI pins before they are enabled.

AP-466

Listing 12-2.
Using The High Speed Input Unit - HSIA.A96

```
$DEBUG ERRORPRINT NOSYMBOLS
;*******************************************************************
; HSIA.A96 - Using The High Speed Input Unit
;*******************************************************************
HSIA    MODULE MAIN,STACKSIZE(20)
$NOLIST INCLUDE (C:INTEL\INCLUDE\80C196.INC)
$LIST

RSEG AT 30H
RSV:        DSW     8                       ;Reserved space in RISM

;HSI.0 and HSI.1 monitor the same signal, HSI.0 captures the time of
;every positive transition and HSI.1 captures the time of every negative
;transition.  Event1 and event2 store the times of each consecutive
;transition.  TIME_TABLE stores the times between each transition.  The
;size of TIME_TABLE is determined by TABLE_SIZE.  All time values are
;based on Timer1.  8 state times = 1 Timer1 count

DSEG
TABLE_SIZE  EQU     0AH                     ;Size of time array
TIME_TABLE: DSW     TABLE_SIZE              ;Array of event time
                                            ;differences
RSEG
EVENT1:     DSW     1                       ;Transition time
EVENT2:     DSW     1                       ;Transition time
TIME:       DSW     1                       ;Time between events
PTR:        DSW     1                       ;Time array pointer
SIZE:       DSW     1

CSEG AT 2004H
DCW         CAL_TIME                        ;Address of HSI Data
                                            ;Available
                                            ;Interrupt Service Routine
CSEG AT 2080H

;Load the stack pointer, disable interrupts, unmask HSI Data Available
;Interrupt, mask all other interrupts and disable HSI.0 and HSI.1

INIT:       LD SP, #100H                    ;Load stack pointer
            DI                              ;Disable interrupts
            LDB INT_MASK, #00000100B        ;Unmask HSI Data Available
            CLRB IMASK1                     ;Mask all other interrupts
            CLRB IOC0                       ;Disable HSI.0 and HSI.1
            LDB IOC1, #10000000B            ;Select HSI Data Available

;Flush the FIFO, enable HSI.0 to capture positive transitions and HSI.1
;to capture negative transitions

FLUSH:      CLR HSI_TIME                    ;Unload one FIFO level
            SKIP R0                         ;Wait 4 state times
            SKIP R0                         ;Wait 4 state times
            JBS IOS1, 7, FLUSH              ;If FIFO is not empty goto
                                            ;flush
            LDB HSI_MODE, #00001001B        ;Set HSI.0 to collect
                                            ;positive transitions and
                                            ;HSI.1 to collect negative
                                            ;transitions
            LD PTR, #TIME_TABLE             ;Initialize time table ptr
            CLR SIZE                        ;Initialize counter
            LDB IOC0, #00000101B            ;Enable HSI.0 and HSI.1

;Save first valid transition time and enable interrupts

WAIT1:      JBC IOS1, 7, WAIT1              ;Wait for capture
            CLR HSI_TIME                    ;Dump 1st capture - invalid
WAIT2:      JBC IOS1, 7, WAIT2              ;Wait for next capture
            LD EVENT1, HSI_TIME             ;Save transition time
            EI                              ;Enable interrupts
            BR $                            ;Wait here for interrupt

;HSI Data Available Interrupt Service Routine - Calculates the time
;between consecutive transitions, and stores the times in TIME_TABLE

CAL_TIME:   PUSHA                           ;Disable interrupts
            LD EVENT2, HSI_TIME             ;Collect transition time
            SUB TIME, EVENT2, EVENT1        ;Calculate time between
                                            ;transitions
            ST TIME, [PTR]+                 ;Store in time table
            LD EVENT1, EVENT2
            INC SIZE                        ;Increment storage counter
            CMP SIZE, #TABLE_SIZE           ;If size and table_size are
            BNE RETURN                      ;not equal goto return
            CLRB IOC0                       ;Disable HSI.0 and HSI.1
RETURN:     POPA                            ;Enable interrupts
            RET                             ;Return
END                                         ;The last line must be end
```

272116-34

AP-466

12.3 Example 3—Using the High Speed Input Unit and the Pulse Width Modulation Output

As in the previous example, Example 3 shown in Listing 12-3 monitors a signal and captures positive and negative transition times. HSI.0 captures positive transition times and HSI.1 captures negative transition times. For every three consecutive transitions the software calculates the low time percentage. The program then generates a PWM output with a duty cycle equal to the low time percentage. Figure 12-1 shows various input signals and the resulting PWM outputs.

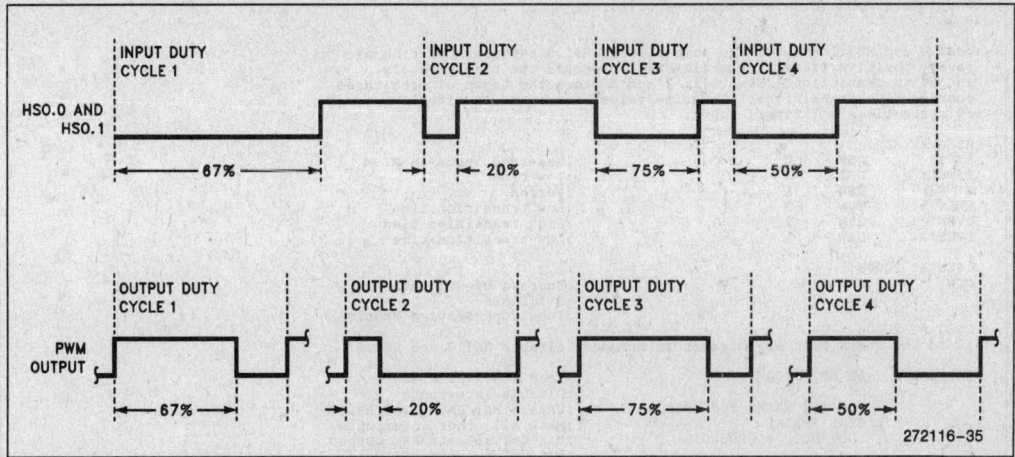

Figure 12-1. Example Input Signals and the Resulting PWM Outputs

AP-466

Listing 12-3.
Using the High Speed Input Unit and The Pulse Width
Modulation Output--HSIB.A96

```
$DEBUG ERRORPRINT NOSYMBOLS
;*********************************************************************
; HSIB.A96 - Using The High Speed Input Unit
;*********************************************************************
HSIB    MODULE MAIN,STACKSIZE(20)
$NOLIST INCLUDE (C:\INTEL\INCLUDE\80C196.INC)
$LIST

;HSI.0 and HSI.1 monitor the same signal, HSI.0 captures the time of
;every positive transition while HSI.1 captures the time of every
;negative transition.  Events 1, 2 and 3 store the times of each three
;consecutive transitions.  The time values are based on timer1.
;8 state times = 1 timer1 count.

        RSEG AT 30
RSV:        DSW     8                   ;Reserved space in RISM
TIME1:      DSL     1                   ;Low time
TIME2:      DSW     1                   ;Period
EVENT1:     DSW     1                   ;Low transition time
EVENT2:     DSW     1                   ;High transition time
EVENT3:     DSW     1                   ;Low transition time

        CSEG AT 2004H
        DCW         CAL_TIME            ;Address of HSI DATA
                                        ;AVAILABLE
                                        ;Interrupt Service Routine
        CSEG AT 2080H
;Load the stack pointer, disable interrupts, disable HSI.0 and HSI.1

INIT:       LD SP, #100H                ;Load stack pointer
            DI                          ;Disable interrupts
            LDB INT_MASK, #00000100B    ;Unmask HSI DATA AVAILABLE
            CLRB IMASK1                 ;Mask all other interrupts
            LDB IOC1, #10000001B        ;Bit 0=1 selects PWM output
                                        ;Bit 7=1 selects HSI Data
                                        ;Available Interrupt
            CLRB IOC0                   ;Disable HSI.0 and HSI.1

;Flush the FIFO, set-up HSI.0 to capture positive transitions and HSI.1
;to capture negative transitions and enable the HSI pins

FLUSH:      CLR HSI_TIME                ;Unload one FIFO level
            SKIP R0                     ;Wait 4 state times
            SKIP R0                     ;Wait 4 state times
            JBS IOS1, 7, FLUSH          ;If FIFO is not empty goto
                                        ;flush
            LDB HSI_MODE, #00001001B    ;Set HSI.0 to collect
                                        ;positive transitions and
                                        ;HSI.1 to collect negative
                                        ;transitions
            LDB IOC0, #00000101B        ;Enable HSI.0 and HSI.1

;Event1 stores the time of the first valid negative transition.  Event2
;stores the next positive transition.

WAIT1:      JBC IOS1, 7, WAIT1          ;Wait for first capture
DUMP:       CLR HSI_TIME                ;Dump capture
WAIT2:      JBC IOS1, 7, WAIT2          ;Wait for next capture
            JBS HSI_STATUS, 0, DUMP     ;If pos transition goto dump
            LD EVENT1, HSI_TIME         ;Save neg transition time
WAIT3:      JBC IOS1, 7, WAIT3          ;Wait for next capture
            LD EVENT2, HSI_TIME         ;Save time pos transition
            EI                          ;Enable interrupts
            BR $
;HSI Data Available Interrupt Service Routine - calculates the low time
;period, % low time and outputs a PWM.  Low time is the difference
;between every positive transition and the preceding negative transition
;Period is the difference between every negative transition.
;% low time = low time / period.  % low time is then used as the duty
;cycle for a PWM output.

CAL_TIME:   PUSHA                       ;Disables interrupts
            LD EVENT3, HSI_TIME         ;Save neg transition time
            SUB TIME1, EVENT2, EVENT1   ;Calculate low time
            SUB TIME2, EVENT3, EVENT1   ;Calculate period
            LD EVENT1, EVENT3
WAIT4:      JBC IOS1, 7, WAIT4          ;Wait for next capture
            LD EVENT2, HSI_TIME         ;Save pos transition time
CAL_PWM:    MUL TIME1, #256D            ;Determine % of the signal
            DIV TIME1, TIME2            ;that is low, set-up pwm
            LDB PWM_CONTROL, TIME1      ;with duty cycle of same %
            POPA                        ;Enable interrupts
            RET                         ;Return
END
```

272116-36

AP-466

12.4 Example 4—Using the High Speed Output Unit to Generate Multiple PWMs

Example 4 shown in Listing 12-4 shows the most common way to generate multiple PWMs using the HSO Unit. This module uses pins HSO.0, HSO.1 and HSO.2 as the PWM outputs. The commands that set each PWM, clear each PWM and reset Timer2 are locked in the CAM.

Since Timer2 is the reference timer, an external source must drive it. The three PWMs generated by this program are shown in Figure 12-2. It is possible to change the waveforms of these PWMs by simply changing the EQU statements at the beginning of the program.

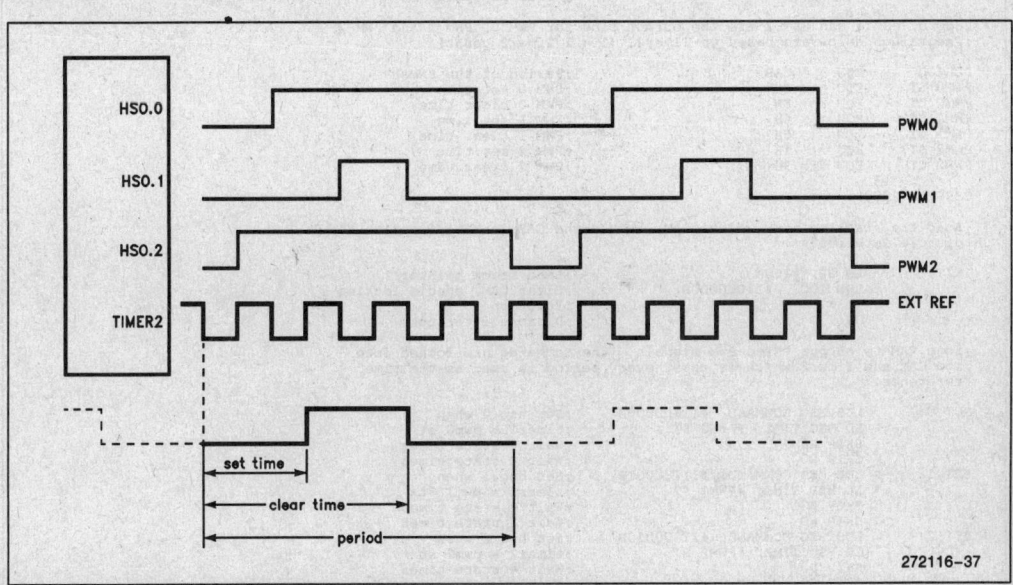

Figure 12-2. Example PWMs

AP-466

Listing 12-4.
Using the High Speed Output Unit to Generate Multiple PWMs – HSOA.A96

```
$DEBUG ERRORPRINT NOSYMBOLS
;*********************************************************************
; HSOA.A96 - Using The High Speed Output Unit
;*********************************************************************
HSOA    MODULE MAIN,STACKSIZE(20)
$NOLIST INCLUDE (C:\INTEL\INCLUDE\80C196.INC)
$LIST

        RSEG AT 30H
RSV:            DSW        8                  ;Reserved space

;HSO.0, HSO.1 and HSO.2 are the output pins for PWM 0, PWM 1 and PWM 2
;The values below are based on Timer2. (1 = 1 Timer2 count)

PERIOD          EQU        0AH                ;Period of the PWMs
PWM0_ST         EQU        2H                 ;PWM 0 set time
PWM0_CT         EQU        8H                 ;PWM 0 clear time
PWM1_ST         EQU        4H                 ;PWM 1 set time
PWM1_CT         EQU        6H                 ;PWM 1 clear time
PWM2_ST         EQU        1H                 ;PWM 2 set time
PWM2_CT         EQU        9D                 ;PWM 2 clear time

        CSEG AT 2080H

;Load the stack pointer, clear CAM, enable the CAM locking function and
;disable interrupts

INIT:           LD SP, #100H                  ;Load stack pointer
                LDB IOC2, #11000000B          ;Clear CAM, enable locking
                                              ;function
                DI                            ;Disable interrupts

;Load CAM to output three PWM signals. The commands are locked into
;the CAM and Timer2 which is reset every period is used as the time
;reference.

SET_0:          LDB HSO_COMMAND, #11100000B   ;Set hso.0 when
                LD HSO_TIME, #PWM0_ST         ;timer2 = pwm0_st
                SKIP R0                       ;Wait 4 state times
                SKIP R0                       ;Wait 4 state times
SET_1:          LDB HSO_COMMAND, #11100001B   ;Set hso.1 when
                LD HSO_TIME, #PWM1_ST         ;timer2 = pwm1_st
                SKIP R0                       ;Wait 4 state times
                SKIP R0                       ;Wait 4 state times
SET_2:          LDB HSO_COMMAND, #11100010B   ;Set hso.2 when
                LD HSO_TIME, #PWM2_ST         ;timer2 = pwm2_st
                SKIP R0                       ;Wait 4 state times
                SKIP R0                       ;Wait 4 state times
CLEAR_0:        LDB HSO_COMMAND, #11000000B   ;Clear hso.0 when
                LD HSO_TIME, #PWM0_CT         ;timer2 = pwm0_ct
                SKIP R0                       ;Wait 4 state times
                SKIP R0                       ;Wait 4 state times
CLEAR_1:        LDB HSO_COMMAND, #11000001B   ;Clear hso.1 when
                LD HSO_TIME, #PWM1_CT         ;timer2 = pwm1_ct
                SKIP R0                       ;Wait 4 state times
                SKIP R0                       ;Wait 4 state times
CLEAR_2:        LDB HSO_COMMAND, #11000010B   ;Clear hso.2 when
                LD HSO_TIME, #PWM2_CT         ;timer2 = pwm2_ct
                SKIP R0                       ;Wait 4 state times
                SKIP R0                       ;Wait 4 state times
RESET:          LDB HSO_COMMAND, #11001110B   ;Reset timer2 when
                LD HSO_TIME, #PERIOD          ;timer2 = period
                BR $
        END
```

272116-38

AP-466

12.5 Example 5—Using the High Speed Output Unit to Generate a Single PWM

Example 5 shown in Listing 12-5 shows another way to generate a single PWM using the HSO Unit. To use this example another module must set-up the PWM period and clear time. This program uses an HSO Interrupt (INT03) to force a call to an Interrupt Service Routine (ISR). The ISR then loads the commands in the CAM: a set command and a clear command. These CAM commands use Timer1 as the reference timer. Since this example does not use locked CAM entries, it is possible to alter the PWM output while the program is running by changing the period and clear time values.

```
Listing 12-5.
Using the High Speed Output Unit to Generate a Single PWM - HSOB.A96

$DEBUG ERRORPRINT NOSYMBOLS
;************************************************************
; HSOB.A96 - Using The High Speed Output Unit
;************************************************************
HSOB    MODULE MAIN,STACKSIZE(20)
$NOLIST INCLUDE (C:\INTEL\INCLUDE\80C196.INC)
$LIST

        RSEG AT 30H
RSV:    DSW     8                       ;Reserved space in RISM

;HSO.0 is the output pin for a PWM.  The signal starts high, has the
;designated PERIOD and is cleared at the designated CLEAR_TIME.  The
;PERIOD and CLEAR_TIME values are determined in another module.  These
;values are based on Timer1 (1 = 1 Timer1 count = 8 state times).

        RSEG
        EXTRN PERIOD, CLEAR_TIME        ;Period and Clear time of PWM
TEMP_TIMER: DSW   1                     ;Time value used for the HSO
                                        ;set and clear commands

        CSEG AT 2006H
        DCW     OUTPUT                  ;Address of HSO
                                        ;Interrupt Service Routine

        CSEG AT 2080H
;Load the stack pointer, clear CAM, unmask HSO interrupt,
;mask all other interrupts and enable interrupt

INIT:   LD  SP, #100H                   ;Load stack pointer
        LDB IOC2, #11000010B            ;Clear the CAM
        LDB INT_MASK, #00001000B        ;Unmask HSO interrupt
        CLRB IMASK1                     ;Mask all other interrupts
        EI                              ;Enable interrupts

;Force a call to output routine

        LD TEMP_TIMER, TIMER1           ;Initialize temp_timer
        CALL OUTPUT
        BR $                            ;Wait here for interrupt

;HSO - Interrupt Service Routine to output signal using HSO.0.

OUTPUT: PUSHA                           ;Disable interrupts
        ADD TEMP_TIMER, PERIOD          ;Temp_timer=temp_timer+period
SET0:   LDB HSO_COMMAND, #00110000B     ;Set HSO.0 when
        LD  HSO_TIME, TEMP_TIMER        ;timer1 = temp_timer + period
        SKIP R0                         ;Wait four state times
        SKIP R0                         ;Wait four state times
CLEAR0: LDB HSO_COMMAND, #00000000B     ;Clear HSO.0 when
        ADD HSO_TIME, TEMP_TIMER, CLEAR_TIME
                                        ;timer1=temp_timer + clr time
        POPA                            ;Enable interrupts
        RET                             ;Return
END
```

272116-39

5-351

12.6 Example 6—Using the A/D Converter

Example 6 shown in Listing 12-6 uses the HSO Unit to start an A/D conversion. Timer 2 is the reference timer so an external source must drive it. The value of SAMPLE__TIME determines how often the HSO will start an A/D Conversion. The Conversion Complete Interrupt forces a call to an Interrupt Service Routine (ISR). The ISR reads the A/D result and reloads the conversion command.

```
Listing 12-6.
Using the A/D Converter - AD.A96

$DEBUG ERRORPRINT NOSYMBOLS
;****************************************************************
;       AD.A96 - Using the A/D Converter
;****************************************************************

AD      MODULE MAIN,STACKSIZE(20)
$NOLIST INCLUDE (C:\INTEL\INCLUDE\80C196.INC)
$LIST

RSEG AT 30H
RSV:        DSW     8                   ;Reserved space in RISM

RSEG
SAMPLE_TIME EQU     170D                ;The HSO will start an A/D
                                        ;conversion every
                                        ;Timer2 = sample_time
SAMPLE:     DSW     1                   ;A/D conversion result
RESULT:     DSW     1                   ;A/D conversion result


CSEG AT 2002H
DCW         GET_RESULT                  ;Address of A/D Conversion
                                        ;Complete
                                        ;Interrupt Service Routine

;Load stack pointer, disable interrupts, enable CAM locking function,
;unmask only the A/D Conversion Complete Interrupt, and enable
;interrupts

CSEG AT 2080H
INIT:       LD   SP, #100H              ;Load stack pointer
            DI                          ;Disable interrupts
            LDB  IOC2, #11000000B       ;Clear CAM, enable locking
                                        ;function
            LDB  INT_MASK, #02H         ;Unmask A/D Conversion Complete
            CLRB IMASK1                 ;Mask all other interrupts
            EI                          ;Enable interrupts

;Set-up an A/D conversion on A/D-channel 0 that the HSO unit will
;trigger.  Load the CAM with a command to start the A/D conversion and
;reset Timer2 every SAMPLE_TIME.

COMMAND:    LDB  AD_COMMAND, #0         ;Conversion on AD0 started by
                                        ;HSO
START_CONV: LDB  HSO_COMMAND, #11001111B ;AD Conversion, locked ,timer2
            LD   HSO_TIME, #SAMPLE_TIME ;Load conversion starting time
            SKIP R0                     ;Wait 4 state times
            SKIP R0                     ;Wait 4 state times
RESET_T2:   LDB  HSO_COMMAND, #11001110B ;Reset timer2 when
            LD   HSO_TIME, #SAMPLE_TIME ;timer2 = sample_time
            BR   $                      ;Wait here for interrupt

;A/D Conversion Complete Interrupt Service Routine - Read the AD_RESULT
;registers and reload the AD_COMMAND register

GET_RESULT: PUSHA                       ;Disable interrupts
            LD   RESULT, AD_RESULT_LO   ;Load ad_result (result 10 MSBs)
            SHR  RESULT, #6             ;Shift result (result 10 LSBs)
            LD   SAMPLE, RESULT         ;Save result in sample
            LDB  AD_COMMAND, #0         ;Conversion on AD0 started by
                                        ;HSO
            POPA                        ;Enable interrupts
            RET                         ;Return
END
```

AP-466

12.7 Example 7—Using the Serial Port

Example 7 shown in Listing 12-7 uses Mode 1, the standard asynchronous mode of the 80C196KB Serial Port, to transmit the message "hello". The program transmits the first byte of the message then enables the TI (Transmit Interrupt). The transmission of the last data bit of the message byte causes a TI. The TI forces a call to an Interrupt Service Routine. The ISR then transmits the next byte of the message and the program control is returned to the main program where it waits for the next TI.

```
Listing 12-7.
Using the Serial Port - SP.A96

$DEBUG ERRORPRINT NOSYMBOLS
;*****************************************************************
;   SP.A96 - Using the Serial Port
;*****************************************************************
Serial_P   MODULE MAIN,STACKSIZE(20)
$NOLIST INCLUDE (C:\INTEL\INCLUDE\80C196.INC)
$LIST

       RSEG AT 30H
RSV:        DSW 8                    ;Reserved Space in RISM

       RSEG
MESS_PTR:   DSW 1                    ;Pointer into message

       CSEG AT 2030H
DCW         TRANSMIT                 ;Address of TI
                                     ;Interrupt Service Routine
       CSEG
MESSAGE1:   DCB         'HELLO'      ;Message to transmit
            DCB         0DH,0AH      ;Carriage return, line feed
MESS1_END   EQU         $            ;Address of end of message

       CSEG AT 2080H

;Load stack pointer, enable TxD pin, unmask TI interrupt, mask all
;other interrupts, set serial port to mode 1, load the baud value for a
;baud rate of 9600 at 12 Mhz and set MSB of baud value to indicate that
;XTAL1 is the clock soure for the baud rate generator

INIT:       LD SP, #100H             ;Load stack pointer
            DI                       ;Disable interrupts
            LD IOC1, #20H            ;Enable TxD pin
              LDB IMASK1, #1         ;Unmask TI interrupt
            CLRB INT_MASK            ;Mask all other interrupts
            LDB SP_CON, #1           ;Set serial port to mode 1
            LDB BAUD_RATE, #77D      ;Load least significant byte of
                                     ;baud value
            LDB BAUD_RATE, #80H      ;Load most significant byte of
                                     ;baud value with MSB = 1 to
                                     ;indicate XTAL1 as the baud
                                     ;rate source
            EI                       ;Enable interrupts

;Send the first byte of message1, the following message bytes are sent
;in the TI interrupt service routine

            LD MESS_PTR, #MESSAGE1   ;Mess_ptr = address of message1
WAIT:       JBC SP_STAT, 3, WAIT     ;Wait till serial buffer is
                                     ;empty
            LDB SBUF, [MESS_PTR]+    ;Send first byte of message
            BR $                     ;Wait here for TI interrupt

;TI Interrupt Service Routine - Check for end of message, if not at
;end of message send the next byte of message1

TRANSMIT:   PUSHA                    ;Disable interrupts
            CMP MESS_PTR, #MESS1_END ;If at message end goto return
            BE RETURN
            LDB SBUF, [MESS_PTR]+    ;Load next byte of message1
RETURN:     POPA                     ;Enable interrupts
            RET                      ;Return

       END                           ;Last line must be end
```

AP-466

13.0 HARDWARE EXAMPLES

Several different combinations of addressing and data bus modes exist on the 80C196KB. External memory is addressable through the AD0–AD15 lines. These lines form a multiplexed 16-bit address and data bus. The standard data bus mode uses a 16-bit data bus. Other data bus modes include an 8-bit only external bus mode, and a data bus mode that can switch dynamically between 8 bits and 16 bits. The address bus is always 16 bits wide. The address/data bus shares pins with ports 3 and 4.

An 8-bit system with EPROM and RAM is shown in Figure 13-1. The EPROM is addressable through the lower half of memory, and the RAM is addressable through the upper half. The diagram in Figure 13-2 shows a simple 16-bit system with 2 EPROMs. The first EPROM contains the even bytes while the second EPROM contains the odd bytes. Shown in Figure 13-3 is a system using the dynamic bus width. The two EPROMs contain the executable code and the single RAM provides for external data storage. Note the system uses AD15 as the Chip Select, and as input to the BUSWIDTH pin to select an 8-bit cycle.

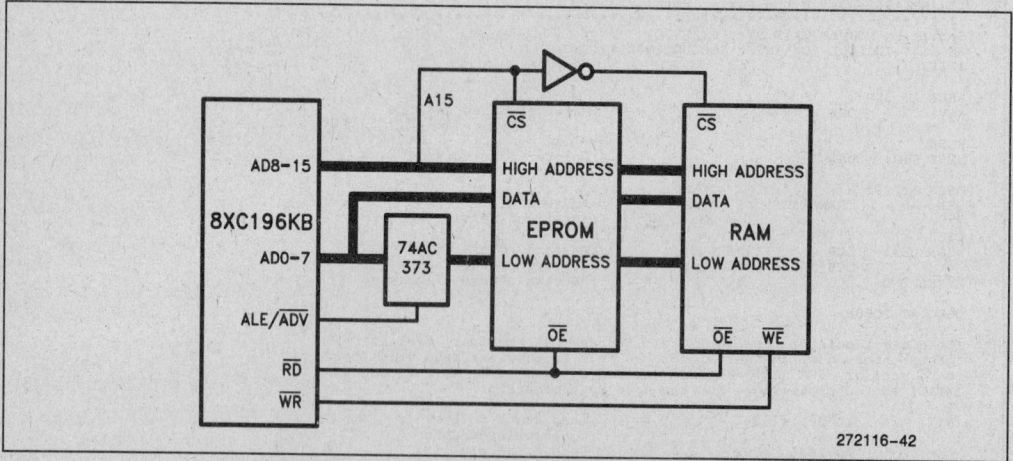

Figure 13-1. 8-Bit System with EPROM and RAM

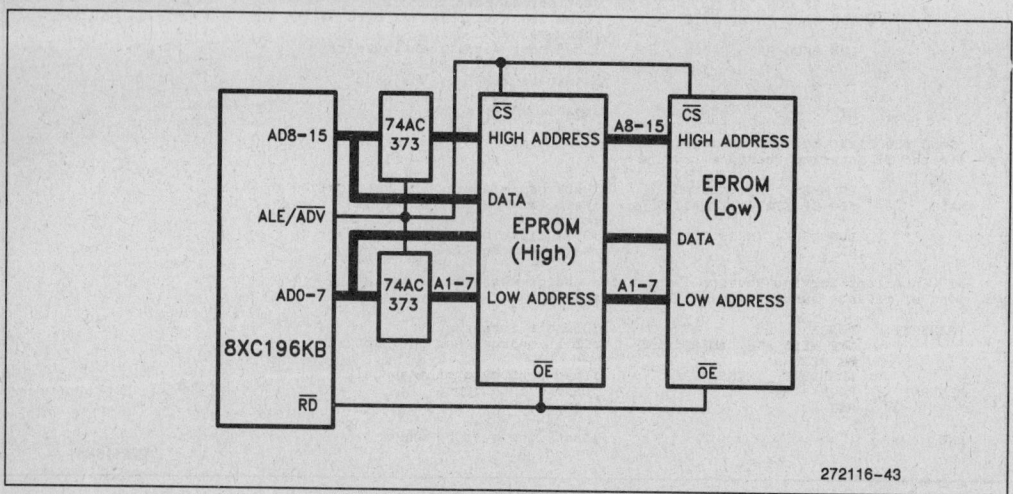

Figure 13-2. 16-Bit System with EPROM

AP-466

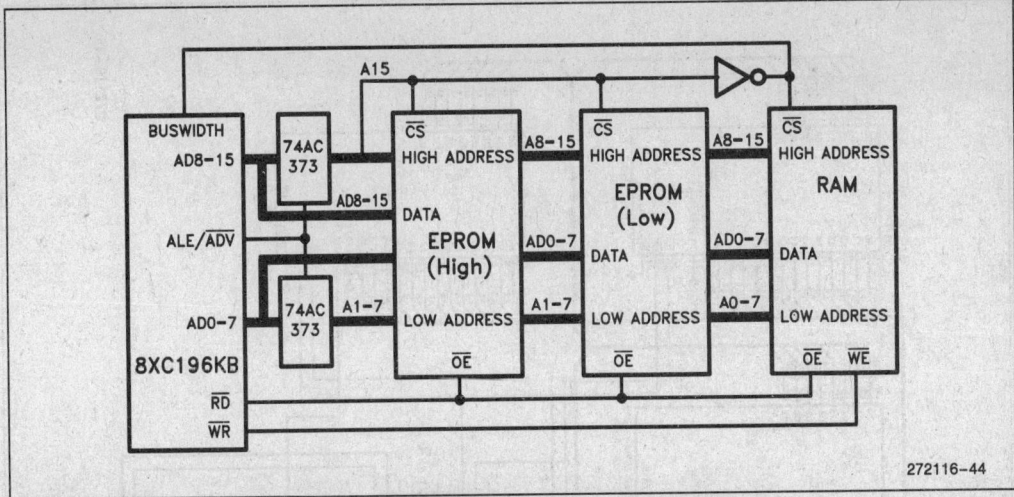

Figure 13-3. 16-Bit System with Dynamic Bus Width

Figure 13-4 is a schematic of a typical minimal system using the 80C196KB. The address/data bus is demultiplexed by latches U3 and U4. U5 and U7 are connected as odd and even bytes of 16-bit wide EPROM. Note that bus address line A0 is not required for these devices, as they are always addressed in increments of 2 bytes (A0 is a don't care). U6 is a byte-wide RAM chip.

Address mapping and BUSWIDTH is determined by U8, a PAL. The RESET signal is generated by an R–C network, U2A, U2B and D2. U2 is a Schmitt trigger which generates a fast edge from the R–C network slow rise time. D2 is used as a "wired or" gate to the RESET pin on the 80C196KB. This is necessary to avoid signal contention as the RESET pin is both an input and an output from the 80C196KB.

AP-466

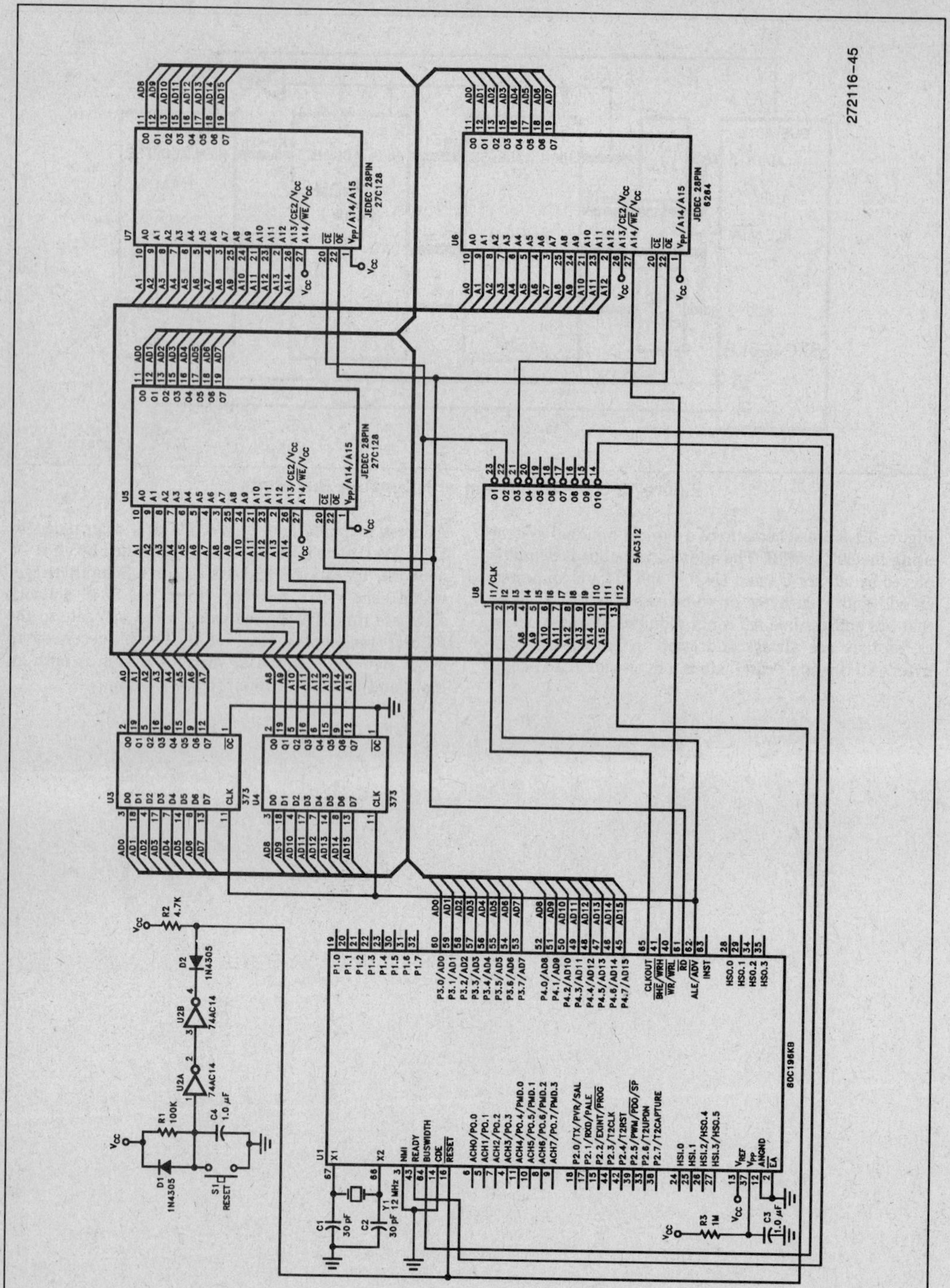

Figure 13-4. Schematic of 16-Bit System with Dynamic Bus Width

AP-466

14.0 PORT RECONSTRUCTION

External memory systems for the 80C196KB use a multiplexed address/data bus (AD0–AD15) which shares pins with I/O Ports 3 and 4. Ports 3 and 4 are read and written at locations 1FFEH and 1FFFH. If $\overline{EA}$ is high, accessing locations 1FFEH and 1FFFH reads/writes to Ports 3 and 4. However, if $\overline{EA}$ is low, locations 1FFEH and 1FFFH act as memory locations, not ports. Thus, to use Ports 3 and 4 under these conditions requires a port reconstruction circuit. Shown in Figure 14-1 is a port reconstruction circuit that uses a memory mapped I/O technique.

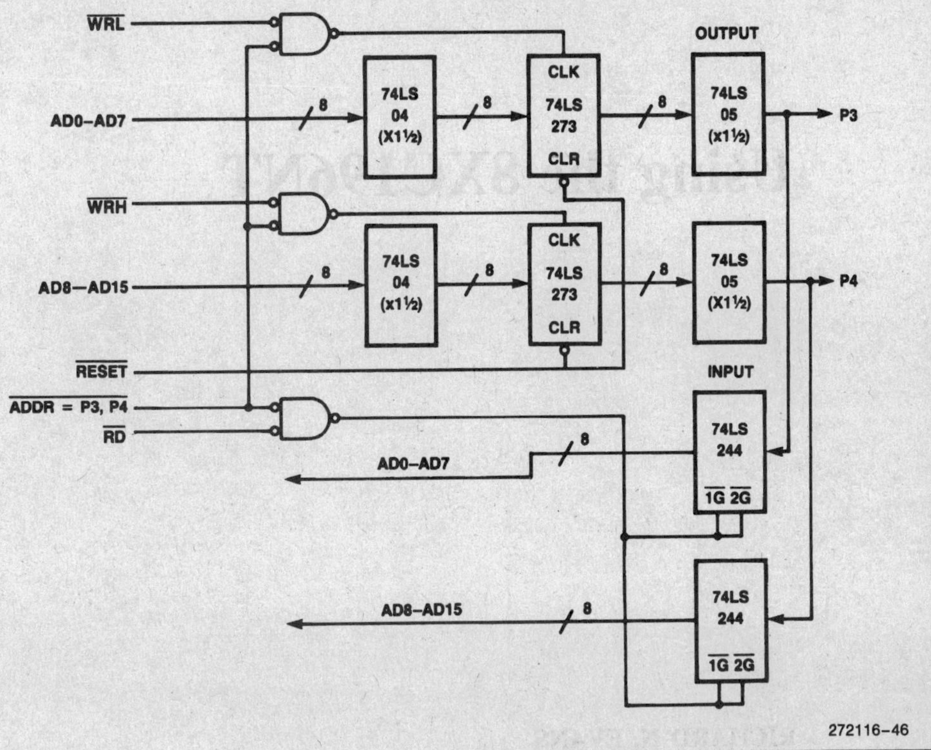

Figure 14-1. I/O Port Reconstruction

15.0 CONCLUSION

This application note presented an overview of the 80C196KB and provided software examples using its key features. Intel supports application development of its 80C196KB with a complete set of development languages and utilities. These tools include ACE196, a macroassembler (ASM96), a PL/M compiler (PLM96), a C compiler (iC96), linker/relocator program (RL96), floating point arithmetic library utility (FPAL96), a librarian utility (LIB96) and object-to-hex utility (OH96). ACE196 software is a PC-based expert system to guide you through detailed documentation training and includes: a hypertext manual, peripheral design modules and an assembler editor. Contact your local sales office for more information on the 80C196KB and its hardware and software development tools.

BIBLIOGRAPHY

1. "1991 16-Bit Embedded Controllers Handbook", Intel Corporation, 1990. Order Number 270646-003.
2. "1991 Embedded Applications Handbook", Intel Corporation, 1990. Order Number 270648-003.
3. AP-248, "Using the 8096, 1991 Embedded Applications Handbook", Intel Corporation, September 1987. Order Number 270648-003.
4. "MCS-96 Macro Assembler User's Guide for DOS Systems", Intel Corporation, 1990. Order Number 122350.
5. "iC-96 Compiler User's Guide for DOS Systems", Intel Corporation, 1990. Order Number 481194.

intel.

AP-475

APPLICATION NOTE

Using the 8XC196NT

RICHARD N. EVANS
CHRISTINE NEFFENGER
APPLICATIONS ENGINEERS

January 1994

Order Number: 272315-001

Using the 8XC196NT

CONTENTS

1.0 INTRODUCTION 5-361

2.0 ARCHITECTURAL OVERVIEW 5-361

3.0 8XC196NT NEW INSTRUCTIONS 5-363
   3.1 ELD/ELDB—Extended Load Word/Byte 5-363
   3.2 EST/ESTB—Extended Store Word/Byte 5-364
   3.3 EBR—Extended Branch 5-365
   3.4 EBMOVI—Interruptable Extended Block Move 5-365
   3.5 ECALL—Extended Subroutine Call 5-366
   3.6 RET—24-Bit Mode Return 5-366
   3.7 EJMP—Extended Jump 5-366

4.0 EPORT 5-366
   4.1 EPORT Gives 20-Bit External Address 5-366
   4.2 EPORT is Address Lines or I/O Pins 5-366
   4.3 EPORT SFRs 5-366
      4.3.1 EP_MODE Register 5-367
      4.3.2 EP_DIR Register 5-367
      4.3.3 EP_REG Register 5-367
      4.3.4 EP_PIN Register 5-368
      4.3.5 Reset Values of EPORT SFRs 5-368
      4.3.6 Accessing EPORT SFRs 5-368
   4.4 EPORT 5-368

5.0 MEMORY MAP 5-369
   5.1 Memory Layout 5-369
   5.2 How the EPORT Affects Memory Accesses 5-369
      5.2.1 The iC Compiler 5-370
      5.2.2 Warning about Changing Pages with EP_REG when the Stack is in External Memory 5-370
   5.3 The Different Memory Maps 5-370
      5.3.1 MODE 16 5-370
      5.3.2 REMAP 5-371
      5.3.3 64K Compatible Mode 5-371
      5.3.4 Example: Using the "64K Compatible Mode" with 96 Kbytes of Data 5-371
      5.3.5 64K Compatible Mode with Page 00h Free 5-374
      5.3.6 Example: Using the 64K Compatible Mode with 128K of External Data 5-374
      5.3.7 24-Bit Mode with EPROM Remapped 5-375
      5.3.8 Example: Using 24-Bit Mode with (EP)ROM Remapped 5-375
      5.3.9 24-Bit Mode 5-376
      5.3.10 Example: Using 24-Bit Mode 5-376
   5.4 Internal RAM 5-377
      5.4.1 Reading the EA Pin and Redirecting Internal RAM Accesses 5-377
   5.5 Wraparound 5-378

6.0 TIMING IMPROVEMENTS 5-382
   6.1 Signals 5-382
   6.2 Conditions 5-382
   6.3 Critical Memory Timings 5-382
   6.4 What Can Be Done to Use Less Expensive Memories and Run at Maximum Speed with Zero Wait States 5-383
   6.5 New Timing Modes 5-383
      6.5.1 Standard Timing (Mode 3) .. 5-384
         6.5.1.1 Mode 3 Timing Specs .. 5-384
      6.5.2 Standard Timing with One Wait State (Mode 0) 5-384
         6.5.2.1 Mode 0 Timing Specs .. 5-384
      6.5.3 Long READ/WRITE with Advanced ALE (Mode 1) 5-384
         6.5.3.1 Mode 1 Timing Specs .. 5-385
      6.5.4 Long READ/WRITE with Advanced ALE and Early Address (Mode 2) 5-385
         6.5.4.1 Mode 2 Timing Specs .. 5-385
   6.6 Given These New Timing Modes, Which Memory Devices Can Be Used with No Wait States? 5-387

CONTENTS PAGE

6.7 Changes to the Bus Control
  Timings 5-387
6.8 8-Bit Bus in Modes 1 and 2 5-387

CONTENTS PAGE

7.0 CHIP CONFIGURATION BYTES ... 5-393
  7.1 CCBs 5-393

8.0 QUESTIONS AND ANSWERS 5-395

AP-475

1.0 INTRODUCTION

The 8XC196NT can address 1 Mbyte of linear address space which is beyond the standard MCS®-96 64 Kbyte address space. Many applications require much memory whether it be from large code sizes due to high level language compilation or from large data tables. The standard MCS-96 family member has 16 address lines which allow linear access to 64 Kbytes of address space. To accommodate a growing need for address space the 8XC196NT was designed with 20 external address lines. The 8XC196NT is an upgrade from the standard MCS-96 family member. There are many similarities and a few differences that must be noted. The same peripheral set exists on the 8XC196NT as on the 8XC196KR. The peripherals on the 8XC196NT and the 8XC196KR are more advanced than the peripherals on the 8X96BH, 8XC196KB, 8XC196KC and 8XC196KD. The instruction set is a superset of the MCS-96 family containing special extended addressing instructions. The bus controller on the 8XC196NT has new modes which allow for slower memories to be utilized resulting in cost savings. An extended address port (EPORT) adds 4 more address lines to the external bus. The EPORT can also be used as an I/O port if the extended address lines are not needed.

2.0 ARCHITECTURAL OVERVIEW

The architecture for the 8XC196NT is consistent with the previous members (see Figure 2-1). The program counter has been extended to 24 bits to accommodate the extended addressing capabilities. The ALU is tied directly to the register RAM which creates a register-register architecture. The 8XC196NT has 1000 bytes of register RAM. Hence, one thousand accumulators (each a byte wide) are possible. This many accumulators minimizes the number of load/store operations. Notice that there are 32 Kbytes of on-chip (EP)ROM available and 512 bytes of internal RAM. The internal RAM can be used just like external RAM to execute code or hold data.

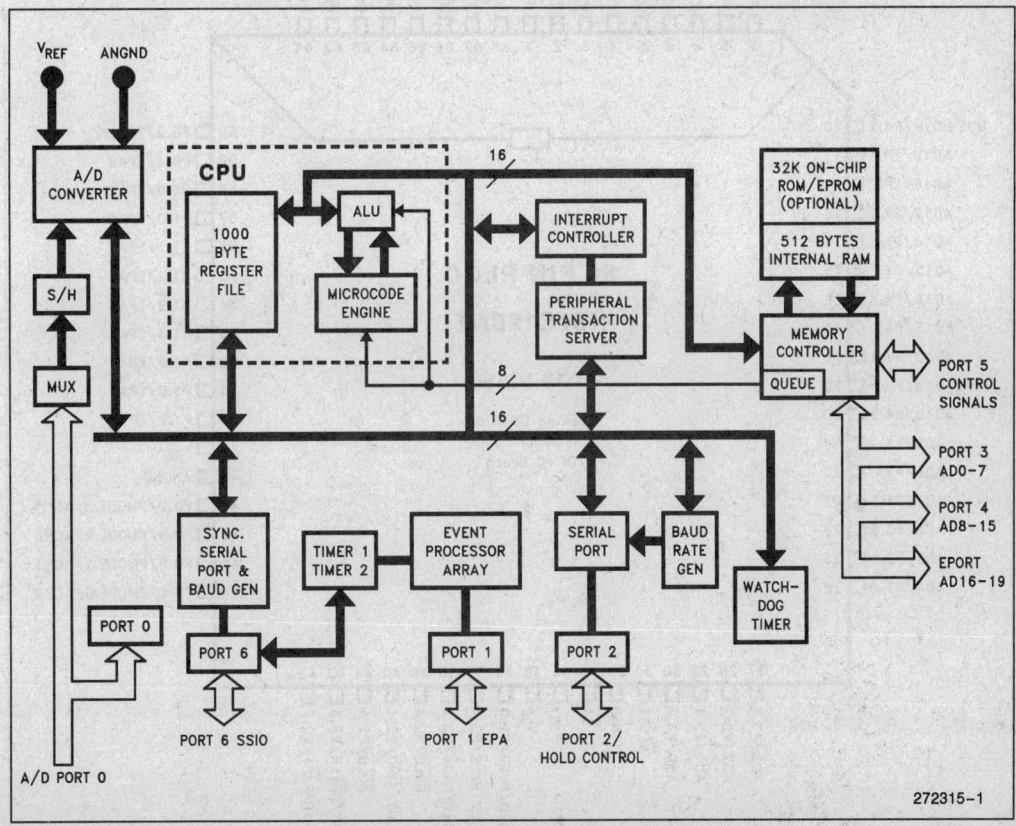

Figure 2-1. 8XC196NT Block Diagram

AP-475

The peripheral set on the 8XC196NT includes the following:

- Serial Port (3 asynchronous modes, 1 synchronous mode)
- SSIO (Synchronous Serial I/O Port with bi-directional clocking with two separate data and two separate clock channels)
- Slave Port
- EPA (Event Processor Array—high speed input capture and output compare) 10 channels
- PTS (Peripheral Transaction Server—microcoded interrupt service routine)
- A/D converter (4 channel 8/10 bit resolution with programmable sample and convert times)
- Two 16-bit timers
- Watchdog Timer
- Dedicated 15-bit Baud Rate Generator
- Extended Address Port (EPORT)

See pin out diagram in Figure 2-2.

For more information on the peripherals consult the 8XC196NT or 8XC196KX user's guides. The next sections go into more detail on how to use the EPORT, the memory map and the bus controller improvements which allow for greater flexibility in choosing memories. Also, code examples are given where needed as well as memory interface diagrams.

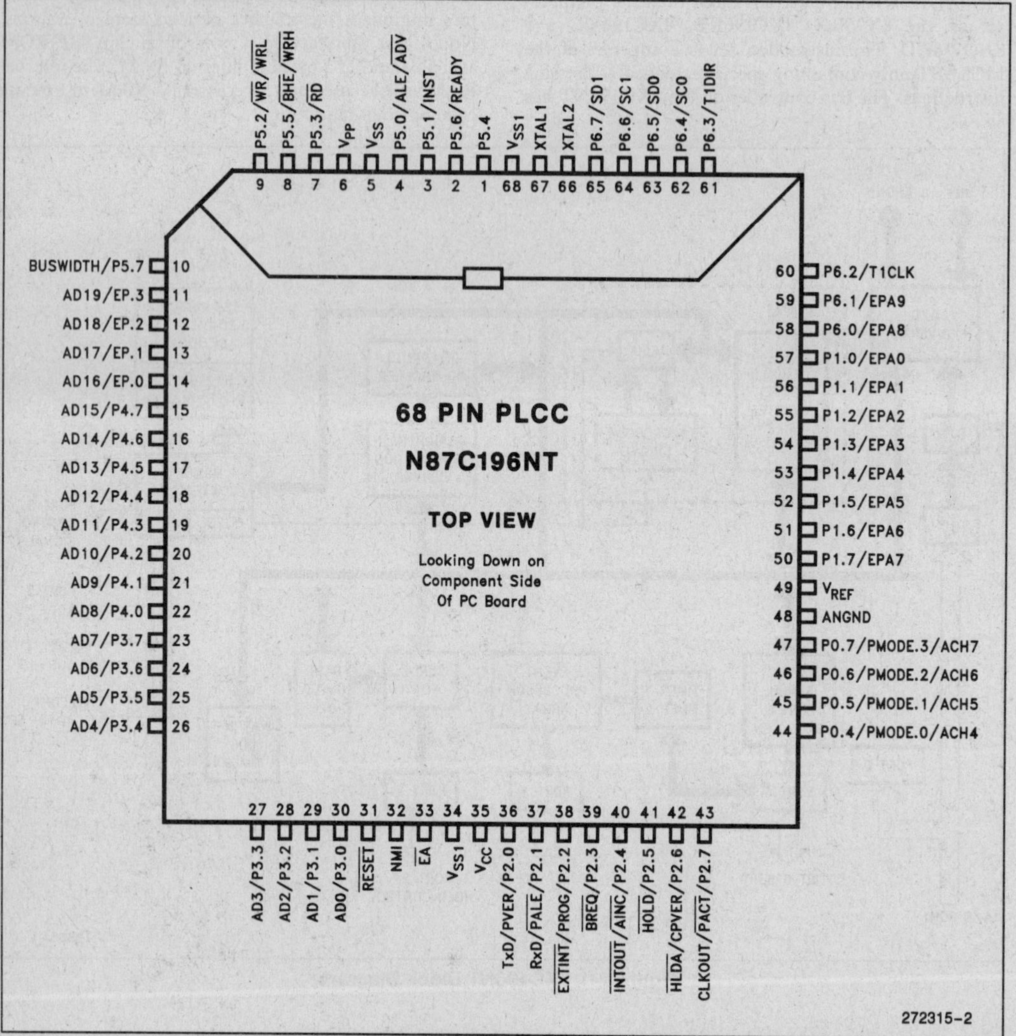

Figure 2-2. 8XC196NT Pin Out Diagram

AP-475

3.0 8XC196NT NEW INSTRUCTIONS

There are a few new instructions for accessing the 1 Mbyte address space. They are listed below and explained in detail in the following pages. When executing in 24-bit mode, instructions which push or pop the PC onto the stack will decrement or increment the stack pointer by four. These instructions include LCALL, SCALL, and RET. RET is explained in the new instruction section.

New Instructions:

    EBMOVI—Interruptable Extended Block Move
    EBR—Extended Branch, Indexed
    ECALL—Extended Subroutine Call
    EJMP—Extended Jump
    ELD/ELDB—Extended Load Word/Byte, Indexed or Indirect
    EST/ESTB—Extended Store Word/Byte, Indexed or Indirect
    RET—24-Bit Mode Return from Subroutine

Assembly Language:
```
      DST    SRC
ELD wreg, waopi
```
where:

wreg   = a word register in the internal register file.

waopi = a word operand 24-bit indirect or indexed addressed. Even address boundary, so LSB = 0 if indirect and LSB = 1 if indirect auto-increment.

Object Code Format:

Instruction	->	Object code format
ELD wreg, [wiop]	->	[E8][wiop 0][wreg]
ELD wreg, [wiop]+	->	[E8][wiop 1][wreg]
ELD wreg, xx[wiop]	->	[E9][wiop][xx][wreg]
ELDB breg, [biop]	->	[EA][biop 0][breg]
ELDB breg, [biop]+	->	[EA][biop 1][breg]
ELDB breg, xx[biop]	->	[EB][biop][xx][breg]

3.1 ELD/ELDB—Extended Load Word/Byte

Operation:
The word/byte contents of the source—indirect, indirect auto-increment, or index addressed—are copied into the register indicated by the destination. The source is located at a 24-bit address.

Example:

```
rseg at 1CH
A:    dsb   1
B:    dsw   2

cseg at 0FF2080h

ld    B,#01FE6h    ; load low word of B with low word of 24-bit address
ldbze B+2,#00h     ; load high word of B with highest byte of 24-bit address
eldb  A,[B]        ; (A) <= (001FE6h), which reads EP_PIN register
```

AP-475   intel.

3.2 EST/ESTB—Extended Store Word/Byte

Operation:

The word/byte contents of the source—indirect, indirect auto-increment*, or index addressed—are copied into the register indicated by the destination. The source is located at a 24-bit address.

Assembly Language:
```
     SRC   DST
EST wreg, wiop
```
where:

wreg = a word register in the internal register file

wiop = a word operand 24-bit indirect or indexed addressed modes. Even address boundary, so LSB = 0 for indirect and LSB = 1 for indirect auto-increment.

Object Code Format:

Instruction	->	Object code format
EST wreg, [wiop]	->	[1C][wiop][wreg]
EST wreg, xx[wiop]	->	[1D][wiop 0][xx][wreg]
EST wreg, xx[wiop]+	->	[1D][wiop 1][xx][wreg]
ESTB breg, [biop]	->	[1E][biop 0][breg]
ESTB breg, [biop]+	->	[1E][biop 1][breg]
ESTB breg, xx[biop]	->	[1F][biop][xx][breg]

Example:

```
    rseg at 1CH
    A:    dsb   1
    B:    dsw   2

    cseg at 0FF2080h
    ldb    A,#055h      ; load A with value
    ld     B,#01FFCh    ; load low word of B with low word of extended address
    ldbze  B+2,#00h     ; load high word of B with highest byte of extended address
    estb   A,[B]        ; (001FFCh) <= 055h, which writes to P3_REG, a location
                        ; unavailable with windowing or with 'stb' if EP_REG not
                        ; set to 00h
```

5-364

AP-475

3.3 EBR—Extended Branch

Operation:

Execution continues at the extended address specified in the operand register.

Assembly Language:
EBR [dwreg]
where:

dwreg = double word register containing 24-bit address of the branch location

Object Code Format:
[E3][dwreg]

Example:

```
rseg at 1CH
B:    dsw   2

cseg at 0FF2080h
 .
 .
 .
ld    B,#2080h
ldbze B+2,#00h    ; load B with external address for execution
ebr   [B]         ; load PC with 24-bit address in B (002080h)
```

3.4 EBMOVI—Interruptable Extended Block Move

Operation:

This instruction is used to move a block of word data from one location in extended memory to another and is interruptable. The source and destination registers are calculated using the indirect auto-increment addressing modes. A long register addresses the source and destination pointers which are stored in adjacent double word registers. The number of transfers is specified in the word register. The blocks of data can reside anywhere in memory, but should not overlap.

Assembly Language:
BMOVI   qwreg,wreg
where:

qwreg = a quad-word register

Object Code Format:
[E4][wreg][dLreg]

Example:

```
rseg at 1CH
ptrs:  dsl  2
count: dsw  1

cseg at 0FF2080h

ld     count,#1000h
ld     ptrs,#4000h
ld     ptrs+2,#0003h
ld     ptrs+4,#3000h
ld     ptrs+6,#0005h
ebmovi ptrs,count    ; moves 1000h words of data from 034000h through
                     ;035000h to 053000h through 054000h
```

AP-475

3.5 ECALL—Extended Subroutine call

Operation:

The contents of the program counter (the return address) are pushed onto the stack*. Then the distance from the end of the instruction to the target label is added to the program counter, effecting the call. The offset from the end of the instruction to the call must be in the range of $-8,388,608$ to $+8,388,607$ inclusive, which is a 24-bit offset.

Assembly Language:
ECALL   label

Object Code Format:
[F1][24-bit offset]

NOTE:
*The PC is pushed onto the stack as 4 bytes or 32-bits.

3.6 RET—24-Bit Mode Return

Operation:

The PC is popped off the stack.

Assembly Language:
RET

Object Code Format: [F0]

NOTE:
Since 32-bits were pushed onto the stack at call of subroutine, 32-bits are popped. Therefore, RET in 24-bit mode will execute the following:
PC <= SP
SP = SP+4

3.7 EJMP—Extended Jump

Operation:

The distance from the end of this instruction to the target label is added to the program counter, effecting the jump. The operand may be any address in the entire address space.

Assembly Language:
EJMP   cadd

Object Code Format:
[E6][24-bit displacement]

4.0 EPORT

4.1 EPORT Gives 20-Bit External Address

The main feature of the 8XC196NT is its ability to address 1 Mbyte of external memory plus over 32 Kbytes of internal memory on the device. This is accomplished using the extended address port, which is the EPORT. The EPORT can be configured as four additional address lines. Therefore, operating the device in 24-bit mode, external memory is accessed with a **20-bit address** (pins: EP.3 → EP.0 and AD15 → AD0). The memory map in Figure 5-4 shows the address range accessible using the 20-bit external memory address. The EPORT replaces four of the A/D channels, therefore the 8XC196NT has only four remaining A/D channels. The pin diagram of the 8XC196NT 68-pin PLCC is shown in Figure 2-2.

4.2 EPORT is Address Lines or I/O Pins

The EPORT can be used as either additional **address lines or I/O pins**. In addition, the port can function as any combination of additional address lines or I/O pins. For example, two of the EPORT pins can be used as address lines for two additional address bits and the other lines for two additional I/O pins. The user must be aware that this configuration as address or I/O can be changed during normal execution using the EPORT control registers. Therefore, caution should be used when changing the control registers of the EPORT.

4.3 EPORT SFRs

The function, direction, and data of the EPORT are controlled by four special function registers (SFRs) which are: EP_MODE (1FE1h), EP_DIR (1FE3h), EP_REG (1FE5h), and EP_PIN (1FE7h). Table 4-1 shows the SFR control of the pins.

AP-475

Table 4-1. EPORT SFRs Control of EPORT Pins

EP_Mode	EP_Dir	EP_Reg	Pull-Up	Pull-Down	Pin Function
x	0	0	Off	On	Output 0
x	0	1	On	Off	Output 1
x	1	0	Off	On	Open-Drain 0
x	1	1	Off	Off	Open-Drain 1 (Input)

4.3.1 EP_MODE REGISTER

The **EP_MODE register** determines the function of the EPORT pins. This register is written as a byte. Each bit of the EP_MODE indicates whether the pin will be a I/O port pin (EP_MODE.x = 0) or an address line pin (EP_MODE.x = 1).

4.3.2 EP_DIR REGISTER

The **EP_DIR register** indicates whether the pin will be an input or open-drain output (EP_DIR.x = 1) or a complementary output (EP_DIR.x = 0). This register is written as a byte.

4.3.3 EP_REG REGISTER

The **EP_REG register** can be used in two different ways. If the pin is configured as an I/O pin, the EP_REG is written with the data to be placed on the pin. If the pin is configured as an address line, the EP_REG will supply the extended address on the EPORT when a 16-bit instruction is executed in 24-bit mode. It should be noted that, although the EP_REG is an 8-bit register, only the lower 4-bits can place data onto the pins while all 8-bits can place an extended address onto the internal extended address bus. This register is written as a byte. If EP_MODE has configured the pins as standard I/O, the value written to the EP_REG will appear immediately on the pins.

For example see code 4-1, if the contents of the EP_REG = 0FFh and a 16-bit instruction is used, the 16-bit address is concatenated to the contents of the EP_REG to form the 24-bit address.

But extended address instructions will drive the extended address specified in the instruction and the EPORT pins will hold these values throughout the bus cycle.

```
Ax      EQU  1Ch
STB     Ax,1FFEh ; if EP_REG = 0FFh (reset value of register) and device in 24-bit mode
              ;     0FF1FFEh <= contents of 1Ch
```

Code 4-1. Writing to the EPORT Register with 16-Bit Addressing

AP-475

4.3.4 EP_PIN REGISTER

The **EP_PIN register** contains the data that is currently on the port pins. This register is read as a byte.

When the EPORT SFRS are to be used as address lines, they should be initialized in the following order:

1. Write to the EP_REG
   — since output address line, write the expected value.
2. Write to the EP_DIR
   — 0 for complementary output (without external pull-up)
   — 1 for open-drain output.
3. Write to the EP_MODE (write FFh since EPORT used for address lines).

4.3.5 RESET VALUES OF EPORT SFRs

The **EPORT registers reset** to the following values: EP_MODE = 0FFh, EP_DIR = 0FFh, EP_REG = 0FFh, EP_PIN = xxh, and the EPORT pins are tri-stated after reset and are weakly pulled high during reset. Also, during the CCB fetch, the EPORT is forced to 0FFh since the CCBs are located in 0FF20xx.

4.3.6 ACCESSING EPORT SFRs

Changing the **values of the EPORT SFRs** is not possible using the windowing feature of the MCS-96 devices.

The EPORT, Ports 3, 4, and 5, and the Slave Port SFRs, which are located in the 1FE0h–1FFFh range, are only accessed using 24-bit instructions. All the other SFR registers, which are located in the 1F00h–1FDF range, can be addressed using 8-bit addressing and the windowing feature.

4.4 EPORT

A **block diagram of the EPORT** is shown in Figure 4-1. The extended address either accesses data using the contents of the extended data address register (EDAR) or executes code using the address in the extended slave program counter (ESPC). If the EP_MODE and EP_DIR registers are configured for the addressing function and code is to be executed or data retrieved from an extended address, this extended address will be placed onto the EPORT pins. If a 16-bit instruction is executed and the device is in 24-bit mode, the contents of the EP_REG will determine the highest byte of the extended address. Therefore, the contents of the EP_REG should contain the correct extended address for the registers in the 16-bit instruction. If the device is in 16-bit mode and the port is configured for the addressing function, the EPORT pins will default to 0Fh. If the EP_MODE and the EP_DIR registers are configured for the I/O function, the contents of the EP_REG register is placed on the EPORT pins and the contents of the EP_PIN register is updated to the current value on the pins.

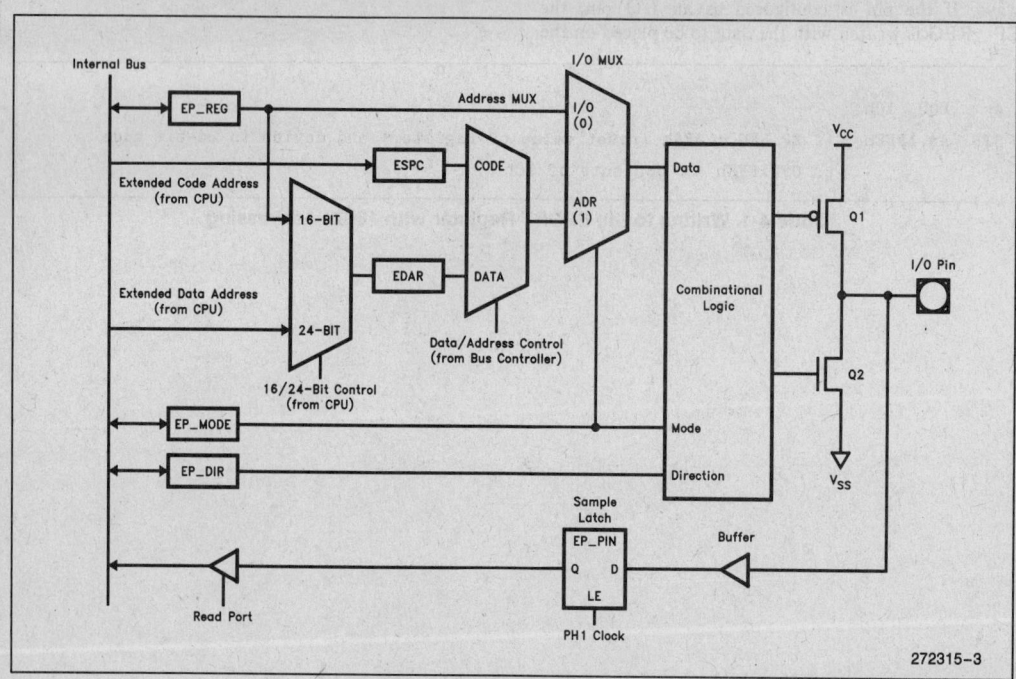

Figure 4-1. EPORT Block Diagram

AP-475

5.0 MEMORY MAP

5.1 Memory Layout

The memory addressing capability of the 8XC196NT is 1 Mbyte of linear address space. Two bits in the chip configuration bytes configure the memory map four different ways. It is conceptually convenient to think of the address space as sixteen 64-Kbyte pages of address space (see Figure 5-5). The lower 8 Kbyte (in page 00h) is specific purpose memory. The specific purpose memory contains the CPU SFRs, the register file, 512 bytes of internal RAM and the peripheral SFRs. The upper 64 Kbyte (page FFh) is where the internal (EP)ROM is located. After RESET, the CCBs are fetched from FF2018h, FF201Ah and FF201Ch. Then the program counter is set to FF2080h where execution begins. Like the previous MCS-96 devices, if $\overline{EA}$ is tied low accesses to locations FF2000h–FF9FFFh go external and access to the internal (EP)ROM is not available. The 512 bytes of internal RAM are mapped to both pages FFh and 00h in locations FF0400h–FF05FFh (and 000400h–0005FFh). In all memory configurations the CPU SFRs (0000h–0017h), peripheral SFRs (1F00h–1FDFh) and Register RAM (0018h–03FFh) are mapped to all pages. Hence, 16-bit loads/stores can be used to access them from any page. When referencing these locations (except page 00h) with extended loads/stores memory access goes external. Note however that the "memory mapped" peripheral SFRs (1FE0h–1FFFh) are only mapped in page 00h (this includes P3, P4, P5, EPORT and the Slave Port; see Figure 5-5, General Memory Map of the 8XC196NT).

5.2 How the EPORT Affects Memory Accesses

The standard 16-bit address/data bus of the MCS-96 family is extended by the extended addressing port (EPORT). The EPORT is 8 bits wide, however only four bits are bonded out to make the extra four address lines. The EPORT can be used for I/O as discussed in the previous EPORT section of this application note.

Understanding how the EPORT is loaded is important. The EPORT block diagram is shown in Figure 4-1. First, the extended data address register (EDAR) is 8 bits wide and concatenated with the 16-bit data address register (DAR) to make a 24-bit data address register. Notice in the EPORT block diagram that the EDAR is loaded from either the EP__REG or the CPU data address bus. When using 16-bit instructions (LD, ST), EP__REG is the source for the EDAR. When using the extended addressing instructions (ELD, EST) the CPU data address bus is the source. When using the 16-bit addressing instructions, the 1 Mbyte of memory can be viewed as sixteen 64 Kbyte memory sections. When it is desired to use the 16-bit addressing instructions on a particular page, use the extended store instruction to initialize EP__REG to that page (see Code 5-1).

The code in Code 5-1 changes the EPORT to 23h. So, when 16-bit instructions are used such as LD, ST, CALL, and JMPs they all refer to the 64 Kbytes of memory in page 23h.

Now suppose that instead of the previous code example, the code in Code 5-2 had been used to change the EPORT.

```
;************ Initializing the EPORT ************

EP_REG      equ     1fe5h

        ldb page,#23h     ;initialize so 16-bit instructions will access page 23h
        estb page,EP_REG  ;use extended store to write to SFR 001fe5h
```

Code 5-1. Initializing the EPORT

```
EP_REG      equ     1fe5h

        ldb page,#23h     ;initialize so 16-bit instructions will access page 23h
        stb page EP_REG   ;use 16-bit store to write to SFR xx1fe5h
```

Code 5-2. Erroneously Initializing the EPORT

If the code in Code 5-2 is executed, where will the register "page" be stored? Refer to the 8XC196NT general memory map (Figure 5-5) and look at locations 001FE0h–001FFFh. These SFRs are ONLY mapped to page 00h. So in the code (Code 5-2) it might not be known what value the EP_REG contained before the "stb" is executed. If the EP_REG contained a "01h", the "page" register would have been stored in location "011FE5h" which is external memory. Therefore, when accessing a peripheral SFR in locations 001FE0h–001FFFh, use the extended store instruction.

It is important to note that the 8XC196NT has 20 address lines. The EPORT register is an 8-bit register. Future devices may bond out the upper four bits of the EPORT register to make a total of 24 address lines. Since internally the (EP)ROM is located in page FFh, you must assemble your (EP)ROM code starting at location FF2080h (where execution begins after reset).

It is a good rule of thumb to set the EP_REG (when the EPORT is configured for address) **to 00h and leave it alone. Hence, all 16-bit loads and stores thereafter will occur in page 00h.** Changing the page via EP_REG should be done with attentiveness.

5.2.1 THE iC COMPILER

The iC compiler assumes that the current page is 00h. So, to remain compatible with the iC compiler, it is recommended to keep the page (via EP_REG) set to 00h.

5.2.2. WARNING ABOUT CHANGING PAGES WITH EP_REG WHEN THE STACK IS IN EXTERNAL MEMORY

If it is desired to use non-extended instructions such as LD, ST, etc. in any page, then the EP_REG can be loaded with the appropriate page value and non-extended instructions will operate within that page. This also applies to stack operations. For example, lets say you set the stack pointer to 0800H in page 00H (external memory). Then you change to page 01H by loading EP_REG with 01H. Now, any stack operation such as PUSH, POP, CALL, ECALL will use the stack pointer in page 01H. So the new stack location will be 010800H. Therefore, if you enter a subroutine while in page 00H, then once in the subroutine you change the EP_REG to any other value and then return from the subroutine, you will return to some unknown location. This is because the stack pointer is now operating in a page other than 00H. Remember the following three rules when coding and when EPORT is configured as address:

1. You must pay careful attention when changing EP_REG when the stack is located in external memory.
2. Before doing any stack operation, make sure EP_REG is loaded with the same page as the stack is in.
3. If the stack is in register RAM then there is no problem since register RAM is mapped to all pages.

5.3 The Different Memory Maps

There are many possible memory map configurations with the 8XC196NT (see Figures 5-6 through 5-9). Two bits in chip configuration byte 2 (CCB2) control the memory map configurations and the number of EPORT lines decoded. These bits are named MODE16 (CCB2.1) and REMAP (CCB2.2). First, these two configuration bits are discussed, then the memory map configurations are explained.

5.3.1 MODE 16

When MODE16 is set to a 1 the extended slave program counter (ESPC) is forced to FFh (see the EPORT block diagram Figure 4-1). The extended slave program counter is also 8 bits wide and is concatenated with the 16-bit program counter (PC) to create a 24-bit wide program counter. The extended program counter can be thought of as holding the page location value of the currently executing code. Hence, code fetches are limited to the 64 Kbyte region in page FFh when MODE16 is set to a 1. **In this mode extended branching instructions (EBR, EJMP, ECALL) do not work and must not be used.**

If MODE16 is set to a 0, then 24-bit mode is entered (see Figures 5-8 and 5-9). Now the extended program counter can be any page value. A simple extended jump instruction across pages changes the extended program counter value to the destination page. For example, if code is executing out of internal (EP)ROM in page FFh, the code can branch to external memory location 003000h by the following instruction (see Code 5-3):

AP-475

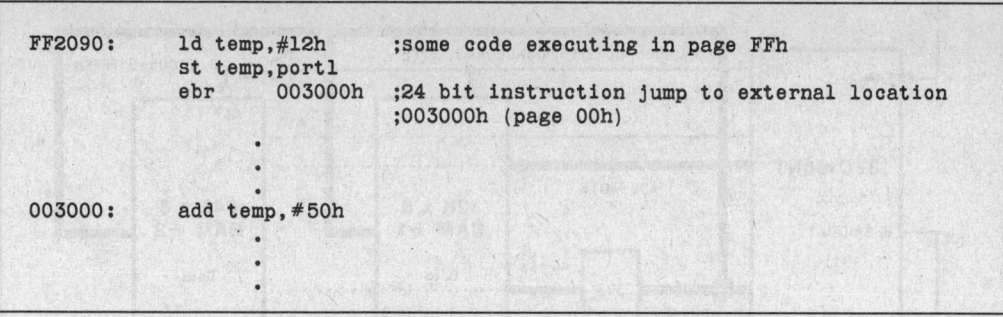

```
FF2090:        ld   temp,#12h      ;some code executing in page FFh
               st   temp,portl
               ebr       003000h  ;24 bit instruction jump to external location
                                  ;003000h (page 00h)
                 .
                 .
                 .
003000:        add  temp,#50h
                 .
                 .
                 .
```

Code 5-3. Using the Extended Branching Instruction

5.3.2 REMAP

The REMAP bit, when set to a 1, maps the internal (EP)ROM to both pages 00h and FFh. See Figures 5-6 and 5-7 for the memory maps with REMAP = 1. The disadvantage of having the (EP)ROM mapped in both pages 00h and FFh is that a 32 Kbyte piece of page 00h is used. However, this may be useful if data tables are stored in (EP)ROM. When the REMAP bit is set to a 0, the internal (EP)ROM is only mapped to page FFh. But, if executing externally (EA low) the REMAP bit is a don't care. Hence, the REMAP bit is ONLY effective when EA is high.

5.3.3 64K COMPATIBLE MODE

Now that the two CCB2 bits MODE16 and REMAP have been defined, we can discuss the different memory configurations mentioned earlier. The first configuration is called 64K compatible mode and its memory map is pictured in Figure 5-6. This mode makes the 8XC196NT completely compatible with the 8XC196KR (EP__REG should be loaded with 00h if complete compatibility is desired). In this mode, MODE16 is set to a 1 so the program counter is limited to a 64K address space and the REMAP bit is set to a 1 so the (EP)ROM is mapped in both page FFh and page 00h. A program written for a 64K MCS-96 device such as the 8XC196KR can be ported over to the 8XC196NT easily. The lower 64 Kbytes of memory looks similar to the 64K MCS-96 devices. If desired, the EPORT lines can be configured as address allowing access to 1 Mbyte of data. Setting the EP__REG to a page value allows use of the 16-bit addressing instructions (i.e. LD, ST) in any page 01h through 0Eh.

5.3.4 EXAMPLE: USING THE "64K COMPATIBLE MODE" WITH 96 KBYTES OF DATA

Figure 5-1 shows the 87C196NT running from internal (EP)ROM in 64K compatible mode. External data accesses are allowed using extended addressing instructions. The first 32 Kbyte RAM is mapped to the locations in page 00h that are not mapped for a specific purpose (see general memory map Figure 5-5). The general purpose spaces in page 00h amount to 32 Kbytes of memory. The 64 Kbyte RAM is mapped to page 01h. The 16-bit instructions (LD, ST) access RAM #1 (if the EP__REG was set to 00h) and the extended instructions access both RAMs. The 16-bit instructions can access RAM #2 if the EP__REG is loaded with 01h.

AP-475

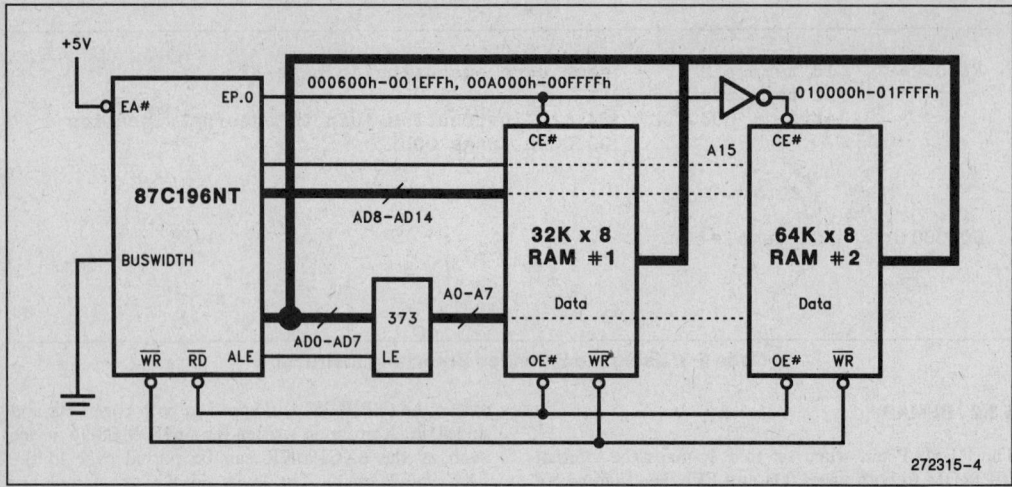

Figure 5-1. 64K Compatible Mode with 96 Kbytes of External Data Space

The code below applies to Figure 5-1 above. There are two subroutines (A and B). In subroutine A (see Code 5-4) page 01h is accessed using 16-bit stores. However, first the EP_REG has to be initialized to page 01h. In addition the subroutine has to restore the page value to EP_REG upon exiting the subroutine. So there is some overhead involved with using 16-bit loads/stores in different pages. Although if many data accesses are done in subroutine A then 16-bit loads/stores would be advantageous since they are faster. The extended loads/stores require an extra bus cycle since the internal bus is 16-bits wide.

In subroutine B (see Code 5-5) the extended instructions are used. Notice the overhead from subroutine A has been eliminated. Subroutine B takes less memory space and is more "readable" since fewer instructions are needed. If time is not critical and subroutine B is not called often to do data accesses then it would be justifiable to use extended instructions. Only in time critical applications where many loads and stores are done would it be advantageous to use 16-bit non-extended instructions.

AP-475

```
                    ;* Accessing data in page 01h using 16-bit instructions
EP_REG          equ 1FE5h
                rseg at 1ch
    temp:       dsw 1
    page:       dsb 1
    current_page: dsb 1
    result:     dsw 1

                cseg at 0FF2080h
                .                               ;Some code
                .
                .
SubA:           pusha                           ;save flags, disable interrupts
                eldb current_page,EP_REG        ;save the current setting of the
                                                ;page
                ldb page,#01h                   ;all 16-bit accesses go to page 01h
                est page,EP_REG                 ;initialize EP_REG for data access
                                                ;in page 01h
                ld temp,#1234h
                st temp,600h                    ;value in "temp" is stored in
                                                ;location 010600h
                add result,temp,#4000h          ;do something with registers
                st result,602h                  ;store result in 010602h
                                                ;more ld/st instructions in page
                                                ;01h
                .
                .
                .
                estb current_page,EP_REG        ;restore page value for calling
                                                ;program
                popa                            ;restore flags and interrupts
                ret
                .                               ;The rest of the code
                .
                .
done:           br done
                end
```

Code 5-4: Accessing Page 01h in "64K Compatible Mode" Using 16-Bit Instructions

AP-475

```
                        ;* Accessing data in page 01h using extended instructions
        EP_REG          equ 1FE5h
                        rseg at 1ch
        temp:           dsw 1
        result:         dsw 1
                        cseg at 0FF2080h
                        .                       ;Somecode
                        .
                        .
SubB:                   pusha                   ;save flags, disable interrupts
                        ld temp,#1234h
                        est temp,010600h        ;value in "temp" is stored in
                                                ;location 010600h
                        add result,temp,#4000h  ;do something with registers
                        est result, 010602h     ;store result in 010602h
                        .                       ;more eld/est instructions
                        .
                        .
                        popa                    ;restore flags and interrupts
                        ret
                        .                       ;The rest of the code
                        .
                        .
done:                   brdone
                        end
```

Code 5-5: Accessing Page 01h in "64K Compatible Mode" Using Extended Instructions

5.3.5 64K COMPATIBLE MODE WITH PAGE 00h FREE

The next memory map is pictured in Figure 5-7. This is the same as the previous mode except that the REMAP bit is set to 0. The program counter is still forced to page FFh since MODE16 = 1. So any jumps beyond the page will stay within page FFh. Page 00h is now available with the exception of some of the lower memory (see the general memory map Figure 5-5). This mode can be used for a program that was written for a 64 Kbyte MCS-96 device, which needs more memory for data.

5.3.6 EXAMPLE: USING THE 64K COMPATIBLE MODE WITH 128K OF EXTERNAL DATA

Since page 00h is free to use (except for SFRs, etc.), this next memory configuration takes advantage of page 00h in 64K compatible mode (see Figure 5-2). The program counter is limited to 64 Kbyte. But, the (EP)ROM is only mapped in page FFh and the 32 Kbyte memory space in page 00h is now free. This allows use of a 64 Kbyte RAM instead of the 32 Kbyte RAM shown in Figure 5-1. Hence, there is a total of 128 Kbytes of external data available to access when using only one EPORT address line.

AP-475

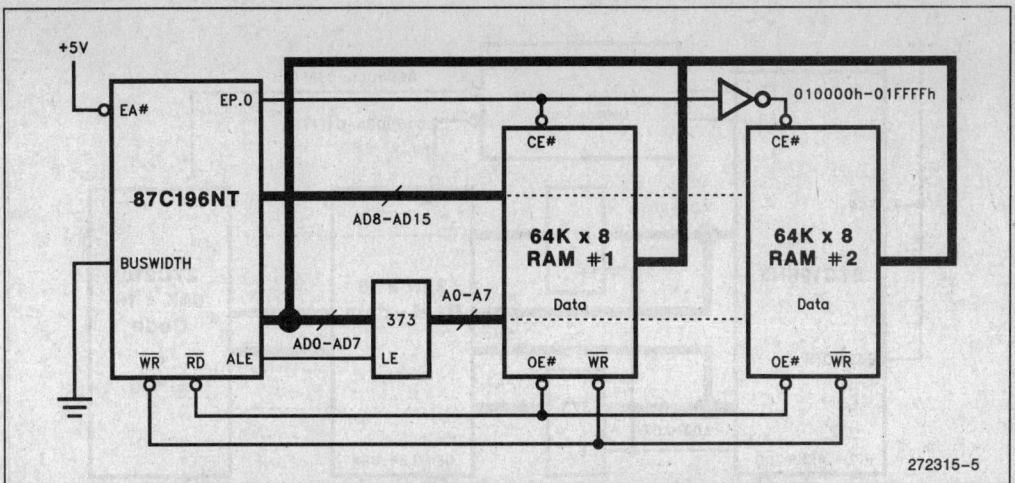

Figure 5-2. 64K Compatible Mode with 128 Kbytes of External Data

5.3.7 24-BIT MODE WITH (EP)ROM REMAPPED

Figure 5-8 shows the third memory map. Here the (EP)ROM is remapped to page 00h as well as page FFh (REMAP = 1) but the program counter is 24 bits wide (MODE16 = 0). Hence, code can be executed from anywhere in the memory space. Remember that 32 Kbytes of memory space in page 00h are dedicated to the internal (EP)ROM which would typically be used to store look-up tables or constants. The ELD/EST instructions work in all modes and always allow access to 1 Mbyte of data.

5.3.8 EXAMPLE: USING 24-BIT MODE WITH (EP)ROM REMAPPED

The third memory configuration is extended addressing with the EPROM remapped (Figure 5-3). In this configuration, MODE 16 = 0 so the program counter is 24 bits wide. This memory configuration could be used when a program was written for the 87C196KR but requires more memory space for code. Notice in Figure 5-3 that there are three pages of external memory used. The RAM (page 01h) is used for external data storage. The external EPROM (pages 02h and 03h) is used for 128 Kbytes of code. So in the example below there are 160 Kbytes of code space (32 Kbytes internal EPROM + 128 Kbytes external EPROM) and 64 Kbytes of data space. Note this time a 16-bit buswidth was used.

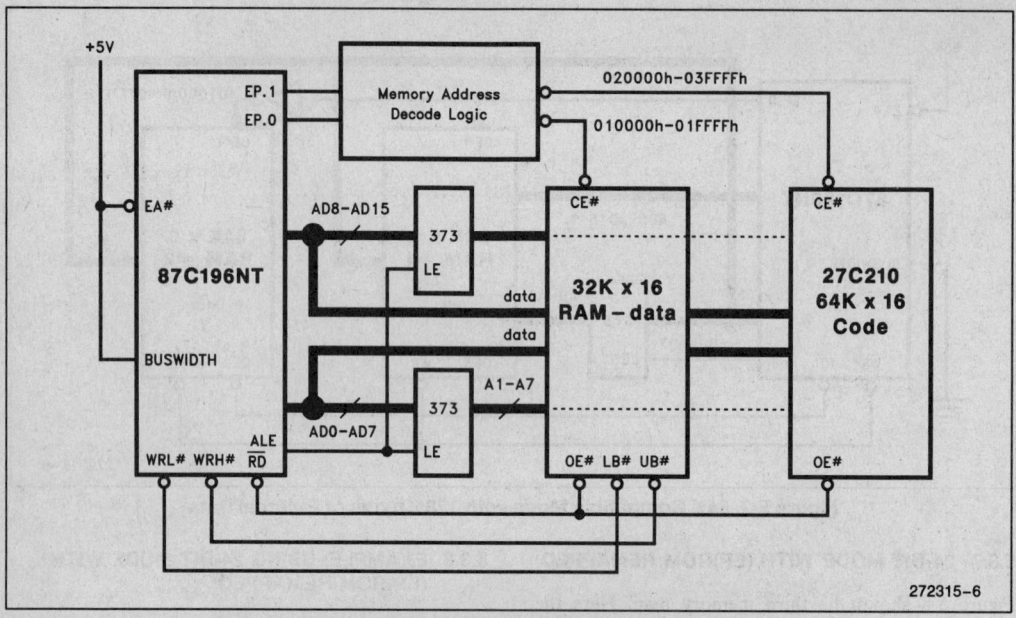

Figure 5-3. Extended Addressing with 64 Kbytes of External EPROM and 32 Kbytes of External RAM (16-Bit Buswidth)

5.3.9 24-BIT MODE

The 24-bit mode is the most liberal of the memory map configurations (see Figure 5-9). The program counter is 24 bits wide and the internal (EP)ROM is only mapped to page FFh. In this mode, code and data can be accessed almost anywhere in memory.

5.3.10 EXAMPLE: USING 24-BIT MODE

Finally, the normal extended addressing mode is shown in Figure 5-4. Here we are in 24-bit mode and the REMAP bit is a don't care since all code accesses go external. Code begins execution in page FFh. The first 64 Kbyte EPROM is used for page FFh. The next 64 Kbyte EPROM is used for page 00h. The 64 Kbyte RAM can be used for data storage; in addition, code can be executed from the RAM. Only two of the EPORT pins need to be decoded. If more memory is needed, then it is easy to decode the additional EPORT pins.

AP-475

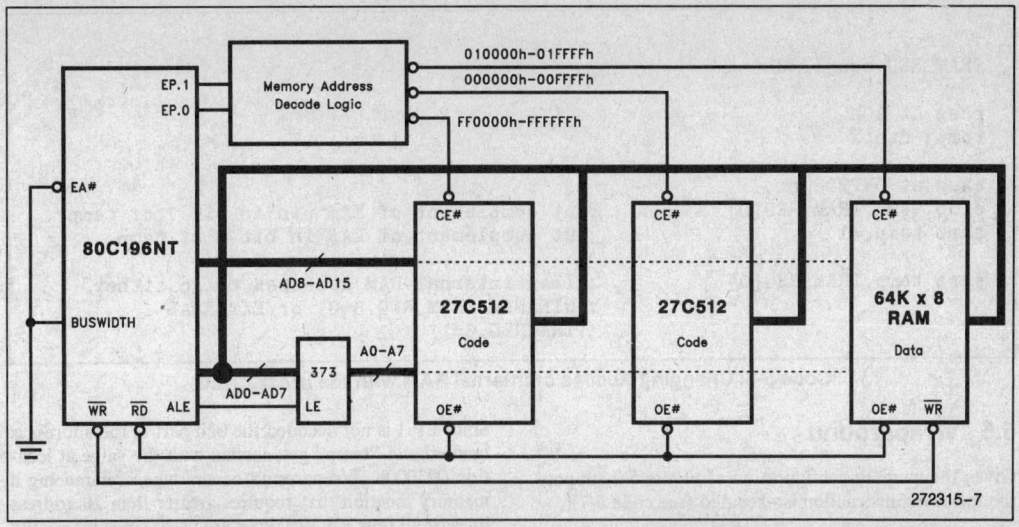

Figure 5-4. Normal Extended Addressing with 128 Kbytes of Code, 64 Kbytes of External Data

5.4 Internal RAM

The 8XC196NT has 512 bytes of internal RAM. This RAM is mapped in both pages FFh and 00h (see Figure 5-5: General Memory Map). The internal RAM is like external RAM that has been brought inside the chip. Hence, the internal RAM can be used to execute code or store data. To access the internal RAM as data, only indexed or indirect addressing can be used. Code can be placed in internal RAM in many ways. For example, if a board executes different code each time it powers up then the boot code can be downloaded via the serial port to the internal RAM.

5.4.1 READING THE EA PIN AND REDIRECTING INTERNAL RAM ACCESSES

It is possible to read the logic level on the $\overline{EA}$ pin via the internal RAM register (IRAM__REG). The format of the IRAM__REG (1FE0h) is shown below:

7	6	5	4	3	2	1	0
EA__STAT	IRAM	0	0	0	0	0	0

EA__STAT: This bit is the complement of the logic level on the $\overline{EA}$ pin.

 = 0 means $\overline{EA}$ = 1 and code accesses in the range FF2000h–FF9FFFh are directed to internal EPROM or ROM.

 = 1 means $\overline{EA}$ = 0 and code accesses in the range FF2000h–FF9FFFh are directed to external memory.

IRAM: direct the internal RAM accesses to external memory

 = 0 means all internal RAM accesses from 400h–5FFh go INTERNAL

 = 1 means all internal RAM accesses from 400h–5FFh go EXTERNAL

Bits 5–0: reserved and should be set to 0

The IRAM__REG is useful when in the design stage and the internal RAM code must be interrogated with a logic analyzer. This can't be accomplished unless all internal RAM accesses are directed to external memory where a logic analyzer can be hooked up. The following initialization code (Code 5-6) can be placed at the beginning of your program to check for internal execution or external execution and configure internal RAM accesses accordingly:

AP-475

```
IRAM_REG equ 1FE0h

rseg at 1Ch
temp: dsb 1

cseg at 0FF2080h
eldb temp,IRAM_REG[0]        ;put complement of EA# pin in bit 7 of temp
shrb temp,#1                 ;put complement of EA# in bit 6 of temp

estb temp,IRAM_REG[0]        ;Allow internal RAM accesses to go either
                             ;INTERNAL(IRAM_REG.6=0) or EXTERNAL
                             ;(IRAMREG.6=1)
```

Code 5-6: Changing Access of Internal RAM with the IRAM__REG

5.5 Wraparound

Given the memory configuration of Figure 5-2 suppose the following instruction is executed (see code 5-7):

```
eld temp, 023000h[0]
```

Code 5-7: An Example of Wraparound

Since EP.1 is not decoded the 02h part of the address is ignored and "temp" gets loaded with the value at location 003000h. Wraparound occurs when referencing a memory location that requires greater than 20 address lines (if all four EPORT lines are used) since internally, extended addresses are 24 bits wide. There is no negative effect of wraparound, just keep it in mind when coding.

AP-475

FFFFFF FFA000	External Memory
FF9FFF FF2000	Internal (EP)ROM or External Memory
FF1FFF FF0600	External Memory
FF05FF FF0400	Internal RAM (mapped to 000400 to 0005FF also)
FF03FF FF0100	External Memory
FF00FF FF0000	Reserved for ICE
FEFFFF 010000	896K of External Memory
00FFFF 00A000	External Memory
009FFF 002000	External Memory or Internal (EP)ROM (depends on remap bit)
001FFF 001FE0	Peripheral Special Function Registers
001FDF 001F00	Peripheral Special Function Registers*
001EFF 000600	External Memory
0005FF 000400	Internal RAM (mapped to FF0400 to FF05FF also)
0003FF 000018	Register RAM*
000017 000000	CPU Special Function Registers*

NOTES:
Code accesses to locations 00000h to 003FFFh go external.
*Accessible in every page using 16-bit addressing (LD, ST). External memory in every page (except 00h) when using extended addressing instructions.

Figure 5-5. General Memory Map of the 8XC196NT

AP-475

FFFFFF / FF0000	• External code and data • 32K Internal (EP)ROM • 512 Bytes of internal RAM (mapped from page 00h)
FEFFFF / 010000	• External data ONLY
00FFFF / 000000	• External data • Remapped internal (EP)ROM • 512 Bytes of internal RAM • SFRs • Register File

Figure 5-6. Memory Map: 64K Compatible Mode

MODE 16 = 1 program counter limited to 64K; no limit to data access
REMAP = 1 internal (EP)ROM mapped in both pages 00h and FFh

FFFFFF / FF0000	• External code and data • 32K Internal (EP)ROM • 512 Bytes of internal RAM (mapped from page 00h)
FEFFFF / 010000	• External data ONLY
00FFFF / 000000	• External data • 512 Bytes of internal RAM • SFRs • Register File

Figure 5-7. Memory Map: 64K Compatible Mode with Page 00h Available

MODE 16 = 1 program counter limited to 64K; no limit to data access
REMAP = 0 internal (EP)ROM mapped in page FFh ONLY

NOTES:
When $\overline{EA}$ is high accesses from FF2000h to FF9FFFh go INTERNAL
When $\overline{EA}$ is low accesses from FF2000h to FF9FFFh go EXTERNAL

AP-475

FFFFFF	• External code and data • 32K Internal (EP)ROM • 512 Bytes of internal RAM (mapped from page 00h)
FF0000	
FEFFFF	
	• External code and data
010000	
00FFFF	• External code and data • Remapped internal (EP)ROM • 512 Bytes of internal RAM • SFRs
000000	• Register File

Figure 5-8. Memory Map: 24-Bit Mode with (EP)ROM Remapped

MODE 16 = 0 program counter is 24 bits wide; no limit to data access
REMAP = 1 internal (EP)ROM mapped in both pages 00h and FFh

FFFFFF	• External code and data • 32K Internal (EP)ROM • 512 Bytes of internal RAM (mapped from page 00h)
FF0000	
FEFFFF	
	• External code and data
010000	
00FFFF	• External code and data • 512 Bytes of internal RAM • SFRs • Register File
000000	

Figure 5-9. Memory Map: 24-Bit Mode

MODE 16 = 0 program counter is 24 bits wide; no limit to data access
REMAP = 0 internal (EP)ROM mapped in page FFh ONLY

NOTES:
When $\overline{EA}$ is high accesses from FF2000h to FF9FFFh go INTERNAL
When $\overline{EA}$ is low accesses from FF2000h to FF9FFFh go EXTERNAL

AP-475

6.0 TIMING IMPROVEMENTS

The 8XC196NT has an enhanced bus controller. The timing improvements as a result of the enhanced bus controller allow the microcontroller to run with no wait states using slower and less expensive memories on the external bus. This section discusses the improvements to the bus controller that allows this flexibility.

6.1 Signals

First, an explanation of the A.C. timing symbols is necessary. Consult the chart below when studying timing diagrams:

Timing Name: T_{WXYZ}

The signals are **W** and **Y**.

The conditions are **X** and **Z**.

A — address
B — bus control signals ($\overline{BHE}$, $\overline{INST}$)
BR — $\overline{BREQ}$ (bus request)
C — CLKOUT
D — data in
G — buswidth
H — $\overline{HOLD}$
HA — $\overline{HLDA}$ (hold acknowledge)
L — ALE/$\overline{ADV}$
Q — data out
R — $\overline{RD}$ (read)
W — $\overline{WR}/\overline{WRH}/\overline{WRL}$
X — XTAL
Y — READY

6.2 Conditions

H — high
L — low
V — valid
X — no longer valid
Z — floating

6.3 Critical Memory Timings

Before discussing the value of the improved bus controller timings, it is necessary to explain the critical memory device timings. The diagram (see Figure 6-1) below illustrates the important memory device READ timing relationships.

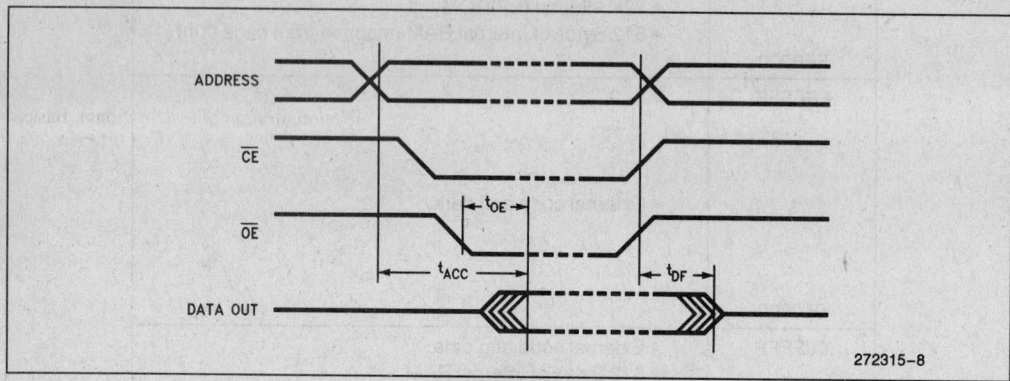

Figure 6-1. Critical Memory Device Timings

AP-475

t_{ACC} — delay time from when the address is valid to when the data output from the memory device is valid.

t_{OE} — delay time from when the output enable of the memory device is asserted to when the data output from the device is valid.

t_{DF} — delay time from when the output enable is deasserted until when the data output from the memory device floats. The smaller this spec is the better because then the microcontroller can drive the next address on the bus sooner.

t_{WP} — the write pulse width

The corresponding MCS-96 BUS READ signals and timings are pictured in Figure 6-2.

T_{AVDV} — address valid to data input valid

T_{RLDV} — read low to data valid

T_{RHDZ} — read high to data float

T_{WLWH} — the write low pulse width (this is the only critical write timing spec)

T_{OSC} — The period of the oscillator or ½ the period of CLOCKOUT. $T_{OSC} = 1/F_{XTAL1}$

Hence, given the above timings, the following relations can be derived:

1. $(t_{ACC}$ + latch delay) must be $< T_{AVDV}$
2. t_{OE} must be $< T_{RLDV}$
3. t_{DF} must be $< T_{RHDZ}$
4. $t_{WP} < T_{WLWH}$

6.4 What Can be Done to Use Less Expensive Memories and Run at Maximum Speed with Zero Wait States?

With the standard bus timings it is difficult for inexpensive memory devices to meet the critical timings of the microcontroller. Therefore, either the microcontroller has to run at a slower clock frequency or more expensive, faster memories must be used.

The new timing modes on the 8XC196NT solve the problem of meeting critical memory timings. The 8XC196NT new bus timing modes allow the microcontroller to run at its maximum specified frequency and use standard (slower) memory devices. The method of solving the problem centers around adjusting the microcontroller's critical bus timings to accommodate slower memory devices. Refer to the critical timings diagrams (Figure 6-1 and 6-2) to conceptualize the following explanation: typically the limiting factor with external memories is the t_{OE} spec (corresponding to T_{RLDV}). If T_{RLDV} is increased enough to meet the t_{OE} spec then the next limiting spec is t_{ACC} (corresponding to T_{AVDV}). However, when T_{AVDV} is relaxed (i.e. increased) the T_{RHDZ} becomes worse (i.e. decreases). Consequently t_{DF} now becomes the limiting factor with the memory device. Hence, there is a tradeoff associated with relaxing the T_{AVDV} spec.

6.5 New Timing Modes

There are four different timing modes available on the 8XC196NT. The modes are: standard timing, standard timing with one wait state, long read/write with advanced ALE, long read/write with advanced address. These modes are selectable by the chip configuration bytes. The chip configuration bytes are loaded into the chip configuration registers after RESET goes high. These bytes configure the microcontroller (see Figure 7-1 for the chip configuration byte definitions). Basically there are two bits in CCB1: MSEL0 and MSEL1 (see Table 6-1) that define the timing modes. A pictorial comparison of these modes is shown in Figure 6-3.

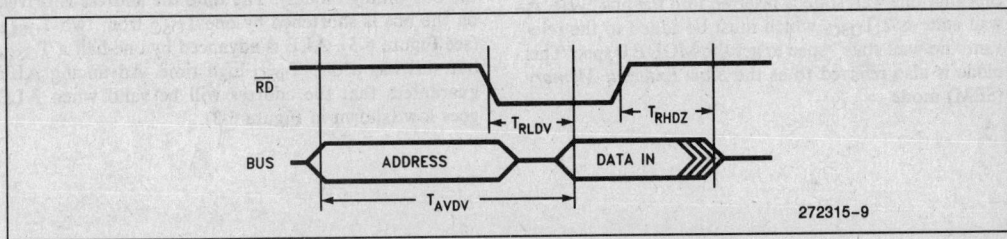

Figure 6-2. Critical 8XC196NT Bus Timings (Read Cycle)

AP-475

Table 6-1. 8XC196NT Bus Timing Mode Selections

MSEL0 (CCB1.6)	MSEL1 (CCB1.7)	Mode	Description
0	0	0	**Standard Timing with One Wait State** inserted into the bus cycle. Also known as Slow External Memory (SEM) mode.
0	1	1	**Long R/W:** advances $\overline{RD}/\overline{WR}$ by 1 T_{OSC} creating a 2 T_{OSC} $\overline{RD}/\overline{WR}$ low time. ALE is also advanced by 0.5 T_{OSC} but ALE high time remains 1 T_{OSC}.
1	0	2	**Early Address:** Same as mode 1 but the address is put on the bus 0.5 T_{OSC} earlier in the bus cycle.
1	1	3	**Standard Timing Mode**

6.5.1 STANDARD TIMING (MODE 3)

The *standard timing* mode configures the bus controller to operate with timings similiar to the 8XC196KR. This mode is the default bus timing mode after RESET. See Figure 6-3 for a pictorial representation of mode 3 compared to modes 1 and 2.

6.5.1.1 Mode 3 Timing Specs

Memory Device Spec	Corresponding 8XC196NT Spec	Time in ns
t_{ACC}	T_{AVDV}	$3 T_{OSC} - 55$ (Max)
t_{DF}	T_{RHDZ}	T_{OSC} (Max)
t_{OE}	T_{RLDV}	$T_{OSC} - 30$ (Max)
t_{WP}	T_{WLWH}	$T_{OSC} - 30$ (Min)

NOTE:
For latest specs consult the current datasheet for the 8XC196NT.

6.5.2 STANDARD TIMING WITH ONE WAIT STATE (MODE 0)

Mode 0 is the same as the *Standard Timing* mode except that one wait state is inserted into the bus cycle. A wait state is 2 T_{OSC}, which must be added to the relevant "no wait state" spec to get the MODE 0 spec. This mode is also referred to as the *Slow External Memory* (SEM) mode.

6.5.2.1 Mode 0 Timing Specs

Memory Device Spec	Corresponding 8XC196NT Spec	Time in ns
t_{ACC}	T_{AVDV}	$5 T_{OSC} - 55$ (Max)
t_{DF}	T_{RHDZ}	T_{OSC} (Max)
t_{OE}	T_{RLDV}	$3 T_{OSC} - 30$ (Max)
t_{WP}	T_{WLWH}	$3 T_{OSC} - 30$ (Min)

NOTE:
For latest specs consult the current datasheet for the 8XC196NT.

6.5.3 LONG READ/WRITE WITH ADVANCED ALE (MODE 1)

Mode 1 improves the t_{OE} spec. Since t_{OE} corresponds to T_{RLDV}, it follows that lengthening the READ (or WRITE) pulse also lengthens T_{RLDV}. Consequently, the memory device has more time to place the data onto the bus. In other words, the t_{OE} spec of the memory device can now be larger which corresponds to a less expensive device. Hence, MODE 1 is called the Long READ/WRITE mode since the $\overline{RD}/\overline{WR}$ signals are advanced by one T_{OSC} (see Figure 6-3, comparison of the bus timing modes). The time the address is driven on the bus is shortened by one T_{OSC} from two T_{OSC}s (see Figure 6-3). ALE is advanced by one-half a T_{OSC}, but still has a one T_{OSC} high time. Advancing ALE guarantees that the address will be valid when ALE goes low (shown in Figure 6-3).

6.5.3.1 Mode 1 Timing Specs

Memory Device Spec	Corresponding 8XC196NT Spec	Time in ns
t_{ACC}	T_{AVDV}	$3\,T_{OSC} - 60$ (Max)
t_{DF}	T_{RHDZ}	T_{OSC} (Max)
t_{OE}	T_{RLDV}	$2\,T_{OSC} - 44$ (Max)
t_{WP}	T_{WLWH}	$2\,T_{OSC} - 20$ (Min)

NOTE:
For latest specs consult the current datasheet for the 8XC196NT.

6.5.4 LONG READ/WRITE WITH ADVANCED ALE AND EARLY ADDRESS (MODE 2)

This mode improves the t_{ACC} spec by lengthening T_{AVDV}. As shown in Figure 6-3, the address is placed on the bus one-half T_{OSC} earlier than the other modes. Therefore, the address is driven for one and a half T_{OSC}s. Since the address is placed on the bus one-half T_{OSC} earlier, the previous data has to be taken off the bus faster. Hence, the T_{RHDZ} spec is shortened (i.e., worse than other modes). In Figure 6-3, the mode 2 A/D bus drawing shows the data output being floated earlier due to the early address. The tightening of T_{RHDZ} (t_{DF}) is a necessary compromise that results from relaxing T_{AVDV}.

6.5.4.1 Mode 2 Timing Specs

Memory Device Spec	Corresponding 8XC196NT Spec	Time in ns
t_{ACC}	T_{AVDV}	$3.5\,T_{OSC} - 55$ (Max)
t_{DF}	T_{RHDZ}	$0.5\,T_{OSC}$ (Max)
t_{OE}	T_{RLDV}	$2\,T_{OSC} - 44$ (Max)
t_{WP}	T_{WLWH}	$2\,T_{OSC} - 20$ (Min)

NOTE:
For latest specs consult the current datasheet for the 8XC196NT.

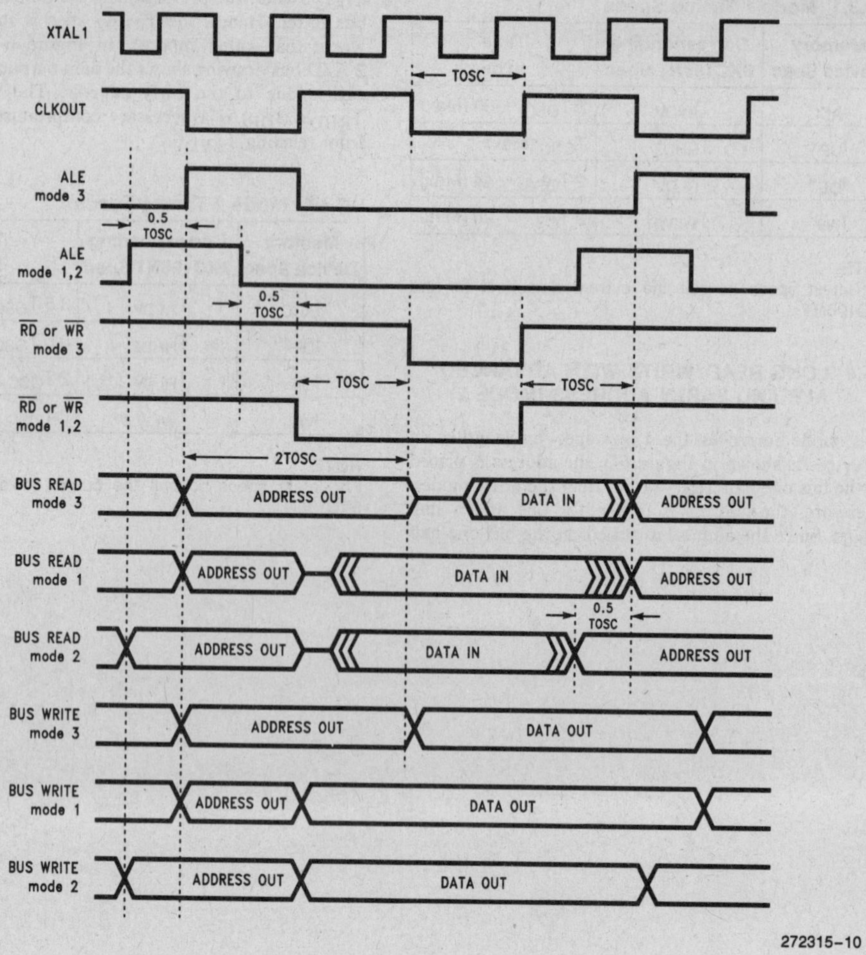

AP-475

Figure 6-3. Comparison of 8XC196NT Bus Timing Modes

NOTE:
Mode 0 is the same as Mode 3 but with one wait state inserted into the bus cycle.

6.6 Given These New Timing Modes, Which Memory Devices Can Be Used with No Wait States?

The timing improvements discussed above allow the memory devices to be used at higher frequencies with no wait states. Included in this application note are four spreadsheets that show the maximum frequency the 8XC196NT can be run at with the given memory device in a given mode. In different modes, the maximum frequency is contingent upon one of the three critical timing specs (i.e., t_{ACC}, t_{OE} or t_{DF}). The spreadsheets show the calculations for each critical timing. For example, it calculates the maximum frequency assuming that t_{ACC} is the limiting spec. Then the spreadsheets calculate the maximum frequency assuming t_{OE} is the limiting spec and so forth. After the maximum frequency is calculated the corresponding 8XC196NT bus timings are calculated based on the maximum frequency just found. For example, in spreadsheet 2, Mode 1 calculations are shown. Three different groups of calculations are done based on either t_{ACC}, t_{OE} and t_{DF}. Notice that the shaded maximum frequency column is under t_{ACC}. That means that t_{ACC} was the limiting spec. Also, the timings t_{ACC}, t_{OE} and t_{DF} are within the limits of the calculated T_{AVDV}, T_{RLDV} and T_{RHDZ} respectively. Notice in the other two columns (t_{OE} and t_{DF}), that the specs t_{ACC}, t_{OE} and t_{DF} do not all meet T_{AVDV}, T_{RLDV} or T_{RHDZ}. The flash memory parts have the same analysis except just t_{OE} and t_{WP} are considered. Also, mode 0, the standard timing mode with one wait state is included for completeness. The last spreadsheet (#5) is a summary of the previous four.

6.7 Changes to the Bus Control Timings

The main control signals affected by the enhanced bus controller are ALE, $\overline{RD}$, and $\overline{WR}$. But, some other control signals changed as well. For example, in modes 1 and 2, $\overline{ADV}$, BHE and INST occur one-half a T_{OSC} earlier to remain consistent with ALE and $\overline{RD}/\overline{WR}$. Also, the $\overline{WRL}/\overline{WRH}$ lengthened the same as $\overline{WR}$.

6.8 8-Bit Bus in Modes 1 and 2

It is required to latch address lines 0 through 15 when running in 8-bit mode when operating in modes 1 (long read/write) and 2 (early address). The reason for the latch is because the upper address lines (A8–A15) are not driven with the address during the write or read portion of the bus cycle. Instead A8–A15 are driven with the data from AD0–AD7 during the write or read cycle.

A latch is not required on the upper address lines A8–A15, when operating in Modes 0 and 3. In these modes the address is driven on A8–A15 during the entire bus cycle. Only a latch on the lower address lines (AD0–AD7) is required.

AP-475

Mode 0

EPROMs	t_{ACC}	t_{OE}	t_{DF}	Based on t_{ACC}				Based on t_{OE}				Based on t_{DF}			
				Max Freq	T_{AVDV}	T_{RLDV}	T_{RHDZ}	Max Freq	T_{AVDV}	T_{RLDV}	T_{RHDZ}	Max Freq	T_{AVDV}	T_{RLDV}	T_{RHDZ}
27C256-200	200	75	55	18.66	200.00	130.80	53.60	28.57	107.00	75.00	35.00	18.18	207.00	135.00	55.00
27C256-150	150	60	50	22.94	150.00	100.80	43.60	33.33	82.00	60.00	30.00	20.00	182.00	120.00	50.00
27C256-120	120	55	30	26.60	120.00	82.80	37.60	35.29	73.67	55.00	28.33	33.33	82.00	60.00	30.00
27C512-200	200	70	60	18.66	200.00	130.80	53.60	30.00	98.67	70.00	33.33	16.67	232.00	150.00	60.00
27C512-150	150	60	50	22.94	150.00	100.80	43.60	33.33	82.00	60.00	30.00	20.00	182.00	120.00	50.00
27C512-120	120	55	30	26.60	120.00	82.80	37.60	35.29	73.67	55.00	28.33	33.33	82.00	60.00	30.00
27C010-200	200	70	60	18.66	200.00	130.80	53.60	30.00	98.67	70.00	33.33	16.67	232.00	150.00	60.00
27C010-150	150	60	50	22.94	150.00	100.80	43.60	33.33	82.00	60.00	30.00	20.00	182.00	120.00	50.00
27C010-120	120	55	30	26.60	120.00	82.80	37.60	35.29	73.67	55.00	28.33	33.33	82.00	60.00	30.00
27C020-200	200	70	60	18.66	200.00	130.80	53.60	30.00	98.67	70.00	33.33	16.67	232.00	150.00	60.00
27C020-150	150	60	50	22.94	150.00	100.80	43.60	33.33	82.00	60.00	30.00	20.00	182.00	120.00	50.00
27C040-200	200	70	60	18.66	200.00	130.80	53.60	30.00	98.67	70.00	33.33	16.67	232.00	150.00	60.00
27C040-150	150	60	50	22.94	150.00	100.80	43.60	33.33	82.00	60.00	30.00	20.00	182.00	120.00	50.00

NOTE: A latch delay of 13 ns is included in the calculations.

Flash	t_{ACC}	t_{OE}	t_{DF}	t_{WP}	Max Freq	T_{AVDV}	T_{RLDV}	T_{RHDZ}	T_{WLWH}
28F256A-150	150	55	35	60	22.94	150.00	100.80	43.60	100.8
28F256A-120	120	50	30	60	26.60	120.00	82.80	37.60	82.8
28F512-150	150	55	35	60	22.94	150.00	100.80	43.60	100.8
28F512-120	120	50	30	60	26.60	120.00	82.80	37.60	82.8
28F010-150	150	55	35	60	22.94	150.00	100.80	43.60	100.8
28F010-120	120	50	30	60	26.60	120.00	82.80	37.60	82.8
28F020-200	200	60	40	60	18.66	200.00	130.80	53.60	130.8
28F020-150	150	55	35	60	22.94	150.00	100.80	43.60	100.8
28F001BX-150	150	55	35	50	22.94	150.00	100.80	43.60	100.8
28F001BX-120	120	50	30	50	26.60	120.00	82.80	37.60	82.8

Spreadsheet 1. Mode 0 Matched Memory Devices

intel

AP-475

Mode 1

EPROMs	t_{ACC}	t_{OE}	t_{DF}	Max Freq	Based on t_{ACC}			Based on t_{OE}			Based on t_{DF}		
					T_{AVDV}	T_{RLDV}	T_{RHDZ}	Max Freq	T_{AVDV}	T_{RLDV}	T_{RHDZ}	Max Freq	T_{AVDV}	T_{RLDV}	T_{RHDZ}
27C256-200	200	75	55	10.99	200.00	138.00	91.00	16.81	105.50	75.00	59.50	18.18	92.00	66.00	55.00
27C256-150	150	60	50	13.45	150.00	104.67	74.33	19.23	83.00	60.00	52.00	20.00	77.00	56.00	50.00
27C256-120	120	55	30	15.54	120.00	84.67	64.33	20.20	75.50	55.00	49.50	33.33	17.00	16.00	30.00
27C512-200	200	70	60	10.99	200.00	138.00	91.00	17.54	98.00	70.00	57.00	16.67	107.00	76.00	60.00
27C512-150	150	60	50	13.45	150.00	104.67	74.33	19.23	83.00	60.00	52.00	20.00	77.00	56.00	50.00
27C512-120	120	55	30	15.54	120.00	84.67	64.33	20.20	75.50	55.00	49.50	33.33	17.00	16.00	30.00
27C010-200	200	60	60	10.99	200.00	138.00	91.00	17.54	98.00	70.00	57.00	16.67	107.00	76.00	60.00
27C010-150	150	60	50	13.45	150.00	104.67	74.33	19.23	83.00	60.00	52.00	20.00	77.00	56.00	50.00
27C010-120	120	55	30	15.54	120.00	84.67	64.33	20.20	75.50	55.00	49.50	33.33	17.00	16.00	30.00
27C020-200	200	70	60	10.99	200.00	138.00	91.00	17.54	98.00	70.00	57.00	16.67	107.00	76.00	60.00
27C020-150	150	60	50	13.45	150.00	104.67	74.33	19.23	83.00	60.00	52.00	20.00	77.00	56.00	50.00
27C040-200	200	70	60	10.99	200.00	138.00	91.00	17.54	98.00	70.00	57.00	16.67	107.00	76.00	60.00
27C040-150	150	60	50	13.45	150.00	104.67	74.33	19.23	83.00	60.00	52.00	20.00	77.00	56.00	50.00

Flash	t_{ACC}	t_{OE}	t_{DF}	t_{WP}	Max Freq	T_{AVDV}	T_{RLDV}	T_{RHDZ}	T_{AVDV}	T_{RLDV}	T_{WLWH}
28F256A-150	150	55	35	60	13.45	150.00	104.67	74.33	104.67	74.33	128.67
28F256A-120	120	50	30	60	15.54	120.00	84.67	64.33	84.67	64.33	108.67
28F512-150	150	55	35	60	13.45	150.00	104.67	74.33	104.67	74.33	128.67
28F512-120	120	50	30	60	15.54	120.00	84.67	64.33	84.67	64.33	108.67
28F010-150	150	55	35	60	13.45	150.00	104.67	74.33	104.67	74.33	128.67
28F010-120	120	50	30	60	15.54	120.00	84.67	64.33	84.67	64.33	108.67
28F020-200	200	60	40	60	10.99	200.00	138.00	91.00	138.00	91.00	162.00
28F020-150	150	55	35	60	13.45	150.00	104.67	74.33	104.67	74.33	128.67
28F001BX-150	150	55	35	50	13.45	150.00	104.67	74.33	104.67	74.33	128.67
28F001BX-120	120	50	30	50	15.54	120.00	84.67	64.33	84.67	64.33	108.67

NOTE: A latch delay of 13 ns is included in the calculations.

Spreadsheet 2. Mode 1 Matched Memory Devices

AP-475

Mode 2

EPROMs	t_{ACC}	t_{OE}	t_{DF}	Based on t_{ACC}					Based on t_{OE}					Based on t_{DF}		
				Max Freq	T_{AVDV}	T_{RLDV}	T_{RHDZ}	Max Freq	T_{AVDV}	T_{RLDV}	T_{RHDZ}	Max Freq	T_{AVDV}	T_{RLDV}	T_{RHDZ}
27C256-200	200	75	55	13.06	200.00	109.14	38.29	16.81	140.25	75.00	29.75	9.09	317.00	176.00	55.00
27C256-150	150	60	50	16.06	150.00	80.57	31.14	19.23	114.00	60.00	26.00	10.00	282.00	156.00	50.00
27C256-120	120	55	30	18.62	120.00	63.43	26.86	20.20	105.25	55.00	24.75	16.67	142.00	76.00	30.00
27C512-200	200	70	60	13.06	200.00	109.14	38.29	17.54	131.50	70.00	28.50	8.33	352.00	196.00	60.00
27C512-150	150	60	50	16.06	150.00	80.57	31.14	19.23	114.00	60.00	26.00	10.00	282.00	156.00	50.00
27C512-120	120	55	30	18.62	120.00	63.43	26.86	20.20	105.25	55.00	24.75	16.67	142.00	76.00	30.00
27C010-200	200	70	60	13.06	200.00	109.14	38.29	17.54	131.50	70.00	28.50	8.33	352.00	196.00	60.00
27C010-150	150	60	50	16.06	150.00	80.57	31.14	19.23	114.00	60.00	26.00	10.00	282.00	156.00	50.00
27C010-120	120	55	30	18.62	120.00	63.43	26.86	20.20	105.25	55.00	24.75	16.67	142.00	76.00	30.00
27C020-200	200	70	60	13.06	200.00	109.14	38.29	17.54	131.50	70.00	28.50	8.33	352.00	196.00	60.00
27C020-150	150	60	50	16.06	150.00	80.57	31.14	19.23	114.00	60.00	26.00	10.00	282.00	156.00	50.00
27C040-200	200	70	60	13.06	200.00	109.14	38.29	17.54	131.50	70.00	28.50	8.33	352.00	196.00	60.00
27C040-150	150	60	50	16.06	150.00	80.57	31.14	19.23	114.00	60.00	26.00	10.00	282.00	156.00	50.00

NOTE: A latch delay of 13 ns is included in the calculations.

Flash	t_{ACC}	t_{OE}	t_{DF}	t_{WP}	Max Freq	T_{AVDV}	T_{RLDV}	T_{RHDZ}	T_{WLWH}
28F256A-150	150	55	35	60	14.29	177.00	96.00	35.00	120.00
28F256A-120	120	50	30	60	16.67	142.00	76.00	30.00	100.00
28F512-150	150	55	35	60	14.29	177.00	96.00	35.00	120.00
26F512-120	120	50	30	60	16.67	142.00	76.00	30.00	100.00
28F010-150	150	55	35	60	14.29	177.00	96.00	35.00	120.00
28F010-120	120	60	30	60	16.67	142.00	76.00	30.00	100.00
28F020-200	200	60	40	60	12.50	212.00	116.00	40.00	140.00
28F020-150	150	55	35	60	14.29	177.00	96.00	35.00	120.00
28F001BX-150	150	55	35	50	14.29	177.00	96.00	35.00	120.00
28F001BX-120	120	50	30	50	16.67	142.00	76.00	30.00	100.00

Spreadsheet 3. Mode 2 Matched Memory Devices

AP-475

Mode 3

EPROMs	t_{ACC}	t_{OE}	t_{DF}	Max Freq	Based on t_{ACC}			Max Freq	Based on t_{OE}			Max Freq	Based on t_{DF}	
					T_{AVDV}	T_{RLDV}	T_{RHDZ}		T_{AVDV}	T_{RLDV}	T_{RHDZ}		T_{AVDV}	T_{RLDV}	T_{RHDZ}
27C256-200	200	75	55	11.19	200.00	59.33	89.33	9.52	247.00	75.00	105.00	18.18	97.00	25.00	55.00
27C256-150	150	60	50	13.76	150.00	42.67	72.67	11.11	202.00	60.00	90.00	20.00	82.00	20.00	50.00
27C256-120	120	55	30	15.96	120.00	32.67	62.67	11.76	187.00	55.00	85.00	33.33	22.00	0.00	30.00
27C512-200	200	70	60	11.19	200.00	59.33	89.33	10.00	232.00	70.00	100.00	16.67	112.00	30.00	60.00
27C512-150	150	60	50	13.76	150.00	42.67	72.67	11.11	202.00	60.00	90.00	20.00	82.00	20.00	50.00
27C512-120	120	55	30	15.96	120.00	32.67	62.67	11.76	187.00	55.00	85.00	33.33	22.00	0.00	30.00
27C010-200	200	70	60	11.19	200.00	59.33	89.33	10.00	232.00	70.00	100.00	16.67	112.00	30.00	60.00
27C010-150	150	60	50	13.76	150.00	42.67	72.67	11.11	202.00	60.00	90.00	20.00	82.00	20.00	50.00
27C010-120	120	55	30	15.96	120.00	32.67	62.67	11.76	187.00	55.00	85.00	33.33	22.00	0.00	30.00
27C020-200	200	70	60	11.19	200.00	59.33	89.33	10.00	232.00	70.00	100.00	16.67	112.00	30.00	60.00
27C020-150	150	60	50	13.76	150.00	42.67	72.67	11.11	202.00	60.00	90.00	20.00	82.00	20.00	50.00
27C040-200	200	70	60	11.19	200.00	59.33	89.33	10.00	232.00	70.00	100.00	16.67	112.00	30.00	60.00
27C040-150	150	60	50	13.76	150.00	42.67	72.67	11.11	202.00	60.00	90.00	20.00	82.00	20.00	50.00

NOTE: A latch delay of 13 ns is included in the calculations.

Flash	t_{ACC}	t_{OE}	t_{DF}	t_{WP}	Max Freq	T_{AVDV}	T_{RLDV}	T_{RHDZ}	T_{WLWH}
28F256A-150	150	55	35	60	11.11	202.00	60.00	90.00	60.00
28F256A-120	120	50	30	60	11.11	202.00	60.00	90.00	60.00
28F512-150	150	55	35	60	11.11	202.00	60.00	90.00	60.00
28F512-120	120	50	30	60	11.11	202.00	60.00	90.00	60.00
28F010-150	150	55	35	60	11.11	202.00	60.00	90.00	60.00
28F010-120	120	60	30	60	11.11	202.00	60.00	90.00	60.00
28F020-200	200	60	40	60	11.11	202.00	60.00	90.00	60.00
28F020-150	150	55	35	60	11.11	202.00	60.00	90.00	60.00
28F001BX-150	150	55	35	50	12.50	172.00	50.00	80.00	50.00
28F001BX-120	120	50	30	50	12.50	172.00	50.00	80.00	50.00

Spreadsheet 4. Mode 3 Matched Memory Devices

AP-475

Summary of Maximum Frequencies at Different Modes

EPROMs	t_{ACC}	t_{OE}	t_{DF}	t_{WP}	Mode 0	Mode 1	Mode 2	Mode 3
27C256-200	200	75	55		18.18	10.99	9.09	9.52
27C256-150	150	60	50		20.00	13.45	10.00	11.11
27C256-120	120	55	30		26.60	15.54	16.67	11.76
27C512-200	200	70	60		16.67	10.99	8.33	10.00
27C512-150	150	60	50		20.00	13.45	10.00	11.11
27C512-120	120	55	30		26.60	15.54	16.67	11.76
27C010-200	200	70	60		16.67	10.99	8.33	10.00
27C010-150	150	60	50		20.00	13.45	10.00	11.11
27C010-120	120	55	30		26.60	15.54	16.67	11.76
27C020-200	200	70	60		16.67	10.99	8.33	10.00
27C020-150	150	60	50		20.00	13.45	10.00	11.11
27C040-200	200	70	60		16.67	10.99	8.33	10.00
27C040-150	150	60	50		20.00	13.45	10.00	11.11
FLASH								
28F256A-150	150	55	35	60	22.94	13.45	14.29	11.11
28F256A-120	120	50	30	60	26.60	15.54	16.67	11.11
28F512-150	150	55	35	60	22.94	13.45	14.29	11.11
28F512-120	120	50	30	60	26.60	15.54	16.67	11.11
28F010-150	150	55	35	60	22.94	13.45	14.29	11.11
28F010-120	120	50	30	60	26.60	15.54	16.67	11.11
28F020-200	200	60	40	60	18.66	10.99	12.50	11.11
28F020-150	150	55	35	60	22.94	13.45	14.29	11.11
28F001BX-150	150	55	35	50	22.94	13.45	14.29	12.50
28F001BX-120	120	50	30	50	26.60	15.54	16.67	12.50

Spreadsheet 5. Compilation of All Modes at Maximum Speeds with Matched Memories

NOTE:
A latch delay of 13 ns is included in the calculations.

AP-475

7.0 CHIP CONFIGURATION BYTES

7.1 CCBs

There are three CCBs on the 8XC196NT: CCB0, CCB1, and CCB2. Like the other devices in the MCS-96 family, following RESET a CCB fetch will occur. If $\overline{EA} = 1$ at the end of RESET, the CCBs are fetched from internal memory. If $\overline{EA} = 0$ at the end of RESET, the CCBs are fetched from external memory. But regardless of the value of $\overline{EA}$, the extended address bus is forced to 0FFh during the CCB fetch. Therefore, the CCBs must be located at 0FF2018h, 0FF201Ah, and 0FF201Ch, respectively, in internal memory ($\overline{EA}=1$). Or if the EPORT is used as an extended address port and $\overline{EA}=0$, the CCBs must be located at xF2018h, xF201Ah, and xF201Ch, respectively, in external memory. As in the 8XC196KR device, after RESET, the 8XC196NT is configured to work in 16-bit mode, independent of the BUSWIDTH input. However, weak holding latches on Port 4 (AD8–AD15) retain the high order address byte on the bus. Therefore, the CCBs are still fetched in 8-bit external systems provided the high byte address of the CCB is 20h. After the CCBs are read and written to the Chip Configuration Registers (CCRs), the bus is configured as either 8-bit, 16-bit, or BUSWIDTH-controlled based on the CCBs. The CCRs are written only during the reset sequence. The device must be reset to change the values of the CCRs.

The bits of the CCBs correspond to the bits of the CCRs. The CCBs and their bits' functions are shown in Figure 7-1. Except for some changes to CCB1 and the addition of CCB2, the functions of CCB0 and CCB1 remain the same as the KR device so the 8XC196KR User's Manual can be referenced. CCB1 has the addition of load CCB2 (LDCCB2) and bus timing mode select (MSEL0–MSEL1). CCB2 provides the means of selecting the mode of the device and the memory mapping which are described in the memory map section.

AP-475

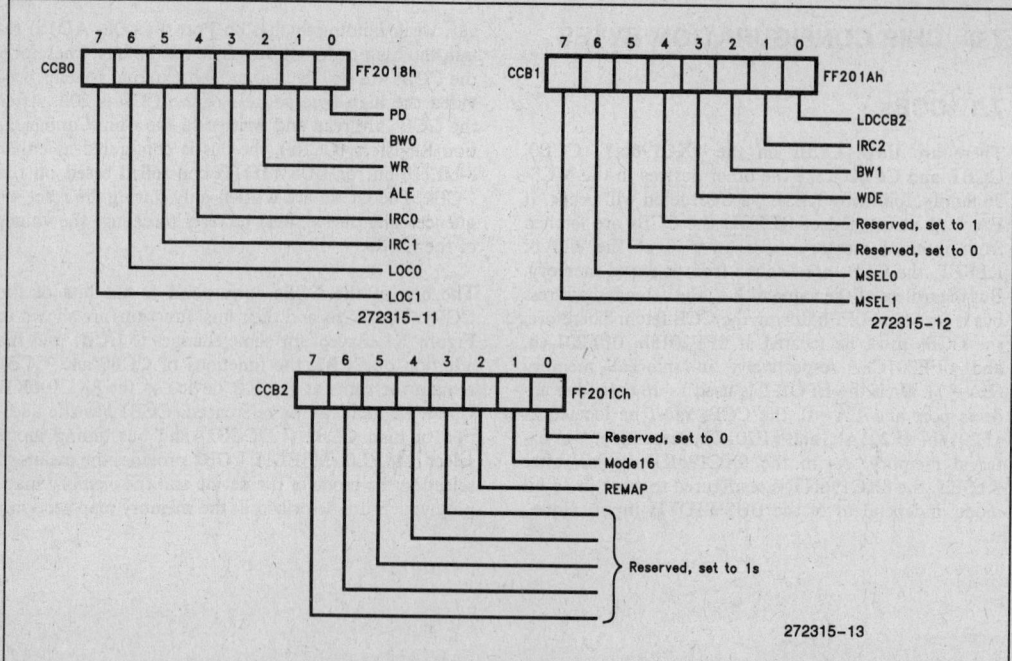

IRC2	IRC1	IRC0	Max Wait States
0	0	0	Zero Wait States
1	0	0	1 Wait State
1	0	1	2 Wait States
1	1	0	3 Wait States
1	1	1	Infinite Wait States

MSEL1	MSEL0	Bus Timing Mode
0	0	Mode 0 (Standard with 1 Wait State)
0	1	Mode 1 (Long R/W—Address Enabled Sooner)
1	0	Mode 2 (Early Address—ALE Rising Edge Occurs Sooner)
1	1	Mode 3 (Standard)

LOC1	LOC0	Function
0	0	Read and Write Protected
0	1	Write Protected Only
1	0	Read Protected Only
1	1	No Protection

BW1	BW0	Bus Width
0	0	ILLEGAL
0	1	16-Bit Only
1	0	8-Bit Only
1	1	BW Pin Controlled

PD = 1 to Enable Powerdown
= 0 to enable Powerdown

WR = 1 for $\overline{WR}/\overline{BHE}$ signals
= 0 for $\overline{WRL}/\overline{WRH}$ signals

ALE = 1 for ALE signal
= 0 for $\overline{ADV}$ signal

REMAP = 1 for remap of internal (EP)ROM to 0FF2000h only
= 0 for remap of internal (EP)ROM to 002000h and 0FF2000h

LDCCB2 = 1 for CCB2 Fetch
= 0 for no CCB2 Fetch

WDE = 0 for WDT always enabled
= 1 for S/W or RST enable WDT

Mode16 = 1 for 16-bit mode
= 0 for 24-bit mode

Figure 7-1. CCB Definitions

8.0 QUESTIONS AND ANSWERS

Q: Where are the interrupt vectors located?

A: The interrupt vectors are located at 0FF2000h to 0FF2013h and 0FF2030h to 0FF203Fh.

Q: If the device is operating in 24-bit mode can the EPORT be used for I/O?

A: Yes, the EP_REG drives a value on the EPORT if the output option is selected by EP_MODE and EP_DIR for a given pin.

Q: Will access to all SFRs always default to page 00h, thus accessible using LD/ST instructions?

A: No, SFRs for the EPORT, Port 3, 4, and 5, and Slave Port can only be accessed with ELD/EST instructions if the current value on the extended address bus is a value other than 00h. All other SFRs can be accessed using the LD/ST instructions and windowing.

Q: Can access to the Register File, located at 00–3FFh, be accomplished using non-extended addressing instructions regardless of current page in EP_REG?

A: Yes, access to Register File always defaults to page 00h.

Q: Are there any special considerations when operating in 24-bit mode and using the stack?

A: Yes, a subroutine call will decrement the SP by 4 and push a 4-byte return address onto the stack. Similarly, the return instruction pops a 4-byte return address and increments SP by 4.

Q: Why is the data being written to 0A000h with a 16-bit instruction actually written to 0FFA000h?

A: The contents of EP_REG is 0FFh. EP_REG must be cleared to 00h or an extended address instruction must be used to write to memory regions in page 00h.

Q: What page does the stack pointer (SP) point to?

A: The value in the EP_REG determines the page that the SP points to. So if SP = 1000h and EP_REG = 01h, the operations on the stack will be performed starting at 011000h.

intel.

AB-32

APPLICATION BRIEF

Upgrade Path from 8096-90 to 8096BH to 80C196

April 1989

Order Number: 270521-001

UPGRADE PATH FROM 8096-90 TO 8096BH TO 80C196

CONTENTS	PAGE
80C196 OVERVIEW	5-399
DESIGN GUIDELINES	5-399

AB-32

Converting applications that use an 8X9X-90 to use an 8X9XBH requires consideration of a few of the BH enhancements. Descriptions of each of the differences between the -90 and the BH follow, along with a discussion of the implications of the change.

$\overline{BHE}$ and INST are latched: The bus control signals $\overline{BHE}$ and INST are valid throughout the bus cycle on 8X9XBH devices. ON -90 devices, these signals need to be latched on the falling edge of ALE.

Byte Read following $\overline{RESET}$ rising: The bus control and buswidth options of 8X9XBH devices are selected by configuration of the chip immediately following the rising edge of $\overline{RESET}$. During the usual 10 state reset sequence, BH parts will perform a byte read of location 2018H to acquire configuration information prior to fetching the first opcode at location 2080H. The 8X9X-90 does not perform this read.

ALE is high while in reset: The $ALE/\overline{ADV}$ pin of the 8X9XBH is driven high while the $\overline{RESET}$ pin is held low. On -90 devices, ALE is driven low while in RESET. Circuits which rely on the state of ALE while RESET is low must be modified. The reset state of ALE was changed to enable implementation of the Chip Configuration Byte read from external memory following the rising edge of RESET.

$\overline{EA}$ is latched on $\overline{RESET}$ rising: The 8X9XBH latches the value of $\overline{EA}$ on the rising edge of $\overline{RESET}$. On -90 devices, $\overline{EA}$ was not latched and could be changed without placing the part in $\overline{RESET}$. This change was necessary to enhance ROM/EPROM security. Circuits that rely on $\overline{EA}$ not being latched must be modified.

A/D speed increased: The 8X95BH and 8X97BH A/D converters complete conversion in 88 state times. On -90 devices with A/D converters, a conversion takes 168 state times. This translates in an increased conversion speed from 42μs on -90 parts to 22μs on BH parts running at 12MHz. Software that relies upon the speed of conversion for timing must be changed. It is also recommended that MCS-96 software be written so as to not be impacted by further changes in A/D conversion speed.

Sample/Hold on A/D: The 8X95BH and 8X97BH have a sample/hold on the input of the A/D converter. 8X9X-90 devices with A/D converters do not have sample/hold circuitry. External analog circuitry which also includes a sample/hold must provide a settled analog input within the first four state times of 8X9XBH conversion.

Duplicate Fetches: The 8X9XBH bus controller was made more aggressive when it comes to instruction fetches in order to minimize the execution speed degradation of using an 8-bit bus. As a result, instruction fetches over a 16-bit bus sometimes occur when there is no space in the prefetch queue to store the fetched opcodes. This requires another instruction fetch from the same address when space in the prefetch queue opens up.

To the external system, these occurrences appear as duplicate instruction fetches. An estimated 10 percent of all instruction fetches will be "duplicates", while overall bus loading will be approximately 65 to 70 percent, compared to an 8X9X-90 bus loading of approximately 55 to 60 percent. Execution speed is not impacted by a duplicate fetch.

Write Pulse Width: The 8X9XBH 16-bit bus write pulse width is one T_{osc} longer than on the 8X9X-90, thus allowing slower memories and peripherals to be used. In order to widen the $\overline{WR}$ pulse width, the time between the end of $\overline{WR}$ and the next ALE was reduced by T_{osc}. Note that the signals $\overline{WRL}$, $\overline{WRH}$, and $\overline{WR}$ with an 8-bit bus are still the same width as on -90 parts.

V_{PP} Replaces V_{BB}: V_{PP} is the programming pin for EPROM devices. Systems that have this connected through a capacitor to ANGND (required on 8X9X-90 parts) do not need to change. ANGND must be held nominally at the same potential as V_{SS}, and V_{PP} must NOT be connected to V_{CC}. High voltage must NEVER be placed on the V_{PP} pin of a ROM device.

While there is almost no reason to do so, an application should not attempt to execute with the EA pin at logic zero and V_{CC} at 5.5 V_{DC} on an 879XBH EPROM device. Additionally, the design should always begin the "out of RESET" code execution from the internal EPROM, immediately after the power-on sequence.

Reserved location warning: Intel reserved addresses can not be used by applications which use 8X9XBH internal ROM/EPROM. The data read from a reserved location is not guaranteed, and a write to any reserved location could cause unpredictable results. When attempting to program Intel Reserved addresses, the data must be OFFFFH to ensure a harmless result.

Intel Reserved locations, when mapped to external memory, must be filled with OFFFFH to ensure compatibility with future parts.

A positive transition on NMI: The 8X9XBH does not clear the Watchdog Timer. The 8X9X-90 does clear the WDT on a positive transition of NMI, and both part vector to external address 0000H.

The following is the latest information on upgrading a NMOS 8096 to a CHMOS 80C196.

The chip which is the CHMOS 8096BH replacement is designated the 80C196. The part can be configured to be pin compatible with the 8096, but because of the process change and other enhancements, it may not be plug compatible in some designs. This is to say that you will not be able to arbitrarily swap out a NMOS 8096 and replace it with the 80C196. However, if a few rules are followed the changes required will be almost painless.

80C196 OVERVIEW

First, some background on the 80C196 is needed. The opcode set is a true superset of the 8096, but some enhancements have been made to the peripherals and timings. The crystal is divided by 2 on the 80C196, instead of 3, as on the 8096. This means that the 80C196 running at 8 MHz will have a 250 ns state time, just like an 8096 running at 12 MHz.

An 80C196 running at 8 MHz will emulate an 8096 at 12 MHz except that some of the instructions and peripherals will operate faster. The instructions which will be speeded up include mul, div, interrupt, call, ret, and jumps. The serial port will require a different baud value and the A to D may not run at exactly the same speed. This means that timing loops which measure instruction speed or A to D completion speed may have to be modified. The bus timings, while not nanosecond for nanosecond compatible, will work in most systems.

DESIGN GUIDELINES

1. Do not use undefined register areas for storage or depend on them to return a specific value if it is not stated in the Embedded Controller. Undefined registers and locations on this, or any other, part should be considered off-limits and reserved for development systems, testing or future use.

2. Do not base timings loops on instruction execution times, as some instructions may execute faster on the 80C196 than on the 8096, even when the 80C196 is slowed down to 8 MHz, its 8096 compatible rate. Counter-type loops should be initialized with values that can easily be changed at compile time.

3. Do not base critical timings on interrupt responses, A to D completions, flag settings, etc. This is for the same reason as above; some of these responses may be slightly different from those on the 8096. Timer 1 is provided for critical timings. With an 8 MHz crystal, it will increment every 2 microseconds, just as an 8096 running at 12 MHz.

4. The serial port baud register values should be easily changeable at compile time. Since the serial port is now capable of running at a higher frequency, a different baud rate value will be needed.

5. The circuitry interfacing to the chip should be capable of interfacing to the 80C196. The I/O lines on 80C196 will look a lot like those on the 80C51.

6. The $\overline{BHE}/\overline{WRH}$ signal in eight bit and write strobe mode will go low for odd byte transfers and high for even byte transfers. The $\overline{WR}/\overline{WRL}$ signal will go low for odd byte transfers and high for even byte transfers. Normally, the $\overline{WR}/\overline{WRL}$ signal should go low for odd and even byte transfers since transfers are on the low byte of the data bus.

7. PUSH and POP operations addressed relative to the stack pointer work differently on the 80C196 than on the 8096. On the 8096, the address is calculated based on the un-updated stack pointer value, on the 80C196, the address is calculated based on the updated value. The only operations effected are: PUSH xx[sp], PUSH [sp], PUSH sp, POP xx[sp], POP [sp], POP sp.

8. The V_{PD} pin on the 8X9X parts is now the CDE (Clock Detect Enable) pin on the 80C196. When tied high, CDE enables a clock speed sensor and will reset the part if the Xtal1 frequency drops below a few hundred KHz. While this is perfect for most production boards, it may be desirable to have a jumper option on this function for evaluation boards.

intel

AB-33
APPLICATION BRIEF

Memory Expansion for the 8096

DOUG YODER
ECO APPLICATIONS ENGINEER

April 1989

Order Number: 270522-001

MEMORY EXPANSION FOR THE 8096

CONTENTS   PAGE

THE 256K SYSTEM 5-403
Hardware 5-403
Software 5-403

THE 544K SYSTEM 5-404
Hardware 5-404
Software 5-404

THE INST PIN 5-404
Instruction Fetches 5-404
Data Reads and Writes 5-404

AB-33

This Application Brief presents two examples of a paging scheme for the 8096, allowing either 256K bytes of total memory, or 544K bytes of total memory. Both systems utilize PORT1 as the output for the upper address lines. Because Interrupt vectors, and other critical sections of code must always be present, addresses 0-7FFFH always refer to the same main page. The PORT1 upper addresses only affect addresses 8000-FFFFH, by slapping several 32K pages in and out.

THE 256K SYSTEM

Hardware

The hardware for the 256K system (see Figures 4 & 5, an example with 128K ROM and 128K RAM) utilizes a 74LS157 quad 2 to 1 multiplexer. The enable pin of the 74LS157 is tied to the inverted A15 signal, which is the latched addr/data 15 (AD15) signal from the 96. In this way, when A15 is low, the 74LS157 is disabled and all its outputs are low. Particularly, MA17 is low, which selects the 27512 and deselects the rams. Also, MA15 and MA16 are low, which guarantee that addresses 0-7FFFH of the 27512 are accessed.

When A15 is high, the 74LS157 is enabled to pass MA15 - MA17 values. The bank select pin of the 74LS157 is connected to the INST pin of the 96. When the INST pin is high, for a code access, INSTA15 - INSTA17 (PORT1.0 - PORT1.2) are used. When INST is low, for a data read or write, DATAA15 - DATAA17 (PORT1.3 - PORT 1.5) are used. This allows for the use of separate pages for code and data without having to change the upper address lines each time. Also, it is possible to select a ROM page for a data table, or load a RAM page with executable code downloaded from another source. PORT1.6 and PORT1.7 can still be used as I/O ports. If a -90 part were used, the INST pin would need to be latched since it is only valid during the address output on the bus pins.

This system was designed to get the maximum amount of memory with a minimum amount of hardware. The amount of ROM and RAM was picked arbitrarily, and could be reconfigured in various ways, however, this may require slight modifications or additions to the decoder circuitry. This setup has a main page at addresses 0-7FFFH, and upper pages 1-7 at addresses 8000-FFFFH. Note that upper page 0 is the same as the main page. The WRL and WRH feature of the BH part was used to allow for byte writes to RAM. If the -90 part were to be used, additional logic would be necessary to generate these signals from WR and BHE.

The RAM chips utilized were NEC uPD43256-15 32K x 8 static rams with an access time of 150ns. The ROMs were Intel 27512 64K x 8 EPROMs with an access time of 200ns. The decoder circuitry used was entirely LS TTL. Using an 8097BH running at 10MHz, there was ample time for address decoding and memory access. Timing analysis showed that 12MHz operation would also be accommodated easily. If slower memories are used, further analysis would be necessary. Also, it would be possible to switch to S TTL to greatly decrease the decoding response time.

Software

When using this system there are several things to keep in mind when preparing the software.

Since ASM96 will only allow addresses from 0-FFFFH, it is necessary to generate each page of code in a separate file. These pages should not be linked together, but rather should each be used to program the proper section of the EPROM associated with that page. The main page routine should be coded with addresses from 0-7FFFH, and each of the upper pages should be coded with addresses from 8000-FFFH. Because linking is not possible, each module should contain a table of constants which defines the symbols used in other modules. These values are easily obtained from the listing file, which can be created using zeros in the table the first time. The addresses of the pages in a 27512 after splitting low and high bytes into 2 EPROMs are shown in Figure 1.

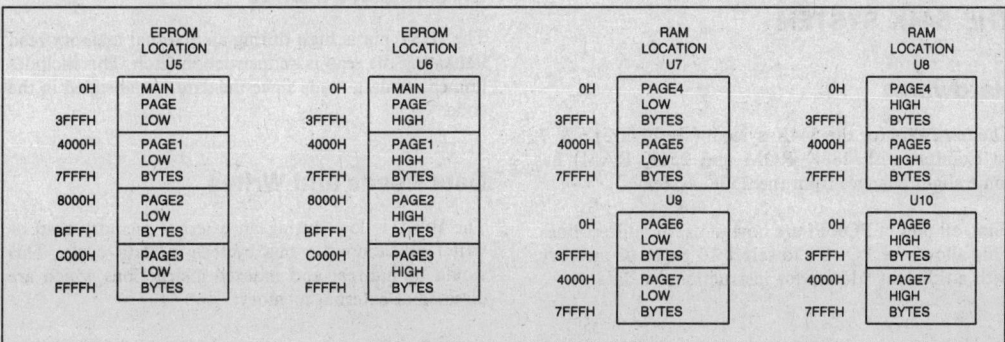

Figure 1. The Current System

AB-33

EPROM LOCATION U5		EPROM LOCATION U6		EPROM LOCATION U7		EPROM LOCATION U8	
0H	MAIN PAGE LOW	0H	MAIN PAGE HIGH	0H	PAGE4 LOW BYTES	0H	PAGE4 HIGH BYTES
3FFFH		3FFFH		3FFFH		3FFFH	
4000H	PAGE1 LOW BYTES	4000H	PAGE1 HIGH BYTES	4000H	PAGE5 LOW BYTES	4000H	PAGE5 HIGH BYTES
7FFFH		7FFFH		7FFFH		7FFFH	
8000H	PAGE2 LOW BYTES	8000H	PAGE2 HIGH BYTES	8000H	PAGE6 LOW BYTES	8000H	PAGE6 HIGH BYTES
BFFFH		BFFFH		BFFFH		BFFFH	
C000H	PAGE3 LOW BYTES	C000H	PAGE3 HIGH BYTES	C000H	PAGE7 LOW BYTES	C000H	PAGE7 HIGH BYTES
FFFFH		FFFFH		FFFFH		FFFFH	

Figure 2. A System Using all EPROMS and no RAM

All changes to the upper instruction addresses of PORT1 must be made by code located in the main page. A listing of subroutines for use in the main page, and a listing of macros for use in all pages is provided. By invoking one of these macros the programmer can easily transfer from one page to another, or select a new data page. The subroutines should not be called directly, they should be entered by using the appropriate macro. The subroutines should be located at the addresses specified, otherwise the macros must be changed as they are written to call an absolute address in the main page. Also, any hardware changes may render the software inoperative.

Because the WRL-WRH feature of the 96BH is used, the correct Chip Configuration Register value of 0FBH must be loaded into the ROMs at address 2018H. This is done in the main code file with the following statements:

```
CSEG AT 2018H

CCR: DCB 0FBH    ;VALUE FOR CHIP
                  CONFIGURATION REGISTER
```

Finally, it is necessary to initialize the DATA address at the start of the program this can be done using the NEW_DATA_PAGE MACRO.

THE 544K SYSTEM

Hardware

The hardware for the 544K system (see Figures 6 & 7, an example with 288K ROM and 256K RAM) has some slight changes from the 256K system.

First, all pins of PORT1 are now in use as address lines. This allows for PORT1 to select 16 pages of memory, with a different address for instructions or data.

Second, 27128 16K x 8 EPROMS have been added for use as the main code page. In this system, the main page is physically separate from upper page 0. The 27128's are selected by A15 being low. The upper pages of memory are selected when A15 is high which enables the 74LS155 demultiplexer which is used for address decoding. When the 74LS155 is disabled, its outputs are all high, which disables all upper memories. The 74LS157 is enabled all the time, to speed up address decoding, as its outputs do not matter when the 74LS155 is disabled.

Software

All rules for the 256K system apply to the 544K system, except that the main page no longer overlaps page 0. However, because all of PORT1 is now in use, different macros and subroutines must now be used. These have been included also.

THE INST PIN

The instruction pin has been verified to work correctly on the 8X9X-90, 8X9XBH, and the 80C196. The functionality of the INST pin is as follows.

Instruction Fetches

The INST pin is high during an external memory read indicating the read is an instruction fetch. This includes immediate data reads since the data is embedded in the code.

Data Reads and Writes

The INST is low during an external memory read or write indicating the bus cycle is a data cycle. This would be indirect and indexed instructions which are directed at external memory.

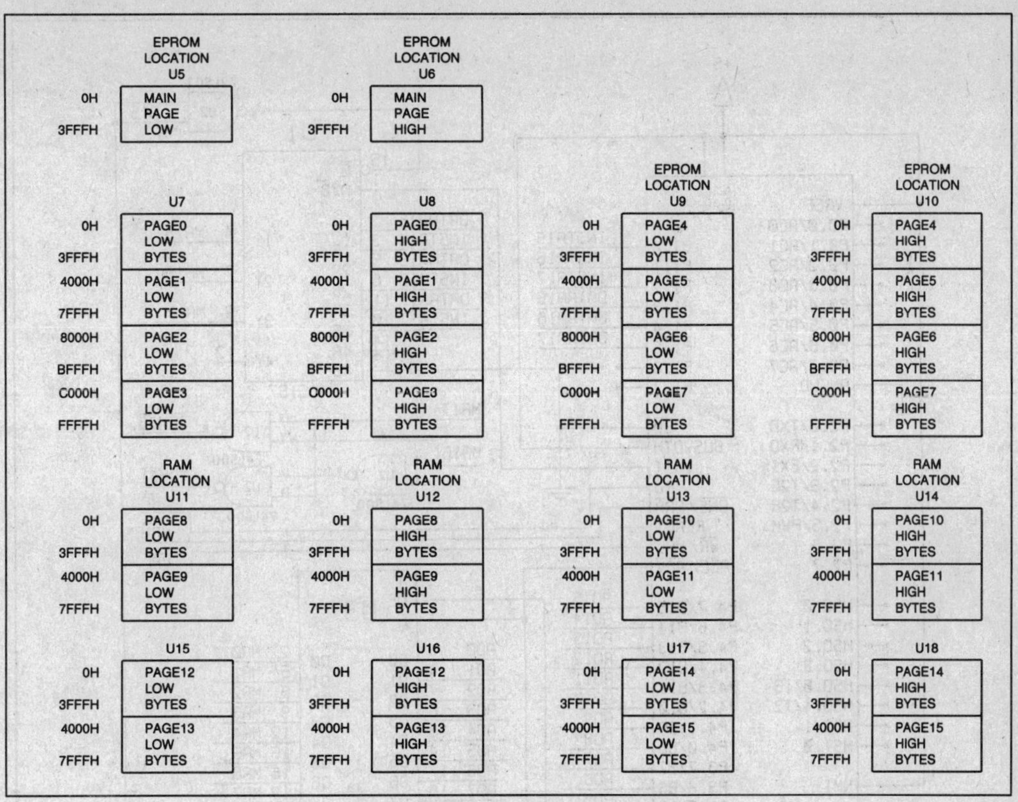

AB-33

	EPROM LOCATION U5		EPROM LOCATION U6					
0H	MAIN PAGE LOW	0H	MAIN PAGE HIGH					
3FFFH		3FFFH						

	U7		U8		EPROM LOCATION U9		EPROM LOCATION U10	
0H	PAGE0 LOW BYTES	0H	PAGE0 HIGH BYTES	0H	PAGE4 LOW BYTES	0H	PAGE4 HIGH BYTES
3FFFH		3FFFH		3FFFH		3FFFH	
4000H	PAGE1 LOW BYTES	4000H	PAGE1 HIGH BYTES	4000H	PAGE5 LOW BYTES	4000H	PAGE5 HIGH BYTES
7FFFH		7FFFH		7FFFH		7FFFH	
8000H	PAGE2 LOW BYTES	8000H	PAGE2 HIGH BYTES	8000H	PAGE6 LOW BYTES	8000H	PAGE6 HIGH BYTES
BFFFH		BFFFH		BFFFH		BFFFH	
C000H	PAGE3 LOW BYTES	C000H	PAGE3 HIGH BYTES	C000H	PAGE7 LOW BYTES	C000H	PAGE7 HIGH BYTES
FFFFH		FFFFH		FFFFH		FFFFH	

	RAM LOCATION U11		RAM LOCATION U12		RAM LOCATION U13		RAM LOCATION U14	
0H	PAGE8 LOW BYTES	0H	PAGE8 HIGH BYTES	0H	PAGE10 LOW BYTES	0H	PAGE10 HIGH BYTES
3FFFH		3FFFH		3FFFH		3FFFH	
4000H	PAGE9 LOW BYTES	4000H	PAGE9 HIGH BYTES	4000H	PAGE11 LOW BYTES	4000H	PAGE11 HIGH BYTES
7FFFH		7FFFH		7FFFH		7FFFH	

	U15		U16		U17		U18	
0H	PAGE12 LOW BYTES	0H	PAGE12 HIGH BYTES	0H	PAGE14 LOW BYTES	0H	PAGE14 HIGH BYTES
3FFFH		3FFFH		3FFFH		3FFFH	
4000H	PAGE13 LOW BYTES	4000H	PAGE13 HIGH BYTES	4000H	PAGE15 LOW BYTES	4000H	PAGE15 HIGH BYTES
7FFFH		7FFFH		7FFFH		7FFFH	

Figure 3. The 544K Memory Map

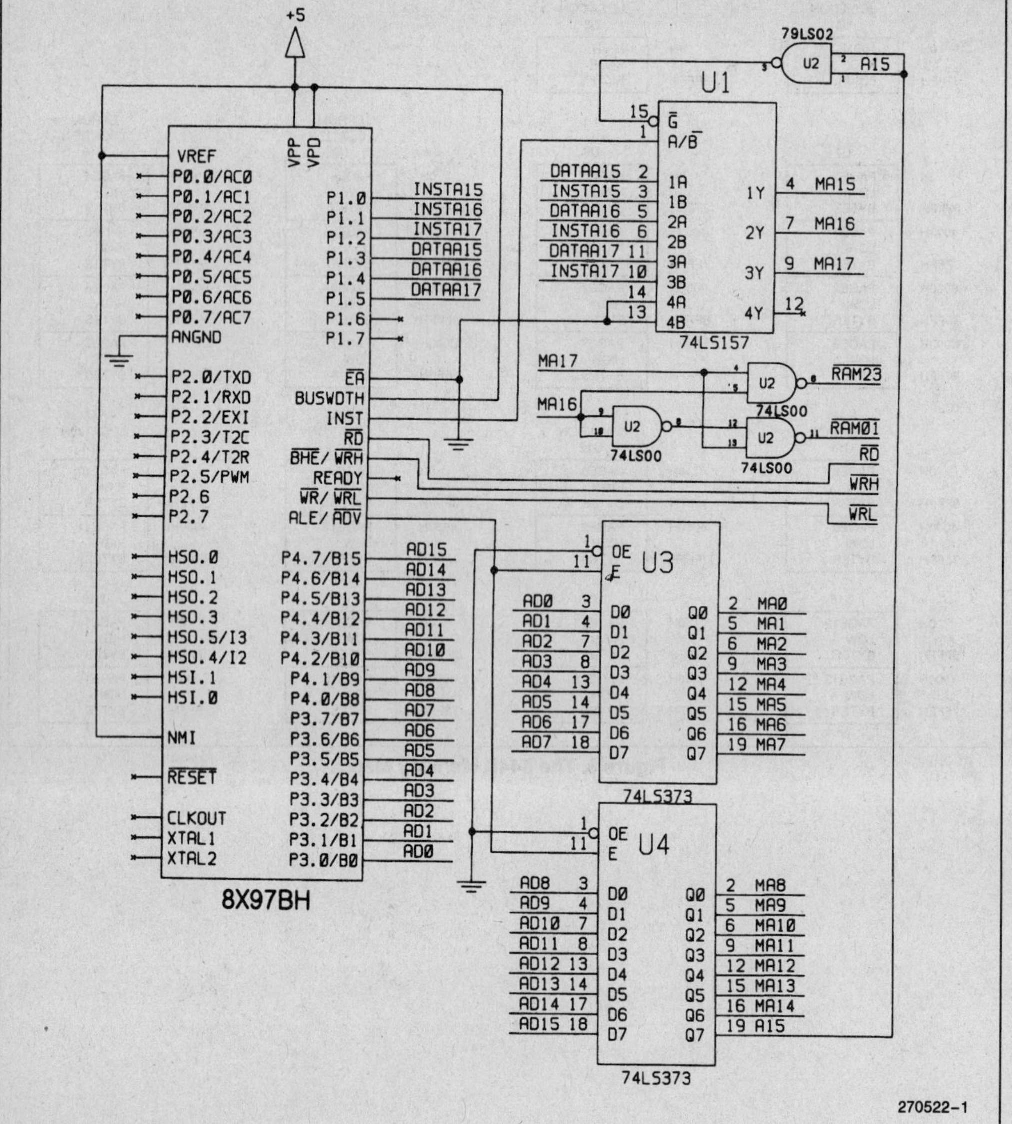

AB-33

Figure 4. 128K ROM + 128K RAM Memory

NOTE:
All other connections should be made as specified in current Embedded Controller Handbook.

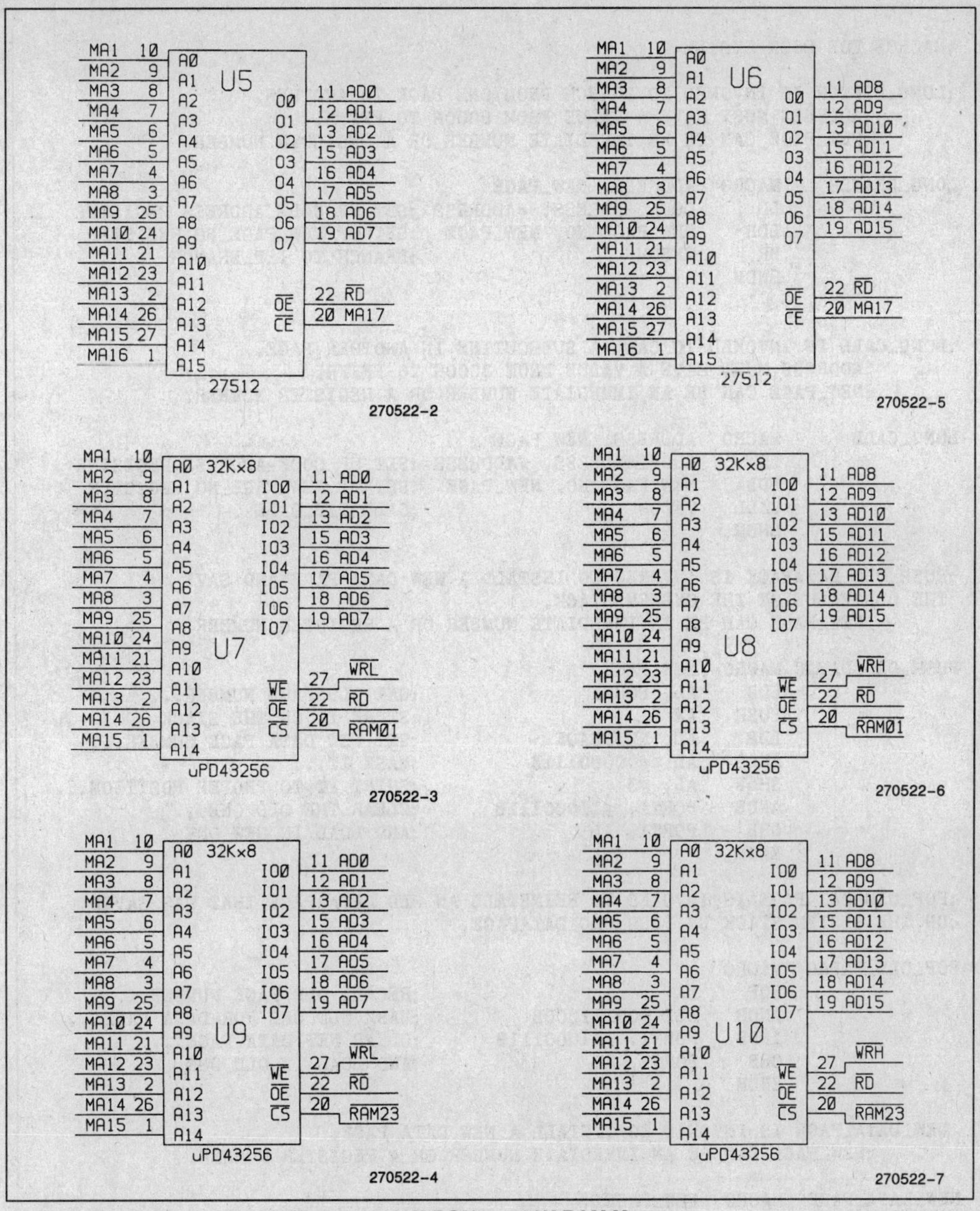

AB-33

Figure 5. 128K ROM + 128K RAM Memory

AB-33

```
;MACROS FOR 256K SYSTEM

;LONG_BRANCH IS INVOKED TO BRANCH FROM ONE PAGE TO ANOTHER.
      ;ADDRESS MUST HAVE A VALUE FROM 8000H TO FFFFH.
      ;NEW_PAGE CAN BE AN IMMEDIATE NUMBER OR A REGISTER NUMBER.

LONG_BRANCH   MACRO   ADDRESS, NEW_PAGE
              LD      CODE_ADDRESS, #ADDRESS    ;SET UP CODE_ADDRESS REGISTER
              LDB     NEW_PAGE_NO, NEW_PAGE     ;SET UP NEW_PAGE_NO REGISTER
              BR      7FF0H                     ;BRANCH TO I_P_BRANCH
              ENDM


;LONG_CALL IS INVOKED TO CALL A SUBROUTINE IN ANOTHER PAGE.
      ;ADDRESS MUST HAVE A VALUE FROM 8000H TO FFFFH.
      ;NEW_PAGE CAN BE AN IMMEDIATE NUMBER OR A REGISTER NUMBER.

LONG_CALL     MACRO   ADDRESS, NEW_PAGE
              LD      CODE_ADDRESS, #ADDRESS    ;SET UP CODE_ADDRESS REGISTER
              LDB     NEW_PAGE_NO, NEW_PAGE     ;SET UP NEW_PAGE_NO REGISTER
              CALL    7FC0H                     ;CALL I_P_CALL
              ENDM

;PUSH_OLD_DATAPAGE IS INVOKED TO INSTALL A NEW DATA PAGE AND SAVE
;THE OLD VALUE ON THE SYSTEM STACK.
      ;NEW_PAGE CAN BE AN IMMEDIATE NUMBER OR A REGISTER NUMBER.

PUSH_OLD_DAPAG MACRO  NEW_PAGE
              LDB     AL, PORT1                 ;GET OLD PAGE NUMBER...
              PUSH    AX                        ;STORE IT ON THE STACK
              LDB     AL, NEW_PAGE              ;GET NEW DATA PAGE NUMBER...
              ANDB    AL, #00000111B            ;MASK IT...
              SHLB    AL, #3                    ;SHIFT IT TO PROPER POSITION...
              ANDB    PORT1, #11000111B         ;CLEAR THE OLD ONE...
              ORB     PORT1, AL                 ;AND LOAD IN NEW ONE
              ENDM

;POP_OLD_DATAPAGE IS INVOKED TO REINSTALL AN OLD DATA PAGE THAT WAS SAVED
;ON THE SYSTEM STACK BY PUSH_OLD_DATAPAGE.

POP_OLD_DAPAG MACRO
              POP     AX                        ;RECALL OLD PAGE NUMBER...
              ANDB    AL, #00111000B            ;MASK OLD ONE FOR DATA PAGE...
              ANDB    PORT1, #11000111B         ;CLEAR NEW DATA PAGE...
              ORB     PORT1, AL                 ;AND LOAD IN OLD ONE
              ENDM

;NEW_DATA_PAGE IS INVOKED TO INSTALL A NEW DATA PAGE.
      ;NEW_PAGE CAN BE AN IMMEDIATE NUMBER OR A REGISTER NUMBER.

NEW_DATA_PAGE MACRO   NEW_PAGE
              LDB     AL, NEW_PAGE              ;GET NEW DATA PAGE NUMBER...
              ANDB    AL, #00000111B            ;MASK IT...
              SHLB    AL #3                     ;SHIFT IT TO PROPER POSITION...
              ANDB    PORT1, #11000111B         ;CLEAR THE OLD ONE...
              ORB     PORT1, AL                 ;AND LOAD IN NEW ONE
              ENDM
```

```
;SUBROUTINES FOR 256K SYSTEM

CSEG AT 7FC0H

;SUBROUTINE:    I_P_CALL
;       THIS SUBROUTINE ALLOWS FOR THE CALLING OF SUBROUTINES LOCATED IN
;       A DIFFERENT PAGE OF MEMORY.
;
;       PARAMETERS:     CODE_ADDRESS, NEW_PAGE_NO
;       SUBROUTINES:    ANY THAT ARE REQUESTED.
;
I_P_CALL:       LDB     AL, PORT1                       ;GET OLD PAGE NUMBER...
                PUSH    AX                              ;STORE IT ON THE STACK
                ANDB    PORT1, #11111000B               ;CLEAR OLD INST PAGE...
                ANDB    NEW_PAGE_NO, #00000111B         ;MASK NEW ONE...
                ORB     PORT1, NEW_PAGE_NO              ;AND LOAD IT IN
                PUSH    #I_P_RETURN                     ;SAVE RETURN ADDRESS...
                BR      [CODE_ADDRESS]                  ;CALL REQUESTED ROUTINE

I_P_RETURN:     POP     AX                              ;RECALL OLD PAGE NUMBER...
                ANDB    PORT1, #11111000B               ;CLEAR NEW INST PAGE...
                ANDB    AL, #00000111B                  ;MASK OLD ONE...
                ORB     PORT1, AL                       ;AND LOAD IT IN
                RET                                     ;RETURN TO CALLING ROUTINE

CSEG AT 7FF0H

;SUBROUTINE:    I_P_BRANCH
;       THIS SUBROUTINE ALLOWS FOR BRANCHING TO LOCATIONS IN A DIFFERENT
;       PAGE OF MEMORY.
;
;       PARAMETERS:     CODE_ADDRESS, NEW_PAGE_NO
;       SUBROUTINES:    NONE
;
I_P_BRANCH:     ANDB    PORT1, #11111000B               ;CLEAR OLD INST PAGE...
                ANDB    NEW_PAGE_NO #00000111B          ;MASK NEW ONE...
                ORB     PORT1, NEW_PAGE_NO              ;AND LOAD IT IN
                BR      [CODE_ADDRESS]                  ;BRANCH TO REQUESTED
ROUTINE
```

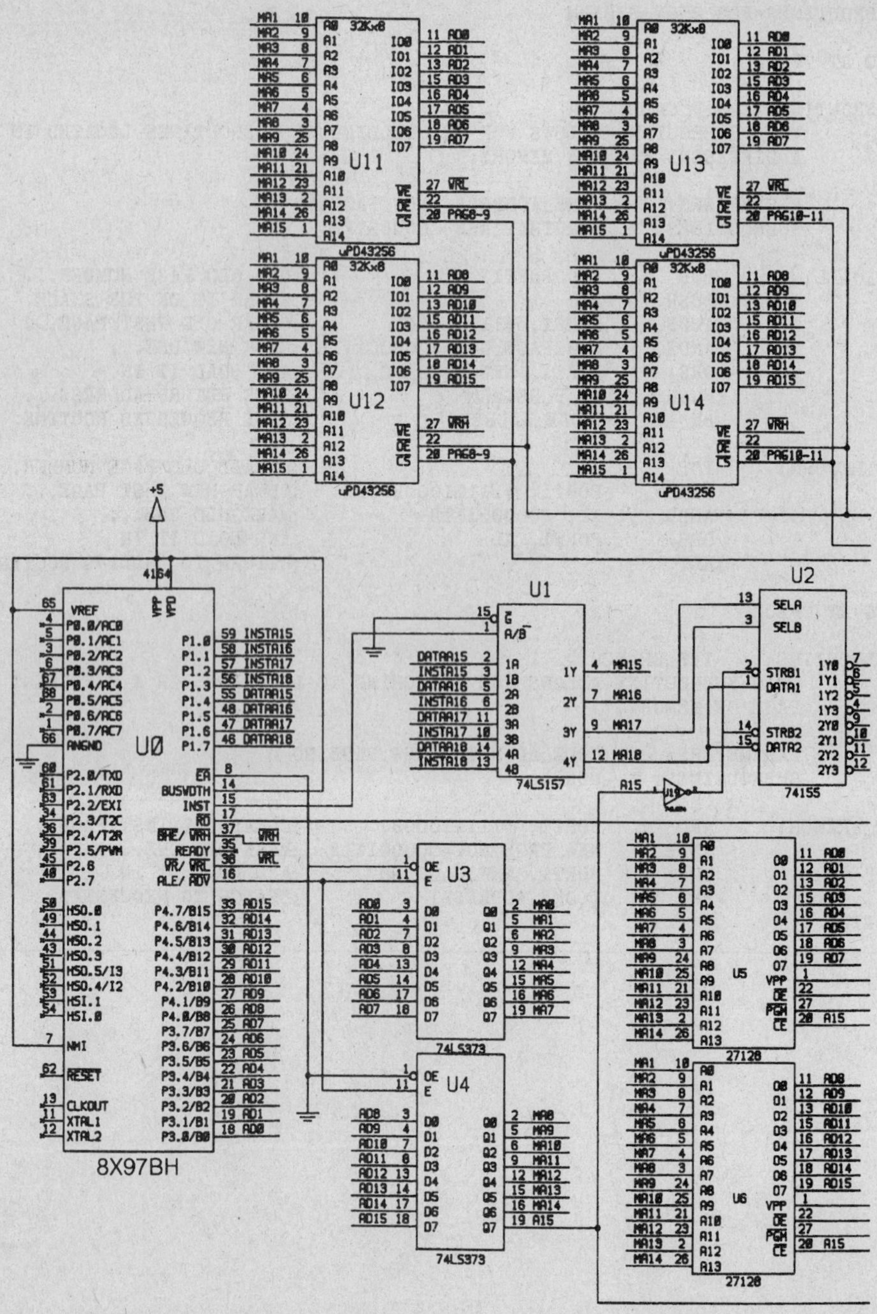

270522-8

NOTE:
All other connections should be made as specified in current Embedded Controller Handbook.

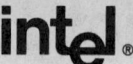

Figure 6. 288K ROM + 256K RAM Memory

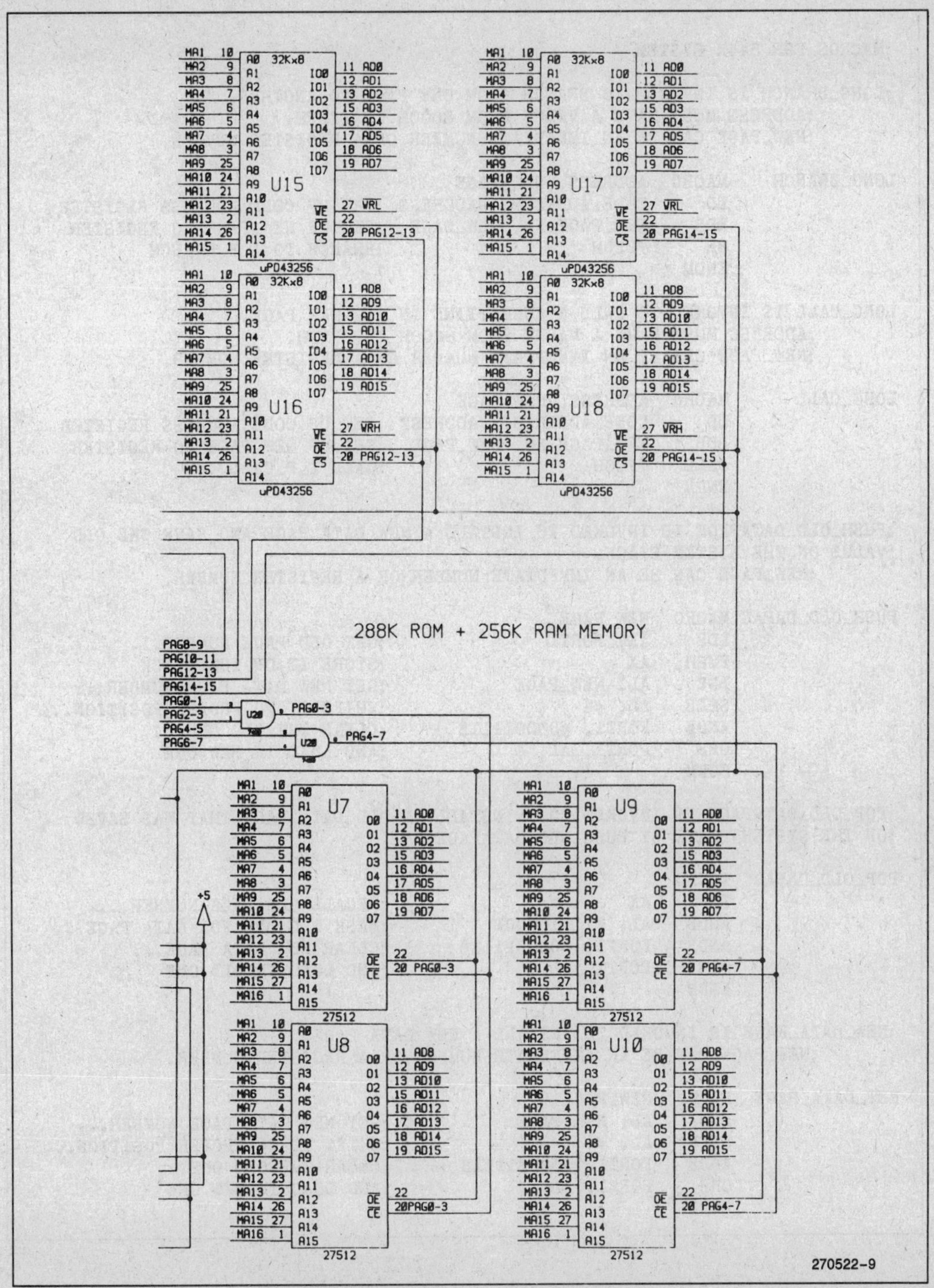

AB-33

Figure 7. 288K ROM + 256K RAM Memory

```
;MACROS FOR 544K SYSTEM

;LONG_BRANCH IS INVOKED TO BRANCH FROM ONE PAGE TO ANOTHER.
        ;ADDRESS MUST HAVE A VALUE FROM 8000H TO FFFFH.
        ;NEW_PAGE CAN BE AN IMMEDIATE NUMBER OR A REGISTER NUMBER.

LONG_BRANCH    MACRO   ADDRESS, NEW_PAGE
               LD      CODE_ADDRESS, #ADDRESS   ;SET UP CODE_ADDRESS REGISTER
               LDB     NEW_PAGE_NO, NEW_PAGE    ;SET UP NEW_PAGE_NO REGISTER
               BR      7FF0H                    ;BRANCH TO I_P_BRANCH
               ENDM

;LONG_CALL IS INVOKED TO CALL A SUBROUTINE IN ANOTHER PAGE.
        ;ADDRESS MUST HAVE A VALUE FROM 8000H TO FFFFH.
        ;NEW_PAGE CAN BE AN IMMEDIATE NUMBER OR A REGISTER NUMBER.

LONG_CALL      MACRO   ADDRESS, NEW_PAGE
               LD      CODE_ADDRESS, #ADDRESS   ;SET UP CODE_ADDRESS REGISTER
               LDB     NEW_PAGE_NO, NEW_PAGE    ;SET UP NEW_PAGE_NO REGISTER
               CALL    7FC0H                    ;CALL I_P_CALL
               ENDM

;PUSH_OLD_DATAPAGE IS INVOKED TO INSTALL A NEW DATA PAGE AND SAVE THE OLD
;VALUE ON THE SYSTEM STACK.
        ;NEW_PAGE CAN BE AN IMMEDIATE NUMBER OR A REGISTER NUMBER.

PUSH_OLD_DAPAG MACRO   NEW_PAGE
               LDB     AL, PORT1                ;GET OLD PAGE NUMBER...
               PUSH    AX                       ;STORE IT ON THE STACK
               LDB     AL, NEW_PAGE             ;GET NEW DATA PAGE NUMBER:..
               SHLB    AL, #4                   ;SHIFT IT TO PROPER POSITION...
               ANDB    PORT1, #00001111B        ;CLEAR THE OLD ONE...
               ORB     PORT1, AL                ;AND LOAD IN NEW ONE
               ENDM

;POP_OLD_DATAPAGE IS INVOKED TO REINSTALL AN OLD DATA PAGE THAT WAS SAVED
;ON THE SYSTEM STACK BY PUSH_OLD_DATAPAGE.

POP_OLD_DAPAG  MACRO
               POP     AX                       ;RECALL OLD PAGE NUMBER...
               ANDB    AL, #11110000B           ;MASK OLD ONE FOR DATA PAGE...
               ANDB    PORT1, #00001111B        ;CLEAR NEW DATA PAGE...
               ORB     PORT1, AL                ;AND LOAD IN OLD ONE
               ENDM

;NEW_DATA_PAGE IS INVOKED TO INSTALL A NEW DATA PAGE.
        ;NEW_PAGE CAN BE AN IMMEDIATE NUMBER OR A REGISTER NUMBER.

NEW_DATA_PAGE  MACRO   NEW_PAGE
               LDB     AL, NEW_PAGE             ;GET NEW DATA PAGE NUMBER...
               SHLB    AL, #4                   ;SHIFT IT TO PROPER POSITION...
               ANDB    PORT1, #00001111B        ;CLEAR THE OLD ONE...
               ORB     PORT1, AL                ;AND LOAD IN NEW ONE
               ENDM
```

AB-33

```
;SUBROUTINES FOR 544K SYSTEM

CSEG AT 7FC0H

;SUBROUTINE:    I_P_CALL
;      THIS SUBROUTINE ALLOWS FOR THE CALLING OF SUBROUTINES LOCATED IN
;      A DIFFERENT PAGE OF MEMORY.
;
;      PARAMETERS:       CODE_ADDRESS, NEW_PAGE_NO
;      SUBROUTINES:      ANY THAT ARE REQUESTED.
;
I_P_CALL:       LDB     AL, PORT1               ;GET OLD PAGE NUMBER...
                PUSH    AX                      ;STORE IT ON THE STACK
                ANDB    PORT1, #11110000B       ;CLEAR OLD INST PAGE...
                ANDB    NEW_PAGE_NO, #00001111B ;MASK NEW ONE...
                ORB     PORT1, NEW_PAGE_NO      ;AND LOAD IT IN
                PUSH    #I_P_RETURN             ;SAVE RETURN ADDRESS...
                BR      [CODE_ADDRESS]          ;CALL REQUESTED ROUTINE

I_P_RETURN:     POP     AX                      ;RECALL OLD PAGE NUMBER...
                ANDB    PORT1, #11110000B       ;CLEAR NEW INST PAGE...
                ANDB    AL, #00001111B          ;MASK OLD ONE...
                ORB     PORT1, AL               ;AND LOAD IT IN
                RET                             ;RETURN TO CALLING ROUTINE

CSEG AT 7FF0H

;SUBROUTINE:    I_P_BRANCH
;      THIS SUBROUTINE ALLOWS FOR BRANCHING TO LOCATIONS IN A DIFFERENT
;      PAGE OF MEMORY.
;
;      PARAMETERS:       CODE_ADDRESS, NEW_PAGE_NO
;      SUBROUTINES:      NONE
;
I_P_BRANCH:     ANDB    PORT1, #11110000B       ;CLEAR OLD INST PAGE...
                ANDB    NEW_PAGE_NO, #00001111B ;MASK NEW ONE...
                ORB     PORT1, NEW_PAGE_NO      ;AND LOAD IT IN
                BR      [CODE_ADDRESS]          ;BRANCH TO REQUESTED ROUTINE
```

AB-34

APPLICATION BRIEF

Integer Square Root Routine for the 8096

LIONEL SMITH
ECO APPLICATIONS ENGINEER

April 1989

Order Number: 270523-001

INTEGER SQUARE ROOT ROUTINE FOR THE 8096

CONTENTS PAGE
Theory 5-416
Practice 5-416
Comments 5-416

AB-34

This Application Brief presents an example of calculating the square root of a 32-bit signed integer.

Theory

Newton showed that the square root can be calculated by repeating the approximation:

$$X_{new} = (R/X_{old} + X_{old})/2 \; ; \; X_{old} = X_{new}$$

where: R is the radicand

X_{old} is the current approximation of the square root

X_{new} is the new approximation

until you get an answer you like. A common technique for deciding whether or not you like the answer is to loop on the approximation until X_{new} stops changing. If you are dealing with real (floating point) numbers this technique can sometimes get you in trouble because it's possible to hang up in the loop with X_{new} alternating between two values. This is not the case with integers. As an example of how it all works, consider taking the square root of 37 with an initial guess (X_{old}) of 1:

$X_{new} = (37/1 + 1)/2 = 19; X_{old} = 19$

$X_{new} = (37/19 + 19)/2 = 10; X_{old} = 10$

$X_{new} = (37/10 + 10)/2 = 6; X_{old} = 6$

$X_{new} = (37/6 + 6)/2 = 6; X_{old} = 6 -$ done!

Note that in integer arithmetic the remainder of a division is ignored and the square root of a number is floored (i.e. the square root is the largest integer which, when multiplied by itself, is less than or equal to the radicand).

Practice

The only significant problem in implementing the square root calculation using this algorithm is that the division of R by X_{old} could easily be a 32 by 32 divide if R is a 32 bit integer. This is ok if you happen to have a 32 by 32 divide instruction, but most 16-bit machines (including the 8096) only provide a 32 by 16 divide. However, a little bit of creative laziness will allow us to squeeze by using the 32 by 16 bit divide on the 8096.

The largest positive integer you can represent with a 32-bit two's complement number is 07fff$ffffh, or 2,147,483,647. The square root of this number is 0b504h, or 46,340. The largest square root that we can generate from a 32-bit radicand can be represented in 16-bits. If we are careful in picking our initial X_{old} we can do all of the divisions with the 32 by 16 divide instruction we have available. Picking the largest possible 16-bit number (0ffffh) will always work although it may slow the calculation down by requiring too many iterations to arrive at the correct result. The algorithm below takes a slightly more intelligent approach. It uses the normalize instruction to figure out how many leading zeros the 32-bit radicand has and picks an initial X_{old} based on this information. If there are 16 or more leading zeros then the radicand is less than 16 bits so an initial X_{old} of 0ffh is chosen. If the radicand is more than 16 bits then the initial X_{old} is calculated by shifting the value 0ffffh by half as many places as there were leading zeros in the radicand. To give credit where credit is due, I first saw this 'trick" in the January 1986 issue of Dr. Dobbs's Journal in a letter from Michael Barr of McGill University.

The routine was timed in a 12.0 Mhz 8096 as it calculated the square roots of all positive 32-bit numbers, the following numbers include the CALL and return sequence and were measured using Timer 1 of the 8096.

Minimum Execution Time:	24 microseconds
Maximum Execution Time:	236 microseconds
Average Execution Time:	102 microseconds

Comments

The program module which follows is part of a collection of routines which perform integer and real arithmetic on a software implemented tagged stack. The top element of the stack is call TOS and is in fixed locations in the register file. Since the square root operation only involves TOS, further details of the stack structure are not shown.

```
MCS-96 MACRO ASSEMBLER    SQRT                                05/12/86 10:44:30 PAGE  1
DOS MCS-96 MACRO ASSEMBLER, V1.1
SOURCE FILE: ROOT2.A96
OBJECT FILE: ROOT2.OBJ
CONTROLS SPECIFIED IN INVOCATION COMMAND: NOSB
ERR LOC  OBJECT        LINE        SOURCE STATEMENT
                         1  ;
                         2  sqrt module
                         3  ;
                         4  ; 32 bit integer square root for the 8096
                         5  ;
                         6  public qstk_isqrt         ;   TOP <- SQUARE_ROOT(TOP)
                         7  extrn interr:entry        ; Integer error routine
                         8  ;
                         9  ;   id stags for stack integer routines
    0019                10  isqrt_id    equ     19h
                        11  ;
                        12  ; error codes
                        13  ;
    0000                14  overflow      equ     00h
    0001                15  paramerr      equ     01h
    0002                16  invalid_input equ     02h
                        17
    001C                18        oseg at 1ch
                        19  ; ===========
    001C                20  ax:     dsw 1
    001C                21  al equ ax:byte
    001D                22  ah equ (ax+1):byte
    001E                23  dx:     dsw 1
    0020                24  cx:     dsw 1
    0022                25  bx:     dsw 1
    0018                26  sp      equ 18h:word
                        27
                        28
    0030                29        oseg at 30h
                        30  ; ===========
    0030                31  qstk_reg:
    0030                32        dsl  1               ; make sure of alignment
    0030                33  next     equ qstk_reg:word  ; pointer to next element in the arg stack.
    0032                34  tos_tag equ (qstk_reg+2):word
    0034                35  tos_value:
    0034                36        dsl  1               ; 32 bit integer
                        37  ;
    0000                38        cseg
                        39  ; ====
                        40  bl  macro param
                        41      bnc   param
                        42      endm
                        43
                        44  bhe macro param
                        45      bc    param
                        46      endm
                        47  $eject
```

AB-34

```
MCS-96 MACRO ASSEMBLER   SQRT                             05/12/86 10:44:30 PAGE   2
ERR  LOC   OBJECT               LINE        SOURCE STATEMENT
     0000                        48         cseg
                                 49    ;    ====
                                 50    ;
     0000                        51    qstk_isqrt:
                                 52    ; Takes the square root of the long integer in TOS
                                 53    ; TOS → Top of argument stack
                                 54    ;    iTOS - iSQRT(TOS)
                                 55    ;
     0020                        56         Xold set cx
     0000 A0341C                 57         ld      ax,tos_value
     0003 A0361E                 58         ld      dx,(tos_value+2)
     0006 371F07                 59         bbc     (dx+1),7,qsi05        ; if (TOS < 0)
     0009 C90119                 60         push    #(isqrt_id*256+paramerr)
     000C EF0000       E         61         call    interr                ;   Call interr.
     000F F0                     62         ret                           ;   Exit
     0010                        63    qsi05:
     0010 0F221C                 64         normal  ax, bx
     0013 DF3B                   65         be      qstk_isqrt0
     0015 991022                 66         cmpb    bx,#16                 ; if (TOS < 2**16)
     0018 DA06                   67         ble     qsi10
     001A A1FF0020               68         ld      Xold, #0ffh            ;   Use 0ffh as first estimate.
     001E 200A                   69         br      qstk_isqrtloop
     0020                        70    qsi10:
     0020 180122                 71         shrb    bx,#1
     0023 A1FFFF20               72         ld      Xold, #0ffffh          ;   Base the first estimate on the
     0027 082220                 73         shr     Xold, bx               ;   number of leading zeroes in TOS.
     002A                        74    qstk_isqrtloop:
     002A A0341C                 75         ld      ax,tos_value           ; do
     002D A0361E                 76         ld      dx,(tos_value+2)
     0030 88201E                 77         cmp     dx,Xold                ;   if (The divide will overflow)
                                 78         bhe     qstk_isqrt_done        ;     The loop is done.
     0035 8C201C                 80         divu    ax,Xold                ;   if ( (ax=TOS/Xold) >= Xold)
     0038 88201C                 81         cmp     ax,Xold                ;     The loop is done.
                                 82         bhe     qstk_isqrt_done
     003D 0122                   84         clr     bx                     ;   Xold=(ax+Xold)/2
     003F 641C20                 85         add     Xold,ax
     0042 A40022                 86         addc    bx,0
     0045 0C0120                 87         shrl    Xold,#1
     0048 27E0                   88         br      qstk_isqrtloop         ; while (The loop is not done)
     004A                        89    qstk_isqrt_done:
     004A A02034                 90         ld      tos_value,Xold         ; TOS=00:Xold
     004D A00036                 91         ld      (tos_value+2),0
     0050                        92    qstk_isqrt0:
     0050 F0                     93         ret                            ; Exit
     0051                        94         end

ASSEMBLY COMPLETED.  NO ERROR(S) FOUND.
```

AB-45

APPLICATION BRIEF

Converting from the 8X9XBH or 8X9XJF to the 8XC196KB

October 1991

Order Number: 272093-001

Converting from the 8X9XBH or 8X9XJF to the 8XC196KB

CONTENTS	PAGE
1.0 INTRODUCTION	5-421
2.0 MEMORY MAP	5-421
3.0 CCB	5-421
4.0 INSTRUCTIONS	5-421
5.0 STACK POINTER	5-421
6.0 INTERRUPTS	5-421
7.0 PWM	5-422
8.0 TIMER1	5-422
9.0 TIMER2	5-422
10.0 HSI	5-422
11.0 HSO	5-422
12.0 SERIAL PORT	5-423
13.0 A/D	5-423
14.0 EPROM PROGRAMMING	5-423
15.0 PINOUT/PIN FUNCTIONS	5-424
16.0 MINIMUM HARDWARE CONSIDERATIONS	5-424
17.0 RESET	5-424
18.0 EXTERNAL MEMORY INTERFACING	5-424
19.0 MODES	5-424
20.0 POWER CONSUMPTION	5-424
21.0 DC CHARACTERISTICS	5-424
22.0 BH, KB ERRATA	5-424
23.0 PACKAGES	5-424

AB-45

1.0 INTRODUCTION

The 8XC196KB is upward compatible with the 8X9XBH and 8X9XJF. The 8XC196KB maintains the same architecture, instruction set and peripheral set as the 8X9XBH and 8X9XJF. It also provides increased performance with lower power consumption and enhanced features.

The purpose of this document is to aid designers who are moving from the 8X9XBH or the 8X9XJF to the 8XC196KB. It assumes a thorough understanding of the 8X9XBH or the 8X9XJF. This document will only identify the differences between the 8X9XBH and 8X9XJF and the 8XC196KB. For more information on any differences consult the current Embedded Microcontrollers and Processors handbook and corresponding data sheets.

For the remainder of this document, the 8X9XBH will be referred to as the "BH", the 8X9XJF as the "JF", and the 8XC196KB as the "KB". Unless otherwise noted, all references to the BH also apply to the JF.

2.0 MEMORY MAP

ON-CHIP ROM/EPROM-The BH ROM and EPROM devices have 8 Kbytes of on-chip memory. The JF has 16 Kbytes. The KB has 8 Kbytes.

ON-CHIP RAM-The BH has 232 bytes of register RAM. The JF has 232 bytes of register RAM plus 256 bytes of executable internal RAM (code RAM). The KB has 232 bytes of register RAM.

RESERVED LOCATIONS-The KB uses some of the reserved locations to support new features.

WINDOW SELECT REGISTER-The Window Select Register on the KB uses a windowing scheme to expand the SFR space to support new features and make the SFR's readable and writable. The available windows are Window 0, Window 14 and Window 15.

3.0 CCB

CCB BIT 0-The KB uses bit 0 in the CCB to enable/disable Power Down mode. This bit is reserved on the BH.

4.0 INSTRUCTIONS

NEW INSTRUCTIONS-There are 6 new instructions on the KB:

1. PUSHA
2. POPA
3. IDLPD
4. CMPL
5. BMOV
6. DJNZW

EXECUTION TIMES-There are 3 oscillator periods per state on the BH. There are 2 oscillator periods per state on the KB. This decreases the instruction execution time. Also, many instructions on the KB require fewer states than on the BH. Timing loops based on instruction execution times should be recalculated for the KB.

FLAGS-The DIV and DIVB instructions leave the overflow flag undefined on the BH. The flag is set or cleared as appropriate on the KB.

5.0 STACK POINTER

OPERATIONS RELATIVE TO THE STACK POINTER (SP)-For indexed and indirect operations relative to the stack pointer (SP), the address is calculated using the un-updated version of the stack pointer on the BH. The KB uses the updated version. For example, the offset for LD TEMP, [SP] and LD TEMP, nn[SP] instructions may need to be changed by a count of 2.

6.0 INTERRUPTS

SHARED INTERRUPTS-On the BH, interrupt vector locations were shared for the RI and TI interrupts, HSI Data Available and HSI FIFO Full interrupts, EXTINT and ACH.7 interrupts, and Timer1 and Timer2 overflow interrupts. The KB supports this interrupt structure and also provides separate interrupts for each event, available under software control.

NEW INTERRUPTS-The KB supports the following new interrupts:

NMI
TRAP
Unimplemented Opcode
EXTINT1
Timer2 Capture
HSI4 (4 or more entries in FIFO)

NMI-On the BH, NMI vectors directly to location 0000H. On the KB it vectors through location 203EH. To be compatible with the BH location 203EH must be loaded with 0000H.

AB-45

NEW STATUS REGISTERS-The KB has INT__PEND1 and INT__MASK1 registers to support the new interrupts.

PRIORITIES-The original interrupts have the same relative priorities on the KB as on the BH. However, the new interrupts all have higher priority than the original interrupts.

PUSHA AND POPA-The KB has two new instructions, PUSHA and POPA, to save the PSW, INT__MASK, INT__MASK1 and WSR on the stack.

INSTRUCTIONS WHICH INHIBIT INTERRUPTS-On the BH the EI, DI, POPF and PUSHF instructions and SIGND, the signed prefix for multiply and divide instructions, inhibit interrupts from being acknowledged until after the next instruction has been executed. On the KB the PUSHA, POPA and TRAP instructions also do this.

INTERRUPT LATENCY-Maximum interrupt latency on the BH is 70 states. This includes 42 states for execution of the longest instruction (NORML) and 24 states for the response time. On the KB the maximum interrupt latency is 61 states. This includes 39 states for the NORML instruction and 18 states for response time.

7.0 PWM

PWM PERIOD-The period of the PWM output is 256 states on the BH. On the KB the pulse width can be 256 states or 512 states, as selected in software.

READING THE PWM-The PWM register can be read on the KB in Window 15.

PWM TIMINGS-The state times of the KB are shorter than the BH. For PWM outputs which require exact timings you may need to recalculate the PWM register value.

8.0 TIMER1

TIMINGS BASED ON TIMER1-The state times on the KB are different than the BH. Any timings based on Timer1 should be recalculated for the KB.

WRITING TO TIMER1-On the BH Timer1 can be changed by writing to location 0CH. Writing any value to location 0CH will set the Timer1 and Timer2 to 0FFFXH. On the KB Timer1 can be programmed by writing to location 0AH in Window 15. This will set Timer1 to the value written to 0AH.

9.0 TIMER2

MAXIMUM TRANSITION SPEED-On the BH the maximum transition speed of inputs to Timer2 is once per eight state times. The maximum transition speed on the KB is once per eight state times in normal mode and once per state time in Fast Increment Mode.

COUNTING UP AND DOWN-Timer2 on the BH only counts up. Timer2 on the KB can count up or down.

T2 OVERFLOW INTERRUPTS-On both devices an overflow on Timer2 can cause an interrupt. The KB can also interrupt when Timer2 crosses the 7FFFH/8000H boundary. An overflow interrupt vectors to location 2000H on the BH. On the KB a Timer2 overflow interrupt can vector to location 2000H or 2038H, as selected in software.

TIMER2 CAPTURE-On the KB the value in Timer2 can be captured into the T2CAPture register. A Timer2 Capture can generate an interrupt.

WRITING TO TIMER2-On the BH Timer2 can be changed by writing to location 0CH. Writing any value to 0CH will set Timer1 and Timer2 to 0FFFXH. On the KB Timer2 can be programmed by writing to location 0CH in Window 0. This will set Timer2 to the value written to 0CH.

10.0 HSI

INTERRUPTS-The BH can generate an interrupt when either the HSI Holding Register contains data or the FIFO contains 6 entries. Both interrupts vector to the same location. The KB, under software control, can vector to the same location for each or to separate locations. The KB can also generate an interrupt when the FIFO contains four entries.

READING AND WRITING THE CONTROL REGISTERS-The HSI__STATUS and HSI__TIME registers can be written to and IOC0 and IOC1 can be read in Window 15 on the KB.

11.0 HSO

LOCKED CAM ENTRIES-HSO entries on the KB can be locked into the CAM. They will occur continually without having to reload the CAM.

CLEARING THE CAM-The entire HSO CAM can be cleared without resetting the device on the KB.

AB-45

STATUS REGISTERS-Status registers on the BH show the current state of the HSO pins and which software timer has interrupted. In addition to these, a new status register is provided on the KB to show which HSO pins have transitioned, if a Timer2 reset has occurred, or if an A/D conversion has started.

READING AND WRITING THE CONTROL REGISTERS-IOS0, IOS1 and IOS2 can be written to and HSO_COMMAND, HSO_TIME and IOC1 and IOC2 can be read in Window 15 on the KB.

12.0 SERIAL PORT

FLAGS-The KB has three new serial port flags:

FE—Framing Error Flag
TXE—Transmitter Empty Flag
OE—Receive Overflow Flag

SP_STAT-SP_STAT supports the new flags on the KB:

KB SP_STAT

7	6	5	4	3	2	1	0
RB8/RPE	RI	TI	FE	TXE	OE	X	X

CLEARING THE FLAGS-On both devices, RI and TI are cleared every time SP_STAT is read. FE and OE are also cleared on the KB. On the KB TXE is also cleared after a transmission.

INTERRUPTS-On the BH the RI and TI interrupts both vector to the same location. The KB, under software control, can vector to the same location for each or to separate locations.

BAUD RATES-The formulas to calculate the baud rate are different on the BH and KB.

READING AND WRITING THE CONTROL REGISTERS-SP_STAT can be written and SP_CON can be read in Window 15 on the KB.

13.0 A/D

CONVERSION TIMES-The BH takes 88 states to complete a conversion. This corresponds to 22 μs at 12 MHz. Because the KB can operate over a wider frequency range, a prescalar can be enabled to adjust the speed of the A/D. The KB takes 91 states to complete a conversion with the prescalar off (22.75 μs at 8 MHz) and 158 states with the prescalar on (26.33 μs at 12 MHz, 19.75 μs at 16 MHz).

SAMPLE WINDOW-The BH has a 4 state sample window. The KB has an 8 state time window with the prescalar off and 15 state sample window with the prescalar on.

14.0 EPROM PROGRAMMING

PROGRAMMING MODES-The KB does not support gang programming using a KB as the master programmer. The programming control signals needed for this mode do not exist on the KB.

PROGRAMMING SIGNALS-The PACT (programming active) signal is multiplexed with HSO.0 on the BH. It is multiplexed with P2.7 on the KB. The KB multiplexes P2.4 with AINC (auto increment signal). Auto increment does not exist on the BH.

PROGRAMMING PULSE WIDTH REGISTER-The KB has a Programming Pulse Width Register (PPW) to determine the width of the programming pulse in the Auto, Auto PCCB and Run-time Programming Modes.

AUTO PROGRAMMING MODE-On the KB in the Auto Programming Mode, the PPW value must be loaded into external location 4014H before the Programming Mode is entered.

SLAVE PROGRAMMING MODE-On the BH in the Slave Programming Mode, the data verify or word dump command must be issued for each address. On the KB the AINC signal can be used to automatically increment the addresses without issuing another command.

RUN-TIME PROGRAMMING-On the BH using run-time programming, the programming pulse width must be programmed in software using a software timer. A "Jump to Self" loop is recommended during programming. On the KB, the PPW controls the programming pulse width. Idle Mode is recommended instead of the "Jump to Self".

ROM DUMP MODE-The ROM Dump Mode is entered the same way on the BH ROM and EPROM and on the KB EPROM. The KB ROM enters the mode differently. On the BH, ROM Dump Mode places indeterminate data at addresses 9000H–91FFH. No data is placed at these addresses on the KB.

SIGNATURE WORDS-The KB contains two words following the Signature Words which can be used to determine the programming voltage.

READ AND WRITE LOCK BITS-On the BH in the Auto, Auto PCCB, and Slave Programming Modes, if either the READ or the WRITE lock bits are programmed in the CCB the device cannot be programmed or verified. On the KB, if either bit is programmed, the device will do a security key verification. If the keys match, the device can be programmed and verified.

AB-45

AC AND DC SPECS-The AC and DC EPROM Programming Characteristics are different for the BH and the KB. Consult the current data sheets for the specifications.

15.0 PINOUT/PIN FUNCTIONS

PIN COMPATIBILITY-The KB is pin compatible with the BH with one exception. Pin 64 (on the PGA package, pin 14 on the PLCC package) is V_{PD} on the BH. On the KB this pin is V_{SS}.

NEW PIN FUNCTION-Several pins have new additional functions on the KB. These pins are listed below.

BH Pin/Function	KB Pin/Function
P2.4/T2RST	P2.4/T2RST/AINC
P2.7/PACT	P2.7/PACT/T2CAPTURE
P2.6	P2.6/T2UP-DN
P1.7	P1.7/$\overline{HOLD}$
P1.6	P1.6/$\overline{HLDA}$
P1.5	P1.5/$\overline{BREQ}$

16.0 MINIMUM HARDWARE CONSIDERATIONS

UNUSED PINS-All unused input pins on the KB must be tied high or low. No input pins can be left floating.

V_{PP}-V_{PP} must be left floating on BH EPROM devices. It must be tied to V_{CC} on all KB devices.

17.0 RESET

INTERNAL RESET TIMING-An internal reset on the BH (software reset or watchdog timer reset) will hold the RESET pin low for at least one state. On the KB, it will hold the RESET pin low for four states.

EXTERNAL RESET TIMING-To externally reset the BH the RESET pin must be held low for at least 10 XTAL1 cycles. The RESET pin must be held low for at least 4 states on the KB.

CAPACITOR ON RESET PIN-If a capacitor between RESET and V_{SS} is used to reset the device, the recommended size of the capacitor is different for the KB.

STATUS DURING RESET-The status of the control registers and the I/O pins during RESET are different on the BH and the KB. Consult the current Embedded Microcontrollers and Processors Handbook for detailed information.

18.0 EXTERNAL MEMORY INTERFACING

AC TIMINGS-The AC Timings for bus operations are different for the BH and the KB. Consult the current data sheets for specifications. Both devices will function with standard ROM/EPROM/Peripheral type memory systems.

$\overline{HOLD}/\overline{HLDA}$-The KB supports a bus exchange protocol ($\overline{HOLD}/\overline{HLDA}$) to allow other devices to gain control of the bus.

19.0 MODES

ENTERING AND EXITING POWERDOWN-Powerdown is entered and exited differently on the BH and the KB.

RAM IN POWERDOWN-The BH maintains the upper 16 bytes of RAM in powerdown mode. The KB maintains all the SFR's, all 232 bytes of RAM and most of the peripherals.

DISABLING POWERDOWN-Powerdown mode can be disabled on the KB.

NEW MODES-The KB has two new modes—Idle and ONCE modes.

20.0 POWER CONSUMPTION

POWER CONSUMPTION-Power consumption on the KB is about 1/10 that of the BH. See the current data sheets for the I_{CC}, I_{IDLE} and I_{PD} specifications.

21.0 DC CHARACTERISTICS

DC SPECS-The DC characteristics on the BH are different than those of the KB. Consult the current data sheets for specifications.

22.0 BH, KB ERRATA

STATUS OF BH, JF AND JF KB ERRATA-Consult the current data sheets for detailed information on BH and KB errata.

23.0 PACKAGES

AVAILABLE PACKAGES-Consult the current data sheets for the available packages.

AB-46

APPLICATION BRIEF

Serial Port Mode 0
8X9XBH/KB/KC/KD

RICHARD N. EVANS
APPLICATIONS ENGINEER

February 1993

Order Number: 272245-001

Serial Port Mode 0
8X9XBH/KB/KC/KD

CONTENTS	PAGE
ABSTRACT	5-427
METHOD OF OPERATION	5-427
Timing Considerations	5-427
Baud Rate	5-427
SETTING UP THE CONTROL REGISTERS	5-428
RECEIVE	5-429

CONTENTS	PAGE
TRANSMIT	5-429
EXAMPLE USING MODE 0	5-429
HARDWARE	5-429
Inverter	5-429
OR Gate	5-429
DIP Switch	5-429
SOFTWARE	5-431

AB-46

ABSTRACT

This application brief explains how to program the MCS®-96 device to operate the serial port in synchronous mode. A 4-bit multiplier which utilizes mode 0 with a port expansion circuit is presented.

METHOD OF OPERATION

The serial port can be operated in a synchronous mode. This mode was intended for port expansion using shift registers. For example, the TXD pin is used to clock both input and output data on RXD. The data is always one byte in length. Whenever a write to the serial port buffer (SBUF) is performed, a train of eight pulses is sent out TXD to clock the outgoing byte. Likewise, whenever SBUF is read, a train of eight pulses is sent out TXD to clock in the byte being read. See the synchronous serial mode timing diagram shown in Figure 1.

Timing Considerations

All timings associated with the serial port are relative to T_{OSC}. Therefore, the timings are fixed whether XTAL1 or T2CLK clocks the baud rate generator.

T_{DVXH} — Input Data Setup to Clock (TXD) Rising Edge. In other words, the data has to be valid at T_{DVXH} before the next TXD pulse rises.

T_{QVXH} — Output Data Setup to Clock (TXD) Rising Edge. The output bit will be valid before the rising edge of the next TXD pulse for T_{QVXH}.

T_{XLXH} — Serial Port Clock Falling Edge to Rising Edge. The low period for the TXD clock cannot be changed. For the 8X9X, T_{XLXH} = 4 T_{OSC} ±50. For KB, KC and KD, T_{XLXH} = 4 T_{OSC} ±50 or 2 T_{OSC} ±50 depending on the baud rate register value.

NOTE:
See the A.C. Characteristics in the datasheets for the timing specifications.

Baud Rate

Baud rate is a misused term. Baud rate is often used interchangeably with bits per second (BPS). This substitution is not always true though. Baud rate is the speed at which packets of information are passed per second. It just so happens that with the MCS-96 family the length of the information packet is 1 bit. Hence, the baud rate measurement is the same as the bits per second (BPS) for the MCS-96 serial port. The MCS-96 has a 15-bit baud rate generator. The most significant bit (bit 15) determines the clock source (XTAL1 or T2CLK). There is a baud rate register (location 0EH). This register is a byte wide. When loading the baud rate register it must be written twice: first, the least significant byte must be written to location 0EH, then the most significant byte. See equation 1 for the baud rate register formula.

$$BAUD\_VALUE = \frac{F_{OSC}}{BAUD\ RATE \times 2} - 1$$

OR

$$= \frac{T2CLK}{BAUD\ RATE}$$

Equation 1: Serial Port Synchronous Mode 0 Baud Rate Register Equations

Setting up the baud rate generator is easy. The example code (code 1) shows how to configure the baud rate generator to run at 9600 baud with a 16 MHz crystal.

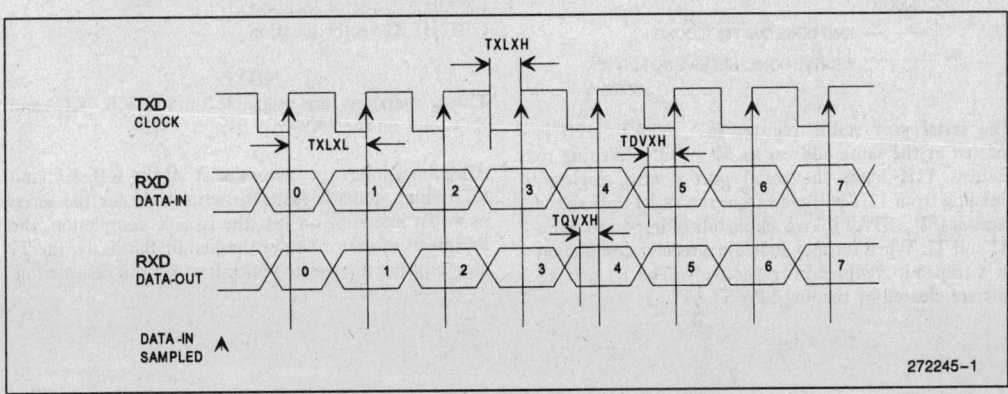

Figure 1. Important Timings for Serial Port Mode 0

AB-46

```
        BAUD_VALUE  EQU   0EH         ; BAUD RATE REGISTER
CSEG AT 2080H
        LDB BAUD_VALUE,40H             ; SET UP BAUD RATE GENERATOR FOR
        LDB BAUD_VALUE,83H             ; FOR 9600 BAUD AT A 16MHz CRYSTAL FREQUENCY
```

Code 1: Setting up Baud Rate Generator in Mode 0

SETTING UP THE CONTROL REGISTERS

(16H) IOC1

```
XX1X-XXXX
   └── SELECT TXD / SELECT P2.0
                                    272245-2
```

There are a few control registers that need to be utilized for mode 0 operation. First, since TXD is shared on the same pin as P2.0, we need to select the TXD function of that pin. This is accomplished by setting bit 5 in IOC1 (16H).

(11H) SP_CON

```
XXXX-XX00
     ││ 00 MODE 0
     ││ 01 MODE 1
     ││ 10 MODE 2
     ││ 11 MODE 3
     └── RECEIVER ENABLE / RECEIVER DISABLE
                                    272245-3
```

In order to set the serial port to operate in mode 0, the serial port control register (SP_CON 11H) needs to be initialized. Bits 0 to 1 set the mode. Hence, setting them to zero enables mode 0. Also, in the SP_CON is the receiver enable bit. Setting this bit (bit 3) enables the receiver (see RECEIVE).

(11H) SP_STAT

```
XXXX-XXXX
     │ └── XMIT DONE / XMIT NOT DONE
     └──── RECEIVE DONE / RECEIVE NOT DONE
                                    272245-4
```

The serial port status register (SP_STAT 11H) is located at the same address as SP_CON. Writing to address 11H loads the serial port control register. Reading from 11H will read from the serial port status register (SP_STAT). Two status bits of importance are RI and TI. When set they indicate a receive completion or a transmit completion respectively. The RI and TI bits are cleared by reading SP_STAT.

(09H) INT_MASK

```
X1XX-XXXX
  └── SERIAL PORT IRPT / S.P. DON'T IRPT
                                    272245-5
```

(200CH) SERIAL PORT interrupt vector location.

NOTE:
This interrupt is available on the 8X9X, KB, KC and KD.

There are two ways to monitor the status of the receiver and/or the transmitter. One is by polling the SP_STAT register (specifically RI and TI), the other is by using interrupts. RI is set whenever the receiver is done receiving one byte in mode 0. Likewise, TI is set whenever the transmitter has sent out one byte in mode 0. If the SERIAL PORT interrupt is masked in, then a rising edge on RI or TI causes the SERIAL PORT interrupt to be taken. The SERIAL PORT interrupt bit in INT_MASK (09H) is the inclusive OR of RI and TI. Hence, either RI or TI can cause a SERIAL PORT interrupt. Therefore, once the interrupt routine is entered, SP_STAT has to be tested to determine which interrupt (RI or TI) occurred.

(12H) INT_MASK1

```
XXXX-XXXX
       │ └── TRANSMIT INTERRUPT
       └──── RECEIVE INTERRUPT
                                    272245-6
```

(2030H) TI vector location
(2032H) RI vector location

NOTE:
These interrupts are available on the KB, KC, and KD—**not** on the 8X9X.

Additional interrupt vectors exist on the KB, KC and KD which make it easier to write code for the serial port. To interrupt on just the receive completion, the RI interrupt vector can be masked in. Similarly, the TI interrupt has a separate vector for transmit completion.

RECEIVE

Reading the SP_STAT register always clears the RI bit and TI bit. If the RI bit is cleared while the RECEIVER ENABLE bit (bit 3 in SP_CON) is high, then another reception is started. Hence, it is possible to start another reception and overwrite the previous one. Therefore, don't poll SP_STAT to monitor the receiver. Use the serial port interrupt, the receive interrupt vector, or INT_PEND1 (KB, KC and KD) to test the RI bit for receive completion.

It is a good programming practice to use the serial port interrupt or the RI interrupt for testing the RI bit. First, load the interrupt vector location with the appropriate ISR routine address. Next, enable the interrupt using either INT_MASK or INT_MASK1 depending on which interrupt is chosen. Now, enable interrupts using the EI instruction. Then, disable the receiver by clearing bit 3 in SP_CON. Now the receiver is in a known state. To start a reception initiate a rising edge on the receiver enable bit (set bit 3 in SP_CON). When the service routine is entered, disable interrupts (i.e., PUSHF or PUSHA) and read SBUF (07H) to obtain the received byte. To start another reception, clear the RI bit by reading SP_STAT. Then, enable interrupts (i.e., POPF or POPA), and return from the interrupt service routine. Clearing the RI bit while the receiver is enabled starts a reception and allows another serial port or receive interrupt to occur. To disable the receiver simply clear the RECEIVER ENABLE bit in SP_CON. See the programming example in the following pages.

TRANSMIT

Transmitting a byte is much more straightforward. First, load SBUF (07H) with the byte to be transmitted. Two methods can be used to detect when transmit completion occurs: polling TI in SP_STAT, or using the serial port interrupt or TI interrupt (KB, KC and KD). Once again, using an interrupt to detect transmit complete is good programming practice.

To set up the transmit interrupt service routine, load the address of the ISR into either the serial port interrupt vector (200CH) or the TI interrupt vector (2030H). As with receive, mask in the appropriate interrupt using either INT_MASK or INT_MASK1. Enable interrupts with EI and load SBUF with the byte to transmit.

When the interrupt service routine is entered disable interrupts (i.e., PUSHF or PUSHA). After the routine is executed another transmit can be started by loading SBUF again. Clear the TI bit in SP_STAT by reading SP_STAT. This action allows another transmit or serial interrupt to occur. Enable interrupts before returning from the service routine (i.e., POPF or POPA). When the next transmit is done, another interrupt occurs (serial or transmit).

EXAMPLE USING MODE 0

A programming example is included to demonstrate most of the above procedures for implementing mode 0. An evaluation board was used in conjunction with an I/O port expansion circuit to test out the following code. The program reads in one byte from an external shift register. Then it multiplies the lower nibble by the upper nibble. The product is transmitted to another external shift register and is displayed on LEDs. The largest product is 0E1H which is 0FH x 0FH.

HARDWARE

The schematic for this example is pictured in Figure 2. The data-in byte is generated by a DIP switch attached to a parallel-in serial-out shift register (74LS165). The output display is simply eight LEDs. The clock (TXD) is used to clock the parallel-in serial-out shift register (74LS165). This (74LS165) register has two modes: a shift mode and a load mode. When the transmit part of the circuit is activated, the 74LS165 is put into LOAD mode so the transmit shift register is not interfered with. To enable the transmit circuit, the TXD clock is gated to the 74LS164 (serial-in parallel-out). The transmit circuit is enabled by the active low signal $\overline{ENABLE}$. The RXD line is used for receiving and transmitting.

Inverter

The inverter (74LS05) has an open-collector output. A weak (15K) pull-up is used at the output. The purpose of the weak pull-up is so the RXD (when used as an output) can drive the data on RXD high or low. If a regular inverter were used, then contention would exist between RXD (when used as an output) and the inverter output. Notice that the input to the inverter is $\overline{QH}$, hence the output of the inverter is the actual data QH.

OR Gate

The OR gate is a switch for the TXD clock. TXD is at one input. The other input is the $\overline{ENABLE}$ line (from P2.6). When the $\overline{ENABLE}$ line is low, TXD passes freely through the OR gate. However, when $\overline{ENABLE}$ is high, the output of the OR gate is always high. As a result there are no transistions at the output of the OR gate and the 74LS164 is not clocked.

DIP Switch

The DIP switch is weakly pulled high (switch off) and strongly driven low (switch on).

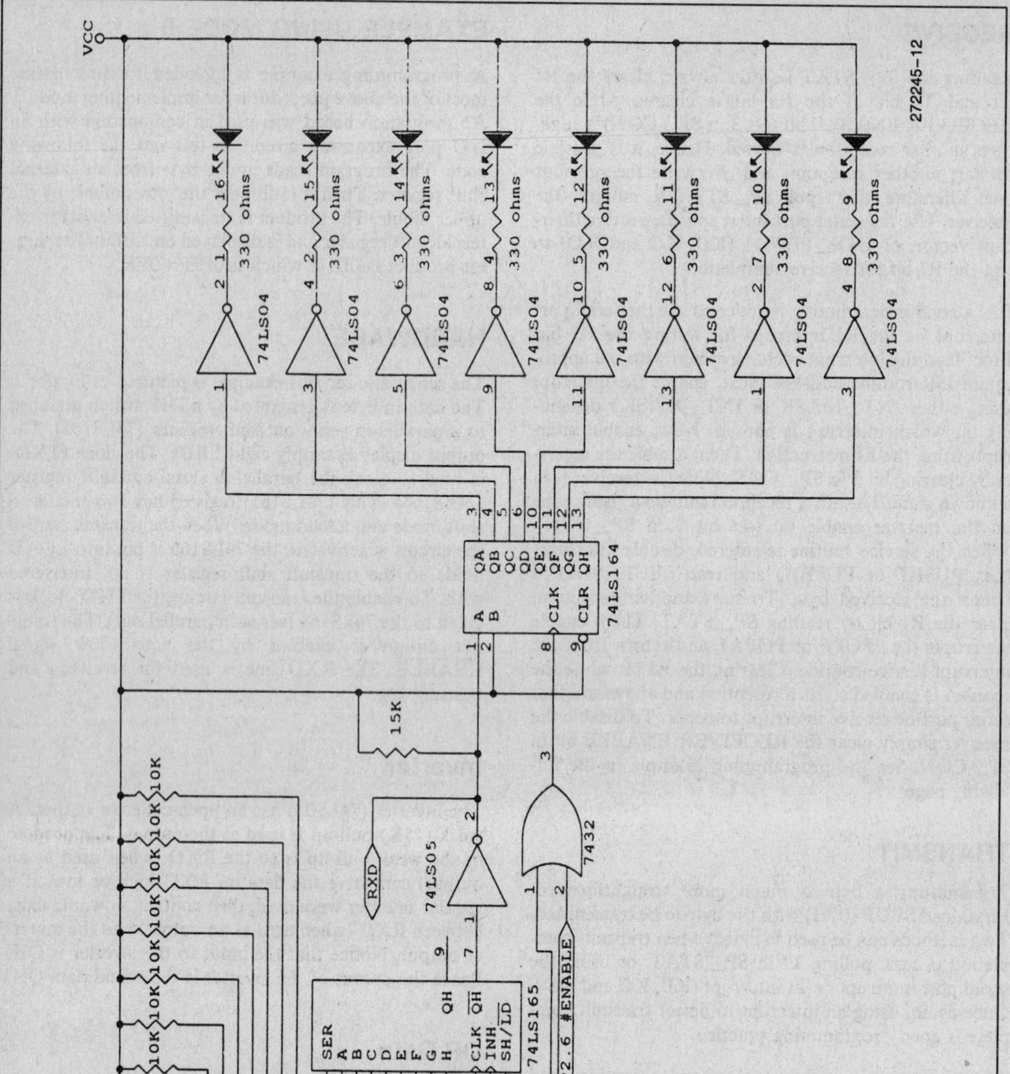

Figure 2. I/O Port Expansion and Example Schematic

SOFTWARE

See the program listing for the software part of this example. Only the serial port interrupt is used in this example. Hence, this program is compatible with 8X9XBH, KB, KC and KD. The flow chart in Figure 3 illustrates the algorithm.

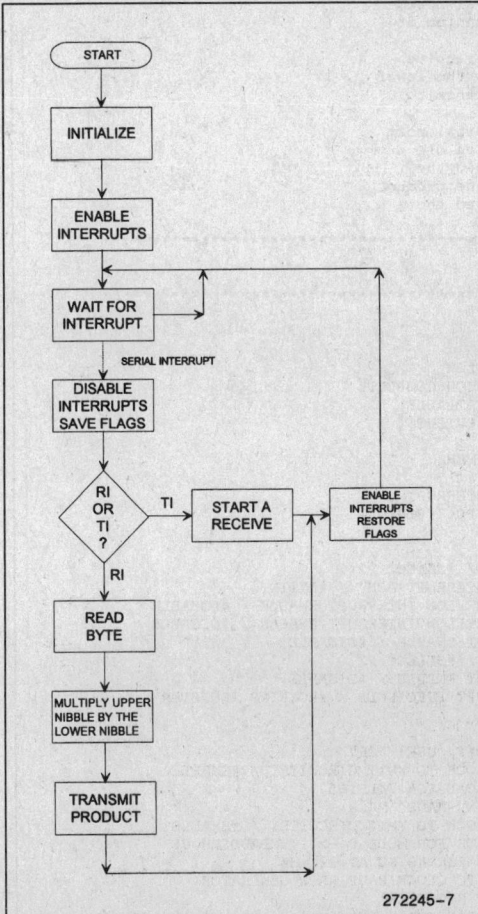

Figure 3. Flowchart of Example Mode 0 Program

During the initialize procedure the control registers are set to a known state. The serial port interrupt is masked in. Then the TXD function is enabled on its respective pin. Next, the baud rate is set. The baud rate generator can be clocked by either XTAL1 or T2CLK.

Now, the first receive is started. The shift register must be loaded with the DIP switch byte. Hence, a procedure is called to load the shift register and to set the register to shift mode. Port 2 is used to output control signals to the shift register and the transmit enable gate. Clearing P2.7 loads the shift register. Setting P2.7 puts the register in shift mode. Furthermore, to allow TXD to clock the transmit shift register P2.6 must be cleared. Setting P2.6 disables the TXD clock to the transmit shift register. Port 2 is diagrammed below:

(10H) PORT 2

```
XXXX-XXXX
     |  |
     |  └── DISABLE CLK TO XMIT / ENABLE CLK TO XMIT
     └───── SHIFT MODE / LOAD REGISTER
```

The next step in starting a receive in this example is to disable the clock to the transmit circuit (see above). P2.6 is set by performing a logical OR. Next, mode 0 is selected and the receiver is disabled by clearing all bits in SP_CON. Now, a rising edge on the REN bit is initiated by setting bit 3 in SP_CON. Finally, SP_STAT is cleared by reading it. Note that a special procedure was used to clear SP_STAT. This routine only needs to be called for the 8X9XBH (see techbit MC3391). The KB, KC and KD can simply do a LDB temp, SP_STAT.

The foreground loop is entered until an interrupt occurs. There is only one interrupt routine—the serial port interrupt service routine. The first step in an interrupt routine is to disable other interrupts and save the flags. Next, the receiver is disabled by clearing SP_CON. Then, the TXD clock to the transmit circuitry is disabled by setting P2.6. The completion bits RI and TI are cleared (call SP_STAT_rd) to allow for the next interrupt. SP_IMAGE is returned from the SP_STAT_rd procedure. SP_IMAGE contains the status of the serial port upon entry into the service routine. The RI bit is tested in SP_IMAGE for receive completion.

If a receive just finished, then a transmit is initiated. First, the received byte is read in. Then, the nibbles are multiplied. The TXD clock to the transmit circuitry is enabled and the transmit is initiated.

Now, if a transmit caused the interrupt, then a receive is started. First, the external shift register is loaded by calling "load_shift_reg". Then, the receiver is enabled. A rising edge on REN starts another reception. The RI bit has already been cleared because SP_STAT_rd was called. Hence, when the interrupt service routine is exited, the POPF enables interrupts and allows for the receive interrupt to occur.

Once again, the foreground loop is entered to await another interrupt.

AB-46

```
$debug
;********************************************************************************
;* TITLE:        Mode 0 demonstration                                            *
;* AUTHOR:       Richard N. Evans                                                *
;* DATE:         March 11, 1992                                                  *
;* DESCRIPTION:                                                                  *
;*      This program demonstrates the receive and transmit                       *
;* functions of mode 0.  The following program is tailored for                   *
;* the 8X9XBH,JF and is upward compatable with the KB and KC.                    *
;* Testing of this program was done on an MCS-96 Eval Board                      *
;* rev 3.1 with a 8096BH, 80C196KB, and 80C196KC running at                      *
;* 12MHz.                                                                        *
;*      The code continually reads a byte from the receive                       *
;* buffer.  It then multiplies the upper nibble by the lower                     *
;* nibble.  Then, it outputs the product via the transmit                        *
;* buffer.  The product is one byte in length.                                   *
;*      One interrupt routine is necessary.  The serial port                     *
;* interrupt is used.  Once entered, either a receive or                         *
;* or transmit is executed.  If a receive done caused the                        *
;* interrupt, then the nibbles are multiplied and the product                    *
;* is trasmitted.  However, if a transmit done caused the                        *
;* interrupt, then a receive is initiated.                                       *
;********************************************************************************

$include (sfrs.equ)
;********************************************************************************

;                    76543210
INT_MASK_MSK   EQU   01000000B
;                    |||||||+-------  TIMER OVERFLOW
;                    ||||||+--------  A/D CONVERSION COMPLETE
;                    |||||+---------  HSI DATA AVAILABLE
;                    ||||+----------  HIGH SPEED OUTPUTS
;                    |||+-----------  HSI.0 PIN
;                    ||+------------  SOFTWARE TIMER
;                    |+-------------  SERIAL PORT
;                    +--------------  EXTERNAL INTERRUPT
;                                     (EXTINT OR P0.7 PIN)

IOC1_MSK       EQU   00100000B
;                    |||||||+-------  SELECT PWM / #SELECT P2.5
;                    ||||||+--------  EXTERNAL INTERRUPT ACH7 / #EXTINT
;                    |||||+---------  TIMER 1 OVERFLOW INTERRUPT ENABLE / #DISABLE
;                    ||||+----------  TIMER 2 OVERFLOW INTERRUPT ENABLE / #DISABLE
;                    |||+-----------  HSO.4 OUTPUT ENABLE / #DISABLE
;                    ||+------------  SELECT TXD / #SELECT P2.0
;                    |+-------------  HSO.5 OUTPUT ENABLE / #DISABLE
;                    +--------------  HSI INTERRUPT FIFO FULL / #HOLDING REGISTER
;                                     LOADED

XMIT_OFF       EQU   01000000B       ;TRANSMIT OFF, USE: "OR"
;                    |+-------------  DISABLE CLOCK TO XMIT CIRCUITRY / #ENABLE
;                    +--------------  SHIFT / #LOAD FOR 74LS165
XMIT_ON        EQU   10111111B       ;TRANSMIT ON, "AND" MASK
;                    +--------------  DISABLE CLOCK TO XMIT CIRCUITRY / #ENABLE
BAUD_RATE_LO   EQU   08H             ;FASTEST RATE FOR MODE 0 -> 1.5MBAUD BH,JF
;                                    ;AND 3MBAUD FOR KB,KC AT 12 MHZ
BAUD_RATE_HI   EQU   80H             ;USE XTAL1 TO CLOCK BAUD RATE GENERATOR
LOAD_SR_MSK    EQU   01111111B       ;LOAD SHIFT REGISTER
;                    +--------------  SHIFT / #LOAD FOR 74LS165
SHIFT          EQU   10000000B       ;PUT SHIFT REG IN SHIFT MODE, USE "OR"
;                    +--------------  SHIFT / #LOAD FOR 74LS165
RB8RPE_MSK     EQU   01111111B       ;MASK FOR SP_STAT RB8/RPE BIT
;                    +--------------  RB8/RPE IN SP_STAT
RI_BNO         EQU   06H             ;BIT NUMBER OF RI IN SP_STAT
TI_BNO         EQU   05H             ;BIT NUMBER OF TI IN SP_STAT
RECV_ENABLE    EQU   00001000B       ;SP_CON
;                    +-------------  RECEIVER ENABLE
NIBBLE_SIZE    EQU   04H             ;THE LENGTH OF A NIBBLE IN BITS
UP_NIBBLE_MSK  EQU   00001111B       ;MASK OFF UPPER NIBBLE OF A BYTE
CODE_START     EQU   2080H           ;STARTING ADDRESS OF CODE
TOP_STACK      EQU   0F0H            ;TOP OF STACK ADDRESS
REGISTER_START EQU   01AH            ;START OF USER REGISTER SPACE
SP_IRPT_VECTOR EQU   200CH           ;SERIAL PORT INTERRUPT VECTOR
```

AB-46

```
;********************************************************************
        rseg    at      REGISTER_START

temp:           dsb     1               ;a temporary register
mltplier:       dsb     1               ;multiplier (upper nibble in byte read in)
                                        ;lower nibble in mltplier byte register
mltplicand:     dsb     1               ;multiplicand (lower nibble in byte read in)
                                        ;lower nibble in mltplicand register
product:        dsw     1               ;lower byte contains product
sp_image:       dsb     1               ;contains serial port status
;********************************************************************
        cseg    at      SP_IRPT_VECTOR
                dcw     serial_isr

;********************************************************************
        cseg    at      CODE_START
                ld      sp,#TOP_STACK           ;set the stack pointer to the top of the stack
                di
                call    init                    ;initialize registers and start reception
                ei
foreground:
                br      foreground              ;wait for interrupt
;********************************************************************
;* serial_isr                                                        *
;*      This routine services the serial port interrupt.  If         *
;* a receive or transmit is done, then the RI and TI bits get        *
;* set and this routine is vectored to.                              *
;*      If a receive caused the interrupt, then the byte is          *
;* read.  The lower and upper nibbles are multiplied together.       *
;* Finally, the product is written to the serial buffer which        *
;* initiates a transmit.                                             *
;*      If a transmit caused the interrupt.  Then that means a       *
;* product was just written out the RXD pin.  So, a receive is       *
;* initiated to get the next byte.                                   *
;*                                                                   *
;* INPUT:        sbuf                                                *
;* OUTPUT:       product, mltplier, mltplicand, port2, sbuf, sp_image *
;* CHANGED:      temp, sp_con, sp_stat, (plus OUTPUT)                *
;********************************************************************
serial_isr:
        pushf                                   ;save flags, disable irpts
        clrb    sp_con                          ;disable the receiver
        ldb     port2,#XMIT_OFF                 ;disable the transmit circuitry
        call    sp_stat_rd                      ;get sp_image
        jbs     sp_image,RI_BNO,get_byte        ;if receive irpt, goto receive routine
        call    load_shift_reg                  ;load shift register, put in shift
        ldb     sp_con,#RECV_ENABLE             ;transmit done so enable receiver
        br      serial_isr_end                  ;exit isr

    get_byte:
        ldb     temp,sbuf                       ;read the received byte
        ldb     mltplier,temp                   ;multiplier is the upper nibble in byte recvd
        shrb    mltplier,#NIBBLE_SIZE           ;shift out the lower nibble and keep upper
        andb    mltplier,#UP_NIBBLE_MSK         ;preserve multiplier nibble
        ldb     mltplicand,temp                 ;get multiplicand nibble from byte
        andb    mltplicand,#UP_NIBBLE_MSK       ;mask off multiplier nibble

        mulb    product,mltplier,mltplicand     ;multiply and get product
        andb    port2,#XMIT_ON                  ;enable clock to transmit circuit, put shift reg
                                                ;in load mode.
        ldb     sbuf,product                    ;start transmission of product

serial_isr_end: popf                            ;restore flags, and enable irpts
        ret                                     ;return to calling procedure
;********************************************************************
;* load_shift_reg                                                    *
;*      This procedure will load the external shift register.  The shift register is a *
;* 74LS165.  A high to low transition on the shift/#load pin, loads the shift register. *
;* Hence, this routine outputs a high to low transition to port 2.  The other bits in *
;* port 2 are preserved.                                             *
;*                                                                   *
;* INPUT:                                                            *
```

272245-10

AB-46

```
;*   OUTPUT:        port2                                                       *
;*   CHANGED:       port2                                                       *
;********************************************************************************
load_shift_reg:
        orb     port2,#SHIFT            ;make shift/#load high
        andb    port2,#LOAD_SR_MSK      ;shift/#load goes low
        orb     port2,#SHIFT            ;put in shift mode
        ret                             ;return to calling procedure

;********************************************************************************
;*   init                                                                       *
;*        This procedure initializes some control registers and starts a receive.*
;*                                                                              *
;*   INPUT:         sp_stat                                                     *
;*   OUTPUT:        port2                                                       *
;*   CHANGED:       int_mask, ioc1, baud_reg, sp_con, sp_stat, port2, temp, sp_image *
;********************************************************************************
init:
        ldb     int_mask,#INT_MASK_MSK  ;allow serial port irpt
        ldb     ioc1,#IOC1_MSK          ;enable txd
        ldb     baud_reg,#BAUD_RATE_LO  ;set the baud rate generator
        ldb     baud_reg,#BAUD_RATE_HI
        call    load_shift_reg          ;load the shift register and put in shift mode
        orb     port2,#XMIT_OFF         ;disable the clock to the transmit circuitry
        clrb    sp_con                  ;Disable receiver
        ldb     sp_con,#RECV_ENABLE     ;enable receiver and put in mode 0, start recept
        call    sp_stat_rd              ;clear RI bit
        ret                             ;return to calling program

;********************************************************************************
;*   sp_stat_rd                                                                 *
;*   This subroutine will clear RI, TI, and RB8 in sp_stat.  The other status bits are *
;*   preserved and returned in sp_image.  This subroutine is meant to replace the *
;*   instruction "ldb sp_image,sp_stat".                                        *
;*                                                                              *
;*   INPUT:         sp_stat                                                     *
;*   OUTPUT:        sp_image                                                    *
;*   CHANGED:       temp, sp_stat, sp_image                                     *
;********************************************************************************
sp_stat_rd:
        clrb    sp_image                ;clear status bits

get_status:
        ldb     temp,sp_stat            ;get current status
        orb     sp_image,temp           ;accumulate status bits

        jbs     temp,RI_BNO,get_status  ;if ti is set, then read again
        jbs     temp,TI_BNO,get_status  ;if ri is set, then read again, otherwise ti
                                        ;and ri are clear

        andb    sp_image,#RB8RPE_MSK    ;clear out the RB8/RPE bit
        orb     sp_image,temp           ;include the most recent copy of RB8/RPE

        ret                             ;return to calling procedure
        end
```

intel ARTICLE REPRINT AR-515

Many applications have throughput time requirements on the order of a few hundred milliseconds, and don't require real-time image analysis.

A Single-Chip Image Processor

A.L. Pai and S.H. Lin, Arizona State University, and David P. Ryan, Intel Corporation

Most of the research efforts on image processing focus on expanding the complexity and dimension of image analysis. Unfortunately, this emphasis results in algorithms that are so computationally intensive that expensive special-purpose vector and pipeline processors are required to evaluate an image fast enough to be considered "real-time." Not all applications, however, have the burdensome requirements of true real-life image analysis. Specifically, applications that have image throughput time requirements of greater than a few hundred milliseconds can use a lower cost, general-purpose microprocessor-based system. Applications that have even slower frame rates are candidates for not only the use of lower cost CPUs, but also allow for replacement of video-rate flash A/D converters with slower, less expensive converters.

Addressing the most cost-sensitive applications, the design described herein uses Intel's 16-bit microcontroller to implement a single-chip image processor. The on-chip 10-bit A/D converter of the controller digitizes the image of a charge injection device (CID) camera, while the chip's 16-bit CPU executes a library of standard vision algorithms and reports the results by passing a few tokens over an on-chip universal asynchronous receiver-transmitter (UART).

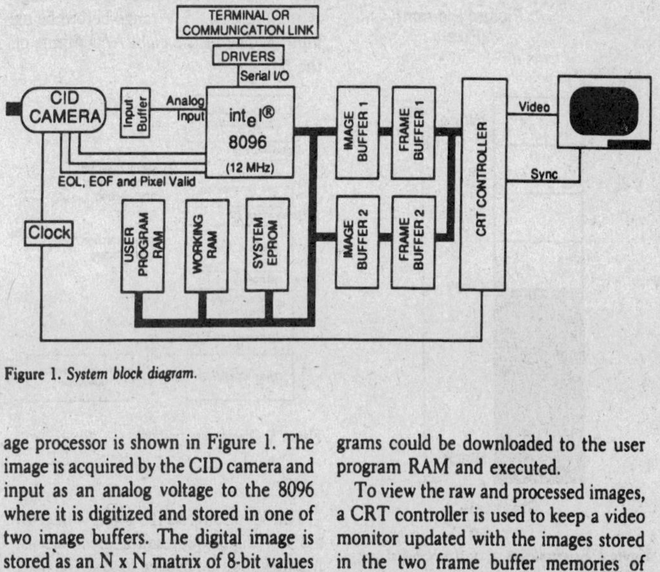

SYSTEM OVERVIEW

A block diagram of the single-chip image processor is shown in Figure 1. The image is acquired by the CID camera and input as an analog voltage to the 8096 where it is digitized and stored in one of two image buffers. The digital image is stored as an N x N matrix of 8-bit values corresponding to the gray level intensity at each picture element (pixel) as shown in Figure 2.

After an image resides in an image buffer, the 8096 can execute a number of standard image processing algorithms available as system monitor commands. These programs perform thresholding and filtering functions on the digital image, and can analyze objects found within the image. If the 8096 were attached to a host system instead of a terminal, custom programs could be downloaded to the user program RAM and executed.

To view the raw and processed images, a CRT controller is used to keep a video monitor updated with the images stored in the two frame buffer memories of Figure 1. The 8096 updates the frame buffers with the data in its image buffers depending upon commands given to the system.

▶ **Hardware.** The system is composed of a 128 x 128 CID camera and Intel's 8096 (with on-chip A/D) for image acquisition and analysis. A standard CRT controller was added for displaying raw and processed images as directed by the 8096. Driving the decision to use a 128 by 128 digital

Figure 1. *System block diagram.*

SENSORS June 1987

AR-515

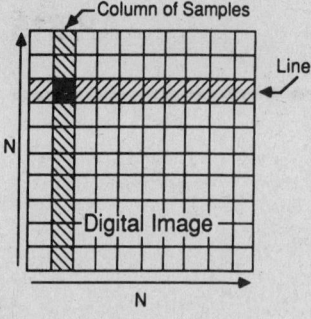

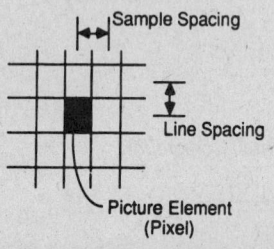

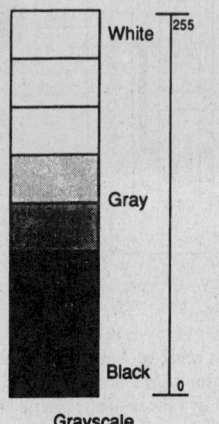

Figure 2. *Representation of an N x N digital image.*

8397 with 3K left. Two 32K x 8 SRAMs are used to provide space for two 16K byte image buffers, a 16K section of working RAM, and space for user-downloadable programs that are invoked by the monitor.

Two 16K byte frame-buffer memories are mapped to the same addresses as the corresponding image buffer used by the 8096. Normally, the frame buffers are mapped to the CRT controller to keep the video monitor updated. However, when the image stored in the image buffer is changed, the 8096 performs a frame-synchronized flyby block move to refresh the frame buffer (50 to 290 ms depending on whether frame synchronization is off or on).

To digitize an image, the 8096 monitors the end-of-line and end-of-frame signals from the CID camera and synchronizes the A/D conversion of the pixel data to a pixel valid signal from the camera. The analog output signal of the camera ranges from 0 to 1 V, corresponding to the gray level intensity at each pixel. This 1 V range is amplified to a 5 V range before being input to one of the eight A/D inputs of the 8096.

The 8096 converts the input voltage to a 10-bit digital representation in 22 µs. Another 18 µs are needed to store the pixel in the image buffer, update pointers, update a counter, and start another conversion. Therefore, the camera is clocked at a rate which results in a new pixel being output every 50 µs.

Although the 8096 converts its analog input to 10 bits, the externally generated analog errors (such as buffer error and noise) led to the decision to use only 8 bits

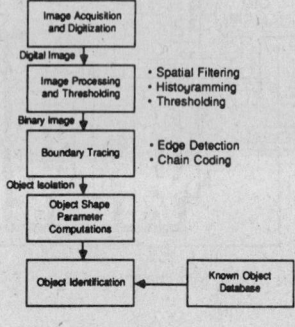

Figure 3. *Object identification.*

of the result. This provides 256 gray levels, and greatly simplifies memory requirements.

▶ **Software.** In addition to the code necessary to digitize images, the system EPROM contains an extensive set of algorithms for digital image acquisition and analysis. Video operations are used to acquire a digitized image. Point and arithmetic operations involve the pixel-by-pixel manipulation of a digital image. Neighborhood operations produce an output image that is the result of a combination of the gray level intensities around a specified neighborhood of each pixel. Measurement operations include the computation of desired parameters of objects located in an image for pattern recognition and other applications. Finally, utility operations are necessary for system operation.

The algorithms present in the system monitor can be used to identify desired objects in a digital image by following the approach shown in Figure 3. Once an image is digitized, it can be enhanced by the application of various image processing techniques including histogramming, thresholding, and spatial filtering to delineate the desired objects. The 8-directional chain code (Figure 4) can then be used to trace the boundaries of objects, and relevant object parameters can be determined and compared with those of a known object database to identify the unknown object.

OBJECT CLASSIFICATION

In the following example, the 8096 performs a binary thresholding operation as described earlier to set the image background to pure white and the objects in the image to pure black. Then the 8096 searches the image for objects. When an object is found, the object boundary is traced and shape analysis is performed. Descriptive information about the object (or objects) is output over the on-chip UART of the 8096 to a terminal, or host computer. The controller, without consulting a host computer, can also be programmed to make the decision to accept or reject an object on a set of prescribed rules.

The sequence of processing for this example, from serial communication reception and interpretation to the reporting of the shape analysis results, takes approximately 1500 ms with an 8096 running at 12 MHz. The time will vary with the size and number of objects in the field of view.

SENSORS June 1987

image was the desire to store and operate upon two images simultaneously while minimizing memory requirements.

The image processing and communications software takes 5K of the 8K bytes allocated to the system monitor space, and would fit in the on-chip ROM space of an

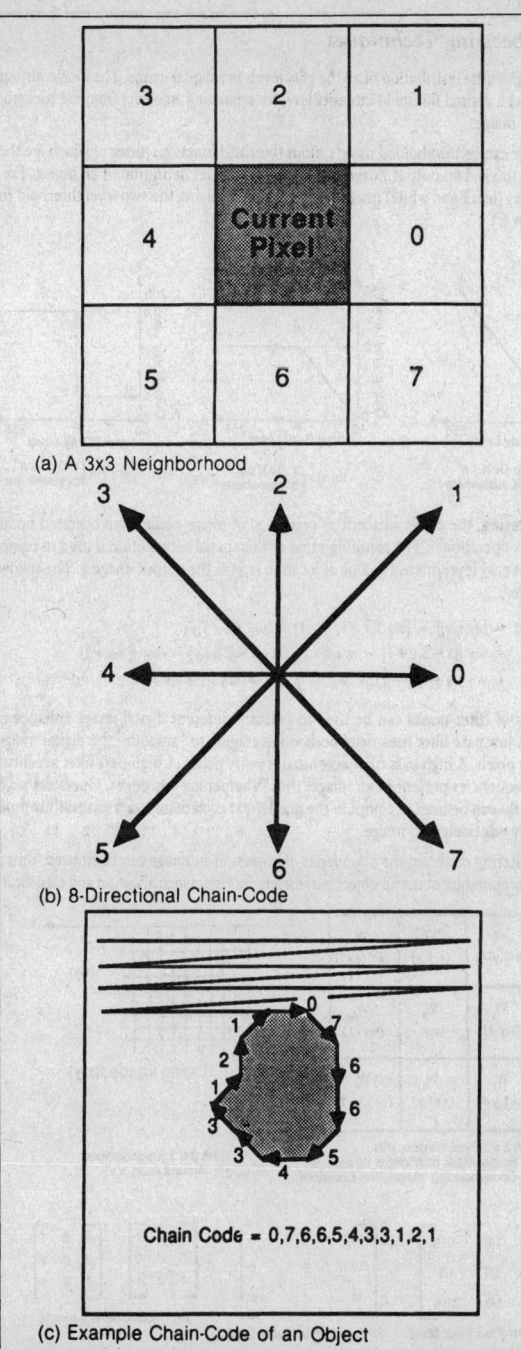

Figure 4. *8-directional boundary chain code.*

Photos 1 through 4 show the original 256 gray level digitized image and resultant binary (two-level) image of a circular object and a square object. (The circle looks like an oval when displayed due to the aspect ratio of the video monitor).

Table 1 summarizes the output of the systems shape analysis program. The objects' perimeter (P), area (A), center of mass coordinates (cx, cy), and the coordinates of the endpoints of each minimum enclosing rectangle are listed.

The rectangularity and circularity of the objects were also calculated and appear in Table 1. The rectangularity of the circle and the square using the actual data were ideal. Although the circularity of the digitized circle is slightly different from ideal (12.416 vs. 12.56), the digitized circle can be distinguished from the digitized square since the circularity of the square is very different from a perfect circle (15.44 vs. 12.56).

From these typical results, it is clear that this image processor can be used to distinguish between and identify objects placed in its field of view.

CONCLUSIONS

If the stringent requirements of "real-time" image processing can be relaxed in favor of substantially reduced sytem cost, a standard 16-bit microcontroller can perform as a stand-alone image processor.

Not only does the design described here demonstrate that a microcontroller can undertake two-dimensional image processing, but the surprising speed with which it accomplishes the processing should lead to the reevaluation of current microprocessor applications for possible cost reduction via microcontrollers.

REFERENCES

1. *Embedded Controller Handbook*, (latest edition). Intel Corporation, Santa Clara, CA.
2. Lin, S.H., A.L. Pai, and D.P. Ryan. A *Microcontroller Based Digital Image Processor*, Proceeding of the Second World Conference on Robotics Research, MS86-766, Society of Manufacturing Engineers, Dearborn, MI.
3. Cunningham, R. "Segmenting Binary Images," *Robotics Age*, Vol. 5, No. 2, July/August 1981.
4. Wilf, J.M. "Chain Code," *Robotics Age*, Vol. 3, No. 2, March/April 1981.
5. Gonzalez, R. and P. Wintz. *Digital Image Processing*, Second Edition, Addison-Wesley Publishing Company, NY, 1987.
6. Fu, S.U., R.C. Gonzalez, and C.S.G. Lee. *Robotics: Control, Sensing, Vision and Intelligence*, McGraw-Hill Book Company, NY 1987.

AR-515

Photo 1. *A digitized image of a circle.*

Photo 2. *A thresholded binary (two-level) image of the same circle. The circle appears oval because of the aspect ratio of the video monitor.*

Photo 3. *A digitized image of a square.*

Photo 4. *A thresholded binary image of the same square.*

7. Castleman, K.R. *Digital Image Processing*, Prentice Hall International, Englewood Cliffs, NJ, 1985.
8. Baxes, G.A. *Digital Image Processing—A Practical Primer*, Prentice Hall International, Englewood Cliffs, NJ, 1984.

Image Processing Techniques

A **histogram** gives the distribution of all the gray levels in a digital image. The image histogram is used to select a desired threshold intensity level for separating an object from the background in the digital image.

A digital image can be **thresholded** using various threshold functions (three of which are shown in the figure) to yield an output image that contains a better definition of an object. For example, a binary (black and white) image is obtained by applying the two-level threshold function shown in (c).

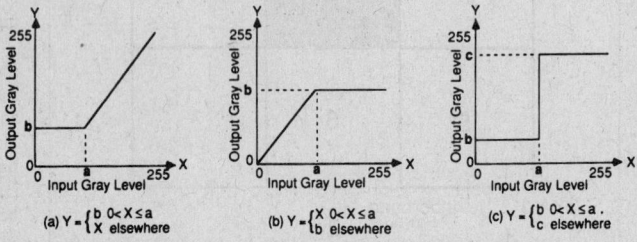

(a) $Y = \begin{cases} b & 0 < X \leq a \\ X & \text{elsewhere} \end{cases}$ (b) $Y = \begin{cases} X & 0 < X \leq a \\ b & \text{elsewhere} \end{cases}$ (c) $Y = \begin{cases} b & 0 < X \leq a \\ c & \text{elsewhere} \end{cases}$

In **spatial filtering**, the pixels adjacent to pixel (x,y) of image plane f are operated upon by the filter mask operation h. The resulting value of this spatial convolution is used to compute a replacement gray level intensity value at location (x,y) in the output image g. The following formula is used:

$$g(x,y) = h[f(x,y)] = [w_1 f(x-1, y-1) + w_2 f(x-1,y)$$
$$+ w_3 f(x-1,y+1) + w_4 f(x,y-1) + w_5 f(x,y) + w_6 f(x,y+1)$$
$$+ w_7 f(x+1, y-1) + w_8 f(x+1,y) + w_9 f(x+1,y+1)]$$

Various types of **filter masks** can be used to perform different digital image enhancement operations. A low-pass filter uses neighborhood averaging to "smooth" the digital image to remove noisy pixels. A high-pass filter accentuates noisy pixels. A high-pass filter accentuates the higher frequencies present in an image, thus "sharpening" its edges. Operators such as the Sobel masks can be used to compute the gradient at each point in an image, thus producing a gradient edge-detected image.

Using such filtering methods, the boundaries of objects in an image can be isolated, thus permitting the computation of useful object parameters for object identification and classification.

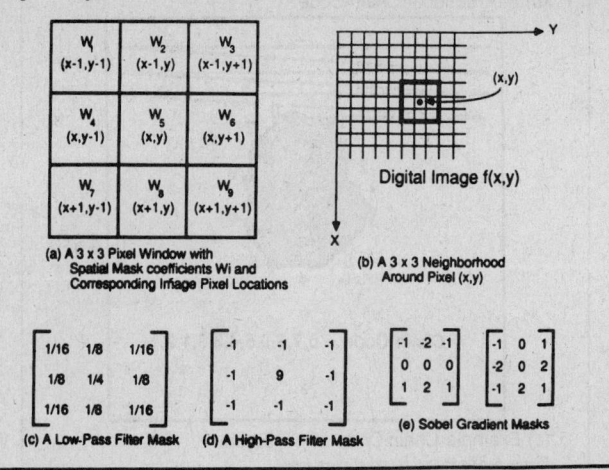

SENSORS June 1987

AR-515

OBJECT	PERIMETER P	AREA A	C.O.M. COORDINATES CX,CY	ENCLOSING RECTANGLE				RECTANGULARITY $R = A_O / A_R$	CIRCULARITY $C = P^2 / A$
				XMAX	XMIN	YMAX	YMIN		
CIRCLE	301	7297	(62,68)	111	15	116	21	0.785	12.416
SQUARE	328	6967	(55,73)	97	14	115	32	1.0	15.440

Table 1. *Example shape analysis output.*

A.L. Pai is an Associate Professor and S.H. Lin is a Ph.D. candidate in the Computer Science Dept., College of Engineering, Arizona State University, Tempe, AZ 85281. **David P. Ryan** is a Senior Applications Engineer for Intel Corp., 5000 W. Chandler Blvd., Chandler, AZ 85226.

Size Parameters

The **horizontal** and **vertical** extent of an object and its minimum enclosing rectangle are easily computed by using the minimum and maximum line and sample numbers.

The **perimeter** (circumferential distance) around an object boundary is obtainable from the boundary chain code by using the formula:
$$P = N_E + \sqrt{2} N_O$$
where N_E and N_O are the number of even and odd steps in the object boundary chain code.

The **area** of an object, which is a convenient measure of object size, is equal to the number of picture elements inside and including its boundary, multiplied by the area of a single pixel.

Shape Parameters

In addition to size parameters, shape parameters can be used to distinguish objects. Some shape parameters that are easily computed are described below.

The formula for computing the **rectangularity** R of an object is:
$$R = A_O / A_R$$
where A_O is the object area and A_R is the area of its minimum enclosing rectangle. R ranges from 0 to 1, with a value of 1.0 for rectangular objects, $\pi/4$ (0.785) for circular objects, and smaller values for slender, curved objects.

The **aspect ratio**, A, which is the ratio of width to length of the minimum enclosing rectangle of an object, is used to distinguish slender objects from roughly square or circular objects.

One of the commonly used **circularity** measures is:
$$C = P^2 / A$$
the ratio of the square of the object perimeter to its area, which reflects the complexity of the object boundary. C has a minimum value of 4π (12.56) for a circular object, while more complex shapes have higher values.

Reprinted from **Sensors, June 1987**
Copyright© 1987 by Helmers Publishing, Inc.
174 Concord St., Peterborough NH 03458
All Rights Reserved

THE MCS®-96 DIAGNOSTICS LIBRARY

Version X1.1

David Ryan
INTEL Corporation
October 1987

© Intel Corporation, 1987

October 1987
Order Number: 270083-002

1.0 INTRODUCTION

In the real time world of microcontroller applications, system failures can be dangerous, and expensive. Preventing them, and understanding them when they occur, is very important to the reliability of any design.

The sources of a system upset are varied. But in general, the failure of a well designed application occurs as a result of either some form of noise, or a hardware failure. The 8096 hardware provides methods of detecting and recovering from the transient noise failures, while the MCS®-96 Diagnostics Library supplies software routines that can help diagnose or detect a failure in system hardware.

Graceful recovery from noise induced failures is possible using the WATCHDOG TIMER. While the 8096-based system is functioning as desired, the executing software periodically resets the WATCHDOG with a special two-byte code. If the WATCHDOG is not reset at least every 16 ms (12 MHz system), a system reset occurs. The two-byte code is a unique password which appears nowhere in the opcode map. This reduces the chance that an erroneous WATCHDOG reset would occur after a system upset.

The 8096 RESET instruction provides another form of protection. Since the opcode for a RESET is 0ffH, protection against the 8096 executing unimplemented external memory is obtained by placing pull-ups on the system bus. The RESET opcode is also the value in erased EPROMs. Therefore, any attempt to execute non-existent memory or an erased EPROM location causes the 8096 to execute the RESET instruction. RESET causes the 8096 to reinitialize itself and provide an external pulse on the RESET pin to reinitialize the system.

Even with the protection afforded by the 8096, a system is rarely complete without checks for hardware failures, both internal and external to the microcontroller. These checks are usually software routines that execute on power-up or periodically to verify that all parts of the system are present and function correctly. The tests generally execute standard check algorithms which are simply re-written in the host's assembly language.

To eliminate the need for every designer of an 8096-based system to write such tests, a collection of modular routines has been developed that any designer could easily use in his system (**General Diagnostics**). In addition, a set of 8096 interrupt service routines was developed for testing 8096 I/O units in a dedicated environment (**The Dynamic Stability Test**). Both sets of programs are contained in the **MCS-96 Diagnostics Library** (DIAG96.LIB).

This library is a collection of software modules that provide a number of ready-made **General Diagnostics** and a specialized MCS-96 diagnostic known as the **Dynamic Stability Test.** The **General Diagnostics** implement frequently used standard test algorithms, while the **Dynamic Stability Test** exercises hardware specific to the 8096.

The library can be considered a software "tool box" from which modules are selected for a variety of run-time diagnostics or laboratory tasks, for example:

- Include a few modules in other programs as a power-up test
- Use a memory module to create a map of external memory
- Use a few modules as a periodic system check
- Develop a simple stand-alone tester
- Build a custom test bed for burn-in, inspection or reliability tests
- Test new background code in an interrupt intensive environment

In addition to easing the development of a program that must perform standard diagnostics or system checks, the library can be a learning tool. Using the proven source code in the library, methods of interrupt management and on-chip peripheral handling can be reviewed to further understand how to use the 8096.

These tests were developed by the 8096 Applications group for experimental use with the 8096. With the programs in this library, the chip has been studied for its functional and asynchronous characteristics.

The **General Diagnostics** should be useful to almost anyone designing an 8096 application. The **Dynamic Stability Test** will be useful to those experimenting with the 8096 in a test environment. Figure 1 shows the modules in the **MCS-96 Diganostics Library**.

1.1 General Diagnostics

The General Purpose Diagnostics consist of 24 programs providing System, ALU and Memory tests. Each of the tests can be called independently, and none require special hardware or impose application limiting constraints.

Two Collected Test programs are also provided so that all tests may be called at once. A third Collected Test program executes a selection of **General Diagnostics** that might be reasonable to include in a typical system power-up.

Section 3 provides a detailed description of the **General Diagnostics**.

1.2 Dynamic Stability Test

The **Dynamic Stability Test** is an integrated set of 11 programs that provide the interrupt service routines necessary to run all forms of MCS-96 I/O concurrently while a user written main task is executing. Virtually all of the chip is made to run simultaneously, with the I/O units responding to asynchronous external events.

Unlike the **General Diagnostics**, the **Dynamic Stability Test** modules must all be linked together, and must run in a specific external environment.

Section 4 provides a detailed description of the **Dynamic Stability Test**.

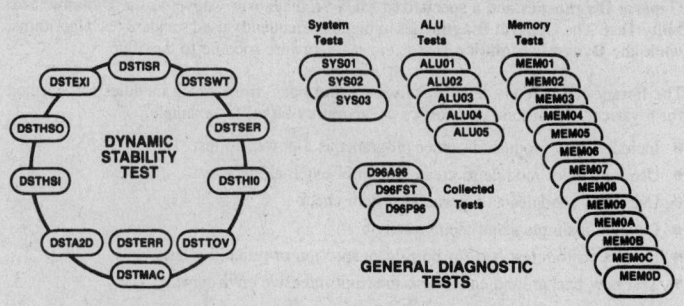

Figure 1. The MCS®-96 Diagnostic Library

1.3 How To Use This Manual

This publication is meant to be a guide for those using any of the programs in the **MCS-96 Diagnostics Library**. On a first pass the entire manual should be skimmed, with more attention paid to Section 2 and the overview sections of Sections 3 & 4. For the casual reader, the overview sections of each chapter should suffice.

Section 2 contains an overview of the general calling conventions to use any test in DIAG96.LIB. The section also describes DIAG96.LIB error reporting conventions and presents some warnings to heed when using this library.

Section 3 describes the classes of **General Diagnostics** and each test in detail.

Section 4 describes the concept of Dynamic Stability and its implementation on the 8096. The section also contains an overview of the tests performed, a description of the constraints placed upon the user-written background task, and detailed descriptions of each interrupt service routine.

The Appendices contain error code and command file descriptions, and of demonstration program listings. Source for the **MCS-96 Diagnostics Library** can be obtained from Insite User's Program Library at the address below. The Insite Catalog order number is AE-17.

Insite User's Program Library
INTEL Corporation DV2-24
2402 W. Beardsley Road
Phoenix, Arizona 85027

With the first-hand knowledge that many problems result from not being able to uncover information lodged in some dark corner of the user manual, information is repeated in the sections where it is pertinent.

MCS®-96

2.0 USING THE LIBRARY

To simplify use of the diagnostics, the tests were developed in a modular fashion and collected in one linkable object file library (DIAG96.LIB). A modular program relies upon only the parameters sent at its invocation and employs standard parameter passing conventions to allow flexibility and uniformity of use. Collecting the modules into a library eliminates the tedium of listing twenty or thirty file names when performing a relocate/link on user developed code. When a program is linked to DIAG96.LIB, only those modules referenced in the user program are drawn from the library for inclusion in the output module.

Since PLM96 conventions were the ones chosen for this set of programs, the **General Diagnostics** are invoked by following the conventions for a PLM96 typed procedure. Parameters are placed on the STACK and the procedure activated via a function reference or explicit CALL. When the test is complete, test data is returned in the special register PLM$REG. The **Dynamic Stability Test** is not PLM96 compatible.

The next section describes the format of the test data that is returned by the diagnostics. Following sections give an overview of how to use a **General Diagnostics** test, how to use **The Dynamic Stability Test,** and what restrictions to keep in mind while using the library.

2.1 Reporting Convention

All DIAG96.LIB tests use the PLM$REG word locations 1CH and 1EH for returning condition codes to the calling program. Within DIAG96.LIB, these locations are the PUBLIC words EREG1 and EREG2. When a test concludes without finding an error, a zero is placed in the high byte of EREG1. If the high byte of EREG1 is non-zero, then some unexpected condition occurred. The low byte of EREG1 always contains the module number of the returning test, and EREG2 contains a detail code if an error was found. The complete listing of EREG1 code meanings and EREG2 meanings is in Appendices A & B.

All modules cease execution upon detection of the first error. The code describing which error was detected (EREG1) follows the format described in Table 1.

Table 1. Error Reporting Format

EREG1 =	nnmx Hex			
where;	nn = 00	if no error was found		
	= 01,...,08H	if an error was found, nn is the error code		
and;	mx = 0xH	for Test =	SYS0x;	$1 \le x \le 03H$
	= 1xH		ALU0x;	$1 \le x \le 05H$
	= 2xH		MEM0x;	$1 \le x \le 0DH$
	= 3xH		D96A96;	$x = 0$
	= 4xH		DSTISR;	$x = 0$
	= 6xH		DSTHSI;	$x = 1$
	= 7xH		DSTHSO;	$x = 0$
	= 8xH		DSTHI0;	$x = 0$
	= 9xH		DSTTOV;	$0 \le x \le 1$
	= 0AxH		DSTEXI;	$x = 0$
	= 0BxH		DSTSER;	$x = 0$
	= 0CxH		DSTA2D;	$x = 0$
	= 0DxH		DSTSWT;	$0 \le x \le 1$
	= 0ExH		D96FST;	$x = 0$
	= 0FxH		D96P96;	$x = 0$

2.2 Using the General Diagnostics

The **General Diagnostics** provide a large set of system, ALU and memory tests that can be used in any combination, independent of system configuration or external circuitry. In addition to allowing for a wide flexibility in how a user's system is externally configured, the tests place minimal requirements on memory maps and interrupt environment.

Except where noted, all tests are interruptible, and maintain Program Status Word and Interrupt Mask integrity. The tests conform to PLM96 conventions, and require only runtime parameters to be passed for such specifics as memory test bounds and ALU test duration. To obtain access to the general diagnostics, the user should declare the needed module names EXTERNAL code segment symbols, and link to:

DIAG96.LIB

The tests are invoked in assembly language by placing the proper parameters on the STACK and CALLing the procedure. In PLM, the tests are run after a function reference is made with the appropriate parameters. The following is an example of an ASM96 call to a memory test:

```
PUSH    #4000h
PUSH    #5000h
CALL    MEM06
CMPB    EREG1+1,0
BNE     Error_Found
```

The diagnostic module called performs a complementary address test on the byte locations between 4000H and 5000H inclusive. If an error is found, the value returned in the word EREG1 will have a non-zero value as its high byte. Also in the case of an error, the MEM06 memory test will place the address of the error in location EREG2. The program D96A96, shown in Appendix D is a working ASM96 example that calls every **General Diagnostic** Test.

The same memory test could be called in a PLM96 program as follows:

```
Response = MEM06(4000h,5000h);
IF Error$Codes.Number > 255 THEN CALL Error$Found;
```

Since the diagnostics return two words in the PLM$REG locations 1CH and 1EH, the function MEM06 would be a PROCEDURE of type LONG. Error$Codes would have to be declared a STRUCTURE AT Response, with the word elements Number and Detail so that the error messages returned by the diagnostic can be stored. Number would contain the EREG1 value returned by the test, and Detail would contain EREG2. Response would have to be DECLARED a double word. The program D96P96, shown in Appendix D is a working PLM96 example that calls every **General Diagnostic**.

The action taken when an error is detected will depend upon the application. For example, the following Error_Found (or Error$Found) routine would output the error codes to a printer or terminal:

```
Error_Found:                    Error$Found: PROCEDURE;
    PUSHF                                    DISABLE
    PUSH    #Message_Ptr_A
    CALL    Send_String                      CALL output (.Message$Ptr$A,
                                                          Error$Codes.Number);
    PUSH    EREG1
    CALL    Send_Hex_Word                    CALL output (.Message$Ptr$B,
    CALL    Send_CR_LF                                    Error$Codes.Detail);
    PUSH    #Message_Ptr_B           Self:   GOTO Self;
    CALL    Send_String
```

(Display continues on next page)

```
        PUSH    EREG2
        CALL    Send_Hex_Word
        CALL    Send_CR_LF
        BR $
```

Message_Ptr_A:
   DCB 27,'ERROR FOUND. Error Number = '

Message_Ptr_B:
   DCB 22,'Error Detail Code is = '

In the Error_Found routine, it is assumed that the subroutines Send_String, Send_Hex_Word, and Send_CR_LF transmit appropriate ASCII codes given the parameters passed to them. Send_String is sent a pointer to a byte string in memory, the first byte of which is the character count. Send_Hex_Word converts the word put on the STACK into the correct four ASCII code bytes and appends the ASCII code for H. Send_CR_LF outputs the ASCII codes to cause a carriage return, followed by a line feed. The PLM routine output would perform similar operations.

2.3 Using the Dynamic Stability Test

The **Dynamic Stability Test** consists of a set of 8096 interrupt service routines that are designed to run while a user-supplied background task executes. The routines are located in the object file library DST96.LIB, which is contained in the master library DIAG96.LIB. To obtain access to the test, the user should invoke the batch file DSTRL.BAT with the background task file name and directory parameters. For example type:

DSTRL \ SOURCE \ BACK

Since the interrupt service routines test 8096 on-chip I/O devices, the part under test must reside in a specified hardware environment. Two such environments are available for use with the **Dynamic Stability Test**. The test may run in either a single chip mode, or a cross-coupled two chip mode. Figures 2 and 3 show the connections required for each configuration. In the single chip mode, output pins are connected to input pins on the same 8096. In the dual chip mode, output pins of one 8096 are connected to the input pins of the other (and vice versa).

To run the test, the user must supply a background task that CALLs an initialization routine (DSTISR) with the specified parameters. After DSTISR returns, the interrupt service routines will begin running. The background task can then perform any function that conforms to the constraints discussed in Section 4. If the user does not wish to write a special background task, one is provided in the module DSTUSR.

The following is an example CALL and a description of the parameters that must be passed to the initialization module (DSTISR).

```
PUSH    <RAM segment1 starting address>
PUSH    <RAM segment1 ending address>
PUSH    <RAM segment2 starting address>
PUSH    <RAM segment2 ending address>
PUSH    <random seed>
PUSH    <random test length>
PUSH    <argument1 for Multiply/Divide Core test>
PUSH    <argument2 for Multiply/Divide Core test>
PUSH    <bit pattern for memory test>
CALL    DSTISR
```

The RAM starting and ending addresses form a memory map for the memory tests that DSTISR runs. The internal RAM is always tested. The random seed is the starting point for ALU tests that execute for as many number pairs as is specified in the random test length parameter. Argument1 and argument2 are the operands for a Multiply/Divide test. The bit pattern parameter is used during a memory test of the internal RAM and the memory segments specified.

Section 4 contains more detailed information on using the **Dynamic Stability Test**, while the next section lists some general restrictions and assumptions that need to be understood to properly use any **MCS-96 Diagnostic Library** module.

2.4 Restrictions and Assumptions

Some general restrictions and assumptions need to be understood before any DIAG96.LIB programs can be successfully used.

- Pay close attention to the warnings about STACK location in the test modules you use. If you use any of the specialized internal register tests, make sure that the STACK is located externally. Do not partition a region of memory that contains your STACK in any memory test, unless you first move the STACK to an area you already tested.

- All **General Diagnostics** assume that the WATCHDOG TIMER is either being RESET by an interrupt service routine created by the user, or that it was never enabled. Only SYS02 ever locks out interrupts for a significant period of time. The amount of time they are locked out depends upon the parameters passed.

- **The Dynamic Stability Test** takes care of the WATCHDOG TIMER within its interrupt service routines. But, do not write to the WATCHDOG before CALLing the initialization subroutine.

- In any Dynamic Stability application, the user's Main Task should not lock out interrupts for more than a few instructions, as the CPU can get quite loaded down with interrupt requests that are very time dependent.

3.0 GENERAL DIAGNOSTICS

The 24 **General Diagnostics** included in DIAG96.LIB provide a good set of basic memory and ALU confidence tests that can be easily linked to application programs.

The **General Diagnostics** allow for a wide flexibility in how a user's system is configured with respect to memory maps and interrupt environment. Except where noted, all tests are interruptible, and maintain Program Status Word and interrupt mask integrity. The tests conform to PLM96 conventions, and require only run-time parameters to be passed for such specifics as memory test bounds and ALU test duration.

The tests are independent to allow specialized diagnostics to be developed as desired. Use just the quick power-up test (SYS02) to verify operation, or use the module that calls all **General Diagnostics** (D96A96) and let it run continuously for months. A module that performs the most common set of tests is also provided (D96FST).

The tests provided are of four classes: System Tests (SYSnn), ALU Tests (ALUnn), Memory Tests (MEMnn), and Collected Tests (D96xxx). To use any of the modules, from zero to ten parameters are PUSHed onto the STACK and the test is CALLed. Results are returned in the two word registers beginning at #1CH. The symbolic names for these locations (EREG1 and EREG2) are made PUBLIC if any DIAG96.LIB module is linked. They also may be referenced in PLM$REG for PLM96 programs.

To obtain access to library modules, the user should declare the needed module names EXTERNAL code segment symbols, and link to:

    DIAG96.LIB

The next few pages contain a brief overview of each of the four classes of tests. Then, the actions of each test are described in more detail.

System Tests

    SYSnn

Common symbol definitions, storage reservations and two common routines are located in SYS01. A reference to any DIAG96.LIB module will cause SYS01 to be linked. SYS02 is meant to be called immediately after a RESET. It checks the special function register status and stack pointer, program status word and timer functionality. SYS03 is a simple program counter test. It does not test the complete range of the counter, and requires external RAM to execute.

    SYS01: Common module
    SYS02: RESET test
    SYS03: Program counter exercise

ALU Tests

    ALUnn

Five ALU modules are provided for checking ALU functionality. All report errors with a code in EREG1/EREG2.

Addition and subtraction are exercised in ALU01. A special eight-word add and subtract

MCS®-96

is executed to test each adder bit with all possible combinations of a bit operation with and without carry-in.

Unsigned byte multiplication is verified by ALU02. This module simply executes all possible unsigned byte multiplications. Although not elegant, the test is effective. It takes six seconds.

A general test of the multiplication and division functions can be made with ALU03. The module executes all possible combinations of signed and unsigned, byte and word, two and three operand Multiplies and Divides using a specially selected table of numbers as operands.

ALU04 extends the ALU03 test by generating pseudo-random test pairs. The user program simply specifies a seed value for the random number generator, and the number of pairs to generate.

ALU05 is the core module for multiply/divide tests. Both ALU03 and ALU04 call ALU05. The user can also call ALU05 by passing a pair of test arguments. The module executes all possible combinations of signed and unsigned, byte and word, two and three operand Multiplies and Divides using the arguments passed as operands.

```
ALU01: Table-driven Addition/Subtraction
ALU02: MULUB (all possible arguments)
ALU03: Table-driven Multiply/Divide
ALU04: Pseudo-random Multiply/Divide
ALU05: Multiply/Divide core module
```

Memory Tests

MEMnn

The DIAG96.LIB MEMnn modules provide tests for register space, external RAM, and ROM. The algorithms used include: walking and galloping ones; walking and galloping zeros; checkerboard patterns; complementary addressing; and checksum verification.

The register tests are in MEM01-MEM05, and MEM0C. With the exception of MEM04, the register tests save the contents of all internal registers except PLM$REG on the STACK before testing, and restore the data when done. If a faulty location is found, its address is reported. MEM04 is a utility which returns the number of bits set in a specified operand.

The external RAM tests are located in MEM06-MEM0A, and MEM0D. They all return a two-word code upon completion. The calling program must partition the RAM to be tested before calling an external RAM test.

Table 2. Memory Tests

Algorithm	Internal Registers	External RAM	ROM
Complementary Address	MEM01	MEM06	
Walking Ones		MEM07	
Walking Ones/Zeros	MEM02	MEM09	
Galloping Ones		MEM08	
Galloping Ones/Zeros	MEM03	MEM0A	
Bit Counter	MEM04		
Checkerboard Pattern	MEM05		
User Specified Pattern	MEM0C	MEM0D	
Checksum	MEM0B	MEM0B	MEM0B

MCS®-96

Collected Tests

D96xxx

The D96xxx set of modules collects together all, or several, of the General Diagnostics and performs them according to the parameters passed. D96A96 is an ASM96 module that calls all tests. D96P96 is a PLM96 module that calls all tests. D96FST is an ASM96 module that calls a logical selection of tests.

```
D96A96:  All tests            / ASM96
D96P96:  All tests            / PLM96
D96FST:  Selection of tests   / ASM96
```

MCS®-96

3.1 System Tests

Common Symbols (SYS01)

Brief Description:

This module contains the global symbol declarations and five utilities used by the **General Diagnostics**.

Assembly Language Calling Sequence:

```
CALL    Get_Psw
   or
CALL    Put_Psw
   or
CALL    Get_Parms
   or
CALL    Stack_Ram
   or
CALL    Restore_Ram
```

Get_Psw Action:

USER_PSW := PSW
EREG1   := 0
EREG2   := 0ffffh

Put_Psw Action:

PSW := USER_PSW

Get_Parms Action:

PARM2 := Last Parameter
         put on the STACK
PARM1 := Next to last parameter
         put on the STACK
USER_PSW := PSW
EREG1   := 0ffffh
EREG2   := 0000h

Stack_Ram Action:

PUSH 1aH;
Ptr := 20H
Do While Ptr<100h;
   PUSH [Ptr] +
End While;

Restore_Ram Action:

Ptr := 0feh;
Do While Ptr>1eh;
   POP [Ptr];
   Ptr: = Ptr-2;
End While;
POP 1aH;

Detailed Description:

A call to any **General Diagnostic** module will cause SYS01 to be linked. This module contains the definition of 4 words of memory used by every module to report errors and store temporary parameters. The STACK routines are used by the internal register tests to save and restore the data in the registers when called. It also INCLUDES an expanded 8096.INC file to provide the PUBLIC declarations of commonly used symbols for the special function registers and constants such as CR and LF.

Nearly all General Diagnostic modules use the routines in SYS01 to save the PSW when called, restore the PSW when returning control to the calling routine, save parameters from the STACK, and initialize the error registers.

System Power-up (SYS02)

Brief Description:

This test is a quick check of the Program Status Word, TIMER1, IOS0, IOS1 and the Interrupt Pending Register. It is meant to be called just after a RESET.

Assembly Language Calling Sequence:

    CALL   SYS02

When Test Passes:

EREG1 := 0002h   EREG2 := 0000h

If Test Fails:

EREG1 := 0102h on unexpected IOS0 or IOS1 — EREG2 := **IOS0** in low byte
                                                                                          IOS1 in high byte
EREG1 := 0202h if **TIMER1** does not change — EREG2 := **TIMER1**
EREG1 := 0302h if Zero register failed   — EREG2 := **PSW** at Failure
EREG1 := 0402h if **PUSHF/POPF** failed   — EREG2 := erroneous value
                                                                                             found
EREG1 := 0502h if Sticky bit failed   — EREG2 := 3fffh if bit did not
                                                                                               set
                                                                                                := 0000h if bit did not
                                                                                                 clear
EREG1 := 0602h if Carry Flag failed   — EREG2 := xxxxh
EREG1 := 0702h on an overflow flag error   — EREG2 := 0002h if flags set
                                                                                             wrong
                                                                                                 := xxxxh flags cleared
                                                                                                 wrong
EREG1 := 0802h if Int. Pending byte failed — EREG2 := offending Int. Pend.
                                                                                              value

Detailed Description:

This module verifies that TIMER1 is changing, then attempts to change the value in the ZERO register. Then, a set of PUSHFs and POPFs is done with test values to verify correct action of these instructions. The carry, sticky and overflow bits in the program status word are then tested. Finally, the Interrupt Pending register bits are tested for their ability to be set and cleared. Any unexpected result is reported.

Any error found having to do with the PUSHF/POPF instructions or the PSW, including Interrupt Pending, will cause interrupts to be disabled before returning to the calling module.

MCS®-96

Program Counter (SYS03)

Brief Description:

This test writes code into a user selected partition of RAM and executes the code. Elapsed time and special registers are checked for correctness.

Assembly Language Calling Sequence:

```
PUSH    <start address>
PUSH    <end address>
CALL    SYS03
```

When Test Passes:

EREG1 := 0003h
EREG2 := 0000h

If Test Fails:

EREG1 := 0103h if test code returned early
EREG2 := Early time

EREG1 := 0203h if test code returned late
EREG2 := Late time

EREG1 := 0303h if count register is incorrect
EREG2 := erroneous counter value

Detailed Description:

This module accepts starting and ending addresses for an external RAM partition, adjusts the boundaries to be double word aligned, and writes three lines of code repeatedly into the partition. The code that is written increments a counter then executes two NOPs every 12 state times. The last byte written into the RAM partition is a RET opcode.

After the RAM partition is adjusted and the code written into the RAM, the test puts a return address on the STACK, stores TIMER1 and CALLs the first byte of the RAM. When the last byte of RAM is executed, program control returns to SYS03. TIMER1 is again stored. The test then compares the elapsed time to the expected elapsed time. The value remaining in the counter is also checked for correctness. Any deviations from expected are reported.

Caution: Since interrupts are locked-out while the code in RAM is executing, partitioning more than 4000h bytes of RAM for this test could cause a WATCHDOG TIMER overflow if the watchdog was started before SYS03 is called.

MCS®-96

3.2 ALU Tests

Add/Subtract (ALU01)

Brief Description:

This routine adds then subtracts two carefully selected eight-word variables and verifies the results.

Assembly Language Calling Sequence:

    CALL   ALU01

When Test Passes:

EREG1 := 0011h
EREG2 := 0000h

If Test Fails:

EREG1 := 0111h on an addition error
       := 0211h on a subtraction error
       := 0311h on a flag error

EREG2 := offending argument on error

Detailed Description:

Two eight-word operands are added together and the results verified. Then, the operands are subtracted and verified. The operands were chosen to exercise every possible combination of two bits and a carry into each bit of the adder. Correctness of the result and the resultant flags is verified.

The operands are:

```
  05555AAAA5555AAAAFFFF0000AAAA5555H
+ 05555AAAAAAAA5555FFFF00005555AAAAH
  0AAAB555500000000FFFE0000FFFFFFFFH

  05555AAAAAAAA5555FFFF00005555AAAAH
- 0AAAA5555AAAA55550000FFFF5555AAAAH
  0AAAB555500000000FFFE0000FFFFFFFFH
```

Some versions of SIM96 do not pass this test.

5-455

MULUB (ALU02)

Brief Description:

This module simply tests the MULUB instruction for all possible combinations of byte multipliers and multiplicands.

Assembly Language Calling Sequence:

```
CALL    ALU02
```

When Test Passes:

EREG1 := 0012h
EREG2 := 0000h

If Test Fails:

EREG1 := 0112h on an error
EREG2 := multiplier/multiplicand

Detailed Description:

This test executes all possible combinations of operands into the MULUB instruction. Results are verified through a method of addition and subtraction as operands cycle. The status of PSW flags is not verified in this routine.

Multiply/Divide Table (ALU03)

Brief Description:

This module sends a specially constructed table of operands through the general Multiply/Divide Core test (ALU05).

Assembly Language Calling Sequence:

```
CALL    ALU03
```

When Test Passes:

EREG1 := 0013h
EREG2 := 0000h

If Test Fails:

EREG1 := 0115h on a signed error
     := 0215h on an unsigned error
     := 0315h on a flag error

EREG2 := offending argument on error

Detailed Description:

This test sends a table of operands through the Multiply/Divide Core test. The 18 operands were selected to exercise all of the hardware multiply and divide control signals.

The operands are:

Arg.1,	Arg.2	Arg.1,	Arg.2
1D99H,	0FFFFH	0FFFH,	9D99H
9D99H,	5555H	5555H,	0E266H
0E266H,	0AAAAH	0AAAAH,	1D99H
1D99H,	5555H	5555H,	9D99H
9D99H,	0AAAAH	0AAAAH,	0E266H
0E266H,	0FFFFH	0FFFFH,	0063H
0063H,	0055H	0055H,	0066H
0066H,	00AAH	00AAH,	0063H
0063H,	00FFH		

Some versions of SIM96 will not pass this test.

Multiply/Divide Random (ALU04)

Brief Description:

This module is a pseudo-random number generator that sends pairs of arguments to the Multiply/Divide Core test (ALU05).

Assembly Language Calling Sequence:

```
PUSH    <seed>
PUSH    <count>
CALL    ALU04
```

When Test Passes:

EREG1 := 0014h
EREG2 := 0000h

If Test Fails:

EREG1 := 0115h on a signed error
      := 0215h on an unsigned error
      := 0315h on a flag error

EREG2 := offending argument on error

Detailed Description:

This module first executes the table driven Multiply/Divide test (ALU03). Then, if passed, pseudo-random argument pairs are generated and fed into the generalized Multiply/Divide Test (ALU05). The parameters passed to ALU04 set the random number seed, and the duration of the test.

There is no restriction on the values passed to the test. However, it must be noted that all possible combinations of signed and unsigned, byte and word, two and three operand Multiply/Divides are done at least twice for each pair of arguments sent to ALU05. Each such test takes from 1 to 5 milliseconds depending upon the arguments. Therefore, if large values for the count parameter are selected, the test will be long. For example, 1000h as a count will take about 12 seconds, depending upon the seed. NOTE: Some versions of SIM96 will not pass this test.

The formula used to generate the number pairs is as follows:

$$X(n+1) = [(0101h + 0001h) * X(n) + 0001h] \text{ MOD } 0ffffh$$
$$\text{where } X(0) = \text{seed}$$

MCS®-96

Multiply/Divide Core (ALU05)

Brief Description:

This test performs a Divide/re-Multiply sequence for all possible combinations of two or three operand, signed or unsigned, byte or word operations using the arguments passed to it as operands. The results are verified.

Assembly Language Calling Sequence:

```
PUSH    <argument1>
PUSH    <argument2>
CALL    ALU05
```

When Test Passes:

EREG1 := 0015h
EREG2 := 0000h

If Test Fails:

EREG1 := 0115h on a signed error
      := 0215h on an unsigned error
      := 0315h on a flag error

EREG2 := offending argument on error

Detailed Description:

This module takes arguments from a calling program and performs upon them all possible combinations of byte or word, two or three operand, signed or unsigned multiplication and division. Argument2 is used to create the high and low words for a word Divide, and the low byte of Argument1 is used as the divisor in a byte Divide.

The test checks multiplication and division by first dividing one operand by the other, then multiplying the quotient by the divisor and adding the remainder. If the result is the original dividend, the operations were correct. However, the possibility of legitimate division overflows must also be considered.

The test first performs a division and checks flag status for correct indication of overflow conditions. If there has been an overflow, the dividend is right shifted by one, the expected result is updated, and the division is performed over. If a division by zero occurred, just the expected result is corrected and the test is continued.

After a division and overflow check/fixup is complete, a re-multiplication occurs and the result verified. Flag status is also verified. If the results are correct, the original operands are reloaded into the test operand registers and the next Divide/re-Multiply combination is begun.

All Divide/Multiply combinations are performed twice. Once with flags set upon entry, and once with flags clear upon entry.

CALLing ALU03 will run a specially selected table of operands through this test. CALLing ALU04 will run a pseudo-random string of operands through this test.

3.3 Memory Tests

Complementary Address (MEM01)
(for registers)

Brief Description:

This module performs a complementary address test on the registers locations 1ah to 0ffh.

Assembly Language Calling Sequence:

    CALL   MEM01

When Test Passes:	If Test Fails:
EREG1 := 0021h	EREG1 := 0121h
EREG2 := 0000h	EREG2 := address of the error

Detailed Description:

This module performs a simple address and integrity test on register locations 1ah-0ffh. The algorithm stores the value NOT(ADDRESS) in the location pointed to by ADDRESS for the range, then loops through memory again to verify the contents.

Caution: If the STACK is partially internal, the STACK POINTER must be pointing at least 260 bytes into external RAM at the time MEM01 is called. The STACK cannot be entirely internal. The arithmetic flags in the PSW are undefined after execution of MEM01.

MCS®-96

Walking Ones/Zeros (MEM02)
(for registers)

Brief Description:

This module performs a Walking Ones and Zeros test on the internal registers 1ah-0ffh.

Assembly Language Calling Sequence:

    CALL   MEM02

When Test Passes: **If Test Fails:**

EREG1 := 0022h   EREG1 := 0122h
EREG1 := 0000h   EREG2 := address of the error

Detailed Description:

This module performs a Walking Ones and Zeros test on the internal registers.

The Walking Ones memory test first loads zero in all locations to be tested. Then, ones are placed in the first byte of memory, followed by a verification of all locations. Next, the first location is zeroed and ones are loaded into the second location. All memory is again verified. This process continues until all locations have been loaded with ones.

The Walking Zeros memory test works exactly like Walking Ones, except that a zero is "walked" through memory filled with ones, instead of ones being walked through a memory filled with zeros.

Caution: If the STACK is partially internal, the STACK POINTER must be pointing at lest 260 bytes into external RAM at the time MEM02 is called. The STACK cannot be entirely internal. The arithmetic flags in the PSW are undefined after execution of MEM02.

Galloping Ones/Zeros (MEM03)
(for registers)

Brief Description:

This module performs a Galloping Ones and Zeros test on the internal registers 1ah-0ffh.

Assembly Language Calling Sequence:

```
CALL    MEM03
```

When Test Passes:	If Test Fails:
EREG1 := 0023h	EREG1 := 0123h
EREG2 := 0000h	EREG2 := address of the error

Detailed Description:

This module performs a Galloping Ones and Zeros test on internal registers.

The Galloping Ones algorithm tests memory by first loading zeros into all locations. Then ones are loaded into the first byte and all memory is verified. The verification is done by alternating reads to the first location and locations through all memory. Next, ones are placed in the second location without altering the first. Verification is again performed by alternating reads to the second location and the rest of memory. This process continues until all locations contain ones.

The Galloping Zeros test is similar to Galloping Ones, except that zeros slowly fill a memory filled with ones. In Galloping Ones, ones slowly fill a memory filled with zeros.

Caution: If the STACK is partially internal, the STACK POINTER must be pointing at least 260 bytes into external RAM at the time MEM03 is called. The STACK cannot be entirely internal. The arithmetic flags in the PSW are undefined after execution of MEM03.

Bits Set (MEM04)

Brief Description:

This module returns the number of bits set in the parameter passed to the routine.

Assembly Language Calling Sequence:

```
PUSH    test_value
CALL    MEM04
```

When All Bits Zero:	When One or More Bits Set:
EREG1 := 0024h	EREG1 := 0124h
EREG2 := 0000h	EREG2 := number of bits set

Detailed Description:

This module returns the number of bits that are set in the low byte of the parameter passed to the test. Any addressing mode may be used to put a value on the STACK, but the parameter on the STACK is treated as an immediate value.

MCS®-96

Checkerboard Pattern (MEM05)
(for registers)

Brief Description:

This module performs a Checkerboard Pattern test on the internal registers 1ah-0ffh.

Assembly Language Calling Sequence:

```
CALL    MEM05
```

When Test Passes:	If Test Fails:
EREG1 := 0025h	EREG1 := 0125h
EREG2 := 0000h	EREG2 := address of the error

Detailed Description:

This module performs a checkerboard test on the internal registers. A checkerboard pattern of ones and zeros is written into the physical rows and columns of the 8096 register space. As the pattern is being written, it is repeatedly verified. After the entire pattern is in place, the memory is verified again, complemented, and re-verified.

Caution: If the STACK is partially internal, the STACK POINTER must be pointing at least 260 bytes into external RAM at the time MEM05 is called. The STACK cannot be entirely internal. The arithmetic flags in the PSW are undefined after execution of MEM05.

Complementary Address (MEM06)

Brief Description:

This module performs a complementary address test on the memory partitioned by user supplied pointers.

Assembly Language Calling Sequence:

```
PUSH    <start address>
PUSH    <end address>
CALL    MEM06
```

When Test Passes:	If Test Fails:
EREG1 := 0026h	EREG1 := 0126h
EREG2 := 0000h	EREG2 := offending address

Detailed Description:

This module performs a simple address and integrity test on RAM locations partitioned by the parameters passed. The algorithm stores the value NOT(ADDRESS) in the location pointed to by ADDRESS for the range, then loops through memory again to verify the contents.

Caution: Do not partition RAM that contains valid STACK elements.

Walking Ones (MEM07)

Brief Description:

This module performs a Walking Ones Test on the memory partitioned by the user.

Assembly Language Calling Sequence:

```
PUSH    <start address>
PUSH    <end address>
CALL    MEM07
```

When Test Passes:

EREG1 := 0027h
EREG2 := 0000h

If Test Fails:

EREG1 := 0127h
EREG2 := offending address

Detailed Description:

This module performs a Walking Ones test on the memory partitioned by the calling program. The Walking Ones memory test first loads zero in all locations to be tested. Then, ones are placed in the first byte of memory, followed by a verification of all locations. Next, the first location is zeroed and ones are loaded into the second location. All memory is again verified. This process continues until all locations have been loaded with ones.

Caution: Do not partition RAM that holds valid elements of the STACK. And, execution time increases non-linearly with memory partition widths.

Galloping Ones (MEM08)

Brief Description:

This module performs a Galloping Ones test on memory partitioned by the calling program.

Assembly Language Calling Sequence:

```
PUSH    <start address>
PUSH    <end address>
CALL    MEM08
```

When Test Passes:

EREG1 := 0028h
EREG2 := 0000h

If Test Fails:

EREG1 := 0128h
EREG2 := offending address

Detailed Description:

This module performs a Galloping Ones test on memory locations partitioned by the calling program.

The Galloping Ones algorithm tests memory by first loading zeros into all locations. Then ones are loaded into the first byte and all memory is verified. The verification is done by alternating reads to the first location and locations through all memory. Next, ones are placed in the second location without altering the first. Verification is again performed by alternating reads to the second location and the rest of memory. This process continues until all locations contain ones.

Caution: Do not partition locations that contain valid elements of the STACK. And, execution time increases non-linearly with memory partition widths.

Walking Ones/Zeros (MEM09)

Brief Description:

This module performs a Walking Ones and Zeros test on the memory locations partitioned by the calling program.

Assembly Language Calling Sequence:

```
PUSH    <start address>
PUSH    <end address>
CALL    MEM09
```

When Test Passes:

EREG1 := 0029h
EREG2 := 0000h

If Test Fails:

EREG1 := 0129h
EREG2 := offending address

Detailed Description:

This module performs a Walking Ones and Zeros test on the memory partitioned by the calling program.

The Walking Ones memory test first loads zero in all locations to be tested. Then, ones are placed in the first byte of memory, followed by a verification of all locations. Next, the first location is zeroed and ones are loaded into the second location. All memory is again verified. This process continues until all locations have been loaded with ones.

The Walking Zeros memory test works exactly like Walking Ones, except that a zero is "walked" through memory filled with ones, instead of ones being walked through a memory filled with zeros.

Caution: Do not partition RAM that contains valid elements of the STACK. And, execution time increases non-linearly with memory partition widths.

Galloping Ones/Zeros (MEM0A)

Brief Description:

This module performs a Galloping Ones and Zeros test on the memory locations partitioned by the calling program.

Assembly Language Calling Sequence:

```
PUSH    <starting address>
PUSH    <ending address>
CALL    MEM0A
```

When Test Passes:

EREG1 := 002Ah
EREG2 := 0000h

If Test Fails:

EREG1 := 012Ah
EREG2 := offending address

Detailed Description:

This module performs a Galloping Ones and Zeros test on memory partitioned by the calling program.

The Galloping Ones algorithm tests memory by first loading zeros into all locations. Then ones are loaded into the first byte and all memory is verified. The verification is done by alternating reads to the first location and locations through all memory. Next, ones are placed in the second location without altering the first. Verification is again performed by alternating reads to the second location and the rest of memory. This process continues until all locations contain ones.

The Galloping Zeros test is similar to Galloping Ones, except that zeros slowly fill a memory filled with ones. In Galloping Ones, ones slowly fill a memory filled with zeros.

Caution: Do not partition RAM that contains valid elements of the STACK. And, execution time increases non-linearly with memory partition widths.

Checksum (MEM0B)

Brief Description:

This module calculates a 16 bit checksum for the memory partition specified by the calling program.

Assembly Language Calling Sequence:

```
PUSH    <starting address>
PUSH    <ending address>
CALL    MEM0B
```

Test Returns:

EREG1 := 012bh
EREG2 := 16-bit checksum

Detailed Description:

This module performs a 16-bit checksum on the region of memory partitioned by the calling program. RAM or ROM may be partitioned. The module is non-destructive to RAM.

User Pattern (MEM0C) (for registers)

Brief Description:

This module performs a Checkerboard Pattern test on the internal registers 1ah-0ffh with a user specified bit pattern.

Assembly Language Calling Sequence:

```
PUSH    <desired bit pattern>
CALL    MEM0C
```

When Test Passes:

EREG1 := 002Ch
EREG2 := 0000h

If Test Fails:

EREG1 := 012Ch
EREG2 := address of the error

Detailed Description:

This module performs a checkerboard test on the internal registers with the bit pattern specified by the calling program. The pattern is written into the physical rows and columns of the 8096 register space. As the pattern is being written, it is repeatedly verified. After the entire pattern is in place, the memory is verified again, complemented, and re-verified.

Caution: If the STACK is partially internal, the STACK POINTER must be pointing at least 260 bytes into external RAM at the time MEM0C is called. The STACK cannot be entirely internal. The arithmetic flags in the PSW are undefined after execution of MEM0C.

User Pattern (MEM0D)

Brief Description:

This module performs a Checkerboard Pattern test on a specified region of memory with a specified pattern of bits.

Assembly Language Calling Sequence:

```
PUSH    <starting address>
PUSH    <ending address>
PUSH    <bit pattern>
CALL    MEM0D
```

When Test Passes:

EREG1 := 002dh
EREG2 := 0000h

If Test Fails:

EREG1 := 012dh
EREG2 := offending address

Detailed Description:

This module performs a checkerboard test on a region of memory that is specified by the calling program using a bit pattern which is also specified. First, the pattern is written into memory. As the pattern is being written, it is repeatedly verified. After the entire pattern is in place, the memory is verified again, complemented, and re-verified.

Caution: Do not partition RAM that contains valid elements of the STACK.

3.4 Collected Tests Modules

ALL Tests in ASM96 (D96A96)

Brief Description:

This module causes every **General Diagnostics** test to execute.

Assembly Language Calling Sequence:

```
PUSH    <RAM segment1 starting address>
PUSH    <RAM segment1 ending address>
PUSH    <RAM segment2 starting address>
PUSH    <RAM segment2 ending address>
PUSH    <random seed>
PUSH    <random test length>
PUSH    <top of code address>
PUSH    <argument1 for Multiply/Divide Core test>
PUSH    <argument2 for Multiply/Divide Core test>
PUSH    <bit pattern for memory test>
CALL    D96A96
```

When Tests All Pass:

EREG1 := 0030h
EREG2 := code checksum

When a Test Fails:

EREG1 := test module error code
EREG2 := test module detail code

Detailed Description:

This module calls all **General Diagnostics** using the parameters passed by the calling program. The parameters needed by the test for proper execution specify two areas of external RAM for memory tests, the ending address of code to be checksummed, the seed and length of the random ALU test, two specific arguments to do the Multiply/Divide Core test, and a bit pattern for memory tests.

Execution speed of this test is highly dependent upon the memory partitions and the length requested for the random ALU test. For example, partitioning 1k and 8k regions of memory, and calling for 1000h random ALU tests, the test takes 3 hours to complete. Testing smaller regions of memory (i.e. 1k and 1k) can reduce test time to a few minutes.

Caution: An external STACK must be used with this test, and it must be in a part of memory outside that partitioned during the CALL.

MCS®-96

ALL Tests in PLM96 (D96P96)

Brief Description:

This module causes every **General Diagnostics** test module to execute.

PLM96 Calling Sequence:

```
D96P96(RAM segment1 starting address,
       RAM segment1 ending address,
       RAM segment2 starting address,
       RAM segment2 ending address,
       random seed, random test length,
       top of code address,
       argument1 for Multiply/Divide Core test,
       argument2 for Multiply/Divide Core test,
       bit pattern for memory tests);
```

When All Tests Pass:

PLMREG   := 00F0h
PLMREG + 2   := 16-bit checksum

When a Test Fails:

PLMREG   := module error code
PLMREG + 2   := module detail code

Detailed Description:

This module calls all **General Diagnostics** using the parameters passed during invocation. The parameters needed by the test for proper execution specify two areas of external RAM for memory tests, the ending address of code to be checksummed, the seed and length of the random ALU test, two specific arguments to do the Multiply/Divide Core test, and a bit pattern for memory tests.

Execution speed of this test is highly dependent upon the memory partitions and the length requested for the random ALU test. For example, partitioning 1k and 8k regions of memory, and calling for 1000h random ALU tests, the test takes 3 hours to complete. Testing smaller regions of memory (i.e. 1k and 1k) can reduce test time to a few minutes.

In his program, the user will have to DECLARE D96P96 an external procedure of the LONG type, with its parameters declared SLOW. The EREG1 and EREG2 values reported by library modules are placed in the long-word location at PLM$REG.

The DECLARations in D96P96 show how any one General Diagnostic Module could be called from a PLM96 program. Each needed module needs to be DECLAREd an external procedure of the LONG type.

Caution: An external STACK must be used with this test, and it must be in a part of memory outside that partitioned during the CALL.

MCS®-96

Selected Tests in ASM (D96FST)

Brief Description:

This is an ASM module that invokes a selected set of **General Diagnostic** tests.

Assembly Language Calling Sequence:

```
PUSH    <RAM segment1 starting address>
PUSH    <RAM segment1 ending address>
PUSH    <RAM segment2 starting address>
PUSH    <RAM segment2 ending address>
PUSH    <random seed>
PUSH    <random test length>
PUSH    <top of code address>
PUSH    <argument1 for Multiply/Divide Core test>
PUSH    <argument2 for Multiply/Divide Core test>
PUSH    <bit pattern for memory test>
CALL    D96FST
```

When Tests All Pass:	When a Test Fails:
EREG1 := 00E0h	EREG1 := test module error code
EREG2 := code checksum	EREG2 := test module detail code

Detailed Description:

This module calls the Power-up and Program Counter tests then all ALU tests. Then, Complementary Address, Galloping Ones/Zeros and Checkerboard tests are run on the internal registers. Finally, Complementary Address and specified pattern tests are done on external memory and the program is checksummed.

The parameters needed by the test for proper execution specify two areas of external RAM for memory tests, the ending address of code to be checksummed, the seed and length of the random ALU test, two specific arguments to do the Multiply/Divide Core test, and a bit pattern for memory tests.

Execution speed of this test is highly dependent upon the memory partitions and the length requested for the random ALU test. For example, partitioning 1k and 8k regions of memory, and calling for 1000h random ALU tests, the test takes about 20 seconds to complete. Testing smaller regions of memory (i.e. 1k and 1k) can reduce test time further.

Caution: An external STACK must be used with this test, and it must be in a part of memory outside that partitioned during the CALL.

4.0 THE DYNAMIC STABILITY TEST

The **Dynamic Stability Test** is a set of interrupt service routines designed to run over a user's background task in either one stand alone 8097, or two 8097s that are cross-coupled. In the stand alone mode, the chip's output pins are hooked to its input pins. In the dual chip mode, each controller's output pins are tied to the input pins of the other. The minimum configuration for each mode are shown in Figures 2 and 3. See Figure 11 for the circuit diagram of a board that can be jumpered for either configuration.

What is Dynamic Stability?

A "Dynamic Stability" test was developed to enable testing of the 8097 in an asynchronous environment. In the one chip mode, HSO events are synchronized with the HSI

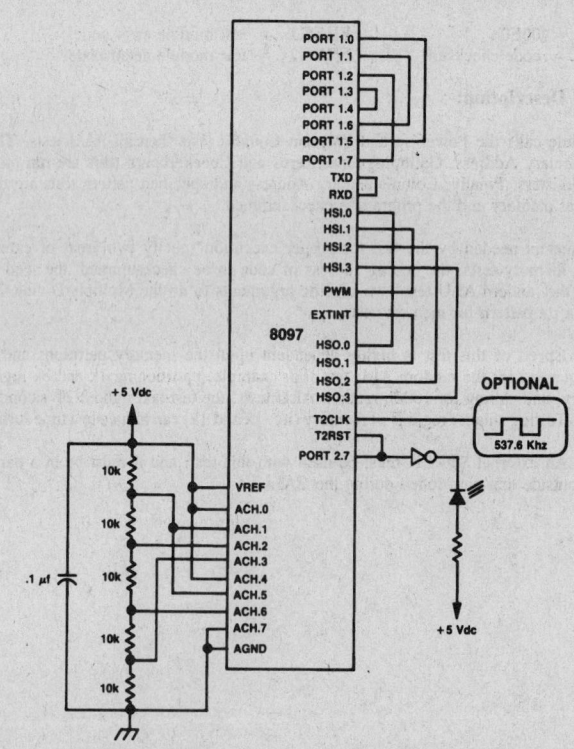

Figure 2. 8097 Strapback Configuration Single Chip Mode

MCS®-96

event capture logic. However, in the cross-coupled mode, HSO events generated by one chip are captured in the HSI unit of another. As long as separate, non-syncronized clock sources are used for each chip, the HSI line events will occur asynchronously to the chip.

To implement a test that could be either stand alone or co-resident without modification, the creation and verification of I/O events needed to be decoupled. Thus the basic structure of the **Dynamic Stability Test** takes the form of a set of I/O Producers causing events that I/O Consumers verify. Figure 4 gives a macro view of the Producer/Consumer relationship.

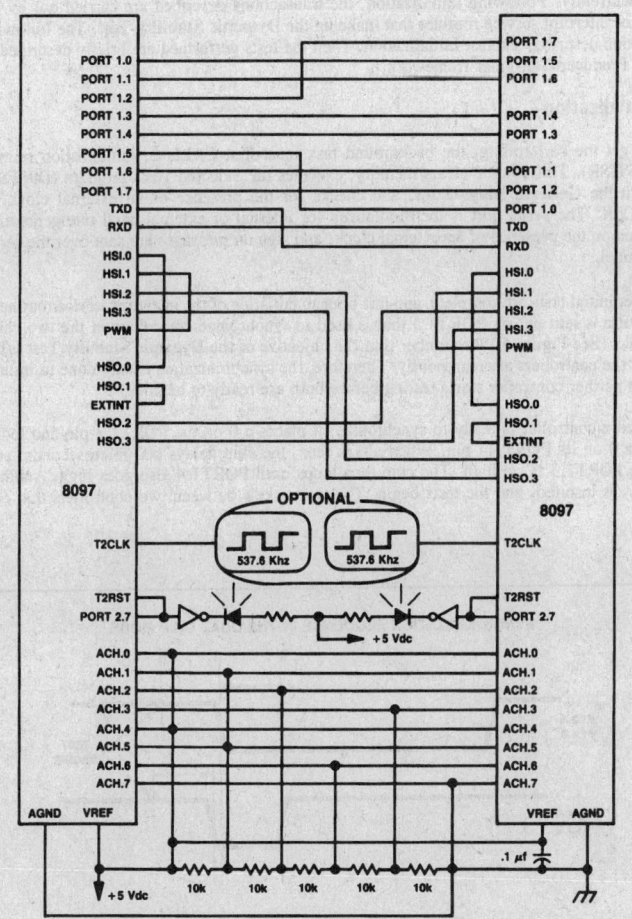

Figure 3. 8097 Strapback Configuration Dual Chip Mode

5-471

MCS®-96

Figure 4. Producer/Consumer Relationship

What Does the Test Do?

Producer/Consumer exchanges were defined to test nearly all of the 8097 I/O capabilities concurrently. Following initialization, the transactions described are carried out by the set of interrupt service routines that make up the **Dynamic Stability Test.** The following section describes the test initialization. Then the tests performed are briefly described in the Producer/Consumer framework.

Initialization

To get the ball rolling, the background task must first CALL an initialization routine (DSTISR). This routine clears memory, executes the Selected Tests program (D96FST) from the **General Diagnostics,** and checks for the presence of an external clock on T2CLK. The serial port is then initialized for internal or external baud rate generation based on the presence of an external clock, and sign on messages are sent over the serial channel.

After initial tests are complete, and just prior to initiation of the interrupt service routines, a pulse is sent out on PORT1.3 that is used to synchronize controllers in the two chip mode. (See Figure 5.) Remember that the objective of the **Dynamic Stability Test** is to test the controllers asynchronously. Therefore, the synchronization is only done to insure that neither controller starts testing before both are ready to begin.

When a controller is ready to synchronize, it places a 0 on the PORT1.3 pin and looks for a 0 on its PORT1.4 pin. When a 0 is seen, the chip delays 600 microseconds, and then PORT1.3 is set high. The chip then loops until PORT1.4 also goes high. Another delay is inserted, and the tests begin. The worst skew between two controllers that can

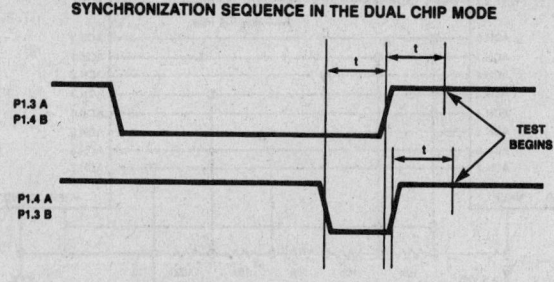

Figure 5. Dual Chip Synchronization

occur using this method is 9 state times (2.25 µs in a 12 Mhz system). However, the skew should average between four and five state times. In any case, the parts will be far from synchronized shortly after the tests begin. This is fine, as long as the tests begin together.

In a one chip system, this process appears as a 600 microsecond pulse on PORT1.3. (See Figure 6.) The tests begin 600 microseconds after the rising edge.

When synchronization is complete, the interrupt service routines are initialized, interrupts are enabled, and control is returned to the background task. At this point, the testing really begins.

Producers and Consumers

The Producer/Consumer exchanges on the 8097 are executed by the interrupt service routines of the **Dynamimc Stability Test**. While some interrupt routines contain an entire Producer or Consumer, some are spread through many routines. Figure 7 shows on a broad level the transactions that occur during test execution. Short descriptions of each Producer and Consumer follow, along with an indication of which interrupt routines contain them.

Serial Producer ●DSTSER● The Serial Producer constantly transmits a table of alphabetic and special characters, and test data which includes the current status of the test and the REAL TIME since reset.

Serial Consumer ●DSTSER● The Serial Consumer monitors the data coming over the serial link to see if all the expected characters are transmitted correctly and in the correct order. Transmission of the test data and the REAL TIME is checked by counting characters between carriage returns.

Port1 Producer ●DSTSWT● The Port1 Producer outputs a series of values on Port1 that are contained in a table constructed to test all possible combinations of input and output of ones and zeros. The test producer executes every 5000h TIMER1 counts via the expiration of Software Timer 1.

Port1 Consumer ●DSTSWT● The Port1 Consumer verifies the patterns appearing on Port1 using a table which contains the expected values. The check executes every 1000h TIMER1 counts via the expiration of Software Timer 2.

A/D Producer ●DSTSWT● The A/D Producer continually starts A/D conversions by loading an HSO command to initiate an A/D. The A/D Producer executes every time Software Timer 0 expires.

A/D Consumer ●DSTA2D● The A/D Consumer verifies the result of conversions initiated by the A/D Producer. It then changes the channel set for conversion and loads an HSO command to cause a Software Timer 0 expiration.

SYNCHRONIZATION PULSE IN THE SINGLE CHIP MODE

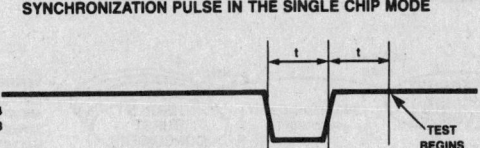

Figure 6. Single Chip Sync Pulse

MCS®-96

External Interrupt Producer •DSTHSO• The External Interrupt Producer causes rising edges on HSO.1, which is tied to EXTINT. This Producer executes every time there has been a falling edge on HSO.1.

External Interrupt Consumer •DSTEXI• The External Interrupt Consumer responds to rising edges on EXTINT. It resets the WATCHDOG TIMER every execution and tests the Test Status Words every 30h executions to see that all tests are running. This Consumer also loads an HSO command to cause a falling edge on HSO.1

PWM Producer •DSTTOV• The PWM Producer executes every time there is a timer overflow. In addition to changing the PWM period, it toggles an LED and checks for unexpected T2CLK overflows. There is no PWM Consumer per se, but the PWM output is tied to HSI.1 which is configured to clock T2CLK. In this way T2CLK counts at a known average rate, and is used by the test in a modulo count fashion to generate a real

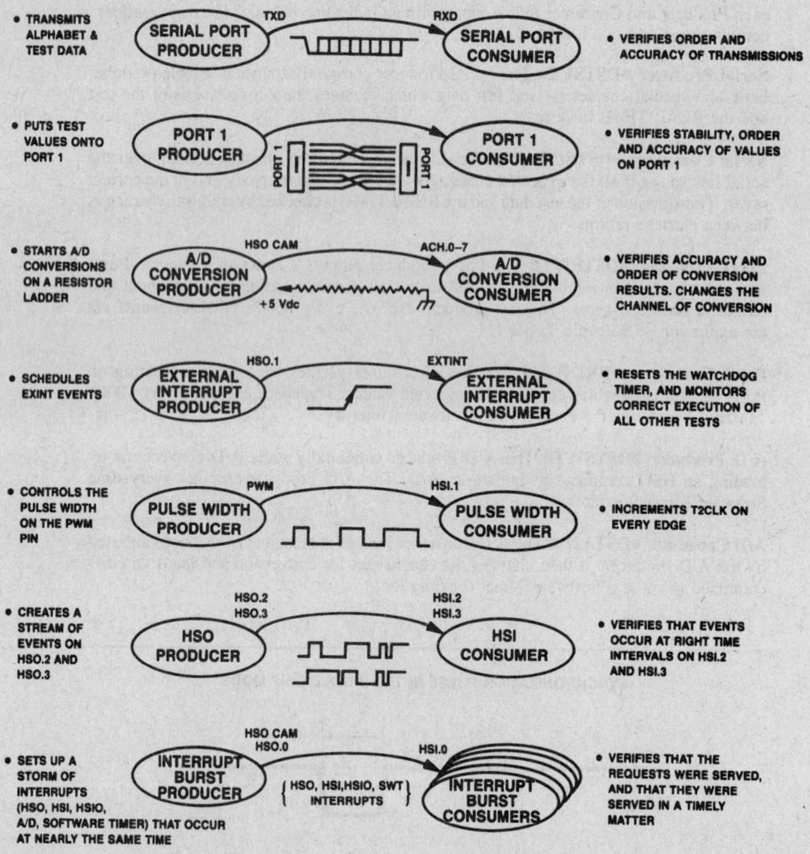

Figure 7. Producer/Consumer Overview

time clock. This module is also expandable to include tests that a user might want to execute only periodically.

HSO Producer ●DSTHSO● The High Speed Output Producer executes every time an HSO event on HSO.2 or HSO.3 occurs. Varying pulse widths are created on the pins using predetermined tables of values. The minimum pulse width is 1000H; the maximum is 0C000H TIMER1 counts.

HSI Consumer ●DSTHSI● The high speed inputs are monitored by the High Speed Input Consumer. The check executes every time an event occurs on HSI.2 or HSI.3. The HSI Consumer verifies that the proper pulse widths appear on the pins, and that the series of pulse widths is in the right order.

Interrupt BURST Producer ●DSTSWT,DSTHI0,DSTHSO,DSTHSO● The previous Producer/Consumer transactions either go between controllers in the dual-chip mode, or stay within the same controller in the single-chip mode. However, there is one **Dynamic Stability Test** that executes invisibly to a co-controller in the dual-chip mode. This test, the Interrupt BURST Test, causes a flood of interrupts that almost fully load the 8097 with interrupt response requests.

The Interrupt BURST Producer causes a complex chain of events that eventually lead to the updating of the REAL TIME Clock. Since the succession of events involves half of the interrupt service routines, the whole process is described here for understanding.

The Big Picture — Each time the REAL TIME Clock is ready to be updated, a BURST of interrupts is setup to occur as close together as possible. Figure 8 shows the sequence of events that occur, their dependency on T2CLK and the commands written into the HSO CAM. If you don't need any more detail, skip "The nitty-gritty".

The nitty-gritty — Every time an the A/D Consumer finishes executing it sets up a Software Timer 0 expiration for TIMER1 = TIMER1 + 2. While T2CLK is between 100h and 600h, the A/D Producer (Software Timer 0) causes a new conversion with an HSO command. If T2CLK is greater than 600h, then an HSO command is loaded to cause a falling edge on HSO.0 instead of causing an A/D conversion to start. This begins the BURST sequence.

The falling edge on HSO.0 causes an HSO interrupt and an HSI interrupt, since HSO.0 is tied to HSI.0. The HSO interrupt loads commands to raise HSO.0 at T2CLK = 1900h and start an A/D at T2CLK = 18ffh. The HSI interrupt loads no HSO commands.

When T2CLK = 18ffh an A/D conversion is begun. When T2CLK = 1900h a rising edge occurs on HSO.0 causing T2CLK to be reset and HSO,HSI and HSI0.0 interrupt requests to be made. At approximately the same time an A/D conversion completes and the A/D Done interrupt request is made.

The HSO interrupt service causes no further events. The HSI interrupt service routing loads an HSO command to cause a Software Timer 3 interrupt at T2CLK = 0ffh. The A/D Consumer loads an HSO command to cause a Software Timer 0 interrupt at TIMER1 = TIMER1 + 2. When the A/D Producer executes it loads a command to start an A/D conversion at T2CLK = 100h. And the HSI.0 interrupt service routine updates the REAL TIME Clock (the real output from this whole mess).

The last interrupt that is serviced from this BURST is a Software Timer 3 expiration. This is the BURST Checker. It verifies that all interrupts occurred within a reasonable time window, but causes no further events if all tests passed.

All these activities keep the HSO CAM almost fully loaded. So, to ensure that CAM overwrites never occur, two precautions were taken. First, one CAM slot was allocated to four of the tests that use the HSO unit, and two slots were allocated for shared use by the Interrupt BURST process and the A/D conversion process.

MCS®-96

The second precaution was to confirm that either the CAM was not full or the HOLDING REGISTER was empty (depending upon the test) before allowing any write to the CAM.

Figure 9 shows the HSO CAM loading over time, with T2CLK as the timebase. External Interrupt, Port1, HSO.2 and HSO.3 events each are allocated the use of one CAM slot all the time. While T2CLK is below 600h, but above 100h, another CAM slot is used by the A/D Done — Start A/D sequence. When T2CLK goes above 600h, two slots are used by the Interrupt BURST process. The BURST events conclude when T2CLK is reset and climbs to 100h. At 100h, the A/D Done — Start A/D sequence being again.

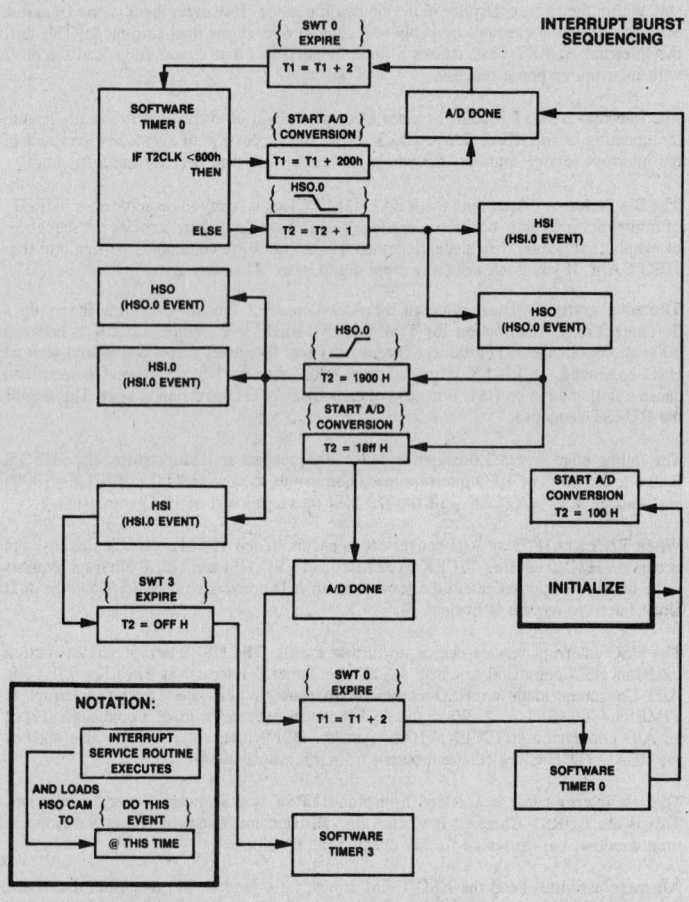

Figure 8. Interrupt BURST Sequencing

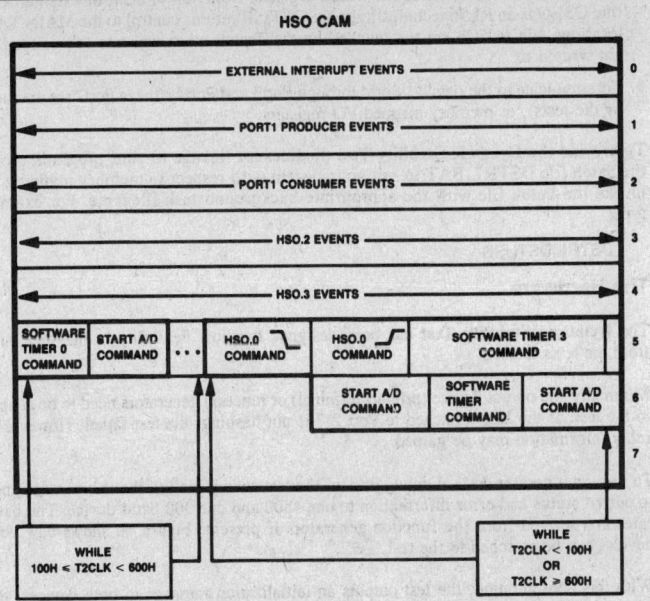

Figure 9. HSO CAM Loading

4.1 How to Use DST96

All program modules that are needed to run the **Dynamic Stability Test** are contained in the DST96 Library (DST96.LIB). This Library is also a part of DIAG96.LIB. To use the test, one or two 8097s must be configured as previously shown. A background task for the Dynamic Stability interrupt service routines must also be provided and linked to DIAG96.LIB. For those who don't wish to write a background task, one is provided (DSTUSR). But, any code may be written which follows some simple rules.

The Software

The software constraints are relatively minor, but they do create incompatibility with PLM96. All background tasks should be written in ASM96.

Minimally, the background task must load the STACK POINTER, PUSH parameters, CALL DSTISR, and go into a loop. Any other code may come after the CALL to DSTISR, as long as:

- Interrupts are never disabled for more than a few instructions;
- No operations to or from special function registers occur (with the exception of reading TIMER1 or T2CLK), and

Other less grave limitations on the main task are that it:

- Be CSEGed at 2080h;

MCS®-96

- Write only to EREG1, EREG2, OSEG registers from 40h to 5Ch, or external RAM, (the OSEG is an RL96 technicality, once DSTISR returns control to the MAIN TASK, locations 40h to 5Ch are not touched by the Tests); other registers can be read, but not written to;

- Communicate to the outside world through Port3 and Port4, (these Ports are untouched by the tests), or memory mapped I/O registers;

To provide the **Dynamic Stability Test** modules for linkage to your program, modify the batch file DSTRL.BAT to suit your system with respect to memory mapping and invoke the batch file with the appropriate background task filename. For example, type:

    DSTRL DSTUSR

The Hardware

The **Dynamic Stability Test** has been designed to allow flexibility in the way output from the tests is used.

Minimally, no output device (printer, terminal) or function generators need to be attached to the test. If the LED attached to Port 2.7 is not flashing, the test failed. However, no other information may be gained.

To support a greater level of debugging (of the test code initially), the test was designed to output status and error information to one 4800 and one 300 baud device. The baud rates are derived from the function generators if present. Figure 10 shows how both devices can be attached to the test.

With this configuration, the test outputs an initialization message to both devices, then selects just the 4800 baud line for monitoring the Serial Port Producer/Consumer transactions. If an error is detected, the 300 baud line is selected for an error information dump.

A diagram of the circuit used in developing the **Dynamic Stabilty Test** appears in Figure 11. It is sufficiently general purpose for use in either the single or double chip modes, with or without printers or terminals attached.

The circuit requires that the 8097 I/O signals be present on an SBE-96 compatible 50 pin connector. The circuit also assumes that the analog voltage reference is provided through the cable. Therefore, if you are using the SBE-96, the jumpers to do this need to be in place (jumper numbers vary with the SBE-96 version).

Figure 12 describes how to jumber the **Dynamic Stability Test** board for one or two chip tests. Figure 13 shows the SBE-96 50 pin connector pinout. The following sections describe in detail the actions of each interrupt service routine in implementing the Producer/Consumer transactions.

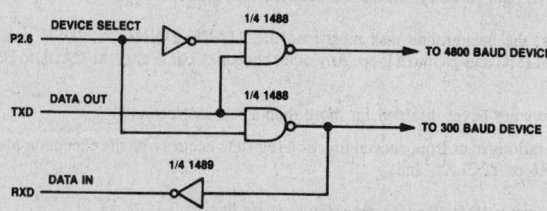

Figure 10. Output Device Selection Circuit

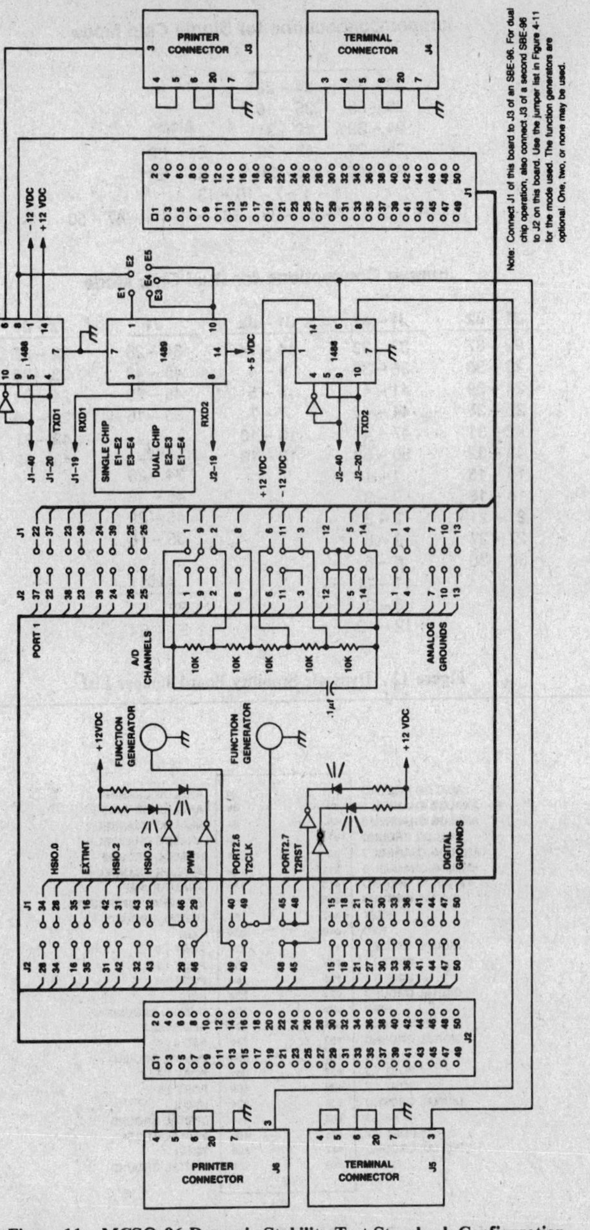

MCS®-96

Figure 11. MCS®-96 Dynamic Stability Test Strapback Configuration

Jumper Connections for Single Chip Mode

J1		Also
22 – 37	34 – 28	
23 – 38	35 – 16	
24 – 39	42 – 31	E1 – E2
25 – 26	43 – 32	E3 – E4
45 – 48	46 – 29	

1 – 4 – 7 – 10 – 13
15 – 18 – 21 – 27 – 30 – 33 – 36 – 41 – 44 – 47 – 50

Jumper Connections for Dual Chip Mode

J1 – J2	J1 – J2	J1 – J2	J1	J2 – J1
22 – 37	33 – 33	14 – 14	34 – 28	22 – 37
23 – 38	36 – 36	4 – 4	45 – 48	23 – 38
24 – 39	41 – 41	5 – 5	46 – 29	24 – 39
25 – 26	44 – 44	7 – 7	35 – 16	25 – 26
42 – 31	47 – 47	10 – 10		42 – 31
43 – 32	50 – 50	13 – 13	**J2**	43 – 32
15 – 15	1 – 1		34 – 28	
18 – 18	9 – 9		45 – 48	
21 – 21	2 – 2		46 – 29	
27 – 27	8 – 8		35 – 16	
30 – 30	6 – 6			
	11 – 11		**Also**	
	3 – 3		E2 – E5	
	12 – 12		E1 – E4	

Figure 12. Dynamic Stability Board Jumper List

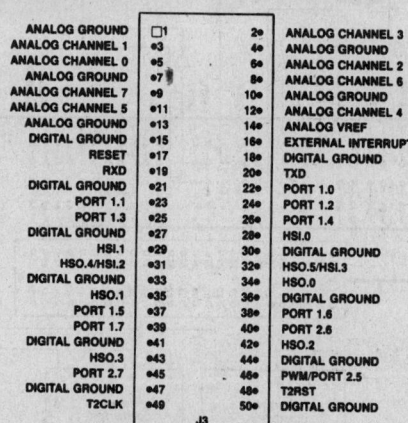

Figure 13. SBE-96 J3 Pinout

4.2 Test Module Descriptions

DST Initialization (DSTISR)

Brief Description:

This module is the invocation and initialization code for the Dynamic Stability Test.

Assembly Language Calling Sequence:

```
PUSH    <RAM segment1 starting address>
PUSH    <RAM segment1 ending address>
PUSH    <RAM segment2 starting address>
PUSH    <RAM segment2 ending address>
PUSH    <random seed>
PUSH    <random test length>
PUSH    <top of code address>
PUSH    <argument1 for Multiply/Divide Core test>
PUSH    <argument2 for Multiply/Divide Core test>
PUSH    <bit pattern for memory test>
CALL    DSTISR
```

When All Tests Pass:

EREG1 := 0040h
EREG2 := 0000h

When a Test Fails:

EREG1 := 0140h on abnormal RESET   EREG2 := TIMER1
EREG1 := 0240h if T2CLK won't change   EREG2 := xxxxh
EREG1 := 0340h if T2RST did not work   EREG2 := xxxxh
EREG1 := 0440h if IOC0.1 did not work   EREG2 := xxxxh

Detailed Description:

This module initializes the registers used by **Dynamic Stability Test** Modules, checks to see if there is an external clock present, tests T2CLK counting and reset functionality, and outputs initialization messages to the two output devices. The selected tests module (D96FST) from the **General Diagnostics** is also executed using the parameters specified.

When all initialization tests are passed, then a synchronization is performed to place the two processors in a dual-chip mode test in close sync. The PORT1 pins are used as to perform the handshaking synchronization. After synchronization, all **Dynamic Stability Tests** are activated and control is returned to the user program.

MCS®-96

External Interrupts (DSTEXI)

Brief Description:

This module executes every time there is a rising edge on the EXTINT pin. The test resets the WATCHDOG TIMER and verifies execution of all Dynamic Stability routines.

If Test Fails:

EREG1 := 01A0h if a test did not execute
EREG2 := Number of Shifts done

Detailed Description:

This routine executes every time there is a rising edge on the EXTINT pin, causing an external interrupt. Each execution, the WATCHDOG TIMER is reset and an HSO command to clear the HSO.1 pin in 1000h TIMER1 counts is loaded into the CAM. The HSO routine that responds to that event will cause HSO.1 to go high, thus causing another vector to DSTEXI.

Every 30h executions of this module, the Test Status Words are NOTed and then NORMaLized to see if any test did not execute. If any bit in the Test Status Words is left set after being complemented, the NORML instruction will leave the most significant bit set, indicating an error. If there was no error, the TSWORDs are cleared. The user can change a mask in DSTEXI to enable checking of any of the currently spare bits in TSWORD. The TSWORD bit map is as follows:

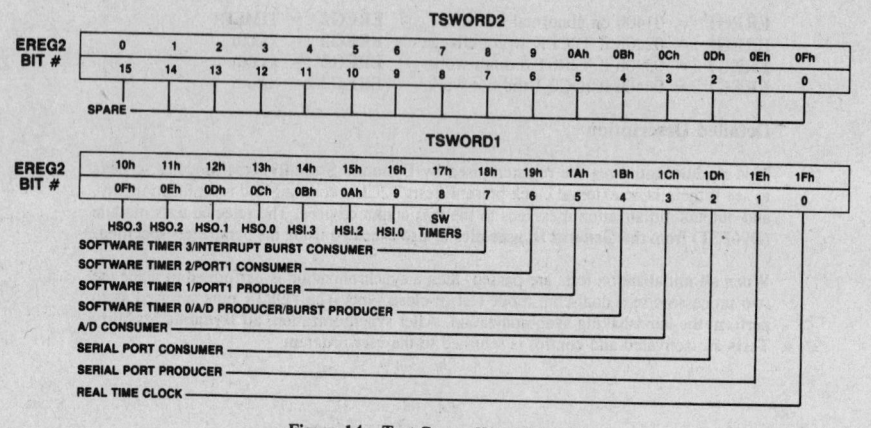

Figure 14. Test Status Word Bit Map

MCS®-96

Serial Port (DSTSER)

Brief Description:

This module contains the Serial Port Consumer and Producer routines for the **Dynamic Stability Tests.** It is executed on every Serial Interrupt.

If Test Fails:

EREG1 := 01B0h if a bad character was received
EREG2 := actual received character

EREG1 := 02B0h if an incorrect number of characters came between carriage returns
EREG2 := actual count

Detailed Description:

This interrupt service routine executes every time there is a Serial Interrupt. The data that is transmitted and checked by the test consists of first, the alphabet and some special characters; second, the current REAL TIME; and finally, the bit representation of the Test Status Words. The receiver verifies the alphabet and funny characters and counts characters until a carriage return. The following is an example of what the output looks like.

ABCDEFGHIJKLMNOPQRSTUVWXYZ*#%&[]@001:23:59.61 111111011101111110001111

The code first checks for a Receive Done flag. If a receive just completed, the receive buffer is emptied and checked for validity. If the received character is a carriage return, then the count since the last carriage return is checked for correctness.

After the receive service has finished, or if there was no receive, DSTSER then checks for the Transmit Done flag. If more transmits can be made, the next data byte is loaded into the transmit buffer. If the data is exhausted, a carriage return is sent, and the routine is set to transmit the first data byte again.

MCS®-96

Software Timers (DSTSWT)

Brief Description:

This module is executed every time a Software Timer Interrupt expires. The routine includes the Port1 Producer and Consumer, the A/D producer, and the Interrupt Burst control and verification code.

If a Test Fails:

EREG1 := 01D0h If an unexpected value is found on Port 1
EREG2 := expected value in high byte, actual value in low byte
EREG1 := 02D0h A/D Done interrupt did not occur within BURST window
EREG2 := Time between A/D done and Software Timer 0
EREG1 := 03D0H REAL TIME update did not occur within BURST window
EREG2 := Time between REAL TIME update and Software Timer 0
EREG1 := 04D0H HSO.0 response did not occur within BURST window
EREG2 := Time between HSO.0 interrupt and Software Timer 0
EREG1 := 05D0H HSI(.0) response did not occur within BURST window
EREG2 := Time between HSI(.0) service and Software Timer 0
EREG1 := 01D1H Invalid T2CLK value reached
EREG2 := T2CLK found
EREG1 := 02D1H Test reached an illegal Software Timer 0 state
EREG2 := the illegal case jump that was made

Detailed Description:

This module is called every time a Software Timer expires and causes and interrupt. Software timers are used by the A/D Done — A/D Trigger Sequence, the Interrupt Burst Sequence, and the Port1 Producer and Port1 Consumer.

When Software Timer 0 expires, a case jump is done on the BURST_STATE variable to sequence the A/D and interrupt BURST process to the appropriate state. Depending upon the value of T2CLK and the state of the A/D converter, either an A/D conversion is initiated or HSO.0 is set to go low to begin the interrupt BURST events.

When Software Timer1 expires, a new value is written to Port1 from a table constructed to test all combinations of input/output states on the quasi-bidirectional port pins. The HSO CAM is also loaded with a command to cause Software Timer1 to overflow again in 5000h TIMER1 counts.

When Software Timer 2 expires, Port1 is read and compared to a table of expected entries. If the value is correct, then an HSO command is loaded into the CAM to cause another Software Timer 2 expiration in 1000h TIMER1 counts. If the value is not correct, the next entry in the Table is checked. If there is still no match, an error is reported. If there is a match, the CAM loading occurs and Software Timer 3 is checked for expiration.

If Software Timer 3 has expired, then the flurry of BURST interrupts should have just occurred. The routine checks to see that each event happened within a reasonable time window. If the checks pass, then the routine exists with no further action.

Real Time Clock (HSI0) (DSTHI0)

Brief Description:

This routine executes every time there is a rising edge on HSI.0 and updates the real time clock value.

When Module Executes:

REAL_TIME := REAL_TIME + .204 seconds

Detailed Description:

This module is the HSI.0 interrupt service routine. On each rising edge of HSI.0, the value in the REAL TIME clock buffer is updated to reflect the passing of 1900h T2CLK counts. Since the PWM output is tied to T2CLK, and the average time between edges is 31.875 μs in a 12 MHz system, then 1900h T2CLK counts represents .204 seconds.

Execution of this module occurs during the interrupt BURST events. No action other than updating the REAL TIME clock is taken in this routine.

High Speed Outputs (DSTHSO)

Brief Description:

This module manages the pulse width outputs on HSO.2 and HSO.3, and causes the Manager test to execute.

Detailed Description:

Every time an HSO command is executed that has the Interrupt bit set, this program executes. The routine manages the pulse widths on HSO lines two and three, and causes the Manager module to execute at the right time.

When a falling edge has been caused on either HSO.2 or HSO.3, DSTHSO loads a command into the CAM to cause a rising edge on the same line at a time that gives the line a low pulse width equal to a predetermined table value. Rising edges cause analogous responses. The tables used cause low and high pulse widths that vary from 1000h and 0C000h. The length of the tables differ by one so that all combinations of low and high table times occur.

When a falling edge was caused on HSO.1, the routine loads a command into the CAM to cause a rising edge on the same line two TIMER1 counts later. Since HSO.1 is tied to the EXTINT pin, rising edges cause the Manager Routine to execute.

MCS®-96

High Speed Inputs (DSTHSI)

Brief Description:

This module does the verification of events on the HSI lines and initiates some interrupt BURST events when appropriate.

If a Test Fails:

EREG1 := 0161h if a high pulse on HSI.2 had an unexpected width
EREG2 := difference between actual and expected pulse width

EREG1 := 0261h if a low pulse on HSI.2 had an unexpected width
EREG2 := difference between actual and expected pulse width

EREG1 := 0361h if a high pulse on HSI.3 had an unexpected width
EREG2 := difference between actual and expected pulse width

EREG1 := 0461h if a low pulse on HSI.3 had an unexpected width
EREG2 := difference between actual and expected pulse width

EREG1 := 0561h if the HSI unit indicated that an HSI.1 event occurred
EREG2 := the time recorded in the FIFO

Detailed Description:

This module executes every time an event is loaded into the HSI Holding Register. Verification of pulse widths on HSI.2 and HSI.3 is done from tables of expected values. Any deviation is reported as an error.

If the test detects a negative transition on HSI.0, then commands are loaded into the HSO CAM to start an A/D at T2CLK = 18ffh and to set HSO.0 high at T2CLK = 1900h. This results in an HSO, HSI, HSI.0 and A/D Done interrupt requests to occur at approximately the same time — approaching a full demand on interrupt service.

When a rising edge on HSI.0 is detected, an HSO command is loaded into the CAM to cause a Software Timer 3 interrupt when T2CLK = 100h. The Software Timer 3 interrupt service will check to see that all burst events happened fast enough.

HSI.1 events are disabled from the FIFO. Any event detected on this line is reported as an error.

A/D Conversion Complete (DSTA2D)

Brief Description:

This module executes every time an A/D conversion is complete. The conversion result is checked for correctness, the A/D converter is setup to convert on the next channel when initiated by an HSO command, and an HSO command to cause a Software Timer 0 expiration is loaded.

If Test Fails:

EREG1 := 01C0h on a conversion error
EREG2 := channel on which error occurred

Detailed Description:

This module executes every time an A/D conversion is complete. The conversion result is checked against a test table for correctness, and the A/D converter is setup to convert on the next channel when initiated by an HSO command. An HSO command to cause a Software Timer 0 expiration in 0002h TIMER1 counts is loaded just prior to exiting the module.

While T2CLK has a value between 100h and 600h, A/D conversions are initiated by the Software Timer 0 Interrupt service routine. When T2CLK goes above 600h, an A/D conversion is initiated by the HSO.0 interrupt service routine.

Given the possibility of additive error in 5% resistors, the conversion is tested to only six bits of accuracy.

Timer Overflows (DSTTOV)

Brief Description:

This module toggles a port pin tied to an LED, manages the PWM output, performs some simple tests, and is expandable to allow inclusion of user written tests.

If Test Fails:

EREG1 := 0190h if T2CLK had an overflow indication
EREG2 := T2CLK a the time the error was found

Detailed Description:

This module executes every time TIMER1 or T2CLK overflow. Only TIMER1 overflows are valid however, so T2CLK overflows are flagged as an error. Each overflow, a new period is loaded into the PWMCONTROL register from a table of pulse periods. If an LED is connected, it will appear to slowly change in intensity. Port2.7 is also toggled in this routine to light another LED.

This interrupt routine can be expanded with special tests that are to execute on a periodic basis. Any of the spare bits in the Test Status Words can also be used by specialized tests. They will be checked by the External Interrupt service routine with a simple change in a bit mask.

MCS®-96

Macro Module (DSTMAC)

Brief Description:

This module contains four macros used by the **Dynamic Stability Test**.

Assembly Language Invocation:

```
SPSTATUS         Temp_Register
   or
SPWAIT           (RI,TI)
   or
BR_ON_ERROR      Label
   or
RESET_WATCHDOG
```

Detailed Description:

The SPSTATUS Macro is used to ORB the Serial Port Status Register to a temp register. The Macro needs to be used to work around a bug in the 809x-90.

The SPWAIT Macro is used to cause program execution to halt and wait for an RI or TI flag, depending upon which is specified.

The BR_ON_ERROR Macro tests the high byte of EREG1 and jumps to the label if the byte is not zero. This can be used every time a **General Diagnostic** completes since the detection of any error will cause the high byte of EREG1 to be non-zero.

The RESET_WATCHDOG Macro does just what it says. The WATCHDOG TIMER is reset by writing the correct sequence to location 0Ah.

To access a DSTMAC macro, this module must be $INCLUDEd.

Error Procedure (DSTERR)

Brief Description:

This module is called if any error is detected in the **Dynamic Stability Test.** Information about the error is output over the serial port, and the test is restarted.

Assembly Language Calling Sequence:

     CALL   Error_Proc

Detailed Description:

This module is CALLed on detection of any error in the **Dynamic Stability Test.** When CALLed, the procedure:

- disables interrupts,
- saves any rapidly changing values (TIMER1,T2CLK,HSO_STATUS, . . .),
- waits for a serial transmit in progress to complete,
- waits for the current serial receive to complete,
- empties eight entries from the HSI_FIFO,
- transmits an open loop sync sequence in case a co-controller is stuck in the sync routine, and
- waits a few hundred milliseconds to ensure that a co-controller has also detected a failure.

After these steps have been taken, the DSTERR de-selects the 4800 baud line, selects the 300 baud line, and outputs error messages. These messages include the Error Code (EREG1), the Detail Code (EREG2), the address of the line in the test which found the error, and the REAL TIME since reset.

Following the error messages, the procedure dumps the data contained in the registers and the external error buffer out over the serial port to the 300 baud device.

Finally, a RST instruction followed by a branch to the RST instruction is executed. If the WATCHDOG TIMER is externally disabled, the test will stay in this loop. If the WATCHDOG TIMER is not disabled, the test chip will reset, and the **Dynamic Stability Test** will reinitialize.

DST Example User Code (DSTUSR)

Brief Description:

This is an example program that initiates the **Dynamic Stability Test** and then executes some **General Diagnostics** as a background task.

Detailed Description:

DSTUSR sends parameters defined at assembly time to the DST initialization routine (DSTISR). When control returns to DSTUSR, the example repeatedly executes ALU01, ALU02, ALU04, ALU05 and MEM0A. It takes two minutes (with the given memory parameters) for the DSTUSR background task to cycle once while interrupts are running.

When creating a custom background task, using this example program as a template will speed development.

MCS®-96

APPENDICES

APPENDIX A • DIAG96.LIB Error Messages by EREG1 Code

APPENDIX B • DIAG96.LIB Error Messages by Module Name

APPENDIX C • Description of DIAG96.LIB Batch Files

APPENDIX D • Example Program Listings
— D96A96
— D96P96
— D96FST
— DSTUSR

APPENDIX A
DIAG96.LIB Error Messages by EREG1 Code

0000   No Message
        EREG2 = 0ffffh
        MODULE = SYS01/Common Symbols

0002   All Tests Passed
        EREG2 = 0000
        MODULE = SYS02/System Power-up

0003   All Tests Passed
        EREG2 = 0000
        MODULE = SYS03/Program Counter

0011   All Tests Passed
        EREG2 = 0000
        MODULE = ALU01/Add/Subtract

0012   All Tests Passed
        EREG2 = 0000
        MODULE = ALU02/MULUB

0013   All Tests Passed
        EREG2 = 0000
        MODULE = ALU03/Multiply/Divide Table

0014   All Tests Passed
        EREG2 = 0000
        MODULE = ALU04/Multiply/Divide Random

0015   All Tests Passed
        EREG2 = 0000
        MODULE = ALU05/Multiply/Divide Core

0021   All Tests Passed
        EREG2 = 0000
        MODULE = MEM01/Complementary Address (Registers)

0022   All Tests Passed
        EREG2 = 0000
        MODULE = MEM02/Walking Ones/Zeros (Registers)

0023   All Tests Passed
        EREG2 = 0000
        MODULE = MEM03/Galloping Ones/Zeros (Registers)

0024   No bits were set in the byte tested
        EREG2 = 0000
        MODULE = MEM04/Bits Set

0025   All Tests Passed
        EREG2 = 0000
        MODULE = MEM05/Checkerboard Pattern (Registers)

0026   All Tests Passed
        EREG2 = 0000
        MODULE = MEM06/Complementary Address

MCS®-96

0027   All Tests Passed
EREG2 = 0000
MODULE = MEM07/Walking Ones

0028   All Tests Passed
EREG2 = 0000
MODULE = MEM08/Galloping Ones

0029   All Tests Passed
EREG2 = 0000
MODULE = MEM09/Walking Ones/Zeros

002A   All Tests Passed
EREG2 = 0000
MODULE = MEM0A/Galloping Ones/Zeros

002C   All Tests Passed
EREG2 = 0000
MODULE = MEM0C/User Pattern (Registers)

002D   All Tests Passed
EREG2 = 0000
MODULE = MEM0D/User Pattern

0030   All Tests Passed, checksum is ready
EREG2 = 16-bit checksum
MODULE = D96A96/ALL Tests in ASM96

0040   Initialization completed satisfactorily
EREG2 = 0000
MODULE = DSTISR/DST Initialization

00E0   All Tests Passed, checksum is over range specified
EREG = 16-bit checksum
MODULE = D96FST/Selected Tests in ASM

00F0   All Tests Passed, checksum is ready
EREG2 = 16-bit checksum
MODULE = D96P96/ALL Tests in PLM96

0102   I/O Status Registers were unexpected
EREG2 = I0S0 in low byte, I0S1 in high byte
MODULE = SYS02/System Power-up

0103   Test Code Returned Early
EREG2 = Early Time
MODULE = SYS03/Program Counter

0111   An Addition error occurred
EREG2 = offending argument when the error occurred
MODULE = ALU01/Add/Subtract

0112   Incorrect multiplication result was detected
EREG2 = Multiplier/Multiplicand
MODULE = ALU02/MULUB

0115   A signed operation failed
EREG2 = offending argument on error
MODULE = ALU03/Multiply/Divide Table

MCS®-96

0115	A signed operation failed EREG2 = offending argument on error MODULE = ALU04/Multiply/Divide Random
0115	A signed operation failed EREG2 = offending argument on error MODULE = ALU05/Multiply/Divide Core
0121	A memory location failed EREG2 = address of the error MODULE = MEM01/Complementary Address (Registers)
0122	A memory location failed EREG2 = address of the error MODULE = MEM02/Walking Ones/Zeros (Registers)
0123	A memory location failed EREG2 = address of the error MODULE = MEM03/Galloping Ones/Zeros (Registers)
0124	At least one bit was set in the byte tested EREG2 = number of bits set MODULE = MEM04/Bits Set
0125	A memory location failed EREG2 = address of the error MODULE = MEM05/Checkerboard Pattern (Registers)
0126	A memory location failed EREG2 = address of error MODULE = MEM06/Complementary Address
0127	A memory location failed EREG2 = address of the error MODULE = MEM07/Walking Ones
0128	A memory location failed EREG2 = address of the error MODULE = MEM08/Galloping Ones
0129	A memory location failed EREG2 = address of the error MODULE = MEM09/Walking Ones/Zero
012A	A memory location failed EREG2 = address of the error MODULE = MEM0A/Galloping Ones/Zeros
012B	16-bit Checksum is ready EREG2 = 16-bit Checksum MODULE = MEM0B/Checksum
012C	A memory location failed EREG2 = address of the error MODULE = MEM0C/User Pattern (Registers)
012D	A memory location failed EREG2 = address of the error MODULE = MEM0D/User Pattern

MCS®-96

0140	An abnormal RESET occurred EREG2 = TIMER1 MODULE = DSTISR/DST Initialization
0161	A high pulse on HSI.2 had an unexpected width EREG2 = difference between actual and expected pulse width MODULE = DSTHSI/High Speed Inputs
0190	An overflow of T2CLK was indicated EREG2 = TIMER1 MODULE = DSTTOV/Timer Overflows
01A0	One or more DST Module did not execute on time EREG2 = Number of SHIFTs done MODULE = DSTEXI/External Interrupt (Supervisor)
01B0	An unexpected serial character was received EREG2 = Bad character received MODULE = DSTSER/Serial Port
01C0	An unexpected A/D conversion result was found EREG2 = Channel number of unexpected result MODULE = DSTA2D/A/D Conversion Complete
01D0	Found unexpected value on PORT1 EREG2 = expected value in high byte, actual in low byte MODULE = DSTSWT/Software Timers
01D1	Invalid T2CLK value reached EREG2 = T2CLK MODULE = DSTSWT/Software Timers
0202	TIMER1 did not change over time EREG2 = TIMER1 MODULE = SYS02/System Power-up
0203	Test Code Returned Late EREG2 = Late Time MODULE = SYS03/Program Counter
0211	A Subtraction error occurred EREG2 = offending argument when the error occurred MODULE = ALU01/Add/Subtract
0215	An unsigned operation failed EREG2 = offending argument on error MODULE = ALU03/Multiply/Divide Table
0215	An unsigned operation failed EREG2 = offending argument on error MODULE = ALU04/Multiply/Divide Random
0215	An unsigned operation failed EREG2 = offending argument on error MODULE = ALU05/Multiply/Divide Core
0240	T2CLK will not change EREG2 = xxxx MODULE = DSTISR/DST Initialization

MCS®-96

0261	A low pulse on HSI.2 had an unexpected width EREG2 = difference between actual and expected pulse width MODULE = DSTHSI/High Speed Inputs
02B0	A carriage return was received out of sequence EREG2 = number of characters since a carriage return MODULE = DSTSER/Serial Port
02D0	A/D Done did not occur within BURST window EREG2 = Time between A/D done and Software Timer 0 MODULE = DSTSWT/Software Timers
02D1	Test reached an illegal Software Timer 0 state EREG2 = Illegal case jump made MODULE = DSTSWT/Software Timers
0302	Zero Register was found to change EREG2 = Program Status Word At Failure MODULE = SYS02/System Power-up
0303	Counter Register contained unexpected value EREG2 = Erroneous Counter Value MODULE = SYS03/Program Counter
0311	A flag error occurred EREG2 = offending argument when the error occurred MODULE = ALU01/Add/Subtract
0315	A flag error occurred EREG2 = offending argument on error MODULE = ALU03/Multiply/Divide Table
0315	A flag error occurred EREG2 = offending argument on error MODULE = ALU04/Multiply/Divide Random
0315	A flag error occurred EREG2 = offending argument on error MODULE = ALU05/Multiply/Divide Core
0340	T2RST pin would not RESET T2CLK EREG2 = xxxx MODULE = DSTISR/DST Initialization
0361	A high pulse on HSI.3 had an unexpected width EREG2 = difference between actual and expected pulse width MODULE = DSTHSI/High Speed Inputs
0391	Illegal Opcode
03D0	REAL TIME update did not occur within BURST window EREG2 = Time between REAL TIME update and Software Timer 0 MODULE = DSTSWT/Software Timers
0402	PUSHF or POPF failed EREG2 = Erroneous PUSHed or POPed value found MODULE = SYS02/System Power-up

MCS®-96

0440   IOC0.1 would not RESET T2CLK
EREG2 = xxxx
MODULE = DSTISR/DST Initialization

0461   A low pulse on HSI.3 had an unexpected width
EREG2 = difference between actual and expected pulse width
MODULE = DSTHSI/High Speed Inputs

04D0   HSO.0 response did not occur within BURST window
EREG2 = Time between HSO.0 update and Software Timer 0
MODULE = DSTSWT/Software Timers

0502   Sticky Bit would not set
EREG2 = 3fffh
MODULE = SYS02/System Power-up

0502   Sticky Bit would not clear
EREG2 = 0000
MODULE = SYS02/System Power-up

0561   HSI unit indicated an HSI.1 event occurred
EREG2 = Time recorded in HSI FIFO
MODULE = DSTHSI/High Speed Inputs

05D0   HSI(.0) response did not occur within BURST window
EREG2 = Time between HSI(.0) service and Software Timer 0
MODULE = DSTSWT/Software Timers

0602   Carry Flag Test Failed
EREG2 = xxxx
MODULE = SYS02/System Power-up

0702   Overflow flags would not set correctly
EREG2 = 0002h
MODULE = SYS02/System Power-up

0702   Overflow flags would not clear correctly
EREG2 = xxxx
MODULE = SYS02/System Power-up

0802   Interrupt Pending Register failed read/write test
EREG2 = offending Interrupt Pending byte
MODULE = SYS02/System Power-up

xx91   (user defined)
EREG2 = (user defined)
MODULE = DSTTOV/Timer Overflows

MCS®-96

APPENDIX B
DIAG96.LIB Error Messages by Module Name

ALU01   Add/Subtract
           0011 All Tests Passed
              EREG2 = 0000

           0111 An Addition error occurred
              EREG2 = offending argument when the error occurred

           0211 A Subtraction error occurred
              EREG2 = offending argument when the error occurred

           0311 A flag error occurred
              EREG2 = offending argument when the error occurred

ALU02   MULUB
           0012 All Tests Passed
              EREG2 = 0000

           0112 Incorrect multiplication result was detected
              EREG2 = Multiplier/Multiplicand

ALU03   Multiply/Divide Table
           0013 All Tests Passed
              EREG2 = 0000

           0115 A signed operation failed
              EREG2 = offending argument on error

           0215 An unsigned operation failed
              EREG2 = offending argument on error

           0315 A flag error occurred
              EREG2 = offending argument on error

ALU04   Multiply/Divide Random
           0014 All Tests Passed
              EREG2 = 0000

           0115 A signed operation failed
              EREG2 = offending argument on error

           0215 An unsigned operation failed
              EREG2 = offending argument on error

           0315 A flag error occurred
              EREG2 = offending argument on error

ALU05   Multiply/Divide Core
           0015 All Tests Passed
              EREG2 = 0000

           0115 A signed operation failed
              EREG2 = offending argument on error

           0215 An unsigned operation failed
              EREG2 = offending argument on error

           0315 A flag error occurred
              EREG2 = offending argument on error

MCS®-96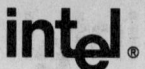

D96A96   All Tests in ASM96
        0030 All Tests Passed, checksum is ready
        EREG2 = 16-bit checksum

D96FST   Selected Tests in ASM
        00E0 All Tests Passed, checksum is over range specified
        EREG2 = 16-bit checksum

D96P96   ALL Tests in PLM96
        00F0 All Tests Passed, checksum is ready
        EREG2 = 16-bit checksum

DSTA2D   A/D Conversion Complete
        01C0 An unexpected A/D conversion result was found
        EREG2 = Channel number of unexpected result

DSTEX1   External Interrupt (Supervisor)
        01A0 One or more DST Module did not execute on time
        EREG2 = Number of SHIFTs done

DSTHSI   High Speed Inputs
        0161 A high pulse on HSI.2 had an unexpected width
        EREG2 = difference between actual and expected pulse width

        0261 A low pulse on HSI.2 had an unexpected width
        EREG2 = difference between actual and expected pulse width

        0361 A high pulse on HSI.3 had an unexpected width
        EREG2 = difference between actual and expected pulse width

        0461 A low pulse on HSI.3 had an unexpected width
        EREG2 = difference between actual and expected pulse width

        0561 HSI unit indicated an HSI.1 event occurred
        EREG2 = Time recorded in HSI FIFO

DSTISR   DST Initialization
        0040 Initialization completed satisfactorily
        EREG2 = 0000

        0140 An abnormal RESET occurred
        EREG2 = TIMER1

        0240 T2CLK will not change
        EREG2 = xxxx

        0340 T2RST pin would not RESET T2CLK
        EREG2 = xxxx

        0440 IOC0.1 would not RESET T2CLK
        EREG2 = xxxx

DSTSER   Serial Port
        01B0 An unexpected serial character was received
        EREG2 = Bad character received

        02B0 A carriage return was received out of sequence
        EREG2 = number of characters since a carriage return

MCS®-96

DSTSWT Software Timers
            01D0 Found unexpected value on PORT1
                EREG2 = expected value in high byte, actual in low byte

            01D1 Invalid T2CLK value reached
                EREG2 = T2CLK

            02D0 A/D Done did not occur within BURST window
                EREG2 = Time between A/D done and Software Timer 0

            02D1 Test reached an illegal Software Timer 0 state
                EREG2 = Illegal case jump made

            03D0 REAL TIME update did not occur within BURST window
                EREG2 = Time between REAL TIME update and Software Timer 0

            04D0 HSO.0 response did not occur within BURST window
                EREG2 = Time between HSO.0 update and Software Timer 0

            05D0 HSI(.0) response did not occur within BURST window
                EREG2 = Time between HSI(.0) service and Software Timer 0

DSTTOV Timer Overflows
            0190 An overflow of T2CLK was indicated
                EREG2 = TIMER1

            xx91 (user defined)
                EREG2 = (user defined)

MEM01   Complementary Address (Registers)
            0021 All Tests Passed
                EREG2 = 0000

            0121 A memory location failed
                EREG2 = address of the error

MEM02   Walking Ones/Zeros (Registers)
            0022 All Tests Passed
                EREG2 = 0000

            0122 A memory location failed
                EREG2 = address of the error

MEM03   Galloping Ones/Zeros (Registers)
            0023 All Tests Passed
                EREG2 = 0000

            0123 A memory location failed
                EREG2 = address of the error

MEM04   Bits Set
            0024 No bits were set in the byte tested
                EREG2 = 0000

            0124 At least one bit was set in the byte tested
                EREG2 = number of bits set

MEM05	Checkerboard Pattern (Registers)	
	0025 All Tests Passed	
	EREG2 = 0000	
	0125 A memory location failed	
	EREG2 = address of the error	
MEM06	Complementary Address	
	0026 All Tests Passed	
	EREG2 = 0000	
	0126 A memory location failed	
	EREG2 = address of error	
MEM07	Walking Ones	
	0027 All Tests Passed	
	EREG2 = 0000	
	0127 A memory location failed	
	EREG2 = address of the error	
MEM08	Galloping Ones	
	0028 All Tests Passed	
	EREG2 = 0000	
	0128 A memory location failed	
	EREG2 = address of the error	
MEM09	Walking Ones/Zeros	
	0029 All Tests Passed	
	EREG2 = 0000	
	0129 A memory location failed	
	EREG2 = address of the error	
MEM0A	Galloping Ones/Zeros	
	002A All Tests Passed	
	EREG2 = 0000	
	012A A memory location failed	
	EREG2 = address of the error	
MEM0B	Checksum	
	012B 16-bit Checksum is ready	
	EREG2 = 16-bit Checksum	
MEM0C	User Pattern (Registers)	
	002C All Tests Passed	
	EREG2 = 0000	
	012C A memory location failed	
	EREG2 = address of the error	
MEM0D	User Pattern	
	002D All Tests Passed	
	EREG2 = 0000	
	012D A memory location failed	
	EREG2 = address of the error	

SYS01   Common Symbols
         0000 No Message
              EREG2 = 0fffh

SYS02   System Power-up
         0002 All Tests Passed
              EREG2 = 0000h

         0102 I/O Status Registers were unexpected
              EREG2 = IOS0 in low byte, IOS1 in high byte

         0202 TIMER1 did not change over time
              EREG2 = TIMER1

         0302 Zero Register was found to change
              EREG2 = Program Status Word At Failure

         0402 PUSHF or POPF failed
              EREG2 = Erroneous PUSHed or POPed value found

         0502 Sticky Bit would not set
              EREG2 = 3fffh

         0502 Sticky Bit would not clear
              EREG2 = 0000

         0602 Carry Flag Test Failed
              EREG2 = xxxx

         0702 Overflow flags would not set correctly
              EREG2 = 0002h

         0702 Overflow flags would not clear correctly
              EREG2 = xxxx

         0802 Interrupt Pending Register failed read/write test
              EREG2 = offending Interrupt Pending byte

SYS03   Program Counter
         0003 All Tests Passed
              EREG2 = 0000

         0103 Test Code Returned Early
              EREG2 = Early Time

         0203 Test Code Returned Late
              EREG2 = Late Time

         0303 Counter Register contained unexpected value
              EREG2 = Erroneous Counter Value

MCS®-96

APPENDIX C
DESCRIPTION OF DIAG96.LIB BATCH FILES

The batch files that come with the library will help speed the process of either linking to the library as is, or revising library programs to suit custom purposes.

Some batch files require a parameter that provides the extensionless name of a user definable variable file to be included in the action of the batch file.

All DIAG96.LIB batch files assume that both the source and destination files reside in the same directory. Given the size of the library, and the fact that all of the files will not fit on one floppy disk, the command files will need to be edited if the user's system is not equipped with a hard disk.

INSTAL.BAT — Used to install the library on a hard disk system. To install the library, create a directory called \ DIAG96 under the main directory, insert disk 1 into drive a: and type:

a:Instal

DST360K.BAT & DST12MEG.BAT — CAUTION: THEE BATCH FILES WILL FORMAT AND DESTROY ALL INFORMATION ON THE FLOPPIES USED. These command files were created to make the DIAG96.LIB disk set. DST360K was created for use with 360K floppy disks and requires three diskettes. DST12MEG was created for use with 1.2M disks and only needs two diskettes. The batch files will prompt you to change disks. MAKE SURE TO ENTER THE CORRECT DISK DRIVE WHEN INVOKING THESE BATCH FILES. ALSO MAKE SURE TO INCLUDE THE DRIVE ID IN THE COMMAND LINE. THESE BATCH FILES FIRST FORMAT THE DISK, AND WE ALL KNOW WHAT WHEN DOS DEFAULTS TO THE HARD DISK!!!!!!!!!!
For example:

DST12MEG a:

SCRUB.BAT — CAUTION: THIS FILE DELETES FILES USING WILDCARDS. All Diagnostic Library related files are delected for the \ DIAG96 directory. SYS?? and MEM?? wildcards are used, so be forewarned. This batch file does not delete itself!!!! To invoke this batch file, type:

Scrub

D96ASM.BAT — Assembles all **General Diagnostic** modules including the PLM compilation of D96P96.P96. To invoke the batch file, get in the \ DIAG96 directory and type:

D96ASM

DSTASM.BAT — Assembles all **Dynamic Stability Test** modules. To invoke the batch file, get in \ DIAG96 directory and type:

DSTASM

D96LP.BAT — Copies all **General Diagnostic list** files to a printer. Invocation must include a device where the printer resides. For example:

D96LP lpt1

DSTLP.BAT — Copies all **Dynamic Stability Test** modules to a printer. Invocation must include a device where the printer resides. For example:

DSTLP.BAT lpt1

LPONLY.BAT — Executes D96LP.BAT and DSTLP.BAT. Invocation must include a device where the printer resides. For example:

LPONLY lpt1

D96LIB.BAT — Deletes the current DIAG96.LIB collection. Also creates a new library of the same name using the files resident in the \DIAG96 directory bearing the **General Diagnostics** names. The DST96.LIB is not altered, and is included in the new DIAG96.LIB. To invoke the batch file, get in the \DIAG96 directory and type:

D96LIB

DSTLIB.BAT — Deletes the current DST96.LIB collection. Also creates a new library of the same name using the files resident in the \DIAG96 directory bearing the **Dynamic Stability Test** names. Since DST96.LIB is included in DIAG96.LIB, DIAG96.LIB is recreated by an invocation of D96LIB.BAT. To invoke this batch file, get in the \DIAG96 directory and type:

DSTLIB

DSTRL.BAT — This batch file is of most interest to **Dynamic Stability Test** users. It links a specified main task to the library. This file makes assumptions about the hardware memory implementation that may not be correct. Therefore minor changes may need to be made to the DSTRL.BAT RL96 invocation statement. A file name without extension must be provided and that file must reside in the \DIAG96 directory. The batch file assumes that the extension of the object file to be linked to the library is .OBJ. For example:

DSTRL Example_task

BLASTP.BAT — This batch file assembles the specified input file, then executes D96ASM.BAT, DSTASM.BAT, LPONLY.BAT, DSTLIB.BAT, and DSTRL.BAT. Then, the listfile output of the user's assembly and the print file of the linkage are copied to the printer specified. The batch file assumes that the input file is in the \DIAG96 directory and has a .A96 extension. For example:

BLASTP Example_ lpt1

BLASTN.BAT — This batch file executes all assemblies, compliations, and linkages executed in BLASTP.BAT, but no copies are sent to the printer. The batch file assumes that the input file is in the \DIAG96 directory and has a .A96 extension. For example:

BLASTN Example_task

REGEN.BAT — Used to regenerate the library when only one module has changed. Specify the module that has changed when invoking this batch file. For example:

REGEN ALU03

MAKPLM.BAT — Used to make an impostor PLM96.LIB. The library created in not a real PLM96.LIB, and will not work with PLM programs. However, it is what is needed to use DIAG96.LIB. To invoke this batch file, get in the \DIAG96 director and type:

MAKPLM

MAKBH.BAT — Used to modify the library to run in an 8X9XBH. The 8X9XBH fails a flag test because of the −90 bug relating to the Z flag on add and subtract with carry is inadvertanly verified by a library test. To invoke this batch file, get in the \DIAG96 directory and type:

MAKBH

D96RL.BAT — A generalized command that links target modules to DIAG96.LIB. It is intended for used when only the **General Diagnostics** are being used. Provide the target object file name and the directory in which it resides. For example:

D96RL \SOURCE\ Example_

MCS®-96

APPENDIX D

Example Program Listings — D96A96

```
SERIES-III MCS-96 MACRO ASSEMBLER, V1.0

SOURCE FILE:  :F5:D96A96.A96
OBJECT FILE:  :F5:D96A96.OBJ
CONTROLS SPECIFIED IN INVOCATION COMMAND: NOGEN DEBUG

ERR LOC  OBJECT            LINE    SOURCE STATEMENT
                            1    ;*************************************************************
                            2    ALL TESTS ASM96.   MODULE STACKSIZE(20)                       0030
                            3    ;*************************************************************
                            4    ;
                            5    ; in order to run this module, the STACK must be ALL external, and the
                            6    ; data ram partitioned for memory test must not include ANY of the STACK
                            7    ;
                            8    ; To call this module
                            9    ;
                           10           PUSH    #<RAM segment1 start address>
                           11           PUSH    #<RAM segment1 ending address>
                           12           PUSH    #<RAM segment2 start address>
                           13           PUSH    #<RAM segment2 ending address>
                           14           PUSH    #<random seed>
                           15           PUSH    #<number of cycles desired for random test>
                           16           PUSH    #<address of the last byte of rom>
                           17           PUSH    #<an argument for mul/div tests>
                           18           PUSH    #<a second argument for mul/div tests>
                           19           PUSH    #<a bit pattern for memory tests>
                           20           CALL    D96A96
                           21    ;
                           22    ; Remember, this test will take a long time if large memory regions are
                           23    ; partitioned, or if a large number of cycles of random test numbers is
                           24    ; requested. For example, with 8Kbytes of Ram in each region the test
                           25    ; executes in 3 hours.
                           26    ;
                           27    ; It is suggested that for large memory tests, that the complimentary
                           28    ; address test be done on the whole region at once. Then, the more
                           29    ; exhaustive tests done on each memory chip in the system.
                           30    ;*************************************************************
                           31                  rseg
                           32
0000                       33           extrn sp,ereq1,ereq2
                           34
                           35                  cseg at 3000h
3000                       36           extrn sys01,sys02,sys03,alu01,alu02,alu03,alu04,alu05
                           37           extrn mem01,mem02,mem03,mem04,mem05,mem06,mem07,mem08
                           38           extrn mem09,mem0a,mem0b,mem0c,mem0d
                           39
                           40           PUBLIC D96A96
                           41           $eject
                           42
                           43    $include (:f3:dstmac.inc)
                           44    ;DST Macros       INCLUDE FILE ;******************************
                           45    ;*************************************************************
                  =1       46    ;                                  ;provides the macro BR ON Error
                  =1       47
                  =1       48
                  =1       49
```

ERR	LOC	OBJECT	LINE	SOURCE STATEMENT			
	0000		104				
			105				
			106	D96A96:			
			107				
	0000	EF0000	108		CALL	sys02	;CALL the System Power Up Test
E			109		BR_ON_ERR	Error_Found	
			110				
	000A	EF0000	114		CALL	alu01	;CALL the Add/Subtract test
E			115		BR_ON_ERR	Error_Found	
			116				
	0014	EF0000	117		CALL	alu02	;CALL the MULUB test
E			121		BR_ON_ERR	Error_Found	
			122				
	001E	EF0000	123		CALL	alu03	;CALL the Multiply/Divide Table
E			124		BR_ON_ERR	Error_Found	;driven test
			128				
			129				
			130				
	0028	CB000C	131		PUSH	0ch[sp]	;PUSH a random seed
E			135				
	002B	CB000C	136		PUSH	0ch[sp]	;PUSH the number of tests desired
	002E	EF0000	137		CALL	alu04	;CALL the Multiply/Divide RanCom test
E			138		BR_ON_ERR	Error_Found	
			139				
	0038	CB0006	140		PUSH	06h[sp]	;PUSH an argument
	003B	CB0006	144		PUSH	06h[sp]	;PUSH another argument
	003E	EF0000	145		CALL	alu05	;CALL the Multiply/Divide Core Test
E			146		BR_ON_ERR	Error_Found	
			147				
			148				
	0048	EF0000	149		CALL	mem01	;CALL a Complementary Address test
E			153		BR_ON_ERR	Error_Found	;on the internal registers
			154				
			155				
	0052	EF0000	156		CALL	mem02	;CALL a Walking 1s/0s test on
E			160		BR_ON_ERR	Error_Found	;the internal registers
			161				
			162				
	005C	EF0000	163		CALL	mem03	;CALL a Galloping 1s/0s test on
E			167		BR_ON_ERR	Error_Found	;the internal registers
			168				
			169				
	0066	CB00	170		PUSH	zero	;PUSH a zero
	0068	EF0000	174		CALL	mem04	;CALL the Bits Set Test
E			175		BR_ON_ERR	Error_Found	
			176				
			177				
	0072	EF0000	178		CALL	mem05	;CALL a Checkerboard Pattern test
E			182		BR_ON_ERR	Error_Found	;for internal registers
			183				
			184				
	007C	CB0014	185		PUSH	14h[sp]	;PUSH the start address
E	007F	CB0014	189		PUSH	14h[sp]	; and the end address of a RAM area
E	0082	EF0000	190		CALL	mem06	; and CALL a Complementary Address test
E			191				
E			192				
			193				

```
ERR LOC  OBJECT         LINE  SOURCE STATEMENT
                        194   BR_ON_ERR    Error_Found
    008C CB0010         198        PUSH    10h[sp]      ;PUSH a second start and end address
  E 008F CB0010         199        PUSH    10h[sp]      ; and repeat the
  E 0092 EF0000         200        CALL    mem06        ;Complementary Address test
                        201
                        202
                        203   BR_ON_ERR    Error_Found
                        207
    009C CB0014         208        PUSH    14h[sp]      ;PUSH a start address
  E 009F CB0014         209        PUSH    14h[sp]      ;PUSH an ending address
  E 00A2 EF0000         210        CALL    mem07        ;CALL a Walking Ones test
                        211
                        212   BR_ON_ERR    Error_Found
                        216
    00AC CB0010         217        PUSH    10h[sp]      ;PUSH the start and end address
  E 00AF CB0010         218        PUSH    10h[sp]      ; for another section of RAM
  E 00B2 EF0000         219        CALL    mem07        ; and repeat the Walking Ones test
                        220
                        221   BR_ON_ERR    Error_Found
                        225
    00BC CB0014         226        PUSH    14h[sp]      ;PUSH a start address
  E 00BF CB0014         227        PUSH    14h[sp]      ;PUSH an ending address
  E 00C2 EF0000         228        CALL    mem08        ;CALL a Galloping Ones test
                        229
                        230   BR_ON_ERR    Error_Found
                        234
    00CC CB0010         235        PUSH    10h[sp]      ;PUSH a second start and end address
  E 00CF CB0010         236        PUSH    10h[sp]      ; for another region of RAM and
  E 00D2 EF0000         237        CALL    mem08        ;CALL the Galloping Ones test again
                        238
                        239
                        240   BR_ON_ERR    Error_Found
                        244
    00DC CB0014         245        PUSH    14h[sp]      ;PUSH the start and end address of
  E 00DF CB0014         246        PUSH    14h[sp]      ; a region of RAM
  E 00E2 EF0000         247        CALL    mem09        ;CALL the Walking 1s/0s test
                        248
                        249   BR_ON_ERR    Error_Found
                        253
    00EC CB0010         254        PUSH    10h[sp]      ;PUSH the start and end address of
  E 00EF CB0010         255        PUSH    10h[sp]      ; another region of RAM
  E 00F2 EF0000         256        CALL    mem09        ;CALL the Walking 1s/0s test again
                        257
                        258
                        259   BR_ON_ERR    Error_Found
                        263
    00FC CB0014         264        PUSH    14h[sp]      ;PUSH the start and end address of
  E 00FF CB0014         265        PUSH    14h[sp]      ; a region of RAM
  E 0102 EF0000         266        CALL    mem0a        ;CALL a Galloping 1s/0s test
                        267
                        268   BR_ON_ERR    Error_Found
                        272
                        273
    010C CB0010         274        PUSH    10h[sp]      ;PUSH the start and end address of
  E 010F CB0010         275        PUSH    10h[sp]      ; another region of RAM
  E 0112 EF0000         276        CALL    mem0a        ;CALL the Galloping 1s/0s test again
                        277
```

```
ERR LOC  OBJECT         LINE     SOURCE STATEMENT
                        278              BR_ON_ERR    Error_Found
                        282
                        283
     011A CB0002        284              PUSH         02h[sp]          ;PUSH a bit pattern to use and
     011D EF0000        285              CALL memØc                    ;CALL the Checkerboard Pattern test
                        286                                            ; for internal registers
                        287              BR_ON_ERR    Error_Found
                        291
     0125 CB0014        292              PUSH         14h[sp]          ;PUSH the start and end address
     0128 CB0014        293              PUSH         14h[sp]          ; of a region of RAM, then
     012B CB0006        294              PUSH         06h[sp]          ;PUSH a bit pattern to use, then
     012E EF0000        295              CALL memØd                    ;CALL the Checkerboard Pattern test
                        296                                            ; for external memory
                        297              BR_ON_ERR    Error_Found
                        301
     0136 CB0010        302              PUSH         10h[sp]          ;PUSH the start and end address
     0139 CB0010        303              PUSH         10h[sp]          ; of another region of RAM, then
     013C CB0006        304              PUSH         06h[sp]          ;PUSH a bit pattern to use, then
     013F EF0000        305              CALL memØd                    ;CALL the Checkerboard Pattern test
                        306                                            ; for external memory
                        307              BR_ON_ERR    Error_Found
                        311
     0147 CB0014        312              PUSH         14h[sp]          ;PUSH a starting address, and
     014A CB0014        313              PUSH         14h[sp]          ;PUSH an ending address for
     014D EF0000        314              CALL sys03                    ; the Program Counter Module
                        315
                        316              BR_ON_ERR    Error_Found
                        320
     0155 CB0010        321              PUSH         10h[sp]          ;PUSH the start and end addresses
     0158 CB0010        322              PUSH         10h[sp]          ; for a second test region for
     015B EF0000        323              CALL sys03                    ; for the Program Counter Module
                        324
                        325              BR_ON_ERR    Error_Found
                        329
     0163 C98020        330              PUSH         #2080h           ;PUSH the code starting address
     0166 CB000A        331              PUSH         0ah[sp]          ;PUSH the ending code address
     0169 EF0000        332              CALL memØb                    ;CALL the Checksum routine
                        333
                        334                                            ;ALL DIAG96 TESTS PASSED
     016C A1300000      335              LD           EREG1,#0030h     ; load the appropriate error code
                        336
     0170 CF0014        337              POP          14h[sp]          ; clean off the stack
     0173 65120000      338              ADD          sp,#12h
     0177 F0            339              RET                           ; return to the calling program
                        340
     0178               341     Error_Found:
                        342
     0178 CF0014        343              POP          14h[sp]          ; clean off the stack
     017B 65120000      344              ADD          sp,#12h
     017F F0            345              RET                           ; return to the calling program
                        346     ;****************************************************
     0180               347              end
```

SYMBOL TABLE LISTING

N A M E	VALUE	ATTRIBUTES
ALL_TESTS_ASM96	----	MODULE STACKSIZE(20)
ALU01	----	CODE EXTERNAL
ALU02	----	CODE EXTERNAL
ALU03	----	CODE EXTERNAL
ALU04	----	CODE EXTERNAL
ALU05	----	CODE EXTERNAL
BR_ON_ERR	----	MACRO
D96A96	0000H	CODE REL PUBLIC ENTRY
EREG1	----	REG EXTERNAL
EREG2	----	REG EXTERNAL
ERROR_FOUND	0178H	CODE REL ENTRY
MACRO_TEMP	0000H	REG REL BYTE
MEM01	----	CODE EXTERNAL
MEM02	----	CODE EXTERNAL
MEM03	----	CODE EXTERNAL
MEM04	----	CODE EXTERNAL
MEM05	----	CODE EXTERNAL
MEM06	----	CODE EXTERNAL
MEM07	----	CODE EXTERNAL
MEM08	----	CODE EXTERNAL
MEM09	----	CODE EXTERNAL
MEM0A	----	CODE EXTERNAL
MEM0B	----	CODE EXTERNAL
MEM0C	----	CODE EXTERNAL
MEM0D	----	CODE EXTERNAL
RESET_WATCHDOG	----	MACRO
RI	0006H	NULL ABS
SP_STAT	----	REG EXTERNAL
SP_STAT	----	REG EXTERNAL
SPSTATUS	----	MACRO
SPWAIT	----	MACRO
SYS01	----	CODE EXTERNAL
SYS02	----	CODE EXTERNAL
SYS03	----	CODE EXTERNAL
TI	0005H	NULL ABS
ZERO	----	REG EXTERNAL

ASSEMBLY COMPLETED, NO ERROR(S) FOUND.

MCS®-96

— D96P96

```
SERIES-III PL/M-96 V1.0 COMPILATION OF MODULE ALLDIAG96TESTS
OBJECT MODULE PLACED IN :F2:D96P96.OBJ
COMPILER INVOKED BY: PLM96.86 :F2:D96P96.P96 CODE DEBUG


  1              All$Diag96$Tests:
                    DO;

  2      1          SYS02: PROCEDURE DWORD EXTERNAL;
  3      2          END SYS02;

  4      1          SYS03: PROCEDURE (parm1,parm2) DWORD EXTERNAL;
  5      2             DECLARE (parm1,parm2) WORD;
  6      2          END SYS03;

  7      1          ALU01: PROCEDURE DWORD EXTERNAL;
  8      2          END ALU01;

  9      1          ALU02: PROCEDURE DWORD EXTERNAL;
 10      2          END ALU02;

 11      1          ALU03: PROCEDURE DWORD EXTERNAL;
 12      2          END ALU03;

 13      1          ALU04: PROCEDURE (parm1,parm2) DWORD EXTERNAL;
 14      2             DECLARE (parm1,parm2) WORD;
 15      2          END ALU04;

 16      1          ALU05: PROCEDURE (parm1,parm2) DWORD EXTERNAL;
 17      2             DECLARE (parm1,parm2) WORD;
 18      2          END ALU05;

 19      1          MEM01: PROCEDURE DWORD EXTERNAL;
 20      2          END MEM01;

 21      1          MEM02: PROCEDURE DWORD EXTERNAL;
 22      2          END MEM02;

 23      1          MEM03: PROCEDURE DWORD EXTERNAL;
 24      2          END MEM03;

 25      1          MEM04: PROCEDURE (parm1) DWORD EXTERNAL;
 26      2             DECLARE (parm1) WORD;
 27      2          END MEM04;

 28      1          MEM05: PROCEDURE DWORD EXTERNAL;
 29      2          END MEM05;

 30      1          MEM06: PROCEDURE (parm1,parm2) DWORD EXTERNAL;
 31      2             DECLARE (parm1,parm2) WORD;
 32      2          END MEM06;

 33      1          MEM07: PROCEDURE (parm1,parm2) DWORD EXTERNAL;
 34      2             DECLARE (parm1,parm2) WORD;
 35      2          END MEM07;
```

MCS®-96

```
36  1       MEM08: PROCEDURE (parm1,parm2) DWORD EXTERNAL;
37  2         DECLARE      (parm1,parm2) WORD;
38  2       END MEM08;

39  1       MEM09: PROCEDURE (parm1,parm2) DWORD EXTERNAL;
40  2         DECLARE      (parm1,parm2) WORD;
41  2       END MEM09;

42  1       MEM0A: PROCEDURE (parm1,parm2) DWORD EXTERNAL;
43  2         DECLARE      (parm1,parm2) WORD;
44  2       END MEM0A;

45  1       MEM0B: PROCEDURE (parm1,parm2) DWORD EXTERNAL;
46  2         DECLARE      (parm1,parm2) WORD;
47  2       END MEM0B;

48  1       MEM0C: PROCEDURE (parm1) DWORD EXTERNAL;
49  2         DECLARE      (parm1) WORD;
50  2       END MEM0C;

51  1       MEM0D: PROCEDURE (parm1,parm2,parm3) DWORD EXTERNAL;
52  2         DECLARE      (parm1,parm2,parm3) WORD;
53  2       END MEM0D;

54  1       DECLARE result DWORD;
55  1       DECLARE error$codes STRUCTURE (number WORD,detail WORD) AT (.result);

56  1       D96P96: PROCEDURE (ram1$start,ram1$stop,
                              ram2$start,ram2$stop,
                              random$seed,random$length,
                              top$of$code,
                              argument1,argument2,
                              bit$pattern) DWORD PUBLIC;

57  2         DECLARE (ram1$start,ram1$stop,
                      ram2$start,ram2$stop,
                      random$seed,random$length,
                      top$of$code,
                      argument1,argument2,
                      bit$pattern) WORD SLOW;

58  2         result=SYS02;
59  2         IF error$codes.number > 255 THEN GOTO end$tests;

61  2         result=ALU01;
62  2         IF error$codes.number > 255 THEN GOTO end$tests;

64  2         result=ALU02;
65  2         IF error$codes.number > 255 THEN GOTO end$tests;

67  2         result=ALU03;
68  2         IF error$codes.number > 255 THEN GOTO end$tests;

70  2         result=ALU04(47efH,1000H);
```

5-510

MCS®-96

```
 71  2      IF error$codes.number > 255 THEN GOTO end$tests;
 73  2      result=ALU05(argument1,argument2);
 74  2      IF error$codes.number > 255 THEN GOTO end$tests;
 76  2      result=MEM01;
 77  2      IF error$codes.number > 255 THEN GOTO end$tests;
 79  2      result=MEM02;
 80  2      IF error$codes.number > 255 THEN GOTO end$tests;
 82  2      result=MEM03;
 83  2      IF error$codes.number > 255 THEN GOTO end$tests;
 85  2      result=MEM04(0);
 86  2      IF error$codes.number > 255 THEN GOTO end$tests;
 88  2      result=MEM05;
 89  2      IF error$codes.number > 255 THEN GOTO end$tests;
 91  2      result=MEM06(ram1$start,ram1$stop);
 92  2      IF error$codes.number > 255 THEN GOTO end$tests;
 94  2      result=MEM06(ram2$start,ram2$stop);
 95  2      IF error$codes.number > 255 THEN GOTO end$tests;
 97  2      result=MEM07(ram1$start,ram1$stop);
 98  2      IF error$codes.number > 255 THEN GOTO end$tests;
100  2      result=MEM07(ram2$start,ram2$stop);
101  2      IF error$codes.number > 255 THEN GOTO end$tests;
103  2      result=MEM08(ram1$start,ram1$stop);
104  2      IF error$codes.number > 255 THEN GOTO end$tests;
106  2      result=MEM08(ram2$start,ram2$stop);
107  2      IF error$codes.number > 255 THEN GOTO end$tests;
109  2      result=MEM09(ram1$start,ram1$stop);
110  2      IF error$codes.number > 255 THEN GOTO end$tests;
112  2      result=MEM09(ram2$start,ram2$stop);
113  2      IF error$codes.number > 255 THEN GOTO end$tests;
115  2      result=MEM0A(ram1$start,ram1$stop);
116  2      IF error$codes.number > 255 THEN GOTO end$tests;
118  2      result=MEM0A(ram2$start,ram2$stop);
119  2      IF error$codes.number > 255 THEN GOTO end$tests;
121  2      result=MEM0C(bit$pattern);
122  2      IF error$codes.number > 255 THEN GOTO end$tests;
124  2      result=MEM0D(ram1$start,ram1$stop,bit$pattern);
125  2      IF error$codes.number > 255 THEN GOTO end$tests;
127  2      result=MEM0D(ram2$start,ram2$stop,bit$pattern);
```

```
128   2          IF error$codes.number > 255 THEN GOTO end$tests;

130   2          result=SYS03(ram1$start,ram1$stop);
131   2          IF error$codes.number > 255 THEN GOTO end$tests;

133   2          result=SYS03(ram2$start,ram2$stop);
134   2          IF error$codes.number > 255 THEN GOTO end$tests;

136   2          result=MEMOB(2080h,top$of$code);

137   2          error$codes.number=00f0h;

138   2   end$tests: RETURN result;

139   2      END D96P96;

140 , 1  END All$Diag96$Tests;
```

MCS®-96

```
                                              ;   STATEMENT    56
0000                    D96P96:
0000   C800              E       PUSH    ?FRAME01
0002   A01806            E       LD      ?FRAME01,SP
                                              ;   STATEMENT    58
0005   EF0000            E       CALL    SYS02
0008   A01E02            R       LD      RESULT+2H,TMP2
000B   A01C00            R       LD      RESULT,TMP0
                                              ;   STATEMENT    59
000E   89FF0000          R       CMP     ERRORCODES,#0FFH
0012   D102                      BNH     00001
                                              ;   STATEMENT    60
0014   2226                      BR      ENDTESTS
                                              ;   STATEMENT    61
0016                    00001:   CALL    ALU01
0016   EF0000            E       CALL    ALU01
0019   A01E02            R       LD      RESULT+2H,TMP2
001C   A01C00            R       LD      RESULT,TMP0
                                              ;   STATEMENT    62
001F   89FF0000          R       CMP     ERRORCODES,#0FFH
0023   D102                      BNH     00002
                                              ;   STATEMENT    63
0025   2215                      BR      ENDTESTS
                                              ;   STATEMENT    64
0027                    00002:   CALL    ALU02
0027   EF0000            E       CALL    ALU02
002A   A01E02            R       LD      RESULT+2H,TMP2
002D   A01C00            R       LD      RESULT,TMP0
                                              ;   STATEMENT    65
0030   89FF0000          R       CMP     ERRORCODES,#0FFH
0034   D102                      BNH     00003
                                              ;   STATEMENT    66
0036   2204                      BR      ENDTESTS
                                              ;   STATEMENT    67
0038                    00003:   CALL    ALU03
0038   EF0000            E       CALL    ALU03
003B   A01E02            R       LD      RESULT+2H,TMP2
003E   A01C00            R       LD      RESULT,TMP0
                                              ;   STATEMENT    68
0041   89FF0000          R       CMP     ERRORCODES,#0FFH
0045   D102                      BNH     00004
                                              ;   STATEMENT    69
0047   21F3                      BR      ENDTESTS
                                              ;   STATEMENT    70
0049                    00004:   PUSH    #47EFH
0049   C9EF47                    PUSH    #1000H
004C   C90010                    CALL    ALU04
004F   EF0000            E       CALL    ALU04
0052   A01E02            R       LD      RESULT+2H,TMP2
0055   A01C00            R       LD      RESULT,TMP0
                                              ;   STATEMENT    71
0058   89FF0000          R       CMP     ERRORCODES,#0FFH
005C   D102                      BNH     00005
                                              ;   STATEMENT    72
005E   21DC                      BR      ENDTESTS
                                              ;   STATEMENT    73
```

5-513

```
0060  CB0008          E         00005:  PUSH  ARGUMENT1[?FRAME01]
0063  CB0006          E                 PUSH  ARGUMENT2[?FRAME01]
0066  EF0000          E                 CALL  ALU05
0069  A01E02          R                 LD    RESULT+2H,TMP2
006C  A01C00          R                 LD    RESULT,TMP0
                                        ;     STATEMENT 74
006F  89FF0000        R                 CMP   ERRORCODES,#0FFH
0073  D102                              BNH   @0006
                                        ;     STATEMENT 75
0075  21C5                              BR    ENDTESTS
                                        ;     STATEMENT 76
0077                          00006:    CALL  MEM01
0077  EF0000          E                 LD    RESULT+2H,TMP2
007A  A01E02          R                 LD    RESULT,TMP0
007D  A01C00          R                 ;     STATEMENT 77
0080  89FF0000        R                 CMP   ERRORCODES,#0FFH
0084  D102                              BNH   @0007
                                        ;     STATEMENT 78
0086  21B4                              BR    ENDTESTS
                                        ;     STATEMENT 79
0088                          00007:    CALL  MEM02
0088  EF0000          E                 LD    RESULT+2H,TMP2
008B  A01E02          R                 LD    RESULT,TMP0
008E  A01C00          R                 ;     STATEMENT 80
0091  89FF0000        R                 CMP   ERRORCODES,#0FFH
0095  D102                              BNH   @0008
                                        ;     STATEMENT 81
0097  21A3                              BR    ENDTESTS
                                        ;     STATEMENT 82
0099                          00008:    CALL  MEM03
0099  EF0000          E                 LD    RESULT+2H,TMP2
009C  A01E02          R                 LD    RESULT,TMP0
009F  A01C00          R                 ;     STATEMENT 83
00A2  89FF0000        R                 CMP   ERRORCODES,#0FFH
00A6  D102                              BNH   @0009
                                        ;     STATEMENT 84
00A8  2192                              BR    ENDTESTS
                                        ;     STATEMENT 85
00AA                          00009:    PUSH  R0
00AA  C800                              CALL  MEM04
00AC  EF0000          E                 LD    RESULT+2H,TMP2
00AF  A01E02          R                 LD    RESULT,TMP0
00B2  A01C00          R                 ;     STATEMENT 86
00B5  89FF0000        R                 CMP   ERRORCODES,#0FFH
00B9  D102                              BNH   @000A
                                        ;     STATEMENT 87
00BB  217F                              BR    ENDTESTS
                                        ;     STATEMENT 88
00BD                          0000A:    CALL  MEM05
00BD  EF0000          E                 LD    RESULT+2H,TMP2
00C0  A01E02          R
```

00C3	A01C00		R	LD	RESULT,TMP0
00C6	89FF0000		R	CMP	ERRORCODES,#0FFH
00CA	D102			BNH	0000B
00CC	216E			BR	ENDTESTS
		0000B:		;	STATEMENT 91
00CE	CB0016		E	PUSH	RAM1START[?FRAME01]
00D1	CB0014		E	PUSH	RAM1STOP[?FRAME01]
00D4	EF0000		E	CALL	MEM06
00D7	A01E02		R	LD	RESULT+2H,TMP2
00DA	A01C00		R	LD	RESULT,TMP0
00DD	89FF0000		R	CMP	ERRORCODES,#0FFH
00E1	D102			BNH	0000C
00E3	2157			BR	ENDTESTS
		0000C:		;	STATEMENT 94
00E5	CB0012		E	PUSH	RAM2START[?FRAME01]
00E8	CB0010		E	PUSH	RAM2STOP[?FRAME01]
00EB	EF0000		E	CALL	MEM06
00EE	A01E02		R	LD	RESULT+2H,TMP2
00F1	A01C00		R	LD	RESULT,TMP0
				;	STATEMENT 95
00F4	89FF0000		R	CMP	ERRORCODES,#0FFH
00F8	D102			BNH	0000D
00FA	2140			BR	ENDTESTS
		0000D:		;	STATEMENT 97
00FC	CB0016		E	PUSH	RAM1START[?FRAME01]
00FF	CB0014		E	PUSH	RAM1STOP[?FRAME01]
0102	EF0000		E	CALL	MEM07
0105	A01E02		R	LD	RESULT+2H,TMP2
0108	A01C00		R	LD	RESULT,TMP0
				;	STATEMENT 98
010B	89FF0000		R	CMP	ERRORCODES,#0FFH
010F	D102			BNH	0000E
0111	2129			BR	ENDTESTS
		0000E:		;	STATEMENT 100
0113	CB0012		E	PUSH	RAM2START[?FRAME01]
0116	CB0010		E	PUSH	RAM2STOP[?FRAME01]
0119	EF0000		E	CALL	MEM07
011C	A01E02		R	LD	RESULT+2H,TMP2
011F	A01C00		R	LD	RESULT,TMP0
				;	STATEMENT 101
0122	89FF0000		R	CMP	ERRORCODES,#0FFH
0126	D102			BNH	0000F
0128	2112			BR	ENDTESTS
		0000F:		;	STATEMENT 103
012A					

```
012A  CB0016        E           PUSH    RAM1START[?FRAME01]
012D  CB0014        E           PUSH    RAM1STOP[?FRAME01]
0130  EF0000        E           CALL    MEM08
0133  A01E02        R           LD      RESULT+2H,TMP2
0136  A01C00        R           LD      RESULT,TMP0
                                ;       STATEMENT  104
0139  89FF0000      R           CMP     ERRORCODES,#0FFH
013D  D102                      BNH     @@010
                                ;       STATEMENT  105
013F  20FB                      BR      ENDTESTS
                                ;       STATEMENT  106
                    @@010:
0141  CB0012        E           PUSH    RAM2START[?FRAME01]
0144  CB0010        E           PUSH    RAM2STOP[?FRAME01]
0147  EF0000        E           CALL    MEM08
014A  A01E02        R           LD      RESULT+2H,TMP2
014D  A01C00        R           LD      RESULT,TMP0
                                ;       STATEMENT  107
0150  89FF0000      R           CMP     ERRORCODES,#0FFH
0154  D102                      BNH     @@011
                                ;       STATEMENT  108
0156  20E4                      BR      ENDTESTS
                                ;       STATEMENT  109
                    @@011:
0158  CB0016        E           PUSH    RAM1START[?FRAME01]
015B  CB0014        E           PUSH    RAM1STOP[?FRAME01]
015E  EF0000        E           CALL    MEM09
0161  A01E02        R           LD      RESULT+2H,TMP2
0164  A01C00        R           LD      RESULT,TMP0
                                ;       STATEMENT  110
0167  89FF0000      R           CMP     ERRORCODES,#0FFH
016B  D102                      BNH     @@012
                                ;       STATEMENT  111
016D  20CD                      BR      ENDTESTS
                                ;       STATEMENT  112
                    @@012:
016F  CB0012        E           PUSH    RAM2START[?FRAME01]
0172  CB0010        E           PUSH    RAM2STOP[?FRAME01]
0175  EF0000        E           CALL    MEM09
0178  A01E02        R           LD      RESULT+2H,TMP2
017B  A01C00        R           LD      RESULT,TMP0
                                ;       STATEMENT  113
017E  89FF0000      R           CMP     ERRORCODES,#0FFH
0182  D102                      BNH     @@013
                                ;       STATEMENT  114
0184  20B6                      BR      ENDTESTS
                                ;       STATEMENT  115
                    @@013:
0186  CB0016        E           PUSH    RAM1START[?FRAME01]
0189  CB0014        E           PUSH    RAM1STOP[?FRAME01]
018C  EF0000        E           CALL    MEM0A
018F  A01E02        R           LD      RESULT+2H,TMP2
0192  A01C00        R           LD      RESULT,TMP0
                                ;       STATEMENT  116
0195  89FF0000      R           CMP     ERRORCODES,#0FFH
0199  D102                      BNH     @@014
```

MCS®-96

```
019B                              ;         STATEMENT   117
019D                              BR        ENDTESTS
019D                              ;         STATEMENT   118
019D          @@014:
01A0  CB0012          E           PUSH      RAM2START[?FRAME01]
01A3  CB0010          E           PUSH      RAM2STOP[?FRAME01]
01A6  EF0000          E           CALL      MEM0A
01A9  A01E02          R           LD        RESULT+2H,TMP2
01AC  A01C00          R           LD        RESULT,TMP0
                                  ;         STATEMENT   119
01AC  89FF0000        R           CMP       ERRORCODES,#0FFH
01B0  D102                        BNH       @@015
                                  ;         STATEMENT   120
01B2  2088                        BR        ENDTESTS
                                  ;         STATEMENT   121
01B4          @@015:
01B4  CB0004          E           PUSH      BITPATTERN[?FRAME01]
01B7  EF0000          E           CALL      MEM0C
01BA  A01E02          R           LD        RESULT+2H,TMP2
01BD  A01C00          R           LD        RESULT,TMP0
                                  ;         STATEMENT   122
01C0  89FF0000        R           CMP       ERRORCODES,#0FFH
01C4  D102                        BNH       @@016
                                  ;         STATEMENT   123
01C6  2074                        BR        ENDTESTS
                                  ;         STATEMENT   124
01C8          @@016:
01C8  CB0016          E           PUSH      RAM1START[?FRAME01]
01CB  CB0014          E           PUSH      RAM1STOP[?FRAME01]
01CE  CB0004          E           PUSH      BITPATTERN[?FRAME01]
01D1  EF0000          E           CALL      MEM0D
01D4  A01E02          R           LD        RESULT+2H,TMP2
01D7  A01C00          R           LD        RESULT,TMP0
                                  ;         STATEMENT   125
01DA  89FF0000        R           CMP       ERRORCODES,#0FFH
01DE  D102                        BNH       @@017
                                  ;         STATEMENT   126
01E0  205A                        BR        ENDTESTS
                                  ;         STATEMENT   127
01E2          @@017:
01E2  CB0012          E           PUSH      RAM2START[?FRAME01]
01E5  CB0010          E           PUSH      RAM2STOP[?FRAME01]
01E8  CB0004          E           PUSH      BITPATTERN[?FRAME01]
01EB  EF0000          E           CALL      MEM0D
01EE  A01E02          R           LD        RESULT+2H,TMP2
01F1  A01C00          R           LD        RESULT,TMP0
                                  ;         STATEMENT   128
01F4  89FF0000        R           CMP       ERRORCODES,#0FFH
01F8  D102                        BNH       @@018
                                  ;         STATEMENT   129
01FA  2040                        BR        ENDTESTS
                                  ;         STATEMENT   130
01FC          @@018:
01FC  CB0016          E           PUSH      RAM1START[?FRAME01]
01FF  CB0014          E           PUSH      RAM1STOP[?FRAME01]
0202  EF0000          E           CALL      SYS03
```

MCS®-96

```
0205  A01E02                  R     LD    RESULT+2H,TMP2
0208  A01C00                  R     LD    RESULT,TMP0
                                    ; STATEMENT    131
020B  B9FF0000                R     CMP   ERRORCODES,#0FFH
020F  D102                          BNH   @0019
0211  2029                          BR    ENDTESTS
                                    ; STATEMENT    132
                                    ; STATEMENT    133
                              @0019:
0213  CB0012                  E     PUSH  RAM2START[?FRAME01]
0216  CB0010                  E     PUSH  RAM2STOP[?FRAME01]
0219  EF0000                  E     CALL  SYS03
021C  A01E02                  R     LD    RESULT+2H,TMP2
021F  A01C00                  R     LD    RESULT,TMP0
                                    ; STATEMENT    134
0222  B9FF0000                R     CMP   ERRORCODES,#0FFH
0226  D102                          BNH   @001A
0228  2012                          BR    ENDTESTS
                                    ; STATEMENT    135
                                    ; STATEMENT    136
                              @001A:
022A  C98020                  E     PUSH  #2080H
022D  CB000A                  E     PUSH  TOPOFCODE[?FRAME01]
0230  EF0000                  E     CALL  MEM0B
0233  A01E02                  R     LD    RESULT+2H,TMP2
0236  A01C00                  R     LD    RESULT,TMP0
                                    ; STATEMENT    137
0239  ADF000                  R     LDBZE ERRORCODES,#0F0H
                                    ; STATEMENT    138
                              ENDTESTS:
023C  A0021E                  R     LD    TMP2,RESULT+2H
023F  A0001C                  R     LD    TMP0,RESULT
0242  CC00                    E     POP   ?FRAME01
0244  A21822                        LD    TMP6,[SP]
0247  65160018                      ADD   SP,#16H
                                    BR    [TMP6]
                                    ; STATEMENT    139
024B  E322                          ; STATEMENT    140
                                    END
```

```
MODULE INFORMATION:

    CODE AREA SIZE           = 024DH   589D
    CONSTANT AREA SIZE       = 0000H     0D
    DATA AREA SIZE           = 0000H     0D
    STATIC REGS AREA SIZE    = 0004H     4D
    OVERLAYABLE REGS AREA SIZE = 0000H   0D
    MAXIMUM STACK SIZE       = 000AH    10D
    183 LINES READ
    0 PROGRAM ERROR MESSAGES

PL/M-96 COMPILATION COMPLETE.    0 WARNINGS,    0 ERRORS
```

```
MCS-96 MACRO ASSEMBLER    SELECTED_TESTS_ASM96

SERIES-III MCS-96 MACRO ASSEMBLER, V1.0

SOURCE FILE:  :F5:D96FST.A96
OBJECT FILE:  :F5:D96FST.OBJ
CONTROLS SPECIFIED IN INVOCATION COMMAND: NOGEN DEBUG


ERR LOC  OBJECT            LINE   SOURCE STATEMENT

                             1    ;****************************************************************
                             2    ; Selected Tests ASM96   MODULE   STACKSIZE(20)              0031
                             3    ;****************************************************************
                             4    ;
                             5    ; In order to run this module, the STACK must be ALL external, and the
                             6    ; data ram partitioned for memory test must not include ANY of the STACK
                             7    ;
                             8    ; To call this module
                             9    ;
                            10    ;        PUSH    #<RAM segment1 start address>
                            11    ;        PUSH    #<RAM segment1 ending address>
                            12    ;        PUSH    #<RAM segment2 start address>
                            13    ;        PUSH    #<RAM segment2 ending address>
                            14    ;        PUSH    #<random seed>
                            15    ;        PUSH    #<number of cycles desired for random test>
                            16    ;        PUSH    #<address of the last byte of rom>
                            17    ;        PUSH    #<an argument for mul/div tests>
                            18    ;        PUSH    #<a second argument for mul/div tests>
                            19    ;        PUSH    #<a bit pattern for memory tests>
                            20    ;        CALL    D96FST
                            21    ;
                            22    ;****************************************************************
                            23    
0000                        24             rseg
                            25    
                            26    extrn sp,ereq1,ereq2
                            27    
0000                        28             cseg
                            29    extrn sys01,sys02,sys03,alu01,alu02,alu03,alu04,alu05
                            30    extrn mem01,mem02,mem03,mem04,mem05,mem06,mem07,mem08
                            31    extrn mem09,mem0a,mem0b,mem0c,mem0d
                            32    
                            33    PUBLIC D96FST
                            34    $eject
```

MCS®-96

```
    ERR LOC  OBJECT          LINE       SOURCE STATEMENT
                              38                ;****************************************************
                              39                $include (:f3:dstmac.inc)
                        =1    40                ;****************************************************
                        =1    41                ;DST Macros      INCLUDE FILE ;************************
                        =1    42                ;****************************************************
                        =1    43
                        =1    44                rseg
                        =1    45
            0000        =1    46                macro_temp: DSB 1
                        =1    47                extrn zero,sp_stat
                        =1    48
            0000        =1    49                cseg
            0005        =1    50                ti equ 5
            0006        =1    51                ri equ 6
                        =1    52
                        =1    53                ;****************************************************
                        =1    54                ;                                     ;macro to reset the watchdog
                        =1    55                RESET_WATCHDOG  MACRO
                        =1    56                                LDB     0ah,#1eh
                        =1    57                                LDB     0ah,#0e1h
                        =1    58                ENDM
                        =1    59                ;****************************************************
                        =1    60
                        =1    61                ;****************************************************
                        =1    62                ;                                     ; macro to read sp_stat to
                        =1    63                SPSTATUS        MACRO   v1            ; work around the ri/ti bug
                        =1    64                                LOCAL   Sp_read       ; on the 8x9x-90.
                        =1    65
                        =1    66                Sp_read:        LDB     macro_temp,sp_stat
                        =1    67                                ORB     v1,macro_temp
                        =1    68                                ANDB    macro_temp,#01100000B
                        =1    69                                JNE     Sp_read
                        =1    70                ENDM
                        =1    71                ;****************************************************
                        =1    72
                        =1    73                ;****************************************************
                        =1    74                ;                                     ; macro to wait for ri/ti set
                        =1    75                SPWAIT          MACRO   v2            ; and avoid 8x9x-90 bug.
                        =1    76                                                      ; NOTE!! this macro won't work
                        =1    77                                                      ; with a full duplex line.
                        =1    78                                JBC     sp_stat,v2,$
                        =1    79                                LDB     zero,sp_stat
                        =1    80
                        =1    81                ENDM
                        =1    82                ;****************************************************
                        =1    83
                        =1    84                ;****************************************************
                        =1    85                ;                                     ; macro to test high byte of
                        =1    86                BR_ON_ERR       MACRO   Label         ; EREG1 and branch away if
                        =1    87                                                      ; the byte is non-zero (which
                        =1    88                                CMPB    ereg1+1h,zero ; means there was an error).
                        =1    89                                BNE     Label
                        =1    90                ENDM
                        =1    91                ;****************************************************
                        =1    92
                        =1    93
                        =1    94
```

5-520

MCS®-96

```
ERR LOC  OBJECT       LINE        SOURCE STATEMENT
    0000              96          D96FST:
                      97
                      98
    0000 EF0000       99              CALL  sys02.A96        ;CALL the Power Up Test
                      100
        E             101             BR_ON_ERR  Error_Found
                      105
    000A EF0000       106             CALL  alu01            ;CALL the Add/Subtract test
                      107
        E             108             BR_ON_ERR  Error_Found
                      112
    0014 EF0000       113             CALL  alu02            ;CALL the MULUB test
                      114
        E             115             BR_ON_ERR  Error_Found
                      119
    001E EF0000       120             CALL  alu03            ;CALL the Multiply/Divide Table
                      121                                    ; driven test
        E             122             BR_ON_ERR  Error_Found
                      126
    0028 CB000C       127             PUSH  0ch[sp]          ;PUSH a seed and test length
    002B CB000C       128             PUSH  0ch[sp]          ; for the random number based
    002E EF0000       129             CALL  alu04            ; Multiply/Divide Random test
                      130
        E             131             BR_ON_ERR  Error_Found
                      135
    0038 CB0006       136             PUSH  06h[sp]          ;PUSH an argument
    003B CB0006       137             PUSH  06h[sp]          ;PUSH another argument
    003E EF0000       138             CALL  alu05            ;CALL the Multiply/Divide Core test
                      139
        E             140             BR_ON_ERR  Error_Found
                      144
    0048 EF0000       145             CALL  mem01            ;CALL the Complementary Address test
                      146                                    ; for internal registers
        E             147             BR_ON_ERR  Error_Found
                      151
    0052 EF0000       152             CALL  mem03            ;CALL the Galloping 1s/0s test
                      153                                    ; for internal registers
        E             154             BR_ON_ERR  Error_Found
                      158
    005C EF0000       159             CALL  mem05            ;CALL the Chekerboard Pattern test
                      160                                    ; for internal registers
        E             161             BR_ON_ERR  Error_Found
                      165
    0066 CB0014       166             PUSH  14h[sp]          ;PUSH a start and end address
    0069 CB0014       167             PUSH  14h[sp]          ; for another region of RAM to conduct
    006C EF0000       168             CALL  mem06            ; the Complementary Address test for
                      169                                    ; external RAM
        E             170             BR_ON_ERR  Error_Found
                      174
    0074 CB0010       175             PUSH  10h[sp]          ;PUSH a start and end address
    0077 CB0010       176             PUSH  10h[sp]          ; for another region of RAM to conduct
    007A EF0000       177             CALL  mem06            ; the Complementary Address test for
                      178                                    ; external RAM
        E             179             BR_ON_ERR  Error_Found
                      183
    0082 CB0014       184             PUSH  14h[sp]          ;PUSH a start and end address
    0085 CB0014       185             PUSH  14h[sp]          ; for a region of RAM, and PUSH
```

5

MCS®-96

```
ERR  LOC   OBJECT        LINE    SOURCE STATEMENT
                          186            PUSH      06h[sp]       ; a bit pattern to use in the
     0088  CB0006      E  187            CALL      mem0d         ; Checkerboard Pattern test for
     008B  EF0000      E  188                                    ; external RAM
                          189    BR_ON_ERR Error_Found
                          193
     0093  CB0010      E  194            PUSH      10h[sp]       ;PUSH a start and end address for
     0096  CB0010      E  195            PUSH      10h[sp]       ; another region of RAM, and PUSH
     0099  CB0006      E  196            PUSH      06h[sp]       ; a bit pattern to use in the
     009C  EF0000      E  197            CALL      mem0d         ; Checkerboard Pattern test for
                          198                                    ; external RAM
                          199    BR_ON_ERR Error_Found
                          203
     00A4  CB0014      E  204            PUSH      14h[sp]       ;PUSH a start and end address
     00A7  CB0014      E  205            PUSH      14h[sp]       ; for a region of RAM to conduct
     00AA  EF0000      E  206            CALL      sys03         ; the Program Counter test
                          207
                          208    BR_ON_ERR Error_Found
                          212
     00B2  CB0010      E  213            PUSH      10h[sp]       ;PUSH a start and end address
     00B5  CB0010      E  214            PUSH      10h[sp]       ; for another region of RAM to conduct
     00B8  EF0000      E  215            CALL      sys03         ; the Program Counter test
                          216
                          217    BR_ON_ERR Error_Found
                          221
     00C0  C98020         222            PUSH      #2080h        ;PUSH the code starting address
     00C3  CB006A      E  223            PUSH      0ah[sp]       ;PUSH the code ending address
     00C6  EF0000      E  224            CALL      mem0b         ; CALL the checksum routine
                          225
     00C9  A1310000       226            LD        ereql,#0031h  ;ALL DIAG96 TESTS PASSED
                          227                                    ; load appropriate error code
                          228
     00CD  CF0014      E  229            POP       14h[sp]       ; clean off the stack
     00D0  65120000    E  230            ADD       sp,#12h
     00D4  F0             231            RET                     ; return to the calling program
                          232
                          233    Error_Found:
                          234
     00D5  CF0014      E  235            POP       14h[sp]       ; clean off the stack
     00D8  65120000    E  236            ADD       sp,#12h
     00DC  F0             237            RET                     ; return to the calling program
                          238
                          239    ;****************************************************************
     00DD                 240    end
```

5-522

SYMBOL TABLE LISTING

N A M E	VALUE	ATTRIBUTES
ALU01	----	CODE EXTERNAL
ALU02	----	CODE EXTERNAL
ALU03	----	CODE EXTERNAL
ALU04	----	CODE EXTERNAL
ALU05	----	CODE EXTERNAL
BR_ON_ERR		MACRO
D96FST	0000H	CODE REL PUBLIC ENTRY
EREG1	----	REG EXTERNAL
EREG2	----	REG EXTERNAL
ERROR_FOUND	00D5H	CODE REL ENTRY
MACRO_TEMP	0000H	REG REL BYTE
MEM01	----	CODE EXTERNAL
MEM02	----	CODE EXTERNAL
MEM03	----	CODE EXTERNAL
MEM04	----	CODE EXTERNAL
MEM05	----	CODE EXTERNAL
MEM06	----	CODE EXTERNAL
MEM07	----	CODE EXTERNAL
MEM08	----	CODE EXTERNAL
MEM09	----	CODE EXTERNAL
MEM0A	----	CODE EXTERNAL
MEM0B	----	CODE EXTERNAL
MEM0C	----	CODE EXTERNAL
MEM0D	----	CODE EXTERNAL
RESET_WATCHDOG		MACRO
RI	0006H	NULL ABS
SELECTED_TESTS_ASM96		MODULE STACKSIZE(20)
SP	----	REG EXTERNAL
SP_STAT	----	REG EXTERNAL
SPSTATUS		MACRO
SPWAIT		MACRO
SYS01	----	CODE EXTERNAL
SYS02	----	CODE EXTERNAL
SYS03	----	CODE EXTERNAL
TI	0005H	NULL ABS
ZERO	----	REG EXTERNAL

ASSEMBLY COMPLETED, NO ERROR(S) FOUND.

MCS®-96

— DSTUSR

```
MCS-96 MACRO ASSEMBLER    DSTUSR

SERIES-III MCS-96 MACRO ASSEMBLER, V1.0

SOURCE FILE:  :F2:DSTUSR.A96
OBJECT FILE:  :F2:DSTUSR.OBJ
CONTROLS SPECIFIED IN INVOCATION COMMAND:  GEN DEBUG

ERR LOC    OBJECT          LINE    SOURCE STATEMENT
                             1     ;*********************************************************
                             2     DSTUSR     MODULE  main,stacksize(2)
                             3     ;*********************************************************
                             4
    0040                     5              oseg at 40h
    0040                     6
                             7     User_Registers: DSB    1ch
    0040                     8              temp    set   User_Registers:WORD
                             9
    0000                    10              rseg
                            11     EXTRN sp,zero,timer1,ereql
                            12
                            13              dseg at 100h
    0100                    14
    0100                    15     DSEG1:   DSB     700h              ;to ensure that the STACK does not get
                            16                                        ; located in an area of RAM that will be
    4200                    17              dseg at 4200h             ; memory tested, reserve those regions
    4200                    18     DSEG2:   DSB     1e00h             ; as data segments.
                            19
                            20
                            21
                            22
                            23              cseg at 2080h
    2080                    24
                            25     extrn alu04,alu01,alu02,mem06,mem0a,error_proc,alu05
                            26     EXTRN DSTISR
                            27
    2080 A1FF0040           28              LD      temp,#0ffh
    2084 E040FD             29              DJNZ    temp,$            ;wait for sbe96 NMIs to stop
                            30
    2087 A1000000   E       31              LD      sp,#STACK
                            32
    208B C90001             33              PUSH    #100h             ;RAM segment1 start address
    208E C9FF07             34              PUSH    #7ffh             ;RAM segment1 end address
    2091 C90042             35              PUSH    #4200h            ;RAM segment2 start address
    2094 C9FF5F             36              PUSH    #5fffh            ;RAM segment2 end address
    2097 C9EF47             37              PUSH    #47efh            ;RAM test length
    209A C90010             38              PUSH    #1000h            ;random seed
    209D C9F33F             39              PUSH    #3fffh            ;top of code address
    20A0 C9429D             40              PUSH    #9d42h            ;an argument for mul/div test
    20A3 C98C77             41              PUSH    #778ch            ;another argument for mul/div test
    20A6 C95A5A             42              PUSH    #5a5ah            ;bit pattern for memory test
    20A9 EF0000     E       43              CALL    DSTISR            ;CALL the Dynamic Stability Test
                            44                                        ; initialization routine
                            45
                            46     Main_Task:
    20AC                    47
    20AC C98080             48              push    #8080h            ;use the multiply/divide core
    20AF C90080             49              push    #8000h            ; test on the arguments
    20B2 EF0000     E       50              call    alu05
                            51
```

```
ERR  LOC    OBJECT        LINE    SOURCE STATEMENT
     20B5   980001         52             cmpb    eregl+1,zero      ; #8000h and #8000h in all
     20B8   DF022074       53             bne     error_found       ; combinations
                                   IJE    $+4
                                   ISJMP          error_found       ; combinations
     20BC   C90080         54             push    #8000h
     20BF   C98080         55             push    #8080h
     20C2   EF0000         56             call    alu05
     20C5   980001       E 57             cmpb    eregl+1,zero
     20C8   DF022064     E 58             bne     error_found
                                   IJE    $+4
                                   ISJMP          error_found
     20CC   C90080         60             push    #8000h
     20CF   C90080         61             push    #8000h
     20D2   EF0000         62             call    alu05
     20D5   980001       E 63             cmpb    eregl+1,zero
     20D8   D756         E 64             bne     error_found
                            65
                            66
     20DA   C98080         67             push    #8000h
     20DD   C90080         68             push    #8000h
     20E0   EF0000         69             call    alu05
     20E3   980001       E 70             cmpb    eregl+1,zero
     20E6   D748         E 71             bne     error_found
                            72
     20E8   C90001         73             push    #100h             ; perform a galloping 1s/0s test
     20EB   C9FF7F         74             push    #7ffh             ; on a small section of RAM
     20EE   EF0000         75             Call    mem0a
     20F1   980001       E 76             cmpb    eregl+1,zero
     20F4   D73A         E 77             bne     error_found
                            78
     20F6   C800           79             push    timerl            ;send a timerl based seed to the
     20F8   C90020         80             push    #2000h            ;random number based multiply/divide
     20FB   EF0000         81             call    alu04             ; test and let it run for a string
     20FE   980001       E 82             cmpb    eregl+1h,zero     ; of 2000h argument pairs
     2101   D72D         E 83             bne     error_found
                            84
     2103   EF0000         85             call    alu01             ;perform the add/subtract test
     2106   980001       E 86             cmpb    eregl+1h,zero
     2109   D725         E 87             bne     error_found
                            88
     210B   C90042         89             push    #4200h            ; perform a Complementary address test
     210E   C9FF5F         90             push    #5fffh            ; on a large section of RAM
     2111   EF0000         91             Call    mem06
     2114   980001       E 92             cmpb    eregl+1,zero
     2117   D717         E 93             bne     error_found
                            94
     2119   EF0000         95             call    alu02             ; perform the MULUB test
     211C   980001       E 96             cmpb    eregl+1h,zero
     211F   D70F         E 97             bne     error_found
                            98
     2121   C800           99             push    timerl            ; send another timerl based seed to
     2123   C90020        100             push    #2000h            ; the random number based multiply/
     2126   EF0000        101             call    alu04             ; divide test
     2129   980001      E 102             cmpb    eregl+1h,zero
     212C   D702        E 103             bne     error_found
                           104
```

MCS-96 MACRO ASSEMBLER   DSTUSR

```
ERR LOC   OBJECT           LINE      SOURCE STATEMENT
    212E  277C              105           BR    Main_task       ; start the main_task tests over
                            106
                            107      Error_found:
    2130  FA                108            di                   ; if an error is found, disable
    2131  EF0000          E 109            CALL  Error_Proc     ; interrupts and call the error
                            110                                 ; procedure in the DST96.LIB.
                            111                                 ; the test that found an error will
                            112                                 ; have placed the appropriate
                            113                                 ; error codes in locations EREG1 and
                            114                                 ; EREG2 for output through Error_Proc
    2134  27FE              115           BR $
                            116      ;***********************************************
                            117
    2136                    118           end
```

M S-96 MACRO ASSEMBLER   DSTUSR

SYMBOL TABLE LISTING
────────────────────

```
N A M E                   VALUE    ATTRIBUTES

ALU01. . . . . . . . . .  ----     CODE EXTERNAL
ALU02. . . . . . . . . .  ----     CODE EXTERNAL
ALU04. . . . . . . . . .  ----     CODE EXTERNAL
ALU05. . . . . . . . . .  ----     CODE EXTERNAL
DSEG1. . . . . . . . . .  0100H    DATA ABS BYTE
DSEG2. . . . . . . . . .  4200H    DATA ABS BYTE
DSTISR . . . . . . . . .  ----     CODE EXTERNAL
DSTUSR . . . . . . . . .  ----     MODULE MAIN STACKSIZE(2)
EREG1. . . . . . . . . .  ----     REG EXTERNAL
ERROR_FOUND. . . . . . .  2130H    CODE ABS ENTRY
ERROR_PROC . . . . . . .  ----     REG EXTERNAL
MAIN_TASK. . . . . . . .  20ACH    CODE ABS ENTRY
MEM06. . . . . . . . . .  ----     CODE EXTERNAL
MEM0A. . . . . . . . . .  ----     CODE EXTERNAL
SP . . . . . . . . . . .  ----     REG EXTERNAL
TEMP . . . . . . . . . .  0040H    OVERLAY ABS WORD
TIMER1 . . . . . . . . .  ----     REG EXTERNAL
USER_REGISTERS . . . . .  0040H    OVERLAY ABS BYTE
ZERO . . . . . . . . . .  ----     REG EXTERNAL
```

ASSEMBLY COMPLETED,   NO ERROR(S) FOUND.

intel.

Embedded Intel386™ Processors

6

intel

AP-442
APPLICATION NOTE

33 MHz 386 System Design Considerations

SHAHZAD BAQAI
KIYOSHI NISHIDE

May 1990

Order Number: 240725-001

33 MHz 386 SYSTEM DESIGN CONSIDERATIONS

CONTENTS	PAGE
1.0 INTRODUCTION	6-3
2.0 HIGH SPEED SYSTEM DESIGN CONSIDERATIONS	6-5
2.1 Overview of High Speed Effects	6-5
2.2 Transmission Line Effects	6-8
2.3 Reflection	6-9
2.4 Cross Talk	6-14
2.5 Skew	6-14
2.6 D.C. Loading	6-15
2.7 A.C. (Capacitive) Loading	6-15
2.8 Derating Curve	6-15
2.9 High Speed Clock Circuits	6-16

CONTENTS	PAGE
3.0 DESIGN EXAMPLE	6-18
3.1 System Architecture for High Speeds	6-18
3.2 CPU Subsystem	6-18
3.3 DRAM Subsystem	6-18
3.4 Cache Subsystem	6-20
3.5 I/O-EPROM Subsystem	6-26
APPENDIX A Schematics	6-30
APPENDIX B State Diagrams and Palcodes	6-41
APPENDIX C Timing Diagrams	6-88
APPENDIX D Timing Equations	6-101
APPENDIX E References	6-111

AP-442

RELATED DOCUMENTATION

This Application Note should be used in conjunction with the 386 DX microprocessor Data Sheet (Order Number 231630-011) and the 386 DX Hardware Reference Manual (Order Number 231732-004). A list of related references is provided in the appendix for getting more information on high speed design issues.

SECTION I. INTRODUCTION

The 386 DX Microprocessor is an advanced 32-bit microprocessor designed using Intel's CHMOS IV process for applications which require very high performance. It is optimized for multitasking operating systems. The 32-bit register and data paths support 32-bit address and data types allowing up to four gigabytes of physical memory and 64 terabytes of virtual memory to be addressed. The integrated memory management and protection architecture includes address translation registers, advanced multitasking hardware and a protection mechanism to support operating systems. In addition, the 386 DX microprocessor allows the simultaneous running of DOS with other operating systems.

Instruction pipelining, on chip address translation and high bus bandwidth ensure short average instruction execution times and high system throughput. To facilitate high performance system hardware designs, the 386 DX microprocessor bus interface offers address pipelining, dynamic data bus sizing and direct byte enable signals for each byte of the data bus.

This Application Note is intended to show how to complete a successful design of a 'Core' system using the 386 DX-33, the 33 MHz clock version. A Core system is a minimum system configuration, in this case comprising the CPU, the 82385 32-bit Cache controller, Dynamic and Static RAM and an I/O mechanism with which to communicate with the CPU.

The Application Note examines the design techniques necessary when executing a design at this frequency. Many of the methods used at lower frequencies, such as 16 MHz and 20 MHz, are no longer valid at this higher frequency. Phenomena, whose effects are negligible at the lower frequencies, must be taken into account in the design. The physical positioning of components relative to each other plays a significant part in the success of the design, since transmission line effects (reflection, radiation) are no longer negligible.

AP-442

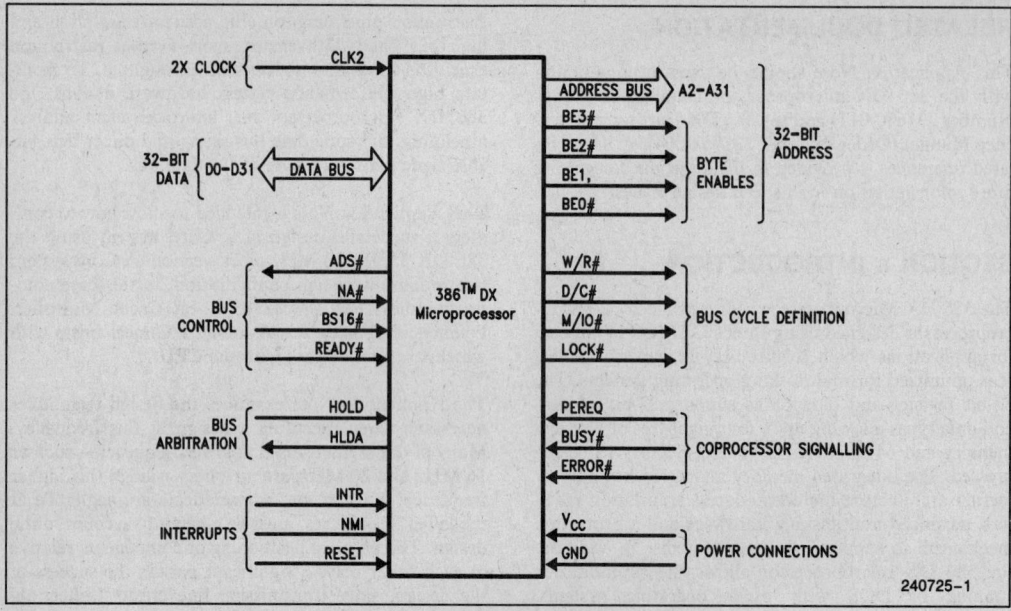

Figure 1-1. Functional Signal Groups

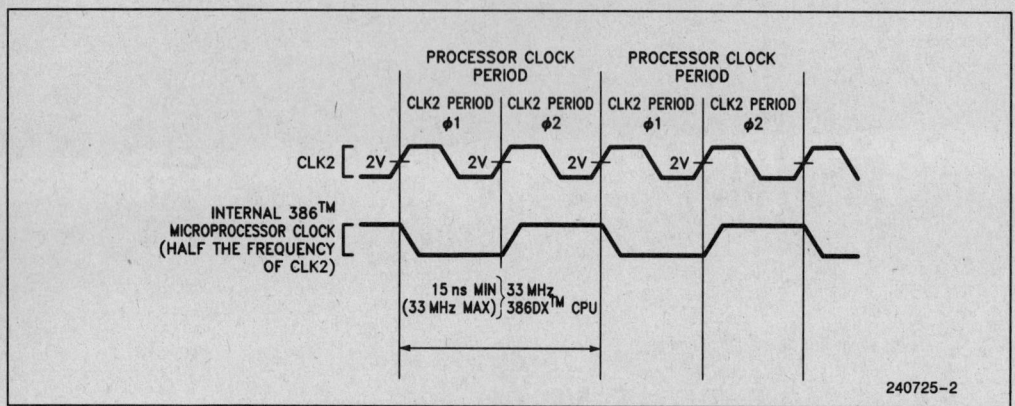

Figure 1-2. CLK2 Signal and Internal Processor Clock

SECTION II. HIGH SPEED SYSTEM DESIGN CONSIDERATIONS

2.1 Overview Of High Speed Effects

This section is included as a brief overview of general issues that are applicable to both higher and lower frequencies of circuit design.

The CHMOS IV 386 DX CPU differs from previous HMOS microprocessors in that its power dissipation is primarily capacitive; there is almost no DC power dissipation. Power dissipation depends mostly on frequency. This fact is used in designs where power consumption is critical.

Power dissipation can be distinguished as either internal (logic) power or I/O (bus) power. Internal power varies with operating frequency and to some extent with wait states and software. Internal power increases with supply voltage also. Process variations in manufacturing affect internal power, although to a lesser extent than with NMOS processes.

I/O power, which accounts for roughly one-fifth of the total power dissipation, varies with frequency and voltage. It also depends on capacitive bus load. Capacitive bus loadings for all output pins are specified in the 386 DX CPU data sheet. The 386 DX CPU output valid delays will increase if these loadings are exceeded. The addressing pattern of the software can affect I/O power by changing the effective frequency at the address pins. The variation in frequency at the data pins tends to be smaller; thus varying data patterns should not cause a significant change in power dissipation.

POWER AND GROUND PLANES

Power and ground planes must be used in 386 DX CPU systems to minimize noise. Power and ground lines have inherent inductance and capacitance, therefore an impedance $z = (L/C)^{*1/2}$. The total characteristic impedance for the power supply can be reduced by adding more lines. This effect is illustrated in 2.1 which shows that two lines in parallel have half the impedance of one. To reduce the impedance even further, the user should add more lines. In the limit, an infinite number of parallel lines, or a plane, results in the lowest impedance. Planes also provide the best distribution of power and ground.

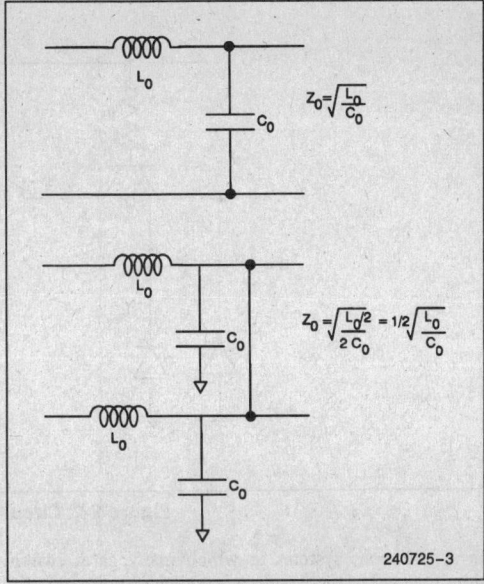

Figure 2-1. Reducing Characteristic Impedance

The 386 DX CPU has 20 V_{CC} pins and 21 V_{SS} (ground) pins. All power and ground pins must be connected to a plane. Ideally, the 386 DX CPU is located at the center of the board, to take full advantage of these planes. Although the 386 DX CPU generally demands less power than the 80286, the possibility of power surges is increased due to higher frequency and pin count. Peak-to-peak noise on V_{CC} relative to V_{SS} should be maintained at no more than 400 mV, and preferably to no more than 200 mV.

DECOUPLING CAPACITORS

The switching activity of one device can propagate to other devices through the power supply. For example, in the TTL NAND gate of Figure 2.2, both Q3 and Q4 transistors are on for a short time when the output is switching. This increased load causes a negative spike on V_{CC} and a positive spike on ground.

AP-442

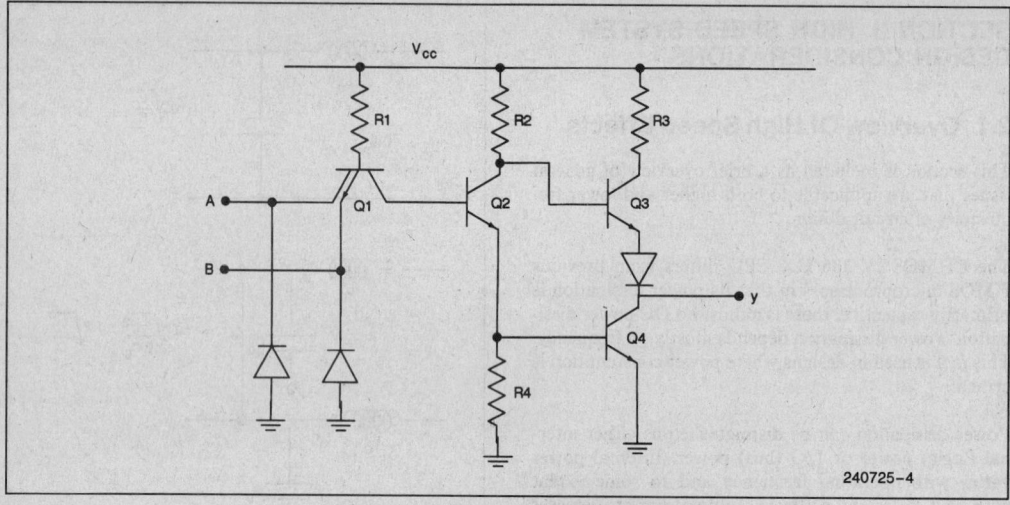

Figure 2-2. Circuit without Decoupling

In synchronous systems in which many gates switch simultaneously, the result is signifcant noise on the power and ground lines.

Decoupling capacitors placed across the device between V_{cc} and ground reduce Voltage spikes by supplying the extra current needed during switching. These capacitors should be placed close to their devices because the inductance or connection lines negates their effect.

When selecting decoupling capacitors, the user should provide 0.01 microfarads for each device and 0.1 microfarads for every 20 gates. Radio-frequency capacitors must be used; they should be distributed evenly over the board to be most effective. In addition, the board should be decoupled from the external supply line with a 2.2 microfarad capacitor.

Chip capacitors (surface-mount) are preferable because they exhibit lower inductance and require less total board space. They should be connected as in Figure 2.3. Leaded capacitors can also be used if the leads are kept as short as possible. Six leaded capacitors are required to match the effectiveness of one chip capacitor, but because only a limited number can fit around the 386 DX, the configuration in Figure 2.4 results.

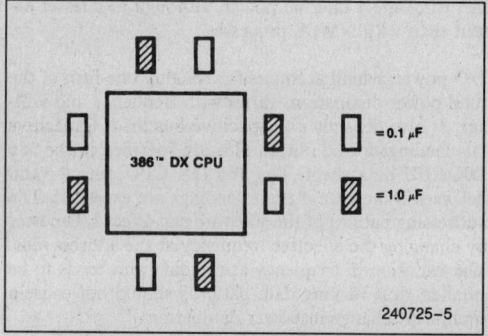

Figure 2-3. Decoupling Chip Capacitors

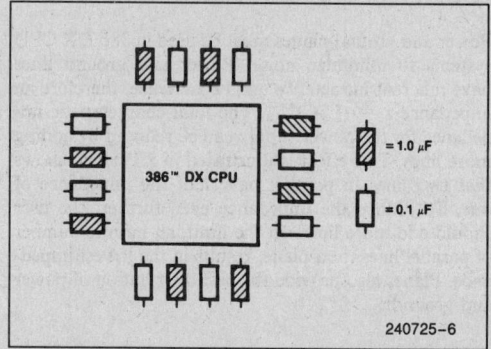

Figure 2-4. Decoupling Leaded Capacitors

HIGH FREQUENCY DESIGN CONSIDERATIONS

At high signal frequencies, the transmission line properties of signal paths in a circuit must be considered. Reflections, interference, and noise become significant in comparison to the high-frequency signals. They can cause false signal transitions, data errors, and input voltage level violations. These errors can be transient and therefore difficult to debug. In this section, some high-frequency design issues are discussed. Their effects and ways to minimize will be introduced in the next section.

REFLECTION AND LINE TERMINATION

Input voltage level violations are usually due to voltage spikes that raise input voltage levels above the maximum limit (overshoot) and below the minimum limit (undershoot). These voltage levels can cause excess current on input gates that results in permanent damage to the device. Even if no damage occurs, most devices are not guaranteed to function as specified if input voltage levels are exceeded.

Signal lines are terminated to minimize signal reflections and prevent overshoot and undershoot. If the round-trip signal path delay is greater than the rise time or fall time of the signal, terminate the line. If the line is not terminated, the signal reaches its high or low level before reflections have time to dissipate, and overshoot and undershoot occur. There are a few termination techniques that are used in different applications, these will be discussed in the next section.

INTERFERENCE

Interference is the result of electrical activity in one conductor causing transient voltages to appear in another conductor. It increases with frequency and closeness of the two conductors.

There are two types of interference to consider in high frequency circuits: electromagnetic interference (EMI) and electrostatic interference (ESI).

EMI (also called crosstalk) is caused by the magnetic field that exists around any current carrying conductor. The magnetic flux from one conductor can induce current in another conductor, resulting in transient voltage. Several precautions can minimize EMI.

Running a ground line between two adjacent lines wherever they traverse a long section of the circuit board. The ground line should be grounded at both ends.

Running ground line between the lines of an address bus or a data bus if either of the following conditions exist.
- The bus is on an external layer of the board.
- The bus is on an internal layer but not sandwiched between power and ground planes that are at most 10 mils away.

Avoiding closed loops in signal paths (see Figure 2.5). Closed loops cause excessive current and create inductive noise, especially in the circuitry enclosed by a loop.

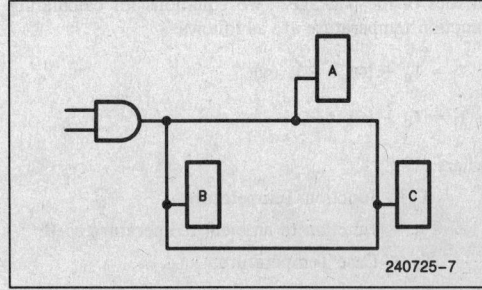

Figure 2-5. Avoid Closed-Loop Signal Paths

ESI is caused by the capacitive coupling of two adjacent conductors. The conductors act as the plates of a capacitor; a charge built up on one induces the opposite charge on the other.

The following steps reduce ESI:

Separating signal lines so that capacitive coupling becomes negligible.

Running a ground line between two lines to cancel the electrostatic fields.

LATCHUP

Latchup is a condition in a CMOS circuit in which V_{CC} becomes shorted to V_{SS}. Intel's CHMOS IV process is immune to latchup under normal operating conditions. Latchup can be triggered when the voltage limits on I/O pins are exceeded, causing internal PN junctions to become forward biased. The following guidelines help prevent latchup:

Observing the maximum rating for input voltage on I/O pins.

Never applying power to an 386 DX CPU pin or a device connected to an 386 DX CPU pin before applying power to the 386 DX CPU itself.

Preventing overshoot and undershoot on I/O pins by adding line termination and by designing to reduce noise and reflection on signal lines.

AP-442

THERMAL CHARACTERISTICS

The thermal specification for the 386 DX CPU defines the maximum case temperature. This section describes how to ensure that an 386 DX CPU system meets this specification.

Thermal specifications for the 386 DX CPU are designed to guarantee a tolerable temperature at the surface of the 386 DX CPU chip. This temperature (called the junction temperature) can be determined from external measurements using the known thermal charactcristics of the package. Two equations for calculating junction temperature are as follows:

$T_j = T_a + (@j_a * PD)$ and

$T_j = T_c + (@j_c * PD)$

where:

T_j = Junction Temperature
$@j_a$ = Junction to ambient temperature coeff.
T_c = Case Temperature
T_a = Ambient Temperature
$@j_c$ = Junction to Case
PD = Power Dissapation temperature coeff.

Case temperature calculations offer several advantages over ambient temperature calculations.

Case temperature is easier to measure accurately than ambient temperature because the measurement is localized to a single point (top center of the package).

The worst-case junction temperature (T_j) is lower when calculated with case temperature for the following reasons:

— The junction-to-case thermal coefficient ($@j_c$) is lower than the junction-to-ambient thermal coefficient ($@j_a$); therefore, calculated junction temperature varies less with power dissipation (PD).

— $@j_c$ is not affected by airflow in the system; $@j_a$ varies with air flow.

With the case-temperature specification, the designer can either set the ambient temperature or use fans to control case temperature. Finned heat sinks or conductive cooling may also be used in environments where the use of fans is precluded. To approximate the case temperature for various environments, the two equations above should be combined by setting the junction temperature equal for both, resulting in this equation:

$$T_a = T_c - ((@j_a - @j_c) * PD)$$

The current data sheet should be consulted to determine the values of @ja (for the system's air flow) and ambient temperature that will yield the desired case temperature. Whatever the conditions are, the case temperature is easy to verify.

2.2 Transmission Line Effects

As a general rule, any interconnection is considered a transmission line when the time required for the signal to travel the length of the interconnection is greater than one-eighth of the signal rise time. (True K. M., "Reflection: Computations and Waveforms, The Interface Handbook", Fairchild Corp, Mountain View, CA, 1975, Ch. 3). As frequencies increase, designers must account for the negative effects associated with transmission lines. The section that follows will attempt to describe these effects and provide some suggestions for minimizing their negative effect on the system.

Before describing each effect, it is important to know how to characterize a trace on different types of transmision lines. This includes knowing the characteristic impedance of a trace, Z_o, and the propagation delay for a given trace, t_{pd}. These parameters will be used in determining what effects must be accounted for and to select component values used in minimizing the effects.

TRANSMISSION LINES TYPES

Although many types of transmission lines (conductors) exist, those most commonly used on the printed circuit boards are microstrip lines, strip lines, printed circuit traces, side-by-side conductors and flat conductors.

MICRO STRIP LINES

The micro strip trace consists of a signal plane that is seperated from a ground plane by a dielectric as shown in Figure 2.6. G-10 fiber-glass epoxy, which is most common, has an $e_r = 5$ where e_r is the dielctric constant of the insulation. Let:

w = the width of the signal line (inches)
t = the thickness of copper
h = the height of dielectric for controlled impedance (inches)

AP-442

The characteristic impedance Z_o, is a function of dielectric constant and the geometry of the board. This is given by:

$$Z_o = (87/(e_r + 1.41)^{1/2}) \ln (5.98/0.8 w + t) \; \Omega$$

where e_r is the relative dielectric constant of the board material.

The propagation delay (t_{pd}) associated with the trace is a function of the dielectric only.

$$t_{pd} = 1.017 (0.475 e_r + 0.67)^{1/2} \; \text{ns/ft}$$

STRIP LINES

A strip line is a strip conductor centered in a dielectric medium between two voltage planes. The characteristic impedance is given by:

$$Z_o = 60/(e_r)^{1/2} \ln (5.98 b/(0.8 W + t)) \; \Omega$$

where b = distance between the planes for the controlled impedance as shown in Figure 2.10

The propagation delay is given by:

$$t_{pd} = 1.017 (e_r)^{1/2} \; \text{ns/ft}$$

Typical values of the characteristic impedance and propagation delay of these types of lines are:

$$Z_O = 50 \Omega$$
$$t_{pd} = 2 \; \text{ns/ft (or 6 in/ns)}$$

2.3 Reflection

The first effect is reflection. As the name indicates it is the reflection of a signal as it propagates down the trace. The reflection results from a mismatch in impedance. The impedance of a transmission line is a function of the geometry of the line, its distance from the ground plane, and the loads long the line. Any discontinuity in the impedance will cause reflections.

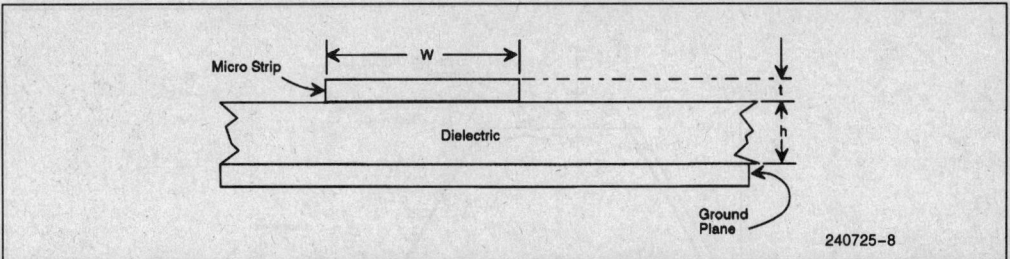

Figure 2-6. Micro Strip Lines

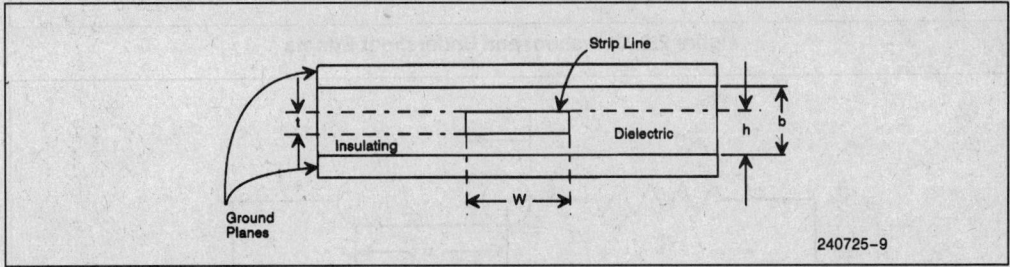

Figure 2-7. Strip Lines

AP-442

Impedance mismatch occurs between the transmission line characteristic impedance and the input or output impedance of the devices that are connected to the line. The result is that the signals are reflected back and forth on the line. These reflections can attentuate or reinforce the signal depending upon the phase relationships. The results of these reflections include overshoot, undershoot, ringing and other undesirable effects.

At lower edge rates, the effects of these reflections are not severe. However at higher rates, the rise time of the signal is short with respect to the propagation delay. Thus it can cause problems as shown in Figure 2-8.

Overshoot occurs when the voltage level exceeds the maximum (upper) limit of the output voltage, while undershoot occurs when the level passes below the minimum (lower) limit. These conditions can cause excess current on the input gates which results in permanent damage to the device.

The amount of reflection voltage can be easily calculated. Figure 2-9 shows a system exhibiting reflections.

The magnitude of a reflection is usually represented in terms of a reflection coefficient. This is illustrated in the following equations:

$$T = v_r/v_i = \text{Reflected voltage/Incident voltage}$$
$$T_{load} = (Z_{load} - Z_O)/(Z_{load} + Z_O)$$
$$T_{source} = (Z_{source} - Z_O)/(Z_{source} + Z_O)$$

Reflections voltage V_r is given by V_i, the voltage incident at the point of the reflections, and the reflection coefficient.

The model transmission line can now be completed. In Figure 2-9, the voltage seen at point A is given by the following equation:

$$V_a = V_s * Z_O/(Z_O + Z_s)$$

This voltage V_a enters the transmission line at "A" and appears at "B" delayed by t_{pd}.

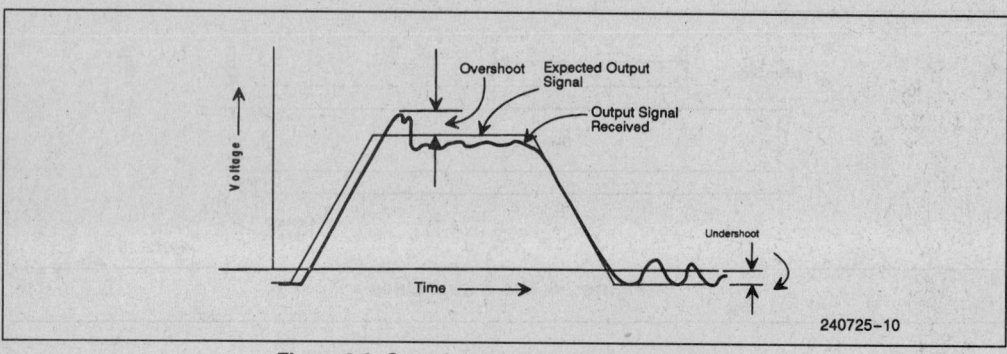

Figure 2-8. Overshoot and Undershoot Effects

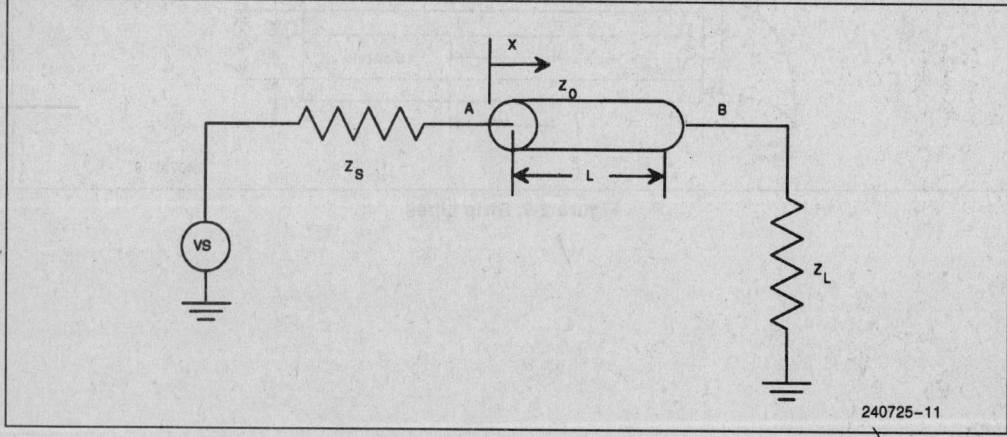

Figure 2-9. Loaded Transmission Line

AP-442

$$V_b(t - x/t) \; H(t - x/v)$$

where $x =$ distance along the transmission line from point "A" and $H(t)$ is the unit step function. The waveform encounters the loads Z_L, and this may cause reflection. The reflected wave enters the transmission line at "B" and appears at point "A" after time delay (t_{pd}):

$$V_{r1} = T_{load} * V_b$$

This phenomenon continues infinitely, but it is negligible after 3 or 4 reflections. Hence:

$$V_{r2} = T_{source} * V_{r1}$$

Each reflected waveform is treated as a seperate source that is independent of the reflection coefficient at that point and the incident waveform. Thus the waveform from any point and on the transmission line and at any given time is as follows:

$$V(x,t) = (Z_O/(Z_O+Z_s)) \; \{V_s(t-(x/v)) \; H(t-(x/v)) + $$
$$T_1 \; [V_s(t-((2L-x)/v) \; H(t-(t-((2L-x)/v)))] + $$
$$T_1 T_s \; [V_s(t-((2L+x)/v) \; H(t-(t-((2L+x)/v)))] + $$
$$T_1{}^2 T_s \; [V_s(t-((4L-x)/v) \; H(t-(t-((4L-x)/v)))] + $$
$$T_1{}^2 T_s{}^2 \; [V_s(t-((4L+x)/v) \; H(t-(t-((4L+x)/v)))] $$
$$+ \ldots \}$$

Each reflection is added to the total voltage through the unit step function $H(t)$. The above equation can be rewritten as follows:

$$V(x,t) = (Z_O/(Z_O+Z_s)) \; \{V_s(t-(t-t_{pd}x) \; H(t-t_{pd}x) + $$
$$T_1 \; [V_s(t-t_{pd}(2L-x)) \; H(t-t_{pd}(2L-x))] + $$
$$T_1 T_s \; [V_s(t-t_{pd}(2L+x)) \; H(t-t_{pd}(2L+x))] + \ldots \}$$

Impedance discontinuity problems are managed by imposing limits and control during the routing phase of the design. Design rules must be observed to control trace geometry, including specification of the trace width and spacing for each layer. This is very important because it ensures the traces are smooth and constant without sharp turns.

HOW TO MINIMIZE

There are several techniques which can be employed to further minimize the effects caused by an impedance mismatch during the layout process:

1. Impedance Matching
2. Daisy Chaining
3. Avoid 90° Corners
4. Minimize the Number of Vias

IMPEDANCE MATCHING

Impedance matching is the process of matching the impedance of the the source or load to the impedance of the trace. This matching is accomplished using a technique called termination. Termination makes the effective source or load impedance, seen by the trace, to be approximately equal to the characteristic impedance of the trace. Before terminating a line one must determine if termination is required. This is done by a simple calculation. If the propagation delay down a trace from source to destination is greater than or equal to one-third the signals rise time, termination is needed. (i. e. $T_{pd} \geq \frac{1}{3} \; t_r$). The rise time is the 0%-100% rise time specified for the source. If this value is specified for 10%-90% or 20%-80%, it must be scaled by multiplying the specified value by 1.25 or 1.67, respectively. The propagation delay is caculated by multiplying the trace propagation delay, t_{pd}, descibed earlier by the trace length.

Once it is determined that termination is needed, use the equation described earlier to calculate the trace's characteristic impedance. The specification sheets for the load can be consulted to determine the load impedance, Z_L. These values are needed to select the component values used to terminate.

The next chore is selecting the type of termination to use. In this section we will examine 4 different techniques and point out the advantages and disadvantages. Figure 2.10 shows the four types of termination and the corresponding component values.

Parallel termination, shown in Figure 2-10(a), is a good technique to maintain the waveform. The waveform at the load is a perfect image of the waveform at the source. In addition there is no added propagation delay associated with this technique. The disadvantage of this technique is that it requires a fair amount of additional power and it is not suggested for characteristic impedances of less than 100 ohms because of the large d.c. current required.

Thevenin termination, shown in Figure 2-10(b), is another option. This technique also requires a large amount of power, but does not have the restrictions for characteristic impedance. This technique is very good at removing overshoot and undershoot while not adding any additional delay. Another advantage is that the trace can be biased toward Vcc or GND by simpling selecting the appropriate resistor values. This can help maintain fast edges on important signal transitions.

AP-442

Name	Circuitry	Advantages	Disadvantages
Parallel	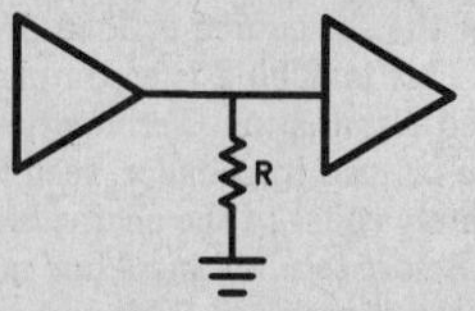 R = Z_O	Waveform at receiver is almost perfect image of input Bipolar/Advanced CMOS No added T_{PD}	High power dissipation $Z_O \geq 100\Omega$, else D.C. current limit
Thevenin	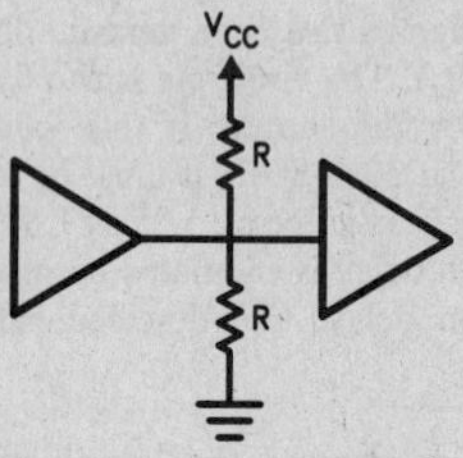 R = 2Z_O	Good overshoot and undershoot suppression Bipolar or Bipolar/CMOS systems No added T_{PD}	High power dissipation

Figure 2-10(a). Termination Techniques

Name	Circuitry	Advantages	Disadvantages
Series	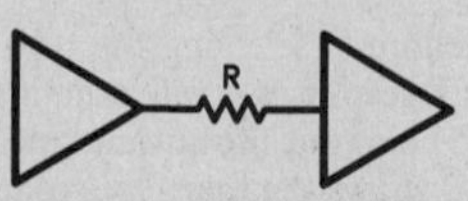 R = Z_O − Z_{OUT}	Low power consumption CMOS—CMOS Systems Easy to adjust signal amplitude to match switching threshold	Added T_{PD}
A.C.	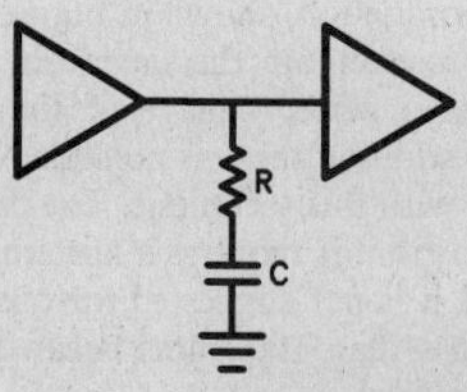 R = Z_O, C = 200 pF–500 pF	Low—medium power dissipation (capacitor blocks D.C. coupling of signal) No added delays High-speed CMOS families	Two added components

Figure 2-10(b). Termination Techniques

Series termination, shown in Figure 2-10(b), is a very easy technique of matching impedance. It only requires on resistor and very little additional power is required. In addition the resistor value can be selected to provide constructive or destructive reflections and thus alter the signal amplitude to match the switching threshold. The major disadvantage of this technique is the added delay it introduces.

The fourth technique is A.C. termination, shown in Figure 2-10(b). It requires a small amount of additional power, this is decreased over parallel termination by the introduction of the capacitor, and adds no extra delay to the path. The major disadvantage is that it requires two extra components.

After examing the systems needs and selecting a termination technique, the impedance values determined earlier, Z_O and Z_L, can be used to determine the component values to implement the termination. These values should be seen as a starting point and may be altered to remove a specific problem experienced on a signal or to bias signals in an appropriate fashion.

DAISY CHAINING

Another technique of minimizing reflections is to daisy-chain signals, shown in Figure 2-11. This means to run a single trace from a source and to distribute the loads along this trace. The alternative is to run multiple traces from the source to each load. Each trace will have reflections of its own and these will be transmitted down the other traces once they have returned to the source. To manage such a system separate termination would be required for each branch. To eliminate these multiple terminators from T-connections, high frequency designs are routed as daisy chains.

Because each gate provides its own impedance load along the chain, it is necessary to distribute these loads evenly along the length of the chain. Hence, the impedance along the chain will change in a series of steps and is easier to match. The overall speed of this line is faster and predictable. Also all loads should be placed at equal distances (regular intervals).

90 DEGREE ANGLES

Eliminating 90° angles also minimizes reflections. It is much more desirable to use 45° or 135° angles as shown in Figure 2-12.

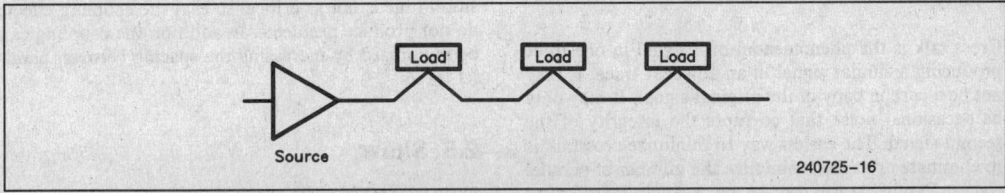

Figure 2-11. Daisy Chaining

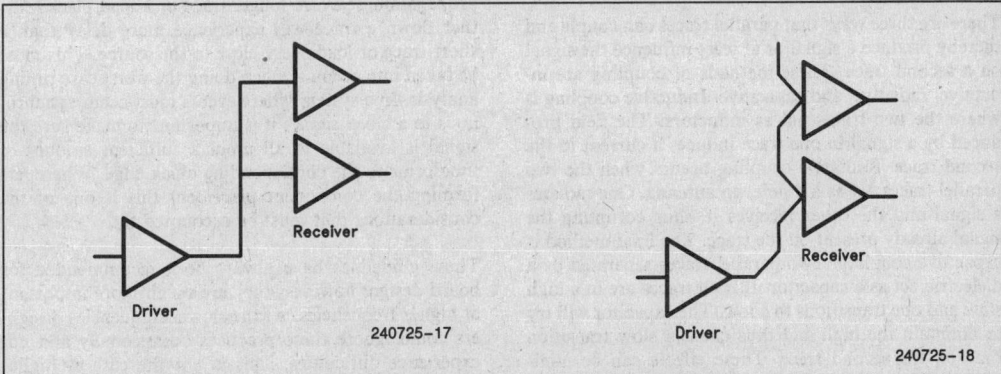

Figure 2-12. Avoiding 90 Degree Angles

VIAS (FEED THROUGH CONNECTIONS)

Another impedance source that degrades high frequency circuit performance is the via. Expert layout techniques can reduce vias to avoid reflection sites on PCBs.

Following these guidelines will not guarantee elimination of all reflections, but they will minimize the number and size.

2.4 Cross Talk

Cross talk is another negative effect of transmission lines. It is a problem at high frequencies because, as operating frequency increase, the signal wavelength become comparable to the length of the interconnections on the PC board. In general, interference such as cross talk, occurs when electrical activity in one conductor causes a transient voltage to appear in another conductor. Main factors that increase interference in any circuit are:

1. Variation of current and voltage in the lines causes frequency interference. This interence increases with increase in frequency.
2. Coupling occurs when conductors are in close proximity.

Cross talk is the phenomenom of a signal in one trace producing a similar signal in an adjacent trace. It may not be a carbon copy of the original signal. It may only be occasional noise that corrupts the integrity of the second signal. The easiest way to minimize crosstalk is to eliminate or at least minimize the number of parallel traces. Parallel traces can be on a single layer or on adjacent signal layers.

There are three ways that parallel traces can couple and thereby produce a signal or at least influence the signal on a second trace. These methods of coupling are inductive, radiative, and capacitive. Inductive coupling is where the two traces act as inductors. The field produced by a signal in one trace induces a current in the second trace. Radiative coupling occurs when the two parallel traces act as a dipole, an antenna. One radiates a signal and the other receives it, thus corupting the signal already present on the trace. The final method is capacitive coupling. Two parallel traces separated by a dielectric act as a capacitor. If both traces are in a high state and one transitions to a low. The capacitor will try to maintain the high and thus cause a slow transition time on the second trace. These effects can be minimized by reducing the number of parallel traces.

HOW TO MINIMIZE

When laying out a board for an high speed 386 DX based system, several guidelines should be followed to minimize crosstalk. Some of them are as follows:

1. To reduce crosstalk, it is necesary to minimize the common impedance paths.
2. Run a ground line between two adjacent lines. The lines should be grounded at both ends.
3. Seperate the address and data busses by a ground line. This technique may however be expensive due to large number of address and data lines.
4. Remove closed loop signal paths which create inductive noise.
5. Capacitive coupling can be reduced by reducing the number of parellel traces. Parallel traces can be minimized by insuring that signals on adjacent signal layers run orthogonal, perpendicular. Ground planes or traces can be inserted to provide shielding. A ground plane between signal layers eliminates any coupling that could occur. On a single trace, a ground trace can be run between traces to prevent coupling.

In some instances it is necessary to run traces parallel to each other. In these cases try to make the distance as short as possible and choose signals in which the transition time is not as critical so that the coupling effects do not produce problems. In addition the coupling can be minimized by increasing the spacing between parallel traces.

2.5 Skew

Skew is another effect of transmission lines. This is very important in a synchronous system. Long traces add propagation delay. A longer trace or a load placed further down a trace will experience more delay than a short trace or loads very close to the source. This must be taken into account when doing the worst case timing analysis. In a system where events must occur synchronous to a clock signal, it is important to make sure the signal is available to all input a sufficient amount of time prior to the corresponding clock edge. When performing the component placement this is one of the considerations that must be accounted for.

These guidelines have always been recommended for board design; however, they are much more important at higher frequencies. At the slower frequencies designers could ignore these practices occassionally and not experience difficulties. This is not the case at higher frequencies.

AP-442

2.6 DC Loading

To maintain proper logic levels, all digital signal outputs have a maximum load, they are capable of driving. DC loading is the constant current required by an input in either the high or the low state. It limits the ability of a device driving the bus to maintain proper logic levels. For a 386 DX based system, a careful analysis must be performed to ensure that in a worst case situation no loading limits are exceeded. Even if a bus is loaded slightly beyond its worst case limit, it might cause problems if a batch of parts whose input loading is close to maximum is encountered. Proper logic level will then fail to be maintained and unreliable operation may result. Marginal loading problems are particularly insidious, since the effect is often erratic operation and non repetitive errors that are extremely difficult to track down. For both the high and low logic levels, the sum of the currents required by all the inputs and the leakage currents of all outputs (drivers) on the bus must be added together. This sum must be less than the output capability of the weakest driver. Since the 386 DX is a CHMOS device having negligible dc loading, the main contributors to dc loading will be the TTL devices.

2.7 AC Loading

The AC or capacitive loading is caused by the input capacitance of each device and limits the speed at which a device driving a bus signal can change the state from high to low or low to high. Designers of microprocessor systems have traditionally calculated load capacitance of their systems by determining the number of devices and their individual capacitance loading attached to a signal plus the amount of trace capacitance. Typically, the trace capacitance was a set "lumped" number of pf (i.e. 2 pf to 3 pf per inch) when it is thought of at all. This lumped method is a general rule-of-thumb which generates a good first pass approximation. For low frequency designs, the lumped method works since system and component margins are large enough to cover any minor differences due to the approximation.

For high frequency designs, the component and system margins are no longer available to the designer. With less than 1 ns of margin, even the amount of trace capacitance can make a circuit path critical.

A more accurate calculation of capacitive loading can be derived by modeling the device loads and system traces as a series of Transmission Lines Theory. Transmission Line Theory provides a more accurate picture of system loading in high frequency systems. In addition, it allows new factors such as inductance and the effect of reflections upon the quality of the signal waveform to be factored into consideration.

2.8 Derating Curve and Its Effects:

A derating curve is a graph that plots the output buffer against the capacitive load. The curve is used to analyze a signal delay without necessitating a simulation every time the processor's loading changes. This graph assumes the lumped capacitance model to calculate the total capacitance. The delay in the graph should be added to the specified AC timing value for the device that is driving the load. The derating curve is different for different devices because each device has different output buffers.

A derating curve is generated by tying the chip's output buffers to a range of capacitors. The voltage and resistance values chosen for the output buffers are at the highest specified temperature and are rising (worst case) values. The value of the capacitors centres around the AC timing values for the chip. For 33 MHz and above, this is 50 pF. Since the AC timing specifications are measured for a signal reaching 1.5 V. A curve is then drawn from kthe range of time and capacitance values, with 50 pF representing the average and with nominal or zero derating. These curves are valid only for 50 pF–150 pF load range. Beyond this range the output buffers are not characterized. The the derating curve for the 386 DX are shown in 2-13. These curves use the lumped capacitance model for circuit capacitance measurements and must be modified slightly when doing worst-case calculations that involve transmission line effects.

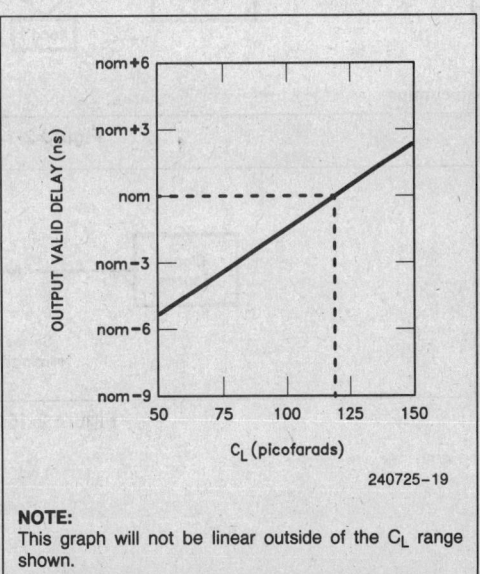

NOTE:
This graph will not be linear outside of the C_L range shown.

Figure 2-13. Typical Output Valid Delay Versus Load Capacitance at Maximum Operating Temperature (C_L = 120 pF)

6-15

2.9 High Speed Clock Circuits

For performance at high frequencies, the clock signal (CLK2) for the 386 DX CPU must be free of noise and within the specifcations listed in the 386 DX CPU data sheet. Achieving the proper clock routing around a 33 MHz printed circuit board is delicate because a myriad of problems, some of them subtle, can arise design guidelines are not followed. For example, fast clock edges cause reflections from high impedance terminations. These reflections can cause significant signal degradation in systems operating at 33 MHz clock rates. This section covers some design guidelines which should be observed to properly lay out the clock lines for efficient 386 DX operation.

- Since the rise/fall time of the clock signal is typically in the range of 2-4 ns, the reflections at this speed could result in undesirable noise and unacceptable signal degradation. The degree of reflections depends on the impedance of the traces of the clock connections. These reflections can be optimized by terminating the CLK2 output with proper terminations and by keeping length of the traces as short as possible. The preferred method is to connect all of the loads via a single trace as shown in Figure 2-14, thus avoiding the extra stubs associated with each load. The loads should be as close to one another as possible. Multiple clock sources should be for distributed loads.

- A less desirable method is the star connection layout in which the clock traces branch to the load as closely as posssible (Figure 2-15). In this layout, the stubs should be kept as short as possible. The maximum allowable length of the traces depends upon the frequency and the total fanout, but the length of all the traces in the star connection should be equal. Lengths of less than one inch are recommended. In this method the CLK2 signal is terminated by a series resistor. The resistor value is calculated by measuring the total capacitive load on the CLK2 signal and referring to Figure 2-16. If the total capacitive load is less than 80 pF, the user should add capacitors to make up the diference. Because of the high frequency of CLK2, the terminating resistor must have low inductance; carbon resistors are recommended.

- Use an oscilloscope to compare the CLK2 waveform with those in Figure 2-17.

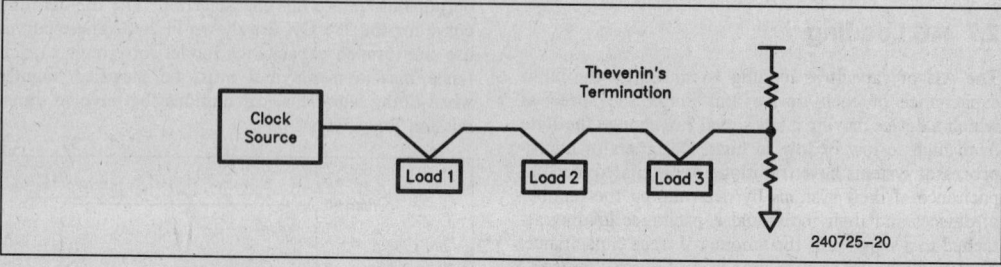

Figure 2-14. Clock Routing

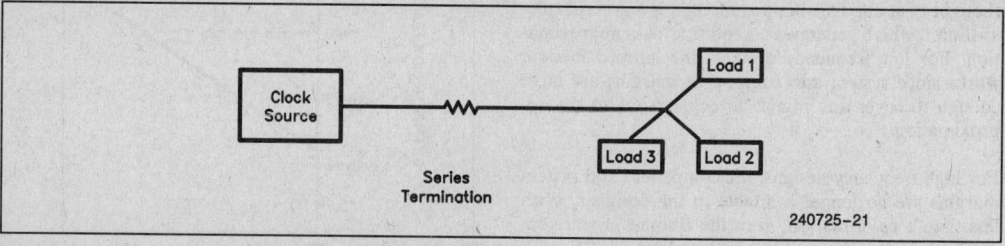

Figure 2-15. Star Connection

AP-442

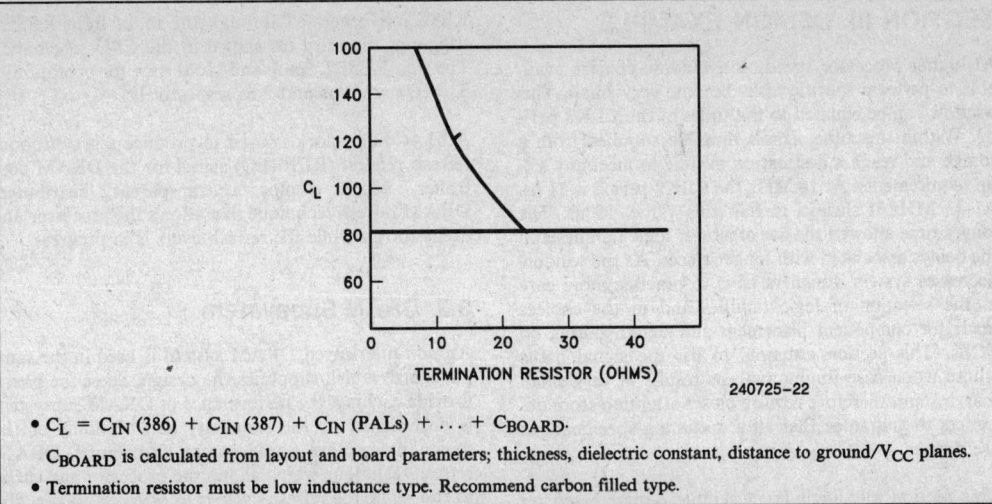

- $C_L = C_{IN}(386) + C_{IN}(387) + C_{IN}(PALs) + \ldots + C_{BOARD}$.

  C_{BOARD} is calculated from layout and board parameters; thickness, dielectric constant, distance to ground/V_{CC} planes.
- Termination resistor must be low inductance type. Recommend carbon filled type.

Figure 2-16. CLK2 Series Termination

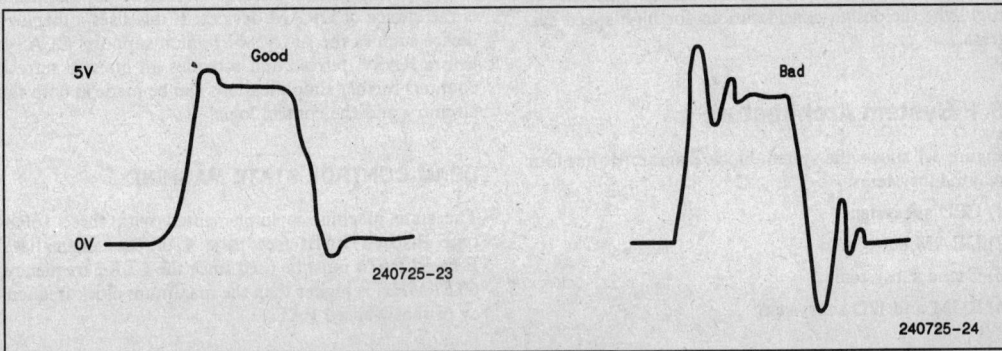

Figure 2-17. CLK2 Waveforms

AP-442

SECTION III. DESIGN EXAMPLE

At higher processor speeds the window of time available to perform specific tasks become very small. This window can be equated to multiples of the CLK2 period. Within this time signals must be supplied from a source and reach a destination in time to meet any set-up requirements. At 16 MHz the CLK2 period is 31 ns. At 33 MHz it shrinks to half this value, 15 ns. The longer time allowed the use of slower logic families and the delays associated with longer traces. As the window decreases system designers have to practice more care in the selection of logic families and in the choices made for component placement and signal routing on PCBs. This section attempts to list the signal paths whose worst case timing analysis results in very small margins and therefore require closer attention from designers to guarantee that all a. c. timing specifications are met.

This section also includes a sample design based on 33 MHz version of the 386 DX. It should not be taken as a recommended design. The circuit is used only to highlight the design considerations for high speed systems.

3.1 System Architecture

Figure 3.1 shows the system block diagram. It has four major subsystems.

1) CPU subsystem
2) DRAM subsystem
3) Cache subsystem
4) ROM and I/O subsystem

The system has 1 megabytes of Page-Mode DRAMS (60 ns RAS access time), 128 kilobytes of EPROMS (200 ns access time), an 8259A-2, and an 82510. The cache subsystem is optional. Schematics and PAL codes are given in appendix A and B respectively.

3.2 CPU Subsystem

The CPU subsystem consists of the 386 DX microprocessor, a clock and reset circuitry, and bus control logic. Clean and proper clock is very important in the designs at high frequencies.

RESET STATE MACHINE

This state machine is used to generate three control signals, namely RESET, REFREQ and CLK. The CLK signal is half of the CPU clock, CLK2 and is used mainly in I/O and EPROM subsystem.

RESET is generated through the input from RESET triggering circuitry (as shown in the CPU schematic). The min RESET Setup and Hold time for operation at 33 MHz are 5 ns and 2 ns respectively.

A 61.44 KHz clock is used to produce a synchronous refresh request (REFREQ) signal for the DRAM controller, which employ a transparent, distributed, DRAM refresh technique that allows the processor and cache to run while the refresh cycle is in progress.

3.3 DRAM Subsystem

An non-interleaved DRAM system is used in the sample board, which simplifies the design. Since the board provide caching, the performance of DRAM subsystem is outweighed by the simplicity and economy of the design. It employs a transparent, distributed, DRAM refresh technique which allows the processor and cache to run while the refresh cycle is in progress. It uses the 3-state capability of the 16R8-7 and the 74ACT258 to multiplex the refresh address. A further consideration is the choice of DRAM devices. If one uses a memory device such as the AAA2801 (which supports a CAS# before RAS# refresh and provides an internal refresh counter) further simplifications can be made in both the circuitry and the control logic.

DRAM CONTROL STATE MACHINE

The state machine is implemented with three 16R8-type E-speed PALs (see page 4 of the schematics). E-speed PALs must be used since the CLK2 frequency, 66.67 MHz, is higher than the maximum clock frequency of the D-speed PALs.

In order to generate DRAM control signals with smallest delay from the CLK2 edges, all state machines are implemented as Moore machines. The state machines flip-flops generate most of the DRAM control signals directly. This is an expensive design approach in terms of hardware but allows signal timings and skews to be fine tuned.

DRAM CYCLES—NO CACHE CONFIGURATION

Pages C-1 through C-4 show examples of DRAM cycles. In order to hide the DRAM page hit-or-miss decision time, the DRAM controller always tries to put the 386 DX in pipelined mode. The first read cycle requires only two wait states since RAS# has been precharged (see page C-1). The second cycle takes only two clock cycles. The second cycle is a pipelined, page-hit read cycle, which is the best case. The third cycle is a pipelined, page-hit write cycle. This cycle requires one wait state. DRAMs capture data at the falling edge of CAS# during Early Write cycles. The 386 DX drives

6-18

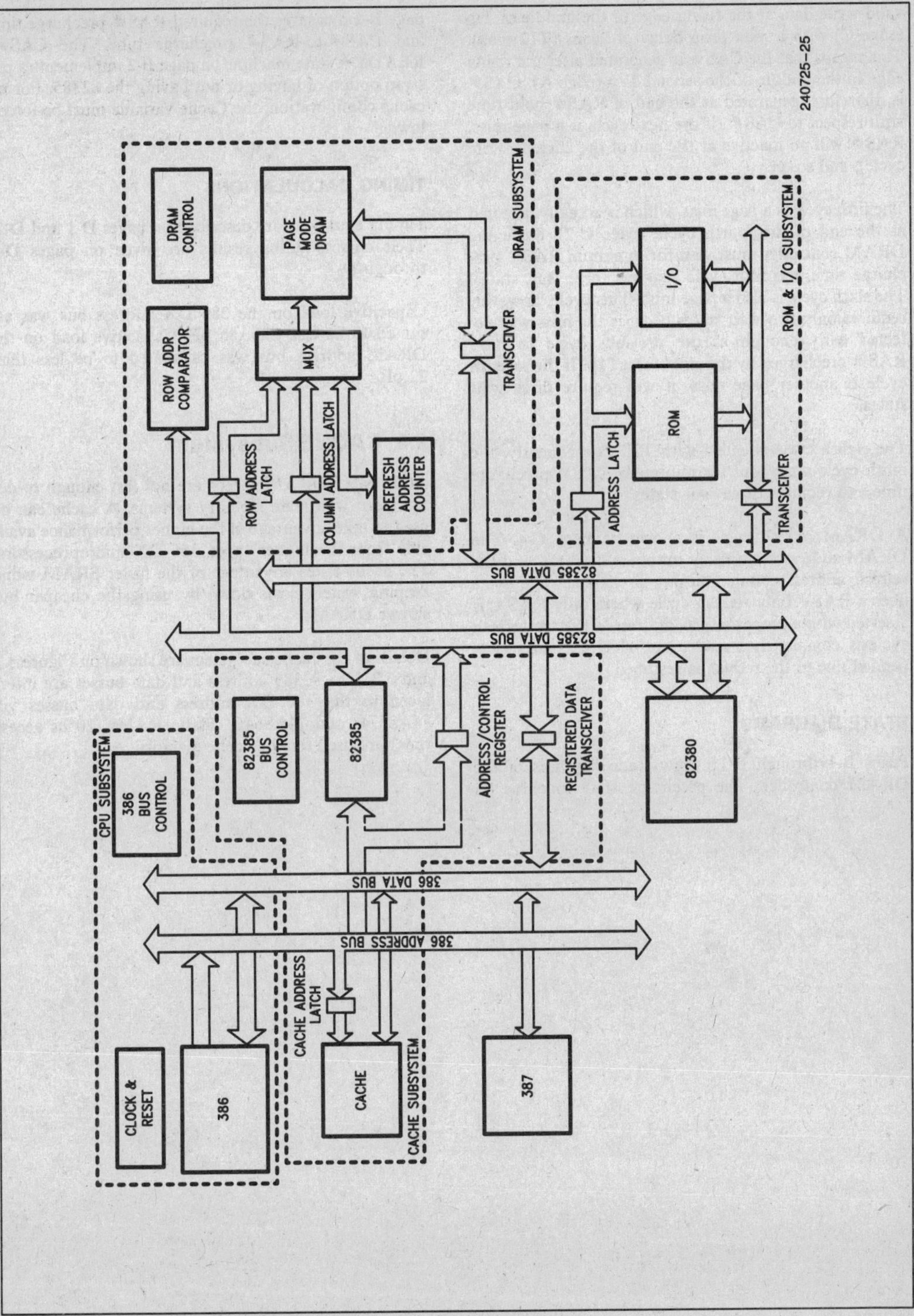

Figure 3-1. Block Diagram

AP-442

valid write data at the rising edge in the middle of Tip (edge C) with a max prop delay of 24 ns (T12 max). This means that the CAS# is generated after the rising edge in the middle of the second T2p (edge A). CAS# is, therefore, generated at the end of RAS# hold time with respect to CAS# (if the next cycle is a page miss, RAS# will go inactive at the end of the current write cycle), and so on.

The fifth cycle is a page miss, which is actually detected at the end of the fourth cycle (page C-2). Since the DRAM controller must wait for minimum RAS# precharge time, the fifth cycle requires three wait states. The sixth cycle is also a page miss. This cycle, however, requires only two wait states because the miss was detected early enough in the previous cycle to have RAS# precharged by the end of the T1p. If the seventh cycle is another page miss, it will require three wait states.

The eighth cycle is ended with T2i. Consequently, the ninth cycle must wait for minimum RAS# precharge time and requires three wait states.

A DRAM refresh cycle is shown on page C-4. The DRAM address multiplexer output is disabled, and the refresh address counter output is enabled. The cycle does a RAS# only refresh cycle where only RAS# is asserted with a proper refresh address. After the refresh cycle is completed, a read cycle which has been suspended due to the refresh is resumed.

STATE DIAGRAMS

Pages B-1 through B-11 show state diagrams of the DRAM controller. The precharge state machine on page B-2 measures the required RAS# precharge time and CAS#-to-RAS# precharge time. The CAS#-READY# state machine on page B-2 implements a pin strap option of having or not having the 82385. For no cache configuration, the Cache variable must be forced low.

TIMING CALCULATIONS

Timing equations are described on pages D-1 and D-2. Their corresponding results are given on pages D-3 through D-7.

Capacitive load on the 386 DX address bus was assumed to be less than 85 pF. Capacitive load on the DRAM address bus was calculated to be less than 22 pF.

3.4 CACHE Subsystem

At 33 MHz DRAM speeds are not fast enough to design zero wait state memory systems. A cache can be used to take advantage of the higher performance available from the higher speed 386 DX microprocessors. The cache takes advantage of the faster SRAM while keeping system costs down by using the cheaper but slower DRAMs.

Details of the cache subsystem are shown on Figure 3.2 and 3.3. The 82385 address and data busses are interfaced to the 386 DX address and data busses via 74AS574s and 74AS646s. Static RAMs (20 ns access time) are used for the cache memory.

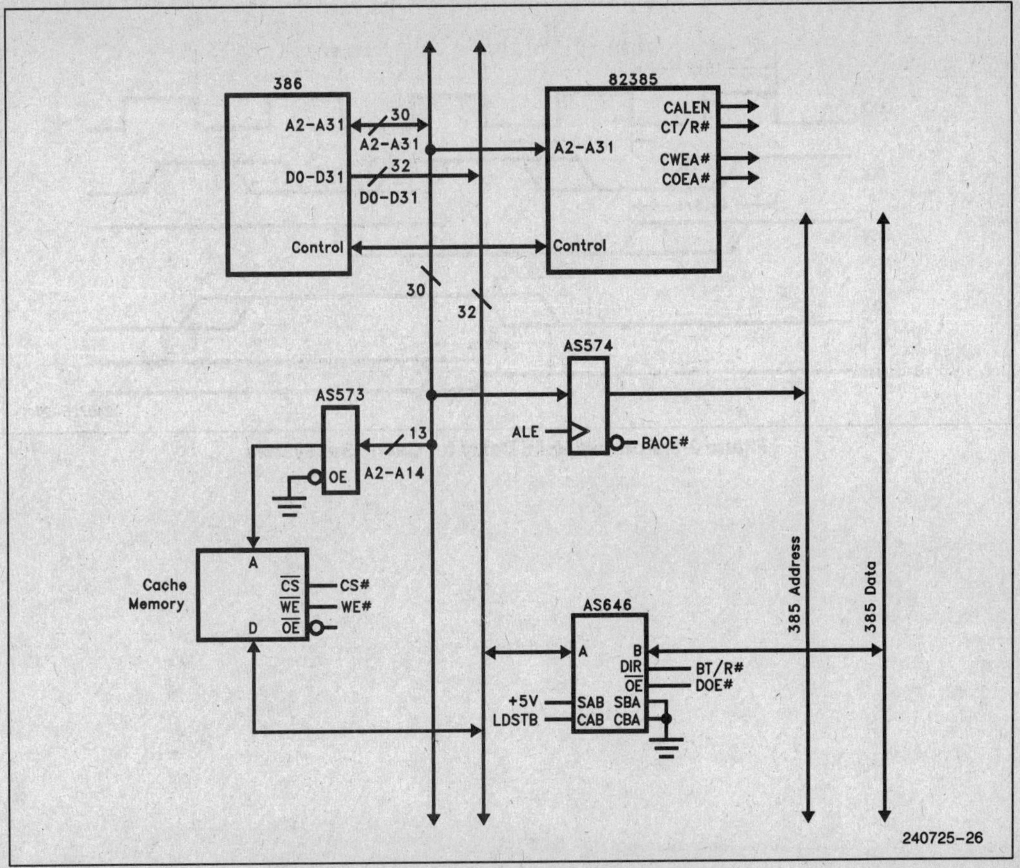

AP-442

Figure 3-2. Block Diagram of Cache Subsystem

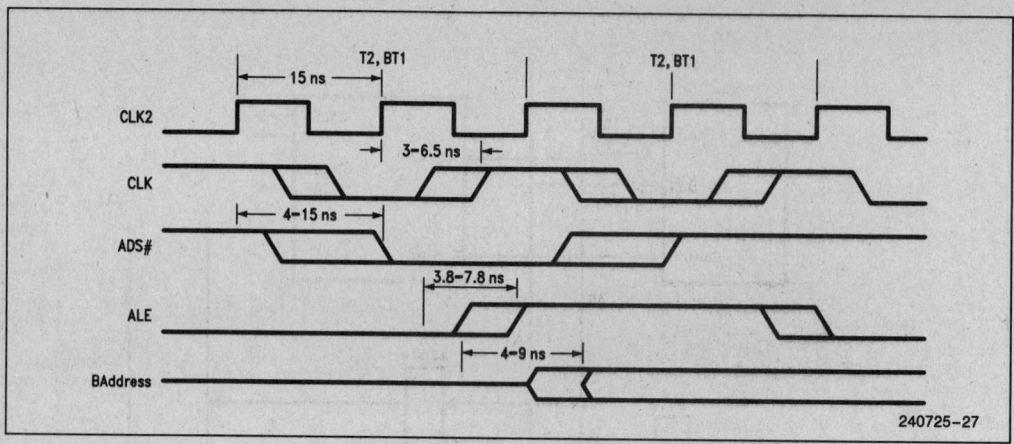

Figure 3-3. Address Valid Delay for Cache Subsystem

AP-442

In selecting SRAM there are several types one can choose to use. Some SRAM require a latch for the address and a transceiver for the data. Others have an OE#, output enable, signal and incorporate the transceiver on chip. The third type is called integrated SRAM and these contain both the latch and the transceiver on chip. However, there are two timing paths that dictate the speed selection within each type. Figure 3.4 shows a typical system configuration using each type.

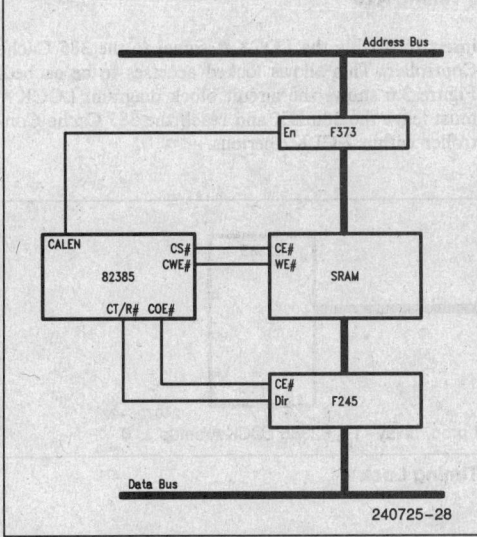

Figure 3.4(a) SRAM w/o OE#

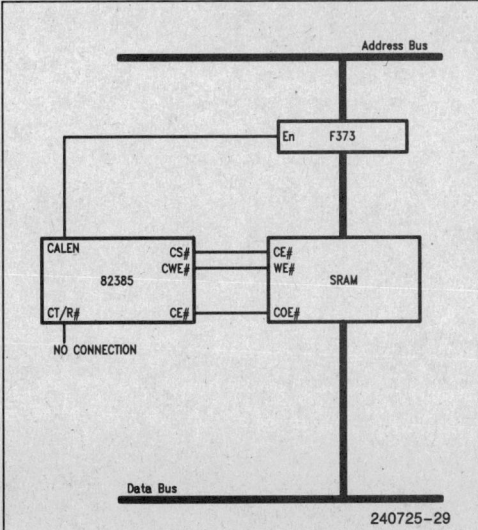

Figure 3.4(b) SRAM with OE# Control

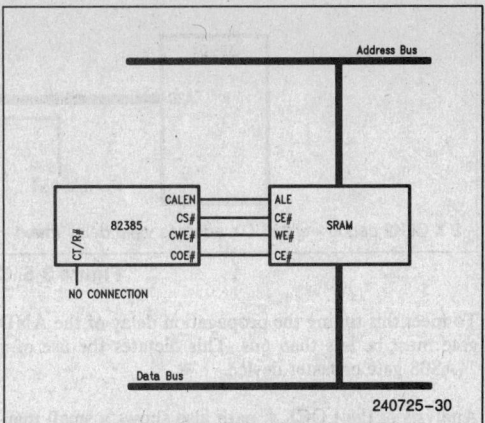

Figure 3-4. (c) Integrated SRAM

The critical times for the SRAM are the SRAM OE# to data delay and the SRAM address to data delay. The following analysis applies to SRAMs with an OE# signal as shown in Figure 3.4b. First examine the path of OE# to data. This path must be completed within 2 CLK periods. The COE# signal from the 385 Cache Controller must be valid and the SRAM must drive data onto the data bus so that the data setup time of the 386 DX CPU is met.

2 X CLK2 period - t_{25b} 82385 COE# valid delay (max) - SRAM access time (OE# to data) - t_{21} 386 DX data setup ≥ 0

Using the specified values from the data sheets reveals that the SRAM must have an OE# to data delay of 10ns or less. The other path is for the address to become available and data to reach the 386 DX CPU. This path has 4 CLK2 periods. The 385 Cache Controller must supply the CALEN signal to pass the address to the SRAM and then the SRAM must drive the data on the data bus so that the data setup time is met on the 386 DX CPU.

4 X CLK2 period - t_{21b} 82385 CALEN valid delay (max) - t_{pd} (x373 latch) - SRAM access time (address to data) - t_{21} 386 DX data setup ≥ 0

Once again using the data sheet the access time can be determined. Depending on the type of transparent latch the SRAM needs an address to data access time of 20ns or 25ns. If an F series 373 is used the faster 20ns SRAM must be used, but if an FCT373a or PCT373a is used the 25ns SRAM is sufficient.

The A_{20} path is another path with a small margin. The reason is the AND gate that many designers insert to provide 1MB wraparound of address in real mode. Figure 3.5 shows the circuit block diagram. A_{20} must leave the 386 DX and reach the 385 Cache Controller within 2 CLK2 periods.

6-23

AP-442

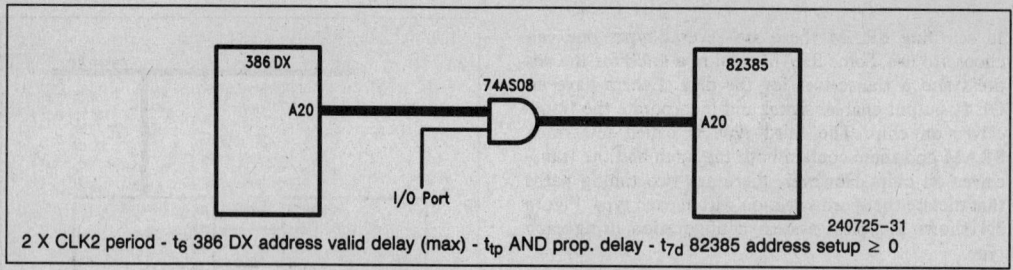

2 X CLK2 period - t_6 386 DX address valid delay (max) - t_{tp} AND prop. delay - t_{7d} 82385 address setup $\geq$ 0

Figure 3-5. Critical Timing A20

To meet this timing the propagation delay of the AND gate must be less than 6ns. This dictates the use of a 74AS08 gate or faster device.

Analysis of the LOCK# path also shows a small margin. The reason is the OR gate that many designers insert to disable the LOCK# signal to the 385 Cache Controller. This allows locked accesses to be cached. Figure 3.6 shows the circuit block diagram. LOCK# must leave the 386 DX and reach the 385 Cache Controller within 2 CLK2 periods.

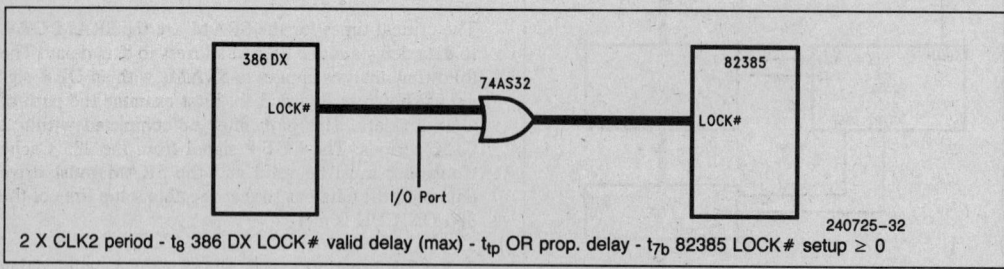

2 X CLK2 period - t_8 386 DX LOCK# valid delay (max) - t_{tp} OR prop. delay - t_{7b} 82385 LOCK# setup $\geq$ 0

Figure 3-6. Critical Timing Lock#

AP-442

To meet this timing the propagation delay of the OR gate must be less than 6ns. This dictates the use of a 74AS32 gate or faster device.

The final path examined here is the NA# path. Recently designers have selected to use an I/O port and an OR gate to disable pipelining selectively. Figure 3.7 shows the circuit block diagram. NA# must leave the 386 DX and reach the 385 Cache Controller within 2 CLK2 periods.

Using the specified values in the appropriate data sheets results in the need for the propagation delay of the OR gate must be no greater than 5.8ns. This dictates the use of a 74AS32 gate or faster device.

This list is not meant to be exhaustive. It is merely meant to highlight a few of the critical timings. Each designer should perform a thorough timing analysis of the system they are designing to verify that all timing requirements are met.

In addition to the specified timing parameters in the data sheets, designers should account for propagation delays introduced by the trace and by capacitive loading. The propagation delay added by the trace is explained in the section on transmission line effects and supplies an equation to determine the amount of delay.

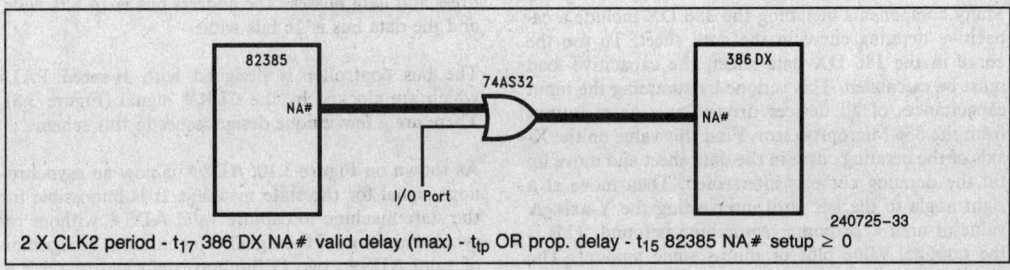

2 X CLK2 period - t_{17} 386 DX NA# valid delay (max) - t_{tp} OR prop. delay - t_{15} 82385 NA# setup ≥ 0

Figure 3-7. Critical Timing NA#

AP-442

Another factor that becomes more important at higher frequencies is loading. DC loading and especially capacitive loading must be considered during the design stage. If the board is to be assembled and tested in stages, then the DC loads should be considered for all configurations of the board. Most termination techniques require additional current. If a board has a marginal loading situation, one is limited in one's choices of termination techniques. If a capacitive loading problem exists, the timing situations can become extremely difficult at higher frequencies. If timing is critical, do not overload the capacitance at which a device was tested. If a device is overloaded, derating must be taken into consideration.

Capacitive loading also introduces a delay on signals. Many components including the 386 DX include a capacitive derating curve in the data sheet. To use the curve in the 386 DX data sheet, the capacitive load must be calculated. This is done by summing the input capacitances of all devices driven by a given output from the 386 Microprocessor. Find this value on the X-axis of the derating curve in the data sheet and move up till the derating curve is intersected. Then move at a right angle to the left until intersecting the Y-axis. A value of nom+ or nom− something is found. This is the nominal value plus or minus some amount. The nominal value is the value found in the data sheet. Add the offset from the curve to this nominal value to get the resulting delay corresponding to the capacitive loading in the system. Note: The trace capacitance was not included in this calculation. It is accounted for in the trace propagation delay mentioned earlier.

DRAM CYCLES WITH 82385 ENABLED

When the 82385 is enabled (the CACHE variable of the state machine on page B-2 is forced High), the DRAM controller inserts one extra wait state in all read cycles. This extra time is needed to allow a cache update cycle to occur after each cache read miss cycle. During a cache update cycle, the read data from DRAMs must propagate through the 74AS646 and the 74F245 (optional) and must be ready for a SRAM write cycle with enough setup time.

Timing diagrams on pages C-5 through C-9 show cache and DRAM cycles.

TIMING CALCULATIONS

Timing equations are found on pages D-8 and D-9. Only tCAS, tRAC, tCAC, tAA, tPC, and tCAP are different in this configuration. Actual values for DRAM timings are found on page D-10.

3.5 I/O - EPROM Subsystem

A block diagram of the I/O-EPROM subsystem is shown on Figure 3.8. This subsystem has separate address and data busses. The address bus is 14 bits wide, and the data bus is 16 bits wide.

The bus controller is designed with B-speed PALs which are clocked by the CLK# signal (Figure 3.8). There are a few unique design issues in this scheme.

As shown on Figure 3.10, ADS# is now an asynchronous signal for the state machine. It is impossible for the state machine to capture valid ADS# without re-synchronization of the signal. To guarantee recognition of valid ADS#, two D flip-flop is clocked by CLK# and provides a synchronous ADS# (or Latched ADS#) which is in phase with the state machine.

The second issue is its asynchronous nature of the state machine output signal. With the state machine running almost asynchronously to CLK2 (B PALs also have a long clock-to-output propagation delay), signals generated by the state machine must be re-synchronized before they are returned to the 386 DX. Signals that go to I/O devices and EPROMs need no re-synchronization since these devices are asynchronous. Signals which require re-synchronization are BS16# and DEN#. Each rising edge of DEN# is synchronized to CLK2 by a J-K flip-flop as shown on Figure 3.9. This is important to avoid bus contention after an I/O or EPROM read-cycle. BS16# is synchronized to CLK2 by D flip-flops.

EPROM and I/O cycle timings are shown on pages C-10 through C-13. The worst case is a write cycle to the 82510 and may require as many as 14 wait states.

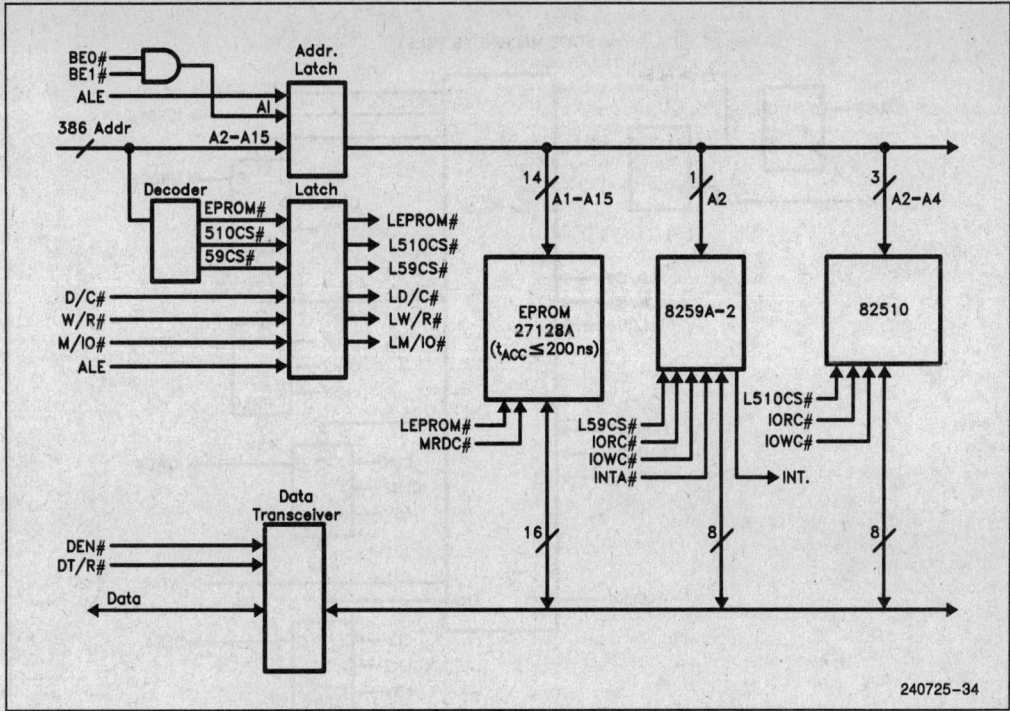

Figure 3-8. Block Diagram of I/O, EPROM Subsystem

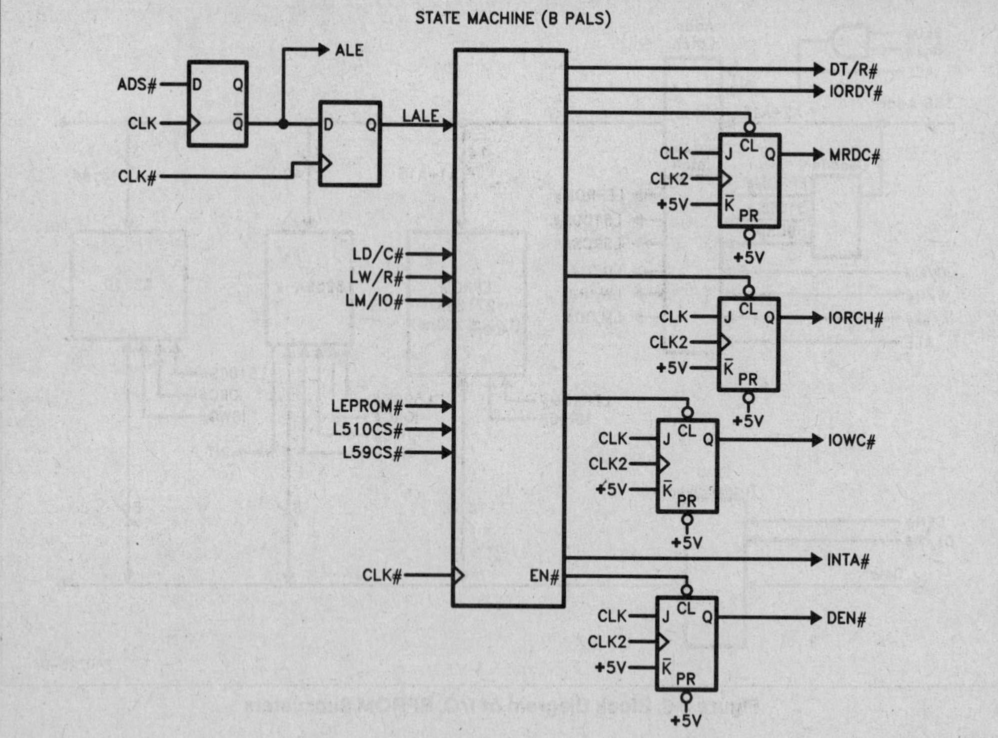

NOTE:
Create BS16# for 386 Using DEN# and EPROM# (Synch to CLK)

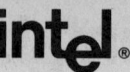

Figure 3-9. Control Logic for I/O, EPROM Subsystem

AP-442

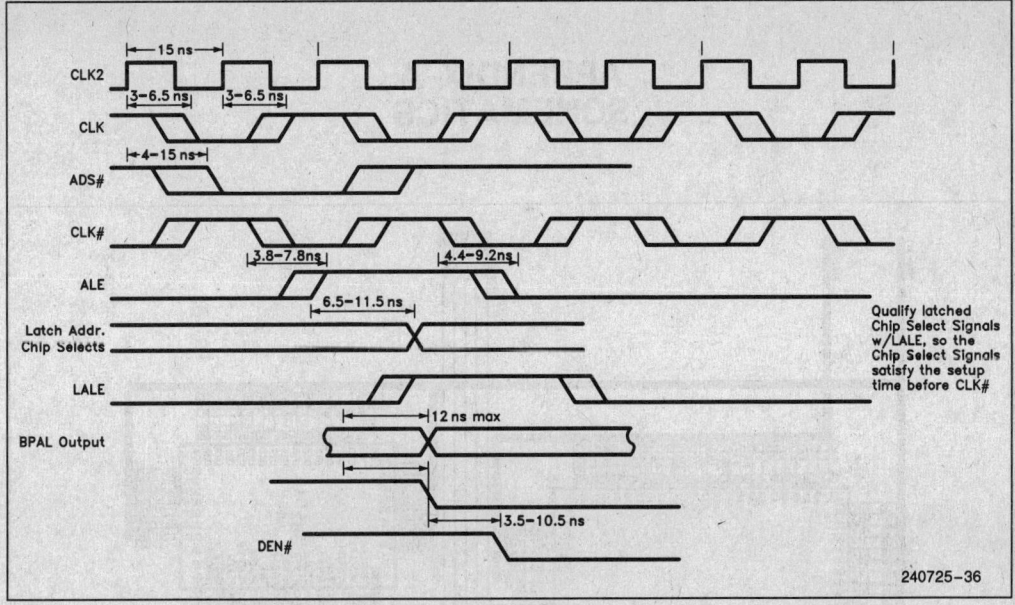

Figure 3-10. ADS# Should Be Synchronized to Guarantee Recognition

AP-442

APPENDIX A
SCHEMATICS

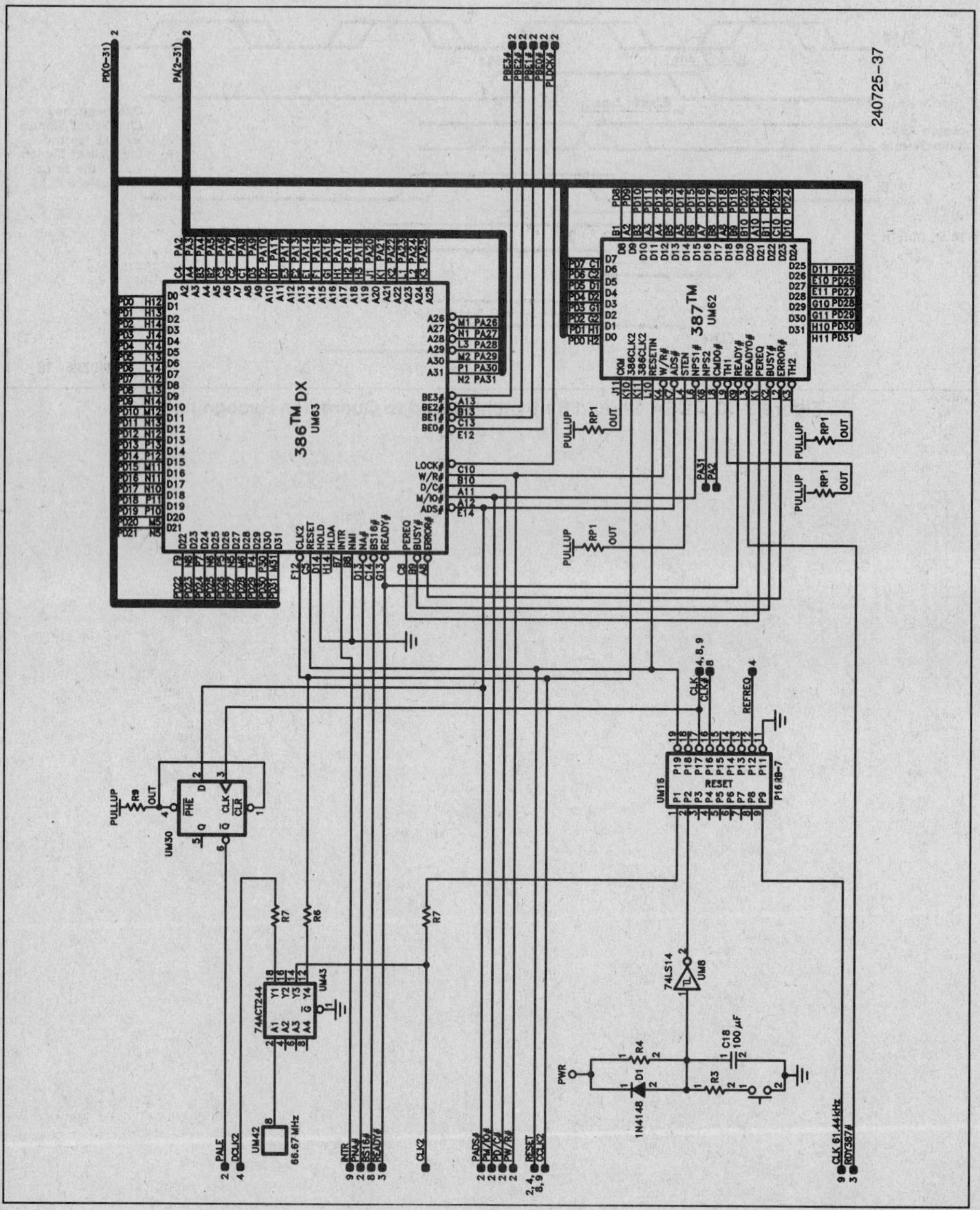

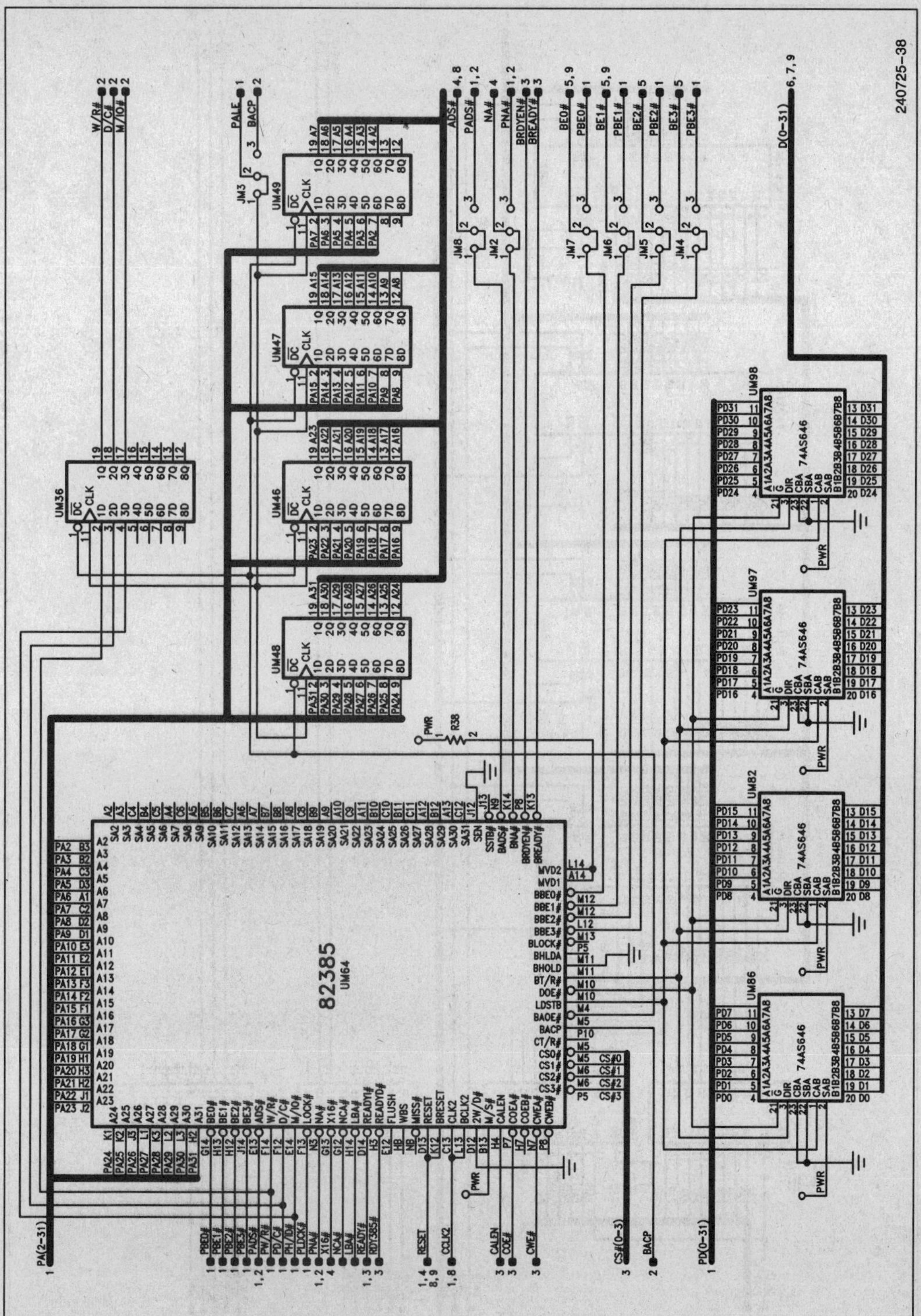

AP-442

6-31

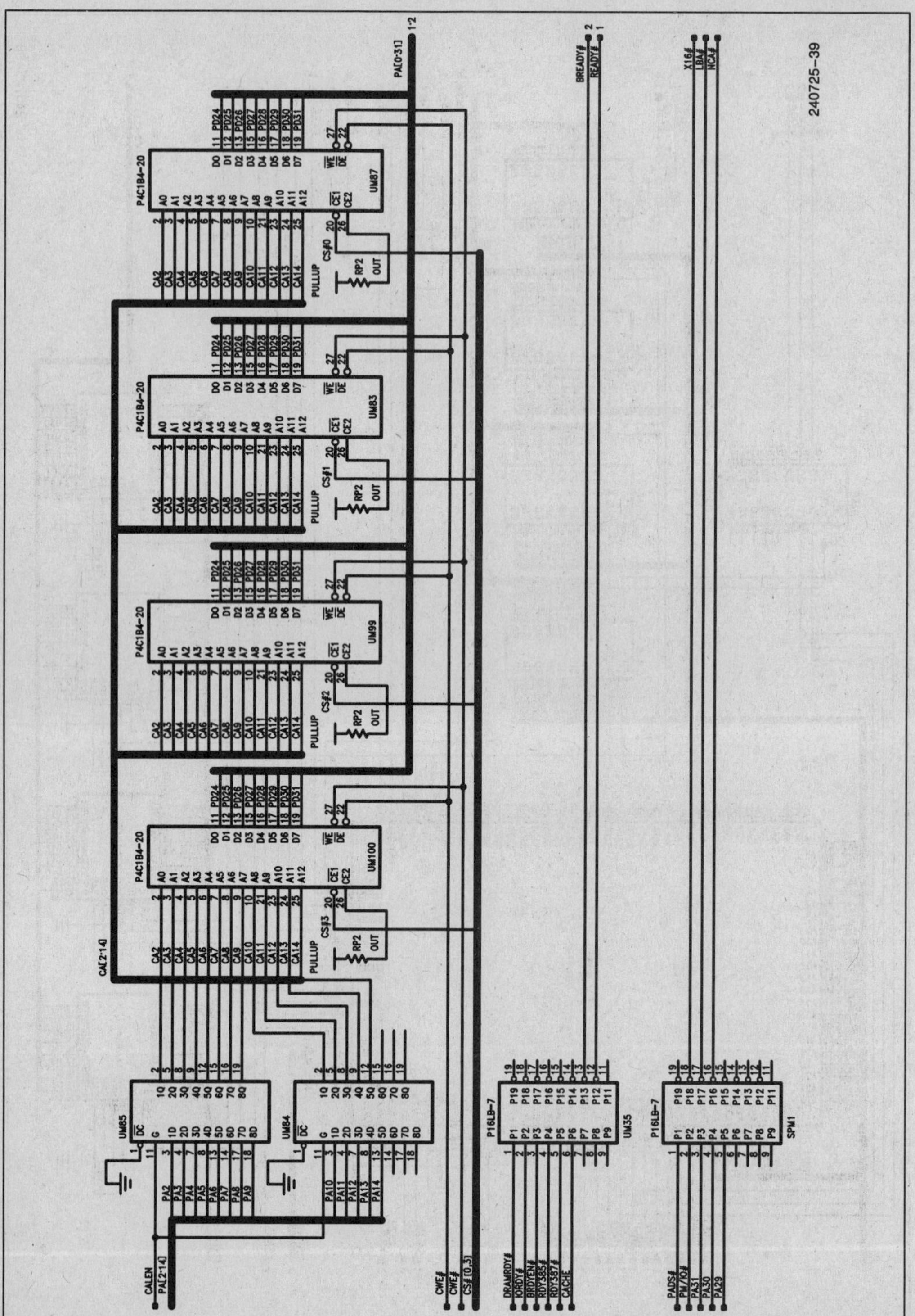

AP-442

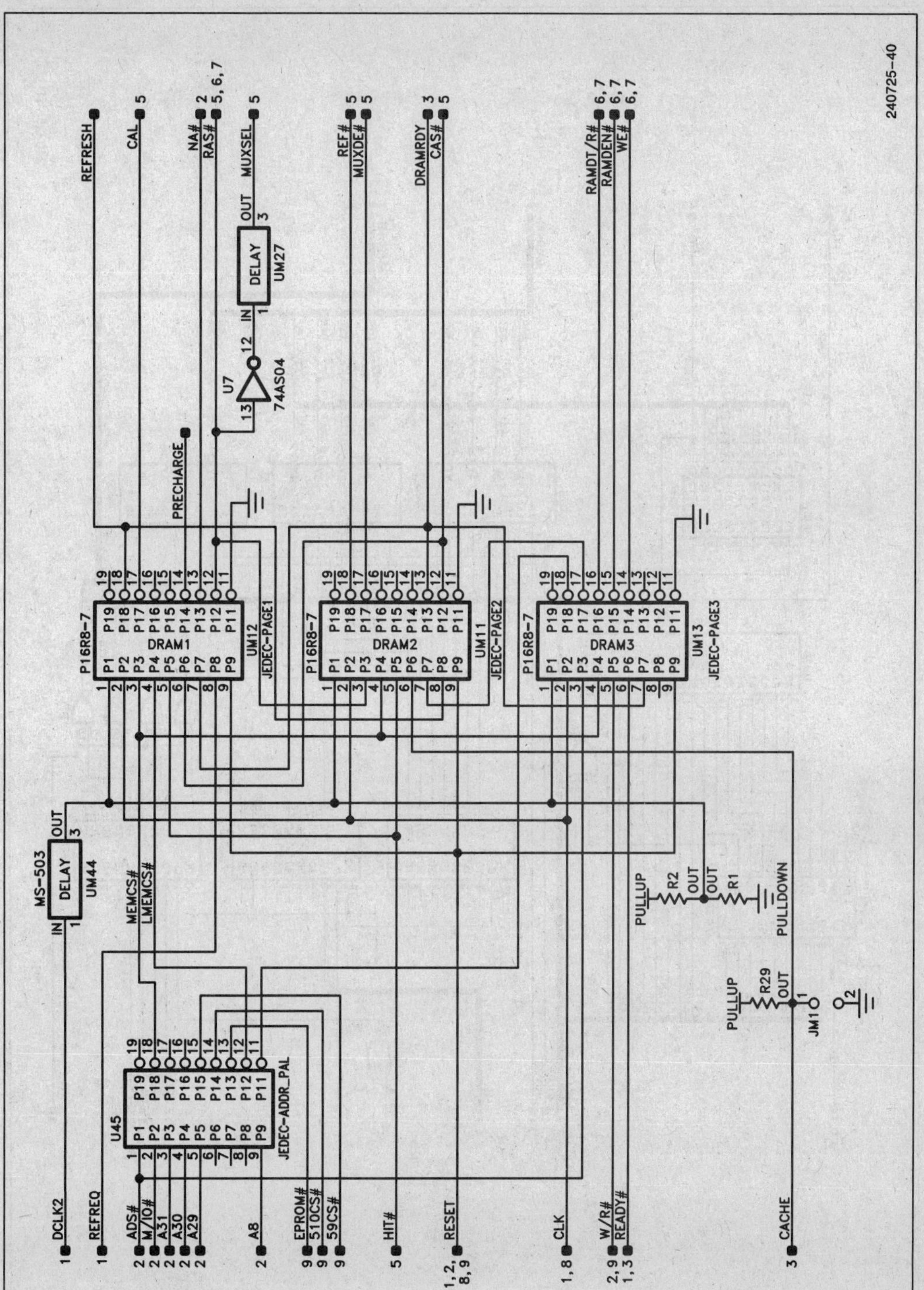

AP-442

240725-40

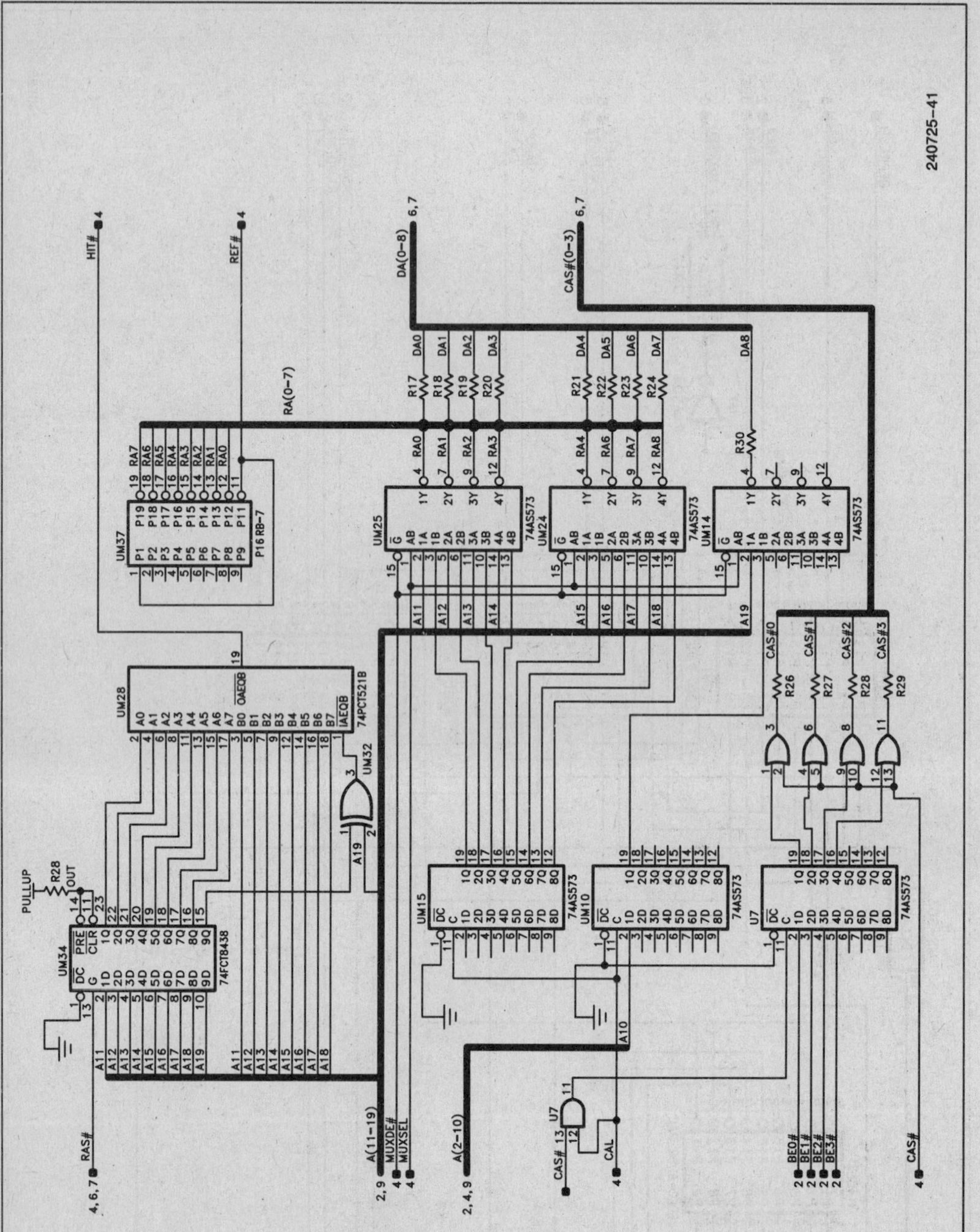

AP-442

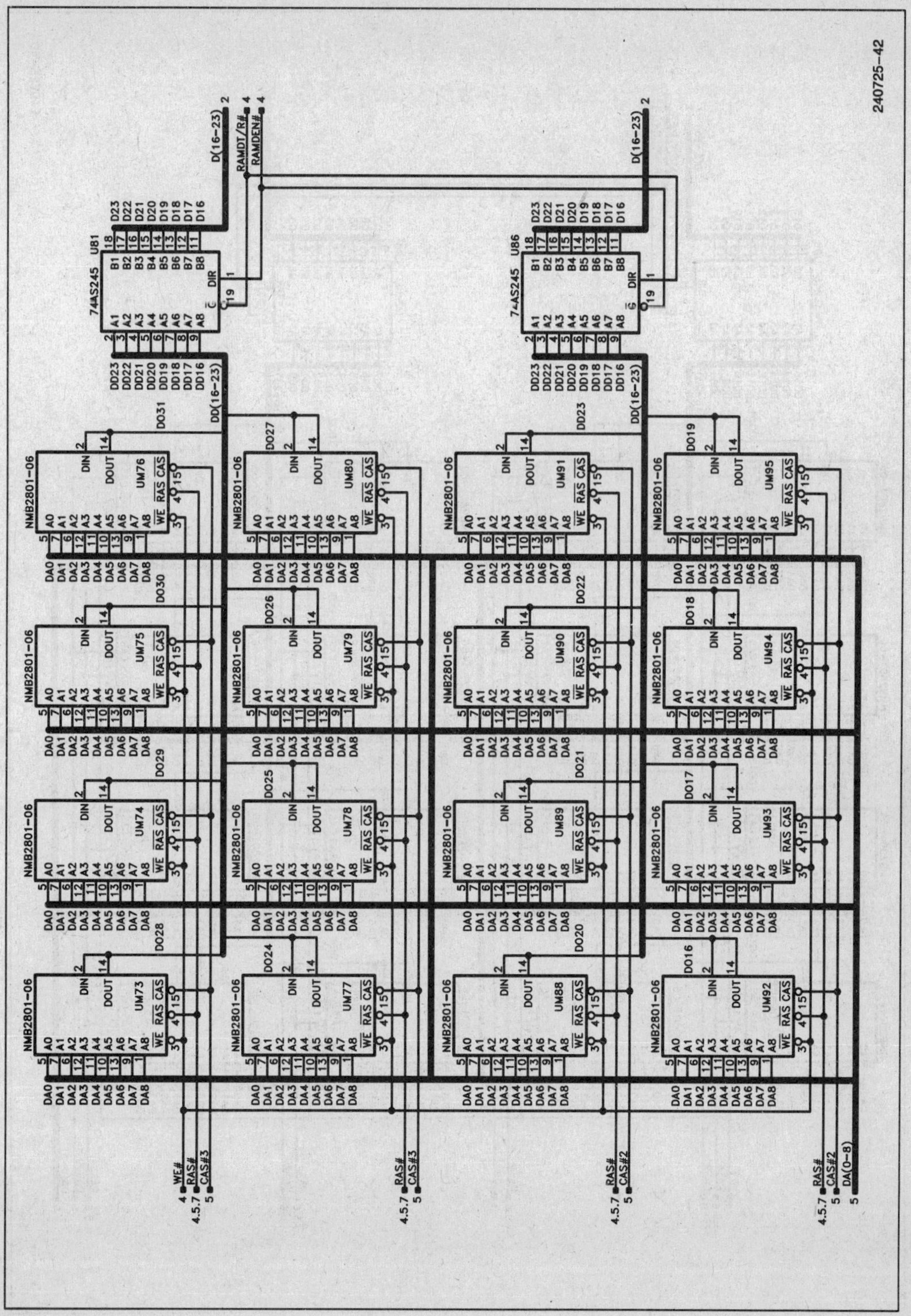

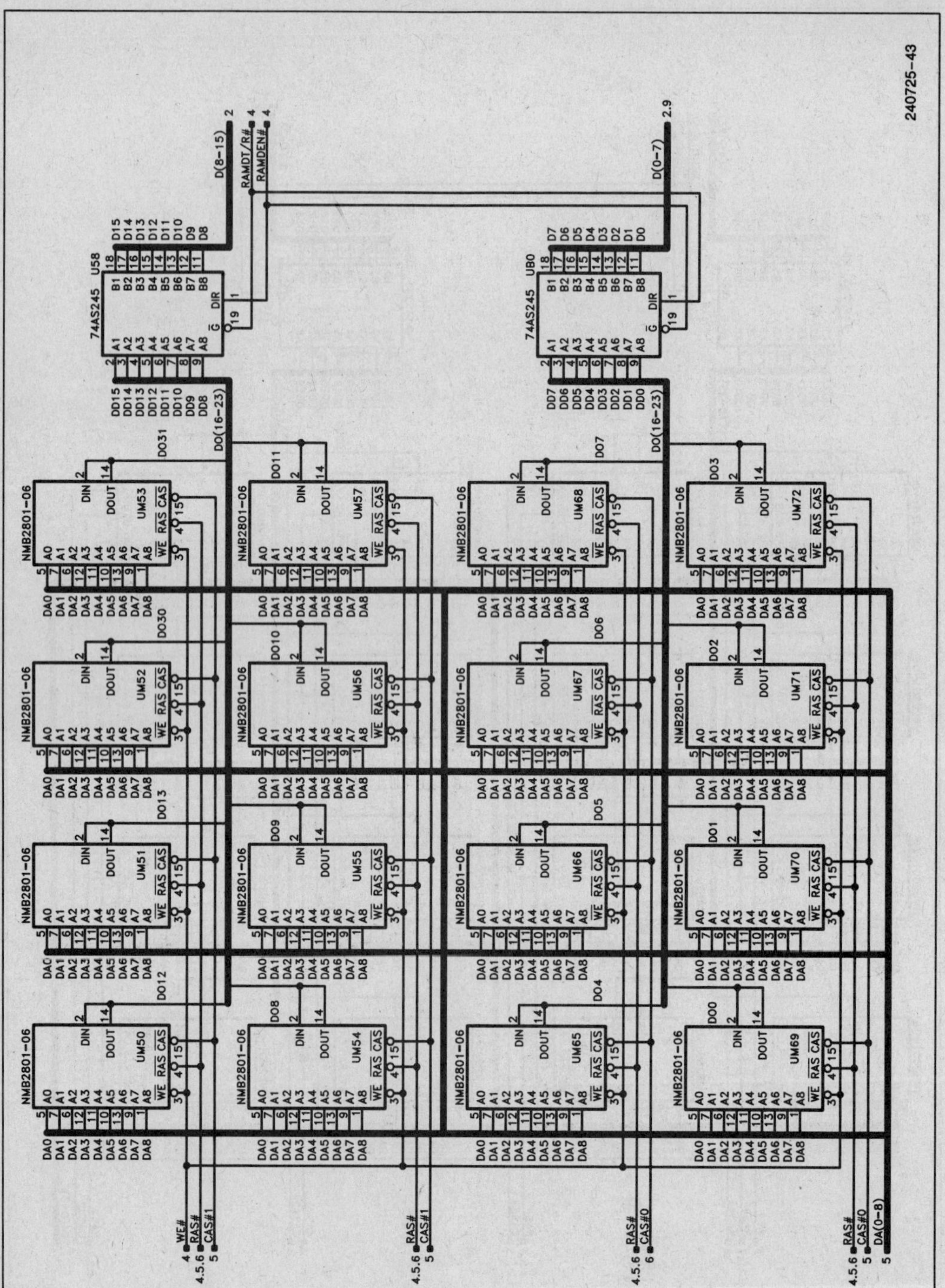

AP-442

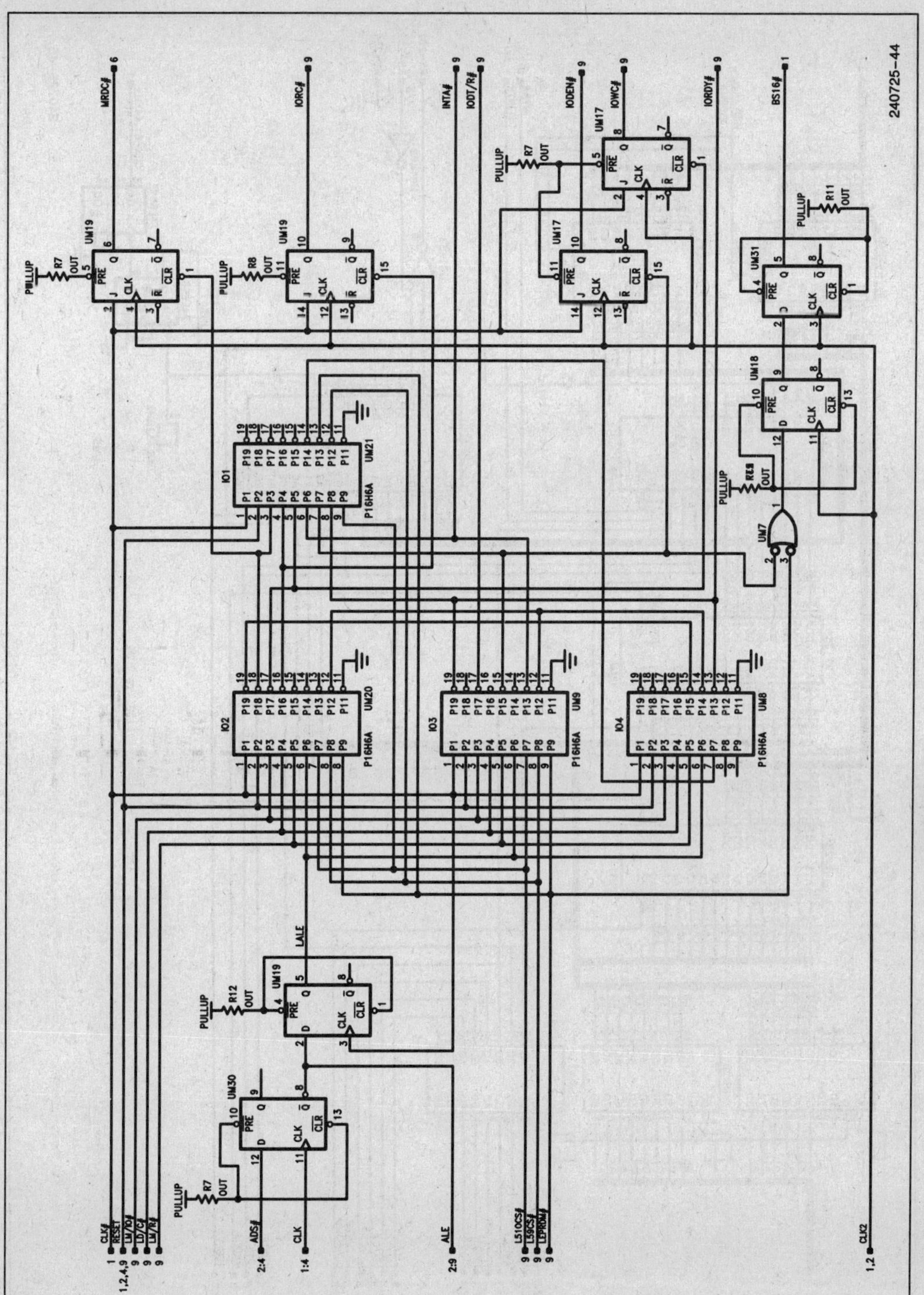

AP-442

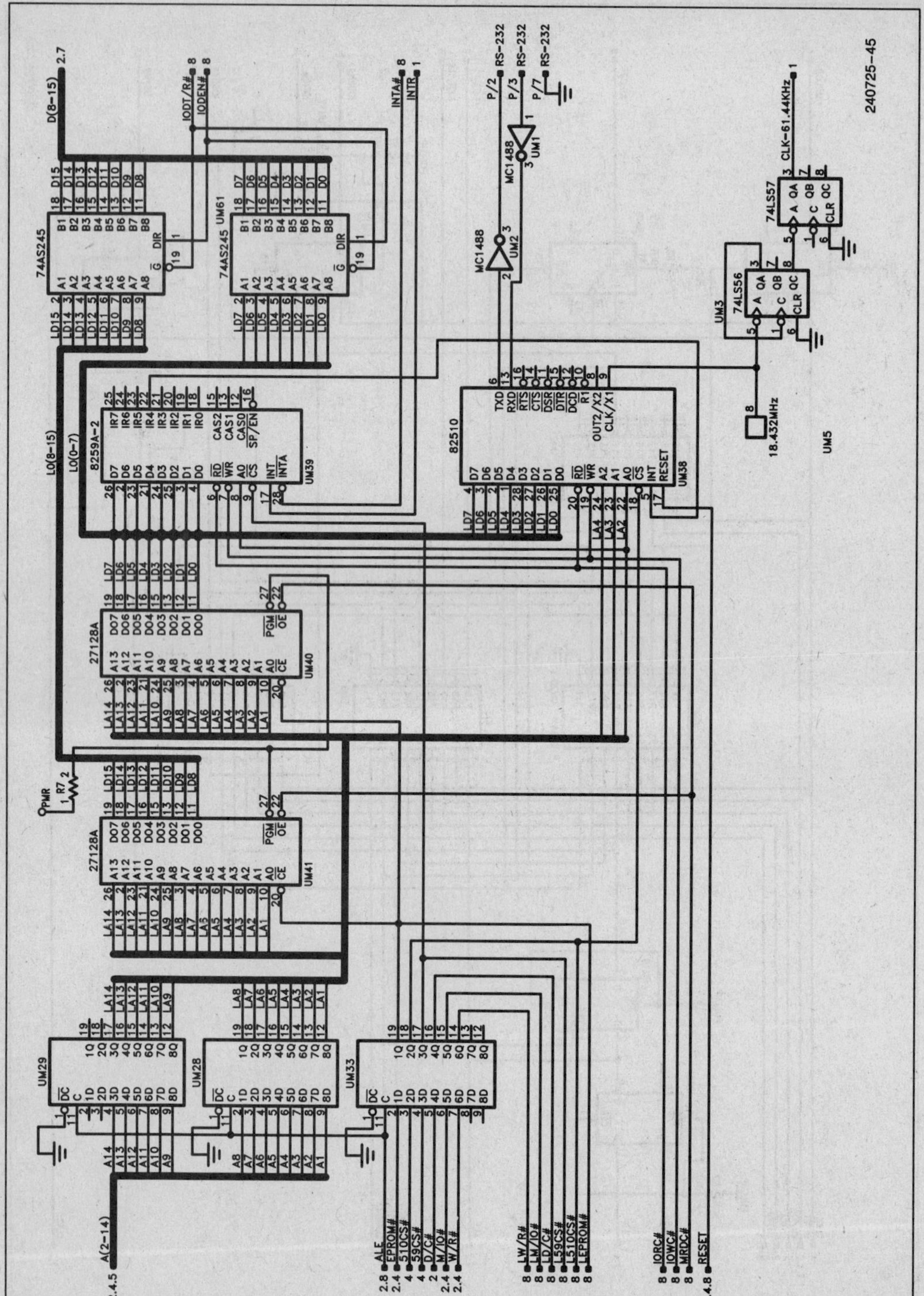

AP-442

intel

AP-442

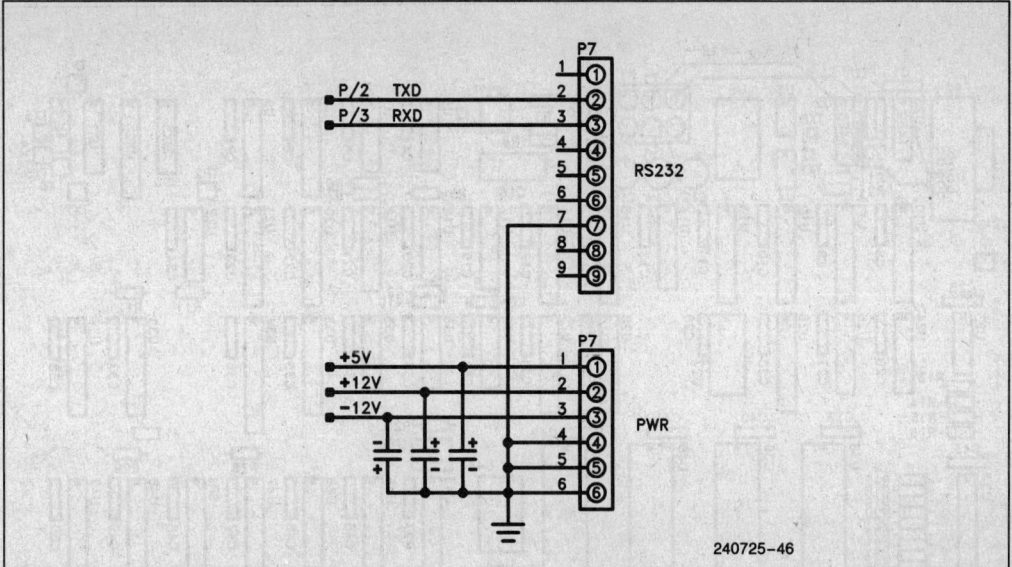

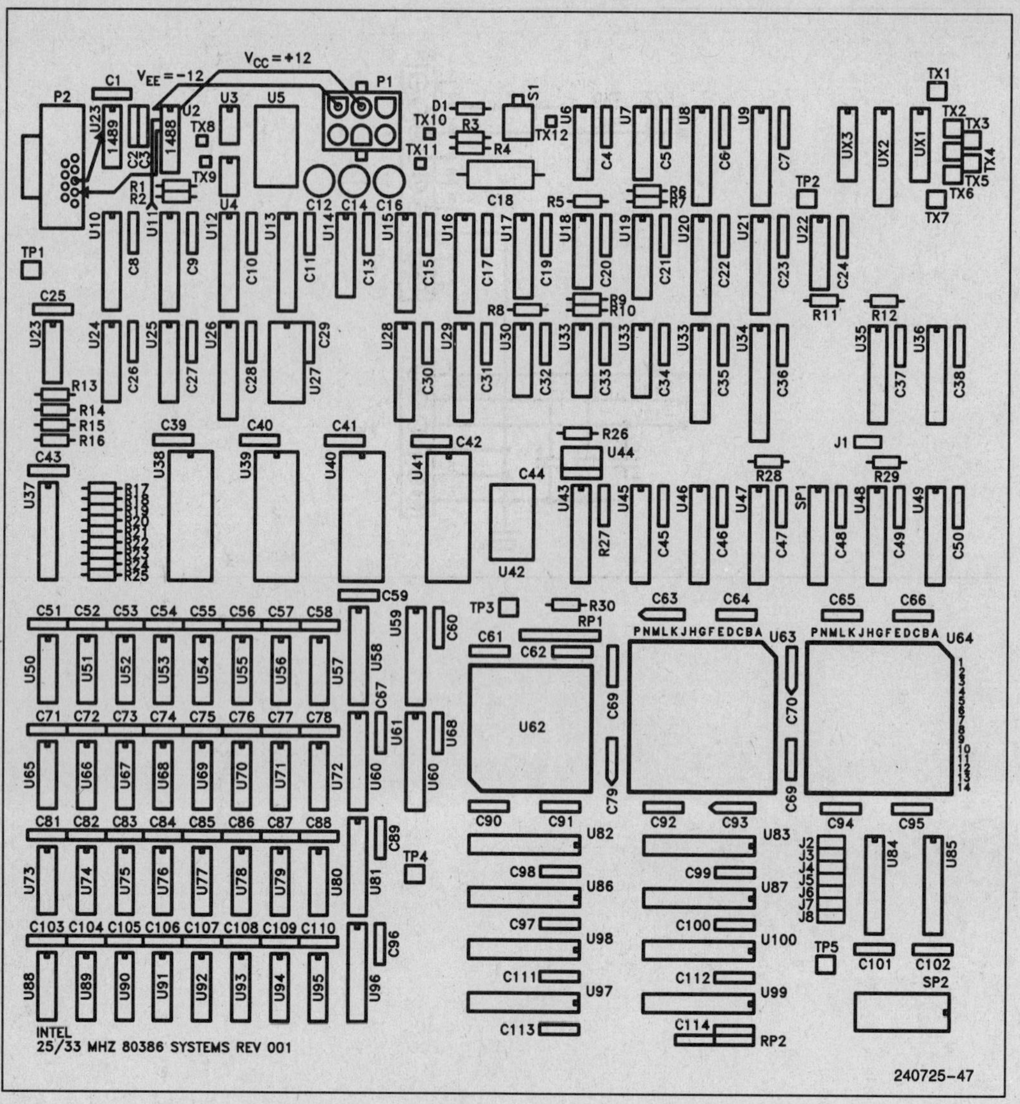

AP-442

AP-442

APPENDIX B
STATE DIAGRAMS AND PALCODES

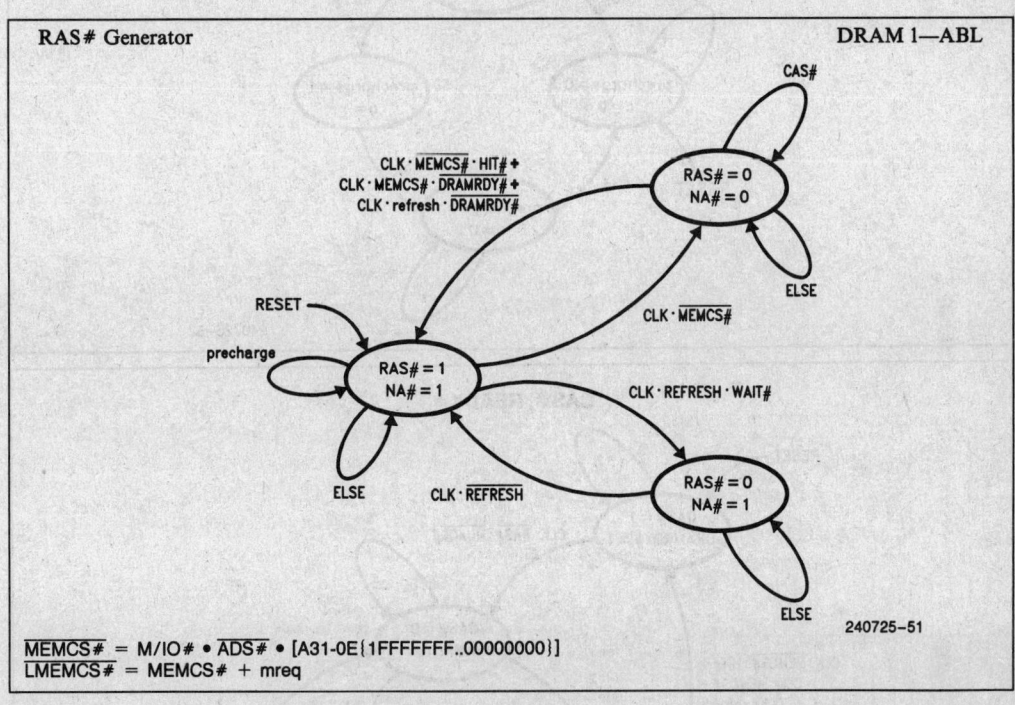

AP-442

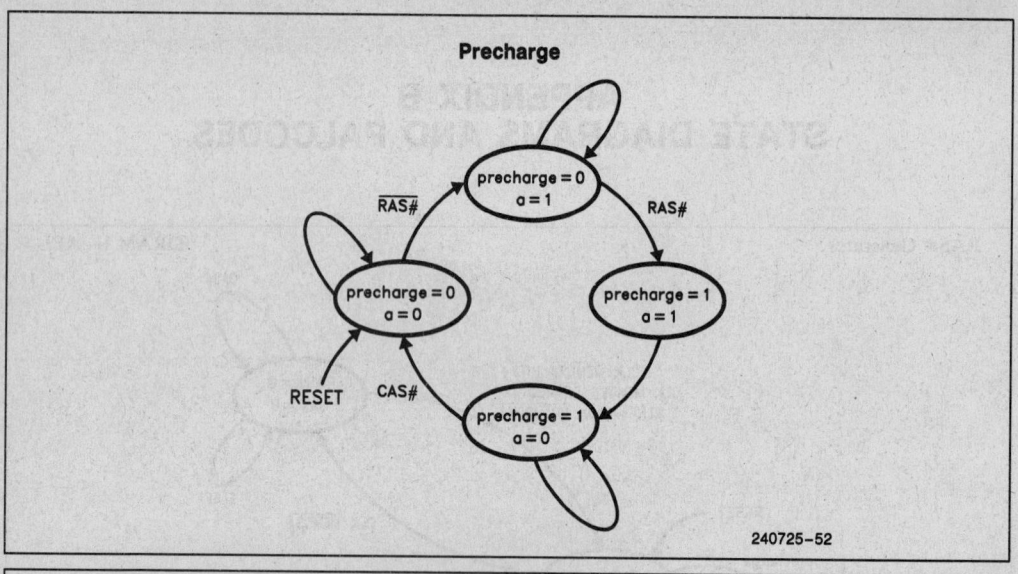

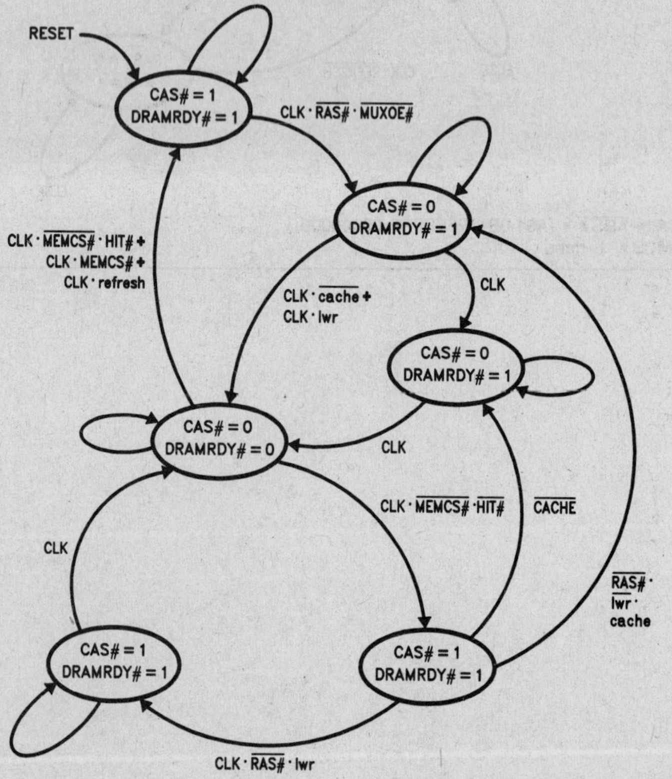

 AP-442

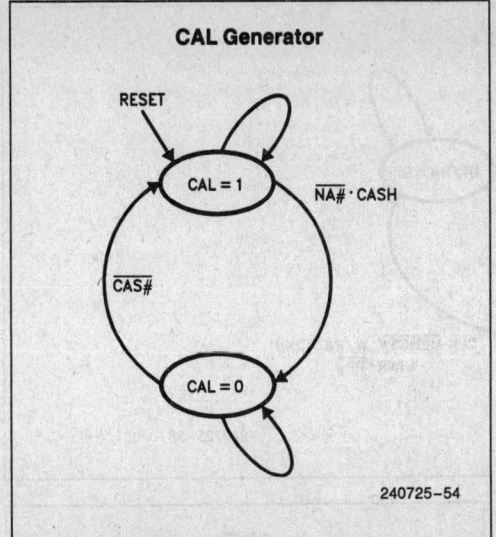

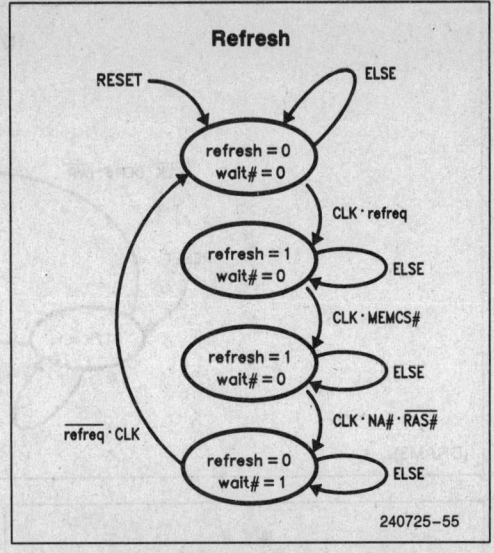

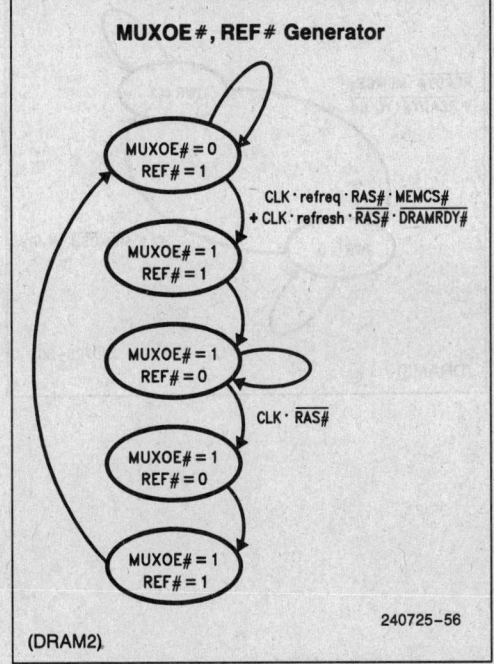

(DRAM2)

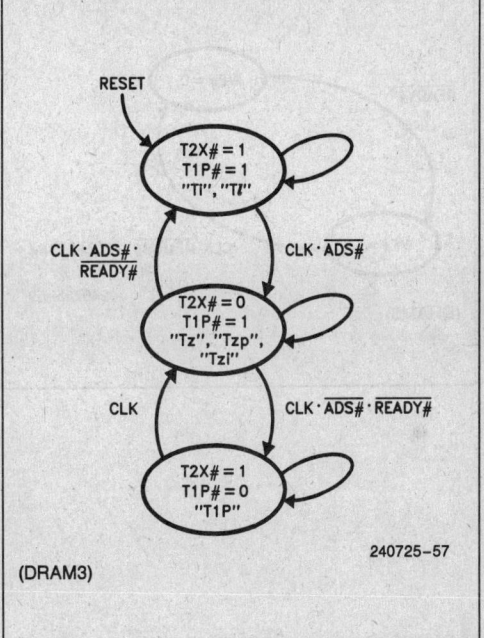

(DRAM3)

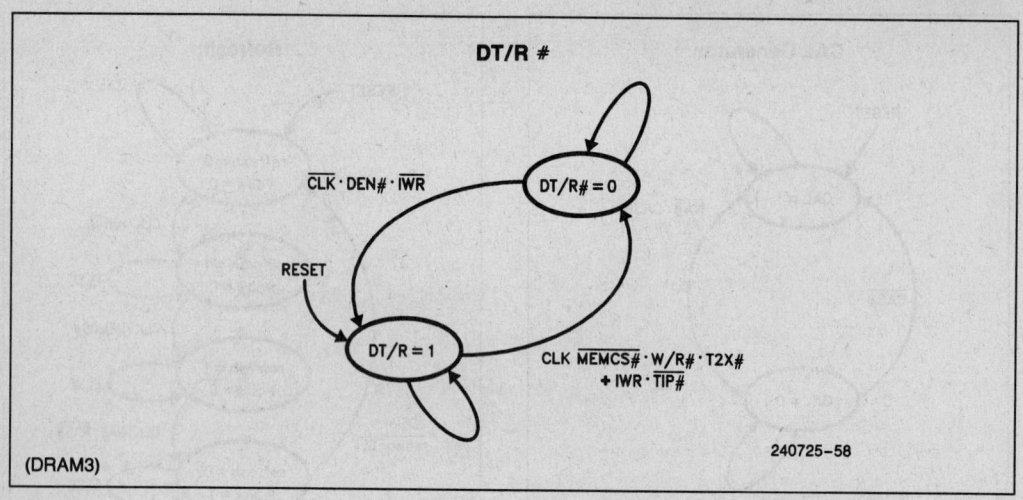
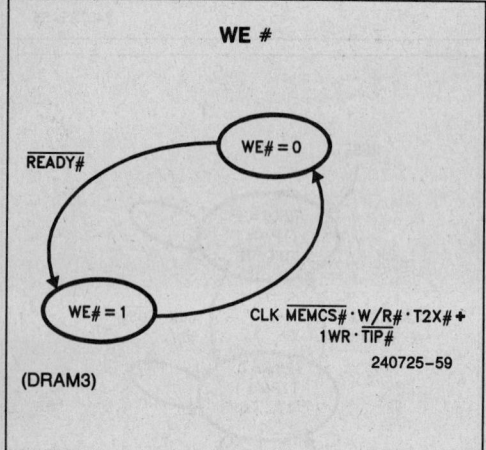
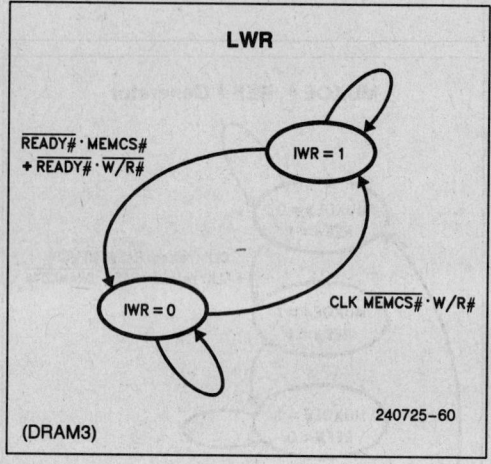

AP-442

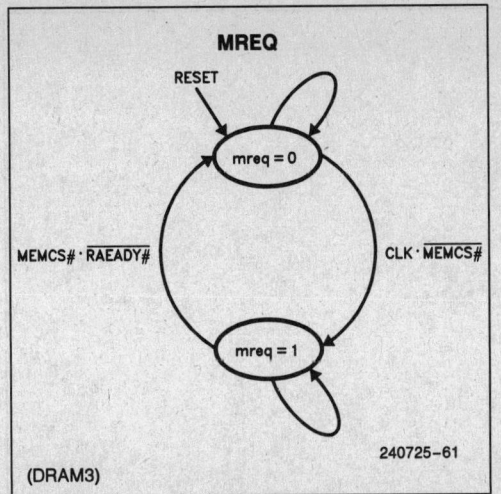

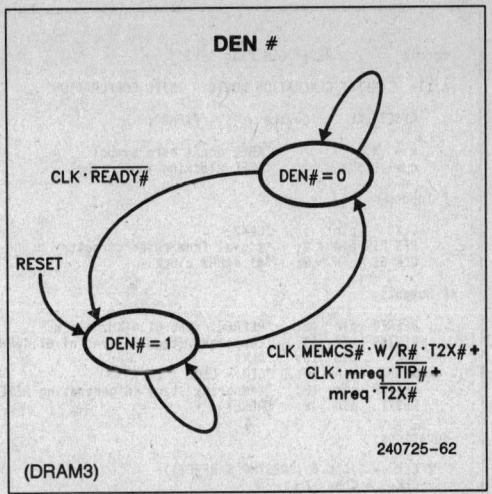

AP-442

```
module          RESET_GEN flag '-r3'
title       'RESET_GENERATION_LOGIC - INTEL CORPORATION'

    RESET_PAL   device      'P16R8';

    x = .X.;            "ABEL don't care symbol
    c = .C.;            "ABEL clocking input sybol

" Inputs

    CLK2      pin  1;   "CLK2
    RESTRIG   pin  2;   "signal from reset circuitry
    CLK_61    pin  9;   "61.44KHz clock

" Outputs

    REFREQ    pin 12;   "REFREQ, sync 61.44KHz clock
    RFQTMP    pin 13;   "temporary stage in sync of 61.44MHz clk
    CLK-      pin 16;   "CLK#
    CLK       pin 17;   "CLK = CLK2 / 2
    RESTMP    pin 18;   "temporary stage in generating RESET
    RESET     pin 19;   "RESET

equations

    CLK    := (!CLK # (!RESTMP & RESET));
    CLK-   := CLK;
    RESTMP := RESTRIG;
    RESET  := RESTMP;
    RFQTMP := CLK_61;
    REFREQ := RFQTMP;


test_vectors

    ([CLK2, CLK_61, RESTRIG, CLK, CLK-, RESTMP, RESET, RFQTMP, REFREQ] ->
     [CLK, CLK-, RESTMP, RESET, RFQTMP, REFREQ])

"    C  C   R   C  C   R   R   R        C  C   R   R   R
"    L  L   E   L  L   E   E   F        L  L   E   E   F
"    K  K   S   K  K   S   S   Q        K  K   S   S   Q
"    2  _   T   _  _   T   E   F        _  _   T   E   F
"       6   R      T   M   T   R        T   T  M   T   R
"       1   I          P       E        M   M  P       E
"           G                  Q                        Q

    [c, x, 1, x, x, x, x, x, x] -> [x, x, 1, x, x, x];
    [c, x, 1, x, x, 1, x, x, x] -> [x, x, 1, 1, x, x];
    [c, x, 0, x, x, 1, x, x, x] -> [x, x, 0, 1, x, x];

    [c, x, x, x, x, 0, 1, x, x] -> [1, x, x, x, x, x];   " clk generation
    [c, x, x, 1, x, x, 0, x, x] -> [0, 1, x, x, x, x];
    [c, x, x, 0, x, x, x, x, x] -> [1, 0, x, x, x, x];
```

240725-48

PAL Codes: RESET

AP-442

```
        [c, x, x, 1, x, 1, x, x, x] -> [0, 1, x, x, x, x];

        [c, x, 0, x, x, x, x, x, x] -> [x, x, 0, x, x, x];   " restmp gen
        [c, x, x, x, x, 0, x, x, x] -> [x, x, x, 0, x, x];   " reset gen
        [c, x, 1, x, x, x, x, x, x] -> [x, x, 1, x, x, x];

        [c, x, x, x, x, 1, x, x, x] -> [x, x, x, 1, x, x];

        [c, 0, x, x, x, x, x, x, x] -> [x, x, x, x, 0, x];   " 61.44KHz clk
        [c, x, x, x, x, x, x, 0, x] -> [x, x, x, x, x, 0];
        [c, 1, x, x, x, x, x, x, x] -> [x, x, x, x, 1, x];
        [c, x, x, x, x, x, x, 1, x] -> [x, x, x, x, x, 1];

end RESET_GEN;
```

240725-49

```
ABEL(tm) 3.10  -  Document Generator         14-Feb-90 09:53 AM
RESET GENERATION LOGIC - INTEL CORPORATION
Equations for Module RESET_GEN

Device RESET_PAL

- Reduced Equations:

    !CLK  := (CLK & !RESET # CLK & RESTMP);

    !CLK- := (!CLK);

    !RESTMP := (!RESTRIG);

    !RESET := (!RESTMP);

    !RFQTMP := (!CLK_61);

    !REFREQ := (!RFQTMP);
```

240725-D4

PAL Codes: RESET (Continued)

AP-442

ABEL 3.10—Document Generator
RESET__GENERATION__LOGIC—INTEL CORPORATION
Chip diagram for Module RESET__GEN

14-Feb-90 09:53 AM

Device RESET__PAL

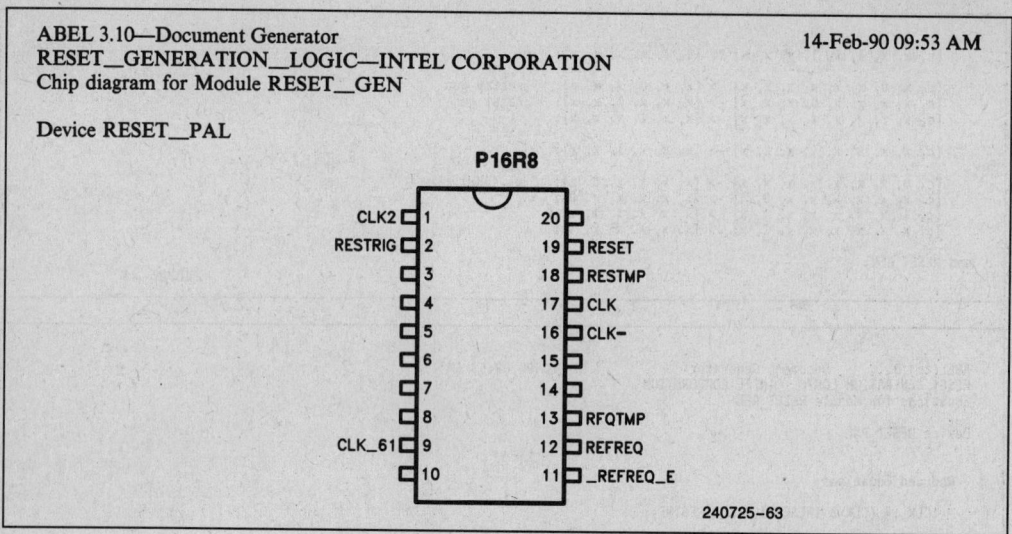

PAL Codes: RESET (Continued)

AP-442

```
module      ADDR_DEC flag '-r3'
title     'ADDRESS_DECODE_LOGIC - INTEL CORPORATION'

  ADDR_PAL    device 'P16L8';

  x = .X.;              "ABEL don't care symbol
  c = .C.;              "ABEL clocking input sybol

" Inputs

  ADS-      pin  1;    "ADS#
  M_IO-     pin  2;    "M/IO#
  A31       pin  3;    "Addr bit 31
  A30            pin  4;    "Addr bit 30
  A29       pin  5;    "Addr bit 29
  A6        pin  9;    "Addr bit 6
  mreq      pin 11;    "Latched memory chip select

" Outputs

  MEMCS-    pin 18;    "Memory chip select
  _59CS-    pin 15;    "8259A chip select
  _510CS-   pin 14;    "82510 chip select
  EPRDM-    pin 13;    "EPROM chip select
  LMEMCS-   pin 12;    "Latched/unlatched memory chip select

equations

  !MEMCS-  = !ADS- & M_IO- & !A31 & !A30 & !A29;
  !LMEMCS- = (!ADS- & M_IO- & !A31 & !A30 & !A29) # mreq;
  !_59CS-  = !M_IO- & !A6;
  !_510CS- = !M_IO- & A6;
  !EPRDM-  = M_IO- & A31 & A30 & A29;


test_vectors

  ([ADS-, M_IO-, A31, A30, A29, A6, mreq, MEMCS-] ->
   [MEMCS-, LMEMCS-, _59CS-, _510CS-, EPRDM-])

"   A  M  A  A  A  m  M      M  L  5  5  E
"   D  3  3  2  6  r  E      E  M  9  1  P
"   S  I  1  0  9     e  M   M  E  C  0  R
"   -  O              q  C   C  M  S  C  D
"      -                 S   S  C  -  S  M
"                        -      S  -  -  -
"                               -

  [1, x, x, x, x, x, 0, 1] -> [1, 1, x, x, x];

  [1, x, x, x, x, x, 1, 1] -> [1, 0, x, x, x]; "LMEMCS-
  [0, 1, 0, 0, 0, x, x, x] -> [0, x, 1, 1, 1];

                                              240725-92
```

```
  [0, 1, 0, 0, 0, x, 0, 0] -> [0, 0, 1, 1, 1];
  [0, 1, 0, 0, 0, x, x, x] -> [0, x, 1, 1, 1];
  [1, x, x, x, x, x, 1, 0] -> [1, 0, x, x, x];

  [1, x, x, x, x, x, x, x] -> [1, x, x, x, x]; "---CS-
  [x, 1, x, x, x, x, x, x] -> [x, x, 1, 1, x];
  [x, 0, x, x, x, x, x, x] -> [1, x, x, 1, 1];
  [x, 1, 0, x, x, x, x, x] -> [x, x, 1, 1, 1];
  [x, 1, x, 0, x, x, x, x] -> [x, x, 1, 1, 1];
  [x, 1, x, x, 0, x, x, x] -> [x, x, 1, 1, 1];
  [x, 1, 1, 0, x, x, x, x] -> [1, x, 1, 1, 1];
  [x, 1, 0, 1, 0, x, x, x] -> [1, x, 1, 1, 1];
  [x, 1, 0, 0, 1, x, x, x] -> [1, x, 1, 1, 1];
  [x, 0, x, x, x, 0, x, x] -> [1, x, 1, 1, 1];
  [x, 0, x, x, x, 1, x, x] -> [1, x, 1, x, 1];

  [x, 1, 1, 1, 1, x, x, x] -> [1, x, 1, 1, 0];
  [0, 1, 0, 0, 0, x, x, x] -> [1, x, 1, 1, 1];
  [1, 1, 0, 0, 0, x, x, x] -> [1, x, 1, 1, 1];
  [0, 0, x, x, x, 0, x, x] -> [1, x, 0, 1, 1];
  [0, 0, x, x, x, 1, x, x] -> [1, x, 1, 0, 1];

end ADDR_DEC;

                                              240725-93
```

PAL Codes: Address Decoder

AP-442

```
ABEL(tm) 3.10  -  Document Generator        14-Feb-90 09:50 AM
ADDRESS_DECODE_LOGIC - INTEL CORPORATION
Equations for Module ADDR_DEC

Device ADDR_PAL

- Reduced Equations:

    !MEMCS- = (!A29 & !A30 & !A31 & !ADS- & M_IO~);

    !LMEMCS- = (mreq # !A29 & !A30 & !A31 & !ADS- & M_IO~);

    !_59CS- = (!A6 & !M_IO~);

    !_510CS- = (A6 & !M_IO~);

    !EPRDM- = (A29 & A30 & A31 & M_IO~);
```

240725-D5

PAL Codes: Address Decoder (Continued)

AP-442

ABEL 3.10—Document Generator
ADDRESS_DECODE_LOGIC—INTEL CORPORATION
Chip diagram for Module ADDR_DEC

14-Feb-90 09:50 AM

Device ADDR_PAL

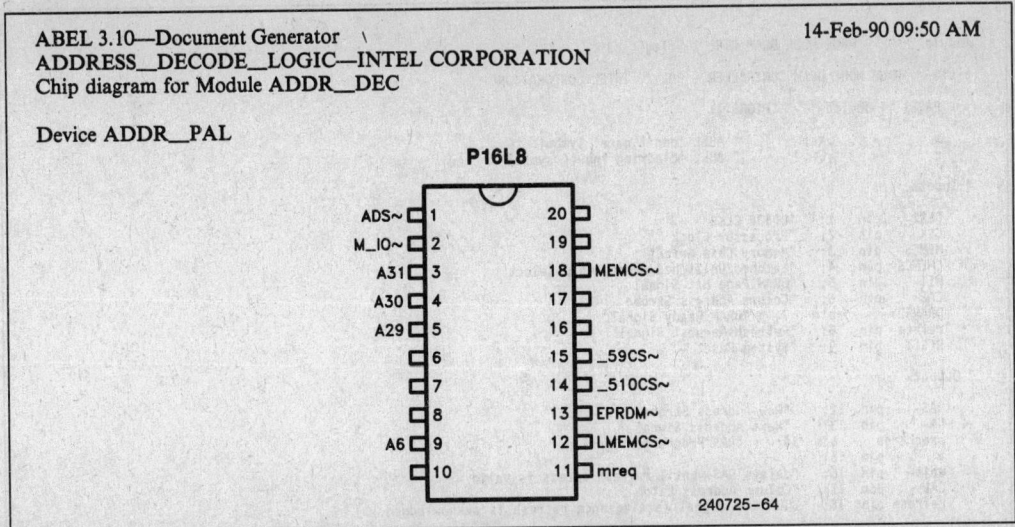

PAL Codes: Address Decoder (Continued)

AP-442

```
module      PAGE_MODE_DRAM_CTRL_1 flag '-r3'
title   'PAGE MODE DRAM CONTROLLER - PAL 1, INTEL CORPORATION'

    PAGE1   device     'P16R8';

    x   =   .X.;    " ABEL 'don't care' symbol
    c   =   .C.;    " ABEL 'clocking input' symbol

" Inputs

    CLK2        pin   1;    "80386 CLK2
    CLK         pin   2;    "Processor Clock
    MEMCS-      pin   3;    "Memory Chip Select
    LMEMCS-     pin   4;    "Latched/Unlatched Memory Chip Select
    HIT-        pin   5;    "DRAM Page Hit Signal
    CAS-        pin   6;    "Column Address Strobe
    DRAMRDY-    pin   7;    "DRAM Ready Signal
    refreq      pin   8;    "Refresh Request Signal
    RESET       pin   9;    "System Reset

" Outputs

    RAS-        pin  12;    "Row Address Strobe
    NA-         pin  13;    "Next Address Signal
    precharge   pin  14;    "RAS Precharge Signal
    a           pin  15;
    wait-       pin  16;    "delays RAS- until refresh adress is valid
    CAL         pin  17;    "Column Address Latch
    refresh     pin  18;    "Refresh Signal (active once refresh is acknowledged.)

    unused      pin  19;    "

state_diagram [RAS-, NA-]

    state [1, 1]:   if precharge then [1, 1] else
                    if (CLK & refresh & wait-) then [0, 1] else
                    if (CLK & !LMEMCS-& !refresh) then [0, 0] else [1, 1];
    state [0, 0]:   if RESET then [1, 1] else
                    if CAS- then [0, 0] else
                    if (CLK & !MEMCS- & HIT- #
                       CLK & MEMCS- & !DRAMRDY- #
                       CLK & refresh & !DRAMRDY-) then [1, 1] else [0, 0];
    state [0, 1]:   if RESET then [1, 1] else
                    if (CLK & !refresh) then [1, 1] else [0, 1];
    state [1, 0]:   goto [1, 1];

state_diagram [precharge, a]

    state [0, 0]:   if (!RAS-) then [0, 1] else [0, 0];
    state [0, 1]:   if (RESET) then [0, 0] else
                    if (RAS-) then [1, 1] else [0, 1];
    state [1, 1]:   goto [1, 0];
    state [1, 0]:   if (CAS-) then [0, 0] else [1, 0];
```

PAL Codes: DRAM 1

AP-442

```
state_diagram [CAL]
    state [1]:      if (!NA- & CAS-) then [0] else [1];
    state [0]:      if (RESET) then [1] else
                        if (!CAS-) then [1] else [0];

state_diagram [refresh, wait-]
    state[0, 0]:    if (CLK & refreq) then [1, 0] else [0, 0];
    state[1, 0]:    if (RESET) then [0,0] else
                        if (CLK & MEMCS-) then [1, 1] else [1, 0];
    state[1, 1]:    if (RESET) then [0,0] else
                        if (CLK & NA- & !RAS-) then [0, 1] else [1, 1];
    state[0, 1]:    if (RESET) then [0,0] else
                        if (CLK & !refreq) then [0, 0] else [0, 1];

test_vectors
    ([CLK2,CLK,MEMCS-,LMEMCS-,HIT-,CAS-,DRAMRDY-,refreq,RESET] ->
     [RAS-,NA-,precharge,CAL,refresh])

"   C  C  M  L  H  C  D  r  R           R  N  p  C  r
"   L  L  E  M  I  A  R  e  E           A  A  r  A  e
"   K  K  M  I  T  S  A  f  S           S  -  e  L  f
"   2     C  E  -  -  M  r  E           -     c     r
"         S  M           R  e  T              h     e
"         -  C           D  q                 a     s
"            S           Y                    r     h
"            -           -                    g
"                                             e

    [c, x, x, x, x, x, 1, x, 1] -> [1, 1, x, 1, 0];
    [c, x, x, x, x, x, 1, x, 1] -> [1, 1, x, 1, 0];
    [c, 1, 1, 1, x, 1, 1, 0, 0] -> [1, 1, x, 1, 0]; "Ti, phase 1
    [c, 0, 1, 1, x, 1, 1, 0, 0] -> [1, 1, x, 1, 0]; "    phase 2
    [c, 1, 1, 1, x, 1, 1, 0, 0] -> [1, 1, x, 1, 0]; "T1, Read, Non-Pipelined
    [c, 0, 0, 0, x, 1, 1, 0, 0] -> [1, 1, 0, 1, 0];
    [c, 1, 0, 0, x, 1, 1, 0, 0] -> [0, 0, 0, 1, 0]; "T2
    [c, 1, 0, 1, x, 1, 1, 0, 0] -> [0, 0, 0, 0, 0];
    [c, 1, 1, 1, x, 1, 1, 0, 0] -> [0, 0, 0, 0, 0]; "T2P
    [c, 0, 0, 0, x, 0, 1, 0, 0] -> [0, 0, 0, 1, 0]; "     Page Hit
    [c, 1, 0, 0, 0, 0, 1, 0, 0] -> [0, 0, 0, 1, 0]; "T2P
    [c, 0, 0, 0, 0, 0, 1, 0, 0] -> [0, 0, 0, 1, 0]; "T1P, Read, Pipelined
    [c, 1, 1, 0, 0, 0, 1, 0, 0] -> [0, 0, 0, 1, 0]; "T2P
    [c, 0, 1, 0, 0, 1, 1, 0, 0] -> [0, 0, 0, 1, 0];
    [c, 1, 0, 0, 0, 0, 1, 0, 0] -> [0, 0, 0, 1, 0]; "T1P, Write
    [c, 0, 1, 0, 0, 1, 1, 0, 0] -> [0, 0, 0, 0, 0];
    [c, 1, 1, 0, 0, 1, 1, 0, 0] -> [0, 0, 0, 0, 0]; "T2P
    [c, 0, 0, 0, 0, 1, 1, 0, 0] -> [0, 0, 0, 0, 0];
    [c, 1, 0, 0, 0, 1, 1, 0, 0] -> [0, 0, 0, 0, 0]; "T2P
    [c, 0, 0, 0, 0, 0, 0, 0, 0] -> [0, 0, 0, 1, 0];
```

240725-95

PAL Codes: DRAM 1 (Continued)

AP-442

```
    [c, 1, 0, 0, 0, 0, 0, 0, 0] -> [0, 0, 0, 1, 0]; "T1P
    [c, 0, 1, 0, 0, 1, 1, 0, 0] -> [0, 0, 0, 0, 0];
    [c, 1, 1, 0, 0, 0, 1, 0, 0] -> [0, 0, 0, 1, 0]; "T2P
    [c, 0, 0, 0, 0, 0, 0, 0, 0] -> [0, 0, 0, 1, 0]; "     Page Miss
    [c, 1, 0, 0, 1, 0, 0, 0, 0] -> [1, 1, 0, 1, 0]; "T1P
    [c, 1, 1, 0, 1, 1, 1, 0, 0] -> [1, 1, 1, 1, 0];
    [c, 1, 1, 0, 1, 1, 1, 0, 0] -> [1, 1, 1, 1, 0]; "T2
    [c, 0, 1, 0, 1, 1, 1, 0, 0] -> [1, 1, 0, 1, 0];
    [c, 1, 1, 0, 1, 1, 1, 0, 0] -> [0, 0, 0, 1, 0]; "T2
    [c, 0, 1, 0, 1, 1, 1, 0, 0] -> [0, 0, 0, 0, 0];
    [c, 1, 1, 0, 1, 1, 1, 0, 0] -> [0, 0, 0, 0, 0]; "T2P
    [c, 0, 0, 0, x, 0, 1, 0, 0] -> [0, 0, 0, 1, 0];
    [c, 1, 0, 0, 1, 0, 1, 0, 0] -> [1, 1, 0, 1, 0]; "T2P
    [c, 0, 0, 0, 1, 0, 0, 0, 0] -> [1, 1, 1, 1, 0];
    [c, 1, 0, 0, 1, 0, 0, 0, 0] -> [1, 1, 1, 1, 0]; "T1P
    [c, 0, 1, 0, 1, 1, 1, 0, 0] -> [1, 1, 0, 1, 0];
    [c, 1, 1, 0, 1, 1, 1, 0, 0] -> [0, 0, 0, 1, 0]; "T2
    [c, 0, 1, 0, 1, 1, 1, 0, 0] -> [0, 0, 0, 0, 0];
    [c, 1, 1, 0, 1, 1, 1, 0, 0] -> [0, 0, 0, 1, 0]; "T2P
    [c, 0, 0, 0, 1, 0, 1, 0, 0] -> [0, 0, 0, 1, 0];
    [c, 1, 0, 0, 0, 0, 1, 0, 0] -> [0, 0, 0, 1, 0]; "T2P
    [c, 0, 0, 0, 0, 0, 0, 0, 0] -> [0, 0, 0, 1, 0];
    [c, 1, 0, 0, 0, 0, 0, 0, 0] -> [0, 0, 0, 1, 0]; "T1P
    [c, 0, 1, 0, 0, 1, 1, 0, 0] -> [0, 0, 0, 0, 0];
    [c, 1, 1, 0, 0, 0, 1, 0, 0] -> [0, 0, 0, 1, 0]; "T2P
    [c, 0, 0, 0, 0, 0, 1, 0, 0] -> [0, 0, 0, 1, 0];
    [c, 1, 0, 0, 0, 0, 0, 0, 0] -> [0, 0, 0, 1, 0]; "T1P
    [c, 0, 1, 0, 0, 1, 1, 0, 0] -> [0, 0, 0, 0, 0];
    [c, 1, 1, 0, 0, 0, 1, 0, 0] -> [0, 0, 0, 1, 0]; "T2i
    [c, 0, 0, 0, 0, 0, 0, 0, 0] -> [0, 0, 0, 1, 0];
    [c, 1, 1, 1, 0, 0, 0, 0, 0] -> [1, 1, 0, 1, 0]; "T1
    [c, 0, 0, 0, x, 1, 1, 0, 0] -> [1, 1, 1, 1, 0];
    [c, 1, 0, 0, x, 1, 1, 0, 0] -> [1, 1, 1, 1, 0]; "T2
    [c, 0, 1, 0, x, 1, 1, 0, 0] -> [1, 1, 0, 1, 0];
    [c, 1, 1, 0, x, 1, 1, 0, 0] -> [0, 0, 0, 1, 0]; "T2
    [c, 0, 1, 0, x, 1, 1, 0, 0] -> [0, 0, 0, 0, 0];
    [c, 1, 1, 0, x, 1, 1, 0, 0] -> [0, 0, 0, 0, 0]; "T2P
    [c, 0, 0, 0, x, 0, 1, 0, 0] -> [0, 0, 0, 1, 0];
    [c, 1, 0, 0, 0, 0, 1, 0, 0] -> [0, 0, 0, 1, 0]; "T2P
    [c, 0, 0, 0, 0, 0, 0, 0, 0] -> [0, 0, 0, 1, 0];
    [c, 1, 0, 0, 0, 0, 0, 0, 0] -> [0, 0, 0, 1, 0]; "T1P
    [c, 0, 1, 0, 0, 1, 1, 0, 0] -> [0, 0, 0, 0, 0];
    [c, 1, 1, 0, 0, 0, 1, 0, 0] -> [0, 0, 0, 1, 0]; "T2P
    [c, 0, 0, 0, 0, 0, 0, 0, 0] -> [0, 0, 0, 1, 0];
    [c, 1, 0, 0, 0, 0, 0, 0, 0] -> [0, 0, 0, 1, 0]; "T1P
    [c, 0, 1, 0, 0, 1, 1, 1, 0] -> [0, 0, 0, 0, 0];
    [c, 1, 1, 0, 0, 0, 1, 1, 0] -> [0, 0, 0, 1, 1]; "T2P
    [c, 0, 0, 0, 0, 0, 0, 1, 0] -> [0, 0, 0, 1, 0];
    [c, 1, 0, 0, 0, 0, 0, 1, 0] -> [1, 1, 0, 1, 1]; "T1P, Refresh
    [c, 0, 1, 0, 0, 1, 1, 1, 0] -> [1, 1, 1, 1, 1];
    [c, 1, 1, 0, 0, 1, 1, 1, 0] -> [1, 1, 1, 1, 1]; "T2
    [c, 0, 1, 0, 0, 1, 1, 1, 0] -> [1, 1, 0, 1, 1];
    [c, 1, 1, 0, 0, 1, 1, 1, 0] -> [0, 1, 0, 1, 1]; "T2
    [c, 0, 1, 0, 0, 1, 1, 0, 0] -> [0, 1, 0, 1, 1];
```
                                                          240725-96

```
    [c, 1, 1, 0, 0, 1, 1, 0, 0] -> [0, 1, 0, 1, 0]; "T2
    [c, 0, 1, 0, 0, 1, 1, 0, 0] -> [0, 1, 0, 1, 0];
    [c, 1, 1, 0, 0, 1, 1, 0, 0] -> [1, 1, 0, 1, 0]; "T2, Pending Read
    [c, 0, 0, 1, 0, 1, 1, 0, 0] -> [1, 1, 1, 1, 0];
    [c, 1, 1, 0, 0, 1, 1, 0, 0] -> [1, 1, 1, 1, 0]; "T2
    [c, 0, 1, 0, 0, 1, 1, 0, 0] -> [1, 1, 0, 1, 0];
    [c, 1, 1, 0, 0, 1, 1, 0, 0] -> [0, 0, 0, 1, 0]; "T2
    [c, 0, 1, 0, 0, 1, 1, 0, 0] -> [0, 0, 0, 0, 0];
    [c, 1, 1, 0, 0, 1, 1, 0, 0] -> [0, 0, 0, 0, 0]; "T2P
    [c, 0, 0, 0, 0, 0, 1, 0, 0] -> [0, 0, 0, 1, 0];
    [c, 1, 0, 0, 0, 0, 1, 0, 0] -> [0, 0, 0, 1, 0]; "T2P
    [c, 0, 0, 0, 0, 0, 0, 0, 0] -> [0, 0, 0, 1, 0];
    [c, 1, 0, 0, 0, 0, 0, 0, 0] -> [0, 0, 0, 1, 0]; "T1P

end PAGE_MODE_DRAM_CTRL_1;
```
                                                          240725-97

PAL Codes: DRAM 1 (Continued)

```
ABEL(tm) 3.10  -  Document Generator          15-Feb-90 05:47 PM
PAGE MODE DRAM CONTROLLER - PAL 1, INTEL CORPORATION
Equations for Module PAGE_MODE_DRAM_CTRL_1

Device PAGE1


- Reduced Equations:

    !RAS- := (NA- & !RAS- & !RESET & refresh
            # DRAMRDY- & !HIT- & !NA- & !RAS- & !RESET
            # DRAMRDY- & MEMCS- & !NA- & !RAS- & !RESET
            # !HIT- & !MEMCS- & !NA- & !RAS- & !RESET & !refresh
            # !CLK & !RAS- & !RESET
            # CAS- & !NA- & !RAS- & !RESET
            # CLK & !LMEMCS- & NA- & RAS- & !precharge & !refresh
            # CLK & NA- & RAS- & !precharge & refresh & wait-);

    !NA- := (DRAMRDY- & !HIT- & !NA- & !RAS- & !RESET
            # DRAMRDY- & MEMCS- & !NA- & !RAS- & !RESET
            # !HIT- & !MEMCS- & !NA- & !RAS- & !RESET & !refresh
            # !CLK & !NA- & !RAS- & !RESET
            # CAS- & !NA- & !RAS- & !RESET
            # CLK & !LMEMCS- & NA- & RAS- & !precharge & !refresh);

    !precharge := (CAS- & !a
                 # !RAS- & !precharge
                 # RESET & !precharge
                 # !a & !precharge);

    !a := (precharge # RESET & a # RAS- & !a);

    !CAL := (!CAL & CAS- & !RESET # CAL & CAS- & !NA-);

    !refresh := (!refresh & wait-
               # CLK & NA- & !RAS- & wait-
               # RESET & refresh
               # !refreq & !refresh
               # !CLK & !refresh);

    !wait- := (CLK & !refreq & !refresh
             # !MEMCS- & !wait-
             # !CLK & !wait-
             # RESET
             # !refresh & !wait-);
```

PAL Codes: DRAM 1 (Continued)

AP-442

ABEL 3.10—Document Generator   15-Feb-90 05:47 PM
PAGE MODE DRAM CONTROLLER—PAL 1, INTEL CORPORATION
Chip diagram for Module PAGE__MODE__CTRL__1

Device PAGE1

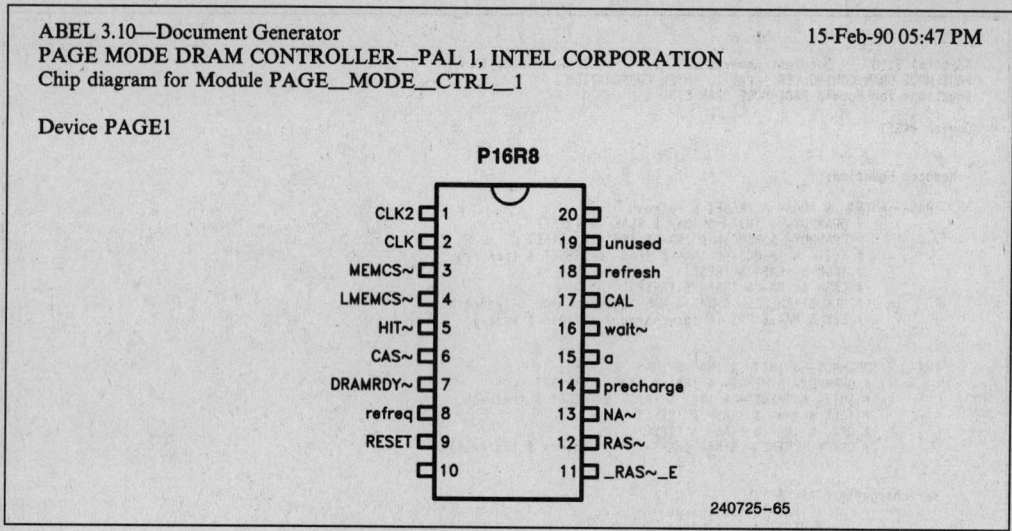

PAL Codes: DRAM 1 (Continued)

AP-442

```
ABEL(tm) 3.10  -  Document Generator          15-Feb-90 06:16 PM
PAGE MODE DRAM CONTROLLER - PAL 2, INTEL CORPORATION
Equations for Module PAGE_MODE_DRAM_CTRL_2

Device PAGE2


- Reduced Equations:

    !CAS- := (CAS- & CLK & DRAMRDY- & !RESET & !a & !b
            # !CACHE & DRAMRDY- & !RESET & a & !b & !lwr
            # DRAMRDY- & !RAS- & !RESET & a & !b & !lwr
            # !CAS- & !CLK & !RESET & a & b
            # !CAS- & DRAMRDY- & !RESET & a
            # CAS- & CLK & DRAMRDY- & !MUXOE- & !RAS- & a & b);

    !DRAMRDY- := (CAS- & CLK & DRAMRDY- & !RESET & !a & !b
               # !CAS- & !CLK & !DRAMRDY- & !RESET & a & b
               # !CAS- & CLK & DRAMRDY- & !RESET & a & !b
               # !CAS- & CLK & DRAMRDY- & !RESET & a & !wr
               # !CACHE & !CAS- & CLK & DRAMRDY- & !RESET & a);

    !a := (CAS- & !CLK & DRAMRDY- & !RESET & !a & !b
        # CAS- & CLK & DRAMRDY- & !RAS- & !RESET & a & !b & lwr);

    !b := (CAS- & !CLK & DRAMRDY- & !RESET & !a & !b
        # CAS- & DRAMRDY- & RAS- & !RESET & a & !b
        # !CACHE & CAS- & DRAMRDY- & !RESET & a & !b
        # CAS- & DRAMRDY- & !RESET & a & !b & lwr
        # !CAS- & CLK & !DRAMRDY- & !MEMCS- & !RAS- & !RESET & a & b &
    !refresh
        # !CAS- & !CLK & DRAMRDY- & !RESET & a & !b
        # CACHE & !CAS- & CLK & DRAMRDY- & !RESET & a & b & !lwr);

    !MUXOE- := (!MUXOE- & !REF-
             # REF- & !r
             # MUXOE- & RESET
             # DRAMRDY- & !MUXOE- & !RAS-
             # !MEMCS- & !MUXOE- & RAS-
             # !MUXOE- & !refresh
             # !CLK & !MUXOE-);


    !REF- := (MUXOE- & !RESET & r);

    !r := (MUXOE- & !REF- & !RESET & !r
        # CLK & MUXOE- & !RAS- & !REF- & !RESET);
```

240725-98

PAL Codes: DRAM 2

AP-442

ABEL 3.10—Document Generator 15-Feb-90 06:16 PM
PAGE MODE DRAM CONTROLLER—PAL 2, INTEL CORPORATION
Chip diagram for Module PAGE__MODE__DRAM__CTRL__2

Device PAGE2

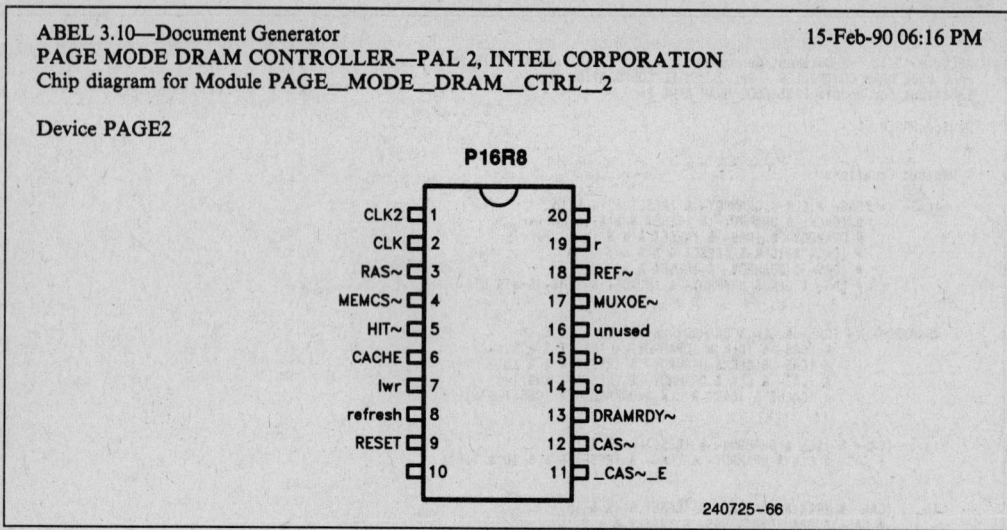

PAL Codes: DRAM 2 (Continued)

AP-442

```
module       PAGE_MODE_DRAM_CTRL_2  flag '-r3'
title  'PAGE MODE DRAM CONTROLLER - PAL 2, INTEL CORPORATION'

    PAGE2      device     'P16R8';

    x     =    .X.;       " ABEL 'don't care' symbol
    c     =    .C.;       " ABEL 'clocking input' symbol

" Inputs

    CLK2      pin   1;    "80386 CLK2
    CLK       pin   2;    "Processor Clock
    RAS-      pin   3;    "Row Address Strobe
    MEMCS-    pin   4;    "Memory Chip Select
    HIT-      pin   5;    "DRAM Page Hit Signal (unused)
    CACHE     pin   6;    "Hi when 385 is used; otherwise, Low
    lwr       pin   7;    "Latched Write/Read
    refresh   pin   8;    "Refresh Signal
    RESET     pin   9;    "System Reset

" Outputs

    CAS-      pin  12;     "Column Address Strobe
    DRAMRDY-       pin 13;    "DRAM Ready
    a         pin  14;     "
    b         pin  15;     "
    unused    pin  16;     "
    MUXOE-    pin  17;     "DRAM Address Multiplexer Output Enable
    REF-      pin  18;     "Enables refresh counter instead of MUX
    r         pin  19;

    cstate  = [CAS-, DRAMRDY-,a, b];
    idle    = [ 1 ,  1    ,1, 1]; "Idle
    start   = [ 0 ,  1    ,1, 1]; "CAS- Active
    wait    = [ 0,   1    ,1, 0]; "CAS- Active, Wait State
    active  = [ 0,   0    ,1, 1]; "CAS- and DRAMRDY- Active
    inactive_1 = [ 1 ,  1    ,1, 0]; "Page Hit, CAS- and DRAMRDY- Inactive
    inactive_2 = [ 1 ,  1    ,0, 0]; "Page Hit, CAS- and DRAMRDY- Inactive
    illegal_a  = [0,0,0,0];
    illegal_b  = [0,0,0,1];
    illegal_c  = [0,0,1,0];
    illegal_d  = [0,1,0,0];
    illegal_e  = [0,1,0,1];
    illegal_f  = [1,0,0,1];
    illegal_g  = [1,0,1,0];
    illegal_h  = [1,0,1,1];
    illegal_i  = [1,1,0,1];
    illegal_j  = [1,0,0,0];

    muxstate  = [MUXOE~, REF~, r];
    enabled = [  0  ,  1   , 1]; "Multiplexer Outputs Enabled
```

240725-99

PAL Codes: DRAM 2 (Continued)

AP-442

```
        disabled_1   = [ 1 , 1  , 1]; "Multiplexer Outputs Disabled
        disabled_2   = [ 1 , 0  , 1]; "Refresh Address Enabled
        disabled_3   = [ 1 , 0  , 0]; "Wait for RAS#
        disabled_4   = [ 1 , 1  , 0]; "Refresh Address Disabled
        illegal_z    = [0,0,0];
        illegal_y    = [0,0,1];
        illegal_x    = [0,1,0];

state_diagram cstate

    state idle:      if (CLK & !RAS- & !MUXOE-) then start else idle;
    state start:     if RESET then idle else
                     if (CLK & !CACHE # CLK & !wr) then active else
                     if CLK then wait else start;
    state wait:      if RESET then idle else
                     if CLK then active else wait;
    state active:    if RESET then idle else
                     if (CLK & !MEMCS- & RAS- #
                        CLK & MEMCS- #
                        CLK & refresh) then idle else
                     if (CLK & !MEMCS- & !RAS-) then inactive_1
                     else active;
    state inactive_1: if RESET then idle else
                     if (CLK & !RAS- & !wr) then inactive_2 else
                     if (!RAS- & !!wr & CACHE) then start else
                     if (!!wr & !CACHE) then wait else
                     inactive_1;
    state inactive_2: if RESET then idle else
                     if CLK then active else inactive_2;
    state illegal_a: goto idle;
    state illegal_b: goto idle;
    state illegal_c: goto idle;
    state illegal_d: goto idle;
    state illegal_e: goto idle;
    state illegal_f: goto idle;
    state illegal_g: goto idle;
    state illegal_h: goto idle;
    state illegal_i: goto idle;
    state illegal_j: goto idle;

state_diagram muxstate

    state enabled:   if (CLK & refresh & RAS- & MEMCS- #
                        CLK & refresh & !RAS- & !DRAMRDY-) then
                     disabled_1 else enabled;
    state disabled_1: if (RESET) then enabled else disabled_2;
    state disabled_2: if (RESET) then enabled else
                     if (CLK & !RAS-) then disabled_3 else disabled_2;
    state disabled_3: if (RESET) then enabled else disabled_4;
    state disabled_4: goto enabled;
    state illegal_z: goto enabled;
    state illegal_y: goto enabled;
    state illegal_x: goto enabled;
```

240725-A0

PAL Codes: DRAM 2 (Continued)

AP-442

```
test_vectors

    ([CLK2,CLK,MEMCS~,lwr,HIT-,RAS~,refresh,RESET,CACHE] ->
     [CAS-,DRAMRDY-,MUXOE-,REF-])

"   C  C  M  l  H  R  r   R  C       C  D  M  R
"   L  L  E  w  I  A  e   E  A       A  R  U  E
"   K  K  M  r  T  S  f   S  C       S  A  X  F
"   2     C  -  -  -  r   E  H       -  M  O  -
"            S           e   T  E           R  E
"            -           s       -           D  -
"                        h       -              -
"                                -
"                                -

    [c, x, x, 0, x, x, x, 1, 0] -> [1, 1, 0, 1]; "Cache disabled
    [c, x, x, 0, x, x, x, 1, 0] -> [1, 1, 0, 1];
    [c, 0, 1, 0, x, 1, 0, 0, 0] -> [1, 1, 0, 1]; "T1
    [c, 1, 1, 0, x, 1, 0, 0, 0] -> [1, 1, 0, 1];
    [c, 0, 0, 0, x, 1, 0, 0, 0] -> [1, 1, 0, 1]; "T1
    [c, 1, 0, 0, x, 1, 0, 0, 0] -> [1, 1, 0, 1];
    [c, 0, 1, 0, x, 0, 0, 0, 0] -> [1, 1, 0, 1]; "T2
    [c, 1, 1, 0, x, 0, 0, 0, 0] -> [0, 1, 0, 1];
    [c, 0, 0, 0, x, 0, 0, 0, 0] -> [0, 1, 0, 1]; "T2P
    [c, 1, 0, 0, 0, 0, 0, 0, 0] -> [0, 0, 0, 1];
    [c, 0, 0, 0, 0, 0, 0, 0, 0] -> [0, 0, 0, 1]; "T2P
    [c, 1, 0, 0, 0, 0, 0, 0, 0] -> [1, 0, 0, 1];
    [c, 0, 1, 0, 0, 0, 0, 0, 0] -> [0, 1, 0, 1]; "T1P
    [c, 1, 1, 0, 0, 0, 0, 0, 0] -> [0, 0, 0, 1];
    [c, 0, 0, 0, 0, 0, 0, 0, 0] -> [0, 0, 0, 1]; "T2P
    [c, 1, 0, 0, 0, 0, 0, 0, 0] -> [1, 1, 0, 1];
    [c, 0, 1, 1, 0, 0, 0, 0, 0] -> [1, 1, 0, 1]; "T1P
    [c, 1, 1, 1, 0, 0, 0, 0, 0] -> [1, 1, 0, 1];
    [c, 0, 0, 1, 0, 0, 0, 0, 0] -> [1, 1, 0, 1]; "T2P
    [c, 1, 0, 1, 0, 0, 0, 0, 0] -> [0, 0, 0, 1];
    [c, 0, 0, 1, 0, 0, 0, 0, 0] -> [0, 0, 0, 1]; "T2p
    [c, 1, 0, 0, 0, 0, 0, 0, 0] -> [1, 1, 0, 1];
    [c, 0, 1, 0, 0, 0, 0, 0, 0] -> [0, 1, 0, 1]; "T1P
    [c, 1, 1, 0, 0, 0, 0, 0, 0] -> [0, 0, 0, 1];
    [c, 0, 0, 0, 0, 0, 0, 0, 0] -> [0, 0, 0, 1]; "T2P
    [c, 1, 0, 0, 1, 1, 0, 0, 0] -> [1, 1, 0, 1];
    [c, 0, 1, 0, 1, 1, 0, 0, 0] -> [1, 1, 0, 1]; "T1P
    [c, 1, 1, 0, 1, 1, 0, 0, 0] -> [1, 1, 0, 1];
    [c, 0, 0, 0, 1, 1, 0, 0, 0] -> [1, 1, 0, 1]; "T2
    [c, 1, 1, 0, 1, 0, 0, 0, 0] -> [1, 1, 0, 1];
    [c, 1, 1, 0, 1, 0, 0, 0, 0] -> [1, 1, 0, 1]; "T2
    [c, 1, 0, 0, x, 0, 0, 0, 0] -> [0, 1, 0, 1];
    [c, 0, 0, 0, x, 0, 0, 0, 0] -> [0, 1, 0, 1]; "T2P
    [c, 1, 0, 0, 1, 0, 0, 0, 0] -> [0, 0, 0, 1];
    [c, 0, 0, 1, 1, 1, 0, 0, 0] -> [0, 0, 0, 1]; "T2P
    [c, 1, 0, 1, 1, 0, 0, 0, 0] -> [1, 1, 0, 1];
    [c, 0, 1, 1, 1, 1, 0, 0, 0] -> [1, 1, 0, 1]; "T1P
    [c, 1, 1, 1, 1, 1, 0, 0, 0] -> [1, 1, 0, 1];
```

240725-A1

PAL Codes: DRAM 2 (Continued)

AP-442

```
[c, 0, 1, 1, 1, 0, 0, 0, 0] -> [1, 1, 0, 1]; "T2
[c, 1, 1, 1, 1, 0, 0, 0, 0] -> [0, 1, 0, 1];
[c, 0, 0, 1, 1, 0, 0, 0, 0] -> [0, 1, 0, 1]; "T2P
[c, 1, 0, 1, 0, 0, 0, 0, 0] -> [0, 0, 0, 1];
[c, 0, 0, 1, 0, 0, 0, 0, 0] -> [0, 0, 0, 1]; "T2P
[c, 1, 0, 0, 0, 0, 0, 0, 0] -> [1, 1, 0, 1];
[c, 0, 1, 0, 0, 0, 0, 0, 0] -> [0, 1, 0, 1]; "T1P
[c, 1, 1, 0, 0, 0, 0, 0, 0] -> [0, 0, 0, 1];
[c, 0, 0, 0, 0, 0, 0, 0, 0] -> [0, 0, 0, 1]; "T2P
[c, 1, 0, 0, 0, 0, 0, 0, 0] -> [1, 1, 0, 1];
[c, 0, 1, 0, 0, 0, 0, 0, 0] -> [0, 1, 0, 1]; "T1P
[c, 1, 1, 0, 0, 0, 0, 0, 0] -> [0, 0, 0, 1];
[c, 0, 1, 0, 0, 0, 0, 0, 0] -> [0, 0, 0, 1]; "T2i
[c, 1, 1, 0, 0, 0, 0, 0, 0] -> [1, 1, 0, 1];
[c, 0, 0, 0, x, 1, 0, 0, 0] -> [1, 1, 0, 1]; "T1
[c, 1, 0, 0, x, 1, 0, 0, 0] -> [1, 1, 0, 1];
[c, 0, 1, 1, x, 1, 0, 0, 0] -> [1, 1, 0, 1]; "T2
[c, 1, 1, 1, x, 1, 0, 0, 0] -> [1, 1, 0, 1];
[c, 0, 1, 1, x, 0, 0, 0, 0] -> [1, 1, 0, 1]; "T2
[c, 1, 1, 1, x, 0, 0, 0, 0] -> [0, 1, 0, 1];
[c, 0, 0, 1, x, 0, 0, 0, 0] -> [0, 1, 0, 1]; "T2P
[c, 1, 0, 1, 0, 0, 0, 0, 0] -> [0, 0, 0, 1];
[c, 0, 0, 1, 0, 0, 0, 0, 0] -> [0, 0, 0, 1]; "T2P
[c, 1, 0, 0, 0, 0, 0, 0, 0] -> [1, 1, 0, 1];
[c, 0, 1, 0, 0, 0, 0, 0, 0] -> [0, 1, 0, 1]; "T1P
[c, 1, 1, 0, 0, 0, 0, 0, 0] -> [0, 0, 0, 1];
[c, 0, 0, 0, 0, 0, 0, 0, 0] -> [0, 0, 0, 1]; "T2P
[c, 1, 0, 0, 0, 0, 0, 0, 0] -> [1, 1, 0, 1];
[c, 0, 1, 0, 0, 0, 0, 0, 0] -> [0, 1, 0, 1]; "T1P
[c, 1, 1, 0, 0, 0, 0, 0, 0] -> [0, 0, 0, 1];
[c, 0, 0, 0, 0, 0, 0, 0, 0] -> [0, 0, 0, 1]; "T2P
[c, 1, 0, 0, 0, 1, 0, 0] -> [1, 1, 1, 1];
[c, 0, 1, 0, 0, 1, 1, 0, 0] -> [1, 1, 1, 0]; "T1P
[c, 1, 1, 0, 0, 1, 1, 0, 0] -> [1, 1, 1, 0];
[c, 0, 1, 0, 0, 1, 1, 0, 0] -> [1, 1, 1, 0]; "T2
[c, 1, 1, 0, 0, 1, 1, 0, 0] -> [1, 1, 1, 0];
[c, 0, 1, 0, 0, 0, 1, 0, 0] -> [1, 1, 1, 0]; "T2
[c, 1, 1, 0, 0, 0, 1, 0, 0] -> [1, 1, 1, 0];
[c, 0, 1, 0, 0, 0, 1, 0, 0] -> [1, 1, 1, 1]; "T2
[c, 1, 1, 0, 0, 0, 0, 0, 0] -> [1, 1, 0, 1];
[c, 0, 1, 0, 0, 1, 0, 0, 0] -> [1, 1, 0, 1]; "T2
[c, 1, 1, 0, 0, 1, 0, 0, 0] -> [1, 1, 0, 1];
[c, 0, 1, 0, 0, 1, 0, 0, 0] -> [1, 1, 0, 1]; "T2
[c, 1, 1, 0, 0, 1, 0, 0, 0] -> [1, 1, 0, 1];
[c, 0, 1, 0, 0, 0, 0, 0, 0] -> [1, 1, 0, 1]; "T2
[c, 1, 1, 0, 0, 0, 0, 0, 0] -> [0, 1, 0, 1];
[c, 0, 0, 0, 0, 0, 0, 0, 0] -> [0, 1, 0, 1]; "T2P
[c, 1, 0, 0, 0, 0, 0, 0, 0] -> [0, 0, 0, 1];
[c, 0, 0, 0, 0, 0, 0, 0, 0] -> [0, 0, 0, 1]; "T2P
[c, 1, 0, 0, 0, 0, 0, 0, 0] -> [1, 1, 0, 1];
[c, 0, 1, 0, 0, 0, 0, 0, 0] -> [0, 1, 0, 1]; "T1P
[c, 1, 1, 0, 0, 0, 0, 0, 0] -> [0, 0, 0, 1];
[c, 0, 0, 0, 0, 0, 0, 0, 0] -> [0, 0, 0, 1]; "T2P
[c, x, x, 0, x, x, x, 1, 1] -> [1, 1, 0, 1]; "Cache eanbled
```

PAL Codes: DRAM 2 (Continued)

AP-442

```
        [c, x, x, 0, x, x, x, 1, 1] -> [1, 1, 0, 1];
        [c, 0, 1, 0, x, 1, 0, 0, 1] -> [1, 1, 0, 1]; "T1
        [c, 1, 1, 0, x, 1, 0, 0, 1] -> [1, 1, 0, 1];
        [c, 0, 0, 0, x, 1, 0, 0, 1] -> [1, 1, 0, 1]; "T1, Read
        [c, 1, 0, 0, x, 1, 0, 0, 1] -> [1, 1, 0, 1];
        [c, 0, 1, 0, x, 0, 0, 0, 1] -> [1, 1, 0, 1]; "T2
        [c, 1, 1, 0, x, 0, 0, 0, 1] -> [0, 1, 0, 1];
        [c, 0, 0, 0, x, 0, 0, 0, 1] -> [0, 1, 0, 1]; "T2P
        [c, 1, 0, 0, 0, 0, 0, 0, 1] -> [0, 1, 0, 1];
        [c, 0, 0, 0, 0, 0, 0, 0, 1] -> [0, 1, 0, 1]; "T2P
        [c, 1, 0, 0, 0, 0, 0, 0, 1] -> [0, 0, 0, 1];
        [c, 0, 0, 0, 0, 0, 0, 0, 1] -> [0, 0, 0, 1]; "T2P
        [c, 1, 0, 0, 0, 0, 0, 0, 1] -> [1, 1, 0, 1];
        [c, 0, 1, 0, 0, 0, 0, 0, 1] -> [0, 1, 0, 1]; "T1P, Read
        [c, 1, 1, 0, 0, 0, 0, 0, 1] -> [0, 1, 0, 1];
        [c, 0, 0, 0, 0, 0, 0, 0, 1] -> [0, 1, 0, 1]; "T2P
        [c, 1, 0, 0, 0, 0, 0, 0, 1] -> [0, 0, 0, 1];
        [c, 0, 0, 0, 0, 0, 0, 0, 1] -> [0, 0, 0, 1]; "T2P
        [c, 1, 0, 0, 0, 0, 0, 0, 1] -> [1, 1, 0, 1];
        [c, 0, 1, 1, 0, 0, 0, 0, 1] -> [1, 1, 0, 1]; "T1P, Write
        [c, 1, 1, 1, 0, 0, 0, 0, 1] -> [1, 1, 0, 1];
        [c, 0, 0, 1, 0, 0, 0, 0, 1] -> [1, 1, 0, 1]; "T2P
        [c, 1, 0, 1, 0, 0, 0, 0, 1] -> [0, 0, 0, 1];
        [c, 0, 0, 1, 0, 0, 0, 0, 1] -> [0, 0, 0, 1]; "T2p
        [c, 1, 0, 0, 0, 0, 0, 0, 1] -> [1, 1, 0, 1];
end PAGE_MODE_DRAM_CTRL_2;
^Z
```

PAL Codes: DRAM 2 (Continued)

AP-442

```
module       PAGE_MODE_DRAM_CTRL_3  flag '-r3'
title   'PAGE MODE DRAM CONTROLLER - PAL 3, INTEL CORPORATION'

    PAGE3     device      'P16R8';

    x      =   .X.;        " ABEL 'don't care' symbol
    c      =   .C.;        " ABEL 'clocking input' symbol

" Inputs

    CLK2     pin   1;   "80386 CLK2
    CLK      pin   2;   "Processor Clock
    ADS-     pin   3;   "Address Strobe
    MEMCS-   pin   4;   "Memory Chip Select
    WR       pin   5;   "Write/Read
    READY-   pin   6;   "System Ready
    DRMRDY-  pin   7;   "DRAM Ready
    unused1  pin   8;
    RESET    pin   9;   "System Reset

" Outputs

    T2X-     pin  12;   "active during T2, T2p, and T2i
    T1P-     pin  13;   "active during T1p
    WE-      pin  14;   "DRAM Write Enable
    DEN-     pin  15;   "DRAM Data Bus Transceiver Enable
    DTR      pin  16;   "DRAM Data Bus Transceiver R/W# Direction signal
    lwr      pin  17;   "Latched Write/Read
    mreq     pin  18;   "Latched Memory Chip Select
    unused2  pin  19;   "

state_diagram [T2X-, T1P-]

    state [1, 1]:    if (CLK & !ADS-) then [0, 1] else [1, 1];
    state [0, 1]:    if RESET then [1, 1] else
                     if (CLK & !ADS- & !READY-) then [1, 0] else
                     if (CLK & ADS- & !READY-) then [1, 1] else [0, 1];
    state [1, 0]:    if RESET then [1, 1] else
                     if (CLK) then [0, 1] else [1, 0];
    state [0, 0]:    goto [1, 1];

state_diagram [WE-]

    state [1]:       if (CLK & !MEMCS- & WR & T2X- #
                     lwr & !T1P-) then [0] else [1];
    state [0]:       if (RESET) then [1] else
                     if (CLK & !READY-) then [1] else [0];

state_diagram [DEN-]

    state [1]:       if (CLK & !MEMCS- & !WR & T2X- #
                     mreq & !T2X- #
                     CLK & mreq & !T1P-) then [0] else [1];
```

240725-A4

PAL Codes: DRAM 3

AP-442

```
        state [0]:      if RESET then [1] else
                        if (CLK & !READY~) then [1] else [0];

state_diagram [DTR]

        state [1]:      if (CLK & !MEMCS~ & WR & T2X~ #
                        lwr & !T1P~) then [0] else [1];
        state [0]:      if (RESET) then [1] else
                        if (!CLK & DEN~ & !lwr) then [1] else [0];

state_diagram [lwr]

        state [0]:      if (CLK & !MEMCS~ & WR) then [1] else [0];
        state [1]:      if (RESET) then [0] else
                        if (!READY~ & MEMCS~ #
                            !READY~ & !WR) then [0] else [1];

state_diagram [mreq]

        state [0]:      if (CLK & !MEMCS~) then [1] else [0];
        state [1]:      if RESET then [0] else
                        if (!READY~ & MEMCS~) then [0] else [1];

test_vectors

        ([CLK2,CLK,ADS~,WR,MEMCS~,READY~,RESET] ->
         [T2X~,T1P~,DEN~,lwr,WE~,DTR, mreq])

"       C C A W M R R          T T D l W D m
"       L L D R E E E          2 1 E w E T r
"       K K S   M A S          X P N r ~ R e
"       2 ~     C D E          ~ ~ ~     ~ q
"               S Y T
"               ~ ~

        [c, x, x, x, x, x, 1] -> [1, 1, 1, 0, 1, 1, x];
        [c, x, x, x, x, x, 1] -> [1, 1, 1, 0, 1, 1, 0];
        [c, 1, 1, x, 1, 1, 0] -> [1, 1, 1, 0, 1, 1, 0];
        [c, 0, 1, x, 1, 1, 0] -> [1, 1, 1, 0, 1, 1, 0]; "Ti
        [c, 1, 1, x, 1, 1, 0] -> [1, 1, 1, 0, 1, 1, 0];
        [c, 0, 0, 0, 0, 1, 0] -> [1, 1, 1, 0, 1, 1, 0]; "T1
        [c, 1, 0, 0, 0, 1, 0] -> [0, 1, 0, 0, 1, 1, 1];
        [c, 0, 0, 0, 1, 1, 0] -> [0, 1, 0, 0, 1, 1, 1]; "T2
        [c, 1, 1, 0, 1, 1, 0] -> [0, 1, 0, 0, 1, 1, 1];
        [c, 0, 0, 0, 0, 1, 0] -> [0, 1, 0, 0, 1, 1, 1]; "T2
        [c, 1, 0, 0, 0, 1, 0] -> [0, 1, 0, 0, 1, 1, 1];
        [c, 0, 0, 0, 0, 0, 0] -> [0, 1, 0, 0, 1, 1, 1]; "T2P
        [c, 1, 0, 0, 0, 0, 0] -> [1, 0, 1, 0, 1, 1, 1];
        [c, 0, 1, 0, 1, 1, 0] -> [1, 0, 1, 0, 1, 1, 1]; "T1P
        [c, 1, 1, 0, 1, 1, 0] -> [0, 1, 0, 0, 1, 1, 1];
        [c, 0, 0, 1, 0, 0, 0] -> [0, 1, 0, 0, 1, 1, 1]; "T2P
        [c, 1, 0, 1, 0, 0, 0] -> [1, 0, 1, 1, 1, 1, 1];
        [c, 0, 1, 1, 1, 1, 0] -> [1, 0, 1, 1, 0, 0, 1]; "T1P
        [c, 1, 1, 1, 1, 1, 0] -> [0, 1, 0, 1, 0, 0, 1];
```

240725-A5

PAL Codes: DRAM 3 (Continued)

AP-442

```
[c, 0, 0, 0, 0, 1, 0] -> [0, 1, 0, 1, 0, 0, 1]; "T2P
[c, 1, 0, 0, 0, 1, 0] -> [0, 1, 0, 1, 0, 0, 1];
[c, 0, 0, 0, 0, 0, 0] -> [0, 1, 0, 0, 0, 0, 1]; "T2P
[c, 1, 0, 0, 0, 0, 0] -> [1, 0, 1, 0, 1, 0, 1];
[c, 0, 1, 0, 1, 1, 0] -> [1, 0, 1, 0, 1, 1, 1]; "T1P
[c, 1, 1, 0, 1, 1, 0] -> [0, 1, 0, 0, 1, 1, 1];
[c, 0, 0, 0, 0, 0, 0] -> [0, 1, 0, 0, 1, 1, 1]; "T2P
[c, 1, 0, 0, 0, 0, 0] -> [1, 0, 1, 0, 1, 1, 1];
[c, 0, 1, 0, 1, 1, 0] -> [1, 0, 1, 0, 1, 1, 1]; "T1p
[c, 1, 1, 0, 1, 1, 0] -> [0, 1, 0, 0, 1, 1, 1];
[c, 0, 1, 0, 1, 1, 0] -> [0, 1, 0, 0, 1, 1, 1]; "T2
[c, 1, 1, 0, 1, 1, 0] -> [0, 1, 0, 0, 1, 1, 1];
[c, 0, 1, 0, 1, 1, 0] -> [0, 1, 0, 0, 1, 1, 1]; "T2
[c, 1, 1, 0, 1, 1, 0] -> [0, 1, 0, 0, 1, 1, 1];
[c, 0, 0, 1, 0, 1, 0] -> [0, 1, 0, 1, 1, 1, 1]; "T2P
[c, 1, 0, 1, 0, 1, 0] -> [0, 1, 0, 1, 1, 1, 1];
[c, 0, 0, 1, 0, 0, 0] -> [0, 1, 0, 1, 1, 1, 1]; "T2p
[c, 1, 0, 1, 0, 0, 0] -> [1, 0, 1, 1, 1, 1, 1];
[c, 0, 1, 1, 1, 1, 0] -> [1, 0, 1, 1, 0, 0, 1]; "T1P
[c, 1, 1, 1, 1, 1, 0] -> [0, 1, 0, 1, 0, 0, 1];
[c, 0, 1, 1, 1, 1, 0] -> [0, 1, 0, 1, 0, 0, 1]; "T2
[c, 1, 1, 1, 1, 1, 0] -> [0, 1, 0, 1, 0, 0, 1];
[c, 0, 0, 0, 0, 1, 0] -> [0, 1, 0, 1, 0, 0, 1]; "T2P
[c, 1, 0, 0, 0, 1, 0] -> [0, 1, 0, 1, 0, 0, 1];
[c, 0, 0, 0, 0, 0, 0] -> [0, 1, 0, 0, 0, 0, 1]; "T2P
[c, 1, 0, 0, 0, 0, 0] -> [1, 0, 1, 0, 1, 0, 1];
[c, 0, 1, 0, 1, 1, 0] -> [1, 0, 1, 0, 1, 1, 1]; "T1P
[c, 1, 1, 0, 1, 1, 0] -> [0, 1, 0, 0, 1, 1, 1];
[c, 0, 0, 0, 0, 0, 0] -> [0, 1, 0, 0, 1, 1, 1]; "T2P
[c, 1, 0, 0, 0, 0, 0] -> [1, 0, 1, 0, 1, 1, 1];
[c, 0, 1, 0, 1, 1, 0] -> [1, 0, 1, 0, 1, 1, 1]; "T1P
[c, 1, 1, 0, 1, 1, 0] -> [0, 1, 0, 0, 1, 1, 1];
[c, 0, 1, 0, 1, 0, 0] -> [0, 1, 0, 0, 1, 1, 0]; "T2i
[c, 1, 1, 0, 1, 0, 0] -> [1, 1, 1, 0, 1, 1, 0];
[c, 0, 0, 1, 0, 1, 0] -> [1, 1, 1, 0, 1, 1, 0]; "T1
[c, 1, 0, 1, 0, 1, 0] -> [0, 1, 1, 1, 0, 0, 1];
[c, 0, 1, 1, 1, 1, 0] -> [0, 1, 0, 1, 0, 0, 1]; "T2
[c, 1, 1, 1, 1, 1, 0] -> [0, 1, 0, 1, 0, 0, 1];
[c, 1, 1, 1, 1, 1, 0] -> [0, 1, 0, 1, 0, 0, 1]; "T2
[c, 1, 1, 1, 1, 1, 0] -> [0, 1, 0, 1, 0, 0, 1];
[c, 0, 0, 0, 0, 1, 0] -> [0, 1, 0, 1, 0, 0, 1]; "T2P
[c, 1, 0, 0, 0, 1, 0] -> [0, 1, 0, 1, 0, 0, 1];
[c, 0, 0, 0, 0, 0, 0] -> [0, 1, 0, 0, 0, 0, 1]; "T2P
[c, 1, 0, 0, 0, 0, 0] -> [1, 0, 1, 0, 1, 0, 1];
[c, 0, 1, 0, 1, 1, 0] -> [1, 0, 1, 0, 1, 1, 1]; "T1P
[c, 1, 1, 0, 1, 1, 0] -> [0, 1, 0, 0, 1, 1, 1];
[c, 0, 0, 0, 0, 0, 0] -> [0, 1, 0, 0, 1, 1, 1]; "T2P
[c, 1, 0, 0, 0, 0, 0] -> [1, 0, 1, 0, 1, 1, 1];
[c, 0, 1, 0, 1, 1, 0] -> [1, 0, 1, 0, 1, 1, 1]; "T1P
[c, 1, 1, 0, 1, 1, 0] -> [0, 1, 0, 0, 1, 1, 1];
[c, 0, 0, 0, 0, 0, 0] -> [0, 1, 0, 0, 1, 1, 1]; "T2P
[c, 1, 0, 0, 0, 0, 0] -> [1, 0, 1, 0, 1, 1, 1];
[c, 0, 1, 0, 1, 1, 0] -> [1, 0, 1, 0, 1, 1, 1]; "T1P
[c, 1, 1, 0, 1, 1, 0] -> [0, 1, 0, 0, 1, 1, 1];
```

```
[c, 0, 1, 0, 1, 1, 0] -> [0, 1, 0, 0, 1, 1, 1]; "T2
[c, 1, 1, 0, 1, 1, 0] -> [0, 1, 0, 0, 1, 1, 1];
[c, 0, 1, 0, 1, 1, 0] -> [0, 1, 0, 0, 1, 1, 1]; "T2
[c, 1, 1, 0, 1, 1, 0] -> [0, 1, 0, 0, 1, 1, 1];
[c, 0, 1, 0, 1, 1, 0] -> [0, 1, 0, 0, 1, 1, 1]; "T2
[c, 1, 1, 0, 1, 1, 0] -> [0, 1, 0, 0, 1, 1, 1];
[c, 0, 1, 0, 1, 1, 0] -> [0, 1, 0, 0, 1, 1, 1]; "T2
[c, 1, 1, 0, 1, 1, 0] -> [0, 1, 0, 0, 1, 1, 1];
[c, 0, 1, 0, 1, 1, 0] -> [0, 1, 0, 0, 1, 1, 1]; "T2
[c, 1, 1, 0, 1, 1, 0] -> [0, 1, 0, 0, 1, 1, 1];
[c, 0, 0, 0, 0, 1, 0] -> [0, 1, 0, 0, 1, 1, 1]; "T2P
[c, 1, 0, 0, 0, 1, 0] -> [0, 1, 0, 0, 1, 1, 1];
[c, 0, 0, 0, 0, 0, 0] -> [0, 1, 0, 0, 1, 1, 1]; "T2P
[c, 1, 0, 0, 0, 0, 0] -> [1, 0, 1, 0, 1, 1, 1];
[c, 0, 1, 0, 1, 1, 0] -> [1, 0, 1, 0, 1, 1, 1]; "T1P
[c, 1, 1, 0, 1, 1, 0] -> [0, 1, 0, 0, 1, 1, 1];
[c, 0, 0, 0, 0, 0, 0] -> [0, 1, 0, 0, 1, 1, 1]; "T2P

end PAGE_MODE_DRAM_CTRL_3;
```

PAL Codes: DRAM 3 (Continued)

AP-442

```
ABEL(tm) 3.10  - Document Generator          14-Feb-90 09:54 AM
PAGE MODE DRAM CONTROLLER - PAL 3, INTEL CORPORATION
Equations for Module PAGE_MODE_DRAM_CTRL_3

Device PAGE3


- Reduced Equations:

    !T2X- := (CLK & !RESET & !T1P- & T2X-
            # READY- & !RESET & T1P- & !T2X-
            # !CLK & !RESET & T1P- & !T2X-
            # !ADS- & CLK & T1P- & T2X-);


    !T1P- := (!CLK & !RESET & !T1P- & T2X-
            # !ADS- & CLK & !READY- & !RESET & T1P- & !T2X-);


    !WE- := (READY- & !RESET & !WE-
           # !CLK & !RESET & !WE-
           # !T1P- & WE- & lwr
           # CLK & !MEMCS- & T2X- & WE- & WR);


    !DEN- := (!DEN- & READY- & !RESET
            # !CLK & !DEN- & !RESET
            # CLK & DEN- & !T1P- & mreq
            # DEN- & !T2X- & mreq
            # CLK & DEN- & !MEMCS- & T2X- & !WR);


    !DTR := (!DTR & !RESET & lwr
           # !DEN- & !DTR & !RESET
           # CLK & !DTR & !RESET
           # DTR & !T1P- & lwr
           # CLK & DTR & !MEMCS- & T2X- & WR);


    !lwr := (!READY- & !WR
           # MEMCS- & !READY-
           # RESET & lwr
           # !WR & !lwr
           # MEMCS- & !lwr
           # !CLK & !lwr);


    !mreq := (MEMCS- & !READY-
            # RESET & mreq
            # MEMCS- & !mreq
            # !CLK & !mreq);
```

240725-A8

PAL Codes: DRAM 3 (Continued)

AP-442

ABEL 3.10—Document Generator 14-Feb-90 09:54 AM
PAGE MODE DRAM CONTROLLER—PAL 3, INTEL CORPORATION
Chip diagram for Module PAGE__MODE__DRAM__CTRL__3

Device PAGE3

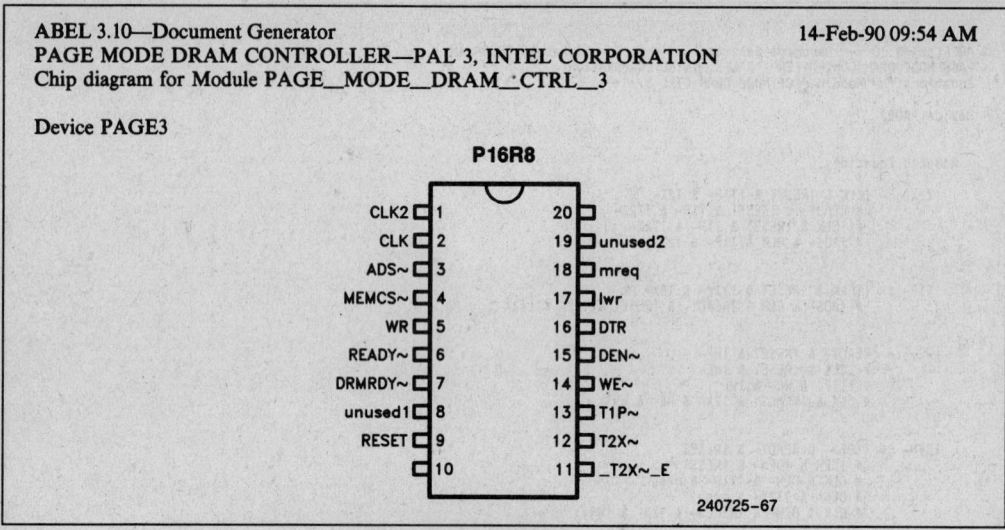

PAL Codes: DRAM 3 (Continued)

AP-442

```
module       PAGE_MODE_DRAM_CTRL_4  flag '-r3'

title   'PAGE MODE DRAM CONTROLLER - PAL 4, INTEL CORPORATION'

    PAGE4    device     'P16R8';

    x     =   .X.;      " ABEL 'don't care' symbol
    c     =   .C.;      " ABEL 'clocking input' symbol

" Inputs

    CLOCK   pin   1;
    D0      pin   2;
    D1      pin   3;
    D2      pin   4;
    D3      pin   5;
    D4      pin   6;
    D5      pin   7;
    D6      pin   8;
    D7      pin   9;
    OE      pin  11;

" Outputs

    A0      pin  12;
    A1      pin  13;
    A2      pin  14;
    A3      pin  15;
    A4      pin  16;
    A5      pin  17;
    A6      pin  18;
    A7      pin  19;

addr = [A7..A0];

equations

    addr := addr + 1;

end PAGE_MODE_DRAM_CTRL_4;
```

240725-A9

PAL Codes: DRAM 4

AP-442

```
ABEL(tm) 3.10  -  Document Generator         14-Feb-90 09:54 AM
PAGE MODE DRAM CONTROLLER - PAL 4, INTEL CORPORATION
Equations for Module PAGE_MODE_DRAM_CTRL_4

Device PAGE4


- Reduced Equations:

    !A7 := (A0 & A1 & A2 & A3 & A4 & A5 & A6 & A7
         #  !A0 & !A7
         #  !A1 & !A7
         #  !A2 & !A7
         #  !A3 & !A7
         #  !A4 & !A7
         #  !A5 & !A7
         #  !A6 & !A7);


    !A6 := (A0 & A1 & A2 & A3 & A4 & A5 & A6
         #  !A0 & !A6
         #  !A1 & !A6
         #  !A2 & !A6
         #  !A3 & !A6
         #  !A4 & !A6
         #  !A5 & !A6);


    !A5 := (A0 & A1 & A2 & A3 & A4 & A5
         #  !A0 & !A5
         #  !A1 & !A5
         #  !A2 & !A5
         #  !A3 & !A5
         #  !A4 & !A5);


    !A4 := (A0 & A1 & A2 & A3 & A4
         #  !A0 & !A4
         #  !A1 & !A4
         #  !A2 & !A4
         #  !A3 & !A4);


    !A3 := (A0 & A1 & A2 & A3 # !A0 & !A3 # !A1 & !A3 # !A2 & !A3);

    !A2 := (A0 & A1 & A2 # !A0 & !A2 # !A1 & !A2);

    !A1 := (A0 & A1 # !A0 & !A1);

    !A0 := (A0);
```

240725-B0

PAL Codes: DRAM 4 (Continued)

AP-442

ABEL 3.10—Document Generator 14-Feb-90 09:54 AM
PAGE MODE DRAM CONTROLLER—PAL 4, INTEL CORPORATION
Chip diagram for Module PAGE__MODE__DRAM__CTRL__4

Device PAGE4

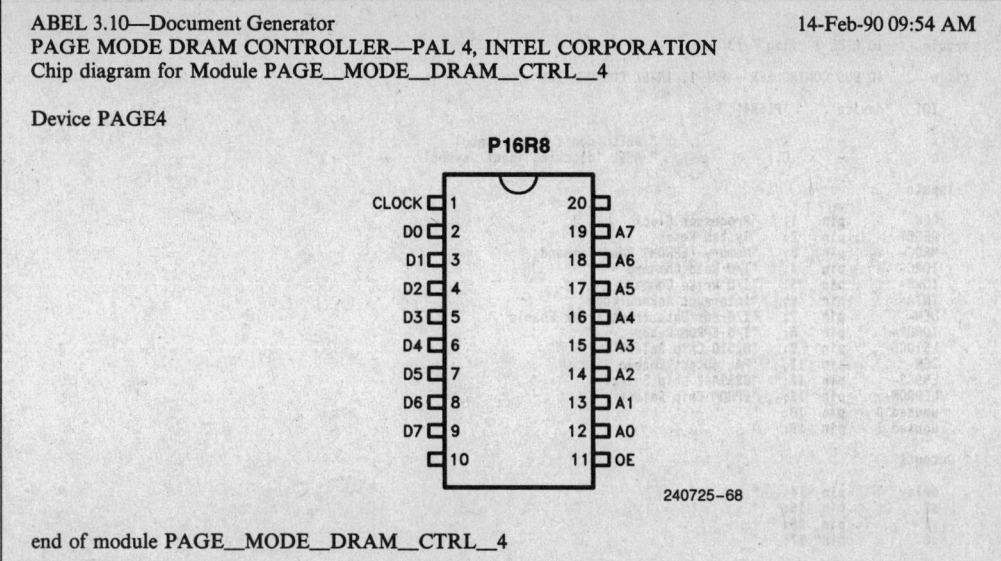

240725-68

end of module PAGE__MODE__DRAM__CTRL__4

PAL Codes: DRAM 4 (Continued)

AP-442

```
module      IO_CTRL_1   flag '-r3'
title       'IO BUS CONTROLLER - PAL 1, INTEL CORPORATION'

    IO1         device      'P16R4';

    x           =           .X.;            " ABEL 'don't care' symbol
    c           =           .C.;            " ABEL 'clocking input' symbol

" Inputs

    CLK         pin 1;      "Processor Clock
    RESET       pin 2;      "System Reset
    MRDC-       pin 3;      "Memory (EPROM) Read Command
    IORC-       pin 4;      "I/O Read Command
    IOWC-       pin 5;      "I/O Write Command
    INTA-       pin 6;      "Interrupt Acknowledge
    DEN-        pin 7;      "I/O Bus Data Transceiver Enable
    IORDY-      pin 8;      "I/O-EPROM Ready
    L510CS-     pin 9;      "82510 Chip Select
    OEN-        pin 11;     "PAL output Enable
    L59CS-      pin 12;     "8259A-2 Chip Select
    LEPROM-     pin 13;     "EPROM Chip Select
    unused_0    pin 18;     "
    unused_1    pin 19;     "

" Outputs

    delay       pin 14;     "
    s2          pin 15;     "
    s1          pin 16;     "
    s0          pin 17;     "

    dstate      =   [delay, s2, s1, s0];
    idle        =   [ 1 , 1 , 1 , 1 ];
    start       =   [ 1 , 1 , 1 , 0 ];
    wait_14     =   [ 1 , 0 , 1 , 0 ];
    wait_13     =   [ 1 , 0 , 1 , 1 ];
    wait_12     =   [ 1 , 0 , 0 , 0 ];
    wait_11     =   [ 1 , 1 , 0 , 0 ];
    wait_10     =   [ 1 , 1 , 0 , 1 ];
    active      =   [ 0 , 1 , 1 , 1 ];

state_diagram dstate

    state idle:     if (!DEN- & !MRDC- # !DEN- & !IORC- #
                        !DEN- & !IOWC- # !DEN- & !INTA-) then start
                    else idle;
    state start:    if (!L510CS- & !IOWC-) then wait_14 else
                    if (!L510CS- & !IORC-) then wait_13 else
                    if (!L59CS- & !IOWC-) then wait_11 else
                    if (!LEPROM- # !L59CS- & !IORC- # !INTA-) then wait_10;
    state wait_14:  goto wait_13;
```

240725-B1

```
    state wait_13:  goto wait_12;
    state wait_12:  goto wait_11;
    state wait_11:  goto wait_10;
    state wait_10:  goto active;
    state active:   if !IORDY- then idle else active;

end IO_CTRL_1;
^Z
```

240725-B2

PAL Codes: IO-1

```
ABEL(tm) 3.10  -  Document Generator       15-Feb-90 06:40 PM
IO BUS CONTROLLER - PAL 1, INTEL CORPORATION
Equations for Module IO_CTRL_1

Device IO1


  Reduced Equations:

    !delay := (IORDY- & !delay & s0 & s1 & s2 # delay & s0 & !s1 & s2);

    !s2 := (delay & s1 & !s2
         # !IORC- & !L510CS- & delay & !s0 & s1
         # !IOWC- & !L510CS- & delay & !s0 & s1);


    !s1 := (delay & !s0 & !s1
         # delay & s0 & s1 & !s2
         # !INTA- & IORC- & IOWC- & delay & !s0 & s2
         # IORC- & IOWC & !LEPROM & delay & !s0 & s1
         # !IORC- & L510CS- & !L59CS- & delay & !s0 & s2
         # !INTA- & L510CS- & delay & !s0 & s2
         # L510CS- & !LEPROM- & delay & !s0 & s2
         # !IOWC- & L510CS- & !L59CS- & delay & !s0 & s2);


    !s0 := (delay & !s0 & !s1 & !s2
         # delay & s0 & s1 & !s2
         # !IOWC- & !L59CS- & delay & !s0 & s1 & s2
         # !IOWC- & !L510CS- & delay & !s0 & s1 & s2
         # !DEN- & !INTA- & delay & s0 & s1
         # !DEN- & !IOWC- & delay & s0 & s1
         # !DEN- & !IORC- & delay & s0 & s1
         # !DEN- & !MRDC- & delay & s0 & s1);
```

240725-B3

PAL Codes: IO-1 (Continued)

AP-442

ABEL 3.10—Document Generator   15-Feb-90 06:40 PM
IO BUS CONTROLLER—PAL 1, INTEL CORPORATION
Chip diagram for Module IO__CTRL__1

Device IO1

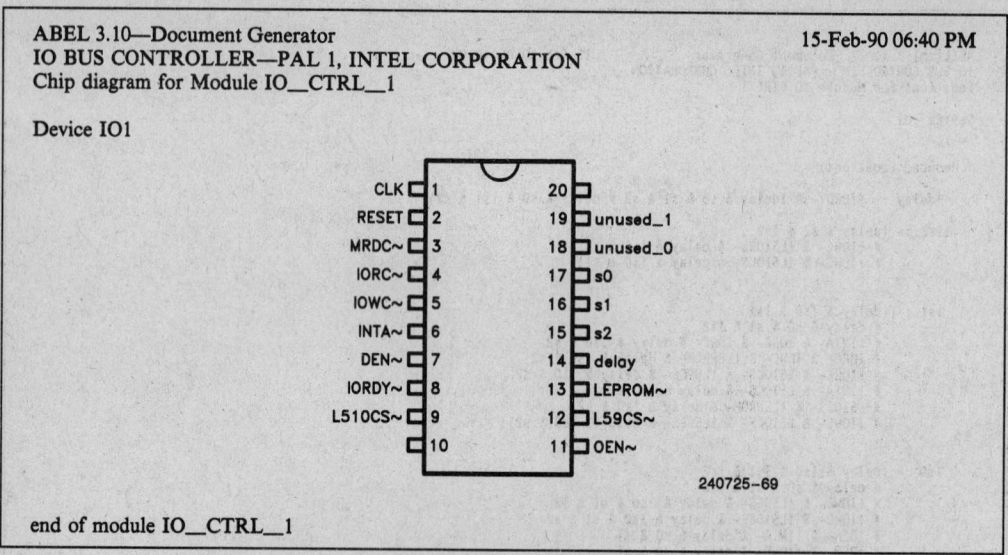

end of module IO__CTRL__1

PAL Codes: IO-1 (Continued)

AP-442

```
module    IO_CTRL_2  flag '-r3'
title     'IO BUS CONTROLLER - PAL 2, INTEL CORPORATION'

    IO2     device      'P16R6';

    x       =   .X.;         " ABEL 'don't care' symbol
    c       =   .C.;         " ABEL 'clocking input' symbol

" Inputs

    CLK       pin  1;    "Processor Clock
    RESET     pin  2;    "System Reset
    LMIO      pin  3;    "Latched M/IO#
    LDC       pin  4;    "Latched D/C#
    LWR       pin  5;    "Latched W/R#
    LALE      pin  6;    "Latched ALE
    L510CS-   pin  7;    "82510 Chip Select
    L59CS-    pin  8;    "8259A-2 Chip Select
    LEPROM-   pin  9;    "EPROM Chip Select
    OEN-      pin 11;    "PAL Output Enable
    rdy-      pin 12;    "I/O-EPROM Ready (n-1)
    rdy510-   pin 19;    "I/O-EPROM Ready (n-2)

" Outputs

    recovery  pin 13;    "I/O Recovery Time
    s1        pin 14;    "
    s0        pin 15;    "
    IORC-     pin 16;    "I/O Read Command
    IOWC-     pin 17;    "I/O Write Command
    MRDC-     pin 18;    "Memory (EPROM) Read Command

    rstate      = [recovery, s1, s0];
    idle        = [ 0  , 1 , 0 ];
    active      = [ 0  , 1 , 1 ];
    inactive_0  = [ 1  , 1 , 1 ];
    inactive_1  = [ 1  , 0 , 1 ];
    inactive_2  = [ 1  , 0 , 0 ];
    inactive_3  = [ 1  , 1 , 0 ];
    illegal_a   = [ 0  , 0 , 0 ];
    illegal_b   = [ 0  , 0 , 1 ];

state_diagram rstate

    state idle:        if (!IORC- # !IOWC-) then active else idle;
    state active:      if (IORC- # IOWC-) then inactive_0 else active;
    state inactive_0:  goto inactive_1;
    state inactive_1:  goto inactive_2;
    state inactive_2:  goto inactive_3;
    state inactive_3:  goto idle;
    state illegal_a:   goto idle;
    state illegal_b:   goto idle;
```

240725-B4

```
state_diagram [IOWC-]

    state [1]: if (!recovery & !LMIO & LDC & LWR & (!L510CS- # !L59CS-))
                   then [0] else [1];
    state [0]: if RESET then [1] else
                   if (!L510CS- & !rdy510- # !rdy-) then [1] else [0];

state_diagram [IORC-]

    state [1]: if (!recovery & !LMIO & LDC & !LWR & (!L510CS- # !L59CS-))
                   then [0] else [1];
    state [0]: if RESET then [1] else
                   if !rdy- then [1] else [0];

state_diagram [MRDC-]

    state [1]: if (LALE & LMIO & !LWR & !LEPROM-) then [0] else [1];
    state [0]: if RESET then [1] else
                   if !rdy- then [1] else [0];

end IO_CTRL_2;

^Z
```

240725-B5

PAL Codes: IO-2

```
ABEL(tm) 3.10  - Document Generator            14-Feb-90 09:34 AM
IO BUS CONTROLLER - PAL 2, INTEL CORPORATION
Equations for Module IO_CTRL_2

Device IO2

- Reduced Equations:

    !recovery := (!recovery & !s1 # !IORC- & !IOWC- & !recovery # !s0 & s1);

    !s1 := (recovery & s0);

    !s0 := (recovery & !s0 # !s1 # IORC- & IOWC- & !s0);

    !IOWC- := (!IOWC- & !RESET & rdy510- & rdy-
              # !IOWC- & L510CS- & !RESET & rdy-
              # IOWC- & !L59CS- & LDC & !LMIO & LWR & !recovery
              # IOWC- & !L510CS- & LDC & !LMIO & LWR & !recovery);

    !IORC- := (!IORC- & !RESET & rdy-
              # IORC- & !L59CS- & LDC & !LMIO & !LWR & !recovery
              # IORC- & !L510CS- & LDC & !LMIO & !LWR & !recovery);

    !MRDC- := (!MRDC- & !RESET & rdy-
              # LALE & !LEPROM- & LMIO & !LWR & MRDC-);
```

PAL Codes: IO-2 (Continued)

AP-442

ABEL 3.10—Document Generator   14-Feb-90 09:34 AM
IO BUS CONTROLLER—PAL 2, INTEL CORPORATION
Chip diagram for Module IO__CTRL__2

Device IO2

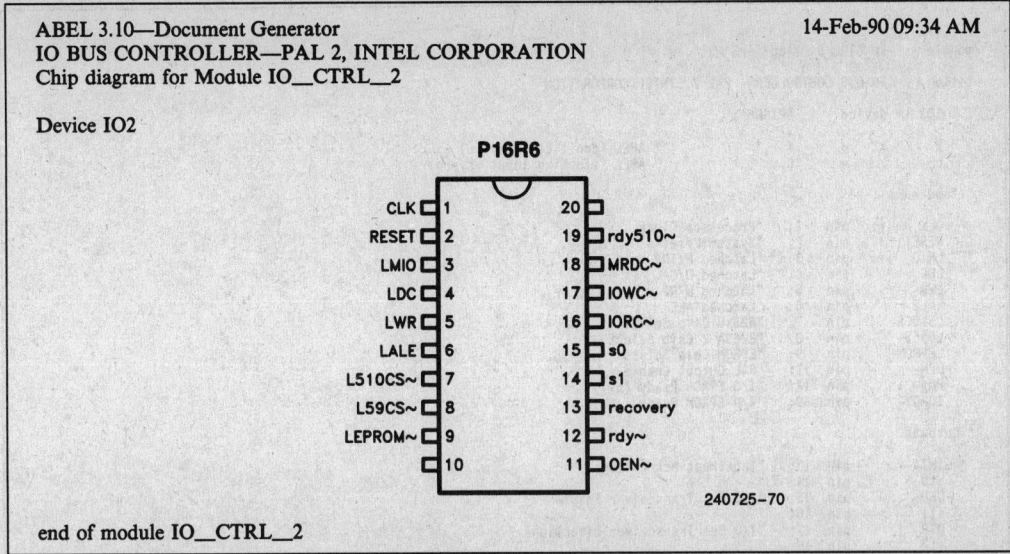

end of module IO__CTRL__2

PAL Codes: IO-2 (Continued)

AP-442

```
module      IO_CTRL_3  flag '-r3'
title      'IO BUS CONTROLLER - PAL 2, INTEL CORPORATION'

   IO3      device    'P16R6';

   x          =       .X.;         " ABEL 'don't care' symbol
   c          =       .C.;         " ABEL 'clocking input' symbol

" Inputs

   CLK        pin     1;    "Processor Clock
   RESET      pin     2;    "System Reset
   LMIO       pin     3;    "Latched M/IO#
   LDC        pin     4;    "Latched D/C#
   LWR        pin     5;    "Latched W/R#
   LALE       pin     6;    "Latched ALE
   L51OCS~    pin     7;    "82510 Chip Select
   L59CS~     pin     8;    "8259A-2 Chip Select
   LEPROM~    pin     9;    "EPROM Chip Select
   OEN~       pin    11;    "PAL Output Enable
   rdy~       pin    12;    "I/O-EPROM Ready (n-1)
   IORDY~     pin    19;    "I/O-EPROM Ready

" Outputs

   INTA~      pin    13;    "Interrupt Acknowledge
   st0        pin    14;    "
   DEN~       pin    15;    "I/O Bus Transceiver Enable
   st1        pin    16;    "
   DTR        pin    17;    "I/O Bus Transceiver Direction
   st2        pin    18;    "

state_diagram [INTA~, st0]

   state [1, 1]: if (!LMIO & !LDC & !LWR & LALE) then [1, 0] else [1, 1];
   state [1, 0]: if RESET then [1, 1] else
                 if !LALE then [0, 0] else [1, 0];
   state [0, 0]: if RESET then [1, 1] else
                 if !rdy~ then [1, 1] else [0, 0];
   state [0, 1]: goto [1, 1];

state_diagram [DEN~, st1]

   state [1, 1]: if LALE & (!LEPROM~ # !L51OCS~ # !L59CS~) then [1, 0] else
                 if !INTA~ then [0, 0] else [1, 1];
   state [1, 0]: if RESET then [1, 1] else
                 if !LALE then [0, 0] else [1, 0];
   state [0, 0]: if RESET then [1, 1] else
                 if !rdy~ then [1, 1] else [0, 0];
   state [0, 1]: goto [1, 1];

state_diagram [DTR, st2]
```

240725-B7

```
   state [1, 1]: if LALE & (!LEPROM~ # !L51OCS~ # !L59CS~) & LWR then [0, 1]
                 else [1, 1];
   state [0, 1]: if RESET then [1, 1] else
                 if !IORDY~ then [0, 0] else [0, 1];
   state [0, 0]: goto [1, 1];
   state [1, 0]: goto [1, 1];
end IO_CTRL_3;
^Z
```

240725-B8

PAL Codes: IO-3

```
ABEL(tm) 3.10  -  Document Generator          15-Feb-90 06:45 PM
IO BUS CONTROLLER - PAL 2, INTEL CORPORATION
Equations for Module IO_CTRL_3

Device IO3

- Reduced Equations:

    !INTA- := (!INTA- & !RESET & rdy- & !st0
             # INTA- & !LALE & !RESET & !st0);


    !st0 := (!RESET & rdy- & !st0
           # INTA- & !RESET & !st0
           # INTA- & LALE & !LDC & !LMIO & !LWR & st0);


    !DEN- := (!DEN- & !RESET & rdy- & !st1
            # DEN- & !LALE & !RESET & !st1
            # DEN- & !INTA- & L510CS- & L59CS- & LEPROM- & st1
            # DEN- & !INTA- & !LALE & st1);


    !st1 := (!RESET & rdy- & !st1
           # DEN- & !RESET & !st1
           # DEN- & !INTA- & st1
           # DEN- & !L59CS- & LALE & st1
           # DEN- & !L510CS- & LALE & st1
           # DEN- & LALE & !LEPROM- & st1);


    !DTR := (!DTR & !RESET & st2
           # DTR & !L59CS- & LALE & LWR & st2
           # DTR & !L510CS- & LALE & LWR & st2
           # DTR & LALE & !LEPROM- & LWR & st2);


    !st2 := (!DTR & !IORDY- & !RESET & st2);

                                                        240725-B9
```

PAL Codes: IO-3 (Continued)

AP-442

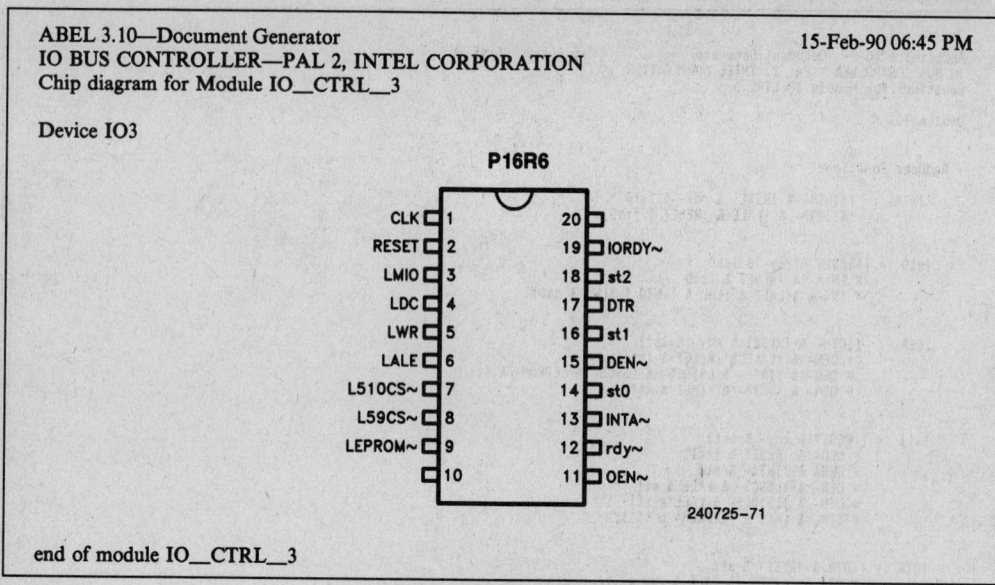

PAL Codes: IO-3 (Continued)

AP-442

```
module   IO_CTRL_4  flag '-r3'
title          'IO BUS CONTROLLER - PAL 2, INTEL CORPORATION'

    IO4      device     'P16R6';

    x        =   .X.;           " ABEL 'don't care' symbol
    c        =   .C.;           " ABEL 'clocking input' symbol

" Inputs

    CLK          pin   1;       "Processor Clock
    RESET        pin   2;       "System Reset
    LMIO         pin   3;       "Latched M/IO#
    LDC          pin   4;       "Latched D/C#
    LWR          pin   5;       "Latched W/R#
    LALE         pin   6;       "Latched ALE
    delay        pin   7;       "Delay Signal for Wait State Generation
    unused_0     pin   8;       "
    unused_1     pin   9;       "
    OEN-         pin  11;       "PAL Output Enable
    unused_3     pin  12;       "
    unused_4     pin  19;       "

" Outputs

    IORDY-       pin  13;       "I/O-EPROM Ready
    rdy-         pin  14;       "I/O-EPROM Ready (n-1)
    rdy510-      pin  15;       "I/O-EPROM Ready (n-2)
    nc_0         pin  16;       "
    nc_1         pin  17;       "
    nc_2         pin  18;       "

    rstate     =  [IORDY-, rdy-, rdy510-];
    idle       =  [  1  ,  1  ,   1    ];
    rdy2       =  [  1  ,  1  ,   0    ];
    rdy1       =  [  1  ,  0  ,   1    ];
    rdy0       =  [  0  ,  1  ,   1    ];
    illegal_a  =  [  1  ,  0  ,   0    ];
    illegal_b  =  [  0  ,  0  ,   0    ];
    illegal_c  =  [  0  ,  0  ,   1    ];
    illegal_d  =  [  0  ,  1  ,   0    ];

state_diagram rstate

    state idle:         if (LMIO & !LDC & LWR & LALE) then rdy1 else
                        if !delay then rdy2 else idle;
    state rdy2:         if RESET then idle else rdy1;
    state rdy1:         if RESET then idle else
                        if !LALE then rdy0 else rdy1;
    state rdy0:         goto idle;
    state illegal_a:    goto idle;
    state illegal_b:    goto idle;
    state illegal_c:    goto idle;
```

240725-C0

PAL Codes: IO-4

AP-442

```
       state illegal_d:    goto idle;
 end IO_CTRL_4;
^Z
```
                                                            240725-C1

```
ABEL(tm) 3.10 - Document Generator         15-Feb-90 06:55 PM
IO BUS CONTROLLER - PAL 2, INTEL CORPORATION
Equations for Module IO_CTRL_4

Device IO4


- Reduced Equations:

    !IORDY- := (IORDY- & !LALE & !RESET & rdy510- & !rdy-);

    !rdy- := (IORDY- & LALE & !RESET & rdy510- & !rdy-
            # IORDY- & !RESET & !rdy510- & rdy-
            # IORDY- & LALE & !LDC & LMIO & LWR & rdy510- & rdy-);

    !rdy510- := (IORDY- & !LALE & !delay & rdy510- & rdy-
               # IORDY- & !LWR & !delay & rdy510- & rdy-
               # IORDY- & LDC & !delay & rdy510- & rdy-
               # IORDY- & !LMIO & !delay & rdy510- & rdy-);
```
                                                            240725-C2

PAL Codes: IO-4 (Continued)

AP-442

ABEL 3.10—Document Generator
IO BUS CONTROLLER—PAL 2, INTEL CORPORATION
Chip diagram for Module IO__CTRL__4

15-Feb-90 06:55 PM

Device IO4

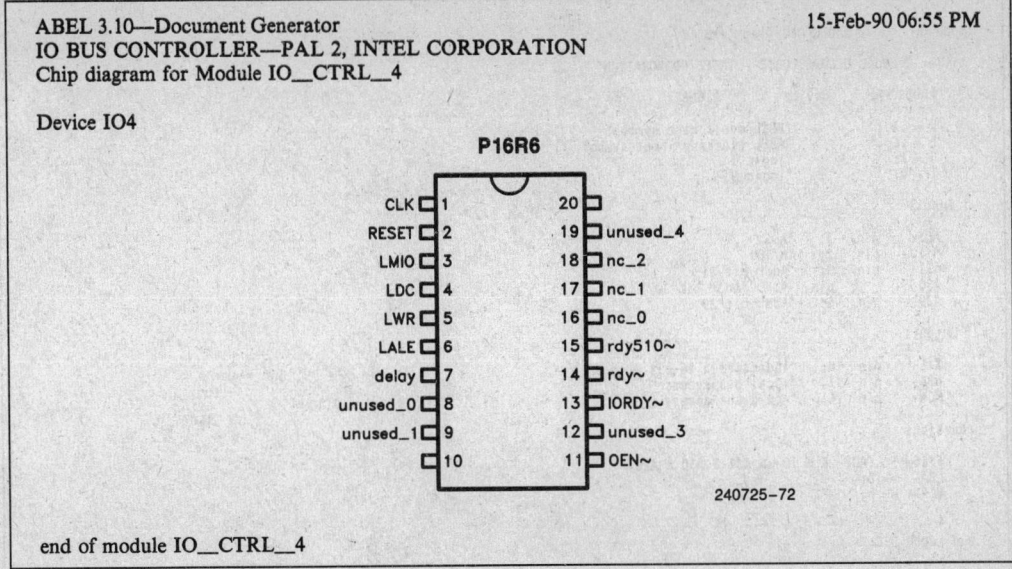

end of module IO__CTRL__4

PAL Codes: IO-4 (Continued)

AP-442

```
module      LADDR_DEC flag '-r3'
title   'LOCAL_DECODE_LOGIC - INTEL CORPORATION'

    LADDR_PAL   device      'P16L8';

    x = .X.;            "ABEL don't care symbol
    c = .C.;            "ABEL clocking input symbol
    h = 1;              "logic 1
    l = 0;              "logic 0

" Inputs

    ADS-    pin  1;     "ADS#
    M_IO-   pin  2;     "M/IO#
    A31     pin  3;     "Addr bit 31
    A30     pin  4;     "Addr bit 30
    A29     pin  5;     "Addr bit 29

" Outputs

    X16-    pin  18;    "indicates a 16-bit access
    LBA-    pin  17;    "local bus access
    NCA-    pin  16;    "non-cache access

equations

    !X16~   = !ADS- & M_IO- & A31 & A30 & A29;
    LBA-    = h;
    NCA-    = h;

end LADDR_DEC;
```

240725-C3

```
ABEL(tm) 3.10  -  Document Generator       14-Feb-90 09:51 AM
LOCAL_DECODE_LOGIC - INTEL CORPORATION
Equations for Module LADDR_DEC

Device LADDR_PAL

- Reduced Equations:

    !X16~ = (A29 & A30 & A31 & !ADS- & M_IO-);

    !LBA- = (0);

    !NCA- = (0);
```

240725-C4

PAL Codes: Local Decoder

AP-442

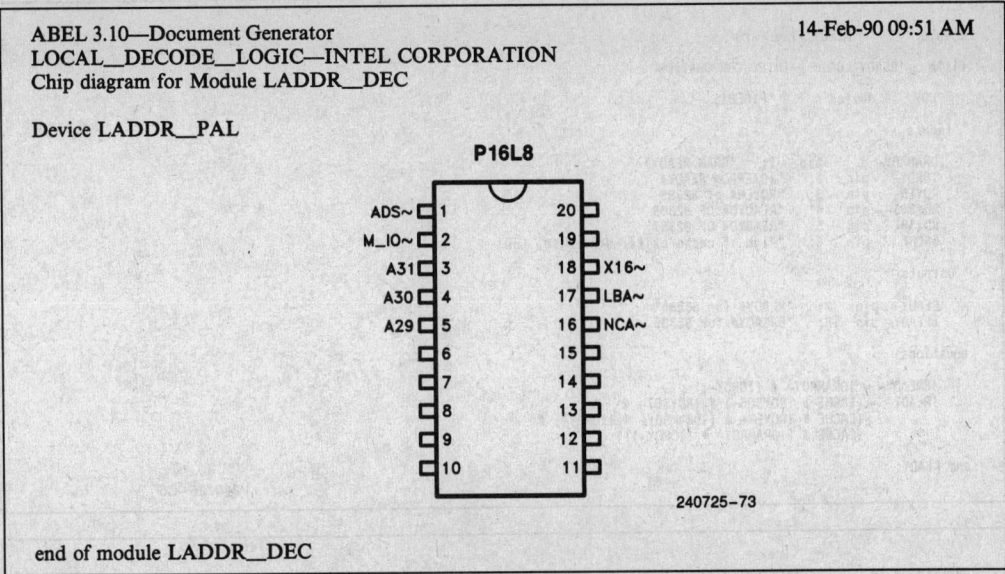

PAL Codes: Local Decoder (Continued)

AP-442

```
module      READY flag '-r3'
title    'READY_LOGIC - INTEL CORPORATION'

   RDY       device       'P16L8';

" Inputs

   DRAMRDY-    pin  1;   "DRAM READY#
   IORDY-      pin  2;   "IO/EPROM READY#
   RDYEN-      pin  3;   "RDYEN# of 82385
   RDY385-     pin  4;   "READYO# OF 82385
   RDY387-     pin  5;   "READYO# OF 82387
   CACHE       pin  6;   "High if cache exits; otherwise, Low

" Outputs

   READY-  pin 12;   "READY# for 80386
   BREADY- pin 13;   "BREADY# for 82385

equations

   !BREADY- = !DRAMRDY- # !IORDY-;
   !READY-  = (CACHE & !RDY385-) # !RDY387- #
              (CACHE & !RDYEN- & (!DRAMRDY- # !IORDY-) #
              !CACHE & (!DRAMRDY- # !IORDY-));

end READY;
```

240725-C5

```
ABEL(tm) 3.10 - Document Generator        15-Feb-90 07:02 PM
READY_LOGIC - INTEL CORPORATION
Equations for Module READY

Device RDY


- Reduced Equations:

    !BREADY- = (!IORDY- # !DRAMRDY-);

    !READY- = (!CACHE & !IORDY-
            # !CACHE & !DRAMRDY-
            # !IORDY- & !RDYEN-
            # !DRAMRDY- & !RDYEN-
            # !RDY387-
            # CACHE & !RDY385-);
```

240725-C6

PAL Codes: Ready

AP-442

ABEL 3.10—Document Generator 15-Feb-90 07:02 PM
READY_LOGIC—INTEL CORPORATION
Chip diagram for Module READY

Device RDY

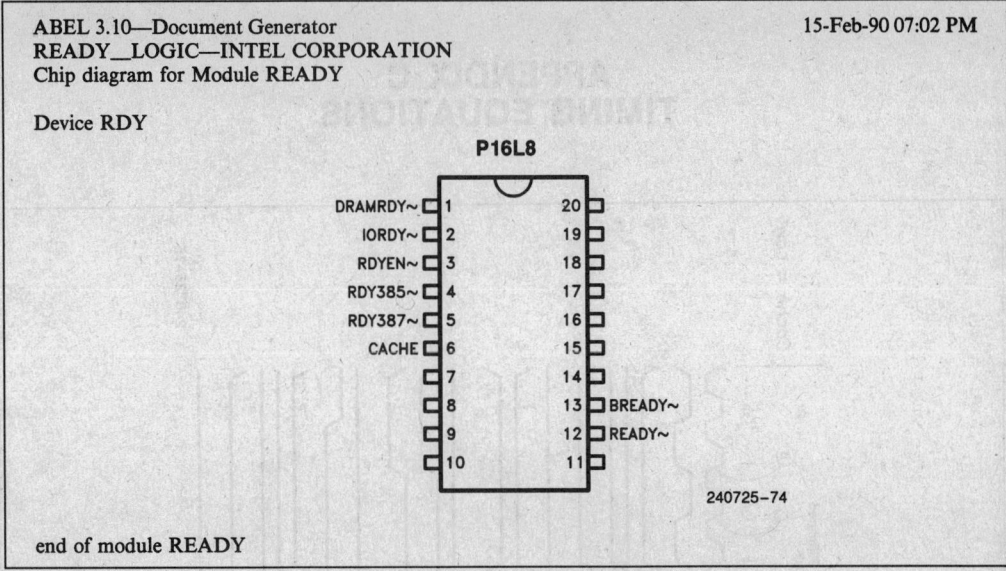

end of module READY

PAL Codes: Ready (Continued)

APPENDIX C
TIMING EQUATIONS

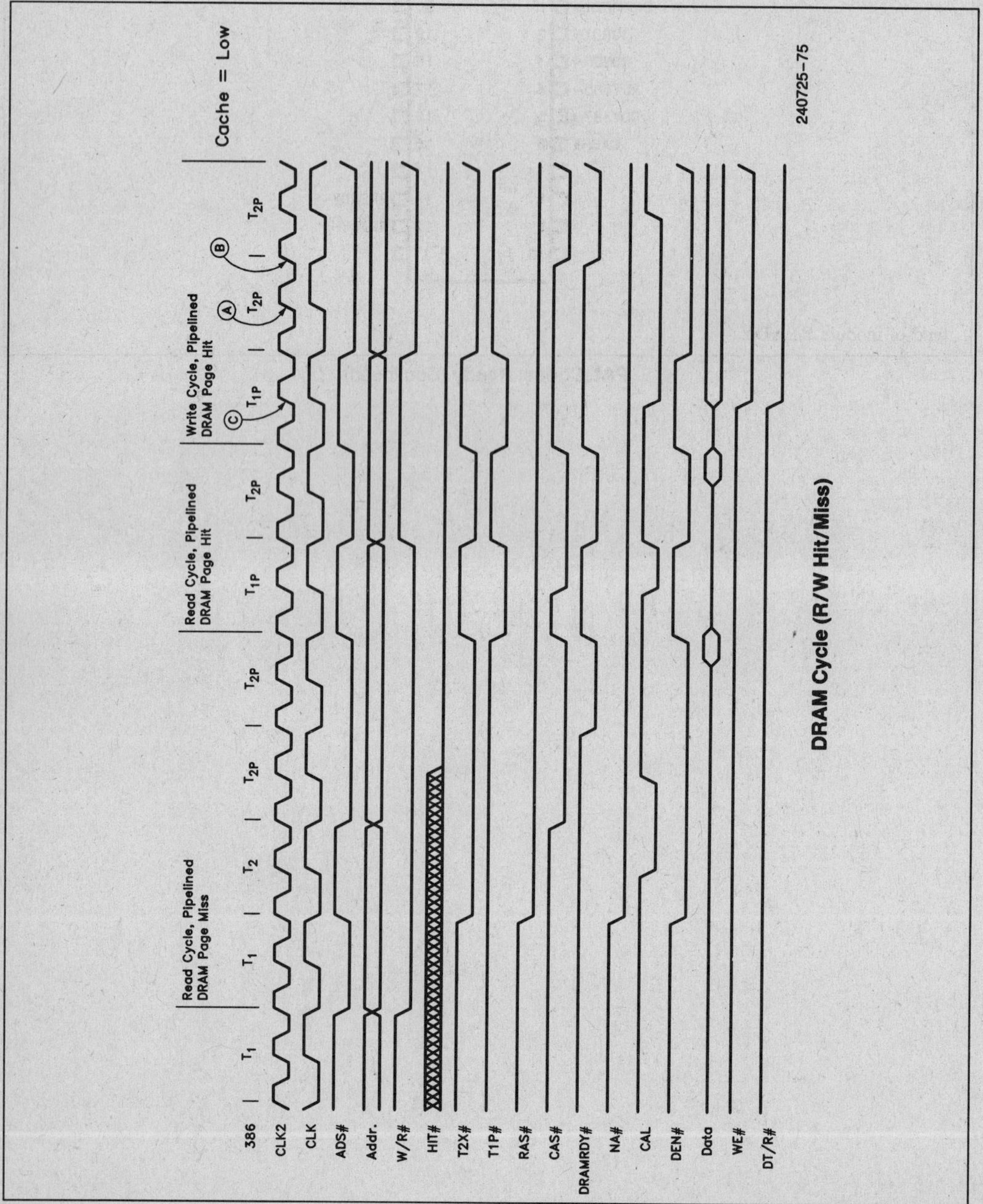

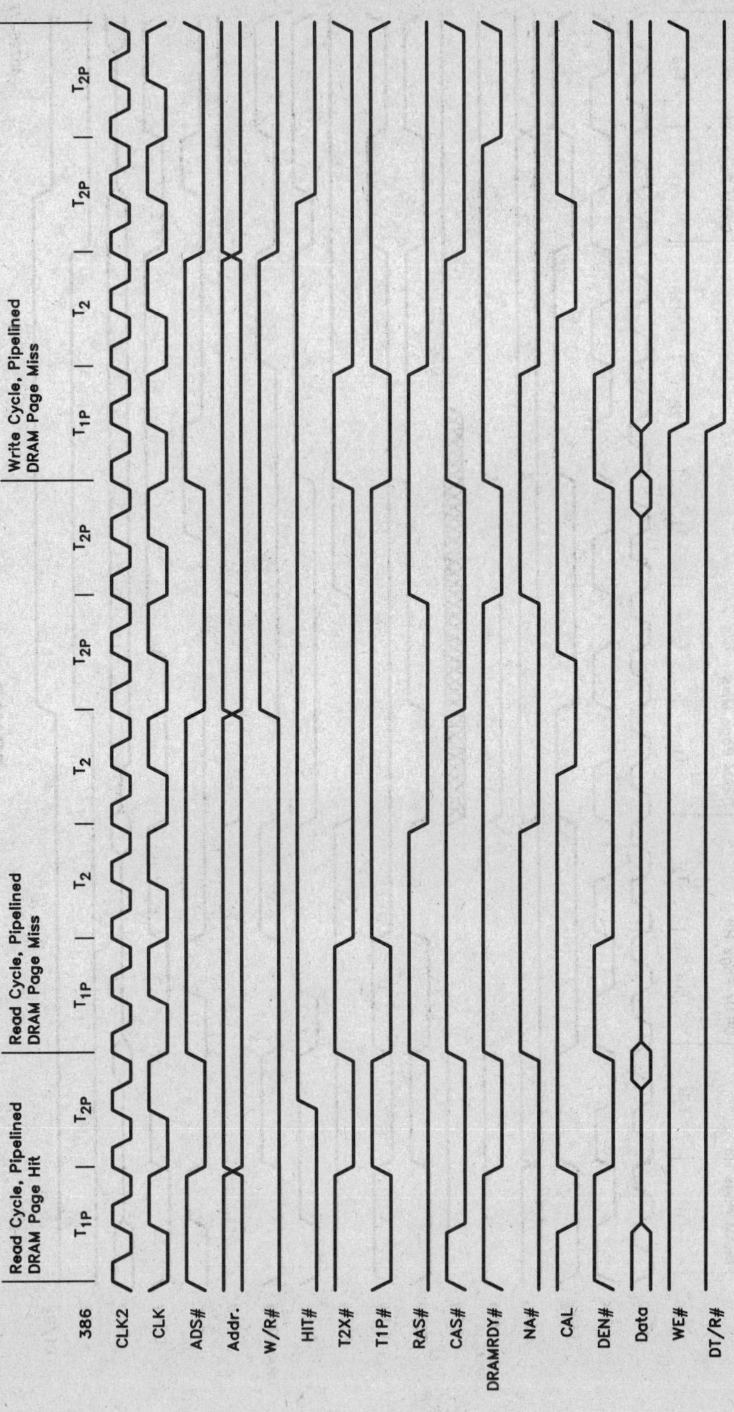

AP-442

DRAM Cycle (Page Miss)

240725-76

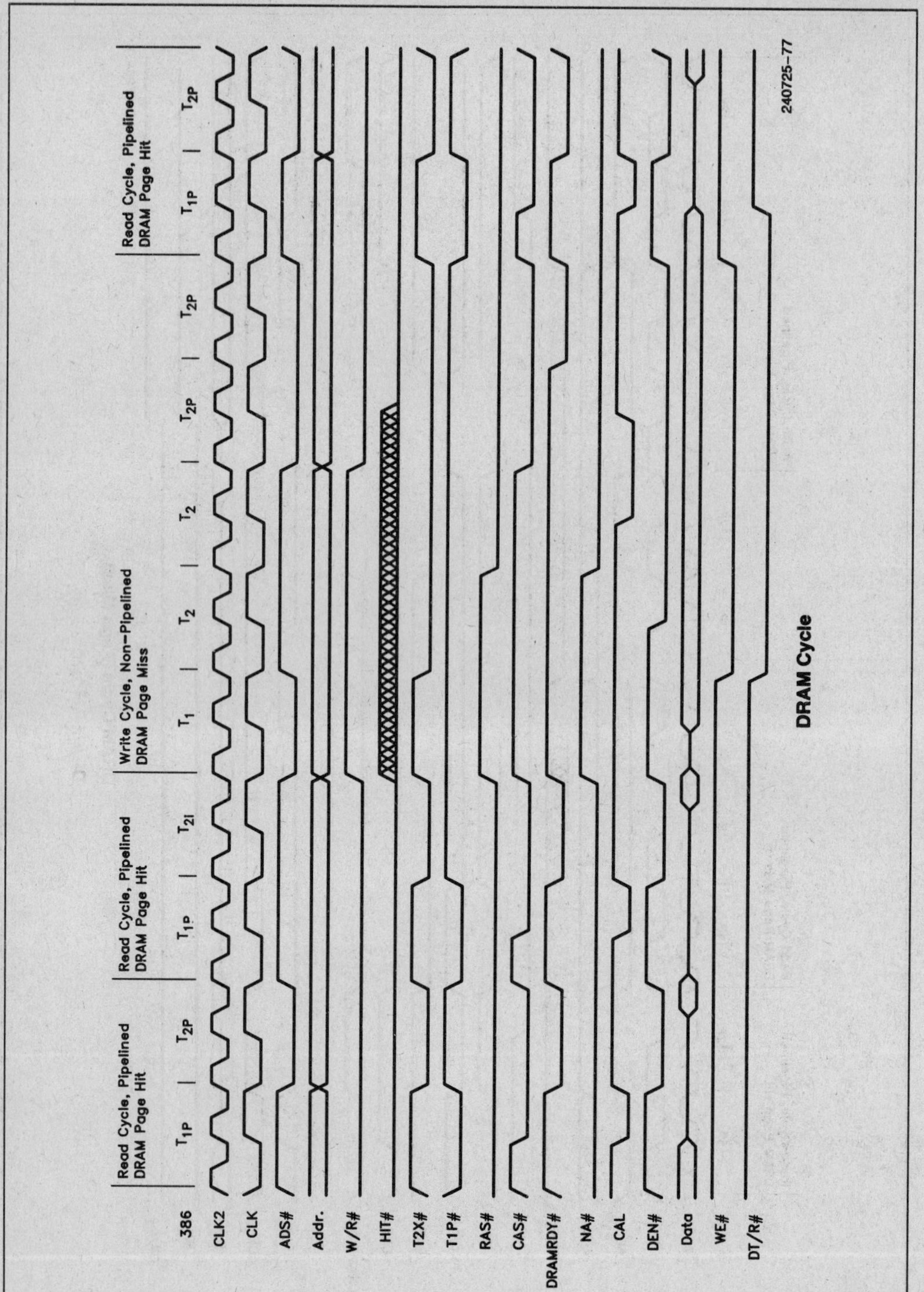

AP-442

DRAM Cycle

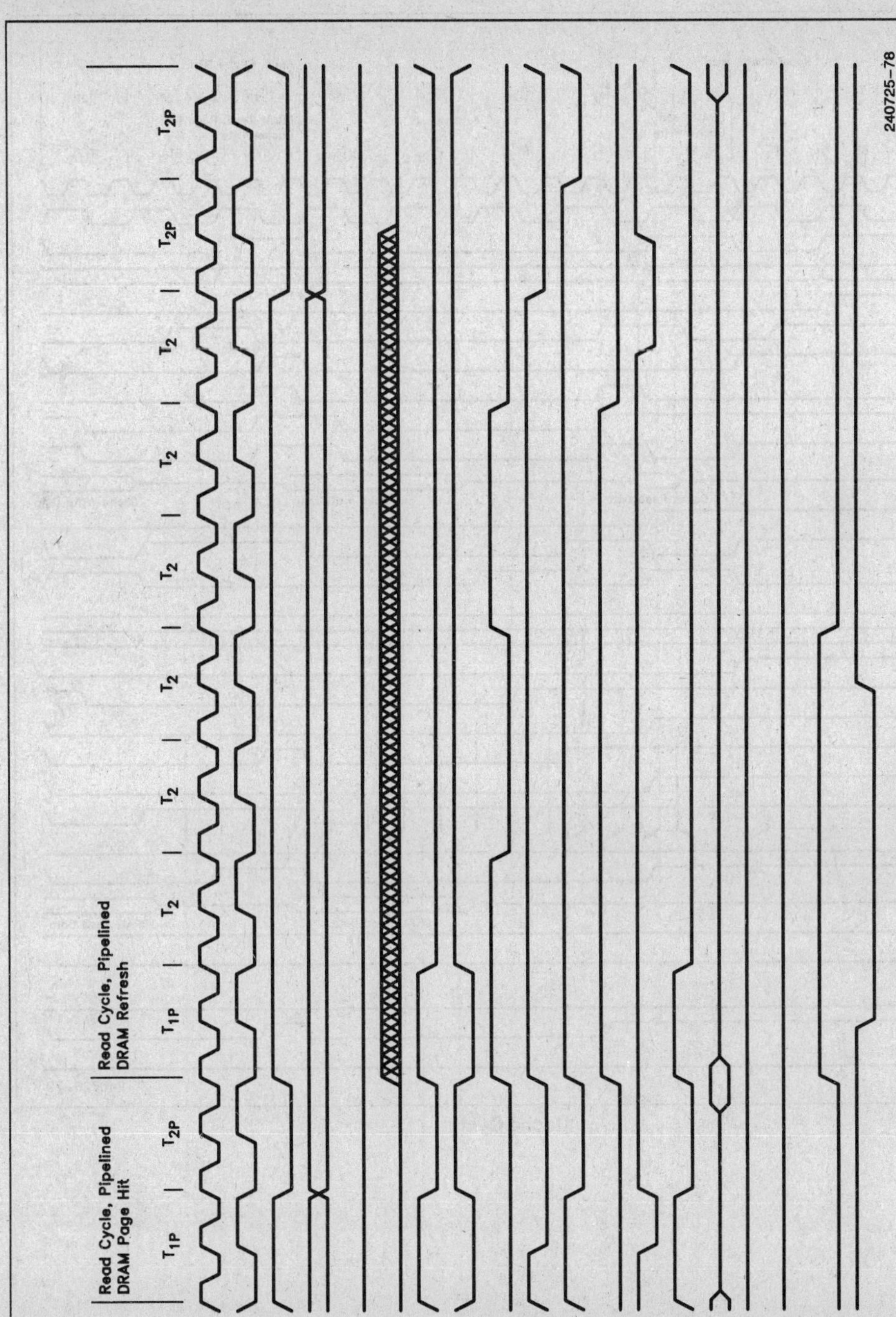

AP-442

DRAM Refresh Cycle

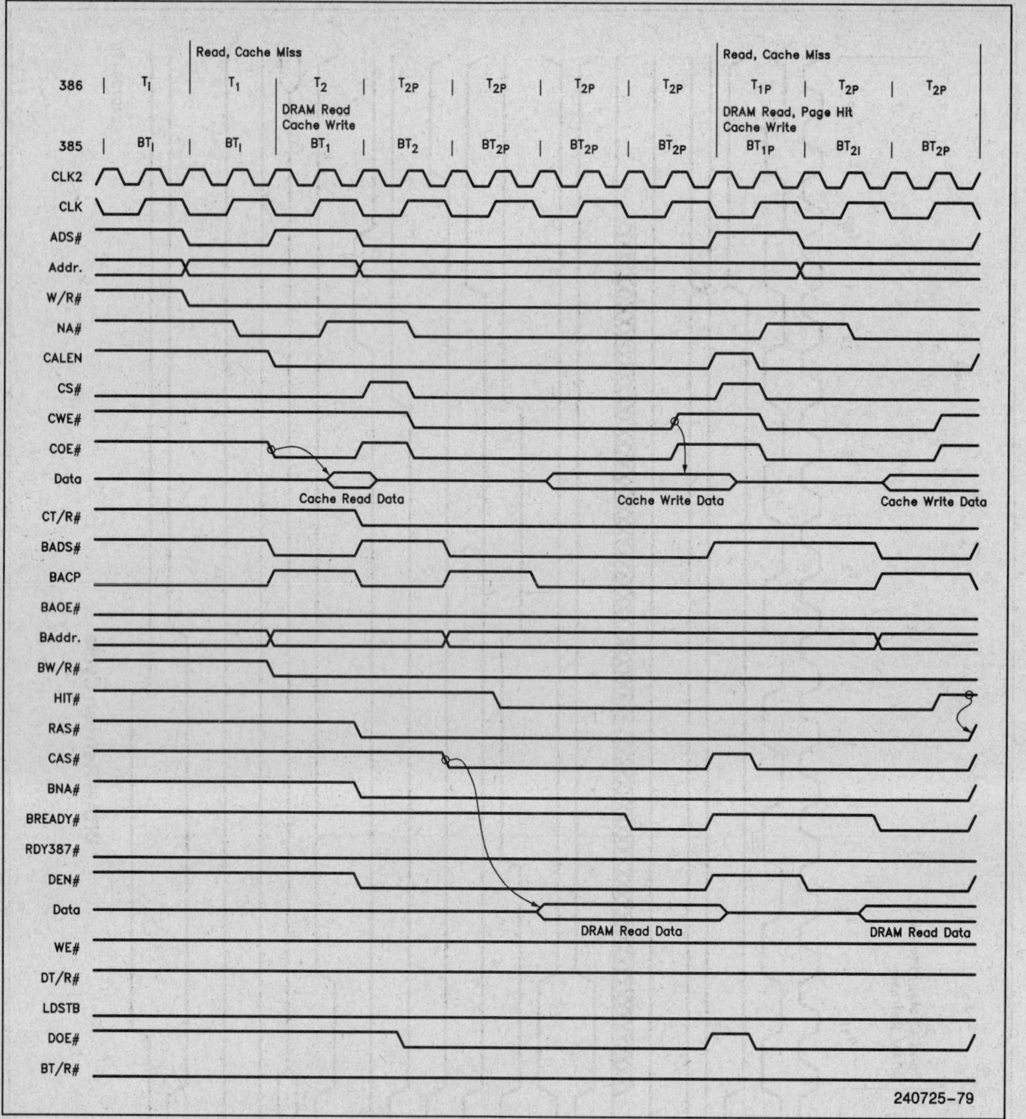

AP-442

Cache Cycle

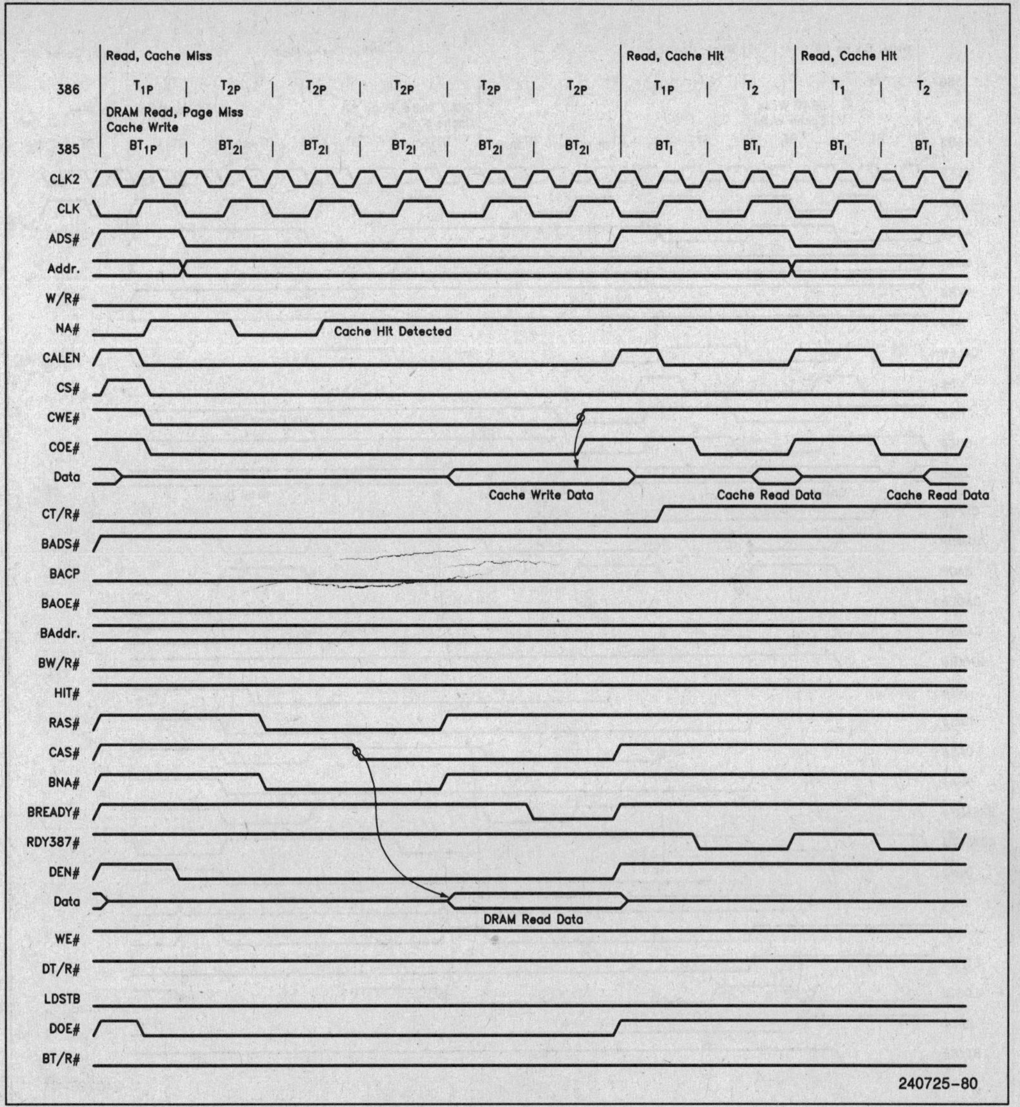

AP-442

Cache Cycle (Continued)

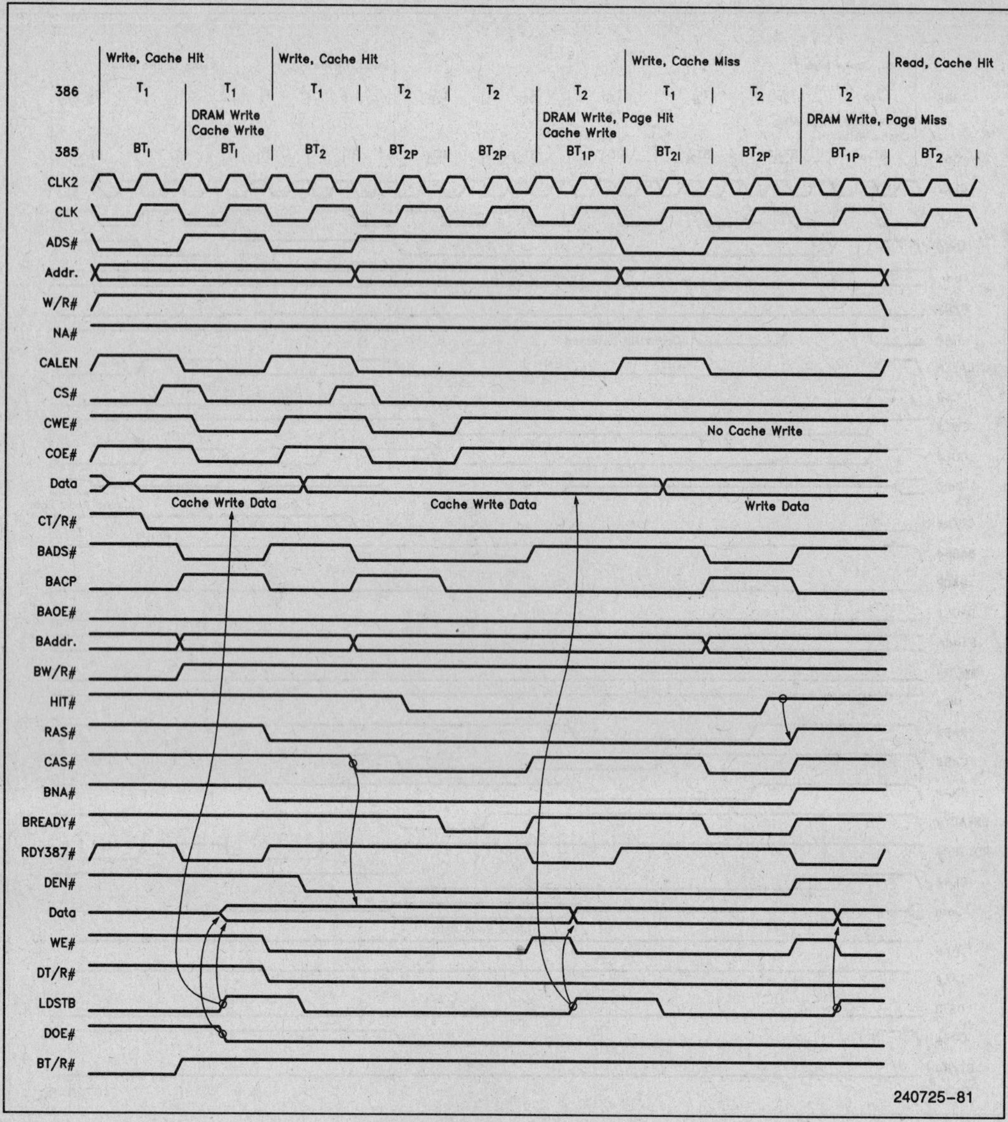

AP-442

Cache Cycle (Continued)

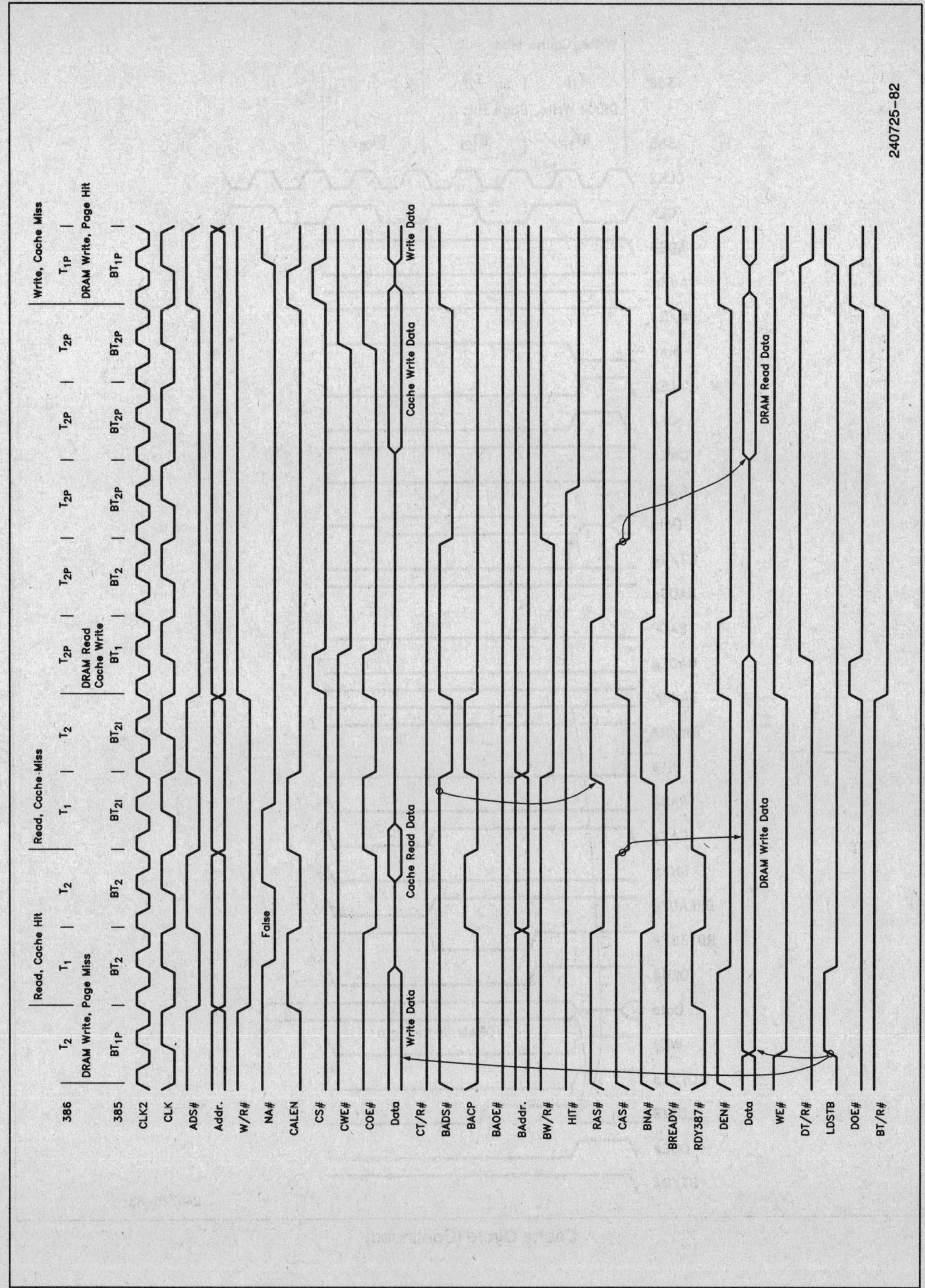

AP-442

Cache Cycle (Continued)

240725-82

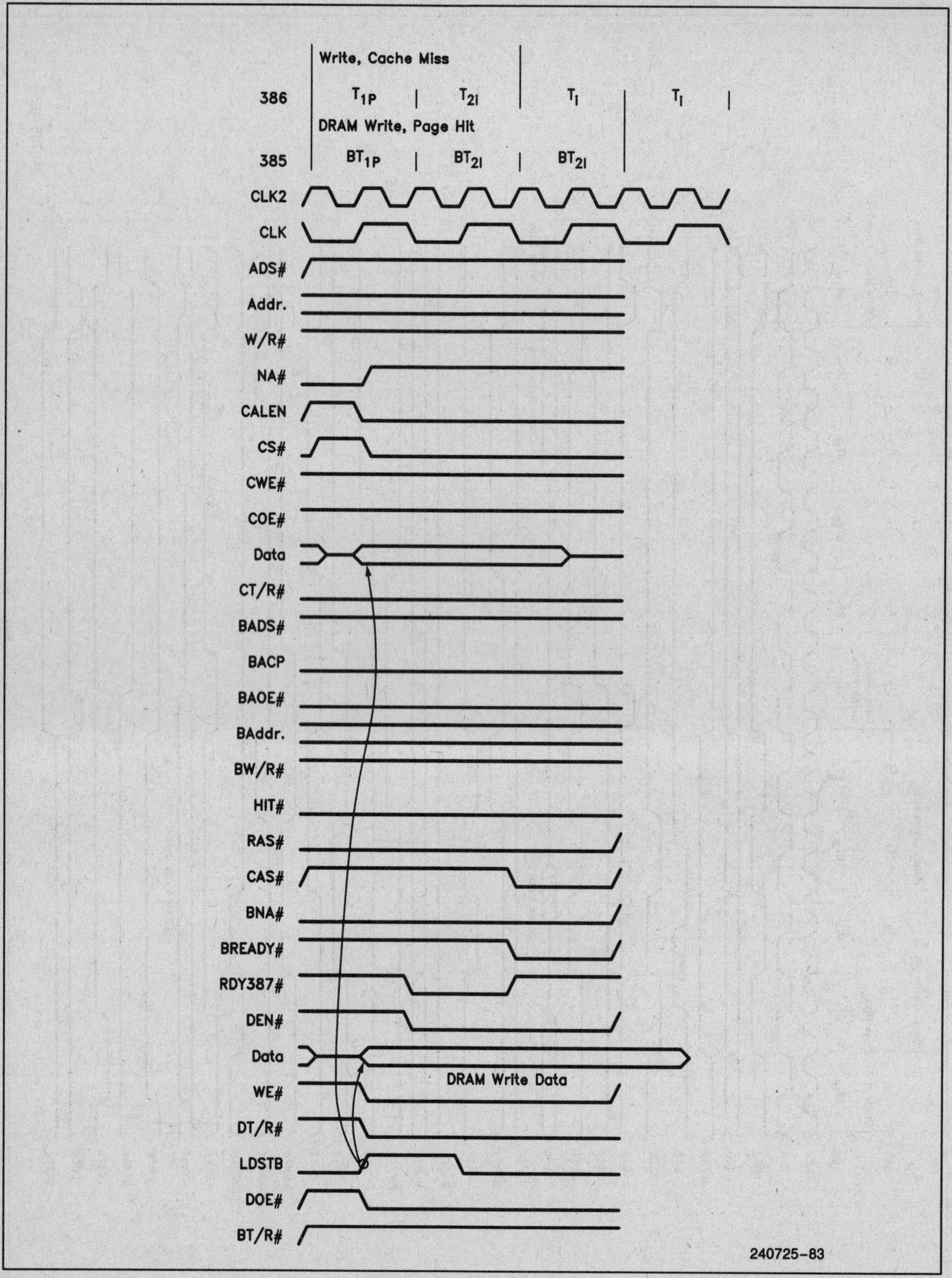

AP-442

Cache Cycle (Continued)

AP-442

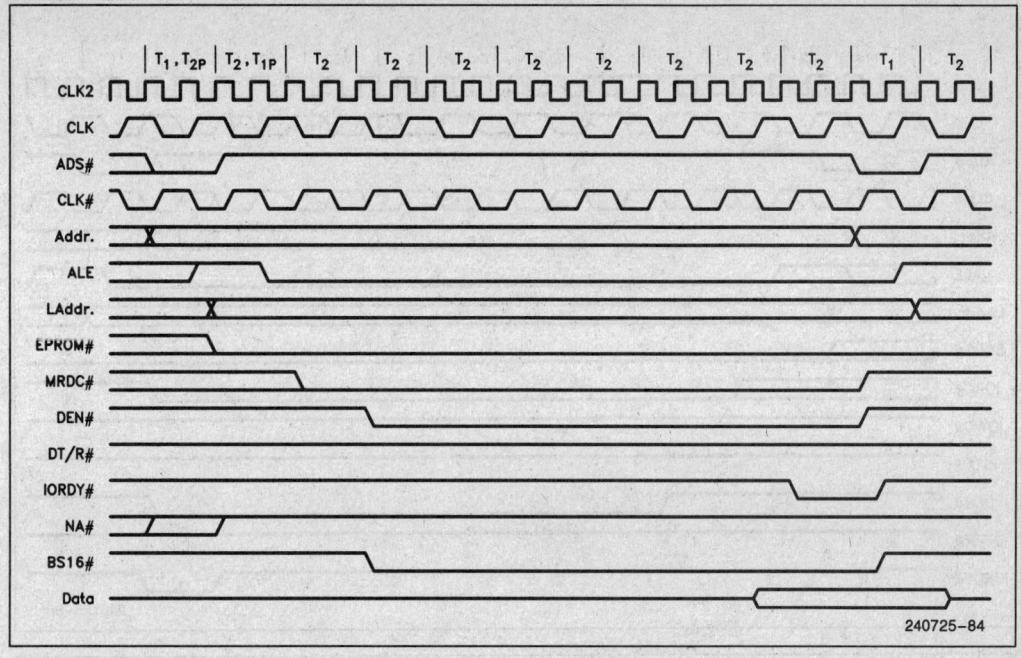

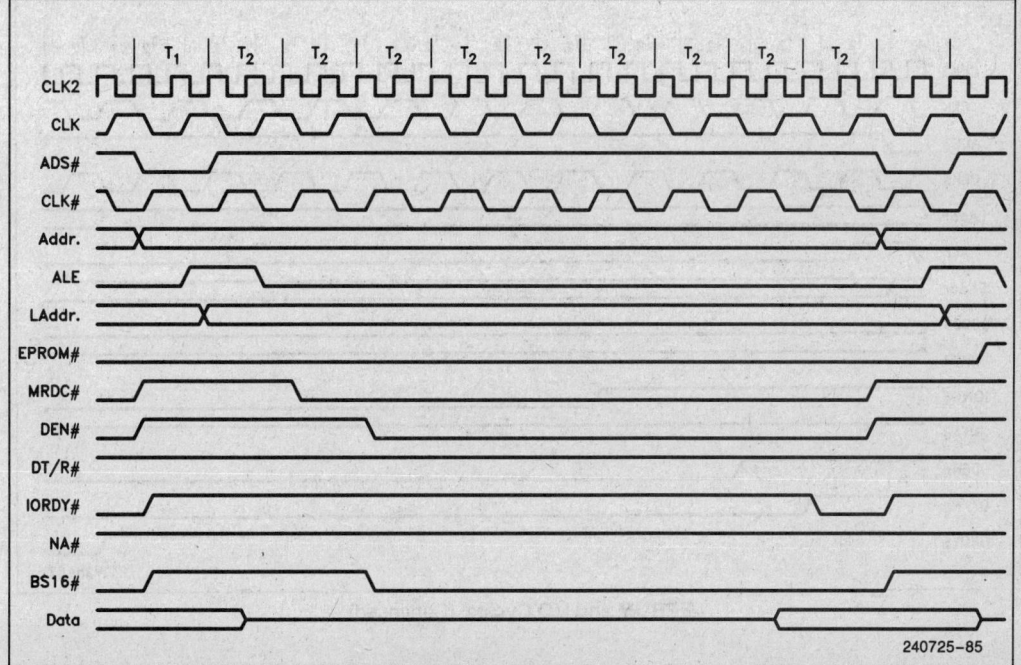

EPROM and I/O Cycles

AP-442

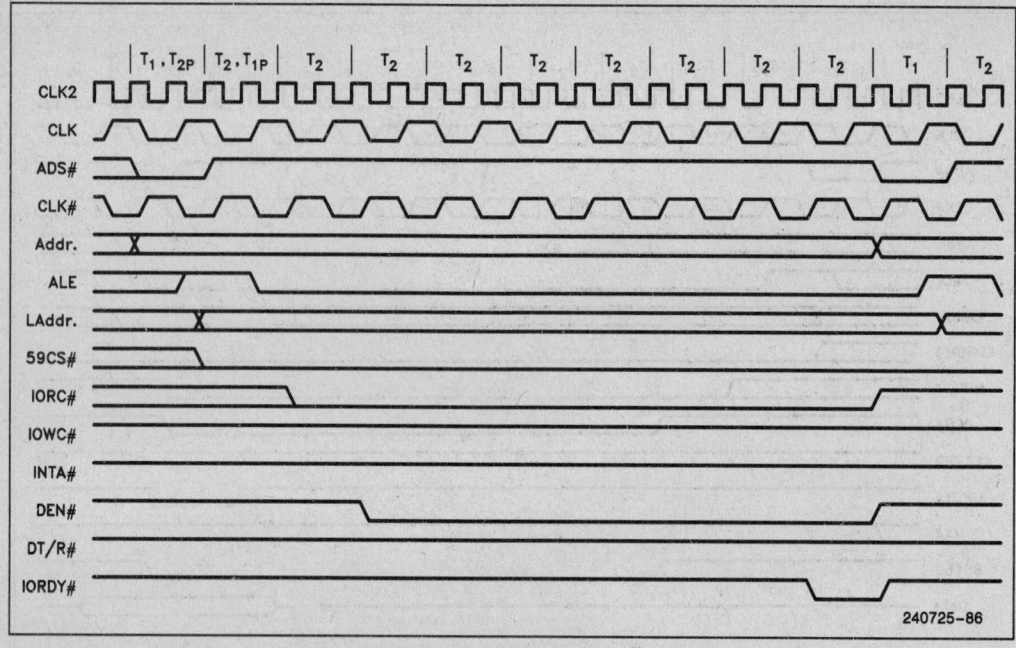

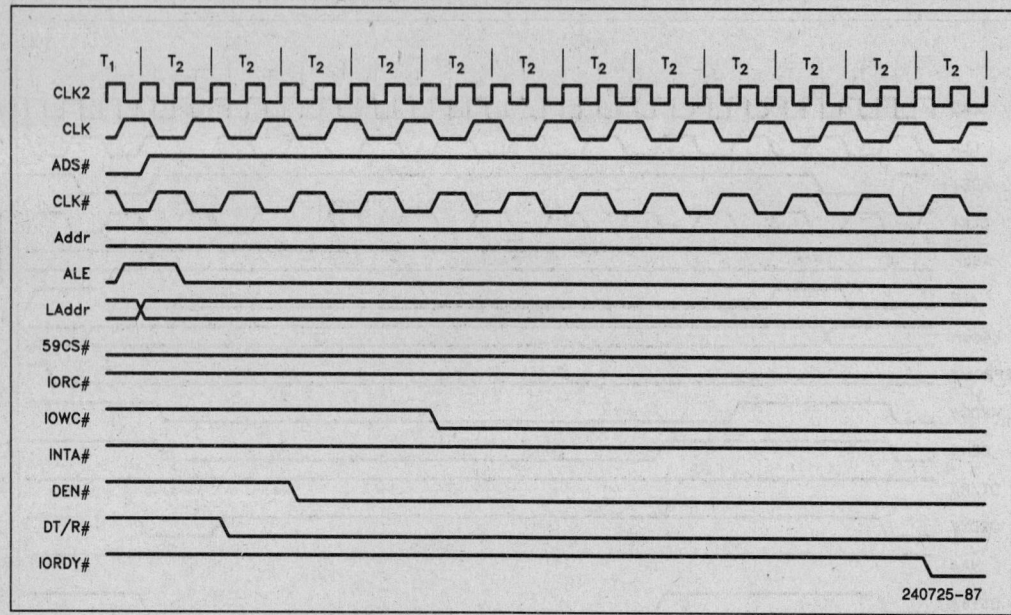

EPROM and I/O Cycles (Continued)

AP-442

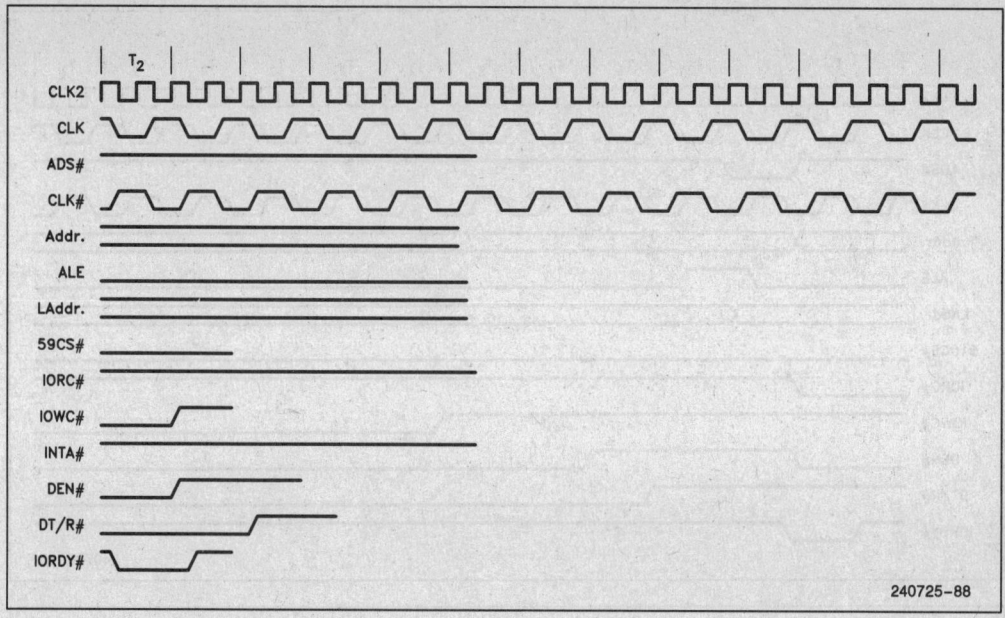

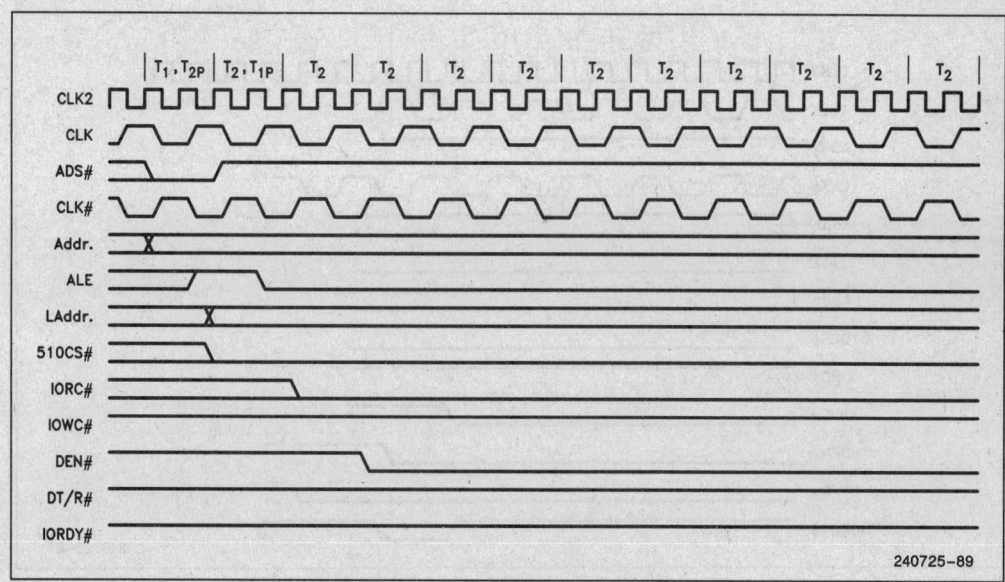

EPROM and I/O Cycles (Continued)

AP-442

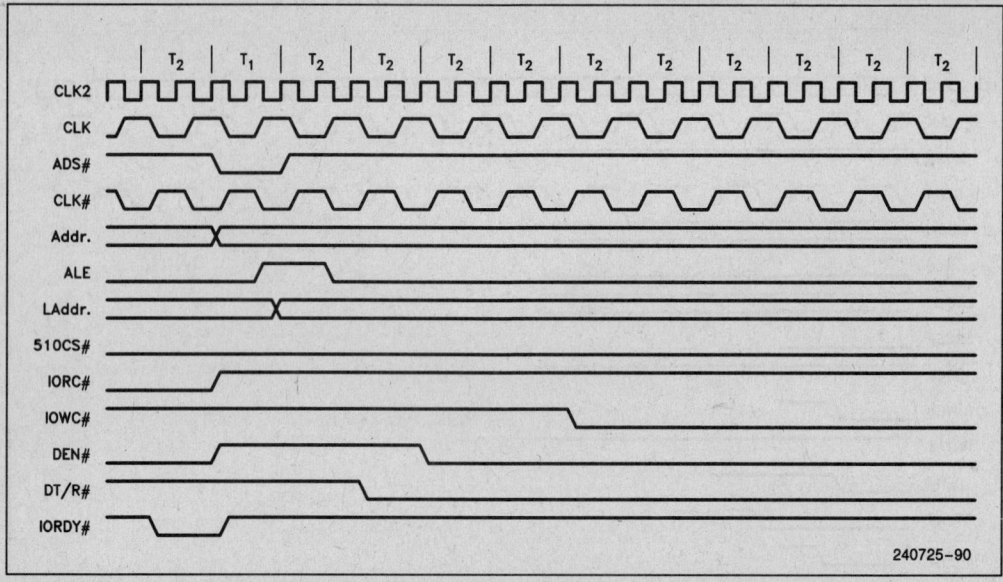

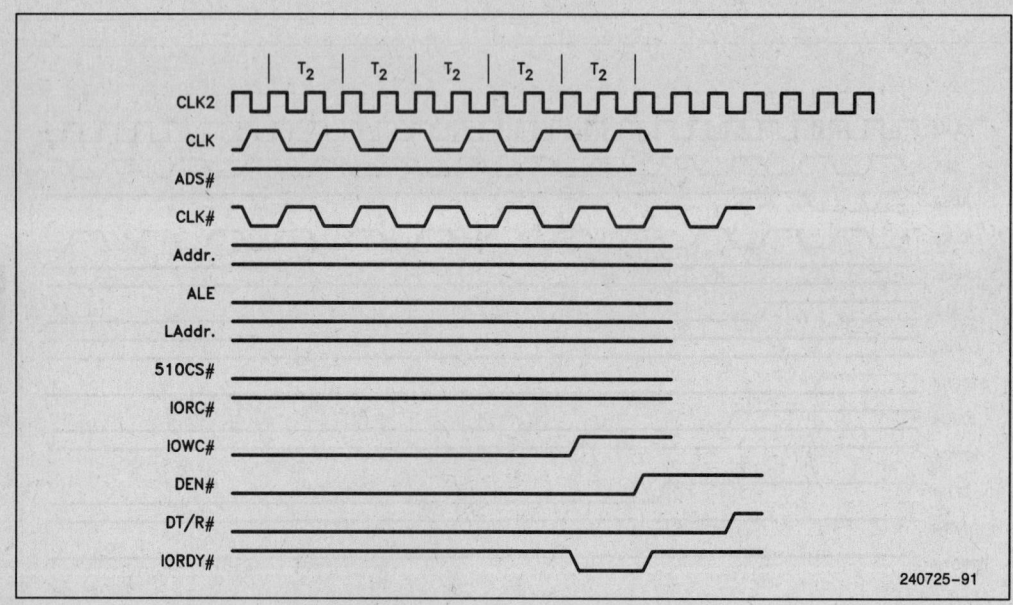

EPROM and I/O Cycles (Continued)

APPENDIX D
TIMING EQUATIONS

EQUATIONS FOR DRAM TIMINGS (NO CACHE CONFIGURATION):

Read and Write Cycles (Common Parameters):

tRC: Random Read or Write Cycle Time

  CLK2 × 10

tRP: RAS# Precharge Time

  CLK2 × 4

tRAS: RAS# Pulse Width

  CLK2 × 4

A random DRAM cycle may have a RAS# pulse which is only four CLK2 periods wide. This is the case if the cycle is followed by Idle cycles (DRAMs not selected or Ti's) or a DRAM page miss.

tCAS (Read): CAS# Pulse Width

  CLK2 × 3

CAS# pulses can be as narrow as three CLK2 cycles during Page Mode read cycles.

tCAS (Write): CAS# Pulse Width

  CLK2 × 2

CAS# pulses can be as narrow as two CLK2 cycles during Page Mode write cycles.

tASC: Column Address Setup Time

  min (CLK2 × 2 + AS32.tphl.min − Delay.max − ACT258.StoZ.tpl.max − ACT258.Cap.Derating, CLK2 × 3 + AS32.tphl.min − t6.max − 386.Cap.Derating − AS373.DtoO.tpd.max − ACT258.ItoZ.tpl.max − ACT258.Cap.Derating)

The Column Address becomes valid as RAS# switches from High to Low or as the 386 address becomes valid while RAS# is already Low (i.e., Page Mode, Pipelined cycles).

tCAH: Column Address Hold Time

  CLK2 + AS373.GtoO.tpd.min + ACT258.ItoZ.tpl.min − AS32.tphl.max

The CAL (Column Address Latch) signal is activated one CLK2 period after the active-going edge of CAS#.

tAR: Column Address Hold Time to RAS#

  CLK2 × 3 + AS373.GtoO.tpd.min + ACT258.ItoZ.tpl.min − RAS.Delay.max

tRCD: RAS# to CAS# Delay Time

  CLK2 × 2 + AS32.tphl.min − RAS.Delay.max

tRAD: RAS# to Column Address Delay Time

  (min) ACT258.StoZ.tphl.min + Delay.min − RAS.Delay.max

  (max) ACT258.StoZ.tphl.max + Delay.max + ACT258.Cap.Derating − RAS.Delay.min

tRSH: RAS# Hold Time

  CLK2 × 2 − AS32.tphl.max + RAS.Delay.min

The worst case occurs when a DRAM Page miss or Idle is detected at the end of the current DRAM Page miss cycle.

tCSH: CAS# Hold Time

  CLK2 × 6 + AS32.tplh.min − RAS.Delay.max

tCRP: CAS# to RAS# Precharge Time

  CLK2 × 2 + RAS.Delay.min − AS32.tplh.max

This is guaranteed by the DRAM control state machine.

tASR: Row Address Setup Time

  CLK2 × 2 − t6.max − 386.Cap.Derating − ACT258.ItoZ.max − ACT258.Cap.Derating + H124.tpd.min + H125.tpd.min + PAL.tco.min + RAS.Delay.min

tRAH: Row Address Hold Time

  ACT258.StoZ.tphl.min + Delay.min − RAS.Delay.max

tT: Transition Time (Rise and Fall)

tREF: Refresh Period

tREF2: Refresh Period

AP-442

Read Cycles:

tRAC: Access Time
  CLK2 × 6 − H124.tpd.max − H125.tpd.max − PAL.tco.max − t21.min − F245.max − RAS.Delay.max

tCAC: Access Time from CAS#
  CLK2 × 3 − H124.tpd.max − H125.tpd.max − PAL.tco.max − AS32.tphl.max − t21.min − F245.max

tAA: Access Time from Address
  CLK2 × 6 − t6.max − 386.Cap.Derating − AS373.DtoO.max − ACT258.ltoZ.tp.max − ACT258.Cap.Derating − t21.min − F245.max

tRCS: Read Command Setup Time
  CLK2 + AS32.tphl.min

tRCH: Read Command Hold Time to CAS#
  CLK2 − AS32.tplh.max

tRRH: Read Command Hold Time to RAS#
  CLK2 − RAS.Delay.max

tOFF: Output Buffer Turn-off Time
  CLK2 × 2 + F245.tzh.min

Write Cycles:

tWCS: Write Command Setup Time
  CLK2 × 3 + AS32.tphl.min

tWCH: Write Command Hold Time
  CLK2 × 2 − AS32.tplh.max

tWCR: Write Command Hold Time to RAS#
  CLK2 × 6 − RAS.Delay.max

tWP: Write Command Pulse Width
  CLK2 × 5

tRWL: Write Command to RAS# Lead Time
  CLK2 × 5 + RAS.Delay.min

tCWL: Write Command to CAS# Lead Time
  CLK2 × 5

tDS: Data-in Setup Time
  CLK2 × 3 + H124.tp.min + H125.tp.min + AS32.tphl.min − T12.max − F245.tp.max

tDH: Data-in Hold Time
  CLK2 × 2 + F245.tpz.min − AS32.tphl.max

tDHR: Data-in Hold Time to RAS#
  CLK2 × 6 + F245.tpz.max + RAS.Delay.min

Page Mode Cycles:

tPC: Page Mode Cycle Time
  CLK2 × 4

tRAPC: Page Mode RAS# Pulse Width
  CLK2 × 4

tRSW: RAS# to Second WE# Delay Time
  CLK2 × 7 − RAS.Delay.max

tCP: CAS# Precharge Time
  CLK2

tWI: Write Invalid Time
  CLK2

tCAP: Access Time from Column Precharge Time
  CLK2 × 4 − H124.tp.max − H125.tp.max − PAL.tco.max − t21.min − F245.max

AP-442

```
80386 A.C. SPECIFICATIONS
                                      80386-33
  Symbol   Parameter                  Minimum  Maximum
  ----------------------------------------------------
           Operating Frequency         8.00    33.33
  t1       CLK2 Period                15.00    62.50
  t2a      CLK2 High Time              6.25
  t2b      CLK2 High Time              4.50
  t3a      CLK2 Low Time               6.25
  t3b      CLK2 Low Time               4.50
  t4       CLK2 Fall Time                       4.00
  t5       CLK2 Rise Time                       4.00
  t6       A2-A31 Valid Delay          4.00    15.00
  t7       A2-A31 Float Delay          4.00    20.00
  t8       BE0#-BE3#, LOCK# Valid Delay 4.00   15.00
  t9       BE0#-BE3#, LOCK# Float Delay 4.00   20.00
  t10      W/R#, M/IO#, D/C#, ADS# Valid Delay 4.00 15.00
  t11      W/R#, M/IO#, D/C#, ADS# Float Delay 4.00 25.00
  t12      D0-D31 Write Data Valid Delay 5.00  24.00
  t13      D0-D31 Float Delay          4.00    17.00
  t14      HLDA Valid Delay            4.00    20.00
  t15      NA# Setup Time              5.00
  t16      NA# Hold Time               3.00
  t17      BS16# Setup Time            5.00
  t18      BS16# Hold Time             3.00
  t19      Ready# Setup Time           7.00
  t20      Ready# Hold Time            4.00
  t21      D0-D31 Read Setup Time      5.00
  t22      D0-D31 Read Hold Time       3.00
  t23      HOLD Setup Time            11.00
  t24      HOLD Hold Time              3.00
  t25      RESET Setup Time            8.00
  t26      RESET Hold Time             3.00
  t27      NMI, INTR Setup Time        5.00
  t28      NMI, INTR Hold Time         5.00
  t29      PEREQ, ERROR#, BUSY# Setup Time 5.00
  t30      PEREQ, ERROR#, BUSY# Hold Time  4.00
==========================================================

  PAL SPECIFICATIONS


  Symbol   Parameter                   Minimum  Maximum
  ----------------------------------------------------

  ts       Input or Feedback Setup Time  7.00
  tco      Clock to Output               3.00    6.50
==========================================================

  ROW ADDRESS LATCH SPECIFICATIONS
  74FCT843B (IDT)
                                       50 pF
  Symbol   Parameter                   Minimum  Maximum
  ----------------------------------------------------

  tplh     Dn to On Propagation Delay    3.00    6.50
  tphl                                   3.00    6.50
  tplh     G to On Propagation Delay     6.00    8.00
  tphl                                   4.00    8.00
  ts       Setup Time                    2.00
  th       Hold Time                     3.00
==========================================================
```

240725-C7

Timings for No Cache Configuration

6-103

AP-442

```
ROW ADDRESS COMPARATOR SPECIFICATIONS
74PCT521B (Performance)

Symbol    Parameter                              Minimum  Maximum
-----------------------------------------------------------------
tplh      An or Bn to Q Propagation Delay         1.50     5.50
tphl                                              1.50     5.50
tplh      I to Q Propagation Delay                1.50     4.60
tphl                                              1.50     4.60
=================================================================

DRAM ADDRESS MULTIPLEXER SPECIFICATIONS
74ACT258

Symbol    Parameter                              Minimum  Maximum
-----------------------------------------------------------------
tplh      S to Zn Propagation Delay               1.00    11.50
tphl                                              1.00    11.00
tplh      E# to Zn Propagation Delay              1.00     9.50
tphl                                              1.00     9.50
tplh      In to Zn Propagation Delay              1.00     9.50
tphl                                              1.00     8.00
=================================================================

DATA TRANSCEIVER SPECIFICATIONS
74F245

Symbol    Parameter                              Minimum  Maximum
-----------------------------------------------------------------
tplh      An to Bn or Bn to An Propagation Delay  2.50     7.00
tphl                                              2.50     7.00
tzh       Output Enable Time                      3.00     8.00
tzl                                               3.50     9.00
tphz      Output Disable Time                     3.00     7.50
tplz                                              2.00     7.50
=================================================================

COLUMN ADDRESS LATCH SPECIFICATIONS
74AS573

Symbol    Parameter                              Minimum  Maximum
-----------------------------------------------------------------
tplh      Dn to On Propagation Delay              3.00     6.00
tphl                                              3.00     6.00
tplh      G to On Propagation Delay               6.00    11.50
tphl                                              4.00     7.50
ts        Setup Time                              2.00
th        Hold Time                               3.00
=================================================================

RAS# DELAY

Symbol    Parameter                              Minimum  Maximum
-----------------------------------------------------------------
tp        Propagation Delay                       0.00     0.00
=================================================================
```

Timings for No Cache Configuration (Continued)

AP-442

```
OR SPECIFICATIONS
74AS32
Symbol   Parameter                               Minimum  Maximum
-------------------------------------------------------------------
tplh     Propagation Delay                        1.00     5.80
tphl                                              1.00     5.80
===================================================================

DRAM TIMING REQUIREMENTS
                                          For 80386-33        Timing Margin (NMB 2801-06)
Symbol   Parameter                       Minimum  Maximum     Minimum  Maximum
-------------------------------------------------------------------

Read and Write Cycles (Common Parameters):
tRC      Random Read or Write Cycle Time  150.00              29.00
tRP      RAS# Precharge Time               60.00               5.00
tRAS     RAS# Pulse Width                  60.00               0.00
tCAS     CAS# Pulse Width (Read)           45.00              34.00
tCAS     CAS# Pulse Width (Write)          30.00              25.00
tASC     Column Address Setup Time          9.70               9.70
tCAH     Column Address Hold Time          14.20               8.20
tAR      Column Address Hold Time to RAS#  50.00              10.00
tRCD     RAS# to CAS# Delay Time           31.00              25.00   14.00
tRAD     RAS# to Column Address Delay Time  5.00    21.30      1.00    6.70
tRSH     RAS# Hold Time                    24.20               9.20
tCSH     CAS# Hold Time                    91.00              51.00
tCRP     CAS# to RAS# Precharge Time       24.20              21.20
tASR     Row Address Setup Time             5.45               3.45
tRAH     Row Address Hold Time              5.00               3.00
tT       Transition Time (Rise and Fall)
tREF     Refresh Period
tREF2    Refresh Period

Read Cycles:
tRAC     Access Time                       68.25               8.25
tCAC     Access Time from CAS#             17.45               6.45
tAA      Access Time from Address          41.20               9.20
tRCS     Read Command Setup Time           16.00              16.00
tRCH     Read Command Hold Time to CAS#     9.20               9.20
tRRH     Read Command Hold Time to RAS#    15.00              15.00
tOFF     Output Buffer Turn-off Time                33.00              16.00

Write Cycles:
tWCS     Write Command Setup Time          46.00              46.00
tWCH     Write Command Hold Time           24.20              19.20
tWCR     Write Command Hold Time to RAS#   90.00              50.00
tWP      Write Command Pulse Width         75.00              70.00
tRWL     Write Command to RAS# Lead Time   75.00              62.00
tCWL     Write Command to CAS# Lead Time   75.00              70.00
tDS      Data-in Setup Time                17.75              17.75
tDH      Data-in Hold Time                 26.20              21.20
tDHR     Data-in Hold Time to RAS#         97.50              57.50

Page Mode Cycles:
tPC      Page Mode Cycle Time              60.00              23.00
tRAPC    Page Mode RAS# Pulse Width        60.00
tRSW     RAS# to Second WE# Delay Time    105.00
tCP      CAS# Precharge Time               15.00              10.00
tWI      Write Invalid Time                15.00
tCAP     Access Time from Column Precharge Time     38.25               4.25
===================================================================
                                                                   240725-C9
```

Timings for No Cache Configuration (Continued)

AP-442

```
ADDRESS DECODER REQUIREMENTS
                                        For 80386-33
Symbol    Parameter                     Minimum  Maximum
---------------------------------------------------------
tpd       Available Propagation Delay            8.75
=========================================================

ROW ADDRESS COMPARATOR REQUIREMENTS
                                        For 80386-33
Symbol    Parameter                     Minimum  Maximum
---------------------------------------------------------
tpd       Available Propagation Delay            8.75
=========================================================

NA# SETUP TIME

Symbol    Parameter                     Minimum  Maximum
---------------------------------------------------------
tNA#      Available NA# Setup Time      5.25
=========================================================

QUAD TTL TO 10KH-ECL TRANSLATOR
MC10H124
Symbol    Parameter                     Minimum  Maximum
---------------------------------------------------------
tpd       Propagation Delay             2.75     3.25
=========================================================

QUAD 10KH-ECL to TTL TRANSLATOR
MC10H125
Symbol    Parameter                     Minimum  Maximum
---------------------------------------------------------
tpd       Propagation Delay             0.00     0.00
=========================================================

DELAY ELEMENT

Symbol    Parameter                     Minimum  Maximum
---------------------------------------------------------
tpd       Propagation Delay             4.00     6.00
=========================================================
```

240725-D0

Timings for No Cache Configuration (Continued)

AP-442

```
DRAM SPECIFICATIONS
             NMB 2801-06           VITELIC V53C256 (70 ns)
Symbol    Minimum   Maximum        Minimum   Maximum
-------------------------------------------------------
tRC       121.00                    130.00
tRP        55.00                     50.00
tRAS       60.00    100000           70.00   75000.00
tCAS       11.00                     15, 20  75000.00
tCAS        5.00
tASC        0.00                      0.00
tCAH        6.00                     15.00
tAR        40.00                     55.00
tRCD        6.00      45.00          25.00      55.00
tRAD        4.00      28.00          20.00      35.00
tRSH       15.00                     15, 25
tCSH       40.00                     70.00
tCRP        3.00                     15.00
tASR        2.00                      0.00
tRAH        2.00                     15.00
tT                                    3.00      25.00
tREF
tREF2
tRAC                  60.00                     70.00
tCAC                  11.00                     15.00
tAA                   32.00                     35.00
tRCS        0.00                      0.00
tRCH        0.00                      5.00
tRRH        0.00                      5.00
tOFF                  17.00                     15.00
tWCS        0.00                      0.00
tWCH        5.00                     15.00
tWCR       40.00                     55.00
tWP         5.00                     15.00
tRWL       13.00                     20.00
tCWL        5.00                     20.00
tDS         0.00                      0.00
tDH         5.00                     15.00
tDHR       40.00                     55.00
tPC        37.00                     50.00
tRAPC
tRSW
tCP         5.00                     15.00
tWI
tCAP                  34.00                     45.00
```

240725-D1

```
CAPACITIVE LOAD TIMING DERATING FOR 74ACT258

Load Capacitance (pF)    Additional Propagation Delay (ns)
----------------------------------------------------------
       60.00              0.26  (p = 0.02625q - 1.3125)
       80.00              0.79
      100.00              0.89  (p = 0.022q - 1.3125)
      120.00              1.33
      140.00              1.77
      160.00              2.21
      180.00              2.65
      200.00              3.09
      220.00              3.83  (p = 0.01666q + 0.1666)
      240.00              4.17
      260.00              4.50
      280.00              4.83
      300.00              5.17
```

```
DRAM ADDRESS BUS TIMING DERATING

Reason                  Capacitive Load (pF)    Additional Propagation Delay (ns)
---------------------------------------------------------------------------------
DRAM Address Inputs           160.00
F258 Output
Microstrip/Strip Lines         60.00
                             ---------
TOTAL                         220.00  ===>                3.80
```

240725-D2

Timings for No Cache Configuration (Continued)

AP-442

EQUATIONS FOR DRAM TIMINGS (82385 Active):

Read and Write Cycles (Common Parameters):

tRC: Random Read or Write Cycle Time

CLK2 × 10

tRP: RAS# Precharge Time

CLK2 × 4

tRAS: RAS# Pulse Width

CLK2 × 4

A random DRAM cycle may have a RAS# pulse which is only four CLK2 periods wide. This is the case if the cycle is followed by Idle cycles (DRAMs not selected or Ti's) or a DRAM page miss.

tCAS (Read): CAS# Pulse Width

CLK2 × 5

CAS# pulses can be as narrow as five CLK2 cycles during Page Mode read cycles.

tCAS (Write): CAS# Pulse Width

CLK2 × 2

CAS# pulses can be as narrow as two CLK2 cycles during Page Mode write cycles.

tASC: Column Address Setup Time

min (CLK2 × 2 + AS32.tphl.min − Delay.max − ACT258.StoZ.tpl.max − ACT258.Cap.Derating, CLK2 × 3 + AS32.tphl.min − t6.max − 386.Cap.Derating − AS373.DtoO.tpd.max − ACT258.ItoZ.tpl.max − ACT258.Cap.Derating)

The Column Address becomes valid as RAS# switches from High to Low or as the 386 address becomes valid while RAS# is already Low (i.e., Page Mode, Pipelined cycles)

tCAH: Column Address Hold Time

CLK2 + AS373.GtoO.tpd.min + ACT258.ItoZ.tpl.min − AS32.tphl.max

The CAL (Column Address Latch) signal is activated one CLK2 period after the active-going edge of CAS#.

tAR: Column Address Hold Time to RAS#

CLK2 × 3 + AS373.GtoO.tpd.min + ACT258.ItoZ.tpl.min − RAS.Delay.max

tRCD: RAS# to CAS# Delay Time

CLK2 × 2 + AS32.tphl.min − RAS.Delay.max

tRAD: RAS# to Column Address Delay Time

(min) ACT258.StoZ.tphl.min + Delay.min − RAS.Delay.max

(max) ACT258.StoZ.tphl.max + Delay.max + ACT258.Cap.Derating − RAS.Delay.min

tRSH: RAS# Hold Time

CLK2 × 2 − AS32.tphl.max + RAS.Delay.min

The worst case occurs when a DRAM Page miss or Idle is detected at the end of the current DRAM Page miss cycle.

tCSH: CAS# Hold Time

CLK2 × 6 + AS32.tphl.min − RAS.Delay.max

tCRP: CAS# to RAS# Precharge Time

CLK2 × 2 + RAS.Delay.min − AS32.tplh.max

This is guaranteed by the DRAM control state machine.

tASR: Row Address Setup Time

CLK2 × 2 − t6.max − 386.Cap.Derating − ACT258.ItoZ.max − ACT258.Cap.Derating + H124.tpd.min + H125.tpd.min + PAL.tco.min + RAS.Delay.min

tRAH: Row Address Hold Time

ACT258.StoZ.tphl.min + Delay.min − RAS.Delay.max

tT: Transition Time (Rise and Fall)

tREF: Refresh Period

tREF2: Refresh Period

AP-442

Read Cycles:

tRAC: Access Time

   CLK2 × 8 − H124.tpd.max − H125.tpd.max − PAL.tco.max − − F245.max − AS646.tpd.max − F245.max − RAS.Delay.max − SRAM.tDW − CLK2 + 385.t22a.min

tCAC: Access Time from CAS#

   CLK2 × 5 − H124.tpd.max − H125.tpd.max − PAL.tco.max − AS32.tphl.max − F245.max − AS646.tpd.max − F245.max − SRAM.tDW − CLK2 + 385.t22a.min

tAA: Access Time from Address

   CLK2 × 8 − t6.max − 386.Cap.Derating − AS373.DtoO.max − ACT258.ItoZ.tp.max − ACT258.Cap.Derating − F245.max − AS646.tpd.max − F245.max − SRAM.tDW − CLK2 + 385.t22a.min

tRCS: Read Command Setup Time

   CLK2 + AS32.tphl.min

tRCH: Read Command Hold Time to CAS#

   CLK2 − AS32.tplh.max

tRRH: Read Command Hold Time to RAS#

   CLK2 − RAS.Delay.max

tOFF: Output Buffer Turn-off Time

   CLK2 × 2 + F245.tzh.min

Write Cycles:

tWCS: Write Command Setup Time

   CLK2 × 3 + AS32.tphl.min

tWCH: Write Command Hold Time

   CLK2 × 2 − AS32.tplh.max

tWCR: Write Command Hold Time to RAS#

   CLK2 × 6 − RAS.Delay.max

tWP: Write Command Pulse Width

   CLK2 × 5

tRWL: Write Command to RAS# Lead Time

   CLK2 × 5 + RAS.Delay.min

tCWL: Write Command to CAS# Lead Time

   CLK2 × 5

tDS: Data-in Setup Time

   CLK2 × 3 + H124.tp.min + H125.tp.min + AS32.tphl.min − − 385.t43c.max − AS646.GotO.tp.max − F245.tp.max

tDH: Data-in Hold Time

   CLK2 × 2 + F245.tpz.min − AS32.tphl.max

tDHR: Data-in Hold Time to RAS#

   CLK2 × 6 + F245.tpz.max + RAS.Delay.min

Page Mode Cycles:

tPC: Page Mode Cycle Time

   CLK2 × 6

tRAPC: Page Mode RAS# Pulse Width

   CLK2 × 4

tRSW: RAS# to Second WE# Delay Time

   CLK2 × 7 − RAS.Delay.max

tCP: CAS# Precharge Time

   CLK2

tWI: Write Invalid Time

   CLK2

tCAP: Access Time from Column Precharge Time

   CLK2 × 6 − H124.tp.max − H125.tp.max − PAL.tco.max − − F245.max − AS646.tpd.max − F245.max − SRAM.tDW − CLK2 + 385.t22a.min

AP-442

```
DRAM TIMING REQUIREMENTS

                                            For 80386-33        Timing Margin (NMB 2801-06)
Symbol    Parameter                         Minimum  Maximum    Minimum  Maximum
-------------------------------------------------------------------------------------
Read and Write Cycles (Common Parameters):
tRC       Random Read or Write Cycle Time   150.00              29.00
tRP       RAS# Precharge Time                60.00               5.00
tRAS      RAS# Pulse Width                   60.00               0.00
tCAS      CAS# Pulse Width (Read)            75.00              64.00
tCAS      CAS# Pulse Width (Write)           30.00              25.00
tASC      Column Address Setup Time           9.70               9.70
tCAH      Column Address Hold Time           14.20               8.20
tAR       Column Address Hold Time to RAS#   50.00              10.00
tRCD      RAS# to CAS# Delay Time            31.00              25.00    14.00
tRAD      RAS# to Column Address Delay Time   5.00   21.30       1.00     6.70
tRSH      RAS# Hold Time                     24.20               9.20
tCSH      CAS# Hold Time                     91.00              51.00
tCRP      CAS# to RAS# Precharge Time        24.20              21.20
tASR      Row Address Setup Time              6.20               4.20
tRAH      Row Address Hold Time               5.00               3.00
tT        Transition Time (Rise and Fall)
tREF      Refresh Period
tREF2     Refresh Period

Read Cycles:
tRAC      Access Time                        67.50               7.50
tCAC      Access Time from CAS#              16.70               5.70
tAA       Access Time from Address           37.70               5.70
tRCS      Read Command Setup Time            20.80              20.80
tRCH      Read Command Hold Time to CAS#      9.20               9.20
tRRH      Read Command Hold Time to RAS#     15.00              15.00
tOFF      Output Buffer Turn-off Time                33.00               16.00

Write Cycles:
tWCS      Write Command Setup Time           46.00              46.00
tWCH      Write Command Hold Time            24.20              19.20
tWCR      Write Command Hold Time to RAS#    90.00              50.00
tWP       Write Command Pulse Width          75.00              70.00
tRWL      Write Command to RAS# Lead Time    75.00              62.00
tCWL      Write Command to CAS# Lead Time    75.00              70.00
tDS       Data-in Setup Time                  9.00               9.00
tDH       Data-in Hold Time                  31.70              26.70
tDHR      Data-in Hold Time to RAS#          97.50              57.50

Page Mode Cycles:
tPC       Page Mode Cycle Time               90.00              53.00
tRAPC     Page Mode RAS# Pulse Width         60.00
tRSW      RAS# to Second WE# Delay Time     105.00
tCP       CAS# Precharge Time                15.00              10.00
tWI       Write Invalid Time                 15.00
tCAP      Access Time from Column Precharge Time      37.50               3.50
```

Timings with Cache Active

APPENDIX E
REFERENCES

REFERENCES

Advanced CMOS Logic Designer's Handbook, Texas Instruments Inc., 1988.

Blood W., *MECL System Design Handbook*, Motorola Corp., 1983.

Keeler R., "High Speed Digital Printed Circuit Boards," *Electronic Packaging & Production*, pp. 140-145, Jan. 1986.

Tomlinson J., "Avoid The Pitfalls of High Speed Logic Design," *Electronic Design*, pp. 75-84, Nov. 9, 1989.

Pace C., "Terminate Bus Lines to Avoid Overshoot and Ringing," *EDN*, pp. 227-234, Sept. 17, 1987.

Royle D., "Rules Tell Whether Interconnections Act Like Transmission Lines," *EDN*, pp. 131-136, June 23, 1988.

Royle D., "Correct Signal Faults by Implementing Line-Analysis Theory," *EDN*, pp. 143-148, June 23, 1988.

Winchester E., "Guidelines Help You Design High-Speed PC Boards," *EDN*, pp. 221-226, Nov. 28, 1985.

Yeargan J. R., Day R. L., and Nguyen T., "Effects of Printed Circuit Board Transmission Lines an Loading on Gate Performance," *IEEE Transactions on Industrial Electronics*, Vol. IE-34, no. 3, pp. 399-405, Aug. 1987.

intel.

AP-513

APPLICATION NOTE

Intel386™ EX CPU POS Terminal Reference Design

AL WEIDNER
SENIOR STAFF ENGINEER

October 1994

Order Number: 272578-001

Intel386™ EX CPU POS TERMINAL REFERENCE DESIGN

CONTENTS

1.0 INTRODUCTION 6-114

2.0 BLOCK DIAGRAM 6-115

3.0 FUNCTIONAL DESCRIPTION OF THE Intel386™ EX MICROPROCESSOR 6-116
   3.1 Clock Generation and Power Management Unit 6-117
   3.2 Chip Select Unit 6-117
   3.3 Interrupt Control Unit 6-117
   3.4 Timer/Counter Unit 6-117
   3.5 Watchdog Timer Unit 6-118
   3.6 Asynchronous Serial I/O Unit 6-118
   3.7 Synchronous Serial I/O Unit 6-118
   3.8 Parallel I/O Unit 6-118
   3.9 DMA and Bus Arbiter Unit 6-118
   3.10 Refresh Control Unit 6-119
   3.11 JTAG Boundary Scan Unit 6-119

4.0 MEMORY 6-120
   4.1 Memory Chip Selects 6-120
   4.2 Memory Map 6-121

5.0 I/O DEVICES 6-122
   5.1 I/O Map 6-122
   5.2 Intel386 EX CPU Internal I/O 6-122
      5.2.1 Interval Timers 6-122
      5.2.2 Refresh Unit 6-122
      5.2.3 Port 92 6-122
      5.2.4 Watch Dog Timer 6-122
      5.2.5 SIO 0 and 1 6-122
      5.2.6 Parallel I/O Ports (Emulated LPTx) 6-123
   5.3 External I/O 6-123
      5.3.1 VGA 6-123
      5.3.2 Keyboard/Mouse 6-124
      5.3.3 RTC 6-124
      5.3.4 IDE 6-124
      5.3.5 PCMCIA Controller 6-124

6.0 HARDWARE INTERRUPTS 6-124

7.0 iFX780 OVERVIEW 6-125
   7.1 Reset Synchronization 6-125
   7.2 Ready Generation 6-125
   7.3 Data Bus Transceiver Control 6-125
   7.4 MNI Setting/Clearing 6-125
   7.5 DRAM Control 6-125
   7.6 Flash Memory/EPROM Control .. 6-125
   7.7 SEB Interface 6-126

8.0 THEORY OF OPERATION 6-126
   8.1 Pin Definition 6-126
   8.2 State Machines 6-128
   8.3 Bus Tracker Description 6-128
   8.4 SEB Description 6-129
   8.5 DRAM Controller Description 6-130
   8.6 Flash Memory/EPROM Control .. 6-132

9.0 FUNCTIONAL TIMING DIAGRAMS 6-133

10.0 TIMING ANALYSIS 6-137
   10.1 DRAM Timing 6-137
   10.2 Flash Memory Timing 6-138
   10.3 Synchronous Expansion Bus (SEB) 6-139

11.0 SYSTEM BIOS 6-141
   11.1 Intel386 EX CPU Configuration 6-141
   11.2 NMI Handler 6-144
   11.3 Parallel Port 6-144
   11.4 Flash Memory Support 6-144

12.0 VGA BIOS 6-144

13.0 iFX780 EQUATIONS 6-144

14.0 SCHEMATICS 6-144

15.0 SUMMARY 6-145

AP-513

1.0 INTRODUCTION

The POS, or Point of Sales, Terminal Reference Design was developed as a working design to enable shorter design cycles by providing a proven platform as a starting point. This design has been built, debugged, and tested. The POS terminal was designed by Intel and highlights the features of the embedded Intel386™ EX Processor and Intel Boot Block Flash Memory. The POS Terminal is available as a Reference Design Kit which contains all necessary technical documentation; the design can be used "as is" or as a building block to enhance a specific solution.

POS terminals are typically characterized by a PC-like platform with a ruggedized housing that is more suitable for retail and service environments ranging from clothing boutiques to fast food restaurants. A POS terminal may also include a keyboard or LCD/CRT touchscreen that is conducive to efficient transaction entry, battery backup, and expanded number of serial ports for the various peripherals such as barcode scanners, magnetic card readers, digital scales, and coin changers. Clearly, the POS terminal hardware architecture is driven by a standardized low-cost PC-like platform; as the terminal costs continue to decrease and valuable features are provided in software/firmware, they will begin to displace simple electronic cash registers (ECR). In general, POS software has been increasingly standardized on a PC-like environment with operating systems such as DOS, UNIX, or other real-time systems; these applications can readily be developed on any PC systems with off-the-shelf tools. The Intel386 architecture is ideal to provide sufficient computing power and low-cost solutions for such POS terminals.

The Intel386 EX processor is a single-chip system utilizing an on-board static Intel386 CX processor core and a host of integrated peripherals, including DMA and interrupt controllers, serial and parallel ports, chip selects, timers/counters and JTAG. Its 26-bit addressing provides a large 64 MB memory address space. The POS Terminal Reference Design also incorporates a number of additional technologies which may be used as building blocks for many applications.

This reference design is intended to include a set of features required for most DOS and Windows based POS terminal applications. It is self-contained with expansion capabilities via a single PCMCIA slot. The design generates a general purpose Synchronous Expansion Bus (SEB) that allows the selected peripherals to be attached to the CPU. Command strobes (IOR#, IOW#, MEMW#, MEMR#, BALE) are generated while status inputs (IOCHRDY, IOCS16#, MEMCS16#) are used in a way similar to the ISA bus. The design uses the SEB to interface to the SVGA graphics controller (Cirrus Logic GD5424), PCMCIA controller (Cirrus Logic PD6710), the IDE disk interface, the RTC (DS1287A) and the keyboard/mouse controller (Intel 82C42PC).

Even though the implementation is mostly PC compatible, some software drivers and BIOS customization are required to handle the reassignment of the interrupts, emulation of the LPT parallel port and other capabilities.

Product Description

The POS reference design is DOS compatible and uses a standard PC-like BIOS. It features several products and technologies:

- Embedded Intel386 EX Processor
- Intel 4 Mb Boot Block Flash Memory
- Complex PLD
- PCMCIA Slot

The POS terminal has the following features:

- Pipelined, Zero Wait state, page mode operation
- Non-pipelined, one wait state, page mode operation
- 1, 4, or 16 MB DRAM
- One single-sided x32 SIMM
- SVGA Local Bus Graphics Controller (512 KB DRAM frame buffer)
- RTC with Extended Battery Backed RAM
- PS/2 Style Keyboard and Mouse Interface
- IDE Hard Disk Interface
- PCMCIA 2.0 (single slot)
- 2 Asynchronous Serial Ports (COM1 and COM2)
- Parallel Printer Port (LPT)

The features of the Intel386 EX CPU are used extensively to eliminate the requirement for a chip set and to minimize external logic. The interrupt controller, chip select unit, wait state generator, SIOs, parallel I/O parts and dynamic bus sizing are all used.

Although the initial stepping of the Intel386 EX CPU does not support pipeline mode, this design anticipates the future steppings, which will allow the full zero wait state performance that pipeline provides.

NOTE:
Although this is a complete functional unit, the design is modular, allowing for addition and modification of features to meet the specific requirements of a target application.

AP-513

2.0 BLOCK DIAGRAM

Figure 1 shows a system block diagram.

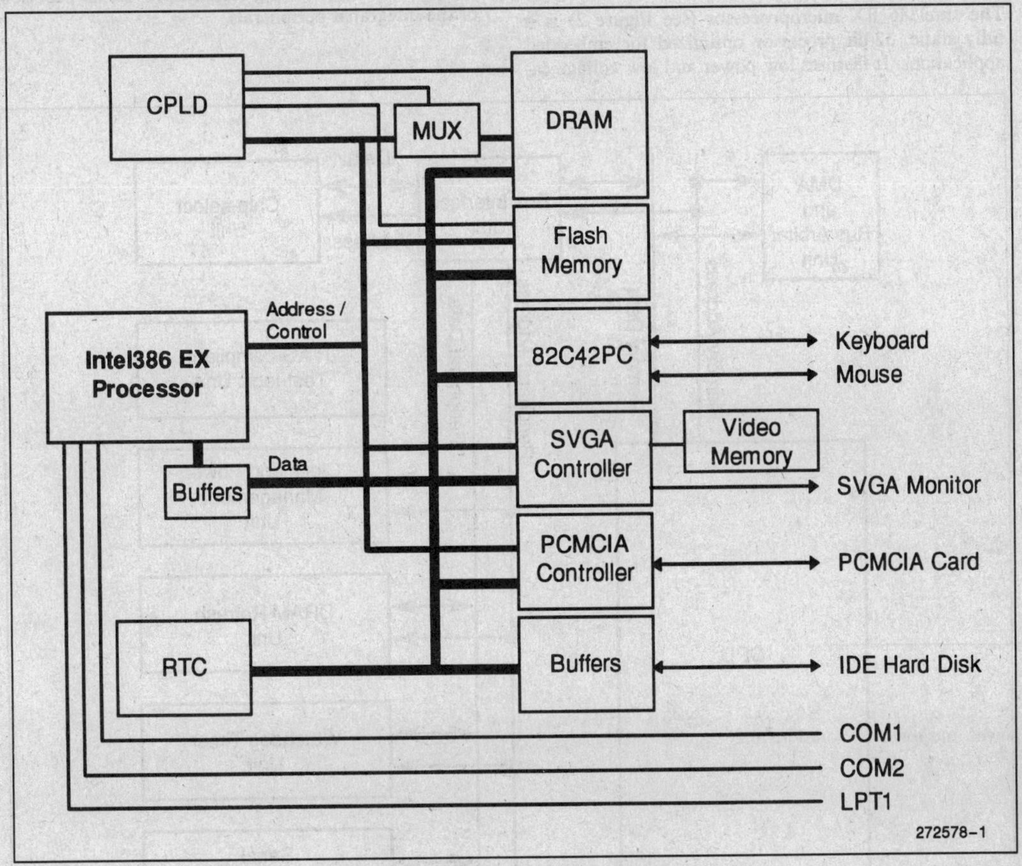

Figure 1. POS Terminal Block Diagram

AP-513

3.0 FUNCTIONAL DESCRIPTION OF THE Intel386™ EX MICROPROCESSOR

The Intel386 EX microprocessor (see Figure 2) is a fully static, 32-bit processor optimized for embedded applications. It features low power and low voltage capabilities, integration of many commonly used DOS-type peripherals, and a 32-bit programming architecture compatible with the large software base of Intel386 processors. The following sections provide an overview of the integrated peripherals.

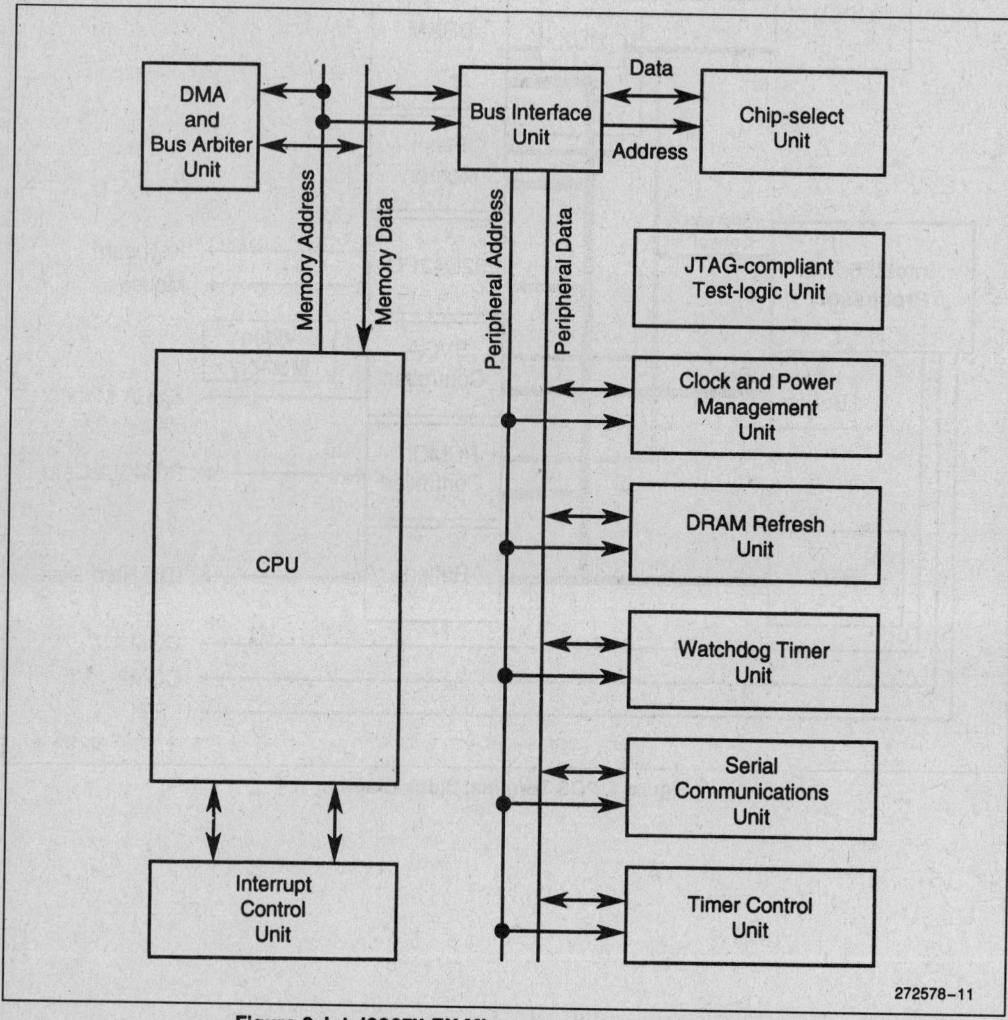

Figure 2. Intel386™ EX Microprocessor Block Diagram

3.1 Clock Generation and Power Management Unit

The clock generation circuit includes a divide-by-two counter, a programmable divider for generating a prescaled clock (PSCLK) and Reset circuitry. The CLK2 input provides the fundamental timing for the chip. It is divided by two internally to generate a 50% duty cycle Phase1 (PH1) and Phase 2 (PH2) for the core and integrated peripherals. For power management, separate clocks are routed to the core (PH1C/PH2C) and the peripheral modules (PH1P/PH2P).

Two Power Management modes are provided for flexible power-saving options. During Idle mode, the clocks to the CPU core are frozen in a known state (PH1C low and PH2C high), while the clocks to the peripherals continue to toggle. In Powerdown mode, the clocks to both core and peripherals are frozen in a known state (PH1C low and PH2C high). The Bus Interface Unit will not honor any DMA, DRAM refresh, or HOLD requests in Powerdown mode because the clocks to the entire device are frozen.

3.2 Chip Select Unit

The Chip Select Unit (CSU) decodes bus cycle address and status information and enables the appropriate chip-selects. The individual chip-selects become valid in the same bus state as the address and become inactive when either a new address is selected or the current bus cycle is complete.

The CSU is divided into eight separate chip-select regions, each of which can enable one of the eight chip-select pins. Each chip-select region can be mapped into memory or I/O space. A memory-mapped chip-select region can start on zero or any $2^{(n+1)}$ Kbyte address location (where n = 0–15, depending upon the mask register). An I/O-mapped chip-select region can start on zero or any $2^{(n+1)}$ byte address (where n = 0–15, depending upon the mask register). The size of the region is also dependent upon the mask used.

3.3 Interrupt Control Unit

The Intel386 EX microprocessor's Interrupt Control Unit (ICU) contains two 8259A modules connected in a cascade mode. The 8259A modules make up the heart of the ICU. These modules are similar to the industry-standard 8259A architecture.

The Interrupt Control Unit directly supports up to eight external (INT7:0) and up to eight internal (IR7:0) interrupt request signals. Pending interrupt requests are posted in the Interrupt Request Register, which contains one bit for each interrupt request signal. When an interrupt request is asserted, the corresponding Interrupt Request Register bit is set. The 8259A module can be programmed to recognize either an active-high level or a positive transition on the interrupt request lines. An internal Priority Resolver decides which pending interrupt request (if more than one exists) is the highest priority, based on the programmed operating mode. The Priority Resolver controls the single interrupt request line to the CPU. The Priority Resolver's default priority scheme places IR0 as the highest priority and IR7 as the lowest. The priority can be modified through software.

Besides the eight interrupt request inputs available to the Intel386 EX microprocessor, additional interrupts can be supported by cascaded external 8259A modules. Up to four external 8259A units can be cascaded to the master through connections to the INT3:0 pins. In this configuration, the interrupt acknowledge (INTA#) signal can be decoded externally using the ADS#, D/C#, R/W#, and M/IO# signals.

3.4 Timer/Counter Unit

The Timer/Counter unit on the Intel386 EX microprocessor has the same basic functionality as the industry-standard 82C54 counter/timer. It provides three independent 16-bit counters, each capable of handling clock inputs up to 8 MHz. This maximum frequency must be considered when programming the input clocks for the counters. Six programmable timer modes allow the timers to be used as event counters, elapsed-time indicators, programmable one-shots, and in many other applications. All modes are software programmable.

AP-513

3.5 Watchdog Timer Unit

The Watchdog Timer (WDT) unit consists of a 32-bit down-counter that decrements every PH1P cycle, allowing up to 4.3 billion count intervals. The WDTOUT pin is driven high for sixteen CLK2 cycles when the down-counter reaches zero (the WDT times out). The WDTOUT signal can be used to reset the chip, to request an interrupt, or to indicate to the user that a ready-hang situation has occurred. The down-counter can also be updated with a user-defined 32-bit reload value under certain conditions. Alternatively, the WDT unit can be used as a bus monitor or as a general-purpose timer.

3.6 Asynchronous Serial I/O Unit

The Intel386 EX microprocessor's asynchronous serial I/O (SIO) unit is a Universal Asynchronous Receiver/Transmitter (UART). Functionally, it is equivalent to the National Semiconductor NS16450 and INS8250. The Intel386 EX microprocessor contains two asynchronous serial channels.

The SIO unit converts serial data characters received from a peripheral device or modem to parallel data and converts parallel data characters received from the CPU to serial data. The CPU can read the status of the serial port at any time during its operation. The status information includes the type and condition of the transfer operations being performed and any errors (parity, framing, overrun, or break interrupt).

Each asynchronous serial channel includes full modem control support (CTS#, RTS#, DSR#, DTR#, RI#, and DCD#) and is completely programmable. The programmable options include character length (5, 6, 7, or 8 bits), stop bits (1, 1.5, or 2), and parity (even, odd, forced, or none). In addition, it contains a programmable baud rate generator capable of DC to 512 Kbaud.

3.7 Synchronous Serial I/O Unit

The Synchronous Serial I/O (SSIO) unit provides for simultaneous, bidirectional communications. It consists of a transmit channel, a receive channel, and a dedicated baud rate generator. The transmit and receive channels can be operated independently (with different clocks) to provide non-lockstep, full-duplex communications; either channel can originate the clocking signal (Master Mode) or receive an externally generated clocking signal (Slave Mode).

The SSIO provides numerous features for ease and flexibility of operation. With a maximum clock input of 12.5 MHz to the baud rate generator (assuming 25 MHz device operation), the SSIO can deliver a baud rate of 6.25 Mbits per second. Each channel is double buffered. The two channels share the baud rate generator and a multiply-by-two transmit and receive clock. The SSIO supports 16-bit serial communications with independently enabled transmit and receive functions and gated interrupt outputs to the interrupt controller.

3.8 Parallel I/O Unit

The Intel386 EX microprocessor has three 8-bit, general-purpose I/O ports. All port pins are bidirectional, with CMOS-level input and outputs. All pins have both a standard operating mode and a peripheral mode (a multiplexed function), and all have similar sets of control registers located in I/O address space. Ports 1 and 2 provide 8 mA of drive capability, while port 3 provides 16 mA.

3.9 DMA and Bus Arbiter Unit

The Intel386 EX microprocessor's DMA controller is a two-channel DMA; each channel operates independently of the other. Within the operation of the individual channels, several different data transfer modes are available. These modes can be combined in various configurations to provide a very versatile DMA controller. Its feature set has enhancements beyond the 8237 DMA family; however, it can be configured such that it can be used in an 8237-like mode. Each channel can transfer data between any combination of memory and I/O with any combination (8 or 16 bits) of data path widths. An internal temporary register that can disassemble or assemble data to or from either an aligned or a nonaligned destination or source optimizes bus bandwidth.

The bus arbiter, a part of the DMA controller, works much like the priority resolving circuitry of a DMA. It receives service requests from the two DMA channels, the external bus master, and the DRAM Refresh controller. The bus arbiter requests bus ownership from the core and resolves priority issues among all active requests when bus mastership is granted.

Each DMA channel consists of three major components: the Requestor, the Target, and the Byte Count. These components are identified by the contents of programmable registers that define the memory or I/O device being serviced by the DMA. The Requestor is the device that requires and requests service from the DMA controller. Only the Requestor is considered capable of initializing or terminating a DMA process. The Target is the device with which the Requestor wishes to communicate. The DMA process considers the Target a slave that is incapable of controlling the process. The Byte Count dictates the amount of data that must be transferred.

3.10 Refresh Control Unit

The Refresh Control Unit (RCU) simplifies dynamic memory controller design with its integrated address and clock counters. Integrating the RCU into the processor allows an external DRAM controller to use chip-selects, wait state logic, and status lines.

The Intel386 EX microprocessor's RCU consists of four basic functions. First, it provides a programmable-interval timer that keeps track of time. Second, it provides the bus arbitration logic to gain control of the bus to run refresh cycles. Third, it contains the logic to generate row addresses to refresh DRAM rows individually. And fourth, it contains the logic to signal the start of a refresh cycle.

Additionally, it contains a 13-bit address counter that forms the refresh address, supporting DRAMs with up to 13 rows of memory cells (13 refresh address bits). This includes all practical DRAM sizes for the Intel386 microprocessor's 64 Mbyte address space.

3.11 JTAG Boundary Scan Unit

The JTAG Boundary Scan Unit provides access to the device pins and to a number of other testable areas on the device. It is fully compliant with the IEEE 1149.1 standard and thus interfaces with five JTAG-dedicated pins: TRST#, TCK, TMS, TDI, and TDO. It contains the Test Access Port (TAP) finite-state machine, a 4-bit instruction register, a 32-bit identification register, a single-bit bypass register, and an 8-bit test mode register. The JTAG unit also contains the necessary logic to generate clock and control signals for the chains that reside outside the JTAG unit itself: the SCANOUT and Boundary Scan chains.

Since the JTAG unit has its own clock and reset signals, it can operate autonomously. Thus, while the rest of the microprocessor is in Reset or Powerdown, the JTAG unit can read or write various register chains. This feature can be used, for example, to write to the test mode register while the rest of the chip is in Reset or Powerdown. Then when the microprocessor exits Reset or Powerdown, it will enter the specified test mode.

AP-513

4.0 MEMORY

Memory accesses are directed to Flash Memory, DRAM or the SEB depending on the Intel386 EX CPU's chip select configuration. System memory is implemented using a single 4 Mbit Boot Block Flash Memory device and a single x32 SIMM socket supporting 1, 4 or 16 Mbyte of DRAM connected as two 16-bit banks with jumpers to select the options. The chip selects are used as follows:

- GCS5# defines the DRAM linear space from address 0 to the DRAM size.
- UCS# defines the Flash Memory space in the upper 512 Kbyte of the 64 MB address range.
- GCS6# provide access to the lower half (up to 256 Kbyte) of the Flash Memory in real memory just below 1 MB.
- Accesses above GCS5# and in the 00A0000h–00FFFFFh range where GCS6# is not generated are directed to the SEB.

SEB memory accesses are in support of the PCMCIA and VGA controllers. The PCMCIA controller "windows" can be configured anywhere in real or extended memory and the VGA frame buffer can be configured to reside in DOS memory (normally 00A0000–00BFFFFh) or as a linear frame buffer in the extended memory area above the DRAM.

4.1 Memory Chip Selects

Table 1 describes the chip select utilization.

It should be noted that the DRAM chip select overlaps the GCS6# and the SEB area in the lower 1 MB of the memory map. The CPLD controlling the DRAM, inhibits DRAM accesses for 00A0000h–00FFFFFh and enables the SEB to be accessed in this region when GCS6# is not active or generates two wait state flash memory access when GCS6# is active.

Table 1. Chip Select Utilization

Chip Select	Device	Address Range (hex)	Wait States	Data Width	Memory Speed (ns)
GCS5#	1 MB DRAM 4 MB DRAM 16 MB DRAM	0000000–00FFFFF 0000000–03FFFFF 0000000–0FFFFFF	0,1,2,3	16	70
UCS#	512 KB FLASH	3F80000–3FFFFFF	2	16	80
GCS6#	128 KB FLASH 256 KB FLASH	00E0000–00FFFFF 00C0000–00FFFFF	2	16	80
None	SEB	00A0000–00DFFFF 00A0000–00BFFFF	8/15(1)	16/8(2)	

NOTES:
1. Default cycles are 15 wait states for 8-bit and 8 wait states for 16-bit.
2. CPLD forces 8-bit if external logic does not assert MEMCS16#.

 **AP-513**

4.2 Memory Map

Figure 3 shows the system memory map.

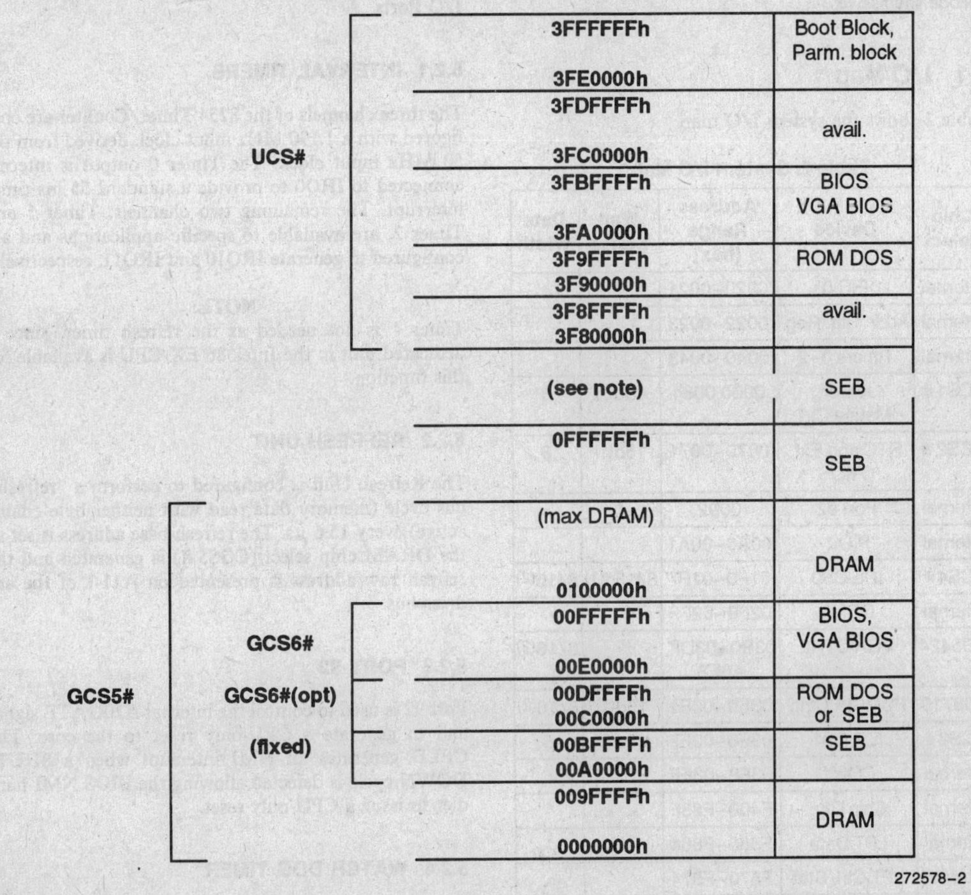

			Address	Region
			3FFFFFFh	Boot Block, Parm. block
	UCS#		3FE0000h	
			3FDFFFFh	avail.
			3FC0000h	
			3FBFFFFh	BIOS VGA BIOS
			3FA0000h	
			3F9FFFFh	ROM DOS
			3F90000h	
			3F8FFFFh	avail.
			3F80000h	
			(see note)	SEB
			0FFFFFFh	SEB
			(max DRAM)	
GCS5#	GCS6#			DRAM
			0100000h	
			00FFFFFh	BIOS, VGA BIOS
	GCS6#(opt)		00E0000h	
			00DFFFFh	ROM DOS or SEB
	(fixed)		00C0000h	
			00BFFFFh	SEB
			00A0000h	
			009FFFFh	DRAM
			0000000h	

272578-2

NOTE:
All memory accesses to areas above GCS5# (DRAM) but below UCS# are directed to the SEB. This allows the flexibility to access the VGA and PCMCIA in extend memory when configured with 16 Mbyte of DRAM.

Figure 3. System Memory Map

AP-513

5.0 I/O DEVICES

The design uses both internal and external I/O mapped peripherals. Some of the external devices require the use of a chip select while others perform the address decode themselves.

5.1 I/O Map

Table 2 shows the system I/O map.

Table 2. System I/O Map

Chip Select	Device	Address Range (hex)	Wait States	Data Width
internal	PIC 0	0020–0021		
internal	Addr. Cfg. Reg.	0022–0023		
internal	Timers 0–2	0040–0043		
GCS1#	Kybd/Mouse Ctrl	0060,0064	15d(1)	8
GCS2#	RTC and Ext. CMOS	0070–0071	15d(1)	8
internal	Port 92	0092		
internal	PIC 1	00A0–00A1		
GCS4#	IDE CS0	01F0–01F7	8/15d(1)	8/16(2)
internal	COM2	02F8–02FF		
GD5424	VGA CTRL	03B0–03DF, 46E8		8/16(2)
PD6710	PCMCIA Ctrlr.	03E0–03E1	15d(1)	8/16(2)
GCS3#	IDE CS1	03F6–03F7	15d(1)	8
internal	COM1	03F8–03FF		
internal	Chip Cfg.	F400–F85F		
internal	LPT Data	F860–F864		
internal	LPT Ctrl/Stat	F870–F874		
internal	Chip Cfg.	F875–F8FF		

NOTES:
1. Default cycles are 15 wait states for 8-bit and 8 wait states for 16-bit.
2. A CPLD forces 8 bit if external logic does not assert IOCS16#.

5.2 Intel386™ EX CPU Internal I/O

The standard internal peripherals that are used in this design include the Interrupt Controllers, Interval Timers, Refresh Unit, the SIOs, Port 92 and the Parallel I/O Ports.

5.2.1 INTERVAL TIMERS

The three channels of the 8254 Timer/Counter are configured with a 1.190 MHz input clock derived from the 50 MHz input clock. The Timer 0 output is internal connected to IRQ0 to provide a standard 55 ms timer interrupt. The remaining two channels, Timer 1 and Timer 2, are available to specific applications and are configured to generate IRQ10 and IRQ11, respectively.

NOTE:
Timer 1 is not needed as the refresh timer, since a dedicated unit in the Intel386 EX CPU is available for this function.

5.2.2 REFRESH UNIT

The Refresh Unit is configured to perform a "refresh" bus cycle (memory data read with neither byte enable active) every 15.6 μs. The refresh base address is set so the DRAM chip select (CGS5#) is generated and the refresh row address is presented on A11-1 of the address bus.

5.2.3 PORT 92

Port 92 is used to control the internal A20GATE signal and to generate a CPU-only reset to the core. The CPLD generates an NMI interrupt when a SHUTDOWN cycle is detected allowing the BIOS NMI handler to issue a CPU-only reset.

5.2.4 WATCH DOG TIMER

The Watch Dog Timer can be used to generate an IRQ15.

5.2.5 SIO 0 and 1

The serial ports are mapped to I/O addresses 3F8h–3FFh (COM1) and 2F8h–2FFh (COM2) are connected to IRQ4 and IRQ3, respectively. COM1 is a "two-wire" interface while COM2 is a full RS232 port. The ports are consistent with the PC's implementation except the input clock is 12.5 MHz (derived from the

AP-513

50 MHz clock). Table 3 shows the divider values and error percentage for some selected baud rates.

Table 3. Divider Values and Error Percentages

Desired Baud Rate	12.5 MHz Clock	
	Divisor Value for 16x Clock	Percent Error
300	2604	0.006
1200	651	0.006
2400	326	0.147
9600	81	0.469
19200	41	0.756
56000	14	0.351
115000	7	2.950

5.2.6 PARALLEL I/O PORTS (EMULATED LPTx)

A combination of the parallel I/O ports in the Intel386 EX CPU are used to implement a Centronix parallel port. It has a subset of the handshake lines typically used by the interface (the SLCT status pin is not available) and the port addresses and bit positions are different from the PC's LPTx port. A custom BIOS and/or driver is required to utilize this port. The Intel386 EX CPU's P1DIR register allows the data port to be bi-directional.

The bits of the CPU's parallel I/O Ports (PI, P2 and P3) that are used for the LPT port are shown in Figure 4.

5.3 External I/O

This design includes a set of interfaces to external peripherals. They include interfaces to VGA controller, an IDE hard disk, an RTC, a buffered PCMCIA slot, a i82C42PC keyboard/mouse controller.

5.3.1 VGA

The display section uses the Cirrus Logic, single chip, CL-GD5424 True Color VGA Controller that includes a palette DAC and a frequency synthesizer. This supports VGA and SVGA functionality with screen resolutions from 640 x 480 up to 1280 x 1024 and from 4 to 16M colors depending on the video DRAM configuration. The design uses one 256K x 16 DRAM to provide a 512 Kbyte frame buffer.

The controller resides on the SEB and is configured in ISA mode. The memory and I/O space used by the VGA controller is a function of its configuration.

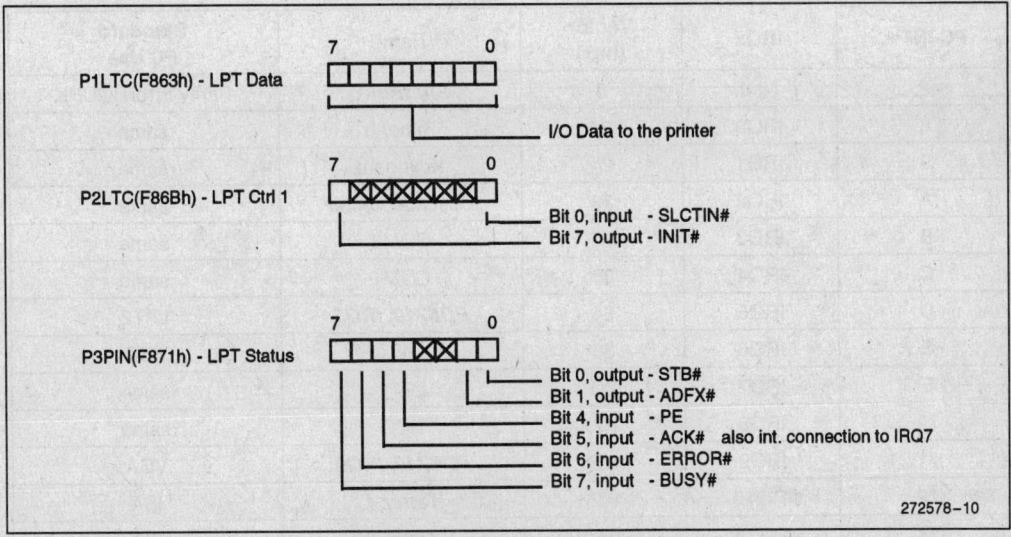

Figure 4. Printer Port Signal Map

5.3.2 KEYBOARD/MOUSE

An Intel 82C42PC micro-controller is used to provide a PS/2 style keyboard/mouse interface. Although it physically resided on the local address and data buses, it requires ISA-like I/O read and write strobes. GCS1# is configured for I/O space 60h and 64h does not use the Ex's wait state generation, therefore accesses are run as the default 8-bit, 15 wait state, SEB I/O cycles.

The keyboard interrupt is connected to IRQ1 and the mouse interrupt to IRQ13 (IRQ12 is used in a PC).

5.3.3 RTC

A Dallas Semiconductor DS1287A provides the real-time clock and the battery backed RAM function normally used in a PC environment. RTC__AS and RTC__DS are generated by the CPLD from GCS2#. The RTC resides on the local data buses and is accessed by SEB cycles to I/O 70h-71h.

The RTC interrupt is connected to IRQ8.

5.3.4 IDE

An IDE interface is implemented using two chip selects from the Intel386 EX CPU. GCS3# is configured for I/O addresses 3F6h-3F7h and used to for HST__CS1#, while GCS4#, I/O addresses 1F0h-1F7h, is used for HST__CS0#. The CPLD is used to control a data bus transceiver and uses (IOCS16#) to determine the access time and the Intel386 EX CPU's bus sizing. These cycles are run at the SEB standard 8 or 15 wait states.

The IDE interrupt is tied to IRQ14.

5.3.5 PCMCIA CONTROLLER

A Cirrus Logic CL-PD6710 is used to support one buffered PCMCIA card slot. Its control registers are mapped to I/O locations 3E0h-3E1h and performs its own decode.

Three of the interrupt outputs of the CL-PD6710 are available. IRQ5, 9 and 14 outputs are tied directly to the Intel386 EX CPU's IRQ5, 9 and 14 inputs. IRQ14 is shared with the IDE interface and allows a PCMCIA ATA disk to be used instead of the IDE disk interface.

6.0 HARDWARE INTERRUPTS

The interrupt mapping is close to that of a PC. Table 4 shows this mapping and where it deviates from a standard PC implementation.

Table 4. Interrupt Mapping

PC INT #	IRQx	Vector (hex)	Name	Standard PC Use
2	NMI	8	*Shutdown*	Parity Error/IOCHK
8	IRQ0	20	Timer 0	same
9	IRQ1	24	Keyboard	same
A	IRQ2	28	Cascade Vector	same
B	IRQ3	2C	COM2	same
C	IRQ4	30	COM1	same
D	IRQ5	34	*PD6710, IRQ5*	LPT2
E	IRQ6	38	nu	FDC
F	IRQ7	3C	LPT1	same
70	IRQ8	1C0	RTC	same
71	IRQ9	1C4	*PD6710, IRQ9*	VGA
72	IRQ10	1C8	*Timer 1*	ISA
73	IRQ11	1CC	*Timer 2*	ISA

AP-513

Table 4. Interrupt Mapping (Continued)

PC INT#	IRQx	Vector (hex)	Name	PC Use
74	IRQ12	1D0	*DMA*	Mouse
75	IRQ13	1D4	*Mouse*	NPX
76	IRQ14	1D8	*IDE or PD6710, IRQ9*	HDC
77	IRQ15	1DC	WDT	ISA

7.0 CPLD OVERVIEW

An Altera FLEXlogic 780 CPLD is used to provide the support required by the Intel386 EX CPU and the peripheral devices. This CPLD is a modular design and provides a set of functions that are likely to be required in many common Intel386 EX CPU designs. Details of the design are included in the "CPLD Theory of Operation" section.

7.1 Reset Synchronization

The RESET signal that goes to the CPU is synchronized with CLK2 to allow the internal state machines to be in sync with the CPU.

7.2 Ready Generation

This logic returns RDY# to terminate any bus cycle that is not claimed by the Intel386 EX CPU (LBA# is inactive). This includes "Halt/Shutdown" cycles, SEB, DRAM and Flash Memory (below 1 MB) access.

- Halt/Shutdown and 16-bit SEB cycles are 8 wait states.
- 8-bit SEB cycles are 15 wait states
  — SEB accesses can be extended with the IOCHRDY signal.
- DRAM access vary from 0 to 3 wait states depending on the access type (i.e., page hit, miss, ...).
- Flash Memory accesses are 2 wait states

The generation of RDY# for all unclaimed accesses allows a simple interface to most ISA peripherals and eliminates the "hang" condition possible when software "polls" various addresses to determine the existence of a resource.

The CPLD drives RDY# any time LBA# is inactive, forcing it high for the cycle immediately after its sample low by the CPU. This allows a large pull-up resistor to be used to sustain the high level while not being driven.

7.3 Data Bus Transceiver Control

A disable signal for a data bus transceiver between the CPU and peripheral devices is generated to eliminate the possibility of a conflict on the data bus when the CPU transitions from a read to a write cycle. The transceiver also provides TTL to CMOS level translation for the Intel386 EX CPU. The transceiver is disabled for all T1, T1P and Ti cycles.

7.4 MNI Setting/Clearing

NMI is generated when a CPU "Shutdown" cycle is detected. The BIOS uses this to issue a CPU-only reset via Port 92. The CPLD includes the logic to reset the NMI by detecting an access to the Reset Vector (UCS#).

7.5 DRAM Control

The DRAM controller was designed to support two-way, page-mode interleaved access to the main memory. It provides access times from 0 to 3 wait states depending on the address sequence from the CPU. The DRAM interface was designed to support a single-sided 256K x 32, 1M x 32 or 4M x 32 symmetric SIMM (equal number of rows and columns) configured as two banks, 16-bits wide (2 RAS, 4 CAS and 1 WE input).

7.6 Flash Memory/EPROM Control

FLASHCS# is generated any cycle where either UCS# or GCS6# is detected and FLSHWE# is generated for write cycles where either UCS# or GCS6# is active. All write access to Flash Memory must be word-wide on even byte boundaries. The V_{PP} programming voltage for the Flash Memory is controlled by a jumper.

AP-513

7.7 SEB Interface

The CPLD generates BALE, MEMR#, MEMW#, IOR#, IOW# and responds to MEMSC16#, IOCS16# and IOCHRDY as required by the external peripheral devices.

8.0 THEORY OF OPERATION

This discussion is limited to the description of the Altera FLEXlogic 780 CPLD and its interface to the other components. For detailed descriptions of the other individual devices, please refer to the appropriate vendor's documentation.

8.1 Pin Definition

Table 5 shows the pin definitions.

Table 5. Pin Definitions

Inputs	
CLK2	2x Input Clock Same As Input to the Intel386™ EX CPU
ADS#	Address Status
W/R#	Write/Read
M/IO#	Memo/IO
D/C#	Data/Command
BHE#	High Byte Enable
BLE#	Low Byte Enable
A[23:10,1]	CPU Address Bus Used for Row Address Compare and Misc. Decodes
UCS#	Upper Chip Select (FLASH at the Top of the Address Space)
GCS6#	General Chip Select 6 (FLASH below 1 MB)
GCS5#	General Chip Select 5 (DRAM 1,4 or 16 MB)
GCS4#	General Chip Select 4 (IDE)
GCS3#	General Chip Select 5 (IDE)
GCS2#	General Chip Select 2 (Partial decode for I/O 60–61, 64–65)
GCS1#	General Chip Select 1 (RTC)
LBA#	Intel386 EX CPU Local Bus Access
PWRGD	Power Good Used to Generate a RESET
SEB Inputs	
IOCHRDY	Used to Extend SEB Cycles
IOCS16#	Indicates a 16-bit SEB I/O Device Is Being Accessed
MEMCS16#	Indicates a 16-bit SEB Memory Device Is Being Accessed
Outputs to the CPU	
RESET	RESET—Synchronized with CLK2, Used to Phase the State Machines
RDY#	READY I/O

AP-513

Table 5. Pin Definitions (Continued)

Outputs to the CPU (Continued)	
NA#	Next Address—Used to Request Pipelining for All DRAM Accesses
BS8#	Bus Size Eight—Used to Indicate an External 8-bit Device Is Being Accessed
NMI	Non Maskable Interrupt—Generated for CPU Shutdown Cycles
Outputs to DRAM	
RASA#	Row Address Strobe to the DRAM Bank A
RASB#	Row Address Strobe to the DRAM Bank B
ROW_SEL#	Enables the ROW Address Register to the DRAM Address Bus
COL_SEL#	Enables the COLUMN Address Register to the DRAM Address Bus
MALE#	Rising Edge Clocks the CPU Address into the ROW/COLUMN Register
CASAH#	Column Address Strobe to the DRAM Bank A, High Byte
CASAL#	Column Address Strobe to the DRAM Bank A, Low Byte
CASBH#	Column Address Strobe to the DRAM Bank B, High Byte
CASBL#	Column Address Strobe to the DRAM Bank B, Low Byte
WE#	Write Enable to Both DRAM Banks
Outputs to Flash Memory	
FLSHCS#	Flash Memory Chip Enable
FLSHWE#	Flash Memory Write Enable
FLSHA18	Most Significant Address Bit to the FLASH
SEB and Misc Outputs	
IOR#	SEB I/O Read Strobe
IOW#	SEB I/O Write Strobe
MEMR#	SEB Memo Read Strobe
MEMW#	SEB Memo Write Strobe
BALE	Address Latch Signal
RTC_AS	Address Strobe to the RTC (IOW to 70h)
RTC_DS	Data Strobe to the RTC (IOR or IOW to 71h)
IDE_ENH#	Enable to the IDE High Byte Data Transceiver
IDE_ENL#	Enable to the IDE Low Byte Data Transceiver
DATA_DE	Disable for Data Bus Transceivers
REFRESH#	Reserved
KBD_CS#	Chip Select to the i82C42PC.

AP-513

8.2 State Machines

Three state machines make up the core of the CPLD:

- The **Bus Tracker** uses ADS# and RDY# to follow the Intel386 EX CPU bus through its various T-states.
- The **DRAM** state machine keeps track of DRAM access states and is used to generate the DRAM control signals and RDY# for DRAM accesses.
- The **SEB** state machine generates various cycles to the external peripherals.

8.3 Bus Tracker Description

Figure 5 shows the bus tracker.

All transitions of the state machine are synchronized with the CPU's internal 1x clock.

This state machine is used to start the SEB state machine, generate the Flash Memory chip select and to detect CPU "shutdown" cycles in order to generate an NMI.

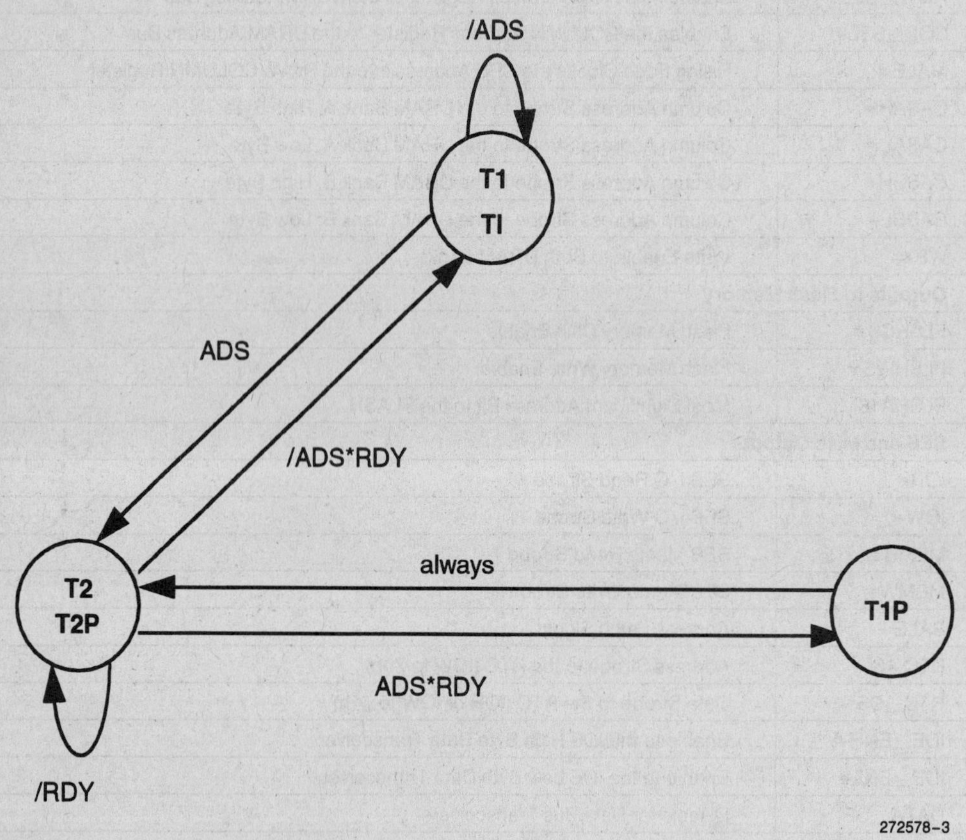

NOTES:
1. The system resets to the T1Ti state waiting for the first access indicated by assertion of ADS.
2. It remains in this state until RDY is asserted.
3. It transitions to T1 if ADS is inactive (non-pipeline) or to T1P if ADS is active (pipeline).

Figure 5. Bus Tracker

AP-513

8.4 SEB Description

Figure 6 shows the SEB state machine.

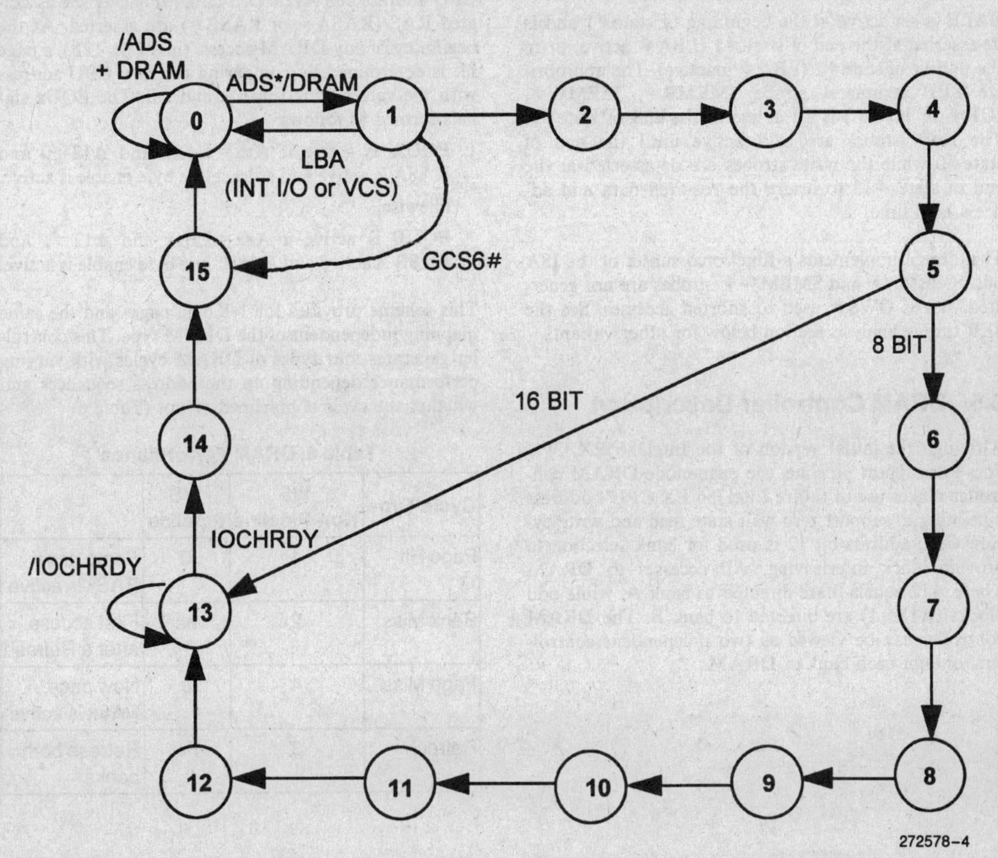

NOTES:
1. A transition from state #0 to state #1 occurs at the end of any T1 or T1P that is not directed to DRAM.
2. LBA# is checked at the end of state #1 to identify internal Intel386 EX CPU I/O accesses and VCS accesses (the Intel386 EX CPU generates the RDY) and returns the state machine to state #0 to await the next bus cycle. Access to flash memory with GCS6# sends the state machine to state #15, providing 2 Wait States. All other cycles are directed to the SEB.
3. In state #5, IOSC16# or MEMCS16# is sampled to determine whether the access is to an 8- or 16-bit device to adjust the wait states.
4. At state #13, IOCHRDY is sampled to allow the accessed device to extend the cycle.
5. RDY# is set active at the end of state #15 for one T-state.

Figure 6. SEB State Machine

AP-513

The dynamic bus sizing capability of the Intel386 EX CPU, via the BS8# signal, is used to provide the 16 bit to 8 bit conversion cycles when an 8 bit device is accessed with a "word" bus cycle.

BALE is set active at the beginning of state #1 and is de-asserted at the end of state #1 (LBA# active) or in the middle of state #2 (LBA# inactive). The appropriate SEB command strobe (MEMR#, MEMW#, IOR# or IOW#) is set active at the end of state #2. The read strobes are held active until the end of state #0 while the write strobes are de-asserted at the end of state #15 to insure the required data and address hold time.

This design implements a functional subset of the ISA bus. SMEMR# and SMEMW# strobes are not generated, nor is OWS# used to shorten accesses. See the SEB timing analysis section below for other variants.

8.5 DRAM Controller Description

Although the initial version of the Intel386 EX CPU does not support pipeline, the page-mode DRAM controller makes use of future Intel386 EX CPU's address pipelining to support zero wait state read and write cycles. CPU address bit 12 is used for bank selection to provide block interleaving. All accesses to DRAM where A12 equals 0 are directed to bank A, while odd blocks (A12=1) are directed to bank B. The DRAM controller can be viewed as two independent controllers, one for each bank of DRAM.

The actual implementation uses a single state machine and two row address registers, one associated with DRAM bank A (LA reg) and the other with DRAM bank B (LB reg). The LA and LB registers save the CPU address bits A[23:13, 11:10] whenever the associated RAS (RASA# or RASB#) are asserted. At the beginning of any DRAM access, (in T1 or T2P), a page hit is determined by comparing the new CPU address with the values stored in LA and LB. The EQUx signals formed as follows:

EQUA is active if Axx=LAxx and A12=0 and RASA is active and at least one byte enable is active.

likewise,

EQUB is active if Axx=LBxx and A12=1 and RASB is active and at least one byte enable is active.

This scheme provides for 1 Kbyte pages and the same mapping independent of the DRAM type. This controller generates four types of DRAM cycles with varying performance depending on the address sequences and whether the cycle is pipelined or not (Table 6).

Table 6. DRAM Performance

Cycle Type	WS Non-Pipeline	WS Pipeline	
Page Hit	1	0	Same page, RASx is active
Bank Miss	2	na	First access after a Refresh
Page Miss	4	3	New page, RASx is active
Refresh	3	na	Refresh both banks

AP-513

Figure 7 details the DRAM controller state machine.

Figure 7. DRAM Controller State Machine

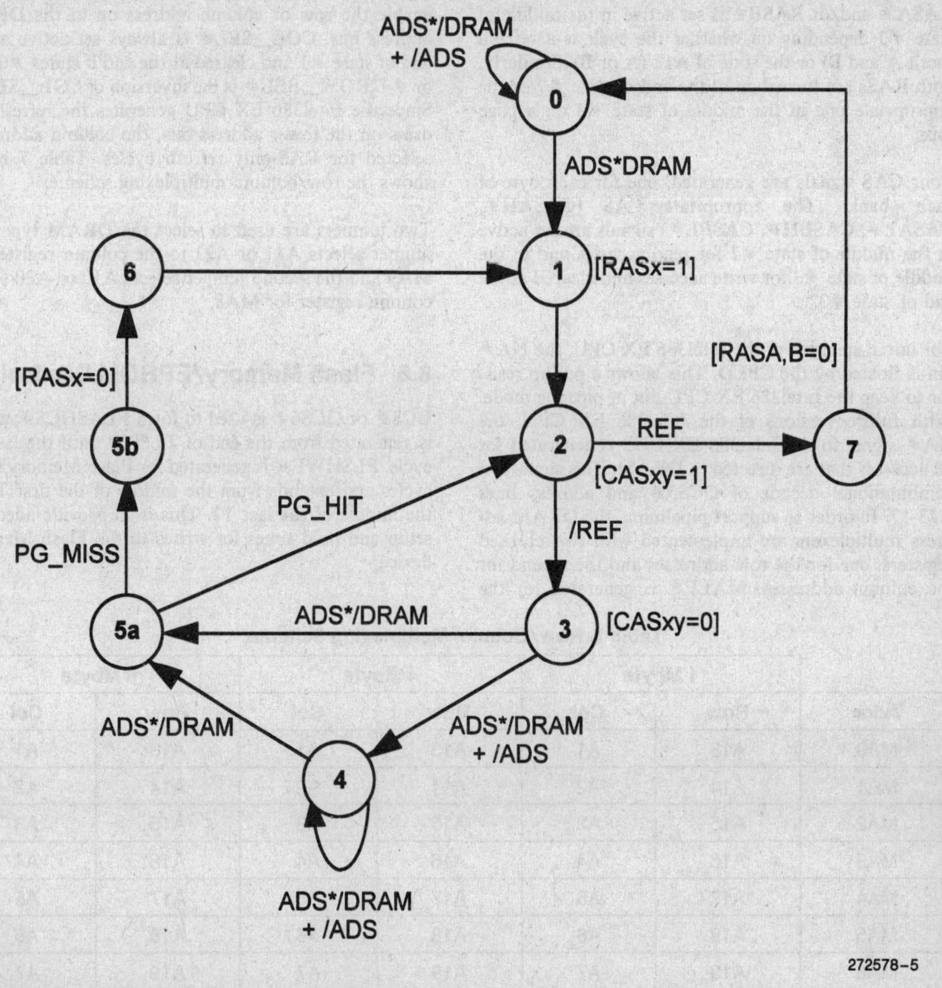

NOTES:
1. State #0 is entered from RESET or after a refresh cycle.
2. When a DRAM access is detected, the state machine advances to state #1 and onto state #2.
3. BHE and BLE are tested to determine if a refresh cycle or a DRAM read/write is to be done.
4. If the cycle is a refresh, the state machine goes through to state #7 and back to #0.
5. If it is a read/write cycle it goes to where a check is made for:
   a. pipeline DRAM access (to #5a)
   b. non-pipeline/non-DRAM cycle (to #4).
6. In state #5a, a check is made for:
   a. a page hit (to #2)
   b. a page miss (to #5b and #6).

AP-513

All the DRAM control signals are generated by this state machine and the current cycle type.

RASA# and/or RASB# is set active in the middle of state #1 depending on whether the cycle is a refresh (both A and B) or the state of A12 (A or B). Similarly, both RASs are turned on at the end of state #7 or the appropriate one in the middle of state #5 on a page miss.

Four CAS signals are generated, one for each byte of each bank. The appropriate CAS (CASAH#, CASAL#, CASBH#, CASBL#) signals are set active in the middle of state #2 for read accesses and in the middle of state #3 for write accesses and cleared at the end of state #3.

For initial stepping of the Intel386 EX CPU, the NA# pin is floated by the CPLD. This allows a pullup resistor to keep the Intel386 EX CPU out of pipeline mode. With future versions of the Intel386 EX CPU, the NA# signal to the Intel386 EX CPU is generated for all accesses that are directed to DRAM. This signal is a combinational decode of GCS5# and address lines A23-17. In order to support pipelining, the DRAM address multiplexers are implemented with two clocked registers, one for the row addresses and the second for the column addresses. MALE# is generated for the second phase of states #0, #3 and #4 to clock the addresses into both registers. Two mutually exclusive signals, ROW_SEL# and COL_SEL#, are used to enable the row or column address on to the DRAM address bus. COL_SEL# is always set active at the end of state #1 and cleared at the end if states #0, #5 or #7. ROW_SEL# is the inversion of COL_SEL#. Since the Intel386 EX CPU generates the refresh address on the lower address bits, the column address is selected for RAS-only refresh cycles. Table 7 below shows the row/column multiplexing scheme.

Two jumpers are used to select the DRAM type: one jumper selects A11 or A23 to the column register for MA9 and the second jumper selects A10 or A20 to the column register for MA8.

8.6 Flash Memory/EPROM Control

UCS# or GCS6# is used to form FLASHCS# which is generated from the end of T1/T1P until the last T2 cycle. FLSHWE# is generated for Flash Memory write cycles and extends from the middle of the first T2 to the middle of the last T2. This is to provide adequate setup and hold times for writes to the Flash Memory device.

Table 7. Row/Column Multiplexing Scheme

Addr	1 Mbyte		4 Mbyte		8 Mbyte	
	Row	Col	Row	Col	Row	Col
MA0	A13	A1	A13	A1	A13	A1
MA1	A14	A2	A14	A2	A14	A2
MA2	A15	A3	A15	A3	A15	A3
MA3	A16	A4	A16	A4	A16	A4
MA4	A17	A5	A17	A5	A17	A5
MA5	A18	A6	A18	A6	A18	A6
MA6	A19	A7	A19	A7	A19	A7
MA7	A10	A8	A20	A8	A20	A8
MA8	A11	A9	A11	A9	A23	A9
MA9	x	x	A21	A10	A21	A10
MA10	x	x	x	x	A22	A11

AP-513

9.0 FUNCTIONAL TIMING DIAGRAMS

The following diagrams show some typical bus cycle sequences to clarify the operation of the state machines described above.

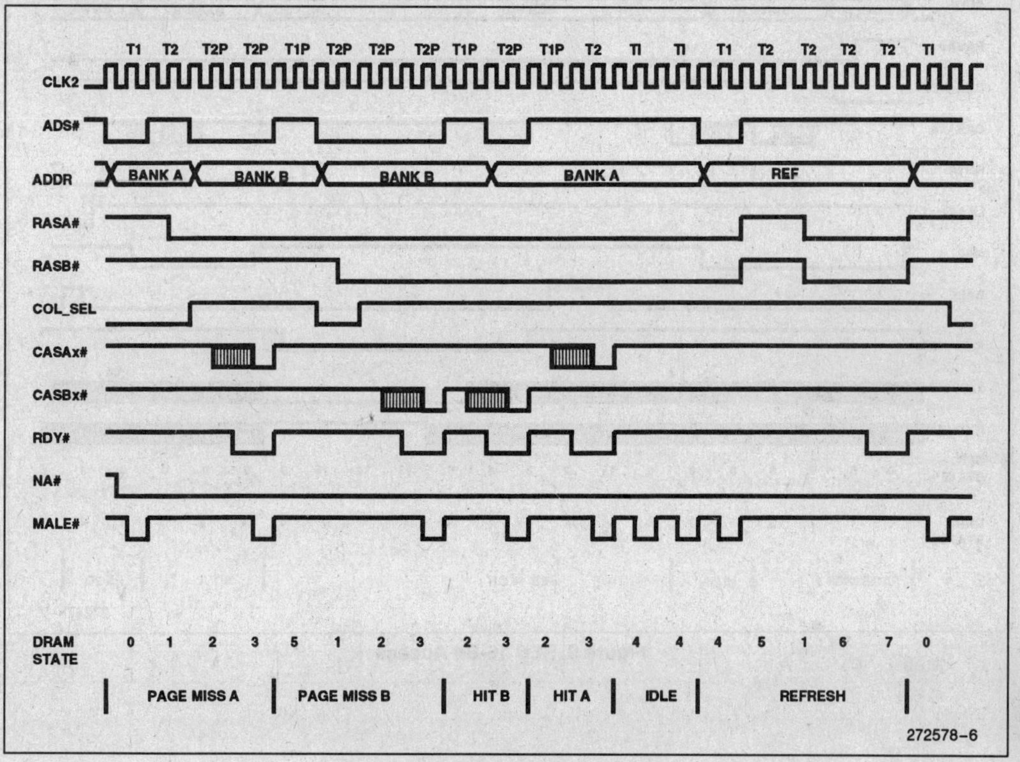

Figure 8. Typical DRAM Accesses

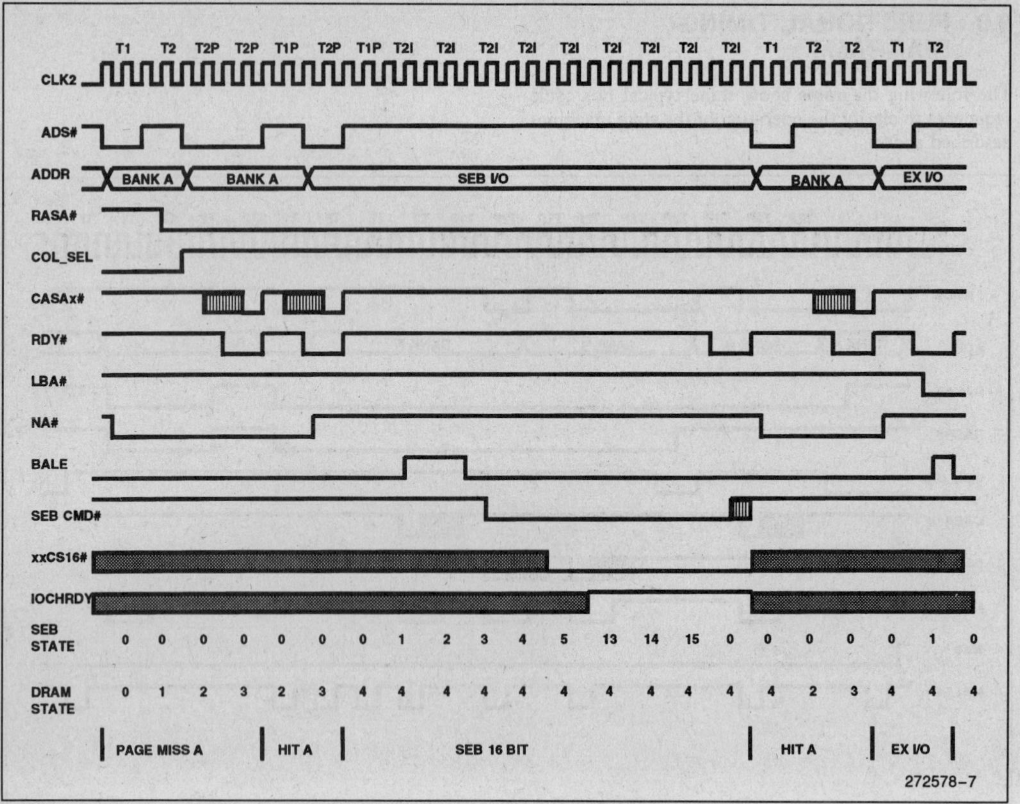

Figure 9. SEB 16-Bit Access

AP-513

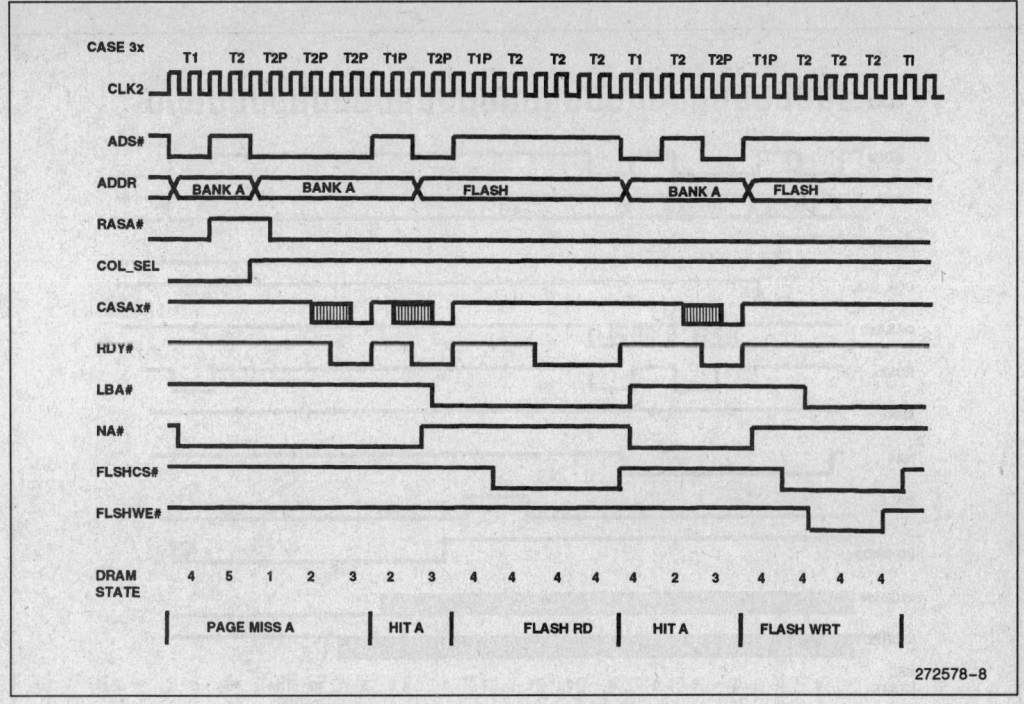

Figure 10. Flash Memory Read/Write Accesses

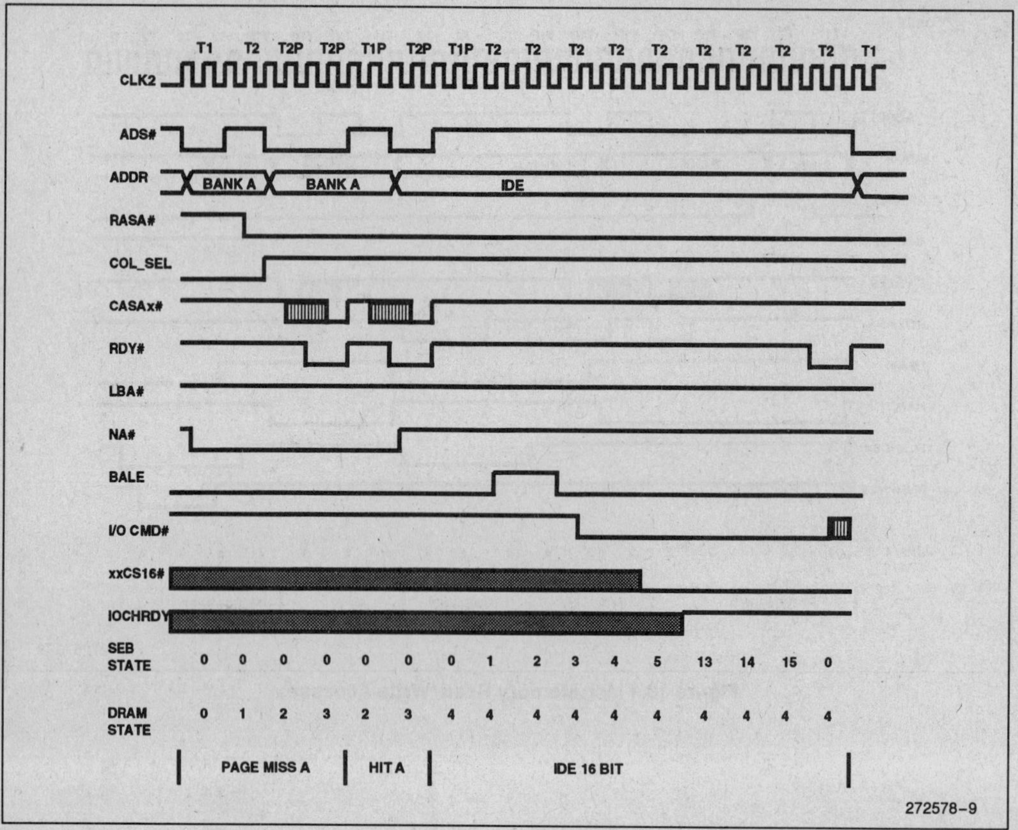

AP-513

Figure 11. IDE Access

AP-513

10.0 TIMING ANALYSIS

The sections below illustrate the system AC timing parameters calculated for this design.

10.1 DRAM Timing

Tables 8 and 9 show the AC timings of the DRAM interface. Shown are the worst case timings for various cycle types including page and non-page, read and write accesses assuming 25 MHz operations with 70 ns DRAMs.

Table 8. DRAM Access Parameters

Symbol	Description	Min (ns)	Max (ns)
Tc	CLK2 Period	20	
TdRAS	CLK2 to RAS# Delay	3	8
TdCAS	CLK2 to CAS# Delay	3	8
TdMALE	CLK2 to MALE# DELAY	3	8
TdMUX	CLK2 to Mux Control	3	8
TdDEN	CLK2 to Data Transceiver Control	3	8
TdWE	CLK2 to WE	3	8
TdMA	MAxx Mux Delay (ACT374)	3	13
TdXD	Data Transceiver A>B (ACT245)	1	13
Tsu	Read Data to CLK2 ↑ Setup (CPU)	7	
TdWD	Write Data Turn On (CPU)	7	30
TdCA	CLK2 to Axx Valid (CPU)	4	28

Table 9. DRAM AC Characteristics vs DRAM Specifications

Symbol	Description	Calc	DRAM Specs	Margin
Trac	Access from RAS#	72	70	2
Tras	RAS# Pulse Width	100	70	30
Trp	RAS# Precharge	60	50	10
Trc1	Read/Write Cycle—Page Miss	160	130	30
Trc2	Read/Write Cycle—Page Hit	80	40	40
Trcd	RAS# to CAS# Delay	35	25	10
TcasR	CAS# Pulse Width—Read	60	20	40
TcasW	CAS# Pulse Width—Write	20	20	0
Tcasp1	CAS# Precharge—Page Miss	100	10	90
Tcasp2	CAS# Precharge—Page Hit	20	10	10
Twcs1	Write Command Setup—Page Miss	95	0	95

AP-513

Table 9. DRAM AC Characteristics vs DRAM Specifications (Continued)

Symbol	Description	Calc	DRAM Specs	Margin
Twcs2	Write Command Setup—Page Hit	55	0	55
Twch	Write Command Hold	15	15	0
Tasr	Row Address Setup	22	0	22
Trah	Row Address Hold	18	10	8
Tasc1	Column Address Setup—Page Miss	2	0	2
Tasc2	Column Address Setup—Page Hit	2	0	2
Tcah	Column Address Hold	18	15	3
Tds1	Write Data Setup—Page Miss	80	0	80
Tds2	Write Data Setup—Page Hit	0	0	0
Tdh	Write Data Hold	20	15	5
Tcac1	Access from CAS#—Read	32	20	12
Tca1	Access from Col. Addr—Page Miss	39	35	4
Tca2	Access from Col. Addr—Page Hit	65	35	30

10.2 Flash Memory Timing

Tables 10 and 11 show the AC timings of the Flash Memory ROM interface programmed for 2 wait states at 25 MHz.

Table 10. Flash Memory Access Parameters

Symbol	Description	Min (ns)	Max (ns)
Tc	CLK2 Period	20	
TdCS	CLK2 to FLSHCS# Delay	3	8
TdWE	CLK2 to FLSHWE# Delay	3	8
TdDEN	CLK2 to Data Transceiver Control	3	8
TdD	Data Transceiver A>B (ACT245)	1	13
Tdsu	Read Data to CLK2 ↑ Setup (CPU)	7	
TdWD	Write Data Turn On (CPU)	7	30
TdCA	CLK2 to Axx Valid (CPU)	4	28
TdRD	CLK2 to RD# Valid (CPU)	4	24

AP-513

Table 11. Flash Memory AC Characteristics vs Flash Memory Specifications

Symbol	Description	Calc	FLASH Specs	Margin
Tavqv	Read Data from Address	112	80	32
Telqv	Read Data from CE#	92	80	12
Tglqv	Read Data from OE#	96	40	56
Tcs	CE# Setup to WE#	25	0	25
Tavwh	Address Setup to WE# ↑	75	50	25
Tdvwh	Write Data Setup to WE# ↑	60	60	0
Twp	WE# Pulse Width	80	50	30
Tdh	Write Data Hold to WE# ↑	13	0	13
Tah	Address Hold to WE# ↑	16	10	6

10.3 Synchronous Expansion Bus (SEB)

The SEB is intended to allow the selected set of peripherals to be used without implementing an entire bus ISA bus. It is an asynchronous bus from the peripherals point of view but is generated synchronous to the Intel386 EX CPU. The bus includes:

- Intel386 EX CPU address line A25–A1, BHE# and BLE#
- Buffered data bus D15–0
- Command strobes, IOR#, IOW#, MEMR#, MEMW#, BALE
- AS and DS for RTC
- Control input IOCHRDY, MEMCS16#, IOCS16#

Table 12 shows the AC parameters and how they relate to the 82C14, 82365SL and IDE interfaces. ISA specifications are listed for reference.

Table 12. SEB Access Parameters

Symbol	Description	Min	Max
Tc	CLK2 Period	20	
TdPLD	CLK2 to FPGA Output	3	8
TsuPLD	FPGA Input to CLK2 Setup	7	
TdD	Data Transceiver A>B (ACT11245)	1	13
TdSU	Read Data to CLK2 ↑ Setup (CPU)	7	
TdWD	Write Data Turn On (CPU)	7	30
TdCA	CLK2 to Axx Valid (CPU)	4	28

AP-513

Table 13. SEB AC Characteristics vs Peripheral Specifications

8 ws/16 bit 15 ws/8 bit		SEB	GD5424		PD6710		IDE Mode 2		82542		051287A	
			SPECS	Margin	SPECS	Margin	SPECS	Margin	SPECS	Margin	SPECS	Margin
TC1	Axx setup to BALE (low)	95	20		30	65						
TC2	Axx setup to CMD# (low)	115	5	110					0	115	20	95
TC3	Axx hold from CMD# (high)—write cycles	16	0	16	0	16			0	16	0	16
TC4	Write data setup to CMD# (low)—(16 bit)	80					30	50				
TC4a	Write data setup to CMD# (high)—(16 bit)	400	5	395	120	280						
TC5	Write data setup to CMD# (low)—(8 bit)	20					20	0				
TC5a	Write data setup to CMD# (high)—(8 bit)	620	5	615	120	500			130	490	100	520
TC6	CMD# (high) to next BALE (high)	49										
TC7	Write data hold from CMD# (high)	44	0	44	0	44	15	29	0	44	0	44
TC8	Read data access from CMD# (low)—(16 bit)	232	60	172			80	152				
TC9	Read data access from CMD# (low)—(8 bit)	472	60	412	130	342	270	202	130	342	120	352
TC10	BALE pulse width	35	20	15								
TC11	CMD# pulse width (16 bit)	260	70	190			100	160				
TC12	CMD# pulse width (8 bit)	500	70	430	140	360	290	210	160	100	125	375
TC13	CMD# inactive*	75	60	15	100	−25					150	−75
TC14	xxCS16# from Axx	205	30	175	40	165						
TC15	IOCHRDY from CMD# (low)—(16 bit)	133	28	105	40	93						
TC16	IOCHRDY from CMD# (low)—(8 bit)	373	28	345	40	333						
TC17	CMD# hold from IOCHRDY (write)	100										
TC18	CMD# hold from IOCHRDY (read)	120										
TC19	Read/Write cycle time*	335	130	205	280	55	240	95			385	−50

* Controlled by S/W

AP-513

11.0 SYSTEM BIOS

The System BIOS is similar to a standard PC BIOS with support for the RTC, PS/2 style mouse/keyboard and the integrated VGA controller. Additional support is required as follows:

- Configuring the Intel386 EX CPU, GD5424 and the PD6710.
- NMI handling to perform a CPU-only reset in case of a Shutdown.
- Parallel Port support
- Flash Memory ROM utilities (jumper on the keyboard controller P14 pin selects normal boot or flash utility)

11.1 Intel386™ EX CPU Configuration

The following table shows the values of the Intel386 EX CPU specific configuration registers:

Table 14. Intel386™ EX CPU Configuration Register Values

Address (hex)	Register	High Byte (hex)	Low Byte (hex)	Description
0022	I/O Remap	—	04	SIO0-1 and DMA into Exp. I/O
F400	GCS0 Low Addr	00	00	Disabled
F402	GCS0 High Addr	00	00	
F404	GCS0 Low Mask	00	00	
F406	GCS0 High Mask	00	00	
F408	GCS1 Low Addr	80	80	0060-0061, 64-65, I/O8
F40A	GCS1 High Addr	00	01	
F40C	GCS1 Low Mask	14	01	
F40E	GCS1 High Mask	00	00	
F410	GCS2 Low Addr	C0	80	0070-0071, I/O8
F412	GCS2 High Addr	00	01	
F414	GCS2 Low Mask	04	01	
F416	GCS2 High Mask	00	00	
F418	GCS3 Low Addr	D8	80	03F6-03F7, I/O8
F41A	GCS3 High Addr	04	0F	
F41C	GCS3 Low Mask	00	01	
F41E	GCS3 High Mask	00	00	
F420	GCS4 Low Addr	C2	80	01F0-01F7, I/O16
F422	GCS4 High Addr	00	07	
F424	GCS4 Low Mask	1C	01	
F426	GCS4 High Mask	00	00	
F428	GCS5 Low Addr	03	80	0000000-0XFFFFF, MEM
F42A	GCS5 High Addr	00	00	
F42C	GCS5 Low Mask	FC	01	

AP-513

Table 14. Intel386™ EX CPU Configuration Register Values (Continued)

Address (hex)	Register	High Byte (hex)	Low Byte (hex)	Description
F42E	GCS5 High Mask	00	0F	1 MB
			3F	4 MB
			FF	16 MB
F430	GCS6 Low Addr	03	80	00E0000–00FFFFF, MEM
F432	GCS6 High Addr	00	0E	
F434	GCS6 Low Mask	FC	01	
F436	GCS6 High Mask	00	01	
F438	UCS Low Addr	03	02	3FE0000–3FFFFFF, MEM, 2WS
F43A	UCS High Addr	03	F8	
F43C	UCS Low Mask	F8	01	
F43E	UCS High Mask	00	07	
F480	SSIO T. Buffer	00	00	Disabled
F482	SSIO R. Buffer	00	00	
F484	SSIO Baud	—	00	
F486	SSIO CON1	—	C0	
F488	SSIO CON2	—	00	
F48A	SSIO CTRL	—	00	
F4A0	REF Base Addr	00	00	Base Addr = 0
F4A2	REF CIR	01	86	~15.6 μs @ 25 MHz
F4A4	REF Ctrl	80	00	Enabled
F4A6	REF Addr	0F	FF	A11–1
F4C0	WDT Reload High	01	00	~670 ms @ 25 MHz
F4C2	WDT Reload Low	00	00	~670 ms @ 25 MHz
F4C4	WDT Cntr High	Read Only	Read Only	
F4C6	WDT Cntr High	Read Only	Read Only	
F4C8	WDT Clr	Read Only	Read Only	LOCKOUT Seq. Reg.
F4CA	WDT Status	—	Read Only	
F4F8	SIO 0	—	—	Remapped to COM1 (3F8–F)
F4FA	SIO 0	—	—	Remapped to COM1 (3F8–F)
F4FC	SIO 0	—	—	Remapped to COM1 (3F8–F)
F4FE	SIO 0	—	—	Remapped to COM1 (3F8–F)
F800	CLK Ctrl	—	00	nu
F802	PSCLK Scaler	00	13	1.190 MHz @ 25 MHz

AP-513

Table 14. Intel386™ EX CPU Configuration Register Values (Continued)

Address (hex)	Register	High Byte (hex)	Low Byte (hex)	Description
F820	Pin Cfg 0	—	00	Port 1x is LPT Data
F822	Pin Cfg 1	—	7E	Port 2[7], Txd, Rxd and GCS4–1, 2[0]
F824	Pin Cfg 2	—	0C	Port 3[7–4], INT1–0, 3[1–0]
F826	Pin Cfg 3	—	1F	GCS6, NPX, GCS5 and SIO1
F830	DMA Cfg	—	88	DMA's Disabled
F832	INT Cfg	—	0F	CAS Disabled, INT7–4
F834	TMR Cfg	—	00	PSCLKs
F836	SIO Cfg	—	47	COM1 (2 pin), SERCLK = 12.5 MHz
F860	P1 Pin	—	Read Only	
F862	P1 LTC	—	XX	LPT Data Out
F864	P1 Dir	—	00	PI[7–0] = Out
F866	nu	—	—	
F868	P2 Pin	—	Read Only	
F86A	P2 LTC	—	00	LPTa, INIT# = 0
F86C	P2 Dir	—	7F	P2[7] = Out
F86E	nu	—	—	
F870	P3 Pin	—	Read Only	
FB72	P3 LTC	—	03	LPTb, ADFX#, STB# = 1
F874	P3 Dir	—	FC	P3[7–4] = In, [1–0] = Out
F8F8	SIO 1	—	—	Remapped to COM2 (2F8–F)
F8FA	SIO 1	—	—	Remapped to COM2 (2F8–F)
F8FC	SIO 1	—	—	Remapped to COM2 (2F8–F)
F8FE	SIO 1	—	-	Remapped to COM2 (2F8–F)

6

AP-513

11.2 NMI Handler

The BIOS should generate a CPU-only reset via Port 92 when an NMI interrupt is detected in order to enable user generated shutdown cycles to cause a reset (PC compatibility).

11.3 Parallel Port

The BIOS supports INT 17h—PRINTER_IO by re-directing/re-shuffling the bits to the parallel I/O ports PI, P2 and P3 and described above.

11.4 Flash Memory Support

There is code in the boot block section of the Flash Memory that allows the contents of any of the parameter or main blocks to be dumps to a host PC or a binary image to be uploaded from the host PC and programmed in the Flash Memory.

The Boot block area of the Flash Memory should contain code to initialize the board and then check the jumper on P14 of the 82C42PC. If the jumper is on (bit equals 0) the code should vector to a Flash Memory programming utility otherwise it will go to the normal PC style POST and boot routines.

The Flash Memory programming utility should provide the capability to attach the POS Terminal's two COM ports to two COM of a host PC running a companion application. One COM port is used for ASCII terminal-like communication to the screen and keyboard of the host while the second COM port provides the data path to upload or download the Flash Memory.

12.0 VGA BIOS

The VGA controller uses the standard VGA BIOS and drives provided by Cirrus Logic.

13.0 CONNECTORS/JUMPERS

JP1		iFX780 V_{PP}
Off		V_{PP} = nc
On		V_{PP} = 12V
JP2	JP3	SIMM Memory Size
1–2	1–2	1 MB
2–3	1–2	4 MB
2–3	2–3	16 MB
JP4		COM1 — 2 wire (Rxd, Txd)
JP5		COM2 — full RS232
JP6		LPTx
JP7		iFX780 Programming Connection
JP8		IDE Disk Connector
JP9		Flash V_{PP}
Off		V_{PP} = 0V
On		V_{PP} = 12V
JP10		BIOS Boot Options
Off		TBD
On		TBD
J1		PS/2 Mouse
J2		PS/2 Keyboard
J4		PCMCIA Slot
J6		VGA Connector

14.0 SCHEMATICS

The latest schematics are available electronically in ORCAD format or in printable Encapsulated Postscript format from the factory.

AP-513

15.0 SUMMARY

The POS reference design has been discussed regarding both hardware and software implementation details. As a DOS-compatible POS terminal, users can easily develop application software on any PC with off the shelf tools. The Intel386 EX CPU process is a highly-integrated embedded CPU with the key peripheral components onboard to build a cost effective yet compact system for POS applications. Some of the key technologies such as Intel boot block Flash Memory, complex PLD use, PCMCIA slot and power management have been discussed. POS terminal architectures and market are well served by embedded Intel architecture processors that can provide for low-cost development, fast time to market, proven support infrastructure, and long life cycles.

The POS has been built, debugged, and tested as a working design.

AP-514

APPLICATION NOTE

Embedded Intel386™ EX Processor Hamilton Hallmark Handheld Terminal (H4T) Reference Design

October 1994

Order Number: 272579-001

EMBEDDED Intel386™ EX PROCESSOR
HAMILTON HALLMARK HANDHELD TERMINAL (H4T)
REFERENCE DESIGN

CONTENTS	PAGE
1.0 INTRODUCTION	6-148
2.0 PRODUCT DESCRIPTION	6-148
3.0 FUNCTIONAL DESCRIPTION OF THE Intel386™ EX MICROPROCESSOR	6-149
3.1 Clock Generation and Power Management Unit	6-150
3.2 Chip Select Unit	6-150
3.3 Interrupt Control Unit	6-150
3.4 Timer/Counter Unit	6-150
3.5 Watchdog Timer Unit	6-151
3.6 Asynchronous Serial I/O Unit	6-151
3.7 Synchronous Serial I/O Unit	6-151
3.8 Parallel I/O Unit	6-151
3.9 DMA and Bus Arbiter Unit	6-151
3.10 Refresh Control Unit	6-152
3.11 JTAG Boundary Scan Unit	6-152
4.0 PARTS SELECTION	6-152
4.1 CPU	6-152
4.2 Memory	6-152
4.3 Data Buffers	6-153
4.4 User Interfaces and Additional Parts	6-153
5.0 POWER SUPPLY CONSIDERATIONS	6-153

CONTENTS	PAGE
6.0 CPLD FUNCTIONALITY	6-154
6.1 Keypad Controller Logic	6-155
6.2 LCD Display Controller	6-155
6.3 PCMCIA Interface	6-158
6.4 Additional Logic	6-158
7.0 PERIPHERALS	6-158
7.1 Barcode Wand Interface	6-158
7.2 RF Module	6-159
8.0 SOFTWARE CONSIDERATIONS	6-159
8.1 I/O Space Configuration	6-160
8.2 Global Chip Select Register Configuration	6-161
8.3 Chip Select Initialization	6-162
8.4 Port Pin Activation	6-163
8.5 Leaving Expanded I/O Space	6-163
8.6 Stack Initialization	6-163
8.7 Serial Port Configuration	6-164
9.0 SUMMARY	6-166
10.0 REFERENCES	6-166
11.0 FILES AVAILABLE ON THE FLOPPY DISK IN THE H4T REFERENCE DESIGN KIT	6-166

AP-514

1.0 INTRODUCTION

The H4T, or Hamilton Hallmark HandHeld Terminal, Reference Design was developed as a working application to enable shorter design cycles by providing a proven platform as a starting point. This design has been built, debugged, and tested. The H4T was designed by Hamilton Hallmark (an Avnet company) with Intel support and highlights the features of the embedded Intel386™ EX processor and Intel Boot Block Flash Memory. The design can be used "as is" or as a building block to enhance a specific solution.

Handheld terminal applications are typically characterized by palm-sized portable devices for specific uses. These vertical applications include portable POS, dataloggers, barcode scanners, communicators, and organizers that are used in a variety of high utility environments, including retail, service, warehouses, inventory control, shipping, package delivery, manufacturing, hospitals, law enforcement, and many others. The Intel386 architecture is ideal to provide sufficient computing power and low-cost solutions for such hand-held terminals. In general, software applications for handheld terminals have become more and more standardized on a PC-like environment with operating systems such as DOS; these applications can readily be developed on any PC systems with off-the-shelf tools.

The Intel386 EX processor is a single-chip system utilizing an on-board static Intel386 CX processor core and a host of integrated peripherals, including DMA and interrupt controllers, serial and parallel ports, chip selects, timers/counters, JTAG, and power/system management features. Its 26-bit addressing provides a large 64 MB memory address space. The H4T reference design also incorporated a number of additional technologies which may be used as building blocks for a myriad of applications.

2.0 PRODUCT DESCRIPTION

The battery powered H4T reference design is DOS compatible and uses a standard PC-like BIOS. It features several products and technologies:
- Embedded Intel386 EX Processor
- Intel 4 Mb Boot Block Flash Memory
- Complex PLD
- PCMCIA Slot
- RF Wireless Communications
- Barcode Wand
- Power Management

The H4T has the following features:
- 5.0V design, can be adapted to 3.3V
- 4x20 character LCD display
- 5x6 keypad and interface
- 1 Mb SRAM, 64 Kb x 16
- 4 Mb Flash Memory, 256 Kb x 16
- 115 Kb/s RF link
- 4.5" x 6.5" x 2" (WxHxD) case size
- Powered by 6 AA-size NiCad batteries, 700 mAh, estimated 20 hrs typical use

The system block diagram is shown in Figure 1. It includes the Intel386 EX processor block, program storage memory, RAM, keypad, barcode input device, alpha numeric LCD display, PCMCIA interface and wireless RF link to a host computer. The device is handheld, battery operated and includes BIOS and embedded ROM-DOS with the PCMCIA slot acting as a solid state disk drive.

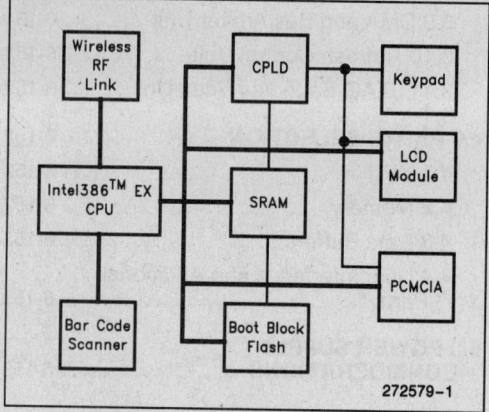

Figure 1. H4T Block Diagram

AP-514

3.0 FUNCTIONAL DESCRIPTION OF THE Intel386™ EX MICROPROCESSOR

The Intel386 EX microprocessor (see Figure 2) is a fully static, 32-bit processor optimized for embedded applications. It features low power and low voltage capabilities, integration of many commonly used DOS-type peripherals, and a 32-bit programming architecture compatible with the large software base of Intel386 processors. The following sections provide an overview of the integrated peripherals.

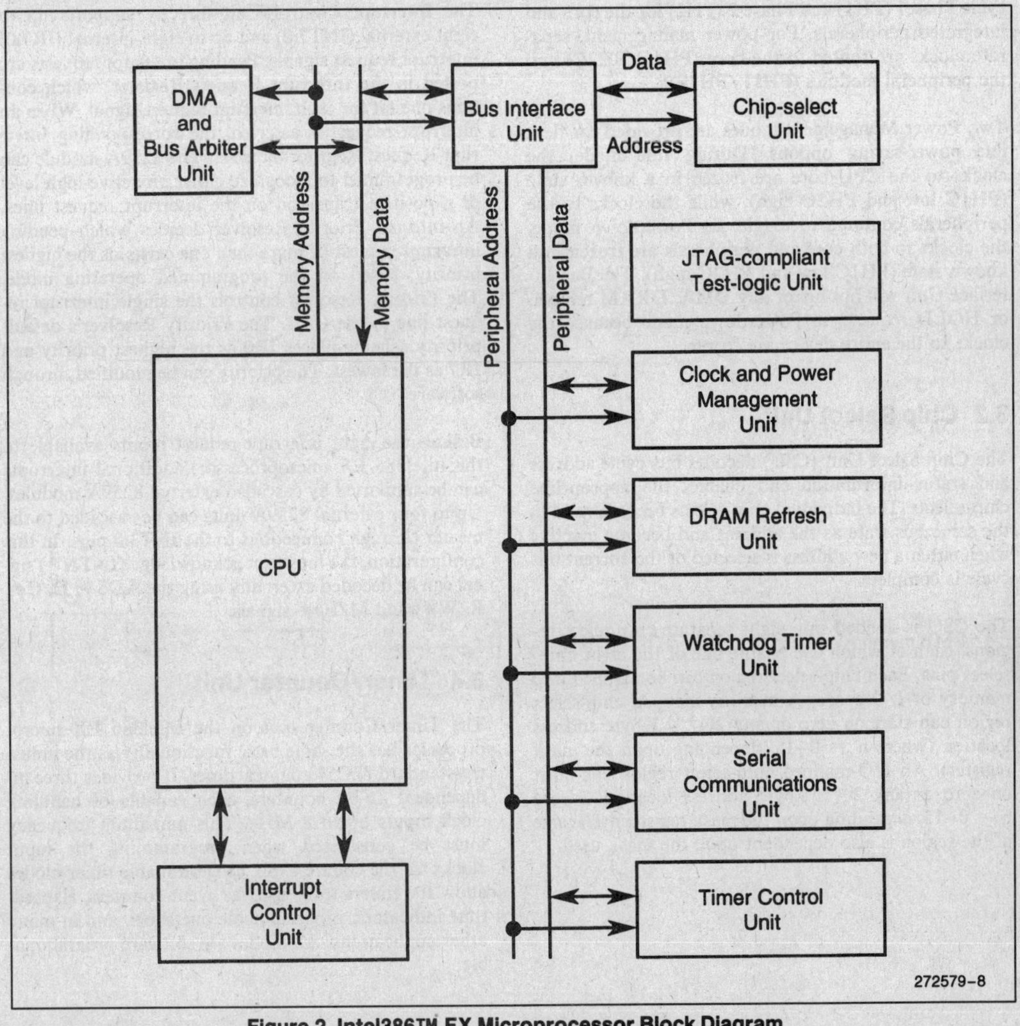

Figure 2. Intel386™ EX Microprocessor Block Diagram

AP-514

3.1 Clock Generation and Power Management Unit

The clock generation circuit includes a divide-by-two counter, a programmable divider for generating a prescaled clock (PSCLK) and Reset circuitry. The CLK2 input provides the fundamental timing for the chip. It is divided by two internally to generate a 50% duty cycle Phase1 (PH1) and Phase 2 (PH2) for the core and integrated peripherals. For power management, separate clocks are routed to the core (PH1C/PH2C) and the peripheral modules (PH1P/PH2P).

Two Power Management modes are provided for flexible power-saving options. During Idle mode, the clocks to the CPU core are frozen in a known state (PH1C low and PH2C high), while the clocks to the peripherals continue to toggle. In Powerdown mode, the clocks to both core and peripherals are frozen in a known state (PH1C low and PH2C high). The Bus Interface Unit will not honor any DMA, DRAM refresh, or HOLD requests in Powerdown mode because the clocks to the entire device are frozen.

3.2 Chip Select Unit

The Chip Select Unit (CSU) decodes bus cycle address and status information and enables the appropriate chip-selects. The individual chip-selects become valid in the same bus state as the address and become inactive when either a new address is selected or the current bus cycle is complete.

The CSU is divided into eight separate chip-select regions, each of which can enable one of the eight chip-select pins. Each chip-select region can be mapped into memory or I/O space. A memory-mapped chip-select region can start on zero or any $2^{(n+1)}$ Kbyte address location (where n = 0–15, depending upon the mask register). An I/O-mapped chip-select region can start on zero or any $2^{(n+1)}$ byte address location (where n = 0–15, depending upon the mask register). The size of the region is also dependent upon the mask used.

3.3 Interrupt Control Unit

The Intel386 EX microprocessor's Interrupt Control Unit (ICU) contains two 8259A modules connected in a cascade mode. The 8259A modules make up the heart of the ICU. These modules are similar to the industry-standard 8259A architecture.

The Interrupt Control Unit directly supports up to eight external (INT7:0) and up to eight internal (IR7:0) interrupt request signals. Pending interrupt requests are posted in the Interrupt Request Register, which contains one bit for each interrupt request signal. When an interrupt request is asserted, the corresponding Interrupt Request Register bit is set. The 8259A module can be programmed to recognize either an active-high level or a positive transition on the interrupt request lines. An internal Priority Resolver decides which pending interrupt request (if more than one exists) is the highest priority, based on the programmed operating mode. The Priority Resolver controls the single interrupt request line to the CPU. The Priority Resolver's default priority scheme places IR0 as the highest priority and IR7 as the lowest. The priority can be modified through software.

Besides the eight interrupt request inputs available to the Intel386 EX microprocessor, additional interrupts can be supported by cascaded external 8259A modules. Up to four external 8259A units can be cascaded to the master through connections to the INT3:0 pins. In this configuration, the interrupt acknowledge (INTA#) signal can be decoded externally using the ADS#, D/C#, R/W#, and M/IO# signals.

3.4 Timer/Counter Unit

The Timer/Counter unit on the Intel386 EX microprocessor has the same basic functionality as the industry-standard 82C54 counter/timer. It provides three independent 16-bit counters, each capable of handling clock inputs up to 8 MHz. This maximum frequency must be considered when programming the input clocks for the counters. Six programmable timer modes allow the timers to be used as event counters, elapsed-time indicators, programmable one-shots, and in many other applications. All modes are software programmable.

3.5 Watchdog Timer Unit

The Watchdog Timer (WDT) unit consists of a 32-bit down-counter that decrements every PH1P cycle, allowing up to 4.3 billion count intervals. The WDTOUT pin is driven high for sixteen CLK2 cycles when the down-counter reaches zero (the WDT times out). The WDTOUT signal can be used to reset the chip, to request an interrupt, or to indicate to the user that a ready-hang situation has occurred. The down-counter can also be updated with a user-defined 32-bit reload value under certain conditions. Alternatively, the WDT unit can be used as a bus monitor or as a general-purpose timer.

3.6 Asynchronous Serial I/O Unit

The Intel386 EX microprocessor's asynchronous serial I/O (SIO) unit is a Universal Asynchronous Receiver/Transmitter (UART). Functionally, it is equivalent to the National Semiconductor NS16450 and INS8250. The Intel386 EX microprocessor contains two asynchronous serial channels.

The SIO unit converts serial data characters received from a peripheral device or modem to parallel data and converts parallel data characters received from the CPU to serial data. The CPU can read the status of the serial port at any time during its operation. The status information includes the type and condition of the transfer operations being performed and any errors (parity, framing, overrun, or break interrupt).

Each asynchronous serial channel includes full modem control support (CTS#, RTS#, DSR#, DTR#, RI#, and DCD#) and is completely programmable. The programmable options include character length (5, 6, 7, or 8 bits), stop bits (1, 1.5, or 2), and parity (even, odd, forced, or none). In addition, it contains a programmable baud rate generator capable of DC to 512 Kbaud.

3.7 Synchronous Serial I/O Unit

The Synchronous Serial I/O (SSIO) unit provides for simultaneous, bidirectional communications. It consists of a transmit channel, a receive channel, and a dedicated baud rate generator. The transmit and receive channels can be operated independently (with different clocks) to provide non-lockstep, full-duplex communications; either channel can originate the clocking signal (Master Mode) or receive an externally generated clocking signal (Slave Mode).

The SSIO provides numerous features for ease and flexibility of operation. With a maximum clock input of 12.5 MHz to the baud rate generator (assuming 25 MHz device operation), the SSIO can deliver a baud rate of 6.25 Mbits per second. Each channel is double buffered. The two channels share the baud rate generator and a multiply-by-two transmit and receive clock. The SSIO supports 16-bit serial communications with independently enabled transmit and receive functions and gated interrupt outputs to the interrupt controller.

3.8 Parallel I/O Unit

The Intel386 EX microprocessor has three 8-bit, general-purpose I/O ports. All port pins are bidirectional, with CMOS-level input and outputs. All pins have both a standard operating mode and a peripheral mode (a multiplexed function), and all have similar sets of control registers located in I/O address space. Ports 1 and 2 provide 8 mA of drive capability, while port 3 provides 16 mA.

3.9 DMA and Bus Arbiter Unit

The Intel386 EX microprocessor's DMA controller is a two-channel DMA; each channel operates independently of the other. Within the operation of the individual channels, several different data transfer modes are available. These modes can be combined in various configurations to provide a very versatile DMA controller. Its feature set has enhancements beyond the 8237 DMA family; however, it can be configured such that it can be used in an 8237-like mode. Each channel can transfer data between any combination of memory and I/O with any combination (8 or 16 bits) of data path widths. An internal temporary register that can disassemble or assemble data to or from either an aligned or a nonaligned destination or source optimizes bus bandwidth.

The bus arbiter, a part of the DMA controller, works much like the priority resolving circuitry of a DMA. It receives service requests from the two DMA channels, the external bus master, and the DRAM Refresh controller. The bus arbiter requests bus ownership from the core and resolves priority issues among all active requests when bus mastership is granted.

AP-514

Each DMA channel consists of three major components: the Requestor, the Target, and the Byte Count. These components are identified by the contents of programmable registers that define the memory or I/O device being serviced by the DMA. The Requestor is the device that requires and requests service from the DMA controller. Only the Requestor is considered capable of initializing or terminating a DMA process. The Target is the device with which the Requestor wishes to communicate. The DMA process considers the Target a slave that is incapable of controlling the process. The Byte Count dictates the amount of data that must be transferred.

3.10 Refresh Control Unit

The Refresh Control Unit (RCU) simplifies dynamic memory controller design with its integrated address and clock counters. Integrating the RCU into the processor allows an external DRAM controller to use chip-selects, wait state logic, and status lines.

The Intel386 EX microprocessor's RCU consists of four basic functions. First, it provides a programmable-interval timer that keeps track of time. Second, it provides the bus arbitration logic to gain control of the bus to run refresh cycles. Third, it contains the logic to generate row addresses to refresh DRAM rows individually. And fourth, it contains the logic to signal the start of a refresh cycle.

Additionally, it contains a 13-bit address counter that forms the refresh address, supporting DRAMs with up to 13 rows of memory cells (13 refresh address bits). This includes all practical DRAM sizes for the Intel386 microprocessor's 64 Mbyte address space.

3.11 JTAG Boundary Scan Unit

The JTAG Boundary Scan Unit provides access to the device pins and to a number of other testable areas on the device. It is fully compliant with the IEEE 1149.1 standard and thus interfaces with five JTAG-dedicated pins: TRST#, TCK, TMS, TDI, and TDO. It contains the Test Access Port (TAP) finite-state machine, a 4-bit instruction register, a 32-bit identification register, a single-bit bypass register, and an 8-bit test mode register. The JTAG unit also contains the necessary logic to generate clock and control signals for the chains that reside outside the JTAG unit itself: the SCANOUT and Boundary Scan chains.

Since the JTAG unit has its own clock and reset signals, it can operate autonomously. Thus, while the rest of the microprocessor is in Reset or Powerdown, the JTAG unit can read or write various register chains. This feature can be used, for example, to write to the test mode register while the rest of the chip is in Reset or Powerdown. Then when the microprocessor exits Reset or Powerdown, it will enter the specified test mode.

4.0 PARTS SELECTION

Successful handheld battery-operated systems must be small, lightweight, reliable, and capable of operating for an extended period of time from a single battery charge. All parts were chosen with these guidelines in mind.

4.1 CPU

The Intel386 EX processor is a single-chip system utilizing an onboard static Intel386 CX processor or core and a host of integrated peripherals, including DMA and interrupt controllers, serial and parallel ports, chip selects, timers and counters, JTAG, power/system management features. Its 26-bit addressing provides 64 MB memory address space.

4.2 Memory

The 28F400BX, a 256Kx16 boot block Flash Memory, is used for program storage in the H4T reference design. The part is compact and capable of holding BIOS, ROM-DOS and initial application program while supporting in circuit reprogrammability.

The system RAM is a Micron Technologies MT5C64K16A, 64Kx16 SRAM. SRAM, rather than DRAM or pseudo-static RAM, was chosen for the system memory for several reasons. First, the small form factor required by a handheld device requires that the physical size of the entire memory sub-system be a minimum. Second, although DRAMs and pseudo-static RAMs would have been less costly in terms of dollars, they both presented an unacceptable trade-off in terms of power consumption. Third, a design criterion was to maximize the operating time per battery charge. Since the 386EX processor is a fully static part, completely stopping the CPU clock whenever processing was not necessary would represent the lowest possible power consumption. However, with the processor completely stopped there would be no mechanism available to accomplish a refresh of RAM contents.

AP-514

The x16 configuration was selected for both the Flash Memory and SRAM in order to eliminate the requirement for generating the BS8# signal, which would have required additional logic, and to reduce the power consumption. (Power consumption for a x16 configuration is significantly lower than that for the x8. This is due to the need for additional bus cycles for both program fetches and 16 bit data read/writes when using parts with the x8 configuration.)

4.3 Data Buffers

The 28F400BX Flash Memory requires data bus buffers to eliminate data bus contention due to data hold time specifications. A 74FCT16245 data bus buffer is used, minimizing board space requirement and part count.

The PCMCIA interface has warm and hot insertion capabilities, and buffers are required to isolate the PCMCIA connector during card insertion and removal. x16 parts were used where possible to reduce part count and minimize PCB space.

4.4 User Interfaces and Additional Parts

The primary user interface is a 5x6 keypad, and the display device is a 4-row by 20-character alphanumeric LCD module. The keypad, LCD module and PCMCIA interfaces require additional logic to generate required timing and control sequences. These functions are implemented in the register-rich Lattice 1024 (CPLD) architecture.

The system requirements also call for an RF link and barcode wand; the H4T reference design implements a National RF module and a Hewlett-Packard HBSW-8200, respectively. These two components are connected to the 2 asynchronous serial ports on the CPU. The RF module requires full RS-232 drive levels, so a Maxim MAX233 is used to provide level translation. **The barcode wand has simple interface requirements.** Data signal output voltage from the barcode wand is 0 to +5V and is inverted. A comparator is used as an invertor to correct this polarity problem. Another comparator, the LP339 quad comparator, generates the reset pulse and drives the FET for power control of the RF module.

5.0 POWER SUPPLY CONSIDERATIONS

A battery pack of six AA size NiCd cells with a total capacity of 700 mAh is used as the power source. These six cells produce a nominal operating voltage of 7.2 volts and "end-of-charge" voltage of 6.0 volts. This allows the use of a step-down switching power supply for the +5 volt power with an efficiency in excess of 90% when averaged over the expected operating conditions. Even though major portions of the design are typically turned off during normal operation, worst case considerations require the power supply to deliver approximately 2 amps peak current at 5 volts. A +12V supply is required for programming a PCMCIA Flash Memory card and the 28F400BX for firmware updates. A Maxim MAX713 is the battery charging controller. This provides a switching constant current battery charger that will charge the battery pack in an hour or less without generating excessive heat. A Maxim MAX746 is used as the +5V supply and a Maxim MAX734 supplies the +12V for Flash Memory programming.

The CPU has sufficient output pins for additional levels of power control. In order to help maximize the operating time per battery charge, the CPU controls the power to the RF module, barcode scanner and the EL backlight for the LCD display, in addition to controlling the V_{PP} voltage for programming the Flash Memory. **Logic level P channel FETs were selected to implement these switches.**

The CPU includes an extremely flexible chip select unit. After reset, the upper chip select is automatically selected with 15 wait states and an internal ready# signal generated. This makes interfacing to the 28F400BX for the boot code completely "glueless". UCS# is used for the chip select, RD# is connected directly to the device. The BYTE# input of the 28F400BX connects to V_{CC} to force the part to respond in 16-bit mode. If 8-bit wide ROMs are chosen for the boot code, the BS8# signal must be generated whenever the ROM is accessed. See Figure 3 for one method of generating the BS8# signal.

AP-514

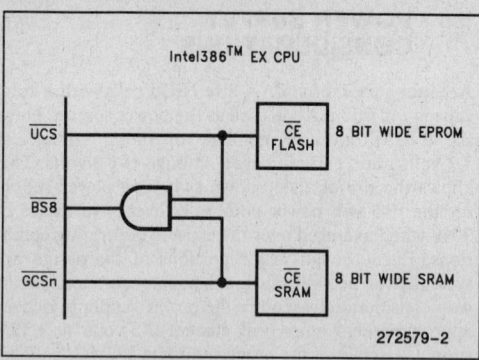

Figure 3. BS8# Generation

When connecting an SRAM to the CPU, WR# timings must be observed. The WR# signal is de-asserted at the same time that the address lines are allowed to change states for the next cycle. This will violate the address hold times for most SRAM devices. Intel386 EX processor designs should qualify WR# with the READY# signal so that when the READY# signal is asserted, the system level WR# signal is de-asserted. Figure 4 shows one method of conditioning the WR# signal with the READY# signal. On the H4T reference design this function is performed within the Lattice 1024 CPLD.

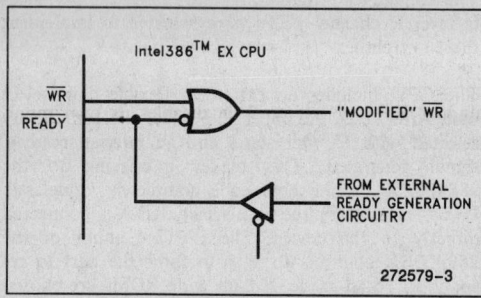

Figure 4. WR# Modification

Although the H4T reference design does not require entry into protected mode to run native code, this may be necessary in many applications. The Intel386 EX processor provides a register on board to cause a fast CPU reset required to support such functions. The PORT92 register resides at address 0092h and is described in the *Intel386™ EX Embedded Microprocessor Hardware Reference Manual*.

In many DOS applications, UCS# is used as the ROM BIOS chip select and is remapped into the 1 MB DOS space for computability. However, entry into protected mode invokes the fast CPU reset which returns the UCS# configuration registers to their initialized state. It is convenient to gate and map an additional GCS# pin (which will not be affected by the fast CPU reset) for protected mode applications. Figure 5 demonstrates a simple method to accomplish this task.

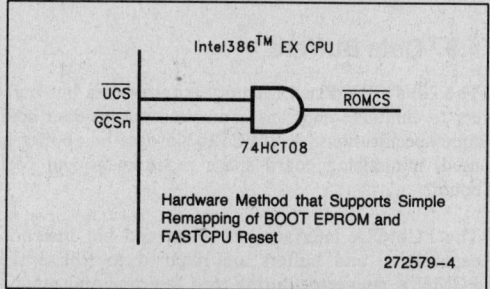

Figure 5. Generating Chip Select for Protected Mode Operation (Port 92 Reset)

6.0 CPLD FUNCTIONALITY

The CPLD has several functions. First, it provides substantial power savings by gating the CPU processor clock. Second, it contains the necessary state machines and control logic to drive the LCD display and row/scan decode circuitry for the keypad. Finally, it provides additional decoding and special functions for the PCMCIA port, protected mode operation, etc. Important functions of the ispLSI 1024 CPLD are detailed above in Figure 6.

In a typical non-static core processor design, the CPU requires a constant clock source and polls I/O during idle or slow periods. In this design, the processor is almost always idle, and simply marks time if special power saving modes are not employed. In order to reduce power consumption to an absolute minimum, the E3X processor clock static clock is completely disabled, restarting only when there is keypad activity. In other applications, this "wake-up" might be generated by a barcode scan or another activity.

AP-514

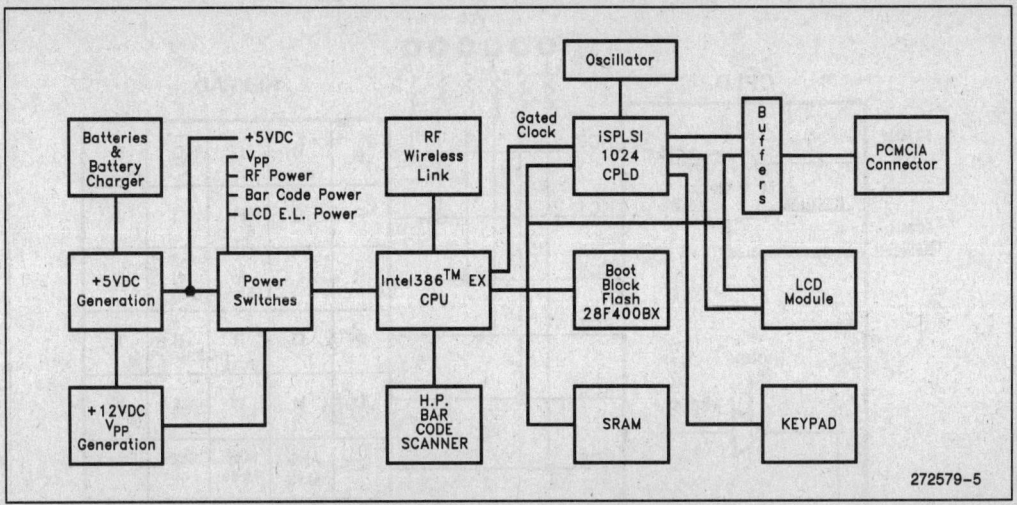

Figure 6. Detailed H4T Functional Block Diagram

As seen both in Figure 7 and Equation 1, a 50MHz clock input signal is gated with the term KR5 to enable the clock to the processor. Once the processor has completed a task, it disables itself under software control by clearing the KR5 signal. The KR5 activate and deactivate operation is described in Section 6.1.

Equation 1

```
FIFTY_QUAL = FIFTYMHZ * KR5
```

6.1 Keypad Controller Logic

The keypad used in the H4T reference design contains 30 keys configured in a 5x6 matrix. There are 6 column decode signals, KC[0:5], which act as inputs to the CPLD and 5 row output lines, KR[0:4], which are driven by the CPLD. Each of the KC lines is pulled high externally.

After initialization, the KR lines are set to a default low state and the processor clock is disabled. When a key is pressed, one or more corresponding KC lines will also be pulled low. A logic term in the CPLD called *KCQUAL* is activated when the change of state is detected. This term sets an internal register bit KR5, enabling the processor's input clock. The processor, now enabled, must scan the keypad to find out which key has been pressed. This is done by generating a delayed I/O read (i.e. longer than the keypad debounce specification) of the buffered KC lines, D[0:5]. If a KC line is still low, the I/O read decodes the keypad column. Each KR bit is then set sequentially by the processor (i.e. walking ones) while the status of the KC signals are monitored. Once the low KC line changes back to a high state, the row decode has been accomplished and the ASCII value assigned to the key is determined via a look-up table in memory. As soon as the processor has completed executing its code, it resets the KR lines (including KR5) to zero, which disables its own input clock. See Equations 2.

6.2 LCD Display Controller

The H4T reference design display is a 20 character by 4 line, 5x7 dot matrix LCD module. Built into the display is an on-board controller with display data RAM, a custom character-generating RAM, and an ASCII character-generating ROM containing 192 characters. It is through the display controller that the CPU can write, read, and set up the module. There is an 11 pin interface consisting of 8 data lines and 3 control signals built into the module to allow for communications between the controller and the CPU. The data lines are buffered by a 74FCT16245 while the three control signals are generated in the CPLD. The control signals are Enable, R/W# (Read/Not Write), and RS (Register

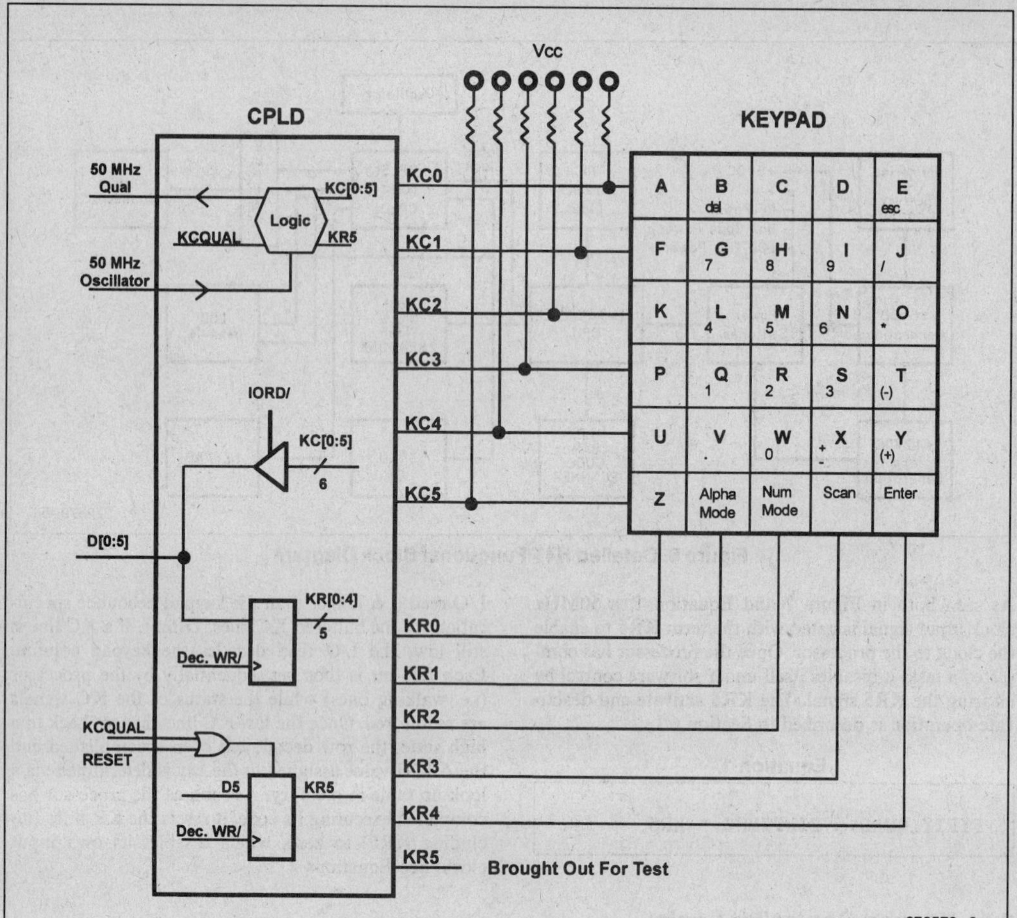

AP-514

Figure 7. Keypad/CPLD Interface

Equations 2

```
KCQUAL          = /(KC0 * KC1 * KC2 * KC3 * KC4 * KC5)
DB[0..5]        = /GCS0 * KC[0..5] * /IORD
DB[0..5].TRST   = /IORD
KR[0..5]        : = D[0..5]
KR[0..4].CLKF   = /GCS0 * /IOWR * FIFTYMHZ      :dec. write
KR5.CLKF        = /GCS0 * /IOWR * FIFTYMHZ      :dec. write
```

6-156

AP-514

Select). R/W# and RS are used by the LCD as a 2-bit code to determine which of four functions to perform as shown in Table 1.

Table 1. LCD Module Control Line Matrix

RS	R/W#	Data	Description
0	0	00000001	Clear Display
		0000001x	Return Cursor Home
		....	
		1xxxxxxx	Character Generator RAM Functions
0	1	Address Counter	Read Busy Flag / Address Counter
1	0	Write Data	Write Data To Character Generator RAM or Data RAM
1	1	Read Data	Read Data From Character Generator RAM or Data RAM

The Enable signal, which has a minimum pulse width of 450 ns, tells the LCD controller to decode the state of R/W# and RS. The CPLD contains a 6-bit resettable counter for creating this signal when the processor performs an I/O read/write operation at address 310-31Fh. In the H4T, GCS1 (Global Chip Select 1) has been initialized for this purpose, and is set for 31 wait states which allows for a normal LCD R/W cycle (1 uS min) without the need for ready generation logic. The Boolean equations used to accomplish the R/W# and RS decode are shown in Equations 3.

LCD initialization code is included as part of the boot source code file H4T.ASM on the floppy disk in the H4T Reference Design Kit. A simplified LCD Display timing diagram is shown in Figure 8.

Equations 3

```
/LCDRS  = /GCS1 * /CA1
/LCDRW  = /GCS1 * /MIO * /WR
LCDENBL     = Q5 * /Q4          ; decoded from 6 bit counter
            + Q5 * /Q3          ; = 560nS at fastest clock frequency
            + Q5 * Q4 * Q3 * /Q2
Q0          := ~ Q0
Q1          := Q1 @ Q0
Q2          := Q2 @ (Q0 * Q1)
Q3          := Q3 @ (Q0 * Q1 * Q2)
Q4          := Q4 @ (Q0 * Q1 * Q2 * Q3)
Q5          := Q5 @ (Q0 * Q1 * Q2 * Q3 * Q4)
Q[0..5].RSTF = GCS1
Q[0..5].CLKF = FIFTYQ
```

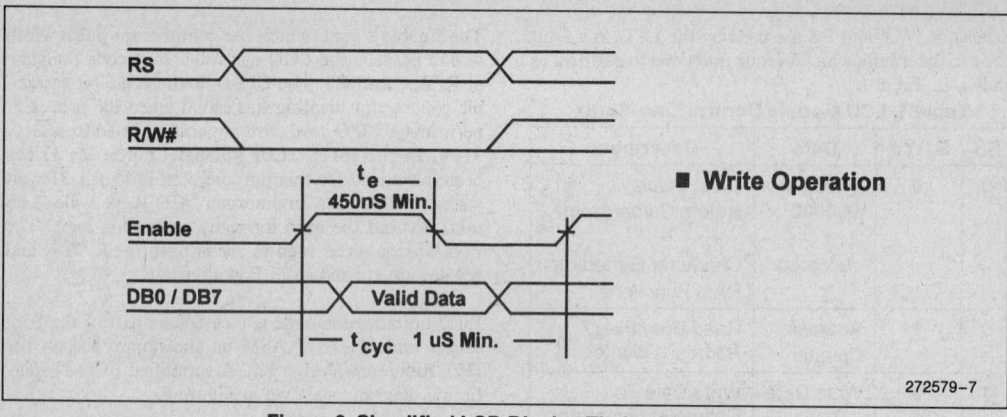

Figure 8. Simplified LCD Display Timing Diagram

6.3 PCMCIA Interface

Communications between the Intel386 EX processor and the PCMCIA port consist of a 16-bit bi-directional buffered data port, with latched addressing and six control signals generated by the CPLD. In order to access the PCMCIA port an I/O Write operation to 330h is used to address the signal ADLATCH which strobes in the upper 10 bits of the port address. Subsequent port operations are accomplished by driving GCS2 which has been initialized as an I/O chip select for address 320h to 32Fh. The CPU accesses the PCMCIA port in a page mode fashion in order to maintain backward compatibility with earlier software applications and the 64K segmentation of the original Intel 8086 microprocessor.

Warm and hot insertion capability is provided by monitoring the two port Card Detect lines, CD1 and CD2. Output buffers are tri-stated until the logical NAND of these two signals (/CD12OUT) is activated. See Equations 4.

Equation 4

```
/PRD     = /GCS2 * /RD
/PWR     = /GCS2 * /WR
/E2      = /GCS2 * /BHE
/E1      = /GCS2 * /BLE
/CD12OUT = /CD1  * /CD2
ADLATCH  = /GCS3 * ADS
```

6.4 Additional Logic

There are a few additional decoded signals created in the CPLD (see Equation 5 below):

ROMCS : Used for accessing the flash memory.
WROUT : Used externally as the write signal.
IORD : Used internally for specifying a read to any I/O port.
IOWR : Used internally for specifying a write to any I/O port.

Equation 5

```
/ROMCS = /GCS4 * /UCS
/WROUT = /WR   * RDY
/IORD  = /MIO  * /RD
/IOWR  = /MIO  * /WROUT
```

7.0 PERIPHERALS

7.1 Barcode Wand Interface

A Hewlett Packard HBSW-8200 Barcode Wand is used as the scanning mechanism due to its simplified RS-232 interface, rugged design, and ease of programming. The wand supports communications rates up to 9600 baud, with programmable start/stop bits. Programming is accomplished by applying power and scanning preset barcodes in the users manual supplied with the wand. The output is straight 7-bit ASCII and no special application programs are needed.

AP-514

7.2 RF Module

The H4T REFERENCE DESIGN incorporates an RF module from National Semiconductor. The AirShare™ module provided a full RS-232C interface and accepts ASCII characters for transmission and reception. Transmission range is limited from 25 feet to 30 feet.

8.0 SOFTWARE CONSIDERATIONS

When the CPU is activated from powerdown, the only chip select line enabled is UCS. As is typical of the Intel architecture processor family, the processor will look for its first instruction at the top of memory, which in this case is 3FFFFF0h (64 MB address space).

The standard first instruction is typically a far jump to a set of initialization routines. For example, in the case of a typical PC BIOS implementation the jump may be executed to the bottom of the current 64K segment where registers and chipsets are initialized. The BIOS ROM is then remapped to the top of the first 1 MB of the processor address range.

The process is similar, with only a few minor modifications to initialize the CPU. The far jump is required, but a few on-board housekeeping tasks must be taken care of before the UCS pin, I/O port, and pin configurations can be initialized and remapped. Compiler directives and macros enable the jump as illustrated below where **FarJmp** is a macro which is called again when re-mapping the UCS pin.

Code Fragment 1

```
;=== This is the hardware entry point after a reset ===

org 0fff0h                      ;top of the 64k flash eprom block

starting_point:
        FarJmp 0f000h, start    ;jump to bottom of block w/offset start

FarJmp macro seg, off           ;the org of start is zero, so
        db    0eah              ;jump is to 0f000:0000
        dw    off
        dw    seg
endm

.code                           ;assembler directive defines beginning of
        org   0h                ;code segment
start:
..................
..................
..................

;**** one more housekeeping chore

        in al, 92h              ;only care about bits 0 and 1
        and al, 0feh            ;bit 0 controls internal core only reset
        or al, 02h              ;bit 1 is A20Gate
        out 92h, al             ;set A20Gate = 1 which drives A20 low
                                ;fast CPU reset (used to access protected mode)
                                ;is disabled
```

AP-514

8.1 I/O Space Configuration

The Intel architecture processor family allows the designer to set aside a specific I/O space which may be up to 64K in length. After reset, all on-board peripherals and registers are initialized to known states, with the serial ports, interrupt controllers, DMAs, and timers all mappped to their standard DOS compatible addresses.

Any of these peripherals, chip selects, and other board functions may be remapped to new I/O address spaces by writing to specific configuration registers as documented below. These configuration registers are internal to the CPU and are mapped into expanded I/O space near the top of the 64K range from F000h to F800h. However, access to the configuration registers is only made available after entering the **expanded I/O space mode** which requires the specific write sequence shown in Code Fragment 2.

This sequence sets the ESE bit, which is required before any other mapping procedures may be invoked. Once the ESE bit has been enabled, DOS compatible peripherals may be remapped out of DOS space by setting the appropriate REMAPCFG register bits, and then altering the associated I/O configuration registers to reflect the starting address and range. Setting of I/O port parameters (serial port baud rates etc.), enabling specific port pins, and mapping of chip selects may also then be accomplished.

The previous code fragment demonstrated how to open the expanded I/O space. Once that is accomplished, the internal peripheral configuration registers may be freely accessed. An example to address internal registers while providing another level of power reduction is shown below. The code used to remap the boot EPROM into a DOS compatible area is shown in Code Fragment 3.

Since this is a bootblock Flash Memory (28F400BX), there are numerous 64K segments with this code residing in the EPROM itself in the last 64K block @ location 70000h to 7FFFFh. Code will continue to execute in the same 64K segment while remapping ROM chip upper select pin (UCS) to the first megabyte of address space for DOS compatibility.

When the CPU is instructed to set the starting (or lower range) address for the UCS to 512K (mov ax, 0008h) the code segment register (CS) is changed to 8000, which corresponds to the first 64K block in the 28F400BX, not the last. Since the next few instructions (see Code Fragment 4) have already been loaded into the pre-fetch cue, an immediate far jump can be initiated to the last 64K, restoring the CS register in the ROM.

Code Fragment 2

```
;open expanded i/o space
;this special procedure is required to set the ESE (Expanded I/O Space
;Enable) bit in the REMAPCFG register

    mov ax,0080h             ' disable interrupts
    xchg al,ah
    out 23h,al
    xchg al,ah
    out 22h,al
    out 22h,ax
```

AP-514

Code Fragment 3

```
;shut off watchdog timer clock reduce power/disable dog

        mov dx, 0f4cah          ;Register: WDTSTATUS
        mov al, 01h             ;Stop all watchdog clocks; set CLKDIS bit
        out dx, al

;remap ucs (28F400bx)
;start address is 80000h region => range 512k bytes (256k words)
;2 wait states

        mov dx,0f438h           ;Register: UCSADL
        mov ax,0302h            ;define UCS as memory CS, bus size = 16
        out dx,ax                       ;disable external ready, 2 wait states
                                ;set lower 5 bits of region address

        mov dx,0f43ah           ;Register: UCSADH
        mov ax,0008h            ;set start address to 512k
        out dx,ax

        mov dx,0f43eh           ;Register: UCSMSKH
        mov ax,03ffh            ;don't mask out any addresses as invalid YET
        out dx,ax

        mov dx,0f43ch           ;Register UCSMSKL
        mov ax,0f801h           ;complete mask.
        out dx,ax               ;Enable chip select
```

Code Fragment 4

```
;currently executing code @ (3FF)F000:offset
;CS was changed to 8000:offset by mov ax, 0008 @ 0f43ah
;Calling the macro FarJmp and passing the parameters F000, offset (The label
;Remap) will reset CS to F000 before pre-fetch cue is empty

        FarJmp 0F000h, Remap
remap:
        mov dx,0f43eh
        mov ax,0007h            ;NOW set range to 512K
        out dx,ax
```

8.2 Global Chip Select Register Configuration

The CPU contains many internal registers which are used to configure devices such as the on-board I/O ports and global chip select registers. The internal registers are mapped into expanded I/O space from f000h to f800h. Once expanded I/O space has been opened, port and global chip select initialization may begin.

The typical process to initialize a global chip select pin requires four I/O writes to 16-bit registers which determine parameters such as bus widths, number of wait states, starting address and address range. The decision to place the chip select in either memory or I/O space is also selected.

AP-514

Table 2. Memory Configuration Register Bit Assignments

Reg. Bit	15	14	13	12	11	10	9	8	7	6	5	4	3	2	1	0
ADH	xx	xx	xx	xx	xx	xx	A25	24	23	22	21	A20	A19	A18	A17	A16
ADL	A15	14	13	12	11	CASM	BS16	MEM	RDY	xx	xx	WS4	WS3	WS2	WS1	WS0
MSKH	xx	xx	xx	xx	xx	xx	A25	24	23	22	21	A20	A19	A18	A17	A16
MSKL	A15	14	13	12	11	CMSM	xx	xx	xx	xx	xx	xx	xx	xx	xx	CSEN

Table 3. I/O Configuration Register Bit Assignments

Reg. Bit	15	14	13	12	11	10	9	8	7	6	5	4	3	2	1	0
ADH	xx	xx	xx	xx	xx	xx	A15	14	13	12	11	10	09	08	07	06
ADL	A05	04	03	02	01	CASM	BS16	MEM	RDY	xx	xx	WS4	WS3	WS2	WS1	WS0
MSKH	xx	xx	xx	xx	xx	xxx	A15	14	13	12	11	10	09	08	07	06
MSKL	A05	04	03	02	01	CMSM	xxx	xxx	xx	xx	xx	xx	xx	xx	xx	CSEN

8.3 Chip Select Initialization

An example of how to configure GCS6 to be the lower memory chip select so on board SRAM can be used to facilitate procedures, data tables, and the stack is shown below. Most of the code fragments will pass parameters to a macro and utilize register names as they appear in the *Embedded Intel386™ Microprocessor Hardware Reference Manual*. An equate statement for each register name may be found in the file EQU.INC which is included on the floppy disk in the H4T Reference Design Kit.

The macro, SetE3XRegWord receives the parameters and performs the functions shown in Code Fragment 5.

Code Fragment 5

```
SetE3XRegWord MACRO reg,val
mov dx, reg        ;move I/O address
                   ;into DX register
mov ax, val
out dx, ax
ENDM
```

The equate statement for GCS6 indicates the extended I/O address for each register.

Code Fragment 6

```
CS6ADL    EQU   0f430h
CS6ADH    EQU   0f432h
CS6MSKL   EQU   0f434h
CS6MSKH   EQU   0f436h
```

The entire initialization of the GCS6 registers is shown in Code Fragment 7.

Code Fragment 7

```
;starting addr = 0k
;region = 256K
;0000:0000 => 3FFF:FFFEh
;2 wait states

SetE3XRegWord      CS6ADL, 0302h
SetE3XRegWord      CS6ADH, 0000h
SetE3XRegWord      CS6MSKH, 0003h
SetE3XRegWord      CS6MSKL, 0f801h
```

A similar process may be utilized to initiate other global chip select pins. Several more examples are shown in the assembly file H4T.ASM, included on the floppy disk in the H4T Reference Design Kit.

AP-514

8.4 Port Pin Activation

Many pins on the CPU have multiple functions. For example, a port pin may be configured for input or output, to act as an open drain driver, or have a specific peripheral related function. Because of this, it is necessary to configure a number on-board port registers to define both the function of the pin and to enable and disable the internal drivers. This is done via the four Port Configuration Registers: PINCFG, P1CFG, P2CFG, and P3CFG.

The series of I/O writes shown in Code Fragment 8 will configure the pins to support the SIO functions, and enable the global chip select functions used in the H4T reference design.

8.5 Leaving Expanded I/O Space

Leaving the expanded I/O space will safeguard the data which has been written to these and other registers. Code to close the expanded I/O space is shown in Code Fragment 9.

Code Fragment 9

```
;close expanded i/o space
        mov  al,00h
        out  23h,al
```

8.6 Stack Initialization

The stack segment is initialized as shown in Code Fragment 10.

Code Fragment 8

```
;**********
;these are byte wide registers and thus, use the macro SetE3XRegByte to
;accomplish the initialization macros are documented in the file MACRO.inc
;
;enable select serial port 0 (COM1) pins through register P1CFG
;RTS0 DTR0 DSR0
;not using DCD0, RI00, LOCK#, or HOLD/HLDA
;**********
SetE3XRegByte P1CFG, 00001110b     ; Was PINCFG0 addr. 0F820h

;enable CTS0, TXD0, RXD0, GCS3-0
SetE3XRegByte P2CFG, 11101111b     ; Was PINCFG1 addr. 0F822h

;enable CTS1, TXD1, DTR1, RTS1 ... RXD1 and DSR1 are enabled by default
SetE3XRegByte PINCFG, 00001111b    ; Was PINCFG3 addr 0F826h

;enable internal reference clock for baud rate generator instead of
;external 1.832mhz source
SetE3XRegByte SIOCFG, 00000011b
```

AP-514

Code Fragment 10

```
;**********
;init stack to live at 3000:0000 where top of stack
;is segment 3000 or 3000 x 10h ==> 30000h
;this is at the top of SRAM (since the stack grows down) and will be
accessed by the GCS6/LCS
;pin initialized earlier
;**********
          mov ax, 2fffh
          mov ss, ax
```

8.7 Serial Port Configuration

The Embedded Intel386 EX processor has two integrated asynchronous serial ports. Each UART is equivalent to the National Semiconductor NS16450 and INS8250A. Upon reset, the CPU comes up in a PC-AT ISA compatible mode, where the serial port and other ISA-compatible peripherals can be found at the normal DOS addresses for COM1 and COM2. (3F8h to 3FFh and 2F8h to 2FFh, respectively). The standard register set for each port is also located at the proper DOS address and is shown below in Table 4.

Table 4. Synchronous I/O Port Registers

SIO 0 Register Addresses (COM1 / DOS Addr.)	SIO 1 Register Addresses (COM2 / DOS Addr.)	DLAB Bit Value	Register Accessed
03F8h	02F8h	0	Receive Buffer (RBRx)
03F8h	02F8h	0	Transmit Buffer (THRx)
03F9h	02F9h	0	Interrupt Enable (IERx)
03F8h	02F8h	1	Divisor Latch / Low Byte
03F9h	02F9h	1	Divisor Latch / High Byte
03FAh	02FAh	X	Interrupt ID (IIRx)
03FBh	02FBh	X	Line Control (LCRx)
03FCh	02FCh	X	Modem Control (MCRx)
03FDh	02FDh	X	Line Status (LSRx)
03FEh	02FEh	X	Modem Status (MSRx)
03FFh	02FFh	X	Scratch Pad (SCRx)

Code to initialize a 16450 is shown in Code Fragment 11. The register names and addresses follow the standard format used in programming a PC I/O card. The example below shows initialization of Port 0 as 9600 baud, no parity, 8 bits data, 1 stop bit.

The same procedure may be used to calculate baud rates and initial control bits for COM2, by using the *ASYNCHRONOUS SERIAL CHANNEL 1 - SLOT 0 (DOS) ADDRESSES* listed in the file EQU.INC, included on the floppy disk in the H4T Reference Design Kit.

NOTE:
If serial ports are relocated to non-DOS space, the *ASYNCHRONOUS SERIAL CHANNEL - SLOT 15* (Non-DOS) registers must be written to (located at F4F8h to F4FFh and F8F8h to F8FFh, respectively). The CPU must be in the expanded I/O mode to access the non-DOS registers.

Table 5. Hamilton Hallmark H4T Memory and I/O Address Map

	Memory or I/O	Starting Address	Ending Address	Wait States	Chip Select
Keypad	I/O	060h	064h	0	GCS0
LCD Module	I/O	310h	31Fh	31	GCS1
PCMCIA READ/WR#	I/O	320h	32Fh	4	GCS2
ADLATCH PCMCIA	I/O	330h	—	0	GCS3
COM1 HP Barcode	I/O	2F8h	2FFh	Polled	Internal to E3X
COM2 RF Module	I/O	3F8h	3FFh	Polled	Internal to E3X
SRAM Data	Memory	00	1FFFFh	0	0
SRAM Stack	Memory	20000h	3FFFFh	0	0
EPROM	Memory	80000h	FFFFFh	2	2

Code Fragment 11

```
;**********
; Initialize Asynchronous Serial Port 0
; internal serial ports are ins8250/NS16450 compatible
;disable interrupts: reset Interrupt Enable Register bits = 00h
;will be using a polled mode

    SetE3XRegByte    IER0D0S,    00h            ;IER0D0S EQU 03F9H

;set communications rate to 9600 baud assuming 20MHZ input clock rate
;Note! The baud rate input clock must equal 16X the final baud rate. The
;input to the baud rate generator on the E3X is equal to
;the processor input clock freqency divided by four,
;or in this example, 5MHZ.
;
;need to produce internal clock rate = 9600 x 16 ==> 153.6khz
;so divisor = 5Mhz / (x) = 153.6khz ==> 32.55
;(will use 33 and accept 1.5% error)
;
;must set DLAB bit high in the Line Control Register in order to access the
;Programmable Baud Rate Generator Divisor latches

    SetE3XRegByte    LCR0D0S,    10000000b      ;addr = 03fbh

;write Programmable Baud Rate Generator.
;set divisor latch register (HI) then divisor latch register (LO)

    SetE3XRegByte    DLH0D0S     00h            ;addr = 03F9h
    SetE3XRegByte    DLL0D0S     33d            ;addr = 03F8h

;Line Control Register
;reset DLAB bit and specify format of communications exchange
;8 bit data    no parity    1 stop bit

    SetE3XRegByte    LCR0D0S,    00000011b      ;addr = 03fbh

;set Modem Control Register bits / turn on DTR and RTS

    SetE3XRegByte    MCR0D0S,    00h            ;addr = 03fch
```

AP-514

9.0 SUMMARY

The H4T Reference Design has been discussed regarding both hardware and software implementation details. Since the H4T is a DOS compatible handheld terminal, users can easily develop application software on any PC with off-the-shelf tools. The Intel386 EX processor is a highly integrated embedded CPU with the key peripheral components onboard to build a cost effective, yet compact system for portable applications. Other key technologies, such as the Intel Boot Block Flash Memory, Complex PLD use, PCMCIA slot, and power management have also been discussed. Handheld terminal architectures and markets are well served by embedded Intel Architecture processors that can provide for low cost development, fast time to market, proven support infrastructure, and long lifecycles.

The H4T has been built, debugged, and tested as a working design. This reference design was developed by Hamilton Hallmark (an Avnet Company) with Intel support.

10.0 REFERENCES

Intel386™ EX Embedded Microprocessor Reference Manual   Order No. 272485-000

Seiko L2014 LCD Data Sheet

National Semiconductor NS16450 Data Sheet

Microsoft MASM 6.11 User's Manual

11.0 FILES AVAILABLE ON THE FLOPPY DISK IN THE H4T REFERENCE DESIGN KIT

H4T.ASM	Boot Source Code
EQU.INC	Equate Include File, used w/H4T.ASM
PROC.INC	Procedure Include File, used w/H4T.ASM
MACRO.INC	Macro Include File, used w/H4T.ASM
H4T.ABL	Abel Source Code for Lattice 1024 CPLD
BOM.DOC	H4T Bill Of Materials
H4T.ZIP	Orcad Schematic Files, Libraries, and Gerber Plot Files

intel®

General Microcontroller

7

AP-125

APPLICATION NOTE

Designing Microcontroller Systems for Electrically Noisy Environments

TOM WILLIAMSON
MCO APPLICATIONS ENGINEER

December 1993

Order Number: 210313-002

DESIGNING MICROCONTROLLER SYSTEMS FOR ELECTRICALLY NOISY ENVIRONMENTS

CONTENTS PAGE

SYMPTOMS OF NOISE PROBLEMS 7-3

TYPES AND SOURCES OF ELECTRICAL NOISE 7-3
Supply Line Transients 7-3
EMP and RFI 7-3
ESD 7-4
Ground Noise 7-4

"RADIATED" AND "CONDUCTED" NOISE 7-4

SIMULATING THE ENVIRONMENT 7-5

TYPES OF FAILURES AND FAILURE MECHANISMS 7-5

THE GAME PLAN 7-6

CURRENT LOOPS 7-6

SHIELDING 7-7
Shielding Against Capacitive Coupling 7-7
Shielding Against Inductive Coupling 7-7
RF Shielding 7-10

GROUNDS 7-11
Safety Ground 7-11
Signal Ground 7-12
Practical Grounding 7-13
Braided Cable 7-13

POWER SUPPLY DISTRIBUTION AND DECOUPLING 7-15
Selecting the Value of the Decoupling Cap 7-16
The Case for On-Board Voltage Regulation 7-17

RECOVERING GRACEFULLY FROM A SOFTWARE UPSET 7-17

SPECIAL PROBLEM AREAS 7-19
ESD 7-19
The Automotive Environment 7-20

PARTING THOUGHTS 7-22

REFERENCES 7-23

AP-125

Digital circuits are often thought of as being immune to noise problems, but really they're not. Noises in digital systems produce software upsets: program jumps to apparently random locations in memory. Noise-induced glitches in the signal lines can cause such problems, but the supply voltage is more sensitive to glitches than the signal lines.

Severe noise conditions, those involving electrostatic discharges, or as found in automotive environments, can do permanent damage to the hardware. Electrostatic discharges can blow a crater in the silicon. In the automotive environment, in ordinary operation, the "12V" power line can shown + and −400V transients.

This Application Note describes some electrical noises and noise environments. Design considerations, along the lines of PCB layout, power supply distribution and decoupling, and shielding and grounding techniques, that may help minimize noise susceptibility are reviewed. Special attention is given to the automotive and ESD environments.

Symptoms of Noise Problems

Noise problems are not usually encountered during the development phase of a microcontroller system. This is because benches rarely simulate the system's intended environment. Noise problems tend not to show up until the system is installed and operating in its intended environment. Then, after a few minutes or hours of normal operation the system finds itself someplace out in left field. Inputs are ignored and outputs are gibberish. The system may respond to a reset, or it may have to be turned off physically and then back on again, at which point it commences operating as though nothing had happened. There may be an obvious cause, such as an electrostatic discharge from somebody's finger to a keyboard or the upset occurs every time a copier machine is turned on or off. Or there may be no obvious cause, and nothing the operator can do will make the upset repeat itself. But a few minutes, or a few hours, or a few days later it happens again.

One symptom of electrical noise problems is randomness, both in the occurrence of the problem and in what the system does in its failure. All operational upsets that occur at seemingly random intervals are not necessarily caused by noise in the system. Marginal VCC, inadequate decoupling, rarely encountered software conditions, or timing coincidences can produce upsets that seem to occur randomly. On the other hand, some noise sources can produce upsets downright periodically. Nevertheless, the more difficult it is to characterize an upset as to cause and effect, the more likely it is to be a noise problem.

Types and Sources of Electrical Noise

The name given to electrical noises other than those that are inherent in the circuit components (such as thermal noise) is EMI: electromagnetic interference. Motors, power switches, fluorescent lights, electrostatic discharges, etc., are sources of EMI. There is a veritable alphabet soup of EMI types, and these are briefly described below.

SUPPLY LINE TRANSIENTS

Anything that switches heavy current loads onto or off of AC or DC power lines will cause large transients in these power lines. Switching an electric typewriter on or off, for example, can put a 1000V spike onto the AC power lines.

The basic mechanism behind supply line transients is shown in Figure 1. The battery represents any power source, AC or DC. The coils represent the line inductance between the power source and the switchable loads R1 and R2. If both loads are drawing current, the line current flowing through the line inductance establishes a magnetic field of some value. Then, when one of the loads is switched off, the field due to that component of the line current collapses, generating transient voltages, v = L(di/dt), which try to maintain the current at its original level. That's called an "inductive kick." Because of contact bounce, transients are generated whether the switch is being opened or closed, but they're worse when the switch is being opened.

An inductive kick of one type or another is involved in most line transients, including those found in the automotive environment. Other mechanisms for line transients exist, involving noise pickup on the lines. The noise voltages are then conducted to a susceptible circuit right along with the power.

EMP AND RFI

Anything that produces arcs or sparks will radiate electromagnetic pulses (EMP) or radio-frequency interference (RFI).

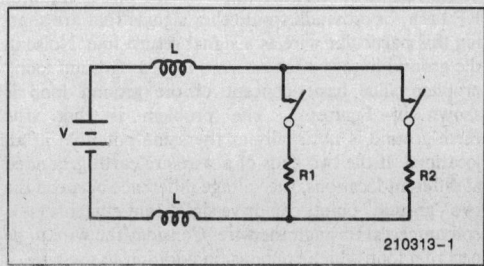

Figure 1. Supply Line Transients

Spark discharges have probably caused more software upsets in digital equipment than any other single noise source. The upsetting mechanism is the EMP produced by the spark. The EMP induces transients in the circuit, which are what actually cause the upset.

Arcs and sparks occur in automotive ignition systems, electric motors, switches, static discharges, etc. Electric motors that have commutator bars produce an arc as the brushes pass from one bar to the next. DC motors and the "universal" (AC/DC) motors that are used to power hand tools are the kinds that have commutator bars. In switches, the same inductive kick that puts transients on the supply lines will cause an opening or closing switch to throw a spark.

ESD

Electrostatic discharge (ESD) is the spark that occurs when a person picks up a static charge from walking across a carpet, and then discharges it into a keyboard, or whatever else can be touched. Walking across a carpet in a dry climate, a person can accumulate a static voltage of 35kV. The current pulse from an electrostatic discharge has an extremely fast risetime — typically, 4A/ns. Figure 2 shows ESD waveforms that have been observed by some investigators of ESD phenomena.

It is enlightening to calculate the L(di/dt) voltage required to drive an ESD current pulse through a couple of inches of straight wire. Two inches of straight wire has about 50 nH of inductance. That's not very much, but using 50 nH for L and 4A/ns for di/dt gives an L(di/dt) drop of about 200V. Recent observations by W.M. King suggest even faster risetimes (Figure 2b) and the occurrence of multiple discharges during a single discharge event.

Obviously, ESD-sensitivity needs to be considered in the design of equipment that is going to be subjected to it, such as office equipment.

GROUND NOISE

Currents in ground lines are another source of noise. These can be 60 Hz currents from the power lines, or RF hash, or crosstalk from other signals that are sharing this particular wire as a signal return line. Noise in the ground lines is often referred to as a "ground loop" problem. The basic concept of the ground loop is shown in Figure 3. The problem is that true earth-ground is not really at the same potential in all locations. If the two ends of a wire are earth-grounded at different locations, the voltage difference between the two "ground" points can drive significant currents (several amperes) through the wire. Consider the wire to be part of a loop which contains, in addition to the wire, a voltage source that represents the difference in potential between the two ground points, and you have the classical "ground loop." By extension, the term is used to refer to any unwanted (and often unexpected) currents in a ground line.

"Radiated" and "Conducted" Noise

Radiated noise is noise that arrives at the victim circuit in the form of electromagnetic radiation, such as EMP and RFI. It causes trouble by inducing extraneous voltages in the circuit. Conducted noise is noise that arrives at the victim circuit already in the form of an extraneous voltage, typically via the AC or DC power lines.

One defends against radiated noise by care in designing layouts and the use of effective shielding techniques. One defends against conducted noise with filters and

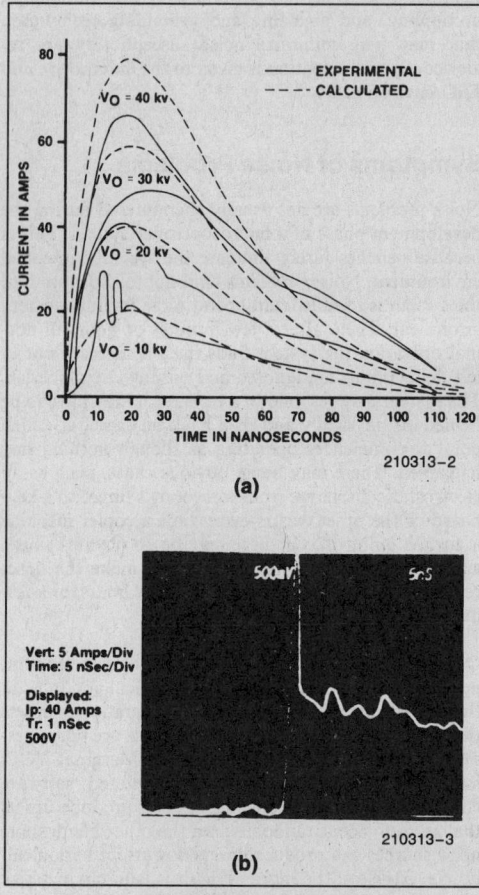

Figure 2. Waveforms of Electrostatic Discharge Currents From a Hand-Held Metallic Object

suppressors, although layouts and grounding techniques are important here, too.

Simulating the Environment

Addressing noise problems after the design of a system has been completed is an expensive proposition. The ill will generated by failures in the field is not cheap either. It's cheaper in the long run to invest a little time and money in learning about noise and noise simulation equipment, so that controlled tests can be made on the bench as the design is developing.

Simulating the intended noise environment is a two-step process: First you have to recognize what the noise environment is, that is, you have to know what kinds of electrical noises are present, and which of them are going to cause trouble. Don't ignore this first step, because it's important. If you invest in an induction coil spark generator just because your application is automotive, you'll be straining at the gnat and swallowing the camel. Spark plug noise is the least of your worries in that environment.

The second step is to generate the electrical noise in a controlled manner. This is usually more difficult than first imagined; one first imagines the simulation in terms of a waveform generator and a few spare parts, and then finds that a wideband power amplifier with a 200V dynamic range is also required. A good source of information on who supplies what noise-simulating equipment is the 1981 "ITEM" Directory and Design Guide (Reference 6).

Types of Failures and Failure Mechanisms

A major problem that EMI can cause in digital systems is intermittent operational malfunction. These software upsets occur when the system is in operation at the time an EMI source is activated, and are usually characterized by a loss of information or a jump in the execution of the program to some random location in memory. The person who has to iron out such problems is tempted to say the program counter went crazy. There is usually no damage to the hardware, and normal operation can resume as soon as the EMI has passed or the source is de-activated. Resuming normal operation usually requires manual or automatic reset, and possibly re-entering of lost information.

Electrostatic discharges from operating personnel can cause not only software upsets, but also permanent ("hard") damage to the system. For this to happen the system doesn't even have to be in operation. Sometimes the permanent damage is latent, meaning the initial damage may be marginal and require further aggravation through operating stress and time before permanent failure takes place. Sometimes too the damage is hidden.

One ESD-related failure mechanism that has been identified has to do with the bias voltage on the substrate of the chip. On some CPU chips the substrate is held at $-2.5V$ by a phase-shift oscillator working into a capacitor/diode clamping circuit. This is called a "charge pump" in chip-design circles. If the substrate wanders too far in either direction, program read errors are noted. Some designs have been known to allow electrostatic discharge currents to flow directly into port pins of an 8048. The resulting damage to the oxide causes an increase in leakage current, which loads down the charge pump, reducing the substrate voltage to a marginal or unacceptable level. The system is then unreliable or completely inoperative until the CPU chip is replaced. But if the CPU chip was subjected to a discharge spark once, it will eventually happen again.

Chips that have a grounded substrate, such as the 8748, can sometimes sustain some oxide damage without actually becoming inoperative. In this case the damage is present, and the increased leakage current is noted; however, since the substrate voltage retains its design value, the damage is largely hidden.

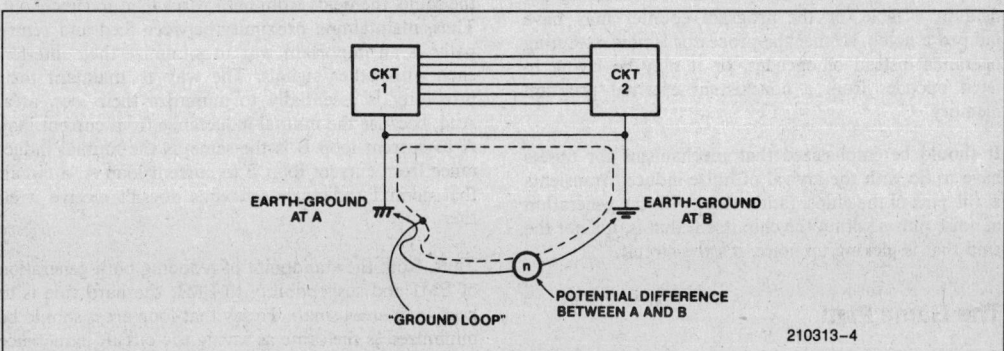

Figure 3. What a Ground Loop Is

AP-125

It must therefore be recognized that connecting port pins unprotected to a keyboard or to anything else that is subject to electrostatic discharges, makes an extremely dangerous configuration. It doesn't make any difference what CPU chip is being used, or who makes it. If it connects unprotected to a keyboard, it will eventually be destroyed. Designing for an ESD-environment will be discussed further on.

We might note here that MOS chips are not the only components that are susceptible to permanent ESD damage. Bipolar and linear chips can also be damaged in this way. PN junctions are subject to a hard failure mechanism called thermal secondary breakdown, in which a current spike, such as from an electrostatic discharge, causes microscopically localized spots in the junction to approach melt temperatures. Low power TTL chips are subject to this type of damage, as are op-amps. Op-amps, in addition, often carry on-chip MOS capacitors which are directly across an external pin combination, and these are susceptible to dielectric breakdown.

We return now to the subject of software upsets. Noise transients can upset the chip through any pin, even an output pin, because every pin on the chip connects to the substrate through a pn junction. However, the most vulnerable pin is probably the VCC line, since it has direct access to all parts of the chip: every register, gate, flip-flop and buffer.

The menu of possible upset mechanisms is quite lengthy. A transient on the substrate at the wrong time will generally cause a program read error. A false level at a control input can cause an extraneous or misdirected opcode fetch. A disturbance on the supply line can flip a bit in the program counter or instruction register. A short interruption or reversal of polarity on the supply line can actually turn the processor off, but not long enough for the power-up reset capacitor to discharge. Thus when the transient ends, the chip starts up again without a reset.

A common failure mode is for the processor to lock itself into a tight loop. Here it may be executing the data in a table, or the program counter may have jumped a notch, so that the processor is now executing operands instead of opcodes, or it may be trying to fetch opcodes from a nonexistent external program memory.

It should be emphasized that mechanisms for upsets have to do with the arrival of noise-induced transients at the pins of the chips, rather than with the generation of noise pulses within the chip itself, that is, it's not the chip that is picking up noise, it's the circuit.

The Game Plan

Prevention is usually cheaper than suppression, so first we'll consider some preventive methods that might help to minimize the generation of noise voltages in the circuit. These methods involve grounding, shielding, and wiring techniques that are directed toward the mechanisms by which noise voltages are generated in the circuit. We'll also discuss methods of decoupling. Then we'll look at some schemes for making a graceful recovery from upsets that occur in spite of preventive measures. Lastly, we'll take another look at two special problem areas: electrostatic discharges and the automotive environment.

Current Loops

The first thing most people learn about electricity is that current won't flow unless it can flow in a closed loop. This simple fact is sometimes temporarily forgotten by the overworked engineer who has spent the past several years mastering the intricacies of the DO loop, the timing loop, the feedback loop, and maybe even the ground loop. The simple current loop probably owes its apparent demise to the invention of the ground symbol. By a stroke of the pen one avoids having to draw the return paths of most of the current loops in the circuit. Then "ground" turns into an infinite current sink, so that any current that flows into it is gone and forgotten. Forgotten it may be, but it's not gone. It must return to its source, so that its path will by all the laws of nature form a closed loop.

The physical geometry of a given current loop is the key to why it generates EMI, why it's susceptible to EMI, and how to shield it. Specifically, it's the area of the loop that matters.

Any flow of current generates a magnetic field whose intensity varies inversely to the distance from the wire that carries the current. Two parallel wires conducting currents $+I$ and $-I$ (as in signal feed and return lines) would generate a nonzero magnetic field near the wires, where the distance from a given point to one wire is noticeably different from the distance to the other wire, but farther away (relative to the wire spacing), where the distances from a given point to either wire are about the same, the fields from both wires tend to cancel out. Thus, maintaining proximity between feed and return paths is an important way to minimize their interference with other signals. The way to maintain their proximity is essentially to minimize their loop area. And, because the mutual inductance from current loop A to current loop B is the same as the mutual inductance from current loop B to current loop A, a circuit that doesn't radiate interference doesn't receive it either.

Thus, from the standpoint of reducing both generation of EMI and susceptibility to EMI, the hard rule is to keep loop areas small. To say that loop areas should be minimized is the same as saying the circuit inductance should be minimized. Inductance is by definition the constant of proportionality between current and the magnetic field it produces: $\phi = LI$. Holding the feed and return wires close together so as to promote field cancellation can be described either as minimizing the loop area or as minimizing L. It's the same thing.

Shielding

There are three basic kinds of shields: shielding against capacitive coupling, shielding against inductive coupling, and RF shielding. Capacitive coupling is electric field coupling, so shielding against it amounts to shielding against electric fields. As will be seen, this is relatively easy. Inductive coupling is magnetic field coupling, so shielding against it is shielding against magnetic fields. This is a little more difficult. Strangely enough, this type of shielding does not in general involve the use of magnetic materials. RF shielding, the classical "metallic barrier" against all sorts of electromagnetic fields, is what most people picture when they think about shielding. Its effectiveness depends partly on the selection of the shielding material, but mostly, as it turns out, on the treatment of its seams and the geometry of its openings.

SHIELDING AGAINST CAPACITIVE COUPLING

Capacitive coupling involves the passage of interfering signals through mutual or stray capacitances that aren't shown on the circuit diagram, but which the experienced engineer knows are there. Capacitive coupling to one's body is what would cause an unstable oscillator to change its frequency when the person reaches his hand over the circuit, for example. More importantly, in a digital system it causes crosstalk in multi-wire cables.

The way to block capacitive coupling is to enclose the circuit or conductor you want to protect in a metal shield. That's called an electrostatic or Faraday shield. If coverage is 100%, the shield does not have to be grounded, but it usually is, to ensure that circuit-to-shield capacitances go to signal reference ground rather than act as feedback and crosstalk elements. Besides, from a mechanical point of view, grounding it is almost inevitable.

A grounded Faraday shield can be used to break capacitive coupling between a noisy circuit and a victim circuit, as shown in Figure 4. Figure 4a shows two circuits capacitively coupled through the stray capacitance between them. In Figure 4b the stray capacitance is intercepted by a grounded Faraday shield, so that interference currents are shunted to ground. For example, a grounded plane can be inserted between PCBs (printed circuit boards) to eliminate most of the capacitive coupling between them.

Another application of the Faraday shield is in the electrostatically shielded transformer. Here, a conducting foil is laid between the primary and secondary coils so as to intercept the capacitive coupling between them. If a system is being upset by AC line transients, this type of transformer may provide the fix. To be effective in this application, the shield must be connected to the greenwire ground.

SHIELDING AGAINST INDUCTIVE COUPLING

With inductive coupling, the physical mechanism involved is a magnetic flux density B from some external interference source that links with a current loop in the victim circuit, and generates a voltage in the loop in accordance with Lenz's law: $v = -NA(dB/dt)$, where in this case $N = 1$ and A is the area of the current loop in the victim circuit.

There are two aspects to defending a circuit against inductive pickup. One aspect is to try to minimize the offensive fields at their source. This is done by minimizing the area of the current loop at the source so as to promote field cancellation, as described in the section on current loops. The other aspect is to minimize the inductive pickup in the victim circuit by minimizing the area of that current loop, since, from Lenz's law, the induced voltage is proportional to this area. So the two aspects really involve the same corrective action: minimize the areas of the current loops. In other words, minimizing the offensiveness of a circuit inherently minimizes its susceptibility.

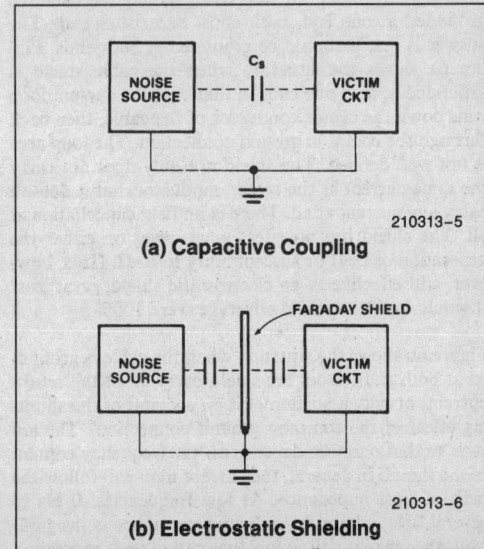

Figure 4. Use of Faraday Shield

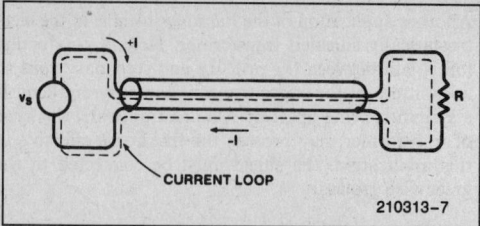

Figure 5. External to the Shield, $\phi = 0$

Shielding against inductive coupling means nothing more nor less than controlling the dimensions of the current loops in the circuit. We must look at four examples of this type of "shielding": the coaxial cable, the twisted pair, the ground plane, and the gridded-ground PCB layout.

The Coaxial Cable—Figure 5 shows a coaxial cable carrying a current I from a signal source to a receiving load. The shield carries the same current as the center conductor. Outside the shield, the magnetic field produced by +I flowing in the center conductor is cancelled by the field produced by −I flowing in the shield. To the extent that the cable is ideal in producing zero external magnetic field, it is immune to inductive pickup from external sources. The cable adds effectively zero area to the loop. This is true only if the shield carries the same current as the center conductor.

In the real world, both the signal source and the receiving load are likely to have one end connected to a common signal ground. In that case, should the cable be grounded at one end, both ends, or neither end? The answer is that it should be grounded at both ends. Figure 6a shows the situation when the cable shield is grounded at only one end. In that case the current loop runs down the center conductor of the cable, then back through the common ground connection. The loop area is not well defined. The shield not only does not carry the same current as the center conductor, but it doesn't carry any current at all. There is no field cancellation at all. The shield has no effect whatsoever on either the generation of EMI or susceptibility to EMI. (It is, however, still effective as an electrostatic shield, or at least it would be if the shield coverage were 100%.)

Figure 6b shows the situation when the cable is grounded at both ends. Does the shield carry all of the return current, or only a portion of it on account of the shunting effect of the common ground connection? The answer to that question depends on the frequency content of the signal. In general, the current loop will follow the path of least impedance. At low frequencies, 0 Hz to several kHz, where the inductive reactance is insignificant, the current will follow the path of least resistance. Above a few kHz, where inductive reactance predominates, the current will follow the path of least inductance. The path of least inductance is the path of

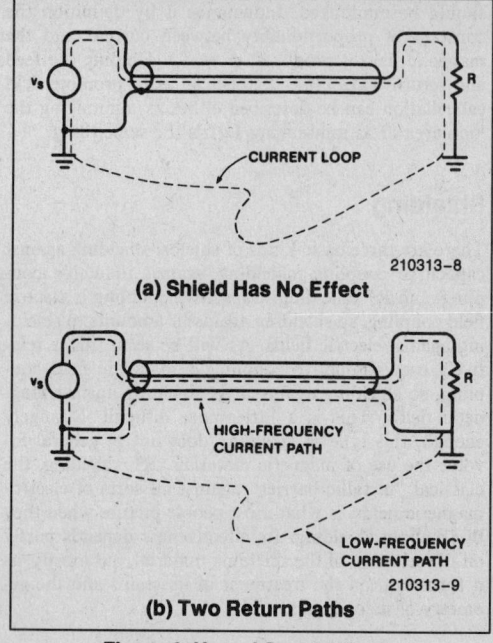

(a) Shield Has No Effect

(b) Two Return Paths

Figure 6. Use of Coaxial Cable

minimum loop area. Hence, for higher frequencies the shield carries virtually the same current as the center conductor, and is therefore effective against both generation and reception of EMI.

Note that we have now introduced the famous "ground loop" problem, as shown in Figure 7a. Fortunately, a digital system has some built-in immunity to moderate ground loop noise. In a noisy environment, however, one can break the ground loop, and still maintain the shielding effectiveness of the coaxial cable, by inserting an optical coupler, as shown in Figure 7b. What the optical coupler does, basically, is allow us to re-define the signal source as being ungrounded, so that that end of the cable need not be grounded, and still lets the shield carry the same current as the center conductor. Obviously, if the signal source weren't grounded in the first place, the optical coupler wouldn't be needed.

The Twisted Pair—A cheaper way to minimize loop area is to run the feed and return wires right next to each other. This isn't as effective as a coaxial cable in minimizing loop area. An ideal coaxial cable adds zero area to the loop, whereas merely keeping the feed and return wires next to each other is bound to add a finite area.

However, two things work to make this cheaper method almost as good as a coaxial cable. First, real coaxial cables are not ideal. If the shield current isn't evenly distributed around the center conductor at every cross-

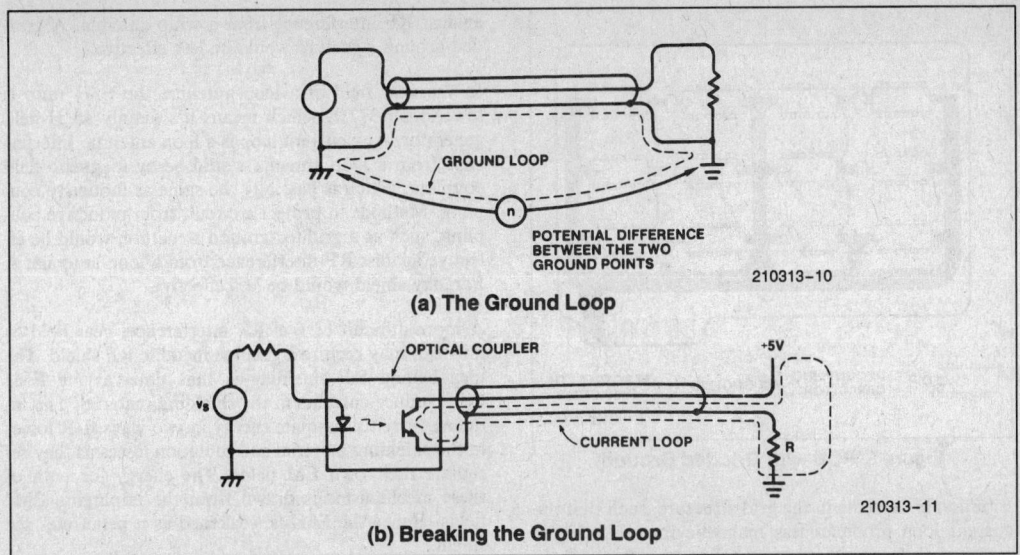

Figure 7. Use of Optical Coupler

section of the cable (it isn't), then field cancellation external to the shield is incomplete. If field cancellation is incomplete, then the effective area added to the loop by the cable isn't zero. Second, in the cheaper method the feed and return wires can be twisted together. This not only maintains their proximity, but the noise picked up in one twist tends to cancel out the noise picked up in the next twist down the line. Thus the "twisted pair" turns out to be about as good a shield against inductive coupling as coaxial cable is.

The twisted pair does not, however, provide electrostatic shielding (i.e., shielding against capacitive coupling). Another operational difference between them is that the coaxial cable works better at higher frequencies. This is primarily because the twisted pair adds more capacitive loading to the signal source than the coaxial cable does. The twisted pair is normally considered useful up to only about 1 MHz, as opposed to near a GHz for the coaxial cable.

The Ground Plane—The best way to minimize loop areas when many current loops are involved is to use a ground plane. A ground plane is a conducting surface that is to serve as a return conductor for all the current loops in the circuit. Normally, it would be one or more layers of a multilayer PCB. All ground points in the circuit go not to a grounded trace on the PCB, but directly to the ground plane. This leaves each current loop in the circuit free to complete itself in whatever configuration yields minimum loop area (for frequencies wherein the ground path impedance is primarily inductive).

Thus, if the feed path for a given signal zigzags its way across the PCB, the return path for this signal is free to zigzag right along beneath it on the ground plane, in such a configuration as to minimize the energy stored in the magnetic field produced by this current loop. Minimal magnetic flux means minimal effective loop area and minimal susceptibility to inductive coupling.

The Gridded-Ground PCB Layout—The next best thing to a ground plane is to lay out the ground traces on a PCB in the form of a grid structure, as shown in Figure 8. Laying horizontal traces on one side of the board and vertical traces on the other side allows the passage of signal and power traces. Wherever vertical and horizontal ground traces cross, they must be connected by a feed-through.

Have we not created here a network of "ground loops"? Yes, in the literal sense of the word, but loops in the ground layout on a PCB are not to be feared. Such inoffensive little loops have never caused as much noise pickup as their avoidance has. Trying to avoid innocent little loops in the ground layout, PCB designers have forced current loops into geometries that could swallow a whale. That is exactly the wrong thing to do.

The gridded ground structure works almost as well as the ground plane, as far as minimizing loop area is concerned. For a given current loop, the primary return path may have to zig once in a while where its feed path zags, but you still get a mathematically optimal dis-

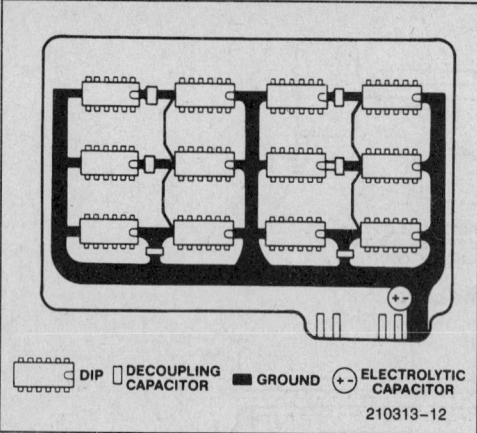

Figure 8. PCB with Gridded Ground

tribution of currents in the grid structure, such that the current loop produces less magnetic flux than if the return path were restrained to follow any single given ground trace. The key to attaining minimum loop areas for all the current loops together is to let the ground currents distribute themselves around the entire area of the board as freely as possible. They want to minimize their own magnetic field. Just let them.

RF SHIELDING

A time-varying electric field generates a time-varying magnetic field, and vice versa. Far from the source of a time-varying EM field, the ratio of the amplitudes of the electric and magnetic fields is always 377Ω. Up close to the source of the fields, however, this ratio can be quite different, and dependent on the nature of the source. Where the ratio is near 377Ω is called the far field, and where the ratio is significantly different from 377Ω is called the near field. The ratio itself is called the wave impedance, E/H.

The near field goes out about 1/6 of a wavelength from the source. At 1 MHz this is about 150 feet, and at 10 MHz it's about 15 feet. That means if an EMI source is in the same room with the victim circuit, it's likely to be a near field problem. The reason this matters is that in the near field an RF interference problem could be almost entirely due to E-field coupling or H-field coupling, and that could influence the choice of an RF shield or whether an RF shield will help at all.

In the near field of a whip antenna, the E/H ratio is higher than 377Ω, which means it's mainly an E-field generator. A wire-wrap post can be a whip antenna. Interference from a whip antenna would be by electric field coupling, which is basically capacitive coupling. Methods to protect a circuit from capacitive coupling, such as a Faraday shield, would be effective against RF interference from a whip antenna. A gridded-ground structure would be less effective.

In the near field of a loop antenna, the E/H ratio is lower than 377Ω, which means it's mainly an H-field generator. Any current loop is a loop antenna. Interference from a loop antenna would be by magnetic field coupling, which is basically the same as inductive coupling. Methods to protect a circuit from inductive coupling, such as a gridded-ground structure, would be effective against RF interference from a loop antenna. A Faraday shield would be less effective.

A more difficult case of RF interference, near field or far field, may require a genuine metallic RF shield. The idea behind RF shielding is that time-varying EMI fields induce currents in the shielding material. The induced currents dissipate energy in two ways: I^2R losses in the shielding material and radiation losses as they re-radiate their own EM fields. The energy for both of these mechanisms is drawn from the impinging EMI fields. Hence the EMI is weakened as it penetrates the shield.

More formally, the I^2R losses are referred to as absorption loss, and the re-radiation is called reflection loss. As it turns out, absorption loss is the primary shielding mechanism for H-fields, and reflection loss is the primary shielding mechanism for E-fields. Reflection loss, being a surface phenomenon, is pretty much independent of the thickness of the shielding material. Both loss mechanisms, however, are dependent on the frequency (ω) of the impinging EMI field, and on the permeability (μ) and conductivity (σ) of the shielding material. These loss mechanisms vary approximately as follows:

$$\text{reflection loss to an E-field (in dB)} \sim \log \frac{\sigma}{\omega \mu}$$

$$\text{absorption loss to an H-field (in dB)} \sim t\sqrt{\omega \sigma \mu}$$

where t is the thickness of the shielding material.

The first expression indicates that E-field shielding is more effective if the shield material is highly conductive, and less effective if the shield if ferromagnetic, and that low-frequency fields are easier to block than high-frequency fields. This is shown in Figure 9.

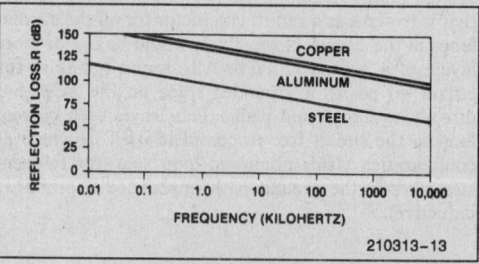

Figure 9. E-Field Shielding

AP-125

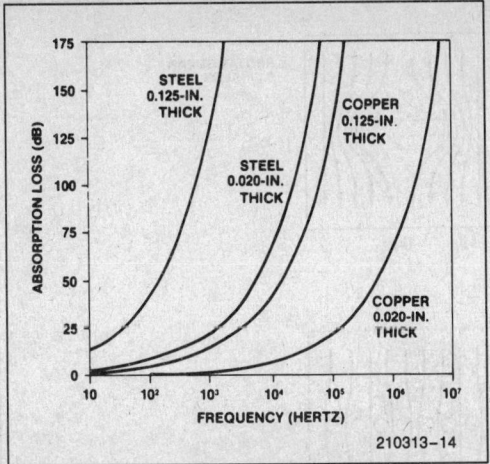

Figure 10. H-Field Shielding

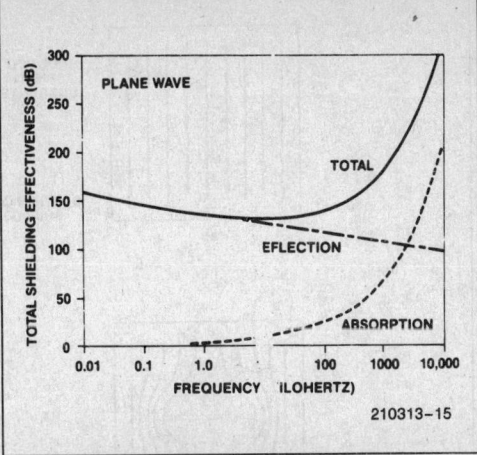

Figure 11. E- and H-Field Shielding

Copper and aluminum both have the same permeability, but copper is slightly more conductive, and so provides slightly greater reflection loss to an E-field. Steel is less effective for two reasons. First, it has a somewhat elevated permeability due to its iron content, and second, as tends to be the case with magnetic materials, it is less conductive.

On the other hand, according to the expression for absorption loss to an H-field, H-field shielding is more effective at higher frequencies and with shield material that has both high conductivity and high permeability. In practice, however, selecting steel for its high permeability involves some compromise in conductivity. But the increase in permeability more than makes up for the decrease in conductivity, as can be seen in Figure 10. This figure also shows the effect of shield thickness.

A composite of E-field and H-field shielding is shown in Figure 11. However, this type of data is meaningful only in the far field. In the near field the EMI could be 90% H-field, in which case the reflection loss is irrelevant. It would be advisable then to beef up the absorption loss, at the expense of reflection loss, by choosing steel. A better conductor than steel might be less expensive, but quite ineffective.

A different shielding mechanism that can be taken advantage of for low frequency magnetic fields is the ability of a high permeability material such as mumetal to divert the field by presenting a very low reluctance path to the magnetic flux. Above a few kHz, however, the permeability of such materials is the same as steel.

In actual fact the selection of a shielding material turns out to be less important than the presence of seams, joints and holes in the physical structure of the enclosure. The shielding mechanisms are related to the induction of currents in the shield material, but the currents must be allowed to flow freely. If they have to detour around slots and holes, as shown in Figure 12, the shield loses much of its effectiveness.

As can be seen in Figure 12, the severity of the detour has less to do with the area of the hole than it does with the geometry of the hole. Comparing Figure 12c with 12d shows that a long narrow discontinuity such as a seam can cause more RF leakage than a line of holes with larger total area. A person who is responsible for designing or selecting rack or chassis enclosures for an EMI environment needs to be familiar with the techniques that are available for maintaining electrical continuity across seams. Information on these techniques is available in the references.

Grounds

There are two kinds of grounds: earth-ground and signal ground. The earth is not an equipotential surface, so earth ground potential varies. That and its other electrical properties are not conducive to its use as a return conductor in a circuit. However, circuits are often connected to earth ground for protection against shock hazards. The other kind of ground, signal ground, is an arbitrarily selected reference node in a circuit—the node with respect to which other node voltages in the circuit are measured.

SAFETY GROUND

The standard 3-wire single-phase AC power distribution system is represented in Figure 13. The white wire is earth-grounded at the service entrance. If a load circuit has a metal enclosure or chassis, and if the black wire develops a short to the enclosure, there will be a shock hazard to operating personnel, unless the enclosure itself is earth-grounded. If the enclosure is earth-

AP-125

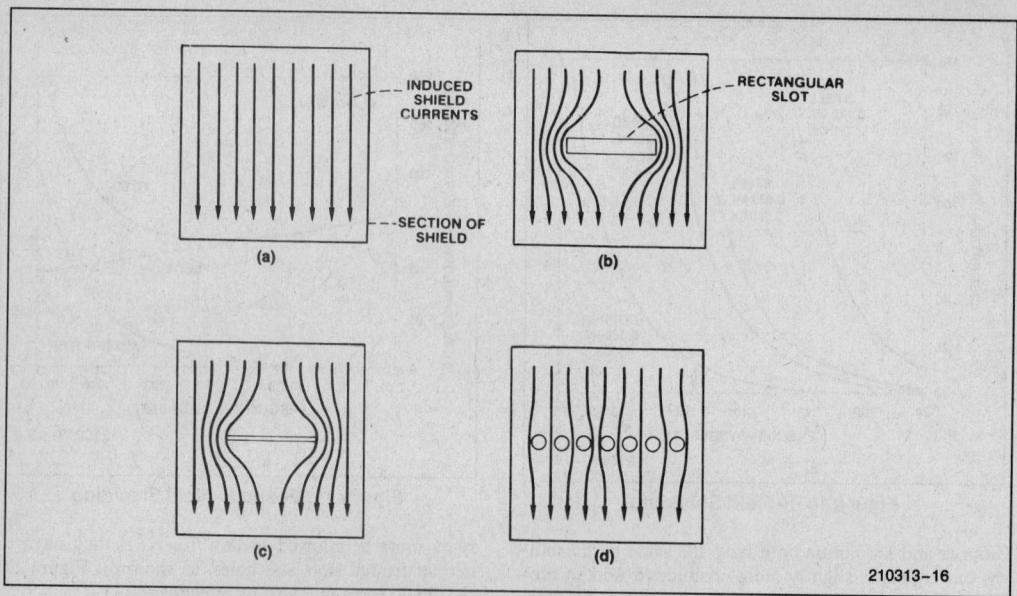

Figure 12. Effect of Shield Discontinuity on Magnetically Induced Shield Current

grounded, a short results in a blown fuse rather than a "hot" enclosure. The earth-ground connection to the enclosure is called a safety ground. The advantage of the 3-wire power system is that it distributes a safety ground along with the power.

Note that the safety-ground wire carries no current, except in case of a fault, so that at least for low frequencies it's at earth-ground potential along its entire length. The white wire, on the other hand, may be several volts off ground, due to the IR drop along its length.

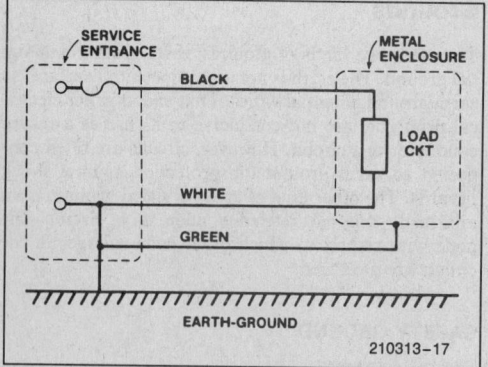

Figure 13. Single-Phase Power Distribution

SIGNAL GROUND

Signal ground is a single point in a circuit that is designated to be the reference node for the circuit. Commonly, wires that connect to this single point are also referred to as "signal ground." In some circles "power supply common" or PSC is the preferred terminology for these conductors. In any case, the manner in which these wires connect to the actual reference point is the basis of distinction among three kinds of signal-ground wiring methods: series, parallel, and multipoint. These methods are shown in Figure 14.

The series connection is pretty common because it's simple and economical. It's the noisiest of the three, however, due to common ground impedance coupling between the circuits. When several circuits share a ground wire, currents from one circuit, flowing through the finite impedance of the common ground line, cause variations in the ground potential of the other circuits. Given that the currents in a digital system tend to be spiked, and that the common impedance is mainly inductive reactance, the variations could be bad enough to cause bit errors in high current or particularly noisy situations.

The parallel connection eliminates common ground impedance problems, but uses a lot of wire. Other disadvantages are that the impedance of the individual ground lines can be very high, and the ground lines themselves can become sources of EMI.

In the multipoint system, ground impedance is minimized by using a ground plane with the various circuits connected to it by very short ground leads. This type of connection would be used mainly in RF circuits above 10 MHz.

PRACTICAL GROUNDING

A combination of series and parallel ground-wiring methods can be used to trade off economic and the various electrical considerations. The idea is to run series connections for circuits that have similar noise properties, and connect them at a single reference point, as in the parallel method, as shown in Figure 15.

In Figure 15, "noisy signal ground" connects to things like motors and relays. Hardware ground is the safety ground connection to chassis, racks, and cabinets. It's a mistake to use the hardware ground as a return path for signal currents because it's fairly noisy (for example, it's the hardware ground that receives an ESD spark) and tends to have high resistance due to joints and seams.

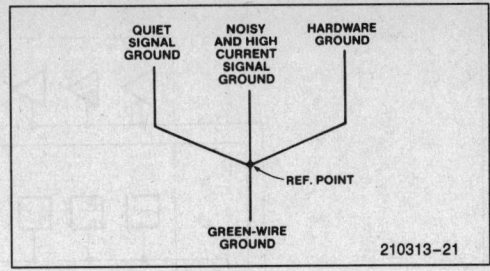

Figure 15. Parallel Connection of Series Grounds

Screws and bolts don't always make good electrical connections because of galvanic action, corrosion, and dirt. These kinds of connections may work well at first, and then cause mysterious maladies as the system ages.

Figure 16 illustrates a grounding system for a 9-track digital tape recorder, showing an application of the series/parallel ground-wiring method.

Figure 17 shows a similar separation of grounds at the PCB level. Currents in multiplexed LED displays tend to put a lot of noise on the ground and supply lines because of the constant switching and changing involved in the scanning process. The segment driver ground is relatively quiet, since it doesn't conduct the LED currents. The digit driver ground is noisier, and should be provided with a separate path to the PCB ground terminal, even if the PCB ground layout is gridded. The LED feed and return current paths should be laid out on opposite sides of the board like parallel flat conductors.

Figure 18 shows right and wrong ways to make ground connections in racks. Note that the safety ground connections from panel to rack are made through ground straps, not panel screws. Rack 1 correctly connects signal ground to rack ground only at the single reference point. Rack 2 incorrectly connects signal ground to rack ground at two points, creating a ground loop around points 1, 2, 3, 4, 1.

Breaking the "electronics ground" connection to point 1 eliminates the ground loop, but leaves signal ground in rack 2 sharing a ground impedance with the relatively noisy hardware ground to the reference point; in fact, it may end up using hardware ground as a return path for signal and power supply currents. This will probably cause more problems than the ground loop.

BRAIDED CABLE

Ground impedance problems can be virtually eliminated by using braided cable. The reduction in impedance is due to skin effect: At higher frequencies the current tends to flow along the surface of a conductor rather

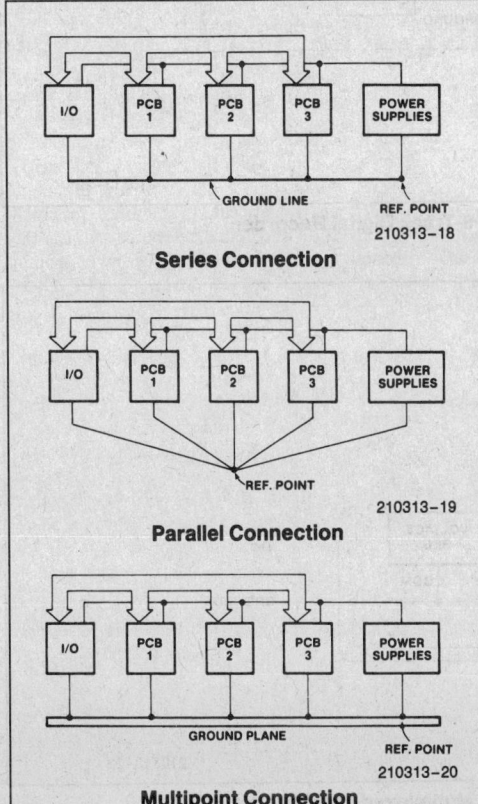

Figure 14. Three Ways to Wire the Grounds

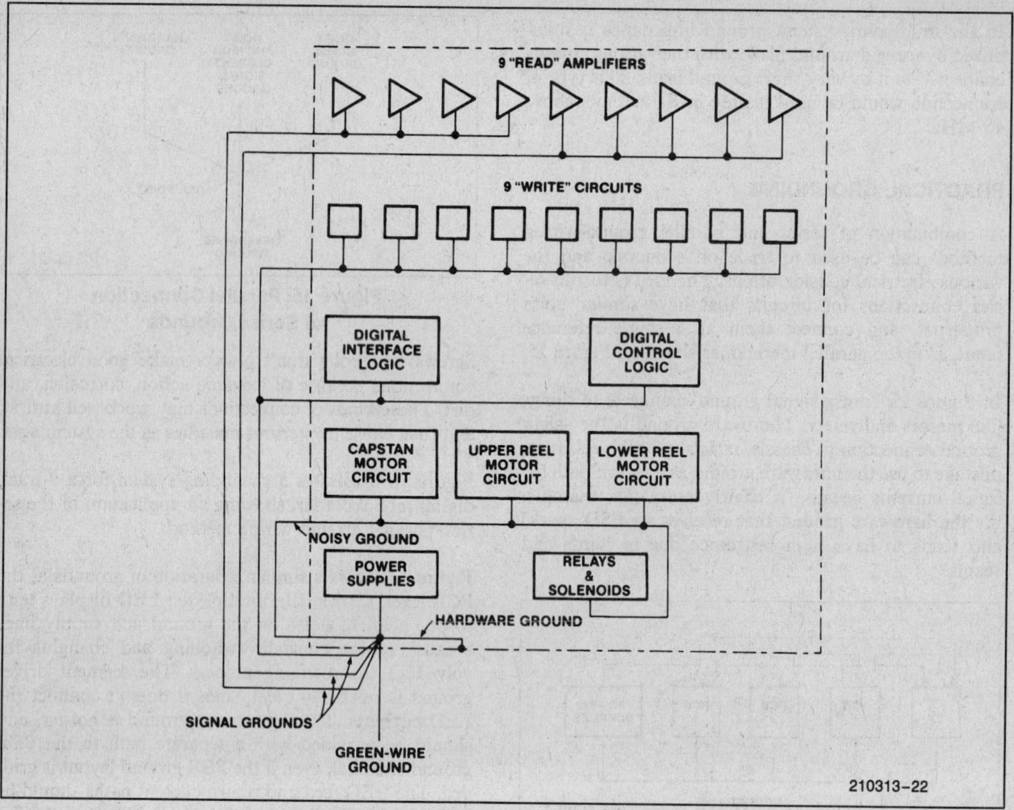

AP-125

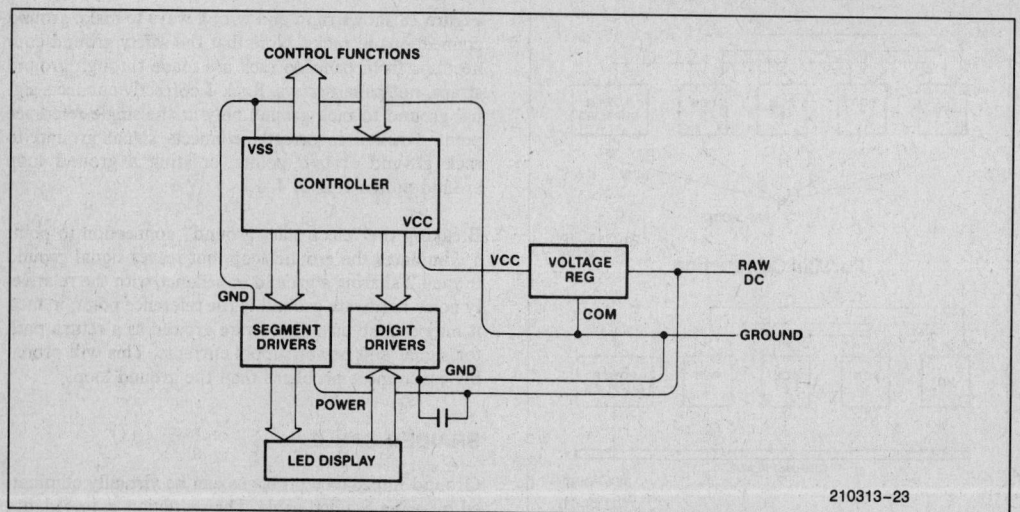

Figure 16. Ground System in a 9-Track Digital Recorder

Figure 17. Separate Ground for Multiplexed LED Display

AP-125

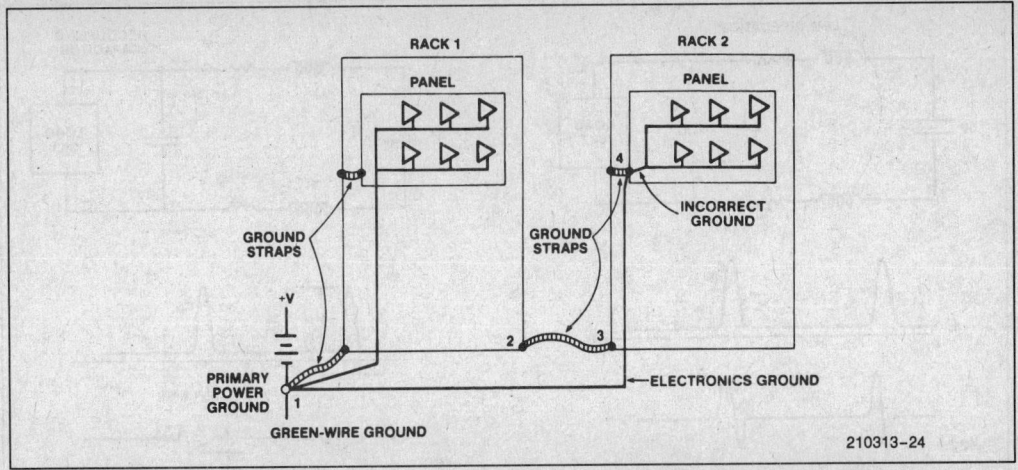

Figure 18. Electronic Circuits Mounted in Equipment Racks Should Have Separate Ground Connections. Rack 1 Shows Correct Grounding, Rack 2 Shows Incorrect Grounding.

than uniformly through its bulk. While this effect tends to increase the impedance of a given conductor, it also indicates the way to minimize impedance, and that is to manipulate the shape of the cross-section so as to provide more surface area. For its bulk, braided cable is almost pure surface.

Power Supply Distribution and Decoupling

The main consideration for power supply distribution lines is, as for signal lines, to minimize the areas of the current loops. But the power supply lines take on an importance that no signal line has when one considers the fact that these lines have access to every PC board in the system. The very extensiveness of the supply current loops makes it difficult to keep loop areas small. And, a noise glitch on a supply line is a glitch delivered to every board in the system.

The power supply provides low-frequency current to the load, but the inductance of the board-to-board and chip-to-chip distribution network makes it difficult for the power supply to maintain VCC specs on the chip while providing the current spikes that a digital system requires. In addition, the power supply current loop is a very large one, which means there will be a lot of noise pick-up. Figure 19a shows a load circuit trying to draw current spikes from a supply voltage through the line impedance. To the VCC waveform shown in that figure should be added the inductive pick-up associated with a large loop area.

Adding a decoupling capacitor solves two problems: The capacitor acts as a nearby source of charge to supply the current spikes through a smaller line impedance, and it defines a much smaller loop area for the higher frequency components of EMI. This is illustrated in Figure 19b, which shows the capacitor supplying the current spike, during which VCC drops from 5V by the amount indicated in the figure. Between current spikes the capacitor recovers through the line impedance.

One should resist the temptation to add a resistor or an inductor to the decoupler so as to form a genuine RC or LC low-pass filter because that slows down the speed with which the decoupler cap can be refreshed. Good filtering and good decoupling are not necessarily the same thing.

The current loop for the higher frequency currents, then, is defined by the decoupling cap and the load circuit, rather than by the power supply and the load circuit. For the decoupling cap to be able to provide the current spikes required by the load, the inductance of this current loop must be kept small, which is the same as saying the loop area must be kept small. This is also the requirement for minimizing inductive pick-up in the loop.

There are two kinds of decoupling caps: board decouplers and chip decouplers. A board decoupler will normally be a 10 to 100 μF electrolytic capacitor placed near to where the power supply enters the PC board, but its placement is relatively non-critical. The purpose of the board decoupler is to refresh the charge on the chip decouplers. The chip decouplers are what actually provide the current spikes to the chips. A chip decoupler will normally be a 0.1 to 1 μF ceramic capacitor placed near the chip and connected to the chip by traces that minimize the area of the loop formed by the cap and the chip. If a chip decoupler is not properly placed on the board, it will be ineffective as a decoupler

7-15

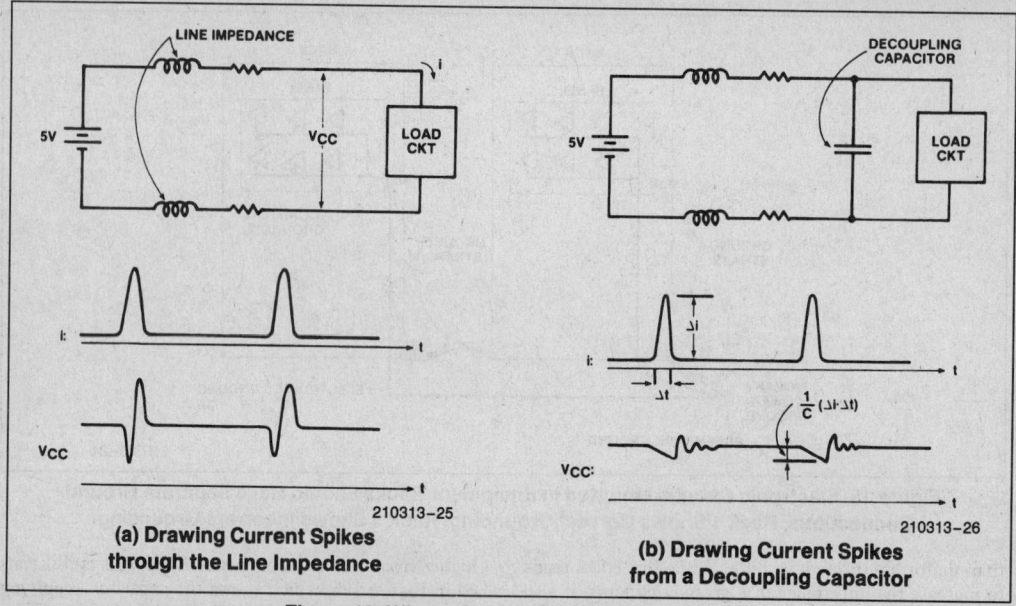

Figure 19. What a Decoupling Capacitor Does

and will serve only to increase the cost of the board. Good and bad placement of decoupling capacitors are illustrated in Figure 20.

Power distribution traces on the PC board need to be laid out so as to obtain minimal area (minimal inductance) in the loops formed by each chip and its decoupler, and by the chip decouplers and the board decoupler. One way to accomplish this goal is to use a power plane. A power plane is the same as a ground plane, but at VCC potential. More economically, a power grid similar to the ground grid previously discussed (Figure 8) can be used. Actually, if the chip decoupling loops are small, other aspects of the power layout are less critical. In other words, power planes and power gridding aren't needed, but power traces *should* be laid in the closest possible proximity to ground traces, prefer-

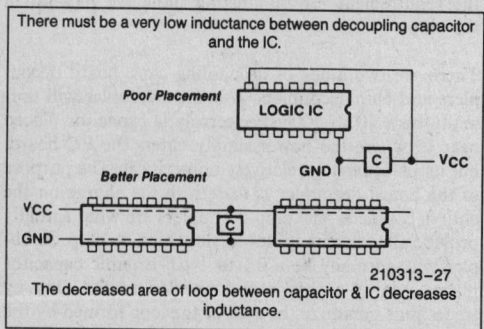

Figure 20. Placement of Decoupling Capacitors

ably so that each power trace is on the direct opposite side of the board from a ground trace.

Special-purpose power supply distribution buses which mount on the PCB are available. The buses use a parallel flat conductor configuration, one conductor being a VCC line and the other a ground line. Used in conjunction with a gridded ground layout, they not only provide a low-inductance distribution system, but can themselves form part of the ground grid, thus facilitating the PCB layout. The buses are available with and without enhanced bus capacitance, under the names Mini/Bus and Q/PAC from Rogers Corp. (5750 E. McKellips, Mesa, AZ 85205).

SELECTING THE VALUE OF THE DECOUPLING CAP

The effectiveness of the decoupling cap has a lot to do with the way the power and ground traces connect this capacitor to the chip. In fact, the area formed by this loop is more important than the value of the capacitance. Then, given that the area of this loop is indeed minimal, it can generally be said that the larger the value of the decoupling cap, the more effective it is, if the cap has a mica, ceramic, glass, or polystyrene dielectric.

It's often said, and not altogether accurately, that the chip decoupler shouldn't have too large a value. There are two reasons for this statement. One is that some capacitors, because of the nature of their dielectrics, tend to become inductive or lossy at higher frequencies. This is true of electrolytic capacitors, but mica, glass,

AP-125

ceramic, and polystyrene dielectrics work well to several hundred MHz. The other reason cited for not using too large a capacitance has to do with lead inductance.

The capacitor with its lead inductance forms a series LC circuit. Below the frequency of series resonance, the net impedance of the combination is capacitive. Above that frequency, the net impedance is inductive. Thus a decoupling capacitor is capacitive only below the frequency of series resonance. The frequency is given by

$$f_0 = \frac{1}{2\pi\sqrt{LC}}$$

where C is the decoupling capacitance and L is the lead inductance between the capacitor and the chip. On a PC board this inductance is determined by the layout, and is the same whether the capacitor dropped into the PCB holes is 0.001 µF or 1 µF. Thus, increasing the capacitance lowers the series resonant frequency. In fact, according to the resonant frequency formula, increasing C by a factor of 100 lowers the resonant frequency by a factor of 10.

Figures quoted on the series resonant frequency of a 0.01 µF capacitor run from 10 to 15 MHz, depending on the lead length. If these numbers were accurate, a 1 µF capacitor in the same position on the board would have a resonant frequency of 1.0 to 1.5 MHz, and as a decoupler would do more harm than good. However, the numbers are based on a presumed inductance of a given length of wire (the lead length). It should be noted that a "length of wire" has no inductance at all, strictly speaking. Only a complete current loop has inductance, and the inductance depends on the geometry of the loop. Figures quoted on the inductance of a length of wire are based on a presumably "very large" loop area, such that the magnetic field produced by the return current has no cancellation effect on the field produced by the current in the given length of wire. Such a loop geometry is not and should not be the case with the decoupling loop.

Figure 21 shows VCC waveforms, measured between pins 40 and 20 (VCC and VSS) of an 8751 CPU, for several conditions of decoupling on a PC board that has a decoupling loop area slightly larger than necessary. These photographs show the effects of increasing the decoupling capacitance and decreasing the area of the decoupling loop. The indications are that a 1 µF capacitor is better than a 0.1 µF capacitor, which in turn is better than nothing, and that the board should have been laid out with more attention paid to the area of the decoupling loop.

Figure 21e was obtained using a special-purpose experimental capacitor designed by Rogers Corp. (Q-Pac Division, Mesa, AZ) for use as a decoupler. It consists of two parallel plates, the length of a 40-pin DIP, separated by a ceramic dielectric. Sandwiched between the CPU chip and the PCB (or between the CPU socket and the PCB), it makes connection to pins 40 and 20, forming a leadless decoupling capacitor. It is obviously a configuration of minimal inductance. Unfortunately, the particular sample tested had only 0.07 µF of capacitance and so was unable to prevent the 1 MHz ripple as effectively as the configuration of Figure 21d. It seems apparent, though, that with more capacitance this part will alleviate a lot of decoupling problems.

THE CASE FOR ON-BOARD VOLTAGE REGULATION

To complicate matters, supply line glitches aren't always picked up in the distribution networks, but can come from the power supply circuit itself. In that case, a well-designed distribution network faithfully delivers the glitch throughout the system. The VCC glitch in Figure 22 was found to be coming from within a bench power supply in response to the EMP produced by an induction coil spark generator that was being used at Intel during a study of noise sensitivity. The VCC glitch is about 400 mV high and some 20 µs in duration. Normal board decoupling techniques were ineffective in removing it, but adding an on-board voltage regulator chip did the job.

Thus, a good case can be made in favor of using a voltage regulator chip on each PCB, instead of doing all the voltage regulation at the supply circuit. This eases requirements on the heat-sinking at the supply circuit, and alleviates much of the distribution and board decoupling headaches. However, it also brings in the possibility that different boards would be operating at slightly different VCC levels due to tolerance in the regulator chips; this then leads to slightly different logic levels from board to board. The implications of that may vary from nothing to latch-up, depending on what kinds of chips are on the boards, and how they react to an input "high" that is perhaps 0.4V higher than local VCC.

Recovering Gracefully from a Software Upset

Even when one follows all the best guidelines for designing for a noisy environment, it's always possible for a noise transient to occur which exceeds the circuit's immunity level. In that case, one can strive at least for a graceful recovery.

Graceful recovery schemes involve additional hardware and/or software which is supposed to return the system to a normal operating mode after a software upset has occurred. Two decisions have to be made: How to recognize when an upset has occurred, and what to do about it.

7-17

AP-125

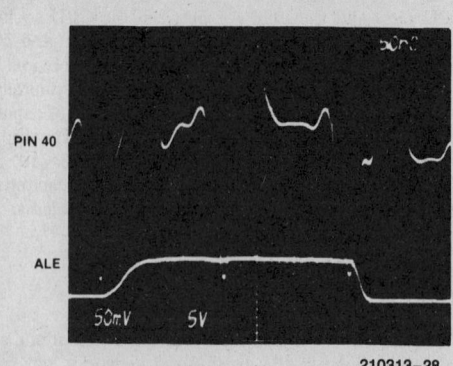

(a) No Decoupling Cap

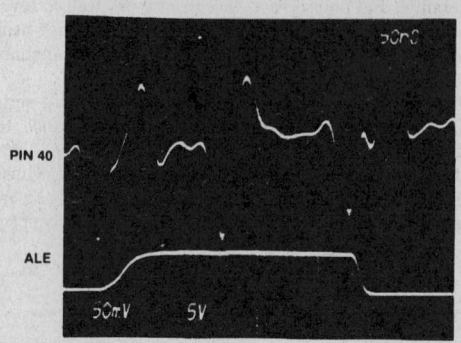

(b) 0.1 μF Decoupler in Place on the PCB

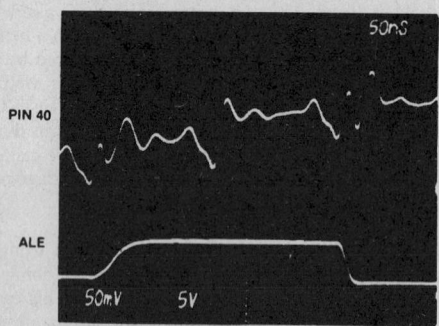

(c) 0.1 μF Decoupler Stretched Directly
from Pin 40 to Pin 20, under the Socket.
(The difference between this and 21b is
due only to the change in loop geometry.
Also shown is the upward slope of a ripple
in VCC. The ripple frequency is
1 MHz, the same as ALE.)

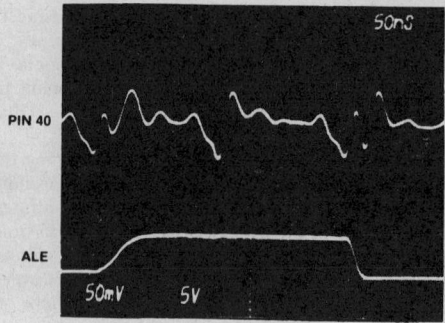

(d) 1.0 μF Decoupler Stretched Directly
from Pin 40 to Pin 20, under the Socket.
(This prevents the 1 MHz ripple, but there's
no reduction in higher frequency components.
Further increases in capacitance
effected no further improvement.)

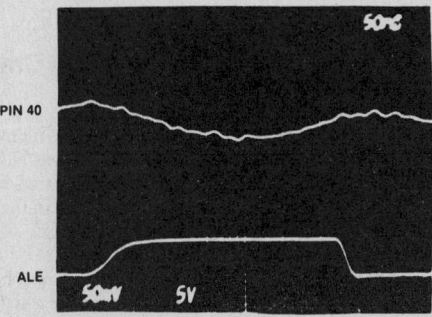

(e) Special-Purpose Decoupling Cap
under Development by Rogers Corp.
(Further discussion in text.)

Figure 21. Noise on VCC Line

AP-125

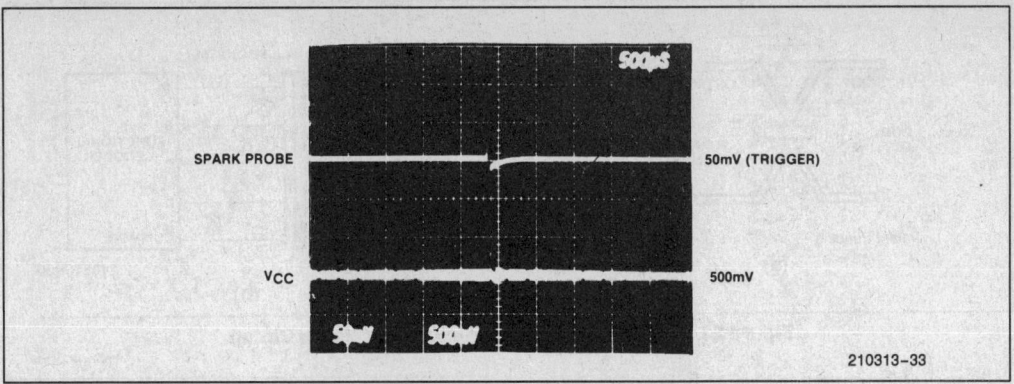

Figure 22. EMP-Induced Glitch

If the designer knows what kinds and combinations of outputs can legally be generated by the system, he can use gates to recognize and flag the occurrence of an illegal state of affairs. The flag can then trigger a jump to a recovery routine which then may check or re-initialize data, perhaps output an error message, or generate a simple reset.

The most reliable scheme is to use a so-called watchdog circuit. Here the CPU is programmed to generate a periodic signal as long as the system is executing instructions in an expected manner. The periodic signal is then used to hold off a circuit that will trigger a jump to a recovery routine. The periodic signal needs to be AC-coupled to the trigger circuit so that a "stuck-at" fault won't continue to hold off the trigger. Then, if the processor locks up someplace, the periodic signal is lost and the watchdog triggers a reset.

In practice, it may be convenient to drive the watchdog circuit with a signal which is being generated anyway by the system. One needs to be careful, however, that an upset does in fact discontinue that signal. Specifically, for example, one could use one of the digit drive signals going to a multiplexed display. But display scanning is often handled in response to a timer-interrupt, which may continue operating even though the main program is in a failure mode. Even so, with a little extra software, the signal can be used to control the watchdog (see Reference 8 on this).

Simpler schemes can work well for simpler systems. For example, if a CPU isn't doing anything but scanning and decoding a keyboard, there's little to lose and much to gain by simply resetting it periodically with an astable multivibrator. It only takes about 13 μs (at 6 MHz) to reset an 8048 if the clock oscillator is already running.

A zero-cost measure is simply to fill all unused program memory with NOPs and JMPs to a recovery routine. The effectiveness of this method is increased by writing the program in segments that are separated by NOPs and JMPs. It's still possible, of course, to get hung up in a data table or something. But you get a lot of protection, for the cost.

Further discussion of graceful recovery schemes can be found in Reference 13.

Special Problem Areas

ESD

MOS chips have some built-in protection against a static charge build-up on the pins, as would occur during normal handling, but there's no protection against the kinds of current levels and rise times that occur in a genuine electrostatic spark. These kinds of discharges can blow a crater in the silicon.

It must be recognized that connecting CPU pins unprotected to a keyboard or to anything else that is subject to electrostatic discharges makes an extremely fragile configuration. Buffering them is the very least one can do. But buffering doesn't completely solve the problem, because then the buffer chips will sustain the damage (even TTL); therefore, one might consider mounting the buffer chips in sockets for ease of replacement.

Transient suppressors, such as the TranZorbs made by General Semiconductor Industries (Tempe, AZ), may in the long run provide the cheapest protection if their "zero inductance" structure is used. The structure and circuit application are shown in Figure 23.

The suppressor element is a pn junction that operates like a Zener diode. Back-to-back units are available for AC operation. The element is more or less an open circuit at normal system voltage (the standoff voltage rating for the device), and conducts like a Zener diode at the clamping voltage.

The lead inductance in the conventional transient suppressor package makes the conventional package essen-

AP-125

Figure 23. "Zero-Inductance" Structure and Use in Circuit

tially useless for protection against ESD pulses, owing to the fast rise of these pulses. The "zero inductance" units are available singly in a 4-pin DIP, and in arrays of four to a 16-pin DIP for PCB level protection. In that application they should be mounted in close proximity to the chips they protect.

In addition, metal enclosures or frames or parts that can receive an ESD spark should be connected by braided cable to the green-wire ground. Because of the ground impedance, ESD current shouldn't be allowed to flow through any signal ground, even if the chips are protected by transient suppressors. A 35 kV ESD spark can always spare a few hundred volts to drive a fast current pulse down a signal ground line if it can't find a braided cable to follow. Think how delighted your 8048 will be to find its VSS pin 250V higher than VCC for a few 10s of nanoseconds.

THE AUTOMOTIVE ENVIRONMENT

The automobile presents an extremely hostile environment for electronic systems. There are several parts to it:

1. Temperature extremes from $-40°C$ to $+125°C$ (under the hood) or $+85°C$ (in the passenger compartment)
2. Electromagnetic pulses from the ignition system
3. Supply line transients that will knock your socks off

One needs to take a long, careful look at the temperature extremes. The allowable storage temperature range for most Intel MOS chips is $-65°C$ to $+150°C$, although some chips have a maximum storage temperature rating of $+125°C$. In operation (or "under bias," as the data sheets say) the allowable ambient temperature range depends on the product grade, as follows:

Grade	Ambient Temperature	
	Min	Max
Commercial	0	70
Industrial	-40	$+85$
Automotive	-40	$+110$
Military	-55	$+125$

The different product grades are actually the same chip, but tested according to different standards. Thus, a given commercial-grade chip might actually pass military temperature requirements, but not have been tested for it. (Of course, there are other differences in grading requirements having to do with packaging, burn-in, traceability, etc.)

In any case, it's apparent that commercial-grade chips can't be used safely in automotive applications, not even in the passenger compartment. Industrial-grade chips can be used in the passenger compartment, and automotive or military chips are required in under-the-hood applications.

Ignition noise, CB radios, and that sort of thing are probably the least of your worries. In a poorly designed system, or in one that has not been adequately tested for the automotive environment, this type of EMI might cause a few software upsets, but not destroy chips.

The major problem, and the one that seems to come as the biggest surprise to most people, is the line transients. Regrettably, the 12V battery is not actually the source of power when the car is running. The charging system is, and it's not very clean. The only time the battery is the real source of power is when the car is first being started, and in that condition the battery terminals may be delivering about 5V or 6V. As follows is a brief description of the major idiosyncracies of the "12V" automotive power line.

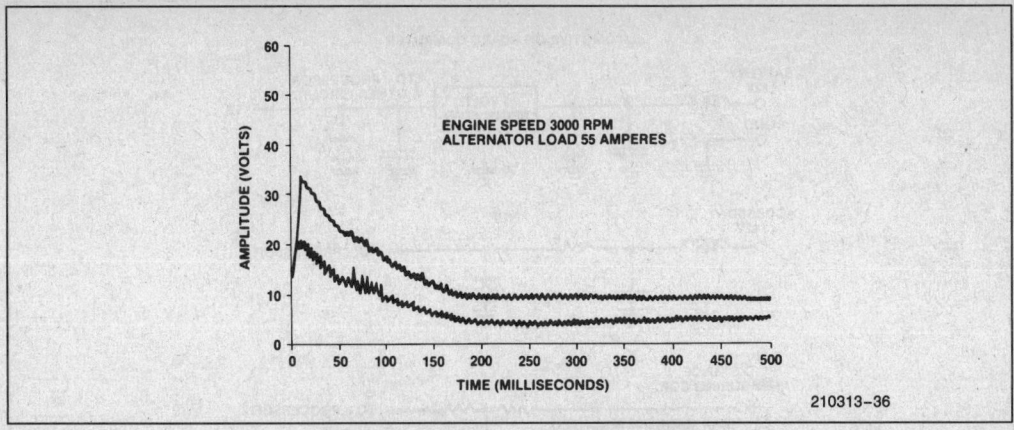

Figure 24. Typical Load Dump Transients

- An abrupt reduction in the alternator load causes a positive voltage transient called "load dump." In a load dump transient the line voltage rises to 20V or 30V in a few μs, then decays exponentially with a time constant of about 100 μs, as shown in Figure 24. Much higher peak voltages and longer decay times have also been reported. The worst case load dump is caused by disconnecting a low battery from the alternator circuit while the alternator is running. Normally this would happen intermittently when the battery terminal connections are defective.

- When the ignition is turned off, as the field excitation decays, the line voltage can go to between -40V and -100V for 100 μs or more.

- Miscellaneous solenoid switching transients, such as the one shown in Figure 25, can drive the line to $+$ or -200V to 400V for several μs.

- Mutual coupling between unshielded wires in long harnesses can induce 100V and 200V transients in unprotected circuits.

What all this adds up to is that people in the business of building systems for automotive applications need a comprehensive testing program. An SAE guideline which describes the automotive environment is available to designers: SAE J1211, "Recommended Environmental Practices for Electronic Equipment Design," *1980 SAE Handbook,* Part 1, pp. 22.80–22.96.

Some suggestions for protecting circuitry are shown in Figure 26. A transient suppressor is placed in front of the regulator chip to protect it. Since the rise times in these transients are not like those in ESD pulses, lead inductance is less critical and conventional devices can be used. The regulator itself is pretty much of a necessity, since a load dump transient is simply not going to be removed by any conventional LC or RC filter.

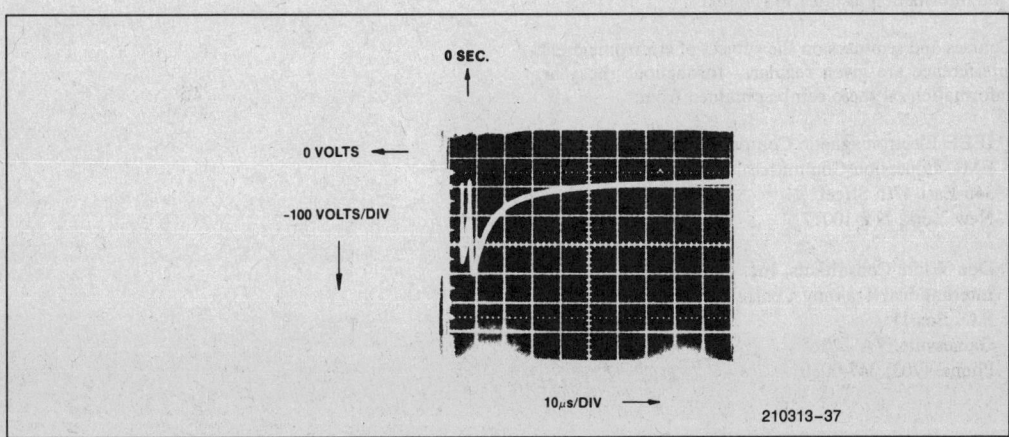

Figure 25. Transient Created by De-energizing an Air Conditioning Clutch Solenoid

AP-125

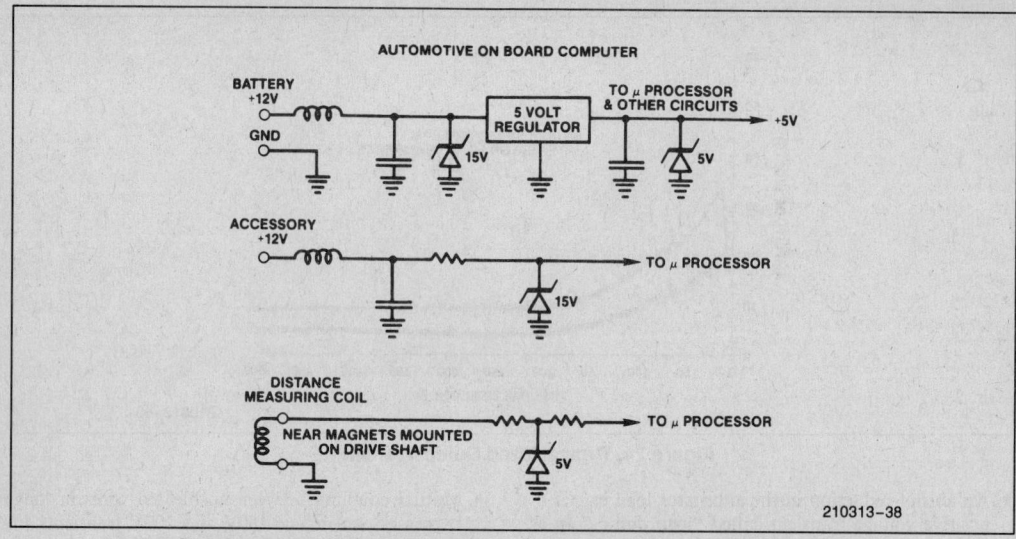

Figure 26. Use of Transient Suppressors in Automotive Applications

Special I/O interfacing is also required, because of the need for high tolerance to voltage transients, input noise, input/output isolation, etc. In addition, switches that are being monitored or driven by these buffers are usually referenced to chassis ground instead of signal ground, and in a car there can be many volts difference between the two. I/O interfacing is discussed in Reference 2.

The EMC Education committee has available a video tape: "Introduction to EMC—A Video Training Tape," by Henry Ott. Don White Consultants offers a series of training courses on many different aspects of electromagnetic compatibility. Most organizations that sponsor EMC courses also offer in-plant presentations.

Parting Thoughts

The main sources of information for this Application Note were the references by Ott and by White. Reference 5 is probably the finest treatment currently available on the subject. The other references provided specific information as cited in the text.

Courses and seminars on the subject of electromagnetic interference are given regularly throughout the year. Information on these can be obtained from:

IEEE Electromagnetic Compatibility Society
EMC Education Committee
345 East 47th Street
New York, NY 10017

Don White Consultants, Inc.
International Training Centre
P.O. Box D
Gainesville, VA 22065
Phone: (703) 347-0030

REFERENCES

1. Clark, O.M., "Electrostatic Discharge Protection Using Silicon Transient Suppressors," *Proceedings of the Electrical Overstress/Electrostatic Discharge Symposium.* Reliability Analysis Center, Rome Air Development Center, 1979.

2. Kearney, M; Shreve, J.; and Vincent, W., "Microprocessor Based Systems in the Automobile: Custom Integrated Circuits Provide an Effective Interface," *Electronic Engine Management and Driveline Control Systems,* SAE Publication SP-481, 810160, pp. 93–102.

3. King, W.M. and Reynolds, D., "Personnel Electrostatic Discharge: Impulse Waveforms Resulting From ESD of Humans Directly and Through Small Hand-Held Metallic Objects Intervening in the Discharge Path," *Proceedings of the IEEE Symposium on Electromagnetic Compatibility,* pp. 577-590, Aug. 1981.

4. Ott, H., "Digital Circuit Grounding and Interconnection," *Proceedings of the IEEE Symposium on Electromagnetic Compatibility,* pp. 292-297, Aug. 1981.

5. Ott, H., *Noise Reduction Techniques in Electronic Systems.* New York: Wiley, 1976.

6. *1981 Interference Technology Engineers' Master (ITEM) Directory and Design Guide.* R. and B. Enterprises, P.O. Box 328, Plymouth Meeting, PA 19426.

7. SAE J1211, "Recommended Environmental Practices for Electronic Equipment Design," *1980 SAE Handbook,* Part 1, pp. 22.80–22.96.

8. Smith, L., "A Watchdog Circuit for Microcomputer Based Systems," *Digital Design,* pp. 78, 79, Nov. 1979.

9. *TranZorb Quick Reference Guide.* General Semiconductor Industries, P.O. Box 3078, Tempe, AZ 85281.

10. Tucker, T.J., "Spark Initiation Requirements of a Secondary Explosive," *Annals of the New York Academy of Sciences,* Vol 152, Article I, pp. 643–653, 1968.

11. White, D., *Electromagnetic Interference and Compatibility, Vol. 3: EMI Control Methods and Techniques.* Don White Consultants, 1973.

12. White, D., *EMI Control in the Design of Printed Circuit Boards and Backplanes.* Don White Consultants, 1981.

13. Yarkoni, B. and Wharton, J., "Designing Reliable Software for Automotive Applications," *SAE Transactions,* 790237, July 1979.

intel

AP-155

APPLICATION NOTE

Oscillators for Microcontrollers

TOM WILLIAMSON
MICROCONTROLLER
TECHNICAL MARKETING

June 1983

Order Number: 230659-001

OSCILLATORS FOR MICROCONTROLLERS

CONTENTS PAGE

INTRODUCTION 7-27

FEEDBACK OSCILLATORS 7-27
Loop Gain 7-27
How Feedback Oscillators Work 7-28
The Positive Reactance Oscillator 7-28

QUARTZ CRYSTALS 7-29
Crystal Parameters 7-29
   Equivalent Circuit 7-29
Load Capacitance 7-30
"Series" vs. "Parallel" Crystals 7-30
Equivalent Series Resistance 7-30
Frequency Tolerance 7-31
Drive Level 7-31

CERAMIC RESONATORS 7-31
Specifications for Ceramic Resonators ... 7-32

OSCILLATOR DESIGN CONSIDERATIONS 7-32
On-Chip Oscillators 7-32
Crystal Specifications 7-32
Oscillation Frequency 7-33
Selection of CX1 and CX2 7-33
   Placement of Components 7-33
   Clocking Other Chips 7-33
External Oscillators 7-34
Gate Oscillators vs. Discrete Devices 7-36
   Fundamental vs. Overtone Operation 7-37
   "Series" vs. "Parallel" Operation 7-37

CONTENTS PAGE

MORE ABOUT USING THE "ON-CHIP" OSCILLATORS 7-37
Oscillator Calculations 7-37
Start-Up Characteristics 7-39
Steady-State Characteristics 7-41
   Pin Capacitance 7-42
   MCS®-51 Oscillator 7-42
   MCS®-48 Oscillator 7-42

CONTENTS PAGE

Pre-Production Tests 7-45
Troubleshooting Oscillator Problems 7-46

APPENDIX A: QUARTZ AND CERAMIC RESONATOR FORMULAS 7-48

APPENDIX B: OSCILLATOR ANALYSIS PROGRAM 7-50

AP-155

INTRODUCTION

Intel's microcontroller families (MCS®-48, MCS®-51, and iACX-96) contain a circuit that is commonly referred to as the "on-chip oscillator". The on-chip circuitry is not itself an oscillator, of course, but an amplifier that is suitable for use as the amplifier part of a feedback oscillator. The data sheets and Microcontroller Handbook show how the on-chip amplifier and several off-chip components can be used to design a working oscillator. With proper selection of off-chip components, these oscillator circuits will perform better than almost any other type of clock oscillator, and by almost any criterion of excellence. The suggested circuits are simple, economical, stable, and reliable.

We offer assistance to our customers in selecting suitable off-chip components to work with the on-chip oscillator circuitry. It should be noted, however, that Intel cannot assume the responsibility of writing specifications for the off-chip components of the complete oscillator circuit, nor of guaranteeing the performance of the finished design in production, anymore than a transistor manufacturer, whose data sheets show a number of suggested amplifier circuits, can assume responsibility for the operation, in production, of any of them.

We are often asked why we don't publish a list of required crystal or ceramic resonator specifications, and recommend values for the other off-chip components. This has been done in the past, but sometimes with consequences that were not intended.

Suppose we suggest a maximum crystal resistance of 30 ohms for some given frequency. Then your crystal supplier tells you the 30-ohm crystals are going to cost twice as much as 50-ohm crystals. Fearing that Intel will not "guarantee operation" with 50-ohm crsytals, you order the expensive ones. In fact, Intel guarantees only what is embodied within an Intel product. Besides, there is no reason why 50-ohm crystals couldn't be used, if the other off-chip components are suitably adjusted.

Should we recommend values for the other off-chip components? Should we do it for 50-ohm crystals or 30-ohm crystals? With respect to what should we optimize their selection? Should we minimize start-up time or maximize frequency stability? In many applications, neither start-up time nor frequency stability are particularly critical, and our "recommendations" are only restricting your system to unnecessary tolerances. It all depends on the application.

Although we will neither "specify" nor "recommend" specific off-chip components, we do offer assistance in these tasks. Intel application engineers are available to provide whatever technical assistance may be needed or desired by our customers in designing with Intel products.

This Application Note is intended to provide such assistance in the design of oscillator circuits for microcontroller systems. Its purpose is to describe in a practical manner how oscillators work, how crystals and ceramic resonators work (and thus how to spec them), and what the on-chip amplifier looks like electronically and what its operating characteristics are. A BASIC program is provided in Appendix II to assist the designer in determining the effects of changing individual parameters. Suggestions are provided for establishing a pre-production test program.

FEEDBACK OSCILLATORS

Loop Gain

Figure 1 shows an amplifier whose output line goes into some passive network. If the input signal to the amplifier is v_1, then the output signal from the amplifier is $v_2 = Av_1$ and the output signal from the passive network is $v_3 = \beta v_2 = \beta A v_1$. Thus βA is the overall gain from terminal 1 to terminal 3.

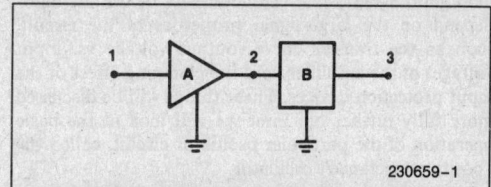

Figure 1. Factors in Loop Gain

Now connect terminal 1 to terminal 3, so that the signal path forms a loop: 1 to 2 to 3, which is also 1. Now we have a feedback loop, and the gain factor βA is called the *loop gain*.

Gain factors are complex numbers. That means they have a magnitude and a phase angle, both of which vary with frequency. When writing a complex number, one must specify both quantities, magnitude and angle. A number whose magnitude is 3, and whose angle is 45 degrees is commonly written this way: $3\angle 45°$. The number 1 is, in complex number notation, $1\angle 0°$, while -1 is $1\angle 180°$.

By closing the feedback loop in Figure 1, we force the equality

$$v_1 = \beta A v_1$$

This equation has two solutions:

1) $v_1 = 0$;

2) $\beta A = 1\angle 0°$.

7-27

In a given circuit, either or both of the solutions may be in effect. In the first solution the circuit is quiescent (no output signal). If you're trying to make an oscillator, a no-signal condition is unacceptable. There are ways to guarantee that the second solution is the one that will be in effect, and that the quiescent condition will be excluded.

How Feedback Oscillators Work

A feedback oscillator amplifies its own noise and feeds it back to itself in exactly the right phase, at the oscillation frequency, to build up and reinforce the desired oscillations. Its ability to do that depends on its loop gain. First, oscillations can occur only at the frequency for which the loop gain has a phase angle of 0 degrees. Second build-up of oscillations will occur only if the loop gain exceeds 1 at the frequency. Build-up continues until nonlinearities in the circuit reduce the average value of the loop gain to exactly 1.

Start-up characteristics depend on the small-signal properties of the circuit, specifically, the small-signal loop gain. Steady-state characteristics of the oscillator depend on the large-signal properties of the circuit, such as the transfer curve (output voltage vs. input voltage) of the amplifier, and the clamping effect of the input protection devices. These things will be discussed more fully further on. First we will look at the basic operation of the particular oscillator circuit, called the "positive reactance" oscillator.

The Positive Reactance Oscillator

Figure 2 shows the configuration of the positive reactance oscillator. The inverting amplifier, working into the impedance of the feedback network, produces an output signal that is nominally 180 degrees out of phase with its input. The feedback network must provide an additional 180 degrees phase shift, such that the overall loop gain has zero (or 360) degrees phase shift at the oscillation frequency.

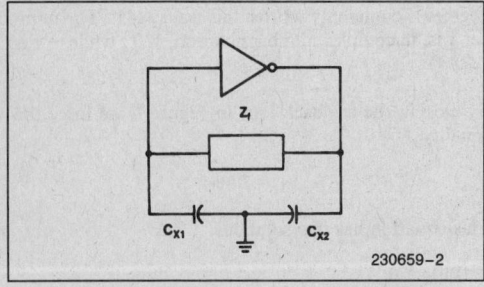

Figure 2. Positive Reactance Oscillator

In order for the loop gain to have zero phase angle it is necessary that the feedback element Z_f have a positive reactance. That is, it must be inductive. Then, the frequency at which the phase angle is zero is approximately the frequency at which

$$X_f = \frac{+1}{\omega C}$$

where X_f is the reactance of Z_f (the total Z_f being $R_f + jX_f$, and C is the series combination of C_{X1} and C_{X2}.

$$C = \frac{C_{X1} C_{X2}}{C_{X1} + C_{X2}}$$

In other words, Z_f and C form a parallel resonant circuit.

If Z_f is an inductor, then $X_f = \omega L$, and the frequency at which the loop gain has zero phase is the frequency at which

$$\omega L = \frac{1}{\omega C}$$

or

$$\omega = \frac{1}{\sqrt{LC}}$$

Normally, Z_f is not an inductor, but it must still have a positive reactance in order for the circuit to oscillate. There are some piezoelectric devices on the market that show a positive reactance, and provide a more stable oscillation frequency than an inductor will. Quartz crystals can be used where the oscillation frequency is critical, and lower cost ceramic resonators can be used where the frequency is less critical.

When the feedback element is a piezoelectric device, this circuit configuration is called a Pierce oscillator. The advantage of piezoelectric resonators lies in their property of providing a wide range of positive reactance values over a very narrow range of frequencies. The reactance will equal $1/\omega C$ at some frequency within this range, so the oscillation frequency will be within the same range. Typically, the width of this range is only 0.3% of the nominal frequency of a quartz crystal, and about 3% of the nominal frequency of a ceramic resonator. With relatively little design effort, frequency accuracies of 0.03% or better can be obtained with quartz crystals, and 0.3% or better with ceramic resonators.

QUARTZ CRYSTALS

The crystal resonator is a thin slice of quartz sandwiched between two electrodes. Electrically, the device looks pretty much like a 5 or 6 pF capacitor, except that over certain ranges of frequencies the crystal has a positive (i.e., inductive) reactance.

The ranges of positive reactance originate in the piezoelectric property of quartz: Squeezing the crystal generates an internal E-field. The effect is reversible: Applying an AC E-field causes the crystal to vibrate. At certain vibrational frequencies there is a mechanical resonance. As the E-field frequency approaches a frequency of mechanical resonance, the measured reactance of the crystal becomes positive, as shown in Figure 3.

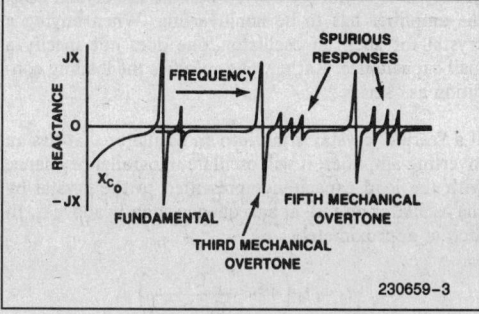

Figure 3. Crystal Reactance vs. Frequency

Typically there are several ranges of frequencies wherein the reactance of the crystal is positive. Each range corresponds to a different mode of vibration in the crystal. The main resonances are the so-called fundamental response and the third and fifth overtone responses.

The overtone responses shouldn't be confused with the harmonics of the fundamental. They're not harmonics, but different vibrational modes. They're not in general at exact integer multiples of the fundamental frequency. There will also be "spurious" responses, occurring typically a few hundred KHz above each main response.

To assure that an oscillator starts in the desired mode on power-up, something must be done to suppress the loop gain in the undesired frequency ranges. The crystal itself provides some protection against unwanted modes of oscillation; too much resistance in that mode, for example. Additionally, junction capacitances in the amplifying devices tend to reduce the gain at higher frequencies, and thus may discriminate against unwanted modes. In some cases a circuit fix is necessary, such as inserting a trap, a phase shifter, or ferrite beads to kill oscillations in unwanted modes.

Crystal Parameters

Equivalent Circuit

Figure 4 shows an equivalent circuit that is used to represent the crystal for circuit analysis.

The R_1-L_1-C_1 branch is called the motivational arm of the crystal. The values of these parameters derive from the mechanical properties of the crystal and are constant for a given mode of vibration. Typical values for various nominal frequencies are shown in Table 1.

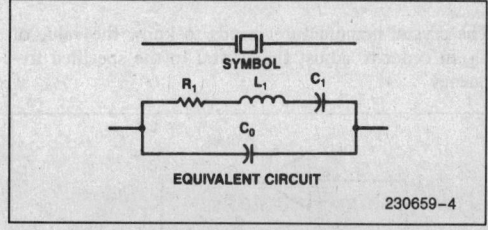

Figure 4. Quartz Crystal: Symbol and Equivalent Circuit

C_0 is called the shunt capacitance of the crystal. This is the capacitance of the crystal's electrodes and the mechanical holder. If one were to measure the reactance of the crystal at a frequency far removed from a resonance frequency, it is the reactance of this capacitance that would be measured. It's normally 3 to 7 pF.

Table 1. Typical Crystal Parameters

Frequency MHz	R_1 ohms	L_1 mH	C_1 pF	C_0 pF
2	100	520	0.012	4
4.608	36	117	0.010	2.9
11.25	19	8.38	0.024	5.4

The series resonant frequency of the crystal is the frequency at which L_1 and C_1 are in resonance. This frequency is given by

$$f_s = \frac{1}{2\pi\sqrt{L_1 C_1}}$$

At this frequency the impedance of the crystal is R_1 in parallel with the reactance of C_0. For most purposes, this impedance is taken to be just R_1, since the reactance of C_0 is so much larger than R_1.

Load Capacitance

A crystal oscillator circuit such as the one shown in Figure 2 (redrawn in Figure 5) operates at the frequency for which the crystal is antiresonant (ie, parallel-resonant) with the total capacitance across the crystal terminals external to the crystal. This total capacitance external to the crystal is called the load capacitance.

As shown in Figure 5, the load capacitance is given by

$$C_L = \frac{C_{X1} C_{X2}}{C_{X1} + C_{X2}} + C_{stray}$$

The crystal manufacturer needs to know the value of C_L in order to adjust the crystal to the specified frequency.

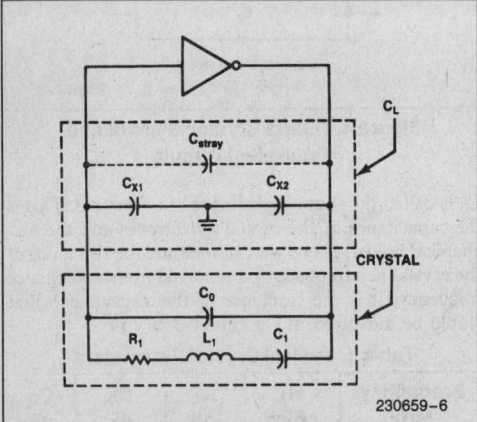

Figure 5. Load Capacitance

The adjustment involves putting the crystal in *series* with the specified C_L, and then "trimming" the crystal to obtain resonance of the series combination of the crystal and C_L at the specified frequency. Because of the high Q of the crystal, the resonant frequency of the series combination of the crystal and C_L is the same as

the antiresonant frequency of the *parallel* combination of the crystal and C_L. This frequency is given by

$$f_a = \frac{1}{2\pi\sqrt{L_1 C_1 (C_L + C_0)/(C_1 + C_L + C_0)}}$$

These frequency formulas are derived (in Appendix A) from the equivalent circuit of the crystal, using the assumptions that the Q of the crystal is extremely high, and that the circuit external to the crystal has no effect on the frequency other than to provide the load capacitance C_L. The latter assumption is not precisely true, but it is close enough for present purposes.

"Series" vs. "Parallel" Crystals

There is no such thing as a "series cut" crystal as opposed to a "parallel cut" crystal. There are different cuts of crystal, having to do with the parameters of its motional arm in various frequency ranges, but there is no special cut for series or parallel operation.

An oscillator is series resonant if the oscillation frequency is f_s of the crystal. To operate the crystal at f_s, the amplifier has to be noninverting. When buying a crystal for such an oscillator, one does not specify a load capacitance. Rather, one specifies the loading condition as "series."

If a "series" crystal is put into an oscillator that has an inverting amplifier, it will oscillate in parallel resonance with the load capacitance presented to the crystal by the oscillator circuit, at a frequency slightly above f_s. In fact, at approximately

$$f_a = f_s \left(1 + \frac{C_1}{2(C_L + C_0)}\right)$$

This frequency would typically be about 0.02% above f_s.

Equivalent Series Resistance

The "series resistance" often listed on quartz crystal data sheets is the real part of the crystal impedance at the crystal's calibration frequency. This will be R1 if the calibration frequency is the series resonant frequency of the crystal. If the crystal is calibrated for parallel resonance with a load capacitance CL, the equivalent series resistance will be

$$ESR = R_1 \left(1 + \frac{C_0}{C_L}\right)^2$$

The crystal manufacturer measures this resistance at the calibration frequency during the same operation in which the crystal is adjusted to the calibration frequency.

Frequency Tolerance

Frequency tolerance as discussed here is not a requirement on the crystal, but on the complete oscillator. There are two types of frequency tolerances on oscillators: frequency *acccuracy* and frequency *stability*. Frequency accuracy refers to the oscillator's ability to run at an exact specified frequency. Frequency stability refers to the constancy of the oscillation frequency.

Frequency accuracy requires mainly that the oscillator circuit present to the crystal the same load capacitance that it was adjusted for. Frequency stability requires mainly that the load capacitance be constant.

In most digital applications the accuracy and stability requirements on the oscillator are so wide that it makes very little difference what load capacitance the crystal was adjusted to, or what load capacitance the circuit actually presents to the crystal. For example, if a crystal was calibrated to a load capacitance of 25 pF, and is used in a circuit whose actual load capacitance is 50 pF, the frequency error on that account would be less than 0.01%.

In a positive reactance oscillator, the crystal only needs to be in the intended response mode for the oscillator to satisfy a 0.5% or better frequency tolerance. That's because for any load capacitance the oscillation frequency is certain to be between the crystal's resonant and antiresonant frequencies.

Phase shifts that take place within the amplifier part of the oscillator will also affect frequency accuracy and stability. These phase shifts can normally be modeled as an "output capacitance" that, in the positive reactance oscillator, parallels C_{X2}. The predictability and constancy of this output capacitance over temperature and device sample will be the limiting factor in determining the tolerances that the circuit is capable of holding.

Drive Level

Drive level refers to the power dissipation in the crystal. There are two reasons for specifying it. One is that the parameters in the equivalent circuit are somewhat dependent on the drive level at which the crystal is calibrated. The other is that if the application circuit exceeds the test drive level by too much, the crystal may be damaged. Note that the terms "test drive level" and "rated drive level" both refer to the drive level at which the crystal is calibrated. Normally, in a microcontroller system, neither the frequency tolerances nor the power levels justify much concern for this specification. Some crystal manufacturers don't even require it for microprocessor crystals.

In a positive reactance oscillator, if one assumes the peak voltage across the crystal to be something in the neighborhood of V_{CC}, the power dissipation can be approximated as

$$P = 2R_1 \, [\pi f \, (C_L + C_0) \, V_{CC}]^2$$

This formula is derived in Appendix A. In a 5V system, P rarely evaluates to more than a milliwatt. Crystals with a standard 1 or 2 mW drive level rating can be used in most digital systems.

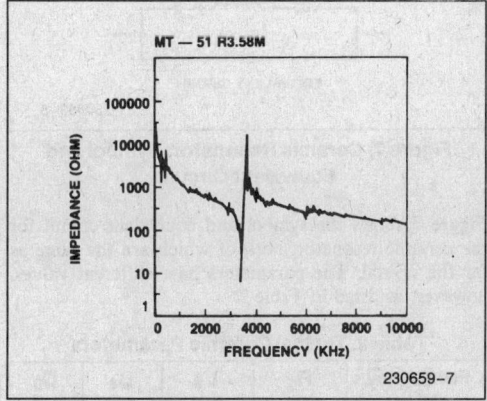

Figure 6. Ceramic Resonator Impedance vs. Frequency (Test Data Supplied by NTK Technical Ceramics)

CERAMIC RESONATORS

Ceramic resonators operate on the same basic principles as a quartz crsytal. Like quartz crsytals, they are piezoelectric, have a reactance versus frequency curve similar to a crystal's, and an equivalent circuit that looks just like a crystal's (with different parameter values, however).

The frequency tolerance of a ceramic resonator is about two orders of magnitude wider than a crystal's, but the ceramic is somewhat cheaper than a crystal. It may be noted for comparison that quartz crystals with relaxed tolerances cost about twice as much as ceramic resonators. For purposes of clocking a microcontroller, the frequency tolerance is often relatively noncritical, and the economic consideration becomes the dominant factor.

Figure 6 shows a graph of impedance magnitude versus frequency for a 3.58 MHz ceramic resonator. (Note that Figure 6 is a graph of $|Z_f|$ versus frequency, where

AP-155

as Figure 3 is a graph of X_f versus frequency.) A number of spurious responses are apparent in Figure 6. The manufacturers state that spurious responses are more prevalent in the lower frequency resonators (kHz range) than in the higher frequency units (MHz range). For our purposes only the MHz range ceramics need to be considered.

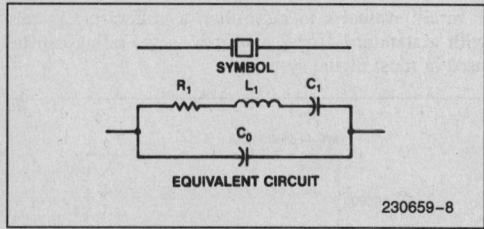

Figure 7. Ceramic Resonator: Symbol and Equivalent Circuit

Figure 7 shows the symbol and equivalent circuit for the ceramic resonator, both of which are the same as for the crystal. The parameters have different values, however, as listed in Table 2.

Table 2. Typical Ceramic Parameters

Frequency MHz	R_1 ohms	L_1 mH	C_1 pF	C_0 pF
3.58	7	0.113	19.6	140
6.0	8	0.094	8.3	60
8.0	7	0.092	4.6	40
11.0	10	0.057	3.9	30

Note that the motional arm of the ceramic resonator tends to have less resistance than the quartz crystal and also a vastly reduced L_1/C_1 ratio. This results in the motional arm having a Q (given by $(1/R_1)\sqrt{L_1/C_1}$) that is typically two orders of magnitude lower than that of a quartz crystal. The lower Q makes for a faster startup of the oscilaltor and for a less closely controlled frequency (meaning that circuitry external to the resonator will have more influence on the frequency than with a quartz crystal).

Another major difference is that the shunt capacitance of the ceramic resonator is an order of magnitude higher than C_0 of the quartz crystal and more dependent on the frequency of the resonator.

The implications of these differences are not all obvious, but some will be indicated in the section on Oscillator Calculations.

Specifications for Ceramic Resonators

Ceramic resonators are easier to specify than quartz crystals. All the vendor wants to know is the desired frequency and the chip you want it to work with. They'll supply the resonators, a circuit diagram showing the positions and values of other external components that may be required and a guarantee that the circuit will work properly at the specified frequency.

OSCILLATOR DESIGN CONSIDERATIONS

Designers of microcontroller systems have a number of options to choose from for clocking the system. The main decision is whether to use the "on-chip" oscillator or an external oscillator. If the choice is to use the on-chip oscillator, what kinds of external components are needed to make it operate as advertised? If the choice is to use an external oscillator, what type of oscillator should it be?

The decisions have to be based on both economic and technical requirements. In this section we'll discuss some of the factors that should be considered.

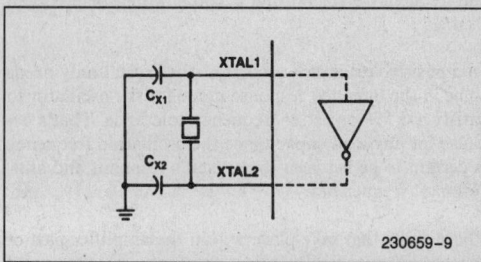

Figure 8. Using the "On-Chip" Oscillator

On-Chip Oscillators

In most cases, the on-chip amplifier with the appropriate external components provides the most economical solution to the clocking problem. Exceptions may arise in severe environments when frequency tolerances are tighter than about 0.01%.

The external components that need to be added are a positive reactance (normally a crystal or ceramic resonator) and the two capacitors C_{X1} and C_{X2}, as shown in Figure 8.

Crystal Specifications

Specifications for an appropriate crystal are not very critical, unless the frequency is. *Any* fundamental-mode crystal of medium or better quality can be used.

AP-155

We are often asked what maximum crystal resistance should be specified. The best answer to this question is the lower the better, but use what's available. The crystal resistance will have some effect on start-up time and steady-state amplitude, but not so much that it can't be compensated for by appropriate selection of the capacitances C_{X1} and C_{X2}.

Similar questions are asked about specifications of load capacitance and shunt capacitance. The best advice we can give is to understand what these parameters mean and how they affect the operation of the circuit (that being the purpose of this Application Note), and then decide for yourself if such specifications are meaningful in your application or not. Normally, they're not, unless your frequency tolerances are tighter than about 0.1%.

Part of the problem is that crystal manufacturers are accustomed to talking "ppm" tolerances with radio engineers and simply won't take your order until you've filled out their list of specifications. It will help if you define your actual frequency tolerance requirements, both for yourself and to the crystal manufacturer. Don't pay for 0.003% crystals if your actual frequency tolerance is 1%.

Oscillation Frequency

The oscillation frequency is determined 99.5% by the crystal and up to about 0.5% by the circuit external to the crystal. The on-chip amplifier has little effect on the frequency, which is as it should be, since the amplifier parameters are temperature and process dependent.

The influence of the on-chip amplifier on the frequency is by means of its input and output (pin-to-ground) capacitances, which parallel C_{X1} and C_{X2}, and the XTAL1-to-XTAL2 (pin-to-pin) capacitance, which parallels the crystal. The input and pin-to-pin capacitances are about 7 pF each. Internal phase deviations from the nominal 180° can be modeled as an output capacitance of 25 to 30 pF. These deviations from the ideal have less effect in the positive reactance oscillator (with the inverting amplifer) than in a comparable series resonant oscillator (with the noninverting amplifier) for two reasons: first, the effect of the output capacitance is lessened, if not swamped, by the off-chip capacitor; secondly, the positive reactance oscillator is less sensitive, frequency-wise, to such phase errors.

Selection of C_{X1} and C_{X2}

Optimal values for the capacitors C_{X1} and C_{X2} depend on whether a quartz crystal or ceramic resonator is being used, and also on application-specific requirements on start-up time and frequency tolerance.

Start-up time is sometimes more critical in microcontroller systems than frequency stability, because of various reset and initialization requirements.

Less commonly, accuracy of the oscillator frequency is also critical, for example, when the oscillator is being used as a time base. As a general rule, fast start-up and stable frequency tend to pull the oscillator design in opposite directions.

Considerations of both start-up time and frequency stability over temperature suggest that C_{X1} and C_{X2} should be about equal and at least 20 pF. (But they don't *have* to be either.) Increasing the value of these capacitances above some 40 or 50 pF improves frequency stability. It also tends to increase the start-up time. There is a maximum value (several hundred pF, depending on the value of R_1 of the quartz or ceramic resonator) above which the oscillator won't start up at all.

If the on-chip amplifier is a simple inverter, such as in the 8051, the user can select values for C_{X1} and C_{X2} between some 20 and 100 pF, depending on whether start-up time or frequency stability is the more critical parameter in a specific application. If the on-chip amplifier is a Schmitt Trigger, such as in the 8048, smaller values of C_{X1} must be used (5 to 30 pF), in order to prevent the oscillator from running in a relaxation mode.

Later sections in this Application Note will discuss the effects of varying C_{X1} and C_{X2} (as well as other parameters), and will have more to say on their selection.

Placement of Components

Noise glitches arriving at XTAL1 or XTAL2 pins at the wrong time can cause a miscount in the internal clock-generating circuitry. These kinds of glitches can be produced through capacitive coupling between the oscillator components and PCB traces carrying digital signals with fast rise and fall times. For this reason, the oscillator components should be mounted close to the chip and have short, direct traces to the XTAL1, XTAL2, and VSS pins.

Clocking Other Chips

There are times when it would be desirable to use the on-chip oscillator to clock other chips in the system.

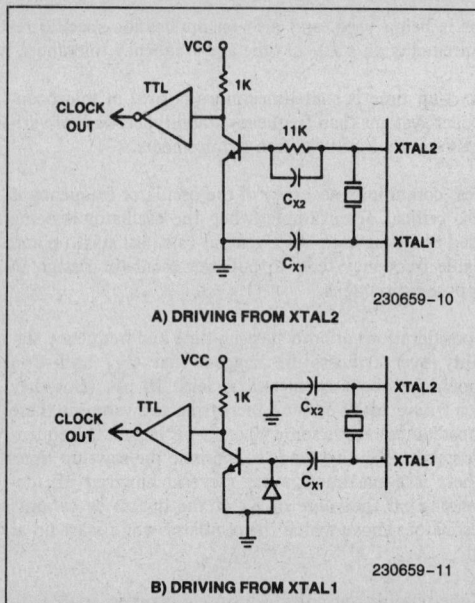

Figure 9. Using the On-Chip Oscillator to Drive Other Chips

This can be done if an appropriate buffer is used. A TTL buffer puts too much load on the on-chip amplifier for reliable start-up. A CMOS buffer (such as the 74HC04) can be used, if it's fast enough and if its VIH and VIL specs are compatible with the available signal amplitudes. Circuits such as shown in Figure 9 might also be considered for these types of applications.

Clock-related signals are available at the TO pin in the MCS-48 products, at ALE in the MCS-48 and MCS-51 lines, and the iACX-96 controllers provide a CLKOUT signal.

External Oscillators

When technical requirements dictate the use of an external oscillator, the external drive requirements for the microcontroller, as published in the data sheet, must be carefully noted. The logic levels are not in general TTL-compatible. And each controller has its idiosyncracies in this regard. The 8048, for example, requires that both XTAL1 and XTAL2 be driven. The 8051 *can* be driven that way, but the data sheet suggest the simpler method of grounding XTAL1 and driving XTAL2. For this method, the driving source must be capable of sinking some current when XTAL2 is being driven low.

For the external oscillator itself, there are basically two choices: ready-made and home-grown.

AP-155

TTL Crystal Clock Oscillator

The HS-100, HS-200, & HS-500 all-metal package series of oscillators are TTL compatible & fit a DIP layout. Standard electrical specifications are shown below. Variations are available for special applications.

Frequency Range: HS-100—3.5 MHz to 30 MHz
HS-200—225 KHz to 3.5 MHz
HS-500—25 MHz to 60 MHz

Frequency Tolerance: ±0.1% Overall 0°C–70°C

Hermetically Sealed Package
Mass spectrometer leak rate max.
1×10^{-8} atmos. cc/sec. of helium

Output Waveform

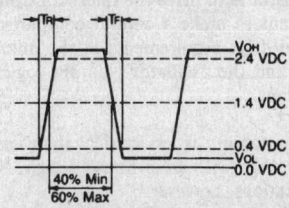

230659-12

	INPUT			
	HS-100		HS-200	HS-500
	3.5 MHz–20 MHz	20+ MHz–30 MHz	225 KHz–4.0 MHz	25 MHz–60 MHz
Supply Voltage (V_{CC})	5V ±10%	5V ±10%	5V ±10%	5V ±10%
Supply Current (I_{CC}) max.	30 mA	40 mA	85 mA	50 mA
	OUTPUT			
	HS-100		HS-200	HS-500
	3.5 MHz–20 MHz	20+ MHz–30 MHz	225 KHz–4.0 MHz	25 MHz–60 MHz
V_{OH} (Logic "1")	+2.4V min.[1]	+2.7V min.[2]	+2.4V min.[1]	+2.7V min.[2]
V_{OL} (Logic "0")	+0.4V max.[3]	+0.5V max.[4]	+0.4V max.[3]	+0.5V max.[4]
Symmetry	60/40%[5]	60/40%[5]	55/45%[5]	60/40%[5]
T_R, T_F (Rise & Fall Time)	< 10 ns[6]	< 5 ns[6]	< 15 ns[6]	< 5 ns[6]
Output Short Circuit Current	18 mA min.	40 mA min.	18 mA min.	40 mA min.
Output Load	1 to 10 TTL Loads[7]	1 to 10 TTL Loads[8]	1 to 10 TTL Loads[7]	1 to 10 TTL Loads[8]

CONDITIONS
[1] I_O source = −400 µA max.
[2] I_O source = −1.0 mA max.
[3] I_O sink = 16.0 mA max.
[4] I_O sink = 20.00 mA max.
[5] V_O = 1.4V
[6] (0.4V to 2.4V)
[7] 1.6 mA per load
[8] 2.0 mA per load

Figure 10. Pre-Packaged Oscillator Data*

*Reprinted with the permission of ©Midland-Ross Corporation 1982.

Prepackaged oscillators are available from most crystal manufacturers, and have the advantage that the system designer can treat the oscillator as a black box whose performance is guaranteed by people who carry many years of experience in designing and building oscillators. Figure 10 shows a typical data sheet for some prepackaged oscillators. Oscillators are also available with complementary outputs.

If the oscillator is to drive the microcontroller directly, one will want to make a careful comparison between the external drive requirements in the microcontroller data sheet and the oscillator's output logic levels and test conditions.

If oscillator stability is less critical than cost, the user may prefer to go with an in-house design. Not without some precautions, however.

It's easy to design oscillators that work. Almost all of them do work, even if the designer isn't too clear on why. The key point here is that *almost* all of them work. The problems begin when the system goes into production, and marginal units commence malfunctioning in the field. Most digital designers, after all, are not very adept at designing oscillators *for production*.

Oscillator design is somewhat of a black art, with the quality of the finished product being *very* dependent on the designer's experience and intuition. For that reason the most important consideration in any design is to have an adequate preproduction test program. Preproduction tests are discussed later in this Application Note. Here we will discuss some of the design options and take a look at some commonly used configurations.

Gate Oscillators versus Discrete Devices

Digital systems designers are understandably reluctant to get involved with discrete devices and their peculiarities (biasing techniques, etc.). Besides, the component count for these circuits tends to be quite a bit higher than what a digital designer is used to seeing for that amount of functionality. Nevertheless, if there are unusual requirements on the accuracy and stability of the clock frequency, it should be noted that discrete device oscillators can be tailored to suit the exact needs of the application and perfected to a level that would be difficult for a gate oscillator to approach.

In most cases, when an external oscillator is needed, the designer tends to rely on some form of a gate oscillator. A TTL inverter with a resistor connecting the output to the input makes a suitable inverting amplifier. The resistor holds the inverter in the transition region between logical high and low, so that at least for start-up purposes the inverter is a linear amplifier.

The feedback resistance has to be quite low, however, since it must conduct current sourced by the input pin without allowing the DC input voltage to get too far above the DC output voltage. For biasing purposes, the feedback resistance should not exceed a few k-ohms. But shunting the crystal with such a low resistance does not encourage start-up.

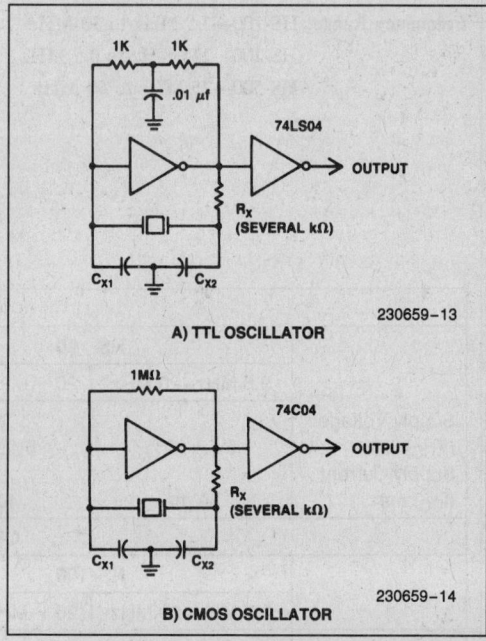

Figure 11. Commonly Used Gate Oscillators

Consequently, the configuration in Figure 11A might be suggested. By breaking R_f into two parts and AC-grounding the midpoint, one achieves the DC feedback required to hold the inverter in its active region, but without the negative signal feedback that is in effect telling the circuit *not* to oscillate. However, this biasing scheme will increase the start-up time, and relaxation-type oscillations are also possible.

A CMOS inverter, such as the 74HC04, might work better in this application, since a larger R_f can be used to hold the inverter in its linear region.

Logic gates tend to have a fairly low output resistance, which destabilizes the oscillator. For that reason a resistor Rx is often added to the feedback network, as shown in Figures 11A and B. At higher frequencies a 20 or 30 pF capacitor is sometimes used in the Rx position, to compensate for some of the internal propagation delay.

Reference 1 contains an excellent discussion of gate oscillators, and a number of design examples.

Fundamental versus Overtone Operation

It's easier to design an oscillator circuit to operate in the resonator's fundamental response mode than to design one for overtone operation. A quartz crystal whose fundamental response mode covers the desired frequency can be obtained up to some 30 MHz. For frequencies above that, the crystal might be used in an overtone mode.

Several problems arise in the design of an overtone oscillator. One is to stop the circuit from oscillating in the fundamental mode, which is what it would really rather do, for a number of reasons, involving both the amplifying device and the crystal. An additional problem with overtone operation is an increased tendency to spurious oscillations. That is because the R_1 of various spurious modes is likely to be about the same as R_1 of the intended overtone response. It may be necessary, as suggested in Reference 1, to specify a "spurious-to-main-response" resistance ratio to avoid the possibility of trouble.

Overtone oscillators are not to be taken lightly. One would be well advised to consult with an engineer who is knowledgeable in the subject during the design phase of such a circuit.

Series versus Parallel Operation

Series resonant oscillators use noninverting amplifiers. To make a noninverting amplifier out of logic gates requires that two inverters be used, as shown in Figure 12.

This type of circuit tends to be inaccurate and unstable in frequency over variations in temperature and V_{CC}. It has a tendency to oscillate at overtones, and to oscillate through C_0 of the crystal or some stray capacitance rather than as controlled by the mechanical resonance of the crystal.

The demon in series resonant oscillators is the phase shift in the amplifier. The series resonant oscillator wants more than just a "noninverting" amplifier—it wants a *zero phase-shift* amplifier. Multistage noninverting amplifiers tend to have a considerably lagging phase shift, such that the crystal reactance must be capacitive in order to bring the total phase shift around the feedback loop back up to 0. In this mode, a "12 MHz" crystal may be running at 8 or 9 MHz. One can put a capacitor in series with the crystal to relieve the crystal of having to produce all of the required phase shift, and bring the oscillation frequency closer to fs. However, to further complicate the situation, the amplifier's phase shift is strongly dependent on frequency, temperature, VCC, and device sample.

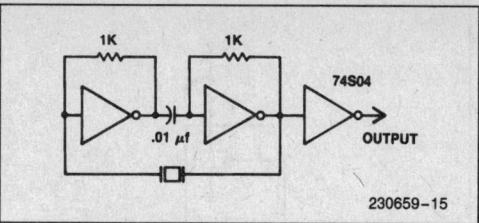

Figure 12. "Series Resonant" Gate Oscillator

Positive reactance oscillators ("parallel resonant") use inverting amplifiers. A single logic inverter can be used for the amplifier, as in Figure 11. The amplifier's phase shift is less critical, compared to a series resonant circuit, and since only one inverter is involved there's less phase error anyway. The oscillation frequency is effectively bounded by the resonant and antiresonant frequencies of the crystal itself. In addition, the feedback network includes capacitors that parallel the input and output terminals of the amplifier, thus reducing the effect of unpredictable capacitances at these points.

MORE ABOUT USING THE "ON-CHIP" OSCILLATORS

In this section we will describe the on-chip inverters on selected microcontrollers in some detail, and discuss criteria for selecting components to work with them. Future data sheets will supplement this discussion with updates and information pertinent to the use of each chip's oscillator circuitry.

Oscillator Calculations

Oscillator design, though aided by theory, is still largely an empirical exercise. The circuit is inherently nonlinear, and the normal analysis parameters vary with instantaneous voltage. In addition, when dealing with the on-chip circuitry, we have FETs being used as resistors, resistors being used as interconnects, distributed delays, input protection devices, parasitic junctions, and processing variations.

Consequently, oscillator calculations are never very precise. They can be useful, however, if they will at least indicate the effects of *variations* in the circuit parameters on start-up time, oscillation frequency, and steady-state amplitude. Start-up time, for example, can be taken as an indication of start-up reliability. If preproduction tests indicate a possible start-up problem, a relatively inexperienced designer can at least be made aware of what parameter may be causing the marginality, and what direction to go in to fix it.

AP-155

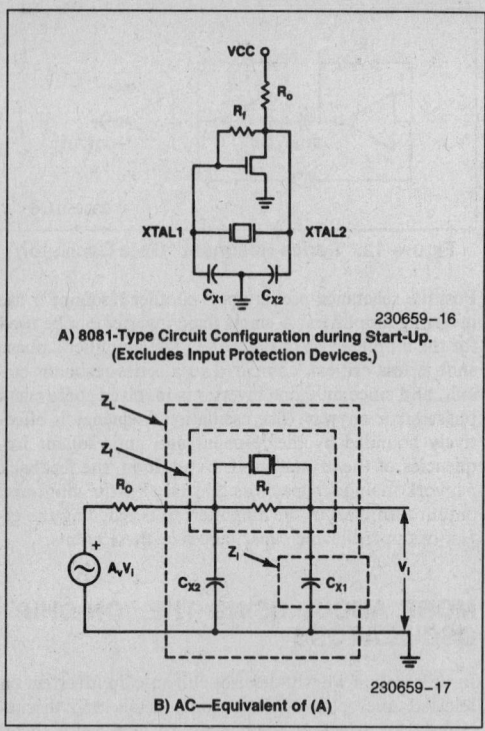

Figure 13. Oscillator Circuit Model Used in Start-Up Calculations

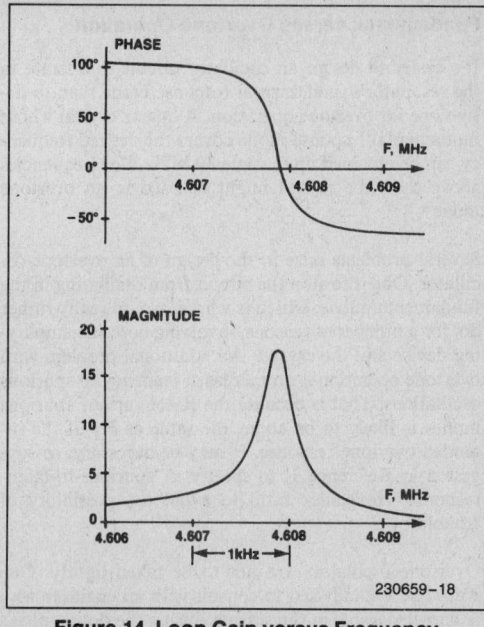

Figure 14. Loop Gain versus Frequency (4.608 MHz Crystal)

The analysis used here is mathematically straightforward but algebraically intractable. That means it's relatively easy to understand and program into a computer, but it will not yield a neat formula that gives, say, steady-state amplitude as a function of this or that list of parameters. A listing of a BASIC program that implements the analysis will be found in Appendix II.

When the circuit is first powered up, and before the oscillations have commenced (and if the oscillations *fail* to commence), the oscillator can be treated as a small signal linear amplifier with feedback. In that case, standard small-signal analysis techniques can be used to determine start-up characteristics. The circuit model used in this analysis is shown in Figure 13.

The circuit approximates that there are no high-frequency effects within the amplifier itslef, such that its high-frequency behavior is dominated by the load impedance Z_L. This is a reasonable approximation for single-stage amplifiers of the type used in 8051-type devices. Then the gain of the amplifier as a function of frequency is

$$A = \frac{A_v Z_L}{Z_L + R_0}$$

The gain of the feedback network is

$$\beta = \frac{Z_i}{Z_i + Z_f}$$

And the loop gain is

$$\beta A = \frac{Z_i}{Z_i + Z_f} \times \frac{A_v Z_L}{Z_L + R_0}$$

The impedances Z_L, Z_f, and Z_i are defined in Figure 13B.

Figure 14 shows the way the loop gain thus calculated (using typical 8051-type parameters and a 4.608 MHz crystal) varies with frequency. The frequency of interest is the one for which the phase of the loop gain is zero. The accepted criterion for start-up is that the magnitude of the loop gain must exceed unity at this frequency. This is the frequency at which the circuit is in resonance. It corresponds very closely with the antiresonant frequency of the motional arm of the crystal in parallel with C_L.

Figure 15 shows the way the loop gain varies with frequency when the parameters of a 3.58 MHz ceramic resonator are used in place of a crystal (the amplifier parameters being typical 8051, as in Figure 14). Note the different frequency scales.

AP-155

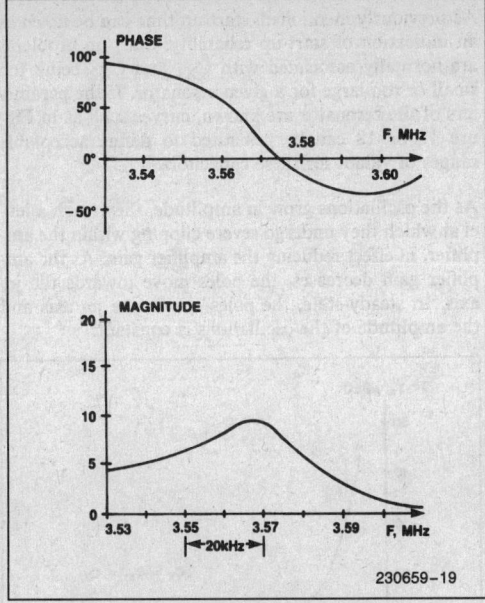

Figure 15. Loop Gain versus Frequency
(3.58 MHz Ceramic)

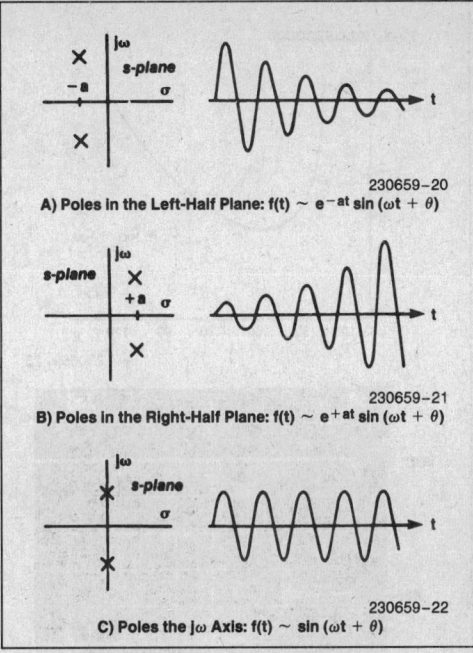

Figure 16. Do You Know Where Your
Poles Are Tonight?

Start-Up Characteristics

It is common, in studies of feedback systems, to examine the behavior of the closed loop gain as a function of complex frequency $s = \sigma + j\omega$; specifically, to determine the location of its poles in the complex plane. A pole is a point on the complex plane where the gain function goes to infinity. Knowledge of its location can be used to predict the response of the system to an input disturbance.

The way that the response function depends on the location of the poles is shown in Figure 16. Poles in the left-half plane cause the response function to take the form of a damped sinusoid. Poles in the right-half plane cause the response function to take the form of an exponentially growing sinusoid. In general,

$$v(t) \sim e^{at} \sin(\omega t + \theta)$$

where a is the real part of the pole frequency. Thus if the pole is in the right-half plane, a is positive and the sinusoid grows. If the pole is in the left-half plane, a is negative and the sinusoid is damped.

The same type of analysis can usefully be applied to oscillators. In this case, however, rather than trying to ensure that the poles are in the left-half plane, we would seek to ensure that they're in the *right*-half plane. An exponentially growing sinusoid is exactly what is wanted from an oscillator that has just been powered up.

The gain function of interest in oscillators is $1/(1 - \beta A)$. Its poles are at the complex frequencies where $\beta A = 1 \angle 0°$, because that value of βA causes the gain function to go to infinity. The oscillator will start up if the real part of the pole frequency is positive. More importantly, the *rate* at which it starts up is indicated by how *much* greater than 0 the real part of the pole frequency is.

The circuit in Figure 13B can be used to find the pole frequencies of the oscillator gain function. All that needs to be done is evaluate the impedances at complex frequencies $\sigma + j\omega$ rather than just at ω, and find the value of $\sigma + j\omega$ for which $\beta A = 1 \angle 0°$. The larger that value of σ is, the faster the oscillator will start up.

Of course, other things besides pole frequencies, things like the VCC rise time, are at work in determining the start-up time. But to the extend that the pole frequencies *do* affect start-up time, we can obtain results like those in Figures 17 and 18.

To obtain these figures the pole frequencies were computed for various values of capacitance C_X from XTAL1 and XTAL2 to ground (thus $C_{X1} = C_{X2} = C_X$). Then a "time constant" for start-up was calculated as $T_s = \dfrac{1}{\sigma}$ where σ is the real part of the pole frequency (rad/sec), and this time constant is plotted versus C_X.

As previously mentioned, start-up time can be taken as an indication of start-up reliability. Start-up problems are normally associated with C_{X1} and C_{X2} being too small or too large for a given resonator. If the parameters of the resonator are known, curves such as in Figure 17 or 18 can be generated to define acceptable ranges of values for these capacitors.

As the oscillations grow in amplitude, they reach a level at which they undergo severe clipping within the amplifier, in effect reducing the amplifier gain. As the amplifier gain decreases, the poles move towards the $j\omega$ axis. In steady-state, the poles are on the $j\omega$ axis and the amplitude of the oscillations is constant.

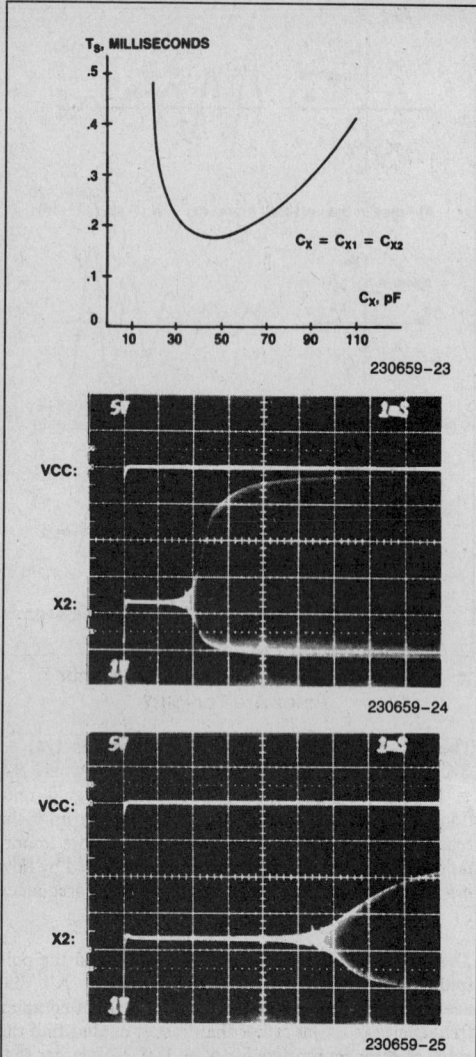

Figure 17. Oscillator Start-Up (4.608 MHz Crystal from Standard Crystal Corp.)

A short time constant means faster start-up. A long time constant means slow start-up. Observations of actual start-ups are shown in the figures. Figure 17 is for a typical 8051 with a 4.608 MHz crystal supplied by Standard Crystal Corp., and Figure 18 is for a typical 8051 with a 3.58 MHz ceramic resonator supplied by NTK Technical Ceramics, Ltd.

It can be seen in Figure 17 that, for this crystal, values of C_X between 30 and 50 pF minimize start-up time, but that the exact value in this range is not particularly important, even if the start-up time itself is critical.

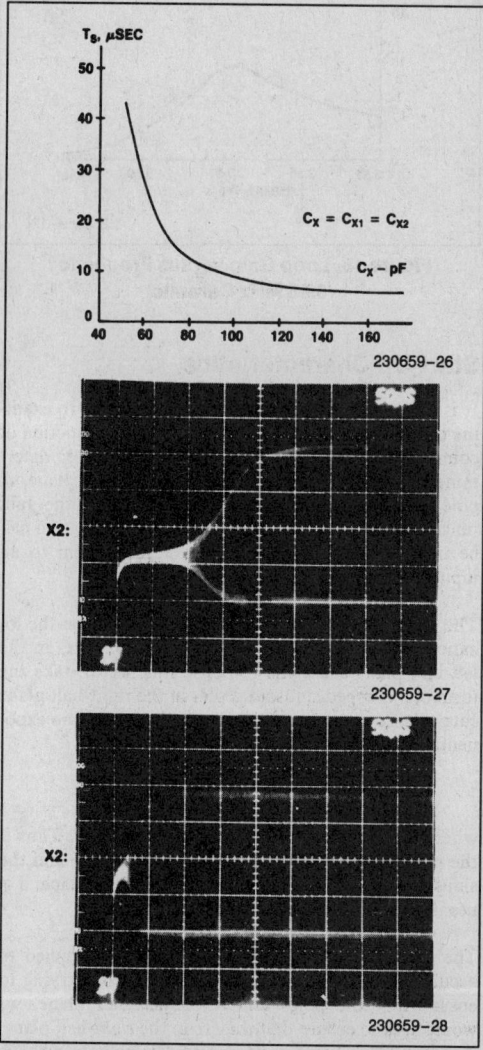

Figure 18. Oscillator Start-Up (3.58 MHz Ceramic Resonator from NTK Technical Ceramics)

AP-155

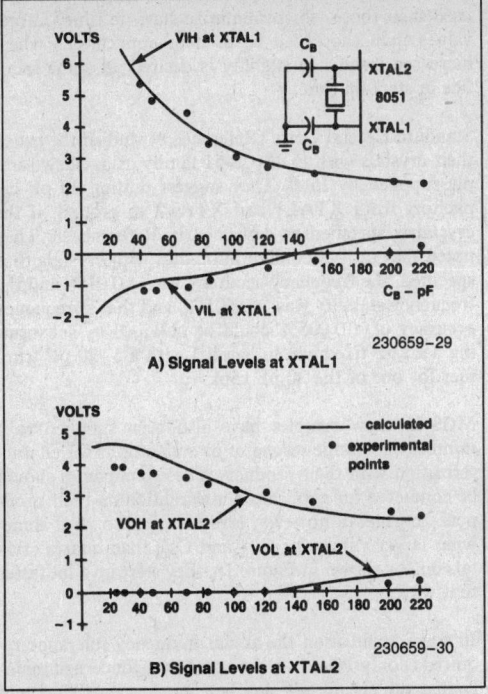

Figure 19. Calculated and Experimental Steady-State Amplitudes vs. Bulk Capacitance from XTAL1 and XTAL2 to Ground

Steady-State Characteristics

Steady-state analysis is greatly complicated by the fact that we are dealing with large signals and nonlinear circuit response. The circuit parameters vary with instantaneous voltage, and a number of clamping and clipping mechanisms come into play. Analyses that take all these things into account are too complicated to be of general use, and analyses that don't take them into account are too inaccurate to justify the effort.

There is a steady-state analysis in Appendix B that takes some of the complications into account and ignores others. Figure 19 shows the way the steady-state amplitudes thus calculated (using typical 8051 parameters and a 4.608 MHz crystal) vary with equal bulk capacitance placed from XTAL1 and XTAL2 to ground. Experimental results are shown for comparison.

The waveform at XTAL1 is a fairly clean sinusoid. Its negative peak is normally somewhat below zero, at a level which is determined mainly by the input protection circuitry at XTAL1.

The input protection circuitry consists of an ohmic resistor and an enhancement-mode FET with the gate and source connected to ground (VSS), as shown in Figure 20 for the 8051, and in Figure 21 for the 8048. Its function is to limit the positive voltage at the gate of the input FET to the avalanche voltage of the drain junction. If the input pin is driven below VSS, the drain and source of the protection FET interchange roles, so its gate is connected to what is now the drain. In this condition the device resembles a diode with the anode connected to VSS.

There is a parasitic pn junction between the ohmic resistor and the substrate. In the ROM parts (8015, 8048, etc.) the substrate is held at approximately $-3V$ by the on-chip back-bias generator. In the EPROM parts (8751, 8748, etc.) the substrate is connected to VSS.

The effect of the input protection circuitry on the oscillator is that if the XTAL1 signal goes negative, its negative peak is clamped to $-V_{DS}$ of the protection FET in the ROM parts, and to about $-0.5V$ in the EPROM parts. These negative voltages on XTAL1 are in this application self-limiting and nondestructive.

The clamping action does, however, raise the DC level at XTAL1, which in turn tends to reduce the positive peak at XTAL2. The waveform at XTAL2 resembles a sinusoid riding on a DC level, and whose negative peaks are clipped off at zero.

Since it's normally the XTAL2 signal that drives the internal clocking circuitry, the question naturally arises as to how large this signal must be to reliably do its job. In fact, the XTAL2 signal doesn't have to meet the same VIH and VIL specifications that an external driver would have to. That's because as long as the oscillator is working, the on-chip amplifier is driving itself through its own 0-to-1 transition region, which is very nearly the same as the 0-to-1 transition region in the internal buffer that follows the oscillator. If some processing variations move the transition level higher or lower, the on-chip amplifier tends to compensate for it by the fact that its own transition level is correspondingly higher or lower. (In the 8096, it's the XTAL1 signal that drives the internal clocking circuitry, but the same concept applies.)

The main concern about the XTAL2 signal amplitude is an indication of the general health of the oscillator. An amplitude of less than about 2.5V peak-to-peak indicates that start-up problems could develop in some units (with low gain) with some crystals (with high R_1). The remedy is to either adjust the values of C_{X1} and/or C_{X2} or use a crystal with a lower R_1.

The amplitudes at XTAL1 and XTAL2 can be adjusted by changing the ratio of the capacitors from XTAL1 and XTAL2 to ground. Increasing the XTAL2 capacitance, for example, decreases the amplitude at XTAL2 and increases the amplitude at XTAL1 by about the same amount. Decreasing both caps increases both amplitudes.

7-41

AP-155

Pin Capacitance

Internal pin-to-ground and pin-to-pin capacitances at XTAL1 and XTAL2 will have some effect on the oscillator. These capacitances are normally taken to be in the range of 5 to 10 pF, but they are extremely difficult to evaluate. Any measurement of one such capacitance will necessarily include effects from the others. One advantage of the positive reactance oscillator is that the pin-to-ground capacitances are paralleled by external bulk capacitors, so a precise determination of their value is unnecessary. We would suggest that there is little justification for more precision than to assign them a value of 7 pF (XTAL1-to-ground and XTAL1-to-XTAL2). This value is probably not in error by more than 3 or 4 pF.

The XTAL2-to-ground capacitance is not entirely "pin capacitance," but more like an "equivalent output capacitance" of some 25 to 30 pF, having to include the effect of internal phase delays. This value will vary to some extent with temperature, processing, and frequency.

MCS®-51 Oscillator

The on-chip amplifier on the HMOS MCS-51 family is shown in Figure 20. The drain load and feedback "resistors" are seen to be field-effect transistors. The drain load FET, R_D, is typically equivalent to about 1K to 3 K-ohms. As an amplifier, the low frequency voltage gain is normally between -10 and -20, and the output resistance is effectively R_D.

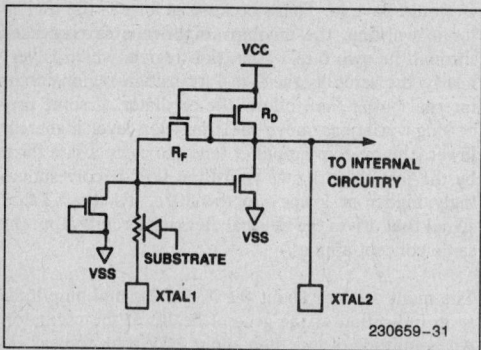

Figure 20. MCS®-51 Oscillator Amplifier

The 80151 oscillator is normally used with equal bulk capacitors placed externally from XTAL1 to ground and from XTAL2 to ground. To determine a reasonable value of capacitance to use in these positions, given a crystal of ceramic resonator of known parameters, one can use the BASIC analysis in Appendix II to generate curves such as in Figures 17 and 18. This procedure will define a range of values that will minimize start-up time. We don't suggest that smaller values be used than those which minimize start-up time. Larger values than those can be used in applications where increased frequency stability is desired, at some sacrifice in start-up time.

Standard Crystal Corp. (Reference 8) studied the use of their crystals with the MCS-51 family using skew sample supplied by Intel. They suggest putting 30 pF capacitors from XTAL1 and XTAL2 to ground, if the crystal is specified as described in Reference 8. They noted that in that configuration and with crystals thus specified, the frequency accuracy was $\pm 0.01\%$ and the frequency stability was $\pm 0.005\%$, and that a frequency accuracy of $\pm 0.005\%$ could be obtained by substituting a 25 pF fixed cap in parallel with a 5–20 pF trimmer for one of the 30 pF caps.

MCS-51 skew samples have also been supplied to a number of ceramic resonator manufacturers for characterization with their products. These companies should be contacted for application information on their products. In general, however, ceramics tend to want somewhat larger values for C_{X1} and C_{X2} than quartz crystals do. As shown in Figure 18, they start up a lot faster that way.

In some application the actual frequency tolerance required is only 1% or so, the user being concerned mainly that the circuit *will* oscillate. In that case, C_{X1} and C_{X2} can be selected rather freely in the range of 20 to 80 pF.

As you can see, "best" values for these components and their tolerances are strongly dependent on the application and its requirements. In any case, their suitability should be verified by environmental testing before the design is submitted to production.

MCS®-48 Oscillator

The NMOS and HMOS MCS-48 oscillator is shown in Figure 21. It differs from the 8051 in that its inverting

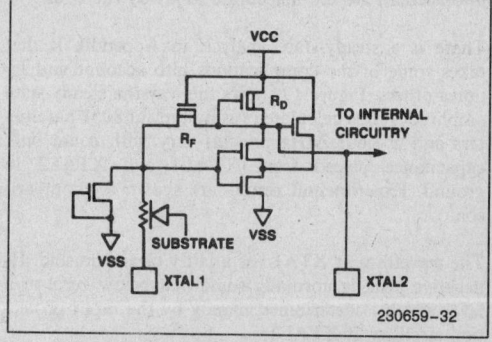

Figure 21. MCS®-48 Oscillator Amplifier

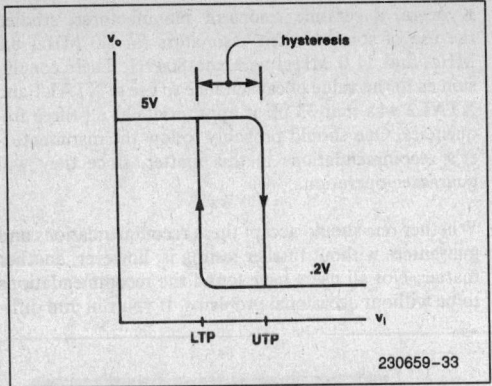

Figure 22. Schmitt Trigger Characteristic

amplifier is a Schmitt Trigger. This configuration was chosen to prevent crosstalk from the TO pin, which is adjacent to the XTAL1 pin.

All Schmitt Trigger circuits exhibit a hysteresis effect, as shown in Figure 22. The hysteresis is what makes it less sensitive to noise. The same hysteresis allows any Schmitt Trigger to be used as a relaxation oscillator. All you have to do is connect a resistor from output to input, and a capacitor from input to ground, and the circuit oscillates in a relaxation mode as follows.

If the Schmitt Trigger output is at a logic high, the capacitor commences charging through the feedback resistor. When the capacitor voltage reaches the upper trigger point (UTP), the Schmitt Trigger output switches to a logic low and the capacitor commences discharging through the same resistor. When the capacitor voltage reaches the lower trigger point (LTP), the Schmitt Trigger output switches to a logic high again, and the sequence repeats. The oscillation frequency is determined by the RC time constant and the hysteresis voltage, UTP-LTP.

The 8048 can oscillate in this mode. It has an internal feedback resistor. All that's needed is an external capacitor from XTAL1 to ground. In fact, if a smaller external feedback resistor is added, an 8048 system could be designed to run in this mode. *Do it at your own risk!* This mode of operation is not tested, specified, documented, or encouraged in any way by Intel for the 8048. Future steppings of the device might have a different type of inverting amplifier (one more like the 8051). The CHMOS members of the MCS-48 family do not use a Schmitt Trigger as the inverting amplifier.

Relaxation oscillations in the 8048 must be avoided, and this is the major objective in selecting the off-chip components needed to complete the oscillator circuit.

When an 8048 is powered up, if VCC has a short rise time, the relaxation mode starts first. The frequency is normally about 50 KHz. The resonator mode builds more slowly, but it eventually takes over and dominates the operation of the cirucit. This is shown in Figure 23A.

Due to processing variations, some units seem to have a harder time coming out of the relaxation mode, particularly at low temperatures. In some cases the resonator oscillations may fail entirely, and leave the device in the relaxation mode. Most units will stick in the relaxation mode at any temperature if C_{X1} is larger than about 50 pF. Therefore, C_{X1} should be chosen with some care, particularly if the system must operate at lower temperatures.

One method that has proven effective in all units to $-40°C$ is to put 5 pF from XTAL1 to ground and 20 pF from XTAL2 to ground. Unfortunately, while this method does discourage the relaxation mode, it is not an optimal choice for the resonator mode. For one thing, it does not swamp the pin capacitance. Also, it makes for a rather high signal level at XTAL1 (8 or 9 volts peak-to-peak).

The question arises as to whether that level of signal at XTAL1 might damage the chip. Not to worry. The negative peaks are self-limiting and nondestructive. The positive peaks could conceivably damage the oxide, but in fact, NMOS chips (eg, 8048) and HMOS chips (eg, 8048H) are tested to a much higher voltage than that. The technology trend, of course, is to thinner oxides, as the devices shrink in size. For an extra margin of safety, the HMOS II chips (eg, 8048AH) have an internal diode clamp at XTAL1 to VCC.

In reality, C_{X1} doesn't have to be quite so small to avoid relaxation oscillations, if the minimum operating temperature is not $-40°C$. For less severe temperature requirements, values of capacitance selected in much the same way as for an 8051 can be used. The circuit should be tested, however, at the system's lowest temperature limit.

Additional security against relaxation oscillations can be obtained by putting a 1M-ohm (or larger) resistor from XTAL1 to VCC. Pulling up the XTAL1 pin this way seems to discourage relaxation oscillations as effectively as any other method (Figure 23B).

Another thing that discourages relaxation oscillations is low VCC. The resonator mode, on the other hand is much less sensitive to VCC. Thus if VCC comes up relatively slowly (several milliseconds rise time), the resonator mode is normally up and running before the relaxation mode starts (in fact, before VCC has even reached operating specs). This is shown in Figure 23C.

A secondary effect of the hysteresis is a shift in the oscillation frequency. At low frequencies, the output signal from an inverter without hysteresis leads (or lags) the input by 180 degrees. The hysteresis in a Schmitt Trigger, however, causes the output to lead the

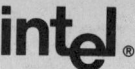

input by less than 180 degrees (or lag by more than 180 degrees), by an amount that depends on the signal amplitude, as shown in Figure 24. At higher frequencies, there are additional phase shifts due to the various reactances in the circuit, but the phase shift due to the hysteresis is still present. Since the total phase shift in the oscillator's loop gain is necessarily 0 or 360 degrees, it is apparent that as the oscillations build up, the frequency has to change to allow the reactances to compensate for the hysteresis. In normal operation, this additional phase shift due to hysteresis does not exceed a few degrees, and the resulting frequency shift is negligible.

Kyocera, a ceramic resonator manufacturer, studied the use of some of their resonators (at 6.0 MHz, 8.0 MHz, and 11.0 MHz) with the 8049H. Their conclusion as to the value of capacitance to use at XTAL1 and XTAL2 was that 33 pF is appropriate at all three frequencies. One should probably follow the manufacturer's recommendations in this matter, since they will guarantee operation.

Whether one should accept these recommendations and guarantees without further testing is, however, another matter. Not all users have found the recommendations to be without occasional problems. If you run into diffi-

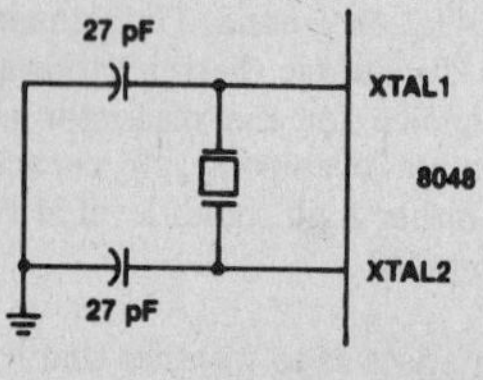

230659-34

A) When VCC Comes Up Fast, Relaxation Oscillations Start First. But Then the Crystal Takes Over.

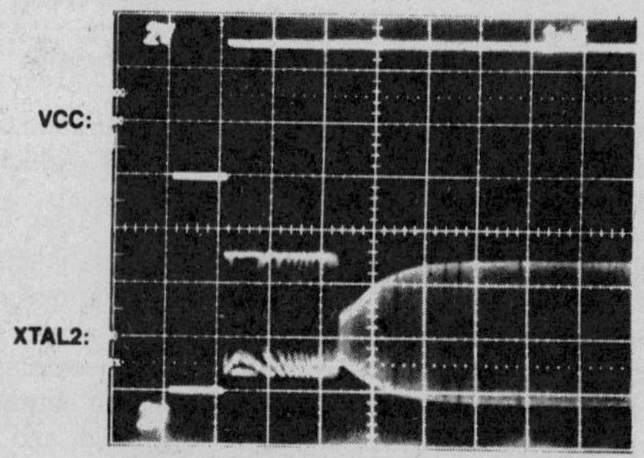

230659-37

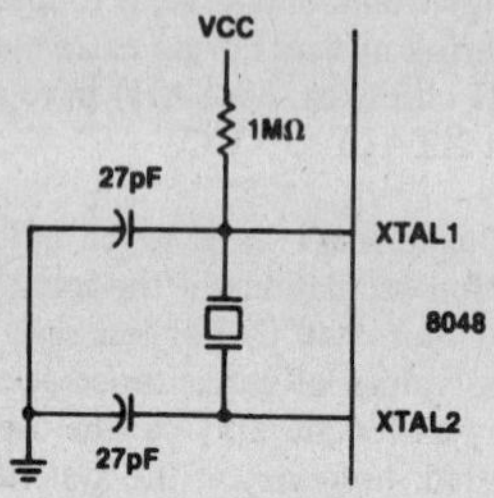

230659-35

B) Weak Pullup (1 MΩ or More) on XTAL1 Discourages Relaxation Mode.

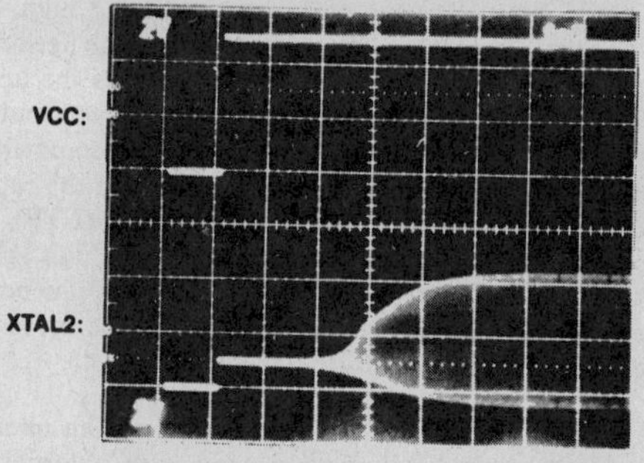

230659-38

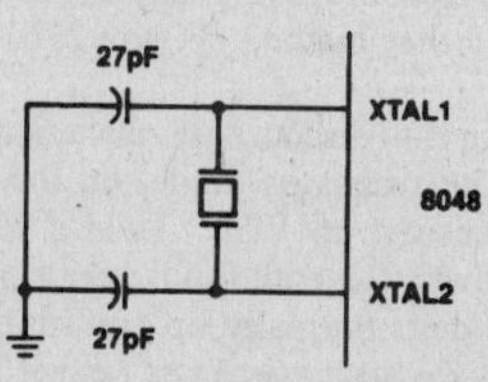

230659-36

C) No Relaxation Oscillations When VCC Comes Up More Slowly.

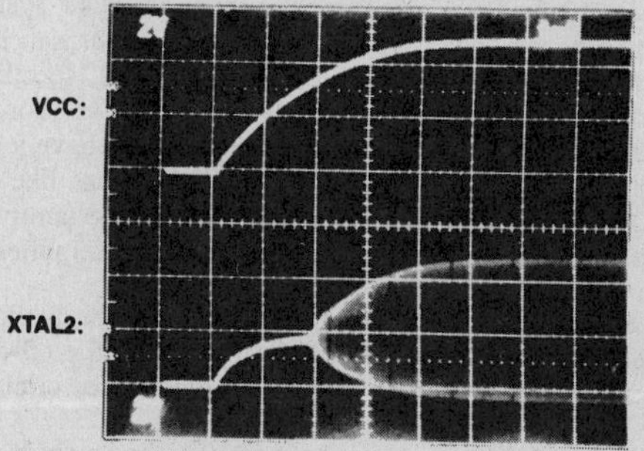

230659-39

Figure 23. Relaxation Oscillations in the 8048

AP-155

culties using their recommendations, both Intel and the ceramic resonator manufacturer want to know about it. It is to their interest, and ours, that such problems be resolved.

It will be helpful to build a test jig that will allow the oscillator circuit to be tested independently of the rest of the system. Both start-up and steady-state characteristics should be tested. Figure 25 shows the circuit that

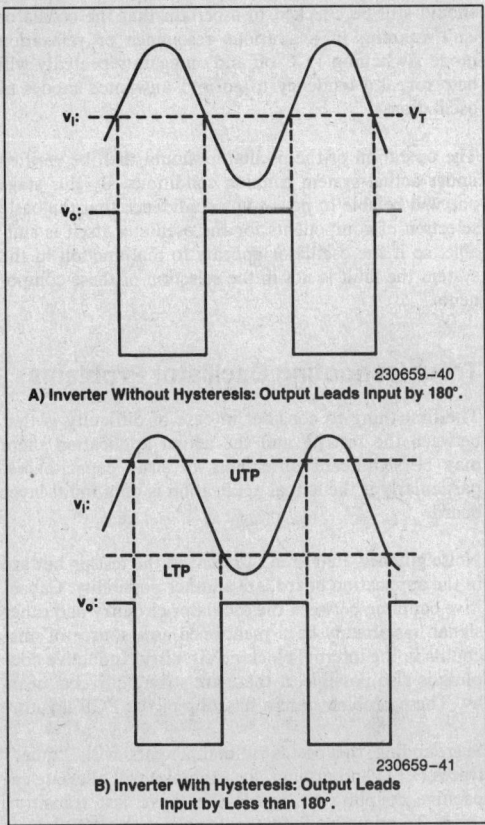

Figure 24. Amplitude—Dependent Phase Shift in Schmitt Trigger

Preproduction Tests

An oscillator design should never be considered ready for production until it has proven its ability to function acceptably well under worst-case environmental conditions and with parameters at their worst-case tolerance limits. Unexpected temperature effects in parts that may already be near their tolerance limits can prevent start-up of an oscillator that works perfectly well on the bench. For example, designers often overlook temperature effects in ceramic capacitors. (Some ceramics are down to 50% of their room-temperature values at $-20°C$ and $+60°C$. The problem here isn't just one of frequency stability, but also involves start-up time and steady-state amplitude. There may also be temperature effects in the resonator and amplifier.

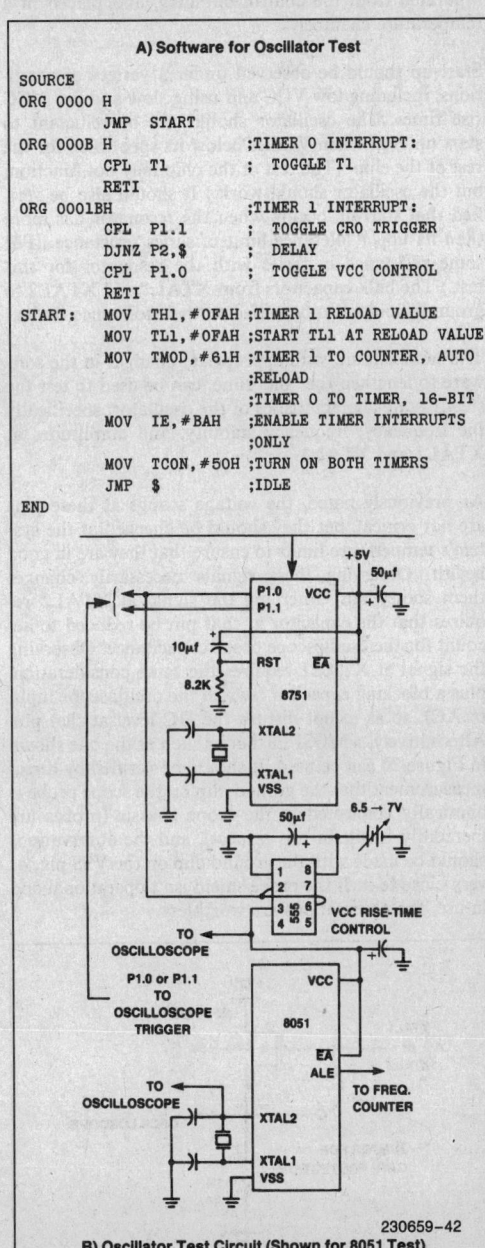

Figure 25. Oscillator Test Circuit and Software

was used to obtain the oscillator start-up photographs in this Application Note. This circuit or a modified version of it would make a convenient test vehicle. The oscillator and its relevant components can be physically separated from the control circuitry, and placed in a temperature chamber.

Start-up should be observed under a variety of conditions, including low VCC and using slow and fast VCC rise times. The oscillator should not be reluctant to start up even when VCC is below its spec value for the rest of the chip. (The rest of the chip may not function, but the oscillator should work.) It should also be verified that start-up occurs when the resonator has more than its upper tolerance limit of series resistance. (Put some resistance in series with the resonator for this test.) The bulk capacitors from XTAL1 and XTAL2 to ground should also be varied to their tolerance limits.

The same circuit, with appropriate changes in the software to lengthen the "on" time, can be used to test the steady-state characteristics of the oscillator, specifically the frequency, frequency stability, and amplitudes at XTAL1 and XTAL2.

As previously noted, the voltage swings at these pins are not critical, but they should be checked at the system's temperature limits to ensure that they are in good health. Observing these signals necessarily changes them somewhat. Observing the signal at XTAL2 requires that the capacitor at that pin be reduced to account for the oscilloscope probe capacitance. Observing the signal at XTAL1 requires the same consideration, plus a blocking capacitor (switch the oscilloscope input to AC), so as to not disturb the DC level at that pin. Alternatively, a MOSFET buffer such as the one shown in Figure 26 can be used. It should be verified by direct measurement that the ground clip on the scope probe is ohmically connected to the scope chassis (probes are incredibly fragile in this respect), and the observations should be made with the ground clip on the VSS pin, or very close to it. If the probe shield isn't operational and in use, the observations are worthless.

Frequency checks should be made with only the oscillator circuitry connected to XTAL1 and XTAL2. The ALE frequency can be counted, and the oscillator frequency derived from that. In systems where the frequency tolerance is only "nominal," the frequency should still be checked to ascertain that the oscillator isn't running in a spurious resonance or relaxation mode. Switching VCC off and on again repeatedly will help reveal a tendency to go into unwanted modes of oscillation.

The operation of the oscillator should then be verified under actual system running conditions. By this stage one will be able to have some confidence that the basic selection of components for the oscillator itself is suitable, so if the oscillator appears to malfunction in the system the fault is not in the selection of these components.

Troubleshooting Oscillator Problems

The first thing to consider in case of difficulty is that between the test jig and the actual application there may be significant differences in stray capacitances, particularly if the actual application is on a multi-layer board.

Noise glitches, that aren't present in the test jig but are in the application board, are another possibility. Capacitive coupling between the oscillator circuitry and other signal has already been mentioned as a source of miscounts in the internal clocking circuitry. Inductive coupling is also possible, if there are strong currents nearby. These problems are a function of the PCB layout.

Surrounding the oscillator components with "quiet" traces (VCC and ground, for example) will alleviate capacitive coupling to signals that have fast transition times. To minimize inductive coupling, the PCB layout should minimize the areas of the loops formed by the oscillator components. These are the loops that should be checked:

XTAL1 through the resonator to XTAL2;
XTAL1 through C_{X1} to the VSS pin;
XTAL2 through C_{X2} to the VSS pin.

It is not unusual to find that the grounded ends of C_{X1} and C_{X2} eventually connect up to the VSS pin only after looping around the farthest ends of the board. Not good.

Finally, it should not be overlooked that software problems sometimes imitate the symptoms of a slow-starting oscillator or incorrect frequency. Never underestimate the perversity of a software problem.

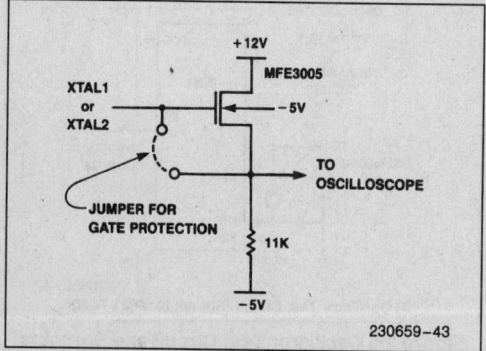

Figure 26. MOSFET Buffer for Observing Oscillator Signals

REFERENCES

1. Frerking, M. E., *Crystal Oscillator Design and Temperature Compensation,* Van Nostrand Reinhold, 1978.

2. Bottom, V., "The Crystal Unit as a Circuit Component," Ch. 7, *Introduction to Quartz Crystal Unit Design,* Van Nostrand Reinhold, 1982.

3. Parzen, B., *Design of Crystal and Other Harmonic Oscillators,* John Wiley & Sons, 1983.

4. Holmbeck, J. D., "Frequency Tolerance Limitations with Logic Gate Clock Oscillators, *31st Annual Frequency Control Symposium,* June, 1977.

5. Roberge, J. K., "Nonlinear Systems," Ch. 6, *Operational Amplifiers: Theory and Practice,* Wiley, 1975.

6. Eaton, S. S. *Timekeeping Advances Through COS/MOS Technology,* RCA Application Note ICAN-6086.

7. Eaton, S. S., *Micropower Crystal-Controlled Oscillator Design Using RCA COS/MOS Inverters,* RCA Application Note ICAN-6539.

8. Fisher, J. B., *Crystal Specifications for the Intel 8031/8051/8751 Microcontrollers,* Standard Crystal Corp. Design Data Note #2F.

9. Murata Mfg. Co., Ltd., *Ceramic Resonator "Ceralock" Application Manual.*

10. Kyoto Ceramic Co., Ltd., *Adaptability Test Between Intel 8049H and Kyocera Ceramic Resonators.*

11. Kyoto Ceramic Co., Ltd., *Technical Data on Ceramic Resonator Model KBR-6.0M, KBR-8.0M, KBR-11.0M Application for 8051 (Intel).*

12. NTK Technical Ceramic Division, NGK Spark Plug Co., Ltd., *NTKK Ceramic Resonator Manual.*

APPENDIX A
QUARTZ AND CERAMIC RESONATOR FORMULAS

Based on the equivalent circuit of the crystal, the impedance of the crystal is

$$Z_{XTAL} = \frac{(R_1 + j\omega L_1 + 1/j\omega C_1)(1/j\omega C_0)}{R_1 + j\omega L_1 + 1/j\omega C_1 + 1/j\omega C_0}$$

After some algebraic manipulation, this calculation can be written in the form

$$Z_{XTAL} = \frac{1}{j\omega(C_1 + C_0)} \cdot \frac{1 - \omega^2 L_1 C_1 + j\omega R_1 C_1}{1 - \omega^2 L_1 C_T + j\omega R_1 C_T}$$

where C_T is the capacitance of C_1 in series with C_0:

$$C_T = \frac{C_1 C_0}{C_1 + C_0}$$

The impedance of the crystal in parallel with an external load capacitance C_L is the same expression, but with $C_0 + C_L$ substituted for C_0:

$$Z_{XTAL \| CL} = \frac{1}{j\omega(C_1 + C_0 + C_L)} \cdot \frac{1 - \omega^2 L_1 C_1 + j\omega R_1 C_1}{1 - \omega^2 L_1 C'_T + j\omega R_1 C'_T}$$

where C'_T is the capacitance of C_1 in series with ($C_0 + C_L$):

$$C'_T = \frac{C_1(C_0 + C_L)}{C_1 + C_0 + C_L}$$

The impedance of the crystal in *series* with the load capacitance is

$$Z_{XTAL + CL} = Z_{XTAL} + \frac{1}{j\omega C_L}$$

$$= \frac{C_L + C_1 + C_0}{j\omega C_L(C_1 + C_0)} \cdot \frac{1 - \omega^2 L_1 C'_T + j\omega R_1 C'_T}{1 - \omega^2 L_1 C_T + j\omega R_1 C_T}$$

where C_T and C'_T are as defined above.

The phase angles of these impedances are readily obtained from the impedance expressions themselves:

$$\theta_{XTAL} = \arctan \frac{\omega R_1 C_1}{1 - \omega^2 L_1 C_1}$$

$$- \arctan \frac{\omega R_1 C_T}{1 - \omega^2 L_1 C_T} - \frac{\pi}{2}$$

$$\theta_{XTAL \| CL} = \arctan \frac{\omega R_1 C_1}{1 - \omega^2 L_1 C_1}$$

$$- \arctan \frac{\omega R_1 C'_T}{1 - \omega^2 L_1 C'_T} - \frac{\pi}{2}$$

$$\theta_{XTAL + CL} = \arctan \frac{\omega R_1 C'_T}{1 - \omega^2 L_1 C'_T}$$

$$- \arctan \frac{\omega R_1 C_T}{1 - \omega^2 L_1 C_T} - \frac{\pi}{2}$$

The resonant ("series resonant") frequency is the frequency at which the phase angle is zero and the impedance is low. The antiresonant ("parallel resonant") frequency is the frequency at which the phase angle is zero and the impedance is high.

Each of the above θ-expressions contains two arctan functions. Setting the denominator of the argument of the first arctan function to zero gives (approximately) the "series resonant" frequency for that configuration. Setting the denominator of the argument of the second arctan function to zero gives (approximately) the "parallel resonant" frequency for that configuration.

For example, the resonant frequency of the crystal is the frequency at which

$$1 - \omega^2 L_1 C_1 = 0$$

Thus

$$\omega_s = \frac{1}{\sqrt{L_1 C_1}}$$

or

$$f_s = \frac{1}{2\pi\sqrt{L_1 C_1}}$$

It will be noted that the series resonant frequency of the "XTAL+CL" configuration (crystal in series with CL) is the same as the parallel resonant frequency of the "XTAL∥CL" configuration (crystal in parallel with C_L). This is the frequency at which

$$1 - \omega^2 L_1 C'_T = 0$$

Thus

$$\omega_a = \frac{1}{\sqrt{L_1 C'_T}}$$

or

$$f_a = \frac{1}{2\pi\sqrt{L_1 C'_T}}$$

This fact is used by crystal manufacturers in the process of calibrating a crystal to a specified load capacitance.

By subtracting the resonant frequency of the crystal from its antiresonant frequency, one can calculate the range of frequencies over which the crystal reactance is positive:

$$f_a - f_s = f_s(\sqrt{1 + C_1/C_0} - 1)$$

$$\approx f_s\left(\frac{C_1}{2C_0}\right)$$

Given typical values for C_1 and C_0, this range can hardly exceed 0.5% of fs. Unless the inverting amplifier in the positive reactance oscillator is doing something very strange indeed, the oscillation frequency is bound to be accurate to that percentage whether the crystal was calibrated for series operation or to any unspecified load capacitance.

Equivalent Series Resistance

ESR is the real part of Z_{XTAL} at the oscillation frequency. The oscillation frequency is the parallel resonant frequency of the "XTAL∥CL" configuration (which is the same as the series resonant frequency of the "XTAL+CL" configuration). Substituting this frequency into the Z_{XTAL} expression yields, after some algebraic manipulation,

$$ESR = \frac{R_1 \left(\frac{C_0 + C_L}{C_L}\right)^2}{1 + \omega^2 C_1^2 \left(\frac{C_0 + C_L}{C_L}\right)^2}$$

$$\approx R_1 \left(1 + \frac{C_0}{C_L}\right)^2$$

Drive Level

The power dissipated by the crystal is $I_1^2 R_1$, where I_1 is the RMS current in the motional arm of the crystal. This current is given by $V_x/|Z_1|$, where V_x is the RMS voltage across the crystal, and $|Z_1|$ is the magnitude of the impedance of the motional arm. At the oscillation frequency, the motional arm is a positive (inductive) reactance in parallel resonance with $(C_0 + C_L)$. Therefore $|Z_1|$ is approximately equal to the magnitude of the reactance of $(C_0 + C_L)$:

$$|Z_1| = \frac{1}{2\pi f (C_0 + C_L)}$$

where f is the oscillation frequency. Then,

$$P = I_1^2 R_1 = \left(\frac{V_x}{|Z_1|}\right)^2 R_1$$

$$= [2\pi f (C_0 + C_L) V_x]^2 R_1$$

The waveform of the voltage across the crystal (XTAL1 to XTAL2) is approximately sinusoidal. If its peak value is VCC, then V_x is $VCC/\sqrt{2}$. Therefore,

$$P = 2R_1 [\pi f (C_0 + C_L) VCC]^2$$

APPENDIX B
OSCILLATOR ANALYSIS PROGRAM

The program is written in BASIC. BASIC is excruciatingly slow, but it has some advantages. For one thing, more people know BASIC than FORTRAN. In addition, a BASIC program is easy to develop, modify, and "fiddle around" with. Another important advantage is that a BASIC program can run on practically any small computer system.

Its slowness is a problem, however. For example, the routine which calculates the "start-up time constant" discussed in the text may take several hours to complete. A person who finds this program useful may prefer to convert it to FORTAN, if the facilities are available.

Limitations of the Program

The program was developed with specific reference to 8051-type oscillator circuitry. That means the on-chip amplifier is a simple inverter, and not a Schmitt Trigger. The 8096, the 80C51, the 80C48 and 80C49 all have simple inverters. The 8096 oscillator is almost identical to the 8051, differing mainly in the input protection circuitry. The CHMOS amplifiers have somewhat different parameters (higher gain, for example), and different transition levels than the 8051.

The MCS-48 family is specifically included in the program only to the extent that the input-output curve used in the steady-state analysis is that of a Schmitt Trigger, if the user identifies the device under analysis as an MCS-48 device. The analysis does not include the voltage dependent phase shift of the Schmitt Trigger.

The clamping action of the input protection circuitry is important in determining the steady-state amplitudes. The steady-state routine accounts for it by setting the negative peak of the XTAL1 signal at a level which depends on the amplitude of the XTAL1 signal in accordance with experimental observations. It's an exercise in curve-fitting. A user may find a different type of curve works better. Later steppings of the chips may behave differently in this respect, having somewhat different types of input protection circuitry.

It should be noted that the analysis ignores a number of important items, such as high-frequency effects in the on-chip circuitry. These effects are difficult to predict, and are no doubt dependent on temperature, frequency, and device sample. However, they can be simulated to a reasonable degree by adding an "output capacitance" of about 20 pF to the circuit model (i.e., in parallel with CX2) as described below.

Notes on Using the Program

The program asks the user to input values for various circuit parameters. First the crystal (or ceramic resonator) parameters are asked for. These are R1, L1, C1, and C0. The manufacturer can supply these values for selected samples. To obtain any kind of correlation between calculation and experiment, the values of these parameters must be known for the specific sample in the test circuit. The value that should be entered for C0 is the C0 of the crystal itself plus an estimated 7 pF to account for the XTAL1-to-XTAL2 pin capacitance, plus any other stray capacitance paralleling the crystal that the user may feel is significant enough to be included.

Then the program asks for the values of the XTAL1-to-ground and XTAL2-to-ground capacitances. For CXTAL1, enter the value of the externally connected bulk capacitor plus an estimated 7 pF for pin capacitance. For CXTAL2, enter the value of the externally connected bulk capacitor plus an estimated 7 pF for pin capacitance plus about 20 pF to simulate high-frequency roll-off and phase shifts in the on-chip circuitry.

Next the program asks for values for the small-signal parameters of the on-chip amplifier. Typically, for the 8051/8751,

Amplifier Gain Magnitude = 15
Feedback Resistance = 2300 KΩ
Output Resistance = 2 KΩ

The same values can be used for MCS-48 (NMOS and HMOS) devices, but they are difficult to verify, because the Schmitt Trigger does not lend itself to small-signal measurements.

AP-155

```
100 DEFDBL C,D,F,G,L,P,R,S,X
200 REM                                                          APRIL 8, 1983
300 REM ***********************************************************************
400 REM
500 REM                    FUNCTIONS
600 REM
700 REM
800 REM  FNZM(R,X) = MAGNITUDE OF A COMPLEX NUMBER, :R+jX:
900 DEF FNZM(R,X) = SQR(R^2+X^2)
1000 REM
1100 REM  FNZP(R,X) = ANGLE OF A COMPLEX NUMBER
1200 REM            = 180/PI*ARCTAN(X/R)            IF R>0
1300 REM            = 180/PI*ARCTAN(X/R) + 180      IF R<0 AND X>0
1400 REM            = 180/PI*ARCTAN(X/R) - 180      IF R<0 AND X<0
1500 DEF FNZP(R,X) = 180/PI*ATN(X/R) - (SGN(R)-1)*SGN(X)*90
1600 REM
1700 REM      INDUCTIVE IMPEDANCE AT COMPLEX FREQUENCY S+jF (HZ)
1800 REM          Z = 2*PI*S*L   + j2*PI*F*L
1900 REM            = FNRL(S,L) + jFNXL(F,L)
2000 DEF FNRL(SL,LL) = 2#*PI*SL*LL
2100 DEF FNXL(FL,LL) = 2#*PI*FL*LL
2200 REM
2300 REM      CAPACITIVE IMPEDANCE AT COMPLEX FREQUENCY S+jF (HZ)
2400 REM          Z = 1/[2*PI*(S+jF)*C]
2500 REM            = S/[2*PI*(S^2+F^2)*C] + j(-F)/[2*PI*(S^2+F^2)*C]
2600 REM            = FNRC(S,F,C) + jFNXC(S,F,C)
2700 DEF FNRC(SC,FC,CC) =  SC/(2#*PI*(SC^2+FC^2)*CC)
2800 DEF FNXC(SC,FC,CC) = -FC/(2#*PI*(SC^2+FC^2)*CC)
2900 REM
3000 REM      RATIO OF TWO COMPLEX NUMBERS
3100 REM          RA+jXA     RA*RB+XA*XB      XA*RB-RA*XB
3200 REM          ------  =  -----------  + j -----------
3300 REM          RB+jXB      RB^2+XB^2        RB^2+XB^2
3400 REM                 = FNRR(RA,XA,RB,XB) + jFNXR(RA,XA,RB,XB)
3500 DEF FNRR(RA,XA,RB,XB) = (RA*RB+XA*XB)/(RB^2+XB^2)
3600 DEF FNXR(RA,XA,RB,XB) = (XA*RB-XB*RA)/(RB^2+XB^2)
3700 REM
3800 REM      PRODUCT OF TWO COMPLEX NUMBERS
3900 REM        (RA+jXA)*(RB+jXB)  =   RA*RB-XA*XB + j(XA*RB+RA*XB)
4000 REM                           = FNRM(RA,XA,RB,XB) + jFNXM(RA,XA,RB,XB)
4100 DEF FNRM(RA,XA,RB,XB) = RA*RB - XA*XB
4200 DEF FNXM(RA,XA,RB,XB) = RA*XB + RB*XA
4300 REM
4400 REM
4500 REM      PARALLEL IMPEDANCES
4600 REM                               (RA+jXA)*(RB+jXB)
4700 REM          (RA+jXA)::(RB+jXB) = -----------------
4800 REM                               RA+RB +j(XA+XB)
4900 REM
5000 REM        RA*(RB^2+XB^2)+RB*(RA^2+XA^2)     XA*(RB^2+XB^2)+XB*(RA^2+XA^2)
5100 REM      = -----------------------------  + j -----------------------------
5200 REM           (RA+RB)^2 + (XA+XB)^2               (RA+RB)^2 + (XA+XB)^2
5300 REM
5400 REM      = FNRP(RA,XA,RB,XB) + jFNXP(RA,XA,RB,XB)
5500 DEF FNRP(RA,XA,RB,XB) = (RA*(RB^2+XB^2) + RB*(RA^2+XA^2))/((RA+RB)^2 + (XA+XB)^2)
5600 DEF FNXP(RA,XA,RB,XB) = (XA*(RB^2+XB^2) + XB*(RA^2+XA^2))/((RA+RB)^2 + (XA+XB)^2)
5700 REM
5800 REM ***********************************************************************
5900 REM
6000 REM                    BEGIN COMPUTATIONS
6100 REM
6200 LET PI = 3.141592654#
6300 REM
6400 REM              DEFINE CIRCUIT PARAMETERS
6500 GOSUB 14500
6600 REM
6700 REM  ESTABLISH NOMINAL RESONANT AND ANTIRESONANT CRYSTAL FREQUENCIES
6800 FS = FIX(1/(2*PI*SQR(L1*C1)))
6900 FA = FIX(1/(2*PI*SQR(L1*C1*CO/(C1+CO))))
7000 PRINT
7100 PRINT "XTAL IS SERIES RESONANT AT ",FS," HZ"
7200 PRINT "           PARALLEL RESONANT AT ";FA;" HZ"
7300 PRINT
7400 PRINT "SELECT: 1. LIST PARAMETERS"
7500 PRINT "        2. CIRCUIT ANALYSIS"
7600 PRINT "        3. OSCILLATION FREQUENCY"
7700 PRINT "        4. START-UP TIME CONSTANT"
7800 PRINT "        5. STEADY-STATE ANALYSIS"
```

AP-155

```
7900 PRINT
8000 INPUT N
8100 IF N=1 THEN PRINT ELSE 8600
8200 REM
8300 REM ----------------- LIST PARAMETERS -----------------------
8400 GOSUB 17100
8500 GOTO 6800
8600 IF N=2 THEN PRINT ELSE 9400
8700 REM
8800 REM ----------------- CIRCUIT ANALYSIS ---------------------
8900 PRINT " FREQUENCY S+JF  TYPE (S),(F) "
9000 INPUT SG,FG
9100 GOSUB 20200
9200 GOSUB 26600
9300 GOTO 6800
9400 IF N=3 THEN 10300 ELSE 11000
9500 REM
9600 REM ----------------- OSCILLATION FREQUENCY -----------------
9700 CL = CX*CY/(CX+CY) + CO
9800 FG = FIX(1/(2*PI*SQR(L1*C1*CL/(C1+CL))))
9900 SG = 0
10000 DF = FIX(10^INT(LOG(FA-FS)/LOG(10)-2)+.5)
10100 DS = 0
10200 RETURN
10300 GOSUB 9700
10400 GOSUB 30300
10500 PRINT
10600 PRINT
10700 PRINT "FREQUENCY AT WHICH LOOP GAIN HAS ZERO PHASE ANGLE:"
10800 GOSUB 26600
10900 GOTO 6800
11000 IF N=4 THEN PRINT ELSE 12200
11100 REM
11200 REM ----------------- START-UP TIME CONSTANT ----------------
11300 PRINT "THIS WILL TAKE SOME TIME    ....."
11400 GOSUB 9700
11500 GOSUB 37700
11600 PRINT
11700 PRINT
11800 PRINT "FREQUENCY AT WHICH LOOP GAIN = 1 AT 0 DEGREES:"
11900 GOSUB 26600
12000 PRINT : PRINT "THIS YIELDS A START-UP TIME CONSTANT OF ";CSNG(1000000!/(2*PI*SG));" MICROSECS"
12100 GOTO 6800
12200 IF N=5 THEN PRINT ELSE 7300
12300 REM
12400 REM ----------------- STEADY-STATE ANALYSIS -----------------
12500 PRINT "STEADY-STATE ANALYSIS"
12600 PRINT
12700 PRINT "SELECT:  1. 8031/8051"
12800 PRINT "         2. 8751"
12900 PRINT "         3. 8035/8039/8040/8048/8049"
13000 PRINT "         4. 8748/8749"
13100 INPUT IC%
13200 IF IC%<1 OR IC%>4 THEN 12600
13300 GOSUB 46900
13400 GOTO 7300
13500 REM   SUBROUTINE BELOW DEFINES INPUT-OUTPUT CURVE OF OSCILLATOR CKT
13600 IF IC%>2 AND VO=5 AND VI<2 THEN RETURN
13700 VO = -10*VI + 15
13800 IF VO>5 THEN VO = 5
13900 IF VO<.2 THEN VO = .2
14000 IF IC%>2 AND VO>2 THEN VO = 5
14100 RETURN
14200 REM
14300 REM ************************************************************
14400 REM
14500 REM          DEFINE CIRCUIT PARAMETERS
14600 REM
14700 INPUT " R1 (OHMS)";R1
14800 INPUT " L1 (HENRY)";L1
14900 INPUT " C1 (PF)";X
15000 C1 = X*1E-12
15100 INPUT " CO (PF)",X
15200 CO = X*1E-12
15300 INPUT " CXTAL1 (PF)";X
15400 CX = X*1E-12
15500 INPUT " CXTAL2 (PF)";X
15600 CY = X*1E-12
```

AP-155

```
15700 INPUT " GAIN FACTOR MAGNITUDE";AV#
15800 INPUT " AMP FEEDBACK RESISTANCE (K-OHMS)";X
15900 RX = X*1000#
16000 INPUT " AMP OUTPUT RESISTANCE (K-OHMS)";X
16100 RO = X*1000#
16200 REM
16300 REM
16400 REM           LIST CURRENT PARAMETER VALUES
16500 GOSUB 17100
16600 RETURN
16700 REM
16800 REM
16900 REM ************************************************************
17000 REM
17100 REM           LIST CURRENT PARAMETER VALUES
17200 REM
17300 PRINT
17400 PRINT "CURRENT PARAMETER VALUES  1. R1 = ";R1;" OHMS"
17500 PRINT "                          2. L1 = ";CSNG(L1);" HENRY"
17600 PRINT "                          3  C1 = ";CSNG(C1*1E+12);" PF"
17700 PRINT "                          4  CO = ";CSNG(CO*1E+12);" PF"
17800 PRINT "                          5. CXTAL1 = ";CSNG(CX*1E+12);" PF"
17900 PRINT "                          6. CXTAL2 = ";CSNG(CY*1E+12);" PF"
18000 PRINT "   7. AMPLIFIER GAIN MAGNITUDE = ";AV#
18100 PRINT "      8.     FEEDBACK RESISTANCE = ";CSNG(RX* 001);" K-OHMS"
18200 PRINT "      9.      OUTPUT RESISTANCE = ";CSNG(RO*.001);" K-OHMS"
18300 PRINT
18400 PRINT "TO CHANGE A PARAMETER VALUE, TYPE (PARAM NO.),(NEW VALUE). "
18500 PRINT "OTHERWISE, TYPE 0,0 "
18600 INPUT N%,X
18700 IF N%=0 THEN RETURN
18800 IF N%=1 THEN R1 = X
18900 IF N%=2 THEN L1 = X
19000 IF N%=3 THEN C1 = X*1E-12
19100 IF N%=4 THEN CO = X*1E-12
19200 IF N%=5 THEN CX = X*1E-12
19300 IF N%=6 THEN CY = X*1E-12
19400 IF N%=7 THEN AV# = X
19500 IF N%=8 THEN RX = X*1000!
19600 IF N%=9 THEN RO = X*1000!
19700 GOTO 17400
19800 REM
19900 REM
20000 REM ************************************************************
20100 REM
20200 REM                CIRCUIT ANALYSIS
20300 REM
20400 REM  This routine calculates the loop gain at complex frequency SG+jFG.
20500 REM
20600 REM  1. Crystal impedance: RE + jXE
20700 REM
20800 X1 = FNXL(FG,L1) + FNXC(SG,FG,C1)
20900 RE = FNRP((R1+FNRL(SG,L1)+FNRC(SG,FG,C1)),X1,FNRC(SG,FG,CO),FNXC(SG,FG,CO))
21000 XE = FNXP((R1+FNRL(SG,L1)+FNRC(SG,FG,C1)),X1,FNRC(SG,FG,CO),FNXC(SG,FG,CO))
21100 REM
21200 REM  2. RF + jXF  = (RE+jXE)!!(amplifier feedback resistance)
21300 REM
21400 RF = FNRP(RX,0,RE,XE)
21500 XF = FNXP(RX,0,RE,XE)
21600 REM
21700 REM  3. Input impedance  Zi = RI + jXI = impedance of CXTAL1
21800 REM
21900 RI = FNRC(SG,FG,CX)
22000 XI = FNXC(SG,FG,CX)
22100 REM
22200 REM  4. Load impedance: ZL = (impedance of CXTAL2)!![(RF+RI)+j(XF+XI)]
22300 REM
22400 RL = FNRP((RF+RI),(XF+XI),FNRC(SG,FG,CY),FNXC(SG,FG,CY))
22500 XL = FNXP((RF+RI),(XF+XI),FNRC(SG,FG,CY),FNXC(SG,FG,CY))
22600 REM
22700 REM  5. Amplifier gain   A = -AV*ZL/(ZL+RO)
22800 REM                        = A(real) + jA(imaginary)
22900 REM
23000 AR# = -AV#*FNRR(RL,XL,(RO+RL),XL)
23100 AI# = -AV#*FNXR(RL,XL,(RO+RL),XL)
23200 REM
23300 REM  6. Feedback ratio   (beta) = (RI)+jXI)/[(RF+RI)+j(XF+XI)]
23400 REM                             = B(real) + jB(imaginary)
```

AP-155

```
23500 REM
23600 BR# = FNRR(RI,XI,(RI+RF),(XI+XF))
23700 BI# = FNXR(RI,XI,(RI+RF),(XI+XF))
23800 REM
23900 REM  7. Amplifier gain in magnitude/phase form: AR+jAI = A at AP degrees
24000 REM
24100 A = FNZM(AR#,AI#)
24200 AP = FNZP(AR#,AI#)
24300 REM
24400 REM  8. (beta) in magnitude/phase form: BR+jBI = B at BP degrees
24500 REM
24600 B = FNZM(BR#,BI#)
24700 BP = FNZP(BR#,BI#)
24800 REM
24900 REM  9. Loop gain: G = (BR+jBI)*(AR+jAI)
25000 REM                   = G(real) + jG(imaginary)
25100 REM
25200 GR = FNRM(AR#,AI#,BR#,BI#)
25300 GI = FNXM(AR#,AI#,BR#,BI#)
25400 REM
25500 REM  10. Loop gain in magnitude/phase form: GR+jGI = AL at AQ degrees
25600 REM
25700 AL = FNZM(GR,GI)
25800 AQ = FNZP(GR,GI)
25900 RETURN
26000 REM
26100 REM
26200 REM *************************************************************
26300 REM
26400 REM              PRINT CIRCUIT ANALYSIS RESULTS
26500 REM
26600 PRINT
26700 PRINT " FREQUENCY = ";SQ;" + J";FQ;" HZ"
26800 PRINT " XTAL IMPEDANCE = ",FNZM(RE,XE);" OHMS AT ";FNZP(RE,XE);" DEGREES"
26900 PRINT "       (RE = ";CSNG(RE);" OHMS)"
27000 PRINT "       (XE = ";CSNG(XE);" OHMS)"
27100 PRINT " LOAD IMPEDANCE = ",FNZM(RL,XL);" OHMS AT ";FNZP(RL,XL);" DEGREES"
27200 PRINT " AMPLIFIER GAIN = ",A;" AT ";AP;" DEGREES"
27300 PRINT " FEEDBACK RATIO = ",B;" AT ";BP;" DEGREES"
27400 PRINT " LOOP GAIN = ";AL;" AT ";AQ;" DEGREES"
27500 RETURN
27600 REM
27700 REM
27800 REM *************************************************************
27900 REM
28000 REM              SEARCH FOR FREQUENCY (S+JF)
28100 REM           AT WHICH LOOP GAIN HAS ZERO PHASE ANGLE
28200 REM
28300 REM  This routine searches for the frequency at which the imaginary part
28400 REM  of the loop gain is zero. The algorithm is as follows:
28500 REM     1. Calculate the sign of the imaginary part of the loop gain (GI).
28600 REM     2. Increment the frequency.
28700 REM     3. Calculate the sign of GI at the incremented frequency.
28800 REM     4. If the sign of GI has not changed, go back to 2.
28900 REM     5. If the sign of GI has changed, and this frequency is within
29000 REM        1Hz of the previous sign-change, exit the routine.
29100 REM     6. Otherwise, divide the frequency increment by -10.
29200 REM     7. Go back to 2.
29300 REM  The routine is entered with the starting frequency SQ+jFQ and
29400 REM  starting increment DS+jDF already defined by the calling program.
29500 REM  In actual use either DS or DF is zero, so the routine searches for
29600 REM  a GI=0 point by incrementing either SQ or FQ while holding the other
29700 REM  constant. It returns control to the calling program with the
29800 REM  incremented part of the frequency being within 1Hz of the actual
29900 REM  GI=0 point.
30000 REM
30100 REM  1. CALCULATE THE SIGN OF THE IMAGINARY PART OF THE LOOP GAIN (GI).
30200 REM
30300 GOSUB 20200
30400 GOSUB 26600
30500 IF GI=0 THEN RETURN
30600 SX% = INT(SGN(GI))
30700 IF SX%=+1 THEN DS = -DS
30800 REM  (REVERSAL OF DS FOR GI>0 IS FOR THE POLE-SEARCH ROUTINE.)
30900 REM
31000 REM  2. INCREMENT THE FREQUENCY.
31100 REM
31200 SP = SQ
```

AP-155

```
31300 FP = FQ
31400 SQ = SQ + DS
31500 FQ = FQ + DF
31600 REM
31700 REM   3. CALCULATE THE SIGN OF GI AT THE INCREMENTED FREQUENCY.
31800 REM
31900 GOSUB 20200
32000 GOSUB 26600
32100 IF INT(SGN(GI))=0 THEN RETURN
32200 REM
32300 REM   4. IF THE SIGN OF GI HAS NOT CHANGED, GO BACK TO 2.
32400 REM
32500 IF SX%+INT(SGN(GI))=0 THEN PRINT ELSE 31400
32600 SX% = -SX%
32700 REM
32800 REM   5. IF THE SIGN OF GI HAS CHANGED, AND IF THIS FREQUENCY IS WITHIN
32900 REM      1HZ OF THE PREVIOUS SIGN-CHANGE, AND IF GI IS NEGATIVE, THEN
33000 REM      EXIT THE ROUTINE. (THE ADDITIONAL REQUIREMENT FOR NEGATIVE GI
33100 REM      IS FOR THE POLE-SEARCH ROUTINE.)
33200 REM
33300 IF ABS(SP-SQ)<1 AND ABS(FP-FQ)<1 AND SX%=-1 THEN RETURN
33400 REM
33500 REM   6. DIVIDE THE FREQUENCY INCREMENT BY -10.
33600 REM
33700 DS = -DS/10#
33800 DF = -DF/10#
33900 REM
34000 REM   7. GO BACK TO 2.
34100 REM
34200 GOTO 31200
34300 REM
34400 REM
34500 REM ****************************************************************
34600 REM
34700 REM                    SEARCH FOR POLE FREQUENCY
34800 REM
34900 REM   This routine searches for the frequency at which the loop gain = 1
35000 REM   at 0 degrees. That frequency is the pole frequency of the closed-
35100 REM   loop gain function. The pole frequency is a complex number, SQ+jFQ
35200 REM   (Hz). Oscillator start-up ensues if SQ>0. The algorithm is based on
35300 REM   the calculated behavior of the phase angle of the loop gain in the
35400 REM   region of interest on the complex plane. The locus of points of zero
35500 REM   phase angle crosses the j-axis at the oscillation frequency and at
35600 REM   some higher frequency. In between these two crossings of the j-axis,
35700 REM   the locus lies in Quadrant I of the complex plane, forming an
35800 REM   approximate parabola which opens to the left. The basic plan is to
35900 REM   follow the locus from where it crosses the j-axis at the oscillation
36000 REM   frequency, into Quadrant I, and find the point on that locus where
36100 REM   the loop gain has a magnitude of 1. The algorithm is as follows:
36200 REM      1. Find the oscillation frequency, 0+jFQ.
36300 REM      2. At this frequency calculate the sign of (AL-1). (AL = magnitude
36400 REM         of loop gain.)
36500 REM      3. Increment FQ.
36600 REM      4. For this value of FQ, find the value of SQ for which the loop
36700 REM         gain has zero phase.
36800 REM      5. For this value of SQ+jFQ, calculate the sign of (AL-1).
36900 REM      6. If the sign of (AL-1) has not changed, go back to 3.
37000 REM      7. If the sign of (AL-1) has changed, and this value of FQ is
37100 REM         within 1Hz of the previous sign-change, exit the routine.
37200 REM      8. Otherwise, divide the FQ-increment by -10.
37300 REM      9. Go back to 3.
37400 REM
37500 REM   1. FIND THE OSCILLATION FREQUENCY, 0+jFQ.
37600 REM
37700 GOSUB 9700
37800 GOSUB 30300
37900 REM
38000 REM   2. AT THIS FREQUENCY, CALCULATE THE SIGN OF (AL-1).
38100 REM
38200 SY% = INT(SGN(AL-1'))
38300 IF SY%=-1 THEN STOP
38400 REM ESTABLISH INITIAL INCREMENTATION VALUE FOR FQ
38500 F1 = FQ
38600 DF = (FA-F1)/10#
38700 GOSUB 30300
38800 DE = (FQ-F1)/10#
38900 DF = 0
39000 FQ = F1
```

```
39100 REM
39200 REM    3. INCREMENT FG.
39300 REM
39400 FG = FG + DE
39500 REM
39600 REM    4. FOR THIS VALUE OF FG, FIND THE VALUE OF SG FOR WHICH THE LOOP
39700 REM       GAIN HAS ZERO PHASE. (THE ROUTINE WHICH DOES THAT NEEDS DF = 0,
39800 REM       SO THAT IT CAN HOLD FG CONSTANT, AND NEEDS AN INITIAL VALUE FOR
39900 REM       DS, WHICH IS ARBITRARILY SET TO DS = 1000.)
40000 REM
40100 DS = 1000#
40200 SG = 0
40300 GOSUB 30300
40400 IF AL=1! THEN RETURN
40500 REM
40600 REM    5. FOR THIS VALUE OF SG+jFG, CALCULATE THE SIGN OF (AL-1).
40700 REM    6. IF THE SIGN OF (AL-1) HAS NOT CHANGED, GO BACK TO 3.
40800 REM
40900 IF SY%+INT(SGN(AL-1!))=0 THEN PRINT ELSE 39400
41000 REM
41100 REM    7. IF THE SIGN OF (AL-1) HAS CHANGED, AND THIS VALUE OF FG IS WITHIN
41200 REM       1HZ OF THE PREVIOUS SIGN-CHANGE, EXIT THE ROUTINE.
41300 REM
41400 IF ABS(F1-FG)<1 THEN RETURN
41500 REM
41600 REM    8. DIVIDE THE FG-INCREMENT BY -10.
41700 REM
41800 DE = -DE/10#
41900 F1 = FG
42000 SY% = -SY%
42100 REM
42200 REM    9. GO BACK TO 3.
42300 REM
42400 GOTO 39400
42500 REM
42600 REM
42700 REM ****************************************************************
42800 REM
42900 REM                   STEADY-STATE ANALYSIS
43000 REM
43100 REM    The circuit model used in this analysis is similar to the one used
43200 REM    in the small-signal analysis, but differs from it in two respects.
43300 REM    First, it includes clamping and clipping effects described in the
43400 REM    text. Second, the voltage source in the Thevenin equivalent of the
43500 REM    amplifier is controlled by the input voltage in accordance with an
43600 REM    input-output curve defined elsewhere in the program.
43700 REM       The analysis applies a sinusoidal input signal of arbitrary
43800 REM    amplitude, at the oscillation frequency, to the XTAL1 pin, then
43900 REM    calculates the resulting waveform from the voltage source. Using
44000 REM    standard Fourier techniques, the fundamental frequency component of
44100 REM    this waveform is extracted. This frequency component is then
44200 REM    multiplied by the factor !ZL/(ZL+RO)!, and the result is taken to be
44300 REM    the signal appearing at the XTAL2 pin. This signal is then
44400 REM    multiplied by the feedback ratio (beta), and the result is taken to
44500 REM    be the signal appearing at the XTAL1 pin. The algorithm is now
44600 REM    repeated using this computed XTAL1 signal as the assumed input
44700 REM    sinusoid. Every time the algorithm is repeated, new values appear at
44800 REM    XTAL1 and XTAL2, but the values change less and less with each
44900 REM    repetition. Eventually they stop changing. This is the steady-state.
45000 REM       The algorithm is as follows:
45100 REM    1. Compute approximate oscillation frequency.
45200 REM    2. Call a circuit analysis at this frequency.
45300 REM    3. Find the quiescent levels at XTAL1 and XTAL2 (to establish the
45400 REM       beginning DC level at XTAL1).
45500 REM    4. Assume an initial amplitude for the XTAL1 signal.
45600 REM    5. Correct the DC level at XTAL1 for clamping effects, if necessary.
45700 REM    6. Using the appropriate input-output curve, extract a DC level and
45800 REM       the fundamental frequency component (multiplying the latter by
45900 REM       !ZL/(ZL+RO)!).
46000 REM    7. Clip off the negative portion of this output signal, if the
46100 REM       negative peak falls below zero.
46200 REM    8. If this signal, multiplied by (beta), differs from the input
46300 REM       amplitude by less than 1mV, or if the algorithm has been repeated
46400 REM       10 times, exit the routine.
46500 REM    9. Otherwise, multiply the XTAL2 amplitude by (beta) and feed it
46600 REM       back to XTAL1, and go back to 5.
46700 REM
46800 REM       1. COMPUTE APPROXIMATE OSCILLATION FREQUENCY.
```

AP-155

```
46900 GOSUB 9700
47000 REM
47100 REM     2. CALL A CIRCUIT ANALYSIS AT THIS FREQUENCY.
47200 GOSUB 20800
47300 PRINT : PRINT : PRINT "ASSUMED OSCILLATION FREQUENCY: "
47400 GOSUB 26600
47500 PRINT : PRINT
47600 REM
47700 REM     3. FIND QUIESCENT POINT
47800 REM  (At quiescence the voltages at XTAL1 and XTAL2 are equal. This
47900 REM    voltage level is found by trial-and-error, based on the input-
48000 REM    output curve, so that a person can change the input-output curve
48100 REM    as desired without having to re-calculate the quiescent point.)
48200 VI = 0
48300 VB = 1
48400 K1 = 1
48500 VI = VI + VB
48600 GOSUB 13600
48700 IF ABS(VO-VI)<.001 THEN 49200
48800 IF K1+SGN(VO-VI)=0 THEN 48900 ELSE 48500
48900 K1 = SGN(VO-VI)
49000 VB = -VB/10
49100 GOTO 48500
49200 VB = VI
49300 PRINT "QUIESCENT POINT = ";VB
49400 REM
49500 REM     4. ASSUME AN INITIAL AMPLITUDE FOR THE XTAL1 SIGNAL.
49600 EI = .01
49700 NR% = 0
49800 REM
49900 REM     5. CORRECT FOR CLAMPING EFFECTS, IF NECESSARY.
50000 REM  (K1 and K2 are curve-fitting parameters for the ROM parts.)
50100 K1 = (2.5-VB)/(3-VB)
50200 K2 = (VB-1.25)/(3-VB)
50300 IF IC%=2 OR IC%=4 THEN IF EI<(VB+.5) THEN EO = VB ELSE EO = EI - .5
50400 IF IC%=1 OR IC%=3 THEN IF EI<(VB+.5) THEN EO = VB ELSE EO = K1*EI+K2
50500 NR% = NR% + 1
50600 REM
50700 REM     6. DERIVE XTAL2 AMPLITUDE
50800 VO = 0
50900 VC = 0
51000 VS = 0
51100 FOR N% = -25 TO +24
51200 VI = EO - EI*COS(PI*N%/25)
51300 GOSUB 13600
51400 VO = VO + VO
51500 VC = VC + VO*COS(PI*N%/25)
51600 VS = VS + VO*SIN(PI*N%/25)
51700 NEXT N%
51800 VO = VO/50
51900 V1 = SQR(VC^2+VS^2)/25*FNZM(RL,XL)/FNZM((RL+RO),XL)
52000 REM
52100 REM     7. CLIP XTAL2 SIGNAL.
52200 IF VO-V1<0 THEN VL = 0 ELSE VL = VO-V1
52300 PRINT : PRINT "XTAL1 SWING = ";EO-EI;" TO ";EO+EI
52400 PRINT "XTAL2 SWING = ";VL;" TO ",VO+V1
52500 REM
52600 REM     8. TEST FOR TERMINATION.
52700 IF ABS(EI-V1*B)<.001 OR NR%=10 THEN RETURN
52800 REM
52900 REM     9. FEED BACK TO XTAL1 AND REPEAT
53000 EI = V1*B
53100 GOTO 50300
```

NORTH AMERICAN SALES OFFICES

ALABAMA

Intel Corp.
4024 Medford Drive
Huntsville 35802
Tel: (205) 883-6137
FAX: (205) 883-4826

ARIZONA

†Intel Corp.
410 North 44th Street
Suite 470
Phoenix 85008
Tel: (800) 628-8686
FAX: (602) 244-0446

CALIFORNIA

Intel Corp.
3550 Watt Avenue
Suite 140
Sacramento 95821
Tel: (800) 628-8686
FAX: (916) 488-1473

†Intel Corp.
9655 Granite Ridge Drive
3rd Floor, Suite 4A
San Diego 92123
Tel: (800) 628-8686
FAX: (619) 467-2460

Intel Corp.
1781 Fox Drive
San Jose 95131
Tel: (800) 628-8686
FAX: (408) 441-9540

*†Intel Corp.
1551 N. Tustin Avenue
Suite 800
Santa Ana 92701
Tel: (800) 628-8686
TWX: 910-595-1114
FAX: (714) 541-9157

†Intel Corp.
15260 Ventura Boulevard
Suite 360
Sherman Oaks 91403
Tel: (800) 628-8686
FAX: (818) 995-6624

Intel Corp.
120 Birmingham
Suite 110-114
Cardiff, CA 92007
Tel: (619) 942-8938
FAX: (619) 942-2849

Intel Corp.
300 N. Continental Blvd.
Suite 100
El Segundo 90245
Tel: (800) 628-8686
FAX: (310) 640-7133

COLORADO

*†Intel Corp.
600 S. Cherry St.
Suite 700
Denver 80222
Tel: (800) 628-8686
TWX: 910-931-2289
FAX: (303) 322-8670

CONNECTICUT

†Intel Corp.
40 Old Ridgebury Road
Suite 311
Danbury 06811
Tel: (800) 628-8686
TWX: 910-576-2867
FAX: (203) 778-2168

FLORIDA

†Intel Corp.
800 Fairway Drive
Suite 160
Deerfield Beach 33441
Tel: (800) 628-8686
FAX: (305) 421-244

Intel Corp.
2250 Lucien Way
Suite 100, Room 8
Maitland 32751
Tel: (800) 628-8686
FAX: (407) 660-1283

GEORGIA

†Intel Corp.
20 Technology Park
Suite 150
Norcross 30092
Tel: (800) 628-8686
FAX: (404) 448-0875

IDAHO

Intel Corp.
9456 Fairview Ave., Suite C
Boise 83704
Tel: (800) 628-8686
FAX: (208) 377-1052

ILLINOIS

*†Intel Corp.
Woodfield Corp. Center III
300 N. Martingale Road
Suite 400
Schaumburg 60173
Tell: (800) 628-8686
FAX: (708) 605-9762

INDIANA

†Intel Corp.
8041 Knue Road
Indianapolis 46250
Tel: (800) 628-8686
FAX: (317) 577-4939

MARYLAND

*†Intel Corp.
131 National Business Parkway
Suite 200
Annapolis Junction 20701
Tel: (800) 628-8686
FAX: (301) 206-3678

MASSACHUSETTS

*†Intel Corp.
Westford Corp. Center
5 Carlisle Road
2nd Floor
Westford 01886
Tel: (800) 628-8686
TWX: 710-343-6333
FAX: (508) 692-7867

MICHIGAN

†Intel Corp.
7071 Orchard Lake Road
Suite 100
West Bloomfield 48322
Tel: (800) 628-8686
FAX: (313) 851-8770

Intel Corp.
32255 N. Western Hwy.
Suite 212, Tri Atria
Farmington Hills 48334
Tel: (800) 628-8686
FAX: (313) 851-8770

MINNESOTA

†Intel Corp.
3500 W. 80th St.
Suite 360
Bloomington 55431
Tel: (800) 628-8686
TWX: 910-576-2867
FAX: (612) 831-6497

NEW JERSEY

Intel Corp.
2001 Route 46, Suite 310
Parsippany 07054-1315
Tel: (800) 628-8686
FAX: (201) 402-4893

*†Intel Corp.
Lincroft Center
125 Half Mile Road
Red Bank 07701
Tel: (800) 628-8686
FAX: (908) 747-0983

NEW YORK

*Intel Corp.
850 Cross Keys Office Park
Fairport 14450
Tel: (800) 628-8686
TWX: 510-253-7391
FAX: (716) 223-2561

*†Intel Corp.
2950 Express Dr. South
Suite 130
Islandia 11722
Tel: (800) 628-8686
TWX: 510-227-6236
FAX: (516) 348-7939

OHIO

*Intel Corp.
56 Milford Dr., Suite 205
Hudson 44236
Tel: (800) 628-8686
FAX: (216) 528-1026

*†Intel Corp.
3401 Park Center Drive
Suite 220
Dayton 45414
Tel: (800) 628-8686
TWX: 810-450-2528
FAX: (513) 890-8658

OKLAHOMA

Intel Corp.
6801 N. Broadway
Suite 115
Oklahoma City 73162
Tel: (800) 628-8686
FAX: (405) 840-9819

OREGON

†Intel Corp.
15254 NW Greenbrier Pkwy.
Building B
Beaverton 97006
Tel: (800) 628-8686
TWX: 910-467-8741
FAX: (503) 645-8181

PENNSYLVANIA

*†Intel Corp.
925 Harvest Drive
Suite 200
Blue Bell 19422
Tel: (800) 628-8686
FAX: (215) 641-0785

SOUTH CAROLINA

Intel Corp.
7403 Parklane Rd., Suite 4
Columbia 29223
Tel: (800) 628-8686
FAX: (803) 788-7999

Intel Corp.
100 Executive Center Drive
Suite 109, B183
Greenville 29615
Tel: (800) 628-8686
FAX: (803) 297-3401

TEXAS

†Intel Corp.
8911 N. Capital of Texas Hwy.
Suite 4230
Austin 78759
Tel: (800) 628-8686
FAX: (512) 338-9335

*†Intel Corp.
5000 Quorum Drive
Suite 750
Dallas 75240
Tel: (800) 628-8686
FAX: (214) 233-1325

*†Intel Corp.
20515 SH 249
Suite 401
Houston 77070
Tel: (800) 628-8686
TWX: 910-881-2490
FAX: (713) 376-2891

UTAH

†Intel Corp.
428 East 6400 South
Suite 135
Murray 84107
Tel: (800) 628-8686
FAX: (801) 268-1457

Intel Corp.
2581 E. Cobblestone Way
Sandy, UT 84093
Tel: (801) 942-8820
FAX: (801) 942-8815

WASHINGTON

†Intel Corp.
2800 156th Avenue SE
Suite 105
Bellevue 98007
Tel: (800) 628-8686
FAX: (206) 746-4495

WISCONSIN

Intel Corp.
400 N. Executive Dr.
Suite 401
Brookfield 53005
Tel: (800) 628-8686
FAX: (414) 789-2746

CANADA

BRITISH COLUMBIA

Intel Semiconductor of
Canada, Ltd.
999 Canada Place
Suite 404, #11
Vancouver V6C 3E2
Tel: (800) 628-8686
FAX: (604) 844-2813

ONTARIO

†Intel Semiconductor of
Canada, Ltd.
2650 Queensview Drive
Suite 250
Ottawa K2B 8H6
Tel: (800) 628-8686
FAX: (613) 820-5936

†Intel Semiconductor of
Canada, Ltd.
190 Attwell Drive
Suite 500
Rexdale M9W 6H8
Tel: (800) 628-8686
FAX: (416) 675-2438

QUEBEC

†Intel Semiconductor of
Canada, Ltd.
1 Rue Holiday, Tour West
Suite 320
Pt. Claire H9R 5N3
Tel: (800) 628-8686
FAX: 514-694-0064

†Sales and Service Office
*Field Application Location